Knopf Publications in Psychology

CONSULTING EDITORS:
David Krech and Richard S. Crutchfield
UNIVERSITY OF CALIFORNIA, BERKELEY

THE CORE SERIES

David Krech and Richard S. Crutchfield
ELEMENTS OF PSYCHOLOGY

THE GENERAL SERIES

Catherine Landreth
THE PSYCHOLOGY OF EARLY CHILDHOOD

ELEMENTS
OF
PSYCHOLOGY

KNOPF CORE SERIES

ELEMENTS
OF
PSYCHOLOGY

by David Krech
and
Richard S. Crutchfield

UNIVERSITY OF CALIFORNIA, BERKELEY

19 *65*

ALFRED A. KNOPF   NEW YORK

L. C. catalog card number: 58-5044
© *David Krech and Richard S. Crutchfield, 1958*

THIS IS A BORZOI BOOK,
PUBLISHED BY ALFRED A. KNOPF, INC.

PUBLISHED 1958; REPRINTED 1958, 1959, 1960, 1961, 1962, 1965², 1966

TO

HILDA

AND

MARY

To the Reader

IN THIS BOOK we have tried to fulfill two objectives. Our first purpose was to organize the various facts, observations, theories, and speculations of psychology so as to stress the inherent harmony existing within the data of psychology. In other words, we have sought to present the science of psychology as an organic whole, indicating at various points the relationships among the different psychological processes. The first chapter provides an "overview" of the entire book. A careful reading of Chapter 1, therefore, will inform the reader of the principles that have guided us and will facilitate his understanding of the material of the book.

We have also attempted to create an effective teaching instrument. In furtherance of this objective we have introduced several devices intended to aid the reader in his study of the material. Among these devices are the *Boxes*, the periodic sections labeled *By way of summary*, and the *Glossaries* at the end of each chapter.

The Boxes contain material of various types. Some of them supplement the main discussion in the text; some contain further illustrative material; some provide the reader with an opportunity to carry out his own demonstration experiments; but most of them present research evidence for the generalizations stated in the text.

The latter may be of particular interest. No science is sounder than its research, and if the reader of this book is to achieve a *critical understanding* of the science of psychology, he must become familiar not only with the "conclusions" of psychology, but also with the research behind these generalizations. This will enable him to understand the conclusions better and to evaluate them critically. The Boxes present enough detail so that the reader can become acquainted with the reasoning, methods, and difficulties of research in psychology. We have also provided the reference for each study described, thus enabling the reader to go to the original source, should any study attract his special interest.

Almost every chapter of a book in science contains two types of material which a student is expected to master: generalizations and specific information. To aid the student we have provided two types of "summaries." Some of the general principles which merit repetition and emphasis are summarized while the discussion of them is still fresh in the mind of the reader—each chapter will be found to contain several "By way of summary" sections. These sections not only repeat and emphasize the principles but attempt to clarify some of their implications.

The more detailed information has been summarized at the end of each chapter in the glossaries. Since the specific concepts and information of any science are summarized by its technical language, definitions of technical terms are important. The technical terms of psychology make up the glossaries in this book. Each term in the glossary is described in some detail so that the student will be aided in his review of the concept covered by the particular term.

The General Glossary repeats each term in the chapter glossaries, without a definition but with an index to the pages where the definition may be found. This should be a good tool for reviewing the entire book.

It is our hope that these various devices will help the reader to grasp and retain the material presented in this book.

Preface

THE PREFACE of a book usually turns out to be the most pleasant chapter to write. This is not only because, in the inverted and realistic logic of book-making, it is the last chapter which needs to be written, but primarily because it is the one chapter where the authors can make explicit their debt to the many people who have helped make the book possible.

We cannot hope to name all who deserve our thanks, but we can, at the very least, indicate those of our friends and colleagues who contributed well beyond the normal call of friendship and good-will.

Of course no book is completely the work of the authors whose names are listed on the title page, and the unnamed authors of this book, as is true of any scientific enterprise, are legion. First among these are the research workers in psychology and the cognate sciences upon whose findings we have attempted to build a systematic approach to the science of human behavior. Since this book is not only a presentation of a body of scientific knowledge and speculation, but is also a teaching instrument, it reflects, we hope, all that we have learned from our students—at Swarthmore College, Bryn Mawr College, Mount Holyoke College, Harvard University, the University of Oslo, the University of Colorado, and the University of California— where we have been privileged to teach and to share with these students the adventure of examining anew, every year, what man has learned about man.

Most immediately, we are indebted to several friends who have read and criticized the first draft of the manuscript in-corporated in this book. Among them is Professor Leo Postman who carefully and painstakingly went over large sections of our manuscript, especially those dealing with perception and learning, and whose helpful criticism has not only saved us from a number of errors, but whose sound scholarship has helped make this book so much the better. Professor Mark R. Rosenzweig has read, and made suggestions relating to, the chapters on physiology and neurology, and has been most generous in helping to design the anatomical illustrations used in those chapters. Professor Edwin E. Ghiselli, through his rare combination of a basic familiarity with the "pure" science of psychology and a mastery of industrial psychology, has made many valuable suggestions which we have not hesitated to incorporate. Professors Paul H. Mussen and John P. McKee have reviewed in a critical and sympathetic manner our chapters on child development, and we have profited from their reviews. Professor Rheem F. Jarrett has gone over our chapter on statistics, and has made several contributions to it. Professor Hans Wallach read and made a number of helpful comments on our chapters of perception, as did Professor Mason Haire, whose interest and kind enthusiasm has encouraged us greatly. And finally, as have so many others, we have profited from the wisdom and encouragement of Professor Robert B. MacLeod.

We have attempted to present in this book an effective teaching instrument. If we have been successful, a large part of the credit properly belongs to the illustrators

ix

and draftsmen who strove to put a number of our notions into interesting, clear, and pleasing graphic form. Mr. Walter Schwarz, the scientific illustrator, has shown infinite patience, a perceptive intelligence, and his usual high order of skill in his execution of the anatomical drawings. Mr. Wolfgang Lederer helped us by his imaginative capacity to translate the "write-ups" of experimental procedure into charming and clear illustrations, and Mrs. Katherine Eardley, who is responsible for the charts, graphs, and some of the line drawings of the book has always been a friend and colleague upon whose patience, talent, and imagination we have drawn liberally. Mr. Herbert Kling, technician of our laboratory, has done yeoman's service in his able photographic and reproductive work.

Miss Jean Pierce was responsible for typing the many, many versions of our manuscript. Her interest, skill, and intelligence made her not only our typist, but our first critical reader and editor. She has helped enormously. Finally, it is with gratitude that we acknowledge our indebtedness to Dr. Ray Ginger, Editor of the College Department of Alfred A. Knopf, Inc., whose careful and sensitive readings improved both how we have had our say, and, at many points, what we have had to say.

We have been most fortunate in the generosity of many individuals who have made available to us original figures, photographs, and manuscripts: Professors Wilder Penfield, Heinrich Klüver, Donald B. Lindsley, Raúl Hernández-Peón, and Per Saugstad.

We wish also to express our most sincere appreciation to the following journals, publishers and individuals who have granted permission to reproduce tables, figures, illustrations, and excerpts:

American Journal of Psychology
American Philosophical Society
American Psychological Association
Appleton-Century-Crofts, Inc.
Archives of Psychology
Mrs. Madison Bentley
British Journal of Psychology
Dodd, Mead & Co.
Dover Publications, Inc.
Genetic Psychology Monographs
Ginn & Company
Harper & Brothers
Henry Holt & Co., Inc.
Houghton Mifflin Company
Journal of Comparative Psychology
Journal of Electroencephalography and Clinical Neurophysiology
Journal of Experimental Psychology
Journal of General Psychology
Journal of Genetic Psychology
Journal of Speech and Hearing Disorders

Liveright Publishing Corp.
The Macmillan Co.
McGraw-Hill Book Co.
W. W. Norton & Company, Inc.
Perception Demonstration Center of Princeton University
Princeton University Press
Psychological Monographs
Psychological Review
Science
Scientific American
Scientific Publishing Company
The Technology Press
University of California Press
University of Chicago Press
University of Wichita Press
D. Van Nostrand Co., Inc.
The Viking Press, Inc.
John Wiley & Sons, Inc.
Yale University Press

Berkeley, California.
September, 1957.

DAVID KRECH
RICHARD S. CRUTCHFIELD

Contents

Contents

Contents

Contents

Contents

Color Plates

(immediately preceding first page of text)

ELEMENTS
OF
PSYCHOLOGY

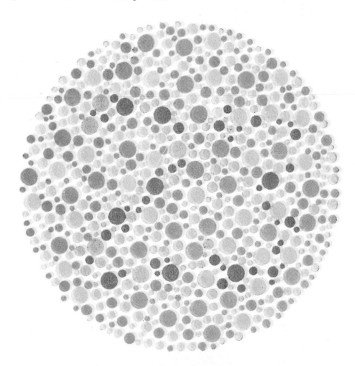

X

I. In order to demonstrate for yourself a change in perception that occurs without your awareness, place a piece of gray paper over the right half of the yellow rectangle. Stare steadily at the fixation mark for 60 seconds. Then remove the gray cover while continuing to look at the fixation mark. How do the left and the right halves of the rectangle look? (See Box 7, p. 25.)

II. One of the plates from the Dvorine Test to detect color blindness. The person with normal color vision sees the numeral 23; the person with red-green color blindness and the totally color-blind person see no numeral at all. (See p. 39.) *Reproduced by permission of the author of the* Dvorine Pseudo-Isochromatic Plates *published by the Scientific Publishing Co., Baltimore, Md.*

III. The color spectrum, produced by the refraction of sunlight through a prism. (See p. 56.)

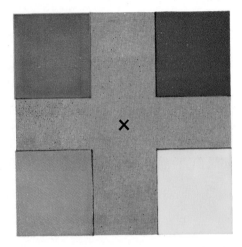 

IV. Fixate the cross in the center of the left figure steadily for about 30 seconds. Then transfer your gaze to the cross in the gray square. What colors are the afterimages you now see in the corners? (See Box 20, p. 76.)

V. Does the blue color look the same in all parts of the figure? It actually *is* the identical color throughout. (See p. 80.) *Reprinted with permission from Ralph M. Evans,* An Introduction to Color, *copyright 1946 by John Wiley & Sons.*

CHAPTER I

The Study of Man

I N STUDYING man, the psychologist resorts to a convenient bit of scientific fiction. He knows perfectly well that a person is a "whole" organism. He knows that he cannot study man in a piecemeal fashion without losing the unity of the man he is describing. But he also knows that he cannot achieve any understanding of man unless he proceeds *as if* man *could* be studied piecemeal. He has no choice, for man-as-a-whole is just too big a piece for any scientist to handle with the instruments and concepts now available. This bit of scientific fiction has proved to be a profitable one, not only for psychology but for all the sciences. Taking a whole, breaking it down into parts, and studying each part intensively is a common method of science. It is the method of *analysis*.

In studying man, then, we first analyze his *perceptions*—how he sees, hears, smells, and feels the world about him. We next concern ourselves with the *motives* and *emotions* of man—his needs, desires, aspirations, fears, and loves. Then we examine man as he attempts to *adapt* to the demands

made upon him—how he solves problems, learns, remembers, and forgets. Finally we consider man as a unique *individual* living in a world of other men—his personality and his relations to society.

But what the psychologist tears asunder, he also seeks to join together. He uses not only the method of analysis, but also the method of *synthesis*, putting the analyzed parts together to recreate an abstracted but scientifically useful facsimile of the original whole. As we progress through this book, we shall attempt synthesis from time to time.

To aid in this task, it will be helpful to get an overview of the entire "plot" of the book and of some of the major principles of each part. In this way we may be able to see more clearly how the findings in each section of the book fit in with those of the other sections. In this first chapter, therefore, we shall present a brief synopsis of what we are to find in the succeeding pages. A careful reading of this first chapter will provide a helpful frame of reference for our inquiry—the study of man.

Perception

Each man lives in his own world. His world is what he experiences—what he perceives, feels, thinks about, and imagines. And what he perceives, feels, thinks about, and imagines depends upon the physical and social environments in which he lives and upon his own biological nature, particularly the way his brain and nervous system work. His world is his own, and different from the worlds of others, because his brain and nervous system and his physical and social environments are not exactly like anyone else's.

How the person *behaves* depends upon this world of his own. To understand his behavior we must first ask: What is the specific nature of his world? We are then in a position to ask: Why is it what it is? How did it come about? What effects does it have on his actions? In brief, we ask the standard questions in the scientist's catechism as he approaches any problem: What? How? Why?

Our first step, therefore, is to describe our worlds as we perceive them. The description of the world about us covers not only the simple attributes of objects—such as their size, shape, color, and location—but also their expressive, meaningful, and changing qualities. Such a description, answering the question "What?" sets the stage for the experimental analysis of the conditions that can account for our perceptions. In other words, we are now ready to seek the answers to the questions "How?" and "Why?"

In accounting for the common perceptions of things, and the individual differences in such perceptions, the experimental evidence indicates that perception is influenced by three main sets of determinants: the physical stimuli falling upon the eyes, ears, nose, and skin of the perceiver; the psychological state of the perceiver; and the physiological equipment of the organism.

Perception and the Stimulus. Perception depends upon the characteristics of the physical stimulus. Thus light waves of a certain frequency will normally evoke in us the sensation of red; light waves of other frequencies will normally evoke other color sensations. A great deal of information is now available which relates the nature of the physical stimulus to the nature of the resulting sensation. But these relationships, expressed in the so-called *psychophysical* laws, are not simple ones. The sensory experiences produced in an observer by the *same* physical stimulus can vary widely, depending, for example, upon the presence of other stimuli.

An example in which the same physical stimulus may lead to different perceptions of size is illustrated by the striking phenomenon of the "moon illusion" experienced by everyone. The full moon when it is just rising above the horizon looks enormous in comparison with the same full moon when it is riding high in the sky. Box 1 describes various scientific attempts to account for this illusion.

Stimuli rarely occur singly (as in a single pin point of light), but mostly in company with a host of other stimuli. Somehow out of this myriad of stimuli a perception results that can best be described as *organized* or patterned. Several generalizations describing this patterning have been suggested from laboratory studies. These generalizations help us to describe how the person perceives order in complex stimulus situations so that his perceptions reflect the realities of the external environment and at the same time permit him to attend to and emphasize those aspects of the environment which are biologically important for him.

BOX 1

What Causes the Moon Illusion?

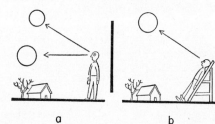

a   b

Hypothesis	*Evaluation of Hypothesis*
1. Denser air at horizon makes moon's image on eye larger by diffusing the light rays.	*Wrong.* Photographs of the moon show no actual physical-size difference at horizon and overhead. The effect must be "psychological."
2. Moon at horizon appears larger because it looks *closer* than when overhead.	*Wrong.* According to principles of size constancy (to be discussed on p. 143) that would mean the horizon moon should look *smaller* than when overhead.
3. The moon appears larger at horizon due to comparison objects on landscape, such as houses, trees, etc.	*Wrong.* The illusion persists when it is set up with artificial "moons" in the dark laboratory where no comparison objects are visible.
4. The smaller apparent size of the moon when seen high in the sky is related to the upward tilt of the eyes in the head when looking upward.	*Right.* When a person lies on a tilted board so that he looks directly at the moon riding high in the sky without having to raise his eyes in their sockets (fig. *b*), the moon looks as large as it does at the horizon when he stands upright (fig. *a*).

We see that many "obvious explanations" do not hold up when put to scientific test. An essential step in scientific understanding of a phenomenon is the finding of consistent relations between the phenomenon (e.g., the change in the apparent size of the moon) and specifiable conditions (e.g., rotation of the eye in the socket). But this is not enough for a satisfactory scientific explanation. We also want to know, to use our present example, *how* the rotation of the eyes in the socket can influence the perceived size of the moon. At the present time we do not have an answer to that question.

BORING, E. G., 1943. The moon illusion. *Amer. J. Physics, 11,* 55–60.

Perception and Psychological State. What the person sees, hears, feels, is influenced by his immediate and temporary states of need, emotion, and "mental set." The thirsty man, the frightened man, and the hunter may perceive the same situation very differently. The more enduring characteristics of the person, such as his personality and his store of experiences, can also help to determine his perception. In this connection psychologists have suggested some generalizations which, it is hoped, can lead to laws relating perception to personality.

Perception and Physiology. A complex sequence of events occurs as a stimulus impinges on a receptor (the eye, ear, nose, etc.), as the receptor initiates a neural impulse to the *sensory* nerves, and as the impulse passes through the nerves to the brain.

The story of physiological processes underlying perception is far from complete. Yet the parts of the story we already know help us to account for many of the complex relationships between stimulus-patterns and perceptual response discovered in the psychologist's laboratory. For example, the receptors themselves are capable of large degrees of integration of stimuli. Our receptors and brain are constantly in action —even when we are "resting"—rather than waiting passively to be thrown into action by outside stimuli. Stimuli, in other words, do not fall on a "quiet" recording instrument. The nervous system is so constructed and so operates that perception is determined by the integrated pattern of activities going on in large parts of the brain— not solely in that part of the brain which receives the messages from the receptors in the first place. We shall find that this integrated activity of the nervous system in perception is a characteristic of the nervous activities involved in motivation and in adaptive behavior as well. Here there is a major generalization to be made about the action of the nervous system.

Motivation and Emotion

So far we have concentrated on the person as a perceiver. But man is not a spectator only. He is also an actor. And when we ask *why* he acts, the answer is usually phrased in terms of motives and emotions: he seeks goals, avoids dangers, feels love. The second main section of the book will take up these important problems of motivation and emotion.

The Self. To begin with we shall examine the nature of the self—the "I" or the "me" who experiences these motives and emotions. The self is an organized and enduring perception in the person's experience. It is a perception with an orderly history of growth and development; it is a perception unique to the individual. The physical body is the most visible aspect of the self, and there are significant ways in which the body is perceived and misperceived. The self is also seen by the person as consisting of more central layers (the "real me") and more peripheral layers (the "unimportant part of me"). The self has various degrees of unity, and can, under certain circumstances, undergo radical changes—as can any other perception. A person's perception of himself can be influenced by his personal experiences and by the demands made upon him by his friends, associates, and society.

The most striking feature of the person's experience of self is his state of motivation. The person perceives disturbances and deficiencies with respect to himself and his surroundings. He feels needs and desires, he sets goals and forms intentions, he exercises choice and will. In response to these felt motivations the person acts. He strives toward goals, he seeks to avoid discomforts and to escape injury.

But this picture is, of course, not complete without the self's central experience of emotion. The specific emotions of man —such as joy, pride, contentment, awe, love, grief, shame, misery—are regularly produced by specific psychological situations. Depending upon their strength and the conditions under which they are aroused, emotions may prove either helpful to the organism's adaptive behavior or harmful.

Patterns of Motives. The nature of man's motives has concerned people over many centuries. As different cultures have held different conceptions of human nature, so have their views of human motivation changed. Man has been regarded as a passive pawn of the fates or the gods, as a machine, as an animal, as a product of society, as a rational being, as an irrational creature. And with each of these differing conceptions the story of man's motives has been rewritten. The modern synthesis of all these views provides for a wide variety of specific motives. Some order can be made out of this variety by viewing all the motives of man as serving four general aims of human behavior: to stay alive, to keep safe, to get enjoyment, to experience change and novelty. In analyzing these motives of man, a distinction can be made between (1) *deficiency* motives, directed at avoiding deficits, deprivations, threats, and disruptions, and (2) *abundancy* motives, concerned with maximizing gratifications and enriching one's experience. (Box 2 describes experimental illustrations of the effects on the human being of insufficient stimulation.) Man's motives, in other words, cannot be described as consisting only of the seeking of food when hungry, safety when frightened, shelter when cold; they also include the seeking of positive goals and varied stimulation.

Arousal of Motives. The arousal of active states of motivation comes about through changes within the body of the organism, through changes in the physical and social environments of the individual, and through the "thoughts" of the person. A motive, once aroused, leads to some sort of action. The nature of the action is in part determined by the strength of the motive. Many ingenious methods have been developed to measure the strength of motives—both in animals and man. With the use of these measuring instruments attempts have been made to relate the strength of the motive to various forms of behavior. Once a motive is aroused and action starts, the motive

may be fulfilled or it may fail of fulfillment. Either event has diverse consequences. Consistent fulfillment of certain motives may "liberate" the person so that "higher" motives may begin to direct his behavior. Failure of fulfillment may narrow his strivings. For example, the starving man can think only of food. However the relation between the strength of motive and adjustive behavior is not a simple one. Too little motivation and too much may be equally harmful. An intensely desired reward may actually disrupt adjustive behavior.

A motive may fail of fulfillment because of obstacles, or because of lacks in the individual or in his environment, or because of conflicts among different motives within the person himself. When this occurs, we speak of frustration. Frustration has many causes and many consequences. Some frustrations may lead to *constructive* effects on goal strivings, others to *disruptive* effects. There are also generalized effects of frustration—effects that can influence the individual's personality and lead to various *defensive* reactions. As we examine the data here, we shall begin to see how the personality of a man is shaped by his failures and successes.

Physiology. Recent research has begun to give us a new understanding of how physiological processes relate to motivation and emotion. Instead of demonstrating, as past evidence seemed to indicate, that motivational and emotional states are dependent upon the "gut" responses of the organism —the reactions of his viscera, his glands, etc.—current research clearly indicates that the initiation and control of motives and emotions are located within the brain itself. Emotional and motivated behavior represents the resultants of visceral *and* cortical factors. Both the "gut" and the brain are involved. Thus again is brought home one

BOX 2

The Distress of Reduced Stimulation

The disturbing effects of severely reducing even simple sensory stimulation, such as lights or sounds, have been studied by Lilly. Naked except for a blacked-out head mask for breathing, he immersed himself in a floating position in a tank of tepid water. Thus variation in sensory stimulation was minimal. At first he felt relaxed, but soon he developed an intense need for "stimulus-action." Despite an intent to remain motionless, "hidden methods" of self-stimulation developed: twitching muscles, stroking one finger with another, etc. If all bodily movements were inhibited, his attention concentrated on the very few remaining stimuli that "became the whole content of consciousness to an almost unbearable degree." (The longest time he or anyone else could "take it" was 3 hours.)

Auditory stimuli were restricted by a foam-rubber pillow covering his ears. Wires were attached to his scalp to permit the experimenter outside to record his brain waves (see p. 483).

Most of the subjects went to sleep soon after entering the cubicle. After waking, they gradually became restless, with spells of acute unpleasant feeling. They appeared eager for stimulation and talked to themselves, sang, whistled, reminisced about past incidents, tried to recall in detail a motion picture they had seen, etc.

The reduced stimulation produced vivid and weird hallucinations, irritability, and childish and disorganized thoughts. There was also a change in the subject's brain waves which was profound enough to lead the experimenters to conclude that a sharp

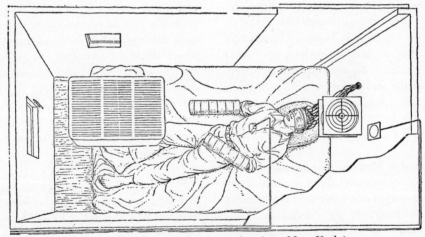

(Copyright 1957 by *Scientific American*, New York.)

In a series of experiments at McGill University, Heron, Doane, and Scott confined themselves (and others) to severely reduced stimulation for several days at a time. The person lay on a bed in a small soundproof cubicle, 24 hours per day, sitting up to eat meals, and being released only to go to the toilet. The room was always lighted. He wore plastic goggles that prevented pattern vision. Touch stimulation was limited by wearing cotton gloves and cardboard cuffs.

reduction in sensory stimulation "can cause disorganization of brain function similar to, and in some respects as great as, that produced by drugs or lesions."

Varied stimulation is necessary for the normal working of the human brain.

HERON, W., DOANE, B. K., and SCOTT, T. H. 1956. Visual disturbances after prolonged perceptual isolation. *Canad. J. Psychol., 10,* 13–18.
LILLY, J. C. 1956. Mental effects of reduction of ordinary levels of physical stimuli on intact healthy persons. *Psychiat. Resch. Repts., 5,* 1–9.

of the major themes of this book: most of man's behavior is integrated behavior.

Adaptive Behavior

Man, then, must find food, shelter, and safety, and must satisfy a myriad of other needs and aspirations. To do this, he must solve problems, learn, remember, think, and acquire skills. To our study of the many worlds of man still another is added—a world inviting him, and requiring him to adapt to it, manipulate it, change it, and create in it.

The third section of the book is concerned with an examination of such adaptive behavior. We find that we cannot understand problem-solving without making extensive use of the perceptual and motivational principles. As we describe adaptive behavior and examine the conditions under which it proceeds, we see that problem-solving is initiated in response to felt needs, is guided by perceptions, and often ends in an intense emotional experience. The relationship between emotion, motivation, and adaptive behavior is both intimate and complex. Indeed it appears that the very process of problem-solving is itself an expression of a basic motive. We frequently behave as if the solution of a problem were a reward in itself. And it even appears that some lower animals share this motive with man. (For an experimental demonstration of this, see Box 3.)

BOX 3

Monkeys Solve a Problem for Its Own Sake

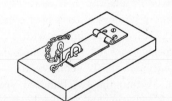

Harlow at the University of Wisconsin has shown that even for monkeys the solution of a problem may carry its own reward. He used the puzzle shown in the figure. The pin and hook had to be opened in that order before the hasp could be raised.

In one experiment 4 rhesus monkeys, Group A, had the assembled puzzle in their home cages for 12 days. Four Group B animals also had the puzzle, but the pin and hook were unassembled and the hasp was raised. They could become familiar with the already-opened puzzle, but there was nothing to solve. From time to time the puzzles in the A cages were checked, and reassembled if they had been opened. On days 13 and 14 all 8 monkeys were given the assembled puzzle for five 5-minute periods.

In these tests the A monkeys opened the puzzle 31 times, averaging less than 30 seconds per solution. The B monkeys opened the puzzle only 4 times, and the *best* score was 60 seconds. The A monkeys had learned to solve the puzzle during the first 12 days and had learned this *without any reward from the experimenter*.

The A monkeys were then given additional tests one at a time. While the animal watched, a raisin was placed in a box, and the assembled puzzle was attached to the box so as to lock it. Then the monkey was released. Now their failures increased strikingly! And a new *kind* of error appeared. In the previous tests without reward the monkeys *never* touched the hasp first; with the food reward, they *always* erred by attacking (literally) the hasp first. The monkeys, when they had the raisin "in mind," could not restrain themselves from a direct attack.

"Personal involvement" and a highly desired reward may sometimes be bad for problem-solving!

HARLOW, H. 1950. Learning motivated by a manipulation drive. *J. exp. Psychol., 40,* 228–34.

Adaptive behavior encompasses an overwhelming variety of different kinds of problems: discovering the cure for cancer, memorizing a list of history dates, designing a bridge, learning the route from home to school, investigating the neurological basis of thought, driving a car, learning to read and write, recalling one's exact whereabouts at 10:00 P.M. on Friday, September 17.

Some of this adaptive behavior can be called "creative problem-solving"; some, "learning."

Creative Problem-Solving. Creative problem-solving refers to adaptive behavior in which something new and original is produced by the person as he attempts to cope with the problems facing him. We shall study, for example, how man goes about the business of *explaining* the events he sees about him, *predicting* events to come, and *inventing* or creating objects of utilitarian and aesthetic value. Experimental work in psychology is beginning to give us a useful set of principles that help us to understand these creative aspects of behavior. We find that there seem to be three basic determinants of creative problem-solving: (1) the nature of the problem, the circumstances under which the problem is presented, and the resulting stimulus-pattern that confronts the person; (2) the nature of the person's previously acquired knowledge (some of which, "badly" acquired, can inhibit creativity); and (3) the personality structure of the problem solver. The laboratory findings on these determinants point to ways of improving our own efforts at creative problem-solving.

Learning. But not all adaptive behavior involves being creative. Many of the problems to be solved in our daily living require nothing more than *re*producing what we have learned to do in the past. We are here dealing with "learning," with such vi-

tally important processes as habit formation, memorizing, skill acquisition, etc. The problem of language and speech is of special interest, and we devote a considerable part of our discussion to the acquisition of language —the characteristic that differentiates man most clearly from all other creatures.

Here again we find many useful descriptive principles that aid in our understanding of man's adaptive behavior, as well as providing us with helpful guides for improving our own learning. The principles of learning, in terms of basic determinants, are found to be quite similar to the principles of creative problem-solving. For "learning" and "creative problem-solving" are not two sharply differentiated kinds of adaptive behavior, but shade into each other.

Physiology. We end this section of the book with an examination of the physiological basis of adaptive behavior. The search for the physiological basis of problem-solving and learning, beginning with the fantastic speculations of the phrenologists, has concentrated fairly consistently on the brain. Within the last hundred years systematic experimental studies have accumulated extensive data that are beginning to "add up" to an interesting and illuminating story of the relation of the "mind" to the brain. Modern experimental methods have made possible the study of the effects of brain destruction on the adaptive behavior of animals, the direct observation of the brains of human surgical patients, the recording of "brain waves" from intact men and animals, etc. But we find that the brain by itself, apart from the rest of the nervous system, is not enough to account for adaptive behavior. The nervous system, by itself, apart from the musculature, is not enough either—for it appears that we "think" with our muscles as well as with our brain. Just as we find that in studying adaptive *behavior* we have to synthesize perception, motivation, and action, so we find that in studying the *physiology* of adaptive behavior we cannot restrict our search to the brain alone. All biological phenomena show integration, but nowhere is this more profoundly true than in the adaptive behavior of living organisms.

The Individual

In the first three sections we shall study man-the-perceiver, man-the-needful, and man-the-problem-solver. But this tripartite division is, as we said in the beginning, merely one of convenience. There is in truth but one individual—who perceives *and* strives *and* thinks. In the final section of the book we shall turn our attention to man-the-individual.

The first notable thing about the individual is that he is *unique*. His pattern of perceptions, motives, emotions, and adaptive behavior is like no one else's. And the most notable thing about a collection of individuals is the compelling fact of individual differences.

Measurement. In order to make a scientific study of the extent and causes of individual differences among men, we must be able to *measure* these individual differences. And the study of statistics permits us to acquire the techniques for such measurement. We shall examine the rationale of some of the fundamental statistical methods, such as those involved in determining averages, variability of scores within a group, and the degree of relationship among different measurements.

As we study the theory and techniques of measurement, we find that we can never measure anything with perfect accuracy— whether it is the length of a table, the personality of a patient in a mental hospital, or the political attitudes of a group of voters.

However we also discover that although the values we obtain from our measurements are only estimates or approximations to the truth, nevertheless we can state the degree of *probability* that our estimates are within some specified distance from the truth. And we thus learn why the scientist must be content with "probable truth" rather than with absolute truth.

The Abilities of Man. Having learned how to measure individual differences among men (and the caution with which all measurements must be regarded), we turn to the study of the facts and theories concerning such differences. Here we must start even before birth, with the heredity of the individual. We shall find that the reproductive system of man guarantees that, except in the case of "identical twins," no two human beings can ever be genetically the same in all respects. Widespread individual differences are thus almost a genetic certainty.

Men differ in many kinds of abilities— such as mechanical, musical, and artistic. All of these have been measured, but perhaps the most important characteristic in which men differ is *intelligence*. We will find that while much progress has been made in the *measurement* of intelligence, we are still not certain about many basic questions regarding intelligence. Is it a single capacity of the person, or is it a cluster or grouping of many different capacities? Is intellectual ability mainly inherited, or is it mainly acquired through training and education after birth?

The distribution of intelligence varies widely from the feeble-minded to the genius. There are numerous studies seeking to determine whether different *groups* or *kinds* of people are more intelligent than others. Thus, differences in intelligence among different racial and national groups, and between the sexes have been investigated. The evidence suggests that, as measured by current intelligence tests, there are consistent differences among such groups in *average* intelligence. But we shall also see that the *interpretation* of these differences is very difficult. At the present time we can only conclude that these differences are due both to hereditary and biological differences and to differences of opportunity and environment among the groups tested.

Growth and Development. The child is father of the man. To understand how the unique personality that is man comes into being we shall continue our study with the growth and development of the child.

Since the behavior of the organism is always limited and directed by its anatomy and physiology, the psychologist's study of the *behavior* of children has gone hand in hand with his study of the growth of the child's *body*. Out of these studies have come several developmental principles relating function (behavior) to structure. These principles tell the story of the development of the human being as a story of integrated changes in structure and function. And we find that in general it is also a story of gradual, systematic unfolding of more and more complex systems. However, adolescence, with its culmination in sexual maturity, seems to represent a sort of "turning point" in this otherwise smooth developmental sequence. We shall examine some of the specific problems involved at this period, with special attention to parent-child relationships.

Personality. Looking at the adult, we shall see again that there are numerous measurable *patterns* of individuality or personality. In trying to account for these different patterns, many *theories* of personality have been developed. In reviewing some of the major ones, we shall find that the chief principles of perception, motivation, and learning, together with the principles of growth and development of the child, are represented to some degree in each one of the theories of personality. It is here that we begin to see that a complete theory of personality will have to encompass all the principles of perception, motivation, and adaptive behavior.

One of the major questions discussed by all theories of personality is how the person handles emotional and motivational conflicts. Different people meet internal conflict in different ways, and it will become clear that the methods of "defensive reaction" adopted by a person are consistent with his over-all personality. We shall also examine the more extreme incapacitating consequences of conflict as found in neuroses and psychoses. This will help us to assess some of the problems of mental health and the treatment of mental disease.

The Individual in Society. From the moment of birth man is surrounded by other people, and thus it is clear that his social environment helps shape his development. Indeed many of the person's problems of adjustment come from his relations to his society. But society is not something independent of the individual, a huge "impersonal" force that pushes man around. Society and its rules and regulations are human products—created by man and changeable by him. Thus we end this book with a look at the individual in society.

An important factor in the person's social functioning is his "social perception," that is, how he perceives other people and groups, how he perceives such social institutions as the church, the state, and the economic structure and such social events as political campaigns, mob action, war, and religious services. We shall find that the principles of the perception of physical stimuli (studied in the first section of the book) enable us to understand many of the more complex phenomena of "social perception."

We shall also find that how a person perceives another person helps to determine how he will feel about him; and, conversely, how a person feels about another will help to determine how he perceives him. This cause-and-effect circle helps us to understand the persistence of racial, national, and religious prejudice. Prejudice toward others is a complex phenomenon. It involves factors of motivation, emotion, adaptive behavior, and personality patterning as well as perceptual factors.

Finally, we shall examine some of the problems the person faces as a member in good standing of a social group—a family, club, school, or nation. The individual is frequently confronted with a difficult problem when he seeks to preserve his personal integrity and independence, while also maintaining his prescribed duties, functions, responsibilities, and loyalties to his group. This is but one aspect of a major problem, perhaps one of the central questions toward which the study of man is directed: Since man is a social animal and cannot live alone, how can the liberty of the individual be maximized and the creativity of the person released *through his relationship with his society?* An understanding of the elements of psychology, insofar as they are helpful in understanding the behavior of man, provides the beginnings of an answer to this question—perhaps the crucial question of our time.

Part One

PERCEPTION

CHAPTER II

The Worlds We Perceive

How the person behaves depends to a large extent on how he perceives the world about him. It is for this reason that many psychologists believe that the study of perception is the beginning of the understanding of man.

The study of perception—what and how man sees, hears, smells, and feels—is an ancient and honorable part of scientific inquiry. It has attracted the attention of physicists, physiologists, neurologists, and psychologists. Each of these groups has had much to contribute to our understanding of perceptual phenomena, and in the succeeding chapters of this section we shall examine their contributions. However, before looking at the evidence from the experimental laboratories in any detail, we must begin our study of perception with a careful description of what people do see, hear, smell, and feel.

Our first step, in other words, is to describe our worlds *as we perceive them*. This means describing the most familiar thing possible to each person—his own world of immediate experience. Because it is so familiar, the description may first seem stale and commonplace. Yet we will soon find, as we take a fresh look at our own worlds and compare them with other people's descriptions of theirs, that we are in for some surprises. Things that we have long taken for granted will appear in a new light, the "obvious explanation" will no longer do, and unexpected questions will be raised. This is but the first step toward the study of perception. It should be clear that this kind of description of one's immediate experience (technically known as *phenomenology*) does not give us an explanation, but serves only as a starting point for an investigation.

We will look first at the "simplest" kind of perception, the perception of physical objects and events. As we do so, we will soon see why the study of perception raises so many basic questions for our understanding of human behavior, and why it has aroused the imagination and wonder of many scientists.

Space and Objects

The first striking thing we notice about our worlds is their *spatial* character. We humans live in a three-dimensional space and find it hard to imagine a world without this spatial character. In our very biological make-up we are basically spatial animals. Our eyes and ears are adapted to the task of bringing us information about *distant* parts of our physical environment; for this reason they are often referred to as "distance receptors." We are remarkably *mobile* animals, moving about quite freely in space. Our brains appear to have the "natural" tendency to construct space, even on the basis of stimulation that is itself not fully spatial. Many patterns of visual stimuli falling on the *flat, two-dimensional* retinas of our eyes result somehow in our experiencing three-dimensional space, that is, depth or distance.

Our world is spatial, but space without content is perceptually meaningless. As we look about us, we see that our space is inhabited by *objects* that are located somewhere in space, are separated from their surroundings, and possess various perceptual properties that distinguish them from other objects. Some of these perceptual properties are simple, e.g., size, shape, texture, color; others are complex.

Size. Objects differ in perceived size from a minuscule, barely perceptible grain of dust, to objects that cover all of the visual field. *A striking fact about perceived size of an object is that it does not depend solely upon the size of the image it casts on the retina of the eye.* A man standing ten feet away looks approximately the same height as when standing twenty feet away, even though the first image on the eye is *twice* the physical size of the second. (See Fig. 1.) The brain somehow "takes account"

of the different distances and preserves the *size constancy* of the object.

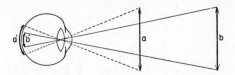

FIG. 1. The diagram shows that two objects of the same size cast retinal images inversely proportional in size to their distances from the eye, a′ being exactly twice b′.

Conversely, as we shall see later when we discuss the experimental investigation of size perception, the same object at a *fixed* distance will not always be perceived as of the *same* size. Different surroundings may make the equal objects look quite different in size, as demonstrated in Figure 2.

Shape. Objects may be of fairly simple shapes—a ball, a book—or of more complex shapes—a typewriter, a tree, a human figure. There are almost limitless dimensions along which perceived shapes may be classified, e.g., circularity, angularity, elongation, symmetry, complexity, etc. And of a single "species" of shape, for instance a triangular shape, there can be any number of variations—there can be an infinite number of geometrically different individual triangles, all of which we recognize as "triangles" while seeing differences among them. And there can be almost endless subtler variations of shape within a single common theme, as witness the eternal preoccupation of painters with the female nude.

Just as we have seen above that there is size constancy in that identical objects at different distances from the observer may look the same size, so there is *shape constancy*, in that an object may look the same shape even when the angle from which it is viewed changes radically. The dinner plates on the table appear round to all the diners, despite the fact that owing to the

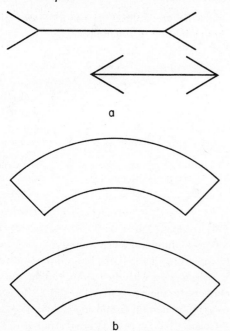

a

b

FIG. 2. Various illusions of size. In *a*, the classical Müller-Lyer illusion, two equal lines appear unequal because of the surrounding arrowheads; in *b*, the lower figure appears larger than the upper figure although both are the same size; in *c*, the three posts are all the same height; in *d*, the two center circles are equal.

level at which they are seated, the images of the plates on the retinas of their eyes are not circles but ellipses of various degrees of fatness and thinness. Somehow the brain "takes account" of the direction of viewing.

But here again, as in the perception of size, constancy is not always the rule. Look at the slightly lopsided circular figure in Figure 3, as it lies on the background of striped lines. You may be surprised to discover, if you make the test, that it is actually a perfect geometric circle. Perceived shape, like perceived size, is influenced by its immediate surroundings.

Texture. Objects also differ perceptually in their textures. Their surfaces may appear rough or smooth, even or uneven, coarse or fine. They may be perceived as shiny,

scratchy, slippery, scaly, silky. As we shall presently note, associated closely with textures are a host of more complex properties—expressive and aesthetic—and because of this the endless permutations and combinations of textural qualities help to provide a livelihood for the clothes designer, the interior decorator, the artist, and others.

Color. The world of color is almost a world in itself. Objects vary in *brightness*, from the whitest snow in full sunlight to the blackest velvet in darkness; they vary in *hue*—red, green, yellow, blue, violet, and all the intermediate shades; they vary in *satu-*

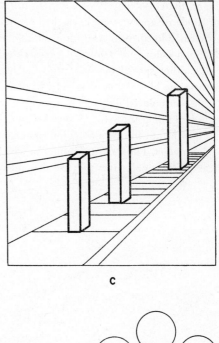

c

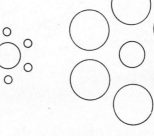

d

ration, from the most washed-out, dilute color to the most intensely concentrated color.

These "standard" three dimensions of color are familiar to everyone, but they are far from sufficient for telling the whole story. A fresh look at the colors around us will reveal other color qualities that relate to the "mode of appearance." All reds of the same hue, brightness, and saturation do not look alike. Under usual conditions of viewing, the colors of objects appear to be relatively solid, opaque, and localized at or on the object's surface. Such colors are known as *surface colors.* When viewed through an aperture that eliminates the contours of the object, the color may have a clearly different mode of appearance, being less opaque, less clearly localized, more filmy in character. Such colors are known as *film colors.* Under other special circumstances, such as viewing the blue sky or a colored haze or a translucent colored liquid, the color appears as though filling the whole space, being neither opaque nor filmy. Such colors are called *volume colors.* The striking manner in which these different color qualities are dependent

upon the precise conditions of viewing is shown in Box 4, where the *same* physical color may be made to appear successively as volume color, film color, and surface color.

Another quality of some colors is that they are *luminous.* A red stoplight is luminous; it glows, appears to give off light, in a manner entirely different from a painted red surface. Our first inclination is to explain this luminous appearance as due to the physical act of light emission. That is, we say it looks luminous because it *is* luminous, as in light bulbs, phosphorescence of the sea, etc. But this explanation will not do. Some objects look luminous even though they themselves do not emit light, but simply *reflect* it, as is the case with the moon at night. And, conversely, the moon may *fail* to look luminous under certain circumstances. See Box 5.

COLOR CONSTANCY. We have noted that the color appearance of an object may widely vary, depending upon its surroundings. But the converse phenomenon of *color constancy* (analogous to size and shape constancies) is also found. A piece of coal in bright sunlight will still appear black; a patch of snow in shadow will still appear white.

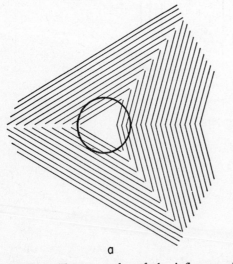

a   b

FIG. 3. Two examples of the influence of surroundings on perceived shape: in *a*, the fig-ure lying on the striped background is an exact circle; in *b* the two inside arcs are identical.

Yet the actual amount of light being reflected from the surface of the coal may be *greater* than that from the snow. Somehow in our perceptions we take account of the conditions of illumination. The color of an object may look about the same through a remarkably wide range of illumination conditions.

Smells, Tastes, Feels, and Sounds. The perceptual properties we have so far mentioned are largely visual in character; these naturally occur to us first, for we are primarily "visual animals." But the objects we perceive have important attributes pertaining to the other senses.

Objects *smell* fragrant or spicy or acrid or pinelike or rotten; or they may be per-

---

BOX 4

How to Change the Color of the Sky

First, look at the deep blue sky in the late afternoon with your back to the sun, observing the quality of the blue color. Then take a piece of white cardboard with a small hole cut in it and look at the same sky through the hole, holding the card so that it is in *shadow*. Finally, hold the card so that *bright sunlight* falls on it and look again at the sky through the hole.

You will note that though the sky color is the same blue hue under these three conditions of viewing, the *quality* of the color is entirely different, varying from "volume" color to "film" color to "surface" color, as a function of the immediate visual surroundings of the patch of sky observed.

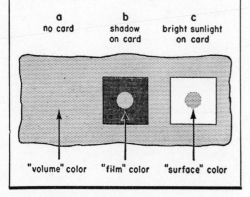

| a | b | c |
| no card | shadow on card | bright sunlight on card |

"volume" color   "film" color   "surface" color

BOX 5

What Makes Moonshine?

Whether an object is perceived as luminous or not depends upon the *relative brightness* of the object and of its immediate surroundings.

The moon looks luminous at night against the dark sky. The *same moon of identical brightness* when viewed against the bright daylight sky appears to be nonluminous and an opaque white in color.

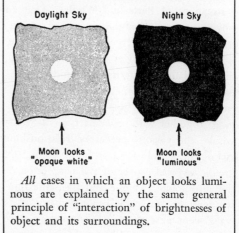

Daylight Sky   Night Sky

Moon looks "opaque white"   Moon looks "luminous"

All cases in which an object looks luminous are explained by the same general principle of "interaction" of brightnesses of object and its surroundings.

Such color constancy is found not only for the brightness of the object, but also for its hue. But constancy is by no means universal or perfect. In Chapter 6 experimental findings will be given that help to explain why constancy exists at some times and not at others.

ceived as odorless. Objects may *taste* sweet or bitter or sour or salty, or like blends of these.

Objects *feel* various ways to us when we touch and handle them. There are many textures, as we described above; also there are properties of lightness or heaviness, warmth or coldness, hardness or softness, brittleness or elasticity, etc., and all degrees and combinations of these.

Objects have different *sounds*. The electric fan whirs, the siren shrieks, the clock ticks, the fire crackles. Sounds vary in several basic dimensions, the most familiar being loudness, pitch, and timbre. Loudness may range from the pin drop to the atomic blast; pitch from that of the bass drum to the flute's tweet; timbre, from the pure tone of the tuning fork to the rich mixture of overtones in a chord of a string quartet.

We often perceive the quality of one object in comparison with similar qualities of other objects; this apple is redder than that one, this chair is smaller than that, this pitch is higher than that. Even lower animals seem to be capable of the perception of relations, as illustrated in *transposition* experiments (see Box 6).

Relations of Parts and Wholes. That an object is perceived as an object at all demonstrates that we perceive relations. The whole object is seen as an organized entity, distinguishable from its surroundings, because its parts are somehow perceptually related to form the whole. Certain parts "belong" together with other parts to make the whole; the various perceived relationships among the wheels, fenders, hood, body, top, are an essential aspect of the perception of the automobile. At one and the same time we perceive the whole car and many of its constituent parts. Our attention may shift around, of course, and in so doing certain parts may be perceptually more outstanding than others; or our attention may even become so narrowly focused on a single part that the perception of other parts and of the car as a whole may momentarily disappear.

The particular manner in which the parts are perceived in relation to one another in forming the whole is technically referred to as the perceived *structure* of the object. Such perceived structure is frequently in close correspondence with the actual physical structure of the environment. As you look at your desk, you may see a pencil, a paper clip, and a book lying side by side on the blotter. You see each as separate from the others. Its parts belong to it and not to the other objects; the eraser of the pencil touches the book, but you do not see it as part of the book but as part of the pencil.

BOX 6

Experiments in Transposition

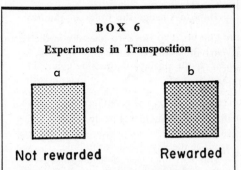

a   b

Not rewarded   **Rewarded**

The subject is taught to choose the medium gray card (b) in preference to the light gray card (a) by regularly finding a reward behind (b). The cards are randomly switched in position so that he cannot learn simply to choose right or left. What happens when card (b) is presented for the first time with a new card (c), a *darker* gray?

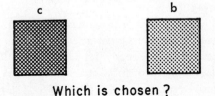

c   b

Which is chosen ?

Card (c) is chosen. Apparently the subject has learned to choose the card that is *relatively* the darker—that is, (b) over (a). Thus, when (b) and (c) are presented, (c) is chosen because it is darker than (b), *even though* (b) has been regularly rewarded. The brightness relationship is "transposed" along the scale of different grays.

Studies giving essentially similar results have been made with chickens, rats, monkeys, children, and with other dimensions, such as size and shape.

On the other hand, the perceived structure of an object may *not* correspond with the actual structure of the physical environment. We may see "objects" that are not there. Everyone has had the experience of lying in a darkened room and seeing a frightening intruder in silhouette, only to discover that this perceived "object" was actually produced through the accidental grouping of the arm of a chair, the jamb of a door, and the sleeve of a coat hanging on the wall.

Every object is perceived to have parts, and the object itself may also be perceived as part of a still larger whole. These part-whole relations may extend indefinitely in both directions: parts may be further differentiated into perceived subparts; wholes may be further grouped into larger perceived wholes.

In later chapters we will examine the question of how perception of the structure of objects comes about, and why the perception sometimes coincides with and at other times violates the nature of the physical structure.

By Way of Summary. Our world is a spatial world. It contains various objects, which are perceived in terms of simple visual attributes, such as size, shape, texture, and color, and attributes of odor, taste, feel, and sound. These perceptual attributes do not necessarily correspond with the *physical* dimensions and properties of the object. The perceived attributes of a given object may vary widely, depending upon the entire stimulus context in which they occur. Visual illusions of size and of shape are dramatic examples of this.

Objects are not perceived in isolation but in relation to other objects. And the very perception of an object depends itself in part upon seeing certain relations among the parts that form the whole; thus the perceived *structure* of an object is the manner in which the parts combine to make up the whole. The perceived structure may differ widely from the actual physical structure of the environment.

Dynamic Properties: Movement and Change

Our "static" description of the perceived world up to this point has ignored Heraclitus' cry, "Flux, flux, all is flux!" for we have said nothing, yet about our perception of movement and change of objects and events.

Movement. In our world things move, and they move in different directions, at different speeds, with different accelerations, and in various manners—smoothly, jerkily, rhythmically. We may see the object moving, or may simply hear it, as when a car goes by outside on the street, or feel it, as when a spider runs across one's arm.

The physical conditions arousing the perception of movement can be specified in considerable detail, as we shall see in later chapters. Here we need only emphasize that although sometimes the basis of the perceived movement is actual physical movement in the environment (the car actually drives by, the spider actually runs on one's skin), in other instances perceived movement occurs for other reasons. For instance, the moon is often seen as moving rapidly behind the clouds, yet we know that the moon is at rest and it is the clouds that are actually moving. When the train stops after a person has been staring out at the moving landscape for a time, he sees the landscape as moving slowly forward, and it is such a compelling illusion of movement that he may believe that the train is actually slowly sliding backward. The moving pictures "move" as convincingly as anyone could desire, yet they consist of nothing more than a rapid succession of still pictures.

Change. Movement is one form of change, and change is a significant perceptual attribute of our world. We may perceive change in location of the object, or change in its structure, or change in its various qualities of size, shape, color, and sound. Usually we can readily identify the nature of the perceived change: the room is suddenly plunged into darkness, the balloon expands, the glass shatters into pieces. But sometimes we are aware of change without being able to specify its concrete nature. A girl we know looks "different" to us now, her appearance has changed; at first we cannot tell why and only later do we realize that her "hairdo" is new.

These are examples of perceived change arising from real change in the environment. But there may be striking cases of perceived change *without* corresponding physical change. Look steadily at the center of Figure 4. At first you may see a dotted Maltese

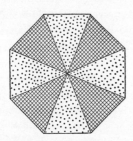

FIG. 4. Keep your eyes steadily fixed on the center of the figure and note the fluctuations between cross and propeller. (After Boring, Langfeld, and Weld, 1948.)

cross lying on a crosshatched background; after a while a marked change suddenly occurs, and now you see a propellerlike cross, and what was previously the "figure" is now the background. With continued inspection the original way of seeing it will reappear, and such fluctuation of this ambiguous object will persist as long as you look at it. No change whatsoever has taken place in the physical stimulus; the basis of the perceived change lies entirely in the functioning of the nervous system.

Objects may undergo pronounced perceptual changes without losing their *identities* as the same objects. In fact, it is just this retention of identity that makes the perception of change possible, for change is a property involving a comparison between what the object *was* and what the same object now *is*.

This points to a distinction between *perception of change* and *change of perception*. It is the former about which we have been talking; the change itself is the experienced fact. The latter refers to something quite different, namely, the case in which the person's perception has changed but he does not perceive the change. (Box 7 provides a surprising demonstration of this.)

Changes in perception, we shall see, are among the most central things that happen in the process of learning, in productive thinking, in the shaping of attitudes and values, in the development of one's personality.

Time. Time is a crucial dimension of our perceived worlds. The qualities of objects and events are often perceived in relation to the ever-present background of time. The time background is often remote and of little or no perceptual consequence; at other times it is more prominent and it may even be the most outstanding feature of the situation.

We perceive time in two quite different ways, as background and as "figure." In the former, time serves as a dimension in terms of which events can be organized together. Tap with your pencil, making successive pairs of taps with very short intervals between the two taps of each pair and with somewhat longer intervals between the pairs. You will perceive a *structuring* of successive sounds, a pattern of pairs sepa-

---

BOX 7

Unnoticed Change in Perception

Using the yellow rectangle shown in Color Plate I, immediately preceding page 1, you can demonstrate for yourself a convincing instance of a change in perception that occurs without your awareness. Take a piece of gray paper and place it over the right half of the yellow rectangle so that the fixation mark is just visible.

Then stare steadily right at the fixation mark, being *careful not to shift your eyes from it,* for a period of one minute. At the end of the minute remove the gray cover from the yellow rectangle, *while continuing without interruption to look at the fixation mark.*

If you are like most people, you will have observed when the cover is removed that the yellow on the left side appears dilute and "washed out" compared with the yellow on the right. What has happened is that during the continuous look at the left side, the perceived color slowly lost its original saturation. Yet most people *are not at all aware of this gradual change as it occurs,* and only realize what a pronounced change has occurred when they see the washed-out yellow beside the unaffected bright yellow on the right after the cover is removed. Perception can change without our perceiving the change!

The *reason* for the gradual dilution of the color with continued exposure will be discussed in Chapter 7, p. 166.

---

rated by intervals, quite analogous to the perception of pairs of dots laid out spatially on a piece of paper.

If you greatly lengthen the interval between the taps, making it say ten seconds, a quite different phenomenon occurs. The structural connection between the taps is weakened; we find ourselves waiting for the next tap and in so doing become aware of the passage or flow of *time.*

This time flow has perceived properties of its own, especially of fastness or slowness of flow: "time flies," "time drags,"

"time stands still." And it may involve impressions of "pressure" or "remorselessness," which are examples of the kinds of expressive qualities of our perceived worlds which will be discussed later.

Perceived time is not the same as real or chronological ("clock") time. The same interval of actual clock time may be perceived as long or short in duration, as slow or fast in flow, depending upon other aspects of the whole situation. To the condemned man the hour before execution may seem to pass like a flash; to the man in a sinking boat the hour before rescue may seem interminable. Facts bearing on the relation of perceived to real time, and the conditions under which we may achieve highly accurate time judgments, will be discussed in Chapter 6.

Quite beyond the perception of time intervals and time flow in our immediate physical environment, there are problems of the much longer sweeps of time, in the past and future, as we look backward and forward in our lives, or even in larger spans of historical time. In later chapters on motivation and on personality we shall deal with these important problems of "time perspective."

Perception of Physical Events

Our description of the perceived world has dealt mainly with objects and relations among objects. This is an appropriate place to look at the perception of physical *events,* for movement and change are inherent aspects of the perception of events. Happenings—movements and changes—constitute events.

Structure of Events. Perceived events, like objects, have structure and location in space and time. Take the following simple example of how we perceive a physical event. We stand in the forest beside a pond. Suddenly the wind begins to blow, and as it blows harder and harder the branch of a tree overhanging the pond begins to sway back and forth. Some leaves come loose and fall into the water, where they float. Then a small twig breaks off its branch and plummets into the water, which splashes, sending a series of concentric ripples out to the edges of the pond. The ripples carry the bobbing leaves up and down as they go. The ripples subside, the surface of the pond smooths out, the wind ceases, and the event is over.

We see that this whole episodic event has a beginning and an end; and it has a structure, in the sense that we see one set of things happening, followed by another set, which is in turn followed by others, etc. Each of the parts of the whole event has its distinctive perceived qualities—such as the whine of the wind and its feel on the face; the pattern of sway of the branches; the size, shape, and speed of the ripples.

As in the case of physical objects, parts of the whole event can often be perceptually differentiated into still smaller subparts; thus we observe the particular flutter of a single leaf on the branch. And conversely, the event we described may be perceived as only part of a still larger event; for instance, it may be merely the first part of a day-long storm that violently agitates the whole forest.

The parts of events are related in specific ways to one another; this constitutes the perceived structure of the event. The twig breaks off and drops *before* the splash of the water, not the reverse. Events are quite typically perceived as having this kind of "logical" structure, in that one happening leads to another in a way that appears "sensible" and "fitting."

There are, to be sure, many perceived events without this "logical" appearance. Sometimes we see a variety of things happening close together in time and in space which do not seem to "make sense"; one thing does not appear to connect in an orderly fashion with another. It is such disarrayed events that we may perceive as sheer "confusion" and chaos. This does not necessarily mean, of course, that the actual physical event is lacking in regularity and order; it simply means that the person fails, for whatever reason, to *perceive* it as having any form of regularity and order. Conversely, perceiving an event as having a "logical" structure is no guarantee that the actual event has it. The continued good health of gambling houses attests to this; the *purely random* sequence of winning numbers in a session of roulette will often be perceived by the confirmed better who plays by an elaborate "system" as having some form of regularity and predictable order. And as we shall see later in connection with the problem of mental disease, a paranoid person suffering delusions of persecution may construct an elaborate "logical" perception of a threatening event that is, in fact, based entirely upon an accidental grouping of unrelated happenings.

Properly speaking, of course, there is no real physical event, merely a continuous flow of physical happenings. That we do tend to *perceive* such a sequence of physical happenings as a unified *event*, an episode with a beginning and an end, depends on the fact that certain physical happenings serve as distinguishing *landmarks*. What we take to be the landmarks depends both on the actual decisive changes in physical stimulus that make certain features "stand out" in our perception and on our "mental set," which disposes us to see particular things as important. When we discuss the principles of perceptual organization (see Chap. 5), we will see some of the determinants of how we break up the continuous stream of physical happenings into perceived events.

The perception of events—how out of a

continuous stream of physical happenings we perceive a unified event—is an extremely important problem. A sequence of physical happenings may be variously organized into events by different people, and this may make for a radical difference in their reactions to the physical happenings. For example, Mr. Anyman at night perceives the sound of a tree against the house followed by a footfall on the porch as a unified event in which a burglar is trying to get into the house. Mrs. Anyman perceives the same two happenings as parts of two entirely separate events—the wind blowing the tree, the neighbor coming to visit.

Music as an Event. Listening to a piece of *music* is a particularly effective example of perception of a physical event. Music, consisting of a pattern of sounds spread out in time, has a definite structure; it has a beginning and an end, it is made up of parts—movements, melodies, solo passages, etc.—and of sub-parts—notes, chords, intervals, etc. The parts are organically related to one another; this part leads to that part and may to a considerable degree be perceived as "requiring" it. Thus a false note may be immediately perceived as wrong. In the music there is movement and change—the melody traces a path, the sound swells and diminishes, rhythms vary.

We have already noted that physical events may be perceived as not "making sense," as confused and chaotic; to some untutored ears extreme examples of modern music may be heard as chaotic, as made up of unrelated parts without discernible structure, in a word, as *noise*.

Expressive and Affective Properties

As we have described it so far, the world we perceive, despite the sizes, shapes, colors, sounds, textures, movements, and changes, seems somewhat "flat." What are missing are the rich expressive attributes of things which provide the real "life" of our experienced worlds. To remedy this serious omission, let us look again at the way we perceive objects and events, this time broadening our description to include more complex and subtle properties.

A certain red color, for instance, may be experienced as more than of a given hue, brightness, and saturation; it may also be seen as "warm," "lively," "advancing." A certain blue may be seen as "cold" and "receding." An elm tree may be perceived as "graceful," an oak as "sturdy." The material of one coat is a checked pattern that looks "jumpy"; another pattern looks "quiet."

In the perception of music, as a case par excellence, such expressive and affective properties are irresistible. One of the most immediate things we perceive in a musical piece is whether it is "plaintive," "gay," "somber," or "powerful," or a complex combination of these and numerous other qualities. The major and minor modes (or "moods") have strikingly different qualities for us, depending entirely upon the particular pattern of notes comprising each scale.

Qualities such as the above are often referred to technically as *physiognomic properties*, the term being derived from the expressive qualities exhibited on the face—the physiognomy—of a person. It is to be emphasized that such perceptual properties—e.g., "gracefulness" of the elm tree—are seen immediately *there* in the object just as much as size and shape are.

There may often be close agreement among perceivers as to the specific physiognomic properties they see in the object. Look at the two drawings in Figure 5. One is named "takete," the other "maluma." Decide which you think is which before reading the legend below the figure.

Aesthetic Qualities. Perceived properties of beauty and ugliness are especially noteworthy among these expressive qualities. The person perceives many objects in his surroundings as beautiful or as ugly, and the aesthetic quality is apprehended by him as something *directly possessed by the object*, not as something he subjectively adds. He looks at a strikingly beautiful woman and in describing her promptly mentions her beauty, perhaps before he mentions her height, coloring, and other simple physical attributes. Only by assuming a deliberate, "hard-boiled," analytical attitude in viewing her may he partly succeed in suppressing her beauty.

He may indeed be prepared to grant that by some other "benighted" person she may not be seen as beautiful, especially by someone from a culture other than his own which stresses different criteria of beauty. But this does not in the least make her look less beautiful to him.

Power Qualities. Objects are perceived as doing things or having the power to do things to other objects. One object is seen as "striking" another, or as "chasing" or "leading" another, or as "attracting" or "threatening" another. Such perceived aspects are referred to as *power qualities*. For the perceiver they are an inalienable part of the immediate appearance of a thing, not simply an intellectual interpretation that he adds. The violent sea pounding heavily at the small boat is immediately perceived as having such "power qualities." So is the gigantic black cloud that hangs "threateningly" over the hilltop.

Perception of Causality. A billiard ball rolls across the table and strikes a second ball, which in turn moves. In observing this event, we perceive the first ball as "causing" the movement of the second; we do not see a mere sequence of neutral, unrelated events. Such perceived "causality" is the most important of power qualities, entering into our perceptions of virtually every event. Complex events may be perceived as organized primarily in terms of "this caused that."

Perceived "causality" may not faithfully mirror *real* causation. Many philosophers have denied the logical existence of causation altogether, asserting that things are merely "correlated" with other things, not "caused" by them. But this logical view does not seem to affect the way we perceive phenomena; we may agree that there is no such thing as "causation," but things still *look* to us as though they cause other things to happen.

FIG. 5. When told that one of the above figures is named "takete" and the other "maluma" almost everyone chooses "maluma" for the upper figure and "takete" for the lower. The consistency among people in pairing these drawings and words, both of which are unfamiliar and meaningless, argues that the visual appearance of the figures and the sounds of the words share certain common physiognomic properties. (From Köhler, W. 1947. *Gestalt Psychology*, rev. ed. New York: Liveright. Figures reproduced by permission of Liveright Publishing Corp. Copyright R 1956 by Liveright Corp.)

How such perceptions come about will be explained in later chapters, where it will be shown that whether or not "causality" is perceived in a given situation is dependent upon the particular arrangement of the physical stimulus events.

Perception of Demands. We are all familiar with the "insistent" quality of some intense stimuli, e.g., the loud, penetrating shrill of a telephone, a brightly flashing light. Such stimuli are deliberately utilized by the advertiser and others as attention-getting devices and warning signals, and they are chosen just because they possess this imperious ability to "demand" or "require" our attention.

We are dealing here with a power quality of an object, not as it is perceived to influence other objects in the field, but as it is perceived to affect *us*. Not only may we perceive certain objects as "demanding" or "repelling" toward other objects, we may also see them as "demanding" or "repelling" toward *ourselves*. A woman may look particularly "inviting" when a man is sexually aroused; the ground may seem to "pull" us down when we stand on a high building; a fatty meat may "repel" when we are sated.

We are coming here to a very important problem of psychology—the problem of *motivation*, why and how we are pushed and pulled into various actions by our environments. When we take up the problems of motivation in later chapters, we will find that these perceptual "power qualities" of objects in our world play a vital role in governing our actions, for it is largely with respect to perceived attractions and repulsions of objects that our motivated behavior is organized.

By Way of Summary. We tend to perceive the continuous stream of physical happenings in the environment as successive *events*, having various structures and attributes. Objects and events are perceived with dynamic attributes of movement and change. Such perceived change is not the same as changes in the percept, which may occur without the person's awareness.

Objects and events are also seen as having complex expressive, affective, and physiognomic properties. There are also power qualities, pertaining to the apparent "causal" relations among objects. All these complex attributes depend upon the entire stimulus-*pattern*, rather than upon single dimensions of the physical stimulus. They are, therefore, just as "real" psychologically as any simpler attribute we perceive, such as size or color.

Identifying Objects

Objects are, of course, perceived as identifiable things. This particular object is perceived as more than a "something" of a certain size, shape, color, and movement; it is a "hippopotamus." The identity is perceived as "there" in the object, like its other qualities.

The perception of identity is intimately bound up with all the other simple and complex perceptual qualities we have already reviewed. The "hippopotamusness" of the object is inseparable from its "lumbering but graceful movement," its "calm humorousness," its "open-mouthed peanut-inviting-ness."

Obviously the perceptions of identity vary widely, depending upon the context in which the object is perceived and the past experience of the person.

Words. The meaning of the passage you have just been reading is given by the words printed on the page. The words have come to convey meanings through complex processes of learning (to be discussed later) which permit us to identify each word and to know what it signifies.

Yet at the same time we must not ignore the striking *physiognomic* characteristics that words as physical stimuli often do have. Onomatopoeia is the familiar case in which the words *sound* like that which they signify: the "babbling" brook, the "swishing" skirt, the "clattering" feet. It has been suggested that in the evolution of language certain words came to represent certain things just because the sounds were similar. Box 8 presents an interesting experiment (which you can try on yourself and on your friends) demonstrating the physiognomic properties of words.

BOX 8

International Physiognomic Properties

Listed below are five common English synonym-antonym pairs, expressing simple qualities. In parallel columns are given the Chinese, Czech, and Hindi translations.

Can you correctly match the foreign words with the English? Try it by guessing which word, *tuñ* or *k'uài*, means "sharp" and which "blunt." Do the same for Czech and Hindi, and for the remaining English pairs.

The first word in the English pair is sometimes the top word in the foreign lists and sometimes the bottom, so that you cannot judge from that.

Do not read what follows the list until you have made all your guesses.

English	Chinese	Czech	Hindi
1. sharp-*blunt*	70 tuñ	83 tupy	83 gothil
	k'uài	špičatý	tez
2. *bright*-dark	90 liang	77 svetly	90 chamakdar
	añ	tmavý	dhundhala
3. *bad*-good	64 huai	57 zlý	31 kharab
	haŏ	hodný	achha
4. soft-*hard*	83 kãng	96 tvrdý	64 sakht
	joú	měkký	narm
5. *sweet*-sour	51 t'ién	25 sladký	70 mitha
	suân	kyselý	khatta

The correct answers are indicated by the italicized word of the English pair, which corresponds with the *top* of the foreign pairs in each case, i. e., "blunt" is *tuñ, tupy, gothil;* "bright" is *liang, svetly,* and *chamakdar;* etc.

The number preceding each foreign pair is the percentage of 86 Harvard and Radcliffe students who made the correct match in a study by Brown, Black, and Horowitz involving 21 such English pairs.

The over-all percentage of correct matches for the 21 pairs was 62 per cent for the Chinese, 62 per cent for Czech, and 61 per cent for Hindi. The chance level of guessing would be 50 per cent, so it is clear that even when entirely ignorant of a language, a person can do better than chance in recognizing the meanings of words expressive of very simple qualities. Although Chinese is *not* an Indo-European language as is English, the per cent of correct matches was as high for it as for Czech and Hindi, which are Indo-European languages. Presumably this is possible because of common physiognomic qualities in the *meaning* and in the *sound* of the word in the development of language.

But note that some of the pairs are matched correctly by almost everyone, whereas others are only slightly above chance, and still others are guesses predominantly in the *wrong* direction. We must conclude that common physiognomic qualities account for only some of the relationship of meanings to sounds of words.

BROWN, R. W., BLACK, A. H., and HOROWITZ, A. E. 1955. Phonetic symbolism in natural languages. *J. abnorm. soc. Psychol., 50,* 388–93.

Unity of the Senses. The perception of *objects* is not completely dependent upon the particular sensory avenue through which they are apprehended, e.g., sense of vision, hearing, touch, etc. This is because more than one sense is typically involved in perceiving objects and because the senses cooperate with and supplement one another. The *taste* of a food depends greatly upon the joint operation of taste and smell receptors; that is why our food is "tasteless" when one has a stopped-up nose.

A given perceptual attribute may be in agreement across several senses, thus an object may *look* large, *sound* large, *feel* large, and even perhaps *smell* large. It may be identically located in space through the eyes, ears, and hands. It may be seen moving,

---

BOX 9

Synesthesia

The most common form of synesthesia is *color hearing*, in which a vivid color image is evoked by a sound, such as a musical note. The tone-color relationships are not identical for different persons, but there are certain general uniformities, e.g., bass notes result in darker colors, treble notes in lighter colors.

For a given individual the relationships of tones and colors may be systematic and fairly permanent. Langfeld studied one person's synesthesia over a seven-year interval with the following results:

(previously associated with green) was given with the pale reddish hue, subjects frequently reported it as *greenish;* if the *low* tone was given with the pale greenish hue it was often seen as *reddish.*

As a further step, two of the subjects were instructed to mix red and green on a color wheel until they achieved a neutral gray. When the high tone was continuously sounded during the color-mixing task, the subjects tended to put in *more red and less green* than normally required for a neutral gray. Conversely, when the low tone was

Musical Note	Color Sensation on First Study	Color Sensation Seven Years Later
c	Red	Red
d♭	Purple	Lavender
d	Violet	Violet
e♭	Soft blue	Thick blue
e	Golden yellow	Sunlight
f	Pink	Pink, apple blossoms
f♯	Green blue	Blue green
g♭	Greener blue	Greener blue
g	Clear blue	Clear sky blue
a	Cold yellow	Clear yellow, hard, not warm
b♭	Orange	Verges on orange
b	Very brilliant coppery	Very brilliant coppery

Another investigator (Howells) succeeded in artificially "conditioning" such color hearing. He presented a low tone accompanied by a red light and a high tone accompanied by a green light 5,000 times each to eight subjects. After this "conditioning" period he presented relatively unsaturated colors, pale but still readily recognizable as reddish or greenish. If the *high* tone

continuously sounded, they tended to put in more green and less red. The hearing of the tone had served as an equivalent of color in the mixing task!

LANGFELD, H. S. 1914. Note on a case of chromaesthesia. *Psychol. Bull., 11,* 113–14.

HOWELLS, T. H. 1944. The experimental development of color-tone synesthesia. *J. exp. Psychol., 34,* 87–103.

heard moving, and felt moving. Sometimes the senses co-operate and agree despite discrepancies in the actual physical situation. When watching the moving picture screen, we hear the voices come right from the location of the moving lips, although the sound actually originates in loud-speakers in quite different places.

Of course, the various sensory domains have their unique and distinctive qualities. Visual experience is not likely to be confused with auditory experience, or smell with touch. However there are surprising interactions of the senses in *synesthesia* (see Box 9), in which stimulation of one kind of sense receptor produces experiences also in a different sense domain.

It is basically through the co-operative action of the senses that we gain a consistent, workable, and "realistic" picture of the physical environment around us. The impressions from the various senses are somehow combined or "organized" to provide this stable picture.

Glossary

brightness. One of the three basic dimensions of color, along with hue and saturation. Brightness varies from black (the least bright) to white (the most bright).

color constancy. The tendency to perceive an object as of the same color regardless of changes in the illumination on the object which alter its physical stimulus properties.

film color. Colors that are seen through apertures and tend to appear less clearly localized and more filmy. One of the modes of appearance of color, along with surface color and volume color.

hue. The color of an object, e.g., blue, red, yellow, green, etc.

phenomenology. The scientific study of immediate experience, in which the person seeks to give a detailed (and naïve) description of the way things look to him.

physiognomic properties. The expressive qualities perceived in an object. Includes aesthetic properties, affective properties, etc.

saturation. The degree of concentration or dilution of the hue of a color.

shape constancy. The tendency to perceive an object as of the same shape regardless of the angle from which it is viewed by the observer and despite differences in the shape of the retinal image. (See also glossary for Chapter 6.)

size constancy. The tendency to perceive an object as of the same size regardless of its distance from the observer and despite differences in size of the retinal image. (See also glossary for Chapter 6.)

structure. The particular manner in which the parts of an object are perceived in relation to one another in forming the whole. This perceived structure may or may not correspond with the physical structure of the object.

surface color. Color that is perceived as relatively opaque and localized at or on the object's surface. One of the modes of appearance of color, along with film color and volume color.

synesthesia. A type of perceptual experience in which stimulation of one kind of sense receptor results in sensations in a completely different sense domain, e.g., a musical sound producing a blue color.

volume color. Color that appears to fill an entire volume of space, being neither opaque nor filmy. One of the modes of appearance of color, along with film color and surface color.

Suggestions for Further Reading

ELLIS, W. D. 1938. *A sourcebook of Gestalt psychology*. New York: Harcourt, Brace.

A rich mine of translated selections from German psychological literature, especially on perception. Includes a selection by Hornbostel on the "unity of the senses."

HARROWER, M. R. 1937. *The psychologist at work*. New York: Harper.

A simple and highly readable introduction to the study of psychology, containing a discussion of the problems raised in accounting for the nature of our naïve perception of the world around us.

KATZ, D. 1935. *The world of colour*. London: Kegan Paul.

An original treatise on the perception of color, including an account of the different modes of appearance of colors.

KÖHLER, W. 1947. *Gestalt psychology* (rev. ed.). New York: Liveright.

Written by one of the founders of Gestalt psychology. Demonstrates the critical significance of the phenomenological approach to the scientific study of perception and behavior.

CHAPTER III

The Many Worlds of Different Perceivers

THE PRECEDING description of the worlds we perceive will be recognized as familiar by everyone. It has dealt with the principal dimensions of all perceived worlds—space, time, structure, objects, movement, change, expression, power qualities. These basic features are found in the perceptions of all people because we have similar nervous systems, because we are exposed to physical environments with many main features in common, and because we must all meet basically similar problems.

Our worlds are, therefore, to a considerable degree, *one world*, and this makes human *communication* possible. Were we not to believe that another person's world is basically similar to our own, we would not feel that we could communicate with him. We live in Hotel Universe, each of us permanently locked in his own private room, tapping out messages on walls to neighboring rooms in the belief that though we can never really visit the other rooms, they are furnished very like our own.

Yet, to extend the metaphor, we come to realize that the rooms are not precisely alike. The rooms of the blind are dark; those of the deaf, silent; and that occupied by our neighbor who belongs to the "other" political party, or church, or nationality, is equipped with viewing or hearing devices that somehow permit him to see or hear things we have never seen or heard.

These differences among people's worlds are often difficult for us to comprehend. Endowed with normal color vision, we may not readily grasp what it means for a color-blind person not to experience color, for it seems so evident to us that color is "right out there" as an inalienable part of the object, along with its shape and size. In teaching a young child to read, we often find it difficult to appreciate that the child

34

does not readily perceive the single letters of the word as grouped. It astonishes us that an Eskimo perceives whale blubber as "appetizing," and that a man can wear skirts in some countries without looking "funny" to others.

It is of the utmost importance that we be constantly alert to variations in perceived physical worlds if we are to achieve a science of perception. We cannot rest content with a study of perception based only upon our "own" perceived world, or even upon the statistically average world. Such studies are useful, but they leave out of consideration the factors making for individual differences. *And we cannot achieve scientific understanding if we neglect any major set of factors.* For this reason much recent research has been concerned with the study of individual differences in perception.

The purpose of this chapter, then, is to clarify the differences among the worlds of different perceivers and to indicate the major sources of such differences. We will discuss (1) differences among various species of organisms; (2) differences due to biological variation among members of the same species—in particular, the human being; (3) differences due to developmental variation in people, especially as related to age, environment, culture, and personality.

By the study of the worlds of other species and other people we may gain an appreciation of the tremendous scope of variation possible in perceived physical worlds. But we may also learn this lesson by an examination of something closer to home—by studying ourselves and by noting the changes that occur from time to time in our own perceived worlds. The final section of this chapter, therefore, will be an account of the *differences in the perceived world of the same individual from time to time*, as influenced by changes in his physiological and psychological states.

Different Worlds of Different Species

The widest variations in perceptions of the physical world are found as we go from one species to another. The bee's view of a flower is quite different from that of the bird, and the bird sees something quite different from the gardener.

These differences are due to the differences among the species in their sensory capacities and in the complexity of their nervous systems. These factors will be discussed in Chapter 7. Here we will merely give some basic illustrative data.

Sensory Capacities. It has been said that no field of biology presents a more varied array than that of the mechanisms for the reception of stimuli by various organisms. As an illustration let us take the specialized mechanism designed to receive and react to light. Special light receptors seem to be found among all living things, even among plants. The many varieties of light receptors can be classified into two main types: the direction eye and the image-forming eye.

The isolated light-sensitive cell of the earthworm is an example of the first; it is an "eye" that can help determine the direction of the light but can form no image. One may speculate that the visual world of the earthworm as it confronts a street scene consists merely of imageless regions of lights and darknesses.

The compound eye (found for example in the bee) is perhaps the simplest of the second main type. It consists of a large number of simple direction eyes, called ommatidia (ranging from about 30 in some insects to 30,000 in others). Each of these direction eyes responds to the light rays

FIG. 6. Two photographs of the same scene, taken in such a way as to represent what the world may look like to different insects. In the top picture the insect's compound eye is made up of many ommatidia. In the bottom picture the eye is made up of fewer ommatidia. (From Uexküll, 1927.)

coming from a given direction, and the total lighted area makes up a mosaic image. The larger the number of direction eyes, the clearer is the image. We may speculate that the worlds of the various insects that have these compound eyes vary somewhat in the fashion illustrated in Figure 6.

The most complicated image-forming eye is the "camera eye" with which various higher animals, including human beings, are equipped. It permits focusing of images at various distances. The details of this eye will be discussed in Chapter 7.

The story of the diversity of light receptors is repeated in all the other kinds of specialized receptors, those sensitive to heat, sound, pressure, and chemicals.

One important difference in receptor mechanisms is in the range of stimuli to which they are sensitive. Not all light energies, or sound waves, or pressures, are capable of producing an effect, that is, *stimulating* the receptor, even if the organism is equipped with a specialized receptor. Thus, for example, only a tiny fraction of the range of physical energy which we call "light waves" can stimulate the eye of man; the light waves outside this tiny band fall upon the eye without effect.

The range of sensitivity is different for each species, overlapping only in part or not at all with the ranges of other species. It is as though each kind of animal has available a different radio set, some of these sets being able to pick up only high-frequency waves, others only waves of low frequencies. The "broadcasting world" of each kind of animal would be quite different even though all were living in the same physical environment. The high-pitched dog whistle calls the dog; the man who blows it does not hear it at all.

Complexity of Nervous System. We see that differences in receptor mechanisms help

to account for much of the diversity among perceived worlds in the animal kingdom. But there is more to it still. Stimulation of receptors is not perception; perception is a product of the organizing functions of the whole nervous system.

Species vary enormously in the complexity of the nervous system. The more complex the nervous system, the more complex the kinds of perceptual organizations of which the organism is capable. For example, there are wide differences among species in the ability to distinguish one stimulus pattern from another (see Box 10). Because of differences in nervous system, the identical physical environment is perceived differently by different species.

Bodily Structure and Habitat. It will be stressed in the following chapter that perception can be regarded as an active process of coping with and adjusting to the environment. We will find that the organism's perceptual world depends upon the bodily structures involved in his motor movements and adjustive acts. Among mobile animals, the very speed and flexibility with which they orient toward a target will affect the resultant perceptions. The bird swoops toward a visual target, man walks, the tortoise crawls; thus the very sequences of events on the eyes of these different animals differ in speed and patterning.

The different bodily structures also help to determine the *selection* of those parts of the total physical environment by which the species will be stimulated. The biological nature of a given species is unique, having been developed through evolutionary selection to be adapted to the particular environmental "niche" it occupies. By virtue of wings the bird is airborne, and has a cursory perspective on things. The fish is eternally immersed in water, subjected to a range of pressures, lights, and chemicals not exactly like those stimulating other species.

BOX 10

The Different Worlds of Bees and Man

The world of the bee has been intensively explored over a period of forty years by the zoologist, von Frisch. Using his methods, Hertz, a psychologist, has shown that the bee can distinguish among complex visual forms.

The method is to arrange two figures on

the top row from each one of the bottom row. But it could *not* distinguish *among* those at the top, or *among* those at the bottom. Thus it could recognize the difference between the solid circle and the hollow square, but not between the circle and the solid triangle.

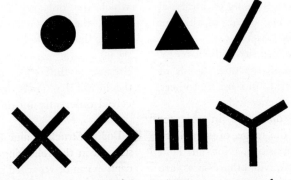

a table, with a dish of sugar-water beside one. After the bee has flown to that figure and tasted the "reward," the dish is removed, and it is then noted whether the bee consistently chooses that figure on the next trials.

By such experimentation it becomes clear that although the bee distinguishes among some patterns among which man distinguishes, it fails to do so among others where man succeeds. For example, tested on the figures shown above, the bee was able to learn to distinguish each of the figures of

What accounts for the difference? Whereas man readily sees each pattern as having a distinctive *shape*, Hertz believes that the most important quality in the bee's perception of a pattern is its degree of "brokenness." Patterns in the top row are all less "broken" than those in the bottom row, but those in the top row are not themselves distinguishable because they all have about the same amount of "brokenness."

HERTZ, M. 1929. *Die Organisation des optischen Feldes bei der Biene. Zeitschr. f. vergl. Physiol.,* 8, 693–748.

Man, too, has his "niche"; his sensory capacities, brain functioning, and physical and physiological constitution are suited to his particular environmental demands, and in turn they determine how he uniquely perceives his environment. It would be well to bear in mind, as an antidote to an exclusively "man-centered" view of the universe, that man, like all creatures, has only a *partial* view of the world, one limited and biased by his particular biological make-up.

Human Worlds with Sensory Deficit

Within a given species, such as human beings, individual members also show remarkably wide variations in their perceived worlds. Not only are there normal individual differences in sensory capacity among men, there are also the more extreme variations resulting from the serious impairment of receptors, as in blindness and deafness.

What does the world of the person with a severe sensory deficit look like?

The World of the Color-Blind. In rare instances a person may be *totally* color-blind (a state of affairs not at all uncommon among some lower animals). This means that he has no experience of differences of hue. His world is portrayed not in Technicolor, but in varying shades of white, gray, and black.

Much more commonly color blindness is partial. Two principal types of partial color blindness are *deuteranopia* and *protanopia*. The first means inability to perceive the difference between red and green; and the second means this same inability plus a weakness in sensitivity to the red end of the spectrum. The possible neurological basis of color blindness will be discussed in Chapter 7.

Although we all have some experience of a world without color, as in black-and-white movies, television, and reproductions of paintings, it is not easy to grasp what it means to be truly color-blind. For a person totally and congenitally color-blind there is not only no color experience now, there is no available memory or imagery of color, since he has *never* had color experience. He must make do with a pallid "language" of color names. He may seem to talk about colors in the same way others do, even though the conception he has of the absent colors is based only on guesses from what others say.

Thus we are often unaware that a person with whom we associate is color-blind, and sometimes he himself is unaware of it. Our world is so constructed that we can get along fairly satisfactorily without the discrimination of color. The color-blind driver stops at the corner even without being able to see the redness of the traffic light because he is able to discriminate the usual *bright-*

ness difference between the green and red lights, and because he remembers the red as being above the green. In coping with our physical worlds, people with sensory defects can often make use of such "vicarious" routes to obtain information.

The exceptions to this rule make dramatic demonstrations. The color-blind person may dress in outlandish color combinations until he learns by rote which garment should go with which. He may make fatal errors in recognizing signals in piloting an aircraft. He may not perceive a familiar figure because certain elements of the figure can be seen as belonging together only by their similarity of hue. This is the basis of the diagnostic tests of color blindness (see Color Plate II immediately preceding page 1).

The color-blind person can occasionally turn the tables on the person with normal vision. Some camouflages used in wartime depend for their effect on color patterns that break up the normal contours of the object being disguised. They may indeed fool the person who sees color, but they may not fool the color-blind.

But there are perhaps even more drastic aspects of the loss of color experience. We have seen in the last chapter that colors have subtle and complex qualities: this red object "advances," looks "hot," looks "cheerful." These expressive aspects of colors are indispensable components of many of our experiences of the world about us, as in aesthetic perceptions. For the color-blind person these are missing, or deficient.

The World of the Blind. We talked first about the world of the color-blind, for this is a short step away from normal visual worlds. Now to take a much longer step, we can explore the world of the *blind*. Some of what we have said about the color-blind applies directly to the blind, only in greater degree.

There is an important distinction to be made between the *congenitally* blind and those who have acquired blindness. For those blind from birth, no visual experience exists—no visual sensation, no visual memory, no visual imagery. And since man is essentially a visual animal, the complete absence of this experience must mean that the perceived world is organized quite differently from the usual way.

The world of the blind is, like everyone else's, a spatial world; but it is a space constructed of movement, of touch, and of sound. Such a space will have many basic similarities to visual space, but there is every reason to suppose that the degree of spatial detail in the world of the congenitally blind is less than that in the world of the seeing.

Despite such limitations, we are struck with how well the blind do perceive and adjust to their environments. Sensitivity to sound, touch, and movement is utilized much more fully by the blind than by those with sight (see Box 11).

Far more than in the case of the color-

BOX 11

"Seeing" with Your Ears

The mystery of how the totally blind person can readily detect and avoid obstacles as he moves around in space has long interested man. An early and favorite explanation was that the blind person develops an uncanny sensitivity to currents of air striking the face and that such cues provide "facial vision" permitting the avoidance of obstacles.

At Cornell University, Dallenbach and his collaborators carried out a series of studies to determine the basis of perception of obstacles by the blind. Using both blind subjects and seeing subjects tested under various experimental conditions, the experimenters were able gradually to eliminate one by one the possible cues for detecting obstacles without vision. For example, when the touch sensitivity of the face to "air currents" was eliminated by covering the head with a felt veil and hat, the subjects could still walk up to a wall and signal correctly just before running into it. Thus touch sensitivity is clearly not necessary to the performance. As a second step the ears were plugged so that auditory cues were eliminated. Under these conditions no subjects succeeded in avoiding running into the wall. Hence auditory cues are clearly essential. This was further demonstrated in an ingenious way by having the *experimenter* walk toward the obstacle carrying a microphone that was connected with headphones

on the subject who sat in a soundproof room. Thus the subject could hear the auditory stimuli impinging on the experimenter as the experimenter approached the obstacle. Under these conditions the subject was able to tell when the experimenter came close to the obstacle. This then is thoroughly convincing evidence that the auditory cues are the essential ones.

Finally, further careful work demonstrated that the particular auditory cues essential for detecting obstacles are reflected sounds of very high frequency, 10,000 cycles per second or more. Thus just as bats flying in total darkness guide themselves by hearing the reflections of very high frequency sound waves as they bounce off obstacles, so the human blind are guided by a similar kind of "sonar." This research has led to the proposal that the blind person carry around a mechanism continuously emitting high frequency sounds. The reflections of these sounds from obstacles in his path would provide him with a continuous supply of auditory "information" about the location of the obstacles. Some research on this proposal has already been carried out.

SUPA, M., COTZIN, M., and DALLENBACH, K. M. 1944. Facial vision: the perception of obstacles by the blind. *Amer. J. Psychol.*, 57, 133–83.
WORCHEL, P., and DALLENBACH, K. M. 1947. Facial vision: perception of obstacles by the deaf-blind. *Amer. J. Psychol.*, 60, 502–53.

blind, the loss of the expressive properties of visual objects by the person who is completely blind can be surmised to restrict the richness and differentiation of his emotional life. Adequate studies of these effects, however, have not as yet been made.

The World of the Deaf. As in the case of other sensory defects, deafness can be partial or complete, congenital or acquired. The world of the completely deaf is a silent world; and for those deaf from birth, a world lacking in memories and images of sound as well as in immediate sensations of sound. The ability to locate an object in space by way of sound is missing, and so are the various warning cues and signals in our physical environment. Usually, however, there are adequate substitutes for such localizations and signals by way of visual, tactual, and other sense avenues.

The congenitally deaf person suffers a great loss by being cut off from the expressive qualities embodied in sound. Music provides some of the most compelling perceptual experiences—of harmonies, rhythms, and melodies. Music has unparalleled power to evoke emotional feelings. All this is missing in the world of the deaf.

The case of *acquired* deafness may be quite different. Beethoven composed some of his greatest work, including the majestic Ninth Symphony, after becoming deaf, but this was only possible because of the richness of musical memory and imagery still left to him.

A World Without Pain. If a person could magically make his world what he would ideally like it to be, he might choose to have it painless. But a world without pain would have serious shortcomings. Physical pain plays an important role in our successful adjustment to the physical environment, and it may have been biologically selected through evolution for just this reason.

We do have actual cases of worlds literally lacking in *physical* pain (see Box 12). We see from them that normal pain is an important cue in helping the person adjust to the dangers of his environment. A new mutant species without pain might soon vanish.

By Way of Summary. One reason for the prominent differences among the perceptual worlds of human beings is the presence of certain sensory deficits. The color-blind person, the totally blind person, the deaf person, all experience somewhat impoverished perceptual worlds. Nevertheless, to a considerable degree they are able to compensate for their defects through other routes of perception. Certain aspects of perceptual experience, such as perception of the expressive and affective qualities of colors and sounds, which necessarily depend upon the integrity of a given sensory system, may not be so readily compensated for.

The World of the Child

Though every adult has passed through the world of childhood, he ordinarily finds it hard to remember how different the world looked to him as a child. This is due, in part, to the continuous process of growth and development of the individual, involving many slight, hardly noticed, step-by-step changes in his world. Thus as adults we may tend to assume that the child's world is not too unlike our own. Except that it is less full of the fund of knowledge and detail that we have acquired over time, we assume that it is simply a smaller, less complicated version of our own, having the same general dimensions and structure.

Careful observations and tests of children's behavior, coupled with study of the children's own descriptions of how things

BOX 12

A World Without Pain

A 19-year-old college girl congenitally insensitive to pain was studied over a nine-month period, being tested in sensory perception, in mental abilities, in personality, etc., by a group of physicians and psychologists at the Duke University Medical School.

Her parents had first noted her defect in infancy when she was badly burned without evidence of pain. She had suffered numerous burns, cuts, and even bone fractures during her life, without discomfort. She had never experienced headaches, menstrual cramps, toothaches, or abdominal pains.

When tested in the laboratory, she was entirely lacking in superficial and deep pain when subjected to pressure, heat, cold, or piercing of the skin.

Otherwise she was physically normal, except for numerous scars on hands, arms, feet, and legs. There was no evidence for suppression of experienced pain: under hypnosis, the girl was given strong suggestion that she would feel pain, but when the painful stimuli were applied to her skin she still gave no sign of pain experience.

Psychological tests showed her to be highly intelligent, and within the normal range in personality characteristics and adjustment. The only striking features of her psychological picture, as revealed in various personality tests, were evidence of some limitations of emotional sensitivity. Yet she was fluent and articulate in expression, and her language about emotions was rich and descriptive. There would seem to be no clear evidence that the lack of pain experiences had interfered with her normal personality development.

She had learned how to use other "cues" than the normal pain in adjusting to the dangers of her environment. But not perfectly: after an auto accident in which her ankle was fractured, she attended a dance, not realizing until the swelling of the foot prevented her from putting on a shoe that anything was amiss.

COHEN, L. D., KIPNIS, D., KUNKLE, E. C., and KUBZANSKY, P. E. 1955. Observations of a person with congenital insensitivity to pain. *J. abnorm. soc. Psychol., 51,* 333–8.

look to them, throw doubt on the above conception.

Body Size and Child's World. To start with the simplest fact, the much smaller physical body of the child affects his perceptions of the environment. We adults have constructed our surroundings to accommodate our own bodily needs, and since the child views things from a much lower height, many physical objects around him loom larger, more imposing, and less within reach. To him, door handles are things to be reached up for, table tops things to be peered at from tiptoe. Because of weaker muscles, he perceives many objects as heavier and stronger than adults do. And relative to his own perceived body size, adults are "giants," seen with qualities of "power" that influence his perception of himself and of other people's selves.

Boundaries of the Child's World. The world in which the child lives is narrower in scope than that of the adult. The boundaries of space and time are much less extended. His world is here and now, rather than there and then. When he sees it raining here, it is "raining everywhere in the world." That exciting event of months ago happened "just yesterday." A promise to do something "a week from now" may really be meaningless to him. The number of things that can be attended to at once and the length of time that the attention can be sustained are far lower for the child.

Organization in the Child's World. With the child's more restricted span of what can be taken in at one time, the simultaneous perception of parts and wholes is limited. The child may lose much of the richness of detailed structure by attending only to the main features of the whole. For instance, the child is far slower than the adult in finding the small object that is camouflaged by being embedded in a larger whole picture (see Fig. 7). And the child is

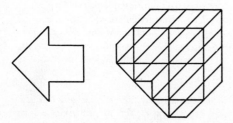

FIG. 7. Can you see the simple figure on the left in the figure on the right?

significantly more susceptible to the Müller-Lyer illusion (see Fig. 2, p. 19), indicating that it is harder for him to isolate the relevant lines to be compared from their context of the surrounding lines forming the arrowheads. Conversely, highly complex figures are probably beyond the child's capacity for organization; he simply may not be able to perceive them at all in the way that the adult immediately does.

There is also evidence that size constancy and other constancies of objects are not present to the same degree in the child's world. These constancies seem to develop gradually, probably as a function both of maturation of the child and of accumulated experience with objects (see Fig. 8). Thus the child may reach for a life-sized statue on a distant building and ask for that "doll." He has not yet been able to take account in an organized way of the various cues of retinal size, distance, etc., which must be incorporated in the achievement of size constancy.

Physiognomic Properties in the Child's World. Expressive and power qualities of

objects and events seem to play a relatively greater role in the child's perceptions than in the adult's. Such qualities are often uppermost for the child. The triangular shape may look "jagged, sharp, and hurtful" before it looks "triangular."

It is a short step from these perceived properties to what has been called *animistic* perception and thinking, often characteristic of the child, in which physical objects are endowed with life, with feelings, and with intentions. The sun is "trying to get through the clouds," the jack is "tired of holding up the car," "the fire is angry."

The basic difference between the adult's world and the child's world is not in the absence or presence of these physiognomic attributes, but in the extent to which they

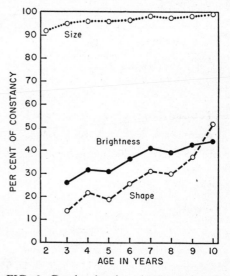

FIG. 8. Graphs showing the increasing degree of size, shape, and brightness constancy in children with increasing age. On the vertical axis is plotted the per cent of constancy achieved by groups of children of the indicated ages. Note that although size constancy is very high even at two years, there is further improvement thereafter, until perfect constancy is achieved at about ten. Brightness and shape constancy are poor to begin with and improve fairly rapidly, although even at ten they fall short of perfect constancy. (Data from Brunswik, 1956.)

may dominate the whole perceptual experience. For the adult, the expressive characteristics of objects are kept in check, and discounted. They are conceived as irrelevant "subjective" factors. But the child, in his immaturity and inexperience, is more at the mercy of these attributes of objects, and they may flood over and swamp his perceptions.

The child's perceptual world may seem to suffer by comparison with the adult's, but there are compensatory values. The very absence of complete objectivity and "realism," and the sensitivity to the influence of physiognomic qualities, are such as to preserve a freshness and spontaneity in the child's view of the world. It has been noted that often the mark of a truly great and original person, whether he is an artist, scientist, inventor, or entrepreneur, is that he has somehow retained as an adult much of the freshness and spontaneity of the "childlike" perception of the world.

Culture, Personality, and Perception

The human race is scattered over the earth in many geographical localities, cultures, and societies. Corresponding to these wide variations in physical and social surroundings, there are variations in the perceived worlds of people. There are differences in the *frequency* of perceptual experiences with certain kinds of objects, and differences in the manner in which the *same* objects are perceived.

For example, there are striking contrasts among societies in how many variants of a class of objects can be perceptually distinguished. A child in the United States may unhesitatingly pick out scores of different makes of cars; an Eskimo child suddenly transported to our highways would see nothing but the grossest differences among them. Were the American child to visit the

Chukchee of the Arctic, he would be bewildered by their easy recognition of two dozen different patterns of reindeer hides and their ready discrimination of slight variations in types of snow. He would also find them sensitized to smells in an extraordinary degree, but almost unable to learn to sort wools into piles of different shades of green.

When the Baganda people of Africa are asked to sort pieces of cardboard of different shapes, sizes, and colors, those who have had little contact with Europeans almost never sort them by color. Moreover, the native language is almost devoid of words for colors. However, those Baganda who have been educated in Western schools perform the test by sorting by colors in much the way we do (Doob, 1956).

Although evidence from anthropological comparisons of perceptual functioning among different cultures is surprisingly scanty, it would seem fairly safe to assume that any differences in perception of simple properties of physical objects are based upon differences in amounts of learning and past experience with such objects, and differences in ability to identify and name objects, rather than upon more basic differences in the general manner of perceptual functioning.

Cultural Values. The cultural *values* placed upon objects, relations, and events may play a significant part in determining how they are perceived. The anthropologist Malinowski (1923) reported, for instance, that in connection with the matrilineal organization of their society, the Trobriand Islanders of New Guinea formerly held to a basic belief that a child can never physically resemble his mother, or his brothers and sisters. Even when to an outsider there was a striking physical resemblance between two brothers, the natives apparently were unable (or unwilling) to detect any resemblance whatsoever. Moreover, there was a contrary tendency to exaggerate the slightest degree of facial resemblance between the father and his children.

Since there is considerable latitude in what aspects of an object the person may *attend to* and emphasize, there may be striking perceptual differences across cultures in this respect. For example, the perceptual experiences when looking at an ink blot are described quite differently by people of various societies. These differences in perceptual emphasis may be interpreted to reflect the cultural values of these people. (See Box 13.)

Personality and the Perceived World. In a sense all that we have previously discussed is embraced in variations in personality—variations in biological make-up, in sensory and brain capacity, in age and experience, in geographical and cultural setting. The unique make-up of the individual—his particular abilities, motives, values, and traits, and the special manner in which these are all patterned—is his personality. Personality is determined by the biological constitution and life experiences of the individual. Thus, as we might expect, associated with personality differences are significant differences in perception of the world. As a matter of fact, it is partly through the study of how an individual perceives the world that psychologists attempt to describe and classify his personality.

There is a growing body of research literature on the relations between personality characteristics and manner of perceiving physical stimuli. Box 14 gives a single example of such research.

Perception and Individual States

It is a commonplace observation that our perception of things may be altered by our knowledge, our motivation, our emotional state, and other physiological conditions.

The effects are both in the perceptual *sensitivity* to objects and in their perceived *properties*.

Influence of Experience. Experience with an object leads to significant shifts in the way it is perceived. Its recognition is easier, it is perceptually organized in a different way, new properties emerge and some old ones disappear. Indeed there is evidence to indicate that even our sensory capacities—the ability to detect and discriminate among stimuli—can be improved with practice. When in later chapters we take up the problem of learning, it will be seen that changes of perception are essential aspects of the learning process.

Influence of Motivation. Scientific understanding of motivational and emotional processes involves study of how motivational states influence perception. The food is more readily noticed and looks more appetizing to the hungry man than to the sated; the female may be perceived quite differently before and after sexual release in the male; the frightened person is more acutely aware of each tiny sound in the lonely house.

Physiological Influences. There are other physiological influences on perceptions, as found, for example, in states of unusual hormonal activity, associated with disease, pregnancy, menstruation, etc. The common belief that the pregnant woman has a more acute sense of smell is false. Experiments indicate that her ability to perceive odors is actually less than normal. But there is a pronounced perceptual effect of another kind; the physiognomic qualities of certain odors are quite different during pregnancy, and so she reacts with more feeling to certain odors when she is pregnant. It is probably this observation which has led people to suppose that she has a more acute sense of smell.

Literature and scientific experimentation

BOX 13

How Ink Blots Are Described in Different Cultures

The Rorschach ink-blot test (see p. 637) is used to study the individual's personality by analyzing his reports of what he sees in a set of standard ink blots. Striking cultural differences in perceptual responses to the blots have been reported.

For example, one study showed that primitive desert Moroccans emphasize tiny *details* of the blots to a much greater degree than do Europeans (Bleuler and Bleuler). Shown below is one of the standard blots, of which a typical description given by European subjects is "two women quarreling." A typical Moroccan response was to identify the tiny, scarcely perceptible marks on the small protrusions at the top of the figure (see arrows) as an alignment of Arab riflemen opposed by a row of Christian warriors.

At the other extreme we find the Samoans, who tend to give relatively few fine-detail responses and a large number of "whole" responses, i.e., perceiving the entire blot as a map, or an animal (Cook). Moreover, the Samoans differ markedly from typical Europeans and other samples of subjects in giving numerous responses to the *white spaces* in the blots, which they perceive as objects rather than holes. For instance, in the blot shown here the middle white area might be seen as an island.

These differences in perceptual emphasis, which can be multiplied in numerous other studies, may reflect the operation of cultural factors in a quite direct way. Moroccan art and religion give great importance to fine details; for the Samoans, white is a symbolic and highly valued color.

All of this does not mean that Moroccans cannot see "wholes," or Samoans "details." The point is that given these ink blots, which are susceptible to many different perceptual organizations, people of different cultures tend to look at them in different ways.

Nor does this "prove" that the "Moroccan personality" is different from the "Samoan personality" and from the "European personality." The problem of designing measures of personality which are equally valid for different cultures is full of pitfalls.

BLEULER, M., and BLEULER, R. 1935. Rorschach's ink-blot tests and racial psychology. *Charact. and Personal., 4,* 97–114.

COOK, T. H. 1942. The application of the Rorschach test to a Samoan group. *Rorsch. Resch. Exch., 6,* 51–60.

agree that there are striking effects on perception produced by drugs and alcohol. The drug marijuana, for instance, may cause colors to be seen as unbelievably bright, and the time sense to be so distorted that an enormous length of time seems involved in the simplest act, such as lifting an arm. Severe chronic alcoholism may be accompanied by periods in which terrifying perceptual experiences occur, such as seeing blood-sucking rats in the room, or feeling worms boring into the skin.

The latter phenomena are cases of *hallucination,* which means a convincing perception of something that is actually not there. Hearing "voices," seeing "visions," etc., are extreme and abnormal hallucinatory experiences; but they differ from more

BOX 14

A Luminous Rod in Darkness Reveals Personality

Everyone has straightened a picture hanging crookedly on the wall by lining it up with the vertical walls of the room. But what if the walls of the room are not vertical? We will probably find that in "straightening" the picture we tilt it somewhat toward the tilt of the walls.

In a series of investigations Witkin and others have used this kind of perceptual situation in studying relations between the personality of the individual and his perception. A "rod-and-frame test" used in such studies is shown in the photograph.

The subject is brought into a dark room and placed before the apparatus. The only visual cues available are the luminous rod and frame. The frame is tilted 28 degrees from the vertical. The subject's task is to set the luminous rod "truly vertical" by turning a knob that controls the rod's tilt.

Each subject is scored by averaging his errors on a number of trials. Some persons are extremely accurate. Some make errors as large as the tilt of the visual frame; that is, what they perceive as vertical is entirely determined by the frame, which is 28 degrees off vertical.

Those making large errors and those making small errors have been compared on a number of personality tests. Significant differences between these extreme groups in various personality traits have been found, as listed below:

Those with large errors tend to

Lack self-insight
Repress impulses
Be suggestible
Have inferiority feelings
Be dependent

Those with small errors tend to

Have self-awareness
Express impulses directly
Resist suggestion
Be self-assured
Be independent

The above is a comparison of the *extremes;* most people fall somewhere in between.

There are also sex differences in performance on this test. For instance, the average error for male students is 7.4 degrees, and for female students, 11.0 degrees.

WITKIN, H. A., LEWIS, H. B., HERTZMAN, M., MACHOVER, K., MEISSNER, P. B., and WAPNER, S. 1954. *Personality through perception.* New York: Harper.

common hallucinatory experiences found in everyone only in intensity, and in the degree to which they are accepted as real. We hear a ringing in the ears, but nothing is out there making the sound; we see a movement in the room out of the corner of our eye, but the room is empty; we feel an "ant" run across our skin, but it is really bare. (A possible neurological basis for some of these impressions is given in Chapter 7.) We have come to accept all these experiences as peculiar misperceptions, recognizing that they do not represent objective reality. Thus, though we have some degree of hallucinatory perception, we are not "hallucinated," as may be persons in states of insanity.

Although the exact physiological and psychological bases of certain other important states of the organism—sleep, hypnotic trances, etc.—are still obscure, there can be no doubt that such states also are associated with marked variations in perception.

The Steps Beyond Description

Our first task in the scientific study of perception has now been completed, namely, the *description* of how the physical world is experienced. The second step is to *account* for the perceptions that have been described. From what we have already seen, we can make the generalization that perception is a function (1) of the characteris-

tics of the *stimulus;* (2) of the *psychological states* of the perceiver, such as motives, emotions, past experiences, illness, age, etc.; and (3) of the *physiological mechanisms* of the perceiver, such as receptors, nerve conductors, and brain.

In the following three chapters we shall examine the facts and principles that show how the stimulus-pattern relates to what is perceived and how the perception is affected by the psychological states of the person. In Chapter 7, which concludes the section on perception, we shall examine the relationship of physiological mechanisms to perception.

In the remaining chapters of the book we shall be repeatedly concerned with the *consequences* of perception in motivation, in learning, and in personality functioning.

Glossary

animistic perception. The perceiving of inanimate objects as having life, feelings, intentions. Often characteristic of the child's perception.

color blindness. A defect in sensitivity to hue. Total color blindness is very rare. Two kinds of partial color blindness are deuteranopia and protanopia.

deuteranopia. Partial color blindness involving the inability to distinguish red and green.

hallucination. A convincing perception of something that is actually not there. Ex-

treme and abnormal hallucinatory experiences may involve hearing "voices," seeing "visions," etc.

protanopia. Partial color blindness involving inability to distinguish red and green plus a weakness in sensitivity to the red end of the spectrum.

Rorschach ink-blot test. A test designed to reveal differences in personality. The person is shown a standard series of ink blots, and reports what he perceives in them. Named for its inventor, the Swiss psychologist, Rorschach.

Suggestions for Further Reading

BLAKE, R. R., and RAMSEY, G. V. (eds.) 1951. *Perception: an approach to personality.* New York: Ronald.

A collection of papers by different authors, touching upon many different aspects of the relation of perception to personality, social, and cultural factors.

PIAGET, J. 1929. *The child's conception of the world.* 1930. *The child's conception of physical causality.* New York: Harcourt, Brace.

Highly original accounts of investigations of the development of mental processes in children.

CHAPTER IV

Physical Stimuli and the Senses

W<small>E ARE</small> immersed in a surging sea of physical energies that make up our physical environment. The energies take many forms—radiant, vibratory, chemical, thermal, mechanical. They vary ceaselessly in concentration and intensity.

We are sensitive instruments moving about in this sea of energies. As the energies play upon us, we register and record. But we are highly *selective* instruments, sensitive to some energies and not to others; and we are active rather than passive instruments, *seeking* information as well as registering it.

The instrument readings are highly complex. They are what we have been describing at length in Chapter 2. And not all of us give the same readings, as we have seen in Chapter 3.

One problem is to determine which readings are related to the different forms of energies. Our perceived worlds are made up of sights, sounds, smells, and feels, and a first scientific task is to determine *how these different sensory experiences are re-*lated to the different physical energies arousing them.*

Psychophysics

The study of these relationships is called *psychophysics*. It was with psychophysics that the history of experimental psychology began about a hundred years ago. Then for the first time physiologists such as Helmholtz inquired scientifically into the systematic relationships between measurable aspects of physical energies and measurable attributes of the sensory experience of the person. This building of an experimental bridge between the two "separate" worlds, physical and mental, was thus the nineteenth-century scientist's approach to the classical "mind-body" problem of philosophy.

Before turning to the facts of psychophysics, we must clarify a number of terms.

The Stimulus. Physical energy that can excite a receptor and thus produce an effect

49

on the organism is called a *stimulus*. If the energy *fails* to produce an effect, it is not properly called a stimulus.

We must, however, distinguish *stimulus* from the *stimulus-object*. A red ball is placed ten feet in front of the child's eyes; it may be called the stimulus-object. It may be objectively described in terms of its physical size, shape, color. It is an object in the environment which is the source of the stimulus.

The visual *stimulus* corresponding to this stimulus-object is the pattern of physical light energies which, emanating from the ball, strike the retina of the eye. The stimulus-object and the stimulus are not the same. For one thing, the light leaving the ball is not identical with the light reaching the eye; as it passes through intervening space its intensity is reduced, it may be mixed with other light, etc. Secondly, the light rays are focused in different ways by the lens of the eye, thus producing different patterns of light on the retina. Thus we see that there are various reasons why a given stimulus-object can give rise to an almost unlimited variety of different stimuli on the receptor surface.

The converse is also true, namely that the very *same* stimulus on the receptor surface can be produced by very *different* stimulus-objects. The retina receives a given pattern of light stimuli, and it can make no difference to the retina *how* these stimuli have been produced. If, without any chair physically present in the environment, the exact pattern of light is produced on the retina which would have been produced by looking at an actual chair, a "chair" will be perceived (see Fig. 9).

Simple and Complex Psychophysics. There are various aspects of the physical stimulus which we can measure, for instance, the frequency and the amplitude of sound waves. It would be convenient to find that

for each such aspect there is a single associated kind of sensory experience. Approximations to such fairly simple relationships do exist. For instance, the greater the frequency of sound waves, the higher the perceived pitch; the greater the amplitude of sound waves, the louder the sound. But even here the relationships are not as simple as was once assumed. Pitch depends upon *both* frequency and amplitude of

FIG. 9. An observer looks with one eye through peephole *a*. The stimulus-object seen on the left from *a* is a chair constructed out of lengths of string. He sees a "chair." Then he looks through peephole *b*. The pieces of string seen on the right from *b* are placed so that the image they cast on the eye is *identical* with the image cast by the other object. Here, too, the person sees a "chair," even though this stimulus-object is very different from the first. (After Kilpatrick, 1952.)

waves, and so does loudness. Our perception is thus a resultant of interaction effects.

Interaction is the rule in psychological processes. But interaction does not mean disorder. We assume that, no matter how complex they may be, the psychophysical relationships are regular and orderly. The task is to discover *what patterns of physical stimuli give rise to what attributes of experience.*

The discovery of these relationships often

requires persistence and ingenuity. For example, the mysterious "homing instinct" of the bird raised a psychophysical problem; namely, what pattern of physical stimuli was the bird perceiving in order to achieve spatial orientation? It required prolonged research to find that the answer seems to lie in a complex combination of stimuli from the earth's magnetic lines of force and the lines of force due to the earth's turning, a solution that had not occurred easily to humans who are themselves not sensitive to such physical forces.

Measuring the Psychophysical Relationship. There is more to the use of an instrument than knowing *what* it measures. The instrument has to be calibrated, so that we can *quantify* the relationships, i.e., know *how much* of what we are measuring. Psychophysics has, therefore, both a qualitative side (which energies result in which attributes of experience?) and a quantitative side (how much energy results in how intense the attribute?).

The Absolute Threshold. The organism is not sensitive to all parts of the possible range of physical energies. Some lights are too dim to see, some sounds too low to hear, some pressures too light to feel. An important psychological problem is the determination of that point in the scale of the intensity of the physical stimulus which separates seeing from not seeing, hearing from not hearing, tasting from not tasting. This point is referred to as the *absolute threshold*.

The threshold is not a single sharp dividing line but a *zone* in which the physical energies gradually move from having no effect, to having partial effect, to having full effect. If we present a very low sound to the ear, it will not be heard. If we gradually increase its intensity, it will come to a place where it is heard once in a while;

as we make it more intense, it will be heard more times; and as we make it still more intense, it will be heard every time. What shall we call the threshold? Is it the lowest point at which the sound might *ever* be heard? Or is it the higher point at which the sound *never fails* to be heard? Or where else?

Obviously, the choice must be somewhat arbitrary. Psychologists have agreed that the absolute threshold will be taken as that point at which the stimulus is perceived *half the time*. It should be clear that the higher the threshold, the less the sensitivity; and the lower the threshold, the greater the sensitivity. There are several different ways that this threshold can be determined. Such measurement techniques are called the *psychophysical methods* (see Box 15).

Measured under the best possible conditions, the absolute thresholds for various stimuli are amazingly low. This means, of course, that the sensitivity of the organism to that energy is very great. Thus, for example, it has been estimated that the physical energy equivalent to *one pin dropping one inch* would, if converted to light energy and properly distributed, be sufficient to stimulate *every one* of the more than four billion human eyes on earth!

Note that we are here talking about thresholds determined under the best possible conditions. Under less favorable conditions the sensitivity is less and the thresholds higher.

This implies, obviously, that the actual thresholds measured on various occasions will differ, depending upon the conditions of the stimulating situation and the conditions of the organism.

The Differential Threshold. We are concerned not only with absolute sensitivity to physical energies, but also with sensitivity to the *differences* in intensity of the energies. The individual may look at two lights

BOX 15

The Psychophysical Methods

Thresholds can be determined by several different methods. Two of the basic ones are described here.

The method of limits. Starting with a stimulus intensity known to be well below threshold, the intensity is gradually increased step by step by the experimenter until that point is reached where the subject reports perceiving the stimulus. Then, starting with an intensity well above threshold, the intensity is gradually decreased step by step until that point is reached where the subject no longer reports perceiving the stimulus. Such ascending and descending series are alternated until a sufficient number of estimates of the "limits" have been obtained.

This method is illustrated in the following data, which show three ascending and three descending series of judgments. "No" means that the stimulus was not perceived, "Yes" that it was. The horizontal bar in each column indicates the stimulus intensity of that "limit" where there is a transition from perceiving to not perceiving, or vice versa.

Note that there is variation among the series in the "limits" obtained. They range from 10.5 to 14.5. The threshold is computed

Stimulus Intensity (arbitrary units)						
7	No		No		No	
8	No		No		No	
9	No		No		No	
10	No		No		No	No ― 10.5
11	No	No ― 11.5	No ― 11.5		No	Yes
12	No ― 12.5	Yes	Yes		No ― 12.5	Yes
13	Yes	Yes			Yes	Yes
14		Yes		No ― 14.5		Yes
15		Yes		Yes		Yes
16		Yes		Yes		Yes
17		Yes		Yes		Yes
18		Yes		Yes		Yes
19		Yes		Yes		Yes

side by side, or first at one and then at the other, or he may look at a gradually changing light. In every case there is the question of whether or not he is able to perceive a difference in the stimuli. If we start with two lights, very slightly different in intensity, the person will be unable to detect a difference. As the difference is made larger, he will sometimes be able to see a difference and sometimes not; and as the difference is made even larger, he may always be able to see the difference. That amount of difference in physical energy just large enough to be perceived, i.e., the just noticeable difference (usually abbreviated j.n.d.), is called the *differential threshold.*

Here again, the convention in psychology is to take as the differential threshold that stimulus difference which will be perceived *exactly half the time.* The psychophysical methods for such determination are similar to those described in Box 15.

As in the case of the absolute threshold, the value of the differential threshold varies widely depending upon the nature of the stimulus and the state of the organism. Moreover, it has a different value for each level of absolute magnitude of the stimulus. For example, the differential threshold for two dim lights is not the same as that for two bright lights.

This latter fact would seem to imply

BOX 15 (continued)

The Psychophysical Methods

as the average of all these obtained "limits," which in this case proves to be 12.2.

The method of constant stimuli. A limited set of stimuli (usually five to eight) which range in intensity are chosen by the experimenter on the basis of rough exploration so that they will bracket the range of intensity from the point where the stimulus will rarely be perceived to the point where it will almost always be perceived. Each of the stimuli is presented for judgment a large number of times (perhaps one hundred) in random order. The subject is to report whether or not he perceives the stimulus. The threshold is computed to be that stimulus intensity which results in a perception of the stimulus *about 50 per cent of the time*.

The method is here illustrated by the same threshold problem used above in the method of limits. First, it was determined roughly that the threshold was in the vicinity of an intensity of 13 units. Five stimuli were then prepared, varying in equal steps from 9 to 17 units. Each of the 5 stimuli was presented 100 times. The graph shows the percentage of times each was perceived and percentage of times not perceived out of the 100 presentations.

The dotted lines show that the threshold

value where the stimulus is perceived 50 per cent of the time is about 12.8. Note that

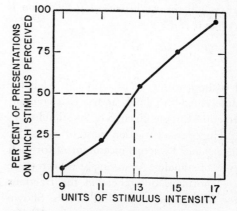

this value is not exactly the same as that obtained by the method of limits. This fact has two implications: first, it indicates the complexity of psychological measurement, even of the simplest functions; second, it indicates that the given psychophysical method used reflects differences in the complex factors determining the threshold. Here we clearly see that *psychological measurement is always relative to the particular method used*, which is true of measurement everywhere in science.

---

that we would have to compute the differential threshold separately for *every* point on a stimulus scale. But a very surprising fact was discovered early in the history of psychophysics which simplified the problem enormously. This fact is that within limits *the differential threshold tends to be a constant fraction of the stimulus intensity*.

Suppose, for example, that the differential threshold for a weight of 50 pounds is one pound; that is, it takes a weight of at least 51 pounds in order to be perceived as heavier. It will then turn out that the differential threshold for a weight of 100 pounds is *two* pounds; that is, for 100

pounds the next heavier weight that can just be perceived as heavier will be 102 pounds. And for a 150 pound weight, the next heavier weight that can be discriminated will prove to be 153 pounds. In each case the differential threshold is the *same* fraction of the stimulus weight: $\frac{1}{50} = \frac{2}{100} = \frac{3}{150} = .02$. This value of .02 tells us that we must add 2 per cent of the original weight before we can experience an increase in its heaviness. Thus, knowing the constant fraction, we can closely estimate what the differential threshold will be for *any* magnitude of stimulus weight.

We have then a kind of "law of relativity" in psychology: The amount of energy which must be added to produce a detectable difference is relative to the amount already there.

Weber's Law. The above facts were first made explicit by the physiologist Weber in 1834, and the mathematical formulation is called *Weber's Law:*

$$\frac{\Delta I}{I} = k$$

I is the intensity of the stimulus, ΔI is the differential threshold, and k is a constant fraction for the given type of stimulus.

The constant fraction must, of course, be determined by actual measurement for each type of stimulus. As we might expect, there are enormous differences in the fractions for different senses and attributes. Shown in Box 16 are some representative Weber fractions.

There is a limitation on Weber's Law. While the law holds fairly well for the middle ranges, at the extremes (e.g., when the light is *very* bright or *very* dim), the Weber fractions may deviate widely from the constant value.

Weber's Law also applies to complex cases of perceptual judgment, such as in comparing objects in their aesthetic qualities. It has even been shown to apply in the rat's discrimination between a long and a short pathway to a goal. (See Box 17.)

By Way of Summary. The *stimulus* is the physical energy that can excite a receptor and produce an effect on the organism. The study of the relationships between the characteristics of the physical stimulus and the resulting sensory experience is called *psychophysics*. There are fairly simple psychophysical relationships as well as complex ones, which depend upon *patterns* of stimuli. The organism is sensitive only to limited parts of the whole range of physical energies. The energies must be above a certain level of intensity for a sensory effect

---

BOX 16

Poor Taste and Good Pitch

The following illustrative Weber fractions [1] have been taken from the work of various investigators. For each stimulus dimension, the absolute level of stimulus intensity at which the Weber fraction was determined is indicated. These are *minimal* values, obtained under optimal conditions of judgment.

Pitch (at 2,000 cycles per second [2]) 1/333
Deep pressure (at 400 grams) 1/77
Visual brightness (at 1,000 photons) 1/62
Lifted weights (at 300 grams) 1/53
Loudness (at 100 decibels, [3] 1,000 cycles per second) 1/11
Smell of rubber (at 200 olfacties) 1/10
Skin pressure (at 5 gram/sq. mm.) 1/7
Taste, saline (at 3 moles/liter) 1/5

The remarkable range in sensitivities of the various senses is well demonstrated, being about seventyfold—from pitch, in which a difference of as little as *one-third of 1 per cent* can be detected, to taste, in which there must be a difference of about 20 per cent before it can be detected.

[1] Listed in Boring, Langfeld, and Weld, 1948
[2] See p. 64.
[3] See Glossary, p. 81.

---

to be produced (the absolute threshold). The organism may also perceive *differences* in stimulus intensities if they are sufficiently great (the differential threshold). The size of the differential threshold for any given sensory attribute, such as loudness, is a constant fraction of the absolute level of stimulus intensity (Weber's Law).

The Physical Stimuli for Vision

The universe is full of radiant energy in the form of electromagnetic waves. The waves vary greatly in length, from cosmic rays of a few trillionths of an inch to radio waves of many miles.

BOX 17

Relativity in the Rat

Yoshioka measured the rat's ability to discriminate shorter from longer paths to food. The rat did not *look* at the two distances, but judged them by running along the paths. The maze used is shown below.

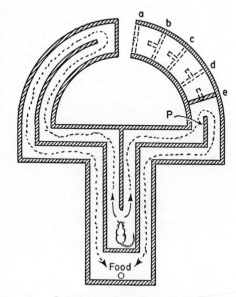

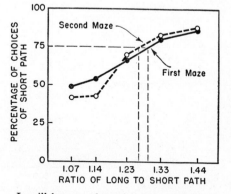

line in the graph below are the percentages of choices (out of 22 trials) of the *shorter* path by each of the five groups.

It will be seen that with the smallest ratio (1.07) there is no preference for the shorter path. As the ratios increase, the choice of the shorter path increases.

The differential threshold would be that ratio value at which the rats chose the shorter path about 75 per cent of the time, that is, halfway between no preference (50 per cent) and perfect preference (100 per cent). This would mean a ratio value of about 1.3.

Now what would happen *if the ratios were kept the same, but the absolute sizes of the differences were doubled?* This was tested by building a second maze exactly like the first, but *twice as big.* Five more groups of rats were run, and the results are shown in the dotted line of the above graph.

The striking finding is that the curves are almost identical, and the estimated difference threshold about the same. Thus the difference in paths that the rat can discriminate is a function of the *relative* lengths not the absolute lengths, and Weber's Law holds true for the laboratory rat judging distances to cheese as it does for the human being judging the loudness of sounds.

Group	Length of Short Path	Length of Long Path	Ratio of Long to Short Path
a	187 inches	200 inches	1.07
b	174 "	200 "	1.14
c	161 "	200 "	1.23
d	148 "	200 "	1.33
e	135 "	200 "	1.44

The rat started at the point where the rat is shown in the maze, choosing either to go left and follow the dotted path to the food, the total distance being 200 inches, or to go right and follow the other dotted path to food, the distance being shorter. Five groups of 10 rats each were tested; for each group the length of the shorter path was different. The shortest path is shown. The path can be lengthened by moving the block from *e* to *d*, etc., and extending the dividing partition, P.

How big did the ratio of the long to the short path have to be for the rat to discriminate between the two? Shown by the solid

YOSHIOKA, J. G. 1929. Weber's law in the discrimination of maze distance by the white rat. *Univ. Calif. Publ. Psychol.*, 4, 155–84.

The stimulus for vision is light waves falling on the eyes. Of the whole range of light waves, only a tiny fraction are capable of arousing visual sensation (see Fig. 10). Above and below this "visible spectrum" there is no visual impression. Within

microns (a millimicron, symbolized by mμ, is one-billionth of a meter) are seen as red light; those of about 400 millimicrons are seen as violet light. Each of the other hues of the spectrum has its own wave length

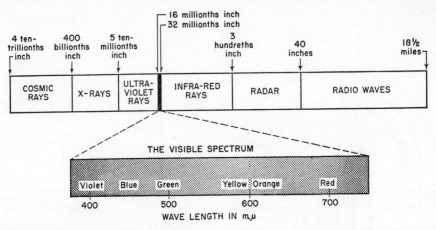

FIG. 10. Here is shown the range of electromagnetic waves, varying from the shortest cosmic rays to the longest radio waves. They are plotted logarithmically in order to condense them on the page. Only the extremely tiny

range between 16 and 32 millionths of an inch is adequate to stimulate vision. As indicated at the bottom of the chart, the *whole* visible spectrum, which includes all the colors we can experience, falls between these narrow limits.

trum" there is no visual impression. Within this visible range the physical characteristics of the light waves are closely related to the principal dimensions of our perception of color—hue, brightness, and saturation.

Hue. If we give people swatches of many colors and ask them to arrange the hues "in an orderly progression," they will closely agree in how they do it: red, orange, yellow, green, blue, violet. It would seem to them clearly "wrong" to put the green between the red and yellow, or the orange beyond the blue. This is true even if we test people who know nothing about the physics of light.

The notable fact is that this perceptual order is identical with the order of the wave lengths of light which give rise to these respective colors, as shown in Figure 10. Wave lengths of about 700 milli-

located somewhere in between these two extremes.

Why there should be this *isomorphism* (same form) of the ordering of perceived colors and of the underlying physical wave lengths is a fascinating and as yet unsolved question. There is a way in which we can experience this progression of colors in nature. When sunlight passes through a prism, it fans out into the familiar color spectrum ranging from red through violet (see Fig. 11 and Color Plate III). The rainbow is a common example where the sunlight is refracted by passing through rain drops serving as prisms.

If we reverse the process and *recombine* the various spectral colors of the rainbow, we once again get the white sunlight. White light, therefore, has no single wave length corresponding to it, and the same is true of some other important colors.

THE COLOR CIRCLE. If we look at the

rainbow, we find a "good" red lacking; the best red is too orangish. Moreover, there are no purples, no browns, no olives, no blacks. These colors are obtained, like white, by *mixture* of wave lengths. Thus a

receptors and brain work, but at present we do not know.

Brightness. Any given hue, such as red, can vary in brightness. Brightness corre-

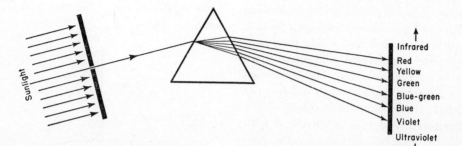

FIG. 11. A ray of sunlight (white light) is refracted by a prism through which it passes in such a way as to be split up into a number of

rays of light of different wave lengths, forming the entire visible color spectrum from red through violet.

"good" red is obtained by combining the wave lengths for orange and violet, purple is obtained by combining those for red and blue. And if we now ask a person to place the purple color somewhere in his orderly perceptual color dimension, he will be in some doubt where it goes, whether below the red or above the violet, or in both places. He can solve the problem by bending his sequence of colors into a circle bringing the two ends together, with purple the connecting link between red and blue (see Fig. 12). Any person facing the problem would probably, sooner or later, "invent" the well-known *color circle*.

PRIMARY COLORS. Certain colors, namely red, yellow, green, and blue, are often called *primary colors* in a psychological analysis of color. This term is used because they appear to the observer to be "pure" rather than "mixtures" of other colors. This "primary" quality is entirely a perceptual phenomenon; there is nothing whatever distinctive in the continuum of physical wave lengths of light at the points corresponding to these primary colors. The answer must lie elsewhere, presumably in the way the

sponds closely with the intensity of the light energies. With greater intensity the colors are brighter, approaching white; with lesser intensities the colors are darker, approaching black.

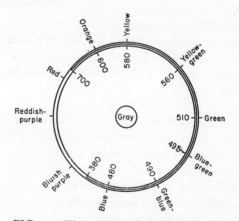

FIG. 12. The color circle, showing placement of various principal hues around its perimeter. The numbers indicate the wave lengths of light corresponding to the hues. Hues on diametrically opposite sides of the circle are complementary, that is, when mixed in equal proportions they yield gray. Colors with wave lengths between 380 and 700 are not found in the physical spectrum, and are obtainable only by the mixing of spectral colors.

Saturation. A color of a given hue and a given brightness may also look more or less *saturated*. That is, it may look more rich and concentrated or more pale, dilute, and washed-out. We can recognize the phenomenon easily by gradually diluting a rich blue water-color paint with water, making it paler and paler tints of blue until no blue at all is discernible. We would then have a completely desaturated color, or what we call an *achromatic* color. The continuum of *grays*, from white through middle gray to black, are the achromatic colors.

Desaturation of hues is correlated with a similar "dilution" of wave lengths, produced by mixing light of different wave lengths. *The greater the number of different wave lengths, the less the saturation.*

The most highly saturated hues are those of a middle level of brightness. As we go toward brighter colors or toward darker colors, the maximal saturation that can be attained is less and less, until on reaching white or black, saturation is zero.

THE COLOR CONE. The student should now be able to take the final step in constructing a geometrical color model adequate to account for all the facts we have observed. This is the well-known *color cone* (actually a double cone) shown in Figure 13.

Color Mixture. The light that strikes the eye is very rarely composed of light of a single wave length; almost always it is a mixture of many wave lengths. This is due to the fact that illumination on objects is mainly from light sources, such as the sun, which emit light waves of various lengths. Only under exceptional laboratory conditions, where there is careful filtering, are we likely to deal with *pure* light of a given single wave length.

The most striking fact about a light mixture is that we do not and cannot *analyze* it into its component parts simply by look-

ing at it—i.e., in our perceptions. We see *only* the single color that results from the mixture. Thus a light mixture is different from some other perceived blends of stimuli. For example, in mixing foods to make a fancy dish, with refined sensitivity we *may* be able to detect the various ingredients.

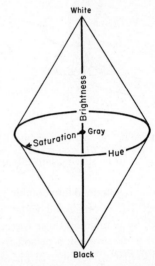

FIG. 13. The color cone. With this three-dimensional model, one can represent each color experience in its three principal attributes of hue, brightness, and saturation. Brightness is represented by distance along the vertical axis, from black through middle gray to white; hue, by the directions of the spokes toward the periphery of the cone; saturation, by the distance from the center axis along the spokes.

There are specific rules by which we can mix colors and predict the resulting hue, brightness, and saturation. These rules have been learned gradually over a long period of time in people's common experience. They have been carefully verified by laboratory experimentation, especially by the use of apparatus that permits controlled combining of colors in measurable amounts. One of the most useful pieces of apparatus for this purpose is the *color wheel* (see Fig. 14).

RULES OF COLOR MIXTURE. It is possible to predict the results of color mixture by direct reference to the relationships among points in the color cone which represent the various component colors.

The following concrete rules of color mixture will be best understood by refer-

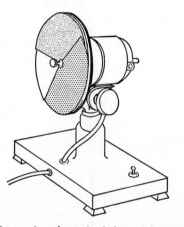

FIG. 14. A color wheel for mixing colors. Discs of colored paper are cut and assembled on the wheel, overlapping so that different sized angular sectors of each color are exposed. When the wheel is rotated rapidly, a completely mixed color is seen instead of the separate component colors. The proportions of mixtures can readily be varied by changing the size of angular sectors of the two or more component colors.

ence to the color cone (Figure 13) and to the illustrations given in Box 18.

1. Two hues mixed in equal amounts will result in a new hue lying on the color circle exactly halfway between the two; if two hues are mixed in unequal amounts, the new hue will be proportionately closer to the more plentiful component.

2. The brightness of the resultant color will be the average of the brightness of the two component colors.

3. The saturation of a mixed color will be less than the average of the saturations of the component colors.

COMPLEMENTARY COLORS. A special case of great significance is the mixture of hues lying exactly opposite each other on the color circle. As the first rule above would

indicate, these hues exactly cancel each other out, yielding an achromatic *gray*. For example, a properly chosen red and green (with wave lengths of about 640 and 490, respectively) will when mixed on a color wheel lose all color (see Box 18). The same is true of a yellow and a blue, and indeed of *any* pair of colors exactly opposite each other on the color circle. Such pairs are known as *complementary colors*. Every color, of course, has its complementary.

MIXTURE OF MORE THAN TWO COLORS. The above rules for mixture apply not only for two, but for *any number* of colors. Given the points on the color cone representing each of the components, we obtain the point representative of the new mixed color simply by taking a kind of "geometrical average" of all the original points. An illustration of this for three colors is shown in Box 18.

It may also have occurred to the reader that *all* hues on the color circle can be manufactured by having *only three* initial colors to mix. (The only proviso is that not all three lie on the same half of the color circle.) For instance, from red, green, and blue, all hues can be mixed. If we simply add white and black to our three chromatic ingredients, we can manufacture *every* color in the color cone, having any desired hue, brightness, and saturation.

The fact that three is the minimal number of required color components has led to various theories of the physiological bases of color vision which assume that there are three specialized retinal receptors for the three different colors (see Chapter 7).

MIXING LIGHT VS. MIXING PAINT. The reader may have detected a contradiction between what has been said about color mixture and his own experiences in mixing colors from a paint box. Yellow and blue, we have said, are complementaries, and when mixed equally yield a gray. But we

BOX 18

Color Mixture

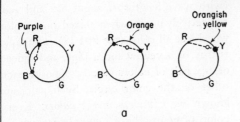

Purple   Orange   Orangish yellow

a

The three color circles (fig. *a*) show, on the left, the mixture of red and blue to produce purple; in the center, the mixture of red and yellow to produce orange; and, on the right, the mixture of a little red and a lot of yellow to produce an orangish-yellow.

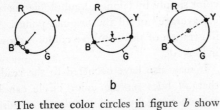

b

The three color circles in figure *b* show how saturation of the resultant mixture is determined by how far apart the original colors are on the color perimeter. On the left, they are close together and the resultant saturation is high, indicated by the length of the arrow. In the center, the saturation is less; and on the right, the saturation is zero, because the two colors are exactly opposite (i.e., complementary) and the resultant mixture must be achromatic.

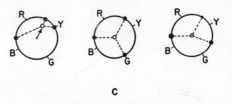

c

Figure *c* shows how *three* colors can be mixed. On the left a moderately saturated hue is obtained. In the center the three colors are equally spaced around the color circle and when mixed in equal amounts yield an achromatic grey. On the right the result is also an achromatic gray, this time produced by a mixture of the appropriate amounts of three colors *not* equally spaced around the color circle.

---

have all mixed yellow and blue paint to get *green*. Moreover, by mixing all the paints of the palette, we get a dirty black, not the white we have specified above. What is the discrepancy? The answer is simple, but it requires us first to examine the manner in which the color of objects is perceived.

The Color of Objects. The perceived color of an object depends upon the light waves that are reflected or emitted from its surface. The differences in physical constitution of objects determine, among other things, the manner in which they will absorb and reflect light. A highly polished surface, such as a mirror, reflects most of the light falling on it; snow reflects a great deal of the light falling on it; dirt reflects less, and coal still less.

Objects also differ in physical constitution in the degree to which they *selectively reflect or absorb light of different wave lengths.* Of all the light waves falling on a given object, some will be more fully absorbed than will others. A ripe tomato in sunlight will absorb most of the wave lengths *except* those around 600 millimicrons, namely, those corresponding to "red" light; hence, what is *reflected* from the tomato and what strikes the eye of the viewer is mainly "red" light and he sees the tomato as red. A "white" object reflects all wave lengths and hence is perceived as white; a "black" object absorbs all wave lengths.

The perceived hue of an object thus depends upon two factors: (1) the wave lengths of the light illuminating it, and (2) the wave lengths of the light it reflects. If the illumination falling on a "red" object contains no "red" wave lengths, the object may look black.

COMBINING AND SUBTRACTING LIGHT WAVES. We can now readily account for the difference in results when we mix lights and mix paints. In the former we are *combining* light waves. In the latter we are *subtracting* light waves, in that we are mixing pigments each of which absorbs different light waves. The resulting pigment mixture absorbs a greater variety of light waves and reflects fewer than does each component pigment alone. Thus, paints act like *filters*.

Visual Sensitivity and Acuity. Sensitivity of the eye to light varies with the intensity and the wave length of light, with the state of the eye, with the point stimulated on the eye, etc.

SENSITIVITY TO INTENSITY. We have already noted that under optimal conditions the smallest intensity of light that the eye can detect is amazingly low. One of the optimal conditions is that the eye be *dark adapted* (see below, p. 76). The longer a person sits in a dark room, the more sensitive his eyes become to light. Sensitivity

to intensity also is a function of the wave length of the light. For example, light of wave length around 500 mμ is more easily seen than light of other wave lengths.

Sensitivity to intensity is dependent upon the part of the retina stimulated. The most sensitive part of the retina lies slightly to one side of the *fovea*, which is the name given to the very center of the retina.

There is one especially interesting anomaly in the sensitivity of different parts of the retina. One part of the retina is completely blind. When you do the demonstration in Figure 15, you will discover this blindness which you may previously not have suspected.

SENSITIVITY TO WAVE LENGTH. Sensitivity to wave length is by no means the same as sensitivity to intensity. In general, there is much greater ability to detect that there *is* light than to detect its color. Thus, at any given wave length, there is a zone of intensities within which we can see light but not color (see Fig. 16).

We have all noticed when sitting in a darkening garden at twilight that the colors of the flowers look different than during the day. During the day the reds and yellows were far brighter than the greens and blues; now at twilight the greens and blues are brighter. As darkness grows more complete, the reds and yellows may completely disappear, long before the shorter-

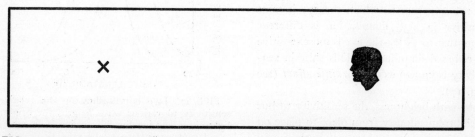

FIG. 15. Hold the book at arm's length, close your left eye, and steadily fixate the cross. Then slowly bring the book toward you. You will find a place at which the head completely disappears. This is because from that distance its image is falling on an insensitive part of the retina known as the *blind spot*. Now bring the book even closer to your face, and the head will reappear. There is, of course, a similar blind spot in the other eye.

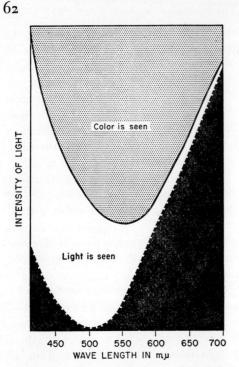

FIG. 16. A chart showing the sensitivity of the human eye to light of different wave lengths. The dotted curve indicates the minimal intensities required at each wave length for *light* to be seen. The solid curve indicates the minimal intensities required at each wave length for *color* to be seen. For the range of intensities lying between the curves, only *achromatic* light is seen.

wave-length colors do. A red rose may look black, while the leaves are still clearly green.

The reason for these shifts in relative brightness of colors is the fact that the part of the spectrum to which the eye is most sensitive in high illumination is different from that to which the eye is most sensitive in reduced illumination. This shift in sensitivity is known as the *Purkinje effect* (see Fig. 17).

As with brightness, the sensitivity to hue varies tremendously from place to place on the retina. Colors are best seen in the foveal region. They are not seen at all in the extreme periphery; everyone is "color blind" at the edge of his visual field. You can

easily demonstrate this by fixating a point in front of you and slowly moving a colored pencil at arm's length from the side of your head, where you cannot at first see it at all, toward the front. You will notice that you can detect the presence of the pencil moving into your visual field long before you can detect its color. Moreover, if the pencil is half yellow and half red, you will find that the yellow can be seen much closer to the periphery than can the red.

VISUAL ACUITY. When we talk about people as having "good" or "poor" vision, it is usually *visual acuity* we are referring to—their ability to differentiate small stimulus differences in the size and shape of objects.

Acuity is measured by testing the individual's ability to make correct discriminations of stimulus differences close to threshold. The conventional eye chart exposes letters or other figures of varying sizes at a standard distance from the viewer. His acuity is measured in terms of his successful identification of the figures, and is commonly expressed as relative to average vision. Thus, 20-20 vision signifies that the person is able to identify stimuli at 20 feet that average vision also identifies at 20 feet.

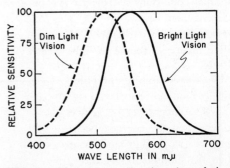

FIG. 17. Two curves showing the relative sensitivity to various wave lengths for bright-light vision and for dim-light vision. The curves are plotted as percentages of maximal sensitivity. For example, in bright light the eye is most sensitive to wave lengths around 550 (a greenish yellow hue); in dim light, to wave lengths around 500 (a green hue).

And 20-40 vision signifies that he must be as close as 20 feet to identify what average vision can identify at 40 feet. For more accurate determinations of visual acuity in the laboratory, other methods are used.

Acuity is not a single, unchanging value. It depends upon many factors. We have seen previously that the retina is anything but homogeneous in its sensitivity. This is true also of acuity, which is increasingly poor as the stimulus moves away from the center of the retina (see Fig. 18). More-

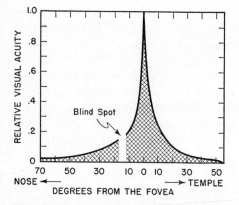

FIG. 18. Diagram showing the varying levels of visual acuity at different places on the retina. Acuity at the fovea is maximal, and it drops sharply as the stimulus moves away from the fovea toward the periphery of the retina. At the blind spot, of course, there is zero acuity.

over, there are tremendous changes in acuity with changes in intensity of illumination.

The relationship of the object to its visual surroundings also plays a significant role in determining level of acuity. Acuity is higher when the contrast between the object and its background is greater, and when the illumination of the surroundings is not too different from that of the object; it is lower when light of high intensity (glare) shines close to the direct line of vision.

Defects of the eye may reduce visual acuity. Thus, in nearsightedness and far-sightedness things clearly discriminated at one distance may be fuzzy and unclear at other distances. The reason has to do with the manner in which the eyeball adjusts or fails to adjust in focusing on the object, as we shall see in Chapter 7.

By Way of Summary. The physical stimuli for vision are radiant energies (electromagnetic waves) striking the eye. The hue of a color depends primarily upon the wave length of the light; the brightness of a color, upon the intensity of the light. Specific hues of the spectrum are related in an orderly way to specific wave lengths of light; some colors not found in the spectrum (such as purple) can be obtained only by color mixture. Color mixture follows certain fairly simple laws. The saturation of a hue depends upon the degree to which it is diluted by mixture with other colors. When the colors are complementary (e.g., yellow and blue), their mixture in equal proportions results in a completely desaturated color—gray. But mixing light involves the "addition" of wave lengths and is quite different from mixing paint, which involves a "subtraction" of wave lengths.

The sensitivity of the eye to light varies with the intensity and the wave length of the light, with the state of adaptation of the eye, and with the region of the retina stimulated. Visual acuity—the ability to see small spatial separations between stimuli—varies, depending upon the part of the retina stimulated, the amount of illumination, the degree of contrast of object and its surroundings, and the presence or absence of defects in the ocular mechanism.

The Physical Stimuli for Sound

The stimuli for sensations of sound are variations in mechanical pressure on the eardrum. In order to understand how these mechanical pressures originate in our physical environment, we must take a short excursion into simple physics.

The Physics of Sound. When a physical object is set into regular vibration (a violin string plucked, a tuning fork struck), the vibrations produce periodic compressions and rarefactions of the surrounding air. These periodic compressions and rarefactions are transmitted through the air in all directions. It is their impact on the eardrum which results in the hearing of sound.

It is convenient to plot the periodic compressions and rarefactions in the graphical form of waves, and hence they are customarily referred to as *sound waves* (see Fig. 19). The two main characteristics of sound waves are frequency and amplitude. The faster the object vibrates, the greater the number of periodic compressions of the air per second. This is known as *frequency* of the sound wave, measured in cycles per second (c.p.s.). The more forceful the vibrations (for instance, the harder the tuning fork is struck), the greater the energy transmitted in the air compressions. This

is known as the *amplitude* of the sound wave.

The frequency of sound waves emitted by a vibrating object remains the same as they travel through the air. The sound waves from a given tuning fork are the same frequency whether close up or far away. But the amplitude of the sound wave decreases as it travels away from the tuning fork. This is because the energy of the wave gradually dissipates as it spreads in all directions.

We now turn to the question of the psychophysical relationship of frequency and amplitude to the auditory experiences of pitch and loudness.

Pitch. Our worlds are full of sounds that vary in *pitch*, all the way from the deepest tone to the highest tone. The rising wail of a siren provides a helpful illustration of variations in pitch and of the stimuli that cause the variations. The sound of the siren is made by directing a jet of air against a revolving disk having a row of holes around its periphery. As the disk moves, the air escapes through the holes in separate puffs. The faster the disk turns,

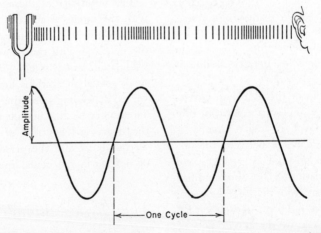

FIG. 19. The successive compressions and rarefactions of the air particles produced by the vibration of a tuning fork. Below is a curve corresponding to these sound waves. The amplitude, or height, of the wave indicates the degree of compression or rarefaction of the air particles. The frequency of sound waves is the number of cycles per second passing a given point.

the greater the rate of puffs, and the higher the pitch of the siren. Thus, *the pitch varies with the frequency of sound waves:* low pitched sounds are evoked by low frequencies and high pitched sounds by high frequencies. As Figure 20 indicates, the relationship between pitch and frequency is not a straight line.

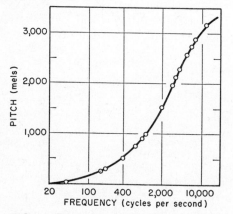

FIG. 20. Graph showing the relation of pitch to frequency of sound waves.

However, as we have earlier emphasized, there is no reason to expect a simple one-to-one relationship between a single dimension of the physical stimulus and a single attribute of sensory experience. Thus, pitch turns out to be determined not only by frequency of the sound waves, but also by their amplitude. The pitch of low-frequency tones drops as the amplitude increases.

Loudness. The sounds we hear vary enormously in *loudness,* from the faintest whisper to the deafening blast. *Loudness varies primarily with the amplitude of the sound waves.* But frequency, too, plays a role. Two tones of equal amplitude but different frequency will not be perceived as identical in loudness.

Complex Attributes as a Function of Wave Mixture. Most of what we have discussed about auditory experiences up to this point

has pertained to the perception of *pure tones.* Pure tones are produced by a regularly vibrating object, such as a tuning fork, which emits waves of a single frequency. Pure tones are rare. Almost always in our physical environments sound waves are mixtures of waves of different frequencies. The sound of a violin string is much more complex than that of a tuning fork, and that of an entire orchestra still more complex. The complexity may come about because the characteristics of the sound-source are such as to emit mixed waves; a violin, for instance, emits not only a basic wave frequency but a large number of other related frequencies, e.g., from the vibration of the wood. The mixture can also come about because there are several different sources of sound emitting waves simultaneously. No matter where the waves come from, they strike the eardrum together and are necessarily mixed there.

The consequences of different forms of wave mixture in auditory experience will now be examined.

TIMBRE AND OVERTONES. The tone of a tuning fork is thin compared with the full, rich tone of a cello. This attribute of tonal quality is usually referred to as *timbre.* It is differences in timbre which enable us readily to distinguish among identical notes played by a violin, a piano, and a flute. Timbre is difficult to analyze, and the most that we can say concerning the psychophysical relationship is that the greater the complexity of mixture of the physical sound waves the richer the timbre.

A perceptive listener can detect tones of higher pitches along with the pitch of the fundamental tone when a musical instrument is played. These are called *overtones.* They are based on concrete properties of the physical stimulus, as described in Figure 21.

DIFFERENTIATION AND MASKING OF TONES. If a person is simultaneously stimulated by two tones of different wave frequencies, for instance, 1,200 and 1,700 cycles per second, he is able to pick out each of these tones. The ease with which this is done will depend upon the degree of separation and the "harmony" of the two tones (see below). It will also depend in an interesting way on their relative loudnesses.

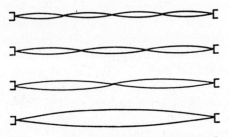

FIG. 21. Diagram showing how a vibrating string also vibrates in halves, thirds, fourths, etc. Each vibrating part produces its own set of waves of higher frequencies, resulting in overtones.

If the lower tone is made considerably louder than the higher tone, it tends to pre-empt attention and become more salient. As the loudness difference becomes even greater, the higher tone may completely disappear, leaving the lower tone as the only one that is heard. This is called *masking*.

DISSONANCE AND CONSONANCE. An extremely important attribute of our auditory world is impression of consonance or dissonance that tonal combinations give. *Consonance* is the quality of harmony, smoothness, or unity of a combination of tones, often experienced as agreeable. *Dissonance* is the reverse of this, a quality of disharmony, ill-fittingness, and lack of unity of a combination of tones, often experienced as disagreeable.

A person will usually have little difficulty in sorting out tonal combinations on the basis of their consonance-dissonance, and he is likely to do it consistently on different occasions. Moreover, many other people will agree closely with his judg-

ments. But there is clear evidence from comparisons of musical judgments in different cultures that there is a great deal of latitude in the manner in which the consonance or dissonance of a specific tonal combination may be perceived. Moreover, people may change their own perceptions of consonance and dissonance with experience and musical training.

Despite these personal and cultural factors, consonance and dissonance are to a considerable degree determined by the pattern of the physical stimulus. If we make up a tonal combination of wave frequencies of 200, 400, 800, and 1,600 cycles per second, it will be heard as high in consonance by most people. If we combine frequencies of 100, 200, 300, 400, 500, etc., this will also tend to be perceived as consonant. Note that the frequencies are all simple multiples of the lowest frequency.

On the other hand, if we combine the following unrelated frequencies—105, 173, 251, 497, 582—the effect is highly likely to be perceived as dissonant. What seems to be the rule in general, therefore, is that the attribute of consonance tends to relate closely to certain mathematical regularities of relationship among the frequencies mixed, and dissonance, conversely, tends to relate to *irregularities* of relationship in the physical wave frequencies.

NOISE. Noise is not merely dissonance carried to an extreme; it is auditory experience that is pretty much removed from the whole tonal sphere. Though we can roughly distinguish some noises with respect to their pitch, for the most part this is difficult and pitch is not a salient aspect of the noise experience. Noises are for this reason sometimes referred to as "atonality," but this would naturally outrage those modern composers whose "atonal" music is to their sophisticated ears anything but noisy.

The physical stimulus for noise is a complex mixture of wave frequencies that bear no simple numerical relationships to one another. The most extreme physical stimulus for noise is that combination which includes *all* the frequencies. This noise is sometimes technically referred to as *white noise*, because of the obvious analogy with white light which includes all wave lengths.

Auditory Sensitivity. Of the whole range of frequencies of sound waves, only a certain band is capable of producing sensations of sound. In man, for instance, the lowest frequency that can be heard is about 20 cycles per second, while the highest is about 20,000 cycles per second. Beyond these limits there is silence.

Auditory sensitivity is a complex function of intensity and frequency. Figure 22 shows how an "auditory area" can be plotted within which all normal hearing occurs.

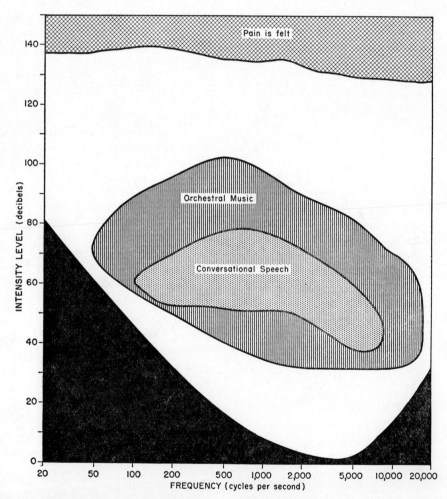

FIG. 22. The auditory area, showing how perception of sound is a function of both intensity and frequency of sound waves. The lower curve shows the minimal intensities required at each frequency in order to hear sound. Above the upper curve the intensities are so great that they produce painful sensation. Between the two curves is the area of hearing. Also shown are the approximate areas of conversational speech and of orchestral music.

Discrimination of pitch and loudness. We have noted previously that the differential threshold, like any threshold, is a function of multiple factors. One of the main determinants of the discrimination of differences in pitch is the level of intensity of the sound. For instance, at frequencies of about 1,000 c.p.s. the ability to distinguish one pitch from another is much better than at lower frequencies.

Conversely, the ability to detect small differences in the loudness of two tones depends partly upon the frequency; sensitivity is greater for tones of middle frequency than for those of higher or lower frequencies.

By Way of Summary. The sensation of sound is dependent upon variations in air pressure at the eardrum. The frequency of the sound wave is closely related to the pitch of the sound; the amplitude of the wave, to the loudness of the sound. But frequency also partially affects loudness; and amplitude, pitch. When there is a mixture of sound waves, the perceived sound has complex qualities, including timbre and overtones, dissonance and consonance.

Auditory sensitivity, like visual sensitivity, is restricted to certain bands of energy intensities; it depends, among other things, upon the intensity and frequency of sound waves.

The Physical Stimuli for Taste and Smell

The senses of taste and smell co-operate closely, the physical stimuli for both are chemical substances, and their receptors are located near each other. For these reasons taste and smell perception are usually discussed together.

Taste. Certain soluble substances placed on the tongue, or in contact with other parts of the mouth and throat, evoke a variety of taste sensations. The classification of these taste sensations is difficult, partly no doubt because of the intimate interaction of odors and tastes in most taste experiences. Usually a *combination* of chemical substances will be applied to the tongue, as in eating food. The resultant mixtures may have new sensory qualities different from the component qualities. Such "blends" especially are likely to vary in subtle physiognomic qualities, e.g., "sharpness," "smoothness."

But taste mixtures, unlike light mixtures, are not always completely unanalyzable fusions. Everyone can recognize some of the different ingredients in a food, and a highly trained expert, such as the tea taster, has remarkable ability to analyze ingredients.

Stimulus relations. Traditionally, the basic components of taste have been identified as sensations of *sweet, sour, bitter,* and *salty*. It is easy to find common chemical stimuli for these four taste attributes: sugar for sweet, hydrochloric acid for sour, quinine for bitter, table salt for salty. But when we seek to specify the precise chemical structure of a substance that can be counted on to evoke the given attribute, we are confronted with a problem as yet unsolved. Substances of extremely different chemical make-up (e.g., sugar and saccharin) may evoke the same taste sensation; substances of highly similar chemical make-up may evoke quite different taste sensations, for instance bitter and sweet.

Smell. The adequate stimuli for sensations of smell are gaseous particles brought into contact with receptors in the upper cavity of the nose. Liquid, incidentally, will not serve. In one classical study the intrepid investigator filled his nasal cavity with Eau de Cologne and found that he could not smell it.

ATTRIBUTES OF ODORS. The bewildering array of experienced odors requires that some attempt be made to classify them, and if possible to represent them in some sort of a model akin to the color cone. This endeavor has been only partially successful. The scheme still most useful is the *smell prism* proposed by Henning in 1916 (see Fig. 23). The scheme assumes that

involve a mixture of chemical substances; thus there is simultaneous stimulation by various odors. There are several consequences of such mixtures. For one thing there may be some degree of fusion of the components, so that an odor blend is perceived. But such fusion, as with taste, is incomplete; with careful attention and training one can often distinguish among the components.

Masking is clearly evident in odor mix-

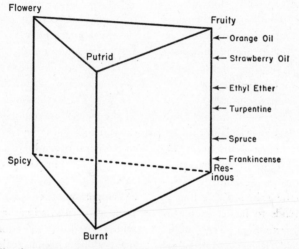

FIG. 23. The smell prism. Though only with moderate consistency, odors can be placed at specific points on the surfaces and edges of the

prism. Shown, for example, are several odors located along the edge between the primary fruity and the resinous odors. (Henning, 1916.)

there are six primary odors (analogous to the primary colors), and that any given odor is some combination of these six, lying at an intermediate point along the edges and surfaces of the smell prism.

As is true of taste, difficulties have been encountered in trying to relate the odor experiences to specifiable chemical structures of the gaseous stimuli. We can only conclude that this scientific task is yet to be accomplished. In Chapter 7 (pp. 183–4) we will see some of the reasons why it is difficult and perhaps *can not* be done.

MIXING OF ODORS. Most things we smell

tures as it is in sound. Where there are large differences in intensity among the component odors, one odor may completely mask another. There may also be a kind of "unmasking." With continued exposure to the stimulus, there is adaptation, that is, decreased intensity of the perceived odor. We may adapt faster to some components of a mixture than to others, so that components first unnoticed through being masked will later emerge. Such qualitative changes in odors are illustrated by the fact that although cheap perfumes smell agreeable at first, they gradually become disagreeable with continued exposure.

The Physical Stimuli for the Skin Senses

Taking together all kinds of sensory qualities aroused in the skin or in deeper tissues, we find a multitude of different experiences. Here, too, there is need for some sort of ordering or classifying of the experiences, but a satisfactory comprehensive "model" has not been found.

One difficulty is probably that all the diverse somesthetic sensations do not naturally go together. Sensations of strain in the muscles and tendons are now studied separately under the heading of the kinesthetic (movement) sense (see below). And the remaining sensations are usually divided up as follows: pressure, pain, warmth, and cold. This division has been encouraged by the search for, and alleged discovery of, specialized receptors for these sensations. (See Chapter 7 for a discussion of the physiological bases of the skin senses.) But at the same time it tends to neglect some of the very common experiences of "itch," "ache," and "tickle." Relatively little research has yet been carried out on these complex attributes of our skin senses. They cannot easily be classed as variants of pressure, pain, temperature, and kinesthetic sensations. They seem to be complex qualities resulting from a *patterning* of pressure and thermal stimuli.

The stimulation of the skin by mechanical pressures and thermal energies reveals that the skin is by no means a uniform receptor. Specific parts of the skin are sensitive to particular kinds of stimuli and insensitive to others. Box 19 indicates how the sensitivity of the skin is mapped.

Pressure Sensation. Objects forced against the skin will arouse sensations of pressure. There are various qualitative as well as quantitative changes in sensation as the force increases, varying from the faintest feeling of touch to the utmost of painful pressure. A mapping of the body's pressure spots indicates that the points sensitive to pressure are distributed very *unevenly* on the body surfaces, with more toward the extremities of the body.

Pain Sensation. The skin may be injured or subjected to extremes of physical energies in a variety of ways, such as by cutting, piercing, and burning, and by the application of heat, certain chemical agents, or electrical current. As in the case of pressure, there are certain spots on the skin where the stimuli are not effective. Here, too, mapping studies have shown that different parts of the body vary appreciably in the density of pain spots. For instance though the tip of the nose is relatively rich in temperature and in touch spots, it is relatively lacking in pain spots.

Temperature Sensation. The stimuli for temperature sensations are thermal energies, whose intensities, of course, vary continuously along a simple scale of physical heat. But our sensory experiences do not vary along a similar intensity scale. Our temperature experiences distinguish warmth from coolness, coolness from cold, heat from warmth. And these are qualitatively, not just quantitatively, different.

COLD AND WARM SPOTS. Some spots on the skin are sensitive to warmth and others to cold. No spot is sensitive to both. If a very hot stimulus is applied to a cold spot, the person may report a sensation of cold; this phenomenon is known as *paradoxical cold*. The opposite phenomenon of paradoxical warmth (a sensation of warmth produced by applying a very cold stimulus to a warm spot) is less well substantiated.

PHYSIOLOGICAL ZERO. Whether a thermal stimulus will evoke a temperature sensation

BOX 19

Mapping Spots on the Skin

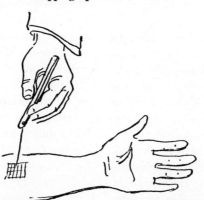

Almost simultaneously (1883–85) three physiologists—Blix in Sweden, Goldscheider in Germany, and Donaldson in America—discovered that there are different "spots" on the skin which are sensitive to stimuli for pressure, pain, warmth, and cold. This is a striking instance of *independent* scientific discovery.

By stamping a grid of fine inked lines on a given part of the skin, the exact location of these spots can be determined by applying a fine hair, or a needle, or a heated rod, etc., and asking the subject to report the resultant sensation. The results of such a mapping study on a small area of the skin are shown below.

LEGEND

- Pressure Spot
◇ Pain Spot
X Warm Spot
o Cold Spot

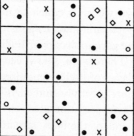

On repeated mappings, do the spots stay in the same place or do they seem to "mi-

grate?" Dallenbach studied this by mapping warm and cold spots on the same grid on the skin on four successive days with the results shown below.

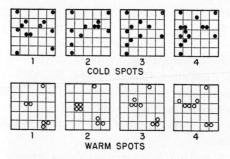

COLD SPOTS

WARM SPOTS

Apparently there is a considerable degree of consistency in location of spots, yet it is far from perfect. Perhaps the problem is in the technical difficulties of the mapping operation, perhaps in the fact that the threshold of sensitivity of the spots varies from time to time. If great care is taken to locate specially sensitive spots, they may prove very dependable on repeated stimulation. One investigator located 36 cold spots with great care and found that only two of them ever failed to give the cold sensation.

DALLENBACH, K. M. 1927. The temperature spots and end organs. *Amer. J. Psychol., 39,* 417.

depends upon the relation of the temperature of the stimulus to the temperature of the skin. This skin temperature is called the *physiological zero*. Stimuli hotter than the physiological zero will produce sensations of warmth; those colder will produce sensations of cold; those close to it will produce no temperature sensations. The physiological zero changes with changes in temperature of the environment and varies for different parts of the body. Therefore, a stimulus of a given temperature can evoke either a hot or a cold sensation. For example, after a person has immersed his left hand in ice water and his right hand in hot water for a while, the skin temperatures of the two hands will be markedly different. If he now puts both hands into the *same* lukewarm water, the water will feel cool to his right hand and warm to his left.

STIMULUS MIXTURE. With extremes of heat and cold sensations pain is also involved, perhaps due to the stimulation of pain receptors. It is sometimes difficult to discriminate between extreme cold and extreme heat, and this may depend upon the fact that an element of pain is common to both.

A striking demonstration that a sensory quality can be evoked by *mixtures* of stimuli that by themselves could not evoke the quality is the arousal of an experience of *heat* by the joint application of *warm* and *cold* stimuli (see Fig. 24). Again we see the importance of interaction effects.

The Physical Stimuli for Internal Bodily Sensations

Pains, aches, spasms, and a whole host of vague and ill-defined "organic" sensations come from organs and tissues of the body. By and large such deep-lying sensations

have not been the subject of intensive psychological investigation. As compared with most other senses, the physical stimuli for these sensations are hard to get at for study.

As we shall see when we turn to problems of motivation in later chapters, some experimental work has been done on the relations of sensations arising from the stomach (hunger pangs, etc.) to states of hunger drive. There has also been some concern with the problem of bodily sensations during states of emotion. But in gen-

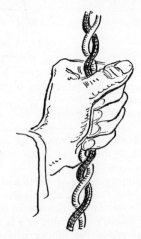

FIG. 24. Warm water and very cold water are circulated separately through the twisted tubes grasped in the person's hand. The combined impression he gets is of *heat*.

eral we must conclude that relatively little systematic knowledge is yet available about the psychophysics of bodily sensations.

There are, however, two particular classes of bodily sensations which have been more carefully studied. These are the *kinesthetic* sensations, which pertain to movements of the body structure, and *vestibular* sensations, which pertain to the orientation of the body in space.

Kinesthetic Sensations. *Kinesthesis* (literally "movement sensitivity") is one of the most basic of our senses. It provides information on the movements of bodily structures, the raising of the arm, the turn of the eyeballs, swallowing, indeed, the whole repertory of motor actions. In addition, it is responsible for the sensations of muscular tension and strain.

The physical stimuli for kinesthetic sensations are mechanical forces affecting receptors in the muscles, tendons, and joints of the body. As the muscles function so that the locations of bodily parts are shifted, various patterns of pressures on these receptors provide the essential information for the guiding of the motor action. As we shall see in later chapters, there is a great deal of interaction between such kinesthetic sensations and other aspects of our perceptual experiences; for example, the perception of visual distance involves, among other things, a complex synthesis of information from the retinas and from the movement of the muscles of the eyeballs. Moreover, we shall see in the chapter on the learning of skills that a critical role is played by the patterning of such kinesthetic sensations.

KINESTHETIC DEFECT. We are normally unappreciative of the role of kinesthetic sensations in our behavior, but their importance is dramatically underlined in cases where they are missing. People may have diseases in which the kinesthetic sensations from parts of the body, such as the legs, are permanently lacking through destruction of the essential sensory nerves. These persons may, for instance, be observed to shuffle as they walk, carefully looking down at the feet. Without such visual guidance of their actions, they would be unable to locomote, for they get no direct kinesthetic information as to what the leg muscles are doing.

Vestibular Sensations. We have been discussing the perception of movements within the body. There is also the perception of spatial movement and orientation of the body as a whole. We are aware of being tilted, whirled, shaken. Much of the time we know "which way is up."

The stimuli for these sensations are accelerative movements of a fluid-filled receptor system located in structures known as the vestibules of the inner ear. For this reason they are referred to as vestibular sensations. (See Chapter 7 for a description of their physiological functioning.)

If the person's body is suddenly tilted from the vertical, the fluids are displaced and sensations of tilt occur. If he is whirled rapidly about, the fluids are displaced in another fashion and sensations of spin are evoked. If his body is suddenly jerked in a linear direction, the fluid displacement evokes a sensation of movement in that direction. These sensations of tilt, spin, and jerk will often occur together in a pattern of complex body-movement perceptions.

It is important to note that it is *acceleration* (i.e., *change* of rate of movement) of the vestibular system which is the critical physical stimulus. Movement at a uniform speed is not a stimulus. We sit in an airplane flying smoothly at 300 miles per hour with no sensation of movement; we are fortunately unaware of our movement in space as the earth whirls us about. But when the speed of movement is suddenly increased or decreased, or the direction abruptly changed, the vestibular sensations are aroused.

Since the receptors in the vestibules of the inner ear send neural impulses to the stomach, a side effect of such movement sensations may be the feelings of inner distress in motion sickness, such as seasickness.

Interaction Effects

We have started our study of the relations of physical stimuli to sensory experience in the narrowest possible way, by dealing with the artificial case of a single stimulus falling on a single "point" (or very restricted area) of a single receptor. In reality the perceptual situation is always more complex than this.

What we generally have is not single, isolated "point" stimulation, but *patterns* of stimulation. The fundamental psychological significance of this fact is that the effect of what happens at one "point" is *not independent* of the effect of what is happening at other "points." The effects of various stimuli *interact* in producing sensory experience, and for this reason we properly speak of *patterns* of physical stimuli.

In seeking to relate patterns of physical stimuli and the resultant sensory experiences, we are taking a step forward in complexity of the psychophysical problem. The patterns of physical stimuli are both spatial and temporal. The spatial patterns come about because of simultaneous stimulation of various parts of a specific receptor, such as the retina of the eye, or the skin of the body. The temporal patterns come about because of the sequence of stimuli falling on a given part.

Temporal Interaction. At any receptor point there is a temporal succession of stimuli. The successive stimuli may be repetitions of the *same* physical energies (that is, homogeneous), or may be *different* physical energies (that is, heterogeneous). The interactions occurring from the successive stimuli can be seen in temporal summation, fusion, and adaptation.

TEMPORAL SUMMATION. A very brief flash of light on the retina may be insufficient to evoke a perceptual effect; it is, as we say, below the threshold (subthreshold). If the same intensity of light is applied for a longer interval, it may become effective as a stimulus, that is, be above the threshold. It appears, therefore, that

the longer the *duration* of a subthreshold intensity, the greater the chance that it may become effective. The above phenomenon is known as *temporal summation.*

Apparently the effect of each momentary stimulus is not entirely independent of stimuli which have just occurred at that receptor "point." There is, instead, a kind of summation effect over time. The basis of such summation is presumably some form of "lag" in the receptor mechanism. That is, the receptor continues to act even after the first stimulus is removed. Thus the effects of the second stimulus are "added to" the aftereffects of the first.

Careful quantitative studies of temporal summation have been made, involving measurements of the reaction to various durations and intensities of light stimuli on the retina. They have led to the formulation that within limits *the effectiveness of a stimulus near the threshold is a product of intensity and duration.* This is known as the Bunsen-Roscoe Law. What it asserts is that a higher intensity for a short exposure may be equal to a lower intensity for a longer exposure. Or, in other words, what counts is the *total amount* of light during the interval.

FLICKER AND FUSION. Another way in which temporal "lag" is clearly shown is in the fact that the sensation accompanying a stimulus lasts for a very brief time *after* the stimulus has ceased.

This can easily be demonstrated by the presentation of an intermittent series of stimuli. If we turn a light on and off at intervals of one second, the observer sees a sequence of lights with dark intervals in between. If we now shorten the on-off intervals, a new phenomenon occurs; there appears to be a "flicker" of the light. If the intervals are made still shorter, the "flicker" disappears and a continuous light is seen.

We speak of this latter phenomenon as

fusion. It is an especially significant case of temporal interaction of stimuli, for out of a series of intermittent stimuli has emerged a quite different sensory impression, that of a continuous light. Obviously, what happens is that the aftereffect of each separate stimulus lasts long enough so that it bridges over the interval until the next stimulus occurs. We encounter the phenomenon repeatedly in our everyday life. The movies give us the undeniable impression of a continuous, unbroken stimulation, yet we know that what is exposed to our eyes is an intermittent series of still photographs with short intervals of darkness in between.

CRITICAL FLICKER FREQUENCY. By gradually increasing the rate of alternation of light and dark, we can determine the threshold rate at which flicker disappears and fusion occurs. This is known as the *critical flicker frequency* (c.f.f.). It, like any threshold value, varies widely depending upon the specific character of the stimulating conditions and of the states of the observer. For example, the c.f.f. is higher the greater the intensity difference between the light and the dark. For an unusual demonstration of this, see Figure 25. The brightness of the surrounding environment also has an influence on the magnitude of c.f.f. There is even some evidence that there are consistent individual differences in c.f.f. which relate to personality variables. People of different personality make-up looking at the same flicker apparatus may see the fusion occurring at quite different speeds.

PERCEPTUAL QUALITIES OF THE FUSION. The perceptual qualities of temporal fusion depend upon the *averaging* of the characteristics of the individual stimuli. In the above simple example there were alternate intensities of light and darkness, and the fusion is a brightness corresponding to an average of these intensities. Mixing of colors on a color wheel (see Fig. 14, p. 59) is an example of fusion.

SENSORY ADAPTATION. We have seen so far that there can be several kinds of temporal interaction of stimuli, e.g., summation of effect and fusion of components. There is another extremely important type of temporal interaction in which a succession of identical stimuli falling on the same re-

FIG. 25. When this figure is rotated at gradually increasing speed on a color wheel, the thin ring continues to flicker after the rest of the black and white field has fused to yield a uniform gray. Through *contrast* the difference between the white and black of the ring has been accentuated by their respective backgrounds. Hence they are slower to fuse. Note the striking fact that the flicker fusion rates for the ring and for the background are different *even though the physical stimulus characteristics of the two are identical.* (Sherrington, 1897.)

ceptor "point" leads to a *decrease* in the effectiveness of the later stimuli. This is known as *sensory adaptation.* (Its physiological basis will be discussed in Chapter 7.) The effect is found in all senses. Some striking examples will now be given.

VISUAL ADAPTATION. We have already demonstrated the marked amount of dilution of a yellow color which occurs as a consequence of fairly short continuous exposures (see Box 7, page 25). We can make similar demonstrations for any hue.

This is sensory adaptation; somehow the eye gets "fatigued" or otherwise changes its sensitivity so that the later stimuli in a continuous stream do not have the same effect as the earlier.

There is also pronounced adaptation to brightness of the visual stimuli. A white or a black surface continuously inspected begins to look grayish. And the most impressive of all visual adaptation effects is found in what are called *light adaptation* and *dark adaptation.* The former is illustrated by our common experience in entering a darkened theater from the bright sunlight; at first we cannot see objects, then after a time we see them very easily. What has happened? In the continuous sunlight the eye had become light adapted, so that it was relatively less sensitive to light stimuli. After some time in the darkness the eye recovered its sensitivity and we could again see. Now on leaving the theater we encounter a different difficulty; the sunlight is so bright that it hurts our eyes and we are "blinded" for a few moments. What has occurred is that after the prolonged absence of bright light the eye has become dark adapted, consequently being very much more sensitive to the full light of day.

The *afterimage* is an interesting instance

BOX 20

Afterimages

Stare steadily at the numeral on the sail in the figure for one minute. Then look at

a plain light surface, such as a wall or a sheet of paper. You may be surprised to see the sailboat projected there. And more surprising is the fact that the black and white areas are now reversed. This is known as a *negative afterimage.* It is called an afterimage because it is a sensation persisting after the original stimulus has been removed. It is called negative because the brightness relationships are reversed.

Negative afterimages are found with hue as well as with brightness. Turn to Color Plate IV immediately preceding page 1.

Fixate the cross in the center of the left figure for about 30 seconds; then transfer your gaze to the cross in the gray square. You will see clear colors in the locations of the four colored patches of the original stimulus, but the colors will now be the *complementaries* of the original hues.

There are also *positive afterimages.* If you look for a moment at a whirling bright light and then close your eyes, you will see the image of the path of the light persisting for some time. The image is positive, in that it appears in the same brightness relationships as the original stimulus.

The explanation of afterimages must lie in the fact that the nervous system continues to be aroused for some time after a stimulus has been withdrawn. Why the afterimage should often be the *negative* of the original stimulus is a fascinating question having to do with the adaptation of the visual nervous system to light (see Chapter 7, p. 165).

It should be noted that afterimage phenomena are by no means restricted solely to vision. There are also auditory afterimages and various tactual afterimages, such as the persistent feeling of pressure on the skin after a pressure stimulus has been withdrawn.

of adaptation phenomena. For a demonstration of this type of image see Box 20.

AUDITORY ADAPTATION. The ear is notably less subject to sensory adaptation than the eye and other sense receptors. Even prolonged exposure to a continuous sound of ordinary intensity shows little effect. But when we move into more intense continuous sounds, such as the high-pitched machinery sound that the factory worker may be exposed to, adaptation does occur, and there is a marked loss of auditory sensitivity.

In Figure 26 are shown the results of an

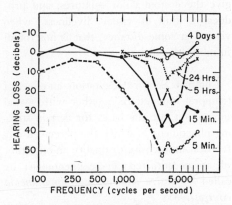

FIG. 26. Curves showing auditory adaptation to *white noise* (a complete mixture of sound waves of all frequencies). Note that the loss is greatest at the higher frequencies, and that the loss is less the longer the time interval after exposure to the stimulus. (Postman and Egan, 1949.)

experiment in which a high intensity *white noise*, which contains all the frequencies in about equal amounts, was continuously experienced. There were marked adaptation effects, which gradually disappeared when tested from 5 minutes to 4 days after cessation of the sound. There were also substantial differences in sensitivity loss for different wave frequencies; sensitivity to high tones was much more affected than sensitivity to low.

ADAPTATION IN THE SKIN SENSES. A modest pressure against the skin will soon not be noticed. For instance, in a 1915 study by von Frey and Goldman, a pressure stimulus was continuously applied at one point on the skin, and its effectiveness was compared with that of similar pressures applied at various comparable points. In three seconds the effect of the first stimulus had dropped to less than one quarter of the initial value.

As compared with pressure, adaptation to pain stimuli is slow. It is difficult to maintain a continuous, unchanging pain stimulus; for one thing, because of body movement in response to the pain, new pain "spots" get stimulated. This is perhaps why we seem to note little or no adaptation to the sensory pains we experience in daily life.

Adaptation to thermal stimuli is a matter of common observation by everyone. The uncomfortably hot bath water soon becomes bearable; the icy plunge into the cold lake soon gives way to a state in which the cold is not felt. If we deal with extremely hot and extremely cold stimuli, however, adaptation does not seem to occur, or occurs only very slowly.

Spatial Interaction. Some of our receptor organs consist of a large number of separate sensitive "points" spread out on the receptor surface. The retina of the eye, containing many light-sensitive cells, is the most important example. The skin of the body is another example. Just as there is highly significant temporal interaction of stimuli, so there is highly significant *spatial interaction*, among the separate sensitive "points" on the receptor surface. Such interaction is exhibited in a number of different ways, in spatial summation, irradiation, and spatial fusion.

SPATIAL SUMMATION. Just as we discovered summation effects of successive stimuli over time, so there is a summation effect of separate stimuli spread over space. The effectiveness of a visual stimulus depends not only on the intensity of the light, but also on the number of retinal points stimulated. Light intensities too weak to be seen when falling on a small retinal area can be seen when falling on a larger area. The effects of light waves falling on different areas of the retina are "added." This phenomenon is known as *spatial summation*. The basis of this and other forms of spatial interaction must lie in the fact that physiologically there are connections among the various receptor "points" (see Chapter 7).

Irradiation. That spatial "spreading" of effect occurs in the retina is suggested by another phenomenon, known as *irradiation*. For example, a white square on a black background appears larger than an equal-sized black square on a white background. It seems that the retinal excitation by the white area "spills over" to some extent into the surrounding retinal areas.

Spatial fusion. There is in spatial interaction an analogue of the fusion we have found in time. Stimuli falling in fairly close spatial proximity on the retina may be seen as separated and with distinct qualities. But if they are even closer together, a new perceptual phenomenon occurs, a sort of "flicker." And if they are brought very close together, *fusion* occurs, and they are no longer seen separately.

Examples of all three stages are common in our everyday experience. In textiles threads of various colors are woven into a pattern. When viewed close up, the separate colors can readily be distinguished. When viewed at a middle distance, an interplay of colors occurs which gives the material a "sparkle," a "liveliness," not seen either when unfused or when completely fused. At a sufficiently great distance, the separate colors completely disappear and a fusion is seen.

The color of the fusion product will be exactly what we would predict from the rules of color mixture previously discussed, even though we are dealing here with spatial rather than temporal mixing. Thus, green and red dots properly chosen will be seen when fused as gray. And separate white and black dots when fused will also be seen as gray.

Seurat (1859–91), the French impressionist painter, invented the technique called "pointillism," in which instead of mixing paints in the traditional way on the palette or canvas, he applied single dots of primary colors over the entire canvas. This method relies upon the spatial fusion of the eye to give the desired color mixtures, and produces a kind of visual "liveliness" when viewed at some distance, that is not found in most other paintings.

Contrast. Sensory adaptation, an effect of temporal interaction, together with spatial interaction, are the bases for certain striking phenomena in which the perceived differences in intensity or quality among stimuli are accentuated. These phenomena are called *successive contrast* and *simultaneous contrast*.

Successive contrast. When the eye has been exposed for some time to a bright stimulus, a darker stimulus following it will look unusually dark. The opposite is also true; a bright stimulus following a dark one will look unusually bright.

There is also successive *chromatic* contrast. After staring for a while at a red surface, a green stimulus looks much greener than usual.

What we note in general, therefore, is that successive contrast occurs when the successive stimuli are of different brightnesses or of opposite (that is, complementary) colors. This can be seen as an instance of sensory adaptation. Since light waves are usually mixed, a green object has a certain proportion of "red" waves; when there is adaptation of the "red" waves because of prolonged exposure to a prior red stimulus, the green object looks greener because the complementary red waves are not so effective as usual.

Although our most noticeable examples of successive contrast are in vision, it is found elsewhere; for instance, in taste. An orange tastes sour after sugar, but sweet after lemon.

SIMULTANEOUS CONTRAST. Look at the silhouetted heads in Figure 27. They seem to vary from light to dark gray. It is hard for most observers to see them as the same gray, yet that is what they are. How can it be that areas of identical brightness look so compellingly different? It is obviously due to the effect of the different surroundings. A given gray is made lighter by dark surroundings and darker by light surroundings. This effect is known as *simultaneous contrast*. As in the case of successive contrast, the general effect is the increase of the difference between two perceived properties.

Similar contrast effects are found with other properties of color, such as hue and saturation. For example, if two small squares of identical gray paper are compared when one is placed on a large red field and the other on a large green field, the former looks distinctly greenish and the latter distinctly reddish.

THE "LAWS" OF CONTRAST. On the basis of detailed investigations in the laboratory it is possible to state a number of generalizations about the *degree* of contrast that will be perceived under various specifiable stimulus conditions. The examples given here pertain to brightness contrast. Similar generalizations hold for contrast of hues.

1. Contrast in an area is greater the larger the difference in *intensity* of the area and its surroundings.

2. Contrast in an area is greater the larger the *relative size* of the surrounding field.

3. Contrast in an area is greater the *closer* the surroundings to the area, being most when the surroundings touch the area.

4. Contrast in an area is greater the *fuzzier the boundary* between the area and the surroundings.

5. Contrast in an area is greater the *less clear the "structure"* of the surfaces of the area and the surroundings. Thus, the contrast effect is greater if the areas look less like surface colors. This can be demonstrated by placing a transparent sheet of tissue paper over the field, so that the surfaces are less distinct. Under these conditions the contrast effect is greatly enhanced.

But we are still far from a complete understanding of the phenomena of contrast. Note, for example, the surprising "failure" of usual contrast effects demonstrated in

FIG. 27. A demonstration of brightness contrast. The heads are all cut from identical gray paper.

Color Plate V immediately preceding page 1.

By Way of Summary. In this chapter we first isolated the principal attributes of each of the senses in order that we might study them in an orderly way. We found that such isolation, though necessary for this kind of experimental analysis, was inadequate because of the central fact of *inter-action* of psychological processes. We therefore took the next step and considered interactions among the events occurring on the single receptor surface, such as the retina of the eye.

We can summarize the effects of sensory interactions occurring at a fairly simple level, as follows:

Stimuli in spatial or temporal proximity may interact so as

(a) to *reinforce* one another (e.g., the summation of subthreshold stimuli in producing a sensation);

(b) to *inhibit* one another (e.g., masking of one sound by another);

(c) to *desensitize* the effect of further stimuli of the same kind (e.g., sensory adaptation);

(d) to *accentuate* the differences between the stimuli (e.g., color contrast);

(e) to *fuse* and produce sensory experiences whose qualities differ from the qualities associated with the individual stimuli (e.g., color mixture).

But we have *two* eyes (and two ears), so there is also interaction occurring among the various receptors of a given sense, such as vision and audition. Furthermore, as we pointed out in discussing "unity of the senses" in Chapter 2, there are important interactions occurring *across* different senses, for instance when the eyes and ears and touch receptors are simultaneously stimulated.

Finally, there is interaction of the patterns of physical stimuli on our various receptors with all the events in the entire nervous system, events that have to do with motivation, emotion, and problem-solving.

In the following chapter on perceptual organization these various higher-order levels of interaction will be explored.

Glossary

absolute threshold. The minimal intensity of a physical stimulus required to stimulate the organism.

acuity. The ability to distinguish small stimulus differences. For instance, visual acuity is the ability to differentiate small details of size and shape of objects. Acuity is not a constant value, but varies depending upon many stimulus factors.

afterimage. The sensation that follows removal of the external light stimulus. The positive afterimage has the same colors as the original percept; the negative afterimage has the opposite colors from the original percept.

brightness. A dimension of visual experience varying from white to black. It is closely correlated with intensity of the light waves.

Bunsen-Roscoe Law. The generalization which states that within limits the effectiveness of a visual stimulus near the threshold is a product of the intensity and duration of the stimulus.

cold spot. A point on the skin which when stimulated, especially by a cold stimulus, evokes a sensation of cold. See also paradoxical cold.

color circle. An arrangement of the various hues around the perimeter of a circle.

color cone. A double cone that serves as a geometrical model adequate for the placement of any color in relation to its hue, saturation, and brightness.

color mixture. The mixture of light of different wave lengths which produces colors different from the component colors, according to certain rules of combination.

color wheel. A device for mixing colors in desired proportions by spinning colored papers of different areas on a wheel at sufficiently high speed so that the colors fuse.

complementary colors. Colors that lie exactly opposite each other on the color circle and which when mixed in equal proportions produce an achromatic gray, e.g. red and green, yellow and blue.

consonance. The quality of harmony, smoothness, or unity of a combination of tones, often experienced as agreeable.

critical flicker frequency (c.f.f.). The frequency of intermittent light flashes necessary to eliminate flicker and produce fusion.

decibel (db.). A unit of measurement which expresses intensity of a sound as a logarithmic function of threshold intensity.

differential threshold. The minimal difference in intensities of two stimuli that can be perceived.

dissonance. A quality of disharmony, ill-fittingness, and lack of unity of a combination of tones, often experienced as disagreeable. The opposite of consonance.

flicker. The visual phenomenon produced by certain rates of intermittent flashing on and off of a stimulus.

fusion. The phenomenon in which a series of successive stimuli produce a continuous, uniform sensation, such as in a rapidly flashing light, or in mixture of colors on a color wheel.

irradiation. The tendency for the retinal stimulation in a given area to spread slightly into the surroundings. Thus, a white square on a black background appears larger than an equal-sized black square on a white background.

kinesthesis. The sense of body movement and muscular strain evoked by mechanical forces affecting receptors in the muscles, tendons, and joints.

masking. The effect of one stimulus in reducing the experience of other stimuli presented simultaneously.

mel. A unit of pitch such that a 1,000-cycle tone sounded at 40 db. above threshold is taken to equal a pitch of 1,000 mels.

method of constant stimuli. A psychophysical method for determining thresholds in which each of a limited number of stimuli is repeatedly presented, and the degree to which each one evokes a sensation is recorded.

method of limits. A psychophysical method for determining thresholds in which a series of stimuli of increasing (or, alternately, of decreasing) intensity is presented, until that point is established at which sensation first occurs (or, alternately, first fails to occur).

overtones. Partial tones in a complex sound which have higher pitch than the fundamental.

paradoxical cold. A sensation of cold evoked when a very hot stimulus is applied to a cold spot on the skin.

pain spots. Points on the skin which when subjected to extreme stimulation such as by cutting, burning, chemicals, or electrical current, give rise to sensations of pain. The density of pain spots varies widely in different parts of the body.

physiological zero. The temperature of the skin. Stimuli hotter than the physiological zero produce sensations of warmth; those colder produce sensations of cold. The physiological zero varies as a function of the temperature of the environment and of the body.

pitch. The attribute of tones in terms of which they may be described as high or low. Closely related to frequency of the sound waves.

pressure spots. Points on the skin which when stimulated by pressure give rise to sensations of pressure, varying from very slight to extreme. Pressure spots are distributed very unevenly on the body surface with more toward the extremities.

primary colors. The colors red, yellow, green, and blue, which appear to the observers "pure" rather than "mixtures" of other colors.

psychophysics. The study of the relationships between the attributes of different sensory experiences and the characteristics of the physical stimuli producing them.

psychophysical methods. Methods for the determination of absolute and differential thresholds, including the method of constant stimuli and the method of limits.

pure tones. Tones produced by simple sound waves of a single frequency, such as by a tuning fork.

Purkinje effect. The shift in relative brightness of colors at the two ends of the spectrum as illumination decreases, e.g., greater relative brightness of reds and yellows in daylight and of blues and greens at twilight.

simultaneous contrast. The tendency for the color of one area to accentuate the complementary color of a neighboring area. The effect is found both with hue and with brightness.

smell prism. A three-dimensional model for the representation of six primary odors and their mixtures.

sound waves. Periodic compressions and rarefactions of the air which, striking the ear, produce sounds. Sound waves have certain frequencies and amplitudes.

spatial summation. The summative effect of separate stimuli spread over space. Thus light intensities too weak to be seen when falling on a small retinal area can be seen when falling on a larger area.

stimulus. Physical energy which excites a receptor and produces an effect on the organism.

stimulus-object. The object in the environment which is the source of the energies that serve as a stimulus.

successive contrast. The tendency for the exposure to one color to cause the accentuation of the complementary color in that same area thereafter. The effect is found both with hue and with brightness.

temporal summation. The phenomenon in which a subthreshold stimulus when continuously applied may summate its effect to produce a response.

vestibular sensations. The sense of balance and movement of the body. The stimuli for these sensations are accelerative movements of semicircular canals of the inner ear.

warm spot. A point on the skin which when stimulated, especially by a hot stimulus, evokes the sensation of heat.

Weber's Law. The principle that the minimal perceptible difference in intensity of two stimuli (ΔI) is a constant fraction (k) of the absolute level of the stimuli (I). Formulated as $\frac{\Delta I}{I} = k$. The constant fraction differs for each given type of stimulus. The law does not hold at the extremes of the stimulus range.

white noise. A complex mixture of sound waves of all frequencies, analogous to white light, which is a mixture of all wave lengths of light.

Suggestions for Further Reading

Boring, E. G. 1942. *Sensation and perception in the history of experimental psychology.* New York: Appleton-Century-Crofts.

An authoritative historical account of the development of experimental research in sensation and perception.

Davis, H. (ed.) 1947. *Hearing and deafness.* New York: Rinehart.

An intelligent layman's guide to the facts about hearing and deafness.

Evans, R. M. 1948. *An introduction to color.* New York: Wiley.

A book on the fundamentals of color

vision and the applications of color. Contains excellent color illustrations.

GELDARD, F. A. 1953. *The human senses.* New York: Wiley.

A textbook treatment of all the senses.

PIRENNE, M. H. 1949. *Vision and the eye.* London: Chapman and Hall.

Fundamentals of vision, presented in a lucid style.

POSTMAN, L., and EGAN, J. P. 1949. *Experimental psychology.* New York: Harper.

A highly readable textbook, including straightforward discussions of the facts about sensation and perception.

WOODWORTH, R. S., and SCHLOSBERG, H. 1954. *Experimental psychology* (rev. ed.). New York: Holt.

A standard and very useful textbook of experimental psychology. Of special interest to the present discussion are its numerous chapters devoted to perception and sensation.

CHAPTER V

Perceptual Organization and Change

Out of a chaos of physical stimuli we achieve order. The previous chapter has shown how man is continuously bombarded by an incredibly complicated array of discrete physical energies, each capable of arousing separate sensory effects. Yet, as Chapters 2 and 3 have described, he *experiences* from this a unified world of meaningful objects and relations. In a word, his perceptions are organized.

Perceptual organization is an achievement. Stimulus data present a "problem" of organization, and the organizing is a kind of "problem-solving." Indeed, as we shall point out in the section on adaptive behavior, many of the characteristics of perceptual organization are found in the complex processes of thinking and learning.

Any stimulus-pattern may give rise to a multitude of perceptual organizations. Only one of these exists at one moment.

The perceiver seems neither to have to intend the particular form of organization nor to be conscious of how it occurs. Perceptual organization occurs *spontaneously*. It takes place without conscious direction, and with a greater speed and sureness than "rational" thought permits.

This is not to underrate the role that conscious thought and deliberate intention do play in perception. Perceptual organization occurs both without and with conscious direction. The person may direct his attention to a particular part of the field. He may search for particular "meanings." He may often be able to produce a particular form of organization if he wishes to.

The task of this chapter is to describe how perceptual organization comes about, and how it changes. In short, it deals with the principles of perceptual organization. We should note that we use the term "organization" to mean both the *process* of organizing the stimulus-pattern, and the *product* of this process, that is, the particular percept achieved.

In discussing the principles of perceptual organization, we shall deal with the processes of *differentiation* of the perceptual field, the processes of *grouping* of parts to form wholes, the operation of perceptual *set*, and the manner in which perceptual organizations *change*.

Differentiation of the Perceptual Field

A man is seated with his head inside a large hollow hemisphere (Fig. 28). Its inner surface is smooth, unmarked, and evenly illuminated by a moderate light in such a way that the stimulation falling on his eyes is entirely uniform. What does he see?

FIG. 28. An experimental method for investigating the perceptual effect of uniform stimulation in the visual field. The inner surface of the hemisphere is completely unmarked and homogeneous. Its level of illumination can be varied.

Laboratory experiments of this kind show that all he sees is a uniform light "mist" fill-

ing an endless space. He cannot tell how far away the surface of the sphere is; in fact, *he perceives no surface at all*. Thus when a receptor (in this case, the eye) receives uniform stimulation, the result is complete lack of perceptual differentiation. This is the simplest possible percept.

When the illumination is made considerably brighter, so that the very fine "grain" of the inner surface of the sphere approaches the threshold of visual acuity, there is at once a perceptual transformation. Now he does see the surface, and it appears to be *localized in space* a short distance in front of him. But the surface itself appears entirely uniform and without detail.

We now do another experiment in which the illumination of the surface is considerably darker at the left side and brighter and brighter across the field to the right side. Despite this gradient from darker to brighter, the field still *looks* evenly lighted throughout.

Finally, a very faint vertical shadow line is exposed through the middle of this field. At once there is a sudden perceptual transformation. A vertical boundary, or *contour*, appears in the middle of the field, and the total field segregates into *two different parts:* the half of the field to the left of the contour is seen as a uniform field of lesser brightness, and the half to the right is seen as a uniform field of greater brightness.

In this simple laboratory demonstration we observe that as a result of gradual systematic changes in the physical stimulus, there is a progression from simple to more complex levels of perceptual differentiation, varying from a field consisting of a completely undifferentiated single quality ("a lightish mist"), through a field containing a single homogeneous surface without structure, to a field divided into two parts. Let us now turn to a more careful consideration of this sequence of events, particularly let us see what accounts for the final differentiation into two parts.

Assimilation and Contrast. The first striking fact to note is that at the intermediate stage, though there was a considerable degree of variation in the intensities of the light stimuli at various points on the retina, the visual field still *looked homogeneous* (see Fig. 29).

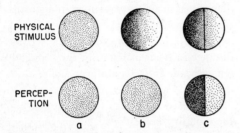

FIG. 29. The upper circles represent the objective illumination conditions on the surface of the hemisphere shown in Figure 28. The corresponding lower circles represent the individual's perception of each of these physical stimulus conditions. In *a*, the homogeneous physical field looks homogeneous. In *b*, despite the gradient of intensity across the field, the field still *looks homogeneous*. In *c*, a faint vertical line in the middle of the hemisphere produces a perception of two different fields, each homogeneous within itself but different in apparent level of illumination.

ASSIMILATION. This tendency toward maximal uniformity and lack of differentiation in perception is known as *assimilation*. Assimilation is one of the most basic of all psychological phenomena, not only in the limited sense in which we find it in perception, but in the broader sense in which we find it in complex processes of thinking and memory, as we shall see later.

Note that the assimilation we have found in our simple experiment was *not* simply due to the fact that all the stimulus differences on the retina were so small as to be below the threshold. We are talking about *large* stimulus differences, which under other circumstances can be readily

perceived. Thus, if the darker and lighter ends of the field were placed side by side, our man would have no difficulty in perceiving them as different.

However the change in intensity of light from one end of the field to the other is gradual and *evenly continuous*. The assimilation tendencies operate throughout the whole field so as to produce a *single* level of perceived brightness which is an average of the light intensities over the whole retina. When the difference between any two adjacent points in the field is below threshold, even though the differences between points farther apart are well above threshold, the over-all homogeneity is produced.

But as the brightness difference from one side of the field to the other becomes even greater, there comes a critical place at which the uniformity can disappear. At this stage, if a boundary or contour of any kind is introduced into the field, the field suddenly divides into the two parts we have described.

Assimilation still occurs for each part separately. Each part is perceived with its own level of uniform brightness. The level of uniform brightness within each part is an average of the light intensities within its own area. Thus the left side of the field is much darker than the right side. This means that a sharp difference in brightness is produced right at the dividing line or contour between the two parts (see Fig. 29*c*). Thus the perceived difference between two adjacent points lying on different sides of the boundary is *maximized*. The net effect is that a continuous gradient of change in the stimulus leads to a perception of discrete steps. We have here a striking demonstration of the important role that contours play in perceptual organization.

CONTRAST. This phenomenon of the perceiving of a difference as greater than that called for by the stimulus intensities is known as *contrast*. We have already encountered examples of it in the form of sensory contrast (see Chapter 4, pages 78–80). Contrast means an accentuation of differences and is, like assimilation, a basic phenomenon in a great many psychological processes beyond perception.

CONTRAST, ASSIMILATION, AND ORGANIZATION. The degrees of contrast and assimilation are governed by the total perceptual organization. In Figure 30 we have a vivid

FIG. 30. First note that the gray ring has a uniform brightness. Now place a long thin object, such as a pencil, along the vertical line so as to divide the ring into two halves. How do the brightness of the two halves of the ring look now? For explanation of this phenomenon, see text.

illustration of how the total organization governs the operation of both contrast and assimilation. Here we see clearly how there

can be tendencies in a given organization pulling in opposing directions. The contrast effects from the black and white would ordinarily make the neutral gray of the ring brighter on the left side and darker on the right. But since the ring is a unified whole, the assimilation effect results in a minimizing of the contrast effects and we perceive a neutral gray throughout. Thus the assimilation effect has overbalanced the contrast effect. When we introduce a contour permitting the *separation* of the whole ring into two parts, the contrast tendencies can be expressed. The left half of the ring now appears to be a uniform lighter gray and the other half a uniform darker gray.

By Way of Summary. We can now see the rough outlines of the story of perceptual differentiation: (1) in perception there is a tendency to minimize stimulus differences; (2) when the stimulus differences exceed a certain level, perceptual differentiation occurs; (3) organizational factors, such as contours, facilitate differentiation; (4) the specific form that differentiation takes is such as to maximize some stimulus differences (contrast) while minimizing others (assimilation).

Figure and Ground. As we look at the parts of any differentiated field, we notice that invariably there is one part that stands out in a distinctive way from the remainder. This part is technically called the *figure*, and the rest is called the *ground*. Figure-ground differentiation is the simplest and most primitive form of perceptual organization.

The distinction between figure and ground is important because their perceptual properties are different. The figure tends to be better defined, better localized, solider, and more integrated, whereas the ground appears to be less well structured, more indefinite. The figure appears to lie in front of or upon the ground, and the ground appears to extend continuously in an unbroken fashion behind the figure. The

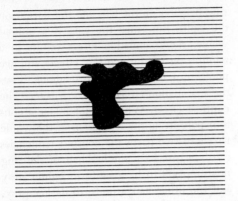

FIG. 31. A simple case of figure and ground.

figure appears to be more the center of attention in the field than does the ground. See Figure 31.

CONTOUR. That we can distinguish a fig-

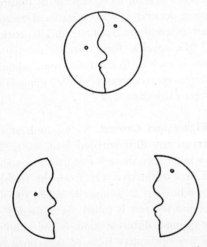

FIG. 32. With continued inspection of the ambiguous drawing at the top, there is fluctuation of figure and ground, so that sometimes the left face is seen and sometimes the right face. The appearance of the common contour between the two faces changes completely, depending upon which figure it momentarily defines. This difference in its appearance is more easily studied when the faces are presented separately, as below. (From Schafer and Murphy, 1943.)

ure at all depends usually upon the existence of a contour separating figure from ground. This contour is clearly perceived as "belonging" to the figure, rather than to the ground, even though it is actually a physical boundary common to both. The contour has the function of providing the distinctive *shape* to the figure. It is striking that as figure-ground reversal occurs, the contour shifts from one figure to the other and the appearance of the contour thus changes markedly. The identical physical contour looks entirely different in the two patterns shown in Figure 32, defining the shapes of the two figures. It is this shifting

FIG. 33. Do you see the white square? If you do, it will appear to be a figure lying on top of the oval black figure that appears to extend continuously beneath. Note that the white square may be seen even though there are no physical contours that completely define it.

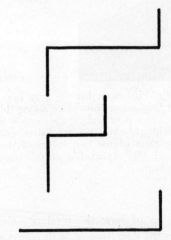

FIG. 34. The block-letter E is seen clearly, despite the missing physical contours.

quality of contour which makes the visual assembling of parts sometimes difficult, as in the pieces of a jigsaw puzzle, which though sharing an identical contour look very different and are not easily matched.

A figure may sometimes be seen even when the physical contours do not completely define it (see Figs. 33 and 34).

This example calls our attention to a general tendency for certain figures to be so organized that they are complete or closed, rather than incomplete. This tendency is known technically as *closure*. There are numerous simple perceptual examples of it, such as the tendency to see as an unbroken whole a circle with a tiny gap in its perimeter.

WHICH WILL BE FIGURE? When we have a stimulus-pattern that can be differentiated into figure and ground, what factors determine which part will tend to be figure and which part ground?

The area of greater stimulus intensity is not necessarily favored as figure. A dark area may be seen as figure on a light ground as well as a similar light area as figure on a dark ground. What seems critical are factors such as the sizes and locations of the two areas. Other things being equal, the *smaller* area and the *more enclosed* area will tend to be seen as figure. Other things

being equal, the *more regular* area will tend to be seen as figure. (See Fig. 35.)

The most powerful factors determining which will be figure and which ground are concerned with the total organizational structure, for instance, the parts of the field are that readily grouped together, the best "sense" that can be made of complex stimulus-patterns, etc. We shall encounter illustrations of these factors throughout the chapter. All manner of "personal" factors having to do with the perceiver's set, motivation, learning, etc., have been shown to play a role in this. Thus, a more "familiar" pattern is likely to be seen as figure. (But see Fig. 36A.)

FIG. 36A. What is this? If you cannot tell after prolonged inspection, turn to Figure 36B. (From W. Brown and H. C. Gilhousen, *College Psychology*. Copyright 1949 by Prentice-Hall, New York.)

And, as noted above, there are periodic reversals of many figure-ground patterns; this implies that there are other kinds of processes in the nervous system that help to determine which will be figure and which ground.

THE UNIVERSALITY OF FIGURE AND GROUND. We have described figure and ground in terms of convenient visual examples. But it should be clearly understood that figure-ground differentiation characterizes *all* perceptual experience, including audition, touch, smell, etc. For instance, if there is a continuous tone of a constant pitch and loudness which is interrupted for a moment by a tone of different pitch or loudness, we hear the brief tone as a "figure" on the "ground" of the continuous tone. And a tiny pebble in one's shoe may be perceived

FIG. 35. This tends to be perceived as wavy white stripes on a black background rather than as black stripes on a white background, even though the total areas of white and black are equal. The reason for this seems to lie in the fact that the white stripes are regular in width, whereas the black stripes are irregular. (From Metzger, 1953.)

Fig. 36B.

German word for "form") psychology.

Max Wertheimer, one of the founders of Gestalt psychology, stated a number of important "grouping principles." He demonstrated these principles with patterns of dots and lines similar to those in Figure 37.

as a "figure" against the otherwise uniform pressure of the foot on the sole.

MULTIPLE FIGURES ON ONE GROUND. There is a strong tendency toward differentiation of a field into only *two* main parts—a single figure and all the rest of the field merging into a single ground. But with complex stimulus-patterns the field invariably contains many figures of equal strength, each capable of being perceived against the common background. For example, there may be a number of dark spots on a white surface, each clearly differentiated from the others and each perceived as a figure.

In such cases there is a tendency to *group* the multiple figures into a smaller number of more inclusive figures. One important instance of this is the so-called *isolation effect.* If in a collection of dots most are black and a few are red, the red dots (technically called the "isolated" items) become more noticeable and may be organized as figure against the background of the black dots.

Since most perceptions are of complex stimulus-patterns rather than of single figures against homogeneous grounds, the analysis of perceptual grouping is an important part of the study of perception.

Perceptual Grouping

The experimental study of the organized nature of perception was initiated primarily by a group of German psychologists in the early part of this century. Their approach has become known as *Gestalt* (the

Grouping by Proximity. Other things being equal, *stimuli that are in closer proximity will have a greater tendency to be grouped.* The proximity may be *spatial* (as illustrated in Fig. 37*a*) or it may be *temporal.* Of a series of flashes of light, the flashes occurring close together in time will tend to be grouped. Stimuli grouped by proximity need not be all of the same sensory mode. Thus, if we hear a loud sound and see a bright light simultaneously, we will tend to perceive them as belonging together as parts of the same event. Grouping by proximity can be seen as an instance of spatial and temporal interaction (see pages 73–8).

This does not assert that stimuli which are close together spatially or temporally *must necessarily* be grouped. As we shall see later, grouping depends upon a host of additional factors, and these may operate so as to prevent neighboring stimuli from being perceived as belonging together.

Grouping by Similarity. Other things being equal, *stimuli that are more similar to one another will have a greater tendency to be grouped* (see Fig. 37*b*). By "similarity" of stimuli is meant that they are alike in various physical attributes, such as intensity, color, size, weight, odor, etc. There are, of course, many dimensions along which stimuli are describable, and for this reason there are numerous possible ways in which two or more stimuli can be called similar or dissimilar. The more attributes the stimuli have in common, the greater the similarity, and hence the greater the grouping tendency.

Grouping by Good Form. Other things being equal, *stimuli that form a good figure will have a tendency to be grouped.* This is a very general formulation intended to embrace a number of more specific variants of the theme, traditionally classified as follows.

1. *Good continuation.* The tendency for elements to go with others in such a way as to permit the continuation of a line, or a curve, or a movement, in the direction that has already been established (see Fig. 37c).

2. *Symmetry.* The favoring of that grouping which will lead to symmetrical or balanced wholes as against asymmetrical ones.

3. *Closure.* The grouping of elements in such a way as to make for a more closed or more complete whole figure.

4. *Common fate.* The favoring of the grouping of those elements that move or change in a common direction, as distinguished from those having other directions of movement or change in the field.

It seems plausible to consider that the percepts resulting from all of the above determinants would be such as to meet the criterion of a good figure, that is, one that tends to be more continuous, more symmetrical, more closed, more unified.

Now the reader will see that a difficulty with this general proposition regarding grouping centers on the crucial phrase "good figure." How can we know which

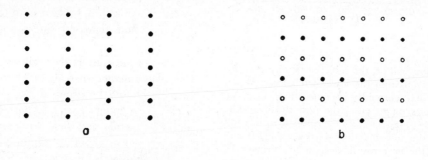

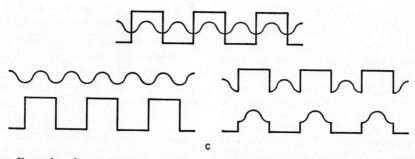

FIG. 37. Examples of grouping. In *a*, the dots are perceived in vertical columns, owing to their greater spatial proximity in the vertical than in the horizontal direction. In *b*, with proximity equal, the rows are perceived as horizontal, owing to grouping by similarity. In *c*, the principle of good continuation results in seeing the upper figure as made up of the two parts shown to the left below, even though logically it might just as well be composed of the two parts shown to the right below, or indeed of any number of other combinations of two or more parts. (Adapted from Wertheimer, 1923.)

BOX 21

How to Measure "Goodness"

Attneave has made an ingenious experimental attack on the problem of measuring the "goodness" of a figure. The subject is given a sheet of graph paper composed of 4,000 tiny squares (50 rows by 80 columns). His task is to guess whether the color of each successive square is black, white, or gray. The experimenter has in mind what the completed figure will look like (fig. a).

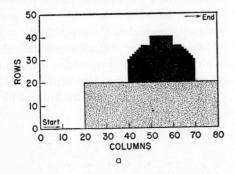

a

Without knowing what the completed figure will be, the subject starts by guessing the square in the lower left corner. When he has correctly identified the color, he moves on to guess the next square to the right. He continues this process to the end of the row and then starts on the left end of the next row above. In this manner he successively guesses each of the 4,000 squares.

On the average, Attneave's subjects made only 15 to 20 wrong guesses for the entire figure. How was this possible? The answer is that the figure was deliberately designed so that knowledge of *parts* of the figure was sufficient to enable the subject to make fairly valid predictions about the remainder of the figure. This was accomplished by making all the white squares contiguous with one another, and similarly the black and the gray squares. Moreover, the contours separating the white, black, and gray areas are simple and regular. Where the figure tapers, it tapers in a regular way. And it has symmetry; after exploring one side, it is easy to predict the other side. Thus, the subject having discovered that the first few squares are white continues to guess white, and he is correct until he hits the gray contour at the 20th column. After one or two errors, he then continues to guess gray. On the next row above, he tends to repeat the pattern of the first.

All these factors of compactness, symmetry, good continuation, etc., are aspects of what is implied by a "good figure." Thus an objective measure of the "goodness" of a figure is the ease with which the subject can predict its total form from minimal information about a part.

Other figures can be similarly tested. For example, figure *b* would prove to be a less "good" figure because the number of errors in guessing would be larger.

Attneave's particular method will not, of course, apply to all kinds of figures or all kinds of perceptual organizations. But it does demonstrate that there are ways in which "goodness" can be objectively determined.

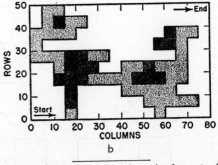

b

ATTNEAVE, F. 1954. Some informational aspects of visual perception. *Psychol. Rev., 61,* 183–93.

configuration of stimuli is "better" than another?

To escape from this difficulty, we need to have *independent* criteria of what is a good figure. Some approach can be made to this; for instance, in the case of "symmetry" there are objective rules we can apply to determine the relative symmetry of various figures. The same is true of simple cases of "closure." (See Box 21 for a relevant experiment.)

But we are far from being able to state such criteria when we deal with the highly complex configurations of our normal perceptual experience. Part of the difficulty stems from the fact of individual differences among perceivers. One man's mess may be another man's order. And this may reflect the important role of *learning and past experience* in the genesis of "good figure."

Competition and Co-operation of Grouping Tendencies. In every stimulus-pattern the elements have some degree of proximity, some degree of similarity, and some degree to which they fit "good form." This means that in every stimulus-pattern all the kinds of grouping tendencies are at work.

The tendencies differ in their respective strengths and in the directions of organization toward which they point. Sometimes they work in the same direction and some-

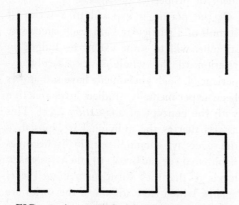

FIG. 38. An example of the competition between grouping by proximity and grouping by closure. The seven lines above tend to fall "naturally" into three pairs and one isolate, by virtue of proximity relations. But the same lines below, with the addition of the short horizontal lines, tend to be grouped by closure with the more distant partner, overriding the influence of proximity.

times they are pitted against one another. An example of the results of such co-operation and competition among grouping tendencies is shown in Figure 38.

A special application of the competition of grouping tendencies is found in the art of camouflage, as represented in the protective coloration and marking of animals in their natural surroundings, and in the warfare of man against man. Camouflage takes advantage of factors such as "good continuation" and "closure" to mask other configurations. Look at Figure 39 and describe it to yourself. Continue to study it for a while and you may suddenly see something surprising. If this experience does not occur, read the legend under the figure.

FIG. 39. If after studying this figure for a while you have not seen what it is, try covering the lower half of the figure.

Determination of Perceptual Qualities by Organization. Grouping processes lead to the formation of wholes made up of parts. These wholes and parts have perceptual qualities, and we shall now see how these qualities are determined by the organization of the field.

Properties of Wholes and Parts. The properties of a whole cannot be considered simply as an adding up of the separate properties of its parts. A round, black dot has no quality of "squareness" about it, yet four such dots arranged in an appropriate spatial *pattern* will together be seen as a "square." It is the *pattern* of the parts which contributes the essential perceptual qualities of the whole.

TRANSPOSITION OF FORMS. A particular organization may be retained, even though the individual elements composing it are changed. In this case we speak of the *transposition* of the form. For instance, the "square" mentioned above can just as easily be built out of white dots, or beans, or any other kind of elements properly distributed in space. The quality of "squareness" is common to all these stimulus-patterns.

There are endless examples of transposition of forms. A melody is recognized as the same when played higher or lower in the scale, providing the *relationships* among the notes remain the same. We have already had occasion to refer to the transposition of relations of stimuli in the experiments on transposition of a brightness relation in animals and children (see p. 22).

Though the form of the whole is determined by the pattern of relationships among the constituent elements, it is also true that the whole is perceived differently depending upon the individual elements. A square composed of four dots is certainly not the same as one made up of four connected lines, or of four pressure points on the skin. A transposed melody may readily be recognized as the same melody, but it may also be recognized as in a different range of pitch or intensity, or as played on a different instrument.

THE PART-WHOLE PRINCIPLE. Just as the properties of wholes are somewhat dependent upon the nature of their constituent elements, so are *the properties of parts dependent upon the nature of the whole.* For example, recall the Müller-Lyer illusion (Fig. 2, p. 19) in which a line looks longer or shorter depending on whether it is part of the open or of the closed arrowhead figure.

We shall find repeatedly in later sections of the book that this part-whole principle generally applies in the more complex psychological functions, e.g., in solving problems and in stereotyped thinking about other persons.

Frame of Reference. The part-whole principle has often been discussed in connection with the concept of *frame of reference.* In the judgment of the perceptual properties of things we typically make use of a standard or a framework that serves as a reference against which the particular property is judged. When we ask how big a thing is, the sizes of the other objects with which it is grouped may serve as a standard. Thus, we saw how two equal circles are seen as very different in size depending upon the sizes of other circles surrounding them (Fig. 2, p. 19). And when we ask how vertical the luminous line in the darkroom is, the tilted luminous square around it serves as a frame of reference, making our judgment of the vertical dependent somewhat upon the angle of the frame (Box 14, p. 47).

ADAPTATION LEVEL. In the previous examples the frame of reference was given by the whole perceptual configuration immediately present. But there may also be *temporal* configurations of stimuli which serve as frame of reference for the judgment of properties of objects.

If the person is exposed to a series of stimuli of a particular kind, each successive stimulus will to some extent be judged in relation to the whole series already experienced. Such phenomena have sometimes been experimentally studied in connection with the concept of *adaptation level.* This asserts that as the individual is exposed to the successive stimuli, he gradually becomes habituated or adapted to their intensity levels, so that they form an "average" level against which later stimuli in the series are judged. But some stimuli play a more important part in determining this "average" than others. *Which* stimuli play the major role depends upon organizational factors. The same stimulus series may thus have very different effects on the perception of a given stimulus (see Box 22).

BOX 22

Adaptation Level

Helson has advanced the theory that a person makes a judgment of the magnitude of any stimulus attribute, such as size, or weight, or loudness, by establishing a sort of subjective or personal scale with respect to which the stimuli are judged. He calls the neutral or medium point of such a scale the *adaptation level*. Stimulus values above the adaptation level are perceived as "large," "heavy," "loud," etc., and those below it are perceived as "small," "light," "soft," etc.

According to Helson's view, the adaptation level is determined by a "pooling" of the values of all the stimuli in the judgment series. It represents the "centering" of the perceiver with respect to the range of stimuli confronting him. This pooling is *not* a mere simple averaging; hence the adaptation level is not the same as the arithmetic mean of the stimulus values in the series. For example, in a weight series ranging from 200 to 400 grams the adaptation level is usually found to be about 250 grams—weights less than 250 are judged to be "light" and those more than 250, "heavy."

The adaptation level constantly changes as a function of all the stimuli acting upon the person at the moment as well as in the past. A single extreme stimulus lying far outside the range of values of the rest of the series may have a pronounced effect in shifting the adaptation level in its direction. For example, in one study the adaptation level of a series of weights ranging from 400 to 600 grams was found to be 475 grams, but when a weight of 900 was introduced a single time, the adaptation level rose to 550 grams.

The mathematical formulations devised by Helson to permit quantitative predictions of adaptation level on the basis of the distribution of stimuli have proved capable of accounting for a wide variety of judgmental data. Indeed Helson believes that *all* kinds of judgments, including social judgments, are capable of being explained by reference to the adaptation-level concept. It is clear, however, that the pooling of stimuli in establishing the adaptation level does not take

place "automatically" without regard for factors of perceptual organization. Through appropriate changes in the person's perception of the situation, the *same* series of stimuli may result in *different* adaptation levels.

An interesting example is given in an experiment by Brown. He first determined the adaptation level for a series of weights ranging from 80 to 144 grams. Then he introduced into the series an additional extreme weight of 242 grams. As Helson would predict, the effect of this one extreme stimulus was substantially to raise the adaptation level. But Brown now made a crucial experimental variation. He presented the same series of weights ranging from 80 to 144 grams, but in this case there was no extreme weight of 242 grams. Instead, he supplied a tray, having a handle like the other weights, which weighed 242 grams. The ostensible purpose of the tray, on which the stimulus weights were loaded, was to enable the experimenter to place them in front of the subject for his judging. After the subject had judged each of the weights, he was asked to pick up the tray and move it out of the way. In this devious fashion the person was made to lift the 242-gram weight along with the regular weights, though not recognizing it as one of the weights. The results clearly showed that *under these conditions, when this heavy weight was perceived as an irrelevant tray rather than as part of the stimulus series, it had no effect on raising the adaptation level.*

In short, whether or not a given stimulus is taken into account in the pooling to arrive at the adaptation level depends upon factors of perceptual organization. And this means that the determinants of adaptation level must be exceedingly complex and not readily accommodated in a simple formula.

HELSON, H. 1947. Adaptation-level as a frame of reference for prediction of psychophysical data. *Amer. J. Psychol.*, 60, 1–29.

BROWN, D. R. 1953. Stimulus similarity and the anchoring of subjective scales. *Amer. J. Psychol.*, 66, 199–214.

Perceptual Set and Organization

Perceptual processes are not disembodied; they occur within an organism that is engaging in activity. Stimuli are organized not only so that they "fit" with one another, but also so that they "fit" the requirements of the perceiver's ongoing activity—what he is thinking, feeling, trying to do. The perceiver's state as he encounters a given stimulus-pattern is never completely "neutral." He brings to the situation various readinesses and expectations that help govern the manner in which the stimuli are perceived and organized. In a word, he is *set* to perceive something more or less specific.

The concept of *set* refers in general to readinesses of the organism to make a particular response. There are various types of sets. A *motor set* is one in which the person is ready for a particular action of his muscles—the runner on his mark is set to sprint. A *mental set* is a readiness for a particular thought process. A *perceptual set* is a readiness for a particular organization of stimuli—after hearing the words "pork and" the man is ready to hear "beans," and so he may hear the word as "beans" even though the word spoken is "greens."

The Determinants of Set. Where do sets come from? What determines whether a particular set will be brought into play at a particular moment in a particular situation?

There are two main determinants of set: (1) *prior experience;* (2) *central factors* in the person, such as needs, emotions, attitudes, and values. It is through the arousal of sets that prior experience and central factors can exercise their all-important influence on thought processes and perception.

Prior Experience and Set. The sheer frequency with which the stimulus-pattern has previously been perceived will help create a set. There are numerous experimental studies bearing on this point. For instance, the more familiar a word, the greater the set toward its perception. Experiments have shown that there is a close relationship between the frequency of usage of words in the English language and the speed of their recognition when presented by tachistoscope for fractions of a second.

An experiment by Henle (1942) shows, however, that mere familiarity will not necessarily create an effective set. She exposed words briefly in a tachistoscope (an optical apparatus that can expose stimuli for precisely timed intervals), some in their normal printwise form and some reversed. Without explicit instruction as to what to expect, subjects were slower to recognize the reversed words than those presented in their more familiar way. But when they were told that reversed words would sometimes be presented, the difference in readiness to identify the printwise and reversed words was greatly reduced. A momentary set, such as induced by instructions, can overcome a set derived from frequency of prior experience.

RECENCY OF PRIOR EXPERIENCE. Experiences that have just occurred will usually have a greater tendency to provide a set in the immediate situation than less recent experiences. Having just seen a particular type of object, the person is more strongly set toward seeing something of that type.

Yet recency and frequency may fail to work as simple determinants of set depending upon the *temporal pattern* of the stimuli. The set that is aroused at the moment reflects the expectation of what should come next in the series of experiences. If there is a patterned sequence of events, such as *a-a-b-a-a-b-a-a*, the set at the next moment is stronger for *b* than for *a*, even

BOX 23

Prior Experience and Organization

Look at the simple geometrical design in figure *a*. Then look at figure *b*. Do you see figure *a* in figure *b*? It is hard to see at once because it is imbedded within the larger figure in such a way as to be deliberately camouflaged, but with careful search you can find it.

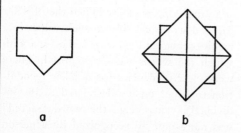

a   b

These are samples of many such figures constructed by the German psychologist Gottschaldt in order to study the effect of prior experience on perception. To determine whether a great deal of familiarity with figure *a* would make it more likely to be seen in figure *b*, he showed figure *a* to one group of subjects 520 times (with instructions to memorize it) and showed it to another group only 3 times. When the subjects were later shown figure *b* and asked to describe it, only about one person in 20 saw the simple figure *a* in it, and *there was no difference between the two groups in tendency to see it*. Gottschaldt concluded that sheer frequency of prior experience with an object does not account for the readiness to perceive it.

However, later experimenters have shown that when dealing with simple figures which are not so completely camouflaged within the larger figure, the amount of prior familiarity with the simple figure *does* help determine ease of recognition. Gottschaldt had chosen a situation in which the stimulus-structure of figure *b* was so strong that

it was unusually difficult for figure *a* to be seen even under favorable conditions.

In other experiments Gottschaldt demonstrated that the temporal pattern of prior stimuli may provide a set that will markedly affect the way a subsequent stimulus is perceived. And in this case he used extremely simple figures, where a minimum of camouflaging was involved. Two groups of subjects looked 40 times in a row at figure *c*, being required to make certain observations about it. Then figure *d* was presented on the 41st trial, and the subjects asked to describe it.

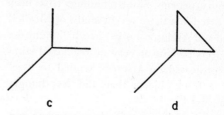

c   d

Group I had been told *beforehand* that an "interrupting" figure would appear *somewhere* in the series. Group II was told *just before* the 41st trial that an "interrupting" figure would appear. The difference between the two groups in their descriptions of figure *d* was striking: 86 per cent of Group I noticed at once that figure *c* was included in figure *d*, whereas *no subject* in Group II saw this. It is clear that since subjects in Group I did not know just where the "interrupting" figure would appear, they were continually expecting figure *c*, and so were set to see it even when slightly camouflaged in figure *d*. Group II was set for a new ("interrupting") figure on the 41st trial and so did *not* see the familiar figure in the new one.

GOTTSCHALDT, K. 1926; 1929. *Über den Einfluss der Erfahrung auf die Wahrnehmung von Figuren. Psychol. Forsch., 8,* 261–317; *12,* 1–87.

though *a* is the more recent and the more frequent. See Box 23 for a description of such studies.

Central Factors and Perceptual Set. Perceptual organization often reflects the central factors in the perceiver, such as his needs, emotions, attitudes, and values. The extent to which this happens depends upon the arousal of appropriate sets by these central factors.

NEEDS. The stronger a state of need in a person, the more strongly he will be perceptually set toward aspects of the field relevant to that need. Many experimental studies have been made of this apparently obvious fact. Beginning with the work of Sanford (1937), hunger has been a favored variable of need in such studies. He showed that incomplete words, e.g., ME__, would be more readily completed as food words, e.g., MEAT, MEAL, by hungry than by non-hungry persons. Similar findings have been reported in a more recent study of McClelland and Atkinson (1948) in which hungrier subjects looking at very unstructured stimuli projected on a screen tended to "see" more food objects than did less hungry subjects.

But there is not a simple one-to-one correspondence between the state of need and the perceptual result. What is critical is the intermediate role of set. Though in general the state of need is likely to arouse an appropriate set, it will fail to do so when the total momentary situation is not such as to favor the emergence of that set. What must always be taken into consideration is the *interaction* of factors of need, stimulus-structure, and set. The very complex manner in which such interactions occur is demonstrated in the study described in Box 24.

EMOTIONS. The emotional state of the person may produce a set affecting processes of perception and thought. For example, in a study by Murray (1933) children at a summer camp judged the characteristics of faces in photographs immediately after a "scary" evening game of "Murder." The amount of "maliciousness" seen by the children in the faces was appreciably greater than they had seen when judging the faces before playing the game of "Murder."

VALUES AND ATTITUDES. A person is likely to be set toward perceiving in accord with his values and attitudes. Postman, Bruner, and McGinnies (1948) used the Allport-Vernon Test of Values (see p. 636) to determine each individual's basic values, such as the relative emphasis upon "religious," "aesthetic," "social," "theoretical," and other aspects of life. Then they briefly exposed words relating to such values in a tachistoscope and measured the ease with which the words were recognized. There were clear tendencies for quicker recognition to occur on words related to the individual's values, e.g., the word "sacred" was more quickly recognized by a person scoring high on "religious" values than by a person having other predominant values. Moreover, there was a tendency for assimilation of stimulus words to the person's values—the person higher on "religious" values might see the word "scared" as "sacred."

But the complexity of the relationship of value and perception is emphasized by the fact that the more valued words are also likely to be those *more frequently experienced* by the person. Thus, Solomon and Howes (1951) demonstrated that the above-obtained relationship between value and recognition threshold largely disappeared when they experimented only with words that were of relatively equal familiarity to the subjects.

The Effects of Set on Perception. The effects of set on perception depend upon (1) the characteristics of the set, (2) the strength of structure of the stimulus-pattern, and (3) the consonance or dissonance between what is "required" by the set and what is "required" by the stimulus-pattern.

CHARACTERISTICS OF SET. Perceptual sets vary in a number of important charac-

BOX 24

Hunger and Skeleton Words

Postman and Crutchfield had 724 undergraduates, some hungry and some not, fill in lists of skeleton words (words with letters omitted). For each skeleton word there were possible both food-related and nonfood-related completions. (For example, PICK___ could be completed as PICKLE or PICKET; ___L_K, as MILK or as SILK.)

The experimenters varied a number of experimental conditions. Among them were:

1. *Induced set toward food words.* To give various groups different amounts of initial set toward food completions, the lists were immediately preceded by set-inducing skeleton words that automatically *forced* a food completion. That is, when the first set-inducing skeleton word was LUN__H, all subjects perceived it as LUNCH, and presumably this provided a certain degree of food set for the solution of succeeding words.

Groups were divided into five degrees of set by varying the number of set-inducing food words from zero to 5, as listed below:

does not "automatically" produce food-related responses. However the degree of hunger does make a difference. The effect of the hunger or non-hunger *varies depending upon the degree of set evoked.*

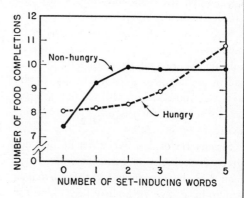

As the graph shows, with *zero* set-inducing words preceding the test words, hungry and non-hungry subjects did not significantly differ in number of food completions given. With *one* set-inducing

		0	1	2	3	5
						LUN_H
						D_SS_RT
					LUN_H	CHE_S_
				LUN_H	D_SS_RT	B_N_NA
			LUN_H	D_SS_RT	CHE_S_	C__KIE
		PICK__	PICK__	PICK__	PICK__	PICK__
		etc.	etc.	etc.	etc.	etc.
		(6.3)	(6.7)	(8.9)	(9.2)	(10.9)

The more the initial set-inducing words, the greater the number of food completions (as shown above by the average number of food completions in the 21-word list for each of the five groups.) Thus an induced set does affect the response.

2. *Degree of hunger.* Half the groups were hungry (as ascertained by their own reports at the end of the experiment, and checked by the number of hours since last meal); the other half were non-hungry.

Taking hungry subjects versus non-hungry subjects, there is *no* difference in number of food completions, the average values being 8.81 and 9.28, respectively. Thus we see that a state of hunger need

word, the non-hungry subjects gave significantly *more* food completions than did the hungry. For the non-hungry subjects the effect of the addition of still more initial set-inducing words was to increase the food completions only slightly. Whereas for the hungry subjects the effect was accelerated with each further set-inducing word. Thus, with *five* such words, the hungry subjects significantly exceeded the non-hungry in food completions.

Can you account for this difference in the shape of the two curves?

POSTMAN, L., and CRUTCHFIELD, R. S. 1952. The interaction of need, set, and stimulus-structure in a cognitive task. *Amer. J. Psychol.*, 65, 196–217.

teristics: how salient they are, how specific they are, how long they last, their relation to other sets.

SALIENCY OF SET. Some sets fully dominate the perceiver's awareness. Mr. Anyman actively searching for a lost key in a cluttered drawer has a salient set to see the key among the odds and ends. Other sets are less salient. While searching for the key, Mr. Anyman may encounter and immediately notice a pen that he has been missing for several days, though he may fail to notice other objects. The set for the key was most salient, the set for the pen less salient, and for the other objects nonexistent.

SPECIFICITY OF SET. Sets differ in their degree of specificity or generality. Mr. Anyman may be searching for the *particular key* to his garage, or he may be looking for *any kind* of key that can be used as a weight for his child's kite.

DURATION OF SET. Sets differ enormously in their duration. Some are extremely brief, lasting only long enough to provide the setting for the next perception. Other sets endure over longer periods. For example, Mrs. Anyman is set 24 hours a day to hear the cry of her baby and she can detect the cry even when others cannot.

MULTIPLICITY OF SETS. In a complex organism many things are going on simultaneously. Thus there are multiple perceptual sets, each with its own characteristics and direction. Some of the directions will be the same; a given perceptual organization will be consistent with several concurrent sets. Some of the directions will be opposed; a given perceptual organization consistent with one set will be inconsistent with others. These multiple sets will sometimes cooperate and sometimes compete. In response to his call the young man may be set to see his girl friend appearing at the window—or her mother! Such competing sets may lead to impaired perceptions.

STRUCTURE OF STIMULUS-PATTERN. Stimulus-patterns may be arranged along a dimension of strength of "structure." A stimulus-pattern is said to be *strongly structured* when the stimuli are clear, intense, simple, and subject to strong grouping factors. A stimulus-pattern is said to be *weakly structured* when the stimuli are barely perceptible, unclear, complex, and not subject to strong grouping factors. A strongly structured stimulus-pattern easily evokes a *stable* perception resistant to change—one in which the figure and ground are firmly established, the parts are seen in a constant relation with one another. A weakly structured stimulus-pattern evokes several alternative perceptions, each one unstable and easily changed. Our world is made up of both strongly structured and weakly structured patterns. *In general, a given set has a greater effect on a weak than on a strong stimulus-structure.*

CONSONANCE OF SET AND STRUCTURE. The perception favored by a given set may exactly fit what would be favored by the stimulus-pattern even in the absence of the set—you are set to hear your name called and it is called. This is extreme *consonance* of set and structure. Conversely, the two may not fit at all—the name they call is entirely unlike yours. This is extreme *dissonance* of set and structure.

Dissonance between the set and the stimulus-structure may result in several different types of perceptual outcomes. We will discuss them in order, starting with those involving least dissonance and proceeding to those with maximal dissonance.

SELECTIVITY. When there are two or more forms of the organization of a stimulus-pattern, each more or less equally probable of occurrence, we have a case in which we speak of an *ambiguous* pattern. The word "right" when heard alone can just as easily be understood as the word

BOX 25

Wife or Mother-in-Law?

Look at figure *a*. What do you see?

a

You may have seen a slightly turned profile of an attractive young woman. Or you may have seen an old hag. (When Boring published this example of an ambiguous stimulus, he termed it the "wife and mother-in-law" picture!) With continued inspection you will be able alternately to see each of the two possible organizations. Normally about 60 per cent of subjects *first* see the young woman, and about 40 per cent the old hag.

In order to test the effect of a *prior set* on how this ambiguous picture is perceived, Leeper performed the following experiment. Two groups of subjects were shown a preliminary series of pictures. Group I saw figure *b* as one of the pictures in the series. Group II saw figure *c* as one of the pictures in the series.

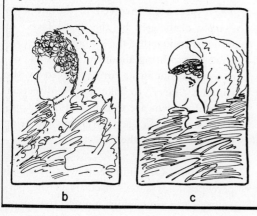

b   **c**

Later both groups were shown the ambiguous version (fig. *a*) and asked to report on what they saw. The effect of the set toward "young woman" or "old hag" induced by the previous exposure of that version was conclusive: 100 per cent of Group I saw the "young woman" in fig. *a*, and 95 per cent of Group II saw the "old hag."

You can perform a similar experiment on yourself. Look first at figure *d*, and then at figure *e*.

d

e

By having first seen the "pirate" in figure *d*, a "pirate" set will have been induced in you, and you will most likely have seen that "pirate" in figure *e*.

Now we are going to induce a different set in you: Look again at figure *e* and you will see a "rabbit"!

LEEPER, R. W. 1935. A study of a neglected portion of the field of learning: the development of sensory organization. *J. genet. Psychol., 46,* 41–75.

"write." The effect of a set is to select among the several alternative possibilities of an ambiguous pattern that particular

---

BOX 26

Chack = chick or check?

Siipola showed words in a tachistoscope for one tenth of a second each. The subject's task was to identify and report the word. Half of her 160 subjects were informed beforehand that the words would have to do with animals or birds; the other half were informed that the words would have to do with travel or transportation. Among the words were six "nonsense" words, so designed that they were fairly close in structure to meaningful words fitting these two categories, as indicated below:

Nonsense word seen in tachisto-scope	*Possible way perception of nonsense word could be distorted to fit*	
	A. animal or bird category	B. travel or trans-portation category
chack	chick	check
sael	seal	sail
wharl	whale	wharf
pasrot	parrot	passport
dack	duck	deck
pengion	penguin	pension

The group instructed to expect animal or bird words responded to the nonsense words with 63 per cent of (A) responses and 11 per cent of (B) responses. Conversely, the other group, instructed to expect travel or transportation words, gave only 14 per cent (A) responses and 74 per cent (B) responses. The subjects perceived the nonsense words in accordance with their respective sets, and they accomplished this by distorting the nonsense word to a meaningful form. For example, the letter "a" in "chack" was altered either to "i" or to "e," and this was done by the subject without his realizing it.

SIIPOLA, E. M. 1935. A study of some effects of preparatory set. *Psychol. Monogr., 46,* #210.

---

perception which is consonant with the set. Box 25 describes an experimental study of this kind of selectivity.

DISTORTION. If the stimulus-structure is fairly close to, but not fully consonant with, the prevailing set, the perception may be "distorted" to fit the set (see Box 26).

In some cases parts of the stimulus-pattern can readily be "fitted" to the form favored by the set, while other parts of the pattern cannot, owing to too great a discrepancy. Even under these circumstances the outcome may be a perception that is fully consistent with the set, and this is accomplished by a complete *suppression* or elimination of the ill-fitting elements of the stimulus-pattern.

COMPROMISE. The perception that occurs is sometimes a compromise between that favored by the set and that favored by the stimulus-pattern. The experiment in Box 27 neatly demonstrates compromise and other ways of resolving the discrepancy between set and structure.

REDIRECTION OF SET. When a strongly structured stimulus-pattern is markedly dissonant with the prevailing set, the effect may be an *accentuation* of the discrepant aspect of the stimulus-pattern. The person becomes clearly aware of the discrepancy and pays special attention to it.

As a consequence there is often a redirection of the prior set (again see Box 27). The expectation involved in the set is so sharply challenged by the "hard facts" of stimulus reality that the set not only proves powerless to bring about the "required" organization, but in its turn is forced by the stimulus "facts" to take a new direction. Set and percept are thus in constant "feedback" interaction, each governing and being governed by the other.

Attention. One important way in which perceptual set shows itself is in the perceiver's *attention*, which is a selective focus-

---

BOX 27

Black Hearts, Red Spades

A neat demonstration of meeting a perceptual problem by either distortion or compromise is given in a study by Bruner and Postman. They exposed playing cards briefly in a tachistoscope, asking the person to name the card. Some of the cards had been especially manufactured with reversed colors of the suit symbols, e.g., a black six of hearts, a red four of spades.

With short exposures most persons *distorted* the false cards to fit their expectation, for example identifying the red four of spades as a four of *hearts,* or as a four of *spades,* without apparently seeing the incongruous color. In other instances, with longer and repeated exposures, the resulting percept coincided neither with the normal expectation nor with the actual stimulus, but rather took a *compromise* or an intermediate form. For example, the red six of spades was reported as a "purplish" six of spades, thus compromising between the actual redness and the expected blackness.

Some persons noticed the abnormalities of the cards almost at once, and everyone was able to do so when the exposures were lengthened or repeated. The effect of this was an accentuation of the abnormal feature, which became the most important aspect of the card.

The accentuation of the abnormal feature, in turn, had the effect of redirecting the prior set; now the person was set for incongruous cards, and more readily recognized them when they occurred.

Different persons meet the same problem in different ways.

BRUNER, J. S., and POSTMAN, L. J. 1949. On the perception of incongruity: a paradigm. *J. Person., 18,* 206–23.

---

til the image of the object falls on the fovea, the lens muscles accommodate so as to bring the image into clearest focus, etc. In trying to hear a faint sound, the person cranes forward, cups his hand behind his ear, and may close his eyes to cut out competing visual stimuli.

FOCUS OF ATTENTION. That part of the perceptual field which is the center or focus of attention is clearer, more salient, more differentiated than other parts. It stands out as "figure" against the rest of the field, which is "ground."

The duration of a given focus of attention is usually brief. There is a constant *shifting of attention* from one part to another. These shifts in visual attention, for instance, may be objectively measured by recording successive eye movements while the person looks at an object. Figure 40 illustrates this.

Attention shifts for several reasons. For one thing, there is in attention, as in all psychological processes, a form of "satiation" (see below, p. 107) which tends to inhibit the continuance of attention in a given direction. Attention will tend to shift "spontaneously" after a period of focus on one part of the field. Moreover, the shifting of attention serves an essential function in the achievement of the total perceptual organization. With complex stimulus-patterns it is impossible for the person to organize the whole in a single glance; there must be successive steps of "exploration" of the pattern, each part or aspect being fixated in turn. We see why it is so important to stress the temporal aspects of perceptual organization, for even with a static stimulus-pattern, adequate perception invariably involves successive shifts of attention. We cannot, in fact, dissociate the temporal pattern of successive fixations on an object from its perceptual organization. This is a cardinal fact for the painter or sculptor, who must deliberately construct his work of art so that the eye of the

ing upon certain parts or aspects of the situation. That which is attended to is the "target" of the perceptual and motor orientations of the person. In looking at an object, for instance, the body swings in the direction of the object, and the ocular mechanism works so that the eyes turn un-

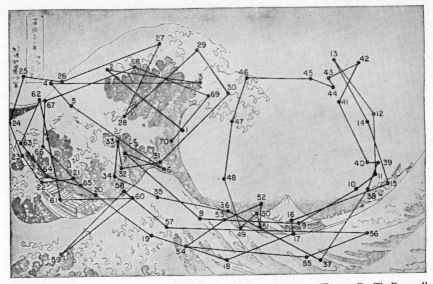

FIG. 40. The successive fixations at various points in looking at a picture, as recorded by a camera which photographed eye-movements of the observer. (From G. T. Buswell, *How People Look at Pictures.* Copyright 1935 by University of Chicago Press, Chicago.)

beholder is "carried" in a predetermined route through the picture or over the statue (again see Fig. 40).

SPAN OF APPREHENSION. Obviously the main necessity for shift of attention is the severe limitation on the sheer amount of material which can be included within the focus of attention at one moment. A "cosmic eye" might apprehend everything in a situation, completely and at once. Man, and lesser organisms, can take in just so much and no more.

One experimental approach to this problem of the maximal scope of the focus of attention is the studies on the *span of apprehension.* This refers to the maximal number of objects that can be immediately perceived, that is, with a duration so brief as to exclude counting or eye movements. Scatter a small number of beans on the tablecloth. Take a very quick glimpse and try to see how many beans there are. You will find, by doing this many times with different numbers of beans, that you will make few errors up to five or six beans,

but with more than that errors will occur. Figure 41 is a graph of the results of a careful experiment of this kind, using a tachistoscope that exposed the stimuli for only one-fifth of a second.

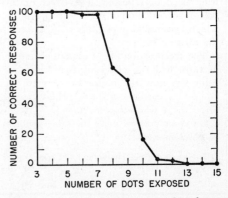

FIG. 41. A curve giving the results of measuring the span of apprehension for one observer, who estimated the number of black dots (varying from 3 to 15) on white cards exposed for split-second intervals in a tachistoscope. It will be noted that although few errors were made up through 7 dots, errors increased sharply beyond that; 11 dots were clearly beyond the span of apprehension (Glanville and Dallenbach, 1929).

DISTRIBUTION OF ATTENTION. The attention of the person at any one moment may be distributed in various ways over the whole field. It can be concentrated at one point, with little attention available for the rest. It may be diffusely spread so that no particular part is primarily in focus. It may be *divided*, the person trying to attend to two or more things simultaneously.

There are strict limits to the extent of such divided attention. The more the division, the more the loss in quality of attention devoted to each part. Evidence for this is given in several kinds of experimental studies. In one of them weak pressure was applied to a finger of each hand and the person had to say which pressure was stronger; at the same instant there was a brief visual exposure of from 3 to 6 lines and the person had to count them. Either task when done alone was so easy as to give nearly perfect performance. But when the two had to be done simultaneously, with divided attention, performance on both was much poorer. Both correct answers were only gotten 12 per cent of the time; one correct answer of the two only 60 per cent of the time.

Often, of course, the person is able to perform marvels of concentration upon a number of tasks in a very short interval of time, as, for example, when the chess master plays fifty games simultaneously. However these are not cases of true simultaneity, but rather of a very rapid shifting of attention back and forth.

ORGANIZATION AND ATTENTION. The limited span of apprehension, and the fact that the greater the division of attention the greater the loss in its quality, emphasize the value of perceptual organization. When parts of the field are organized into larger wholes, the attention required to perceive them effectively is less than when the parts must be attended to separately.

By the *grouping* of objects, the span of apprehension may be extended. If nine beans fall into three clusters of three beans each, they may be correctly seen. This is a simple illustration of the general point that organization has the function of enabling the perceiver to cope with more material.

This is seen in a more significant way in the development of skills (see Chapter 16). A well-trained activity does not have to be attended to, for the very reason that the integrated whole is so put together that it can run off without attention to its individual parts.

This is how it is possible for us to perceive complex situations with the merest glance. The necessry organizations are already available and the stimuli "fit" into them without need for careful attention to each. This, of course, makes for great efficeincy, but it may also result in error when certain details are wrong, but go unnoticed because they "fit" well enough into the orgauization, and cannot be picked out without careful attention. (You may not have noticed three printing errors in this paragraph, being so absorbed in the meaningful organization of the content that slight errors in letters did not emerge above threshold, particularly because the wrong letters did not seriously violate the proper structural appearance of the words. This is the so-called "proof-reader's illusion.")

DETERMINANTS OF ATTENTION. Attention is commonly spoken of as either *voluntary* or *involuntary*. The former pertains to cases in which the individual seems to have "freedom" in determining his own focus of attention, in deliberately choosing what to attend to. How this is possible and what is really meant by something being "voluntary" is a difficult question that we will take up later under the topic of motivation.

Involuntary attention pertains to cases in which the person seems less the agent choosing the direction of his attention, and more the pawn of "forces" that *require* him to attend this way or that. Some of the determinants of involuntary attention have to do with the goal-directed behavior of the person. The attention of the starving man is drawn irresistibly to the food in the restaurant window. Other determinants are related to the more enduring characteristics of the stimulus-objects in the environment; these may be such as "naturally" to attract, demand, seize, and compel his attention, despite what other activity is going on and despite what he seeks "voluntarily" to attend to.

The *attention-demanding* properties of stimuli have been extensively studied by the experimentalist in the laboratory and by the applied practitioner in advertising, in dress design, etc. The important stimulus factors can be summarized as follows: *intensity*, the shriek of the fire siren; *repetition*, the television commercial; *isolation*, the single word of advertising on the white magazine page; *movement and change*, the wigwag at the railroad crossing; *novelty*, the extreme design of the latest car model; *incongruity*, the woman smoking a cigar.

By Way of Summary. Perceptual organization depends heavily upon the *set* of the perceiver. Sets are determined mainly by prior experience, by temporal sequences of stimuli, and by the perceiver's needs, emotions, attitudes, and values. The frequency with which a percept has previously occurred will help to make for a set toward it. But this factor of familiarity can be overcome by other factors, such as a momentary set induced by instructions. Other things being equal, the states of need of the person are likely to give a set toward a need-relevant perception. But this effect is not "automatic"; a state of need may fail to affect perception when other contrary factors are at work.

The effects of sets on perception depend upon their saliency, specificity, duration, and relation to other sets. The effects depend also upon the strength of structure of the stimulus-pattern—a strong structure is more resistant to the effects of set than a weak structure. When the set is dissonant with the stimulus-pattern, there may be several types of perceptual outcome: selectivity of the best "fitting" organization from several possible alternatives, distortion of the pattern to fit the set, compromise between the form favored by set and that favored by the stimulus-pattern, redirection of the set to fit the stimulus-pattern.

What is in the focus of *attention* is the clearest and most differentiated percept in the field. Attention continuously shifts, inasmuch as there is a gradual "satiation" of any prolonged percept and there is a limited span of what can be taken in with a single focus of attention. With divided attention, perceptual discrimination is poorer. Attention can be either voluntary or involuntary, the latter resulting from certain attention-demanding properties of the stimulus itself.

Changes in Perceptual Organization

Up to this point we have been chiefly concerned with the factors determining the establishment of a perceptual organization. But a perception once established can undergo change. Some changes in perception occur with changes in the stimulus-pattern. Other changes in perception occur even though the stimulus-pattern remains constant.

Perceptual Changes with Constant Stimulus-Pattern. There are many cases in which "spontaneous" oscillation between two or more alternative forms of organizing a given stimulus-pattern will occur. Simple figure-ground alternations are common, as we have seen above. For laboratory study more complex patterns have been designed in which there are two main possibilities of perceptual organization, each of which has a fairly equal likelihood. These are called *reversible figures.*

REVERSIBLE FIGURES. In Figure 42 are shown two classical examples of reversible

figure. We cannot assume that simpler, more symmetrical, and generally "better" forms will always prevail. Box 28 gives an example.

To some extent "spontaneous" fluctuations in perceptual organization can be deliberately controlled by the perceiver. In many cases the person may "force" the fluctuation by shifting his visual fixation,

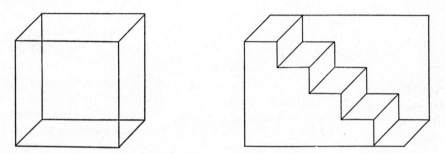

FIG. 42. Two classical examples of reversible figures, the Necker Cube and the reversible staircase.

figures, the Necker Cube and the reversible staircase. By fixating the Necker Cube, it will be observed that after seeing it for a while in one way, another way of seeing it will suddenly emerge, without forewarning. With further continued inspection, these two forms will alternate more or less regularly. Studies have shown that the rate of alternation tends to increase as the person continues to stare at the figure.

The ease of such reversals depends upon the specific form of the stimulus-pattern. If the "forces" making for each alternative are approximately equalized, the reversals are more rapid. If the "forces" favoring one alternative greatly outweigh those favoring the other, the reversals may be less frequent, and the duration of the less favored form will be much shorter.

The striking thing is that with long enough inspection, the simpler and "better" figure does transform into the less good

thus changing the actual stimulus-pattern on the eye. For example, it is well known that in the Necker Cube the point of fixation on the figure will help to determine which of the alternatives will be seen.

Satiation of Organization. But there may be something besides this, for these changes often occur without intention. It has been suggested that there are internal processes which eventually inhibit the preferred organization, so that the less favored organization occurs as the "next best thing."

It is assumed that oscillation of alternative forms occurs through the gradual accumulation of satiation as one form persists. When the satiation reaches a high enough level, the first form is inhibited and the second form appears. The second form in turn gradually satiates as the first form recovers from satiation, and eventually the first form reappears, and so on.

BOX 28

Distortion Through Reversal

The wire object is held about a foot away and viewed with one eye closed. At first it is seen correctly with the larger square face, ABCD, in front (see first figure). But with

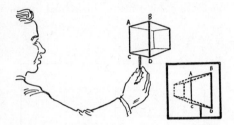

monocular vision it is not easy to tell which of the thin wires are in front of others. Thus the stimulus-pattern is a somewhat ambiguous one, and a spontaneous perceptual reversal soon takes place, just as in the case of the Necker Cube (Fig. 42). The smaller face now appears to be in front, as though the wire object were actually as shown in the insert. With continued inspection there is an oscillation between these two ways of perceiving the object.

If, while it is being seen in the *reversed phase* with the smaller face appearing to be in front, the wire object is slowly rotated by twirling the holder in the fingers, an astonishing thing occurs. The wire object appears to undergo a radical transformation in shape as it rotates. The square faces deform into trapezoidal shapes and then back into squares as the object turns. Once begun, these strange contortions tend to persist as long as the object is rotated. This striking phenomenon is very surprising to the observer. How can it be explained?

The reasons for the illusion can be grasped by a careful study of the stimulus-patterns that change on the retina as the object turns. The top row of the second figure diagrams the successive retinal images cast by the wire object as it turns from a position where the larger square face is actually in front to a position toward the side. It actually turns in a counterclockwise direction as indicated by the arrows. If

this is the direction in which it is perceived as turning, under these circumstances shape constancy operates, and what the observer sees is the rigid wire object rotating in space, its square faces remaining squares as they turn.

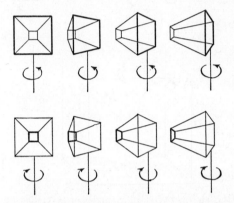

But under the conditions of *reversal*, the smaller face appears to be in front and the larger in back. Thus as the wire object actually rotates in a counterclockwise direction it *appears* to rotate in a clockwise direction, and the successive retinal images cast by the smaller face appear as diagrammed in the bottom row of the second figure. The consequence is that the wire object loses its rigid form, and the square faces undergo the improbable contortions as indicated.

Such contortions destroy the simple, symmetrical shape of the wire object, and it might be expected that for this reason the reversed perspective would be very unstable, and that as soon as the object began turning, the percept would "snap back" to its original (and objectively correct) form. But the highly significant fact that we have noted above is that once the rotation is started with the percept in the reversed phase, that perceptual organization *persists* despite the queer distortions in perceived shape that it entails.

This is a convincing demonstration that the *simpler* and *more familiar* perceptual organization will not necessarily occur in preference to an unusual and complex one.

Experiments have supported this interpretation by showing that if one alternative is deliberately *over*satiated by prolonged inspection of this form in isolation, the second (and normally less favored) form will immediately occur when the complete ambiguous figure is presented. By following the instructions in Figure 43, you can repeat

count for a phenomenon known as *figural aftereffects*. In vision, and probably in other sensory fields also, the prolonged exposure of a stimulus-pattern leads to some sort of change in the receptor or the nervous system so that new stimulus-patterns falling on the same region of the receptor shortly afterward are perceived in a systematically

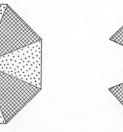

a   b   c

FIG. 43. In *b* is reproduced the ambiguous drawing encountered earlier in the book. Whether the cross or the propeller tends more readily to be seen can be influenced by prior fixation of either figure *a* or figure *c*. Look at *a* for sixty seconds, carefully fixating the center. Then fixate the center of *b*. You will tend to see the alternative figure. The experiment can be repeated by first fixating on *c*, in which case the opposite version of *b* will be immediately favored. (From Boring, E. G., Langfeld, H. S., and Weld, H. P. 1948. *Foundations of psychology*. New York: Wiley. Figures reproduced by permission of John Wiley & Sons, Inc.)

one of the experiments on yourself. Box 29 describes another experiment, one pertaining to oscillations of direction of perceived movement.

Another indication of the effect, which has not been studied systematically, is the subtle changes in appearance of a stimulus-object during prolonged exposure. If we stare at a printed word for some time, it begins to look "queer," as if it were spelled incorrectly, etc., though usually we cannot say just wherein the difference lies. The same is true of the repeated hearing of a word. Try saying the word "book" out loud over and over again. You will note that the word begins to sound completely meaningless.

Figural aftereffects. The underlying mechanism of such satiation of organization is not yet understood. Some experimenters have suggested that satiation can also ac-

distorted fashion. Box 30 describes some experiments of this sort.

Perceptual Changes with Changes in Stimulus-Pattern. Up to this point we have discussed perceptual changes occurring with *constant* stimulus-pattern. We now turn to perceptual changes taking place as a consequence of changes in the stimulus-pattern.

On the basis of various studies of such changes we can formulate a number of tentative generalizations summarizing the experimental findings:

1. *Change in perceptual organization tends to be minimal.* When there are changes in a stimulus-pattern, there are numerous kinds of perceptual changes that may occur; the tendency is for the fewest to occur. Some parts of the percept will be more affected than others; some parts may not change at all. In other words, not only will the total amount of change be minimal, the

BOX 29

Satiation of Downward Movement

A continuous paper tape with 45° lines drawn on it moves constantly downward at a slow rate. It is viewed by the person through the square aperture cut in the large cardboard shield in front of it (see fig. *a*).

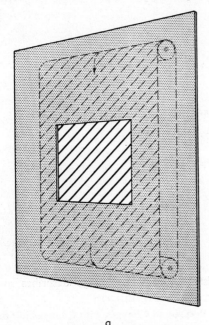

a

Under these circumstances the direction of perceived movement of the lines is *ambiguous;* they can be seen as moving vertically downward or as moving horizontally to the right. Subjects almost always tend first to see the downward movement. But with continued inspection there is a shift to the horizontal direction, and then an oscillation between these two directions of movement.

If we assume that these oscillations are caused by a gradual accumulation of "satiation" as the movement continues in a given direction, we should be able to change the perceptual sequence by deliberately over-satiating on one of the alternatives. Wallach conducted such an experiment by requiring the subject first to inspect for several minutes a moving paper tape on which were drawn lines that could *only* be seen as moving downward (see fig. *b*). Then when the

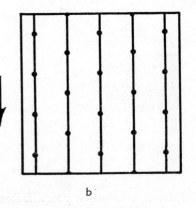

b

subject was shown figure *a*, he immediately tended to see the movement in the horizontal direction, rather than in the usual vertical direction. Apparently, the "satiation" for downward movement produced by inspection of figure *b* built up resistance to seeing movement in that direction, and thus the alternative horizontal direction was favored.

WALLACH, H. 1935. *Über visuell wahrgenommene Bewegungsrichtung. Psychol. Forsch., 20,* 325–80.

number of *types* of changes in the organization will be minimal.

The following is an experimental example of this minimal change. In a dark room a rotating luminous rod is viewed through an opening in the form of an ellipse. Thus when the visible part of the rod rotates, it constantly changes its length, contrac-

ting and elongating as it passes the short and long axes of the ellipse (see Fig. 44*a*). Thus on the retina we have *two* continuous stimulus changes, corresponding to the rotation of the rod and to the change in length of the rod. But actually that is not what the observer *sees.* He sees the rod *remaining the same unchanging length* while it rotates *in*

BOX 30

Figural Aftereffects

Fixate the cross in figure *a* steadily without moving your eyes for about 60 seconds. Then at once shift your eyes to the cross in figure *b*, and, while keeping your fixation, observe the appearance of the four squares.

equal. The distortion of figure *b* has been produced by the prior inspection of figure *a*.

On the basis of many similar experiments at Swarthmore College, Köhler and Wallach have proposed that these distortions can be described in terms of a *displacement* effect caused by satiation. When a figure has been cast for a short while in a given area of the retina, there is a kind of "satiation" which causes new figures cast near that retinal area to be displaced away from it. Thus in the above demonstration the perceived distortion of the squares in figure *a* can be understood by their displacement away from the places where the inspection figures had been previously exposed. Figure *c* schematizes the relationship by showing how figures *a* and *b* would appear if combined. The two left-hand squares are pushed apart and the two right-hand squares are pushed together.

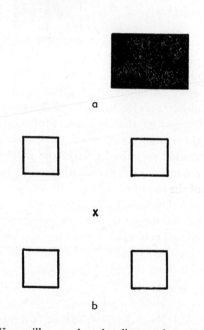

a

b

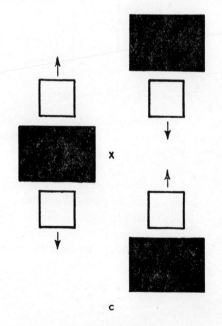

c

You will note that the distance between the two left-hand squares appears to be greater than that between the two right-hand squares. Actually the distances are

Köhler, W., and Wallach, H. 1944. Figural after-effects. *Proc. Amer. phil. Soc., 88,* 269–357. (Figures reproduced by permission of the authors and the American Philosophical Society.)

a plane tilted at an angle from the frontal plane (see Fig. 44*b*). Two continuous changes in the stimulus-pattern (the rotation

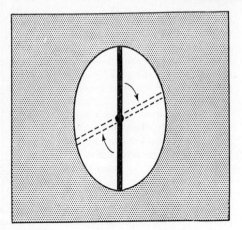

a

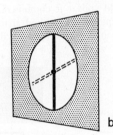

b

FIG. 44. For explanation, see text.

and the contracting and elongating of length) are perceived as *one* continuous change (the rotation in a tilted plane).

2. *Other things being equal more strongly organized parts of the field resist change longer than do weaker parts.* We have seen above (p. 100) that perceptual organizations vary in their structural strength. For instance, the figure tends to be more strongly structured than the ground.

If our only criterion for strength is a tendency to resist change, our statement is circular. We must, therefore, review some of the factors making for "stronger" or "weaker" structures. Briefly, we have seen that a percept is more strongly organized when the stimuli are clearer (that is, far

above threshold) and when the patterning is such that more of the grouping tendencies co-operate to produce the organization. In addition, the set, past experience, emotional state, and motivations of the perceiver may influence the strength of structures in the percept.

Let us look at a simple illustration involving primarily the first set of factors. If we look at two ballons of equal size side by side in a completely dark room, each balloon evenly illuminated, we perceive them as being at the same distance away. As one of the balloons is slowly inflated to a larger size, what happens on the retina is a change in size of the image of that balloon, the image of the other balloon remaining unchanged. However we do *not* see the two balloons as remaining in their same location and one of them expanding (a valid perception of what objectively happens out there). Instead, *it appears that the balloon being inflated slowly comes toward us— without changing its size.*

This is in accordance with our second generalization. The stimuli that normally make possible our judgment of how far away an object is (e.g., placement of the object relative to surroundings) are weak because of the darkness. This means that the spatial location of the balloons is a weakly organized part of the percept. On the other hand, the stimuli for the judgment of the size of the lighted balloons are clearer, and thus size is a more strongly organized part of the percept. In accordance with our second generalization, the perceptual change that occurs maintains the size of the object and shifts its location in space.

3. *Adjustment to stimulus change is often accomplished by the separation of parts of the field.* A particularly strong percept in the field may often be maintained without change, through a reorganization that somehow removes or insulates that percept from its surroundings—surroundings that would

tend to produce change in it. Thus the percept gets established as a more independent "sub-system" from the total "system" of the field. This so-called "separation of systems" is a fundamental characteristic of all psychological processes. We shall encounter it repeatedly in later topics of thinking, remembering, learning, motivation, growth, and personality change.

If we present a uniform green field to one eye and a uniform red field to the other, the person will experience a fluctuation of the visual field. Sometimes it will appear red and sometimes green, but not both at the same time. We speak of *retinal rivalry.* Apparently what occurs is that if the two fields do not readily fuse into one whole by combining the stimuli from both eyes, only one field will be seen at a time. If the two tendencies are about equal, there should be an oscillation; if the tendencies of one are much stronger, that one will predominate most of the time.

This is a simple case of color. But the same phenomenon can be demonstrated with complex stimulus-patterns. If we expose two quite different pictures to the two eyes, fusion cannot occur, and there will be retinal oscillation. Thus the perceptual organization of the visual field alters periodically even though the total stimulus-pattern remains unchanged.

We see here a good example of the manner in which a resolution of a difficult perceptual problem is achieved. If fusion cannot occur, the next best thing is to "give each separate organization its chance" in turn, thus preserving essential simplicity of the pattern, yet incorporating both parts within a whole extended through time. "Separation of systems," we see, can occur in the temporal as well as the spatial dimension.

4. Perceptual reorganization often occurs by sudden, stepwise transformations. Perceptual changes are sometimes gradual quantitative modifications of the attributes of percepts. Thus the object may move gradually closer, or get gradually larger; the shape of the object may gradually alter; the relations among objects may gradually change. But often the changes are not of this form, but are instead sudden, discontinuous "leaps" from one qualitative form to another. At one instant the organization looks this way, at the next moment that way. And the two appearances are sometimes so qualitatively unlike that it is hard to believe that the difference came about by only a slight quantitative change in the stimulus-pattern, or some other slight shift in "forces."

These sudden qualitative "leaps" are commonplace in natural phenomena. When we titrate a colorless solution in the chemistry laboratory, letting drop after drop of acid fall into the solution, there will come a point when with one more drop the solution changes suddenly and wholly to a red color. The enormous stresses deep in the earth may gradually build up without any noteworthy alteration on the surface, but suddenly as the stresses exceed a critical threshold, an earthquake comes and in a moment the landscape may be radically transformed.

Not alone in perception, but throughout psychological processes of all kinds, we find manifestations of this "principle." Tiny shifts in the "forces" of a situation may be sufficient to upset the balance of forces in a radical manner. This is true in shifts in emotional states, in motivational psychodynamics, in learning and thinking, in the crises of pathological "breakdowns" of persons under stress, etc. The concept of the "straw that breaks the camel's back" has basic theoretical support.

5. Change of perceptual organization often involves the creation of new forms. Every man is a creator who makes perceptual order out of stimulus chaos. This re-

BOX 31

Creative Perceiving

The illusion of movement described in Box 29, page 110, has been used by Wallach to study perceptual reorganization. A continuous paper tape moving slowly downward is viewed by observers through an aperture. On the tape is drawn a grid of 45°-angle lines. The left half of each line is black and the right half is red, as indicated by the dotted parts in figure *a.*

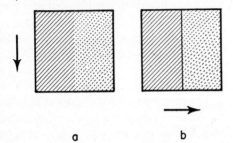

a   b

The movement is first perceived as a grid of half black–half red lines moving downward. After several minutes the "satiation" produced by this downward movement builds up a strong tendency for the movement to shift to the sideways direction. But this shift is inhibited by the fact that the lines would then have to be perceived in an unlikely way as *changing color* from black to red as they move to the right past the center. Hence the downward movement continues for a much longer time than it does under the conditions of Box 29. Finally, however, the problem of accommodating the growing tendency to shift from the downward movement is accomplished by the perceiver through a "creative" perceptual reorganization. He suddenly sees the black lines as moving sideways and as they reach the center *they pass behind a*

transparent red surface. This red transparency is perceptually "invented." It is clearly seen as a separate surface lying in front of the paper on which the black lines are drawn, and a vertical contour is seen in the center of the aperture, defining the edge of the red transparency, as indicated in figure *b.*

An even more complicated effect is obtained by showing a grid of lines that end in a scalloped edge (fig. *c*). Now the difficulty of seeing sideways movement is even greater than before because the lines have "nowhere to go." But for many observers a remarkable perceptual solution does spontaneously occur. They see the field as separated into two parts: (1) the set of lines moving sideways, (2) a white surface with a scalloped edge which *moves downward,* while the lines pass behind it (fig. *d*).

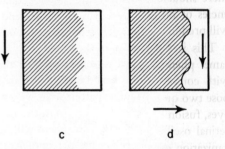

c   d

The restructuring occurs suddenly and without the perceiver's foresight or intention. He is surprised when it happens. It is "creative" in achieving a novel configuration that accommodates the requirements of the stimulus-pattern through the separation of the total into parts and the "invention" of new parts.

WALLACH, H. 1935. *Über visuell wahrgenommene Bewegungsrichtung. Psychol. Forsch.,* 20, 325–80.

quires the construction of a perceptual world, and this construction is often marked by "creative" ways in which stimulus-patterns are organized and reorganized. (See Box 31 for a striking demonstration.)

That such perceptual reorganizations may properly be designated as creative rests also

upon the fact that the new organization arrived at is *not* one previously in the perceiver's repertory. The new organization may appear *for the first time* as a result of the need for "making sense" of this stimulus situation. Moreover, as with all essentially creative acts, the new organization accommodates the necessary data in an economical and elegant way. And, too, perceptual creativity, like a great deal of the creativity in higher realms, may occur without intention and without clear awareness by the person of just how it is brought about.

By Way of Summary. Changes in perceptual organization may occur "spontaneously," without actual change in the physical stimulus-pattern, such as in reversible figures. This is partly due to the self-satiation of a given percept, which gradually accumulates the longer it endures.

When there are actual changes in the physical stimulus-pattern, perceptual changes also tend to occur. But the changes in perception are not simply a direct mirroring of the stimulus changes; they tend to be minimal, and to involve changes first in the more weakly organized parts of the percept. The perceptual changes often take the form of a separation of parts of the whole field. This may occur by sudden, stepwise transformations, often involving the creation of entirely novel percepts.

Glossary

adaptation level. A subjective level established by the person as a standard in making judgments, derived from a "pooling" or "averaging" of a series of similar stimuli he has experienced. For example, what is regarded as a neutral weight will be determined by the other weights that the person has lifted; weights above it will be judged "heavy" and those below it "light."

ambiguous stimulus-pattern. A stimulus-pattern that lends itself to two or more forms of perceptual organization, each more or less equally probable of occurrence.

assimilation. The tendency for the difference in intensities of adjacent parts of a field to be minimized in perception. Often these differences, even though above the threshold, are not seen at all. The effect is opposite to that observed in *contrast* phenomena, in which differences are maximized.

attention. The focusing of perception involving a heightened awareness of a limited part of the perceptual field.

closure. The tendency for certain figures to be so perceived that they are complete or closed, rather than incomplete or unclosed. For example, a circle with a tiny gap may be seen as an unbroken whole.

common fate. The tendency for the perceptual grouping of those stimulus elements that move or change in a common direction, as distinguished from other directions of movement or change in the field.

consonance of set and structure. A "fitting" of the perception favored by a given set with the perception that would be favored by the stimulus-pattern even in the absence of the set.

contour. A line of demarcation separating one part of a perceptual field from adjacent parts. Perceived as "belonging" to the figure, it provides the distinctive shape to it. Nevertheless contour and figure are not identical, since the very same physical contour looks entirely different when belonging to two different figures.

dissonance of set and structure. The lack of "fit" between the perception favored by a given set and the perception that would be favored by the stimulus-pattern alone, i.e., in the absence of the set.

figure. The part of the perceptual field which stands out on the background of the remainder of the field.

figural aftereffect. Refers to the fact that after prolonged exposure to one stimulus pattern, a new stimulus pattern falling on the same region of the receptor shortly thereafter will be perceived in a distorted manner. Some experiments have suggested that this phenomenon is related to self-satiation.

frame of reference. The standard or framework that serves as a reference against which a particular perceptual property is judged. For example, the apparent angle of objects in a room is partly determined by the angle of the surrounding walls. The frame of reference effect can be seen as an instance of the part-whole principle.

Gestalt psychology. An approach to the experimental study of the organized nature of perception, initiated by a group of German psychologists, including Wertheimer, Koffka, and Köhler. *Gestalt* is the German word for "form."

good continuation. The tendency for stimulus elements to be perceptually grouped in such a way as to permit the continuation of a line, or a curve, or a movement, in the direction that has already been established.

good figure. The characteristic of a certain pattern of stimuli having qualities of good continuation, symmetry, closure, unity, etc. The so-called "Law of grouping by good figure" states that perceptual grouping of elements will be favored in the direction of forming a good figure.

ground. The part of the perceptual field which serves as background for the figure. It appears to be less clearly structured than the figure, and less the focus of attention.

involuntary attention. Attention that seems to result from the characteristics of the stimulus rather than the intention of the observer. Some important attention-demanding properties of stimuli are intensity, repetition, isolation, movement and change, novelty and incongruity.

isolation effect. The tendency for the "minority" elements of a stimulus-pattern (those that are different from the majority of the elements) to stand out as a grouped figure against the "ground" of the majority elements.

part-whole principle. The principle that the perceived properties of a part of a stimulus pattern are largely determined by the whole pattern of stimuli. This part-whole principle has been applied to more complex psychological functions as well as to perception.

principle of proximity. The tendency, other things being equal, for stimuli close together in space or time to be perceived as grouped into a single whole.

principle of similarity. The tendency, other things being equal, for stimuli with similar attributes to be perceived as grouped into a single whole.

retinal rivalry. The fluctuation in the appearance of the visual field when the two eyes are separately stimulated with incompatible colors or patterns.

reversible figure. Stimulus-patterns that give rise to a "spontaneous" oscillation between two or more alternative perceptual organizations. The Necker Cube is a classical example of a reversible figure.

satiation. The tendency for the prolongation of a particular stimulus-pattern to produce inhibitions to the continuation of the percept, and a tendency to change to an alternative form of organization, such as in reversible figures.

separation of systems. In perception, refers to the observation that some parts of a percept may get established as relatively independent "sub-systems" of the percept, such that they will be relatively immune to the factors causing change in the rest of the percept.

set. A readiness of the organism to make a particular response or class of responses. Motor sets are readiness for particular actions; mental sets, for particular thought processes; perceptual sets, for particular organizations of stimuli.

span of apprehension. The maximal number of objects or items that can be immediately perceived with an exposure so brief as to exclude counting or eye movements.

The span of apprehension is increased by the grouping of the items.

stepwise transformation. Sudden, apparently discontinuous changes as opposed to gradual changes. Stepwise transformations are found frequently in perception, in shifts in emotional states, and in problem-solving.

strength of stimulus-structure. Stimulus-patterns may be arranged along a dimension of strength of structure. A stimulus-pattern is said to be strongly structured when the stimuli are clear, intense, simple, and subject to strong grouping factors. A stimulus-pattern is said to be weakly structured when the stimuli are barely perceptible, unclear, complex, and not subject to strong grouping factors.

symmetry. The tendency for the perceptual grouping of those stimulus elements that will result in symmetrical or balanced wholes as against asymmetrical ones.

tachistoscope. An apparatus for the controlled presentation of visual stimuli for very short intervals of time—as brief as one hundredth of a second.

transposition. The recognition of a stimulus-pattern as the same as another stimulus-pattern, even though the elements are different. This is based on the maintaining of an identical relationship among the stimuli in the two patterns, for instance as in the transposition of a melody on the keyboard.

Suggestions for Further Reading

ALLPORT, F. H. 1955. *Theories of perception and the concept of structure.* New York: Wiley.

An extremely valuable critical review of the main theories of perception, including approaches that stress the influence of set and personal factors.

ELLIS, W. D. 1938. *A sourcebook of Gestalt psychology.* New York: Harcourt, Brace.

A rich mine of translated selections from German psychological literature, especially on perception. Contains important selections from the writings of Wertheimer, Gottschaldt, and others.

KOFFKA, K. 1935. *Principles of Gestalt psychology.* New York: Harcourt, Brace.

A detailed presentation of many facts and theories concerning perceptual organization as considered from a Gestalt point of view, by one of the founders of Gestalt psychology. Difficult but rewarding reading.

METZGER, W. 1953. *Gesetze des Sehens.* Frankfurt am Main: Waldemar Kramer.

A full account of the facts of perceptual organization. Not available in English translation, but well worth study in the original.

CHAPTER VI

Movement, Time, Space, and Objects

THE WORLD we live in is a world of space, of time, of movement. In space are objects with which we must effectively cope. We must know where they are located in space, how distant from us and from other objects. We must know when they appear and how long they last. We must know whether or not they are moving, in what direction, and how fast. We must know how large they are, and what shape and color and weight.

Our ability to achieve such effective perceptions of movement, time, space, and objects depends upon an orderly integration of very complex stimulus-patterns in a manner that follows the principles of perceptual organization and change presented in the preceding chapter.

Visual Movement

The perception of visual movement is one of the most fascinating topics in the study of perception. Like many basic phenomena, the seeing of movement of things in our environment at first seems to present no particular problems. *Question:* Why do we see the object move? *Answer:* Simply because the object *does* move, and in moving it changes its location in physical space; as we note these changes, we "see" the movement. Now this "simple answer" is no answer at all, for it implies that our perception of movement is a direct "mirroring" of physical movement. But this is *not* the case. Physical movement of an object often fails to produce a perception of movement of the object, and movement is often seen where there is no physical movement at all.

Induced Movement. Recall the illusion of the moon appearing to move swiftly behind the clouds. This illustrates both that a truly moving object (the clouds) may fail to be seen as moving, and that an object truly at rest (the moon) may be seen as in motion. The moving object is said to "induce" an appearance of movement in the other object, and so we refer to this phenomenon as *induced movement*.

To understand this phenomenon, let us

first analyze the stimulus situation. On the retina there is an image of the moon and an image of the clouds. As the clouds physically move, the distance between these retinal images changes. It is this change in distance between the two images on the retina which constitutes the stimulus for perceived movement.

If *all* the information we have is that the two things are displaced relative to one another, the situation is ambiguous from the perceiver's point of view. Either one, or both, might actually be moving. Which, then, is perceived as moving?

seen is exactly what was seen before—the rectangle is seen at rest and the dot as moving to the right! (c) The rectangle is moved to the left and simultaneously the dot is moved to the right. Once again, what is *seen* is the rectangle at rest and the dot as moving to the right.

Here we have observed a striking case in which three *different* physical movements result in an *identical* perception of movement. The reason should be obvious. It is because the change in retinal stimulus for the three situations is identical.

Logically, any one of three perceptions

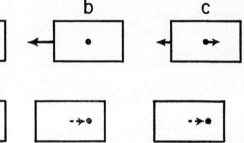

FIG. 45. Three experimental situations producing induced movement. The dot and rectangle can be moved independently of one another. The solid arrow indicates physical movement and the dotted arrow, perceived movement. In *a*, only the dot physically moves; in *b*, only the rectangle moves; and in *c*, both rectangle and dot move. Yet in all cases the *perceived* movement is the *same:* the dot appears to move and the rectangle appears to remain at rest. Three *different* physical movements result in an *identical* perception of movement.

Let us go into the darkroom where we can experiment with a very simple stimulus situation. On the wall is a luminous outline of a rectangle and within it a dot of light. The rectangle and the dot are mounted separately so that they can be moved independently of one another. We will do three experiments (see Fig. 45).

(a) The rectangle is fixed in place and the dot moved slowly to the right. The dot is seen as moving to the right and the rectangle as being at rest. Here the perception does correspond with the physical situation. (b) The dot is fixed in place and the rectangle is moved to the left. Now the perception fails to correspond to reality, for what is

might have occurred in all three experiments—a rectangle at rest and a dot moving, a dot at rest and a rectangle moving to the left, a rectangle moving to the left and a dot moving simultaneously to the right. The fact that the third of these perceptions never occurs is a further illustration of our generalization (p. 109) that change in perceptual organization tends to be minimal: one part (the framework) remains fixed, and *all* the movement is ascribed to the other part (the dot).

Further laboratory experiments indicate what factors cause one stimulus-object to be favored as framework over another stimulus-object. In brief, an object is more likely to be seen as moving with respect to another object if it is smaller, more enclosed, or more figurelike. Moreover, the object that is *fixated* is more likely to move.

The *meaning* of the stimulus-objects sometimes plays a role in induced movement. Thus, if two dots of light are exposed in darkness one above the other and either one is given a horizontal movement back and forth, we have an ambiguous situation. Either the upper dot or the lower dot can be seen as moving relative to the other. If the person is told that he is seeing a "metronome," the *upper* dot appears to move. If he is told that it is a "pendulum," the *lower* dot appears to move. (See Fig. 46.) Here we see how the perceiver's set

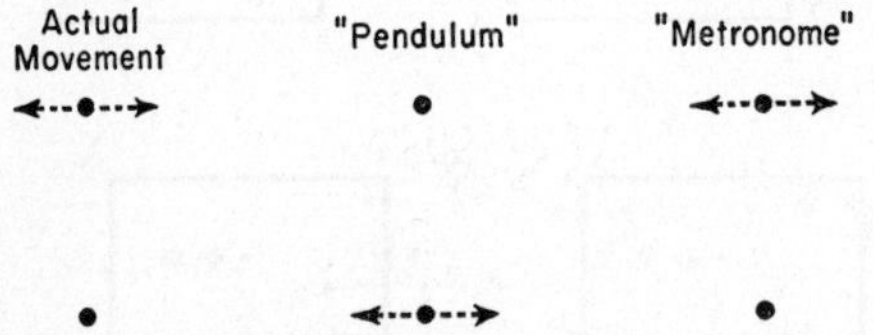

Actual
Movement   "Pendulum"   "Metronome"

◄--●--►   ●   ◄--●--►

       ●   ◄--●--►   ●

FIG. 46. For explanation, see text. (Carr and Hardy, 1920.)

selects between the two alternatives of an ambiguous stimulus-pattern the one that is consonant with the set (p. 100).

Of course, most real situations have more than the two parts with which we have been concerned. Each additional part may serve as framework for the other parts, and thus we get very complex interactions of figure and frame. In Box 32 is described a further series of darkroom experiments in which *three* elements in the field are displaced with respect to one another. In this case there may be several different directions of induced movement simultaneously. Just which relative displacements lead to induced movement and which do not depends upon the perceptual organization of the field.

It should be emphasized that induced movement is not different for the perceiver from "real" movement. If the frame-

work conditions are such that the object seen as moving is the one actually moving, we may be inclined to call it "true" movement perception; but if the framework conditions are such that the movement is induced in another object, actually immobile, we are inclined to regard it as an "illusion." In truth, the mechanism is identical in both cases. For "real" movement is also perceived only by virtue of the fact that there is spatial displacement of the stimulus with respect to some larger framework.

Apparent Movement. Everyone knows that a completely convincing impression of movement can be given by a rapid succession of still pictures, as in the movies. Here we have the case where there is no actual *continuous* physical displacement of stimuli with respect to one another. What there is, simply, is a rapid sequence of stimulus-patterns each of which differs slightly from the ones preceding and following. What is seen is an unbroken movement rather than a series of discrete, static images. This kind of temporal fusion is what is called *apparent movement* (sometimes referred to technically as stroboscopic movement or the phi phenomenon).

Take a simple laboratory demonstration. Two lights are mounted a few inches apart. The left one is turned on for an instant and then off. A second or two later the right light is turned on and off. What the observer perceives is the simple *succession* of one light and then another light. If the time interval between the two lights is gradually shortened, at a certain interval a surprising perceptual transformation occurs. Now it appears as though the light on the left *moves across* the intervening space to the right. Finally, as the time interval is made very short, the impression of movement disappears and instead the two lights are seen appearing *simultaneously,* each in its own place.

BOX 32

Induced Movement and Perceptual Organization

Induced movement depends upon the way the perceptual field is divided up into parts. A moving object may not induce movement in another object if the two are not perceptually connected. The following demonstration makes this clear.

In a darkroom a luminous dot is mounted on the wall. Surrounding it are a luminous rectangle and a luminous circle, so arranged that they can be moved independently with respect to one another.

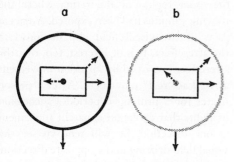

In figure *a* the circle moves physically downward, the rectangle moves physically to the right, and the dot remains stationary. The solid arrows indicate the direction of *physical* movement and the dotted arrows the direction of *perceived* movement. As the dotted arrows show, the rectangle is seen to move diagonally upward to the right, and the dot is seen to move *horizontally to the left*. This movement of the dot is paradoxical. The dot should *logically* move diagonally upward to the left, being given an induced movement to the left by the rec-

tangle and an induced movement upward by the circle.

How can this be explained? The answer seems to be that the total perceptual pattern gets differentiated into two *separate* systems or parts: (1) the system made up of the circle containing the rectangle, (2) the system made up of the rectangle containing the dot. *All* of the inducing influence of the movement of the circle impinges on the rectangle only, none on the dot. In other words, the effects are contained within one system and do not reach over into the other system. The outcome is the rectangle-and-dot system seen moving *as a whole* diagonally upward to the right within the circle, while simultaneously within and with respect to the rectangle the dot moves horizontally to the left.

That induced movement depends upon the way the perceptual field is organized is demonstrated by the following experiment.

In the situation depicted in figure *b*, the color of the dot and the circle is now made *red*, leaving the rectangle white as before. Now the induced movement of the dot appears different from what it was in figure *a*. As figure *b* indicates, the dot is here seen to move *diagonally upward to the left*. Because of similarity of color, the dot and the circle are *grouped* together, thus the separation of the two systems has been somewhat diminished. Now the movement of the circle has some inducing effect on the dot.

DUNCKER, K. 1938. Induced movement. In Ellis, W. D., *A source book of Gestalt psychology*, New York: Harcourt, Brace.

By virtue of a simple *quantitative* change in the length of the time interval between the two stimulus events, there have been produced *three qualitatively different perceptual experiences*—succession, movement, and simultaneity. What is even more noteworthy is that the apparent movement is clearly seen as occurring through the empty

space between the two stimulus locations. Here we have not only the fact that there may be movement perceived when there is no physical movement, but the more surprising fact that an object can be seen as moving in a place *where there is no stimulus on the retina at all*.

We have here, then, a remarkable demonstration of temporal interaction effects (see p. 74). Not only are the qualities of one set of stimuli modified by the relation to other stimuli, but the interaction "creates" something altogether new.

It is natural to suppose that the apparent movement is explained by the fact that as the eyes move from the one stimulus to the other, their turning somehow gives the impression of movement. This is readily disproved by the fact that movement can be seen in *opposite directions* simultaneously (see Fig. 47). Moreover, the "phi phenome-

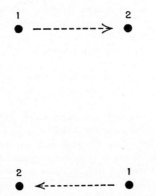

FIG. 47. The lights numbered 1 flash simultaneously, followed a fraction of a second later by lights numbered 2, which flash simultaneously. The observer sees movement to the right between the top pair of lights, and *at the same time* movement to the left between the bottom pair.

non" is also found in other senses. In touch, for instance, if light pressures are applied successively at two nearby points there will be an impression of movement of the stimulus along the skin from the one place to the other. A click in one ear followed an instant later by a click in the other ear may be heard as a single click moving through the head.

The stimulus conditions that govern the occurrence of apparent movement have been expressed in a number of "laws" of apparent movement. Box 33 describes these "laws," as well as certain striking examples of how the organization of the field determines characteristics of the movement, for instance, its direction.

Aftereffect Movement. We mentioned in Chapter 2 a well-known "illusion" of perceived movement which comes about as an aftereffect of continued exposure to a moving stimulus: the landscape seems to slide forward after the train comes to rest. Another demonstration of aftereffect movement is given by whirling the spiral shown in Figure 48.

Aftereffect movement is not restricted to the exact region of the retina where the moving stimulus had been exposed. Adjacent parts of the visual field also demonstrate the aftereffect. It is of interest, too, that the aftereffect is evoked by *apparent* movement as well as "real" movement. After a person fixates for a prolonged period a succession of lights that evoke an apparent movement in one direction, he will tend to see the visual field drifting in the opposite direction. An illusion can have an aftereffect!

FIG. 48. After the spiral has been observed rotating in a clockwise direction for some time and is then stopped, it appears to bulge outward toward the observer. After a counterclockwise spin, it will appear to bulge inward.

BOX 33

Factors in Apparent Movement

Three stimulus factors determining the *threshold* for apparent movement are (a) the distance between the two stimuli, (b) the time interval of the succession, and (c) the intensity of the stimuli. Korte experimentally varied these factors and formulated three "laws" which state that to obtain optimal movement:

1. The greater the distance between the two stimuli, the greater must be their intensity (if the time interval is constant), or the greater the time interval (if intensity is constant).

2. The greater the intensity, the greater must be the distance apart, or the less the time interval.

3. The greater the time interval, the greater must be the distance apart, or the less the intensity.

Grouping factors play a major role in determining the *direction* of the apparent movement. In figure *a*, light (1) goes on and off, followed shortly by lights (2) and (3), which go on and off simultaneously. The movement could go from (1) to either (2) or (3). Experiments show that it tends to go to (2), which is the nearer, in accord with the principle of grouping by proximity. In figure *b*, with proximity equal, the movement goes from (1) to (3) rather than to (2) because of the greater similarity of (1) and (3)—the principle of grouping by similarity. In figure *c*, the movement tends to take the curved path of the channeling contours, rather than to cut directly across the shortest distance from (1) to (2)—the principle of good continuation.

The shape and spatial arrangements of the successive stimuli may make it difficult or impossible to see a straight linear movement from one to the other. More complex apparent movements may then result. For instance, in figure *d* the line is seen to *rotate* through an angle from the vertical to the horizontal, and in figure *e* movement occurs in the *third dimension*, that is, the inverted V-shaped figure is seen to swing down and "flop over" into the reverse orientation.

KORTE, A. 1915. *Kinematoskopische Untersuchungen. Zeitsch. f. Psych.*, 72, 194–296.

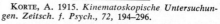

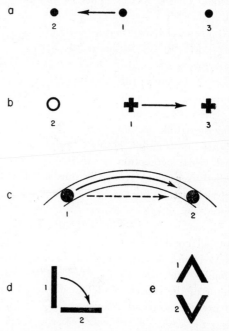

Autokinetic Movement. Return once again to our darkroom. As we look at a tiny *stationary* dot of light which is the only visible stimulus, we notice an astonishing thing. The stationary light appears to *move*, sometimes in this direction sometimes in that, sometimes slowly, sometimes more rapidly. As we watch it for a considerable

time, it may execute large sweeping movements, or move erratically in a jerky fashion. The extent of the movement can be very great. If we point our outstretched finger at the light as it moves, we will be amazed to find (when the room is suddenly illuminated) that our finger may be pointing as much as 30 degrees from where the dot of light actually is. *Knowing* that the light is really stationary does not change the effect. Moreover, the movement is seen as "real" movement, and a naïve observer believes that the dot actually does physically move.

This is known as *autokinetic* ("self-generated") movement. The essential stimulus condition for its occurrence is the absence of visual framework for the dot of light. As soon as other visual features are introduced close by into the field, e.g., a line, or other dots, etc., the autokinetic movement appreciably decreases, and if we make the visual field very complex, for example by turning on the room's lights, it disappears altogether.

The complete explanation for autokinetic movement is yet to be established. Eye movements play a role. So do various postures of the body; the direction and extent of the movement can be influenced markedly by the way the eyeballs, the head, the neck, and the trunk are rotated away from the normal line of vision. Thus we have evidence that visual perception is affected by kinesthetic sensations from the muscles. Perceptual interaction cuts across the various senses.

Moreover, in view of the fact that the optimal condition for the movement is a simple, "unstructured" or weakly structured stimulus-field, we should expect that the factor of the perceiver's *set* would be able to exercise a strong influence. This is indeed the case. Experiments (Sherif, 1935) have shown that the amount of movement is readily influenced by the suggestions of other persons. Moreover, there are large individual differences in the movement which seem to be related to the personality of the perceiver.

Autokinetic movement provides in a nutshell a demonstration of the basic fact that any perceptual phenomenon, even one as simple as this, is a function of a whole host of different potential influences, ranging from the pattern of the stimulus to deep central determinants in the person.

Organization and the Direction and Speed of Movement. The *direction* of visual movement is principally governed by organizational factors. We have already demonstrated this in the induced movement experiments (Box 32), where it was seen that direction of induced movement of an object depends upon which framework is functionally connected with the object in question.

Let us mention two additional examples. If a moving line is viewed through an aperture, the shape of the aperture will help to determine the direction of perceived movement (see Fig. 49). Another quite

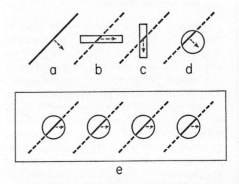

FIG. 49. The 45-degree-angle line sweeps across the visual field; see *a*. When it is viewed through an aperture so that only a segment of the moving line is visible, the direction it appears to move (indicated by the dotted arrows) is wholly determined by the shape of the aperture. In *b*, it appears to move horizontally, and in *c*, vertically, thus conforming to the main edges of the aperture. In *d*, the movement is at a 45-degree angle downward toward the right. But if a series of such circular apertures is presented in a horizontal row, as in *e*, and the line passes successively behind them, it appears to move in a *horizontal* direction.

different example, in Figure 50, shows how a complex combination of movements in different directions may be so unified as to yield a simplification of the whole pattern.

SPEED OF MOVEMENT. Things are seen to move with different speeds. The perceived speed depends for one thing, of course, on the actual physical speed of the object in space. In general, we do achieve a fairly accurate judgment of real speed, otherwise our highways would be even more cluttered with wrecks and our baseball batters would more often strike out. But there are limits to this. Some physical movements are so slow that we cannot discern them—the continuous growth of the plant's leaves may only be seen when we use a very slow camera. Some are so fast that we miss them altogether—the rifle bullet whizzes by our unseeing eyes.

Within the discernible range, perceived speed of movement depends upon the vis-

ual context. Objectively equal speeds may be seen as extremely different in different frameworks. See Figure 51 for an experimental demonstration.

FIG. 51. Behind each of two apertures is observed an endless paper tape moving downward. On the tape is printed a row of dots. The larger aperture is exactly *twice* the size of the smaller, and the dots on its tape are twice as large and twice as far apart. The observer's task is to adjust the speeds of the tapes until the dots in the two apertures *appear* to be moving at equal speeds. It turns out that the physical speed of movement of the tape behind the large aperture must be just about *twice* the speed of the smaller, for equality of phenomenal speed. (After Brown, 1931.)

The speed of movement is apprehended *directly*. We can make a very good judgment of the speed of an object while being quite unable to judge the distance through which it moves or the time it takes.

Perceived Causality in Movement. Movements are perceived not only as having certain directions and speeds but also as having more complex attributes. We commented earlier on the fact that we often have the vivid perceptual impression that certain moving objects interact "causally" with other objects. This rolling ball strikes one at rest and appears to set it into motion; the movement of the first is experi-

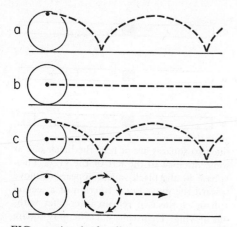

FIG. 50. A wheel rolls slowly along a table in a completely dark room. On its rim a small light is attached. The observer sees the light moving in a cycloid path as shown in *a*. In *b* the light is attached only at the hub and the observer sees it move along a straight horizontal path. What does he see when these two conditions are combined, with one light on the rim and one on the hub? It might be expected that he would see both the cycloid and the horizontal movements occurring together as schematized in *c*. But in fact what he sees is a "simpler" and more unified pattern of movement as schematized in *d*. The rim light is seen as rotating around the hub light as a center, while this whole "system" of rim and hub lights moves horizontally; the previous cycloid movement is entirely absent.

BOX 34

Perception of Causality

The Belgian psychologist Michotte has conducted a series of laboratory experiments designed to specify the stimulus conditions that give rise to different impressions of physical causality in movement.

On a cardboard disc he drew two thick curved lines, one black and one gray (see diagram). The disc was mounted vertically on an axle so that it could be slowly rotated.

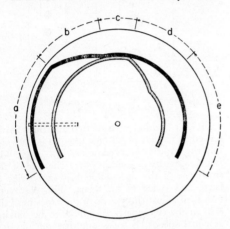

In front of the disc he placed a large shield, which hid the disc except for what the observer could see through a small horizontal slot cut in the shield (the dotted slot in the diagram). In the position that the disc was shown, all the observer could see were two small squares, one black and one gray.

By slowly rotating the disc counterclock-

wise, the experimenter could make the two squares appear to move along the slot, the pattern of movements being governed by the particular shapes of the pathways of the two lines drawn on the disc. In the diagram above, the dotted lines around the periphery of the disc and the letters *a* through *e* indicate the five different phases of movement of the squares as the disc turns once. The figure below shows the sequence of events as seen by the observer. At first (phase *a*)

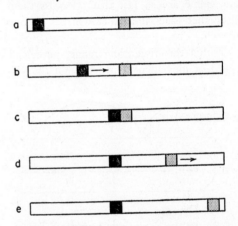

the two squares are at rest, the black one at some distance to the left of the gray. Then (phase *b*) the black square appears to move toward the gray. For a fraction of a second (phase *c*) the two remain in contact without moving. Then (phase *d*) the gray square

enced as somehow transferred to the second.

Now we should be clear that we are here concerned not with genuine physical causality, but with *perceived* causality. In other words, the problem of perceived causality is no different from any other psychophysical problem, such as the relation of perceived color to physical attributes of light stimuli.

Box 34 illustrates how such psychophysical studies of perceived causality can be made.

By Way of Summary. The perception of visual movement is not explained simply by real physical movement of stimuli in the environment. In *induced* movement, for example, the movement is seen when two objects are displaced relative to one another; but the one seen moving is not necessarily the one actually moving. In *apparent* movement a convincing impression of movement is given when there is no real movement at all, but merely a temporal succession of static stimuli, as in motion pictures. *After-*

BOX 34 (continued)

Perception of Causality

moves off to the right while the black one remains at rest. Finally (phase *e*), the gray one comes to rest, some distance to the right of the black.

In the basic experiment illustrated above, observers reported that there was a clear impression that the movement of the black object "caused" the subsequent movement of the gray object. This was not experienced by them as a mere *inference*, but as a *direct perception*.

Michotte then systematically varied the stimulus conditions by changing the pathways of the lines drawn on the disc. In this manner he studied the influence of variations in (1) speed of movement of the black square, (2) the distance it traveled before reaching the gray, (3) the duration of contact between the two squares, (4) the subsequent speed of movement of the gray square after contact was broken.

From perceptions reported by observers under these different stimulus-patterns of movement, Michotte discovered that there were two distinctly different types of perceived causality: "launching," in which the black object appeared to set the gray object into motion by transferring its force of motion to the gray; and "releasing," in which the role of the black object appeared to be only that of causing the gray to move by unleashing or "triggering" a *latent* force of motion already in the gray, without any accompanying impression of a transfer of

force of motion from the black to the gray.

By carefully varying the number of milliseconds (thousandths of a second) that the black and gray remained in contact (phase *c*), he found that below a certain number of milliseconds, "launching" was invariably seen, whereas above a certain number of milliseconds, "releasing" was invariably seen.

Some of his findings are quite different from what "commonsense" might lead us to predict. For example, if an object moves at a given speed and strikes another object, which then moves *faster* than the original speed of the first, we would be inclined to infer that the second object must have had a latent source of motion within it that was simply "released" or "triggered" by contact with the first object. Yet Michotte found that such "releasing" was *not* what observers perceived under these stimulus conditions, until the movement of the gray object reached a speed almost *twice* that of the black. Below this speed, even though the gray object moved substantially faster than the black, the impression was purely that of "launching." Here, then, is still another indication of the general point that the phenomena of perception are not merely "rational" representations of what our logic tells us.

MICHOTTE, A. 1954. *La perception de la causalité.* 2nd ed. Louvain: Publication Universitaires de Louvain.

effect movement is another form of illusory movement occurring in the reverse direction as a carry-over of a prolonged viewing of real movement. *Autokinetic* movement is an illusory movement occurring when a single stationary spot of light is seen in an otherwise dark room. In all these kinds of movement "illusory" movement is not distinguishable by the observer from physically real movement.

The speed and direction of perceived movement is strongly influenced by per-

ceptual organization of the entire field. Moving objects are often seen as having complex attributes, such as "causality," which are governed by specifiable features of the stimulus-pattern rather than being "rationally" determined.

The Perception of Time

Time, like space, is so much with us that we take it for granted. Though it is a necessary framework within which all events occur, as with many general frameworks we are not always aware of it. We become aware of it only when our attention is particularly drawn to it, when we are waiting, when we are keeping appointments, when we look at clocks.

Time is an attribute of a perceptual configuration, not an elementary sensory impression. There is no sense receptor for time. It is misleading, therefore, to think that the stimulus for perceived time is the passage of *physical* time. Physical time is, of course, one of the factors entering into the total determination of perceived time, but it is only one of many, and what counts is how all the factors interact in the total organization of the situation.

There is a clearly experienced difference between short intervals of time (a few seconds) and longer intervals (minutes and hours). In the former we *perceive* the time directly; in the latter we *judge* what the duration has been since something happened. The accuracy of perception of short time intervals is dependent upon numerous factors. For instance, there are systematic tendencies to overestimate intervals of less than about one second and to underestimate intervals of more than one second. Whether the interval seems short or long depends in part upon what goes on during the interval. If two clicks mark off an interval of silence (an *unfilled* interval), it will be perceived as shorter than the same physical interval during which a continuous series of clicks is presented (a *filled* interval). And curiously enough, a meaningful sentence will be perceived as of shorter duration than an equivalent sequence of nonsense syllables. It might be argued that the nonsense items being not yet organized present a series with many more discrete parts than does a meaningful sentence, and hence the interval is *more filled*, and thus seems longer.

Time Orientation. When we deal with much longer time intervals—minutes, hours, and even days—we are not concerned with a purely perceptual question, but with a question of *judgment*. That is, we judge the duration of time in relation to specific events, e.g., how many minutes have passed since the telephone rang, how long will it be before we eat. The accuracy of judgment of time duration depends upon two main kinds of factors, events in the external environment and events within the person himself.

The external events may pertain explicitly to time—we can look at a timepiece, or at the angle of the sun in the sky. Or they can be in the form of habitual cues. The remarkable ability of some individuals to awaken at a specified time in the morning has been found to depend upon cues of which the person may himself be entirely unaware, such as the onset of daylight, the sounds of traffic, or the steps of the neighbor.

Yet it is clear that even in the complete absence of such external cues, there is considerable accuracy of time orientation. In one experiment a man spent four days in complete isolation in a soundproof room, doing what he wished. At irregular intervals he telephoned to the experimenter his estimates of the time of day. During the first day the man's "personal clock" gained more than four hours. Then it began to return to proper pace, and by the end of the four-day isolation his guess of the time was only forty minutes in error. How was this possible in the complete absence of the habitual external cues? Obviously, he was responding to certain cues from inside the body, such as sleepiness, hunger, or pressure to eliminate.

There are large individual differences in the apparent speed of passage of time. Experiments have shown that for children of 10, a given interval of time may seem to pass as much as five times as rapidly as for an adult of 60. And within the individual there are tremendous variations from situation to situation, depending upon his mental and physiological states. In depressed states of mind, time slows down, as it does also when the person is experiencing frustration and failure. Coffee and tea speed up our subjective time; quinine and certain other drugs may retard it. It has been experimentally proved that the higher the body temperature, the slower time seems to pass. For a patient with a very high fever an interval of 20 minutes seemed to be hours long.

Time Perspective. Our ability to judge the duration of time permits us to develop a time dimension—a time framework within which events can be fairly accurately placed. Present events define a particular place in the time dimension; events remembered from the past are placed earlier in this dimension, and events expected in the future are placed later. This general perception of the relations of past, present, and future is technically known as *time perspective*.

Time perspective has been relatively little investigated. But casual evidence would seem clearly to suggest that time perspectives vary enormously for different individuals, at different ages, and in different situations. For Sergeant Anyman in the front lines under enemy attack, the time perspective is narrow; the past is not in his mind and the only future is the next few hours of battle. The next day, lying wounded in the hospital, his time perspective expands; thoughts of his boyhood and of the many years to come may be much with him. We shall see later, in our discussion of motivation, how important time perspective is in the determination of our value-systems and much of our general behavior.

The Perception of Space

It has already been pointed out that we are basically spatial animals, and our problem now is to explain how our perception of space comes about. We experience space through hearing, touching, moving, seeing. These different sensory experiences do not lead to different spaces, but to a *single unified space*. In this same single space we can see objects localized at different places, can hear them localized, can feel them localized. The various senses provide different avenues to the perceiving of this unified space; it is just as appropriate to say that we *hear* space as that we see space and feel space.

The perceptual problem is one of the synthesis of information from all these sources, since there is not always perfect agreement among the impressions of space provided by the different senses. For instance, there are striking cases of discrepancies between our feeling of space and our seeing of it. When we move about in the complete darkness, the size and arrangement of a room may seem quite different to us from when we can see it. But in general there is a high degree of harmonization of the cues from the different senses. The firm impression of space derived from these harmonious cues may be a correct perception of space or an incorrect perception of space.

Space Through Sounds. One way we can perceive space is through the localization of sounds. To localize sounds in space requires that we perceive both their distance and their direction.

Distance of Sounds. Distance is perceptually determined by a number of characteristics of the sound waves. The major stimulus characteristic is the amplitude of the sound waves reaching the ear. Loud sounds tend to be heard as coming from a closer object and soft sounds as coming from a more distant object. Often while we are listening, the intensity of the sound changes, and our perception of its distance changes correspondingly. As the sound grows louder, it is heard to approach; as the sound grows softer, it seems to recede.

As a complex sound wave travels through the air, its complexity diminishes. For example, the sound waves reaching the ear from a violin at a distance are less complex than those reaching the ear from a violin nearby. We should recall that the complexity of sound waves determines the perceived *timbre*. Owing to these facts, timbre serves as another factor determining the localization of sounds. The more complex a sound, the closer to the perceiver is it likely to be localized.

A number of other stimulus factors also contribute to perceived distance. A sound that has more space-filling "volume" is heard as closer, as is also one that dominates over other competing sounds.

Aside from these stimulus factors, there are the very important factors of set and meaning. We hear sounds at distances we expect, and in accord with our interpretation of their sources. All these diverse cues of stimulus, set, and meaning are synthesized according to the principles of organization discussed in the previous chapter.

Direction of Sounds. Under normal conditions most of us possess an almost uncanny ability to locate the direction of the source of sounds simply by hearing them, even without the benefit of other cues. To understand the way this is accomplished, we must first stress the difficulty of identifying the direction of a sound when using only *one* ear.

As we have seen, sound waves are agitations of the air spreading out in all directions from a sound source. The fact that the air in contact with the eardrum is agitated carries no "message" as to the direction from which the agitation traveled. If a single ear is stimulated by sound waves coming from either one of two similar sources at the same distance but in different directions from the perceiver, the effects of the two sets of sound waves on the ear are identical. The person cannot distinguish a difference in direction of the two.

BINAURAL CUES. But with *both* ears sounds may be localized with great accuracy. The cues making possible sound localization by two ears are called *binaural cues*.

The nature of binaural cues has been systematically investigated by fixing the person's head in a sound cage and requiring him to judge the direction of sounds presented at various locations on the surface of the surrounding sphere (see Fig. 52).

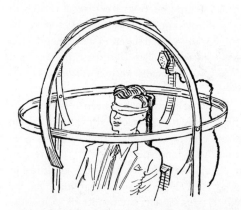

FIG. 52. A sound-cage used to investigate sound localization. The loud-speaker can be placed at any desired point on the sphere surrounding the person's head, which is held motionless by a head-holder.

When a sound is presented to the right or left of the median plane (the vertical plane passing through the middle of the head from front to back), the person correctly hears the sound as coming from that side. Analysis of the physical situation shows that the two ears are differently stimulated by a sound coming from the right side than by a sound coming from the left side. If the sound originates on the right side, it reaches the right ear a split second sooner than it does the left ear. This slight *time difference* provides an essential cue to direction. Since under optimal circumstances the error in location of a sound direction is only 1 or 2 degrees (out of the 360-degree circle surrounding the head), the organism must be able to take account of amazingly tiny time differences. Careful experiments demonstrate that when the time difference at the two ears is as little as *30 millionths of a second,* the side from which the sound comes can be correctly identified. Obviously this time difference is far shorter than what can be consciously recognized by the person; the effect occurs through an "automatic" integrating process in the auditory nervous system, as we shall see in Chapter 7.

A check on the hypothesis that direction is dependent upon the time difference at the two ears is provided by experiments with the *pseudophone*. This apparatus reverses the time of arrival of the sounds at the two ears (see Fig. 53). Under these artificial conditions the sound that is ac-

FIG. 53. The pseudophone. A sound coming from the right side would normally first strike the right ear and then the left, but the tubes of the pseudophone divert it so that it reaches the left ear first. The effect is to reverse the perceived direction of the sound, so that it appears to come from the left side. (Young, 1928.)

tually on the right is heard as coming from the left.

Similar experiments can be conducted in a more refined way by using earphones that deliver sounds separately to the two ears. It has been found from studies for example, that if a click in the right earphone precedes the click in the left earphone by more than about three thousandths of a second, the person hears two successive clicks, the first on the right, the second on the left. If the interval is shortened, the clicks fuse, and he hears a single click that seems to come from the right. As the time difference is shortened even further, the location of the fused click appears to move toward the left, and when the clicks are simultaneous, the single sound is heard as though located in space in the median plane.

There is a second important cue arising from the stimulus difference at the two ears when a sound is to one side. This is the *intensity difference*. A sound source on one side of the head will deliver a slightly more intense sound to the ear on that side. This is primarily caused by the sound "shadow" cast by the head; sound waves that have to pass around the head are somewhat disrupted and their intensity slightly reduced. Careful experiments show that these slight intensity differences are sufficient to help us to locate correctly to left or right.

If the sound comes from anywhere in the median plane, *it strikes the two ears simultaneously and with equal intensity,* and thus is heard as being *somewhere* in the median plane. But the person cannot tell where in the plane it is; it may be in front, in back, above, or below. This is, then, a "plane of confusion."

Similarly, for sounds to one side of the median plane, there is a "cone of confusion" (see Fig. 54). The person can tell from which side the sound comes, but he cannot discriminate among the sounds originating at the many points on the surface of the cone. The reason is obvious: since all points on the cone are the same distance farther from one ear than from the other, a sound

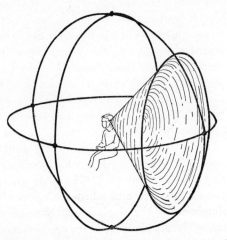

FIG. 54. No matter at what point a sound originates on a conical surface like the one illustrated, it is always the same distance farther from one ear than from the other. Accordingly, though the hearer can tell from which side the sound comes, he cannot discriminate among the many possible locations. (After Boring, Langfeld, and Weld, 1948.)

originating at any point on the cone will provide the *same difference* in stimuli at the two ears.

Thus the two binaural cues of difference in time and intensity are not sufficient to enable localization from all possible directions. And yet such localization is possible. How can it be accomplished? The main additional stimulus factor is *head movement*.

HEAD MOVEMENTS. Normally, when we are trying to localize sounds, we move our heads, often so slightly that it is not noticeable. These head movements produce *different temporal patterns of stimulation* at the two ears, and this enables us to discriminate among sounds that are otherwise indistinguishable as to direction. Rotating one's head from right to left enables one to tell a sound directly in front from one

directly in back; for as the head turns leftward, a sound from in front arrives relatively sooner and louder at the right ear than at the left. Similarly, by tilting one's head from side to side, one can tell a sound directly above from one directly below. The combination of angles of head movement and of changes of stimulation pattern at the two ears "pins down" the exact location of a sound source. In Box 35 are described some beautiful experimental demonstrations of this.

OTHER CUES. Other kinds of factors also play a decisive role in sound localization. When a visual stimulus occurs simultaneously with an auditory stimulus, they tend to be localized at the same place in space. This is an instance of grouping by proximity. Thus we hear the sound as though coming from the lips of the person on the movie screen, even though the sound source may actually be far to one side of the screen. This depends also, of course, upon the factors of learning and expectation (set), which play a major role in sound localization as they do in all forms of perceptual organization.

Taken together, all these facts about localization of sounds provide an excellent illustration of how perceptual organization works in the "solution" of the problem of space. Stimulus information from both ears, as well as from other receptor systems, is synthesized in an orderly, efficient, and "spontaneous" fashion to provide a compelling impression of auditory space. We turn now to visual space, where the same kind of story will be repeated and extended.

The Perception of Visual Depth

The retina of the eye is virtually a flat surface, and the light energies that fall upon it are thus spread out in two dimensions

---

BOX 35

Locating Sounds by Head Movement

Wallach has conducted an experiment in which the sound source is constantly kept directly in front of the head. The sound source moves automatically as the head turns, much as with the donkey with a carrot suspended from a pole attached to its head. There is a continuous buzz from the sound source, and the person tries to locate it in space, being permitted to turn his head only to right and left. Thus the person gets kinesthetic cues that his head is moving, but at the same time there is no change in the auditory stimuli at the two ears.

The person hears the sound directly *overhead*. This is an entirely sensible "fitting together" of the two facts that there is movement of the head, yet the sounds at the two ears do not change. For, as we can readily see, this is precisely the stimulus situation that prevails when the sound is *actually* directly overhead. Here we see, then, a demonstration of the elegant workings of the perceptual system.

A further very striking fact is that the system is concerned with *phenomenal* relations, not necessarily with actual stimulus events. The figure illustrates the set-up. The individual is seated on a stool inside the striped drum. His head is fixed and a sound is presented continuously and directly in front of him. The striped drum is set into motion; this gives the person the impression that he is whirling about, although he is actually completely at rest. *Where does he hear the sound?*

Here again the astute reader will be able to figure out the necessary outcome. Again the sound is heard directly *overhead*. And this is so despite the fact that the head is *stationary* and the auditory stimuli at the two ears do not change, a situation that would normally lead to hearing the sound directly in *front*. What has happened,

obviously, is that the *subjective impression* of movement when combined with the fact of no auditory stimulus changes at the two ears can be made simple "sense" of only by perceiving the sound as coming from directly overhead.

WALLACH, H. 1940. The role of head movements and vestibular and visual cues in sound localization. *J. exp. Psychol.*, 27, 339–68.

---

only. We might expect then that visual experience would consist of a similar two-dimensional space, flat, without depth. But

this is never the case; space is *always* seen as tri-dimensional, even under very simple stimulus circumstance—where the man in the hollow hemisphere (p. 85) saw only a homogeneous surface, he still saw it at some distance away in the third dimension.

Perception of depth seems to be a "natural" accompaniment of perceptual organization. For instance, in figure-ground separation the figure is pushed forward while the ground is thrust backward. Here we have the simplest and most primitive depth experience, an effect that helps maintain the separation.

The particular manner in which depth experience does occur and the stimulus-patterns for its arousal will be discussed under the main headings of monocular and binocular cues.

Monocular Cues for Depth. "In the world of the blind, the one-eyed man is king." For even a man with a solitary eye can achieve the marvels of seeing, and among these is the seeing of depth. Normally, depth perception requires two eyes, just as the perception of direction of sounds requires two ears. But whereas with only one ear it is not possible to localize sounds, with one eye visual depth perception can be achieved through various *monocular cues* for depth, some pertaining to the visual pattern, some to the muscle adjustments of the eye, some to head movements.

Cues from the visual pattern. To achieve the impression of depth solely from a visual pattern on a flat canvas is the problem faced by the artist. We all know how successful this can be. At one point when stress in art was on realistic representation, the "eye-fooling" (*trompe-l'oeil*) painters vied with one another in the use of devices to simulate depth, and one triumphed by painting "velvet curtains" on his picture so convincingly that his discomfited rival reached out to draw back these "curtains," thinking to see the painting beneath.

Figure 55 illustrates some of the following features of a flat visual pattern which give it the appearance of depth by making the objects appear to be at different distances from the observer.

(1) *Interposition.* An object that partly covers another object tends to be seen as the closer. (2) *Relative size.* The larger of two objects tends to be seen as the closer. (3) *Relative height.* The lower of two objects tends to be seen as the nearer. (4) *Relative clearness.* The clearer and more detailed the object, the closer it tends to be seen. (5) *Linear perspective.* The greater the convergence of lines, the more distant the impression. (6) *Light and shadow.* Certain patterns of light and shadow favor the depth impression.

It has been proposed by Gibson (1950) that most or all of the above cues can be

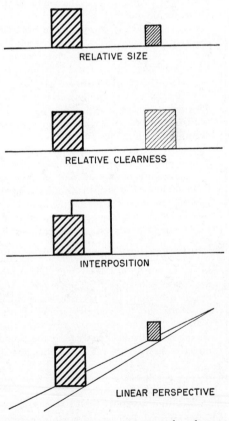

FIG. 55. Some monocular cues for the perception of depth.

BOX 36

Depth Through Gradients

In our normal viewing of the three-dimensional enviroment, we see various surfaces that extend outward in depth from us, such as the ground on which we stand, the walls, floors, and ceilings of the room. On the retina the surfaces are projected as flat images. These surfaces typically have *textures*. Owing to the geometry of the spatial situation, a uniform texture on the physical surface gets projected on the retina in such a way that *the greater the distance away, the greater the density of the texture in the retinal pattern*. This is shown in the figure below. In brief, there are *gradients* of tex-

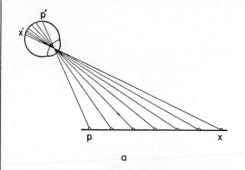

a

ture in the flat retinal pattern which correspond to the real physical distance dimension.

Gibson argues that these gradients of texture provide the adequate stimulus for perception of depth. He illustrates this with a number of flat drawings that have various texture gradients which give a clear impres-

sion of depth. In figure *b* is an array of spots in which sizes of the spots and distances between them decrease regularly toward the top of the drawing. That is, there is an increasing gradient of texture density. The result is a strong impression of a continuous receding plane. In contrast, figure *c* has a

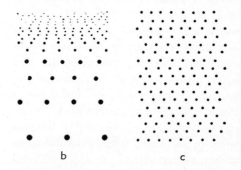

b   c

perfectly regular spacing of dots, that is, a zero gradient, and it is seen as a vertical plane without depth.

Gibson offers similar illustrations indicating that other depth cues are merely special cases of stimulus gradients on the retina. In the case of *relative clearness* the light from distant objects in the environment is more diffused by the time it reaches the eye than is the light from nearby objects, with the result that there is a gradient of clearness among their corresponding images on the retina.

GIBSON, J. J. 1950. *The perception of the visual world.* Boston: Houghton Mifflin.

subsumed under a more general concept of *stimulus gradient.* Box 36 gives specific examples.

ACCOMMODATION. The light rays coming from an object at which we are looking get focused by the lens system of the eye in such a way as to achieve the clearest image. This *accommodation* is accomplished by the pull of the eye muscles that shape the lens into the appropriate curvature. To

focus on a distant object, the lens must be flattened; and to focus on a nearby object, made rounder. Thus when one looks at a close object, such as a book held in one's hand, the amount of accommodation is quite different from when one looks at a more distant object.

The kinesthetic sensations from the different amounts of pull of eye muscles thus provide cues as to the distance of the object. However, since beyond a few feet there is no significant difference in the amount of accommodation, this cue is effective in depth perception only for short distances.

RELATIVE MOVEMENT. The above cues from the stimulus-pattern refer to what happens at a single moment in time. Another kind of cue is given by the *temporal* pattern of visual stimuli that occurs when the head moves from side to side. If we look at a flat picture, of course the relations among objects within the picture do not change with the movement. But for objects with actual depth differences among them, head movements do make for a change in the stimulus-pattern when the objects are viewed from successively different angles. In particular, as the head moves to the left, nearer objects are displaced relatively to the right and farther objects relatively to the left of one another. This *relative movement*, sometimes called *movement parallax*, is a powerful monocular cue for depth.

Binocular Cues for Depth. We have just seen that when the one-eyed man moves his head, he gets different images of the object. When we look with *both* eyes—in binocular vision—we get different images of the object without head movements, since each eye looks at the object from a slightly different angle. The difference in images on the two eyes is known as *retinal disparity*.

RETINAL DISPARITY. To the maximal degree possible the perceiver seeks to harmonize and synthesize all available cues. The two different retinal images are brought together and fused wherever possible. We have already noted the fact (page 113) that the retinal images may not fuse, but may oscillate from one to the other (retinal rivalry). The degree to which fusion rather than rivalry occurs depends upon the consonance or dissonance of the two images. If they can be fitted together to produce a single unified field, that is favored. One critical way in which such unification can often occur is through the creation of an object that has perceived depth; out of two simultaneous and slightly different images, each of which is two-dimensional, a new fused image is achieved that has depth.

It is these facts that make possible the *stereoscopic* devices for giving the impression of depth in viewing flat photographs. (See Box 37 for an explanation of how the stereoscope works.)

CONVERGENCE. As we have seen in the stereoscope, the eyes swing their lines of sight toward one another in looking at an object. This is called *convergence*. The kinesthetic sensations arising from the muscles controlling the swing of the eyes may give some additional information as to whether the object is near or far. The effect is not, of course, a *conscious* one.

When the objects are far away, the lines of sight become almost parallel and the amount of convergence insignificant; for distances greater than 50 or 60 feet the convergence cue is not effective in aiding the perception of depth.

The Synthesis of Depth Cues. We have analyzed the monocular and binocular cues for depth one at a time. But the most compelling and full-bodied experience of depth comes when many cues work simultaneously.

There are often situations in which the cues are not harmonious, for instance, where there are oddities in the spatial arrangements of objects, where the illumination is unusual, where the stimulus-pattern is poorly structured. In such situations the various cues may tend in contradictory directions, competing rather than co-operating, and the impression of depth may

BOX 37

The Stereoscope and 3-D

Since binocular disparity is such a powerful depth cue, it should be possible to produce an artificial impression of depth by giving each eye a slightly different picture and making the eyes converge as they would if looking at the real three-dimensional object.

This reasoning led the English physicist Wheatstone to invent the *stereoscope* in 1838. There are several different types. The most common is the prism stereoscope shown in the figures. The two flat pictures, p_1 and p_2, are presented to the two eyes separately. The partition prevents each eye from seeing the picture intended for the other eye. The light rays from the pictures are bent by the prisms so that they seem to reach the eyes from a three-dimensional

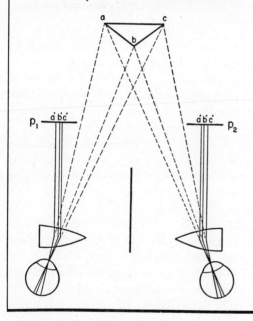

object, *abc*, on which the eyes are converged. The distances between *a*, *b*, and *c*, differ slightly in pictures p_1 and p_2, as the retinal images would if the person were actually looking at the real object.

The necessary photographs can be taken by moving the camera into two successive positions, or more simply with the stereo-camera now in common use which has two lenses and takes two pictures simultaneously from slightly different angles. The lenses can be placed somewhat wider apart than the eyes actually are, and this accentuates the depth impression.

The so-called 3-D movies, which had a recent short-lived vogue, are produced by a somewhat different stereoscopic device. Two disparate views are projected on the screen by light polarized in two different planes. The person wears Polaroid frames so that each eye receives only the appropriate picture. The resultant three-dimensional effect is astonishing, as viewers will testify who "dodged" objects thrown toward the audience and observed new depth to feminine charms.

It should be noted that other currently popular devices to give depth impression in the movies are based on entirely different principles, primarily those involving monocular cues. In Cinerama, for example, the depth impression is achieved by the use of a very large, curved screen on which three closely co-ordinated and synchronized pictures are projected from three angles. The spectator seems to be surrounded by the picture, and the various gradients of texture, movement, etc., together with multiple sound sources (stereophonic sound), are especially effective in stimulating depth.

thereby be weakened or altered. This kind of situation can be artificially induced in the laboratory in order to study the way cues interact. For instance, by pitting the cue of interposition against the cue of relative size, we can distort the depth perception of objects. Figure 56, on the next page, presents an interesting illustration from an experiment where this distortion of depth was successfully achieved.

The perception of depth, therefore, cannot be thought of as a simple summation of the various cues. In general, the perceptual process seems to weigh the various cues

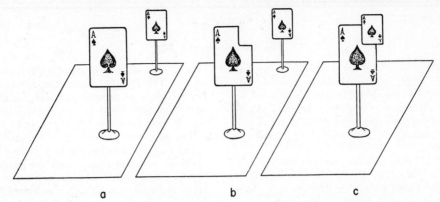

a   b   c

FIG. 56. In a dark room two playing cards are attached vertically to stands, one placed closer to the observer and the other more distant. Only the cards are visible, and the observer views them with one eye, thus being restricted to monocular depth cues. As illustrated in *a*, the cue of relative size (and perhaps other monocular cues) clearly makes the distant card *look* more distant. Then a corner is clipped from the nearer card, as shown in *b*, and the stand holding the farther card is moved to the left so that in the observer's retinal image its edges exactly fit the cutout edges of the nearer card. As shown in *c*, the effect is clearly to make the more distant card now *appear to be in front* of the closer card. The cue of interposition contradicts and is sufficiently powerful to overcome the cue of relative size, thus resulting in a distorted perception of the two cards.

and in this way derives a "reasonable" percept of space. The perceiver, however, does not do this in a deliberate or conscious fashion.

The Origins of Space

How it comes about that these cues can be integrated to yield a perceived space is a question that has beset philosophers and scientists for centuries. Is this something gradually *learned* through the organism's adjustment to its environment, or is it "given" through the *inherent nature* of the organism? The former is an *empiristic*, and the latter a *nativistic* interpretation. Both positions have been vigorously argued.

The weight of the experimental evidence, which is far from satisfactory as yet, would seem to favor a synthesis of the empiristic and nativistic emphases.

Experimental Findings on Animals. That space can be perceived by organisms with-

out specific learning is clearly shown by the fact that insects give every evidence of simple space orientation in the absence of prior experience. There is some evidence that the same is true of more complex organisms, such as the rat (see Box 38).

But even if the perception of space does not *require* learning, this does not, of course, rule out the critical role of learning in extending and refining our space perception. The organism moves continuously about in its physical environment and gains an enormous amount of information about the relationships of various kinds of cues to depth. It seems unquestionable that such experience contributes significantly to the full achievement of depth perception. Take, for instance, some of the monocular cues for depth, such as relative size, relative clearness, lights and shadows. It would seem obvious that the sensible relationship between these cues and the actual physical situation is partly based on learning; of two objects, the one that looks dimmer and less detailed also looks more distant because

BOX 38

A Look Before a Leap

An experiment by Lashley and Russell showed that rats, too, seem to be able immediately to perceive visual space without the benefit of prior experience. They raised 13 rats in complete darkness from birth until the age of 100 days (rat adulthood). The only visual experience the rats had during this whole period was the few seconds of very dim illumination each day when their cages were opened for feeding.

On the critical day of the rats' first experience of full light the experimenters tested the rats' orientation to visual space. This was done by placing each rat on a high pedestal and urging it to jump the gap to a platform a short distance away on which food was available. After brief preliminary training at this fixed distance so that the rats were accustomed to jumping, the distance between the pedestal and the food platform was varied over a range of a few inches to several feet. The accuracy of the rat's perception of the changing distances was measured by the force of its leaps toward the platform; that is, it was assumed that if the animal were perceiving the distances properly, a large gap should result in a proportionately stronger jump than a small gap. The force of the jump was recorded by the swing of a pointer attached to the platform and set into motion by the impetus of the leap.

Even though the rats were far from uniformly successful in hitting the platform, it was convincingly clear that they did discriminate among the different visual distances. The graph, which plots the average

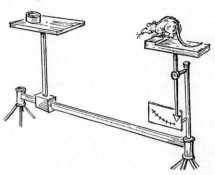

force of jump against the distance to the platform, shows that the rats regulated the impetus of their leaps in fairly good accordance with the actual distance. The performance of these rats raised in darkness was virtually the same as that of rats who had been raised in the normal way.

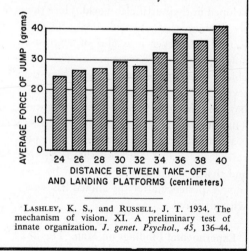

LASHLEY, K. S., and RUSSELL, J. T. 1934. The mechanism of vision. XI. A preliminary test of innate organization. *J. genet. Psychol., 45,* 136–44.

we have incessantly experienced this "fact" about the real environment. Shadows below an object make it appear convex in depth because we are accustomed to light from above in our real worlds.

Yet it is important to note that the sensible connection between the way the cues work and what they ought to mean may not *necessarily* prove that such relation-

ships must be learned afresh by each organism. Evolutionary development of the species within the given kind of physical environment may have *selected* genetically for a biological make-up of organism in which the proper cues are inherently built-in to the nervous system. What we need are experiments to determine whether the meanings of the cues depend upon the specific life experiences of the particular organism.

Hess (1950) has performed one illustrative experiment of this kind, designed to determine whether the depth cue of shadow does indeed depend upon the organism's early discovery that objects are generally lighted from above. He raised chickens from the time of hatching in an artificial world in which all lighting was uniformly *from below* rather than above (by using wire floors). At seven weeks he tested their depth perception by exposing vertical cards on which were realistic photographs of pieces of grain taken in two ways—(1) lighted from above, (2) lighted from below. When the hungry chickens pecked at the "grains," they tended to favor those with lighting from below, in accord with the experience of depth they had developed in their artificial world. Here there is evidence that cues of depth may be learned. However it is also of interest to note that in further experiments, when chicks were tested at *younger* ages than seven weeks, they responded somewhat more in accord with *overhead* lighting. Thus it appears that to begin with there is a "natural" tendency for depth to be perceived in accord with overhead lighting and that this can only be reversed by contrary experience after the animal has somewhat matured.

Experimental Findings on Man. The likelihood is that man, because of his higher biological development, is more flexible in the learning and relearning of depth cues. It certainly seems likely, for instance, that the acquired *meanings* of stimulus-patterns, their identification as "objects," will be accompanied by impressions of depth not intrinsically found in the stimulus-pattern. A flat drawing of a normally three-dimensional object will readily take on depth because of such acquired meaning. And fac-

tors of set will also play a central role in the impression of depth.

Experiments on the effect of changing the normal relations of the visual space cues to the auditory and kinesthetic space cues have been done with human beings. A classical experiment of this kind was conducted by Stratton in 1897, in which for eight days he wore special glasses that inverted the visual field. The flexibility of the perceptual system in adjusting to this radical change of cue relationships is described in Box 39.

By Way of Summary. On the basis of all the available evidence the following generalizations may be made:

(1) Primitive tri-dimensional space perception is a product of the way the nervous system works—no learning is necessary. In other words, when the organism's eyes and ears are properly stimulated, the percept of space occurs naturally and spontaneously, just as, for instance, the stimulation of the retina by light of various wave lengths gives rise naturally and spontaneously to different color sensations without learning.

(2) Perception of space is not necessarily fully present at the organism's birth, but may develop gradually with the physiological *maturation* of the nervous system. This process of growth may be required in order to permit the various sensory systems that participate in the unified perception of space to develop the necessary connections. Different kinds of organisms differ widely in the speed of this maturation process.

(3) The complex differentiation and organization of perceived space is a product both of primitive, inherent tendencies and of the learning of the relationships and meaning of cues through past experience. How the organism adjusts and readjusts in its spatial world depends upon these factors of past experience.

BOX 39

The Upside-Down World of Psychologists

The effects of continuously wearing a lens system that inverts the visual field was first studied by George M. Stratton in 1897 at the University of California (whose psychological laboratory he founded). He wore the lenses for 8 days on the right eye only; the left eye was kept blindfolded. The optical effect was to turn the whole visual field completely upside down, and to reverse it from right to left.

Stratton reported severe immediate disorientation on donning the lenses. The co-ordination of vision and body movement was badly disrupted. He reached in the wrong direction for visually perceived objects, and heard sounds coming from the opposite side from their visually perceived source. A great deal of trial-and-error groping was required to accomplish simple acts, such as placing a fork in the food and conveying it to the mouth. After about three days the disorientation lessened and by the end of the eight days the new visual-motor co-ordinations became quite good. As the days passed, he even became less and less aware that the visual scene was upside down. When the lenses were finally removed, some further disorientation was again noticed, but it lasted only briefly.

In a recent repetition (Snyder and Pronko) the inverting lenses were worn for 30 days, and careful comparative tests of visual-motor co-ordination were made before, during, and after the period of inversion. In one of the tests the subject had to sort cards rapidly into appropriate boxes. Time in seconds for completion of the task was recorded. Five trials per day were carried out for 17 sessions before the lenses were worn, for 28 sessions during their wearing, and for 4 sessions after their removal. The graph shows the average time scores for these sessions. Note the enormous

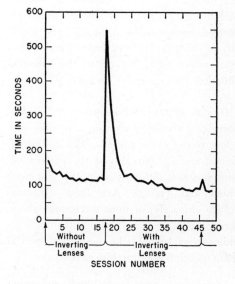

slowing down in the task performance after the lenses were first put on, the fairly rapid readjustment during the period of inversion, and the slight and very brief further disruption when the lenses were removed.

Toward the end of the experiment the subject was asked whether a scene from a tall building looked "upside down" to him. He replied:

"I wish you hadn't asked me. Things were all right until you popped the question at me. Now, when I recall how they *did* look *before* I put on these lenses, I must answer that they do look upside down *now*. But until the moment that you asked me I was absolutely unaware of it and hadn't given a thought to the question of whether things were right side up or upside down."

STRATTON, G. M. 1897. Vision without inversion of the retinal image. *Psychol. Rev., 4,* 341–60.

SNYDER, F. W., and PRONKO, N. H. 1952. *Vision with spatial inversion.* Wichita, Kansas: Univ. of Wichita Press.

Object Perception

As we have repeatedly stressed, our organized perceptions are of *objects*, not of separate and disembodied stimulus properties. And in order to perceive and identify objects, we must be able to take account of *patterns* of stimuli produced by the object. There are two major questions to be considered about this perception of objects. First, does the perception require specific learning of the relationships of the various given stimulus-patterns, or does it occur without the necessity of learning? Second, how can the properties and identity of objects remain perceptually *constant* even when many features of the stimulus situation are radically changed?

Origins of Object Perception. When we perceive an object, we not only take account of the pattern of visual stimuli or of tactual stimuli, but also of the pattern of stimuli *across* different senses, for instance, visual and tactual. Are these patterns "given" innately, or must we acquire them through experience? The English empiricist philosopher John Locke considered such a basic question posed to him as follows:

"Suppose a man born blind, and now adult, and taught by his touch to distinguish between a cube and a sphere of the same metal, and nighly of the same bigness, so as to tell, when he felt one and the other, which is the cube, which the sphere. Suppose then the cube and sphere placed on a table, and the blind man to be made to see; query, Whether by his sight, before he touched them, he could now distinguish and tell which is the globe, which the cube?"

In commenting on this question later, Bishop Berkeley pointed out that though the man might know it was a cube by its square surfaces:

". . . the ideas of sight are all new perceptions, to which there are no names annexed in his mind; he cannot therefore understand what is said to him concerning them: and to ask of the two bodies he saw placed on the table, which was the sphere, which the cube, were to him a question downright bantering and unintelligible."

It may not have occurred to these men that a concrete *experimental* answer was ever likely to be given to their hypothetical question, but that is what has indeed been partly achieved by the study of patients blinded by cataracts from birth, who later had the cataracts removed surgically and then reported on their visual perceptions on first seeing. The facts described in Box 40 illuminate many issues about the origins of space perception and also indicate that many questions are yet unresolved.

These facts provide strong evidence for both nativistic and empiristic factors in the development of object perception. Unquestionably, there are certain primitive aspects of object perception, such as figure-ground differentiation, which occur without prior experience. But unmistakably, too, the more complex aspects of object perception do require a period of learning.

Object Constancy. We stressed in Chapter 2 that our perceptual experience of our worlds is characterized by an enormous degree of constancy in the over-all characteristics of objects. Mr. Anyman is perceived as Mr. Anyman with his characteristic body proportions whether he is seen lying down, standing upright, or balancing on his head. A dictionary is seen as the same massive tome from every angle of observation. The adaptive value of this *object constancy* is obvious. By maintaining a stable and consistent perception of an object despite wide variations in the conditions under which we encounter it, we are able to cope more effectively with our environments.

Constancy of any property—whether it is size, or shape, or brightness, or weight, or whatever—depends upon unchanging *relationships* among the relevant elements in the total stimulus-pattern. Without such invariant stimulus relationships, constancy

BOX 40

Suppose a Man Born Blind . . .

Some adults have been blind from birth because of cataracts on both eyes. This congenital blindness can be ended by surgical means. When the bandages are removed and the person has vision for the first time in his life, what does he see?

Senden has compiled the published reports of the visual experiences of 66 such cataract cases. The reported facts are not fully substantiated and the tests of perception used were imperfect. Nevertheless there is fairly consistent agreement on the following facts:

1. On first vision, the person does not immediately experience the kind of orderly visual world seen by the normal person. He is at first greatly *confused* by the bewildering array of unfamiliar visual stimuli.

2. All is not sheer stimulus chaos, however, for he at once sees *unitary figures*, differentiated from their backgrounds.

3. Moreover, he is at once able to *fixate* the figures and scan them, and to *follow* moving figures with his eyes.

4. But he is unable to *identify* objects by vision alone—even objects long familiar to him through his sense of touch. He may report that a short stick and a long stick look somehow "different," but he does not know which is "long" and which "short," even though if allowed to feel them he can tell

at once. Though thoroughly acquainted with tactual differences between curved and straight, square and round, thick and thin, he cannot apply these concepts at once to visual objects. And he cannot correctly name visual objects that are highly familiar to him through touch, such as knives, keys, and faces.

5. It may require days, weeks, or months for the patient to come to identify and *name* objects correctly. For instance, a square and a triangle may be discriminated only after some weeks of practice with them, painstakingly counting the corners.

6. The difficulty of learning to discriminate in the new visual world is shown, also, by the inability to *generalize*. Even after the name of the visual object has been learned, its recognition is readily destroyed by changing it slightly or putting it into a new setting. A white square successfully learned may not be correctly recognized as a square when it is turned over to its yellow side. Yet it should be emphasized that this is not due to a difficulty in discriminating colors, *per se*. There is not a single case in which there is difficulty in learning color names.

SENDEN, M. V. 1932. *Raum und Gestaltauffassung bei operierten Blindgeborenen vor und nach Operation.* Leipzig: Barth.

fails. Constancy can thus be seen as another instance of transposition (see p. 93).

The particular stimulus relationships that are relevant differ, of course, from one property to another. The essential factors in size constancy, for instance, are retinal size and apparent distance.

Size Constancy. The visual size of an object obviously depends, in part, on the size of the retinal image it casts. Moreover, whenever we perceive an "object," we necessarily perceive it as at some certain distance, through the operation of the depth

cues discussed above. Therefore, there are two main "facts" that determine the perception of the size of an object: (1) the *actual* size of the retinal image, (2) the *apparent* distance of the object. These two "facts" are integrated to yield the resultant percept—an object perceived as of a certain size and at a certain distance. Of two objects that appear to be at the same distance from the observer, the object casting the smaller retinal image looks smaller. Of two objects casting the same-size retinal image, the object that appears closer looks smaller.

A simple demonstration of this can be done by the reader. Fixate a one-inch square of white paper on a dark background about 10 inches away from your eyes. After a brief inspection a good afterimage of the square will be formed. Then look at some light surface about the same distance away, and note that the size of the afterimage as it appears to be projected on that surface is the size of the original square. Now look at a more distant surface, such as the wall of the room. Here you will note that the afterimage appears much larger. Careful comparisons have shown that the perceived size of the afterimage is exactly determined by the distance between the eye and the surface on which the image appears to be projected. This is known technically as *Emmert's Law.* For instance, an afterimage projected on a surface ten times as far away as the original stimulus will look ten times as large as the original stimulus, even though the retinal image remains the same. (See Fig. 57.)

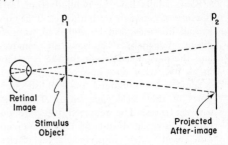

FIG. 57. Illustration of Emmert's Law. See text.

It is important to understand that perceived size is determined by the *apparent* distance of the object, and not the real physical distance. An object that is actually far away but looks as if it were close will be seen as smaller. Look at Figure 58. We

FIG. 58. Freaks? Or illusion? See Box 41.

see a room containing a shrunken woman and an oversized child. In this a circus room showing side-show freaks, or are our eyes somehow deceiving us? Box 41 gives the answer.

The above demonstrations show us how the two cues of retinal size and apparent distance jointly determine perceived size of an object. Neither cue can properly be regarded as more primary than the other. We do not *first* detect the distance of an object and *then* infer its size from the size of the retinal image; nor do we do the opposite. *The two cues work together simultaneously as a system.* The recognition of this kind of systematic relationship of

---

BOX 41

The Distorted Room

The figure shows what an observer sees when he looks with one eye through a peephole into the room. It looks to him like a normal, rectangular room, but the two people in its far corners look weirdly distorted in size.

The room has been deliberately constructed so as to mislead the perceiver. It is actually very *asymmetrical,* one corner being three times as far away as the other; all dimensions are chosen so as to be exact geometrical projections of a normal, rectangular room viewed from the observer's eye.

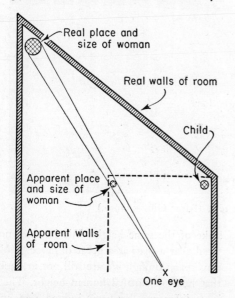

Real place and size of woman

Real walls of room

Child

Apparent place and size of woman

Apparent walls of room

x
One eye

The binocular depth cues are all eliminated by requiring the person to look through the peephole with one eye. And the cue of accommodation is ineffective at this distance. On the basis of retinal pattern alone, he cannot tell how far away the parts of the room actually are. A real rectangular room and also any number of distorted rooms could give this same retinal pattern. His most natural assumption is that the room is a normal rectangular one of the kind with which he is most familiar, and since the stimulus-pattern is consistent with this interpretation, that is how he sees it.

But the consequence of this is that objects inside the room must assume perceived sizes appropriate to the perceived size and shape of the room. Hence the child looks much taller than the woman.

Space perception involves more than a single sense modality; it involves the harmonizing of information from all the senses. To what extent is there flexibility in the manner in which the various cues are synthesized and modified in accordance with changes in the stimulus situation? Subjects were permitted to explore the distorted room with a long pointer while they continued to watch. As they did so, the room tended to lose its "illusory" symmetrical character and to assume its correct shape, with one corner much closer than the other. Here is a convincing example of how kinesthetic cues contradict and bring about a change in the visual depth organization. Yet we must remember that the stimulus situation was a highly ambiguous one, in which many alternative visual organizations were possible, and therefore it may have been relatively easy for the kinesthetic cues to overcome the visual ones.

cues in perception paves the way for our understanding of the phenomenon of *constancy.*

To a truly astonishing degree, a given object looks the same size to us even though we are near it or far away. When the object is farther away, its retinal image is smaller, so why should we not see the object as smaller? The answer has already been given in what we have said about the working together of retinal size and distance as a single perceptual system. As an object moves away its retinal size *decreases* but its apparent distance, as determined by the distance cues, *increases.* To the extent that the *relation* between these two "facts" remains the same, i.e., as retinal

ous distances. The observer looked at a distant stake and then at a set of nearby stakes of varying heights, attempting to pick out the one that was the same height as the distant one (see Fig. 59). Gibson found that his observers could succeed in this task with great accuracy even when the distant stake was a half mile away, where it was scarcely perceptible. A standard 71″ stake set at 14, 224, and 784 yards from the observer, was judged on the average to be 71.9″, 75.8″, 75.9″, respectively.

It should be noted that although the observer was able to judge the size of the very distant stake quite accurately, it did not "look" the same size to him as a nearby

FIG. 59. For explanation, see text. (After Gibson, 1950.)

size decreases there is a proportional increase in apparent distance, the perceived size remains the same.

The remarkable degree to which size constancy holds, even over very large distances, is demonstrated in an experiment by Gibson (1950). In flat, open terrain he placed vertical stakes in the ground at vari-

stake of the same height. We have all noticed that a man at a great distance "looks tiny" even though we are still not in doubt that he is of normal human height. There is a difference between judged size and phenomenal size. Close up, the two are indistinguishable. A chair five feet away actually "looks" the same size as an identical chair ten feet away, even though the first retinal image is twice the size of the second. It may take a deliberate act of analytical looking to see them as different. This is what the painter does in determining the retinal sizes of objects at different depths in the landscape by holding his pencil at arm's length and marking the various objects off on it.

The Gibson findings pertained to a situation in which the distance cues were good ones, even up to half a mile. There were obvious gradients of textures in the terrain, linear perspectives, and lights and shadow. But what if distance cues are poor? We should expect size constancy to break down, since the *apparent* distance depends upon these cues. A demonstration of this under controlled laboratory conditions is given in the study described in Box 42.

When distance cues are weak, perceived size may be mainly determined by the *meaning* of the object. For instance, in an experiment by Ittelson (1951) playing cards of normal size, half size, and double size were placed at the same distance from the observer. He looked with one eye through a peephole at the cards and reported on their perceived sizes and distances. The perceptual process "solved" the problem by maintaining the "normal" size of the cards and adjusting the perceived distances to fit. The perceiver saw all the cards as of "normal" size, but at various distances; the half-size card was seen twice as far away as the standard card, and the double-size card was seen as half as far away. In other words, in this situation in which distance cues were extremely impoverished, prior experience with normal sizes of playing cards provided the essential cue to perceived size.

The influence of prior experience with the object on its perceived size is strictly limited by the strength of structure of the stimulus-pattern (see p. 100). We have already noted that in the distorted room experiment (Box 41) human bodies take on very eccentric sizes. An even more startling perception utterly incongruous with knowledge and past experience is readily produced when the observer watches a person walk across the distorted room from one corner to the other. He is perceived as *swelling threefold in size!* And by similar means the observer can easily be made to see water "flowing uphill." However there is some evidence that if the observer assumes a particular set which emphasizes an accurate perception of the real size of the object, the effect of the distorted room may be diminished. One experimenter reports that when the person walking across the room was the observer's wife, the illusion was markedly decreased, and size constancy maintained!

SHAPE CONSTANCY. We have already pointed to the fact that a plate looks "round" to us even when it is tilted and the image it casts on our retina is therefore elliptical. The essential factors here are the shape of the retinal image and the apparent tilt of the object. The apparent tilt of the object is provided by various cues from the object and its surroundings. When we look at a tilted object the texture of its surface appears denser toward the farther end of the object; and, as we have seen (Box 36), such texture gradients can provide information about tilt, independent of the shape of the retinal image. Impoverished cues of tilt will, of course, tend to reduce shape constancy.

LOUDNESS CONSTANCY. Constancies are not restricted to the visual sphere, but are found in all types of properties of objects. For example, we exhibit a considerable degree of loudness constancy. This means that our perception of the actual loudness of the *sound source* is fairly consistent even though we may be close to the object or far away from it. The essential factors

BOX 42

How to Destroy Size Constancy

In an experiment by Holway and Boring at Harvard University the observer was stationed at the intersection of two long darkened corridors. An adjustable lighted disc was placed 10 feet distant in one corridor. Standard discs were placed at several distances varying from 10 to 120 feet in the other corridor. The standard discs were of such size as to cast the same size retinal image no matter what their distance from the observer's eye. The task was to set the adjustable disc to look the same size as the standard disc (see diagram).

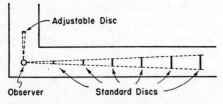

Four experimental conditions were compared. The amount of constancy exhibited in each condition is shown in the graph. The top dotted line is drawn to show what

the judgments would ideally be for *perfect* constancy; that is, the adjusted size of the comparison disc would be exactly the same as that of the standard disc regardless of distance. The horizontal dotted line at the bottom indicates *zero* constancy; that is, the adjusted size of the comparison disc would always be set to the size of the standard disc at 10 feet, regardless of where the standard disc actually was placed.

First, the person looked in the normal way with *both eyes*. As shown in the graph, the achievement of size constancy was excellent, being very close to the perfect level of constancy represented by the top dotted line (actually exceeding it slightly).

Second, the person was restricted to *monocular* vision. Even with the binocular depth cues thus eliminated, constancy was still almost as great as before.

Third, the person looked through a small *peephole;* this eliminated still more depth cues having to do with head movement, etc. Now there was a sharp drop in constancy.

Fourth, in addition to the monocular viewing through the peephole, drapes were placed on the walls to *eliminate reflections* from the stimuli. As a consequence, constancy became even poorer.

A final step, taken in a later study by Lichten and Lurie, was to use all the above restrictions of cues plus *screens* that cut out all the visual field of the corridors except the discs themselves. Under these most extreme conditions of elimination of depth stimuli, size constancy completely disappeared, the size judgments approximating the zero level of constancy represented by the bottom dotted line.

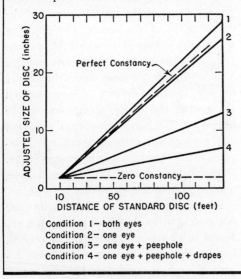

Condition 1 — both eyes
Condition 2 — one eye
Condition 3 — one eye + peephole
Condition 4 — one eye + peephole + drapes

HOLWAY, A. H., and BORING, E. G. 1941. Determinants of apparent visual size with distance variant. *Amer. J. Psychol., 54,* 21–37.

LICHTEN, W., and LURIE, S. 1950. A new technique for the study of perceived size. *Amer. J. Psychol., 63,* 281–2.

are two: (1) the amplitude of the sound waves striking the ear, (2) the apparent distance of the sound source. The apparent

distance of the sound source depends upon the various factors discussed on page 130. If our perception of the distance is poor, we may not be able to judge the loudness of the sound source with any accuracy.

BRIGHTNESS CONSTANCY. In each of the previous examples of constancy a factor of apparent distance from the object was involved. This is not always one of the essential factors in the invariant stimulus relationship in constancies. For example, when we turn to brightness constancy, the factors have to do with (1) the intensity of the light rays emitted from the object

by varying the proportions of white and black sectors. He keeps adjusting the wheel until the observer reports that it matches the brightness of the one in the light. Under these conditions the match proves to be very close; the amounts of white in the two color wheels are almost identical. Yet the actual stimulus fact is that the intensity of light reaching the observer's eye from the shadowed wheel is radically less than that from the other wheel. The explana-

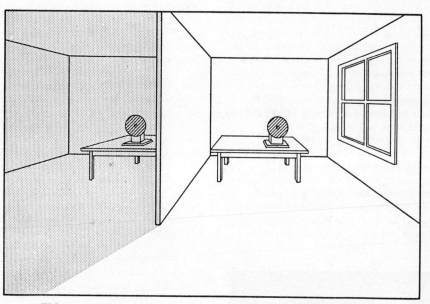

FIG. 60. An experimental setup for the study of brightness constancy.

and (2) the intensity of the illumination of the object and its surroundings.

We have already seen that snow in deep shade looks white and coal in sunlight black, even though the intensity of light striking the eye from the former is less than the latter. Careful experimental analyses of the means by which this can occur have been carried out in the laboratory. A typical set-up is shown in Figure 60. The observer looks at two gray color wheels, one of which is in full sunlight and the other in shadow. The brightness of the wheel in shadow can be altered by the experimenter

tion is that the perceived brightness depends not upon the light coming from the object only, but upon the *relationship* of this light to the light coming from the surroundings of the object, that is, the wall against which the color wheel is viewed. While it is true that on the lighted side the illumination of both wheel and background are higher than on the shadowed side, the *ratio* of illumination of the wheel to that of the background is the same on both sides. It is this invariant proportional relationship between the light from the object and its background that is the major

BOX 43

Brightness Ratios and Constancy

In order to investigate brightness constancy as a function of the relative illumination of an area and its surroundings, Wallach at Swarthmore College performed the following experiment. In a laboratory darkroom he set up four projectors side by side, each casting a beam of light of the same intensity on a white wall. In front of three of the projectors he placed *episcotisters*, which are rapidly spinning discs with slots of different sizes cut in them so that specified fractions of the total light from the projectors can pass through. The size of the episcotister opening in angular degrees is thus a measure of the amount of illumination of the image projected on the wall. For example, a full opening of 360 degrees would mean full light, an opening of 180 degrees would mean half light, and so on.

One projector was set up so as to cast a *ring* of light of 360 degrees intensity. A second projector cast a *spot* of light just large enough to fill the area inside the ring. The illumination of this spot was 180 degrees, or exactly half that of its surrounding ring. The ring and spot arrangement is schematized on the left-hand side of the figure.

On the same wall to the right, the other two projectors were directed so that they cast a similar ring-spot pair. But the intensity of illumination in this ring was only 90 degrees. In front of the fourth projector, which cast the spot, was placed an *adjustable* episcotister. It could be continuously manipulated by the subject so as to change the size of the episcotister opening and hence to vary the amount of light of the enclosed spot (indicated by "?" in the figure).

The experiment was carried out in an otherwise completely dark room so that the subject had no light stimuli except those already described. He was instructed to view the two enclosed spots and to adjust the episcotister controlling the illumination of the one on the right until it looked to him exactly equal in brightness to the spot on the left. Several trials were taken for each subject in order to obtain a reliable estimate of the setting.

It was Wallach's hypothesis that under these special circumstances the apparent brightness of an area is entirely determined by the *ratio* of the illumination of the area and the illumination of its immediate surroundings. In other words he assumed that the *absolute* level of illumination of the area had no importance and that only the *relative* illumination level counted. Since the spot on the left had exactly half the illumination of its surrounding ring (180 degrees as opposed to 360 degrees), the prediction was that the spot on the right when adjusted to look equal to that on the left would also have an illumination just half that of *its* surrounding ring. Since the surrounding ring on the right was 90 degrees, it was predicted that when the spot had an illumination of 45 degrees it would appear to be as bright as the spot on the left, i.e., 45:90::180:360.

The results confirmed his hypothesis. The subjects' average setting of the illumination of the right-hand spot was 42 degrees, a very close approximation to the expected value of 45 degrees. Thus, though the two spots were viewed simultaneously and the one on the left was physically illuminated to a degree *four times* that on the right, *they were perceived as of equivalent brightness*.

Under these simplified stimulus conditions, therefore, brightness constancy seems to be a pure matter of *ratios* of brightnesses of the stimuli and their surroundings.

WALLACH, H. 1948. Brightness constancy and the nature of achromatic colors. *J. exp. Psychol., 38,* 310–24.

determinant of brightness constancy. A striking experimental demonstration of this is given in Box 43.

It is sometimes assumed that brightness constancy means that the observer takes "rational" account of the illumination conditions and perceives objects accordingly. This is not the case. It makes little difference whether the person is aware or unaware of the *actual* illumination conditions.

To dramatize how good brightness constancy is under most normal conditions of viewing, we might show how downright poor it is when we interfere with this essential relationship of brightnesses in the stimulus-pattern. Suspend a square of black velvet somewhat in front of a moderately lighted wall. It looks black. Now throw a bright illumination on the velvet in such a way that none of the added illumination falls on the background wall. The velvet now at once and irresistibly looks *white*.

Constancy as Achievement. Though mere knowledge of the actual situation may not be critical in the determination of constancy, this is not to minimize the important role that the learning and intention on the part of the perceiver do play. We have already seen that set can influence the degree of constancy. The observer can deliberately try to minimize constancy by paying attention to the retinal size cue and neglecting the distance cue, or by concentrating on the sheer loudness of sound at his ears without reference to the apparent distance of its source, or by judging the brightness of the light rays from the surface of the object independent of the surroundings.

Seeing the size of something without being influenced by how far away it is located is a neat and exceedingly difficult trick. Often the observer makes various "implicit" assumptions that affect his perception despite his intention. A striking example is the *size-weight illusion* (see Box 44).

The conclusion is that our perception tends under natural circumstances to be "object-directed" rather than "stimulus-directed." That is, we customarily seek to achieve an accurate perception not of the isolated stimulus attribute, but rather of the whole object. The functional value of this is obvious, inasmuch as it is with whole objects in our environment that we must cope. In order to see objects, we must necessarily take account of *patterns* of stimuli, not isolated stimulus attributes, and in so doing we are enabled to achieve perceptual *constancy* of the objects.

By Way of Summary. The question of how we come to be able to perceive objects in the first place is a complicated one. The experimental evidence gives some support both to the view that simple object perception is innately given and to the contrary view that it comes about only through specific learning.

Our perception of objects is characterized by a great deal of *constancy*, that is, the object is perceived as of the same constant size, shape, color, even though it is viewed from different distances, from different angles, in different illuminations. Object constancy seems to depend upon the maintenance of certain *invariant relationships* among parts of the stimulus-pattern. In size constancy there is the working together of the cues of size of retinal image and of apparent distance of the object. On the other hand, size constancy of objects can be radically distorted by appropriate changes in the critical relationships in the stimulus-pattern. In shape constancy the relevant invariant relationships are between shape of the retinal image and the apparent angle of viewing the object. In loudness constancy they are the amplitude of the sound waves striking the ear and the ap-

BOX 44

Pound of Feathers, Pound of Lead

A most surprising illusion can be demonstrated with two rectangular wooden blocks. One is 1½″ x 1½″ x 2½″ and the other 3″ x 3″ x 5″, or exactly eight times the volume of the first. Concealed inside each block are pieces of lead so adjusted that the total weight of each block is exactly 300 grams. Each block can be hefted by placing the forefinger inside the metal ring on its top.

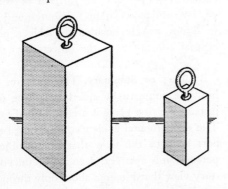

The subject is informed that the larger block weighs 300 grams. He is asked to heft the larger block and then the smaller block and to judge the latter's weight in grams. The striking fact is that virtually all persons perceive the smaller block to be *substantially heavier* than the larger block even though the two are exactly equal in weight. For instance, in a study of 100 military officers (Crutchfield, Woodworth, and Albrecht) the average judgment of weight of the smaller was 750 grams, about 2½ times the correct weight. For some of the officers the overestimate was as much as seven times!

This phenomenon is known as the *size-weight illusion.* A common explanation of the illusion is that the person "expects" the smaller block to be *lighter* than the larger (because of the obvious size difference), and the *contrast* of this prior expectation with the actual weight of the smaller when hefted makes it seem *heavier.* But this ex-planation is entirely inconsistent with the fact that the illusion persists almost as strongly after the blocks have been repeatedly hefted, and even after the person weighs them on a scales. Mere "knowledge" of the objective facts is insufficient to destroy the illusion. Further results show that even when the subject is instructed to "pay no attention" to the relative sizes of the blocks and to concentrate, in making his judgment, only on the feeling of their weights, the illusion is as great as before. And if a subject first looks at the blocks and then closes his eyes when hefting them, the illusion is equally great.

Brunswik has suggested that what may be happening is that the person, although attempting to judge *weight*, is implicitly taking *density* (weight per cubic inch) into account. Since the small block is one-eighth the size of the large block but weighs exactly the same, the *density* of the small block is eight times that of the larger. The person in judging the weight of the small block may partly be influenced by his perception of its density. In this way the smaller and denser block is judged heavier. Brunswik has supported this explanation by finding that subjects who are carefully instructed to pay attention to the attribute of "weight" and to avoid the attribute of "density" exhibit less than normal amounts of the size-weight illusion.

The age-old conundrum "which is heavier, a pound of feathers or a pound of lead?" is the mental counterpart of the perceptual size-weight illusion. The unwary person answers that a pound of lead is obviously heavier, his judgment being implicitly affected by the relative densities of the objects.

CRUTCHFIELD, R. S., WOODWORTH, D. G., and ALBRECHT, R. E. 1955. *Perceptual performance and the effective person.* San Antonio: Air Force Personnel and Training Research Center.

BRUNSWIK, E. 1956. *Perception and the representative design of psychological experiments.* Berkeley: Univ. of California Press.

parent distance of the sound source. In brightness constancy the relevant factors have to do mainly with an invariant ratio of the brightness of the object to its immediate surroundings. Factors of set also play a significant role in governing constancy. Though the person tends naturally,

in his attempt to achieve a workable perception of a stable environment, to be "object directed," and hence likely to perceive with high constancy, he can also be "stimulus directed," in which case constancy is greatly weakened. Thus, constancy depends partly upon the perceiver's goal.

Glossary

accommodation. The readjustment in the focusing power of the eye so as to maintain a sharp image on the retina even when the distance between the eye and the object is constantly changing.

aftereffect movement. An illusion of perceived movement in which an object actually at rest appears to move in a direction opposite to the direction of a prolonged real movement of the stimulus field. For example, when the train comes to a halt, the landscape seems to move forward.

apparent movement (phi phenomenon). The illusory movement from one stimulus location to another as a function of the temporal sequence of the stimuli. An example is the motion pictures. Also known as stroboscopic movement.

autokinetic movement. An illusion of movement of a stationary dot of light in an otherwise dark room. The effect is enhanced by the absence of visual framework.

binaural cues. The stimulus cues occurring at the two ears which make sound localization possible. The identical sound waves starting at one source have different characteristics when they reach the two ears. The principal binaural cues have to do with the time differences and intensity differences of the sound waves at the two ears.

binocular depth cues. The stimulus factors that aid in the perception of depth, dependent upon the functioning of both eyes. The two principal binocular cues are retinal disparity and convergence.

brightness constancy. The tendency to perceive an object as of the same brightness despite wide variations in the intensity of illumination. Brightness constancy seems to depend mainly upon an invariant relation between the intensity of light emitted from the object and the intensity of light emitted from its surroundings.

convergence. The rotation of the eyes toward one another in looking at an object in depth. The closer the object, the greater the angle of convergence. Convergence is a cue for depth perception which becomes ineffective at distances greater than 50–60 feet, at which the lines of sight become almost parallel.

Emmert's Law. The exact proportionality of the perceived size of an afterimage to the distance between the eye and the surface on which the image appears to be projected. The same afterimage projected on a wall 10 times as far away as the original stimulus is seen 10 times as large.

induced movement. The appearance of movement in an object actually at rest produced by the movement of other objects in its surroundings. For instance, the moving clouds induce perceived movement in the moon.

interposition. A monocular depth cue. Refers to the situation in which one object is seen as partly covering a second object. In this case the second object is seen as the farther away.

linear perspective. A monocular depth cue. Refers to the convergence of lines in the visual field.

loudness constancy. The perception of the

actual loudness of a sound source in a fairly constant way, even though the observer may be close to the object or far away from it. It depends on the relationship between amplitude of the sound waves striking the ear and the apparent distance of the sound source.

monocular depth cues. The stimulus characteristics that lead to an impression of visual depth with one eye. Monocular cues from the visual pattern include interposition, relative size, relative height, relative clearness, linear perspective, and light and shadow. Other monocular cues are accommodation and relative movement.

object constancy. The tendency for objects to be perceived in an established and a consistent way despite wide variations in the conditions under which they are viewed.

perceived causality. Experiencing one moving physical object as "causing" the movement of another. For example, a rolling ball that strikes another may be perceived to "cause" the subsequent movement of the second ball. This phenomenal causality is a function of the particular configuration of stimulus events. *Perceived* causality is to be differentiated from genuine *physical* causality.

pseudophone. An apparatus that reverses the time of arrival of sounds at the two ears. Under these artificial conditions a sound actually on the left is heard as coming from the right.

relative movement (movement parallax). The relative visual displacement of nearer objects to the right and farther objects to the left as the head moves to the left.

retinal disparity. The difference in retinal images on the two eyes when looking at an object in depth, produced by the slightly different angle at which each eye looks at the object.

shape constancy. The tendency for the shape of an object to be perceived correctly even though it is tilted in such a way that the retinal image it casts on the eye is of a different shape from the object itself. It depends upon the relation of the shape of the retinal image and the apparent plane of the object.

size constancy. The tendency for a given object to be perceived as of the same size despite wide variations in distance of the object from the observer. It depends upon the relation between the retinal size and the apparent distance of the object.

size-weight illusion. Of two similar objects objectively equal in weight, the smaller is perceived as heavier. The illusion is not appreciably reduced by knowledge of the actual weights.

stereoscope. A device making possible the impression of depth in viewing a flat picture. It is accomplished by presenting separate and slightly different pictures to each eye, corresponding to the retinal images that would have occurred in each eye had the actual three-dimensional scene been viewed.

stimulus gradient. A variation in stimulus intensity or quality in the perceptual field. Stimulus gradients serve as important cues to perception of depth.

time perspective. The general temporal framework including past, present, and future in which the person perceives events. Time perspectives vary enormously in different individuals, at different ages, and in different situations.

Suggestions for Further Reading

CARR, H. A. 1935. *An introduction to space perception.* New York: Longmans.

   A comprehensive review of the earlier research and theorizing on the perception of space.

GIBSON, J. J. 1950. *The perception of the visual world.* Boston: Houghton Mifflin.

   A highly stimulating and original treatment of many problems of visual perception, especially as related to problems of depth perception. Presents many experimental demonstrations.

LAWRENCE, M. 1949. *Studies in human behavior*. Princeton, N.J.: Princeton Univ. Press.

A manual of unusually interesting laboratory demonstrations on the perception of depth and related aspects.

MICHOTTE, A. 1954. *La perception de la causalité* (2nd ed.). Louvain: Publication Universitaires de Louvain.

A thought-provoking presentation of numerous experiments on the perception of physical causality. Unfortunately not available in English translation.

WOODWORTH, R. S., and SCHLOSBERG, H. 1954. *Experimental psychology* (rev. ed.). New York: Holt.

A standard and very useful textbook of experimental psychology, including considerable data on the perception of movement, space, and objects.

CHAPTER VII

Physiological Basis of Perception

IN CHAPTERS 2 and 3, as we described the basic attributes of our perceived world, it became increasingly clear that the familiar hides many puzzles. The major puzzle seemed to be that sometimes the same stimulus results in different perceptions; and sometimes different stimuli result in the same perceptions. In Chapters 4, 5, and 6 we examined the specific relationships between physical stimulus and perception. We found three recurrent themes in these relationships: complexity, interaction, and integration.

In order to shed further light on the complex relations between stimulus-pattern and perception, we must consider the *physiological processes* that intervene between stimulus and perception. This is the objective of the present chapter.

There is one consideration that the reader should keep in mind as he studies the material which we discuss here. The facts about the physiological processes underlying perception are not fully known, and much of what we think we know is probably wrong. Again and again, in the present chapter, we will have to say "We do not know . . . ," "We can only guess . . . ," "We assume. . . ." Herein lies the fascination of physiological psychology, for we are not repeating an oft- and well-told tale of someone else's past adventures; we are participating in an attempt to explore the unknown.

Note: Before continuing with this chapter, the reader is urged to examine the material in Figures 61, 62, and 63 on the following pages. From time to time we will have occasion to refer to these figures in more detail. At this stage it is recommended that the reader merely familiarize himself with the *general* "geography" of the brain as presented in these figures.

Visual Perception

We have already seen in Chapter 4 how complex are the relationships between the light stimulus and the visual experience. It should not come as a surprise to us, therefore, to find that the sequence of physio-

156

logical events that occur between the moment a light stimulus impinges on the retina and the moment we react with a visual experience is exceedingly complicated.

To describe the physiological mechanisms involved in visual perception, we must describe how the light rays from the outside stimulus-object enter through the cornea of the eye and are focused so as to cast an image on the retina; how these focused light rays then trigger off a neurological reaction in the retina; how this process is propagated to the individual's brain; and how his brain reacts to these incoming signals. The simplest perception involves all of these processes.

For purposes of simplification we can divide these events into four stages involving four major physiological mechanisms: (1) the *optical* mechanism, (2) the *photosensitive* mechanism, (3) the *conduction* mechanism, and (4) the *central* mechanism. Each of these is functionally related to the other three.

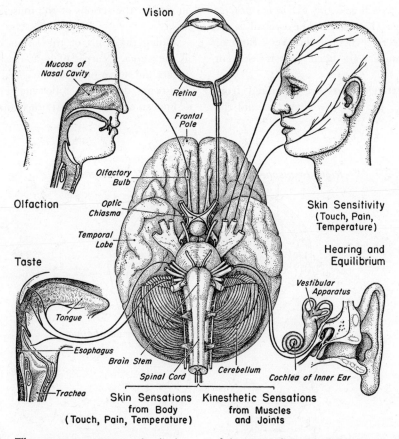

Vision

Mucosa of
Nasal Cavity

Retina

Frontal
Pole

Olfactory
Bulb

Olfaction

Optic
Chiasma

Skin Sensitivity
(Touch, Pain,
Temperature)

Temporal
Lobe

**Hearing and
Equilibrium**

Taste

Vestibular
Apparatus

Tongue

Esophagus

Brain Stem

Spinal Cord   Cerebellum   Cochlea of Inner Ear

Trachea

**Skin Sensations
from Body**
(Touch, Pain, Temperature)

**Kinesthetic Sensations
from Muscles
and Joints**

FIG. 61. The sensory routes to the brain. Here we see the brain from beneath so as to get a good view of the routes over which neural messages travel from our sense receptors into the brain. While our sensory system and brain are bilaterally symmetrical (we have two eyes, two sensory areas for smell, two ears), this diagram shows only one route for each of the types of sensory organ.

Note that the nerves that carry neural messages from the eyes, nose, tongue, ears, face, and vestibular apparatus go directly to the brain, i.e., not via the spinal cord. The nerves that carry impulses from the skin, muscles, and joints of the rest of the body enter the brain via connections in the spinal cord.

The Optical Mechanism. As we have already pointed out, virtually all living things have special mechanisms for the reception of light. In this chapter we shall restrict ourselves to the type of eye found among the higher vertebrates including man.

STRUCTURE. A semidiagrammatic drawing of the human eye is shown in Figure 64. The eyeball is enveloped by a tough skin called the *sclera*. The sclera is white and opaque (the "white of the eye"), except in one area, the *cornea*, where it is clear and transparent. Attached to the outside of each eyeball are the *extrinsic muscles* of the eye (Fig. 64*d*). The eyeball is divided into two unequal chambers. Both of these chambers are filled with transparent fluids.

The two chambers are separated from each other by the *crystalline lens* and the *ciliary muscles*. The former is a transparent structure shaped somewhat like a convex lens. It is attached to the ciliary muscles in such a manner that changes in the curvature of the lens (and, therefore, in focusing power) are produced when the ciliary muscles are contracted or relaxed.

Within the smaller cavity, and lying on the lens, is found the *iris*, a delicate fibrous structure (colored blue or brown or gray, etc., in different people) that has a circular opening in its center. This opening (called the *pupil*) can be increased or decreased in size by the actions of the muscles of the iris.

Lining the walls of the larger chamber is the *retina*, a carpet of light-sensitive elements and nerve fibers that we shall discuss in greater detail in a following section.

FOCUSING AND ACCOMMODATION. When

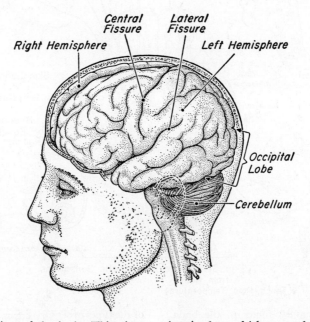

FIG. 62. Side view of the brain. This view shows the general geography of the surface of the brain, some of its major landmarks, and the relation of these to the various parts of the face and head. Only the left half of the brain (labeled "left hemisphere") is fully shown. The right hemisphere is barely indicated, but can be imagined as a fairly exact duplicate of the left hemisphere. The cerebellum also has two hemispheres.

Note the heavily convoluted nature of the brain's surface and the deep fissures that demarcate the cortex of the brain into a number of major areas.

light from an outside object enters the cornea, the rays are refracted (bent) toward each other. As the rays continue through the crystalline lens, the rays are bent further, so that in a perfectly formed eye, the combined action of the cornea and lens will bring a bundle of rays from an outside point to a focus on the retina. The fact that the focusing power of the lens can constantly be readjusted by changing its curvature makes possible the maintenance of a sharp image on the retina, even under conditions of changing distance between the object and the retina. (Compare Figs. 64*b*

and *c*.) This readjustment in focusing power of the eye is called *accommodation*. (See pages 135–6 for a discussion of the role of accommodation in the perception of distance.)

Human eyes are not always found perfectly formed. The focusing mechanisms can go wrong in various ways, as in nearsightedness and farsightedness (in which the lens cannot adjust properly as it does in Figs. 64*b* and *c*) and in astigmatism (in which the lens or cornea is not uniformly shaped). When this happens, the perceived world changes radically. There is one in-

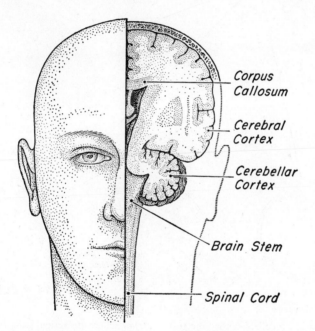

Corpus
Callosum

Cerebral
Cortex

Cerebellar
Cortex

Brain Stem

Spinal Cord

FIG. 63. Front view of sectioned brain. This view of the brain is approximately what we would see if we sectioned the head about half way back from the face. Note specially the part of the brain labeled *cerebral cortex*. This is the outer "rind," "bark," or covering of the brain. It consists almost entirely of brain cells with their interconnecting fibers. The brain cells give the cortex its characteristic gray color (the "gray matter"). The *subcortical* parts of the brain (the parts underneath the cortex) have a whitish appearance. Note again that the cortex does not form a tightly stretched covering, but is highly convoluted. The con-

voluted form of the cortex permits a very large surface or cortical area within the skull cavity.

The *corpus callosum* is a great band of fibers that go from one hemisphere of the brain to the other. The dark area underneath the corpus callosum is a *ventrical*—a cavity continuous with the central canal in the spinal cord, and normally filled with spinal fluid.

Note that the cerebellum also has a cortex or "cerebellar cortex." The *brain stem* is a continuation of the spinal cord and contains within it various structures that play crucial roles in the control of behavior.

teresting case in which a defect in the focusing mechanism may actually "improve" perception. Not all wave lengths of light can pass through the cornea and the lens. Some of the ultraviolet waves, near the normally visible spectrum, are *absorbed* by the lens and never reach the retina. For this reason objects that give off only ultraviolet radiations are invisible to normal eyes. People who have had the lenses removed because of cataracts may occasionally see such objects because the ultraviolet radiations *do* get through to their retinas.

Convergence. The extrinsic muscles of the eye play a crucial role in our perception of three-dimensional space. As we have seen in Chapter 6 (p. 134), a person, even with one eye, may be able to perceive relative distances of different objects in his

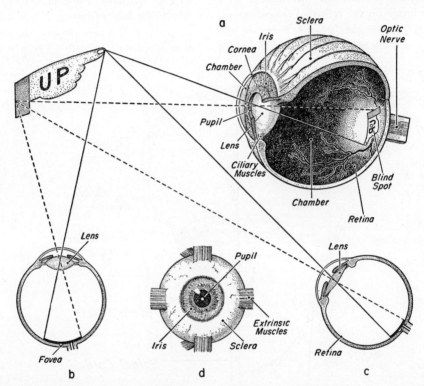

FIG. 64. The optical mechanism. See the text for a detailed explanation and description of the various parts of the eyeball. Note especially the following:

1. The object in the visual field when projected on the retina is reversed both horizontally and vertically: the *left* part of the object (the cuff of the sleeve) is projected on the *right* half of the retina, the *right* part of the object (the index finger) is projected on the *left* half of the retina; and the object as a whole is projected upside down.

2. The diagram is drawn so that the eye is focused directly on the "P" of the word "UP." Therefore part of the "U" falls on the *blind*

spot where no retinal cells are present. (See p. 163.)

3. The farther away the eye is from an object, the flatter is the lens. Compare the lens of the eye in the lower right-hand corner with that in the lower left-hand corner. (See p. 159.)

4. The farther away the eye is from the object, the smaller is the retinal image cast by the object. Compare the retinal image on the eye in the lower right-hand corner with that in the lower left-hand corner.

5. The *fovea* is a thinned-out section of the retina, and when the eye is looking directly at an object, the fovea will be in the center of the image cast.

physical world. When he uses two eyes, his perception of space and distance becomes much more accurate. Each eye views an object from a slightly different direction and sees aspects of a solid object that the other eye cannot see. But because of this, the images focused on the retinas of the two eyes are not identical (see Fig.

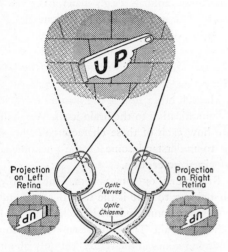

FIG. 65. The *visual field* (the area seen) of one eye does not coincide with the visual field of the other eye. The amount of overlap is shown by the heavy shading on the brick wall. This means that each eye sees a slightly different picture when both eyes converge on the same stimulus-object. This is illustrated by showing the difference between the projection of the brick wall on the two retinas. Note the differences between the two retinal images carefully. The hand is on the extreme right side of the image in the right eye and on the extreme left side of the image in the left eye. The right eye sees more of the brick wall to the right of the index finger, while the left eye sees more of the brick wall to the left of the cuff. The left eye can see the back of the raised cuff, which is hidden from view of the right eye. Both eyes together can see more of the object than either eye alone. This permits perception of depth, or solidarity of the object. The light rays from the left side of the brick wall (indicated by dotted lines) fall on the *right sides of both eyes*, while the light rays from the right side of the brick wall (indicated by solid lines) fall on the *left sides of both eyes* —the corresponding parts of the brick wall fall on corresponding sides of each of the two retinas.

65). These different images (retinal disparity) evoke two different patterns of neural responses in the retinas and therefore in the brain. Somehow these two sets of patterns are combined in the brain (we do not really know how) so as to yield a single three-dimensional perception of the object.

In order to achieve this three-dimensional perception, the images must fall on "corresponding parts" of the two retinas. The right-hand sides of both eyes, for example, are corresponding parts. If the images do not fall on corresponding parts then double vision may result. When we look straight ahead at an object, light from the right side of the object will fall on the left half of each retina, and light from the left side of the object will fall on the right half of each retina. (See Fig. 65.) But this will happen only if the two eyes are properly directed at the object, i.e., if they *converge* on the object. This convergence of the eyes is carried out by action of the extrinsic eye muscles that control the rotation of the eyes in their orbits. Occasionally these muscles are paralyzed by disease or injury. In that event double vision results. You can demonstrate this on yourself by a very simple experiment. Gaze steadily at an object some distance away. You see one image. Now press lightly on the side of one eye. Eventually the single image you see will break up into two images. What you have done is to shift the eye so that the images from the object fall on noncorresponding parts of the retinas. The proper functioning of the extrinsic muscles, then, is vitally important for three-dimensional vision.

The degree to which the two eyes must converge in order to secure a single perception will vary with the distance of the object from the perceiver. We know that in accommodation the focusing power of the lens must also vary with the distance of the object from the perceiver if we are to get a sharp image on the retina. Normally there is some kind of "coupling" between the convergence and accommodation mechanisms so that as the curvature of the lens is changed, the eyes converge appropriately. This "coupling" is made possible by the interchange in the brain of neural signals between the ciliary muscles controlling the lens and the extrinsic muscles of the eyes.

It should be clear that the proper association between accommodation and convergence (and, therefore, the perception of depth) is upset by incorrect muscular balance between the two eyes, by the presence of refractive errors induced by the cornea or lens, or by a nervous system, including the brain, that is not functioning properly because of injury, disease, or drugs (for example, alcohol). The *integrative* action of man's nervous system is of primary importance for visual perception even at the level of the optical mechanism. We shall find again and again, as we follow this story, that we do not "see" with our eyes alone—but with our brain as well.

PUPILLARY BEHAVIOR. The response of the eye to a light stimulus depends, among other things, upon the amount of light that reaches the retina. This, in turn, is controlled to a considerable degree by the size of the pupillary opening. Soon after the eye is exposed to light (about ¼ of a second later), the size of the pupil begins to decrease. The speed with which it decreases and the final size it attains depend upon the intensity of the light, the duration of the light, the part of the retina stimulated, etc. In general, the more intense the light, the smaller the pupil becomes. As the iris opens or closes (i.e., the pupil dilates or contracts), the amount of light reaching the retina is increased or decreased. The size of the pupil serves as a protective buffer to sudden changes in intensity.

The Photosensitive Mechanism. The *retina* is a delicate, almost perfectly transparent membrane composed of photosensitive nerve cells and their connecting cells. Some animals (e.g., the horned lizard) possess only one kind of photosensitive cell called *rods;* some animals (e.g., turtles) have only another kind called *cones;* and still other animals (e.g., man) have both kinds. The names "rods" and "cones" suggest the different shapes of the cells, but these cells also differ in their functions, in the way they are distributed over the entire retina, in the way they are connected with each other, and in the manner of their communication to the brain itself. We shall see how each of these characteristics helps us to understand some of the phenomena of visual perception.

STRUCTURE OF THE RETINA. One of the first things to note is the way the rods and cones are connected with each other and with the brain. There are about 125 million rods and cones in the retina, but only about one million optic nerve fibers that leave the retina. This means that many rods and cones must share common nerve fibers to the brain. Examples of the three major types of connections between the retinal cells and the brain are shown in Figure 66. The most direct transmission is found among the cones and never among the rods. Where it exists, the cone is connected with a "midget bipolar cell" that is in turn connected with a ganglion cell that transmits the neural impulse directly along the optic nerve into the brain. These cones are thus said to have a "private line" to the brain. (Fig. 66a). That this "private line" is open to interference will be shown later. Next, we have transmission systems in which several cones feed into a common bipolar cell (called "mop" or "brush" bipolars). These bipolars, in turn, feed into a ganglion cell and then into the brain. Similar systems are also found for the rods. These systems might be thought of as "family party lines" —several neighboring cones (or rods) share a line to the brain (Fig. 66*b*). Finally, we have mixed rod-cone systems, in which a number of rods *and* cones share a common bipolar cell. This we might call a "public party line" to the brain (Fig. 66*c*).

In addition to the connections between the photosensitive cells and the brain, we have various other connecting cells in the retina. These permit interactions among

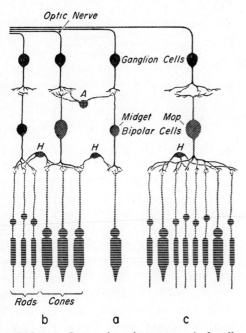

FIG. 66. Connections between retinal cells and brain. Diagrammatic representation of the three major types of connections between the rods and cones of the retina and the brain. In *a* is shown the transmission system typical of the cones in the *fovea*. Here each cone has its own midget bipolar cell which then connects with the optic nerve which, in turn, leads directly to the brain. What the text calls the "family party line" type of connection is shown in *b*. Here a group of rods *or* cones share one bipolar cell. The mixed transmission system, typical of the periphery of the retina, is illustrated in *c*. A mixed group of rods *and* cones may share one bipolar cell.

The little cells labeled "H" and "A" connect one part of the retina with another, giving us the anatomical basis for interaction on the retinal level.

neighboring cones, neighboring rods, and between rods and cones. *The retina, in other words, is not like a "switchboard" of isolated photosensitive elements. It is constructed so as to be capable of a large degree of integration.*

DISTRIBUTION OF RODS AND CONES. The rods and cones are not distributed in a uniform way over the entire retina. Figure 67 indicates the manner of their distribution in the human retina. The *fovea*, which is taken as the center of the retina, consists of very thin and very closely packed cones. Each cone in the fovea has its own "private line" to the brain.

As we move outward from the fovea, we find a rapid decrease in the number of cones and a correspondingly rapid increase in the number of rods. The absolute number of rods comes to a peak, as can be seen from the figure, just to the side of the fovea, and then drops. At the periphery there are very few cones present. As we move toward the periphery another important change occurs. Each ganglion cell serves more and more photosensitive cells. In other words, there are more and more "party lines."

All the fibers of the ganglion cells meet in one bundle just to one side of the fovea. This bundle, the *optic nerve*, leaves the retina through an opening in the eyeball (see Fig. 64). Since there are no rods or cones at this point, light waves falling here cannot result in any neural impulses and, therefore, in any visual perception. This is the simple explanation of the "mysterious" *blind spot* that some of you discovered for the first time on page 61.

PHOTOCHEMISTRY OF THE RETINA. It is assumed that rods and cones contain chemicals that are very sensitive to light. One of these, in the rods, has already been identified, and is known by the name "visual purple." When light falls on these chemicals, they begin to decompose, and in so

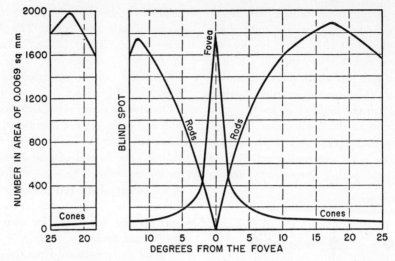

FIG. 67. This diagram shows the number of rods and cones at various distances from the fovea. Note that the number of cones drops rapidly with increasing distance from the fovea and the number of rods increases, reaching peaks at about 20° from the fovea. (Adapted from Bartley, 1951, based on data from Østerberg, 1935.)

doing they initiate activity in the rods and cones. As soon as the light-sensitive substances start to decompose, fresh light-sensitive material begins to be produced, with the result that the sensitivity of the rods or cones is restored. However, continued stimulation of a specific group of retinal cells may deplete them of the light-sensitive chemical (the decomposition running ahead of the manufacture of fresh material), making these cells temporarily less reactive to light.

The rods and cones do not react equally to light waves. Among the ways they differ are the following three: (1) cones are more sensitive to the longer wave lengths, rods to the shorter; (2) light waves have to be more intense to stimulate a cone than a rod; (3) stimulation of the cones by different wave lengths results in qualitatively different experiences of hues, while stimulation of the rods gives the experience only of brightness ("lighter" or "darker"). The idea that the rods and cones differ in function is called the *duplicity theory*.

COLOR AND COLOR VISION. There are several theories about the relation between color vision and cone function, but at the moment none of them fits all the facts. This is a very active research field, and we may soon be able to decide among them. There are, at present, two major contenders: the *triple-receptor theory* and the *polychromatic theory*. According to the triple-receptor theory, there is specialization among the cones in their ability to respond to different parts of the physical spectrum. Some cones are said to respond only to red, some only to green, and some only to blue. According to the polychromatic theory, there are not three specialized groups of cones, but many groups (perhaps as many as seven), each sensitive to a restricted band of frequencies.

The physiological explanation for color blindness would vary, of course, according to the theory held, but the general pattern of the explanation would be common for most theories. Since all theories agree that the cones are essential for the perception of color, all theories assume that color blindness involves some defect in these specialized sensory cells. Actually there is good experimental evidence for this assumption. The specific *type* of color blindness (see p. 39) would be explained differently by the various theories. The triple-receptor theory would have only three different specialized types of cones which could "go wrong." This theory would explain all different kinds of color blindness in terms of the malfunctioning or nonexistence of any one or any combination of three kinds of cells. For example, in one kind of color blindness the person sees no hue at the red end of the spectrum. One explanation is that such a person lacks red-sensitive cones. The polychromatic theory would explain the different types of color blindness by reference to the malfunctioning of one (or several) of seven different kinds of cells.

It might be noted that the polychromatic theory enjoys the greatest favor among the researchers in the field of vision, and seems to have the best experimental support, especially from electrophysiological studies.

ELECTROPHYSIOLOGY OF THE RETINA. When a nerve fiber is in action, electrical changes occur in, or around, the fiber. By measuring these electrical changes, we can measure the activity of nerve cells and their fibers. For example, with suitable electrodes attached to the fibers from the rods and cones, we can pick up electrical changes on our recording instrument whenever we illuminate the retina. In this way we can study, in great detail, how the rods and cones in the retina respond to light stimulation.

Among the findings from such experimentation we can list the following three: (1) The greater the intensity of the light, the more rapid the firing rate of the rods and cones. That is, an intense point of light will stimulate a single rod to initiate a large number of neural impulses per second; a weak light will result in many fewer neural impulses. (2) Rods and cones seem to be capable of "spontaneous" discharge, and initiate neural impulses, from time to time, even in the absence of stimulation by light waves. (3) The response in one fiber can be *inhibited* or stopped by stimulating a neighboring receptor. Here again we see that the retina is an interdependent structure, in which what happens in one area affects the events occurring in other areas.

SENSITIVITY, ADAPTATION, AND ACUITY. We pointed out on page 63 that thresholds of absolute and differential sensitivity are complex functions of many factors—the intensity and wave lengths of light, the locality of the retina stimulated, the state of dark-adaptation of the eye, etc. In terms of anatomy and physiology, why should this be so?

Photochemical studies of the retinal elements tell us that before a retinal cell can respond to light, it must have an adequate supply of photosensitive chemicals. The supply of these chemicals is lowered when the retina is stimulated by light. It is clear therefore that a dark-adapted eye (one that has been shielded from light) will have more adequate supplies of photosensitive chemicals than an eye that has been continuously stimulated by light waves. Insofar as this is true, we must expect that the dark-adapted eye will be more sensitive, i.e., more ready to respond to light, than the eye that is not dark-adapted (see p. 76).

In much the same way we can understand negative afterimages (Box 20, p. 76). If we fixate a black and white figure and then look at a gray wall, we experience an afterimage with the black-white relationships of the original figure reversed. During the initial fixation the retinal elements upon which the intense light from the white areas falls gradually become depleted of the photosensitive substance. This does not happen for the retinal elements upon which the weaker light from the black areas falls. Immediately after fixation of the black and white figure, the retina is stimulated over-all by the relatively weak light from the gray wall. Now the already depleted retinal elements (corresponding to the original white part of the figure) will show little response; the undepleted elements (corresponding to the original black part of the figure) will show a relatively large response. Therefore what had previously been seen as brighter will now be seen as darker, and what had previously been seen as darker will now be seen as brighter.

The reader should now be able to explain the phenomenon illustrated in Box 7, p. 25. The same kind of reasoning is involved with the additional assumption that "yellow" light waves stimulate a specialized group of receptor cells (an assumption that many color theories make). To work out the explanation, the reader must ask himself the following questions: What effect does fixation of the left-hand part of the figure have upon the photosensitive chemicals in the "yellow" retinal receptors? Will all the "yellow" receptors of the eye be equally affected?

The fact that the fovea contains many thin cones, tightly packed together, permits us to understand why our visual *acuity* is best in the fovea and becomes poorer as we leave the fovea. Two closely spaced points of light stimulating closely neighboring cones in the fovea, each with its "private line" to the brain, can send two distinct patterns of signals to the brain. Outside the fovea the cones become interspersed with rods, their diameter increases, "party-line" communication with the brain becomes the rule. And *now* two closely spaced points of light may stimulate only one photosensitive element; or even if they

should stimulate two elements, these two elements will send only *one neural impulse* over their common "party line." Therefore visual *acuity*, the ability to differentiate small details, becomes poorer as we leave the fovea.

Much the same facts help us to understand a less familiar, and at first puzzling, visual experience. When we observe a very faint star in the sky, it is easier to see it if we do not look directly at it, but fixate slightly to one side of it. Indeed, if the star is very faint, it will disappear when we look *directly* at it. This suggests that, contrary to what we found in visual acuity, visual *sensitivity* (or absolute threshold) is better just off the fovea than it is at the fovea.

To understand this, we must recall that as we leave the fovea the number of rods rises very rapidly from zero to a peak of about 1,900 per .0069 sq. mm. (see Fig. 67) at a point about 20° off the fovea. And rods, it will be recalled, are more sensitive to weak light than are cones. It therefore follows that light sensitivity will be highest at 20° *off* the fovea.

There is an additional reason for the greater sensitivity of this area. We have seen that a weak light results in a very low rate of neural impulses being fired by an individual rod or cone. This low frequency rate feeding into the bipolar cell may not be enough to fire the ganglion cell fed by a single cone or rod. These impulses, therefore, never get beyond the bipolar cells. However, if a *number* of rods and cones funneled their impulses into one common "party" bipolar cell, the *sum* of the neural impulses arriving at the ganglion cell could be enough to fire that cell and send a message off to the brain. Since "party line" communication is absent in the fovea, but increasingly present outside the fovea, we have here another explanation for the increased sensitivity of the periphery. This may also provide us with a physiological explanation for the *summation* effect we have observed in Chapter 4, page 78. In any event it is for these various reasons that under conditions of poor illumination it is much better *not* to look directly at the stimulus-object, but rather to let the image fall slightly to one side of the fovea.

The distribution of rods and cones in the retina also permits us to understand why our *color* vision is better when we look at a colored stimulus-object with the fovea than when we see it from the periphery. Actually, as we have noted, everyone is color blind at the extreme periphery (p. 62), where there are so very few cones.

PURKINJE PHENOMENON. Finally, the findings that cones and rods differ in their sensitivity to light help us to understand the *Purkinje phenomenon* (see p. 62). We must first recall three facts: (1) cones are more sensitive to longer wave lengths, and rods to shorter wave lengths; (2) rods are more sensitive to less intense light than are cones; (3) the brightness of an object will be determined by the number of cones and rods stimulated.

Consider two objects—one red (long wave length) and another blue (short wave length). Let us assume that the red object, in bright illumination, is brighter than the blue object. The red object owes its brightness to the fact that its light waves are stimulating many cones and relatively fewer rods (fact 1, above). The blue object owes its brightness to the fact that its light waves are stimulating relatively fewer cones but many rods. Now suppose we gradually diminish the over-all intensity of the light. As we do so, the number of cones (whether "belonging to" the red or blue objects) stimulated will begin to decrease, but this will not be as true for the rods (fact 2, above). This must mean that the total number of retinal elements stimulated by the red object will decrease at a more rapid rate than the total number of retinal elements stimulated by the blue object. Gradually, then, as illumination is decreased, the brightness of *both* objects will fall, but that of the red object will fall faster. Eventually a point will come when the blue object is brighter than the red object. This is the Purkinje phenomenon—objects of different hues change in their comparative brightness as illumination decreases. If the illumination is lowered still further, only the rods will respond and neither hue—blue nor red—will be seen, only objects of different intensities. In the dark all cats are gray.

INTERACTION EFFECTS IN VISION. We can begin our understanding of the perceptual effects of stimuli that are in spatial or temporal proximity when we remember (1) that the retina is not built like a switchboard of isolated elements, but has cells *connecting* one part with another; and (2) that activity in one element can *inhibit* activity in neighboring elements or summate with activities in neighboring elements.

Two stimulus-objects may be physically isolated in the real world, but the neural responses evoked by their isolated images in the retina may be *interrelated*. The brain may never actually receive sets of isolated signals corresponding to the isolated stimulus-objects. The photosensitive apparatus *itself* may begin the combining and organizing process. Thus the summation and irradiation effects observed in visual perception (see pp. 77-8) can be understood in terms of the interconnecting cells of the retina.

The observation that a retinal cell, in action, can block its neighboring cell from reacting to light suggests a possible neurological explanation for the perceptual phenomenon of simultaneous contrast (see p. 79). Here the explanation may run something like this: The cells stimulated by the *bright* patch of color may inhibit the action of the neighboring cells being stimulated by the gray patch. The result would be that the light from the gray patch would activate fewer retinal elements when the gray patch is next to a bright patch than when it is alone in the visual field. The brighter the white patch is, the greater would be this inhibitory effect. This would mean that two equal gray patches surrounded by two *different* white patches appear to be of different brightness because the *grays* would be differentially "muted." Conversely, a gray surrounded by black looks brighter than a gray surrounded by white because the first gray is less inhibited by its neighboring black.

The Conduction Mechanism. The optic nerve consists of bundles of nerve fibers from the ganglion cells. These fibers conduct the neural impulses originating in the rods and cones to the cortex of the brain. There are three major way stations that we must consider in this conduction pathway —the *optic chiasma*, the *geniculate bodies*, and the *occipital lobes* of the brain. There is, in addition, a special way station, the reticular formation, which we will discuss later. The events that take place at these three stations have important psychological implications.

THE OPTIC CHIASMA. After the optic nerves from each eye enter the cranium, they converge and meet at the very base of the brain. This meeting place is called the "optic chiasma," and here the bundles of nerve fibers making up each optic nerve are re-sorted before they continue on into the brain. The re-sorting accomplishes two things, as can readily be seen from Figure 68. In the first place, fibers from the right-hand side of both retinas (corresponding parts) are bundled together and go to the right half of the brain; and fibers from the left-hand side of both retinas (corresponding parts), to the left side of the brain. Light from objects on the *left* side of the visual field forms an image on the right side of both retinas. This means that the *two* images from objects on the left side send signals to the *same* side of the brain.

FIG. 68. The visual system. The sketch of the brain in the upper left corner outlines the route of the optic tract from the optic chiasma to the occipital lobes. Use this to orient yourself for the larger drawing that gives the details of this route. Note specially the following:

1. The light rays from the left side of the brick wall (indicated by dotted lines) fall on the right sides of both eyes, while the light rays from the right side of the brick wall (indicated by solid lines) fall on the left sides of both eyes—the corresponding parts of the brick wall fall on corresponding sides of each of the two retinas.

2. The fibers from the *right sides of each retina* (indicated by the dotted lines from the retinas to the occipital areas) end up on the right occipital lobe of the brain; the fibers from the *left side of each retina* (indicated by solid lines) end up on the left occipital lobe. This means that the *left visual field* is represented on the right side of the brain, the right visual field, on the left side of the brain. Only half of the visual object (but as seen by *both* eyes) is projected on each occipital lobe. Of course we

experience only one integrated object. For example, the cuff (greatly diminished in size) together with the letter "U" are projected on the right occipital lobe, the fingers together with the letter "P" are projected on the left occipital lobe. Nevertheless we perceive a single hand with the word "UP" on the background of a brick wall. Just how this integration across the two halves of the brain takes place to give us this unified perception is at present unknown.

3. The distortions of the projections on the occipital lobes follows from the fact that the fovea is more richly connected with the occipital lobes (via their "private lines") than any other part of the retina. Since, in the above diagram, the eyes are supposed to be fixated at a point midway between the letters "U" and "P" on the brick wall, the two inner parts of these letters fall on the foveas and are therefore given detailed representation in the lobes, while the rest of the picture gets less representation and is therefore shown diminished in size.

For discussion of the other parts of the visual system pictured here (optic chiasma, geniculate bodies, reticular formation), see the text.

Brain Split Longitudinally

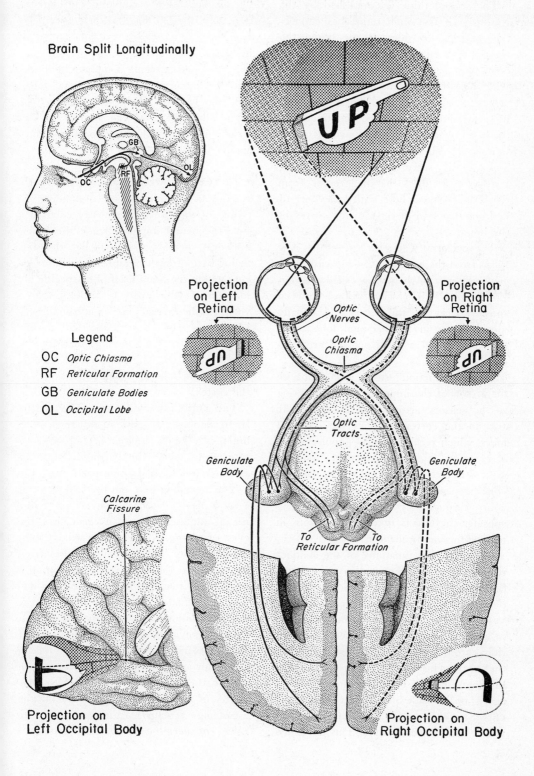

Legend

OC *Optic Chiasma*
RF *Reticular Formation*
GB *Geniculate Bodies*
OL *Occipital Lobe*

Projection
on Left
Retina

*Optic
Nerves*

*Optic
Chiasma*

Projection
on Right
Retina

*Optic
Tracts*

*Geniculate
Body*

*Geniculate
Body*

Calcarine
Fissure

*To
Reticular Formation*

To

Projection on
Left Occipital Body

Projection on
Right Occipital Body

The second thing accomplished by the re-sorting is that each retina has connections with *both* sides of the brain; the right half of each retina with the right side of the brain, and the left half of each retina with the left side of the brain.

THE GENICULATE BODIES. These two bundles of reshuffled fibers then continue into the brain, where they end in two masses of brain cells called the "geniculate bodies." These bodies serve as relay and shunting stations. The fibers that have come from the retina connect here with a new set of neurons that lead directly to the cortex of the brain.

THE OCCIPITAL LOBES OF THE BRAIN. The fibers from the geniculate bodies end up in a specific part of the cortex called the "occipital lobes." The connections between specific areas on the retina and equally specific areas in the occipital lobes have been fairly well worked out and are indicated in Figure 68.

Our "conduction" story is ended with the arrival of the impulses from the retina to the sensory area of the cortex. (Any area in the cortex, such as the occipital lobes, which receives neural impulses from a receptor organ, is called a "sensory area.") Before we turn to a discussion of what happens in the brain as these impulses course through its various structures, let us consider the effects of different lesions in the conduction mechanism.

BLINDNESS. The anatomy of the conduction pathway of the visual system is such that damage in various portions of the optic pathway will cause different kinds of visual defects. This enables the physician to locate lesions fairly accurately. Destruction of one optic nerve before it reaches the optic chiasma will cause complete blindness in that eye. Destruction of the nerves on one side *after* it leaves the optic chiasma will cause blindness in *half* of the visual field of each eye. This is called "hemianopia." For example, if the destruction is on the left side, the person will be unable to see objects to the right of where he fixates. Of course if both optic pathways are cut or destroyed, complete blindness results. Destruction of the occipital lobes will also lead to blindness—whether total or not depends upon the amount of destruction and whether one or both lobes are involved.

The Central Mechanisms. We have already seen that some of the organizing activities of the visual system may occur before the neural impulses reach the brain. However there is good evidence that the major part of such organizing activity occurs within the brain itself. The specific allocation of which part of the brain does what, and how the "what" is accomplished, is not too well known. We will discuss briefly some of the functions that are believed to be determined by two subparts of the brain—the reticular formation and the cortex.

THE RETICULAR FORMATION. The reticular formation, a structure of the lower midbrain, is a highly interconnected network of neurons which can be divided into an *ascending* and a *descending* part.

The ascending part can be thought of as a kind of *central station* at which arrive neural impulses from many receptors, the eyes, ears, nose, skin, etc. Thus fibers from the geniculate bodies carry impulses from the retina to the reticular formation. Impulses *from* this formation are, in turn, diffusely conducted to various parts of the brain, including the cortex (see Fig. 69).

Our knowledge about the functions of the reticular formation is extremely recent, and while many of the "facts" are still in dispute, the following can be said with some degree of safety. Neural impulses from the ascending reticular formation *serve to arouse or alert the cortex.* Such arousal is essential before normal perception can take place. Experiments have indicated that if the ascending reticular system is prevented (by cutting, drugging, or otherwise interfering with the pathways of the reticular system) from sending on neural impulses to the cortex, the individual either loses consciousness, goes off into a deep coma, falls into a deep sleep, or, in any event, has great difficulty in responding to stimuli from the outside world. Even though the neural impulses from his retina, for example, do reach his occipital lobes directly from the geniculate bodies, the individual cannot sustain his visual perceptions *unless impulses from the ascending reticular formation are diffusely discharged into his cortex at the same time.*

This basic observation has many impli-

cations for perception. For example, an impulse from the *retina*, when it is shunted into the ascending reticular formation, can alert the whole cortex, so that the cortex can respond more adequately to an impulse *from the ear.* Thus stimulation by one sensory mode (vision) can facilitate perception in another sensory mode (audition). The fact that an impulse initiated by a light, for example, not only goes directly to the cortex, but can also set off the ascending reticular formation, suggests that light waves from an object can act as a "sensory stimulus" and an "alerter" at the same time. Here perhaps is the physiological basis for the "attention-demanding character" of objects (see p. 106).

THE DESCENDING RETICULAR FORMATION. The descending reticular formation re-

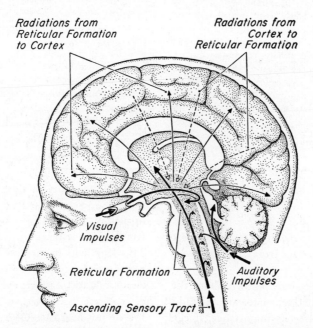

Radiations from
Reticular Formation
to Cortex

Radiations from
Cortex to
Reticular Formation

Visual
Impulses

Reticular Formation

Auditory
Impulses

Ascending Sensory Tract

FIG. 69. This diagram indicates some of the relations between the reticular formation and the cerebral cortex. Note that the neural impulses from the sensory organs (ear, eye, skin, etc.) not only go directly to the cortex but also enter the ascending reticular formation through branch lines. From the ascending reticular formation impulses are sent diffusely to cover much of the cortex. Note also that impulses radiate *from* the cortex to the descending reticular formation. From the descending reticular formation these impulses are sent back to some of the lower brain centers that receive incoming sensory impulses. It is clear from this diagram why the reticular formation has been called the "central pool" for sensory impulses.

BOX 45

Deafened by Intense Visual Gaze

Physiologists Hernández-Peón, Scherrer, and Jouvet, with the help of a cat and two mice, tested the possibility that there exists a neurological mechanism which can *block "unimportant" sensory signals from ever reaching the cortex.* Stainless steel electrodes were implanted into a cat's cochlear nucleus (the ear's first relay station, see p. 179) through a small hole bored in the skull. From these, wires led off to an apparatus that recorded electrical activity at the site of the electrodes. A week after the cat had been thus prepared, the following tests were made: (1) short clicks were sounded over a loud-speaker near the cat; (2) two mice, in a closed bottle, were placed before the cat; (3) the mice were then removed from the room. As can be seen from the photographs, when the cat is relaxed, the click responses in the cochlear nucleus are large. This means that the neural impulses from the ear are reaching the cochlear nucleus, then continue through the lower brain centers and finally reach the cortex. At this point the cat "hears" the clicks from the loud-speaker. As soon as the mice are brought in, the cat immediately fixates the mice and seems to be giving them all his attention. Now the click responses are practically abolished! The neural impulses from the ear have been *blocked at, or before, the* *cochlear nucleus.* This means that the cat probably cannot hear the clicks because the neural impulses *never reach his cortex.* When the mice are removed, the cat relaxes again, and the click response reappears at full strength in the cochlear nucleus.

In a related experiment it was demonstrated that an olfactory stimulus that attracted the animal's attention could produce similar blocking effects. Fish odors were delivered through tubes and when the cat attentively sniffed at these odors, the electrical activity at the cochlear nucleus was almost completely abolished despite the fact that the loud-speaker was sounding away at full force. Here again we have evidence that an inhibitory mechanism exists in the brain which operates during attention to select only certain sensory impulses for transmission to the cortex, and to block others.

From other evidence it seems that this blocking is accomplished by neural impulses that come down through the descending reticular formation from the cortex. The cat's intense visual or olfactory activity sends down signals that prevent auditory stimuli from reaching his cortex.

HERNÁNDEZ-PEÓN, R., SCHERRER, H., and JOUVET, M. 1956. Modification of electrical activity in cochlear nucleus during "attention" in unanesthetized cats. *Science, 123,* 331–2.

ceives impulses from the cortex and then sends impulses to the various fibers coming up from the receptors. That is, neural signals coming *down from the cortex* meet the signals coming *up from the eyes, ears, skin,* etc.

Even less is definitely known about the descending formation, but we already know enough to see its importance. It can be shown that neural impulses originating from one sensory area of the brain can set off impulses in the descending reticular formation which will *block* other sensory impulses from reaching the cortex. For example, an impulse that comes down from the occipital lobes of the brain (the visual center) through the descending reticular formation can prevent impulses coming up from the ear from ever reaching the cortex. This can help us to understand the very common experience of not hearing someone speak to us when all our attention is directed at watching an object intently. We do not hear the person because, for the moment, *we are literally deafened by our intense visual gaze!* (See Box 45 for an interesting illustrative experiment.) This function of the descending reticular formation may also help us to understand many of the phenomena of shifts of attention (see

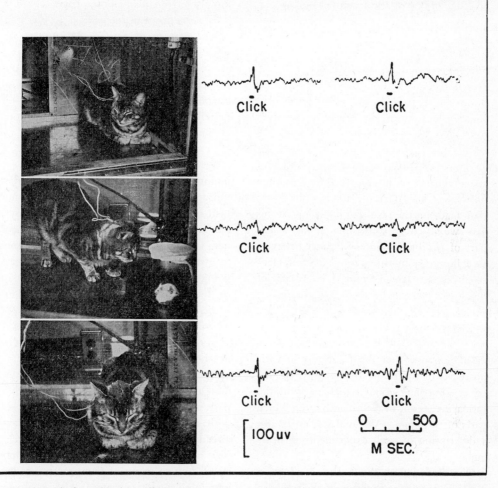

Click   Click

Click   Click

Click   Click

[100 uv

0 ____ 500
M SEC.

p. 103) and the selective effects of set on perception (see p. 98).

Some psychologists have been so impressed by the way the reticular formations work that they consider them to be the neurological mechanisms that underlie attention, motivation, and consciousness. Again we must point out that research in this field has but recently begun and we should be cautious about interpretations, but it does seem possible that many insights into why we behave the way we do will come from this research within the next few years.

How THE CORTEX WORKS. Psychologists, neurologists, physiologists, and anatomists have spent many years studying the way the cortex works. Ingenious and highly technical methods have been worked out for studies, and a great deal of specific information has been obtained. However, when we attempt to answer the basic question of just how an organized, meaningful visual perception is finally achieved from the neural impulses that reach the brain from the retina, we must confess that we do not know. We *do* know that our former explanations—explanations that were found in the textbooks of a very few years ago—are probably wrong; and we *can* make a few general statements about the integrative operations of the brain.

There are two major research techniques that have been used, on animals and man, in the study of brain function. (1) In the *ablation* techniques, different parts of the receptor organs, conduction system, or brain are destroyed, and observations are then made on the behavior of the organism. (2) The *electrophysiological* techniques are of two types. In the first, the brain of an animal or man is exposed surgically, and specific parts of it are stimulated with a mild electrical current. Observations are then made on the resulting behavior. In this way we discover something about which part of the brain controls which behavior (see Box 46). In the second type of electrophysiological technique, various parts of the lower nervous system (the receptors, or segments of the conduction system) are stimulated in one way or another, and records are made of the nature of the electrical responses that finally appear in various parts of the brain. In this way we discover something about which parts of the retina, say, result in neural activity in which parts of the brain. (We will see, on p. 181, a description of such experiments in hearing.)

Our knowledge about the conduction mechanism and the function of the reticular formation comes from much work with these and allied techniques. These studies seem to warrant the following additional general statements about brain function and perception. (1) *In man at least, the occipital lobes must be activated before any visual perception occurs.* In other words, the cortex must function in visual perception. This does *not* imply, however, that the occipital lobes alone are responsible, or even adequate, for visual perception. The brain is such a well-interconnected system that impulses received by the occipital lobes spread to almost every other part of the brain and, in turn, are influenced by impulses from many other parts. (2) *The final perception is determined by the integrated pattern of activity of most of the cortex and perhaps even of the rest of the brain.* The very fact that so many of our perceptual attributes reflect the results of learning (which must somehow be represented in the brain) demands the operation of much of the brain in perception.

By Way of Summary. One of the very important generalizations that the reader can achieve about the anatomy of the human nervous system is that the *entire* system is constructed in an interrelated manner. Our nervous system is not analogous to a network of insulated telephone wires going from receptors to specific areas of the brain and then directly to muscles. This is the view that was once held and that we now know to be wrong. There are *many places* (in the receptor organs themselves, in the conduction paths, in the brain) where what happens in one part of the system modifies what happens in another part. And it is precisely this fact, together with all the specific information we have already gained about the nervous system, that may eventually enable us to understand why so many of our perceptions are integrated, organized, and full of meanings, memories, emotional overtones—in short, why we perceive the world the way we do.

Auditory Perception

The sequence of physiological events taking place when we hear is no less complicated than that occurring when we see. Here we must trace the story of how sound waves in the air become converted into vibrations of the *eardrum*, then into movements of levers in the *middle* ear, then into waves of fluid in the *inner* ear,

BOX 46

"Mapping" the Functions of a Human Brain

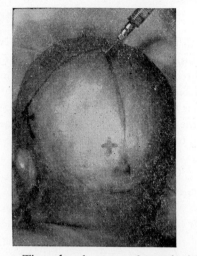
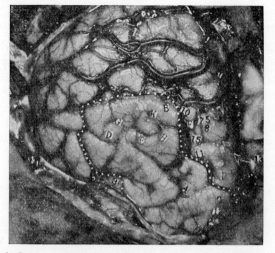

The best-known electrophysiological studies on the human brain are those of Wilder Penfield, McGill University's famous brain surgeon. He and his associates have now reported on about 400 brain operations, mostly on epileptic patients. When a patient requires surgery, a "craniotomy" is performed, i.e., a bone flap is cut into the scalp (see left fig.) and the brain is exposed to view. Done under local anesthesia, the patient is conscious throughout the operation. The surgical problem is to remove every bit of abnormal tissue with minimal interference to the functioning of the brain.

To discover how much tissue he can safely remove, the surgeon stimulates a point on the cortex with a weak electrical current. A numbered ticket is placed on the spot stimulated, and the corresponding response is recorded. The entire area is explored in this fashion, and the surgeon soon has a "map" of the functions of the brain to guide his surgery. Let us describe, very briefly, one of his cases.

Case C. J. 18-year-old boy suffering from epileptic seizures. Craniotomy was carried out and left occipital lobe exposed. From various diagnostic tests it appeared desirable to remove the cortex indicated by dotted white lines (see

right fig.). "Mapping" of surrounding cortex was then carried out. Here are some of the responses of the boy when the various points on his cortex were stimulated: *Point 2:* "A ball of light, all colors." *Point 3:* "Flashing in my eyes." *Point 4:* "Tiny colored lights which were moving." *Point 8:* "There was a short spot in the right eye."

Many similar investigations lead Penfield to the following conclusions: (1) Removal of the primary visual sensory area of the cortex results in complete blindness on that side. (2) Electrical stimulation of the occipital area alone results in very elementary visual experiences—fuzzy lights, shadows, and colors—but there are no well-defined visual images of objects. Much more of the brain than the primary visual centers of the cortex is involved in the perception of objects.

P.S. The operation was carried out on C. J. Complete right blindness was produced, but C. J. no longer suffered from epileptic seizures.

PENFIELD, W., and RASMUSSEN, T. 1950. *The cerebral cortex of man.* New York: The Macmillan Co. Figures reproduced by permission of The Macmillan Company. Copyright 1950 by The Macmillan Company.

and finally into neural impulses in the phonoreceptor elements. We must again follow the neural impulses to the brain and examine what happens there. Our story this time will be somewhat easier in the telling simply because much of what we had to say for visual perception will also hold for auditory perception.

Again we shall divide these events into four major stages dealing with (1) the physical mechanism; (2) the phonosensitive mechanism; (3) the conduction mechanism; and (4) the central mechanism.

a somewhat schematized drawing of all three. The outer ear includes the auricle (which has but a minor function for man— except for those of us who can wiggle it) and the ear canal. Separating the ear canal from the middle ear is a thin membrane, the eardrum. The middle ear, the area between the eardrum and the inner ear, contains three little bones (ossicles) forming a chain from the eardrum to the window of the inner ear. The inner ear consists of two parts, the *vestibular apparatus* (which has nothing to do with hearing and will be dis-

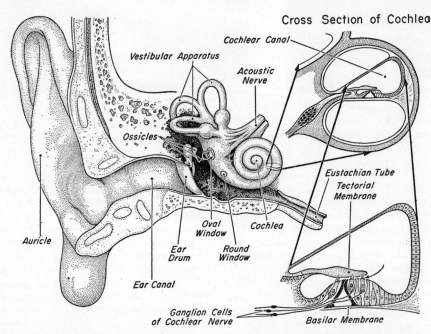

FIG. 70. Cross section of the ear. Here we have a semidiagrammatic representation of the outer, middle, and inner ears, together with a

view of the cross section of the cochlea and an enlarged diagram of the basilar membrane. For detailed description, see text.

The Physical Mechanism. The stimulus for hearing is, of course, the sound wave (see p. 64). When a sound wave enters the outer ear, a series of events is set off which eventually leads to an auditory perception.

STRUCTURE OF THE EAR. The ear consists of three parts: the *outer ear*, the *middle ear*, and the *inner ear*. Figure 70 represents

cussed later) and a coiled, divided, fluid-filled tube, the *cochlea*. One end of the cochlea is closed off by the third ossicle at the *oval window* and the other end by a thin membrane at the *round window*. This coiled tube is divided into two major channels by a partition called the *cochlear canal* (or *duct*), which is filled with a jellylike fluid. In the cochlear canal are contained the actual sensory elements whereby the mechanical stimuli are converted to neural impulses.

FROM SOUND WAVES TO FLUID WAVES. A sound wave from the outside is conducted by the ear canal to the eardrum. This causes the eardrum to vibrate with the same frequency as the impinging wave. The vibrations of the eardrum are transmitted through the middle ear by the chain of ossicles, ending with in-and-out movements of the last ossicle against the oval window of the inner ear. As the ossicle moves in and out, it intermittently puts pressure on the fluid in the cochlear canal. Since the other end of the cochlear canal (the round window) is stopped with a thin membrane, the alternating pressure on the fluid in the canal causes the membrane to bulge in and out, and fluid motions are set up in the liquid of the cochlear canal. In this way the sound waves set up by a vibrating object (e.g., a violin string) in the outside world are eventually transformed into corresponding liquid pressure waves in the inner ear.

However the ossicles do not transmit the vibrations of the eardrum perfectly. This helps to account for some of the distortion of our perception of sounds. For example, if a pure tone is very intense, the simple wave form is distorted in transmission in the ear and we hear it as a complex tone.

The Phonosensitive Mechanism. The sensory cells of audition, called *hair cells*, are all found inside the cochlear canal. The hair cells rest upon the *basilar membrane*. (See Fig. 70.) As the basilar membrane is agitated by the pressure waves set up in the fluid of the cochlea, the hair cells are pushed against or away from a mass of gelatinous material, the *tectorial membrane*. When pushed against the tectorial membrane, the hair cells are temporarily squeezed out of shape. This deformation stimulates the nerve fibers in these cells and a neural impulse is set up.

Before going on to a description of the conduction mechanism, we might stop to indicate how the anatomical and physiological facts we have already discussed can contribute to our understanding of some of the phenomena of auditory perception.

LOUDNESS. The attribute of loudness in perception depends upon the "intensity" of neural discharges reaching the brain. Whether a sound wave from the outside will set up a neural impulse depends, among other things, on whether the basilar membrane is sufficiently agitated by the wave motion of the liquid in the inner ear to deform the hair cells. It should be obvious that an intense sound wave will set the eardrum into vibrations of greater excursion than a less intense sound wave. This in turn means that an intense sound wave will be transformed into an intense pressure wave in the liquid of the inner ear; a less intense sound wave will result in a less intense pressure wave. It is equally obvious that a more intense pressure wave will result in a greater displacement of the basilar membrane than a less intense wave.

At this point we must bring in an additional fact which, at first glance, appears to offer difficulties in explaining how a greater displacement of the basilar membrane can be translated into a more "intense" neural discharge to the brain. Any hair cell when it becomes deformed *will fire with a constant intensity*. It does not matter whether it is very much deformed or only slightly deformed. If it is deformed enough to fire, it "gives its all." This is true of all neural cells—they either do not fire at all, or they fire with maximum intensity. This is the so-called *all-or-none* law of neural discharge. How then can the degree of displacement of the basilar membrane determine the "intensity" of the neural discharge to the brain? The solution to this difficulty is an interesting and simple one. With greater displacement of the basilar membrane, a larger *number* of sensory cells are deformed. Therefore the *sum* of the neural impulses that reach the brain is correspondingly large.

The relationship between *intensity* of stimulus, *number* of neural elements stimulated, and *intensity* of sensation is a general relationship that holds for all modes—vision, audition, olfaction, etc.

PITCH. We already know that sound waves of different frequencies are perceived as differing in pitch. The perceived attribute of pitch depends upon different patterns of neural impulses reaching the brain. The question we must answer here is how differences in *frequencies* of sound waves evoke different patterns of neural impulses in the brain. To answer this question, we must introduce one more fact about the pressure waves in the liquid of the cochlea. When a sound wave of a given frequency is transformed into its corresponding pressure wave, the resulting pressure wave has a characteristic history. As it proceeds from the oval window through the cochlea, it gradually builds up its pressure against the cochlea, reaches a maximum point, and then fairly rapidly subsides to almost zero. (The analogy to a wave at the shore is clear.) Pressure waves initiated by sound waves of *different frequencies* will reach their maximum pressure at *different points* along the cochlea. Thus, for example, a pressure wave initiated by a sound wave of 300 cycles per second will reach its maximum pressure point at a distance of about 26 millimeters from the oval window; a sound wave of 200 c.p.s. will reach its maximum at a distance of 28 mm. In general, waves in the cochlea initiated by high-frequency sound waves will reach their maximum pressure and stimulate the hair cells near the oval window; waves of low frequency will stim-

ulate the hair cells farther along. Thus differences in *frequency* of sound waves are transformed into differences in the *spatial location* of the sensory cells that are stimulated. The brain, in other words, will receive neural messages from one set of sensory cells when a high-frequency sound wave hits the ear, and from another set of sensory cells when a low-frequency sound wave stimulates the ear. In this way the ear sorts out the different frequencies and permits us to discriminate one pitch from another (see Fig. 71).

ABNORMAL HEARING. We might first mention an "abnormal" auditory phenomenon that all of us have experienced at one time or another—*tinnitus*, or ringing in the ears, when there are no outside sources for such noises. Just as we have seen that there is constant activity in the retinal cells of the eye, so there is spontaneous activity in the hair cells of the inner ear. The faint ringing noise we all hear in a very quiet room is probably due to this normal spontaneous activity. Such ringing can at times become loud and annoying. This may occur after long exposure to a very loud sound, in certain cases of progressive deafness, and in other diseases. In the first case (a common one for the healthy ear) what happens is that the prolonged loud sound results in a mild injury to some of the hair cells; they remain deformed and continue to send off neural impulses. They seem to recover quickly from this, the ringing disappears, and no ill effects remain. Where ringing persists, it is assumed that there is some constant irritant at work among the hair cells.

Another interesting abnormality in hearing is found in instances of partial tone deafness, for instance, where the individual is incapable of hearing high tones. This has an explanation analogous to the one for partial color blindness. As a result of fatigue, disease, injury, or degeneration, one part of the cochlea, or one group of hair cells, may not be functioning, temporarily or permanently.

The Conduction Mechanism. The auditory nerve conducts neural impulses from the hair cells in the cochlea to the brain. Of particular interest is the peculiar arrangement of the various fibers that make up the auditory nerve, the five major relay stations through which the nerve passes, and finally the terminal area in the cortex. Each plays an important role in perception.

THE AUDITORY NERVE. The human auditory nerve is a bundle of about 30,000 separate nerve fibers stemming from the hair cells. The separate fibers in the auditory nerve are bundled together in a complex

but orderly fashion. The fibers that come from about the middle of the cochlea make up the central core of the bundle; the fibers that come from the oval window end are twisted one way around this core, and the fibers that come from the apex area of the cochlea are twisted the opposite way around this core. For the entire length of the auditory nerve, the spatial separation of high-, middle-, and low-tone neural elements that we found in the cochlea is *preserved up to the very termination of the system in the cortex.*

THE FIRST RELAY STATION. Soon after leaving the internal ear the auditory nerve enters the lower brain stem and terminates at its first relay station, the *cochlear nuclei* (see Fig. 71). Here the fibers make new

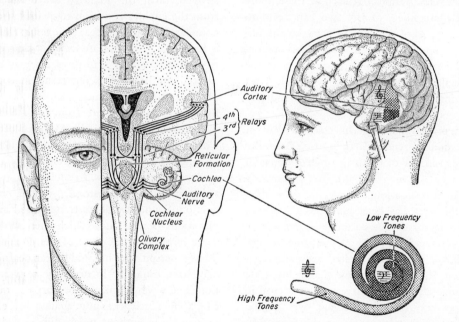

FIG. 71. This diagram illustrates the conduction pathway of the auditory impulses from the cochlea to the cerebral cortex. Note how close the cochlea of the inner ear is to the cochlear nucleus, the first relay station within the brain. (The reader should also refer back to Fig. 61 to locate the point of entrance of the auditory nerve into the brain.) The gradient of shading in the cochlea represents the gradient of tone localization in that organ. The

higher frequency tones stimulate the sensory cells at one end, the lower frequency at the other. Note also the point-for-point projection of the cochlea on the cortex. That is, nerve impulses from the cochlea stimulated by high frequency tones end deeply within the fold of the cortex, and those from low frequency terminate on the surface of the fold. The outer part of the auditory cortex has been pulled down to show this.

connections, some of them with fibers that go on to the next relay station *on the same side* of the brain, and some of them with fibers that *cross over* to the next relay station on the other side.

THE SECOND RELAY STATION. This next relay station is called the *olivary complex.* Here, for the first time, there are opportunities for *interaction* between the fibers coming from the left ear and those coming from the right ear. However, as can be seen from Figure 71, *some* fibers from each ear go through the olivary complex without connecting up with fibers from the other ear.

ASCENT TO THE CORTEX. After leaving the olivary complex, the fibers go up the two ascending tracts and pass through two more relay stations. At each of these, more and more fibers of the two ears seem to interact. Also, somewhere between the olivary complex and the next relay station, fibers from each ear carry impulses to the reticular formation (see pages 170–3). After leaving the last relay station, the auditory fibers end in the cortex.

AUDITORY AREA OF THE CORTEX. Most of the auditory sensory area in man's brain lies hidden in one of the major convolutions of the cortex (see Fig. 71). As a result of much investigation the specific geography of this area has been fairly well mapped. Two major findings should be noticed in this connection: (1) as was true of the auditory *nerve,* the spatial separation between the high-, middle-, and low-tone sensory elements is fairly well preserved in the cortex; (2) the crossing over of the fibers which takes place as the two auditory nerves ascend the brain is such that each ear is somewhat *better* represented on the other side of the brain than on its own side. The significance of this crossing over merits discussion. We have already seen that in vision each side of the visual *field* is represented on the opposite side of the

brain. This means that an object on the *right* side of the visual field is represented on the *left* side of the brain. We now see that the same is true for audition. A sound coming from the right side of the auditory field is better represented on the *left* side of the brain than it is on the right side. Finally, as we shall soon see, the nerves which carry impulses from the skin surface show almost complete crossing over, so that a touch on the right hand results in cortical activity on the left side of the brain. Thus, a buzzing insect, alighting on the right hand, sends neural impulses from the ear, skin, and eye to the *same* (left) side of the brain. We hear, feel, and see the insect on the right hand.

DEAFNESS. If a cochlear canal is destroyed, or if the auditory nerve leading from the cochlea is destroyed at its source, complete deafness on that side results. This is known as "nerve deafness." But destruction of one of the pathways after it has entered the brain does not result in complete deafness, since each pathway, as we have seen, carries fibers from both cochleas. Disease of the middle ear may cause what is known as "transmission deafness" by interfering with the movements of the eardrum or the ossicles. In such cases, partial hearing may be restored by·bone conduction. Sound waves are transformed into vibrations of the skull which then set up wave motions in the fluid of the cochleas. Thus a person who has middle-ear deafness may have difficulty in ordinary conversation, but when he places the earpiece of a telephone receiver firmly against his ear, he may hear without much difficulty, because the sounds are conducted through the bones of the head. Many hearing aids work on this principle. In complete nerve deafness, however, no hearing aid will help.

Central Mechanisms. As in the case of vision, much of our information about the central mechanism in audition comes from ablation and electrophysiological studies. The latter have been especially successful in helping us to "spell out" the physiological basis of many perceptual phenomena in hearing.

BINAURAL INTERACTION. We saw in the last chapter that our ability to detect whether a sound is to our right or left, in front of us or behind us, above or below us, depends upon the difference in stimulation at the two ears by sound waves coming from a single object. (Note the similarities and differences between the situation with the ears, and that with the eyes in retinal disparity, p. 136.)

In the visual system this difference between the two retinas seems to be integrated at the cortical levels. In the ear, however, it seems that neural impulses coming from one ear and those coming from the other ("binaural interaction") begin their interaction long before they reach the cortex. The electrophysiological studies of a psychologist, Rosenzweig (using the cat as the experimental subject), not only help to answer the question of where the neural integration occurs, but describe the neurophysiological bases for other perceptual phenomena. We shall therefore present his studies (1954) as illustrative experiments in this field.

ELECTROPHYSIOLOGICAL STUDIES. The experimental method used can be described very briefly. After the cat is anesthetized, the animal's skull is surgically opened, exposing the brain to view. Needle electrodes are inserted into that part of the brain which is to be investigated (e.g., into the auditory sensory cortex, or the olivary complex). The needle electrodes are connected through an amplifier to an oscilloscope equipped with a motion-picture camera. The entire apparatus can detect, magnify, portray, and photograph very weak electrical currents so that any neural impulse that arrives at the point where the needle electrode is inserted will be picked up and recorded. The cat wears a set of earphones that permit the experimenter to stimulate either ear independently. In the experiment each ear may be stimulated with a single click of *equal* intensity but the click in one ear may be made to occur a thousandth of a second before the other; or both ears may be stimulated *simultaneously*, but one click may be a bit more intense than the other; or only one ear may be stimulated. In this way the experimenter can reproduce the stimulus-patterns that give rise to auditory localization (see p. 131). In every instance, of course, the resulting electrical responses in various parts of the brain are recorded.

The results of many such experiments have led to the following conclusions:

1. No binaural interaction is detected at the cochlear nuclei (stimulating the *right* ear has no effect on the neural responses at the *left* cochlear nucleus).

2. Some binaural interaction begins as soon as the olivary complex is reached (stimulating the right ear does have an effect on the left olivary complex).

3. The degree of interaction increases at each succeeding relay station.

The significance of these findings seems to be that the nervous system as a whole, not only the "higher" centers, is built for interaction. Long before the impulses from the receptors reach the cortex, they begin to create a patterned, integrated set of responses.

Another important finding is that when the stimulation at both ears is identical in time and intensity, the cortical activity at the two hemispheres is identical; when the stimulation is made to differ at the two ears in time or intensity, the cortical activity comes to differ between the two hemispheres. And the greater the difference in stimulation at the two ears, the greater the difference in activity at the two hemispheres. Since *perception* involves cortical activity, these different cortical patterns help us to understand how the perception of the direction of sound is dependent upon different stimulation at the two ears.

It appears that the data from psychological, physical, chemical, anatomical, and neural-physiological research are beginning to "mesh" in the study of man's most important senses—vision and hearing. An adequate outline of the complete story of visual and auditory perception may not be too far away.

Perception of Taste and Smell

The senses of vision and hearing (the primary senses for the perception of space) are probably the most important senses for man, since he is a spatial animal. That is why we have described them in a relatively detailed manner. However it is clear that taste and smell also contribute considerably to our ability to survive and to the richness of our perceptual world. The reasons why taste and smell perception are usually treated together have been indicated on page 67, and we shall follow this grouping in discussing their physiological bases.

Taste. We shall restrict ourselves to a discussion of the receptor organs for taste with only a brief discussion of the conduction and central mechanisms, primarily because the study of the latter has been so complicated by technical difficulties as to make a simple presentation of the details impossible.

TASTE BUDS. The receptors for taste are mostly concentrated in certain areas of the tongue, but they are also found in the mucous membrane of the throat, larynx, and soft palate. There are regions of the tongue (along the sides) which have no taste receptors and are therefore completely "taste-blind." (These would be appropriate places for the bitter pills that many of us have occasion to swallow from time to time.) The number, kind, and efficiency of taste receptors differ from person to person and within the same person, and this helps us to understand some of the individual differences in taste sensitivity.

The taste receptor consists of a number of taste-sensitive cells and supporting cells grouped together into a *taste bud*. The opening of the bud (*taste pore*) in the mucous membrane permits chemicals to reach the taste-sensitive cells. Around each of the taste-sensitive cells are wound endings of the *taste nerves* (see Fig. 72). Chem-

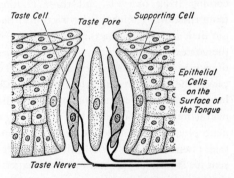

FIG. 72. Here we have a diagrammatic representation of a taste bud. These structures, consisting of a number of *taste cells*, endings of *taste nerves*, and *supporting cells*, are found scattered in the tongue with an opening to the surface of the tongue. This opening is called a *taste pore*. When a chemical substance, dissolved by the fluid on the surface of the tongue and in the mouth, enters the taste bud through the taste pore and stimulates the taste cells, the taste nerves (which wind about the taste cells) carry a neural impulse to the brain.

ical substances (found in food, for example) are usually first dissolved in the saliva, and when they reach the taste-sensitive cells, they initiate a neural reaction in the cells. The neural impulse is transmitted to the endings of the taste nerves, which conduct the neural impulses to the brain.

Electrophysiological studies of single taste-nerve fibers show that different fibers are particularly sensitive to different chemicals. But this relationship between stimulus and neural response is not a simple one. One fiber seems to respond most actively when it is stimulated by hydrochloric acid (sour), sugar (sweet), or quinine (bitter); another fiber responds to sour, salt, and bitter chemical stimuli; and still another, only to sweet, sour, and salt, etc. It appears, in other words, that there are not specialized taste buds for each of the four so-called basic taste categories, salt, sour, bitter, and sweet (see p. 68). Our ability to perceive a specific taste is determined by the *pattern* of stimulated receptors. For example, sugar will stimulate the first and third sets of fibers described above but not the second, while quinine will stimulate the first and second but not the third. The perception of a "sweet-and-sour" flavor in food is *not* the result of the stimulation of "sweet" receptors *plus* "sour" receptors, but, most probably, of the activity of a distinct pattern of receptors. Again we find patterns of responses in our nervous system rather than isolated point-by-point responses or simple "additive" responses.

CONDUCTION AND CENTRAL NEURAL PROCESSES. The nerve fibers from the taste buds do not travel to the brain in a single fiber bundle. The taste nerve fibers from the front of the tongue, the back of the tongue, and from the throat and larynx divide into several bundles and travel along in company with fibers from various skin sensory nerves (see Fig. 74). All these bundles seem to send impulses to the same general area of the cortex. Ablation studies indicate, however, that the removal of this part of the cortex does not make the individual "taste-blind," but merely reduces his taste sensitivity.

Smell. There are two outstanding attributes of smell which merit particular attention: its sensitivity and its rate of adaptation. The sense of smell is exceedingly sensitive. In terms of the concentration of molecules necessary to stimulate the receptors it has been estimated that the sense of smell is 10,000 times as sensitive as taste. This is compensated for (frequently to our great relief) by the ease with which our sense of smell becomes adapted so that a substance that originally provoked a very strong odor soon loses its effectiveness. (See p. 69.)

OLFACTORY RECEPTORS. The olfactory receptors are found in the mucous membrane on each side of the upper part of the nasal cavity. These receptors are fairly long, columnar-shaped cells. From one end of these cells delicate hairs project into the fluid covering of the mucous membrane, and from the other end protrude long threads, which are the fibers of the olfactory nerve (see Fig. 73). When particles of gas reach the mucous membrane of the nose, they are dissolved by the fluid covering and then stimulate the olfactory cells into neural activity.

Recent electrophysiological studies seem to show that there is odor specificity for different olfactory nerve cells; some cells seem to respond to one group of chemicals, others to a different group. (Note that the specificity is to groups of chemicals, rather than to single chemicals.) If this specificity can be clearly established, we may be able to account for the strong adaptation effect to specific odors in olfactory perception. Presumably the excessive stimulation of one specific and limited group of olfactory cells may throw that group out of commission temporarily and thus make the perceiver "smell-blind" for that group of odors.

CONDUCTION AND CENTRAL NEURAL PROCESSES. The olfactory nerve fibers leave the sensory cells and ascend through tiny openings in the base of the skull and very soon reach the *olfactory bulb*. (See Fig. 73.) Here the arrangements of interconnections among the fibers is varied and complex, but two interesting characteristics should be noted. (1) There are many opportunities provided for interaction among the different fibers. The fact that interaction may occur so early and so extensively may help to explain why psychologists have never had much success in their attempt to construct a "smell prism" (see p. 69). (2) Circuitous pathways are provided, so that a kind of reverberating circuit can be established. That is, a neural impulse coming from an olfactory cell reaches the olfactory bulb, where it stimulates a fiber that carries the signal to the brain; *at the same*

time it sends back a signal via a shunt-line fiber, to some of the preceding cells at an earlier relay station (called "glomerulus"). These cells can then send a second signal on through the olfactory bulb to the brain. Thus *one* stimulation of the olfactory cell can send several signals to the brain; and this may account, in part, for the extreme sensitivity of the nose even to very weak stimuli.

The neural impulses travel into the brain from the olfactory bulb in bundles of fibers known as the *olfactory tracts* (see Figs. 61 and 73). Once they enter the brain the locations of subsequent pathways are so complex and little understood that no attempt will be made here to describe them. Even the location of the olfactory sensory area in the cortex is not completely certain.

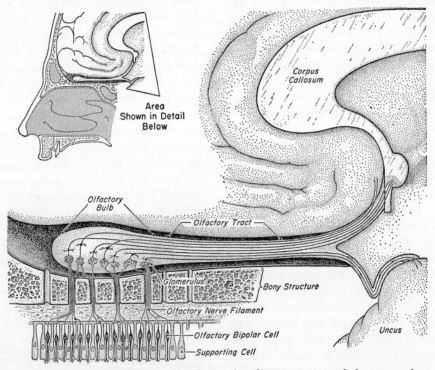

FIG. 73. The receptors for smell. For details of the operation of the olfactory receptor, see the text. Note specially the following structures: the *olfactory bipolar cells* (sensory cells for olfaction), the *olfactory bulb*, the *glomeruli*, the *olfactory tract*, and the *uncus*, the part of the brain which receives many of the fibers from the olfactory tract. See Fig. 61 to help you localize the position of the olfactory bulb in relation to the rest of the brain.

Perception of Our Bodies in Space

We can all perceive the position of our own bodies in space. Although we may err in varying degrees under various circumstances, in general we know whether our bodies are bent, upright, moving, or stationary; we also perceive whether our muscles are relaxed or taut.

The perception of body position and body movement is made possible by two anatomically separate but highly co-ordinated physiological mechanisms, the *kinesthetic* sensory system and the *vestibular system* of the inner ear.

The Kinesthetic System. The receptors for kinesthesis are specialized sensory cells that are found in muscles, tendons, and joints. It is their neural impulses that make possible our perception of the movements of our limbs, and of the contraction and relaxation of our muscles.

RECEPTORS, CONDUCTORS, AND CENTRAL MECHANISM. The kinesthetic receptors are usually found in the form of "spindles." A spindle consists of one or more muscle (or tendon) fibers, each of which is supplied with a large sensory fiber (which carries impulses to the brain) and a small motor fiber (which brings impulses *from* the brain). All of these are enclosed in a tissue capsule and the entire spindle is surrounded by fluid as it lies in the muscle, tendon, or joint. (See Fig. 74.)

The sensory fibers of the spindle vary in the structure of their endings; some coil around the muscle fibers, whereas some have spraylike endings. It has been assumed that these different endings pick up different kinds of stimulation. Some spindles send impulses only when the muscle is lengthened as a result of relaxation, and some only when it is in tension as a result of contraction.

The kinesthetic nerve fibers travel from the spindle cells into the spinal cord where they make connections for various important reflexes. They then ascend the spinal cord, following pathways adjacent to those of the skin senses (see p. 189), and then go into the cerebrum and cerebellum, where they end in the cortex of each. (See Fig. 74.)

The Semicircular Canals. The inner ear, it will be remembered, contains the *vestibular apparatus,* which has little to do with hearing but much to do with our sense of balance or equilibrium. The vestibular apparatus of each inner ear consists of three small liquid-filled canals, each of which is in the form of a half circle. Within each canal are found various sensory cells, each equipped with a hair tuft, which respond to the wave motions of the fluid in the canals. (See Fig. 75.)

The vestibular nerve, which carries the impulses from the sensory cells of the vestibular apparatus, enters the brain stem next to the auditory nerve. In the brain stem the nerve fibers seem to end in masses of gray matter (called the *vestibular nuclei*) within the reticular formation. From here messages are relayed to muscles of the eye, to the viscera, and to the cerebellum. Although impulses also reach the cerebral cortex, the direct pathway is unknown.

The familiar symptoms of seasickness seem to be caused by overstimulation of the vestibular system which, it has just been pointed out, relays messages to the viscera. Rapid or prolonged rotation or other movements may produce dizziness, nausea, and vomiting. Much the same pattern of symptoms may also be produced by various diseases that overstimulate the vestibular system. Thus an inflammation that affects the vestibular system of one side and results in constant stimulation on that side may result in dizziness or nausea.

The kinesthetic and vestibular systems, so highly co-ordinated, make possible not only specific perceptions of muscle or head movements, but contribute to the over-all general perception of our own bodies. The perception of specific muscle movements is extremely important in skilled performances, as we shall see in Chapter 16. The general perception of our body, as being graceful or awkward, relaxed or tense, helps

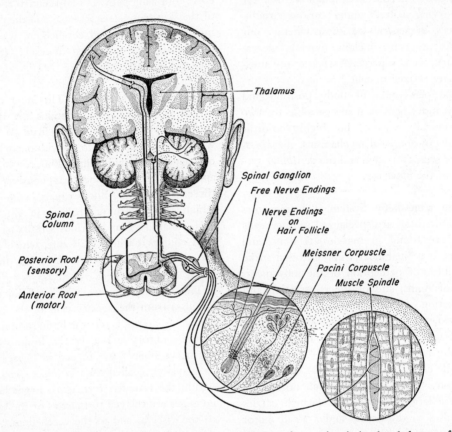

Thalamus

Spinal Ganglion
Free Nerve Endings

Nerve Endings
on
Hair Follicle

Meissner Corpuscle
Pacini Corpuscle
Muscle Spindle

Spinal
Column

Posterior Root
(sensory)

Anterior Root
(motor)

FIG. 74. Here we have a diagrammatic representation of the receptors, conduction pathways, and central mechanisms for kinesthetic perception and the perception of touch, pressure, temperature, and pain. Note that the nerve fibers from the various skin and muscle receptors enter the spinal cord through the *posterior root*, where their cell bodies are located in the *spinal ganglion*. From there they enter the spinal column itself, some making a connection with fibers that cross over immediately to the other side of the spinal cord, while the rest ascend the spinal cord on the same side. In the brain stem, those fibers that have remained on the same side send off some branches to the cerebellum, and the rest of the fibers cross over to the other side. Another important relay station is in the thalamus of the opposite side, where all the fibers coming from the skin senses make their last connection before ending up in the cerebral cortex. The net result is that the skin receptors of one side of the body are represented in the cerebellum of the same side and in the cerebral cortex of the opposite side.

The *anterior root* of the spinal cord is the pathway through which the motor fibers (not shown in this diagram) make their exit from the spinal cord to the muscles of the body. These motor fibers originate in the brain, travel down the spinal cord, leave the spinal cord (at various levels) through the anterior roots, and go on to stimulate and set into action the different muscles of the body.

to determine our own body percept, which we will discuss in the next chapter.

The Skin Senses

The sensations of touch, temperature, pressure, and pain are thought of as origi-nating from receptors in the skin, and are therefore called the cutaneous (skin) sensations. These cutaneous sensations, together with the proprioceptive sensations described in the previous section, are sometimes combined under the term somesthetic (body) sensations.

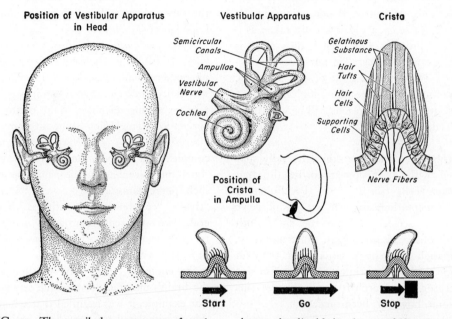

FIG. 75. The vestibular apparatus of each inner ear consists of three small liquid-filled *semicircular canals*. These three canals correspond to the three planes of the space in which we move about: up-down, forward-backward, right-left. The base of each canal is enlarged into an *ampulla*. Each ampulla has within it the *crista*. The crista contains the *hair cells*. These hair cells lie between the supporting cells and bear on their free ends long *hair tufts* embedded in a gelatinous substance. The fluid in the canal, when it is moved, bends the gelatinous substance and the hair tufts. The bending of the hair tufts stimulates the hair cells, which then send neural impulses through their nerve fibers to the brain and to the stomach—which is also supplied by the vestibular nerve.

At the bottom of the figure is a representation of activity in the crista during various head movements. When the head starts moving or turning, the liquid at first lags behind, bending the hair tufts in the *opposite* direction. This is similar to your being thrown *back* when the automobile you are riding in suddenly starts *forward*.) As the movement of the head con-tinues, the liquid in the canal "catches up" with the movement of the head and the hair tufts become erect again. As long as the head is moving in a constant direction and at a constant speed, the hair tufts will remain erect. (This is similar to the way you remain seated erect as long as the automobile is traveling smoothly, without jerks and without turning.) When the head movement *stops*, the inertia of the liquid carries it forward and the hair tufts are again bent, this time in the *forward* direction. It is for these reasons that we get neural impulses from the vestibular apparatus only when the motion of the head is changed, i.e., starts, turns, suddenly increases or decreases in speed, and stops. As long as we are moving at a constant rate, the brain receives no impulses from the vestibular apparatus. Frequent stops and starts or changes in direction or speed of movement (as in a "bumpy" airplane or a rocking boat) will repeatedly deform the hair tufts, stimulate the hair cells, and send a series of impulses to the brain and viscera. This may result in "seasickness"—dizziness, nausea, vomiting.

From a biological point of view these sensations of warmth and cold, touch, pressure, and pain are critically important to us. However when we come to a discussion of the physiological bases of these cutaneous perceptions, we find ourselves in the peculiar position of seeming to know much less today than we did ten or fifteen years ago. This, of course, is not unique in the history of science and is usually taken as a sign of progress. For what it does mean is that we have at least rid ourselves of misconceptions. In the light of this situation, our discussion of the physiological bases of the cutaneous perceptions will be very brief indeed.

The Receptors. The skin is liberally supplied with what appear to be different sensory cells (see Fig. 74). Psychological experiments indicate that we can perceive different sensations from the skin. Both these observations suggest, quite naturally, that each different sensation from the skin is initiated by the stimulation of a different receptor. The search for such relationships has not, however, been successful.

"BASIC" SENSATIONS AND "BASIC" RECEPTORS. A few years ago it was more or less generally accepted that the "hair bulbs" and Meissner corpuscles were responsible for the sensation of light touch, the "free nerve endings" for pain, and the Pucinian corpuscles for deep touch or pressure, and various types were nominated at one time or another for the sensations of warmth and cold.

As research continued, as new and more refined neurological and electrophysiological methods were brought into use, one by one these receptor organs seemed to lose their assigned specificity. Most recent research even seems to suggest that the purely *anatomical* differences among the various types of cutaneous sensory nerves are not as profound as was once thought. Al-

though many textbooks in psychology and physiology still teach the doctrine of specificity among the nerve endings in the skin, many experimentalists today are unwilling to ascribe *any* specificity to any one type of sensory cell in the skin. The two nerve endings that seem to be holding on longest to the claim of specificity in function are the "free nerve endings" for pain and the Pucinian corpuscles for pressure.

"COMPLEX" SKIN PERCEPTIONS AND RECEPTORS. There is a whole set of perceptual phenomena which has always bedeviled the specificity doctrine, even when it was most popular among scientists. Many of the skin perceptions (including some of the most interesting ones) are very much more complex than the sensations of cold, warmth, touch, pressure, and simple pain. These are such perceptions as "wetness," "oiliness," "tickle," "roughness," "smoothness." In general, two different approaches were attempted in dealing with these perceptions. (1) The assumption was made that the more complex perceptions resulted from the brain's integration of simple sensations. For example, it was assumed that when the skin is stimulated by water, the brain first responds with separate and independent sensations of cold and touch, and then, as a *next* step, the brain adds these sensations together and arrives at the perception of wetness. However this hypothesis was never given sufficiently valid experimental support to make it stick. (2) Some theorists have even suggested that there are specialized receptor organs for each of these complex perceptions—a "tickle receptor," a "wetness receptor," etc. But here again, no experimental data could be found to support the hypothesis.

ONE CURRENT VIEW. Recent detailed microscopic work has suggested, as has already been indicated, that the various sensory cells in the skin cannot be safely classified into basically different structures.

However these sensory cells can be safely classified into different categories on the basis of the distance they lie from the surface of the skin, and on the basis of the specific skin areas in which they are found (lips, finger tips, hairy skin, etc.). Furthermore, several experimenters have shown that when heat is applied to the hairy surface of the skin, a whole range of perceptions can be evoked which merge into each other almost imperceptibly—warmth, itch, prick, sting, and pain.

All of this has suggested the view that the different sensations or perceptions are determined by the *pattern of stimulation* of the skin sense organs. Thus, the same kind of skin receptor will evoke two different sensations, depending on whether it is found in the finger tip or in the lip; or a deep-lying free nerve ending will evoke different sensations from a superficially lying free nerve ending; or the stimulation of several hair cells simultaneously will evoke a different sensation from the stimulation of these hair cells one after another.

Conductors and Central Mechanisms. The fibers from the various skin receptors travel to the brain along much the same path that the kinesthetic fibers use. They both enter the spinal column, both show almost complete crossing over, both make important junctions with other fibers in the thalamus, and both end up in approximately the same area of the cortex. (See Fig. 74.)

Experiments and clinical observations clearly show that when the fibers from the skin receptors are cut (either deliberately or by accident), sensations from areas of the skin served by those fibers disappear; we can no longer feel touch, heat, pain, tickle, or wetness. This not only confirms the theory that the skin receptors we have been discussing are responsible for cutaneous perception; it also has important medical uses. Occasionally there occur severe cases of intractable pain (in some of the advanced cases of cancer, or in severe injuries) that cannot be alleviated by the usual methods. In such instances the surgeon will deliberately cut the skin fibers to the brain. Pain will then immediately disappear, but so also will many of the other skin sensations.

In general, then, it appears that the cutaneous perceptions are served by the same kind of physiological mechanisms which lie at the base of our other perceptions. While the more recent, nonspecificity hypothesis discussed above may be vague and may lack the clarity of the older specificity theory, several points should be remembered by the reader. (1) Both hypotheses depend upon the same specialized group of receptor cells (one merely makes finer distinctions than the other within this group); and (2) both hypotheses depend upon a specialized conduction pathway. In these respects, then, both hypotheses fit the general pattern of the physiological mechanisms of perception which have been described in this chapter. In addition it should be pointed out that this newest proposal, emphasizing *pattern of stimulation,* is consistent with many of the things we know about the structure and functioning of the nervous system and with many of the things we know about the relations between stimulus-patterns and response in perception.

Neural Basis of Sense Qualities

We started our discussion of perception in Chapter 2 by pointing to the many different sensory qualities we experience—visual, auditory, olfactory, gustatory, cutaneous, etc. We now face the question of the neural basis for these *qualitative* differences in our experience. How can the brain tell the difference between, say, a light and a sound on the basis of the neural impulses it receives? .

The "Specific Sense Energy" Doctrine. One of the early attempts to answer this question was formulated by the German physiologist, Johannes Müller, in about 1825 and has come to be known as the doctrine of "specific sense energies." According to a common interpretation of this position, the differences in qualities of perception are determined by the receptors from which the neural impulses *originate.* For example, *any* impulse originating in the retina, whether as a result of electrical stimulation, slow pressure, or light waves, will give us the sensation of light.

There is one major difficulty with this position. As far as we know, neural impulses are alike, no matter from what receptors they originate. A nerve impulse started by a beam of green light is physi-

cally and chemically indistinguishable from one started by a piece of sugar on the tongue, by the notes of Beethoven's Fifth Symphony as they reach our ears, or by a bug crawling down one's neck. The question remains: How do we distinguish these *qualitatively different experiences* if they depend upon *qualitatively identical physical chemical events?*

The "Localization" Answer. A more recent attempt to deal with this problem is in terms of the brain areas in which the neural impulses *end.* As we have seen, the neural impulses from any one receptor (the retina, the cochlea, the skin) have fairly specific "reception centers" or terminal areas in the cortex. Figure 76 depicts the sensory reception areas that can be seen from a top view of the brain. The localization answer would then be that when the auditory sensory area of the brain is thrown

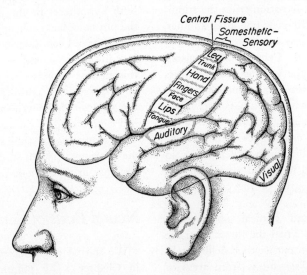

FIG. 76. Sensory representation on the cortex. When looking down on the cortex, three major sensory areas can be distinguished. These are the areas where the nerve fibers from the various sense organs from the body terminate in the cortex. The three areas are the visual area, the auditory area, and the somesthetic-sensory area. The latter lies directly behind the central fissure. Note that the hand and fingers as well as the face-lips-tongue parts occupy the major portion of this area.

This figure, showing the *terminal areas* of the sensory routes, should be studied in conjunction with Fig. 61 showing the sensory routes as they *enter* the brain. The leg and trunk areas have relatively little representation in the cortex.

into action, we experience sound; when the visual area is activated, we experience vision. And it does not matter how these areas have been activated. For example, we have seen (Box 46) that stimulation of the occipital areas by an electrical current applied directly to the brain will result in the sensation of light.

The localization hypothesis is adhered to by most workers in the field. However the complexity of the problem is indicated by some of the other data we have examined.

In some instances the *pattern* of stimulation seems to be more important than the specific sense organ or cortical area stimulated. The same "hot spot" can give rise to a sensation of heat or of cold.

In any event, the fact that the nerve impulses are electrochemical events having the same physical character in all nerve cells, despite the differences in sense qualities they evoke, presents psychologists, physiologists, and philosophers alike with a fundamental problem.

Glossary

ablation technique. A research technique used in neurology and physiological psychology. Different parts of the sensory receptors, neural conduction system, or the brain are destroyed, and observations are then made on the behavior of the animal.

all-or-none law. A term referring to the fact that every neural cell fires with its maximum intensity. Any single burst of a neural cell is fired at maximum intensity no matter how intense may be the stimulus that initiates the firing.

ampulla. The enlarged base of the semicircular canal in the vestibular apparatus. There are three ampullas corresponding to the three semicircular canals. Each ampulla has within it the crista.

anterior root of spinal cord. Carries the *motor* fibers from the spinal cord out to the various muscles of the body. Sometimes called the motor root of the spinal cord.

auditory cortex. The area of the cortex which receives impulses from the ear via the auditory tract. Lies just below the lateral fissure. Only a small part of this area can be seen from the surface of the brain.

auditory (acoustic, cochlear) nerve. A bundle of about 30,000 separate nerve fibers stemming from the hair cells in the cochlear duct. This bundle leaves the internal ear, enters the lower brain stem, and finds its first relay station in the cochlear nuclei.

auricle. The projecting, external part of the outer ear. Sometimes called the *pinna*.

basilar membrane. A membrane in the cochlear duct upon which rest the hair cells.

binaural interaction. Referring to the effects of the neural influences coming from the fiber of one ear upon the neural activity in the fiber coming from the other ear.

bipolar cell. A neural element that carries impulses from rods and cones to the ganglion cells. Two types of bipolar cells are differentiated in the visual system: *Midget* bipolars, which are supplied by single cones; and *Mop* bipolars, which make connections with several rods and cones.

brain stem. The lowest part of the brain, continuous with the spinal cord. The brain stem is, however, quite different from the spinal cord. Most of the cranial nerves arise or end in the brain stem. The cerebellum has many connections there. The reticular formation is formed there. Some of the vital functions (breathing, etc.) are controlled through centers of the brain stem.

central fissure. One of the major depressions on the dorsal surface of the brain. The portion of the brain in front of the central fissure is called the frontal lobe.

The area behind the central fissure and above the lateral fissure is called the parietal lobe. The strip of cortex directly behind the central fissure is the somesthetic-sensory area of the cortex.

central mechanism. A general term referring to the various anatomical and physiological mechanisms of the entire brain. This includes the brain stem, the other subcortical structures, and the cortex.

cerebellum. The "little brain," just behind the lower portions of the cerebral hemispheres and separated from them by a fissure. It is divided into hemispheres. The cerebellum is connected with the spinal cord, brain stem, and cerebral hemispheres. Like the cerebral hemispheres, the cerebellum has a cortex of gray matter and an interior of both white and gray matter. The cerebellum plays a very important role in the co-ordination of muscular activity.

cerebral hemispheres. The two symmetrical halves of the cerebrum. The two halves are partially separated by a deep fissure at the mid-line. They are united by bands of nerves crossing from one side to the other. The most prominent of these bands is the corpus callosum.

cerebrum. The brain as a whole can be divided into three major parts: the cerebrum, the cerebellum, and the brain stem. The cerebrum is the largest of the three and consists of the hemispheres making up the anterior and upper part of the brain.

ciliary muscles. These muscles are attached to the lens of the eye, and their contraction and relaxation produce changes in the curvature of the lens.

cochlea. A coiled, divided, fluid-filled tube containing the sensory elements involved in hearing. One end of the cochlea is closed off by the third ossicle at the cochlea's oval window; the other end, by a thin membrane at the cochlea's round window.

cochlear canal (or duct). The partition structure dividing the cochlea into two major channels. It is filled with a jellylike fluid and contains the hair cells, the sensory elements whereby the wave motion of the cochlear fluids is converted into neural impulses.

cochlear nuclei. The first relay or synapse centers on the route of the auditory nerve from the inner ear to the cortex. Located in brain stem.

conduction mechanism. A general term referring to the various anatomical and physiological mechanisms involved in conducting neural impulses from receptor organs to the cortex.

cones. Specialized cone-shaped cells in the retina. These cells are sensitive to light waves and initiate a neural impulse when light waves impinge upon them. Cones are specially sensitive to differences in light-wave *length*. Stimulation of cones gives rise to the experience of hue.

cornea. A clear and transparent area of the sclera making up the frontal surface of the eyeball.

corpus callosum. A great band of fibers connecting the cerebral hemispheres.

cortex. Anatomically, the word "cortex" refers to the outer part of an organ. Thus we have the cerebral cortex, a large mass of cell bodies (gray matter) lying in folds as a thick outer part of the cerebrum. Similarly, we have the cerebellar cortex, consisting of a gray-matter covering of the cerebellum.

cranial nerves. The nerves carrying neural impulses to and from the eyes, nose, tongue, ears, face, and vestibular apparatus. The cranial nerves enter the brain stem directly without going through the spinal cord.

crista. The structure within the ampulla of the vestibular apparatus, containing the vestibular hair cells.

crystalline lens. A transparent structure of the eye shaped somewhat like a convex lens and capable of change in shape by the stretching action of the ciliary muscles. The lens focuses light waves from the outside onto the retina. The lens itself is held in place through attachment to the ciliary processes.

cutaneous sensations. The skin sensations: touch, pain, warmth, cold, superficial pressure.

duplicity theory. The theory that rods and cones differ in function: the rods being primarily sensitive to intensity of light waves and the cones to differences in wave length. Thus the rods help us discriminate brightness differences; the cones, hue differences.

ear canal. The opening from the outer ear to the eardrum. Conducts sound waves from the outside to the middle ear.

eardrum. A thin membrane separating the ear canal from the middle ear. Sound waves striking the eardrum cause it to vibrate.

electrophysiological technique. Used in neurology and physiological psychology. Based on two observations: (1) When a nerve fiber is in action, electrical changes occur in or around the fiber. By measuring these electrical changes with appropriate instruments, therefore, we can learn much about neural action. (2) Stimulation of a nerve cell by an electrical current applied to that cell or group of cells can initiate neural impulses. Corresponding to these observations the electrophysiological technique can be divided into two types: (1) Parts of the nervous system are stimulated (in various ways) and observations are made of the resulting electrical responses in the brain. (2) Specific areas of the brain are stimulated with a mild electrical current and observations are made of the resulting experience or behavior.

eustachian tube. A cavity connecting the middle ear with the pharynx. The eustachian tube is usually closed at the pharynx end, but it opens when we swallow or yawn. In this way the pressure in the middle ear is equalized with the atmospheric pressure on the outside.

extrinsic muscles. Muscles attached to the outside of each eyeball permitting controlled rotation of the eyeball in its socket.

fovea. A central part of the retina consisting of very thin and closely packed cones. Each cone in the fovea has its own midget bipolar cell. There are no rods in the fovea. Because of its composition the fovea is the area of the retina capable of greatest visual acuity and most efficient in hue discrimination.

free nerve endings. Endings of nerve fibers in the skin, unassociated with any coverings of connective tissue. Assumed to be responsible for sensations of pain.

ganglion cell. A neural cell receiving impulses from rods and cones via an intervening bipolar cell and transmitting these impulses to the brain.

geniculate bodies. Mass of brain cells serving as relay stations for the optic nerve. The fibers from the ganglion cells at the retina connect at the geniculate bodies with a new set of neurons. Some of these neurons then lead to the cerebral cortex, and some to the reticular formation.

glomerulus. A relay station in the olfactory bulb where nerve fibers from the olfactory cells make synapses with fibers in the olfactory bulb.

hair bulbs. Receptor organs in the skin consisting of nerve endings wound around the roots of hair. Assumed to be partially responsible for sensations of light touch.

hair cells (auditory). The sensory cells of audition. These cells convert the wave motion of the cochlear fluids into neural impulses. The hair cells are found in the cochlear duct and rest upon the basilar membrane.

inner ear. The innermost section of the hearing apparatus. It consists of two parts: the vestibular apparatus and the cochlea.

iris. A delicate, colored, fibrous structure that lies on the lens and has a circular opening (the pupil) in its center. The actions of the muscles of the iris can increase or decrease the size of the central opening.

lateral fissure. A deep depression on the side surface of the cerebrum. The area of the cerebrum below the lateral fissure is called the temporal lobe. The area above the lateral fissure is called the parietal lobe.

Meissner corpuscle. Receptor organs in the skin lying fairly close to the surface and assumed to be responsible for the sensation of light touch. Named after the German histologist, George Meissner.

midbrain. The upper part of the brain stem.

middle ear. A cavity between the outer and inner ear. Contains the three ossicles. The middle-ear cavity opens into the eustachian tube.

motor fibers. Fibers carrying neural impulses from the brain to the muscles of the body.

nerve deafness. Deafness resulting from injury to the cochlea or auditory nerve. Most elderly people suffer from some degree of nerve deafness. If the auditory nerve is completely destroyed, no hearing aid can help.

occipital lobes. The sensory areas of the cortex where fibers from the geniculate bodies terminate. These areas, because they are the primary receptor areas for impulses from the eyes, are called the visual projection areas or the visual-sensory areas of the cortex.

olfactory bipolar cells. The sensory cell for olfaction. These are fairly long, columnar-shaped cells from one end of which delicate hairs project into the fluid covering of the mucuous membrane, and from the other end protrude long fibers making up the olfactory nerve. When particles of gas, dissolved by the mucuos of the nose, reach these cells, neural impulses are initiated.

olfactory bulb. A mass of cells and fibers resting on the base of the skull and into which the olfactory nerve fibers enter. Here the fibers connect with other fibers that form the olfactory tract into the brain.

olfactory tract. Bundles of fibers going from the olfactory bulb into the brain and terminating at the uncus.

olivary complex. The second relay or synapse center on the route of the auditory nerve from the inner ear to the cortex. Located in the brain stem.

optic chiasma. The meeting place of the optic nerves from the two eyes. Located at the base of the brain. At the optic chiasma the crossing over of the optic nerves takes place.

optic nerve; optic tract. A bundle of nerve fibers of the ganglion cells carrying neural impulses from the rods and cones to the brain. This bundle leaves the retina through an opening in the eyeball called the blind spot. The portion of this conduction pathway lying between the retina and the optic chiasma is called the optic nerve; beyond the optic chiasma it is called the optic tract.

optical mechanism. A general term referring to the various anatomical and physiological mechanisms involved in conducting light waves from the outside world and focusing them on the retina. Specifically, the structures and function of the cornea, lens, ciliary muscles, iris, extrinsic muscles.

oscilloscope. An instrument that converts electrical currents into visible wavelike patterns. This permits us to see and photograph changes in electrical activity. When used with an amplifier, very weak electrical currents can be detected and photographed for study. Used extensively in electrophysiological studies.

ossicles. The three bones forming a chain from the ear drum to the oval window of the cochlea. They transmit vibrations of the ear drum to the fluid in the cochlea.

outer ear. The outermost and only visible part of the hearing apparatus. Includes the auricles and the ear canals.

oval window. An opening in the cochlea into which is fitted the last of the three bones leading from the ear drum. It is the vibration of this ossicle in the oval window which sets the fluid in the cochlea into wavelike motion.

phonosensitive mechanism. A general term referring to the various anatomical and physiological mechanisms involved in the initiation of neural impulses in the inner ear. Specifically, the operation of the hair cells in the cochlear canal and the function of the basilar membrane.

photosensitive mechanism. A general term referring to the various anatomical and physiological mechanisms involved in the conversion of light waves into neural activity. Specifically, this term refers to the nature, distribution, and functions of the rods and cones.

polychromatic theory. A theory designed to give a physiological basis for color vision, laws of color mixing, color blindness, etc. According to this theory there are approximately seven groups of cones in the retina, each group especially sensitive to a somewhat restricted band of frequencies of light waves.

posterior root of spinal cord. Carries the sensory fibers from the various receptors into the spinal cord. Sometimes called the sensory root of the spinal cord.

Pucinian corpuscles. Receptor organs lying deep in the skin, consisting of nerve endings surrounded by layers of connective tissue. Assumed to be responsible for sensations of deep touch or pressure. Named after the Italian anatomist, Filippo Pacini, who is known for his studies of peripheral receptors.

pupil. The circular opening in the center of the iris. The pupil is not a structure. It is the "hole" in the "doughnut."

reticular formation. A network of neurons in the brain stem divided into an ascending and descending column. The ascending column receives impulses from many receptors and sends them up to the cortex in a diffuse discharge. The descending column receives impulses from the cortex, including impulses from the sensory areas.

retina. A layer of light-sensitive elements (rods and cones) and nerve fibers. It lines the inner wall of the large chamber of the eyeball.

rods. Specialized rodlike cells in the retina. These cells are sensitive to light waves and initiate a neural impulse when light waves impinge upon them. Rods are primarily responsive to changes in the intensity of light waves. Stimulation of the rods gives rise to the experience of brightness but not of hue.

round window. An opening in the cochlea across which is stretched a thin membrane. As the pressure on the cochlear fluid (coming from vibrations at the oval window) eventually is brought to bear on this membrane, the membrane bulges in and out, permitting the fluid in the cochlea to express itself as wave motion.

sclera. A white opaque skin enveloping the eyeball. The frontal surface of the sclera becomes clear and transparent and is known as the *cornea*.

semicircular canals. Three small liquid-filled canals in the vestibular apparatus. Each of these canals is in the shape of a semicircle and is oriented in a different plane in space: up-down, left-right, forward-backward. The semicircular canals contain sensitive hair cells in a structure known as the crista.

sensory area of cortex. Any area in the cortex, such as the occipital lobes, which is a major reception area for neural impulses from a sensory receptor.

sensory fibers. Fibers that carry neural impulses *from* sense organs.

somesthetic. Pertaining to the soma or body, hence somesthetic sensations refer to skin and muscular sensations; somesthetic nerves refer to the fibers carrying neural impulses from the skin receptors and the muscle and tendon spindles to the brain. Somesthetic-sensory cortical area refers to the area of the cortex where the impulses from the somesthetic sense organs terminate. This area lies directly behind the central fissure on the surface of the brain.

specific sense energies. The name given to the theory, first formulated by Johannes Müller in about 1825, that the differences in qualities of perception are determined by the *receptors* from which the neural impulses originate. For example, *any* impulse originating in the retina, whether as a result of electrical stimulation, pressure, or light waves, will give the sensation of light.

spinal column. The part of the nervous system encased in the backbone. It serves as a pathway for the conduction of somesthetic-sensory impulses to the brain and motor impulses from the brain to the muscles.

spinal ganglion. The nerve fibers from the various skin and muscle receptors have their cell bodies in the posterior root of the spinal cord. The collection of these cell bodies makes a bulge in the posterior root and this collection is called the spinal ganglion.

spindles. Structures found in muscles and tendons. Consist of one or more muscle fibers (or tendon fibers), supplied with a large sensory fiber and a small motor fiber. The whole is enclosed in a tissue capsule and surrounded by fluid. Stimulation of this spindle initiates impulses to the brain, and makes possible our perception of muscle stress and movement.

supporting cells. Cells found in many receptor organs (nose, ear, taste buds) whose major function seems to be structural. They are not sensitive to the various stimuli but merely help support the structure.

taste buds. The receptors for taste, mostly concentrated in the tongue. A taste bud consists of taste-sensitive cells and supporting cells, arranged in a bud shape and having an opening to the mucous fluid on the tongue. The opening is referred to as a taste pore.

taste nerves. The nerves conducting neural impulses from the taste buds to the brain. The endings of the taste nerve are wound around each of the taste-sensitive cells in the taste bud. The taste nerves do not travel to the brain in a single fiber bundle, but divide up into several bundles and travel along in company with fibers from various skin sensory nerves.

tectorial membrane. A mass of gelatinous matter resting above the tufts of the hair cells in the cochlear duct. Important in helping convert the wave motion of the cochlear fluid into neural impulses. When the hair cells are pushed against the tectorial membrane, the hair cells are temporarily squeezed out of shape. This deformation stimulates the nerve fibers in the hair cells and a neural impulse is initiated.

thalamus. An area in the brain, lying beneath the corpus callosum. It forms an important station in the relaying of impulses from the sense organs of the body and from the cerebellum to the cerebral cortex.

tinnitus. The condition of hearing a ringing in the ears when there is no outside source for such sounds.

transmission deafness. Deafness due to the interference of the movements of the eardrum or of the ossicles. In these cases partial hearing may be restored through the transmission of vibrations by the skull. Many hearing aids work on this principle.

triple-receptor theory. A theory designed to give a physiological basis for color vision, laws of color mixing, color blindness, etc. According to this theory there are three specialized types of cones. Some cones are assumed to respond only to red, some only to green, and some only to blue.

uncus. The part of the brain which receives the impulses from the olfactory sense organs via the olfactory tract. This area lies at the base of the brain near the optic chiasma.

ventrical (in brain). A cavity in the brain continuous with the central canal in the spinal cord. Normally the brain ventricals are filled with spinal fluid.

vestibular. Referring to that part of the inner ear involved in our sense of balance or equilibrium. Hence "vestibular apparatus" refers to the semicircular canals and their allied structure; "vestibular nerve" refers to the fibers that carry the impulses from the sensory cells in the semicircular canals to the brain; "vestibular nuclei" refers to the masses of gray matter in the brain stem where the vestibular nerve ends.

vestibular hair cells. The sensory cells of the vestibular apparatus. Each hair cell bears on its free end a long hair tuft that is embedded in the gelatinous substance of the crista. When the gelatinous substance is displaced by action of the fluids in the semicircular canals, the hair tufts are bent, and this stimulates the hair cells, which then send neural impulses through their nerve fibers to the brain and viscera. The hair cells are bent only when there is a *change* in the movement of the head.

visual purple. A chemical found in the rods which decomposes when light waves impinge upon the rod. The decomposition of this chemical is assumed to initiate nerve currents in the rods.

Suggestions for Further Reading

GARDNER, E. 1952. *Fundamentals of neurology* (rev. ed.). Philadelphia: Saunders.

A presentation of the basic principles of the nervous system with emphasis upon the human being. Clearly written and well illustrated. The following chapters of Gardner's book may prove of special help in supplementing our present chapter: 7, 9, 11, 12, 18.

MORGAN, C. T., and STELLAR, E. 1950. *Physiological psychology*. New York: McGraw-Hill.

An introductory textbook, simply written.

PENFIELD, W., and RASMUSSEN, T. 1950. *The cerebral cortex of man.* New York: Macmillan.

One of the world's most eminent brain surgeons, together with his colleague, describes results of electrical stimulation of the human cerebral cortex in conscious subjects. Most of the observations were done on epileptic patients who required brain surgery. Many extremely interesting case histories are presented.

STEVENS, S. S. (ed.) 1951. *Handbook of experimental psychology*. New York: Wiley.

A standard reference book for psychologists. Not easy reading, but valuable for intensive study. Contains excellent summaries of the physiology of the nervous system. The book includes twelve chapters devoted to sensory mechanisms and sensory processes, each written by an authority in the field.

Part Two

MOTIVATION AND EMOTION

CHAPTER VIII

The Self

"ALL the world's a stage," and the descriptive accounts of our worlds of experience up to this point have concentrated mainly on the scenery, leaving out the central character, the *self*. The person says, "I see, I feel, I want"; and he says, "The sound strikes me, people look at me."

We turn now to a study of this principal actor, the self. By calling it the "actor," we stress its most important feature, namely that it *acts*. It is the self that is seen as seeking goals, avoiding dangers, doing things to the environment. The perception of the self in action is basic to an understanding of the problems of motivation and emotion with which this Part is concerned.

Plan of Part II. In this chapter we shall examine the nature of the self, the "lifespace" of the self, and the motivated states of the self in the immediate situation. The following chapter extends the discussion of the self to emotional experiences.

Having laid the groundwork for the analysis of motivation by this description of the *experiencing* of self in action, we shall take up the problem of motivated *behavior* in the three remaining chapters. Chapter 10 reviews different conceptions of human motivation and describes the varieties of motives. Chapter 11 explores the dynamics of motivated behavior and the frustration of motives. Finally, Chapter 12 examines the underlying physiology and neurology of motivational and emotional processes.

The Self. The self is the "I" or the "me" of which the person is aware in his thoughts, feelings, and actions. However the self is not a perception alone, nor a general feeling, nor a "pure" thought. It is all of these simultaneously. It is, to coin an inelegant term, a "perfink," that is, an integrated process involving *per*ceiving, *f*eeling, and th*ink*ing. It is no different in principle from other complex entities existing in our experience. These, too, are the organized products of complex patterns of percepts, feelings, thoughts.

But the self is vastly more complex than any other entity we experience, and generally the most important, though we shall see that its significance varies markedly from situation to situation.

CHARACTERISTICS OF THE SELF. The self is perceived as constructed of interrelated parts; it has various properties, especially those pertaining to its relations with other objects and people. The way it is experienced at any given moment depends upon the specific situation. It may be the center of our attention or experienced only peripherally; it may be experienced in varying states of disruption and distress, and as having needs and desires, as feeling emotions, intentions, and obligations, as being involved in goal-seeking and other actions. And, paradoxically, it may be the object of the person's *own* scrutiny, evaluations, and attitudes. Indeed, one of man's unique distinctions, setting him off most sharply from other animals, may be just this extraordinary capacity *to look at himself.*

Like any other enduring entity in the person's world, the self has a natural history of development. It grows from primitive beginnings in infant consciousness, it develops gradually, it undergoes changes, some slight, some drastic; it may even disintegrate under stress. The story of *how* the self develops and *why* each person's self is unique will be taken up in Part IV.

SELF, EGO, PERSONALITY, ORGANISM. It may be helpful at this point to clarify the distinction between self, as we are defining it, and certain related concepts. The term *ego* has sometimes been used to refer to what we are calling "self," but we will reserve the term "ego" for the particular meaning given it in the psychoanalytical use by Freud (see p. 618).

Nor is self the same as *personality.* As we shall see in Chapter 23, the term "personality" properly refers to the *entire* psychological structure of the person—his abilities, traits, motives, habits, cognitions. *Everything* that a psychologist can say about

the individual defines the personality. Of the whole personality, the self is but one part, namely, that which the individual experiences as "self." And, as we shall see later, a critical concern of the personality psychologist is to determine just how the "self" part of the personality relates to the rest.

Finally, self must be distinguished from *organism.* The organism is what the scientist defines as a biological entity, objectively observable, and the subject of study by the physiologist, the geneticist, and the neurologist, as well as by the psychologist.

Perception of the Body. The most material and visible part of the self is one's physical *body*. Like any other object in the person's physical environment, his own body is perceived through the various senses. Being necessarily close to our eyes, parts of the body occupy large areas of our visual field. Sounds of our body functioning, lips smacking, stomach rumbling, hands clapping, are also nearby. We see and hear a lot of ourselves! We also smell ourselves, though not as fully as do others, owing to the advantages or disadvantages of fast odor adaptation. When we explore our surroundings with our hands, we often touch and feel parts of our own bodies. In a circumstantial way, so to speak, our bodies necessarily come to occupy a central role in our perceptions.

Body perception is so firmly established that even drastic changes in the body may not at once result in corresponding changes in body percept. A dramatic illustration of this is the "phantom limb" phenomenon (see Box 47).

THE BODY INSIDE. The body is not only perceived through external receptors—eyes, ears, nose, skin—but also through internal receptors, which provide unique information about the *inner* environment and functioning of the body. Some of these recep-

BOX 47

The Phantom Limb

After a person has suffered the amputation of an arm or a leg, he may continue to feel that the limb is there. He may feel itching in it; he may feel he can still move it, and even momentarily forget that it is gone and try to use it.

These experiences of "phantom limbs" are almost universal in cases of amputation. Sometimes they are of brief duration, and sometimes they endure throughout the rest of the person's life. They often undergo gradual change in their perceived character. For example, Katz has reported that a phantom hand may gradually shrink and move up into the stump so that finally it is experienced as a small hand embedded there. He has also observed that "If an amputee walks up to a wall, the phantom limb seems to go through it . . . the law of impermeability of matter does not seem to hold."

Simmel has studied phantoms in patients with leprosy, for whom parts of the body such as the fingers and toes gradually disappear through absorption. The loss is very gradual, often extending for ten years or more, and is generally painless. After interviewing 18 patients, she concluded that the mere loss of digits through absorption does not result in phantoms, but when there is amputation of the remnants of the fingers or toes following such gradual absorption, the phantoms do appear. The striking fact is that the phantoms do not reproduce merely the remnants that were surgically removed; *they are phantoms of the whole*

digits prior to the beginning of absorption.

The following is an excerpt from her records for one amputee: "When woke from anesthesia, tried to reach for foot. Phantom persists, patient still 'forgets,' steps on phantom and falls. Can wiggle phantom toes."

KATZ, D. 1950. *Gestalt psychology.* New York: Ronald Press.

SIMMEL, M. L. 1956. Phantoms in patients with leprosy and in elderly digital amputees. *Amer. J. Psychol., 69,* 529–45.

tors are distributed widely throughout the internal organs, for example in the stomach walls, and they provide a rich complex of sensations of pressure and tension, of ache and pain, of heat and cold. Others are embedded in the muscles, joints, and tendons, and provide the sensations of stress and strain from which perceptions of posture and movement are derived.

These various sensations arising from the internal receptors are not chaotic and unrelated. We do not merely sense pain; we perceive that we have a headache, or a sore thumb. We do not merely sense uncomfortable pressure; we perceive that we have an overfull bladder. We do not merely sense muscle strain; we perceive that our legs are moving, or that our necks are twisting. These body percepts are organized with others derived from our seeing, hearing, smelling, and touching the body, to form a total unified perception of the body. Our body perception is unique among all perceptions of physical objects in this one particular—the combination of impressions of both the inner and outer aspects of the object.

THE BODY AS OBJECT AND AS INSTRUMENT. The topic of body perception may be confusing because of a failure to distinguish between the body as an object perceived and the body as an instrument for perception. If we look at our feet, we perceive them as part of the body. The eyes, which are part of the physical body, are here serving as the instrument *for* the perception. In this case we do not perceive the eyes. The eyes, too, can in their turn be perceived as parts of the body, as when we look at them in the mirror or touch them with our fingers or feel the sensations of their rotation or their smarting. For proper psychological analysis, these two aspects— perceiving the body and perceiving with the body—must be kept separate.

PROPERTIES OF THE BODY-PERCEPT. As in the case of any kind of physical object, we perceive our own bodies as having certain sizes, shapes, textures, colors. We also perceive our bodies as having "structure," that is, as being made up of various parts and of various relationships among these parts. Our bodies are also endowed with important attributes of more complex kinds; a person may perceive his body as powerful or puny, as beautiful or ugly, as awkward or graceful. Moreover, there are power qualities in body perception. We perceive our bodies as affecting other things, or as having the power to do so. We perceive "causality" in the manner the body interacts with the environment.

The particular *way* the person perceives his physical body—whether distorted or not—may have important psychological consequences for him. An adolescent may

exaggerate the awkwardness of his movements and become unduly self-conscious; a woman may be overly sensitive about her weight and indulge in zealous reducing campaigns; a small boy may be deluded into perceiving himself as much taller than he really is; a person may develop a "narcissistic" love and admiration of his own body to the exclusion of more usual directions of love. It is clear that perception of the body relates intimately to perception of larger aspects of the *self*.

BODY AND SELF. The body is normally experienced as a part or aspect of the self, often constituting its outer boundary. But there are many situations in which body and self are not coextensive.

Many persons have had the experience of lying in bed just after awakening and seeing their feet "down there" as though they were external objects, not part of themselves. Even amputations of parts of the body may not be perceived as amputations of the self, although there are cases in which the loss of a highly prized part, such as the hands of a musician, may really be experienced as partial destruction of self.

Though we do not usually even think of the possibility that a person can experience physical pain as not *his*, there is ample evidence that this does happen under abnormal circumstances. In cases of hysteria, in hypnotic states, during prolonged torture, peculiar transformations of self-perception may occur. Among these may be the separation of pain from self. Somehow it is as though the pain were still there as part of a person's perception of the body, but it is not *his* pain, and hence seems more bearable.

When we ask a person to say just exactly *where* he feels the center of self to be, he almost invariably locates it somewhere inside his body. Most commonly he apprehends it as somewhere "in the head" or "in back of the eyes." Perhaps this is what we should expect in the light of the fact that we are basically "visual animals," having our most important commerce with the environment through our eyes. There is some indication that congenitally blind persons, in contrast, may feel their selves more centered in their fingers. However it is also likely that cultural factors play a large role. In some cultures the self may character-

istically be located in the chest region— "the heart is the seat of the soul."

Yet we also know that there is remarkable flexibility in the different mental *perspectives* that the person can assume in viewing the world. It is possible to "put oneself" in other places and other times. The same is true of our spatial perspective on our own physical bodies. As Box 48

BOX 48

The Self Inside or Outside?

An experimental demonstration of the fact that people can assume different perspectives for the self in relation to the body can be given in the following way. With his finger, the experimenter traces a symbol on the forehead of the subject, whose eyes are closed. He asks the subject to say what symbol was traced.

In one demonstration the experimenter traced a script capital ε (see fig. *a*). This symbol was deliberately chosen because its mirror image is a ɜ. Logically, then, it can be identified as an ε or a ɜ. What did the person report? If he "viewed" the symbol as though he were "looking out" at it from inside his head, he would have perceived

on his forehead from either the "inside" or the "outside" perspective. Thus if a series of numerals (not reversible) is first traced on the forehead so that the person comes to expect numerals, the ε is perceived as a ɜ.

It is also of interest to note that there are pronounced individual differences in readi-

b

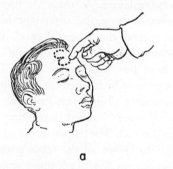

a

ness to perceive from the "inside" or the "outside" when no prior set is given. For example, in one demonstration 76 per cent of a group of 202 student subjects reported the symbol as a ɜ (that is, in accord with an "inside" perspective), whereas 24 per cent reported it as ε. Moreover, the tendency to see the symbol in the latter way (that is, according to an "outside" perspective) was clearly more pronounced in the male than in the female students. Perhaps here is confirmation of the common notion that females (at least in our culture) tend to be more "subjective" in their outlook than do males!

it as a ɜ (see fig. *b*). If he "viewed" the symbol as though he were looking at his own forehead from the outside, as the experimenter was, he would have reported it to be an ε.

It turns out that, given an appropriate set, any person can perceive the symbol traced illustrates, we sometimes experience the self "as though" *outside* the body.

There are various well-recognized ways in which self and body are completely dissociated objects in perception. In Yoga the person trains himself to take attitudes of mind in which body and self are not the same. In aging, we may think of *ourselves* as eternally young, in bodies that are physically growing old, ugly, and decrepit, thinking of ourselves as somehow imprisoned within "this mortal coil." And the belief in life after death—of the perpetuation of personal identity after the death of the physical body—of course depends upon an acceptance of this potential separation of body and self.

The Conception of Self. The individual perceives himself as being a certain "kind of person," as having certain traits, habits, characteristic patterns of behavior; as possessing certain abilities, skills, knowledge; as holding various beliefs, values, attitudes; as being directed toward certain goals, aims, and aspirations. And he perceives himself, too, in the ways he is related to his surroundings—what objects he possesses, what social groups he belongs to, what his social status and roles are, how he is regarded in the eyes of other people.

All these things together make up his total self-conception. The way they are put together, organized, is the structure of his self-conception. As we shall see in Part IV, the qualities and structure of each individual's self-conception are unique, a product of his particular development.

Yet there are at least two general things that can be said about the structure of all people's self-conceptions.

CENTRAL AND PERIPHERAL LAYERS. For everyone, some parts of the self are felt to be more central, closer to the "essential core" of self; other parts of the self are felt to be more peripheral or superficial.

And even beyond the boundaries of the self, some external objects are felt to be more closely related to self and others to be more remote.

For example, one's material possessions, such as cars, houses, furniture, are often close to self. We feel proud of our car, take loving care of it, defend it against calumny, almost seem to regard it as an "extension" of self. Yet it can be maligned or destroyed without one's feeling the same degree of self-damage that might occur, say, if one's creation, such as a textbook, were maligned or destroyed. One's work tends to be closer to the basic self-conception than more material things, for the work is an expression of the self.

One's reputation is generally a prized part of self. "Who steals my purse, steals trash; but he that filches my good name . . . makes me poor indeed." The reputation may, however, be intimately dependent upon one's financial status; the stolen purse may *be* the stolen name; the blow to self may be unendurable (witness the wave of suicides among bankrupt men in the Great Depression).

The self, like an onion, is made up of successive layers. As these are successively penetrated from the outermost layer, the most central, the "essential core" of self, is approached. And when finally the last layer has been penetrated, then what? Like the onion, of which there is nothing more central after all its layers have been peeled, the self once "tracked down" may not be there after all. The "essential me" is perhaps a fiction. When all the other parts of self are somehow destroyed, this essential core, too, may be gone.

We may honestly *feel* that the more peripheral parts of our self-structure are not really us, are not really necessary to us. We may say that social status is not important to us, nor are the opinions of others; we may disavow the importance to us of material possessions, physical beauty, good clothes; we may say that our overt behavior does not really reflect what we are basically like, what we really stand for, really value. And we may sometimes be right. The difficulty is that the importance of various parts of the self is hard to assess while we still comfortably possess them. But suppose that Mr. Anyman is in fact stripped of successive layers: all his external possessions are lost in a financial crash, his reputation and social status are destroyed, he is deprived of family and friends, his very clothes are stolen, what then remains of Mr. Anyman's self? As we shall see when we turn to individual differences in personality, there would be wide differences among persons of different cultures, social groups, and developmental circumstances, in what the residual self would be after these successive catastrophies. For some persons, there would be *nothing* after these "peripheral" layers were gone; the person would completely collapse in death, or in a vegetablelike stupor. For others, there might result a single sheer unadulterated passion for revenge, alone constituting the meaning of "self." For others, there would remain more central layers, something still intact—a basic set of beliefs, a transcendant faith.

"HIGHER" AND "LOWER" LEVELS OF SELF. Just as the individual tends to evaluate the other objects in his world as "good" or "bad," so he regards some parts of the self as more desirable and some as less desirable. He feels that it is "good" that he is kind, tolerant, unselfish; he feels it is "bad" that he is lazy, weak, irrational. It is "good" that he masters and controls his impulses; "bad" that he gives in to them. It is "good" that he succeeds in his work, tries to do better, keeps healthy, feels happy; it is "bad" that he fails, gives up, feels ill and unhappy.

Many things seem to him neither "high"

nor "low," but simply neutral with respect to value. For example, most people regard it as neither "good" nor "bad" that they sleep, have a certain physical height, know the alphabet, move at a certain rate, like to eat. But it is also striking that any one of these, and probably any other aspect of one's self, *can* in some circumstances come to be regarded as "higher" or "lower."

This distinction between "higher" and "lower" levels of self is age-old. The particular terms in which it has been cast have reflected the religious and cultural climate of the times. For some Greek philosophers, soul, mind, and body were assumed to be a descending hierarchy of parts of the self. And there have been endless other variants —animal nature vs. spiritual nature, blind instinct vs. rational thought, evil impulses vs. good impulses. More recently, there is the Freudian hierarchy of Id, Ego, and Superego (see p. 618).

The individual's particular conceptions of what is "higher" and what "lower," and indeed the very conception that there is such a distinction as "higher" vs. "lower," are provided by the culture and social group in which he develops. On the other hand, anthropological, historical, and sociological evidence suggests that such evaluations of levels of self may not be universal. In some cultural settings the self lacks such distinctions, because the whole nature of self is vastly different, the person being less a separate entity and more a part of a larger social grouping. Distinctions of level are unnecessary, inasmuch as the "goodness" or "badness" of the individual's behavior is not *his* voluntary concern, but rather the concern of the society of which he is merely the passive instrument.

THE SELF-IDEAL. Especially significant among cultural influences is the setting of standards of conduct. Parents and others help to shape the developing self-structure in the child by pointing out what he *should* and *should not* do, what he *should* and *should not* be like. Rewards and punishments help to accentuate the difference between "desirable" and "undesirable" aspects of self.

Thus the individual comes to develop an enduring conception of what he *ought* to be like. This aspect of his whole self-picture has been called the *self-ideal* (or ideal self). It defines the "highest" level in the hierarchy of the self. It provides a standard against which the rest of the self may be evaluated. As we shall see presently, this comparison of one's actual behavior with the ideal self is a basic determinant of motivation and emotional experience.

But the ideal self by no means necessarily constitutes a part that is the most central to the self. For some individuals, the ideal self exists as a fairly remote part, playing a minor role in behavior. For others, there is a greater degree of unification of ideal self and rest of self; what he does, feels, and believes is consistent with his ideal self.

UNITY OF SELF-STRUCTURE. The self-conception, then, is composed of many differentiated parts and aspects, organized into a whole. Like any structure, the self may be strongly or weakly unified.

In some persons the various parts of self fit together closely and harmoniously. The person experiences his thoughts, feelings, impulses, acts, as comprising a meaningful and orderly whole; they all make "sense" with respect to his entire nature—his traits, skills, motives, values, and social roles.

Other people may experience many of their thoughts, feelings, impulses and acts as somehow unrelated, discrepant, dissonant, contradictory to one another.

Most persons experience neither of these extremes of unity or disunity. Their selves are apprehended as complicated structures, some parts of which are more tightly organized and others less so. And there may be several different, more or less discon-

nected, "subsystems" within the entire self-structure, each unified in itself, but not with the others. An example of this is the partial separation of "good self" from "bad self" mentioned above. In extreme cases the separation of such "subsystems" in the self-structure may become so acute that the entire structure becomes fractionated, and the person may experience two or more "selves" that are entirely alien to one another. (See Box 49 for a discussion of such multiple personalities.)

CONTINUITY OF SELF-IDENTITY. The self, like many other entities, is experienced as enduring over time, remaining constant in some respects and changing in others. What is most striking is that the *identity* of the self is preserved over time. We perceive ourselves as the *same* persons we have been since birth, and we expect to remain the same until death, and perhaps even after. We do, of course, recognize various changes in our selves as we develop, but even though the changes have been so drastic as to leave virtually no property unaltered, we still experience ourselves as the same persons. It is like Great-Grandfather's Ax, which is regarded by Mr. Anyman as the *same* ax that great-grandfather had, even though in the intervening years its head and shaft have each been worn out and replaced several times, so that no part now is literally the same part great-grandfather handled.

There are exceptional cases, on the other hand, in which the continuity of self-identity may be temporarily or permanently lost through radical changes in the individual's circumstances. And, to a lesser degree, we all know that there are times in life when we feel ourselves to be very different persons from what we once were—there is a curious experience of both continuity and change at the same time.

This continuity of self-identity is reinforced by various distinguishing features of

---

BOX 49

One Body, Multiple "Selves"

Although the Dr. Jekyll–Mr. Hyde syndrome has long been a popular literary theme, authentic cases of such multiple "selves" within the same body are extremely rare in psychiatric records, totaling probably not more than 100 in all. The dramatic characteristics of cases of so-called *multiple personality* make up for their rarity.

The patient typically manifests two fairly complete and distinct patterns of personality. (Sometimes more than two patterns may coexist; in the classical case of Miss Beauchamp, described by Morton Prince, five distinct "selves" were identified.) The patterns are likely to be of contrasting character: one "self" may be well-behaved, conventional, and inhibited, while the alternate "self" may be loud, boisterous, and unrestrained.

The alternations from one self to another may occur frequently and within short periods of time, or more rarely and over much longer periods. There appear to be two main types of cases. In one type the alternate phases of the self are highly compartmentalized; while in one phase the person exhibits no memory of his other self. In the second type the alternate phases are not so fully independent of one another; for example, though the person while in phase A may be entirely ignorant of the existence of phase B, while in phase B he is well aware of the existence of phase A.

Thigpen and Cleckley have described a case that was discovered recently. Eve White, a young mother suffering from severe headaches, came for psychotherapy. She was an earnest, quiet, "well-bred," and feminine woman, conscientious but some-what passive and lacking in spontaneity. During therapy it was discovered that she would sometimes undergo a radical transformation in personality. In the character of Eve Black she was lively, michievous, egocentric, and less "well-bred." As Eve Black she was fully aware of the existence of Eve White, but as Eve White she was entirely ignorant of Eve Black. (Still a third "self," named Jane, was later observed by the therapist.)

Investigation showed that Eve White and Eve Black had "inhabited" the same body since childhood. Repeatedly, Eve Black had gotten into trouble and left Eve White to suffer the consequences.

The sharp and genuine separation of the two patterns of personality was confirmed by various psychological and physiological tests taken during the two phases. Tests of handwriting, of brain waves (see p. 483), and of personality attributes all showed marked differences between Eve White and Eve Black, of a magnitude that might be expected in studying two actually different individuals.

It should be emphasized that such a multiple personality is not a condition wholly unconnected with other abnormal phenomena in which there are extreme dissociative tendencies in the person, for instance, cases of amnesia, etc. Indeed, there are dissociative tendencies of lesser degree found frequently in everyone, and of considerable degree found in most people under severely stressful circumstances.

PRINCE, M. 1930. *The dissociation of personality* (2nd ed.). New York: Longmans, Green.

THIGPEN, C. H., and CLECKLEY, H. M. 1957. *The three faces of Eve*. New York: McGraw-Hill.

---

the self which enable the individual to organize the entity over time. One's name is a permanent "marker" of self, and there are many other external supports of self-continuity, such as one's body, physical belongings, clothes, house, etc. Among the most critical of these is the behavior of other people toward oneself. Self-identity is partly defined by how other people behave toward one; radical changes in the behavior of others may result in marked transformations of self-identity, accompanied by stages of disorganization of the self, in which there is severe confusion about self-identity.

By Way of Summary. The self is a subjectively experienced entity, an integration of percepts, feelings, and thoughts. It is not the same as the ego or the personality, being simply an aspect of the latter. The most material part of the self is the physical body, which is both an object *of* perception and an instrument *for* perception. Under special circumstances the body and self may be perceived as somewhat, or even completely, separated.

The person's total self-conception consists of many diverse qualities—traits, habits, abilities, motives, social roles and status, etc. The self-conception is typically characterized by more central and more peripheral parts, and by "higher" and "lower" parts, the former being related to the self-ideal. The self-structure may be weakly or strongly organized; its parts may form a harmonious whole, or may be somewhat dissonant with one another. Normally there is continuity of self-identity over long periods of time, supported by the person's recognizable body, name, material possessions, social position, etc. But there may also under special conditions be marked disruptions of usual self-structure and disturbances in self-identity.

Self and the Life-Space

The self is never, of course, perceived in a vacuum. It is always perceived as existing within the total psychological environment that the person experiences. We will call this the *life-space*, using Lewin's (1935) term.

The Life-Space. The life-space is the individual's total conception of the worlds in which he exists. It is the universe of space and time in which the person conceives that he can or might move about, either physically, or through social mobility, or through flights of fancy, thought, and memory. It includes his knowledge, beliefs, and memories and his view of the past and future as well as of the present; and it may include domains of life reached after mortal "death"—heaven and hell, paradise and purgatory. It is not, of course, the same as the actual physical and social environments described by the outside observer. It is what exists subjectively for the person. His life-space may correspond in some ways with the actual external environments, but it also deviates from them in radical degree, and varies markedly from the life-spaces of other people.

The life-space of some persons is of limitless scope, stretching off endlessly into the cosmos, into the dim mists of prehistory and remote future. For other persons, the life-space is narrowly limited, a "cozy" place, where there is no unknown.

DIFFERENTIATION OF THE LIFE-SPACE. Not only are there marked differences in the scope of life-spaces, there are also differences in the degree of differentiation of the total life-space, and of its parts. For some people there are fewer kinds of people, fewer places, fewer facts, fewer distinctions of all kinds among things. For other people, there exists an extremely rich variety of different things, awareness of refined distinctions, subtle nuances.

Some of the areas of knowledge for the person may be highly differentiated: he knows an enormous number of things about sailing a ship, or cooking, or comparative religions. Other areas may be scarcely differentiated at all: he has only the vaguest notions of the differences among the many countries of Africa and Asia, thinks that all "jazz" music is the same.

STRUCTURE OF THE LIFE-SPACE. People differ widely in the degree of unification of their life-spaces. For some, there is a high degree of organization of the various parts; their worlds are tidy systems, "everything in its place and a place for everything."

The person with a mature and sophisticated outlook, or a set of cardinal values, or a well-developed philosophy of life, may see his world in a unified way. But so may the narrow-minded bigot who views everything in life in the light of a single overriding prejudice that all progressive things are dangerous radicalism, or that all conservative things are dangerously reactionary, or that all people different from himself are inferior.

Other people may have a far less unified life-space. The relations among things are unclear, changeable, inconsistent. Many aspects of their experience may seem to them only distantly related to other things, or entirely unrelated. The world is kaleidoscopic, fragmented.

There may be considerable degrees of unity in certain areas of knowledge, but no connections between the areas. And this compartmentalization, resulting in what is sometimes referred to as "logic-tight compartments," may permit all sorts of basic inconsistencies among things existing side by side. For example, religious inquisitors could zealously burn heretics for the "glory of God"; the sternest advocate of free enterprise may seek to restrain competition in his own industry; the hard-headed scientist may be the gullible mark of the soft-headed theory outside his own field.

REGIONS OF THE LIFE-SPACE. The life-space can be thought of as made up of a large number of "regions," that is, all the kinds of conditions, places, and activities of which the person is aware. For example, there are the "regions" of playing tennis, reading Hamlet, making love, being elected president of the women's club, taking a rocket ship to Mars, going to Hades, having a full stomach, and so on, in endless profusion.

It is with respect to the nature of these regions that we can understand many things about the *motivation* of the person. The "regions" vary in their attractiveness for him. Some of them are positive, being conditions and activities that the person regards as desirable, as satisfying, as valuable, to be approached. Others are negative, being regarded as undesirable, repelling, to be avoided. The greater proportion of "regions" are neutral, being neither attractive nor repelling, felt neither as sought after nor to be avoided.

The perceived pathways to these regions are of different kinds. Some of the regions can be reached through physical locomotion, others by "social locomotion"—as in "getting to know the right people"—and still others by abstract thought or imagination or "remembrance of things past."

Some regions are perceived as near at hand and easily accessible to the self, others as remote and hard to get to, and still others as entirely inaccessible.

SPACE OF FREE MOVEMENT. The proportion of all the regions in the person's life-space which are regarded by him as accessible determines what he feels to be the size of his "space of free movement." This size varies extremely widely among different individuals and among different social classes and cultures. For the prosperous, educated, healthy person living in a permissive social climate, the space of free movement is enormous; for the underprivileged person, the sick, the incompetent, or the victim of social discrimination and injustice, the space of free movement may be severely shrunken.

A person's impression of the size of his space of free movement is a vital factor in his motivation and adjustment, as we shall see later. It is especially noteworthy that the sense of constriction of the space of free movement may have less to do with the number of *actually* accessible regions than with the number of *potentially* accessible regions. The man of low status who lives in a strict caste society, and who recognizes the fact that upward social mobility is impossible, is not likely to feel as constricted as the man of low status living in a society whose official ideology includes the ideal of equal opportunity for all, but which actually denies opportunity on grounds of prejudice.

Place of Self in the Life-Space. Although it is generally the case that the self is the most salient and highly differentiated entity in the life-space, it does not necessarily follow that the self is always located at the exact *center* of the life-space. The more self-centered or egocentric the person, the more it is true that his life-space is so constructed that, like the ancient conception of the earth in the cosmos, everything pivots around the self. (See Box 50.) Things are more highly differentiated the closer they are to the self; the universe is conceived as though "made for my use," and its meaning lies basically in how it serves *me*. What counts is the present moment, the immediate here and now.

For other persons, the self may be placed quite far from the center. Like the Copernican view of the earth in the solar system, the self is a minor object rotating about a larger central object. The midpoint of history does not lie just here and now where the self is; the center of the physical universe is not here at my body, but rather, the body is merely at one tiny point on Earth, a single planet of the sun, itself lying at the fringe of a twirling pin-wheel galaxy, only one of billions of galaxies in endless space.

TIME-PERSPECTIVE. In connection with the perception of time (p. 129) it was mentioned that the person typically apprehends himself as located somewhere within a larger framework of time. The future

lies ahead, the past behind. He has a *time-perspective*.

For some persons, the time-perspective is long; for others, short. For some, the future is highly structured, each successive stage fitted into its proper place; for others, the future is unclear. For some, the life-space ends abruptly at the point where death for the self is foreseen; for others, the life-space goes on, and death of the self is but a single episode in the stretch of time. For some, the future is bright and attractive; things are getting better, "progress" is the keynote. For others, the past was the golden time; the world is "getting worse."

These various aspects of the individual's time-perspective are of central importance in understanding his motivations. The dejection of the aged person for whom retirement means simply "no more future"; the unrealistic behavior of the person who lives on past glories, such as the former college football star for whom youth was the real time of life and for whom, now that it has passed, nothing is important—these are cases in which motivation is negatively affected by particular time-perspectives. And, conversely, the enthusiasm of youth for whom nothing is impossible, the active involvement of the older person for whom every moment of life left is precious for what there is yet to experience and accomplish, the untroubled drive of the person whose own death is but an incident in the total world pattern and for whom activity is directed at the welfare of those who will exist after him—these are cases of positive motivation which depend upon particular time-perspectives.

The *clarity* of structure of the time-perspective of the life-space plays a critical role in motivation. Studies of morale show that individuals and groups act more effectively when there is clarity as to the steps that lie ahead, just what leads to what,

BOX 50

A Girl Describes Her Office

Wertheimer has reported his experience in talking with a young woman about the office in which she worked. In answer to his request that she describe the activities of her office, she replied in the following vein:

"Well," she said, "there are a number of people in the office. I have to do directly with a Mr. A, a Mr. B, and a Mr. C, who often come to my desk, ask questions, bring me letters, etc. There are others in the office with whom I do not have to do directly. Mr. A has dealings with a Mr. D, Mr. B with a Mr. E, and Mr. C with a Mr. F. D and E also have dealings with each other; so do E and F. Let me see, that makes six people in the office besides myself." (Fig. *a* is a diagram of her description.)

from Mr. E, Mr. E from Mr. B, and Mr. F from Mr. E." (She was apparently logical-minded, and was trying to tell the whole story. Fig. *b* adds arrows to fig. *a* to indicate the directions of authority.)

Wertheimer being by this time somewhat confused (as the reader probably is) then had a hunch, and asked, "So Mr. B is your boss and you are directly below him, and so is Mr. E?" "Yes," she said.

Why was the young woman's description so confusing? What she stated had been correct in every detail, but the difficulty was that she had described the office as though *centered about herself*. In so doing she had given a picture of the structural organization that was in violation of its logical hierarchy, with the boss at the center and herself in a secondary status (see fig. *c*).

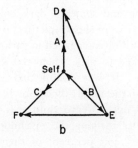

a

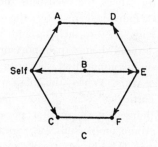

c

Wertheimer then asked, "Are you the boss?" "Oh no," she answered. "Do you give orders to anyone?" "Oh yes, I sometimes give orders to Mr. A and to Mr. C. I get orders from Mr. B; Mr. D gets them

b

P.S. Sometime later Wertheimer asked one of her office coworkers how she was getting along.

"Quite nicely," he said. "She is a fine person. But we are not certain whether her job will last very long. She has a funny way of behaving toward the others and even toward her work. She seems to relate all things to herself, as if she were always the center of the situation, even in business matters when nobody is thinking of her personally. That is not good for business."

WERTHEIMER, M. 1945. *Productive thinking.* New York: Harper. Excerpts reproduced by permission of Harper and Brothers. Copyright 1945 by Harper and Brothers.

where they are on the pathway to goals, etc. And, conversely, such studies demonstrate that demoralization results from lack of clarity, when the individual or the group does not know where it is going, is not able to understand the relevance and place of the particular activity of the moment in the larger framework of progress toward remote goals.

SHARPNESS OF BOUNDARIES OF SELF AND LIFE-SPACE. In some people the self has many connections with the surroundings. In others the self is more sharply separated; the person sees the surroundings foreign to the self as full of dangers and threats.

These differences in closeness of self and life-space are especially obvious in reference to other people. The individual may feel himself to be unfriendly with, alien to, cut off from those about him and from society at large. He may feel no interest in or concern for others; the "bell tolls" not for him. Other individuals may feel themselves friendly with, close to, helping and helped by those around them. An important phenomenon in this connection is identification.

IDENTIFICATION. When the person perceives a particular form of close involvement of himself with another person or with a group of persons, we speak of *identification*. The boy normally identifies with his parents, especially with his father; the man identifies with the fellow employees in his office. The degree of identification can vary widely, from a strong and enduring identification, such as exists among close friends and family members, to a diluted and temporary state, such as when the movie-goer feels an identification with the hero on the screen.

Among the various kinds of perceived relationships between the self and other people, identification is distinguished by the fact that what happens to the other person is to some degree equivalent psychologically to its happening to oneself. Thus an achievement of the father's is to some extent felt by the boy as his achievement, a tragedy befalling the fellow employee is to some extent felt as one's own. In brief, it is as though the self were somewhat "extended out" to include other persons.

We shall have occasion in discussing personality development (see Chapter 23) to see the critical significance of the phenomenon of identification in the growth and socialization of the person. We shall find there that the developmental determinants of identification are exceedingly complex. At this point we need only mention several perceptual determinants. Principles of grouping by proximity and by similarity (see p. 90) may help to account for identification. It is commonplace that our identifications are strongest with persons and groups in close proximity to us. We may feel a sense of deep sympathy and concern in reading of a tragic accident occurring to a person in our own town, but our glance at the newspaper may scarcely pause at an item telling of the death of thousands in a flood in a remote foreign country.

The factor of similarity is also powerful. Other things being equal, it seems that we identify most readily with those perceived to be like ourselves (or like our self-ideal). The bases of the perceived similarity may be of many kinds—sex, age, group membership, skin color, etc. For example, Clark and Clark (1939) studied Negro children aged 3 to 5, some of whom were of light coloring and some of dark coloring. The children were shown pictures of white and Negro children engaged in various activities and asked to pick "themselves" out in the pictures. It was found that the darker-skinned the child, the more likely he was to pick out a Negro child in the picture as "himself." Among the 33 children of light coloring, 36.5 per cent of their identifications were with Negro children; whereas among the 54 children of dark coloring, 56.4 per cent of their identifications were with Negroes.

The Psychological Situation. At any single moment the person actually experiences only a limited and selected aspect of his total potential life-space. The particular configuration of self and world as he actually experiences it at a given moment is called his *psychological situation.*

The psychological situation is what *he* experiences at the moment, not what the outside observer defines as the objective situation. His psychological situation may be far removed from the present objective environment; he may be living for a moment in the past, or anticipating the future, or dreaming. The blush that just now floods his face may bear no relation to the objective situation of the moment; he may be reliving a past episode in which he now sees himself as having been ridiculous.

The specific character of the psychological situation depends, of course, upon the patterns of external and internal stimuli playing upon the person at the moment, and how they are organized in connection with the activated processes in his nervous system. As these stimuli and processes continuously change from moment to moment, the psychological situation continuously changes. But the succession of situations is not disorderly. Each momentary situation tends to be experienced as a part of a larger temporal unity, a whole episode with meaningful continuity from moment to moment.

However there may be interruptions of this continuity. Sudden intrusions of new stimuli or new processes may produce radical changes in the situation; the old episode may be broken off incomplete and later returned to after the interrupting episode has run its course.

OVERLAPPING SITUATIONS. Moreover, owing to the very complexity of human mental processes, the person may be in several *overlapping situations* simultaneously. The blushing man may be reliving that past experience, while at the same time continuing to be somewhat aware of his immediate objective surroundings. While reminiscing, he is still paying some attention to the machine he is operating, and still has an ear partly bent in the direction of the conversation of his fellow workers.

Typically, one of the several simultaneous situations has greater momentary salience in his attention, being "figure" on the "ground" of the others. But there is also rapid shifting back and forth, with this one now more salient than that one. And there is, of course, *interaction* across the boundaries of these overlapping situations. Each helps shape and change the others. The half-heard derisive tone of the conversation by his fellow workers fits in with and reinforces the past embarrassing social situation that he is now recalling; the feeling of shame engendered in that situation makes his hands tremble as they now operate the machine; and the sudden intrusion of a new factor, such as the entrance of the boss, abruptly obliterates the several psychological situations existing the moment before and institutes a wholly new one.

By Way of Summary. The life-space is the total psychological world in which the person exists, including past, present, and future, concrete and abstract, real and unreal. Individuals differ widely in the scope and richness of differentiation of the life-space, and in the unity of its structure. The life-space is made up of large numbers of regions (activities), some of which are positive goals and some of which are things to be avoided. How accessible these regions appear to be to the person varies widely.

The self, though usually the most important part of the life-space, does not necessarily lie at its very center. Time-perspectives in the life-space vary greatly and have intimate bearing on the person's attitudes and motives. The sense of involvment of self with other people and objects in the life-space is known as identification. Identifications are complexly determined, with factors of perceptual grouping playing an important role.

That aspect of the life-space experienced most saliently at any one moment is called the psychological situation. Its make-up depends upon the total momentary pattern of stimulation, both internal and external. The person may be in several overlapping situations simultaneously, and this has significant consequences for his behavior, since usually there is interaction among the various psychological situations.

Motives and the Self

The most striking feature of the person's experience in most psychological situations is his state of motivation. The person perceives disturbances and deficiencies with respect to himself and his surroundings, feels needs and desires, sets goals and forms intentions, exercises choice and will, and engages in actions. Intimately involved in all these aspects of motivation are his emotional experiences.

Disturbances and Deficiencies. In some psychological situations all is quiescence, order, sufficiency. But these situations are exceptional. Most of the time the person is aware of various kinds and amounts of discomforts, disturbances, and deficits.

DISTURBANCES OF SELF. Many of these disturbances are perceived as conditions of the *self*, especially of the body. The person may feel himself anxious, irritated, agitated, gloomy, "empty." He may feel aches and pains, fatigue, stomach pangs, tense muscles, etc. These are generally unpleasant feelings, though often only mildly so. They are often perceived as related to, or "signaling," lacks and deficiencies. The stomach pang is perceived as meaning a lack of food in the body; fatigue is perceived as a lack of rest.

The person also perceives various disturbances and deficiencies that involve the relation of the self to the surroundings. He sees that the speeding car is about to hit him, that he is standing close to a disgusting object, that the chair on which he is sitting is about to tip over. He may also perceive that he has not completed the task he was working on, that he does not have enough money in his bank account to cover his bills, that he does not know the answer to the problem he sees.

Especially, he perceives disturbances and deficiencies in his relations with other people. He sees himself left out of the party, feels dominated by another individual, feels that others do not appreciate him, or that he does not understand them, sees himself as "out of step" with his group.

Finally, he may perceive various disturbances and deficiencies existing in the objects and events in his surroundings that have no direct relationship to himself. That is, they are not *his* disturbances or deficiencies, but are "out there." He sees that someone has left a job unfinished, that the ladder is not properly braced against the wall, that a pedestrian is about to be hit by a car, that a child is crying in distress.

We must carefully distinguish his *perceived* disturbance from what might be *objectively* defined as a disturbance or deficiency. His body may actually have a food deficiency without his perceiving it; the two people he observes may be quarreling but he may not realize it. Conversely, the disturbance or deficiency he perceives may have no objective correspondence; he may feel that he is disliked by someone who actually likes him.

Needs. Merely perceiving disruptions and deficiencies of self and of surroundings is *not* motivation. To become motivated, the person must *first feel a necessity to remove, allay, or correct the condition.* Such feelings of necessity are called *needs.* The person may feel a *need* to soothe the pain, replenish the food in his body, dodge an oncoming car, finish the incomplete task, join the party.

It should be noted that the term "need" is used in many different ways by psychologists. Some refer to the actual *organic* deficits or requirements of the body as "physiological or biological needs." Others reserve the term for the *experiencing* of deficit conditions, speaking of "felt needs." Throughout this book the term "need" will be used only in the latter sense.

Needs involve the person's feeling that *he* is obliged or compelled to do something about the sensed disruption or deficiency. Discomforts and disruptions that are seen as pertaining closely to oneself are more likely to evoke such needs than are those that are more remote. Thus body pains, emotional states, and external threats to self are likely to be the source of needs. But even disruptions seen as close to self may not evoke needs in all situations. The person may recognize that he is tired, or hungry, or sneered at, or whatever, without feeling that *he* is obliged to do anything about it. This is especially the case when he is involved in other activities that take precedence, or when he sees the disruption as part of a larger pattern of events that will eventually reduce the disruption without involving himself. The arousal of needs depends upon the particular way the whole situation is perceived by the person.

When we identify with another person, we acquire a sense of involvement in his fate. *His* disruption or distress may evoke needs in *us*—we feel obliged to take remedial action to help the situation. But identification is not always essential. Sometimes when we watch a mere acquaintance or even a stranger solving a problem, we feel a compelling urge to intercede and to make for him the "obvious" move that he fails to see. We are thus highly "task-involved"; we feel a need for completion or solution of the task, but not at all because we perceive the task as having any direct relevance for *ourselves.*

The intensity of the perceived discomfort or the magnitude of the disruption or deficiency is a significant factor in the arousal of needs. There is a threshold below which the perceived disruption is not sufficient to evoke the need to cope with it; once exceeding this threshold, the disruption will arouse the need. Needs, therefore, are essentially what we might call "deficiency drives." They are in the service of removal of unwanted conditions; their aim is to re-establish a condition of quiescence, sufficiency, equilibrium, which has been temporarily disrupted. Needs persist only as long as the disrupted conditions continue to be *perceived;* for example, if an organic deficit still remains but is for any reason not perceived, the need disappears.

However not all behavior is directed by feelings of necessity to remove discomforts and deficiencies. The story of motivation is more than the story of seeking quiescence, sufficiency, equilibrium. This becomes clear when we consider "desires."

Desires. *Desires* are feelings of wish, appetite, yen, urge, which the person experiences as directed toward certain objects or conditions. He feels desires to kiss his girl, to master the theory of relativity, to see novel things and faraway places; he feels desires to learn Spanish, to drive a racing car, to go to the movies, to eat a bowl of French onion soup.

The person thinks of these activities as capable of providing pleasure, gratification, "fun." They are not perceived by him as arising from states of discomfort, deficit, or disruption, as are needs. They often occur more or less "spontaneously" or as a result of his thinking about, or being reminded of, or perceiving the desired thing. He perceives the thing as desired *in its own right*. To put it crassly, desires are pleasure-bent, needs are pain-avoidant—using the terms "pleasure" and "pain" as broadly as possible.

The important distinction between needs and desires, as the two main classes of motivational forces, is readily confused because of the way that needs and desires *may be intimately related*. For example, a *need* for food will often be connected with a *desire* for food. The stomach pang may make us aware of a deficiency, and we feel the need to allay it with food; the idea of food may at the same time strike us as very attractive and desirable, not as needed to allay hunger but as a source of gratification. Indeed, many of our desires have come into being just through a process of need-fulfillment. That is, the actions taken to reduce the unwanted state have been discovered to be pleasurable, and the person may then come to desire them in their own right, quite apart from need-states.

Another basic connection of needs and desires rests on the happy circumstance that the fulfillment of needs tends to be a source of pleasure. That is, the acts allaying a discomfort, correcting a disruption, or removing a deficiency, are likely to be enjoyed. Tension-reduction is a source of pleasure. There is no essential reason why this *must* be the case. Sometimes, indeed, it is not; many cases of need-fulfillment are not themselves particularly enjoyed, and sometimes tension-reduction can be unpleasant. Eating with a painful sore throat may reduce hunger, but it gives no enjoyment.

It is also the case that desires may lead into needs. An insistent desire, becoming more and more intense without achieving gratification, may be converted into a *need*. Now the person seeks gratification not as anticipated pleasure, but as needed relief.

BY WAY OF SUMMARY. Needs arise when the person experiences a deficit or disruption of states of self and surroundings, and feels the necessity to correct the upset conditions. Needs are not the same as the objective requirements of the body and the environment; whether and in what manner a need gets aroused depends upon the particular way the whole immediate situation is perceived. Desires are feelings of appetite, wish, urge, with respect to pleasurable activities. They are not, like needs, based on deficits. Needs and desires may, however, often merge—one leading to the other. But even though needs and desires are often connected, they must be distinguished. This distinction between needs and desires is a vital one for our understanding of motivation. It helps us to do justice to the richness and complexity of our motivational experience, as we shall see in Chapter 10. It helps us to avoid the common error of assuming that all motivation is in the service of avoidance or removal of unwanted conditions. It thus preserves for our picture of motivation the proper balance of both positive and negative forces, of both appetite and aversion, of both pleasure and pain, of both "abundancy drives" and "deficiency drives."

Goals. The person perceives in his surroundings *goals* capable of removing his needs and fulfilling his desires. When he feels thirsty, drinking from the nearby drinking fountain is a goal. When he feels a need for company, being at the bridge party is a goal. When he feels a desire for some pleasurable reading, reading a particular book in his library becomes his goal.

The drinking fountain, bridge party, and book are *goal-objects;* drinking the water, being at the party, reading the book, are the *goal activities.*

The perceiving of goals depends mainly upon the person's past experience. He has learned what goals will satisfy a given need; usually he has learned that any of several different goals will do so. Among these, certain goals will be seen by him as more appropriate than the others, having more easily, regularly, and fully reduced that need in the past—or fulfilled that desire.

But there is also the matter of *preference.* Of a number of alternative goals, more or less equally adequate for the fulfillment of a given need or desire, he prefers some to others. He anticipates that some will be more pleasurable than others, quite aside from mere functional utility. His hunger pangs can be allayed by eating any number of different foods, but he prefers the fried grasshoppers to the beefsteak, or the blue cheese to ice cream—again depending upon his past training and experience.

Often, of course, the range of alternative goals that will satisfy a given need or desire may be quite limited. It is this girl and no other that he wants to love and be loved by; it is that particular book that he wants to read, and no other will do; it is to be the champion discus thrower that he ardently seeks, not champion sprinter, swimmer, or chess player.

A given need or desire arises, of course, in a concrete psychological situation. Thus the actual perception of goals will depend on the availability and accessibility of different possible goals in the surroundings. Other things being equal, that which is now within a person's purview will be seized upon as the appropriate goal. He studies the available menu and selects the best thing offered, even though it may be much less preferred than other things he can imagine. And the attractiveness of the

goal is heavily dependent upon its relative preference to others now available. The best immediately available food, or book, or girl, or achievement may be highly prized and eagerly sought, even though at other times, in company of better goals, this goal would appear to the person to be inferior and unattractive.

PATHWAYS TO GOALS. Not only does a person perceive goals; he also perceives pathways to them. How he sees the pathways depends upon the entire situation. On the basis of past experience he has come to develop "cognitive maps" of his world, which tell him what leads to what, how to get from here to there. He may see the pathways as clear or unclear, short or long, easy or difficult. He may see them as made up of many successive parts, or "steps," or of few.

He also sees *barriers* that must be surmounted in reaching the goal. They may be physical obstacles, such as fences; or they may be social obstacles, such as having the wrong ancestry to qualify for a desired position, or they may be obstacles in thought processes, such as not knowing how to use logarithms.

The most striking thing about perception of goals and pathways is the change in appearance of goal-objects and other relevant parts of the surroundings in connection with the needs and desires. As the need or desire becomes more intense, the attractiveness of the goal-object or goal activity grows; once attained, its attractiveness may disappear, or even turn to downright unattractiveness. Barriers to goals may take on negative appearance, which persists until they are overcome. And there is the important phenomenon of emergence of *subgoals.* The pathways to goals are often perceived as organized into a number of subparts, each of which constitutes an intermediate subgoal to be attained on the way to the ultimate goal. These subgoals take on many of the perceived characteristics of goals; they are attractive and sought after, and attaining them provides gratification. Sometimes, indeed, they can become goals in their own right, independent of the goals that they originally served. For example, for a student seeking admission to medical school, high course grades may at first be a subgoal; but he may come to seek high grades for the gratification they provide in themselves.

LEVEL OF ASPIRATION. There is not only the intention to attain a certain goal, but also the intention to achieve it in a certain way, within a certain time, with a certain degree of effort, and at a certain level of performance.

Particularly in those tasks that pertain to feelings of self-achievement, the person sets a standard toward which he aims, a *level of aspiration.* The sprinter aims at running 100 yards in 9.2 seconds, the student at getting a B in the course. The aim is to get the feelings of satisfaction associated with successful achievement of the self.

There are many factors determining the setting of the particular level of aspiration. The natural tendency is to set it as high as possible, so that it will yield the maximal gratification. Yet there is the restraining tendency not to set it too high, for fear of failure. Usually there is a fairly realistic balancing of these two tendencies, in the way the person appraises the situation. He sets the level high enough to bring feeling of success and yet not so high as to preclude the likelihood of achieving it. His past experiences of performance on this kind of task play a major role. The new level of aspiration is set in accordance with the past discrepancies between levels of aspiration and of actual performance. Having fallen short, he now reduces the level of aspiration; having reached or exceeded his aim, he now raises his level of aspiration. Gen-

erally, the new level is set so that it is somewhat, but not too far, above the previous level of actual performance.

But there are other determinants too. Perceiving the standards of one's own group, or of other groups, plays a large role. By seeing what others aspire to and do, an individual's own level is affected. Sometimes he is brought to set his own level too high, and fails, "playing out of his own league." At other times he may set it too low and succeed too easily without the real feeling of gratification. The bright student who aims only at the "gentleman's C" gets no real sense of gratification from it.

There are enormous individual differences in setting levels of aspiration. There are those who are afraid of failure and never set the level high enough; there are those who are "unrealistic" about their abilities and set it always too high; there are those who attain a mature balance between the two extremes. (See Box 51.)

Will, Conflict, and Choice. Intentions, good or bad, are not enough. For action to occur, there must be a linkage of intention with initiation of action; the set toward goals must be translated into actual striving; the clutch must be engaged. This brings us to one of the most difficult problems of human motivation, the problem of *will.*

Mr. Anyman may lie abed in the morning, needing to get up, intending to get up, and yet failing to get up. "The spirit is willing, but the flesh is weak." We are all familiar with this frequent gap between our motive state and our action. We refer to it commonly as a lack of "will power," and more technically as *abulia.*

But calling it "will power" is no explanation. "Will power" is not a trait of the person, such as his physical strength or his intelligence. It is a characteristic of the way

BOX 51

Setting the Level of Aspiration

The level of aspiration established by the individual with regard to his performance on a given task is determined by many different kinds of factors:

1. Some factors have to do with the *objective nature of the task* as perceived by the person. Recognizing a task as actually difficult, he will, other things being equal, tend to set his sights lower than for a task that is recognized as relatively easy.

2. The person's appraisal of the difficulty of a task is obviously closely related to his *past experiences of success or failure* with the task. These past performances serve to form a kind of "adaptation level" with respect to which the next probable level of performance can be judged. There is also considerable transfer from other past experiences of success and failure, the degree of transfer depending upon how similar the present task is perceived to be to the previous tasks.

3. Another significant factor is the extent to which the person feels himself *involved* in the task. With high self-involvement the person is more sensitive to considerations of personal success and failure, and his level of aspiration will be altered accordingly. Experimental studies show that the higher the self-involvement in the task, the smaller the role played by the objective features of the task in setting the level of aspiration. Moreover, with higher self-involvement, there is a greater *generality* of the person's level of aspiration. That is, the person is more likely to set his levels of aspiration either consistently high or consistently low over a wide range of quite varied kinds of tasks.

4. The level of aspiration is significantly influenced by the external *norms* of performance and aspiration established by the person's group or by other groups. These norms constitute frames of reference for his judgment of his own performance. Numerous experiments show that the level of aspiration set by an individual on a task can be markedly raised or lowered by informing him (rightly or wrongly) of the relatively low or high performances and intentions of the group. Not all groups, of course, are equally effective in influencing a person's level of aspiration. For a group norm to be effective, it must pertain to a group that has psychological significance for the individual.

5. Finally, characteristic tendencies in the individual's setting of levels of aspiration are closely related to various dimensions of his personality.

A study of fourth-, fifth-, and sixth-grade children by Pauline Sears at Yale University throws light on some of the above points. Children were chosen for study in accordance with their school records of success or failure in arithmetic and reading. In the laboratory they were presented with arithmetic and reading tasks. The level of aspiration on these tasks was obtained by asking the child to estimate, after finishing one page of exercises, how long the next page would take him.

The findings show that the child's setting of his level af aspiration on the laboratory tasks was closely related to his past history of success or failure with that same kind of school material. For example, children who had been successful in arithmetic tended to "raise their sights" as they passed from page to page of the laboratory arithmetic test. But the levels they set were "reasonable," in that they indicated rather modest expectations of improvement from trial to trial. On the other hand, children with some failure in school with the given subject matter tended to set their levels of aspiration in quite a different way. Some of them tended to set the level far too low, expressing no likelihood that they would do better, or even as well, on next trials. Others tended to set the level of aspiration unreasonably high, far beyond what could be realistically expected of them.

SEARS, P. S. 1940. Levels of aspiration of academically successful and unsuccessful children. *J. abn. soc. Psychol.*, *35*, 498–536.

an individual behaves in a given situation. In order to understand it, we must look at the whole motivational situation.

We have talked so far about needs and desires, goals and intentions, without reference to the critical fact that many *different* needs, desires, goals, and intentions may occur at the same time. The human being is enormously complex, and his world of immediate experience simultaneously contains many needs and desires, many goals and intentions, many pathways to goals, many positive and negative features of his surroundings.

Thus he experiences *conflict*. He feels drawn in several contradictory directions at once. The degree of experienced conflict ranges from that scarcely perceptible to the utmost of paralyzing stress. The *behavioral* consequences of conflict and how conflict can be resolved will be treated in Chapter 11. In the present connection we need point out only that many cases of apparent lack of "will power" are actually cases of conflict in which one set of tendencies becomes strong enough to dominate other opposing tendencies. Mr. Anyman, reading of the suspicious link between smoking and lung cancer, firmly resolves to give up cigarettes. But despite this resolve he soon succumbs to the temptation to smoke. The reason is not that he failed to exercise sufficient "will power," but that the tendencies impelling him to smoke (for sheer pleasure, escape from nervousness, social participation, or whatever) become at the moment strong enough to override his fear of cancer.

In addition to direct conflict within the single immediate situation, there is the significant factor of *overlapping situations*, which we have already described. The person may experience two or more situations simultaneously, each having less potency than a single situation can have. The man lying abed may "see" himself getting up to eat breakfast and simultaneously "see" himself deep in luxurious sleep. But he may also with half his attention be thinking about a problem that he is trying to solve, or recalling his adventures of the evening before. The diffusion of his attention among the several situations further reduces the likelihood that he will act on *any* of his intentions. His failure to rise is not a matter of lack of "will power," but a consequence of diffusion of attention.

A closely related aspect of this problem is the phenomenon of "inhibitory reflection." The person may spend a good deal of his time reflecting or "introspecting" on the situation he is in instead of acting. The result is often to *alter the perspective* within which the immediate situation is viewed. For example, the immediate act is weighed in terms of a long-range time perspective ("Why get up today, we'll all die sooner or later anyway?"); its value is depreciated ("Why should I get up and vote, it is only one vote in millions?"); the clarity of its rightness is obscured ("If I get out of bed, how do I know that there may not be some bad news awaiting me?"). These are all demoralizing thoughts, inhibiting of action, and, in the extreme, making a virtue of passivity. The classic epitome is Hamlet, in whom

> . . . *the native hue of resolution*
> *Is sicklied o'er with the pale cast of thought,*
> *And enterprises of great pith and moment*
> *With this regard their currents turn awry,*
> *And lose the name of action.*

There is also the paralysis of perfectionism. The man who must have a perfectly satisfactory situation, who must be perfectly sure of the outcome, perfectly sure of his rightness, perfectly sure that he has looked at all sides of the question, is a man who cannot act. *Why* an individual compulsively demands perfection, why he suffers the inhibition of undue reflection, why he experiences overlapping situations rather than one, are questions pertaining to his unique development and personality.

Here we can point out one central factor that makes the person able to take action, to exercise will. It is his perception of the *necessity to make imperfect choices.* His recognition of the fact that he *must* choose, that he must always choose without complete knowledge, that every choice inevitably involves a sacrifice of something else —these are favoring elements for the expression of will.

"FREE WILL." But *can* we really choose, really exercise will? This is the eternal question of *free will.* We must distinguish at once between the person's *perception* that he has or has not free will, and the larger philosophical question of the existence or nonexistence of free will. Our concern here is solely with the former, which is a more limited perceptual issue.

Clearly the person often does regard himself as having free will. The very reason for the endurance of the concepts of will and free will in the face of relentless attack from some thinkers is that we *do* regularly experience ourselves as engaging in what seems to us voluntary action. We may be utterly deluded. Were we to know enough, we might see that the specific choice made is completely predictable on the basis of our total make-up and the total situation facing us, just as by knowing all the stimulus conditions and the set of the observer, the psychologist can predict the specific perception that occurs.

Yet the "fiction" of freedom, if it is fiction, is strongly with us. We agonize over our choices, feel guilt if we make the "wrong" ones. We do not behave as if we were really convinced that we have no freedom. It has been said that man's only

freedom really consists in his ability to make gracefully the choice that he *has* to make; but even this implies that he still exercises some real choice.

DETERMINANTS OF "FREE WILL." One main factor that helps to account for man's perception of free will is the enormous complexity of his experience. It seems likely that the larger the range and diversity of things he is aware of—the more possibilities he sees, the more extensive his time-perspectives, the more kinds of needs and desires he feels—the more likely he is to have the impression of being freely *able* to choose and decide. This is probably due to his greater difficulty in perceiving the actual cause-and-effect relations in complex situations. The less clear the perceived causation, the greater the latitude for seeing the situation not as determined, but as open to the forces of free choice.

The extent of perceived "space of free movement" (see p. 211) is another factor that helps to determine his own sense of free will. The man who sees his physical, social, and conceptual environments as full of accessible regions may perceive himself as not only free on the outside, but free on the "inside" too.

COMPULSION. The distinction between external and internal freedom becomes particularly clear when we turn to the opposite of freedom, that is, *compulsion.* We constantly experience objects and events and people as requiring us to do things. The father orders the child to obey; the storm drives us inside the house; the social role requires that the person follow etiquette. All these situations are seen as demands *on* the self, arising externally to the self, essentially "alien" to the self. We *need* to fulfill these demands, but we certainly do not *desire* to do so.

Such demands come mostly from the external surroundings, but they may also be experienced as coming from our own

BOX 52

Goal Gradient in the Rat

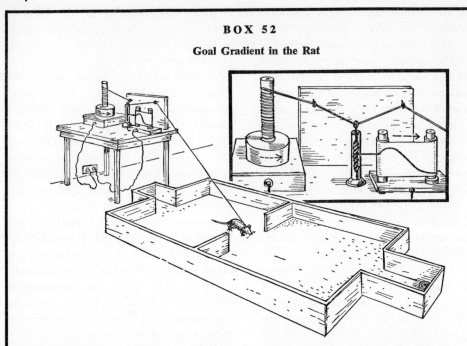

In 1935 at the University of Chicago, Krech developed a method for measuring the strength of the rat's goal-directed motivation.

The rat ran from the starting chamber to the food box wearing a harness to which a restraining string was attached. The string was played out at a slow constant rate as it unwound from a cylinder rotated by an electrically driven motor. The rat could not proceed through the box faster than the motor played out the string, no matter how much force he exerted. The string passed through a hook mechanism attached to a fixed spring in such a manner that when the animal strained against the string the spring was stretched. This in turn moved a stylus that made a continuous record on a moving roll of waxed paper of the amount of force exerted at each moment by the rat in tugging against the harness toward the goal. Thus, as shown in the drawing, the rat "wrote" its own record of its striving toward the goal.

A typical record for one rat is shown in the first graph.

Two points are noteworthy:

(1) There appears to be evidence of lessening of tension as the rat enters the "goal-region" (food box) even before the actual goal-object (food) is obtained.

(2) The dip in strength of pull in the middle is determined by the side partitions, which do not in any way provide an obstacle for the animal. Apparently they serve as a kind of perceptual "landmark"

bodies. An intense and incessant body need may appear to get somehow "externalized," to be outside our real self. It makes demands on "us" and, if sufficiently intense, may compel us to act in its behalf; we may feel ourselves "at the mercy of," "enslaved by," our bodily demands. Moreover, such demands may appear to come from parts of the self which are also somehow "externalized." The gnawing conscience of our better self compels us to act in certain ways.

All these cases of demands—from the surroundings, from the body, from the conscience—may indeed compel us, but still we retain the impression of some "inner" free-

BOX 52 (continued)

Goal Gradient in the Rat

and function somewhat as a "subgoal." Arrival at this subgoal is accompanied by a temporary lessening in the pull, which is resumed in its full vigor once past this point. When the side partitions are removed, animals no longer give any sign of lessening in pull at that point.

In the second graph is illustrated the effect of progressive satiation of hunger drive on the *gradient* of pull toward the goal. Six consecutive trials were given with three minutes of feeding in the food box after each trial. The graph shows a record of

trials 1 and 6. Note that on trial 1 the animal pulled strongly almost from the very beginning, whereas by trial 6, when he had had 15 minutes of eating, the animal began at a low level and only gradually reached a fairly high level as the goal was closely approached. The attractiveness of food, even for a satiated animal, increases as he gets closer to it.

KRECH, D. 1935. Measurement of tension. Paper read at Symposium on Topological Psychology, Bryn Mawr College.

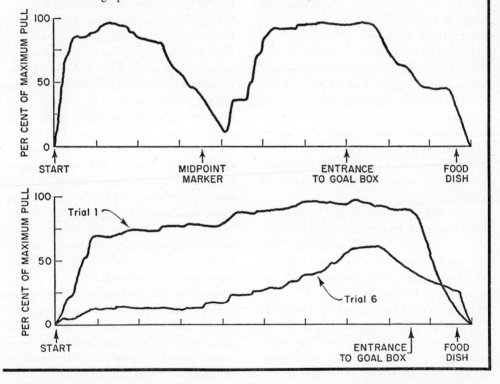

dom; it is still "I" who am voluntarily fulfilling these demands, and there is still the possibility of refusing to meet them. But this "inner" freedom, too, can be lost. We may experience impulses that rise in us and actions in accord with them that occur *without any sense of involvement of our own wills.* We feel ourselves powerless

in the grip of these "autonomous" forces.

For instance, there are the so-called *obsessions,* such as recurrent and unavoidable obsessive thoughts in the insane person that he has committed the "unpardonable sin," or the more trivial obsession of the man in the street with a tune that he cannot get out of his mind. Then there are the so-called *compulsions*, such as repetitive washing of the hands in a mentally unbalanced person, or the careful avoidance of stepping on cracks in the sidewalk as we walk down the street.

It should be emphasized, however, that owing to the basic tendency to make sensible order of our experiences, such "irrational" appearing impulses and acts quickly give way to interpretations that make them "rational" in the individual's own mind, regardless of how irrational they may continue to look to the outside observer. The hand-washing is "to remove invisible microbes"; the avoidance of stepping on cracks is a "game."

BY WAY OF SUMMARY. The problem of translating intentions into action is the problem of will. Failure of "will power" can be understood, at least in part, as due to conflicts among opposing motives, to the existence of overlapping psychological situations that dilute the person's effective involvement in any one of the situations, to the inhibitory effect of excessive introspective thought, to an unrealistic standard of perfectionism.

Quite aside from the larger question of the actuality of free will, the person does tend to *perceive* himself as having "free will" to exercise choice and to carry out intentions. Other things being equal, the person tends to feel himself "free" when he has a more differentiated life-space and a greater perceived "space of free movement." Contrary to this sense of "free will" is the sense of being compelled, which may be perceived as arising *externally* to the self in the form of forces from the environment or from other people, or as arising *inwardly*, as when the person feels emotionally driven by "irrational" obsessions and compulsions.

The Self in Action. Finally, we must consider the person's experiences of himself as *acting*, as actually moving in the direction of the sought-after goals. As action proceeds, the perceived situation continuously changes; for as the person arrives at each new point on the path to the goal, he sees the situation in a somewhat altered perspective. He may perceive that the path to the goal is not as easy or as difficult as he had assumed, that the goal itself is more or less attractive than he had thought, that other competing goals have entered the picture. All such changes will modify the motivational condition from moment to moment, and his subsequent action may therefore take new directions and new forms.

Once having overcome all the barriers to the goal, the person may experience a sharp drop in tension, even *before* the actual goal activity takes place. The alcoholic who has desperately striven and finally succeeded in getting money to buy the craved drink may, once the glass is finally in his hand, delay the actual drinking, being able to relax and savor the knowledge that nothing can keep him from it. (His perception of being safely in the goal-region may of course be faulty: "There's many a slip 'twixt the cup and the lip.")

Box 52 describes an experimental study in which changes of tension along the path to the goal and on reaching the goal-region are objectively measured.

Attaining the goal may result in various feelings. The person may feel a sense of success and gratification; or he may feel "let down." Such feelings may derive from a new perspective on the entire situation, including a retrospective look, which makes the goal appear less desirable, the effort less necessary, the cost too great.

One particular reason for this negative reappraisal comes, of course, from the fact that once the consummatory activity takes place, the need or desire tends to be reduced or entirely abolished. And as this happens, the attractive quality of the goal-object may undergo a sharp change, with its attractive features diminishing, perhaps even being swamped by its previously hidden bad features.

But what about the cases in which the person fails to reach the goal? He may fall short through an "unrealistic" setting of level of aspiration, through failure to perceive an accessible pathway, through the unforeseen intrusion of barriers and conflicting goals. Now the person experiences feelings of frustration and failure, which may be accompanied by an intensification of the feelings of needs and desires, or, conversely, their change or disappearance. What happens in the behavior and experience of the person when he fails to achieve the goal will be treated fully in Chapter 11.

Glossary

abulia. Impairment of ability to initiate voluntary action and make decisions.

barrier. Something perceived by the person as an obstacle to goal-attainment. Barriers may be physical obstacles, social obstacles, or "inner" obstacles in the person's mental processes.

compulsion. The experiencing of an irresistible impulse to act in a certain way, even though the act may be recognized by the person as irrational and undesirable.

desire. A feeling of appetite, wish, or urge, which the person experiences as directed toward certain objects, conditions, or activities. Desires are not the same as needs. They derive not from states of perceived deficits, but from the perception of the thing as capable of providing gratification or pleasure in its own right. Desires can be said to provide the "positive" element to the motivational picture of man.

free will. The impression experienced by the person that he is free to make choices and to initiate voluntary acts. The psychological question of such *perception* of "free will" is to be distinguished from the broader philosophical question of the actuality of free will.

goal. A condition or activity perceived by the person as capable of removing his need or fulfilling his desire. Goal-*objects* are those objects in the environment toward which the motivated action is directed (e.g., food); goal *activities* are the intended actions with respect to the goal-object (e.g., eating the food).

identification. The phenomenon in which the person perceives and feels a particular form of close involvement of self with another person (or group). The self is experienced as though "extended out" to include the other person, and what befalls the other is to some extent felt as happening to oneself. Identifications are learned as part of psychological development. They are partly governed by perceptual organization, such as through grouping by similarity and by proximity.

level of aspiration. The standard of performance which the person sets for himself in a given goal-directed activity. Feelings of success or failure are determined by the relation between level of aspiration and the subsequent level of actual performance. Level of aspiration is determined by many factors, including one's past experience of success or failure in the given activity and the norms established by social groups.

life-space. The individual's total conception of the worlds in which he exists and behaves. It includes his percepts, knowledge, and beliefs; his forward and backward time-perspectives; things abstract as well as concrete, unreal as well as real.

multiple personality. A rare disorder involving the existence of two or more fairly separate "selves" within the same individual. The alternate selves are likely to be very different in traits, and the person during one phase may have no memory of the other dissociated phases.

need. The person's experience of a disruption or deficiency in the self, or in the surroundings, requiring action to remove, allay, or correct the condition. Need, in this usage, refers to an experienced psychological state rather than to an objective requirement in the person's body. Needs may or may not coincide with objective body requirements, depending upon the total psychological situation. Needs are in the service of removal of deficit conditions; their aim is to re-establish a condition of psychological equilibrium. They are different from, though often intimately related to, *desires.*

obsession. A recurrent and unavoidable thought, often disturbing and unwelcome to the person.

overlapping psychological situations. Two or more psychological situations that exist simultaneously for the individual. The several situations may differ in the proportion of the person's attention they command, and hence in the degree to which they determine his behavior.

pathways to goals. The routes that the person perceives will lead him to goals. The pathways may involve actual physical locomotion or other kinds of motor activity, or purely mental acts.

personality. The entire psychological structure of the individual, including his abilities, traits, motives, habits, cognitions, and their complex patterns. In short, everything that the psychologist can say about the given individual is part of the definition of his personality.

phantom limb. The commonly experienced feeling of the person whose limb has been amputated, that the limb is still there. The illusion may persist indefinitely.

psychological situation. The person's immediate experience of his self and life-space. It is subjectively defined, rather than as an outside observer would define it. The psychological situation changes from moment to moment in relation to the continuous changes in the pattern of external and internal stimuli.

regions of the life-space. All the potential activities, of whatever kind, in which the person can conceive of engaging. Some regions are attractive, some are negative, most are neutral in value. Not all regions of the life-space are equally accessible (see "space of free movement").

self. The "I" or "me" of which the person is aware in his thoughts, feelings, and actions. The self, like any other perceived object, has a structure with various properties, and is subject to development and change. The term "self" is to be distinguished from the terms "ego," "personality," and "organism." The self is but one part of the total personality of the individual.

self-ideal. The person's enduring conception of what he *ought* to be like, of how he *ought* to act. It provides a standard against which the rest of the self may be evaluated, and this comparison is a basic determinant of motivational and emotional experiences. The self-ideal is a product of psychological development, and is significantly influenced by social factors.

space of free movement. The person's subjective impression of the amount of freedom he has to move about in his life-space. The size of space of free movement is determined less by the *absolute* number of accessible regions than by the number of such regions *relative* to the number perceived by him as *potentially* but not actually accessible.

subgoal. A distinguishable part of a pathway to a goal which is perceived as being necessary to attain in order to reach the ultimate goal. Subgoals may come through experience to serve as goals in their own right.

will. The ability to make choices and to initiate voluntary action. Will is not a trait of the individual but a characteristic of behavior in a given situation. It tends to be manifested more strongly the less the conflict of forces, and the less the diffusion of attention among overlapping psychological situations.

Suggestions for Further Reading

LEWIN, K. 1935. *Dynamic theory of personality.* New York: McGraw-Hill.

The highly influential first report in English of the theories and experiments of Lewin and his associates on psychological conflict, tension, etc. Contains discussion of the self and the life-space.

MURPHY, G. 1947. *Personality: a biosocial approach to origins and structure.* New York: Harper.

A comprehensive treatment of the topic, including an excellent discussion of the concept of the self.

SHERIF, M., and CANTRIL, H. 1947. *The psychology of ego-involvements.* New York: Wiley.

A stimulating review and discussion of a great deal of research and theory about motivational involvement of the self. Includes discussion of the formation, change, and breakdown of the self.

SYMONDS, P. M. 1951. *The ego and the self.* New York: Appleton-Century-Crofts.

A detailed account of the concepts of ego and self, with particular stress on their dynamic aspects.

CHAPTER IX

Emotions of Man

Among the most central of our experiences of the self are the emotions. We feel anger, fear, joy, and grief; we feel guilt, pride and shame, misery and contentment, awe and wonder, love and hate.

In its broadest psychological meaning the term *emotion* refers to a stirred-up state of the organism, reflected in three quite different ways: (1) emotional experience, e.g., the person feels angry; (2) emotional behavior, e.g., he curses and attacks his tormentor; (3) physiological changes in the body, e.g., the blood rushes to his face, the heart beats faster, etc. These three aspects are intimately related, as we shall presently see. In this chapter, however, our concern is primarily with *emotional experience*. In Chapters 10 and 11 we will take up the behavioral consequences of motivational and emotional states, and in Chapter 12 their physiological aspects.

The Dimensions of Emotional Experience.
To bring some order into a description of

the bewildering array of emotional experiences is a formidable task. One way to approach it is to look for a limited number of general "dimensions" that are involved in the description of all emotional experiences. Four such general "dimensions" are intensity of feeling, level of tension, hedonic tone, and degree of complexity.

Intensity of feeling. Emotional experiences range in intensity of feeling all the way from the barely noticed tinge of a momentary mood to the most powerful of passions. Anger may vary from a faint vexation to a violent rage; joy, from a mild contentment to a sweeping ecstasy. The greater the intensity, the greater the tendency for the entire self to be involved, to be in the "grip" of the emotion.

Level of tension. Although we tend to think of all emotions in terms of feelings of agitation and upset, it is clear that emotional experiences vary widely in the level of tension involved. Tension refers to the *impulse toward action*. The person feels impelled to attack the frustrating barrier, to flee from the threatening object, to dance with delight. Here we have the "active" emotions. The more "passive" or "quiet" emotions may not involve such impulse to action; the sad person may sit without desiring to move, the contented one does not feel driven to act. "Active" and "passive" emotions are equally central to the person, equally involving the self. The difference between them lies in the degree of associated excitement and the strength of the impulse to action.

Intensity of feeling and level of tension are often correlated. A high degree of tension is very likely to mean a more intense feeling. But acute intensity may also be found in emotions with little tension as, for instance, in a profound depression.

HEDONIC TONE. Emotional experiences vary widely in their pleasantness or unpleasantness, that is, in what is technically called their *hedonic tone*. Feelings of grief, of shame, of fear, of remorse, are clearly unpleasant, while feelings of joy, pride, contentment, reverence, are as clearly pleasant. Some emotions are less clearly placed on a hedonic continuum. A feeling of pity, or of wonder, or of surprise, may be neither clearly pleasant nor clearly unpleasant.

The intensity of the feeling will, of course, affect the hedonic tone. A faint anger may not be particularly unpleasant, but a state of rage is unpleasant. And there are interesting paradoxes in which an emotion usually felt as pleasant may become so intense as to be unpleasant, e.g., hunger; or in which a mild negative emotion may be felt as pleasurable, e.g., a satisfying sorrow, a titillating fear ("You frighten me, Sir," said the maiden to her masterful suitor, "but that is not enough for marriage!").

DEGREE OF COMPLEXITY. These latter paradoxes point to the important fact that emotional experiences are often highly complex, being *patterns of diverse feelings*. We often feel ourselves in an "indescrib-able" state of emotion, and it is this very complexity of elements which makes it impossible for us to say just how an emotional experience feels, or whether it is pleasant or unpleasant. In contrast, a great many of our emotional experiences are simple and uncomplicated; we feel a pure fright at the earthquake, a pure elation in sudden good fortune, a pure grief in the death of our beloved dog.

Description of Emotions. It is the poets, the playwrights, the novelists, who have made the bravest attempts at concrete descriptions of emotional experience. It is to their literature that we usually go for accounts of what it is to feel jealousy, terror, remorse, guilt, ecstasy. Yet despite the richness of language, there is something lacking in even the best of literary descriptions. The writer's skill achieves only a skeleton of the full-bodied experience as we ourselves feel it; the richness and subtlety of the emotional experience defy available language.

In a laboratory method for describing emotions the subject is asked to characterize various emotions in a common set of physiognomic terms which depart from the usual language of description and seek to capture the feeling in words that can serve as *indicators* rather than as direct characterizations. Box 53 describes a study of this kind.

SITUATIONAL CONTEXT. One of the difficulties with all such attempts to describe emotions is that the emotions are abstracted from their situational context. Emotions occur as essential and inseparable aspects of all experiences. It is not the feeling of fear that we should seek to describe, but a particular experience of fear as it occurs in a specific situation, what the person perceives, feels, and thinks about. For again we are dealing with a "perfink" (see p. 201). It is in just this way, by

BOX 53

"Red" Envy, "Green" Grief

Is *fear* "rough" or "smooth," "wet" or "dry," "angular" or "rounded," "soft" or "loud," "empty" or "full," "green" or "red"? In a study by Block, subjects were asked such questions about a list of 15 emotions: love, anger, envy, humiliation, nostalgia, pride, fear, boredom, contentment, sympathy, grief, worry, elation, guilt, anticipation. His aim was to investigate the way different emotions appear to people through the use of physiognomic terms (see p. 27) not normally applied to the description of emotions. It was assumed that the use of this procedure would result in a more valid phenomenology of emotions than could be achieved through usual descriptions, as these are likely to be colored by mere verbal conventions and stereotypes.

Forty male and 48 female college students were asked to characterize each of the 15 emotions with respect to a set of 20 pairs of physiognomic terms. In general, there was found to be rather high agreement in the way the subjects characterized each of the different emotions. Men and women were analyzed separately, and it turned out that with the exception of the emotion of *grief* the correspondence of descriptions between men and women was very high. In the case of grief, aside from the many terms on which men and women agreed, women used such terms as "low," "green," "weak," "smooth," and "rounded," while men characterized it as "high," "red," "strong," "rough," and "angular."

The degree of similarity or dissimilarity of descriptions of each emotion with every other one was computed statistically. There were wide differences in similarity found among the emotions. For instance, guilt and worry were described in highly similar physiognomic terms, as were envy and fear, elation and love. Conversely, there was extreme dissimilarity among certain other pairs, such as guilt and contentment, boredom and love, nostalgia and anger. And for still other pairs the relationship was about zero; that is, the emotions seemed neither similar to one another in their physiognomic connotations, nor dissimilar. Examples were fear and boredom, sympathy and pride, guilt and nostalgia.

It should be stressed that mere conventional verbal usage in the description of emotions would probably not account for the findings. For one thing, we do not have well-established verbal conventions for referring to most emotional feelings. And the few conventions we do have may not coincide with the physiognomic terms we actually use in making phenomenological descriptions of emotions. For example, *envy* turned out to be characterized more frequently as "red" than as "green."

A preliminary *cross-cultural comparison* was made by administering the same procedure to a sample of male and female subjects in Norway. It was found that in general the descriptions of emotions by the American and Norwegian subjects were highly similar. However there were certain striking differences between the two cultural groups in the degree of relationship among pairs of emotions. For example, among Americans, *grief* and *guilt* were described in highly similar terms, whereas among Norwegians the two were seen as unrelated. This finding may illustrate an effective approach to the cross-cultural study of values and attitudes.

BLOCK, J. 1957. Studies in the phenomenology of emotion. *J. abnorm. soc. Psychol.,* 54, 358–63.

describing emotions in a context, that writers have best contributed to the description of emotions.

In a given fear-provoking situation the person may see himself threatened by a gun, feel impelled to run, see dangerous parts and safe parts of the surroundings, and feel tight constriction of the chest and a "freezing" of the legs; and accompanying all this he will experience a feeling of fear which language cannot describe. All this together makes up the fear experience; with some of these elements changed or removed, the fear experience is different, or may not be fear at all. Let us turn, then, to a more detailed discussion of the main types of components that make up the whole emotional experience. We will discuss bodily feelings, feelings of impulses to action, and, very broadly, the perceptions and thoughts about the immediate situation, the surrounding objects and events, and their relation to the self.

BODILY FEELINGS. Salient in our emotional experiences are states of our physical bodies. We feel tenseness, dryness of the throat, heart jumping, dizziness, sweating, and weakness of limbs. And we feel our bodies engaging in various involuntary actions—crying, laughing, trembling, making startle responses. This rich complex of organic and kinesthetic perceptions suffuses the emotional experience. These effects may be barely noticeable or overwhelming; and they may be apprehended as central to the whole emotional experience or rather peripheral to it.

By deliberately starting certain voluntary bodily responses, such as laughing and crying, the appropriate emotion may sometimes be induced. The same is true of certain postures that go with emotional experience; cringing and shrinking may sometimes evoke at least a faint feeling of anxiety; smiling may tend to make for a pleasant feeling, frowning for irritation. In this way the actor may through portraying the emotion actually feel it to some degree. Presumably the ability of the bodily posture and expression to induce an appropriate emotional experience rests upon the fact that such bodily expressions are, through past learning or instinctive patterning, characteristic parts of the whole emotion.

The mere existence of a certain set of bodily feelings will not in and of itself evoke the emotion. The situation must be one that is readily capable of being perceived in the appropriate way, and the effect of the bodily feelings is to sensitize the person to seeing the situation in that appropriate way. Thus the woman slicing onions will usually cry without feeling grief; but if she has just been ill-treated by her husband, the flow of tears from the onions may quickly evoke a genuine emotion of grief. (See Box 54.)

EMPATHY, SYMPATHY, COMPLEMENTARITY. To the extent that the perceptions of one's bodily states can induce emotions, there is a sort of "self-induction" of emotion. Similarly, when we perceive other people's external bodily expressions of emotion, the same emotion may be induced in ourselves. Here we might speak of "emotional contagion." There does seem to be ample evidence of such "contagion": the wailing of other mourners induces grief in us; the laughing child makes us laugh too; the posture of fear in another may strike fear in ourselves. When we have "caught" the emotion of the other and express it ourselves, we say that we *empathize* with the other. Yet here, too, the presence or absence of a situation that can be meaningfully related to the specific emotion plays an important part. If we cannot see what the other person is afraid of, or crying about, we will probably remain unaffected.

When we do not perceive the situation the way the other person does, his emotional expression may stir no similar emotion in us, even if we identify closely with him. What we *will* often feel in such cases is a *sympathetic* emotion—the mother feels protective tenderness when her frightened child cries. We may also, of course, feel a *complementary* emotion, depending upon how *we* perceive the situation. If we perceive the anger of the other person as caused by and directed at us, our feeling is not so likely to be anger as fear. And if we see a person being shamed, we may not feel an empathic shame, but rather a

BOX 54

"Cold" Emotion

The critical role of the perceived situation in governing the experience of emotion is shown in an ingenious way by the following experiment by Marañon. Adrenaline was injected into the blood stream of human subjects in a neutral laboratory situation. As we shall see in Chapter 12, the effect of adrenaline is to produce some of the kinds of physiological upsets which are normally found in cases of strong emotion. What, then, would be the effect of producing such physiological upsets by the adrenaline injection when there is no external situation appropriate to evoke an emotion?

The subjects reported that they perceived the physiological effects, such as palpitations, trembling, etc. But they described the experience as a peculiar one, lacking genuine emotional quality. It was experienced as a kind of "cold" emotion, pale copies of previous emotional experiences. The subjects described their feelings in remarks such as: "I feel as if afraid," "I feel as if I had a great fright, yet am calm."

Here we have a simple case where the situation was not of such a nature psychologically as to evoke a true emotion, and though an artificially induced bodily upset was highly similar to the physiological changes in real emotional states, it was not *by itself* sufficient to evoke a genuine feeling of emotion.

The reader might speculate on the results of a hypothetical experiment in which adrenaline would be injected while the person was in a situation not entirely neutral in emotion-evoking power. That is, the situation, though not quite adequate to arouse an emotional response, would, with a little intensification, be capable of doing so. What, under these circumstances, would be the effect of the adrenaline? Might the threshold for arousal of the emotion be lowered?

MARAÑON, G. 1924. *Revue française d'endocrinologie, 2,* 301.

sense of anger at the person causing the shame.

EMOTIONAL ACTION. To a considerable degree the specific character of the emotional experience is provided by the particular actions that we find ourselves exhibiting. McDougall (1923) was one of the first to stress the close integration of emotion and action (which he believed to be instinctive in origin), pointing out that fear and flight, anger and attack, maternal feeling and protective action, naturally go together as parts of unitary behavior patterns.

UNCLEAR SITUATIONS. We have been stressing the theme that emotional states of the self are apprehended by the person as meaningfully related to certain concrete features of the immediate situation; he feels his fear as related to that pointed gun, his joy as stemming from that examination successfully passed, his aesthetic excitement as caused by that painting, his sexual passion as directed at that girl. But there are often emotional states in which the reference to the situation is much less clear, or in which the emotional state seems to be experienced as unconnected with the situation. For instance, the person feels anxiety, but it is anxiety without any clear cognitive content; he cannot say why he feels anxious or what there is to be anxious about. (This is sometimes called "free-floating" anxiety.)

The more intense such unconnected emotional feelings, the less likely they are to remain unconnected. What tends to happen, as we should expect from our knowledge about the ever-insistent perceptual organizing tendencies of the individual, is that the emotional experience is made "sensible" with respect to the whole situation. In brief, the person comes to "attach" the emotion to an appropriate aspect of the situation, if need be through "inventing" a situation. For example, the feeling of anger which wells up gradually in the person as a consequence of a series of mild annoyances, and which is not at first experienced by him as relevant to anything that he can identify, is now suddenly experienced as anger directed at a store clerk who has been "impolite."

BY WAY OF SUMMARY. Emotional experience is an organized pattern of feelings as contributed to by the perception of bodily states and processes, the perception of expression of the emotions, and the perception of adjustive actions.

The nature of the particular emotion is determined by the particular psychological situation.

Situational Analysis of Specific Emotions. In view of the infinite variety of situations that exist for the person, his emotional experiences would seem to defy classification. Yet our language does have terms for specific emotions and these do point in a useful way to certain general "types" of emotional experiences which we readily distinguish in our experience. Although each experience of "anger," for example, is in some degree different from every other experience of "anger," there does seem to be something common to all "anger experiences." This justifies a search for a particular pattern of situational determinants to be found in all such instances, for we assume that there is a *necessary relationship between the situational pattern and the emotion evoked.*

As we have already noted, the primary elements that comprise the pattern of the immediate situation include needs and desires, intentions and striving toward goals, the objects and events in the surroundings, and the place of self and these objects and events in the entire life-space as now perceived.

As we now analyze specific emotions, we will find that each of these situational features plays a larger or smaller role. Thus for certain emotions, say remorse, it is the backward time-perspective that is crucial (what we *should have done*—or should not have done); for certain emotions, say joy,

it is the *outcome* of goal-directed striving which is the critical factor.

It is convenient to discuss emotions in the following six main classes, starting with the most primary and goal-directed:

1) *Primary emotions*, e.g., joy, fear, anger, grief
2) *Emotions pertaining to sensory stimulation*, e.g., pain, disgust, horror, delight
3) *Emotions pertaining to self-appraisal*, e.g., shame, pride, guilt
4) *Emotions pertaining to other people*, e.g., love, hate, pity
5) *Appreciative emotions*, e.g., humor, beauty, wonder
6) *Moods*, e.g., sadness, anxiety, elation

Primary Emotions

Joy, anger, fear, and grief are often referred to as the most basic or primary emotions. They are so designated for several reasons. They appear early in the development of the individual; the situations that evoke them are basically simple; they are intimately involved with aroused, goal-striving activity, and hence likely to be found with high degrees of associated tension.

There is a tendency to view emotions as disruptive and handicapping. This tendency overstresses the undesirable aspects of emotion. Emotions have desirable aspects too. Let us therefore accentuate the positive by starting our discussion with joy.

Joy. The essential situational condition for joy is that the person is striving toward a goal and attains it. The intensity of the joy depends upon the level of tension which had built up in the person in the course of the motivated act. Where there is an unimportant goal, the emotion may be no more than mild satisfaction; for an extremely important goal, the result may be transports of joy.

The joy is the emotional counterpart of the release of tension with goal-attainment. Thus *suddenness* with which the goal is achieved and tension released affects the intensity of the joy. When a person wins a game easily, he may feel only mild elation; but winning a game at the last instant, when all seemed lost, may evoke an ecstatic feeling.

This is not to say that the feeling of joy that comes when the child gets the new toy is identical with the feeling of joy that comes when an Archimedes solves a baffling problem. Nor is the savage joy of the person who sees his enemy struck down the same as the ecstatic joy of the religious experience.

But our concern here is not with all the specific goal achievements that can lead to joy, or with the nuances of joyous feeling. The main point is to see that it is goal-attainment and tension release that are the essential situational determinants.

Anger. The essential condition for arousing anger is the *blocking* of goal-attainment, especially where there is persistent frustration of goal-attainment, with the gradual accumulation of tension. At first there may be nothing more than a slight feeling of exasperation or vexation; with prolonged frustration the person may become truly angry, and eventually reach a state of rage or fury.

Not all cases of thwarting of one's goals will lead to anger. As we shall see in Chapter 11 and also in Chapter 24, thwarting has many different possible consequences, of which anger is but one. A great deal seems to depend upon the extent to which there is an identifiable barrier to goal achievement. If the person simply cannot see what is preventing his goal achievement, anger is not so likely to occur; but if he sees (rightly or wrongly) an obstacle that is causing the trouble, and particularly if the thwarting seems to him somehow "unreasonable" or "deliberate" or "malicious," anger is more likely to occur and to be expressed in aggressive action against the thwarting object.

Fear. Joy and anger are, in a sense, emotions of "approach," that is, they involve goal-striving. Fear, on the other hand, is an emotion of "avoidance," involving an escape from danger. And because the world is full of potential dangers, fear is a very commonly experienced emotion. Some observers of human nature have even made it the core of human behavior; in their view, "It is fear that makes the world go round."

The essential situation for the onset of fear is the perception of a dangerous object or condition that threatens us. The key fact in the situation seems to be the *lack of power or capability of the person to handle the threat.* If he does not know how to ward it off, or especially if he sees his escape route blocked, fear is induced. The profoundest terror can be induced by a feeling of powerlessness in the grip of overwhelming forces, such as an earthquake or other natural cataclysms, or—on a more modest scale—a father's harsh threats as they appear to the child.

In due course we may become habituated to dangerous objects, living close to them without alarm; this happens because we have learned how to cope with them. But if the immediate situation changes, so that our well-established means for handling them are disrupted, fear emerges.

It is especially noteworthy that unexpected alterations in our usual surroundings can induce fear. It is as though we have organized our worlds in such a way as to protect ourselves, and any disruption in the order may cause us immediate

BOX 55

The Fear of the Strange in the Chimpanzee

In a series of experiments at the Yerkes Laboratories of Primate Biology, Hebb tested the fear responses of 30 chimpanzees when confronted with strange and unfamiliar objects.

Among the objects used were an ape head, a skull, a human head (from a window-display dummy), anesthetized chimpanzees, pictures, toy animals. These test objects were presented to the chimpanzee while he was in his home cage. The animal was lured to the front of his cage by an offer of a small amount of food. The hinged top of a box was then lifted, exposing one of the test objects. "Fear" was ascribed to the chimpanzee if definite signs of withdrawal from the object were observed. Accompanying such withdrawal were signs of unusual excitement such as erection of hair, screaming, threatening gestures, etc.

From the data it is clear that *either* a lack of responsiveness in a whole animal (the anesthetized chimps), *or* the lack of a body when the head is seen, is the most effective determiner of fear.

Hebb's explanation is somewhat along these lines: (1) Through past learning the chimpanzee comes to expect certain events when stimulated by an object (e.g., when seeing a head, he "expects" to see the rest of the body). (2) Neurologically, this means that as a result of stimulation by such an object, a *co-ordinated sequence of neural*

events is started in the animal's brain. (3) The immediate source of fear is a *disruption* of this patterned sequence. Fear is thus seen as a direct result of *profound disorganization of cerebral processes.* (4) Strange, dead, or mutilated bodies arouse perceptual and intellectual processes that are *incompatible* with an already ongoing pattern of activities, and the result is *fear*.

The fear reaction—withdrawal or flight—tends to restore "cerebral equilibrium" by removing the animal from the whole complex of disrupting and incompatible stimuli.

HEBB, D. O. 1946. On the nature of fear. *Psychol. Rev., 53,* 259–76.

---

apprehension. It is commonplace that a young child is often made anxious and apprehensive by changes in his customary surroundings. The "terror of the unknown" is not merely a literary expression, for it is universally found that the strange, the unfamiliar, may cause dread in its viewers. This is a very primitive reaction, for we note it also in animals (see Box 55).

It is with fear, perhaps more than with any other emotion, that contagion by others is most acute. Seeing and hearing others in a state of terror will often induce panic in

the onlooker even when there is nothing else in his situation to account for it.

An important component in many fear situations is the *future time-perspective*, that is, we anticipate what is going to happen and by dwelling upon it in our thoughts may work up a severe state of anticipatory dread. The worst torture may sometimes be that which assails the prisoner in his cell before he is taken to the torture chamber; dentists know all about this!

Such anticipation of impending threat is typically felt as *anxiety*. The limitless possibilities of imagined future events provide us with endless fuel for anxiety. Moreover, the very complexity of the worlds in which we live is such as to make it hard for most people to be sure they have protected themselves against all possible danger.

STARTLE. Many years ago Watson (1924) experimented with fear in young infants, and concluded that the sudden loss of body support and sudden loud sounds were the critical stimuli. Since his day, laboratory psychologists have experimented extensively with effects of inducing the so-called *startle-respon*se—which we have all studied less elegantly by saying "Boo!" They have been especially interested in the pattern of physiological upsets and bodily expressions during startle, on the assumption that the pattern resembles that during fear and that studying it is a simple way of studying the effects of fear. It is obvious that when suddenly startled, we often feel a momentary fright. Yet we cannot equate startle and fear; there are many instances in which the startle fails to arouse fear, perhaps arousing a quite different response, such as laughter.

The sudden stimulus may "trigger off" the emotion of fear when the rest of the situation predisposes toward its arousal. Note the difference in emotional effects of loudly saying "Boo!" in the ear of an unsuspecting person when he is reading a suspense-thriller at night, and when he is sitting in a football stadium watching the game. In the former situation this may well lead to fear; in the latter it is more likely to lead to surprise, laughter, annoyance, or nothing whatever.

Grief. Joy, anger, and fear have to do with the seeking of goals or the escape from dangers. Grief is concerned with the *loss* of something sought or valued. The intensity depends upon the value; usually the most profound grief comes from the

loss of loved persons, and deep feelings of grief may come also from the loss of prized possessions. These are cases of intense and enduring grief; there are all shades of grief, down to the merest feeling of disappointment or regret.

Joy, anger, and fear are typically "active" emotions, involving large amounts of tension. Grief is often typically "quiet," less characterized by tension and activity. Yet there are obvious cases in which the grief is expressed in crying and other active expressions. A person who sees his loved one endangered and seeks to protect her may be thrown into the most violent of griefs if she is lost. And on a much less profound scale, the player who has lost a close game may burst into tears, or the child who has seen a desired toy destroyed may show an outburst of grief. There is often a "delayed" reaction in cases of bereavement. First, the person experiences a sense of shock, with a "numbness"; he, and those around him, may be surprised that he seems to feel no real emotion. This is typically followed by a period in which the realization of the loss becomes clearer and now the person may find himself experiencing genuine transports of grief, with a high degree of tension and active expression.

It would seem probable that this grief occurs because of the flow of thoughts that envisage the many ways in which the loss of the loved one forever prevents many things desired and needed. And as the person comes from moment to moment into contact with all sorts of objects that remind him of the loved one—his clothes, his books, his photographs—there is repeated accentuation of the significance of the loss: the child's toys ("We loved to play together, and never again can we play together"); the books ("He wanted so to learn to read and I wanted to help him, but now it is too late"). And with the whiplash of each newly perceived aspect of the loss comes the renewed burst of grief. Even long after the emotion has disappeared, when suddenly the person comes upon a forgotten possession of the dead one, he is once again grief-stricken. We see again the critical significance of situational factors in determining the emotion.

As with all emotions, the bare essential of loss of something valued is far from the entire story. For we know of many cases in which the loss of something valued is *not* accompanied by grief. In some cultures the death of a loved one is an occasion for quiet joy; the loved one has joined "his fathers," has gone to the "happy hunting ground." And thus it seems clear that what is critical is *how* the loss is perceived, and in what larger context. The immediacy of the personal loss may be dwarfed by the wider perspectives: the dead one is now happier, is "waiting for me to join him after the grave"; and on a more trivial scale of griefs, this lost game is but one of many more to be played, this broken toy can be replaced by a better one.

Though we have classified grief as a primary emotion, along with joy, anger, and fear, it appears to be a somewhat less primitive emotion. It is not at all clear how extensively grief occurs in animals lower than man. And in children, too, grief comes later than the other primary emotions. It would seem that there is a greater complexity of the essential situation involved in grief, a greater element of the recognition of the loss and its consequences, a greater dependence on the *future* in one's time-perspective. This may exceed the mental grasp of the animal or young child.

An additional factor is especially relevant to the emotion of grief. To a greater extent than is true of joy, anger, and fear, the situational pattern evoking grief involves concrete *objects*. Without the concrete thing that is valued and lost, there is no grief. In joy, anger, and fear objects may

also play a role, but with less necessity. We may feel an indeterminant joy, an unconnected anger, a fear "of we know not what," but grief pertains to a particular object. There is probably no "free-floating" grief.

Emotions Pertaining to Sensory Stimulation

In this class of emotional experiences are those that more clearly pertain to pleasant and unpleasant sensory stimulation by objects. The stimulation may be mild or intense. The resulting emotional feeling tends to be directed toward the positive or negative object.

Pain. Physical pain is the most important case of intense physical stimulation leading to emotional arousal. At low intensities the pain sensation may be perceived as peripheral to the self, and it may evoke neither an emotional feeling nor an avoidant action. At higher intensities an unpleasant emotional state is aroused, and with extreme pain may come the most acute emotional agitation.

One's *understanding* of the "pain situation" has much to do with the intensity of emotional arousal. Painful emotion is often reinforced by fear. An internal pain whose source we do not understand may be intensely agitating, especially if we are prone to think it has the dread significance, for example, of cancer. Once the pain is diagnosed as harmless, the intensity of the painful emotion may greatly subside.

The painful emotion has parallels with the emotion of fear, in that both are maximized by the blocking, or apparent blocking, of avoidance, and both are minimized by a sense of being capable of dealing with the conditions arousing them.

Disgust. There are various kinds of objects which when seen, smelled, tasted, or touched arouse *disgust*—acute unpleasant feelings, involving strong avoidance tendencies and marked sensations of bodily upset, such as nausea and vomiting. Here again it is the *closeness of contact* with the self which is all-important. In our culture slimy objects, such as slugs, tend to evoke strong disgust. The feeling is much stronger when the object is not merely seen, but placed in contact with the skin.

Note that by disgust we mean only this primary emotion that includes the essential bodily sensations of nausea and related upsets. In popular parlance the term is often used more generally to refer to any kind of aversive feeling: "She is a disgusting person," or "I'm disgusted with myself." But these emotions are more complex and will be considered later under classes of emotions pertaining to self and to other people. It is true, of course, that authentic feelings of disgust are sometimes aroused by other people as stimulus-objects. In some cultures, being actually touched by a person of lower or "unclean" caste might evoke genuine disgust and even nausea. Obviously, cultural standards and specific past experience of the individual play a major role in determining what objects will evoke genuine disgust.

Displeasures. Pain and disgust tend to incorporate clear feelings of bodily upset as essential parts of the emotional experience. Beyond these two more explicit negative emotions there is a large, ill-defined class of unpleasant emotional experiences that pertain to a tremendous array of negative stimulus-objects. For want of a better term we call these *displeasures*. They are feelings of aversion, dislike, discomfort, and distress which are directed mainly at the negative stimulus-object.

They range in intensity from minor irritations and annoyances (see Box 56) to extreme *horror*, which is induced by the witnessing of profoundly affecting events, particularly events involving terrible accidents, maiming of bodies, destruction of objects. The degree of one's feeling of involvement or identification with the people or objects determines the intensity of the horror. To see a loved person killed or imminently endangered, or to see one's valued property destroyed as in a fire, induces strong horror. And, as is true of fear and disgust, the horror is accentuated by the feeling that one is helpless to intercede in the event.

Delights. A vast array of objects and events have the power to evoke pleasurable feelings in us. We may call these emotional experiences *delights*, in contradistinction to the *displeasures* above. They vary in intensity from minor enjoyments, satisfactions, and likings to the utmost ecstasy.

The emotions of delight are not to be confused with joy, as we have described it. They are not feelings of sudden relief from tension, rather they are positive *enjoyments*. They often, of course, involve feelings of excitement, but the excitement is an intrinsic aspect of the delight, not a prior condition for its arousal.

The sources of delights, like those of displeasures, are well-nigh inexhaustible. Some are the pleasant sensations in the body as it is touched, stroked, or caressed. Some come from perceptions of body movement and functioning—delights in muscular activity, rhythmical dancing, singing—and from the feelings associated with mild degrees of body need—pleasant hungers, pleasant weariness.

Other sensory delights pertain to external objects, their textures, colors, shapes; their sounds, tastes, smells. And there are limitless varieties of activities surrounding and engaging us that give us enjoyment—play-

BOX 56

How to Be Annoyed 507 Ways

In 1928 Cason studied common annoyances as experienced in a sample of over a thousand persons of both sexes, varying in age from 10 to 90 years, representing wide ranges of intelligence, wealth, physical characteristics, race, religion, and locality (all American). The subjects rated 507 common annoyances on a rating scale varying from "extremely annoying" to "not annoying." These 507 common annoyances represented the careful distillation of over 21,000 collected from large groups of people.

It was Cason's belief that in the ordinary affairs of civilized man the simple and often trivial annoyances and irritations have far greater significance for people's adjustment than do the more violent forms of emotion which have been more widely studied. He concerned himself with annoyances that were concrete and objective, especially those having an irrational aspect. Some of the annoyances were strong enough to be classed as cases of anger; others were matters of disgust; still others included an element of fear.

These 507 annoyances were classified into five groupings with most of them falling into the category "human behavior." The five categories and the percentage of annoyances in each category was as follows:

	Per Cent
Human behavior	59.0
Nonhuman things and activities, exclusive of clothes	18.8
Clothes and manner of dress	12.5
Alterable physical characteristics of people	5.3
Persisting physical characteristics of people	4.4
	100.0

Some of the 507 annoyances are listed below. In each case the average annoyance score is shown for both males and females. The possible range is from 0 to 30.

It will be seen that a great many of the annoyances are probably not unique to the year 1928, but persist today. On the other hand, certain ones clearly indicate changes of custom and standards even in that short period. It would be interesting to compare such a list with a list of annoyances found, say, among the Bantu of Africa. Some of the 507 annoyances might appear everywhere as basic human annoyances, but most would probably be found to be specific to the cultural setting.

CASON, H. 1930. Common annoyances: A psychological study of every-day aversions and irritations. *Psychol. Monog., 40,* No. 2, 1–218.

AVERAGE SCORES FOR SOME SPECIFIC ANNOYANCES

Annoyance	*Male*	*Female*
A person coughing in my face	28.5	29.3
To see or hear an animal being cruelly treated by a person	28.0	28.3
The odor of garbage	24.0	25.5
A person in an automobile I am driving telling me how to drive	23.0	18.5
To have to get off the sidewalk to pass people who are taking up all the room	21.3	19.0
To see a person picking his (or her) teeth	15.3	21.3
To see a woman smoking a cigarette in public	16.5	18.3
To be held very close by my dancing partner	6.8	19.3
A beggar asking me for some money in a public place	14.0	10.8
To find a newspaper disarranged when I begin to read it	11.8	9.5
To see bobbed hair on a woman over 40	10.5	8.3

ing games, reading, thinking, sports, pleasant work, the ballet, the burlesque, the ball game.

Emotions Pertaining to Self-Appraisal

Feelings of success and failure, of shame, pride, guilt, remorse, are emotions in which the essential determinants have to do with the person's perception of his own behavior *in relation to various standards of behavior.* It would appear doubtful that lower animals can experience such emotions, since they lack the capability of perceiving standards of conduct and their own actions in relation to them. And it seems quite clear that these emotions appear only gradually in the human child; the infant does not feel shame, and it may take quite a while before the child is able to experience remorse.

Feelings of Success and Failure. The attainment of goals and the attendant release of tension result, as we have seen, in joyful emotion. But beyond this is the more complicated situation in which there is perception of the quality of our *performance* compared with our *intentions.* Feelings of success and satisfaction do not necessarily accompany accomplishment of the task. These feelings occur only to the extent that the person's attention is centered on his achievement, and they are determined by his *level of aspiration* (see pp. 220–1). If he perceives that he has reached or exceeded his level of aspiration, an emotion of satisfaction is engendered. If he feels that he has fallen short of it, a sense of failure and a feeling of dejection is aroused.

Success and failure must be defined in terms of the person's *own* perceptions, his own level of aspiration. He may feel that he has succeeded when others would judge he has not; and he may feel that he has failed when others would judge him successful. As we have already seen in discussing level of aspiration, he may come to perceive that he has set his aimed-at level too low, so that even when he achieves it, he will feel despondent. Outward success may taste like "ashes in the mouth," and this feeling will be intensified by the contrast he perceives between the praises accorded him by others and his own inner judgment of failure.

This is not, of course, to say that whenever he perceives his performance as falling short of his standard, the result will be the dejected emotions of failure. As we shall see in later chapters, there are many resources of self-defense against the feelings of failure, and his emotions may be quite different—resentment of others who succeed, anger at self, etc.

Although it is the inner-personal rather than the external-social standards of performance which directly determine what will be failure for him and what success, it is clear that social factors play an enormous role in shaping these inner standards. The person comes to set and adjust his standards in some degree of meaningful relation with those of other people; for one thing, he is often competing with others, and the common evaluation of performance is strongly pressed upon him. Moreover, the very nature of social living makes him especially conscious of the judgments that others are constantly making about him. The very perception of one's self is highly dependent upon one's perception of the social world.

Pride and Shame. When successes or failures of goal-achievement are perceived by the person as signifying basic accomplishments or defects *of the self*, deeper and more central emotions of pride or shame may be engendered. In general, the feeling of *pride* results from the person's perception that his behavior is in accord with what is called for by his ideal-self conception. Conversely, the feeling of *shame* results from his perception that his behavior falls short of what is required by his ideal picture of self.

Merely perceiving that there is a discrepancy between self and ideal self is not always, however, a sufficient condition for emotions of shame. Individuals may come to have a realistic acceptance of the gap between self and ideal self, just as in the level-of-aspiration experiments some subjects feel no sense of failure in falling short of their level of aspiration. They apparently are able to recognize the reasonableness of performance short of the ideal, coupled with a persistent effort toward the ideal; in short, they exhibit a common-sense acceptance of the fallibility of human nature, in themselves as well as in others.

On the other hand, there are strong forces in society designed to make the individual continuously evaluate his behavior and conduct with respect to the dictates of ideal self, and thus the emotions of pride and shame are especially likely to be aroused in a social setting, such as in a group. For example, as part of the social training of children, parents and others deliberately try to *induce* such self-evaluative attitudes in them. They may say to the errant child, "Aren't you ashamed of yourself?" "Do you think you have behaved the way you know is right?" Or they may call his attention to the "model" behavior of another child in the situation: "Why can't you act the way Johnny does?"

These are obvious and direct applications of *external social standards* of self-appraisal and conduct. To a very considerable extent external standards eventually become *internalized*. Standards that were originally perceived by the person as outside himself are now seen as his own; that is, they form an enduring part of the person's self, no longer dependent upon the application of actual social forces.

INTERNALIZED SOCIAL STANDARDS. There are, of course, all degrees and varieties of such "internalization." For some people and some cultures, standards of conduct are not highly "internalized"; the *external signs of approval or disapproval* of the group continue to be the main determinants. The person feels shame when the group expresses its disapproval of his conduct, and pride when it expresses approval. The phrase "loss of face" neatly expresses this close dependence of shame on outer social evaluation.

For other individuals and cultures the ideal self is thoroughly "internalized." The person carries his code as part of himself, and is affected by it regardless of the immediate presence or absence of outer social evaluations. He does not need to have others ask if he feels ashamed of his conduct, for he asks himself; he needs no one to look askance, for he sees himself as though through the perspective of others. The man secretly shamed may still feel "loss of face" and commit hara-kiri.

We should not exaggerate the extreme of either the external or the "internal" status of the self standards. Most people experience both sets of forces. In privacy the individual does not revert to an asocial outlook, nor is he in public by any means subject exclusively to the evaluations of those around him.

Certain aspects of the ideal-self picture are especially vulnerable to direct social evaluations. The external "trappings" of social status, such as social position and possessions, are examples. Physical appearance is, of course, a powerful instance. The most agonizing emotion of shame may be induced in the adolescent because of the belief that others see him or her as gawky, or pimply, or wearing the wrong kind of clothes, instead of the accepted adolescent "uniform"—blue jeans and saddle shoes, cashmere and pearls, or whatever local custom dictates.

Guilt and Remorse. Emotions of guilt and of shame are not the same, though they are often closely linked. *Guilt* is a feeling of wrongdoing, of violation, which is generally experienced as distressing or painful. The essential circumstances evoking the emotion have to do with the perception of one's own action in a situation as discrepant from the "right" or "moral" or "ethical" action required by the situation.

The emotion of guilt may be slight and fleeting, a mere "twinge of conscience." Or, at the other extreme, it may be a prolonged torture of "agonizing appraisal." The milder degrees of guilt feelings may even at times be somewhat pleasant and exhilarative in tone. This is not surprising in the light of the fact that when the person violates what he perceives as "right," it is often simply because of the more powerful force of positive pleasures to be gained. As anthropologists and others have pointed out, moral prohibition tends to be created by society just *because* there is social necessity for restraint of certain activities that are themselves desirable. But this is by no means the entire story. The very imposition of the prohibition may have the paradoxical effect of making the thing appear attractive to the person: "Forbidden fruits are sweetest." Moreover, the very act of violation is often in itself satisfying because it is experienced as a successful defiance of outer authority, an expression of autonomy and power of self.

The basic question of the *source* of the individual's belief in the "rightness" or "wrongness" of certain acts we cannot consider at this point (see Chapter 23). But given the fact that he *does* perceive acts in this way, the emotion of guilt flows directly from his perceived transgression of the morality.

SPECIFICITY OF GUILT. It is important here to understand that there are wide differences in the way a person perceives the guilt-inducing situation. He may see quite specifically just what is "required" of him, and recognize quite clearly how he has violated this requirement. His consequent feeling of guilt is likely to be directly and explicitly attached to the action: "I feel guilty because I allowed the store clerk to give me too much change." But other situations may be far more complex and his perceptions unclear as to exactly what is required and how his actions relate to it. The resulting guilt feeling may not be so explicitly connected with a given act or given feature of the situation. We may all feel a vague and perhaps even intense guilt when the world is thrown into war. There is a kind of "free-floating" guilt, just as there is "free-floating" anxiety. Indeed, one of the marked features of such ill-defined and "irrational-appearing" guilt feelings is their anxiety component; the person feels an anxious guilt in which he is not quite clear about just where and why the feelings of fear or dread or distress appear, nor about how he can modify his behavior to prevent the guilt feeling. Like the prisoner in Kafka's novel, *The Trial*, he knows not what crime he is charged with.

It is especially in cases of ill-defined guilt feelings that the person tends to perceive the guilt as attaching deeply to *himself*; it is not so much that any one of his *acts* is bad, but that *he* is a bad person. The profoundest and most agitating of guilt emotions—such as those found in the fanatically self-punishing or in the insane—are of this sort; the self is seen as the focal point and basic source of the guilty action.

OBJECTIFICATION OF GUILT. There are significant differences in the extent to which the guilt is experienced as "objecti-fied." At one extreme it may be perceived as arising sheerly in connection with a particular action. Though the self is seen as an essential agent in the whole act, *the act is not a basic characteristic of the self*, but something rather peripheral to it. At the other extreme is the guilt experienced as the Sin of Self, *my* evil nature, the "bad me"; the wrong act did not simply *involve* me, but it was *caused* by me.

The distinction between the different types of guilt feelings also bears intimately on the matter of how these feelings are removed. Feelings of guilt which are more "objectified" (that is, explicitly connected with specific acts) are presumably easier to slough off; they are less likely to persist in one's self-conception. It has sometimes been said that Catholic confession and absolution of sins achieves this purpose; the person goes forth feeling "cleansed" of guilty feel-ing. Acts of expiation required by the priest are *acts* that can cancel out or rectify the bad act. In some of the harsher forms of Protestantism, on the other hand, the per-son may be forced to "live with" his guilt, to feel it continuously and be punished by it; forced to acknowledge his basic sin from which there is redemption only through removing the sin *from himself*, through faith and good works, or from which there is *no* redemption, the Sin being Original.

GUILT VS. SHAME. The fact that guilt can be experienced as "objectified" and not basically related to one's real self-concep-tion helps to explain the distinction be-tween guilt and shame. Feelings of guilt *without* associated feelings of shame can readily occur when the person feels the guilt as peripheral to his real self—the fact that he engaged in the bad action bears in no way on his essential self-conception. This is especially so in the common case in which the person does not rationally accept the external moral standard, but nonetheless is sufficiently subject to its emotional force that a transgression will evoke the sense of guilt.

Conversely, there can be feelings of shame *without* associated feelings of guilt; indeed this is perhaps the more common condition. A man may feel shame when caught using the wrong fork at an elegant dinner party, but not guilt. His shame stems from a sense of having made a fool of himself in the eyes of others or of having failed to live up to his ideal self-picture of the "sophisticate." But there is no cause for feelings of guilt, since there has been no violation of moral standards.

Suppose, on the other hand, that he has been caught *stealing* one of the forks from the dinner table. Now we would expect him to experience a combination of feelings of shame *and* guilt. There are many kinds of situations in which these two emotions may be found associated. Another kind of example is seen in the case in which there is a perception that it is "wrong" or "sinful" or "immoral" to fail to live up to one's ideal-self picture. Thus, a child may be brought up by his parents to feel that he has a moral obligation to live up fully to the ideal-self, for otherwise he will not have paid his debt to them for their love and care. If he should then fail, he is both shamed *and* guilty. And, too, there are cul-tures that particularly stress the moral rightness of "making the most of oneself," of attaining one's ideals, which are usually, of course, those promulgated by the soci-ety itself. In these cultural settings the in-dividual who fails is likely to feel a com-bined shame and guilt; the child who fails the school test may thus feel "guilty," as may the neurotic who fails to adjust well to society, and the woman who chooses a career and fails to maintain her (or soci-ety's) ideal of the wife and the mother.

REMORSE. Remorse, from the Latin "to bite again," is the emotion of guilt which arises when we look back to our action in a previous situation and feel the distressing awareness of a bad act. Its tone is never, as with some other forms of guilt feeling, pleasant; remorse is a painful experience, often, indeed, more acute than the guilty emotion that may have occurred at the time of the action itself. It is not necessary, of course, that guilt *was* originally felt. It is often only in retrospect that the nature and consequences of one's action are seen in a particular light as violations of what is "right." This may be due to the later chance to perceive the actual consequences, or to the absence now of the pleasure-seeking aspects of the momentary motivation which may at the time have served to conceal the moral requirements of the situation.

Moreover, the momentary guilty action is often perceived by the person as coming from an uncontrollable, "irrational" impulse, in the grip of which he was powerless. The strength of that impulse is not likely to be fully reinstated in his recollection of the situation, and this, too, may make the act seem later to be more blameworthy.

The intensity of remorseful feelings can be extreme, even years after the event. One source of the intense agitation that may accompany remorse is the awareness of one's powerlessness to rectify one's earlier action. "It is too late; there is nothing I can now do to make it right!" It is this factor of the backward time-perspective of the remorse-inducing situation which is most critical.

By Way of Summary. Some of the emotions most central to the person's motivational life are those arising from his perception of his behavior in relation to his standards of behavior as set by himself and by other people. Feelings of success or failure are evoked by performances reaching or falling short of his level of aspiration. If these feelings of success or failure are also seen by him as indicative of basic attainments or deficiencies of the *self*, deeper emotions of pride or shame may be engendered. This is especially true when the evaluative standards are "internalized," as in the self-ideal.

Emotions of guilt arise from a perception of one's violation of a "moral" requirement. The guilt feeling may often be ill-defined as to its exact source. Sometimes the guilt is more objectified, pertaining to a "bad" *act;* at other times it is more subjectified, pertaining to a "bad" *me.* In the latter case the guilt feeling is likely to be compounded with an emotion of shame, inasmuch as the person perceives the guilty action as implying a failure to live up to his ideal self-conception of conduct. But closely linked though they often are, shame and guilt are not the same emotion.

Feelings of Self-Consciousness. There are many social situations in which the person is acutely aware of being in the immediate focus of attention of other people—he feels self-conscious as he wears the new moustache, or enters the crowded room, or addresses the audience, or spills coffee on his hostess's table, or sits down to play the piano. His perception is, of course, often in error, for the other people may not really be looking at him at all. There is a common tendency to exaggerate other people's interest in oneself, stemming from the predominant saliency of self in one's own life-space—it is not only hard to see ourselves as others see us, it is also hard *not* to see ourselves as they do *not* see us! A sense of self-importance may exaggerate the belief, but so may a sense of inferiority, timidity, shyness.

Because a person sees the attention of others directed at him, he is attentive to himself. If he perceives their attitude as critical, or likely to be critical, the feeling engendered may be a painful *embarrassment*. He feels awkward, ill at ease, acutely aware of his appearance, his clothes, his movements, his manner. The emotional agitation, for instance in stage fright, may sometimes be severe; he experiences feelings of utmost confusion, paralysis of thought and action. And his very perception of these incapacities in the situation further reinforces the feeling of distress.

But the emotional consequences may be quite the reverse. The same objective situation may be perceived in an entirely different light. He may perceive (rightly or wrongly) an attitude of admiration, respect, and positive interest in him on the part of the other people; they are for the moment his "captive audience" before whom he "performs." The accompanying emotional feelings are pleasant in tone, and may reach a considerable degree of elation. These are often reinforced by feelings of satisfaction as the person judges that he has succeeded in the "performance." Sometimes, of course, the "success" entails simply holding the attention of the others, regardless of the quality of their attitudes. The boy may "show off" before his fellows by reckless deeds; the adolescent may need to attract attention—the hot-rodder, the zoot-suiter, the goldfish-swallower. And in pathological cases adults may commit bizarre acts and even horrifying crimes in order to bask in the light of public attention.

Emotions Pertaining to Other People

Much of our emotional experience pertains to the relations of self to other people as objects in our surroundings, the feelings being directed toward them. Such feelings toward people (and other external objects) often become crystallized over time in the form of enduring emotional predispositions or attitudes.

Love. By the word *love* we refer both to an enduring emotional disposition toward another person, and to the immediate feeling of strong emotion in the presence of that person.

The feelings of love take many forms, depending upon the particular nature of the perceived relationship of object and self. The tender and protective feelings central in maternal love clearly flow from the perception of the child as weaker and needful of help. The excitement and elation found in "romantic love" come from the desire and anticipation of being together, the idealized imagining of shared delights. The strong element of sexual excitement, found in some emotions of love, obviously derives from the person's perception of the sexual adequacy of the other person to his own sexual desires. The love of the child for his mother may include basic elements of feelings of need for protection and help. And there may even be in the emotion of love pronounced elements of submissiveness and fear, such as that aroused in the child by the powerful father.

The emotions of love may vary in all these and many other forms; the intensities of experience may range from mild to profound, the degree of tension from the most serene affection to the most violent of agitated passion. What, then, is common to all, that makes us call them love? The core of the feeling in love seems to be the feeling of being drawn to the other, desiring to be drawn. Clearly too, the self is apprehended as closely identified with him. Furthermore, there is an essential feeling of *devotion* of self to the other. As seen from the point of view of the person, his love is always and necessarily "unselfish," for otherwise it is not of the stuff of love. Whether it is *really* unselfish, as judged by an impartial observer, is quite another matter. We have all seen cases that we would call selfish, for instance the "love" of a demanding and possessive mother for her daughter.

Moreover, the intensity of the arousal depends upon such other factors as the accessibility or inaccessibility of the loved object. ("Absence makes the heart grow fonder," but only so long as it is not a case of "Out of sight, out of mind!") The unattained loved one is loved the more fiercely; the thwarting of one's heart's desire, to be in contact with the loved person, leads to increased tension and intensified feeling.

ROMANTIC LOVE. "Romantic love" has a large element of this thwarting of complete contact, and it is not surprising that it occurs most in those who are held apart. But once the goal is attained, sooner or later the honeymoon is over, and there is less likelihood of the "romantic love" persisting. It is not that there is disillusion, although this too can happen; it is more that there is a change in the psychological situation, which no longer provides the setting for "romantic love." The barriers separating the lovers are gone, the goal has been reached; the shared delights can no longer be idealized in imagination.

We have already seen in other emotions that the change in such situational elements results in changes in the emotional experience. The girl who had foreseen marriage as a never-ending idyllic romance, with a *chronic* emotional intensity at the courtship level, had unwittingly assumed that the psychological situation would forever remain unchanged. She now finds that the kind of emotional love aroused by the mate is not nearly so chronically intense and that the nature of "married love" is quite different.

SELF-LOVE. It is a remarkable fact that love, like many other emotional feelings, may be aroused by and directed at one's own self. The goddess Nemesis caused Narcissus to fall in love with his own reflection in the water, and the name *narcissism* is applied to feelings of self-love. Presumably everyone has such feelings to some degree, but there are cases of people for whom self-love is the most intense love they experience. Sometimes such self-love has a clearly sexual element, as found in those instances of autoerotic behavior in which the person's fantasy experience is not of sexual relations with others, but is centered on his own body alone.

Jealousy. Jealousy would seem to have few peers among the emotions in the range and sweep of its potential components. Where else is to be found the thwarted love, the anger, hate, and anguish; the sense of being rejected, scorned, derided; the feeling of failure, dejection, and even shame?

The essential situational pattern for the emotion of jealousy is the perception of the loved one as turning affection to another person rather than to oneself. The existence of a *rival* (real or imagined) is the indispensable factor. Let the glance of the loved one rest ever so fleetingly on another, and the jealous agitation may emerge.

The intensity of jealousy often seems disproportionate to the situation; like Othello, the person is highly predisposed to the emotion on slightest provocation. The individual's predisposition toward jealousy depends upon several factors. One factor is, of course, the intensity of the love, especially where the needs and desires persistently fail of satisfaction because the love is not reciprocated. Another factor is the person's feeling of a blow to his self-esteem, seeing the rival valued by the loved one over himself. The more insecure the person's self-conception, the more likely this factor is to play a larger role. If he tends to have doubts about the measuring up of his actual self to his ideal self, he is especially "set" toward seeing evidence of this discrepancy. We have already noted how such a perceptual set can predispose a person to see in minimal stimuli (for instance, his loved one's glance at another) support for such an interpretation of personal shortcoming.

We have referred mostly to jealousy as evinced in adult love relations. Another important form is found in the close emotional relations of family members. The child may feel an intense jealousy of the new baby, feeling that the parent's attention and love have been turned away from him to the new one. The husband may feel jealousy of a new baby, perceiving that the wife's attention has been displaced from him. The child may feel jealousy of the relation between his mother and father, perceiving the father as a rival for the affections of the mother. This, of course, is involved in the well-known *Oedipus complex,* described by Freud (see p. 620).

Envy. Another form of negative emotion of self that depends upon relation with another person is *envy*. The essential stimulus conditions are simple: we perceive another person as possessing something that we covet for ourselves. Yet this is apparently not the whole pattern, for it does not explain why we sometimes feel envy under such circumstances and why we sometimes do not.

One factor is the intensity of the desire for the object; if the desire is weak, we are less likely to feel envy of the person, but instead may merely feel a sense of minor frustration in not having the thing. Another factor is that envy is more likely to occur when the situation is perceived as one of *scarcity* of the wanted thing, so that possession of the wanted thing by the other person *prevents* us from having it. This factor is accentuated where there is some possibility of seeing *inequity* in the other person's having it and not ourselves. This would be the case, for example, when someone else *in one's own position* possesses something, and when it is seen as acquired not through his own merit or special situation, but "unfairly." This points to a third factor that may play a significant role. The person must occupy a central place in our life-space (see p. 210). A prior negative attitude toward the person may predispose us to feel the resentment toward him which is often a main component of the envious emotion. But even a positive attitude toward him, when we identify with him, may also accentuate envy.

We do not feel the same degree of envy of the good fortune of a person quite remote from us, for example, when we read that the Maharajah of Japore has been given a birthday present of his weight in platinum. But if the good fortune descends upon a brother, we may feel intense envy. The Maharajah of Japore is not a salient part of our life-space, and the things happening to him are not readily accessible regions of our life-space. But the brother is salient, and we see his fortune as potentially accessible to us. And as we have seen (p. 212), a potentially accessible region that is denied to us may engender negative feelings.

Hate. Hate, like love, involves the two characteristics of an enduring disposition and a periodically aroused intense emotional feeling. The obvious conditions for arousal of the hate experience have to do with the exposure of self to the hated person or object. The feeling of hate is accentuated in situations that tend to arouse other negative emotions as well. Being blocked in one's goal-striving, being threatened, being made jealous or envious, will serve to intensify the emotion of hate. What seems to happen is that all these negative emotions are readily funneled to a single target in the situation. Almost any person who is already endowed with some negative properties will readily become the target of this emotion.

The essential core of the emotion of hate is the desire to destroy the hated object. Hate is not simply a feeling of dislike, aversion, or loathing with respect to the object, for these feelings would simply lead to an avoidance tendency. We do not seek to destroy what we dislike; we merely avoid it. But hate is essentially an emotion involving approach. We seek out the hated object, cannot rid ourselves of obsessive thoughts about it, and do not rest satisfied until we have destroyed it.

The hated person must necessarily be perceived as playing a central role in our life-space. Just as we can be jealous only of a person psychologically close to us, so we can hate only a person psychologically close to us. In some cases, such as traditional family feuds or pathological fixations, persistent hate may come to take on some of the attributes of a positive feature of the person's life-space. He "nurses" his hate, savors it, channels much attention and effort toward it. And if his aim is finally achieved and the hated object destroyed, he may feel a sense of *loss*. The hated object had actually become a central and needed object, *giving meaning to the person's world*. It had enabled him to organize a stable set of beliefs and attitudes around this negative value. "Love thy enemy" may have more than one meaning!

SELF-HATE. Just as there is self-love, so there is self-hate. The person can find many aspects of himself which are repugnant, he can perceive that attainment of his goals is being blocked by his own defects, his own cowardice, his own sin, his own stupidity.

And since he is unable to escape from himself as he would normally seek to escape from such aversions, a persistent feeling of self-hate develops. As with any hate, the core of self-hate is a desire to destroy and hurt; he humiliates himself, punishes himself, mentally and physically, and may even ultimately kill himself.

A special instance of self-hate may be seen in the person who through accident of birth or upbringing is forced to identify with a group he dislikes, such as a religious or racial minority group, or a particular economic class. He may dislike the group because its values are not his own—the rich man's son who does not believe in unequal distribution of wealth, the poor man's son who is ashamed of his "low" origins; or because he accepts the standards of the majority—the Jew who shares the anti-Semitism of the society in which he lives. The effect of forced identification with the group may be that he comes to hate his own group—the group with which he is irrevocably identified—and to hate himself as a member of this group.

Other Emotional Feelings Toward People. Among the emotions pertaining to other people, love, hate, envy, and jealousy have high degrees of tension. The person is actively motivated, is seeking things that the other people may provide or deny. Hence these emotions are especially characterized by agitation, excitement, and upset.

There are other kinds of emotional feelings toward people that are usually less self-involving, less connected with goal-seeking. Typically, they involve one's *evaluations* of the other person. For this reason they are closely related to what we call *attitudes*, that is, enduring predispositions to perceive and to be affected by given objects, including people. Attitudes, as we have seen, are also components of love and hate. As with other types of attitudes, emotional feelings toward other people are either positive or negative.

POSITIVE FEELINGS. Feelings of liking toward another person may exist in many shades of intensity, from the passionate devotion of love to the milder affection of friendship. The closer the perceived identification of self with the other, the more intense the feeling is likely to be (and, in turn, greater liking tends to reinforce the feeling of identification). Obviously, the feeling of liking relates closely to the perception of the other person as having desirable qualities, especially those that are contained in one's own self-picture or ideal-self picture.

However the relationship between perception of self and of other is not simple. A person seen by us as very similar to ourselves may not be especially liked, for we may see in him the things that we dislike or hate in ourselves. And if we see him as having the traits making up our own ideal-self conception, this, too, may make us less than enthusiastic in our liking for him. For we may see in him a reminder of our own shortcomings, a constant reproach. We may feel a keen *admiration* for him, without an equally intense liking.

It appears that it is in seeing the other person as very like ourselves in both self and aspiration, as having both our weaknesses and our strengths, that we come to feel the most intense liking. And it would also appear that it is in this situation that we can feel the greatest identification with another, as especially manifested in feelings of *sympathy* for him. It is harder to feel the same quality of sympathetic glow for one highly admired; it is as though the admired one is somewhat remote or distant from self. To feel real sympathy for a hero or a god, it seems necessary to bring him down to a more "human" level, and by this almost every individual means his own level, for what indeed is more "human" than oneself?

If we see the other person as having what we consider inferior qualities, and yet we like him, the quality of our other feelings for him is different. It is harder to identify with him. Our feeling, instead of being sympathy with his distress, is one of *pity*. The fervent expression "There, but for the grace of God, go I" has a ring of self-satisfied superiority; we may pity the unfortunate, but it is not easy to think of ourselves as really like him.

There are other aspects to the importance of identification in determining our feelings toward another. It is doubtless true that love often blinds us to the imperfections of our beloved, but once these imperfections *are* perceived, they may result in especially severe feelings of criticism. It is as though the failure or bad conduct of the person with whom we have identified is felt as our *own* failure or bad conduct. In addition to the effects of identification, the bad conduct of the loved one has more saliency because the loved one himself is a salient object. For these reasons, the defects take on greater importance and arouse a more intense feeling of condemnation than would be attached to the same behavior by someone not identified with. But the feelings of criticism and condemnation may still be positive in tone, rather than negative. We feel a sense of "being let down," but with it there may be an underlying quality of "understanding" and "forgivingness." This is by no means always the case. Just as a person may feel intense negative emotions of guilt and shame and hate about himself, so he may feel unforgiving anger toward the person with whom he closely identifies. In due course, under these latter circumstances, the identification is likely to weaken or be totally destroyed.

Liking and identification often have the result of bringing us into closer contact with the other person. The consequence of this is a greater opportunity to perceive new traits and aspects of the person, and this in a wider sampling of situations. This experience has a feedback effect on the emotional feeling. It may be either positive feedback, in which the more one knows, the more good things one finds and the intenser the liking becomes ("to know is to love"); or negative feedback, in which the more one discovers, the less likeable the person seems ("familiarity breeds contempt").

NEGATIVE FEELINGS. Feelings of dislike toward other persons may vary in degree from the faintest aversion to the deepest hate. The basic determinants of the dislike are the perceptions of negative qualities in the person. These may pertain to failures of the other to meet one's own sense of values, or they may be more directly related to his being seen as threatening to oneself or interfering with the achievement of one's goals.

As with the positive feelings, the intensity of dislike will depend upon the closeness of self-involvement. There is a phenomenon that might be called *negative involvement,* in which the self is seen as directly opposed to the other person, being in conflict with him, standing for contradictory values. And such negative involvement means that one is more intensely affected by that person than by a neutral person. Negative involvement may occur because the self and other are perceived as grouped in some manner, seen as existing in some form of forced relationship with each other. For instance, the person may dislike or hate the members of his own family, and yet because of social and other factors he experiences them as closely but negatively involved with self. The same may be true of disliked fellow team members or work groups, or, on a wider scale, of one's disliked fellow citizens. Negative involvement may also occur when the other person, though not a member of one's group, is perceived as a barrier or "threat" to one's goals.

It should not be assumed that negative involvement is greatest with persons *least similar* to oneself. Indeed, the strongest negative involvement may occur with those who are quite similar to oneself in many ways, but dissimilar in certain critical negative aspects. In order for two things to appear most dissimilar or incongruous, they must be perceived as closely *alike* in many ways, thus accentuating the essential ways in which they *differ.* If they are entirely unlike, they are simply not compared. In the same fashion, it is the person seen as quite like oneself who can be the target of our bitterest feelings.

As with positive feelings, the specific qualities of negative feelings depend partly on the perceived superiority or inferiority of the other person relative to oneself. Toward a disliked person regarded as inferior or weak, the feeling may be *scorn,* disdain, contempt; toward a disliked person regarded as superior or strong, the feeling may be one of *resentment.* And if the disliked person is seen as neither particularly superior nor inferior, the feeling may be one of *antipathy* and lack of sympathy.

To dislike a person often means to avoid him. The consequence of this is the loss of opportunities to reappraise him. Thus dislike has a "built-in" mechanism that may serve to perpetuate dislike by preventing favorable evidence from appearing.

By Way of Summary. It appears that many of the emotions involving evaluative attitudes toward other people can be roughly located on a single two-dimensional "map," one axis being the degree of liking or disliking of the person, and the other axis the level of perceived superiority or inferiority of the person relative to oneself. Figure 77 demonstrates this for some of the principal emotions.

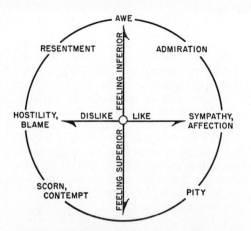

FIG. 77. A "map" of emotional attitudes toward other persons permitting the placement of each emotion with respect to two dimensions. Thus, resentment and admiration involve the same degree of inferiority feeling but are on opposite sides of the like-dislike dimension.

The Appreciative Emotions

We turn now to a cluster of emotions characterized by the person's appreciative orientation toward objects and events in his world, and toward his own place in the "cosmic scheme of things."

Humor and Laughter. The complex of feelings which includes amusement and mirth has been a subject of vast study by psychologists, philosophers, writers, and others. The common core of such feelings is pleasant in tone, but there are wide varieties of feelings loosely referred to under the topic of humor, each having its own unique feeling quality: wit, comedy, satire, jest, burlesque, etc. It is for this reason that the many hopeful attempts to discover a single pattern of situational determinants for humor have been futile.

Furthermore, there has been some confusion between a particular mode of *ex-pression* of a feeling of humor, namely laughter, and the nature of the inner *experience* being expressed. There is no *single* laughter response, but many, differing in quality and detail. The person may roar with laughter, or merely chuckle; he may shriek, giggle, titter, snicker, cackle, crow, guffaw. The particular quality of each of these laughters reflects the differences in the entire situation that is evoking the laughter. *Laughter*, like every other motor response of the organism, may be evoked by a very large number of different, and often unrelated, stimulus conditions. Laughter may have little or nothing to do with humor. It may not express delight, but a mere overflow of tension in painful situations, as in "hysterical laughter" or "nervous laughter," or when a child is tickled and the "threat" of the attack arouses tensions that are released through laughter (note that the person cannot succeed in inducing laughter by tickling *himself*). It may express the sudden release of tension which comes with goal-attainment, the laughter expressing a feeling of joy. It may reflect a general elation and sense of well-being in the person, which make the threshold for laughter low.

THEORIES OF HUMOR. Just as we have noted that there is no single pattern of situational determinants for humor, so we find that no single theory is adequate to account for the different kinds of humor experiences. Among the many theories of humor, two have been given considerable attention.

The first theory suggests that humor permits the person to express superiority, aggression, or sexuality in a socially acceptable manner, and to defend himself against the threat of reality. The essential occasion for humor, according to this theory, is the perception of the discomfiture of a disliked or hated person, institution, or practice. Here laughter expresses triumph,

BOX 57

Death, Sex, and Humor

Much of the psychological speculation on the bases of humor has been summed up by Flugel, who discusses, among others, the following motivational functions served by humor:

1. *Expression of superiority.* Many instances of humor express the person's attitudes of superiority toward others. Thomas Hobbes long ago stated it when he characterized laughter as ". . . sudden glory arising from some eminency in ourselves by comparison with the infirmity of others . . ." A great many jokes have this readily recognizable element of implied contempt or derision with respect to minority groups, for instance jokes aimed at the "drunken Irish," or the "dumb farmer," or the "uneducated Negro."

2. *Expression of aggression.* Humor is, of course, a highly convenient vehicle for the expression of aggressions in safe, socially acceptable, and somewhat indirect manner. (The parallel has been pointed out of the facial expressions involved in smiling and in sneering, and in smiling and in baring the teeth!) Sometimes the humor lies in aggressions felt toward those of superior status, or of manifest self-importance. The pompous person who slips on a banana peel may evoke hilarity; a cripple in the same situation may not.

The aggression is usually directed outwardly, as in the frequent anti-Semitic jokes. But it may also be directed at oneself, as in the anti-Semitic jokes told by Jews themselves. And the outward and inward directions of aggression may sometimes be

neatly combined. A Jewish cardplayer abuses his partner: "What sort of a fellow are you to sit down to play cards with the sort of fellow who sits down to play cards with a fellow like you?"

3. *Expression of sexuality.* The obvious elements of sexuality and obscenity contained in many jokes indicate that humor offers a ready avenue for the expression of such socially tabooed thoughts. Flugel comments that the sex joke is often in the nature of a "seduction" of the listener, that is, he is invited, as it were, to "participate" in the sexual transgression.

4. *Defense against reality.* There is always an essential aspect of "playfulness" and unreality in humor. The point is that the humor may serve the person as a way of protecting himself against the pains and threats of reality. Thus, we may laugh to prevent ourselves from feeling personally humiliated; or to protect ourselves from being too painfully touched by the tragic misfortunes of others. And there is the so-called "gallows humor," in which the person jokes while in desperate straits as a way of fending off the grim reality. The condemned criminal being asked, "Isn't there anything you'd like to say before they pull the rope?" replies, "Yes, tell the judge maybe he done a good thing after all; this is gonna be a mighty good lesson to me."

Humor, we see, is all things to all men.

FLUGEL, J. C. 1954. Humor and laughter. In *Handbook of social psychology*, G. Lindzey (ed.) Cambridge, Mass.: Addison-Wesley.

superiority, derision, or contempt. (See Box 57.)

The second theory regards perception of *incongruity* as the core of the humor situation. Incongruity means that the parts of a situation are somehow not "fitting." What we call "fitting" depends partly, of course, upon our past experience. The fact that we sometimes find the unusual customs, or clothes, or manners of people in foreign

lands a source of humor is due to the element of incongruity. That which is new to us often seems incongruous. But it is not the novelty that is responsible for the humor. There is nothing funny about seeing a completely new thing; what is required is that we see old things in new and unexpected *relations*. And even more, there must be something that tends to lead us first in one direction, and then abruptly takes us in a contradictory direction. The element of *surprise,* the unexpected twist, is the thing. The *in*congruous is not simply *non*congruous.

To ride through the hot, dry desert and suddenly encounter a naked baby crawling on the sands may be an occasion for surprise, but scarcely for humor. It may evoke pity or even horror. But if a group of top-hatted gentlemen, wearing school ties and Bikini swim suits is met, it may be funny. The critical aspect is that the situation as we first see it (the hot, dry desert) leads to expectations that are suddenly violated by a quite contradictory event which does not itself evoke feelings inconsistent with the feelings of delight and humor.

The more fully the initial expectation can be built up, the better; and the sharper the incongruity, the better. This is, of course, the core of telling a joke. There is a prolonged and gradual build-up of a direction, with growing tension as the event proceeds, and at the final moment the direction suddenly shifts, the person is surprised, and the tension released. Only faint humor is likely to attach to cases in which there is the mere sudden shift in direction. What is required to bring the humor to its peak is to make the final outcome "fit." That is, the punch line of the joke must be such as to make perfect "sense" of all that went before; it is only that the listener was being misled.

Aesthetic Feelings. The complex emotional experiences aroused by aesthetic objects and situations have been relatively little studied by psychologists, though they have been described by countless writers. That the aesthetic feeling is pleasurable is obvious, and its intensity may range from a quiet delight to an ecstatic joy. But this is far from the whole story; otherwise the aesthetic delight would be undifferentiable from any other. There are often also strong components of feeling an astonishing "rightness" or "completeness," as though just now at this instant one has a kind of "insight" into the whole. The mathematician who sees a "beautiful" solution, the scientist or thinker who gets the "beautiful" idea, may experience such an authentic aesthetic emotion.

It should be noted that it is not merely in respect to "official" works of art that the aesthetic feelings arise. They may come anywhere, anytime. Most of the work of the experimental aesthetician has, of course, been directed at the concrete attributes of a work of art which render it beautiful. Little attention has been given to the total situational analysis of the aesthetic perception itself, including art object *and* self.

Wonder and Awe. Feelings of wonder and awe are aroused by situations involving objects, forces, events, which are seen as overwhelming, strange, astonishing, inexplicable. In particular, it is the experiencing of these objects and events as large, powerful, and mysterious beyond the comprehension of the self which renders them wonderful and awesome. The vastness of the Grand Canyon compels an emotion of wonder and awe in its viewer; so does the mighty storm. The man alone standing beneath starry heavens may be filled with wonder and awe, especially as he contemplates the scope of the universe and is aware of his own puniness within it.

Whatever makes the self loom larger in the situation serves to reduce the wonder and awe. The mother anxiously watching lest her child fall over the brink doubtless feels little of the wonder of the Grand Canyon. The contemplative man beneath the starry heavens who becomes acutely conscious of an itch finds it hard to scratch his body and feel the mysteries of the cosmos at the same moment.

To the extent that the self is felt as

helpless in confrontation with the powerful object or event, there may also be engendered an emotion of fear or dread. And a sense that the powerful object though beneficent is remote, inaccessible, somehow exalted, adds a component feeling of solemn respect and deference, a feeling of *reverence.*

THE VARIETIES OF RELIGIOUS EXPERIENCE. The discussion of wonder, awe, and reverence leads us naturally to the important phenomena of *religious emotions.* In all human societies men have experienced powerful emotions in connection with their conceptions of divine and supernatural forces, whether in the form of one God, or many gods, of the Supreme Being, the Universal Spirit, the Absolute. More than fifty years ago, William James wrote an unsurpassed book that analyzed these powerful religious emotions (see Box 58).

Loneliness. The man standing alone beneath the starry heavens may first feel wonder, being conscious of the vastness of the universe in comparison with self. But this feeling is fragile, the focus of attention on self tends to increase, and the result in his experience may be an intensification of the boundary between self and rest of the world. The very vastness of the universe may thus serve to make him feel cut off and isolated, lost within the whole, in such a way as to produce a strong feeling of *loneliness.*

The mere presence of others is not enough to overcome the feeling of loneliness. The most intense feelings of loneliness

---

BOX 58

Religious Emotions

The psychological complexity of the "religious sentiment" was aptly described by William James in the following passage:

"In the psychologies and in the philosophies of religion, we find the authors attempting to specify just what entity it [the 'religious sentiment'] is. One man allies it to the feeling of dependence; one makes it a derivative from fear; others connect it with the sexual life; others still identify it with the feeling of the infinite; and so on. Such different ways of conceiving it ought of themselves to arouse doubt as to whether it possibly can be one specific thing; and the moment we are willing to treat the term 'religious sentiment' as a collective name for the many sentiments which religious objects may arouse in alternation, we see that it probably contains nothing whatever of a psychologically specific nature. There is religious fear, religious love, religious awe, religious joy, and so forth. But religious love is only man's natural emotion of love directed to a religious object; religious fear is only the ordinary fear of commerce, so to speak, the common quaking of the human breast, in so far as the notion of divine retribution may arouse it; religious awe is the same organic thrill which we feel in a forest at twilight, or in a mountain gorge; only this time it comes over us at the thought of our supernatural relations; and similarly of all the varied sentiments which may be called into play in the lives of religious persons. As concrete states of mind, made up of a feeling *plus* a specific sort of object, religious emotions are of course psychic entities distinguishable from other concrete emotions; but there is no ground for assuming a simple abstract 'religious emotion' to exist as a distinct elementary mental affection by itself, present in every religious experience without exception. . . . There thus seems to be no one elementary religious emotion, but only a common storehouse of emotions upon which religious objects may draw. . . ."

JAMES, W. 1902. *The varieties of religious experience.* New York: Longmans, Green.

are often evoked when the individual is in the very midst of others, the "lonely crowd." The feeling of loneliness can be avoided only when there is a grouping or identification of oneself with others.

Moods

The pervasive and transitory emotional states that are called *moods* give an affective coloring to our entire momentary experience. They are the keys in which experience is rendered, like the major and minor in music. The mood tends to swamp everything, often being felt as pertaining not only to the self but to the surroundings as well, which are perceived to be endowed with the same mood quality. To the melancholy person, the world looks melancholy; to the happy person, "All's right with the world."

Moods are chiefly distinguished by the fact that there is little explicit awareness of their basis in concrete aspects of the situation. We feel moods of melancholy, relaxed contentment, or "high spirits" without being able to identify just what they stem from in the immediate situation. We are often puzzled as to what action to take to dispel the bad mood or prolong the good one. We suddenly find ourselves a prey to unaccountable moods, and they may "hang on" despite all sorts of changes in our immediate situation; and then, just as suddenly, they may evaporate.

Varieties of Moods. Just because of the lack of connection with specific features of

the immediate situation, the precise quality of any single mood is difficult to pin down. Yet there are two principal features of most mood states which stand out: (1) degree of tension, (2) pleasantness or unpleasantness. Types of moods seem to come in contrasting pairs. We naturally think of an *elated* mood as contrasted with a *depressed* mood, a *happy* mood with a *sad* mood, a *calm* one with a *tense* one.

A rough topography of mood states can be drawn by taking into account two factors: pleasantness or unpleasantness, and degree of tension, in the manner shown in Table 1. It will be seen that with the pleasant moods arranged in order of decreasing tension, their unpleasant opposite-numbers fall into just the reverse order of increasing tension.

But this rough analysis does not do justice to the endless nuances and subtle gradations among moods. A morose mood may be sour, gloomy, sullen, bitter; a sad mood may be flavored with nostalgia; a tense mood may be colored with anxiety; a gay mood may be cheerful, frivolous, lighthearted.

Determinants of Moods. Such subtleties of mood coloring, and the fluidity of their changes, point to the fact that the essential situational determinants are highly complex. However, relatively little research has been directed at the specific conditions under which different moods appear, change, and disappear.

It seems likely that the reason for the lack of perceived connection of the mood with specific features of the situation is

TABLE 1

	Pleasant Mood		Unpleasant Mood	
(*High tension*)	Elated	vs.	Depressed	(*Low tension*)
	Gay	vs.	Morose	
	Happy	vs.	Sad	
	Contented	vs.	Discontented	
(*Low tension*)	Calm	vs.	Tense	(*High tension*)

that no single aspect of the situation clearly dominates the rest. Numerous complex determinants are simultaneously at work, tending to affect the person in diverse directions. No single feature of the situation is powerful enough to dominate the person's perception. He experiences an over-all feeling that represents all the effects in an unanalyzable pattern.

Our perceptions, as we have amply demonstrated in previous chapters, tend to take realistic account of the outer stimulus conditions, and at times it is the very *contrast* between the way outer things look and our inner mood that accentuates the mood. We may be further oppressed by the contrast between the "somberness" of our own mood and the "brightness" of the day or the "cheeriness" of those around us. At other times the very *agreement* between mood and appearance of surroundings reinforces the mood; the bleak countryside matches our bleak mood, or the gay music our mood of gaiety. And, indeed, the matching "mood" of the environment provides a way of making "sense" of one's otherwise unaccountable mood. The reason I may give for my depression is the disquieting stories of war and disasters that fill the front pages of the daily newspaper.

However, just as a slight change in some one aspect of the painting or symphony or social event may suddenly give it an entirely different cast, so a slight change in some aspect of the individual's immediate situation may produce a sudden, and to him, unaccountable swing in mood.

The Dynamics of Emotional Experience

In the continuous stream of our conscious life emotional experiences are in constant flux. A feeling of awed wonder under the starry heavens gradually shifts to loneliness. A fervent affection for the loved one is abruptly transformed into an equally hot jealousy. A feeling of irritation gradually becomes one of anger and then rage, culminating in a violent outburst and a subsequent feeling of calm.

In this latter example the abrupt change in emotional feeling paralleled the sudden overflow of tension. But not all tension reduction is sudden. Sometimes when the goal has not been attained, or when a violent outburst has not been precipitated, there is a very slow decay of tension. With such slow decay may go various shifts in emotional quality. An unpleasant feeling of frustrated incompletion, of irritability, is a common consequence. For instance, it may be experienced by the woman who has been brought to a high pitch of sexual excitement with a failure to achieve orgasm, or by an angry person who finds himself unable to provoke the target of his angry attack into a satisfying responsiveness (when it may not happen that the soft answer "turneth away wrath" but rather "provoketh thwarted fury").

The duration of some emotional states is extremely brief, a mere flash of resentful feeling come and gone before it can be fully experienced; in episodes of fully developed anger, or grief, or shame, or humor, the duration may be a matter of minutes or hours; and a mood of contentment or of despondency may persist relatively unbroken over a period of days, or even longer. We are here referring to the duration of the immediate experience of the emotion, not to the duration of the concomitant attitude. Obviously, many of our emotional attitudes toward objects and persons endure over long periods of our lives, but the momentary experiencing of them comes and goes as the immediate situation changes.

Our objective at this point is to account for these continuous shifts in immediate emotional experience.

Determinants of Shifts in Emotional Experience. The value of the situational analysis of emotions now becomes clear: such an analysis, if complete, enables us to predict, and even to some extent to control, the shifts in emotional experience. For the essence of the given emotional experience is its lawful connection with the unique situational pattern in which it arises. As aspects of the situation change, the emotion must correspondingly shift in an orderly way. The *reasons* that the situation changes are, of course, many.

ENVIRONMENTAL CHANGES. The person's external environment constantly undergoes change. The environmental change may originate in outside forces or in the person's own behavior. In either event this change in the environment tends to produce changes in the way the situation appears to him, with associated shifts in emotional experience. The angry attack may destroy the frustrating barrier; the paralyzing fear may deliver the person right into the grasp of the dangerous object. And it is especially in connection with emotions directed at other people that such feedback on the environment works. The man's jealousy may actually drive his loved one into the arms of his rival; a feeling of hate may evoke a reciprocal attitude of hate in the other; a feeling of admiration may spur the admired one to even greater accomplishments.

PERCEPTUAL INTENSIFICATION. As a consequence of the emotional state itself, the person's perceptions of the situation change. To the frightened man, all sorts of formerly neutral objects now look dangerous and further increase his anxiety; the loved one looks even more desirable and accentuates the ardor; the embarrassed person "sees" everyone looking at him and is further embarrassed. There are perceptual effects other than mere intensification of the same emotion. For example, feeling anger toward someone may make you "perceive" faults in him, and this in turn may lead to a feeling of scorn in place of the anger.

IDEATIONAL FLOW. Emotional experiences, we have said before, are "perfinks," involving thoughts as well as percepts and feelings. Thus an emotion can "trigger off" a chain of thoughts that will in turn redirect the emotional experience. The feeling of failure in a given task may bring the person to think about his more general shortcomings, engendering a feeling of shame; this reminds him of wasted opportunities for bettering himself in the past which his family had provided, and a feeling of remorse arises. But the end is not yet in sight: the backward time-perspective reminds him of his disliked successful brother, and he feels a sense of hatred, etc. And all this flow of shifting emotional experience may have occurred in a shorter time than it takes to describe.

Obviously we cannot foresee the exact succession of emotional shifts that will occur for a given person. The "pathways" of successive "perfinks" differ from one person to the next, and from time to time in the same person. Yet there is a considerable degree of regularity for any one individual in the structure of such emotional "pathways." Thus, for one person there may be a much higher probability of states of anger being immediately succeeded by states of shame, while for another person the greater likelihood may be that anger will be succeeded by such emotions as resentment or fear.

SATIATION OF EMOTIONAL EXPERIENCE. There may be a phenomenon of *satiation* in emotional experience akin to that found in perception, with prolonged exposure of a stimulus-pattern. If so, one basis of ultimate shift in a prolonged emotional state would be the gradual "fatiguing" or "blunting" of the affect with the passage of time. After a siege of uninterrupted grief, the well of tears runs dry. In time, shame subsides. Humor eventually dulls. This depends partly upon changes in the situation. The joke is not so funny when it is repeated, because its "unexpected" twist is no longer unexpected.

But there is probably also a genuine satiation effect that occurs even without situational change. This effect can be circumvented, in order to prolong the emotion, only by the expedient of thinking of new aspects of the situation which will evoke the feeling, or finding new supporting stimuli for the emotion. The mourner may deliberately remind himself of all the ways in which his bereavement will affect him; the abject person may continue to lash himself with shame by forcing himself to think of all the possible ways in which he is disgraced; the sexual excitement may be maintained by seeking ever-novel and stimulating sexual activity.

The Control of Emotional Experience. Knowing some of the determinants of emotional shift makes it possible to approach the problem of emotional *control*, both of our own emotions and of those of others. We must distinguish at once between control of the outward *expression* of the emotion and control of the *experience* of the emotion.

EMOTIONAL EXPRESSION. In common language when we talk about the "need for emotional control," it is often the outward expression to which we refer. The stiff upper lip, the brave smile, the gritted teeth, are all meant to conceal the inner turmoil. And, in the interests of civilized living with one's fellow men, the angry impulse to strike out is to be curbed, the sexual impulse to be restrained. (Some of the difficulties in recognizing what emotion a person is expressing are discussed in Box 59.)

Undoubtedly, such control of outward emotional expression and impulse to action does have some effect as well on the inner emotional experience. For instance, it is likely that by inhibiting the bodily expression, the intensity of the emotional feeling will sometimes be reduced. But there may be unintended and more far-reaching effects of such outward control. The curbing of the socially undesirable impulse may actually accentuate the emotional desire, or its thwarting may lead to anger, resentment, and hate toward the frustrating agents. And the persistent inhibition of emotional expression may come to produce a permanent and deep-seated apathy or a loss of spontaneity in the person's emotional life.

SITUATION CONTROL. What, then, is a more effective way of control of emotional experience? Since we have seen that the arousal of emotional experiences depends upon the immediate situational pattern, the answer is to change the situation appropriately. Situational manipulation is the key to emotional control, and it can apply to the control both of our own emotions and of those of people around us.

Of course, this is what we naturally do all the time. We can reduce our shame by dwelling in our thoughts on superior aspects of self, or by comparing our own inadequacies with those of much worse people; we can diminish embarrassment in a stressful social situation by telling a joke that makes everyone laugh and diverts their critical attention from us (perhaps the psychological basis for the well-established tradition of the funny story to open a speech); we cool our momentary anger by counting to ten (or some larger number) to give ourselves time to see the situation in a somewhat different way. We take the

BOX 59

Recognizing Emotional Expression

Common human experience over the ages would seem to give undeniable proof that people are generally able to recognize the emotions that other people are experiencing simply by observing the expression of the face, gestures, etc. On the other hand there is also ample evidence of failure to identify emotional expressions. The grin reflecting nervous fear may be mistaken for pleasure; the set face and pallor may indicate anger rather than pain or determination.

There have been numerous experiments designed to ascertain just how accurately observers can judge the emotions of others on the basis of outward expression alone. Some of the main findings are:

1. The pattern of facial expression of a given emotion tends to be highly variable among different individuals. In one of the earlier studies Landis photographed subjects' faces while they engaged in the following types of genuine emotion-evoking situations: smelling ammonia, hearing a loud noise, viewing pornographic pictures, listening to music, writing out an account of an embarrassing event that had once been experienced, decapitating a rat with a dull knife, getting an electric shock, etc. On the basis of detailed mapping of the movements of the facial musculature during each of the induced emotions, he concluded that for none of the emotions was there a common expressive pattern among his subjects. On the basis of facial expression alone, the different emotions could presumably not be distinguished by an observer.

Part of the reason for this surprising finding may be that Landis included few if any really pleasant emotions in his study; other evidence shows that the most reliable discrimination among emotional expressions is found in expression of the pleasant as against the unpleasant. Moreover, of course, Landis restricted himself to facial expression alone, and to an analytical study of the details of the expression rather than making judgments based upon the total perceptual impression of the face.

2. The latter approach was used by several investigators who asked observers to name the emotion expressed in each of a number of still photographs of faces. The photographs were obtained by having professional actors *pose* and intentionally portray the designated emotions. The results showed that observers, though able to some extent to identify the posed emotions correctly, tended to make large errors. Some pairs of emotions were rarely confused, e.g., love and contempt; other pairs were very frequently confused, e.g., fear and anger. It is important to note that with such *posed* photographs the role of deliberate social communication is large. Success in recognizing facial expressions of emotion under this circumstance may tell us something about the *social* perception of emotions, but little about the distinguishing expression of emotions when the individual is alone and not seeking to communicate his emotional state to others.

Incidentally, certain facial features prove to be more expressive of emotions than others. Dunlap cut photographs in half, so that the eyes and the mouth could be judged separately. He found that the *mouth* provides far more informative cues about the person's emotion than do the *eyes*—despite conventional belief to the contrary.

3. As greater numbers of expressive cues are added to those of facial expression, accuracy of emotional identification greatly increases. Additional cues have to do with vocalization, bodily posture, gestures, etc.

All such cues are governed by cultural learning. The gestures accompanying a given emotion may be entirely different in a native Italian and a native Icelander. If after spilling soup on us a Japanese waiter smiles, should we take offense because he appears to be feeling "derision" toward us? Perhaps not, if we understand that for the Japanese the smile in this situation is the proper way for him to express his feeling of having been foolish and clumsy!

LANDIS, C. 1924. Studies of emotional reactions. II. General behavior and facial expression. *J. comp. Psychol.*, 4, 447–501.

DUNLAP, K. 1927. The role of eye-muscles and mouth-muscles in the expression of the emotions. *Genet. Psychol. Monog.*, 2, No. 3.

sting out of fear, guilt, dejection, by seeking to place them in our minds in a much wider time-perspective and life-space perspective: What does this really count for in my total life? What possible difference will this make a year from now?

One particularly powerful method of control is to discover ways in which the situation can provide the self with greater "space of free movement" (see p. 211). Our frustration is diverted from the channel of anger if we can see other possible routes to the goal; our fear is reduced if we can see a possible escape hatch. An interesting illustration of the latter is the device invented by a dentist to allay his patients' excessive emotion of anticipated pain. He provided a buzzer that the patient could sound whenever he wanted the dentist to stop drilling, and the mere provision of this potential avenue of escape from pain greatly reduced the customary emotional attacks, even if the patient made no use of the buzzer at all!

This is not to say that we are always successful in such efforts to control the emotions of others and self. Our attempts to allay our guilt by seeking to place the event in a wider life-perspective may lead us, if we are thus brought to consider the real uselessness of our entire lives, to an even more profound guilt or despair. The character of a particular situation may be so strongly effective that deliberate attempts to alter it are fruitless: a terror-stricken man is in no condition to seek to control his emotion. When the emotion stems from very strong emotional attitudes in the person, it is difficult to bring about the appropriate situational changes. We see this in prejudice or in love.

Emotion—Disruptive or Facilitative. What is the basis of the interest in emotional control? From society's point of view, control is important because it inhibits *actions* that are often socially injurious, such as aggression. From the individual's point of view, control of emotional *states* has been regarded as desirable because it protects him from the disruptive consequences of emotion on his adjustments to his environment.

That emotional states often do have disruptive effects on our goal-attainments is familiar to all of us. It is so clear that some psychologists have asserted that the effect of emotion is *always* negative and disruptive. Their argument is that where emotion is involved, rational processes are necessarily disturbed, and that this must always be regarded as detrimental to goal-attainment. Other psychologists do not take quite as dim a view of the value of emotions. While agreeing that emotions are often disruptive of rational processes, they point to their value in energizing the action of the organism.

EMERGENCY EFFECTS. Bodily changes accompanying emotions such as anger and fear have been described by Cannon (1929) as *emergency reactions*. His theory is that these bodily changes—increased breathing rate, blood pressure, muscle tension, etc.—mobilize the organism for prompt and vigorous action. The details of this conception are given in Chapter 12. The frightened man can run faster from his pursuers, the enraged man can attack his enemy more ferociously. In this way the bodily accompaniments of emotion can help achieve one's goal.

However there is a limited utility to this. The frightened man, in his haste, may not perceive a more effective way of escaping from his pursuer; the enraged man may be led recklessly to attack an enemy very much stronger than he is and thus be defeated no matter how ferociously his rage permits him to fight.

Taken together the facts seem to lead to the following generalizations: (1) For such active emotions as anger and fear, the emotion may help to make possible more vigorous motor responses. (2) Intense anger and fear may interfere with *rational* processes. (3) Whether emotion is facilitative or disruptive depends upon the particular character of the situation. To illustrate: On the one hand, there is the tennis player who, becoming angry, loses the fine co-ordination of muscular control necessary for a good game; on the other hand, we have the Olympic 16-pound shot-put champion who reports that he works himself up just before his stupendous heaves by deliberately making himself feel hate for someone. Similarly, there is the political leader whose hatred of a neighboring country is so intense that it prevents him from reaching an agreement with this neighbor—an agreement that would be of real advantage to his own country. Opposite in effectiveness is the righteously angry man who carries others with him through the very force of his outraged convictions on the issue.

ENDURING EFFECTS. We can also raise questions concerning the desirability or undesirability of consequences of the less active emotions, that is, those involving a smaller component of bodily energy and motor action. In general, when we deal with these less active emotions, we are less concerned with the *immediate* disruptive or facilitative consequences on adjustment to the situation—as we are with fear and rage—and more concerned with far-reaching effects on the person's behavior. What, then, about the consequences of emotions, for example, of love, of pride?

Love may certainly detract from the person's rational processes. His ability to describe and judge the loved one in an objective way may be impaired. But, on the other hand, the love also may increase his understanding of the other by making him more patient of faults of the other, more interested in discovering more about the other. The love may tend to broaden his life-space and to widen his perspectives.

Feelings of excessive pride may lead the person astray; through vanity or arrogance he may lose perspective on himself: "Pride goeth before the fall." But, conversely, pride may serve as a strong support of worth-while endeavor.

In Part IV, when we consider the emotional development of the person and his life adjustments, we shall see the particular manner in which emotions may serve both beneficial and detrimental ends.

Glossary

appreciative emotions. A class of emotions (e.g., humor, beauty, wonder) characterized by the person's appreciative orientation toward objects and events in his world and toward his own place in the "cosmic scheme of things."

emotion. A stirred-up state of the organism, reflected variously in emotional experience (the *feeling* of the emotion), in emotional behavior, and in certain patterns of physiological change.

emotions pertaining to other people. A class of emotions arising mainly in connection with the person's perceived relations with other people, the feelings (e.g., love, envy, pity), being directed toward them. Such feelings often become crystallized in the form of enduring emotional predispositions, or attitudes.

emotions pertaining to self-appraisal. A class of emotions (e.g., shame, pride, guilt) in which the essential determinants have to do with the person's perception of his own behavior in relation to various standards of behavior and conduct, both external and internal.

emotions pertaining to sensory stimulation. A class of emotions (e.g., pain, disgust, delight) which most clearly pertain to pleasant or unpleasant sensory stimulation by objects.

empathy. Feeling the same emotion that is being expressed by another person, (e.g., feeling fear when another person shows signs of fright). To be distinguished from *sympathy*.

hedonic tone. That aspect of emotional experience having to do with the degree of pleasantness or unpleasantness of the emotional feeling.

moods. Pervasive and transitory emotional states (e.g., sadness, anxiety, elation) that tend to give an affective coloring to the entire momentary experience of the person.

narcissism. Feelings of self-love, often containing an erotic component.

negative involvement. The perception of a close and "forced" involvement or relationship between oneself and another person (or group) toward whom one has negative feelings.

primary emotions. The class of emotions (e.g., joy, anger, fear, grief) usually regarded as most basic, simple, and primitive, and typically associated with goal-striving and high degrees of tension.

startle-response. The pattern of bodily reactions occurring as a result of sudden, intense stimulation, such as a loud sound. The startle-response is not identical with a fear reaction.

sympathy. The experiencing of a positive emotion pertaining to the emotional state or circumstance of another person, such as the mother's feeling of protective tenderness toward her frightened child. Sympathy tends to be greater the greater the identification with the other person. To be distinguished from *empathy*.

Suggestions for Further Reading

CANNON, W. B. 1929. *Bodily changes in pain, hunger, fear, and rage* (2nd ed.). New York: Appleton-Century-Crofts.

An account of classical experiments on some of the physiological accompaniments of emotional states.

DUNBAR, F. 1954. *Emotions and bodily changes* (4th ed.). New York: Columbia Univ. Press.

A detailed account of the research literature on psychosomatic relationships.

REYMERT, M. L. (ed.). 1950. *Feelings and emotions.* New York: McGraw-Hill.

A symposium of numerous authorities in the field.

RUCKMICK, C. A. 1936. *The psychology of feeling and emotion.* New York: McGraw-Hill.

A textbook giving a review of earlier research and theories of emotion.

YOUNG, P. T. 1943. *Emotion in man and animal.* New York: Wiley.

A broad textbook treatment of the psychological problems of emotion.

CHAPTER X

Motives of Man

MAN has had an ageless preoccupation with his own motives and with the motives of others. Beginning with that primal crime story, the murder of Abel, there has been a detective search for the "reason" for the behavior, the *motive*.

This search is an expression of a need to make sense of the events in one's world. A complicated series of behaviors of another organism can be "understood" by ascribing to the organism a *motive*. And by motive in this sense, one means what the organism is trying to do, is trying to bring about.

Conceptions of Man's Nature

The kinds of answers given in the search for man's motives have differed widely from time to time, from culture to culture. The "explanations" have been a function of the then prevailing *conception of man's nature and of his place in the universe*. The various conceptions are not to be regarded merely as "antique curiosities." We shall discover that, however inadequate each

was in accounting for the full complexity of human motivation, it nonetheless contained an essential germ of truth; and that the modern account of human motivation really reflects, though in altered form, each of the prior conceptions.

Man, the Pawn of Fates. Man has often been thought of as a passive instrument of supernatural forces outside himself. These supernatural forces have assumed many forms and guises, but they have been similar in being seen as the real locus of man's motivation. It is they that move him to action. The gods of Olympus join in rivalry and conflict with one another, using man as a pawn in their own designs. The Three Fates determine his destiny, spinning, and snipping the thread of life. His motives are not *his*, but theirs. He is the mere battleground of supernatural forces. In some conceptions the forces of good and evil grapple for his soul; in others, inscrutable forces lay out a predetermined track that man fatalistically trudges, unable to deviate from it.

Motivation in this conception is *outside* the person, and indeed outside a lawful and deterministic framework. In this perspective the problem of motivation is not really a scientific problem, for there is no way the scientist can measure or control the supernatural forces that motivate man.

To a certain degree, however, man *could* do things that would serve to cope with the demands of these outer forces; he could placate the spirits by various rituals. The belief that man could placate the gods implied that he understood something about their emotions and motives. The gods of Olympus, for example, were endowed with very human traits, desires, emotions, and frailties. Thus the ancient Greeks knew a lot about motivation, but their "explanation" of human motivation was somehow "projected" onto the gods. Of course, the same has been true of many quite different cultures. The so-called "primitive," too, accounted for behavior in this external way. This did not prevent him from noting regularities in the way that particular states of the person result in particular actions.

Man, the Rational Master. The area of man's control in the universe broadened gradually until we find other conceptions in which the fates are completely banished and man reigns. *He* is the master of his fate; his wants and desires, his goals and purposes, are *his;* and the explanation of his behavior is to be found inside himself. Man is the thinker, the decider, the reasoner, the actor. We behave as we do because we take account of our situation, calculate and weigh consequences, and finally act in accord with a rational analysis. The locus of motivation is now in the *mind*, the laws of motivation are laws of rational process, we choose what we do, and we do what we choose. We have free will.

The objectives of such application of ra-

tional processes may vary, of course. The person's conduct may be governed by his intention to maximize pleasures and minimize pains (so-called *hedonism*); or by intentions to serve his own self-interest (*egoism*) or the interests of others (*altruism*); or by the seeking of religious redemption and salvation.

Such a rationalistic conception of human nature and motivation could not, of course, fail to take some account of the physical world and the physical body. The question of the connection between Mind and Body (the Mental and the Physical Worlds) entered the motivational problem. Thus Descartes, the French philosopher, sought to segregate each in its own separate sphere, locating some of the motivational forces in the physical world, as part of the physical nature of the beast, and others in the mental world. He postulated that these two kinds of motivational forces were somehow co-ordinated through the pineal gland, an organ in the brain.

Man, the Machine. But such a halfway measure was not satisfactory to those whose conception of man was such as completely to abolish mental factors and to explain motivation entirely in terms of physical forces. They conceived of man as a *machine*, a more complex apparatus than other physical machines, but a machine nonetheless.

The problem of motivation became, in a way, superfluous, for we do not ask what motivates a simple machine. Our explanation of its working pertains to the various mechanisms, each of which when set into motion produces an effect and in turn sets other mechanisms into operation. We do not ask about the motivation of the doorbell. We are satisfied to account for its behavior in terms of the pushing of the switch, the flow of electric current through the wires, the vibration of the clapper caused by magnets, and the sound of the clapper on the bell ringer.

Man, too, was conceived of in this "push-button" model: physical energies (*stimuli*) strike the receptors, impulses are relayed from the receptors through the nervous system, to the muscles, which move (make *responses*). Thus the whole picture of behavior was the sequence of stimuli and responses, and understanding it consisted in understanding what stimuli resulted in what responses, and how. And the latter question was to be answered simply in terms of the arrangement of the inner mechanisms, that is, just how the "wires" were connected up.

There is something highly attractive about this model, for it dispenses with embarrassing and complex questions of "motivation" and suggests that the final complete description of man's behavior is just the kind of untangling of the inner mechanisms that would be involved in trying to figure out how a complicated machine works.

Certain features of the behavior of organisms do indeed seem to lend themselves to this kind of simple-machine conception, especially *reflexes* and *tropisms*.

REFLEXES. We are all familiar with the knee-jerk reflex, which is tested routinely by the doctor to determine whether the nervous system is functioning properly. This simple, involuntary, and apparently "automatic" muscle movement seems, at first sight, to be a clear example of mechanical or machinelike behavior. The "button" is pushed (the knee is tapped), the impulse is sent from the knee through the spinal cord, and back to the leg muscles, and the "machine operates" (the leg jerks). Questions about mind, purpose, goal, seem entirely superfluous.

Of course, behavior is usually much more complicated than the knee-jerk, but more complicated behavior was explained by assuming a very large number of simple reflex mechanisms, connected together to provide the final response of the organic "machine." One reflex response was conceived to serve as the stimulus for the next reflex response, and a long chain of reflexes accounted for a whole behavioral sequence.

However plausible such an account might seem for innate behavior, it is inadequate for complex behavior that reflects learning and involves much more than the running off of an innately built-in sequence of simple reflexes. This embarrassment was removed with the conception of the "conditioned reflex" (see Chapter 15) in which by simple association new stimulus-response connections could be established in the "organic machine."

TROPISMS. A somewhat similar approach to the mechanistic view of man was given by the study of so-called *tropisms*, observed in insects and lower animals. These are co-ordinated "forced movements" that occur in response to the stimulus situation.

Such tropisms (from the Greek word for "turning") are commonplace: the sunflower turns throughout the day in such a way that it always faces the sun; the moth is drawn toward the flame; the cockroach scuttles from the light. These are innate "forced movements." They serve a *biological survival function* in that through them the organism is brought into effective orientation with its physical environment, but a tropism is action not involving foreknowledge, purpose, or goal.

The effective orientation is produced by an innate internal mechanism that makes the organism respond to outer stimulation in a specific way. The mechanisms may be conceived of in very simplified terms (Fig. 78).

Regardless of the simplicity or complexity of the inner "machinery"—and it is presumably much more complicated when dealing with the tropisms of higher animals

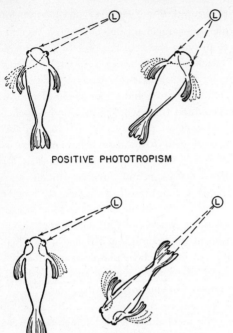

POSITIVE PHOTOTROPISM

NEGATIVE PHOTOTROPISM

FIG. 78. A schematic representation of positive and negative phototropism in a hypothetical "fish." Light falling on the "eye" results in stimulation to the "fins" by way of the "nerves" indicated by the lines connecting "eyes" and "fins." In the case of a *positive* phototropism the nerves are crossed so that a greater intensity of light on the right "eye" activates the left "fin" and the animal is swung toward the light; then, with both "eyes" equally stimulated, it is propelled toward the light. In the case of *negative* phototropism the nerve connections are not crossed and now a greater intensity of light on the right "eye" activates the right "fin" so that the animal is swung away from the light; then, with both "eyes" equally stimulated, it is propelled away from the light.

—the essential thing is that the behavior is elicited and guided by the stimulus environment (see Box 60).

It should be noted that the tropistic conception of behavior is a step beyond that based upon mere reflexes, in that it deals with a *pattern of stimulation*, not a single stimulus, and a *pattern of behavior*, not a single response. In this sense it avoids something of the narrow, segmental view of behavior that characterizes the reflex approach.

SIMPLE MACHINES VS. PHYSICAL SYSTEMS. It should be stressed that what we have been describing under the conception of man as a machine pertains to a view of a very simple machine. This should not be confused with the more general conception of a physical *system*. The essence of a simple machine is that there are rigidly connected parts, whose *fixed paths of movement* are closely channeled by surrounding constraints (e.g., a piston within its cylinder walls). But this is not the only model of a physical system. The movements in the solar system, for example, are subject to exact laws of physics, yet the movement of a planet is not within an unchangeably fixed path. Whereas the piston within its cylinder walls can only move up or down or remain at rest, the movement of a planet represents the resolution of the whole field of gravitational forces derived from its relation to the movements and masses of all the other objects in the solar system. Alteration in the other objects will produce an immediate and *varying* readjustment in the planet's movement. In this sense the solar system is a *dynamic physical system*—a change in any one part of the system results in compensating and equalizing changes in other parts.

The concept of man as a machine has gradually moved from the notion of man as a simple machine with rigidly connected parts, to the modern notion of the organism as a dynamic physical system with flexible self-adjusting capacities.

Man, the Animal. Darwin was by no means the first to conceive of man as an animal. But his statement of the theory of biological evolution caused a re-examination of man's concept of himself and of the universe which reached to the widest borders of thought and whose effects rever-

BOX 60

The Rat as a Tropistic Machine

A number of years ago Crozier and Pincus carried out a series of studies purporting to show that even mammals exhibit tropistic responses. They found that there appears to be a negative phototropism in young rats. When one eye is stimulated by light in 9- to 14-day-old rats, the animal moves in a circle or spiral away from the stimulation. When two eyes are stimulated by unequal intensities of light, the animal tends to orient by moving away from the stronger illumination until the intensities at the two eyes are equalized.

Another finding was that young rats would creep up an inclined plane at an angle (see fig., angle *b*) systematically re-

Angle *a*	Angle *b*
15°	32.6°
20°	44.5°
25°	52.9°
30°	57.4°
35°	64.0°
40°	69.8°
50°	77.9°
60°	84.7°
70°	88.3°

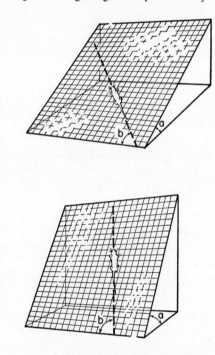

It was their belief that this mathematical relationship of creeping behavior to tilt of the plane was proof of a tropistic response in which there was a tendency on the part of the rat to move in a direction that provided symmetrical stimulation on the body from gravitational and other forces.

One particularly striking study by these experimenters was to combine the gravitational stimulus with a light stimulus provided by shining a light down the inclined plane. The purpose was to see whether the new path would be a simple resultant of the two separate paths predicted for the tropism to avoid light and the gravitational tropism. Crozier and Pincus reported that the behavior of the rats in this situation did indeed confirm their mathematical predictions. In their words, the study "affords proof that in the compounding of the two kinds of excitation the rat is behaving as a machine."

Later investigators, however, have presented findings that throw doubt on the adequacy of the simple tropistic explanation, indicating that factors of postural reflexes and of learning may account for the results, and that there are large individual differences among rats, with substantial deviations from the mathematical predictions.

The rat may be a machine, but it is not a simple tropistic one.

lated to the angle of tilt of the plane (angle *a*). The investigators found the following average values for angles *a* and *b*, and proposed a mathematical formula that described a consistent relationship between changes in the values of *b* and corresponding changes in the values of *a*.

CROZIER, W. J., and PINCUS, G. 1926. The geotropic conduct of young rats. *J. gen. Physiol.*, 10, 257–69.

CROZIER, W. J., and PINCUS, G. 1927. On the equilibration of geotropic and phototropic excitation in the rat. *J. gen. Physiol.*, 10, 419–24.

berated in controversy for many years.

One of the effects of Darwinism was the search for common qualities in the behavior of man and that of lower animals. Simpler explanations of man's behavior were sought in the model of animal behavior; and this greater attention to animal behavior led to a much broader view of the complexity of that behavior itself. Thus evolution involved not only the "descent of man" but also an "ascent" of lower animals. It was observed that many "lower" animals, too, engage in goal-directed action, express emotions, prefer monogamous sexual relationships, show maternal tenderness for their young, get frustrated and "neurotic," "reason" and display "hypotheses" in problem-solving, co-operate with others. The effect of such observations was to throw doubt on the need for peculiarly "human" explanations of man's behavior.

INNATE DRIVES. What was considered really basic about motivation (human or other) was a set of simple biological *drives* that set the organism into action. These drives were intimately related to physiological requirements of the body and of its survival, the requirements for food, water, oxygen, avoidance of painful stimuli, and the like. Presumably, these innate drives came into being through evolutionary processes of natural selection, and in this manner they came to serve the necessary functions of survival of the organism. The explanation of motivated action was largely reduced to an explanation of just how the drives are brought into play, their effects on behavior, and their subsequent removal. For instance, the depletion of food substances in the body leads to a state of unrest in the animal; he engages in activity, finds and eats food; his body is replenished, and his drive reduced.

DERIVED DRIVES. From this point of view, all other motivation was considered *secondary* and as deriving from these basic

bodily drives. The individual learns how to reduce these drives, and in so learning comes to develop *acquired drives.* For example, while seeking a mate to satisfy a sex drive, he may learn that social prestige helps. He therefore gradually acquires a drive for prestige. The drive for prestige, from this point of view, may be understood as a drive in the service of a basic sex drive. Complex motivation was thus analyzed as an elaboration of innate biological tendencies.

INSTINCTS. The innate biological tendencies were sometimes termed *instincts.* The wasp burying the paralyzed caterpillar beside her eggs so that the young when hatched will be supplied with meat, and the ant milking the aphid, are illustrations of instincts. These and many more wondrous behaviors of insects and animals were explained as caused by inborn patterns of the nervous system which when activated result in these complicated behavior sequences. Thus an instinct is more than an innate drive. It refers to both the drive and the appropriate activity to satisfy the drive. Man, the animal, was also conceived of as being driven in part by biological instincts.

Man, the Social Product. At first sight it seems that we are adopting a very different conception of man when we explain his nature and his behavior as products of the society and culture in which he is born and lives. In that conception the origins of his motives are in the requirements of his social group. *Man mirrors his culture;* his motives, his desires, his goals, his purposes, are reflections of what the society needs.

Curiously enough, Darwinian thinking had its influence here too. Man is a *social* animal, as well as a biological animal. Just as there was natural selection in the evolutionary process which led to a human being with human motivations, so, it is assumed, there is social selection and social evolution in which human nature comes to be such that societies survive and fulfill the functions of group living.

The conception of man as a social product allows a place for the basic physiological drives that are the minimal requirements for biological survival. For example, the requirement for food is met in every society, but the *specific manner* in which it enters into the motivational picture of the individual is determined by his society and varies widely. The value placed upon fulfilling the food need, what it is connected with, the particular methods for getting and consuming food, the particular kinds of food consumed—all these have been shown by anthropologists and sociologists to exhibit an endless variation. What is common is simply that the food requirement is met.

CULTURAL RELATIVISM. The emphasis upon man as a social product has been strongly reflected in the doctrine of *cultural relativism*, which, among other things, asserts that human values can only be understood as relative to the culture. We cannot say that this is "good" and that "bad" in any universal sense; but only that this is "good" in *this* culture and "bad" in *that*. The "human nature" of one culture is not necessarily the "human nature" of another.

In this view, the individual learns the ways of his culture as he seeks to satisfy his primitive physiological demands. He internalizes the customs, rituals, and values of his society, and his motivational structure is mainly shaped by these social influences. The biological drives are thus given the minimal role that will permit the organism to survive, and everything else is conceived as being socially derived.

SOCIAL DETERMINISM. The conception of man as a social product is often closely associated with a stress on social determinism. This doctrine asserts that there are "laws" of societies, of social organizations, and of historical trends that transcend individual "human nature." That is, the individual is considered as merely a unit, or part, of the larger social system, taking his direction and fulfilling his narrow roles as dictated by the requirements of the system as a whole. He is the cork bobbing powerlessly on the surging stream of history, the cog in the machine, the mere tool through which inexorable forces of economic determinism express themselves.

The notion of "social determinism" leads us back again to the conception of man as a prey to motivational forces over which he has little control. But with "social determinism" Mr. Anyman is even unaware of the specific determinants of his motives; only the professional student of society can trace these.

Man, the Unconscious Being. Closely allied to the above conception is the view that man's basic motives are *unconscious*. He is unaware of the real reasons for much of his behavior. The real reasons are deep-seated "instinctual" tendencies, which are manifested in complex and often devious ways. His choices and actions are not the outcome of a rational analysis of the situation, a deliberate weighing of consequences. In this sense, his actions are "irrational." As in the case of the conception of the rational man, the motives of the unconscious man are all in himself, but the manner in which they govern his behavior and experience is entirely different. He really neither chooses what he does, nor does what he chooses.

This does not mean that he fails to make "sense" of his behavior. He experiences needs and desires, goals and intentions, and he tends to see most of his behavior as meaningfully related to them. But the "motives" he consciously experiences are often elaborate false fronts for the real "unconscious motives," and his "understanding" of his motivation is merely rationalization.

Although there have been many historical forerunners of such views, it was in Sigmund Freud that the conception came to fullest flower. Like the impact of Darwin, that of Freud has been immense, spreading to the outermost reaches of our conceptions of man, its force still far from spent. Freud's theories are embodied in what is called *psychoanalysis.* As we have already suggested, his views combine many of the points that are involved in the other conceptions of man which we have discussed. His theories aim not only at an explanation of human motivation, but at the wider problems of accounting for the total personality. We will postpone a detailed description of his theories until Part IV (see specially pp. 618-20).

By Way of Summary. We have briefly surveyed a number of conceptions of man's nature, some older, some newer. Each has its merits and its defects. What, then, shall we conclude about man's nature?

It would seem that we must say *all* of these things (and presently more), for in truth man *is* at once both biological animal and social product, both master and servant of fate, both rational and irrational, both driver and driven. His behavior can be fully explained only by placing each aspect in its proper perspective. Of all the dynamic physical systems constituting the universe, man is the most complex.

All these various conceptions of man's nature continue to be reflected in the ways we think about our present-day problems of society—war, racial tensions, depression, crime. Take, for instance, the juvenile delinquent. He may be variously regarded as the innocent victim of older associates who "made him" misbehave; or as a legally responsible person, capable of freely choosing between right and wrong; or as a person with an instinctively "bad" character; or as a case of failure of society to socialize properly; or as an unwilling victim of irrational impulses, a "crazy mixed-up kid" requiring psychotherapy. Each of these ways of looking at him reflects a particular conception of human motivation.

As we proceed to a more detailed account of the problems of motivation, we shall find recurrent echoes of the various conceptions of man's nature.

The Identifying of Motives

As we have already seen in Chapter 8, a *motive* is a need or desire coupled with the intention to attain an appropriate goal. A hunger need is not alone the motive, nor is food the motive; the motive is to seek and eat food to relieve the hunger need. To identify a person's specific motives, it is necessary to infer the specific needs, desires, and goals that he experiences. One way of doing this is to *study his behavior* and to infer his needs and desires from the systematic character of the behavior, and his goals from the effects that his behavior brings about. The other way is to ask the person to *tell* us what his needs, desires, and goals are. These two methods are supplementary, and both are required. As we shall see, each of them presents special difficulties.

Inferring Motives from Behavior. In trying to infer motives from behavior, we are confronted with the necessity of making sense of a bewildering stream of continuous activity of the individual. The *full* record of Anyman's behavior during but a single day—every muscle twitch, every grunt, every jog in blood pressure—would constitute a mountain of data, unmanageable for analysis.

What we must do, therefore, is to study his behavior selectively, not taking account of every detail but looking instead for organized sequences of behavior. One way of doing this is to describe his behavior in terms of *episodes*—beginning with the individual in one psychological situation, following through what appears to be a directed sequence of actions, and terminating with the individual in an altered psychological situation.

BEHAVIOR EPISODES. Episodes may be short and simple, or long and complex. Episodes may be completed or interrupted. Finally, of course, episodes may overlap. A long complex episode may overlap with several short ones.

We can never be certain where one episode starts and another ends. In a sense, breaking up the continuous stream of behavior into episodes is a somewhat artificial procedure, justified only because we must cut down behavior "to size" if we are to analyze it at all.

In any event, from an analysis of episodes we attempt to infer the specific motives of the person. For instance, an episode might begin at the breakfast table when Mr. Anyman remarks enthusiastically to his wife about the charms of the woman they met the evening before. After his departure for work, Mrs. Anyman gets dressed, runs for the train to town, and searches for and buys a new spring hat. When her husband returns from work, he tells her how well she is looking, kisses her tenderly, and Mrs. Anyman's episode ends. We might guess that the change in her situation that has occurred from the beginning to the end of the episode is that Mr. Anyman was at first perceived as admiring another woman and now is admiring *her*. Thus we would be inclined to infer that Mrs. Anyman's motive in this episode was to regain her husband's attention and to satisfy her need for being admired. But we

could be wrong. She may have been motivated to punish her husband for his faithlessness by charging an expensive hat. Or she may simply have been gratifying a desire to enjoy wearing a new hat. Or it may have been a combination of all these.

We see that it is often difficult to be sure exactly what motive or motives the behavior episode reflects merely from observing the effects produced by the behavior. The reasons for this are several.

RANDOM BEHAVIOR—SYSTEMATIC EFFECTS. For one thing, quite systematic and repeatable effects may be brought about "circumstantially" through *random behavior*. By random behavior we mean a series of unorganized responses, forming no consistent pattern, having no constant direction. That is, the direction of each successive response is unconnected with the responses that precede and follow. From the point of view of the observer, each response is unpredictable, pure "chance." How, then, is it possible for such random behavior *regularly* to result in the repeated production of a given end effect? An experimental illustration will help.

Take a horizontal glass tube that is filled with water, hot at one end and cold at the other. Place a number of a certain type of microorganism in the tube at the hot end. These organisms are stimulated by heat to swim; the higher the temperature, the more vigorous the swimming. After a while we will observe a striking fact: *all* the organisms are now concentrated at the cold end and *none* is left at the hot end. That is how they will stay. And if we return them to the hot end, again in due course they will all congregate at the cold end.

Observing this behavior episode, we would probably be inclined to infer in the organisms a "goal" of getting to the cold water. But we could be quite wrong. By looking more closely at one of these organism's behavior at each successive moment in the hot water, we would be surprised to discover that the direction of its movement is *exactly as likely to be toward the hotter water as toward the cooler*. The effect of the heat stimulus is simply to cause the organism to keep swimming. The *direction* of swimming is entirely random. Eventually, by pure chance the organism will swim into the cold water. Here there is no further stimulus to swim, and it will remain at rest in the cold water. Sooner or later, by pure chance, *all* the organisms must thus congregate motionless at the cold end of the tube. And no matter how often the whole experiment is repeated, the same final outcome will occur. Yet this systematic effect occurs without the organisms having a *goal* of getting to the cold water. They may, of course, be said to have a motive, namely, "to swim when hot." But that is far different from saying that they have a motive "to seek cold water in order to escape from heat." (The reader may be struck by an interesting parallel between the collective behavior of this swarm of microorganisms and certain cases of human social action in which a common social end is regularly brought about by the behavior of many persons, each of whom is individually motivated in unique ways.)

CONSISTENT BEHAVIOR—DIFFERENT MOTIVES. But even if we should observe a less primitive organism in our tube of water and find that at each moment it *consistently* swims in the direction of the cold end, we might be wrong in inferring a motive to "seek the cold water." For instance, we might later observe that even when the water is *equal* in temperature throughout the tube, the organism still swims directly to what had been the cold end. Controlled experimentation might then reveal that the water at that end contained a food chemical attractive to the hungry organism.

Clearly, in such a case, we would have been wrong originally in inferring a motive to avoid the hot water by getting to the cold. For the real motive would have been to get to the food at one end in order to remove hunger. This is a simple illustration of the fact that the same apparent pattern of directed behavior may serve one or another of several quite different systematic functions. This can be abundantly demonstrated in human behavior, for example, in Mrs. Anyman's hat-buying described above.

ONE MOTIVE—MULTIPLE EFFECTS. There is a further complication in inferring motives from behavior. Again observing our organisms swimming in the hot water, we see that at least two entirely different changes in situation of the individual have been produced by its activity: (1) it has shifted from hot to cold water; (2) it is now in close spatial proximity to all the other individuals. What has happened is that the swimming activity, whose main effect was to get to cool water, also has a *side effect*, namely, that of bringing all the organisms together. And this side effect will occur just as regularly as the main effect, whenever the experiment is repeated.

Obviously, therefore, the observer might make a serious error in inference, if he inferred that the organism's motive was "to seek company so as to gratify a gregarious need." This kind of organism may have no such need at all. (Again the reader may be struck with this source of danger in making ill-tested inferences about the "social motivation" of individuals in a group, merely on the basis of the group behavior.)

Inferring Motives from Verbal Reports. The second approach to inferring motives is to ask the person to *tell* what needs and desires he is experiencing, what goals he is seeking. This would seem to be the most obvious method and the one least fraught with error. Yet it, too, presents serious difficulties. We cannot ask infants to describe their motives, nor can we ask people unable to communicate because of disease or mental imbalance. Even if the person can talk, we cannot be sure that he is giving a reliable report of what he is experiencing. He may be in an extremely complex situation with multiple motivational determinants, and unable to give a clear report of his complex feelings. Or he may simply lie, being unwilling to expose his motives to the outsider.

A more basic difficulty is that even if he faithfully reports his motives as he clearly perceives them, we may find that his reported motives do not correspond with what is revealed in his behavior as analyzed by the outside observer. It is just this lack of correspondence between the experienced motive and the behavior which has helped give rise to the concept of "unconscious motivation."

Unconscious Motivation. In exploring the various conceptions of man's nature, we observed that the notion of man as "irrational," as "unconsciously motivated," is a particularly influential one.

It is undeniable that in a great deal of behavior the person's own perceptions of his actions do not coincide with those of an external observer. The assumption is that the trained observer grasps the "true reason," while the person does not. The observer frequently has the advantage of studying behavior dispassionately, and he may be able to note consistencies in behavior and its effects of which the behaving person is unaware. On the basis of these consistencies the observer can infer unconscious motives.

This is not to say, however, that the external observer is *always* right. His interpretation may be biased by his own outlook. Moreover, the observer may be deceived by sheer *accidental* regularities in behavior and consequences. He sees a man repeatedly losing one job after another, apparently without reason, and infers that the man has an "unconscious unwillingness to take care of his family." Yet the man's job failures may be entirely circumstantial; for instance, employers tend to dislike the shape of his nose, or he is basically not skillful enough, though competent on the surface. If the observer takes account of these additional facts, the regularity of job-loss may no longer call for a motivational explanation—conscious or unconscious.

TWO MEANINGS OF UNCONSCIOUS MOTIVATION. Assuming that the observer does correctly see a meaningful and consistent pattern to the person's behavior, a pattern of which the person is unaware, we presumably have a case of unconscious motivation. But there are still two main possible interpretations of what "unconscious" means. It is essential that we understand the difference between the two, for they are at the base of two critically different theories of, or approaches to, motivation.

(1) By unconscious motivation is sometimes meant that the person has an "unconscious need" and is "unconsciously seeking" an "unconscious goal." For example, we may say that "He unconsciously feels inferior and, without realizing it, he constantly criticizes his wife in order to make himself feel better." This meaning of unconscious motivation extends concepts from the *conscious life* into a separate realm of inferred "unconscious life." The "unconscious" is conceived here as a separate mental state, having many properties analogous to conscious experience, such as feelings, thoughts, emotions, needs, purposes, etc.; indeed, there is a strong implication that the "unconscious" is a separate agent of action in conflict with the "conscious."

(2) In the second meaning of unconscious there is no assumption of duplicate "mental lives"—a conscious one and an unconscious one. There is no such thing as "unconscious" needs, desires, intentions, goals, hopes and fears. These terms, by very definition, refer only to *consciously* experienced states of the organism. What is implied by this second meaning of unconscious motivation is that the person is unaware of the *effects* of his actions. For example, we may say that "He is unconscious of the fact that his constant criticism of his wife makes him feel better." Compare this statement carefully with the previous one. Though they sound much alike, their motivational implications are quite different. What is meant here is that though the way he experiences the needs and goals and purposes of his action does not involve an *intention* to humble his wife, his behavior does have that *effect.* Why then does the man act in such a way as to humble his wife, if this is not his intention? A possible answer is that his actions result from patterns of well-established habitual behavior, which repeatedly run off without any attention or awareness on his part.

This second view would argue that it would be simplest, therefore, to do away with the term "unconscious motivation" altogether since there is nothing unconscious that has the distinguishing earmarks of goal-directed behavior. We may properly speak, instead, of unconscious *effects*—and then seek the "cause" of such effects and the behavior that brings them about in the past experiences of the person, in his pattern of habitual acts, in stimulus-response relationships, in the state of his nervous system.

MOTIVE AND "CAUSE." It is often assumed that where no "conscious motive" seems to account for the behavior, we must find an "unconscious motive." This assumption is the result of a confusion between "motive" and "cause."

Motive is not synonymous with "cause." A complete statement of the causation of any bit of behavior must include factors of perception, thinking, and learning, as well as specification of the general situation and the multitude of stimuli playing upon the organism.

There is not necessarily a motive for every bit of behavior of the organism. This eye-wink, this snuffle, this tapping of the finger, this laughter is certainly caused, but it may not be a pattern of *goal-directed action in the service of a need or desire;* it may merely be a random expression of excitement, or a reflex response to a simple stimulus, or a rote habit.

What all this implies, of course, is that there are many different sizes of units or levels of analysis of behavior data, varying from what has been called the "molecular" (the smallest unit) to the "molar" (the larger unit). Obviously it follows that the account of motivation the psychologist gives will depend heavily upon the size of the behavior unit he studies.

Coping Behavior. When we consider large chunks of an individual's stream of activity, marked off in behavior episodes, we generally find the individual engaged in goal-directed action in the interests of satisfying needs and desires. Characteristically, such "molar" behavior involves the seeking of means to the goal, adaptability in the choice among alternative means, and the solving of problems necessary to circumvent barriers to the goal. Thus we refer to it as *coping behavior.*

Coping behavior necessarily involves concentrated attention by the individual; he must constantly be aware of what he is after and of how to go about getting it. Consciousness is, indeed, the very mark of the process of coping. For, as we have indicated in the foregoing discussion of "unconscious motivation," it may be doubted that there can be any such thing as purposeful striving, involving the solution of problems, the discovery and selection of means to a goal, etc., that can go on "unconsciously." Coping is concious.

Habitual Behavior. But not all aspects of the person's behavior are characterized by such coping. Indeed, the greater proportion of behavior is not. As we look at somewhat smaller, "molecular," chunks of behavior, constituting only *parts* of the person's total on-going activity, we observe the regular running off of various highly organized and well-practiced response patterns, elicited by specific stimuli. We have here what may be called *habitual behavior*.

Habitual behavior is not characterized by the adaptive flexibility that distinguishes coping behavior. It can be thought of rather as routine response patterns, acquired through learning, which are "automatically" called forth and performed with minimal conscious attention by the person. Such habits are often in the nature of "instruments" or "tools," functioning as parts of larger patterns of coping behavior. It should be stressed that in the *development* of the habitual behavior—in the learning of the habit—consciousness was once necessarily involved. Moreover, a habitual behavior pattern blocked in its normal routine execution may, of course, once again come into the focus of consciousness, as renewed coping behavior to circumvent the block is required.

Expressive Behavior. It is also possible to observe the person's behavior from the point of view of what it *expresses* about him, about his inner states. The concern is neither with goal-seeking patterns nor with habit patterns, but with the *manner* in which he behaves—how rapidly he moves, how tensely he speaks, how loudly he laughs, how quietly he sits.

Such *expressive behaviors* are not usually motivated, that is, they are not themselves directed at attaining goals and satisfying needs. They are simply manifestations of what is going on in the person, his states of tension or release of tension, his emotional feelings, his conflicts. And much of the time the person is not conscious of these expressive behaviors. It is for these reasons that the study of expressive behaviors is one of the major tools of the personality psychologist in his task of understanding the inner and often unconscious states of the individual.

It should be added, however, that expressive behaviors may sometimes be motivated. The person may *intend* to express his inner state in order to communicate it to other people: he laughs to show his feeling of appreciation of the joke (or his pretended appreciation of a poor joke), he knits his brow to show thought, gesticulates to show excitement. Moreover, beyond this communicative function the expressive behaviors may be motivated toward the inherent satisfactions and stimulations they provide. The expressive movements in dancing, in walking, in shouting, may be goals in themselves.

By Way of Summary. In attempting to identify the nature of the person's motives from his behavior, it is necessary to describe his behavior in terms of *episodes*, in which some sort of change in the situation is brought about by what the person does. The difficulty in making such inferences is that there may be systematic changes in the situation produced by purely "random" (not goal-directed) behavior. Moreover, the same consistent pattern of behavior may reflect quite different underlying motives. And, further, a single motive may lead to a number of different kinds of incidental changes in the situation, some of which may be mistaken as reflecting the real motive.

Another approach is to infer motives from the person's verbal report of what he subjectively experiences as his motivations. A basic difficulty here is that there may be a discrepancy between the motive he reports and what an external observer would judge his motive to be on the basis of his behavior. This is especially the case in so-called "unconscious" motivation.

Two quite different meanings attach to the concept of unconscious motivation. One suggests that the person's directed behavior can be governed by needs and desires, goals and intentions, of which he is entirely unaware, in much the same manner that conscious motivation regulates behavior. The other meaning stops short of this assumption of a separate unconscious sphere of psychological functioning. It suggests instead that unconscious motivation refers to cases in which the person's behavior brings about systematic effects of which he is unaware, owing to patterns of well-established *habitual* behavior, capable of running off without his attention. Such habitual behavior is to be distinguished from *coping* behavior, in which the person in full consciousness seeks adaptive ways of attaining an intended goal. *Expressive* behavior resembles habitual behavior in that neither is consciously goal-directed, but differs from it in being indirectly indicative of underlying states of motivation in the person.

The Varieties of Motives

Bearing in mind the difficulties in identifying motives, we turn now to a review of the varieties of motives. Were we to allow for every finest shading and nuance of motives among all the different people on earth, we would find the number of separate human motives running well into the billions. But to bring some order into the picture, we must ignore the detailed differences and concentrate upon the common features. We must seek to find a limited set of groupings of motives that will encompass the behavior of most people.

The best way to do this is to look for the most general aims of human behavior, whether in child or adult, in modern man or Hottentot. It would appear that every activity of the individual can be regarded as governed by one or a combination of four general aims: *survival, security, satisfaction, stimulation.* He aims to stay alive, to keep safe, to feel enjoyments, to experience new stimuli.

Deficiency and Abundancy Motivation. Two of these aims—survival and security —express *deficiency motivation,* which is characterized by *needs* to remove deficit, disruption, discomfort, to avoid or escape from danger, threat, anxiety. In short, it is tension-reductive.

The other two general aims—satisfaction and stimulation—express *abundancy motivation,* which is characterized by *desires* to experience enjoyments, to get gratifications, to know, understand, learn, and discover, to seek novelty, to create and achieve. Tension-reduction is not its aim. Indeed, it may involve the seeking of tension-*increase.*

Every individual is characterized by both deficiency and abundancy motivations. But the relative weighting of the two varies widely among individuals. Some persons are mainly dominated by their needs, with desires impoverished; in others, needs may be subsidiary and desires have full range. Almost every concrete activity we find people engaged in can express either deficiency motivation or abundancy motivation or both. Even when engaged in the same activity—such as playing games, building a bridge, chairing a committee, or making love—the motivational *meaning* of the activity is quite different for a person chiefly dominated by deficiency motivation and a person chiefly governed by the abundancy aims of satisfaction and stimulation.

Classes of Specific Motives. Survival, security, satisfaction, stimulation, are descriptive abstractions, within each of which are found many specific motives.

One convenient classification of the specific motives falling under each general aim is into those pertaining primarily (1) to the person's *body*, (2) to his *relations with the environment*, (3) to his *relations*

with other people, (4) to his *self.* (See Table 2.)

For example, the survival aim is not merely tied up with specific body motives. It also involves maintaining an environment that can provide the necessary supplies, maintaining workable relations with fellow men on whom one is physically dependent, and maintaining a sufficiently favorable self-conception so that one *wants* to go on living.

The Complexity of Motives. Every individual in every culture is in some degree characterized by the classes of motives listed in Table 2. But there are enormous

TABLE 2

The Human Motives

Listed in this table are some of the principal human motives, classified under the general aims of survival and security (deficiency motives) and satisfaction and stimulation (abundancy motives). Under these general headings the motives are further classified according to whether they mainly pertain to the body, to relations with the environment, to relations with other people, or to the self.

	Survival and Security (deficiency motives)	*Satisfaction and Stimulation* (abundancy motives)
Pertaining to the body	Avoiding of hunger, thirst, oxygen lack, excess heat and cold, pain, overfull bladder and colon, fatigue, overtense muscles, illness and other disagreeable bodily states, etc.	Attaining pleasurable sensory experiences of tastes, smells, sounds, etc.; sexual pleasure; bodily comfort; exercise of muscles, rhythmical body movements, etc.
Pertaining to relations with environment	Avoiding of dangerous objects and horrible, ugly, and disgusting objects; seeking objects necessary to future survival and security; maintaining a stable, clear, certain environment, etc.	Attaining enjoyable possessions; constructing and inventing objects; understanding the environment; solving problems; playing games; seeking environmental novelty and change, etc.
Pertaining to relations with other people	Avoiding interpersonal conflict and hostility; maintaining group membership, prestige, and status; being taken care of by others; conforming to group standards and values; gaining power and dominance over others, etc.	Attaining love and positive identifications with people and groups; enjoying other people's company; helping and understanding other people; being independent, etc.
Pertaining to the self	Avoiding feelings of inferiority and failure in comparing the self with others or with the ideal self; avoiding loss of identity; avoiding feelings of shame, guilt, fear, anxiety, sadness, etc.	Attaining feelings of self-respect and self-confidence; expressing onself; feeling sense of achievement; feeling challenged; establishing moral and other values; discovering meaningful place of self in the universe.

individual differences in the specific content and form of actual motives, in their relative importance in the person's life, and in the particular ways they are manifested in behavior.

The "same" motive in two different persons is rarely the same. Many alternative goal-objects are equivalent in reducing a need, but they are far from equivalent in the particular satisfactions they yield. Moreover, motives are rarely found singly. Almost every activity is an expression of many motives, and the "same" type of activity, e.g., eating, may represent in different individuals very different constellations of motives.

These points can be illustrated by four important forms of common human activity: eating, sex, self-assertive behavior, and action provoked by curiosity. They are activities chosen for discussion because of their universal existence, because they reveal the essential complexity of motives, and because they illustrate the four basic human aims of survival, satisfaction, security, and stimulation.

Eating—a Survival Motive. Eating has obvious survival aims. All men eat food, or else perish. Mainly, of course, this behavior expresses a *hunger motive*, arising from the needs felt when the body is depleted of necessary substances.

The intensity and importance of the hunger motive vary enormously among individuals. For some deprived people on earth, hunger is a chronic state, rarely absent. It provides the main focus of life, everything else is subsidiary to it. For more fortunate people, hunger comes and goes, regularly satisfied. For still others, such as the chef always nibbling at the food around him, the hunger state may hardly ever be intensely aroused.

Physiological factors obviously play a major role in determining the onset of hunger. In general, the longer a person is deprived of food, the greater is his hunger, although this is by no means a simple relationship, as we shall see in Chapter 12. Factors other than food deprivation also help to determine the onset of hunger. The ongoing activities of the person may temporarily inhibit the hunger feeling; appropriate external stimuli may arouse it, e.g., a look at the clock, the smell of cooking. And there are established *rhythms* of hunger varying widely among people. In some cultures only one meal a day is eaten, and apparently hunger appears only once daily. Our own cultural preference for three square meals a day is but one possible rhythmic pattern, and even it is giving way to a pattern of light breakfasts, coffee-breaks, lunch, and dinner.

The goal-object of the hunger motive is food. Everyone knows the story of the incredible array of foods that different people eat. Foods favored by one person may be regarded by another as abhorrent. Cultural factors play a large role, but physiological factors sometimes underlie the cultural. The Eskimo's appetite for whale blubber is not just what the culture dictates, but partly what is required by the body in an extremely cold climate.

There are other kinds of evidence that physiological factors help to govern food preferences. In "free-feeding" experiments (Davis, 1928) young children were permitted to eat any foods, in whatever amounts they wished, from a large selection of more than thirty foods of all kinds, presented on a tray. The results over a period of six months or more clearly indicated that the children's free choices constituted a very healthy diet. Presumably their taste preferences were to some extent being determined by underlying physiological requirements for the various food substances.

The pregnant woman's insistent desire

for pickles at 3 A.M. is probably tied up with hormonal states of the body. There are all sorts of specific deficits that require specific foods for their satisfaction (see Box 61).

OTHER MOTIVES FOR EATING. There is much eating behavior that involves no perception of a state of body hunger at all. It is not the *need* for food but the *desire* for a certain food which impels the person to act. He is not hungry; he seeks the pleasure that will come from tasting and eating the particular food. The Roman aristocrats who took emetics in order to continue the banquet provide a bizarre demonstration of eating as a "satisfaction" motive. There can also be seeking after *novelty* in foods— a "stimulation" motive.

But this does not exhaust the complexity of eating behavior. The motives for eating may be far removed from need or desire for *food*. We eat in social situations in close connection with other activities. We may eat with conspicuous consumption or conspicuous waste to discomfit social rivals or to gain prestige; there is religious cannibalism in which the enemy is eaten in order to gain his strength. On the side of the inhibition of eating, there is the child's refusal to eat, which may serve as an attention-getting device, and prolonged fasting, which may be used as an instrument of passive political resistance.

In brief, eating behavior represents a profusion of motives, some closely related to hunger, others entirely unrelated.

Sexual Behavior—a Satisfaction Motive. Sexual behavior is primarily governed by a satisfaction motive. Though, like hunger, it is related to physiological factors, it is less closely linked with survival value than is hunger. Failure of sexual satisfaction is not lethal to the individual, nor, indeed, to preservation of the species.

There are wide individual variations in the intensity of the sex motives. For some individuals they are a main preoccupation; for others they are virtually absent. And in the course of the individual's life there are marked changes in their importance. Childhood sexuality is less intense than that of the adolescent; and as one ages, sexuality tends to diminish. But the individual differences are large. In some persons sexual drives remain vigorous even in old age.

That physiological factors are important will be seen in Chapter 12, in connection with evidence that sexual activity shows variations related to concentration of sex hormones in the body. Yet it appears that such hormonal factors are not all-important, especially in human beings. To a far greater extent the arousal of sexual activity comes from external and ideational stimuli, which serve to produce the feeling of sexual excitement.

The goal of much sexual activity is clearly satisfaction of the sexual desire. Sexual desires can be both general and specific. In an intensely aroused state of sexual excitement the person can be relieved by almost any form of sexual climax or orgasm. On the other hand, just as there are specific hungers, so are there "specific lusts." It is not merely simple sexual release of any kind that is the usual goal of the sex motive, but consummation of a particular sex act with a particular mate.

VARIETIES OF SEXUAL EXPERIENCE. The objects of sexual desire vary among cultures and among individuals within cultures. Most typically the objects are persons of the opposite sex. Yet there are cultures in which the amount of homosexuality is considerable. Occasionally the objects of sexual desire are not people, but animals and inanimate things.

Just as various customs regulate the expression of eating behavior, so too various customs regulate sexual behavior. There are wide cultural differences in the freedom

BOX 61

On Appetites, Specific and "Perverted"

Extensive laboratory experiments with animals plus observations on human beings give conclusive evidence of the existence of a number of distinguishable, and more or less independent, appetites for specific food substances. Among those that have been definitely identified are appetites for protein, fat, carbohydrate, sodium, phosphorus, calcium, and the vitamin B complex. If the organism is deprived of any of these indispensable substances, a heightened appetite for it soon develops. With prolonged deprivation, the appetite may take the form of an insistent craving.

The example of vitamin B is especially instructive. Numerous studies have shown that if rats are fed a diet deficient in vitamin B, they quickly develop a strong preference for foods or liquids containing the vitamin. For instance, in a study by Richter and his associates rats were made deficient in vitamin B. Then a dozen different containers filled with different foods and solutions were placed in their cages, one of the containers having a solution of vitamin B. The rats immediately located and drank from that container. They fiercely resisted attempts by the experimenter to remove the bottle from the cage, holding fast to it with teeth and paws.

Another example: Rats whose adrenal glands are surgically removed will die within 10 to 15 days unless large quantities of salt are ingested, owing to the excessive loss of salt through the urine. But if these rats are given free access to a salt solution, they will drink it in sufficiently large amounts to maintain the body's salt balance and keep alive. Moreover, it appears that the adrenalectomized rat has a *lower threshold* than normal rats for discriminating very tiny concentrations of salt solution.

If the usual forms of a needed food are not accessible, "perverted" appetites may be manifested. For instance, cattle living in regions where the feed is deficient in phosphorus will eat bones lying on the ground, or may even capture small animals and eat their bones. Lacking bones, the cow may eat leather or wood, or even stones and earth. A human being suffering from hookworm disease may eat paper, chalk, earth, and hair.

Despite ample evidence of specific appetites governed by specific physiological requirements, it should not be concluded that there is an inevitable and perfect congruence of deficit and appetite. The physiological factors are but one of many. Factors of learning, of habit, of cultural norms, play equally large roles in governing specific appetites. Often these factors may lead to food preferences detrimental to the organism. A classical case is the polished rice diet of many Oriental peoples. When the polishing of rice (which removes the coatings rich in vitamin B) became common and preferred, the disease *beriberi*, caused by vitamin B deficiency, became widespread. Appetite in this case was a treacherous guide to body requirement.

The manner in which habit can override the physiological requirement in determining food preferences is also shown experimentally by Scott and Verney. They deprived rats of vitamin B and then offered a licorice-flavored food containing the vitamin and another food not containing it. As we would expect from Richter's findings above, the rats chose the vitamin-laden food, even though they do not normally like licorice flavor. Once the habit of choosing the licorice food was well established, the experimenters removed the vitamin from it and placed it in the other food. The rats continued for some time to choose the licorice-flavored food over the food that now contained the vitamin, even though they still suffered a severe vitamin deficiency. Ultimately, however, the rats did switch to the new vitamin-laden food.

Richter, C. P., Holt, L. E., and Barelare, B. 1937. Vitamin B₁ craving in rats. *Science, 86,* 354–5.

Scott, E. M., and Verney, E. L. 1949. Self-selection of diet. IX. The appetite for thiamine. *J. Nutrition, 37,* 81–92.

or inhibition of sexual behavior in children, in unmarried young people, and in married people outside the marriage bond. There are diverse taboos concerning the objects of sexual activity, the situations in which sexual behavior is carried out, the particular forms of the sexual act. For instance, the very postures of the sexual act which are considered "wrong" in one civilization may be considered the only "right" forms in another. And for another example, in virtually every society there are *incest taboos* that prohibit sexual behavior with respect to members of one's "family." But there is no agreement among cultures in the *definition* of "family"; in some cultures intercourse between uncles and nieces is not considered incestuous, in others it is punished by death. In our society, marriage of second cousins is perfectly acceptable, in other societies it is incest.

There is often a "double standard" of sexual conduct. What is considered normal and proper for a man is not permissible for a woman and vice versa. In our culture, for instance, female chastity is regarded as more important than male chastity; on the other hand homosexuality in the female does not usually arouse the same intense condemnation as in the male.

OTHER MOTIVES FOR SEX BEHAVIOR. These cultural and individual differences emphasize again that there is a great deal more involved in sexual behavior than simply the release from sexual tension or the attaining of sexual satisfaction. The fact is that there is an enormous complex of related motives at work. Quite aside from the more clearly sensual aspects, sexual behavior can be mainly concerned with needs and desires to do things to and for other people. The main motive may be to show love and affection, or to dominate and overpower, or to hurt sadistically, or to demean and show contempt for the other. Or the sexual behavior may fulfill needs and desires of the self, for instance, to feel loved, to belong, to be submissive to the other, to be hurt masochistically, to be self-expressive, to build up self-confidence in one's masculinity or prove one's femininity.

There are almost endless other possible purposes: to conceive children, to perpetuate political dynasties, to earn money, to placate enemies, to rebel against one's parents, to be patriotic (the girl who gives herself to the soldier who is off to the wars). Indeed it would appear that a "sexual history" of the world would not fall far short of an account of all its diverse activities. For sexual behavior reflects each of the general aims of survival, security, satisfaction, and stimulation; it involves the body, the environment, other people, and the self; it is both deficiency and abundancy motivation; it is in the service of good ends and bad, high purposes and low.

Self-assertive Behavior—a Security Motive. As we watch the individual's behavior toward other people, we see him leading them, giving orders, pushing his way into line, running for office, trying to beat competitors, wearing medals, driving luxurious cars that are too long to be parked on the street, monopolizing conversations, pulling the strings in a big organization, refusing to do what his fellows do, attacking authority figures. In short, we see him engaging in *self-assertive behavior*. All these diverse activities may express needs and desires to make his presence known and felt, to stand out.

These needs and desires pertain especially to his relations with other persons and with social groups. But they also pertain in some degree to the maintaining and enhancing of his own self-picture, regardless of how others may see him. Thus self-assertive behavior is often basically expressive of a security motive.

These assertive behaviors may be governed by motives far removed from other people and self. Exercising leadership may be in the interests of securing one's group from attack; refusing to do what others do may stem from a conviction that they are wrong. As with eating behavior and sexual behavior, and any other major activity, assertive behavior may serve diverse aims, express diverse needs and desires, take endless forms.

Among the more important aspects of self-assertive behavior that have been studied by psychologists are *dominance, prestige,* and *power.*

DOMINANCE. As we look at any social group, we observe that some members are ascendant over the rest. They more frequently take the lead, give orders, dominate the group activities. They may take the best seats in the room, the best food from the table, the biggest portion of the loot from the bank robbery. They are more likely to be able to criticize and attack their fellows without reprisal.

Such dominance hierarchies are determined by numerous individual factors, including the dominant person's greater size, strength, energy, power, or competence; his personality traits of self-confidence, persuasiveness, poise, vigor. They are also determined by numerous social factors having to do with cultural beliefs about the role of the adult vis-à-vis the child, the male vis-à-vis the female, the "upper-class" person vis-à-vis the "lower-class" person. Many dominance hierarchies are, of course, formalized and legalized by society, as in the chain of military command, the diplomatic protocol, the established relations between employer and employee.

But these social factors often give way to the more powerful individual factors. The experienced top sergeant may dominate his officer; the aggressive worker may intimidate his boss; the wife may "wear the pants" and henpeck the husband.

As the term implies, henpecking is found in the barnyard. Studies of flocks of chickens reveal that there are definite, well-established *pecking orders* among them: Chicken A normally pecks Chicken B, B pecks C, C pecks D, etc. When a hen lower in the hierarchy is injected with the male sex hormone, her dominance behavior may be increased, and a new pecking order established in which she will be in a higher position. Such a new order once established is likely to persist long after the hormonal effects have worn off—a striking illustration of the interaction of physiological and social factors in motivation.

Goats, dogs, monkeys, and many other animals have been found to exhibit such dominance hierarchies. The male is often though not invariably dominant over the female in the various species. But even where the male is normally dominant, there are conditions in which the female may assume the more dominant role (during sexual receptivity or while caring for the young). Box 62 shows how dominance behavior may be experimentally manipulated.

PRESTIGE. The striving for prestige and status takes many forms that are so familiar that we need not review them here. The bases of prestige and status may be one's material possessions, achievements, social position, ancestry, skin color, age.

Prestige and status are conferred on the individual by other people, and his feelings of needs and desires for prestige and status thus depend significantly upon how he thinks other people regard him. But it is not merely people in general who are important to him. There are certain groups whose recognition and esteem he especially values.

We are immersed in a constant cultural atmosphere of prestige- and status-seeking, and it is hard for most of us not to see it as an essential and inherent part of human nature. Our Western culture, like many

BOX 62

Changing the Dominance of Monkeys

An experimental attempt to modify the dominance hierarchy in a group of monkeys through training some of the monkeys to make avoidance responses toward one member of the group was carried out by Miller, Murphy, and Mirsky. Over a period of 20 months they observed the behavior of a group of 8 male and 2 female monkeys, and determined the dominance hierarchy within the group on a number of occasions. The hierarchy was found to be quite stable over time.

Monkey 53, who was consistently low in the dominance hierarchy, was chosen to be the special experimental animal. It was placed in a compartment visible to Monkey 57. As soon as Monkey 53 became visible, Monkey 57 was given an electric shock. The shock continued until the monkey pressed a lever. Not only did this eliminate the shock, it also removed Monkey 53 from view by dropping a door between them. After a number of such trials Monkey 57 learned to press the lever as soon as Monkey 53 came into view. It had learned an avoidance response to Monkey 53. All the other monkeys in the group were in turn given this avoidance training to Monkey 53.

The issue was to see how this learned avoidance to an animal previously low in the dominance hierarchy would affect the dominance relations in the normal group situation. The accompanying figure shows clearly that Monkey 53 increased markedly in dominance as the training went on. Moreover, the monkeys who in the early part of the experiment were not conditioned to Monkey 53 also showed changes in their dominance relationships with it. For example, after three conditioning periods in which only two of the animals had been trained to avoid Monkey 53, the latter's dominance status exceeded not only that of those two, but of four others as well. (The animals conditioned to avoid Monkey 53 are indicated by crosshatched circles.)

The entire dominance hierarchy in the group of 10 animals was somewhat affected by the upward shift of this one animal. That is, the dominance relations among pairs of animals *not* including Monkey 53 were different before and after the experimental training period. This is interesting incidental evidence of the complexity of group dynamics, even in monkeys.

MILLER, R. E., MURPHY, J. V., and MIRSKY, I. A. 1955. The modification of social dominance in a group of monkeys by interanimal conditioning. *J. comp. physiol. Psychol.*, *48*, 392–6.

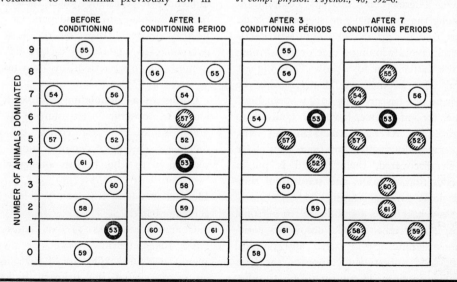

cultures, seems to place heavy stress on the values of prestige and status.

This is not to say that our culture is necessarily as prestige- and status-centered as it possibly could be. Anthropologists have made a comforting study of the Kwakiutl Indians of the Pacific Northwest Coast among whom the strivings for prestige and status assume proportions matched only by special social segments of our own population. These Indians collect food, blankets, and other goods in order to invite their social rivals to a ceremonial *potlatch*, which is the occasion for them to pile all their possessions on the fire and burn them. The prestige acquired is proportional to the goods destroyed, and the discomfited social rivals must bide their time until they can be hosts and give an even bigger potlatch to reassert their status.

Yet anthropologists tell us that such values (whether as exemplified by the Kwakiutl Indians or by us) are not universal. It is reported, for example, that among the Arapesh of New Guinea, self-assertiveness is virtually nonexistent. Among the Zuni of New Mexico values of prestige and status appear to be entirely alien. There is no obvious competition among the individuals, no seeking to stand out from the group. The Zuni will deliberately avoid winning a race or performing a test faster than his fellows. His highest praise for another would presumably be that no one has anything to say about him! We, too, of course, have our contests to locate Mr. Average American and Mrs. Average Housewife, but once they have been discovered, their reward is public recognition, prestige, and status, and they are never "average" again.

Power. The need and desire for personal power over other people, despite its enormous significance in social and political affairs, is, unfortunately, one of the least studied motives. Though it relates to other aspects of self-assertiveness, such as dominance and prestige, it is clearly something different. For the striking fact about power is that it may be fully gratified without social recognition. The essential part is that the individual feels that *he* is the agent of influence and control of other people and of events, so he may be fully satisfied to be the anonymous "power behind the throne." He need not get recognition, nor does he require that he dominate other people in face-to-face relations.

It is certainly true that power often brings with it a whole host of other kinds of rewards, such as wealth, prestige, and security. But these do not account for the power drive itself. The corporation executive who owns very little stock in his company may nonetheless be strongly motivated to build it up as though it were his own property. The satisfactions come not from ownership but may come partly from the power he wields over the destiny of the corporate body.

The drive for power may be expressed also in the person's seeking of *autonomy*. His desire is not so much to influence other people as to make himself free of their influence; he seeks the power to resist, to remain inviolate, to be independent. And he may desire *self-mastery*, the power to overcome, to control, to dictate his own impulses, his own actions, his own fate.

Curiosity—a Stimulation Motive. It has long been observed that animals spend a good deal of time and energy exploring their surroundings, demonstrating what may look to the human observer like "curiosity" or "interest in novel things." How is the drive for such activity to be accounted for?

Curiosity and least effort. Those who stress the deficiency aspect of motives would explain "exploratory" behavior as an expression of the primary biological drives, such as for food, sexual release, and safety. That is, the animal is assumed to "explore" only because he seeks to survive, to find a mate, and to be safe. If these primary needs were satisfied, he would not be driven to explore. The general conception of animal (and human) nature contained in this explanation is that an organism is motivated to learn only so much as is minimally required for biological survival. An organism is "curious" only when a basic bodily need requires fulfillment; an organism is governed by a *law of least effort*—only that minimal energy will be expressed which will suffice to survive. In its extreme caricature this view of motivation leads to a picture of the ideal state of existence as that of the "happy vegetable," "the complacent cow." Certainly there is ample evidence that animals and human beings do often exhibit curiosity only in order to satisfy basic needs. But is *all* exploratory and curiosity behavior to be accounted for in this way?

CURIOSITY AND MAXIMAL STIMULATION. The more recent experimental evidence from the animal laboratory, to say nothing of the mass of age-old human observation, clearly contradicts this extreme view. Rats demonstrate a great deal of exploratory behavior when there seems to be no pressing internal drive to be served; they will cross an electrified grid and suffer an electric shock when the only "reward" is the opportunity to explore a new maze (see Box 67, p. 302). Monkeys will eagerly solve puzzle problems with no extrinsic reward (as we have seen in Box 3, p. 9). The detrimental effects on human subjects resulting from prolonged reduction of sensory stimulation have already been described in Box 2, p. 8. In brief, there seems to be convincing evidence for a powerful tendency to seek novelty, to explore the unknown, and generally to *maximize* stimulation, rather than to minimize

it. And this is not merely in the service of reducing perceptual disorder so that primary needs can better be met; it is a matter of reaching out to encompass more and more of the world and continuously to extend its horizons. This is a psychological economy of *abundance* rather than one of *scarcity*, as is implied in the other conception.

The reader may quite reasonably object that there are many contrary cases in which the individual seems *not* to exhibit any intrinsic tendency to explore. Instead he puts forth no more effort than the very minimum necessary for the achievement of the goal. All of us are familiar with such cases. We even find times when this is the way we ourselves seem to behave.

It is doubtless true that the "law of least effort" pertains to much of our behavior. When we have an urgent motive, we seek to attain the goal as rapidly and as effortlessly as possible. But often such minimal activity gives the individual more freedom to pursue other aims, including that of maximizing stimulation and satisfying curiosity. The man who can efficiently, and with least effort, take care of his primitive survival requirements has that much more energy to devote to exploration and extension of his world. The student who puts forth no more effort than the very minimum that will permit him to "pass," may then have more energy and time to explore and extend his social and athletic worlds.

But when we find that an absence of curiosity is a *pervasive* and enduring characteristic of the person, we may assume that his life circumstances have been such as to preclude its "natural" development and expression. The underprivileged man who has always been forced to an utter preoccupation with the satisfying of primitive survival needs will have had no opportunity for the emergence of curiosity drives. The "luxury" of curiosity is less potent than the "necessities" of life. And even if a man has had the opportunity for the development of curiosity drives, they may not endure, because he may have been "punished" for expressing them. There are many social pressures against curiosity; exploration and curiosity may often mean painful consequences, and for some people the anxiety-producing effects of facing the unknown may be too great to tolerate.

Interrelations of Motives. As we have said, specific motives are unique to the in-dividual. The individual's motives influence one another: the particular set of motives he has, their relative strengths, and the pattern of their relationships all help to determine the character of each specific motive.

Full understanding of the individual's motives requires, therefore, that we know something about how they gradually came into being as he developed, and the role they now play in his entire personality. These problems will be considered in the final section of the book.

Glossary

abundancy motivation. Characterized by *desires* to experience enjoyments, to get gratifications, to understand and discover, to seek novelty, to strive to achieve and create. It includes the general aims of satisfaction and stimulation. As contrasted with deficiency motivation, it may often involve the seeking of tension *increase,* rather than of tension-reduction.

altruism. Directing one's behavior toward ends aiding the interests and welfare of other people.

behavior episode. An organized sequence of behavior, characterized by a more or less constant direction of actions serving to move the person from one psychological situation to another.

coping behavior. Behavior that is concerned with the attainment of goals in the satisfaction of needs or desires and is characterized by adaptability in discovering and using means of reaching the goals. It requires the conscious attention of the person. To be distinguished from *habitual behavior.*

cultural relativism. The doctrine that asserts that human motives, values, and actions are entirely relative to the particular culture in which they occur. Thus, the "human nature" of one culture is alleged to be different from the "human nature" of another.

deficiency motivation. Characterized by *needs* to remove deficits and disruptions, and to avoid or escape danger and threat. It includes the general aims of survival and security. Deficiency motivation is tension-reductive in its aim and thus is to be distinguished from abundancy motivation.

dominance. The tendency toward assertiveness and ascendancy by an individual in his relations with other individuals. In groups, animal as well as human, there are typically well-established dominance hierarchies, or "pecking orders," determined by such factors as the traits, past experience, and physiological makeup of the individuals, the cultural and social influences in the group.

drives. Aroused states of the organism, related to physiological requirements of the body, which set the organism into action. In one view of motivation, drives are considered to be innate biological tendencies, on the basis of which all complex motivation is developed through learning, taking the form of derived or *acquired* drives. In other views of motivation, drives are regarded as but a limited segment of the whole of the motivational energies of the organism.

dynamic physical system. A physical system in which a change in any one part of the system results in compensating and equalizing changes in other parts. To be contrasted with the simple machine.

egoism. Directing one's behavior toward ends that serve self-interest.

expressive behavior. Behavior seen from the point of view of what it expresses about the inner states of the person. Has to do with the manner, style, or quality of responses (e.g., handwriting, tempo of movements), rather than with their goal-directed character.

habitual behavior. Behavior that consists of well-practiced sequences of responses, elicited by a certain pattern of stimulation, and capable of "going off" with the minimal awareness of the person. To be distinguished from *coping behavior.*

hedonism. Directing one's behavior toward ends of the maximizing of pleasure and the minimizing of pain.

incest taboo. A social prohibition against sexual relations among members of an immediate family or kinship group, such as between brother and sister, or father and daughter. Found almost universally, the taboo differs widely from culture to culture in the definition of what constitutes the "family."

instinct. Innate patterns of behavior elicited by certain stimuli, and fulfilling certain basic biological functions for the organism. Refers both to the drive and to the activity appropriate to satisfy the drive.

law of least effort. The view that the organism will tend to expend only that minimal energy which will suffice to reach the goals of basic survival.

motive. A need or desire coupled with the intention to attain an appropriate goal. In accounting for behavior, motive is not synonymous with "cause."

power. An aspect of the motivation of self-assertiveness, related to but not the same as dominance or prestige. The essential attribute of the goal of power is the person's feeling of being the agent of influence and control over other people and over events, regardless of whether or not this entails public recognition of his power. The desire for power may also be expressed in the seeking of personal autonomy and self-mastery.

prestige. The goal of prestige is an aspect of the motivation of self-assertive behavior. Prestige is conferred on the individual by other people, and the concrete bases for attaining prestige are very diverse. There are wide cultural differences in the value placed upon prestige and in the criteria for determining it.

random behavior. A series of unorganized responses, forming no consistent pattern, having no constant direction toward an end.

reflex. A simple, involuntary, and unlearned response of a particular part of the body to a particular stimulus, such as the knee-jerk to a blow on the knee, or the contraction of the pupil of the eye to light.

satisfaction motives. The general class of motives concerned with the aim of attaining desired pleasures of all kinds, that is, enjoyments of activities for their own sake, quite aside from their relevance to needs of survival and security.

security motives. The general class of motives concerned with the aim of avoiding dangers, minimizing threats, establishing and maintaining a safe environment, safe relations with other people, a secure self-conception, etc.

self-assertive behavior. Behavior motivated by the intention of making the self stand out, be noticed and deferred to by others, generally with the aim of obtaining and maintaining a secure picture of self in one's own eyes and the eyes of others.

social determinism. The doctrine which asserts that there are laws of societies transcending laws of individual "human nature." The individual's behavior is considered to be dictated mainly by the requirements and characteristics of the social system as a whole.

stimulation motives. The general class of motives concerned with the aim of maximizing stimulation, change and novelty, exploration, and extension of the person's world.

survival motives. The general class of motives concerned with the aim of keeping alive (e.g., fulfilling biological requirements for food).

tropisms. Unlearned movements of an organism, serving to orient it in such a way that a certain distribution of stimuli is achieved. Tropisms (from the Greek word for "turning") are of many types, for instance, the *negative phototropism* of the cockroach running from the light, and the *negative geotropism* of the baby rat in climbing an inclined plane.

unconscious motivation. Two quite different uses of the term are: (1) Pertaining to a form of motivated behavior in which the person is unaware of his needs and desires, intentions and goals; that is, he engages in unconscious coping—solving problems, adaptively circumventing barriers, etc.—in order to achieve unconscious ends. (2) Pertaining to behavior that serves to bring about ends of which the person is unaware, for instance, in habitual acts whose consequences, though regular and functionally significant, are not the result of directed coping behavior by the person. The latter view of unconscious motivation differs significantly from the former by its denial of the possibility of "unconscious" striving of an adaptive nature, such as found in "conscious" motivation, and thus by its implication that whenever behavior involves adaptive and purposive *coping*, it is necessarily conscious.

Suggestions for Further Reading

FORD, C. S., and BEACH, F. A. 1951. *Patterns of sexual behavior*. New York: Hoeber.

A comparative study of sexual motives and practices in different animals and in different human societies.

KLINEBERG, O. 1954. *Social psychology* (2nd ed.). New York: Holt.

Contains a clearly written discussion of the problem of instinctive and social origin of motives.

McDOUGALL, W. 1923. *An introduction to social psychology* (15th ed.). Boston: Luce.

The classical book representing the theory of the instinctive basis of human motivation.

MASLOW, A. H. 1954. *Motivation and personality*. New York: Harper.

A persuasive argument for greater emphasis upon positive human motives, presenting a formulation of a developmental theory of motives.

TINBERGEN, N. 1951. *The study of instincts*. London: Oxford Univ. Press.

A fascinating account of research on animal instincts.

CHAPTER XI

Fulfillment and Frustration of Motives

A MAN's many motives exist in him as "latent" or potential determiners of behavior capable of being aroused in appropriate situations. At any one moment only a very few of all these "latent" motives are in an aroused state. When aroused, they are experienced by him in the form of needs, desires, and goals, and thus they direct his immediate behavior.

In this chapter we shall consider how motives get aroused, how they are then fulfilled, how they may be frustrated, and what constructive and disruptive effects follow both fulfillment and frustration.

The Arousal of Motive States

In the light of the discussion in the previous chapters, it will be no surprise to learn that the instigators of aroused motive states are complex. Some have to do with internal conditions of the body, others with conditions of the external environment, and still others with the flow of thoughts in the person's mind.

Instigators from the Internal Environment. At least as early as the time of the Greek philosopher Hippocrates, it was recognized that when an organism is disturbed from its "normal" state, it tends to return to it, provided the disturbance is not too great. In 1900 Charles Richet, a French physiologist, stated this point as follows:

"The living being is stable. It must be so in order not to be destroyed, dissolved or disintegrated by the colossal forces, often adverse, which surround it. By an apparent contradiction it maintains its stability only if it is excitable and capable of modifying itself according to external stimuli and adjusting its response to the stimulation. In a sense, it is a necessary condition for the true stability of the organism."

The stimuli that must be adjusted to

come not only from the external environment, but also from the "internal environment," that is, the physiological states of the body.

HOMEOSTASIS. In 1932 Walter Cannon wrote an influential book on *The Wisdom of the Body,* describing the remarkable manner in which the physiological system functions as a whole in order to maintain equilibrium of conditions necessary to keep the organism alive. This self-regulating process he called "homeostasis."

He described the "automatic" physiological mechanisms by which the volume of blood and the concentrations of sugar, salt, oxygen, and carbon dioxide in the blood are kept constant; by which the temperature of the body is maintained within narrow permissible limits; by which foreign particles and invading organisms are removed from the blood stream. These mechanisms are "automatic" in the sense that they occur without the awareness and voluntary action of the person.

Obviously, the physiological system cannot alone do some things required for maintaining body balances. Food and oxygen and water must be continually brought in from the outside; waste products must be delivered to the outside. It is true that the body functions automatically to a remarkable degree even in these respects. If food and water are not introduced, the body makes temporary use of reservoirs of fat and of water in body tissues. Amazingly wide variations in temperature of the external environment can be tolerated, at least temporarily, through the automatic body adjustments of sweating, shivering, panting.

But sooner or later the automatic homeostatic mechanisms can no longer alone maintain the necessary "steady states" in the body. It is at this critical juncture that the organism must be aroused to take "voluntary" action to correct the body deficits

and disturbances, or else it will perish (unless some good Samaritan, such as the infant's mother, steps in and does something to correct it for him).

BODY NEEDS. The various body needs, such as for food, water, oxygen, elimination, rest, and warmth, are thus instigated when the deficits or disturbances reach dangerous levels. It has been phrased this way: "Needs are deficits become conscious."

There is a tremendous variety of body needs, for there are many specific ways in which essential homeostasis can be disrupted. In each case, with sufficient imbalance, there may be an incitement of motivated action by the whole organism to correct the condition. Some imbalances will lead to the emergence of unusual and "unnatural" or "artificial" needs. For example, calcium deficiency may lead to a bizarre "calcium hunger" in rare cases. The drug addict alters his physiological functioning so that the body comes to require a certain amount of the drug. Withholding the drug may result in the most acute and distressing states of need. Box 63 describes the creation of such an "artifical" or induced motive.

Not every form of severe physiological imbalance leads to the arousal of a specific need. The person may simply feel vaguely sick or "queer," or he may feel nothing out of the way, even though vital functions are being fatally impaired, as in certain kinds of cancer.

Obviously, the functions most likely to require periodic voluntary action, such as supplying food or adjusting temperature, are those that through biological development have come to be connected with readily aroused and explicit needs.

A discussion of the specific physiological *mechanisms* through which these body states arouse the appropriate motive will be reserved for the next chapter.

DEPRIVATION SCHEDULES. The onset of these bodily needs is, of course, closely

BOX 63

Morphine Addiction in Chimpanzees

At the Yale Laboratories of Primate Biology, Spragg experimentally induced morphine addiction in four young chimpanzees. Injections, with a hypodermic syringe, were made in an injection room near the living cages, twice daily at 9 A.M. and 5 P.M. The period during which the injections were regularly given varied among the chimpanzees from six weeks to thirteen months.

From three to seven weeks after injections began, there appeared the first signs of *physiological* dependence on the drug. As the hour for injections approached, the animals would show a pattern of symptoms commonly found when the drug is withheld from human addicts: yawning, restlessness, excess salivation, lethargy, crying, and irritability.

After a further period there began to appear clear evidence of *need* for the drug. Genuine addiction began to manifest itself. Behavioral evidence for the existence of the need was convincing. For example, as the regular hour for injection approached, the animal would show signs of excitement and eagerness, would struggle to get out of its cage, would lead the experimenter down the corridor and into the injection room, would sometimes voluntarily get on the table and assume the usual posture for receiving the hypodermic needle. Moreover, if the animal were led away from the injection room by the experimenter without getting the drug,

it showed obvious signs of distress and frustration. All of these signs of desire completely disappeared after the injection was given and did not reappear until the animal had again been without the drug for some time.

As another step, Spragg placed the animals in a situation in which they could freely choose between a black box containing food or a white box containing the hypodermic syringe. When the animals had been recently injected, the choice of the food box predominated, but when the animals had been deprived of *both* food and morphine for approximately 18 hours, the choice of the white box containing the hypodermic syringe predominated. When they were deliberately frustrated in getting at the two kinds of reward boxes, the animals spent more time trying to get at the syringe box. Further experiments showed that the white box served as a more effective reward-object for inducing the animal to solve problems than did the food box.

It is clear that a strong drive was induced in these animals through the upsetting of their normal physiological functioning by repeated injection of the drug. Thus we see that "artificial" needs may take on all the characteristics of primary survival drives.

SPRAGG, S. D. S. 1940. Morphine addiction in chimpanzees. *Comp. Psychol. Monogr.*, 15, No. 7.

related to the circumstances surrounding the intake and output of products from the outer environment. The longer the time since the animal was supplied with water, for instance, the more likely the arousal of the related motive state of thirst. Experimenters have often manipulated the hours or days of *deprivation* of such needed substances as a way of experimentally controlling the degree of motivation—a rat can be spoken of as 8 hours hungry, 24 hours hungry, etc. However, it should at once be emphasized that there is *not* a

simple straight-line relationship between hours of deprivation and intensity of motive arousal.

The relationship between deprivation time and intensity of motive must be determined by experiment for each motive separately. Thus, 24 hours food deprivation is not as critical as 24 hours of water deprivation, nor as 24 *seconds* of oxygen deprivation!

CYCLICAL ONSET. It has also been observed that the onset of some motive states is regularly periodic. There are rhythmic cycles in which the arousal of the motive reaches its peak at certain times. These are readily observed in connection with *activity cycles* in some animals. (See Box 64.) It appears that cycles of periodic motive arousal are partly a function of the physiological processes themselves and partly a function of various stimulus "cues" through

which the animal has learned to "expect" the motive state to appear at that time.

Instigators from the External Environment. The stimuli arising from various objects and events in the external environment serve as important instigators of motive states. In some cases the objects or

---

BOX 64

Cycle of Activity and the Female in Heat

The general activity of an organism can be used as an indicator of aroused motive state. One device for measuring such activity is the activity wheel, a revolving drum (see figure). The animal, in this case the rat,

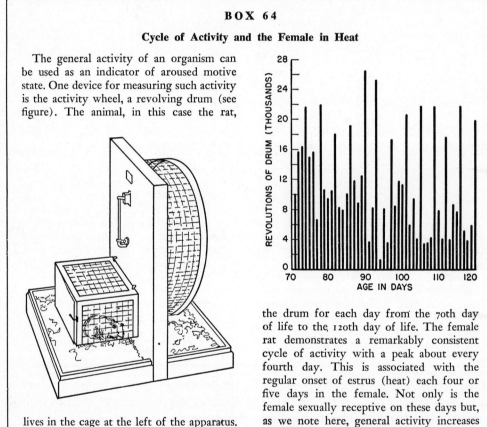

lives in the cage at the left of the apparatus. A door permits the animal to enter and run in the revolving drum. The number of revolutions is recorded by a counter. The living cage is small, so that most of the animal's activity will be in the drum.

Richter at Johns Hopkins University has for many years carried out extensive studies of cycles of activity measured in this manner. The data for one normal female rat in one of his studies are given in the graph. It shows the total number of revolutions of

the drum for each day from the 70th day of life to the 120th day of life. The female rat demonstrates a remarkably consistent cycle of activity with a peak about every fourth day. This is associated with the regular onset of estrus (heat) each four or five days in the female. Not only is the female sexually receptive on these days but, as we note here, general activity increases to many times the level of intervening days.

Further evidence that this periodically aroused motive state is indeed instigated by internal conditions is shown by the fact that removal of both ovaries results in a prompt 60 to 95 per cent drop in activity and a complete disappearance of the regular cycle.

RICHTER, C. P. 1932. Symposium: Contributions of psychology to the understanding of problems of personality and behavior. IV. Biological foundation of personality differences. *Amer. J. Orthopsychiat.*, 2, 345–54.

events are such as to arouse desires and needs that were not aroused the moment before the stimulation occurred. These objects and events may have pronounced effects in directing behavior even when there is complete satiety of inner bodily needs. (Box 65 gives a striking experimental

jerky running movements of the female rat in heat will arouse sexual excitement in the male, even though he may never before have been exposed to this particular stimulus-pattern. It is the particular *pattern of movement*, and not other stimuli from the receptive female, such as odor, which is

---

BOX 65

Social Eating in Hens

The German psychologist, Bayer, carried out experimental studies of the influence of social and physical stimulus factors on the eating behavior of chickens. In one set of studies a hen is allowed to eat from a large heap of grain until she stops. Then a second hungry hen is brought and begins to peck from the heap. The first hen then resumes pecking at once even though she has already eaten to full satisfaction; she may thus eat an additional 60 per cent or more under the social influence of the second hen. The amount of such facilitation of the hunger motive is further increased if *three* hungry hens are introduced after the hen has stopped eating. Conversely, it should be noted that if the experiment is reversed so that three hungry hens together eat from the heap of grain to full satisfaction and a fourth hungry hen is then brought into the group and starts pecking, this is not a sufficient stimulus to induce the three hens to

eat further.

Other experiments of Bayer demonstrate that the persistence of eating depends upon the physical stimulus characteristics of the pile of grain. In one experiment, for example, the hen is placed before a heap of 100 grains of wheat of which she eats 50, leaving the rest untouched. If the same hen in the same degree of hunger is confronted with a larger original heap, she will eat a larger absolute amount of the wheat.

In a further experiment a hen ate to full satisfaction from a heap of grain. Then the remaining food was removed with a brush and immediately replaced. When this was done, the hen invariably resumed eating. With some hens this procedure could be repeated eight times or more and the net result was to increase the total amount eaten in the session by as much as 67 per cent.

BAYER, E. 1929. *Beiträge zur Zweikomponoten-theorie des Hungers. Z. Psychol., 112,* 1–54.

---

demonstration.) In other cases they may serve to heighten or prolong a motive state already aroused.

Both innate and learning factors are involved in the power of external instigators to arouse motive states. In lower animals it is certain that there are stimulus-patterns that will arouse motives without the benefit of past experience with the stimuli. We have already seen (Box 55) that chimpanzees are set into a state of acute fear by the sight of a headless animal, even though they have never seen one before. And, for another example, the peculiar

the crucial instigator: a small bundle of rags pulled along the floor in imitation of the spasmodic jerky running of the female in heat will serve to arouse the sexual excitement and pursuit in the deluded male.

It is equally clear that past experience with stimulus-patterns plays a tremendous role in the development of their motive-arousing potential. The human being has learned a vast repertory of "cues," "symbols," or "signals" that arouse the motive state, which before learning would not have had the power to do so.

In Chapter 8 we saw how various deficits

and disruptions in the external environment may evoke the feeling of needs and hence directed action to correct or remove them. Where do these environmental deficits and disruptions come from? Clearly they come about because something in the physical environment gets out of kilter.

"HOMEOSTASIS" OF THE PHYSICAL ENVIRONMENT. We may think of a rough analogy in the external environment, to Cannon's homeostasis of the internal environment. The organism's environment is a highly complex physical system, exhibiting all sorts of regularities in which there is considerable "self-regulation" of events. For instance, growing plants absorb the toxic carbon dioxide in the atmosphere emitted by animals; the plants convert the carbon dioxide to oxygen, thus maintaining its required supply in the air, and by their very growth providing food and shelter for the animals. The individual has come to adjust to this external system in such a way that his existence in it is with the least expenditure of energy, with the least amount of attentive involvement. Partly this adjustment is through *learning to anticipate* regularities of physical phenomena (for instance, preparing for the winter), through developing firm conceptions of cause and effect, etc. Partly, also, the organism (especially man) *selects* and *constructs* a "self-regulative" environment.

"HOMEOSTASIS" OF THE SOCIAL ENVIRONMENT. Such construction is especially evident in the *society* that man develops as a way of living with his fellow men. Society is a system consisting of a complex pattern of interactions among people. Each member plays his established *roles* in interacting with others, and performs specialized jobs. Society's very reason for being is that it does have "self-regulating" properties; when something goes wrong at one point in the total system, other parts of the system adjust through built-in ways in such

a manner as to restore an equilibrium to the whole. For example, most nations and other social organizations have an established governmental system. If the official leader dies, his replacement is immediate; in this way a leaderless period of transition and a disruptive struggle for power is avoided. We can therefore speak by loose analogy of a kind of "homeostasis" of the social system.

In this "homeostatic social environment" most of the essentials for individual survival are also taken care of automatically. We take these so for granted that they even tend to become depersonalized; we come, as it were, to think of garbage collection, products in stores, electric power, telephones, and newspapers, as somehow "automatically" there, and only when they fail us do we become acutely aware of their dependence on the integrity of the social system. When a breakdown occurs, latent motives are aroused in the individual. If the supply of electric power is suddenly lacking, owing to a strike of maintenance workers in the power plant, the individual is suddenly confronted with an unusual deficit in his normal surroundings and aroused into motivated activity directed toward getting light and heat and toward solving "labor problems." The lacks of light, power, and smooth labor relations have now become "deficiencies made conscious," and motives are aroused.

As we move on to somewhat less "physical" aspects of our social environments, the point becomes even more interesting. A social system provides its members with all sorts of basic "social necessities"—positions, statuses, roles, and identities. When the system breaks down in some degree or at some point, however, the individual may suddenly be confronted with deficits and disruptions that arouse his "social motives." He now has to *cope*, no longer being able merely to *perform* the routinized acts of status, of roles, and of identities along the well-marked tracks of social custom. The man who has firm status has no aroused need for status. But when the status is disrupted or threatened, he may "need" it intensely.

The liberating value of homeostatic systems in body, environment, and society is expressed by Cannon (1939):

"Bodily homeostasis, as we have learned, results in liberating those functions of the nervous system that adapt the organism to new situations, from the necessity of paying routine attention to the management of the details of bare existence. Without homeostatic devices we should be in constant danger of disaster, unless we were always on the alert to correct voluntarily what normally is corrected automatically. With homeostatic devices, however, that keep essential bodily processes steady, we as individuals are free from such slavery—free to enter into agreeable relations with our fellows, free to enjoy beautiful things, to explore and understand the wonders of the world about us, to develop new ideas and interests, and to work and play, untrammeled by anxieties concerning our bodily affairs. . . . [Otherwise] it would be like limiting social activities because of domestic duties, or excluding foreign relations because of troubles in the interior. . . . The main service of social homeostasis would be to support bodily homeostasis. It would therefore help release the highest activities of the nervous system for adventure and achievement. With essential needs assured, the priceless unessentials could be freely sought." (From Walter B. Cannon, *The Wisdom of the Body*, rev. ed. New York: Norton, 1939. Copyright 1939 by W. W. Norton & Co., Inc.)

Ideational Instigators of Motive States. Even when the individual sits quiescent, unaffected by inner and outer stimuli, he is still subject to arousal of motive states. This is because he has a constant flow of ideas, thoughts, and images that are somehow produced and directed by "autonomous" processes of the nervous system and are not dependent upon the input of particular stimulus-patterns. Observed from without, the quiescent man may suddenly, and without apparent "cause," go into action. This "spontaneous" activity is, of course, "caused"; its determinants exist in the brain as a function of the incessant activity that occurs within it (see Chapter 18). We are all fully accustomed to the phenomenon in ourselves. As we sit "wrapped in thought," ideas occur to us that may at once serve to instigate an aroused motive state.

Often these motive states are followed by a directed sequence of thought, ending in the disappearance of that state, the whole episode transpiring without overt action. The person is behaving entirely on a level of irreality, or fantasy, or "inner thought." Nocturnal dreams are of this stuff. The ideationally instigated motive state may also, of course, lead to overt action: the person thinks of succulent food, his hunger is intensified, and he is not satisfied until real food is found and eaten.

Interaction of Instigators. So far we have talked separately about internal, external, and ideational instigators of aroused motives. There is actually, of course, an enormous amount of *interaction* among these various types of instigators.

The motive-arousing effect of an external stimulus may be greatly magnified by the concurrent effect of an internal stimulus, and vice versa, even though neither alone may be powerful enough to activate the motive. (See Box 66 for a striking illustration of the interaction of external and internal factors.)

Similarly, the ideational processes are

BOX 66

Maternal Behavior in the Rat

Among the many interrelated maternal behaviors of the mother rat, such as nursing, cleaning, and defending her young, is the interesting phenomenon of *retrieving*. If the baby rats (called "pups") are placed a few feet outside the nest, the mother rat will rush forth and drag them back to the nest.

Wiesner and Sheard at the University of Edinburgh have made careful experimental studies of this retrieving behavior. As a measure of strength of retrieving they used the number of pups that the mother would retrieve successively in a five-minute interval. (The retrieving response is apparently not weakened by its consummation. Retrieving will continue almost indefinitely as rapidly as the pups are placed in the test situation. For instance, in one case a mother rat retrieved 58 pups in seven minutes.)

The investigators studied the change in the retrieving score under different experimental conditions. For instance, they found that retrieving was very high during the days immediately following birth of the young, but as the days went by, the retrieving score steadily decreased. Careful analysis demonstrated that the relevant factor accounting for this gradual decline in retrieving response did not have to do simply with the length of time since the mother had given birth. Rather, the critical factor was the gradual change in the *appearance* of the pups as they grew older. Thus, after retrieving had declined—because the "matured" pups no longer were adequate retrieving stimuli for the mother—new-born pups of other mothers were placed in the test situation; the maternal rat vigorously retrieved them, even though they were not her own. If these pups were then allowed to grow up, the retrieving again diminished. By periodically providing the mother with new-born young, the experimenters were able to maintain the retrieving response at a high

level for an indefinite period (429 days in one of the rats). We see, therefore, that a continuous stimulus can maintain the aroused motive state even after the conditions that first aroused it have long disappeared.

It was also discovered that if the decline in retrieving has gone too far, the introduction of new-born young will not be an adequate stimulus to restore the original high level of retrieving response.

Wiesner and Sheard then tested the effects of injecting various gonadotropic hormones (see Chapter 12) under various conditions. The following significant facts should be mentioned:

(1) The hormones greatly increase the mother rat's sensitivity to the arousal of retrieving.

(2) Virgin females, which normally do not retrieve, retrieve actively when injected.

(3) Even *male* rats will retrieve young when injected with the maternal hormones, though they never exhibit this behavior under other circumstances.

(4) The range in types of objects that the maternal rats will retrieve is greatly widened with injection. For instance, guinea pigs and mice will be actively retrieved. So will rabbits considerably larger than the mother rat herself. And indeed a small bundle of rags moved in a jerky fashion will be readily retrieved.

We see in these results a remarkable demonstration of the interaction between internal and external instigators of motive states. It is also of interest to see that what we may take to be simply an "instinct" can be experimentally analyzed in terms of its systematic determinants.

WIESNER, B. P., and SHEARD, N. M. 1933. *Maternal behavior in the rat.* London: Oliver and Boyd.

more likely to come up with a particular motive-evoking "thought" when there is appropriate minimal stimulation from the external or internal environment, or both.

Conversely, the presence of such a "thought" is likely to reinforce the effect of an external or an internal stimulus. The fleeting "thought" of food might not alone be sufficient to arouse an active hunger motive, but taken together with the barely felt stomach pang and the dimly heard clatter of dishes it may do so.

By Way of Summary. Aroused motive states may be instigated in various ways. One source of instigation is the internal environment of the body. A breakdown of the homeostatic regulators of body processes may result in the person's taking goal-directed action aimed at restoring the internal equilibrium. Another source of motive instigation is objects and conditions in the external environment. Certain objects may have incentive character for the person, either learned or innate. The physical and social environments may, somewhat analogously to the body environment, suffer breakdowns in the normal "homeostatic" regulation of events, thus leading to the requirement of motivated action by the person. There may also be instigation arising from the flow of ideas in the person's mental life. All these types of instigators *interact* in a complex fashion, depending upon the entire momentary situation, and this is one reason why the analysis of motivation has proved such a baffling problem for scientific study.

Stimulus factors normally capable of activating a given motive state may fail to do so, owing to the fact that the organism is already in another highly aroused motive state. Some motive states appear to take precedence over others. That is, if they are activated, the other motives cannot readily appear. The insistently hungry man may be relatively unsusceptible to the arousal of love or achievement motives.

The Measurement of Motives

In order to study motivational processes scientifically, we must be able to *measure*

motives. We would like to be able to state in objective, quantitative terms the strength of an aroused motive at any particular moment. By strength, we mean its power to affect and direct the person's behavior.

Only by having such measurements, however crude, can we make meaningful statements about the relations of motives to specific aspects of behavior, e.g., how degree of motivation affects learning performance. Measurement is required also in order to *compare* the effects of different motives. Which motive is the most effective in producing learning? Of two conflicting motives, which will determine the action? Measurement of motives is often indispensable to an understanding of the individual's behavior.

Problems in Motive Measurement. The measurement of motives has proved to be one of the most baffling tasks facing the psychologist. This is true for the physiological psychologist in the animal laboratory, the experimental psychologist studying human learning, the industrial psychologist concerned with work morale, and the clinical psychologist seeking to appraise the forces underlying neurosis.

The difficulties stem from the essential complexity of the human organism. In measuring motives, we must consider the following points:

1. The measurement must be *indirect*. There is yet no direct way to measure a motive in the way that we measure the length of a table, by laying a ruler along it. Instead, the strength of the motive must be *inferred* through measuring the observable behavior elicited by the motive.

2. Owing to the fact that there may be all sorts of external and internal suppressions and inhibitions to the direct outward expression of a motive, measurement of a motive may be possible only through the use of concealed and subtle indicators re-

vealed in the unconscious behavior of the person. The measurement of such indicators raises specially formidable problems. Indeed, a special method of psychological measurement—the so-called projective techniques—have been developed to deal with these problems.

3. The inference of motive strength from behavior leads to another difficulty since there are numerous *different* behavioral manifestations of an aroused motive. An aroused hunger motive may manifest itself in persistent efforts directed at the goal (How hard will the person work to get food?), in consummatory behavior with respect to the goal-object (How much food will he eat?), in perceptual behavior (How are his perceptions of food-related objects changed?), in expressive actions (How restless is he as mealtime approaches?). There are numerous alternative behavioral measures of the same aroused motive, and since these different measures will not exactly agree, which is the best measure?

4. Aroused motives never occur singly, but always in concert with others. Since the observable effects of the several motives may look much alike, it may be difficult to know *which* motive is being measured. Does the person's quest of a high grade on the examination express an achievement motive or an avoidance of punishment for failure?

Moreover, the concurrent motives may co-operate or compete with the given motive, and this means that the measured strength of the motive is always *relative* to the strengths of the other motives.

5. Finally, the very act of measurement tends to change the motive state while it is being measured. This is a common measurement problem among other sciences, but it is specially acute in psychology in which the organism is so sensitive to changes in its situation. For example, in trying to measure the strength of a person's hunger motive by seeing how much effort he puts forth to reach food, it is necessary to put obstacles in his path. But this affects the motive; the very existence of the obstacles may cause him to perceive the food as more attractive, and this alters the strength of the hunger.

Methods of Measurement. Many concrete methods of measurement have been developed to deal with the problem—with more or less success. Some of these were adapted directly to the purpose of measuring animal drives, others human motives. We will consider measures having to do both with the overt behavior of the person and with the person's reported experience of motive states.

Among the behavioral measures there are those that have to do with consummatory behavior, with habitual behavior, with coping behavior, and with expressive behavior.

Measures of Consummatory Behavior. It is obvious that the way the individual behaves with the goal-object once he has attained it—that is, his consummatory behavior—should tell us something about the strength of the motive that impelled him toward it. The man who eats great amounts, with desperate urgency and carelessness of "manners," is presumably more intensely hunger-driven than the person who listlessly toys with his food. This assumes, of course, that other things are equal, i.e., that the two men are subject to the same kind of social and situational pressures, have the same normal habits of eating, the same standards of etiquette, etc.

But a difficulty with consummatory behavior as a measure is that it often does not really represent the strength of the drive to get to the goal. We noted earlier that once achieved a goal may look quite different to the person, more attractive or less so; or once he has entered the goal-region, the consummatory response may not show "urgency" even though the motive may have been strong (see p. 226).

A more serious *practical* shortcoming of this method is that it requires that the individual actually reach the goal. In a great many of the cases in which psychologists wish to measure motives, the individual cannot actually get to the goal, or not at least at the time the measurement must be taken.

Measures of Habitual Behavior. For many motives the organism has learned well-organized goal-directed responses; once the motive is instigated, the organism directly expresses these responses. The several measurable characteristics of such habitual goal-directed behavior provide valuable indicators of motive strength.

Speed and vigor of response. Anyone watching a boy dawdling on his way to school feels some confidence that he can estimate the weakness of the school-directed motivation. The same principle has been used in measuring the motivation of rats by recording the speed of their running down alleyways to food or other goal-objects. On the assumption that the rats "know" the food is at the end and that they have developed equally organized habits of running down the alleyway when properly instigated, differences in speed are taken as indicators of differences in motivation.

The vigor or force of the response may also indicate strength of motive. The uninterested worker tugs ineffectually to move the heavy rock; another man shows "superhuman" strength in lifting the overturned car from the crushed victim beneath. Again with rats in alleyways directed toward a goal, a useful measurement of force and vigor can be obtained

by attaching a harness to the rat and recording the power of its pull against a steel spring. An experimental use of this method has been described in Box 52, page 224.

Although speed and vigor of response can be useful measurement methods for animals under some circumstances, they are not generally useful for measuring human motivation, inasmuch as most human motives do not express themselves in simple and direct muscular straining toward the goal-object.

Obstruction method. Many of these methods are combined in the *obstruction method*, one of the classical procedures for measuring animal drives. What is done is to place a negative or painful barrier on the path to the goal, and to record the frequency with which the animal will overcome this obstacle to get to the goal; he is given a tiny bit of the reward each time he reaches the goal and then returned to the starting place. Box 67 describes this obstruction technique and gives some data obtained with it.

Accuracy of performance. The zeal with which a well-practiced habitual response is motivated should be revealed partly in the care and accuracy of the performance. It has been shown, for instance, that rats that have learned a maze will make more errors in running it when they are less highly motivated (see Fig. 79). But with very *high* motive levels, the performance may be disrupted, and the number of errors will again increase.

Measures of Coping Behavior. When the individual is still learning how to get to the goal, that is, when he is engaged in *coping* rather than the performance of habitual goal-directed behavior, it might seem likely that a measure of his motivation would be given by the speed and efficiency of his learning. Unfortunately, this assumption is far too simple. As we shall see in

BOX 67

Ordeal by Electric Shock

Warden at Columbia University, following earlier work by Moss, developed the Obstruction Box technique for measuring the strength of animal drives. The floor plan of the apparatus (see fig.) shows the starting chamber where the rat is placed, the passage, which has an electrified grid on the floor, and the compartment, which contains the goal object.

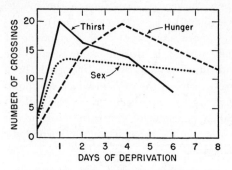

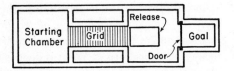

For measuring the strength of a particular drive, for instance, sex, an incentive object—in this case a female rat in heat—is placed in the goal compartment. The male rat is placed in the entrance compartment and permitted to run across the electric grid. As it steps on the release plate, the door to the female in the goal box opens. The moment the male comes in contact with the female, he is picked up and returned to the entrance compartment. This testing procedure is continued for a period of 20 minutes. The strength of the motive is measured by the number of crossings in the standard 20-minute period.

Warden and other investigators have used this standardized technique to compare the strength of various motives of the rat. For example, it has been found that the number of crossings in a 20-minute period increases as a function of number of hours of deprivation of food, or of water, or of a female in heat (for the male). The maximum number of crossings occurs after fewer days of deprivation for thirst than for hunger. With very prolonged deprivation the number of crossings decreases, presumably owing to the weakened bodily state of the animal. There is little drop, however, in the case of the sex drive. (See graph.)

Taking maximal values for each, it appears that thirst is slightly stronger than hunger and that the sexual drive is some-

what less strong than thirst and hunger. But it is perhaps most striking that maternal drive, as measured by the number of crossings of the electric grid made by the mother rat to get to her litter in the goal box, is stronger than all the others.

The exploratory drive of rats was also measured by counting the frequency of crossings of the electric grid to get to an unfamiliar maze, attached to the goal box, containing sawdust and other objects calculated to elicit exploratory activity.

Taking maximal values from several different studies, the comparative strengths of the several drives are indicated by the following number of crossings:

Maternal	22.5
Thirst	20.5
Hunger	18.0
Sex	13.5
Exploratory	6.0

It should be noted that this method of measuring drives places the animal in a conflict situation. Thus it is highly likely that the above figures are not fully reliable as indicators of relative strength of animal drives. It may well be that the electric shock itself has a different frustrating effect on the different motives. Moreover, it has been pointed out that if one uses other intervals of time to count crossings, such as 5 minutes or 10 minutes rather than the standard 20 minutes, the relative ordering of the drives may somewhat change.

WARDEN, C. J. 1931. *Animal motivation studies: The albino rat.* New York: Columbia Univ. Press.
Moss, F. A. 1924. Study of animal drives. *J. exp. Psychol.,* 7, 165–85.

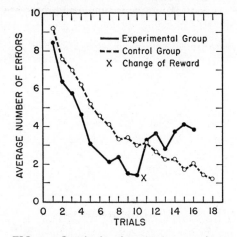

FIG. 79. Graph showing the increase in errors made by rats in running a maze, as a consequence of reduced motivation. One group of rats was taught to run the maze with bran mash as the food reward. Errors rapidly diminished until by the 10th day performance was nearly perfect. On the 11th day the highly desired bran mash was replaced by much less preferred sunflower seeds. On subsequent trials the rats showed a sharp increase in errors, presumably as a consequence of the reduced incentive to run the maze.

The dotted curve shows the errors made by a control group given sunflower seeds as reward from the very beginning. Note that sunflower seeds do serve as an adequate incentive for these rats; thus, for the experimental group, the lower incentive quality of the sunflower seeds can be explained by the contrast with their prior experience in the maze with the more preferred bran mash. (Elliott, 1928.)

the next section of the book (especially pp. 392–4), the relations between motivation and learning are highly complex. Too little motivation may indeed lead to slow learning, but so may too much motivation. Moreover, it may even be that learning can occur without any goal-directed motivation.

By and large, therefore, strength of motives has not been successfully measured through the speed and efficiency of coping behavior.

Measures of Expressive and Perceptual Behavior. Expressive behavior, while not clearly goal-directed, mirrors motivational and emotional states of the organism and for this reason provides another possible route to the measurement of motive strength. A significant advantage here is that expressive behavior, since it is not goal-directed, can often be recorded without affecting the situation of the organism, and this circumvents one of the cardinal difficulties in motive measurement. The relevant expressive behaviors include motor activity, perceptual behavior, and fantasy behavior.

ACTIVITY LEVEL. One indicator of motive state may be the sheer level of activity exhibited. The use of the *activity wheel* to measure drive strength in animals was described in Box 64. It should be noted that we are dealing here with undirected, i.e., random, activity. The behavior itself cannot, therefore, provide an indication of *what* motive is aroused. This can be done by studying specific cycles of activity which occur at different times and under different stimulus conditions.

Normally we do not confine human beings to activity wheels, but in a less mechanical way we do tend to use activity level as an indicator of motive strength. We infer that the very restless person, moving constantly about, has something on his mind, is somehow driven. If we observe the restlessness in a particular situation, such as when the girl is waiting for her date to phone, or when the student is waiting to hear the examination results announced, we may come closer to inferring *what* motive we are measuring.

Over-all activity is a poor measure for many emotions, such as grief and anxiety. A more informative kind of expressive behavior in the human being is found in the complex patterns of bodily posture, facial expression, gesticulations, vocalizations. (But see Box 59, p. 261.)

Especially important is the degree of muscular tension. Often the strong motive is held in check, and the level of muscular tension provides a good index of the motive strength.

PERCEPTUAL BEHAVIOR. The strength of motivation may sometimes be revealed by the perceptual behavior of the person, with or without his awareness of what his perceptions tell about his motives. For example, the threshold for recognizing goal-related objects can be taken as a measure of motive strength, on the assumption that the stronger the motive, the lower the threshold.

However, recalling some of the complex determinants of perceptual performance, the reader will see that perceptual thresholds reflect a good deal more than mere motive arousal, and that therefore this approach to measurement of motive strength has its serious pitfalls.

FANTASY BEHAVIOR. The content of the person's ideational flow, including his dreams and fantasies, reflects aroused motive states, often in ways of which he is quite unaware. By studying the saliency and frequency of themes running through the fantasy behavior, it is possible to arrive at an estimate of the strength of motive states relevant to such themes. A method using standardized materials to evoke the overt fantasies has been applied in the measurement of various human needs (see Box 68).

Measures Based on Self-ratings. Rating scales have proved to be useful instruments of measurement in social psychology, industrial psychology, and personality assessment. (Their applications will be discussed in Chapter 23). The rating scale can also be applied to the problem of measuring motive strength by asking the person to rate the strength of his own motives. For example, he may rate himself on a 5-point scale of hunger, varying from "acutely hungry" to "not the slightest bit hungry."

When the motive is simple and there are no complications in making the report, this rating method may have value. But it is highly susceptible to some of the difficulties already discussed. Especially, there is the fact that the very act of making the self-rating is likely to change the motive state. And because of the various suppressions and inhibitions on the outward report of one's motives, the self-rating may be highly unreliable.

The Fulfillment of Motives

Fortunately for the well-being of most organisms, the great proportion of aroused motive states result in direct and unhindered goal-attainment. The goal is clearly perceived, the path to it is clearly marked, the appropriate actions occur smoothly and effectively. Thus the need is removed, or the desire satisfied, and the motive state disappears. This pattern of tension increase followed by prompt tension-reduction is so commonplace in our continuous flow of experience that we pay little attention to it: that a hungry man bites food is not "news," and it does not seem to make "interesting psychology." However the fulfillment of aroused motives poses problems that merit study.

Goal-attainment and tension-reduction are *not always identical*. The person may discover that the goal was not really appropriate to the needs and desires, and be left with unresolved tension. Conversely, there are numerous alternative ways that the tension may be reduced without goal-attainment.

INDIRECT SATISFACTION OF NEED. The deficit or disruption underlying a need may be corrected independently of the person's goal-striving. Homeostatic processes in the body may succeed in restoring the deficit, and the need will subside without further

BOX 68

Measuring the Achievement Motive

Making use of fantasy behavior, McClelland and his associates have developed ways of measuring various human motives, for example, the *achievement motive*. As stimuli to evoke fantasy behavior, they present pictures of simple situations which are similar to the pictures of Murray's Thematic Apperception Test (see p. 637). For instance, one picture shows a young man standing on a sidewalk with a broom in his hand and looking off into the distance; another shows two men working at a machine; another, a boy seated at a desk with a book in front of him.

After being informed that the test is one of creative imagination, the person is asked to write a brief story about each of the pictures, covering questions such as: What is happening? What has led up to this situation? What is being thought? What will happen?

The stories are scored for the frequency and saliency of ideas pertaining to success, getting ahead in life, accomplishing things, etc. Below are two excerpts from stories written by different subjects about the picture of the young man holding a broom:

"The boy works in the grocery store. He has just graduated from high school and hasn't enough money to go to college. He is standing there thinking about how long it will take him to save enough to get his education. He doesn't want to remain a store clerk all his life, and wants to make something of himself."

"It seems that this young man has been told by his father to clean up the sidewalk. This has prevented him from going off to the beach for the day with his pals. He is watching them go off in their car and is feeling left out and sore at his father."

The first story would earn a high score on achievement motive, the second, a low score.

Applying the test to various samples of young American adults, the investigators found large and consistent individual differences in achievement motive scores. Further experiments demonstrated that the scores so obtained are meaningfully related to the person's achievement behavior in other situations, to the degree to which the achievement motive is actively aroused at the moment, to the life history of the person, etc.

1. For example, it was found that the level of achievement motive characteristic of the person as measured by this test correlates with his behavior on laboratory tasks involving sustained effort. On a task requiring the solution of anagram problems, subjects scoring high on achievement motive continued to accelerate in rate of production of solutions throughout the experimental period, whereas low achievement subjects showed no increase in rate.

2. The level of achievement motive scores elicited at a given moment could be successfully manipulated by the experimenters through the set given to the subjects in taking the test. Thus, in one study two groups of 39 male college students were given the test under the following contrasted conditions:

Relaxed condition. The subjects were led to believe that they were merely aiding in the standardization of some tests of creative imagination; the experimenter behaved in an easy-going manner; he did not ask the subjects to sign their names.

Achievement-oriented condition. The subjects were led to believe that the tests were for the measurement of their intelligence, and that they were being administered in order to enable the military services to discover men of high leadership ability.

The results showed that achievement themes occurred more than twice as frequently in the stories elicited in the latter condition than in the former.

3. Male college students having characteristically high achievement scores were found to have backgrounds of life history and family attitudes somewhat distinguishable from those of students with low achievement scores.

McClelland, D. C., Atkinson, J. W., Clark, R. A., and Lowell, E. L. 1953. *The achievement motive.* New York: Appleton-Century-Crofts.

action. Events in the environment may themselves correct the disruption toward which the person's adjustive action had been directed, and again the underlying need will disappear.

Sometimes such truncated motive episodes may leave the person with a sense of "incompleteness": he had got himself worked up for, and launched on, a course of goal-directed action and then been left "up in the air." This residual tension is most likely to occur when the motive is a complicated one and achievement of the goal really means more than just the removal of a particular need. For example, the boy who goes into heroic action to save his drowning dog may feel "let down" when the dog swims to safety; it is true that the need to save the dog was resolved, but the boy's tensions remained because he had still not gratified the desire to demonstrate his bravery.

REDUCTION BY OTHER MOTIVES. Midway through a goal-directed action there may be a sharp change in the situation which requires a complete shift in the person's directions of activity. The initial motive now gets shunted aside by a more urgent one. Though the tensions related to the first may to some extent persist, they may gradually simply *dissipate* with the passage of time, so that when the person is free to return to the original activity, he no longer has the inclination.

The tension of the initial, interrupted motive may also, of course, get *combined* with that of the new intruding motive, reinforcing its strength. Attainment of the new and different goal can reduce the initial tension by discharge through the other activity. This may occur without the person's awareness of the fate of the original tension.

Enduring Effects of Fulfillment. The principal *immediate* effect of fulfillment of the aroused motive is reduction of tension, and this liberates the organism's attention and energies for other activities. It is also of some interest to consider what the more *enduring* effects of fulfillment may be.

HABITUAL BEHAVIOR. One effect of fulfillment is to strengthen the structure of the motive. That is, repeated successful goal-attainment makes the whole action-pattern more and more *habitual*. The person has to pay less and less attention to the whole sequence of events, and eventually it runs off smoothly with minimal or no awareness. The effect of this is that the person is made more ready for other kinds of problem-solving; but also he is rendered less flexible in this particular behavior pattern.

POTENCY OF MOTIVES. But what about the effect of repeated fulfillment on the *readiness* for the motive to be aroused? There are two quite opposite directions of possible effect. One is for repeated fulfillment to *increase* the readiness, the other is for it to *decrease* the readiness.

If the person is experiencing only minimal satisfactions of most of his motives, the constant gratification of one particular motive may result in a *fixation* on it. That is, he becomes more and more susceptible to its arousal. A man whose needs for love, genuine respect from others, and high self-regard are not fulfilled, but whose need for power over others can be readily gratified, will tend to seek constant power gratification. This motive may become the most potent of his motives, existing in an almost permanent state of arousal.

On the other hand, if he is attaining gratification of most of his motives, living a life of motivational abundance rather than scarcity, the regular fulfillment of any one motive is likely to be less important to him. As we shall see later in our discussion of the development of the individual's motives (see pp. 626–8), such gradual decline in prepotency of any single motive makes possible the emergence of new and "higher-order" motives, for example, the search for knowledge.

Frustration of Motives

It is the cases in which there is *frustration* of goal-attainment that stand out in our experience; it is the man striving but failing to bite the food that makes "news." Frustration refers to the blocking or thwarting of goal-attainment. Frustration is a *state of the organism*, not an external condition. The mere existence of barriers will not necessarily mean frustration. If our goal-directed action somehow takes account of the external interference without impairment of our goal-attainment, there is no frustration. Conversely, frustration may occur without external interference. The person may merely *imagine* a barrier that will serve to disrupt his goal-attainment and cause genuine frustration.

Sources of Frustration. The blocking or thwarting of goal-attainment can occur for many different reasons. Some have to do with *lacks* and *losses* in the environment, physical or social. The thirsty man on the desert is frustrated by the sheer lack of water to drink; the desire of a young person in a remote part of the world to get a college education may be frustrated by the lack of schools. The man may be frustrated by the loss of his job, or by the loss of prestige in the eyes of his fellows.

It should be emphasized again that frustration refers to the aroused motive states. The mere fact that there are objective lacks in one's environment will not produce frustration, unless the person is motivated to get the things that are lacking. It often happens that the frustration appears only when the person first learns of the possibility of having or doing certain things and then perceives the objective environmental lacks as preventing his action. The increase in attractive potential regions of his life-space is not accompanied by a comparable increase in space of free movement (see p. 211). The desert dweller may not be frustrated by lack of books or indoor plumbing until someone tells him about them and arouses a need or desire in him.

Very frequently, of course, the things lacked are not the goals in themselves, but things that are necessary for the satisfaction of other motives. The lack of money may mean a frustration of countless motives.

OBSTACLES. Another source of frustration is *obstacles* in the environment, that is, things that serve as barriers to goal-attainment. Jail bars are frustrating to the man who wants freedom; the restrictive rules of a social club are frustrating to the man who wants membership. There are significant differences in the frustrating effects of lacks and losses on the one hand, and obstacles on the other. As we shall see presently, barriers can become the focus of particular attention, emotional centering, and attack; where there is merely the *absence* of something needed, such focusing and attack is not possible, and the frustrating effects must take other directions.

Here again, obstacles are not frustrating except insofar as they serve to block aroused motives. It is a particularly striking fact about society that it may both induce and thwart motives in its members. The Negro in America may be aided by democratic society in developing goals of self-improvement, education, creative accomplishment, and the like, but at the same time the society (or some segments of it) may, through the restrictions and segregations related to skin color, place obstacles in the way of these attainments.

It is significant that segregation practices

were *less stringent* under slavery than in many localities today. The segregation and restrictive practices are obstacles deliberately imposed by some white people *because* of the new aspirations of the Negro. The strength of the obstacle is kept adjusted to the strength of the goal-striving. The equivalent in a physical setting would be a barrier that got more resistant the more strongly the person tried to surmount it. It is easy for us to imagine how intensely frustrating such a physical obstacle would be, and we are not surprised at the intensity of frustration and strong negative emotion aroused by such social obstacles.

Conflict. Since most of the time the person experiences two or more simultaneous motives each requiring different action, *conflict* is almost always present in some degree. If the actions called for by the several motives are the same or highly compatible, there will be little or no conflict. But most of the time the direction of activity of one motive is contradictory to that of other motives. The essence of conflict is simply that the person cannot go in two different directions at once.

The conflict may be among alternative *needs and desires,* among alternative *goal-objects,* or among alternative *means* to the goal.

PATTERNS OF CONFLICT. Conflict situations, as analyzed by Lewin (1935), fall into one of three basic patterns: approach-approach, avoidance-avoidance, and approach-avoidance.

The *approach-approach* conflict is that between two positive goal-objects. This is likely to be the least painful of conflict situations, for the person can choose between two desirable things. However it is also true that choosing one necessitates losing the other, and this can be a source of quite intense conflict. The man trying to decide which of two girls to propose

to, or which of two jobs to take, can get himself into a state of prolonged and tortured indecision. The more nearly equal the two goals, the greater the conflict will be, and the person may remain poised indecisively halfway between the two. But it is an *unstable* equilibrium. As we have already seen (p. 224), there is a goal-gradient phenomenon in which the attractiveness of a goal-object *increases* as it is approached. Thus, as soon as he makes a tentative move toward one goal-object, its compelling force increases slightly while the other goal-object loses attractiveness slightly. The result is that the pulls on the person are now unbalanced, and he will move ever more energetically to the nearer goal (see Fig. 80).

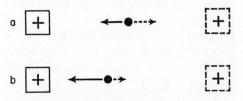

FIG. 80. The approach-approach conflict situation. An unstable equilibrium (*a*), in which a step toward either goal is sufficient (*b*) to resolve the conflict by further enhancing the attractiveness of that goal in preference to the other.

The *avoidance-avoidance* conflict is that between two negative things which the person seeks simultaneously to avoid. Obviously if there is nothing more in the situation than the two negatives, there is little in the way of conflict; the person will simply leave the whole situation. But the real minus-minus conflict is the case in which there are only the two alternatives, and he *must* choose one or the other. It is a case of the lesser of the two evils, the devil or the deep blue sea. For example, the man is required by his employer to choose between the unwelcome alternatives of being transferred to a branch office in a city he dislikes or resigning from the firm.

In this situation the equilibrium tends to be a *stable* one, that is, the person stays as long as possible balanced between the two negatives. The reason is that there is also a *negative* goal-gradient. The repulsion by a negative object grows less the greater its distance from the person. Thus, as he takes a step away from one of the two, its repellent force is less; yet this brings him a step nearer the other object whose negative force is then greater, and he is pushed back again (see Fig. 81).

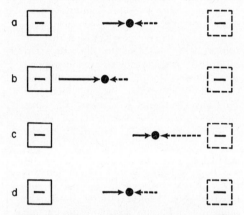

FIG. 81. The avoidance-avoidance conflict situation. A stable equilibrium (*a*) in which a step away from one object (*b*) is immediately redressed by the increased negativity of the object toward which the step is taken (*c*), thus serving to bring the person back to the original point of equilibrium (*d*).

If there is no requirement that the person move, he will stay forever suspended between the two negatives, wavering one way and the other but never moving very far toward either. But usually there is another force in the situation, such as the passage of time, which *requires* him eventually to decide between the two. For instance, the employer may insist that the man decide on his job move by a certain date.

The *approach-avoidance* conflict is likely to be the most agitating of all. Here the person is both attracted and repelled in the *same* direction. This may come about be-

cause the goal-object itself has both positive and negative features, as in the case of a job that pays well but involves living in an undesirable city. This is called an *ambivalent* goal-object. Or it may be because the path to the positive goal necessitates going through a negative region; for instance, the rat must run across the electric grid to get the reward (see Box 67), the alcoholic must go through the distress of going "on the wagon" in order to get back his self-respect. There is also the case in which the positive goal comes first, but is inevitably followed by something negative: the stolen jam means a later spanking; the binge means the hang-over; the forbidden pleasure means the subsequent loss of self-respect.

The approach-avoidance conflict also results in a kind of stable equilibrium, in that at a certain distance from the goal the positive and negative forces balance, and a step closer or away tends to make the individual return to the point of equilibrium (see Fig. 82). Experimental attempts have been made to determine the point of equilibrium in such situations (see Box 69).

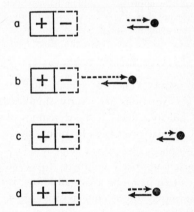

FIG. 82. The approach-avoidance conflict situation. A stable equilibrium (*a*) in which a step toward (or away from) the goal (*b*) produces compensating changes in the relative strengths of the positive and negative forces (*c*), so that the person is returned to the original point of equilibrium (*d*).

BOX 69

Gradients of Approach and Avoidance

Using a method somewhat similar to that described in Box 52, p. 224, Brown measured the strength of a rat's pull toward a food goal, and also the strength of pull away from a point at which it had received an electric shock. By recording the strength of pull at two distances—30 and 170 centimeters from the food (or shock)—it was possible to determine the *gradient* of force of pull for both the approach and the avoidance tendencies.

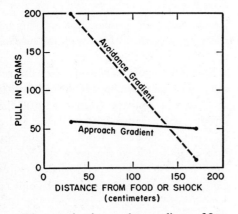

PULL IN GRAMS

Avoidance Gradient

Approach Gradient

DISTANCE FROM FOOD OR SHOCK
(centimeters)

The graph shows the gradients. Note that the approach gradient is very flat, indicating that the attractiveness of the goal is only slightly less at the distant point than at the nearer point. On the other hand, the

avoidance gradient is very steep, so that though there is strenuous pull away from the region of the electric shock when close to it, the amount of pull is almost zero at a distance of 170 centimeters. At the point where the two gradients cross one another (roughly 130 centimeters from the goal), the tendencies to approach and to avoid are presumably about equal.

An earlier finding by Miller confirms this assumption. He first trained rats to run along an alley to a food box and then gave them an electric shock while they were eating there. On the next occasion that the animals were placed in the alley, they ran toward the goal but slowed up and stopped at a point short of the goal. Presumably this was the point where the approach and avoidance tendencies were equal. By varying the intensity of hunger or of shock, it was found that the distance from the goal where the animal would stop could be appropriately manipulated. When the rat was hungrier, the point of equilibrium was closer to the goal; when the rat had suffered a more painful electric shock, the point of equilibrium was more distant.

BROWN, J. S. 1948. Gradients of approach and avoidance responses and their relation to motivation. *J. comp. physiol. Psychol.*, 41, 450–65.

MILLER, N. E. 1944. Experimental studies of conflict. (In Hunt, J. McV., ed. *Personality and the behavior disorders.* New York: Ronald, 431–65.)

DISCUSSION. The foregoing analyses of conflict situations are overly simplified, as they fail to reflect all the dynamics of the motivational processes. In many situations the simple goal-gradient does not hold. In approach-approach conflicts, for example, what often happens, as we all know, is that as we move toward one positive goal, the idea of the incipient loss of the other makes it appear more desirable than before, and we are then swung back to it. This vacillation can go on for some time. Thus, for instance, the man goes on his way to propose to one girl, but as he walks he thinks

of all the to-be-lost charms of the other, and this halts him in his tracks. The real point of all this is that when there is a case of mutual exclusion of positive things, there is more to it than which goal is the more attractive. For if by having one, the other is irretrievably lost, each alternative takes on a certain *negative* character in addition to its positive character, and the equilibrium is not so unstable as before.

Most conflicts are likely to include more than two goals, more than two possible directions of action. The man choosing between the two jobs sees positive and negative features to both, and may indeed see other possibilities that involve taking neither of the two jobs between which he cannot decide. Moreover, situations are not usually so "neat" as all this. It is not necessarily certain that taking this job or this wife will forever preclude the alternative. It is often the more realistic case that there has to be a postponement of one goal in favor of the other, or a putting off of an immediate gratification in favor of a later one. The degree to which this is possible for the person depends greatly upon his time-perspective (see p. 212). For instance, in the shorter time-perspective of the child, a conflict may be more acute than in that of the adult, because in the child's perception of the situation the choice is "forever."

However, this is not by any means to underrate the importance of conflicts in which the situation *is* seen by the person as starkly a case of this choice or that. People frequently find themselves in situations that have no more options than this.

It should also be said that this kind of analysis of conflict situations gives relatively little weight to dynamic aspects of motivational processes. That is, it does not give full range to the kinds of modifications which occur in the motives as a result of the conflict. The very existence of conflict makes the various goals and pathways to them look different, and this in turn modifies the conflict in various directions. We turn now to some of these important dynamic consequences of frustration and conflict.

Frustration and Tension. The degree of tension produced by frustration is a function of (1) the strength of aroused motives and (2) the power and persistence of the blockage. The thwarting of weak motive states produces less tension than the thwarting of strong motive states. Partial frustration, such as a mere slowing

down in the normal rate of progress toward the goal, produces less tension than does a complete frustration. And the longer the frustration persists, the greater the tension that is built up.

When the frustration arises from the conflict of motives, the more equally balanced the opposing motives are, or the greater the strength of the opposing motives, the greater will be the tension.

Prolongation of the frustration results in constantly increasing tension because the needs or desires may be growing stronger with the passage of time. Often there is an urgency imposed by the passage of time itself. This urgency stems from the fact that the delay in satisfying the present aroused motive states may mean a delay in satisfying other motive states that are due to arise. For instance, the man frustrated in his desire for promotions in his job may not only feel deprived of the prestige of the promotion, but may see that his failure to be promoted will also frustrate his desire to get married or to provide for his children's education. Thus the longer he remains frustrated, the greater the tension becomes.

The effects of the increased tension are of many kinds, some constructive, some destructive. Whether they are constructive or destructive depends heavily upon the level of tension.

Constructive Effects of Frustration

Frustration is commonly regarded as "bad" for the person. The destructive effects of frustration tend to occupy the attention of psychologists and laymen alike. There has been less stress on the fact that as frustration or conflict begin to build up tension, the changes occurring in the psychological situation may *facilitate* goal-attainment.

The increased tension has the effect of focusing the organism's attention more firmly on the particular motive state. It becomes more salient and other concurrent motive states may diminish in potency. Irrelevant and distracting features of the whole field may drop out. The attractiveness of the goal may be enhanced by the frustration ("The grass is greener on the other side of the fence").

Intensified Striving. All these effects lead to direct attempts to reach the goal by intensified striving. Within limits, the greater the blockage, the greater the mobilization of effort to overcome it. We are all well acquainted with the manner in which the "challenge" offered by the thwarting of our goal-directed efforts produces a more intense "response." Indeed, it is probably *only* when there is some blocking of goal-attainment that motive strength reaches its fullest height. Without blockage, the activity is more or less "habitual," and only peripherally motivated.

Later, when we consider the more permanent motives of the person and the more chronic frustrations of these motives, we shall see that the intensified striving may take the form of *compensatory* acts involving large parts of the personality. Thus a Teddy Roosevelt, physically puny as a

---

BOX 70

What Is an Effective Substitute?

A number of investigators, primarily stimulated by the theorizing of Kurt Lewin, have studied experimentally the question of what kind of activity will serve as an effective substitute for an activity that has been blocked. The basic experimental technique rests upon the phenomenon of voluntary resumption of an interrupted activity: if the person undertakes a task and is interrupted before he completes it, he will tend voluntarily to resume working at the task when he is later given the opportunity; another task that follows the interrupted task and is completed may, to some extent and under some circumstances, serve as a substitute for the interrupted task. The *substitute value* of a task is measured by the tendency to resume the interrupted task when given an opportunity. High resumption rate means that the intervening task had little substitute value; low resumption rate means that it had much substitute value.

Using this design, Henle was able to show that the manner in which the substitute task is *perceptually organized* with the interrupted task helps to determine its degree of substitute value. In one experiment she varied the extent to which the interrupted and substitute tasks were perceived as connected, by varying their degree of *isolation* from other tasks in the whole series. There were two groups of subjects. For the first group, the five tasks in the series were all of the same type, namely, jigsaw puzzles. The fourth puzzle was interrupted, and the tendency to resume work on the fourth after completion of the fifth was recorded. The resumption proved to be high, that is, the substitute value of the fifth task for the interrupted task was low.

The second group of subjects also had five tasks. The last two were identical with the last two in the other group, but the first three tasks were of a different type, namely, paper-and-pencil mazes. Again the fourth task was interrupted and its later

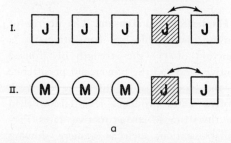

a

youth, may devote a major part of his life activities to building up his physical strength.

Such intensified striving will often result in breaking through the barrier, or overcoming the conflict. But if the barrier is too strong and the compensatory action fails, other types of adjustive action may follow.

Changing the Means to Goals. The person may take a new look at the whole situation and reconsider whether his previous goal-directed action was the most appropriate one for attaining the goal. The enhanced tension may serve to highlight features of the situation which he had not seen, partic-

ularly as he is forced to search more widely for alternate pathways to the goal.

Whether alternative paths will be seen by the person under these circumstances is a complex topic that we will discuss in Chapter 14, on creative problem-solving. Here we need only note that a moderate increase in tension often does result in finding a new path to the goal and overcoming the frustration. But we should also anticipate the later discussion by pointing out that the level of tension must not be too high.

Substitution of Goals. Just as the person may find an alternative path to the goal,

---

BOX 70 (continued)

What Is an Effective Substitute?

resumption recorded. The design for the two groups is schematized in figure *a;* the squares represent jigsaw puzzles (J), the circles represent mazes (M), and the cross-hatched figure means the task was interrupted.

According to principles of perceptual isolation, tasks four and five should be experienced as more closely connected in the second condition than in the first, inasmuch as they tend to stand out against the "background" of the initial three dissimilar tasks. Thus, the substitute value of task five should be greater in the second condition than in the first, and this is just what the results showed: the resumption of the interrupted task was appreciably less in the second condition than in the first.

In another variation, Henle showed that substitute value is greater when the interrupted and substitute tasks are in immediate temporal *proximity* than when separated from one another in time. Three tasks were presented, two completed and one interrupted. For one group of 14 subjects, the interrupted task (a jigsaw puzzle) came first, followed by a dissimilar task (a maze), which was completed, and then by a similar task (another jigsaw puzzle), which was

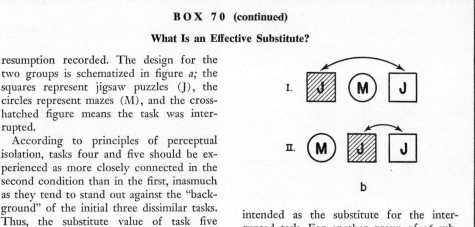

b

intended as the substitute for the interrupted task. For another group of 16 subjects the same tasks were given but the order was changed, so that the interrupted task came second, just before the substitute task. The design is schematized in figure *b*.

In the first group 64 per cent of the subjects resumed the interrupted task whereas in the second group only 25 per cent did so. Thus, the substitute value of a task is clearly greater when it is in close proximity to the task for which it is to serve as substitute.

LEWIN, K. 1935. *A dynamic theory of personality.* New York: McGraw-Hill.
HENLE, MARY. 1942. An experimental investigation of dynamic and structural determinants of substitution. *Contrib. psychol. Theory,* 2, No. 3.

so he may find an alternative goal that will satisfy the need or desire. The effect of the increased tension is to make him search more widely and hence to increase the likelihood that he will perceive an available substitute. Moreover, the increased tension will make the alternatives appear more attractive.

However it is rare that the substitute goal will have the identical properties of the original goal, or be exactly equal in desirability. There will probably be some sacrifice involved in taking the substitute, and some of the initial tension may remain unresolved (see Box 70).

Redefining the Situation. If intensified striving, changing of means, and substitution of goals do not succeed in resolving the frustration or conflict, more fundamental changes in the situation may occur.

One obvious way of removing conflict, its consequent frustration, and increased tension is to make choices among the alternatives. As we have seen, sometimes the choice is an absolute one; in other cases the person decides to attain this goal first, and later that one. In either case the increased tension helps to force a choice—and choice in conflict situations is adaptive behavior. The tension has brought about a redefining of the situation, so that the conflict is eliminated.

The redefining of the situation may be such that things which were separate and opposing are now consolidated and harmonious. For instance, man's separate and conflicting desires to be self-assertive and to retain the love of the group are synthesized into an effort to be elected to the leadership of the group, which will satisfy both initial desires.

In general, such redefining of a situation involving frustration means that new elements are introduced into the situation by the person, or that he broadens the perceived context of the specific situation. This may occur in a sudden "insightful" way, or it may be a more gradual alteration when the frustration is chronic. As we shall see in discussions of personality development (Chapter 23), the redefining may involve changes in self-perception, changes in group identification, changes in attitudes and values.

The Sequence of Constructive Effects. Intensified striving is likely to come first, and the more fundamental changes in the situations, last. It can readily be seen that as we move from the first to the last, there is a shift from the more direct and more circumscribed ways of coping with the frustration, to the less direct and more far-reaching ways.

Although this ordering is by no means absolute or invariable, it does represent a common sequence of constructive attempts under frustration and conflict.

Disruptive Effects of Frustration

If the constructive effects of frustration and conflict fail to bring about goal-attainment, the tension continues to increase. Eventually it will reach levels at which its effects are no longer facilitative, but *disruptive* of the goal-directed activity.

The reasons for this are several. For one thing, the increased mobilization of energy may become so great as to exceed what is appropriate for the task; the person may try *too hard* and thus disrupt the fine coordination of effort. For another thing, the extreme tension may result in *cognitive narrowing;* the person focuses his attention so completely on the blocked pathways or the inaccessible goal that he is "blinded" to the existence of alternative pathways or substitute goals. And, finally, the increased tension is often accompanied by *emotional agitation,* which interferes with the rational processes of deliberation and choice: he gets "rattled," panicky, loses control.

Frustration Tolerance. In short, there is a kind of threshold level beyond which the tension results in qualitatively different kinds of effect on behavior. We may call this threshold the *frustration tolerance.* An individual may experience a considerable degree and persistence of frustration and conflict without exhibiting signs of disorganization or disruption. He may continue to strive toward the goal, look for new paths or substitute goals, and seek to make realistic and rational choices. But with still further increase in tension, he may become overly agitated, emotionally upset, and no longer able to cope in constructive ways with the problem situation. We would say that he has exceeded his frustration tolerance.

Frustration tolerance is clearly not a fixed quantity of tension, but a variable quantity, depending upon the person and the situation. In one situation the individual may be able to withstand a great deal more tension than in another. In part this will depend upon what he has just been experiencing in previous situations, and what he anticipates will happen next. Two different individuals in the same frustrating situation may exhibit quite different frustration tolerances.

Once the tension level approaches and exceeds the critical tolerance, several main kinds of disruptive effects of the frustration make their appearance—aggression, escape, disorganization of behavior.

Frustration and Aggression. The most striking disruptive effect of frustration is the aggressive response it elicits. We have already seen that the emotion of anger is aroused by blockage of goal-attainment.

This is part of the whole pattern of aggression produced by frustration. Aggression can be viewed in its simplest form as a kind of direct attack upon the obstacle or barrier, and in this sense it is really an adaptive behavior. As we have pointed out (see p. 263), the anger may have emergency value. Yet aggression is more often deleterious in that it prevents the person from coping effectively with the barrier. The aggression readily gets too intense and out of control, and the barrier requires a more subtle approach than the frontal attack induced by anger. Moreover, the frustration may not stem from an identifiable barrier at all, but may be a mere lack or loss, or a conflict with another motive. Under these circumstances there is no "logical" object to attack, and the aggression may be diffused over many objects, some quite unconnected with the frustration. This *generalization* of aggression becomes greater the more intense the frustration and the less clear and available the sources of the frustration. The person may strike out wildly, attacking anything in his reach.

DISPLACEMENT OF AGGRESSION. There may be reasons why the person cannot express aggression directly at the source of frustration. The source may itself be dangerous; for instance, the child does not dare attack the father who has frustrated him. Or there may be various social standards concerning the proper objects of aggression. It may be considered wrong to kick one's mother, even though she has been the insistent source of frustration, or to hit one smaller than oneself, or to berate a sick person, or to criticize the president of one's country.

In such cases the aggression may get *displaced* to other objects. That is, the aggression, instead of being directed at the perceived source of frustration, is directed elsewhere, often toward entirely innocent objects or people, as "scapegoats" (see Box 71).

BOX 71

Frustration and Aggression

Miller and Bugelski at Yale University carried out a study of the effects of frustration which occurred in a real-life setting. Boys at a summer camp were required to take part in a long and uninteresting testing session that was deliberately made to run overtime so that the boys were compelled to miss their weekly trip to the local theater, considered by them to be a high point of the week. As the session continued and it began to be clear to the boys that they would be forced to miss the movie, they began to show frustration. By the end of the session the situation had turned into a genuinely frustrating one for them.

All the boys were given brief attitude scales before and after the testing session. Half of them rated their attitudes toward Mexicans before, and toward Japanese after, the session; the other half, toward Japanese before and toward Mexicans after the session.

It was found that after the frustrating testing session the attitudes toward Mexicans and Japanese were much more unfavorable than before the session. Here we see a clear instance of frustration leading to an aggressive reaction, but an aggressive reaction of a quite indirect sort. The boys did not express direct aggression toward the real source of their frustration, namely those administering the long examination. Instead, their aggressions were expressed in hostile attitudes toward remote objects (Mexicans and Japanese), and through the channel of mere verbal expression, not through overt action. This constituted a kind of scapegoating as a function of aggression.

MILLER, N. E., and BUGELSKI, R. 1948. Minor studies of aggression: II. The influence of frustrations imposed by the in-group on attitudes expressed toward out-groups. *J. Psychol., 25,* 437–52.

DISCUSSION. There are several cautions to be borne in mind in interpreting the relations between frustration and aggression. For one thing, *not all* aggression is necessarily derived from frustration. There are numerous reasons why people may seek to attack and injure other people—for gain, for defense, for sadistic pleasure—in which frustration plays no vital role. Of course, many motives of gain, of defense, and of sadism may relate to other kinds of frustration in the person, but they need not. Perhaps a good deal of the answer is given by the characteristics of the aggressive act. If aggression involves anger, it is likely that frustration is its root.

For another thing, frustration does not *have* to lead to aggression. There are many frustrating situations in which there is no evidence of aggression whatsoever, and instead there are tendencies to escape or disorganization of behavior.

Although aggressive outbursts tend to interfere with immediate goal-seeking, there is also an important *catharsis* that often accompanies the aggression. After the sudden and violent release of tension in the angry outburst, the person may be temporarily able to see the situation clearly again, and even perhaps to attain the goal. In this sense, the aggression may be thought to serve as a kind of safety valve; when the tension reaches a critical level, it is dissipated through aggression, rather than permitted to build up a bigger "head of steam," which might result in other more damaging consequences.

Frustration and Escape Reaction. A second major disruptive effect of frustration is the tendency to escape from the frustrating situation. The man caught in the dilemma of deciding which of two attractive girls to marry may finally "leave the

BOX 72

Frustration and Regression in Children

At the University of Iowa Barker, Dembo, and Lewin studied the effects of frustration on the deterioration in constructiveness of children's play. Thirty children between two and five years of age were observed individually while playing with a standardized set of toys. (See fig. *a*.)

b

a

Observers rated the level of constructiveness of each child's play. By constructiveness was meant the extent to which the play showed imagination, elaboration, and well-structured activities. For example, sitting on the floor and connecting and disconnecting a truck and trailer is rated low in constructiveness, whereas carrying out an extensive "trip" in which the truck and trailer take part in a series of events is rated high in constructiveness.

It was found that there was a close relationship between the constructiveness of play and the mental age of the child. Thus it was possible to score constructiveness of play in terms of "mental-age units," that is, in terms of the constructiveness appropriate to children of a given mental age.

The frustration was experimentally created by permitting the children to play briefly with fascinating new toys available in a part of the experimental room normally closed off, and then bringing the child back into the regular play area and locking a wire screen that was interposed between the child and the fascinating toys. (See fig. *b*.)

The effect of the frustration was studied by comparing the constructiveness of the child's play with the original standardized toys before and after the frustration.

In general, there was a marked decrease in constructiveness of play. On the average, the constructiveness regressed by an amount equivalent to 17.3 months of mental age. In other words, following frustration, the child played at a constructiveness level characteristic of a child of about one and a half years younger.

In addition, "barrier" behavior and "escape" behavior were observed. Some children would approach the barrier and reach through the meshes of the screen, or would make efforts to leave the room altogether. The children who showed a great deal of "barrier" and "escape" behavior also showed much greater regression (on the average, about 24 months) when they *did* play with the standard toys again. The children who showed very little "barrier" and "escape" behavior regressed only four months on the average. Indeed, in some of the latter cases there was even an *increase* in subsequent constructiveness of play.

As the experimenters remark, "the lowering of constructiveness of play is similar to the change in behavior occurring under conditions of high emotionality where restless movements, stereotyped repetition of sentences, and stuttering are frequent. Both changes involve reduction in degree of differentiation and level of hierarchical organization within a unit of activity, and a certain lack of realism."

BARKER, R., DEMBO, T., LEWIN, K. 1941. Frustration and regression: an experiment with young children. *Univ. of Iowa Studies in Child Welfare,* 18, No. 1.

field" altogether, escaping into an unhappy permanent bachelordom.

Though such escape may provide relief from the excessive tension, the escape is a disruptive act, in that it prevents the attainment of the goal. It should be clear that this escape reaction is not the same as a fear-induced flight from dangerous objects. The escape may, of course, be only temporary. For, as we have already seen in the discussion of approach-avoidance conflicts, the organism may vacillate at a point of uneasy equilibrium, not entirely removed from the positive goal, and yet not too close to the negative object.

Escape reactions from various frustrations and conflicts may assume drastic and bizarre forms, affecting the person's overall adjustments. These will be discussed in Chap. 24.

Although there is no invariable sequence of disruptive events that occurs in a given episode involving severe frustration, quite commonly the aggressive reaction appears first, and the escape reaction later. If escape does not occur, or if the situation is such as not to permit escape, a further disruptive effect may ensue in the form of disorganization of the behavior pattern.

Frustration and Behavior Disorganization. Behavior patterns vary in their level of organization. The more highly organized patterns involve greater complexity, greater flexibility, greater adaptability. At the other extreme are the completely disorganized patterns, which are entirely lacking in adaptability to goal-attainment. Frustration tends to produce disorganization of the behavior pattern. The degree of decline in level of organization depends upon the intensity of the frustration and its related tension.

With moderate amounts of frustration, the decline in organization may be relatively slight. An experimental demonstra-

tion of this is given in Box 72, where it is shown that children's play behavior regresses to a somewhat lower level of maturity as a consequence of the thwarting of their desires to reach new and fascinating toys.

With more intense frustration, behavior may show more radical drops in level of organization. Thus, rats under extreme frustration in a problem-solving situation may develop stereotyped and rigid forms of response, wholly maladaptive with respect to the goal-attainment (see Box 73).

Finally, the disorganization may be so complete that every vestige of control and adaptability disappears. The acute temper tantrum of the child, the utter incoherence and confusion of behavior sometimes seen in the intensely frustrated person, are examples.

By Way of Summary. When it is not too intense, frustration may lead to various constructive effects aiding goal-attainment. For one thing, the thwarting may induce intensified striving to overcome the barrier. For another thing, it may induce various kinds of adaptive readjustments to the situation, including the recognition of alternative paths to the goal, the substitution of a different and accessible goal for the inaccessible one, and the redefining of the whole situation in such a manner that the conflict is eliminated without further serious consequences.

The threshold level of tension above which the frustration leads to disruptive rather than constructive effects is known as the frustration tolerance. It varies widely in level among individuals and in a given individual from situation to situation. The disruptive effects take various forms: aggression, which may be directed at the barrier or displaced to innocent objects; escape reactions; disorganization of behavior, often involving regression and stereotypy.

BOX 73

Frustration and Fixation

The effect of frustration coupled with punishment on problem-solving behavior in the rat has been experimentally studied by Maier, Glaser, and Klee. Rats were placed on a pedestal in a jumping stand (see Fig. 105, p. 437), facing two doors, one locked and the other unlocked. If the animal jumped against the locked door, it bumped its nose and fell into a net below; if it jumped against the unlocked door, it was able to get through to food. A black card with a white circle on it was affixed to one door, and a white card with a black circle to the other door.

In the usual learning problems one card always marks the unlocked door, which is randomly switched between left and right. The rat's task is to learn to jump to the "correct" card. This is fairly readily learned.

In the present experiment, however, the investigators deliberately frustrated the rat by making the problem *insoluble*. This they did by arranging it so that each card was rewarded 50 per cent of the time and punished 50 per cent of the time, regardless of whether it was on the right or on the left. Moreover, they forced the rat to jump from the pedestal by giving it an electric shock there.

Under these circumstances most animals soon came to develop a fixed habit of jumping either always to the left or always to the right. This form of stereotyped behavior is just as "good" as any other pattern of jumping, inasmuch as the animal will in any case get 50 per cent reward and 50 per cent punishment. (Some animals developed other forms of stereotyped responses, such as jumping always at the dividing post *between* the two doors—a kind of ineffectual "compromise.")

That the stereotyped habit became inflexible and maladaptive to changes in the situation was clearly shown when the experimenters made the problem actually soluble. This was done by regularly punishing the side on which the rat was fixated and unlocking the door on the opposite side. Under these circumstances the rat persisted in jumping to the same side on which it was fixated, even though it was now punished every time. This stereotyped behavior lasted for hundreds of successive trials. It persisted *even after the door on the other side was entirely removed so that the rat could plainly see that jumping to that side would give access to the food.*

Here on the rat level we seem to have rigidly stereotyped behavior, experimentally induced through prolonged frustration, that looks remarkably like the compulsory fixated habits, ineradicable through usual means, that are often observed in human beings.

———

MAIER, N. R. F., GLASER, N. M., and KLEE, J. B. 1940. Studies of abnormal behavior in the rat. III. The development of behavior fixations through frustration *J. exp. Psychol., 26,* 521–46.

Indirect Effects of Frustration

Up to this point we have been concerned only with the *direct* constructive and disruptive effects of frustration and conflict on the aroused motives being frustrated. But the motivational dynamics are far more complex than this. The organism is a unified system in which effects have *their* effects in turn, and so on, and in due course

feed back on, and further influence, the original state of affairs. This circular character of processes helps to make motivation, especially human motivation, the fascinating puzzle that it is.

Diffusion of Effects. It is when we study the *indirect* results of frustration and conflict that we become most conscious of these all-important feed-back consequences. The indirect results come about because the effects of frustration tend to *diffuse* and *generalize,* affecting all of the person's perception and behavior.

The indirect effects may themselves be *constructive.* The man who has experienced many frustrations and conflicts may come to perceive that the world is really full of hard problems and hard decisions. If he has successfully coped with his past frustrations, he may generalize these experiences into the confident belief that he will be able to handle future problems. It is partly through such repeated mastering of frustrations that the person's level of frustration tolerance (see p. 315) is gradually established at a higher level.

The diffused effects of frustration are also often *destructive.* The man enraged by frustration on one problem is not likely to approach other problems coolly, calmly, and effectively. Thus the original disruption frustrates other motives, and this in turn produces an even greater tension state. This also helps to account for the *interaction* of tensions accompanying different aroused motive states. A series of unrelated and minor frustrating experiences can result in a final powerful outburst by the person. That is why we often observe the person showing an upset far out of proportion to the minor frustration of the immediate situation he is in ("the last straw").

Frustration and Anxiety. The very existence of a frustration or conflict and the particular way a man responds to it may subject him to the punishment or threats of society, or to painful feelings of guilt, or to the threats of loss of self-esteem. All of these threats or punishments arouse in him feelings of *anxiety.*

AGGRESSION AND ANXIETY. A good example of the inducing of anxiety as a consequence of frustration concerns the expression of aggression. As we have seen, if the source of frustration is a dangerous and punishing agent, the person is placed in a new conflict between the need to express the aggression and the fear of doing so. Under these circumstances there may be displacement of aggression to a safer target. Such displaced aggression, however, is not likely to provide the full relief that would be obtained in attacking the actual source of frustration. But even displaced aggression may not be available to the person. Society may place strong prohibitions on the expression of aggression in *any* form. The child may learn that he will be punished for aggressive acts; the adult may fully have incorporated the culture's values of nonaggressiveness. Thus the impulse to aggress as a natural product of the original frustration is itself frustrated, and the total tension in the person thereby further heightened.

However the individual may still harbor the need or impulse to aggress. This is likely to be accompanied by acute feelings of anxiety, stemming from the danger of punishment for the aggressive *impulse.* The induced anxiety state is likely to cause still further interference with the person's goal-directed actions, with further frustration of them, and still more anxiety. Frustration, aggression, and anxiety are all interlinked in a vicious circle.

FAILURE AND ANXIETY. Another important root of anxiety in frustration comes from the threats to self-esteem contingent upon the failures of goal-attainment. The frustration of goal-attainment means *more* than that the particular need is not satisfied. It may also be perceived by the person as meaning that *he* has failed, is inferior, incompetent, and weak. Or he may believe that other people regard it that way. Thus he suffers the painful threat of loss of self-esteem and loss of prestige. These threats engender anxiety, and here we have another vicious circle—frustration, failure, anxiety, further frustration.

The extent to which frustration does lead to such anxiety will depend, of course, upon the specific nature of the frustrating situation. It will be recalled that some frustrations result from sheer lacks and losses in the environment. Such frustrations are not likely to arouse anxiety, for the individual does not perceive them as reflecting invidiously on his own reputation or self-picture. The lacks and losses are *objective*, not in any way his responsibility. Though he may be severely frustrated, he

---

BOX 74

Memory for Unfinished Tasks

In 1927, Zeigarnik at the University of Berlin compared the readiness to recall completed tasks and unfinished tasks. Her subjects were given a series of 20 simple tasks, such as molding an animal from clay, naming twelve cities beginning with K, combining the pieces of a jigsaw puzzle, punching holes in a sheet of paper, etc. The subject was permitted to finish half of the tasks. On each of the remaining tasks he was "accidentally" interrupted midway through the task, and the task was left unfinished while he went on to the next. The subjects did not realize that the interruptions were deliberately contrived by the experimenter. The tasks that were interrupted were scattered randomly throughout the series.

As soon as the series was over, the subject was asked to *recall* all the tasks. Subjects could rarely recall all twenty tasks, and so the experimenter could determine whether there was a greater recall for the completed or for the uncompleted tasks. Of a total of 138 subjects, Zeigarnik found that 110 (or 80 per cent) recalled more uncompleted tasks, 17 recalled more completed tasks, and 11 recalled both kinds equally. The superior recall of uncompleted tasks is known as the *Zeigarnik effect*.

Further analysis showed that the effect was greater for more engrossing tasks and for those interrupted shortly before they would have been completed. Zeigarnik's explanation was that the tension set up in relation to the task activity persisted when the goal was not achieved and this persisting tension favored recall. If the recall was not given until 24 hours after the experimental session, the Zeigarnik effect was found to have disappeared completely. (That is, there was no greater recall of the uncompleted than of the completed tasks.) The short duration of the tension is not surprising in view of the relative triviality of the task.

A later study by Lewis and Franklin used the Zeigarnik technique with two groups of subjects. Subjects in one group were led to understand that their performance on the tasks was in the nature of a test of their ability; thus this group was presumably *self-involved*. The other group was "simply helping the experimenter standardize some tasks," and hence could be regarded as *task-oriented*.

The differences between the two groups were striking. Of the 12 subjects in the task-oriented group, 10 (or 83 per cent) recalled more uncompleted tasks, confirming Zeigarnik's results. But of the 12 ego-involved subjects, 11 recalled a preponderance of *completed tasks*. We see here that the effect of the tension resulting from frustration of the goal-directed action can differ in direction depending upon the nature of the motivation and the manner in which the situation is perceived. When the subject is task-oriented, the incompletion may merely signify something left to be done. When he is ego-involved, the incompletion may be taken to signify personal failure, and completion to signify personal success. He therefore remembers more of the completed, i.e., "successful," tasks.

Zeigarnik, B. 1927. *Über das Behalten von erledigten und unerledigten Handlungen. Psychologische Forschung, 9,* 1–85.

Lewis, H. B., and Franklin, M. 1944. An experimental study of the role of the ego in work. II. The significance of task-orientation in work. *J. exp. Psychol., 34,* 195–215.

is not likely to develop the kind of anxiety that comes when he perceives the source of frustration to be himself. When he feels that it is *his* stupidity, his inferiority, his indecisiveness that causes the frustration, the anxiety is likely to be high.

We should, therefore, expect a significant difference in the effects of frustration when the person is *task*-involved and when he is *self*-involved (see pp. 359–60). Box 74 describes experimental comparisons.

ANXIETY AND DEFENSE. The crucial significance of the relation between frustration and anxiety is that anxiety leads the person to exhibit various *defensive* effects of frustration and conflict. These effects are to be distinguished from the more immediate constructive and disruptive effects

already discussed. They are reactions to the anxiety produced by the frustration, rather than to the initial frustration itself. They can be described as ways in which the person behaves in order to reduce or to avoid the anxiety. For this reason they are often referred to as mechanisms of self-defense or *defense mechanisms*. For example, in *rationalization* the person may reduce the anxiety attached to failure in a task by finding "good excuses" to account for the failure. In *repression* the person may avoid the anxiety by "forgetting" the frustrating episode. There are many different types of defense mechanisms. We will postpone discussion of them until Chapter 24, where the entire problem of the individual's adjustment will be considered.

Glossary

activity cycle. Cyclical fluctuations in the level of general activity of an animal, reflecting rises and falls in motivational state. The activity cycles are partly a function of external stimuli, and partly of changes in physiological condition, for instance, the 4-day cycle of activity in the female rat associated with estrus.

activity wheel. A revolving wire drum within which an animal, such as a rat, is confined. When the animal runs, the drum revolves and the amount of activity is recorded in revolutions. Used as a measure of motive strength.

aggression. Attack upon an obstacle or barrier to goal-attainment, or upon an object to which the aggression is displaced. Aggression may take many different forms —physical and verbal, real and fantasied. The frustration-aggression hypothesis states that all aggression stems from frustration (but does not imply the converse, that frustration always leads to aggression).

ambivalent object. An object that combines both positive and negative features for the

person, producing conflict behavior of approach to and avoidance of the object.

anxiety. A state of apprehension felt by the person, in which the source is usually not as specifically perceived as in fear; it often pertains to anticipations of future danger, such as punishment, or threats to self-esteem. Anxiety typically leads to defensive reactions intended to allay or avoid the anxiety.

catharsis. A dispelling of tension and anxiety through emotional outburst or through other avenues. It helps the individual to restore his perspective, to regain control of his behavior, and to cope with problems adaptively.

cognitive narrowing. A narrowing of perception or attention to limited parts of a situation, often as a consequence of extreme tension in the person. Tends to be accompanied by poorer adaptability in solving problems and attaining goals.

conflict. The experiencing of two or more simultaneous motives requiring incompatible actions. The conflict may be among alternative needs and desires, among alternative goal-objects, or among alternative means to a goal. Conflict situations fall into one of three basic patterns: approach-approach, avoidance-avoidance, approach-avoidance.

consummatory behavior. The behavior exhibited by the organism in commerce with a goal-object (e.g., drinking the water, reading the book) and associated with which there is a reduction of the need or desire.

deprivation schedule. The withholding of biologically required substances from the animal, in order to control its motives for experimental purposes. For example, the rat may be deprived of water for varying numbers of hours in order to induce different degrees of thirst.

displacement of aggression. The channeling of aggressive impulses toward targets other than the direct source of frustration. This is sometimes manifested in "scapegoating." The targets of displacement may be people or groups or even inanimate objects. Displacement frequently occurs because of the inaccessibility of the real source of frustration or because of the fear of attacking it.

escape reaction. The tendency to leave a frustrating situation when the frustration tolerance has been exceeded. Such escape reactions are generally regarded as disruptive, in that the failure to cope directly with the problem situation may itself lead to further adjustment difficulties for the person.

fixation. The establishment of a rigid pattern of response in a given situation, a pattern which prevents the individual from making the kinds of adaptive adjustments that are required by changes in the situation. Such fixation is frequently the product of the high levels of tension associated with severe conflict.

frustration. The blocking or thwarting of goal-attainment. Frustration is defined in terms of the state of the organism, rather than in terms of the external conditions. A person may be frustrated by an imaginary barrier, and may fail to be frustrated by a real barrier. Depending upon the level of frustration, its consequences in behavior may be either constructive or disruptive.

frustration tolerance. The threshold for the maximal amount of frustration which the individual can accommodate without developing disruptive or disorganized patterns of behavior. Frustration tolerance is a variable, rather than a fixed, quantity, its level depending upon the characteristics of the person and the nature of the situation.

homeostasis. The maintenance of steady physiological states of the body through self-regulating mechanisms. For example, the maintenance of uniform body temperature, or the maintenance of specific concentrations of substances in the blood. The mechanisms function without the awareness and voluntary action of the person. It is when the homeostatic mechanisms are no longer able to regulate the body conditions that the organism's *motives* may be aroused, with voluntary remedial action ensuing.

instigators of aroused motives. The factors that help to induce an aroused motivational state, including the stimuli from the internal environment of the body, the stimuli from the external environment, both physical and social, and the stimuli arising from the person's flow of thoughts. All these kinds of instigators *interact* in producing the aroused motive state.

obstruction method. The measurement of the strength of an animal's motive by measuring the readiness with which it will cross an electrified grid in order to reach an appropriate goal-object.

regression. A decline in the level of organization of behavior, as a consequence of frustration.

substitution of goals. The searching for and accepting of alternative goals to satisfy a need or desire when the original goal is unattainable. Whether an alternative goal will in fact serve as a satisfactory substitute for the original goal depends upon numerous factors, including the degree to which there is perceptual grouping of the alternative and original goals.

Zeigarnik effect. The phenomenon that an uncompleted task or activity will tend to be better recalled later than will a completed task. The effect is found only when the person is *task-involved*. When he is *self-involved*, the effect may disappear, or may even be reversed.

Suggestions for Further Reading

CANNON, W. B. 1939. *The wisdom of the body* (rev. ed.). New York: Norton.

A well-written presentation of the author's concept of homeostasis.

DOLLARD, J.; DOOB, L. W.; MILLER, N. E.; MOWRER, O. H.; SEARS, R. R.; FORD, C. S.; HOVLAND, C. I.; and SOLLENBERGER, R. T. 1939. *Frustration and aggression.* New Haven: Yale Univ. Press.

Provides experimental evidence and theoretical explanation of the relation between frustration and aggression.

LEWIN, K. 1935. *Dynamic theory of personality.* New York: McGraw-Hill.

Contains Lewin's classical discussion of the varieties of psychological conflict and their theoretical implications.

McCLELLAND, D. C. (ed.). 1955. *Studies in motivation.* New York: Appleton-Century-Crofts.

Numerous contributions by various authors on problems of human and animal motivation.

MAIER, N. R. F. 1949. *Frustration: a study of behavior without a goal.* New York: McGraw-Hill.

An account of research on frustration, with special emphasis on its relationship to stereotypy of behavior.

YOUNG, P. T. 1936. *Motivation of behavior.* New York: Wiley.

A textbook with wide coverage of the experimental research on many aspects of motivation.

CHAPTER XII

Physiology, Motives, and Emotion

THE LIVING organism is in a constantly aroused state. Momentary chemical instabilities are being continuously adjusted; hormones are being secreted into the blood stream and carried to various bodily organs, which respond to their arrival with muscular contractions and relaxations; and the nervous system is everywhere firing and conducting impulses.

A large part of this activity is never consciously experienced by the person. No conscious effort on Mr. Anyman's part is required to direct and co-ordinate this myriad of reactions that maintain in his body an extremely high degree of homeostasis (see p. 292). Mr. Anyman is unaware of the chemical interchanges going on in his body to maintain a stable acidity level in his blood. Yet a very slight shift toward greater acidity than the level appropriate for Mr. Anyman would result in his coma and death; a shift toward greater alkalinity, and he would be thrown into convulsive fits.

Many of the mechanisms that maintain this high degree of constancy are relatively simple and function more or less on their own. For example, the sugar concentration of the blood is regulated by the liver, which takes up excess glucose from the blood, stores it in the form of glycogen, and releases it when the blood-sugar level begins to fall. *Even after removal from the body* the isolated liver in the laboratory flask will continue to take up glucose from its surrounding medium and store it as glycogen.

But such independent action is not the usual picture. Integration and co-ordination, involving larger and larger segments of the organism, are the more typical story. The mechanisms that maintain bodily homeostasis can be classified into three levels of increasing complexity and co-ordination: (1) relatively autonomous effects involving a single system; (2) co-ordinated and integrated events involving many component systems; and (3) the gross muscular "actions" that provide the body with supplies from the outside and remove the organism from external injury.

Normally, we reserve the terms "motive"

and "emotion" for bodily responses of this third level of complexity. However it should be clear that the observable behavior in motivation and emotion represents but a *part* of all the physiological events involved. What we observe when we see a man fighting for his life is only a small segment, overwhelming as it may appear, of the thousands of chemical, hormonal, and neural reactions going on within him. We see the eruption of the volcano; the major part of the activity is hidden from view. To understand the physiology of motivation and emotions, we must examine many of the "hidden" events. And when we examine the internal and external events, we find a beautifully integrated complex of processes.

These processes range from changes in chemical composition of the blood to highly skilled muscular movements of legs, arms, and hands. To integrate these varied processes, three regulatory systems are at work: (1) the cerebrospinal nervous system, (2) the autonomic nervous system, and (3) the endocrine glands.

The Cerebrospinal Nervous System

We are already familiar with some of the major parts of the *cerebrospinal nervous system*. This is the system that includes the sensory nerves of the peripheral sense organs and the muscles, the brain, the motor nerves, and the spinal column. In general, the cerebrospinal nervous system functions to bring information to the brain (perception), to integrate this information (thinking, learning, and problem-solving), and to control the person's actions in his adjustments to his environment. Obviously all this is of major importance in motivated and emotional behavior. But there are vari-

ous special parts of the brain which are of particular significance in the study of motivation and emotion. Perhaps the most important of these is the *hypothalamus*.

The Hypothalamus. Scientific interest in the hypothalamus began only in the twentieth century, yet so much has already been discovered about its functions that many scientists are ready to credit the hypothalamus with the major responsibility for integrating and controlling our motivational and emotional life.

The hypothalamus is a relatively small specialized collection of nuclei of brain cells lying at the base of the brain, immediately behind the optic chiasma. (See Fig. 83.) It receives neural impulses from a number of sources, including the frontal poles of the cerebral hemispheres and the visceral organs of the body. In turn it sends impulses back up to the cortex and down to various visceral bodies. The descending tracts give off branches that lead into the reticular formation. All told, the hypothalamus is in an extremely strategic position, mediating between the cortex, and other parts of the brain and the viscera.

Among the controlling functions ascribed to the hypothalamus on the basis of much experimental and clinical work are the following: metabolic rate, water excretion, breathing, heart activity, temperature regulation, blood pressure, eating, drinking, and many aspects of emotional behavior.

The Hunger Motive. As the nutrient content of the body is depleted, the various organs (e.g., the liver) that have stored up the previous excesses (e.g., glycogen) replenish the blood stream. However this cannot go on indefinitely since the stored supply itself becomes depleted. At some point the autonomous homeostatic processes prove inadequate and a larger segment of the body becomes involved. The organism gets "hungry." It seeks and eats food and in this way replenishes the various organs of the body so that the autonomous homeostatic mechanisms can take over again. What is the physiological mechanism of this "hunger motive"?

Recent experimental work has demonstrated that the hypothalamus plays an important role in this process. The control of the hunger motive does not seem to lie in the stomach or blood stream alone. The control of eating seems to be in "appetite centers" located within very specific parts of the hypothalamus. Thus, destruction of the ventromedial nucleus of the hypothalamus leads to voracious eating. (See Fig. 83.)

Animals with such lesions frequently be-

come savage and vicious (as we shall soon see), but so voracious is their appetite that they will sometimes forget their animosity for their keeper in their desire for food. If enough food is given to them, they quickly become obese, in some instances increasing their weight by as much as 150 per cent. (See Fig. 84.)

What is the relation of these findings to the hunger motive? In the normal human being "hunger pangs" are frequently correlated with an empty stomach, or a low blood sugar (depletion of nutrient elements in the blood), or general weakness (see Box 75). None of these conditions seem to be necessary for animals with hypothalamic lesions, since they will continue to eat heartily after being amply fed.

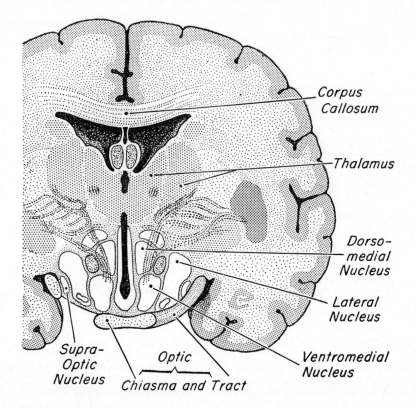

Corpus Callosum

Thalamus

Dorso-medial Nucleus

Lateral Nucleus

Ventromedial Nucleus

Supra-Optic Nucleus

Optic Chiasma and Tract

FIG. 83. The *hypothalamus* consists of the collection of nuclei (colored white) at the base of the brain. The nuclei to which frequent reference will be made in the discussion are labeled: the dorsomedial, lateral, supraoptic, and ventromedial.

What appears to happen might be phrased somewhat along the following lines. Normally the instigators of the hunger motive are of various sorts. They may be the contractions of the empty stomach or the physiological changes that occur with a drop in the nutritional content of the blood. When these conditions occur, neural impulses from the contracting stomach, and perhaps chemical processes from the blood, stimulate the brain so that the individual perceives that he is "hungry"; he looks for food and eats it when it becomes available. The cessation of this "eating pattern" is, however, *controlled* by a fairly specific neural mechanism in the hypothalamus, the ventromedial nucleus. When this neural mechanism is destroyed, the eating pattern is no longer under such regulation and it

"goes haywire." That the center for the *initiation* of the eating pattern is also located somewhere in the hypothalamus is indicated by the fact that destruction of certain other specific hypothalamic areas —the *lateral nucleus* (see Fig. 85)—*inhibits* eating. The stomach may be empty, the blood sugar low, weakness even unto death may set in, but the animal will not eat.

It is of interest to note that human patients with tumors in the hypothalamus will sometimes display a severe loss of appetite, and it has also been suggested that some instances of obesity among people may very well indicate other hypothalamic tumors.

Of major significance is the clear indication that the physiological basis of the

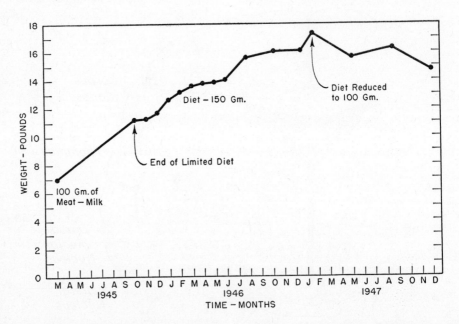

FIG. 84. Obesity and hypothalamic lesions in the cat. The figure gives the 34-month postoperative weight record of an animal that had the ventromedial nucleus of its hypothalamus destroyed in March, 1945. Not only was its appetite increased after the operation, but apparently its metabolism had also been slowed down so that it was able to increase its weight by 4 pounds during the first 8 months on a restricted

diet of 100 gm. When the diet was increased to 150 gm, the cat continued to gain weight, reaching 17 pounds by February, 1947. From that point on it was able to maintain a weight of 15 to 17 pounds even though now restricted to 100 gm. of food daily. The hypothalamus not only controls eating, but plays an important role in general metabolic rate as well. (Adapted from Ingram, 1952.)

BOX 75

How Do We Know We Are Hungry?

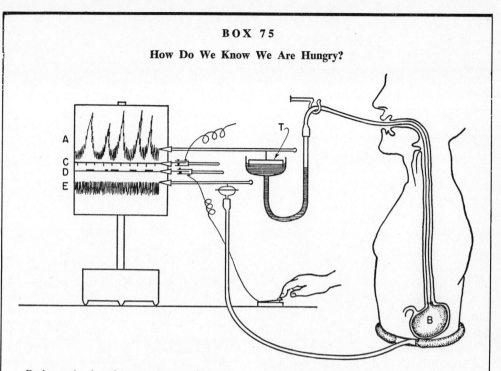

Perhaps the best-known theory that accounts for the origin of hunger sensations is Cannon's "local" stimulus theory: the hunger sensations result from strong contractions of the stomach walls. In 1912 one of his research colleagues, A. L. Washburn, offered his services to test this theory. Washburn first accustomed himself to swallowing a balloon attached to a tube. A key was available at his right hand, and a pneumograph (a rubber tube) was placed around his middle. All of these led to writing instruments placed against a revolving smoked drum (see fig.). As the stomach contracted, the air from the balloon (B) raised the float (T) that moved the writing instrument, recording at A the movements of the stomach wall. Every time Washburn felt a hunger pang, he pressed the key, recording his hunger sensation at D. His breathing movements were recorded from the pneumograph at E. The records were taken after several hours of deprivation from food.

As can be seen, Washburn's hunger pangs occurred at about the time the stomach contraction reached its peak. The smooth breathing record (E) proves that the record at A does not result from the activity of the abdominal wall.

The evidence seems clear, but contradictory evidence is also clear. For example: In 1931 Wangensteen and Carlson of the Cancer Institute of the University of Minnesota Hospital reported the case of a patient whose entire stomach had been removed because of a cancerous growth. Ten months after the operation the patient stated that he felt in the best of health, that he became hungry frequently, that after eating he was no longer hungry, and that his hunger sensations felt no different from prior to the operation. He was induced to swallow a balloon (à la Washburn) and records were taken. A tracing after 8 hours of starvation revealed practically no intestinal activity although the patient reported that he was very hungry and needed food.

Sensations of normal hunger occur with stomach contractions—and without them. Mr. Anyman knows when he is hungry, but the scientist does not know how he knows.

CANNON, W. B., and WASHBURN, A. C. 1912. An explanation of hunger. *Amer. J. Physiol., 29,* 441–54.
WANGENSTEEN, O. H., and CARLSON, H. A. 1931. Hunger sensations in a patient after total gastrectomy. *Proceedings of the Society for Experimental Biology and Medicine, 28,* 545–7.

"perfink" (see p. 201) we call hunger is not simply an empty stomach, or a depletion of nutrient substances in the body, but involves fairly complicated neural mechanisms in the brain.

The Thirst Motive. Water is a greater immediate requirement of man than is food. Men have gone without food for thirty days or more (using up their internally stored food), but they cannot survive long without taking in fresh supplies of water. How long a man can last without drinking depends upon the external conditions. In a hot desert the lack of water may bring about death within a few hours.

A number of attempts have been made to identify the physiological conditions and sense organs involved in the "thirst motive." The most recent evidence seems to point to the hypothalamus as the locus for the initiation of thirst and drinking.

THE DRY-MOUTH THEORY. Cannon, having proposed the local-stimulus theory of hunger instigation (see Box 75), suggested that the instigator for thirst was also a local stimulus: the drying of the mouth and throat. He assumed that with the drying of the mouth, nerve impulses pass to the cortex, resulting in the sensation of thirst and putting the organism into a state of readiness to seek and drink water. Cannon reported that when he administered the drug atropine (which stops the flow of saliva and makes the mouth dry) to himself, he experienced thirst, even though there was no reduction of body water.

However a number of experimental facts soon appeared that could not be encompassed by this theory: Dogs that are given atropine drink no more than their normal daily quantity of water. Pilocarpine, a drug that causes a large increase in saliva flow and thus keeps the throat and mouth con-

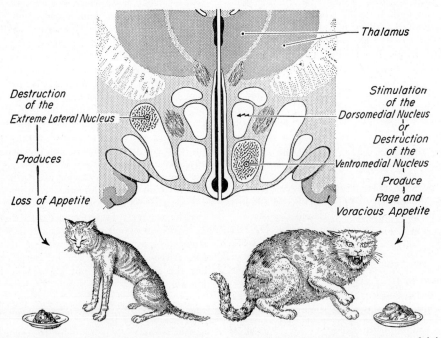

Destruction
of the
Extreme Lateral Nucleus

Produces

Loss of Appetite

Thalamus

Stimulation
of the
Dorsomedial Nucleus
or
Destruction
of the
Ventromedial Nucleus

Produce

Rage and
Voracious Appetite

FIG. 85. This figure summarizes the results of a number of experiments on the cat. It portrays the relationship between destruction and electrical stimulation of various key nuclei in the hypothalamus and rage, and eating behavior. (Adapted from Ingram, 1956.)

stantly wet, fails to lessen the desire for water.

If it is not the localized dryness of the mouth and throat which arouses the thirst motive, what then? We know, of course, that thirst is somehow related to dehydration of the body. There are, however, two kinds of dehydration. *Absolute dehydration* refers to a decrease in the level of water in the body to less than normal (as through sweating). *Relative dehydration* refers to a state in which there is less than the normal amount of water relative to the amount of salt. The body may actually have more water than is normal, but if the salt content has been increased to an even greater degree, the proportion of water to salt is less than normal and a condition of relative dehydration exists. When Mr. Anyman eats a salted pretzel, be brings about a condition of relative dehydration and soon becomes thirsty—and our vendors of beer take advantage of this fact by offering free pretzels with orders of beer.

THE BEER AND PRETZEL THEORY. The concept of relative dehydration has led to the formulation of an alternative theory to Cannon's "dry-mouth" theory—a theory that Wolf (1956) has called the "beer and pretzel" theory of thirst. According to this theory the nervous system contains specialized cells called "osmoreceptors." When these receptors shrink as a consequence of absolute or relative dehydration, nerve impulses from them pass to the cortex, produce the sensation of thirst, and instigate a readiness to look for and drink water.

Recent evidence suggests that these postulated osmoreceptors (their existence has not yet been definitely established) are located in the hypothalamus. Thus Anderson, a Swedish physiologist, reported in 1952 that injection of a microscopic amount of a salt solution directly into the supraoptic nucleus of the hypothalamus (see Fig. 83) of the goat caused immediate drinking

of water. The same injection into other areas of the brain did not have this effect. Further work indicated that destruction of this "drinking center" resulted in a refusal of the animals to drink at all.

Again we see the crucial part played by the hypothalamus in motivation.

The Cerebrospinal Nervous System and Emotion. The instigation of intense emotional behavior has traditionally been ascribed to the viscera. As we shall see later in this chapter, the visceral organs are very much involved in emotional behavior. However evidence accumulated from ablation (destruction) studies and stimulation studies (in which various parts of the brain are stimulated electrically and the behavior of the individual noted) indicates that initiation and control of emotional behavior is to be found primarily within the brain structures, especially in the cerebral cortex, the hypothalamus, and the reticular formation.

RAGE. In 1892 Goltz, a German physiologist, noted that dogs whose cerebral cortex had been removed surgically ("decorticate dogs") were quick to display anger and rage: growling, barking, and general attack behavior. In 1925 Cannon made similar but more extensive observations with decorticate cats, and since then many experimenters have confirmed his findings. Cannon called the anger or rage seen in decorticate animals "sham rage" because it did not seem to be evoked by the usual situational determinants of these emotions (see Chapter 9). It was not directed against any specific target and would go off "automatically" when the animal was handled (no matter how gently) or even if its cage was touched. This rage was usually short-lived and would cease almost as soon as the stimulus was withdrawn. However, while it lasted, it seemed very much like the real thing: barking, growling, snarling, and snapping in dogs; erection of hair, hissing, spitting, biting, striking with unsheathed claws in cats.

The theory was proposed that the hypothalamus contains a release mechanism for rage and that this release mechanism is normally restrained by the cortex. When the cortex is removed, no restraining control on this hypothalamic center is possible, and therefore the slightest stimulation will release the rage pattern.

Further experimental work has supported the hypothalamic theory of rage by identifying within the hypothalamus a center for the initiation of rage and another center for the inhibition of rage. *Electrical stimulation* of the dorsomedial nucleus changes a friendly, tame cat into a raging beast. We seem to have here a center for the initiation of rage. *Destruction* of the ventromedial nucleus (the area whose destruction results also in excessive eating) creates a permanently vicious animal. Here we seem to have a "rage inhibitory center." (See Fig. 85.)

Rage is not, then, only a "gut reaction." A good part of the instigation, control, and co-ordination of the intense rage response is to be found within the brain, primarily in the cerebral cortex and the hypothalamus.

CONTROLLING EMOTIONALITY BY DRUGS. In discussing the functions of the hypothalamus, we pointed to its importance in the control of breathing, heart rate, blood pressure, etc. As we know, all these bodily changes accompany various emotional states of excitement. Presumably, therefore, any drug that could inhibit the activities of the hypothalamus would also tend to "tranquilize" the person, i.e., would tend to keep his blood pressure down, maintain his breathing at a normal rate, and control his heart activity.

It is in this way that we can understand the action of some of the recent "tranquilizing" drugs (reserpine and chlorpromazine), which have been found so effective in calming excited mental patients and in relaxing the very tense person. Reserpine is an extract from the snakeroot plant (named "Rauwolfia" for a sixteenth-century German physician), which has been used in India for centuries as a "calming" drug. Chlorpromazine is a synthetic drug developed by biochemists. Experiments on animals indicate that these two drugs inhibit the action of the hypothalamus so as to lower the body temperature, reduce blood pressure, and prevent agitated behavior.

THE RETICULAR FORMATION. These drugs affect not only the hypothalamus, but also another very important part of the cerebrospinal nervous system—the reticular formation. It will be remembered that the reticular formation acts to arouse or alert the cortex so that the cortex can respond actively to outside stimulation (see p. 170). It has been shown that chlorpromazine, in small doses, blocks the reticular formation from sending its "arousal" impulses to the cortex, and therefore tends to calm a hyperexcitable person. (See Box 76.) This is merely one indication of the important role the reticular formation can play in the initiation and control of general emotionality.

WAKEFULNESS AND SLEEP. The reticular formation also plays an important part in determining the person's susceptibility to emotional or motivational arousal. This is seen in the role of the reticular formation in the sleep mechanism of the brain. The emotional person, the motivated person, is, of course, the awake person. The student who falls asleep during his lectures is hardly describable as a highly motivated student.

The phenomenon of sleep is a rather complicated one. There exist, for example, periodic sleep rhythms. Mr. Anyman will tend to "feel sleepy" when his regular bedtime approaches, regardless of what may

BOX 76

Tranquilizing Drugs and the Arousal of the Brain

Himwich and Rinaldi of the Galesburg (Illinois) State Hospital studied the effect of the tranquilizing drugs on the brain through analyzing "brain waves" of rabbits. Brain waves are the electrical phenomena that accompany neural activity in the cortex. With an instrument that picks up minute electrical waves we can detect and record the pattern of this activity. Under normal conditions the relaxed cortex shows a rhythmic series of waves, about 10 per second. (See p. 483 for a more detailed treatment of brain waves.) When the organism is stimulated by a pinch on the skin, the reticular formation sends up "arousing" impulses to the cortex and the rhythmic waves are *suppressed* (see fig. *a*). The brain is now alerted to incoming information.

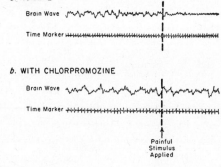

a. NORMAL

Brain Wave

Time Marker

b. WITH CHLORPROMOZINE

Brain Wave

Time Marker

Painful
Stimulus
Applied

If small doses of chlorpromazine are first given, the painful stimulus will *not* produce the brain-wave changes that indicate brain arousal. In figure *b* (with chlorpromazine) the pattern remains unchanged even after painful stimulation. From such experiments Himwich suggests that

. . . in a human patient chlorpromazine inhibits the activating system (reticular system), preventing some stimuli from rising to the level of the cerebral cortex. It thereby places a block between the environment and its influence on the mind. The individual is rendered more aloof from his surroundings. A psychotic is insulated against the terrifying creations of his imagination. A normal person is made less sensitive to troublesome situations which would ordinarily arouse a strongly emotional response. . . .

But the story of tranquilizing drugs is not quite this simple. The same investigators found that *large* doses of chlorpromazine stimulated the reticular system into *action!* Nevertheless chlorpromazine in large doses has a calming effect upon a patient.

It is clear that there is still much to be learned about the action of the tranquilizing drugs.

HIMWICH, H. E. 1955. The new psychiatric drugs. *Scientific American*, 193, 80–6.

be going on about him. It is assumed that he has become "conditioned" to a temporal rhythm (see Chapter 15 for a discussion of conditioning). Fatigue products in the body and metabolic changes may also be factors inducing sleep. There is also *neural* control of sleep in which the reticular formation, together with the hypothalamus, plays an important role.

Normally a person will remain awake as long as he receives a certain level of stimulation. If the noise is loud enough, the lights bright enough, his muscles active enough, he will stay awake, alert, and responsive to motivational and emotional arousal. On the other hand, if the level of stimulation to his cortex from his senses is low (a low sound level, dim lights, relaxed muscles), he may become drowsy, fall asleep, and no longer be available to normally adequate emotional and motivational stimuli. But at this point the reticular formation can come to his rescue. If the reticular system receives enough impulses from these low-level stimuli, it will discharge to the cortex and maintain wakefulness. In other words, the reticular system is able to maintain wakefulness at levels of stimulation which would not ordinarily activate the cortex. We do not always have to be in a room where the radio is going full blast and the light shining brightly to remain awake.

Experimentation with animals has demonstrated that destruction of the reticular formation results in a comatose or somnolent animal. For it there no longer remain problems of motivation or emotion.

By Way of Summary. The more recent experimental data concerning the instigation and control of hunger, thirst, and rage give the brain (especially the hypothalamus) an important role to play in motivation and emotion. (See Box 77 for additional evidence.) Former theories located the initiation and control of hunger and thirst and anger in the viscera—in the stomach, the mouth, the heart, and other internal organs. Modern research is finding these instigators in the brain. As research in physiology and psychology progresses, the cerebrospinal nervous system takes on an increasing importance for the *total* behavior of the person—not only for his perceptual and cognitive life. It is becoming clear that no sharp distinction can be drawn between the emotional and intellectual life of the person. We are indeed dealing with "perfinks" whenever we deal with *any* aspect of behavior—whether it is the beast or the saint within us.

However we must not, by the same token, exaggerate the role of the cerebrospinal nervous system. The viscera of man and his hormonal system also play significant parts.

The Autonomic Nervous System

With the arousal of motivation and emotion many "automatic" events, which normally go along unnoticed in their smooth functioning, play an increased role and intrude themselves upon our awareness. In fear, Mr. Anyman feels the heightened beating of his heart, his increased breathing rate, the blanching of his facial blood vessels (the "pallor of fear"), the Rabelaisian effect upon his bowels and bladder; in shame he is aware of the flushing of his facial blood vessels (the "blush of shame"); in grief he is aware of the action of his tear glands.

So impressive are the activities of the heart, blood vessels, respiratory muscles, and secretory glands in the aroused motivational-emotional state that many experimenters have attempted to measure emotion solely in terms of them.

While the cerebrospinal nervous system plays an important role in these processes, the major control and regulation of these "automatic" visceral processes is maintained through a specialized part of the nervous system. This part is called, appropriately enough, the *autonomic nervous system.*

In the early years of the nineteenth century a French physiologist, Bichat, first suggested that the controlling activities of the entire nervous system could be divided into a "voluntary" and an "involuntary" part. By about 1920 (primarily as the result of the work of an American physiologist, Langley) the existence of two specialized (yet interrelated) nervous systems was well established. What Bichat had called the "involuntary" nervous system was clearly described and further subdivided. One part of the involuntary system was named the *sympathetic* nervous system, and another part, the *parasympathetic*. Both systems together Langley called the "autonomic nervous system," as opposed to the cerebrospinal nervous system. Langley's terminology and divisions have been widely adopted and are in common use today.

The Sympathetic System. The sympathetic nervous system centers about two

BOX 77

"Rewarding" Brain Centers

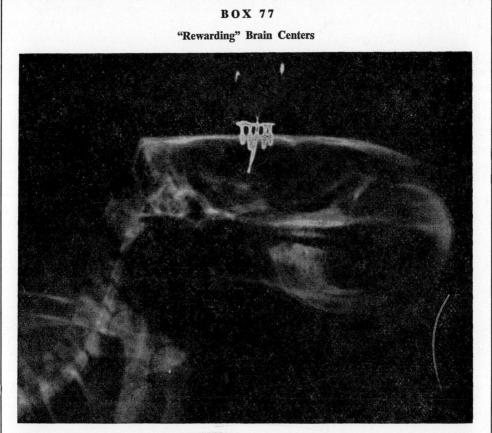

The crucial role of brain activity in "motivated behavior" is dramatically illustrated in an experiment by Olds and Milner, performed at McGill University in 1954.

Fine wire electrodes were permanently inserted through the skull into various lower brain centers of 15 rats. The accompanying figure is an X-ray photograph showing the electrodes in place in an intact rat. During the testing sessions wires were attached to the outside of the electrodes. These wires, in turn, were connected to a lever in the experimental box (where the rats were placed, individually, for testing) and to an electrical stimulator. When the current was on, every time the rat depressed the lever a weak alternating current was delivered to his brain. The rat could stimulate his brain electrically by depressing the lever in his box. The animals were tested with the current on, and then with the current off.

The results seem conclusive. When the current was on, the rat pressed the lever with great frequency and persistence. Some rats made as many as 1,920 presses per hour, or about 1 every 2 seconds. When the current was off, they soon stopped pressing the lever.

Later experiments by Olds demonstrated that rats will even learn to run through a maze if at the end of the maze they get an opportunity to stimulate their brains electrically!

The initiation of purposive behavior is indeed a complicated affair. Even the rat is impelled by more than an empty stomach, a depleted water supply, or hormonal pressures. There seem to be specific brain centers whose stimulation alone is enough to result in a "primary rewarding effect" for the animal.

OLDS, J., and MILNER, P. 1954. Positive reinforcement produced by electrical stimulation of septal area and other regions of rat brain. *J. comp. & physiol. Psychol.*, 47, 419–27.

chains of ganglions running along the sides of the spinal cord. Figure 86 presents one of these two chains. The ganglion cells are supplied by nerve fibers from the spinal cord, called "preganglionic neurons." A single preganglionic neuron makes contact with many sympathetic ganglia. The ganglion cells of the sympathetic system are thus built to facilitate *widespread discharge.*

Since the ganglia of the sympathetic system are connected with the visceral organs, this means that many visceral organs can be thrown into co-ordinated activity when any one part of the sympathetic system is stimulated. For example, when a nervous impulse comes down the spinal cord from the hypothalamus and goes across a preganglionic neuron to the ganglia of the

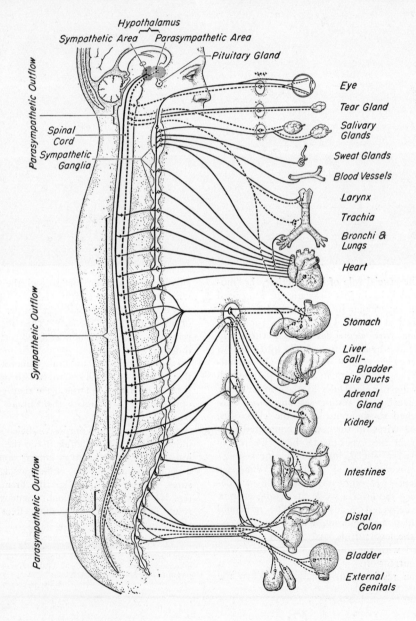

sympathetic system, the following *pattern* of visceral responses occurs simultaneously: dilation of the pupil, increase in heart rate, rise in blood pressure, rerouting of the blood from the skin and stomach to the muscles of the limbs, inhibition of the peristaltic movements of the stomach, etc. All these reactions, taken as a whole, prepare the organism for *emergency action*—for flight or fight. This automatic, unconscious, and uncontrollable series of visceral reactions has been *initiated* by a signal from the hypothalamus but has been *patterned* and put into execution by the structure of the sympathetic nervous system.

The Parasympathetic System. The parasympathetic fibers supply the same visceral organs as do the sympathetic. But, as can be seen from Figure 86, there is one important difference in their structures. The parasympathetic system is somewhat more specific and discriminating in its connections with the visceral organs than is the sympathetic. For example, the stimulation of the parasympathetic nerve that supplies the tear glands results in stimulation of the tear glands *only*, not of many other visceral organs as well.

The effects of stimulation by the two systems are *opposite in direction*. For ex-ample, stimulation of the heart by the sympathetic system accelerates the heart; stimulation by the parasympathetic system slows it down. Thus most visceral organs are supplied by two nervous systems, each having an opposite effect. This is called *reciprocal innervation*. Reciprocal innervation gives us a built-in neurological mechanism for homeostatic control. As one nerve accelerates the heart beyond normal, we have another nerve whose stimulation can slow it down again to the normal rate.

STRIATED AND SMOOTH MUSCLE. The heart, stomach, glands, have their own muscular fibers. These organs, as is true of the limbs, fingers, trunk, can react only through muscular movements. However the skeletal muscles (limbs, etc.) and the muscles of the viscera are structurally different. Under the microscope the skeletal muscles appear to have horizontal markings across the fibers and are therefore called the *striated* muscles. The visceral muscles are called *smooth* muscles. We therefore speak of two muscle systems, the striated or skeletal system, and the smooth or visceral system.

Cerebrospinal and Autonomic Interconnections. As we have already seen, the sympathetic and parasympathetic systems are

---

FIG. 86. Here we have a semidiagrammatic representation of the hypothalamus, the spinal cord, the sympathetic nervous system, and the parasympathetic nervous system. The solid lines represent the sympathetic system, the dotted lines the parasympathetic system.

Consider first the sympathetic system. A nervous impulse originates in the lower part of the hypothalamus. From there it descends the spinal cord and at some point about halfway down the cord (the area labeled "sympathetic outflow") it connects with *preganglionic neurons* and leaves the cord (indicated by small arrow signs). The preganglionic neuron then enters one of the sympathetic ganglia, where it makes several connections. The nervous impulse then travels up and down the chain of ganglia, making contact with many sympathetic ganglia.

This means that when one preganglionic neuron is thrown into action, many ganglia are excited. From these ganglia, postganglionic neurons extend to the various visceral organs—sweat glands, blood vessels, heart, external genitals.

Now consider the parasympathetic system. Here, too, the nervous impulse originates in the hypothalamus, but in its upper part. From there it descends the spinal cord and leaves the cord at one of two levels (the areas labeled "parasympathetic outflow"). From here the impulse is conducted to the same visceral organs supplied by the sympathetic system. Note, however, that for the most part any single fiber of the parasympathetic system serves relatively fewer visceral organs than does any single fiber of the sympathetic system.

triggered off by the preganglionic neurons that come from the spinal cord. These preganglionic neurons, in turn, receive impulses from the cerebrospinal system by way of the hypothalamus.

The hypothalamus is involved in almost all patterned visceral reactions. Injury to the hypothalamus can result in disturbances in stomach reactions, metabolic functions, temperature regulation. Because of this, the hypothalamus has sometimes been called the "head ganglion" of the autonomic system. The close relationship between the hypothalamus and the autonomic system is seen from the following rather disquieting fact: When a surgeon operates in the region of the hypothalamus, he puts some strain on the tissue there. Simply tugging on this tissue is likely to cause such intense changes in heart rate, blood pressure, body temperature, that one authority (Guyton, 1956) estimates that 40 per cent of the mortality rate from hypothalamus operations is due to these factors alone.

When we remember that the hypothalamus, in turn, is connected with the cortex as well as with other centers of the brain, we can see that the brain controls the viscera! Again the moral is driven home that the organism is an integrated system.

Bodily Changes in Emotion. Many of the visceral reactions accompanying emotional states are unobservable to the naked eye. The development of ingenious measurement instruments—polygraphs, amplifiers, oscillographs—has made possible the detection and precise recording of many of these visceral events. The study of bodily changes during emotion has many theoretical and medical and other practical applications. Perhaps the two most commonly used (and most sensitive) measures of bodily effects of emotion are the changes in the electrical characteristics of the skin and the variations in blood pressure.

GALVANIC SKIN RESPONSE. It was early discovered that under emotional or motivational stress the electrical properties of the skin undergo change. If a very weak electrical current (one that cannot be felt by the person) is passed through the skin and the resistance of the skin to the passage of this current is measured with a galvanometer, it is found that *under emotional stress the resistance drops.* When Anyman is in an emotional state, his skin becomes a better conductor of electricity.

It was later found that the change in the electrical properties of the skin could be measured without passing an outside current through the skin. Stress or excitement alone can lead to a change in the electrical potential of the skin.

The change in skin resistance, or in electrical potential, has been known by many names, some of them still in use. Among the more common are galvanic skin response (abbreviated to GSR) and psychogalvanic reflex (PGR).

In one way or another these changes are related to sweating. When the skin sweats, it becomes a better electrical conductor, as is true of any wet conductor. If, therefore, at such a time a current is passed through the skin, it will show a lowered resistance. In the case of skin potential (in which no outside current is used) two theories have been proposed. One is that secretion of sweat brings about an electrochemical effect in the skin which produces a change in electrical potential. The other theory considers the change in electrical potential as a muscular effect. Since we know that every time a muscle contracts a small electrical current is created, we should find, according to this theory, that when the smooth muscles of the sweat glands contract, the "skin" potential also changes. In other words, what we record when we measure skin potentials is really the potentials created by the contraction of the smooth muscles of the sweat glands. Whichever theory is correct (or even if both theories are sound), the action of the sweat glands is obviously involved in the GSR.

Physiological and anatomical evidence indicates that the sweat glands are supplied exclusively by the sympathetic nervous system. Therefore, any time there is a change in the GSR, there must have been sympathetic nervous system activity. Since the sympathetic nervous system is thrown into action when the individual is under stress, a change in the GSR indicates emotional or motivational arousal. It is for this reason that the GSR has become such a popular measure of emotionality. It is a specially valuable indicator of emotionality because the person is not conscious of the changes in his skin, cannot do anything to inhibit them, and for this reason would find it difficult to deceive the instrument.

A major difficulty with the GSR as a measure of emotionality stems from the firm interrelationship between the cerebrospinal and autonomic nervous systems. Almost any sensory stimulus (flashing a light in the eye) or concentrated mental activity may also be accompanied by changes in GSR. The activity of the autonomic nervous system and changes in the GSR are not, then, restricted to "emotional states." Whether we are experiencing the emotions of sex or rage, or showing mental alertness on a high intellectual plane, our brain and sweat glands are involved.

BLOOD PRESSURE. The heart contracts and expands as its muscles contract and expand rhythmically. As the blood leaves the heart, it is pumped out in spurts into the constraining arteries. The pressure of the blood as it courses through the circulatory system can change, with astonishing rapidity, when the person becomes emotional. The simplest device for measuring the pressure of the blood flow is the sphygmomanometer (see Fig. 87).

The regulation of blood flow and blood pressure is partially controlled through various hormonal elements secreted from the adrenals, and partially through the movements of the skeletal muscles that help to force blood through some of the peripheral vessels (e.g., stamping our feet to keep warm). However the major controlling mechanism is the autonomic nervous system.

Most of the blood vessels of the body are supplied mainly by the sympathetic nerves, although a few are supplied by both the sympathetic and the parasympathetic. These autonomic nerves can do two things. They can change the diameter of the arteries (relaxing or constricting the smooth muscles that surround them) and they can alter the force and rate of the heart stroke. Both effects will change the blood pressure and control the supply of blood to various parts of the body. By constricting the blood vessels in some parts of the body (say in the stomach walls) and dilating the blood vessels in other parts (say in the limbs), they can cause the blood to flow rapidly and in large quantities from the constricted parts of the system to the dilated parts. In this way the most active tissues (the muscles of Anyman's limbs when he is frightened and turns to run away from a threatening situation) receive a quickly mobilized and plentiful supply of blood—just when they need it most.

It is precisely because of these effects that changes in blood pressure and blood flow are considered as the best bodily indicators of the preparatory or *emergency* functions performed by the autonomic nervous system. Many other autonomic effects of emotion can also be interpreted as providing immediate sources of energy for emergency action. Since a situation that requires a sudden and sustained action on the part of an organism is also one that arouses an "emotional" response, Cannon as we have already noted, has suggested that the role of emotions and their accompanying visceral reactions is to facilitate emergency action. This concept is frequently referred to as the *emergency theory of emotions*.

Whatever the functional value of blood pressure changes in keeping Mr. Anyman from harm, it is clear that almost every emotional state is accompanied by noticeable changes (usually increases) in blood pressure. Physicians keep this in mind when measuring the blood pressure of their patients. Entering a physician's office for a medical examination may provoke, in some patients, an anxiety state that can raise their blood pressures considerably.

OTHER BODILY CHANGES. Many other bodily changes accompany emotion. Among them are changes in the rate, depth, and pattern of breathing; dilation and contraction of the pupil of the eye; changes in the chemical constitution of the blood, saliva, and urine; over-all metabolic changes in the body; and changes in the chemical and mechanical action of the stomach and intestines (see Box 78). All these effects are controlled by the integrated actions of the cerebrospinal nervous system, the autonomic nervous system, and the hormonal system.

An important problem in this area concerns the specificity of the bodily changes that accompany emotion. Here the ques-

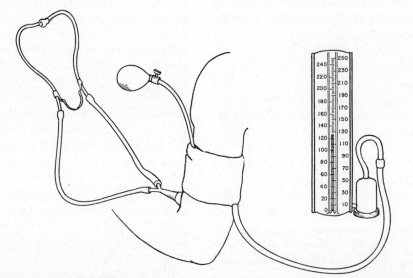

FIG. 87. The sphygmomanometer can measure the two kinds of pressure in a major artery, *systolic* and *diastolic*. Systolic pressure is the maximum pressure shown by the blood during the contraction phase of the heart, diastolic is the minimum pressure shown during the expansion phase. In measuring these with a sphygmomanometer, a rubber tube, connected to an air bulb, is first wound around the person's arm; the diaphragm of a stethoscope is then placed on the arm just below the tube. Air is pumped into the rubber tube until circulation in the artery is blocked off by the pressure of the tube. When this point has been reached, the heart sounds can no longer be heard through the stethoscope. The pressure is then gradually released until the first pulse sounds are heard again. Now the pressure of the blood is just strong enough to break through the pressure exerted on the artery by the tube tied around the arm. At this point we read off from the mercury column (connected with the rubber tube) how much pressure is being applied to the rubber tube encircling the arm. This is the systolic pressure. Then the pressure in the tube is further decreased. As this happens the pulse sounds disappear again, the blood begins to course more freely, and only muffled sounds are heard. We have now reached the diastolic blood pressure.

BOX 78

Psychological Factors and Gastric Ulcers in the Rat

Bodily changes that accompany emotional states may cause permanent damage to the body. It has long been believed that stomach ulcers may be due, at least in part, to the constant irritation and stimulation of the gastrointestinal tract consequent upon emotional stress. In 1956 Sawrey and Weisz, at the University of Colorado Medical School, succeeded in inducing experimental gastric ulcers in rats by placing the rats in a "conflict situation."

The apparatus consisted of three large rectangular boxes with brass-rod grid floors. Each box contained a food platform at one end and a water bottle at the other. The grid floor was divided electrically into 3 equal sections. The 2 sections next to the food and water were kept continuously charged, the center portion, uncharged.

Nine animals (3 in each box) were placed in the uncharged section and left to live in the box for 30 days. During every 48th hour the shock was turned off and the rats were allowed to eat and drink at will. During the other 47 hours the animals had to cross one of the charged sections of the floor to get food or water. In this way a strong approach-avoidance conflict was produced: the rats sought to *approach* the goals but at the same time held back because of the fear of shock.

A control group of 5 rats was kept on a 47-hour hunger and thirst schedule for 30 days in their home cages in order to observe the effects of food and water deprivation alone. Both the control and "conflict" rats were sacrificed and autopsied at the end of the 30-day period.

No evidence of gastric ulcers was found among the 5 control animals. Among 6 of the 9 "conflict" animals numerous ulcers were found in the lower region of the stomach. Actually, 2 of these 6 rats died before the experiment was over because of extensive stomach hemorrhages.

Later experiments indicated that shock plus hunger (without conflict) could account for some but not all of the results. Psychological conflict *per se* contributed greatly to ulcer formation.

If the rat's stomach is that sensitive to bodily expressions of emotion, what about Mr. Anyman's stomach?

SAWREY, W. L., and WEISZ, J. D. 1956. An experimental method of producing gastric ulcers. *J. comp. physiol. Psychol.*, 49, 269–70.

SAWREY, W. L., CONGER, J. J., and TURREL, E. S. 1956. An experimental investigation of the role of psychological factors in the production of gastric ulcers in rats. *J. comp. physiol. Psychol.*, 49, 457–61.

---

tion is: does each different emotional experience (hate, fear, love) have a different pattern of autonomic effects? Until fairly recently it was believed that the bodily changes were diffuse and nondifferentiating among the different emotions. More recent research, taking advantage of our increased knowledge of the functioning of the sympathetic and parasympathetic systems, holds out promise that we will find a somewhat different pattern of autonomic responses for different groups of emotional states. This research development is, however, too recent to permit us to answer the question with any certainty.

THE LIE DETECTOR. One practical application of the findings that emotional stress is accompanied by measurable but involuntary and frequently unconscious bodily changes has been in police work and lie detection.

The so-called "lie detector" consists of several pieces of apparatus simultaneously recording many of the autonomic bodily changes. The theory of the lie detector is simple enough. Since the GSR, blood pressure, heart rate, and respiration (the four most commonly used indices) show changes with emotional stress, it is argued that if a culprit is asked questions the truthful answers to which can have dire consequences for him, he will be thrown into an emotional state. Therefore, while he may control his *verbal* answers to these questions, he cannot control his *autonomic* "answers." His words may deceive, but his GSR, his blood pressure, and his heart beats will bear witness against him.

This method, however, is far from foolproof. *Any* emotional response, whether of an innocent or a guilty person, will be accompanied by similar patterns of autonomic changes. A lie detector cannot differentiate clearly between the lie of the guilty person and the fear of the unjustly accused person.

To avoid this difficulty several techniques have been used. One of these is to attempt to ask questions that are provoking to the guilty person and not to the innocent. Suppose a man has been picked up by the police on the suspicion of having poisoned his neighbor with arsenic. Suppose, further, that the police have been able to determine that the arsenic was bought at the Well-being Drug Store. Presumably only the police, the drug clerk, and the murderer know this fact. The suspect, during his questioning, may be asked, among other things, whether he is familiar with the Natty Clothing Store, the Fuming Cigar Store, and the Well-being Drug Store. The supposition is that if he is innocent, he will show no more changes in his autonomic responses to being asked about the drug store than about the clothing or the cigar store. On the other hand, if he is guilty, the question about the drug store will evoke a greater change in his GSR, blood pressure, heart rate, and respiration.

But all these techniques are not without possibilities of error. Suspect Anyman may be carrying on an extracurricular affair with the cosmetic clerk at the Well-being Drug Store and may therefore show an emotional response to the question—but

still be completely innocent of murder. All that a lie detector can detect (at present) is an emotional reaction to a question; it cannot detect lies *as such*. Nevertheless, in the hands of a skilled operator, and with due caution in the interpretation of results, the lie detector has proved to be a great aid in modern police work.

Theories of Emotion. An emotion always includes two components: there is an emotional feeling and there is a pattern of visceral and skeletal bodily reactions. Several theories have been suggested that seek to describe the temporal sequence of the cortical and the muscular events that occur in this aroused state. That is, these theories attempt to state which comes first—the feeling or the bodily reaction. One of the early attempted answers was the James-Lange theory. This theory was formulated by William James, the American psychologist, in 1884, and almost simultaneously (1885), but independently, by the Danish physiologist, Carl Lange.

THE JAMES-LANGE THEORY. Figure 88 diagrams the interrelationships between the cortex and the bodily changes as envisaged by the James-Lange theory. Let us take the case of Mr. Anyman encountering a bear. According to this theory the bear first stimulates one of Mr. Anyman's sensory receptors, say the eye (R). Sensory impulses are then sent from the retina to the cortex (along path 1). When these impulses reach the cortex, Mr. Anyman perceives a bear, but this conscious experience has no emotional feeling. However Mr. Anyman may perceive the bear as a dangerous animal and decide that something must be done about it. As soon as this happens, motor impulses from the cortex are sent down through the spinal cord (path 2) to the skeletal muscles (Sk M) and smooth muscles (V) of the body. The skeletal muscles will be thrown into activity and so will the

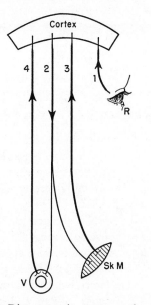

FIG. 88. Diagrammatic representation of the James-Lange theory. For explanation see text. (Adapted from Cannon, 1931.)

smooth muscles. Mr. Anyman, in other words, will turn and run, his blood pressure will rise, his pupils dilate, his heart beat will increase in rate, and his sweat glands will begin to secrete. When *these* events occur, another set of sensory impulses, this time from the skeletal and smooth muscles, will be initiated. When these sensory impulses reach the cortex (along paths 3 and 4), Mr. Anyman will *perceive* that he is running, will become aware of his increased heart beat, his increased breathing rate, his sweating, etc. It is the perception of these bodily events, according to James, which *is* the emotional feeling.

The James-Lange theory, then, gives the bodily changes (skeletal- and smooth-muscle effects) priority over the conscious awareness as far as temporal sequence is concerned.

THE CANNON-BARD THEORY. In 1927 Walter Cannon suggested an alternative

theory. Cannon's theory was taken up by another physiologist, Philip Bard, who revised Cannon's formulation and then did much experimental work in support of the theory. This theory has become known as the Cannon-Bard theory. Current thinking seems to favor a modernized variant of the Cannon-Bard theory over the James-Lange theory.

Figure 89 diagrams the relationships as envisaged by a modern statement of the Cannon-Bard theory. Again let us suddenly confront Mr. Anyman with an uncaged, unleashed bear.

The bear stimulates the retina of Mr. Anyman. The consequent sensory neural impulses start toward the cortex. En route to the cortex (path 1) they pass through the thalamus and also send off fibers to the hypothalamus. Once they reach these areas, any one of several events may occur. The neurons of the thalamic-hypothalamic complex will be thrown into a *state of readiness* to send their signals down to the

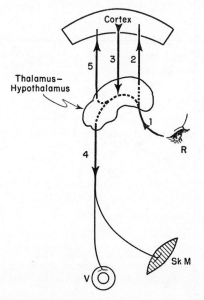

FIG. 89. Diagrammatic representation of the Cannon-Bard theory. For explanation see text. (Adapted from Cannon, 1931.)

skeletal muscles and the viscera. At the same time, impulses from the thalamus (path 2) will reach the cortex and Mr. Anyman will perceive that a bear is out there in front of him. When Mr. Anyman perceives the bear, one of two things can happen. He may decide that the bear is not really dangerous. In that event his cortex will send down signals to the thalamic-hypothalamic complex (path 3) which *inhibit* the hypothalamus from discharging its impulses into the viscera. On the other hand, he may decide that the bear *is* dangerous. In that event, the "at the ready" pattern of discharge in the hypothalamus will not be inhibited but discharged to various bodily organs (through path 4). When this occurs Mr. Anyman runs, sweats, increases his breathing rate, etc. *At the same time* the thalamus sends neural signals up to the cortex (path 5). When these signals from the hypothalamus reach the cortex, the feeling of emotion is added to the perception of the bear.

Certain very strong emotional stimuli (e.g., sudden loud noises) are capable of *directly exciting* the discharge from the hypothalamus in spite of cortical inhibition. A common instance of this may be found in the "startle" response. In this case the pathway would be from 1 directly to 4 and 5.

It will be seen that according to this theory, the emotional feeling and bodily reactions occur *simultaneously*, and both are initiated by the lower brain centers.

Whatever the sequence of events, it is clear that in both theories the cortex plays an important role in the aroused motivational-emotional state. Emotion is not under the sole jurisdiction of the autonomic system.

The Autonomic and Endocrine Systems. Just as we have seen that the autonomic nervous system is co-ordinated with the cerebrospinal nervous system, so is it with the endocrine or hormonal system. At some points, indeed, the autonomic system operates in a "hormonal manner." The sympathetic nerves secrete or produce chemicals that act very much like adrenaline—the hormone produced by a part of the adrenal gland. These chemicals are diffused into the visceral organs where the nerve ends, and stimulate the organ to action. Consequently the effects of stimulating a visceral organ (e.g., the heart) via a sympathetic nerve are very similar to the effects obtained by injecting adrenaline into the system.

Not only do the autonomic nerves secrete hormonelike substances, but they also control the activity of many of the endocrine glands themselves. Clearly there is a very intimate interrelationship between the autonomic nervous system and the hormonal, or endocrine system.

The Endocrine System

The organism contains a number of glands that manufacture various chemical products. Some of these glands have *ducts*, or outlets, which direct these products into specific and localized areas of the body. Examples of these are the tear glands, which secrete tears into the eyes, and the salivary glands, which secrete saliva into the mouth. Other glands have no ducts, but secrete their products directly into the blood stream, which then carries these chemical products, called hormones, throughout the system. These glands are called *ductless glands* or *endocrine glands*.

Among the endocrine glands important for behavior are the gonads, the thyroid, the pituitary, and the adrenals (see Fig. 90). In general, we can distinguish two different systems of control of these glands: (1) Some of the glands (e.g., the anterior lobe of the pituitary gland, the thyroid gland,

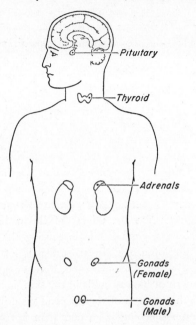

FIG. 90. The location of the major endocrine glands involved in emotions and motivation.

and the gonads) form a self-regulating and co-ordinated system. For example, certain hormonal secretions of the pituitary gland control the activity of the thyroid and the gonads. In turn, the hormones produced by the thyroid and gonads determine the rate of production of these pituitary gland hormones. (2) Some of the endocrine glands (e.g., the adrenal medulla) are dependent upon their connections with the autonomic nervous system for their stimulation and control.

The hormonal secretions of the endocrine glands, as they are carried through the body by the blood stream, call forth many different kinds of reactions from the visceral organs into which they diffuse. As far as their influence on behavior is concerned, these reactions are of two general types. On the one hand they have a temporary effect upon immediate behavior. For example, adrenaline has the same emergency and energizing effect, during fear, which the autonomic nervous system has.

On the other hand, the constant and regulated secretions of the endocrine glands have long-lasting effects, helping to determine the general level of energy, the general level of sex drive, etc. They are the biochemical mechanisms that help to determine our *continuing* motivational and emotional structure.

The Gonads. The gonads, or sex glands (the *testes* in the male, the *ovaries* in the female) have both glandular and nonglandular functions. Their nonglandular function is the production of germ cells (spermatazoa in the male and ova or eggs in the female). Their hormonal function is the secreting of the so-called sex hormones. We shall discuss germ-cell production in Chapter 21, and restrict our discussion here to hormonal functions.

THE TESTES. The testes produce several hormones, among them *testosterone*, the male sex hormone. It should be noted that the normal testes also produce *estrogen*, the female sex hormone. Very little is known about the function of estrogen in the male. Some endocrinologists have suggested that when too much estrogen is produced in the male, it leads to feminine characteristics in the bodily development and behavior of the male. But the evidence for this is not very convincing.

Testosterone and *androsterone* (another male sex hormone whose site of production is not definitely established) are both called *androgens*, and they seem to have three major functions: (1) They speed up the growth of the male sex organs, and thus prepare the individual for normal male sexual behavior and reproduction. (2) They initiate and regulate the development of "secondary sex characteristics." (3) They help to determine the sex drive and sexual behavior of the person.

Among the secondary sex characteristics that testosterone controls are the following: it determines the growth and distribution of hair on the body; it stimulates the enlargement of the larynx (Adam's apple), with a consequent change in the voice of the boy so that he develops the typical masculine bass voice; it controls the skeletal proportions of the body; it increases the thickness of the skin of the body and tends to give it a rough texture. These and similar changes can be seen to occur with great rapidity during adolescence, when there is a great increase of testosterone secretion. An indication of the role of testosterone in these bodily changes is seen in castration effects. If the male sex glands are removed prior to maturity, the secondary sex characteristics will not develop in the male. But if testosterone is administered in time, normal male development does take place.

The production of testosterone is regulated by hormones from the pituitary gland. These hormones are called *luteinizing hormones*. The quantity of testosterone secreted by the gonads varies approximately in proportion to the amount of the luteinizing hormones available in the blood stream. But there is a reciprocal relationship between the activity of the anterior pituitary gland and the gonads. That is, the amount of the luteinizing hormone which is secreted by the pituitary gland depends upon the amount of testosterone available. An interesting illustration of this is seen in castration. When the male is castrated, with a consequent radical decrease of testosterone in his system, the anterior pituitary glands begin to produce greatly increased quantities of its hormone—in a vain "attempt" to stimulate the production of testosterone. Here we have a nice illustration of the balanced interplay that is characteristic of the self-regulatory type of hormonal control.

THE OVARIES. The ovaries produce two types of hormones: *estrogens* and *progesterone*. Estrogen is the female "opposite number" of testosterone. Estrogen is responsible for the growth of the female sex organs, the development of the girl's secondary sex characteristics, and for partial control of the sex drive. Estrogen causes fat deposits in the breast, promotes the growth of the breast's milk-producing mechanisms, and in general is responsible for the characteristic appearance of the mature female breast. It also controls the fat deposits on the thighs, causing the broadened hips characteristic of the feminine figure. It has been suggested that estrogen, in opposition to the effects of the male sex hormones, plays a role in causing the skin to develop a special texture that is soft and usually very smooth, and induces a rich growth of blood vessels in the skin, increasing the warmth of the skin and resulting in greater bleeding from cuts than is true of men.

Progesterone, the other female sex hormone, seems to be primarily concerned with the immediate preparation of the uterus for pregnancy and of the breasts for lactation. The production of both female sex hormones is controlled in much the same manner as are the male sex hormones, by a reciprocal relationship with the hormones of the anterior pituitary gland.

THE SEXUAL MOTIVE. The magnitude of the sex drive in the male and female is at least partially related to the rate of secretion of the sex hormones. But this seems to be more true of the lower animals than it is of the primates and especially of the human being. For example: Removal of the sex glands of the rat during infancy prevents the appearance of mating reactions in adulthood. Removal of the sex glands during adulthood results in a gradual loss of sexual activity in the male rat, and an immediate loss of sexual responsiveness in the female. However normal sexual responsiveness can be recovered by proper hormonal treatment (see Fig. 91).

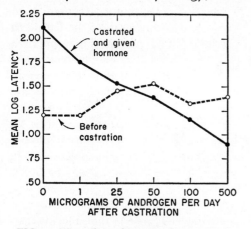

FIG. 91. The effect of hormonal treatment on copulatory behavior of castrated male rats. "Mean log latency" refers to the interval of time which elapsed between the introduction of a receptive female and the occurrence of the first copulation. After castration and with no treatment (zero on the horizontal scale) the mean log latency ran from about 1.25 (prior to castration) to well over 2.00. With 1 microgram of androgen per day, the latency dropped to 1.72. In general, the speed with which coitus is initiated by the castrated male depends upon the amount of the male hormone given. With 500 micrograms per day the mean log latency of the castrate is even less than that of the normal. (After Beach, 1951.)

The story for the human being is somewhat different. Prepuberal castrated men are rarely, if ever, capable of complete sexual response, although *some* sexual activity is present. In adult men removal of the testes sometimes causes marked reduction in sex drive, but very frequently no change is experienced in sexual behavior for as long as 20 years after the operation. It appears that in some men testicular hormone is not necessary for normal sexual activity.

Two general principles may be formulated: (1) Gonadal hormones are essential for the normal *development* of sexuality and responsible to a lesser degree for the continuing level of the drive. (2) As we go up the evolutionary scale from the lower mammals to the human being there is a progressive relaxation of the hormonal control over sexuality. This second principle suggests that other controlling mechanisms take over in the higher animal forms. There is a host of physiological factors which contribute toward sexual responsiveness. Among these are the general metabolism of the individual and the controlling influence of the cerebrospinal nervous system.

It has been shown that an insufficient diet can delay the onset of adult sexual behavior in the rat. Observations made on the behavior and attitudes of prisoners of war and concentration-camp inmates who are forced to live on inadequate diets and are almost constantly in a state of hunger show that they have a marked decrease in sexual interest.

But of major interest is the role of the cerebrospinal nervous system. Experimental evidence indicates quite clearly that sexual behavior is intimately dependent upon the activities of various cortical areas and of the hypothalamus. For one thing, the sexual act is a complicated one, demanding the co-ordination of various skeletal muscles, vascular changes, and other autonomically controlled bodily processes. The integration of these processes becomes increasingly dependent upon the cortex as we go up the evolutionary scale. It is obvious, for example, that the initiating stimulus for the sex act is frequently an ideational or perceptual one. It is therefore not very surprising that with increased cortical destruction there is frequently found a decreasing inclination or even ability to perform the sex act. (See Fig. 92.)

For another thing, the cortex can also *inhibit* the sexual response, which seems to be *released* by other brain centers. Schreiner and Kling (1953) found that destruction in the cat of parts of the brain resulted in an extreme state of *continuous hypersexuality* in the animals. Their interpretation of these results suggests that de-

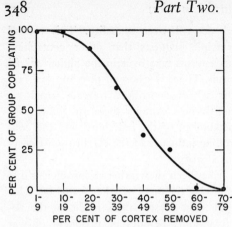

FIG. 92. The effects of cortical injury on the mating behavior of male rats. Each point represents a separate group of animals and indicates the per cent of that group which continued to copulate after cortical destruction. Destruction of less than 20 per cent of the cortex affected very few animals. Destruction of 50 to 59 per cent of the cortex completely eliminated mating in 75 per cent of the rats. No rat with 60 per cent or more of his cortex destroyed was observed to copulate. (It is of interest to note that female rats continue to mate despite *total* decortication.) (After Beach, 1951.)

struction of these brain areas removes the controlling mechanism in the brain which regulates sexual behavior.

Sexual motivation, perhaps more than any other motive of whose physiology we have even an inkling, is dependent upon every integrating mechanism in the body—the cerebrospinal nervous system, the autonomic nervous system, and the hormonal system. Both physiological and psychological evidence testify to the complex interrelationships involved in the sex motive. Sex is certainly not simply a hormonal response. It, too, is a "perfink."

As is true of most hormones, the sex hormones are not limited, in their effectiveness, to sexual behavior alone. We have already seen this in discussing the secondary sex characteristics, which are controlled by the sex hormones. Another illustration is found in the *menopause* or climacteric. The menopause is a condition that occurs in women normally at about the age of fifty (although there are wide individual age differences). At this time there is a diminution in the rate of secretion of the ovarian hormones. When this happens, menstruation ceases, and the ovaries, uterus, mammary glands, and vagina begin to atrophy. Frequently, but not always, this is accompanied by a series of general physiological and emotional upsets—depression, anxiety, unrest. Recent evidence suggests that many of the emotional upsets are partly due to "psychological" factors, as well as to the change in the endocrine balance resulting from the decrease in sex hormone secretion.

The Thyroid Gland. The hormone released by the thyroid gland has a general and continuous effect on the body, and a series of specific effects on the viscera during emotional excitement. The most general effect of the thyroid hormone is to increase tremendously the metabolic activities of almost all cells of the body. As a consequence, greatly increased thyroid hormone production almost always decreases body weight, while greatly decreased secretion increases weight. These effects are especially noticeable in various thyroid gland abnormalities. With *hyperthyroidism*—a condition of continuous excessive thyroid hormone production with a corresponding enlargement of the thyroid glands—a disturbance in skeletal growth may occur. With *hypothyroidism*—a condition of chronic insufficient production—the rate of growth is slowed down, and various pathological conditions may result.

CRETINISM. Extreme hypothyroidism before birth and during infancy and childhood results in a pathological condition called *cretinism.* The individual is dwarfed and various growth abnormalities are present, such as a protruding stomach, enlarged tongue, and dry, cold skin. Mental growth is also retarded and the cretin child will be feeble-minded. Treatment of the cretin child at any time after birth will usually result in a normal return of physical growth. However, unless the cretin is treated very soon after birth, his mental growth will be permanently retarded. This is probably due to the fact that the development of the brain cells immediately after birth is very rapid. Any inadequacy in the metabolism of the brain cells during the first few months of life may, therefore, be permanently injurious. Here we have another illustration of the interaction between the hormonal system and the highest levels of the cerebrospinal nervous system.

THYROID HORMONE AND EMOTIONAL EXCITEMENT. Following or accompanying emotional excitement there is an increased secretion of the thyroid hormone into the blood stream. The effect of this increased supply is manifold. Among other things it tends to raise the blood pressure, increase the rate and depth of breathing, speed up the heart rate, and make the person generally irritable and "nervous." We have here much the same picture that results from stimulation of the autonomic nervous system. And, indeed, the experimental and clinical evidence indicates that there is a close connection between the activity of the thyroid gland and the autonomic nervous system. This connection, however, is a somewhat indirect one, operating via the pituitary gland.

The sympathetic nervous system can stimulate the pituitary gland into the secretion of a *thyrotropic hormone.* This hormone, in turn, stimulates the thyroid gland, which then secretes its hormone. One would expect, then, that continuous emotional stress can result in continuous excess secretion of thyroid hormone. Clinical evidence supports this reasoning. A large percentage of people who develop "thyrotoxic goiter"—an enlargement of the thyroid due to its constant activity—do so after prolonged and serious emotional disturbance. Again we see that the bodily effects of "psychic disturbance" may be lasting ones.

The Pituitary Gland. The anterior and posterior pituitary glands seem to be two quite separate glands lying close to each other. As far as is known, no functional relationship exists between the two. The *posterior* gland is completely controlled by the hypothalamus, and its major hormone, the *antidiuretic hormone,* functions primarily to control the rate and volume of urination. Thus when no antidiuretic hormone is produced, the urine volume excreted per day ranges between 10 and 15 quarts instead of the normal 1½ quarts. Under emotional stress (where there is hypothalamic activity) therefore, large and rapid changes in the urinary activity of the person may occur. Some emotional upsets may inhibit the secretion of the antidiuretic hormone, resulting in frequent and excessive urination; other emotional states may stimulate the secretion of the hormone, causing the urinary outflow to be scanty.

THE ANTERIOR PITUITARY GLAND. We have already seen how important the anterior pituitary gland is in the control of the gonads and the thyroid. Six different hormones have been found to be secreted by the anterior pituitary. These hormones control, among other things, general bodily growth, the secretions of the adrenal cortex (see below), the secretions of the sex hormones, and the secretions of the thyroid. Each of the six hormones is specific as far as its targets are concerned.

The control of the activities of this gland is as complicated as its functions. To some degree it seems to be controlled by the hypothalamus and the autonomic nervous system. To a larger degree it is controlled, as we have seen, by the very glands which it itself controls. Because of its crucial over-all regulating function with regard to some of the most important glands in the body, the anterior pituitary has been called the "master gland" or the "sentinel gland."

The Adrenals. The adrenal gland is made up of two quite distinct parts: the *adrenal cortex* and the *adrenal medulla*. The adrenal medulla comprises the core of the gland and secretes two hormones: *epinephrine* and *nor-epinephrine*. The adrenal cortex is constructed very much like an envelope around the adrenal medulla and supplies still another series of hormones to the body. The functions of these various hormones differ considerably.

THE ADRENAL CORTEX. The adrenal cortex secretes three types of hormones, including male and female sex hormones. For a long time little was known concerning these hormones except that they were somehow essential for life, since animals whose adrenals were removed invariably died. More recent research has been able to spell out some of the functions of these hormones, but their effect on motivational and emotional behavior is still in doubt.

Although the adrenal sex hormones are similar to, or identical with, those secreted by the gonads, they seem to perform no significant sexual function in the normal person. In abnormal cases they are important. Sometimes tumors of the adrenal cortex develop, and these tumors can then secrete tremendous quantities of the adrenal cortex sex hormones. Usually the effect of these hormones is to masculinize the person. In the female it may induce many masculine secondary sex characteristics, such as a bass voice, loss of hair on the head, and growth of a beard. In the male child precocious sexual development may take place. The possible effects on personality which can result from these changes are obvious.

THE ADRENAL MEDULLA. The two hormones secreted by the adrenal medulla are chemically quite similar but have somewhat different physiological effects. Epinephrine constricts some blood vessels and dilates others (such as those in the muscles), while nor-epinephrine constricts all the blood vessels of the body. This means, for instance, that nor-epinephrine causes a greater rise in blood pressure than does epinephrine.

When epinephrine and nor-epinephrine (usually secreted in constant proportion) come into contact with smooth muscle fibers, their effect is exactly the same as the effect of stimulating these muscle fibers via the sympathetic nervous system. A common phrase is to say that the hormonal secretions from the adrenal medulla *mimic* sympathetic nerve stimulation. The function of the adrenal medulla seems to be to support the actions of the rest of the sympathetic nervous system. In fear, for example, both systems work together to prepare the person for emergency actions.

However these hormones have a *longer lasting* effect than stimulation by the sympathetic nerves. The chemical substance that is diffused in the visceral organs by the sympathetic nerve endings loses its effectiveness within 10 to 30 seconds after liberation from the nerve. The effectiveness of the epinephrine–nor-epinephrine mixture, on the other hand, lasts about 2 to 3 minutes. Here we see a very nice co-operative relationship between the two systems in preparing the body for emergency action. The sympathetic nerves stimulate the visceral organs and the adrenal glands simultaneously. Thus the visceral organs are put into immediate emergency action by the temporarily effective stimulation of the sympathetic nerves, and then reinforced by the later arrival of the more effective and longer lasting adrenal hormones via the blood stream.

Individual Variation. The notion that "normal" people have "normal" hormonal levels of activity does not correspond with the data. From the available evidence it seems clear that each person has a distinctive endocrine pattern. Even among so-called "normal" people, one endocrine gland can show as much as a 35-fold variation from person to person. (See Box 79.) As one biochemist (Williams, 1956) puts it, "The endocrine patterns of different people appear to be fully as diverse as are the habitations in which human beings live."

Personality and Hormones. Perhaps nowhere is the fact of individual differences among people more striking than in their emotional patterns of behavior. We have the calm, the excitable, the aggressive, the submissive, and many other "types" of people. When the role of hormones in emotional and motivational behavior first became apparent, together with the recog-

nition of individual variations in the "hormonal equipment" of people, it was believed that the key to the understanding of the different emotional patterns among people would be found in an analysis of their endocrine systems. Continued research in this field, however, has tempered this enthusiasm. The evidence, on the whole, indicates that there is no easily discovered relationship between variations in hormonal functioning and patterns of emotionality.

It is obvious that the endocrine system plays an important role in emotional and motivational behavior. But the effectiveness of any one hormone is determined by the *pattern* of endocrine substances, not by any one hormone alone. The influence of an excessive amount of the sex hormones may be affected by the availability of the thyroid, pituitary, and adrenal hormones. We cannot, therefore, expect to find simple relationships between the amount of any one hormone and patterns of behavior. But

---

BOX 79

Biochemical Individuality

In an extremely interesting book on biochemical individuality, R. J. Williams, a biochemist of the University of Texas, presents data on the individual biochemical make-up of man and beast. The following illustrative human data are taken from his study.

The thyroid. Normal thyroid glands vary in weight from 8 to 50 grams, and their shapes are also extremely variable. Corresponding to this anatomical variation is an even larger variability in the gland's secretory activities.

The sex glands. Ovaries in normal females vary in weight from 2 to 10 grams. Some female infants are born with ovaries containing 30,000 ova, others with ovaries containing more than 10 times that number. Estrogen output of these glands also varies greatly. Testes in males range in weight from 10 to 45 grams. One study has shown that the male sex hormone output varies

from 0.2 to 7.0 milligrams per day—a 35-fold range among normal men.

The pituitary gland. Some people have pituitaries weighing but 350 milligrams, others 1,100 milligrams. In some people the anterior lobe comprises 56 per cent of the total weight of the gland; in others it accounts for 92 per cent. There is equally wide variation in the hormone output of this "master gland."

The adrenals. The adrenal glands vary in weight from about 7 to 20 grams. The adrenal cortex varies in its thickness from 0.5 to 5.0 millimeters, and it is assumed that there is a corresponding 10-fold variation in the activity of the cortex.

Each of us has his own distinctive pattern of endocrine gland activity. People *are* different.

WILLIAMS, R. J. 1956. *Biochemical individuality.* New York: Wiley.

more than that, we have seen that the endocrine system is but one system among several that control emotional and motivated behavior. The autonomic nervous system and the cerebrospinal nervous system also play significant roles. Finally, we must remember that the individual is a product not only of his internal environment but also of his external environment—his cultural background and history of experiences. A discussion of personality, therefore, must be reserved for the last part of the book.

Glossary

adrenals. Consist of two distinct parts. The *adrenal cortex* secretes three types of hormones, including male and female sex hormone. The *adrenal medulla*, comprising the core of the gland, secretes *epinephrine* and *nor-epinephrine*, and plays an important role in controlling the visceral accompaniments of emotion.

androgens. The general name for the male sex hormones. Includes testosterone and androsterone.

androsterone. A male sex hormone whose site of production is not definitely established. Seems to have the same effects as does testosterone.

antidiuritic hormone. A hormone secreted by the posterior pituitary gland. It functions primarily to control the rate and volume of urination. Emotional upset may inhibit secretion of the hormone, resulting in frequent and excessive urination.

autonomic nervous system. The nervous system that supplies the visceral organs and is mainly responsible for the automatic responses of the body. The autonomic system is comprised of two subsystems—the sympathetic and the parasympathetic.

Cannon-Bard theory. A theory proposed by Cannon and modified somewhat by Bard to the effect that the emotional *feeling* and the body *reaction* occur simultaneously, and that both of them are initiated by the lower brain centers of the thalamus and hypothalamus. To be contrasted with the James-Lange theory.

cerebrospinal nervous system. That part of the nervous system which includes the sensory nerves, the brain, the spinal column, and the motor nerves. Sometimes the term "central nervous system" (C.N.S.) is used to refer to this system. The cerebrospinal nervous system is to be differentiated from the autonomic nervous system.

cretinism. A pathological condition due to extreme and chronic hypothyroidism during early life. The individual is dwarfed, typically shows a protruding stomach, enlarged tongue, and dry, cold skin. Mental growth is retarded. Early thyroid treatment of the cretin child will usually result in return of normal physical and mental growth.

dehydration. There are two forms of dehydration of body tissue, either of which may initiate thirst sensations. *Absolute dehydration* refers to a decrease in the level of water in the body to less than normal; *relative dehydration* refers to a state in which there is less than the normal amount of water relative to the amount of salt.

dorsomedial nucleus. A hypothalamic nucleus. Electrical stimulation of this nucleus evokes violent rage responses.

emergency theory of emotions. The theory which states that the evolutionary role of the emotions, with their accompanying visceral reactions, is the facilitation of emergency action in times of danger.

endocrine system. A term referring to the *ductless* glands of the body and their reactions. Ductless glands are organs of the body which manufacture chemical compounds called *hormones*, and secrete these hormones directly into the blood stream. Another name for the endocrine system is the *hormonal system*.

epinephrine—nor-epinephrine. Two chemically similar hormones secreted by the adrenal medulla. These hormones have somewhat different effects on the visceral organs, but in general their combined effect is the same as the effect of stimulating the visceral organs via the sympathetic nervous system; and they are therefore said to "mimic" the sympathetic nervous system.

estrogen. The female sex hormone manufactured and secreted by the ovaries. Seems to be partly responsible for the growth of the female sex organs, development of female secondary sex characteristics, and for control of the sex drive.

galvanic skin response. Change in the electrical potential of the skin. This often occurs during emotional excitement. Known by many other names, among them the psychogalvanic reflex (PGR).

gonads. The sex glands. In the male they are known as the *testes*, in the female as the *ovaries*.

hormones. Chemical compounds manufactured by the endocrine glands and secreted into the blood stream. The hormones, carried by the blood stream to the visceral organs of the body, can stimulate these organs into activity or can inhibit their activity.

hyperthyroidism. A condition of continuous *excessive* thyroid hormone production.

hypothalamus. A collection of specialized nuclei of brain cells lying at the base of the brain, immediately behind the optic chiasma. It receives neural impulses from a number of sources, including the frontal poles of the cerebral hemispheres, the thalamus, and the visceral organs of the body. In turn, it sends impulses to the cortex and through the autonomic system to the visceral organs, as well as to the reticular formation.

hypothyroidism. A condition of chronic *insufficient* thyroid hormone production. Extreme hypothyroidism before birth and during infancy and childhood results in a pathological condition called *cretinism*.

James-Lange theory. A theory independently proposed by William James of America and Carl Lange of Denmark to the effect that bodily changes *precede* the feeling of emotion and that it is the perception of bodily changes that *is* the emotional feeling. This theory is to be contrasted with the Cannon-Bard theory.

lateral nucleus. A hypothalamic nucleus whose destruction inhibits eating.

luteinizing hormones. A hormone secreted by the pituitary gland. The more luteinizing hormones available in the blood stream, the greater is the quantity of testosterone secreted by the testes.

menopause. A condition occurring in women normally at about the age of fifty, at which time there is a diminution in rate of secretion of ovarian hormone, cessation of menstruation, and the beginning of the atrophy of the ovaries, uterus, mammary glands, and vagina.

osmoreceptors. Postulated specialized cells in the hypothalamus presumed to be responsible for the initiation of sensory impulses evoking the sensation of thirst. The osmoreceptors are supposed to be stimulated into action when they shrink as a consequence of absolute or relative dehydration.

ovaries. Female sex glands. Have both glandular and nonglandular functions. Their nonglandular function is the production of ova, or eggs. Their glandular function is the manufacture and secretion of the sex hormones, among them estrogen and progesterone.

parasympathetic nervous system. Part of the autonomic nervous system. The parasympathetic system supplies the visceral organs via nerve fibers from the spinal cord, and is somewhat more specific in its discharge to these organs than is the sympathetic system.

pituitary gland. Consists of apparently two distinct glands. The *posterior* pituitary seems to be completely controlled by the hypothalamus, and its major hormone is the *antidiuretic* hormone. The *anterior* pituitary is controlled partly by the hypothalamus and partly by the other endocrine glands. It secretes six different hormones which control, among other things, general bodily growth, secretions of the adrenal cortex, sex glands, and thyroid. Sometimes referred to as "the master gland."

progesterone. A female sex hormone produced by the ovaries, and primarily concerned with the preparation of the uterus for pregnancy and with the breasts for lactation.

reciprocal innervation. Refers to the fact that most of the visceral organs of the body are supplied by two nervous systems—the sympathetic and the parasympathetic—whose effects on any one organ are *opposite* in direction. That is, where the sympathetic accelerates action, the parasympathetic decelerates.

secondary sex characteristics. The characteristics that distinguish the appearance and other nonreproductive differences of the male and female (e.g., distribution of hair, sound of voice, skeletal proportions of body, thickness of skin).

sham rage. The "anger" or "rage" responses shown by decorticate animals when touched or handled. These responses are so called because they are not evoked by the usual situational determinants of rage, are not directed against any specific target, and cease almost as soon as the stimulation of the animal is withdrawn.

smooth muscles. The muscles of the body controlling the contractions of the visceral organs.

sphygmomanometer. A device for measuring the systolic and diastolic pressure of blood flow in a major artery. Systolic pressure is the *maximum* pressure shown by the blood during the contraction phase of the heart; diastolic is the *minimum* pressure during the expansion phase.

striated muscles. The skeletal muscles of the body responsible for movement of limbs, etc. So called because under the microscope the muscles appear to have hori-

zontal lines running across the fibers. Sometimes called the "skeletal muscles."

sympathetic nervous system. Part of the autonomic nervous system. The sympathetic nervous system consists of two chains of ganglions running along the side of the spinal cord, and the fibers coming to and leaving these ganglia. The ganglion cells are supplied by nerve fibers from the spinal cord, called "preganglionic" neurones; they supply, in turn, various visceral organs, through connections with the post-ganglionic neurone. The sympathetic nervous system is built for widespread discharge.

testes. Male sex glands. Have both glandular and nonglandular functions. Their nonglandular function is the production of spermatozoa. Their glandular function is the manufacture and secretion of the sex hormones, among them *testosterone* (the male sex hormone) and *estrogen* (the female sex hormone).

testosterone. The male sex hormone, produced by the testes. Seems to be important in speeding up growth of the male sex organs; controls development of secondary sex characteristics, and helps to determine the sexual activity of the individual.

thyroid gland. A ductless gland whose hormones have general and specific effects. They increase metabolic action of almost all body cells, raise blood pressure, speed up heart rate, etc. The rate of production of thyroid hormone is in part controlled by a pituitary hormone called the thyrotropic hormone.

thyrotropic hormone. A hormone of the pituitary gland which controls, in part, the manufacture and secretion of thyroid hormones.

ventromedial nucleus. A hypothalamic nucleus that is involved in eating and emotional behavior. Destruction of the ventromedial nucleus results in voracious eating, and turns tame animals into savage and vicious ones.

Suggestions for Further Reading

BEACH, F. 1948. *Hormones and behavior.* New York: Hoeber.

A comprehensive survey of the research done on the effects of hormones on behavior.

MORGAN, C. T., and STELLAR, E. 1950. *Physiological psychology.* New York: McGraw-Hill.

An introductory textbook, simply written, covering some of the material discussed in the present chapter.

STEVENS, S. S. (ed.). 1951. *Handbook of experimental psychology.* New York: Wiley.

Three chapters in this standard reference book provide valuable summaries of material: Chapter 6 on *homeostasis*, by E. W. Dempsey of the Harvard Medical School; Chapter 12 on the physiological basis of *sexual and maternal behavior*, by F. A. Beach, psychologist of Yale University; and Chapter 14, by D. B. Lindsley, psychologist of the University of California, which presents current theoretical thinking on the physiology of *emotion*.

WILLIAMS, R. J. 1956. *Biochemical individuality.* New York: Wiley.

A comprehensive summary of individual differences in the hormonal compositions of man, written by a biochemist who has pioneered in this study and who has initiated the concept of "chemical anthropology."

Part Three

ADAPTIVE BEHAVIOR

CHAPTER XIII

The World of Problems

MAN must find food, shelter, and safety, and satisfy many other needs and aspirations. To do this, man must solve problems, learn, remember, think, and acquire skills—in a word he must *behave adaptively*. We must, therefore, add to the previous pictures of the many worlds of man, still another—a world inviting and demanding that he adapt to it, manipulate it, change it, and create in it.

The next five chapters will examine this adaptive behavior. Here as in Parts I and II, our first step is to describe the *experience* of man as he seeks to find ways and means of satisfying his needs.

Initiation of Adaptive Behavior

Adaptive behavior begins, most typically, when the person perceives a problem. It is obvious that unless the person "sees" a problem, he will not set about solving it. But to say that a man "sees" a problem is not to imply that the situation exists as a problem "out there" in the outside world. We have already seen in Part I that any percept is an *achievement*—reflecting the perceiver's needs as well as the immediate stimulus situation. Whether or not something will be perceived as a problem depends upon the stimulus-pattern (and to the extent that it does, the problem is "out there") and the motives of the perceiver (and to the extent that this is the case, the problem is "within" the perceiver).

Before continuing, turn to Figure 93 and follow the directions given with it.

Ego- and Task-Orientation. The two most obvious characteristics of our experience when we "have" a problem are the attributes of motive and barrier. We first begin to behave adaptively, to seek resolutions, when we experience a frustration of a need or desire. We are "ego-involved" in the problem. But, as we have already pointed out (Chapter 8), the arousal of a need does not require involvement of the self, or feelings of frustration.

FIG. 93. Look at the above drawing carefully. What is going on there? As you keep looking at it, try to remember your stream of thoughts. Spend as long as you wish at it. After you have finished with it, return to the text. As you continue reading, you will soon find out what this is all about.

We often start to think and to solve problems simply when we encounter a problem to be solved. Perhaps this is what is meant when someone says he likes to work on problems "just for the hell of it." Task-oriented experiences in problem-solving, thinking, and creative activities of all kinds are just as genuine, and perhaps just as common, as problem-solving experiences that stem from frustration and self-involvement, and merit equally our scientific attention.

When you looked at Figure 93, you may have seen a problem: how was Youngster Anyman to straighten out the painting hanging askew on the wall? When, in addition, some of you noticed the chair upon which Youngster could stand in order to reach the picture, you had gone ahead and solved the problem. All of this was done without instructions and without personal involvement or frustration. In such an instance, where one's personal needs play very little role, we speak of "task-oriented"

problem-solving. Upon experimental analysis it may very well be seen that the ultimate cause of "task-oriented" problem-solving can be traced to the motivational state of the perceiver. Nevertheless, in the immediate *experiences* of the perceiver the self does not play a salient part as he starts working on the problem.

Changing Perceptions of the Problem

As we start working on a problem and continue working away at it, our perceptions undergo continuous change. When bodily movement or manipulation of physical objects is involved (as in finding a certain house on a street, painting a picture, repairing a typewriter), the relations among the physical objects change and so do our perceptions. But even when we remain seated at a desk as we try to recall the name of an acquaintance, as we try to think through a good ending to the story we are writing, or as we attempt to solve mentally a mathematical problem, we find that the attributes and objects of our perceptual field are ever changing.

A complete, running description of our perceptions as we struggle with a problem would consist of a *stream* of ever-changing perceptions of the problem.

Discontinuities in Perception. This "stream of perceptions" is a very curious stream. There are *discontinuities* in it; it seems to disappear and go underground for short or long stretches. Even the most complete account of our experiences in solving a problem will often indicate that there are "conscious lapses," large time intervals during which the person does not seem to be "thinking" or "working" on his problem at all, and yet substantial progress seems to be made. Occasionally, progress seems to be made even while he is asleep. After such a "silent" period the solution may suddenly appear or substantial progress may be made. Because of this, these lapses in the stream of the perceptions of the problem have been labeled "incubation periods."

The moment we make a significant advance toward the solution, whether following an incubation period or not, we do have vivid and relevant experiences. With certain problems the striking changes in perception, as far as the problem solver is concerned, *are* the advance. He suddenly "sees" a solution—or partial solution.

THE QUICKLY SOLVED PROBLEM. The course of the stream differs tremendously from problem to problem. With easy problems we may find that very soon after we have perceived the problem, we have the solution. At most, in these cases, we can distinguish only two major perceptual "episodes": the initial percept and the final perception of the solution. It is as if here the stream of problem-perceptions can be described as a short, straight line with only two easily identifiable points.

THE DIFFICULT PROBLEM. Quite the contrary seems to be true of very difficult and so-called "creative" problem-solving. With difficult problems, where the solution comes only after a great deal of work, we can often distinguish (scattered among the "silent" periods) several major changes in perception: the initial perception; one or more "turning-point" percepts; and, finally, the solution percept. The turning-point percepts accompany some fairly sudden significant advance toward the final solution. Very rarely in creative problem-solving do we experience a smooth and continuous advance toward our goal. To continue our analogy, it is as if the stream of our perceptions of the problem has several major bends to be rounded before we finally sail home.

PROBLEMS WITHOUT DISCONTINUITIES. There are many instances of learning, as in memorizing a vocabulary list, in which the stream of perceptions seems to consist of minimal, steady, and cumulative changes. The perceptions at the end of the process are quite different from those at the beginning. The word *trottoir* may seem queer and somewhat ludicrous when we start our French lessons. Later it looks "right." But nowhere has the learner experienced any high points, any *sudden* changes in his perceptions of the word.

Changes in Perceptual Content. As we continue along the course of problem-solving, the perceived objects undergo changes in their physiognomic attributes, the meanings of the objects change, and the very formulation of the problem as we perceive it may be revised.

CHANGES IN PHYSIOGNOMIC ATTRIBUTES. As we continue working away at a problem, there is an increase in the *affective* qualities of the perceptual objects. The block is perceived with increasingly negative attributes, and the goal becomes more and more attractive. In some instances the self develops into so dominating an object in the perceptual field that it becomes the central point of reference. For example, the block is perceived not only as a barrier to the goal but as a personal affront.

Even if the self did not play a salient part at the beginning of problem-solving (as in task-oriented problem-solving), it very often enters into the later perceptual content. We may become "ego-involved" as we make advances or as we fail to make advances in solution of the problem. The problem now becomes a personal matter, and *we* experience dejection as we fail to make progress, *we* experience exhilaration as we suddenly see a major "break" in a mathematical problem. Feelings of achievement, of glow, of self-approval, can become dominant even in the most task-oriented problem-solving and among the "coldest" of "hard-headed thinkers."

CHANGES IN MEANINGS OF OBJECTS. As we make progress toward a solution, we find that objects change in their *meanings* for us. A limb of a tree, initially perceived with the meaning of a "limb of a tree," may now be seen as "a-long-rake-if-broken-from-the-tree"; a penny, initially perceived as a relatively worthless coin, may now be perceived as an efficient conductor of electricity; a piece of ice, initially perceived as cold and wet, may now be perceived as something that can be molded into the shape of a lens and used to focus the sun's rays to start a fire. Indeed, the perceived meanings of the same objects that make up the initial and later perceptions may be so different that it sometimes seems to the person as if entirely different objects are involved.

REFORMULATION OF THE PROBLEM. Related to the changes in meanings of objects is the change in *formulation* of the problem. This sometimes involves a change in the person's perception of the barrier. Youngster Anyman may suddenly perceive that lack of money rather than the niggardliness of his mother blocks gratification of his desire for an electric train. He now reformulates his task as that of earning money rather than cajoling his mother.

Sometimes the barrier is a creation of our own perceptual processes. As we work on the problem, we may suddenly see that what we had perceived as a block is not a block at all. Once this initial perception is changed, the entire problem changes its character. (For an illustration of this, look at Box 80.) Why problems are formulated wrongly and why the change in formulation finally does take place (if ever it does) are questions discussed in the next chapter. The significant thing here is that many blocks to the satisfaction of our own needs

and desires are of "our own making," created by our own perceptual processes.

Perceiving the Solution

As we approach the solution of a difficult problem, or of one whose solution has

---

BOX 80

Can You Solve This?

Starting anywhere you wish, draw four *straight* lines that will pass through every one of the nine dots, without lifting your pencil from the paper.

$$\begin{matrix} \bullet & \bullet & \bullet \\ \bullet & \bullet & \bullet \\ \bullet & \bullet & \bullet \end{matrix}$$

Do not read the rest of this Box until you have attempted to solve the problem. If after two minutes you have not solved the problem, read the following "hints."

The nine dots tend to be perceived as a square. But there are no boundary lines to prevent your drawing a line *extending beyond* the "perceived" edge of the "square." Nothing was ever said about staying within the "perceived confines" of the nine dots, yet the organizing nature of perception is such as to lead you to see a block to the movements of your pencil, where no block exists in fact.

been unaccountably evading us, we sometimes experience characteristic changes in perception, feelings, and even emotional excitement. One such experience occurs just prior to the solution, and the feeling can perhaps best be characterized as the "almost-there" feeling. We "see" and yet do not see the solution. It is an "on-the-tip-of-our-tongue" feeling. We feel, rather than precisely know, what should be done, but somehow we cannot phrase it, or make it concrete. It is the sort of feeling of which William James has said, the solution "tin-

gles, it trembles ɔn the verge, but does not come." The form of the solution is perceived, but it is a "contentless" form. For some vivid descriptions of such experiences see Box 81.

The most easily recognized experience in the entire stream of experiences accompanying problem-solving is the one that occasionally occurs at the very moment of solution.

The "Aha!" Experience. The unique "solution experience" does not always occur.

BOX 81

A Poet and a Psychologist Describe the "Almost-There"

In the following passages we have two descriptions of the "almost-there" experience. Both of them come from highly creative people: Paul Valéry, the French poet, and William James, the founder of American psychology.

PAUL VALÉRY: "There is that one where the man whose business is writing experiences a kind of flash—for this intellectual life, anything but passive, is really made of fragments; it is in a way composed of elements very brief, yet felt to be rich in possibilities, which do not illuminate the whole mind, which indicate to the mind, rather, that there are forms completely new which it is sure to be able to possess after a certain amount of work. Sometimes I have observed this moment when a sensation arrives at the mind; it is a gleam of light, not so much illuminating as dazzling. This arrival calls attention, points, rather than illuminates, and in fine, is itself an enigma which carries with it the assurance that it can be postponed. You say, 'I see, and then tomorrow I shall see more.' There is an activity, a special sensitization; soon you will go into the dark-room and the picture will be seen to emerge." (*Quoted in* Hadamard.)

*   *   *

WILLIAM JAMES: "Suppose we try to recall a forgotten name. The state of our consciousness is peculiar. There is a gap therein; but no mere gap. It is a gap that is intensely active. A sort of wraith of the name is in it, beckoning us in a given direction, making us at moments tingle with the sense of our closeness, and then letting us sink back without the longed-for term. If wrong names are proposed to us, this singularly definite gap acts immediately so as to negate them. They do not fit into its mould. And the gap of one word does not feel like the gap of another, all empty of content as both might seem necessarily to be when described as gaps. . . . But the feeling of an absence is *toto coelo* other than the absence of a feeling. It is an intense feeling. The rhythm of a lost word may be there without a sound to clothe it; or the evanescent sense of something which is the initial vowel or consonant may mock us fitfully, without growing more distinct. Every one must know the tantalizing effect of the blank rhythm of some forgotten verse, restlessly dancing in one's mind, striving to be filled out with words." (*From James*, Principles of Psychology.)

HADAMARD, J. 1949. *Psychology of invention in the mathematical field*. Princeton: Princeton Univ. Press. Reprinted by permission from Dover Publications, Inc., New York. $1.25 paper.
JAMES, W. 1890. *Principles of psychology*. New York: Holt.

But when it does, it is unmistakably different from most of our other experiences. It is sudden, it is complete, it is intense. When we attempt to communicate our experiences at such a moment, we make liberal use of such descriptive words as "suddenly," "like a flash," "dazzling." We often cry out with an explosive, "That's it!" "Of course!" "Oh sure!" If we had happened to be a Greek mathematician named Archimedes who had just found the solution to King Hiero's problem of assaying the gold content of his crown, we would (or so goes the ancient story) have leaped from the tub in a rush of joy and run through the streets shouting loudly to the world (in classical Greek, of course), "I have found it, I have found it!" We are referring to the "insight" experience.

Even the psychologist's more technical descriptions of this experience frequently call upon vivid words. The Gestalt psychologists (see p. 90) who have emphasized "insight" in their description of problem-solving, frequently refer to it as "the Aha! experience." (See Box 82.)

Although we are interested at this point only in describing this experience and not in explaining it, we should note several points:

1. Not all learning and problem-solving ends with this sudden and intense experience. As we have already suggested, memorizing a list of history dates, or working out an arithmetic problem by well-known methods, seems to be devoid of this exhilarating sensation. Even with such problems it is possible that we have minor "aha!" experiences, but if we do, they are too pale a copy of the real thing to be noticed.

2. Insights can come when solving simple as well as complex problems. Mr. Anyman, remembering the name of the girl who sat next to him thirty years earlier in Grade 3B

BOX 82

The Aha! Experience—as Seen by a Psychologist and Her Subject

The "aha!" phenomenon as seen by the psychologist looking on, and as reported by one person undergoing the experience, is found in an experiment by Helen Durkin at Columbia University.

Each subject was given a puzzle, with the instructions: "As you solve, please think aloud. Express every idea as it comes to you as you work even if it seems irrelevant. Try to tell me also how you feel about it as you go along. My chief interest is to find out as fully as possible just what goes on in your mind as you work."

Here is Durkin's description of her subjects' behavior at the moment of sudden reorganization of their perceptions—usually just before they solved the puzzle:

"A short pause of peculiarly quiet intentness which sometimes involved an appearance of great tension, and at others seemed to be merely a cessation of all visible activity. The tension seemed to be one of suspense rather than of effort.

This pause ending either in an explosively expressed elation, or in relieved relaxation.

There was a tendency to jump to the conclusion, with considerable certainty, that the solution had been arrived at, even when the subject was not at all sure of the details."

The following brief excerpt is taken from the "thinking-out-loud" of one of Durkin's subjects:

"Oh, I saw it before I moved it. It came suddenly upon me as from the outside and I felt absolutely sure. Just like a flash and I knew I was right. Wasn't conscious of it . . . didn't reason about it—it came to me from the outside."

DURKIN, H. 1937. Trial-and-error, gradual analysis, and sudden re-organization. *Arch. Psychol.*, 30, #210.

(after vainly trying to do so for twenty minutes) may feel the same dazzling uplift that Archimedes felt.

3. Insights can be partial. The "aha!" experience can accompany some of the intermediate steps in the course of solving a complex problem. This means that any one problem-solving process may contain *several* "aha!" experiences.

4. "Aha!" experiences can accompany objectively *wrong* solutions. We may feel all the excitement of an insight and yet discover in the next moment, or on the next day, that our perception of the real world was wrong and that our solution will not work. This emphasizes again the point that we are using the word "insight" *as a description of an experience*, not as a synonym for a solution. Insight frequently accompanies a real solution, but it may also accompany a "false solution."

Images and Thinking

What is the *content* of our experience when we try to "think through" a problem? We can distinguish two kinds or types of objects in our experience at such a time. First, there are the percepts of objects that exist in our present physical world: high fences, locked doors, empty pockets, long lists of written numbers, crying children. Second, there are images of objects not immediately present in our physical world. As we attempt to recall the birthdate of our mother, we can "see" her, although she may long since have died. As the novelist ponders over his next episode, he may "see" his hero—a never-never hero who has yet to walk this earth. Where the object was once perceived but is not present before us now, we speak of *memory images*; where it has never existed, we speak of *created images*.

It must be emphasized that at the moment we are not concerned with the explanation of why or how we experience images, but only with the crucially important fact that much of our experience as we think through a problem consists of images of objects that are not physically present and that may not exist anywhere in the physical world.

Similarities Between Images and Percepts. These images are as real and as rich and as varied as any other of our experiences. There are many qualitatively different kinds of images. Just as we can see, hear, smell, taste, or feel physically existing objects, so can we "see" objects that are not there; "hear" music when none is being played; "smell" foods that we have not had for years; and see, hear, and feel "the silken, sad, uncertain rustling of each purple curtain" as we read Edgar Allan Poe.

We found that individuals differ in perceptual capacity, some excelling in vision, some in hearing, some in smell. So do we find important individual differences in imagery capacity and preferences. Two major findings have come out of the scientific study of such individual differences.

1. Individuals appear to differ greatly in the *vividness* of their imagery. The classic study in this area is represented by Sir Francis Galton's "breakfast table" investigation in the 1880's. He asked each of his subjects to recall his breakfast table as he had sat down to it in the morning and to report what he experienced—whether the imaged objects were colored naturally, whether they were distinct, well-defined, etc. Galton received many different reports, ranging from a report of images as vivid as the original perceptions of the real objects to a report of no images at all. These results have been amply confirmed since then.

2. Individuals differ in their favored mode of imagery. Some people have images that are predominantly visual (they are re-

ferred to as "visualists"), others, images that are predominantly auditory ("audiles"), etc. An "audile," for example, has auditory images of any object he tries to remember. If he thinks of his friend, his first image is the sound of his friend's voice. Most people, however, seem to be of the "mixed types" with perhaps some tendency to favor one mode over the other in their imagery. (See Box 83.)

Differences Between Images and Percepts. Despite the similarities between images and ordinary perceptions, most of us can usually (when we are not hallucinating) tell the difference between them quite easily. On what basis can we do this? There have been several suggestions.

One suggestion is that the image is usually less *vivid* and less clearly experienced than is the perception of a real object. This is generally true, and in many instances the vividness of our perception enables us to tell the difference between something we are "imaging" and something we are actually seeing or hearing. However, this does not hold for all people, or for anyone all the time. Many of us have, on occasion, experienced detailed, clear, and vivid images—no less clear and vivid than the perceptions of a real object. Again it is Sir Francis Galton who tells of the astonishingly detailed and precise imagery of an eminent scientist of his time:

"Mr. Flinders Petrie . . . informs me that he habitually works out sums by aid of an imaginary slide rule, which he sets in the desired way and reads off mentally. He does not usually visualize the whole rule but only that part of it with which he is at the moment concerned." (Quoted in Humphrey, 1948.)

We do not have to depend only upon such informal reports. There is available careful experimental evidence that demonstrates the high degree of vividness and

---

BOX 83

The Images of Albert Einstein

Since the days of Galton there has been a continuing interest in the imagery of scientists as they work on problems. Non-psychologists have collected much valuable data in this field. One of the most recent of such collections is found in a book by the mathematician Jacques Hadamard. He believes that "The mental pictures of mathematicians . . . are most frequently visual, but they may also be of another kind—for instance, kinetic. There can also be auditive ones." Among the mathematicians whom Hadamard included in his study was Albert Einstein. The following excerpt from a letter of Einstein to Hadamard gives us an extraordinarily interesting account of Einstein's thought processes as he himself experienced them:

"The words of the language, as they are written or spoken, do not seem to play any role in my mechanism of thought. The psychical entities which serve as elements in thought are certain signs and more or less clear images which can be 'voluntarily' reproduced and combined . . . this combinatory play seems to be the essential feature in productive thought—before there is any connection with logical construction in words or other kinds of signs which can be communicated to others. The above mentioned elements are, in my case, of visual and some of muscular type. Conventional words or other signs have to be sought for laboriously only in a secondary stage, when the above mentioned associative play is sufficiently established and can be reproduced at will."

HADAMARD, J. 1949. *Psychology of invention in the mathematical field.* Princeton: Princeton Univ. Press. Reprinted by permission from Dover Publications, Inc., New York.

precision possible in images. Box 84, for instance, presents some illustrations of a particularly detailed kind of image, the *eidetic image*. While differences in vividness can sometimes help us to know whether we are experiencing an image or the perception of a real object, this is not a fool-proof guide.

Another suggestion is that the difference

BOX 84

Photographically Clear Images

The most vividly detailed of all images is the "eidetic image." Many experimental investigations (especially those by the German psychologist Jaensch) have been devoted to eidetic images, first described in 1907. The reports given here are taken from a Stanford University experiment by Heinrich Klüver.

The subject was first allowed to look for a very brief period of time at one of the silhouettes shown below. The silhouette was then removed, and the subject looked at a blank gray cardboard screen. He was asked what he "saw" there. The following excerpts are taken from Klüver's reports on one of his woman subjects after she had observed the following figure for 30 seconds.

Subject "sees" the alligator with a "curly tail"; "that kid" with mouth and eyes; "the big tree at the right"; "a couple of palm trees" in the background. "The little boy and the alligator are most distinct"; counts eighteen teeth in the lower jaw of the alligator (correct!). "I don't see the feet at all; they are in the water. I see two forelegs and one hind leg. Two trees in the background having one trunk." (And many other details.)

His report on the same woman *3 months after* she had seen the following figure for 30 seconds was as follows:

Subject "sees" "woman with the umbrella in her right hand. She is standing like that" (indicates position correctly). "The man at the right has lost his cigar; it has fallen to the ground. There is a little man standing beside the woman. To the right is a theater. Above the door I see 'Entra.' At the left of the door there is a poster. Before the door there is a lantern pole. The globe appears to be in the form of a hexagon. In the background there is a church. In the foreground I see three dogs. They are black, only the right one and the left one have white collars. The dog on the left has a curled tail. His mouth is open." This protocol goes on and on with many more accurately described details of the original silhouette).

Eidetic imagery is found more frequently among children than adults. An "eidetiker" will say that he "sees" the image, yet he also realizes that the object is not before him.

KLÜVER, H. 1926. An experimental study of the eidetic type. *Genet. Psychol. Monogr., 1* 71–230.

between the two lies in their "fluidity." Thus, the perception of a real object is determined to a considerable extent by stimulus properties of the object. Images, on the other hand, are more fluid. A visual image is sometimes localized "in the head"; it can be shifted from spot to spot at will, sometimes being organized together with one group of objects, sometimes with another. (Remember Albert Einstein's reference to the "combinatory play" among his images?) It can even be "seen" inside an opaque object. It can readily be experienced as twice its original size, or warped out of shape, or variable in its color.

The final reply to the question of how we can tell whether we are experiencing a perception of a real object or an image seems to be that we *cannot* always tell. The various differences we have listed are important guides and usually sufficient, but experimental work has led to the conclusion that there is no sharp boundary between the qualities of the perception of a real object and the qualities of an image. This has been demonstrated by showing that people can be fooled into taking an image for a real object and a real object for an image. (See Box 85.) It seems clear from laboratory experiments and general observation that it is the over-all conditions of the situation, the perceiver's alertness and his expectations,

---

BOX 85

The Real Becomes the Imagined

In 1910, C. W. Perky at Cornell University reported the following experiment: She prepared cardboard forms with their centers cut out in the shape of a book, a banana, an orange, a leaf, and a lemon. These forms could be so placed that when a lantern was turned on, colored light would shine through the cutout forms and the corresponding colored figure would be cast on the ground-glass window. (See fig.)

The subject was seated facing the window, with the lantern turned off. He was asked to fixate the screen while he "imagined" a colored object—"for instance, a tomato." He was then to describe his "image" if any image took shape. After these instructions, the lamp was turned on (unbeknown to the subject) with an intensity *below* the minimum necessary for vi-

sion. Then, very slowly, the intensity was stepped up, until it was *well beyond the previously determined minimum for actual vision.* As soon as the subject began to describe his "image," the lamp was turned off, and after he had finished his description, he was requested to "imagine" another object —"for instance, a book." The objects actually cast on the screen were a red tomato, a blue book, a deep yellow banana, an orange orange, a green leaf, and a light yellow lemon.

All the subjects (19 sophomores and 8 graduate students) believed that they were imagining the objects and their appropriate colors, and yet not one of them "imagined" the object until the illumination had gone well above the minimum required for normal perception. *They were seeing actual objects, but believed that they were "imagining" them.* When the subject was asked whether he was "quite sure that he had imagined all these things," the question aroused surprise and indignation. Sophomores and graduate students in psychology alike had mistaken the perception of a real object for an image!

PERKY, C. W. 1910. An experimental study of imagination. *Amer. J. Psychol.,* 21, 422–52.

which determine whether he will recognize an image as different from the perception of a real object. These seem much more important than any set of specific attributes of the two experiences.

JAMES' "STREAM OF CONSCIOUSNESS." William James called attention to the fact that while we may experience images during our mental processes, many of these images are neither definite nor long-lasting. He likened our experience to an ever-flowing stream in which one image shades imperceptibly into another among the ever-changing contents of our consciousness. "Every image in the mind," he pointed out, "is steeped and dyed in the free water that flows around it. . . . The significance, the value, of the image is all in this halo or penumbra that surrounds and escorts it." Thus when we recall the "form" of an opera or the theme of a book, when we "have in mind" a scientific or philosophical or religious principle, we do not experience a definite image or even a series of definite images. Instead, we experience a *continuous flux* of "glimpses" of relationships and "snatches" of images.

"Imageless Thought." At the beginning of the present century many German, French, English, and American psychologists were involved in a long and often bitterly waged controversy over the question of "imageless thought"—whether people could think without images. Those who said they could not insisted that people who did not report images were simply not reporting adequately, that they were not well-trained enough to notice the fleeting images. Those who said they could, believed that *all* thinking was imageless; the content of thinking, they felt, was "thoughts," and where images *were* present, they played no important role. The imageless-thought battle ended with "no decision." Psychologists agreed that images are sometimes present—but

they had become interested in other "more tangible" descriptions of adaptive behavior.

By Way of Summary. It seems clear that much of our thinking, problem-solving, invention, and creativity is accompanied by definitely structured percepts and images. Some psychologists have even maintained that one could describe the entire memory, thinking, and problem-solving process solely in terms of the organization and reorganization of these perceptions. While modern experimental psychology is convinced of the inadequacy of such an approach, the description of the contents of our experience during problem-solving has well demonstrated its value. It has suggested many fruitful experimental approaches to the study of creative problem-solving as well as to the study of the physiological basis of adaptive behavior, as we will see in the following chapters.

The experiences of many people—perhaps most—consist of some sort of imagery; images of things once seen and now no longer present, and images of things never actually seen, heard, or felt. These images, no matter what their history, are often experienced as vivid, detailed, and clear. In this way our perceptual world frequently transcends the space and time limitations of our physical world, and aids us in the solution of problems.

Varieties of Adaptive Behavior

We will find as we continue, in the succeeding chapters, with the experimental study of adaptive behavior that we will be required to lean heavily upon the preceding two parts of the book. This is a reflection of the fact that we cannot understand problem-solving and learning without making extensive use of our perceptual and motivational principles. At times it almost seems that the so-called thinking or remembering process consists of nothing but perceptual and motivational processes.

"Rational" vs. "Emotional" Thinking. Mr. Anyman tends to see the "intellectual" side of man as divorced from his "emotional" side. Many of us seem to speak as though the two *should* be separated, even if they often are not. We say that "he lets his emotions run away with his thoughts," or we are quick to use the term "wishful thinking" as a derogatory one to indicate that a man's thinking was directed by his hopes or fears rather than by his "rational", intellectual processes. This oversimplifies the situation considerably. The truth of the matter is that all thinking, learning, and problem-solving are resultants *both* of perceptual processes and of processes of motivation and emotion. We have seen that problem-solving is conceived in perceptual and motivational experiences, develops with an accompanying series of changes in these experiences, and often ends in a genuinely emotional outburst. The hypothalamus as well as the cortex is involved in thinking. This is true of the objective, "scientific" thinker as it is of anyone else who seeks to solve puzzling problems and circumvent obstacles to goals.

Need for Classification. Man's adaptive behavior encompasses an overwhelming variety of activities. The study of how we *memorize,* how we acquire *habits,* how we develop *skills,* how we form *concepts,* how we *think*—are all parts of the study of "adaptive behavior." This enormous variety suggests one of the very first difficulties facing the psychologist as he approaches the study of adaptive behavior: how does one go about studying such a hodgepodge of things? This question is not confined to the Walrus who wished to talk of shoes, ships, sealing wax, cabbages and kings—or

to the psychologist who wishes to treat, under the same rubric of "adaptive behavior," rote memory, learning, the inventions of the engineer, and the elegance of mathematical thought.

All sciences run up against precisely the same problem, and all of them have adopted the same solution: combine and conquer—classify into a small number of groups and then study the *groups* rather than the myriad of individuals. The creatures that hop, run, jump, walk, crawl, fly, soar, burrow, sway, float, and swim—upon the earth and in the heavens above and in the waters below—are as numberless as the stars and as varied as man's intelligence can comprehend. How could the biologist possibly study so many different kinds of beings, and how was he to relate one to every other when there are so many "ones" and so many "others?" The solution was: classification. The swarms of differently fashioned bits of life were grouped and combined into kingdoms, phyla, classes, orders, families, genuses, and species. Life then became possible for the biologist. He had reduced the bewildering kaleidoscopic universe into a manageably few categories within which the individuals had some *common* characteristic. Now he could neglect the individual, study the common characteristics of each *category* intensively, and examine relations among these few *groups* rather than among the millions of individuals.

A Twofold Classification. As is true of any set of events, adaptive behavior can be classified in many ways. Each way has its merits, its difficulties, and reflects the theoretical preferences of the classifier. In the chapters that follow we shall classify adaptive behavior into the two major categories of *creative problem-solving* and *learning.*

Creative problem-solving refers to adaptive behavior in which the individual attempts new and original solutions as he copes with some problem that faces him. The term "productive thinking," as commonly used, is a fairly good synonym for the kinds of processes we shall study under the first category. But not all adaptive behavior involves being creative. Many of the exigencies we face in our daily environment require nothing more than *reproducing* what we have learned to do in the past. The acquisition of specified behavior patterns through a training process, their retention, and their role in adaptive behavior,

is what we shall study under the second category, *learning*. This category encompasses such processes as are commonly called "habit formation" and "rote memorizing" and the learning of skills.

These categories are not sharply differentiated, but shade into each other. Indeed, some kinds of problem-solving can just as rationally be placed in one as in the other. To study science requires the tolerance of this kind of ambiguity. Science has no neat black-and-white differentiations.

Glossary

"aha!" experience. An intense experience occasionally accompanying the sudden realization of how a problem can be solved. This experience may accompany false solutions as well as valid ones. The term "insight" is sometimes used for this experience.

created image. An experience (visual, auditory, etc.) of an object that has never existed as a stimulus-object for the person undergoing the experience. An "imagined" object.

"ego-oriented" problem-solving. A problem-solving process in which the person experiences feelings of need, desire, or frustration.

eidetic image. A particularly vivid and detailed memory image. Found more frequently among children than among adults. May be evoked at will sometimes months after the original viewing of the stimulus-object.

imageless thought. The belief that thinking can proceed in the absence of imagery— or, in its more extreme form, the thesis that imagery plays no role in thinking.

memory image. An experience (visual, auditory, etc.) of an object that has once existed as a stimulus-object for the person but is now not present in his visual field.

"task-oriented" problem-solving. A problem-solving process in which the person does not experience any feeling of personal need or frustration.

Suggestions for Further Reading

HADAMARD, J. 1949. *Psychology of invention in the mathematical field.* Princeton: Princeton Univ. Press.

An interesting series of essays on creative thinking in science, with special analysis of the experiences of mathematicians as they go about solving problems.

JAMES, W. 1890. *Principles of psychology.* New York: Holt.

This classic book, written by the founder of American psychology, may still be read with profit by all students of

psychology. Of special interest for the material of this chapter are James' treatments of "the stream of thought" and "imagination"—Chapters 9 and 18.

WERTHEIMER, M. 1945. *Productive thinking.* New York: Harper.

Essays and demonstration experiments in creative thinking. Written by one of the founders of Gestalt psychology, it presents an interesting account of the perceptual approach to problem-solving and thinking.

CHAPTER XIV

Creative Problem-Solving

THE CREATIVE problem-solver produces *new* and *original* solutions. Whether the same thing has been previously produced by someone else does not matter —it need only be a first occurrence within the person's life. Neither, of course, does the new creation have to "work"; it may be a wrong solution, but still one that is novel and original.

The "importance" of the creative solution may also vary tremendously. The creation may be a new way of packaging ink, a new theory of gravity, a new solution to international conflict, or a new football play (see Box 86).

Although all the problem-solving behavior we will examine in this chapter is presumably creative, it is obvious that the types of problems will vary among themselves in many important particulars. It is therefore necessary, for purposes of analysis, to make some subgroupings among them. The classification we shall use divides creative problem-solving into three major categories: explanation, prediction, and invention.

Explanation, Prediction, and Invention

The three major types of creative problem-solving situations can be distinguished by the different goals involved in each. In explanation, the goal is to seek an understanding of *why a specified event has occurred*. In prediction, certain conditions are given and the goal is to understand the consequences of these conditions, *to anticipate an event that has not yet happened*. In invention, the goal is to *create a novel set of conditions that will result in a specified event*.

NOTE: *Before continuing, turn to Box 87, page 374 and follow the instructions there.*

Explanation. Problems in explanation have given rise to some of the most inspiring creative achievements of the human mind. The work of Galileo, Copernicus, Newton, and Einstein, for example, belongs to this category. But even for Mr. Anyman, explanation problems are prob-

BOX 86

The Rat and Creative Problem-Solving

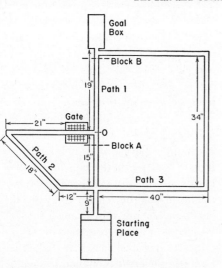

First the rats were given *preliminary training*. Animals deprived of food for 24 hours were placed in the starting box and permitted to find their way to the food box. They were given ten such trials per day. They soon learned (after trying the various paths) to take the shortest path to the food. The experimenters then *blocked* Path 1 at point A, and when this was done, the rats would turn back to the choice point and almost always (about 93 per cent of the time) take Path 2.

In the *test run* the block was *for the first time* placed in the common section of Paths 1 and 2 (at point B). Now when the rats backed out of Path 1, they did not take Path 2, but took Path 3—the longest path, *but the only one now open to the food box.* Of the 15 rats in this experiment, 14 behaved in this way.

Backing out of Path 1 and taking Path 3 was a relatively new and original solution— and one that seemed to the human psychologists observing the rats' behavior to show "insight" and "inference"—or what we are tempted to call "creative problem-solving."

Many psychologists maintain that even the rat is capable of creative problem-solving. In 1930 Tolman and Honzik at the University of California reported their classical experiment on "insight" in the rat.

The apparatus, an "elevated maze," presented three paths to the food box. Path 1 was the shortest, 2 the next shortest, and 3 the longest. Paths 1 and 2 had a common final segment that Path 3 did not share.

Tolman, E. C., and Honzik, C. H. 1930. 'Insight' in rats. *Univ. Calif. Publ. Psychol., 4*, 215–32.

ably the most commonly experienced. They most readily give rise to erroneous solutions and, paradoxically, are often the easiest to solve of all three types. (You will have seen one instance of this if you have followed the instructions in Boxes 87, 88, and 89.) Because all of us are so familiar with explanation (who has not tried to explain an event *after* it has happened?) we will first examine explanation and then point out the differences between it and prediction and invention. We will find that all three types involve the same general pyschological processes.

CAUSAL RELATIONS. The most elemental form of explanation is almost a pure perceptual act. We know from Chapter 5 that the *perception* of "cause" is a fairly compelling one and that it can be seen as an instance of the grouping phenomenon in perception. The "cause" will often be immediately perceived in the event itself. Frequently we do not feel that we have done any *thinking;* we just *see* the "cause" out there. One might say that "to see is to explain."

Very often, of course, these primitive explanations are completely wrong. Many of them are even judged as wrong by the person himself, and sometimes at the very moment he is "perceiving the cause." As has been pointed out:

"Someone comes home of an evening. A gust of wind slams the door shut behind him. At the same moment at the other end of the corridor, the light goes on in a room whose door is ajar. Although one knew ever so well that no causal connection exists between the door's blowing shut, and the light's going on, that rather some one in the room has turned on the light, by chance at exactly the same moment—still he would be unable to escape the compelling impression of causal relationship." (Duncker, 1945.)

EXPLANATIONS AND THE STIMULUS-PATTERN. To understand why the perception of cause is so basic and why these primitive explanations frequently go wrong, we must first remind ourselves of the stimulus factors that influence our causal perceptions. Among these factors are those of similarity and proximity (see Chapter 5). Events *a* and *b* will tend to be seen as causally related if they occur simultaneously or within a very brief period of time, if they are close to each other in space, or if they resemble

each other in shape or form. In Duncker's illustration the simultaneous occurrence of the door's blowing shut and the light's going on results in a "compelling causal relationship" in perception. We have been "trapped" into a wrong explanation by the operation of a simple perceptual law. The experiments of Michotte (discussed in Box 34, p. 126) provide other illustrations of how the perception of cause is determined by certain features of the stimulus-pattern. Very frequently when we observe two events in close spatial or temporal proximity we "jump" to the conclusion that the events are causally connected.

The history of science is filled with illustrations of just this. In medicine it leads frequently to the treatment of symptoms rather than of real causes. A variant of this is seen in the error (common to some scientists as well as to Mr. Anyman) of arguing to cause-and-effect from the observations of a "correlation." We may observe that whenever juvenile delinquency becomes common, the divorce rates also increase;

BOX 87

Invention

The above diagram was drawn from a description of one of Székely's experiments performed at the University of Stockholm. In his experiment actual objects similar to those pictured above were placed on a table in front of the subject, and he was given instructions somewhat like the following: "Using *only* these objects see if you can

balance the wooden plank on the edge of the prism in such a way that after a few minutes the edge labeled A will tip down *automatically*, i.e., without being touched, or blown upon, or the table shaken, etc." Székely reports that the vast majority of his subjects required several minutes and "considerable mental effort" to solve this problem. Pretend that you are one of his subjects and that you actually have these objects before you. Can you solve the problem in *two minutes?* Time yourself. *After two minutes, whether you have solved it or not, please turn the page to Box 88 and follow the instructions there.*

SZÉKELY, L. 1950. Knowledge and thinking. *Acta Psychologica, 7,* 1–24.

and whenever juvenile delinquency decreases, so does the divorce rate (this means that there is a "correlation" between juvenile delinquency and divorce rates); and from this we might argue that juvenile delinquency must be caused by broken homes. Actually, of course, this causal relationship may not be true at all. Both juvenile delinquency and divorce may be caused by some *other* factor, such as economic or social upheaval.

In our efforts to explain an event we may be victimized in a second way by the stimulus situation. The event presents such a dominating pattern of stimuli that we tend to focus all or most of our attention on the event itself. But often the specific event may not present for "perceptual inspection" the objects important for the explanation, and, therefore, we are at a disadvantage in our attempt to discover the explanation. For example: the explanation of a child's temper tantrum may involve factors that are far removed, in time and space, from the immediate situation that preceded the tantrum. It may involve the parents' relation to each other, the child's relations to his friends.

On the other hand, the event may present *too many* objects. If many superfluous objects and events are present, or if the objects have many irrelevant attributes attached to them, the important relationships among the relevant objects become difficult to see, and the solution is delayed (see p. 43 for this kind of effect in simple perception).

"MENTAL DAZZLE." The disturbing effects that "excess stimuli" can have on problem-solving were investigated experimentally by David Katz, a German psychologist. He presented groups of school children with simple arithmetic calculations to perform—addition and subtraction. Some groups worked with undenominated numbers (e.g., 10.50 plus 13.25 plus 6.89 . . .);

other groups worked with numbers preceded by a familiar denomination (e.g., $10.50 plus $13.25 plus $6.89 . . .); and still others, with numbers carrying an unfamiliar designation (e.g., Kr.10.50 plus Kr. 13.25 plus Kr.6.89). He found that (a) the addition of a monetary designation increased the difficulty of calculation, and (b) this difficulty became still greater when a foreign denomination was used. Katz repeated parts of this experiment with adults and found that even with adults, denominated numbers increased the time of addition by 12 per cent! Apparently, adding one irrelevant or unfamiliar feature to so simple and familiar a task as addition or subtraction is enough to produce what Katz called "mental dazzle."

"Mental dazzle," concludes Katz, "appears particularly well suited to emphasize the contrast between logic, which deals with the formal connections between the objects of thinking, and the defective manner in which those objects actually are comprehended."

EXPLANATIONS AND PAST LEARNING. The same object can be perceived with many different meanings; and frequently, of course, it is only when we see a particular attribute of an object that we can achieve the explanation. For example, in Székely's experiment (Box 89) the explanation lies within the candle. However, we can see a candle with the meaning of "a solid physical object with constant weight," or as a "source of light." Neither of these meanings will help us at all in our explanation. Only when we see that a characteristic of a burning candle is that it loses weight can we achieve the proper explanation.

The number and kinds of meanings which we can attach to any one object depend upon *how much* we have learned about it and the *way* we have acquired the knowledge. There are methods of learning which make knowledge readily accessible for vari-

---

BOX 88

Prediction

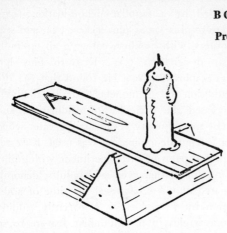

This diagram shows another problem that Székely used in his experiment. This time we have a problem in "prediction." When the objects had been arranged as illustrated above, the experimenter asked the subject: "What will happen if the can-

dle were to be lighted?" Different subjects, of course, were used for this problem than for the "invention" problem of Box 87. Székely found that this problem was somewhat easier to solve than the preceding one, but it still took some doing. Of course you have an advantage over Székely's subjects since you have already attempted to solve the invention problem. However, if you have not solved the preceding problem, see what you can do with this one. Pretend that you actually have the above setup before you. Can you predict what will happen if the candle were to be lighted? *Can you say why?* Time yourself. You have but *one* minute.

After one minute, whether you have solved this problem or not, please turn the page to Box 89 and follow the instructions there.

---

ous problems, and there are ways of learning which limit the availability of knowledge.

BENEFICIAL EFFECTS OF THESE FACTORS. Paradoxically, many of the very same factors that make explanations so difficult to arrive at, also make them easy to achieve. For a specific example, let us return, for a moment, to Box 89. Note how the very perception of the event to be explained almost "forces" the correct explanation upon us. As a consequence of the *perception of the objective event* (no force is seen being applied to the long end, which tips down, and a burning candle is on the short end, which tips up), of *one bit of recalled knowledge* (the end that goes up must be lighter in weight than the end that goes down), and the operation of the *principle of proximity* (the burning candle is on the end that must be lighter), we have almost arrived at our final solution: the explanation "must be" in the candle!

The significance of this illustration lies in

the fact that very frequently in "real life" an event *does* provide most of the material necessary for the achievement of an adequate explanation. The elements of a causal relationship *are* frequently found close to each other in space or time, or similar to each other in certain characteristics. In other words there is some degree of correspondence between cause and effect in the outside world and what happens in our perceptions.

Prediction. Prediction has as its goal the *understanding of a future event.* This immediately rules out sheer "guessing," even should the guess turn out to be correct. To be sure, "guessing" frequently occurs in problem-solving, but it does not qualify as creative problem-solving.

Our definition specifies two things about the prediction problem: (1) the *event* must be one that has not yet occurred; and (2) the *antecedent conditions* of the event must be understood. These two characteristics are important because they determine the differences between explanation and prediction problems.

In explanation, the stimulus-pattern confronting the problem-solver is fairly clearly specified—specific objects have been observed to do specific things in specific sequences and proximities. The stimulus-pattern in the *prediction problem* is much more "impoverished." All one sees is a situation whose outcome has not yet occurred.

What is the significance of this difference between the two types of stimulus-patterns?

ROLE OF STIMULUS STRUCTURE. The specificity and degree of structure of the stimulus-pattern does much to determine perceptual organization. Where there is a paucity of stimulus-objects, our perceptions are much more governed by our mental set and memories than is the case where the stimulus-pattern presents many specific and clearly structured stimulus-objects. (See p. 100.)

We have pointed out that perceptual processes operate, by and large, to give us a true and workable picture of the relationships among physical objects. Some *explanation* problems are "easy" ones, therefore, because the stimulus-pattern consists of concretely defined objects and their interactions. In these we can quite readily achieve the "correct" perception of the event, even a novel event.

In *prediction*, on the other hand, the objects and the relations among them are so relatively few and undefined that the stimulus conditions will not, with the same degree of probability, "force" the correct organization. In Székely's experiment we have an experimental illustration of this. The subjects who attempted to explain an event did much better than the subjects who attempted to predict *the very same event*.

Since the explanation problem presents us with a fairly well-specified stimulus-

pattern, it should be relatively *difficult* to break away from the first solution we attempt even if this solution is wrong. The first solution, it must be remembered, is the one most clearly determined by the stimulus-pattern. We are, as it were, "bound" by the stimulus-pattern. On the other hand, the prediction problem, by presenting relatively few stimuli, should make it easier for us to break away from any solution that does not work. There are not enough stimuli to make us "stimulus-bound."

Experiments have supported such an analysis. For instance, experiments on "functional fixity" have shown that when a person actually sees an object functioning in one way, it becomes more difficult to perceive other possible uses for that object. The consequence is that problem-solving is interfered with (see Box 90).

STIMULUS STRUCTURE AND PERSONALITY. While a stimulus-pattern that presents relatively few defined objects may give one an *opportunity* to organize and reorganize, many people do not seem able to take advantage of the opportunity. Some people seem to be "thrown" by a stimulus-pattern that does not immediately result in a clear and specific perceptual organization. Once having achieved a solution to an "ambiguous" structure, they cling to it tenaciously. This seems to be characteristic of their entire personality pattern. While many people do not react with this extreme lack of flexibility, there are large individual differences in the ease with which people can shift from one formulation of an ambiguous structure to another.

As we go from problems with more concrete and clearly defined stimulus-patterns to problems with less well-defined ones, personality factors and individual differences play an increasingly large role, and the analysis becomes even more definitely one of the interplay of motivational, emotional, and perceptual processes.

BOX 89

Explanation

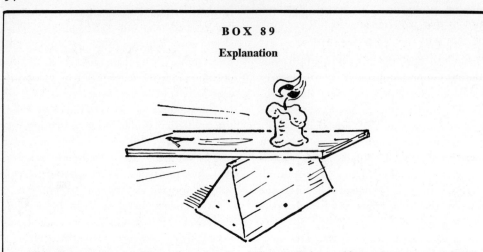

This diagram shows still another of Szé-kely's experimental problems. This time we have a problem in "explanation." In his experiment the above arrangement was set up and the experimenter lit the candle. After a few minutes the lever tipped over so that the edge labeled "A" touched the table top. Székely's subjects, after having seen this occur, were then asked to *explain why it occurred*. This problem was relatively easy for Székely's subjects—but not a "cinch" for all of them. Again you have a considerable advantage over his subjects because of your having wrestled with the two previous problems. However, if you have not solved the preceding problems, try this one. Pretend that you have actually seen the event described above. Can you explain *why* the plank tipped down after the candle had burned for a few minutes?

Invention. We have defined the invention problem as one in which the goal of the problem-solver is to arrange a novel set of conditions which will result in some desired event. Defined thus, invention encompasses a wide range of problems. The problem of Box 87; combining colors and forms into an oil painting; arranging wheels, gears, and spouts to make a new catsup-bottle filler; devising a new system of mathematics; writing a novel, a symphony, or a slogan —these are all inventions. What distinguishes an invention from an explanation or prediction is the fact that invention receives fewer guides to its solution from the stimulus situation, and makes heavier demands upon the resources of the person.

INVENTION AND THE "GIVEN" MATERIAL. Most prediction problems are defined by the nature of their "givens." The predictor focuses his attention on the givens, and it is an understanding of these objects and their interrelationships which will give him his solution.

The inventor must also pay attention to the givens of his problem. For instance, a writer may be given (or set for himself) the problem of writing a comedy about a Presidential election; the chemist may take as his problem the development of a cooking oil made from the vegetable products of a certain country or province. In Box 87 the reader was given certain materials to work with. But the inventor's problem is to bring about a specified future event. His attention, therefore, must also be focused upon the to-be-achieved event. No inventor sets out to "create"—he always sets out to create a specific something. But this "specific something" has not yet happened, and therein lies much of the inventor's difficulty.

If the problem is to invent "Sensies" (movies that will transmit to the audience not only what the actors say, but also what the actors feel, taste, and smell), then it is "Sensies" that will determine the materials and devices the inventor must work with. But our inventor's "Sensies" do not exist. "Sensies" never have existed. "Sensies"

BOX 90

Functional Fixity—A Barrier to Creative Problem-Solving

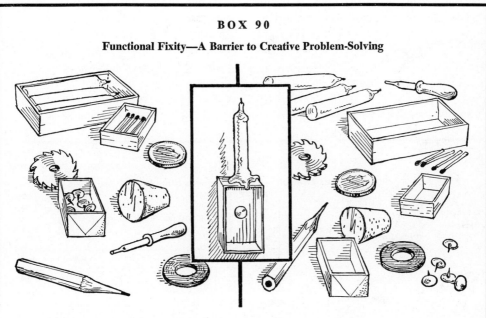

a   b

The German psychologist, Karl Duncker, first proposed the concept of "functional fixity" in about 1930, and he illustrated it with a few simple experiments. Because these experiments were done with so few subjects, several American psychologists repeated them, and they obtained results similar to those of Duncker. One such experiment is that of Adamson at Stanford University.

The task: mount three candles vertically on a soft wooden screen, using any object available on the table. Among the objects are three cardboard boxes, five matches, and five thumbtacks. *The solution:* mount one candle on each box by melting wax on the box, stick the candle to it, and then tack the boxes to the screen. (See central portion of sketch.)

For one group (29 college students), the candles, matches, and tacks were placed *in* the three boxes before they were presented to the subjects (fig. *a*). Thus *the boxes*

were seen functioning as containers, whereas in the solution of the problem the boxes would have to be seen as "*supports*" or "*shelves*." For the second group (28 subjects), the boxes were empty and placed among the other objects (fig. *b*). Here the boxes were not seen functioning as containers. Twenty minutes were allowed for the solution.

Of the first group, only 12 of the subjects (or 41 per cent) were able to solve the problem—apparently the remaining subjects of this group could not perceive the boxes with the meaning of "platform" or "shelf." Of the second group, 24 (or 86 per cent) were able to solve the problem.

These results give striking evidence that functional fixity may be an important barrier in creative problem-solving.

ADAMSON, R. E. 1952. Functional fixedness as related to problem-solving. *J. exp. Psychol.,* 44, 288–91.

therefore do not constitute a "stimulus-pattern" that can give much guidance to the inventor.

To be sure, sometimes the specific thing that the inventor seeks to achieve may not be as foreign to his experience as "Sensies." Something similar to it may have occurred in the past. For example: the feeling of strength through delicate beauty has already been expressed in stone in Michelangelo's "David," and the sculptor may have this in mind as he attacks his own block of stone. But "David" can have only limited value as a guide for the sculptor, because his problem is to create something new and original.

While the inventor's stimulus-pattern is the least structured, it must nevertheless be an extensive one. This in turn increases his difficulties. (See Box 91.) The painter must be aware of the tremendous range of colors, shapes, and materials which can be manipulated and arranged; the writer must be aware of a host of characters, events, and

---

BOX 91

The Inventor's Difficulty—An Ambiguous Stimulus-Pattern

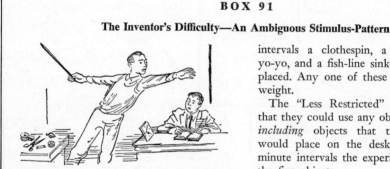

Battersby, Teuber, and Bender at New York University tested the problem-solving of men under three specifications of stimulus conditions. Although they were primarily interested in comparing brain-injured people with normal people, we shall consider here their results only on the uninjured men.

The Maier "string problem" was used. Each subject entered a room in which was a desk, a table, and two strings hanging from the ceiling. His task was to tie the strings together, although they were too far apart to permit reaching one while grasping the other. The solution: attach a weight to one string, give it a swing, run over to the other, catch the first string when it swings close, and then tie them together.

The "Restricted" group was told that they could use only the objects provided by the experimenter. Upon completion of instructions the experimenter placed scissors on the desk. At successive two-minute intervals a clothespin, a small pulley, a yo-yo, and a fish-line sinker were similarly placed. Any one of these could serve as a weight.

The "Less Restricted" group was told that they could use any object in the room, *including* objects that the experimenter would place on the desk. Again at two-minute intervals the experimenter provided the five objects.

For the "Unrestricted" group the five objects were on the *table* when the subject entered the room, but his attention was not drawn to them. The subjects were instructed to use any object *in the room*.

Thus for the "Restricted" group the experimenter pointed to the specific objects relevant to the solution; for the "Less Restricted," this pointing was more ambiguous ("use *any* object including . . . "); for the "Unrestricted," there was no pointing.

The "Restricted" group solved the problem in 2.4 minutes (average); the "Less Restricted," in 7.5 minutes; and the "Unrestricted," in 15.2 minutes.

The analogy to the situation facing the Inventor is clear. The Inventor's goal does not specify the objects that will help him to achieve his goal, and insofar as this is true, his problem is magnified in difficulty.

BATTERSBY, W. S., TEUBER, H. L., and BENDER, M. B. 1953. Problem-solving behavior in men with frontal or occipital brain injuries. *J. Psychol., 35,* 329–51.

places which can be organized into different situations and episodes; the creative engineer must know a great deal about pulleys and gears and levers that can be combined.

Determinants of Creative Problem-Solving

In describing explanation, prediction, and invention, we sketched an outline of the creative problem-solving process. We found three basic determinants affecting this process: (1) the nature of the stimulus-pattern; (2) the nature of the previously acquired knowledge; and (3) the personality structure of the problem solver. We shall now examine the operation of these determinants in some detail.

The Stimulus-Pattern. If we can specify how the stimulus-pattern facilitates or inhibits creative problem-solving, we can use this information to improve our problem-solving. The major interest in a scientific analysis is the understanding it gives us, but a scientific understanding also has practical implications, and we shall examine some possible practical uses of this analysis presently. As one eminent theoretician in psychology (Kurt Lewin) used to point out: there is nothing so practical as a good theory.

SPATIAL ORGANIZATION. We have already pointed out that the spatial arrangement of stimulus-objects in terms of proximity influences the perception of cause and therefore the problem-solving process. What role do the other spatial patternings that have been found effective in perception (see Chapter 5) play in inhibiting or facilitating the problem-solving process? Psychologists have not done enough experiments to enable us to answer this question with certainty. The Gestalt psychologists, who have

been primarily interested in this problem, have mainly sought to demonstrate that the problem-solving process is *in general* analogous to the perceptual process, and that the concepts of perceptual reorganization can be applied profitably to an analysis of the problem-solving process.

For example, in the study described in Box 91 the prediction that the ability to *solve problems,* such as the Maier string problem, would be correlated with the ability to *perceive hidden figures* in the Gottschaldt test, which requires perceptual reorganizing (see Box 23, p. 97), was also tested. The results are in accordance with the prediction. The men who were good at solving the string problem were also good at reorganizing the Gottschaldt figures; those who were poor in the one were also poor in the other. This sort of general finding supports the practice of including perceptual items in intelligence tests and tests of "creative ability."

Some experimentation has been done on the effect of *specific* stimulus-patterns on problem-solving, with encouraging results. On the basis of the experiments that are available, we can state as a reasonable hypothesis that *the spatial arrangement of the objects and events of a problem situation can facilitate or hinder the achievement of a solution in much the same way that it facilitates or hinders the achievement of a perceptual organization.*

When the objects relevant to the solution of a problem are in the visual field of the perceiver, the problem will be more readily solved than when they cannot be perceived simultaneously. (See Box 92 for an experimental demonstration of this.)

Another factor concerns the spatial *subgrouping of the elements* of the problem material. Thus if the solution requires that object A be seen as a part of object X, and A is so placed as to be seen as a part of object Y, the solution may be impeded.

BOX 92

When a Stick Is Not a Rake

Just prior to the outbreak of World War I, Wolfgang Köhler, one of the founders of Gestalt psychology, had gone from the University of Berlin to do some field studies at the Anthropoid Station on the island of Tenerife. With the outbreak of the war Köhler, as a German national, was interned at Tenerife by the Spanish government, and he was forced to remain there from 1913 to 1917. Out of his internment came his famous book, *The Mentality of Apes.* Among other things Köhler studied was the use by the chimpanzee of implements in solving problems. One of the observations from this group of studies is described below.

Tschego, an adult female chimpanzee, was tested for her ability to use sticks as rakes to pull in food from outside her cage. One simple factor that determined whether she could or could not do so was the *spatial location* of the implement in relation to the food. Even a stick that she had *often* used as a rake lost all "instrumental value" if it was not visible to Tschego when she was gazing directly at the food!

Köhler summarizes: "I have used every means at my disposal to attract Tschego's attention to the sticks in the back of her cage and she did look straight at them; but in doing so she turned her back on the objective, and so the sticks remained meaningless to her . . . at the same time, *sticks*—and other substitutes—*which she beheld in the direction of her objective, were made use of without any hesitation*, and she devoured what food she could reach with relish."

KÖHLER, W. 1925. *The mentality of apes.* New York: Harcourt, Brace.

(See the demonstration problem in Fig. 94.) This effect can be accentuated by familiarity with the objects. Frequently the solution to a problem requires that we interpret a familiar object in a novel manner. When the object is located among other objects that have been seen together in the past (e.g., a hammer is shown in the surroundings of nails and boards), it will tend to inhibit the novel interpretation (e.g., it will be more difficult to see that the hammer might also be used as a measuring stick).

These and other factors suggest that we should be able, by proper spatial rearrangement of objects, to change a difficult problem into an easy one, or an easy one into a difficult one. This points to a very simple practical suggestion for improving problem-solving efficiency for certain types of problems: The problem solver does not usually face an immovable array of materials and objects. He is allowed to manipulate and rearrange them. (When this is not possible physically, he can imagine their rearrangement.) By deliberately trying out various spatial arrangements and not remaining fixated on the initial one, he increases the probability of arriving, *by chance alone*, at an arrangement facilitating the solution. We will see later that the general principle implicit in this "hint to the problem-solver"

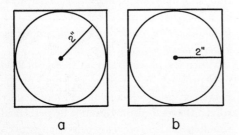

a   b

FIG. 94. A square is drawn so that it just encloses a circle. The *circle* has a radius of 2 inches. What is the area of the *square?* Both *a* and *b* give the same information, but *b* is easier to solve. Why?

In *a* the radius is so placed as to make it difficult to perceive it as "part of" the square. In *b* the radius can more easily be seen as "part of" the square.

has been experimentally tested with encouraging results.

TEMPORAL ORGANIZATION. Some problems present us with temporally as well as spatially patterned objects—some parts of the problem situation precede other parts. How does the temporal organization of such problems affect the ease or difficulty of solution?

We have seen that temporal patterning of stimuli can affect simple sensation and perception, as shown by the phenomena of adaptation, fusion, temporal summation, etc. (Chapter 4). In addition, we discussed another important perceptual effect of temporal patterning significant for our present discussion—"set." In Chapter 5 we saw that if we are presented with several objects in succession, the perceptual attributes of the later objects reflect the influence of the earlier objects.

The influence of "sets" on problem-solving has been studied extensively, and the basic experiment in this field is the one by Luchins (see Box 93). His results (corroborated by many later studies) indicate that solving a number of problems by one method of attack tends to trap the person into using the same method of attack on later problems, even though the method is now inappropriate.

Some of the other attributes of temporal patterning (groupings in time, time intervals between events, etc.) have also been studied in creative problem-solving. Using Luchin's technique, Kendler, Greenberg, and Richman (1952) showed that if the training problems were all "massed" (given to the subjects one immediately after another), the induced set was stronger than if the training problems were "distributed" (presented with a three-minute interval between each training problem). Again the effect of the *temporal-grouping* factor in problem-solving is analogous to that in perception.

On the basis of such experimental investigations, and guided by theoretical consideration, we can state as a reasonable hypothesis a companion generalization to the one in the previous discussion: *the temporal sequence of objects and events of a problem situation can facilitate or hinder the achievement of a solution in much the same way that it can facilitate or hinder the achievement of a perceptual organization.*

This hypothesis has much the same practical implication that the first one has. For many problems the temporal sequence is within our control. For example, many problems require the solution of a *series* of subproblems. In such cases there are several ways in which we can vary the temporal patterning.

We may have a choice between starting with where we wish to end, or starting with where we are at the moment. In the first instance we start by analyzing the *goal*. We ask, "Suppose we did achieve the goal, how would things be different—what subproblems would we have solved, etc.?" This in turn would determine the sequence of problems, and we would work back to the beginning. In the second instance we start by analyzing the *present situation,* see the implications of the given conditions and layout, and attack the various subproblems in a "forward direction." In some instances it may even be preferable to start in the middle, i.e., we can say "Let us assume I can solve the first four subproblems involved, and I now have arrived at such-and-such a point. Where can I go from here?" (This leaves for some later time the solution of the first four subproblems.) For different kinds of problems, certain temporal sequences may prove more efficient than others. The advice of the backwoods Vermonter who said, in response to the tourist's request for information on how to get to St. Johnsbury, "If I were you, I wouldn't start from here!" may be sound advice for

BOX 93

Practice Makes Blindness

Luchins while at New York University investigated the following question: *"Several problems, all solvable by one somewhat complex procedure, are presented in succession. If afterwards a similar task is given which can be solved by a more direct and simple method, will the individual be blinded to this direct possibility?"* Adapting a technique previously used at the University of Berlin, Luchins carried out a series of *Einstellung* (mental set) experiments to answer this question.

The task: obtain a required volume of water, given certain empty jars for measures. The following table presents the basic 8 problems used.

Problem	Given Empty Jars Holding No. of Quarts as Listed			Obtain the Following No. of Quarts of Water
1	29	3		20
2	21	127	3	100
3	14	163	25	99
4	18	43	10	5
5	9	42	6	21
6	20	59	4	31
7	23	49	3	20
8	15	39	3	18

Problem 1 was an illustrative problem; problems 2 through 6 were "training problems," 7 and 8 were "critical test problems." Problem 1 is presented and the solution shown diagrammatically (fig. *a*). Problem 2 is next shown and the answer is again dia-

grammed (fig. *b*), and explained: "One fills the 127-quart jar and from it fills the 21-quart jar once and the 3-quart jar twice. In the 127-quart jar there then remains 100

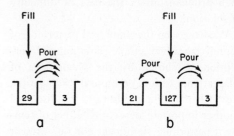

a   b

quarts of water." The method that solves problems 2 through 6 may also be used in 7 and 8. *But* problem 7 may be solved *more directly* by subtracting 3 from 23, and problem 8 by adding 3 to 15.

An experimental group was given problems 1 through 8 in succession (at intervals of about 2½ minutes). A control group went from problem 1 to problems 7 and 8, skipping problems 2 through 6.

In the table below are shown results on the critical test problems (7 and 8) from one experiment done with college students. The experimental subjects gave far fewer direct solutions. Thus, previous success with one technique can blind a person to simpler solutions.

LUCHINS, A. S. 1942. Mechanization in problem-solving. *Psychol. Monogr., 54,* No. 6.

Group	No. of Subjects	Per Cent Indirect Solutions	Per Cent Direct Solutions	Per Cent Other Solutions or Complete Failures
Control	57	0	100	0
Experimental	79	81	17	2

the problem-solver. Unlike the bewildered tourist, we do *not* always have to start from "here."

Sometimes our temporal sequence may be the most efficient, but the time intervals between the solution of one set of sub-

problems and the start of another may be too short, or too long. Here it may help to vary the tempo of our work on any one problem. In some cases it may be preferable to work away at the various subproblems until we will have solved them all; in other cases we may want to take frequent breaks. Again, our knowledge about the effects of temporal ordering is not specific enough to permit us to say which we should do for any one specific problem, but it is clear that the *timing* between subproblems can be important, and, therefore, whenever we do get "stuck," varying our timing may help.

SALIENCY. We have already pointed out that the problem-event is so dominating (salient) that we tend to focus all or most of our attention on the specific objects presented. But cognizance of *only* the specific objects present may be insufficient for the solution (see p. 375). To deal with this possibility, it is reasonable (even if paradoxical) to *reduce* the attention you pay to the problem you wish to solve! There are several ways to do it. (1) Take a break. Forget this problem for a while and work on other problems. When you return to the original problem, your previous excess involvement with the immediately present objects may not be as dominating. (2) Seek a *related* problem and attempt to solve it, even if you are not primarily interested in the related problem. The stimulus-pattern of the related problem may include the objects that are necessary for the solution of the original problem. Perhaps it is for this reason that "reasoning by analogy" is often fruitful (see Box 94).

Generalizing Our Practical Suggestions. We have suggested several specific tactics aimed at improving problem-solving: (1) try out various spatial arrangements of the material you have to work with; (2) try out various temporal patterns of the subproblems you have to attack; (3) try solving other analogous or related problems first. The question was raised by Maier whether such suggestions must be specific to the problem being attacked, or whether

general suggestions that warn against the danger of becoming "stuck" with one method of attack can facilitate problem-solving. To answer this question, Maier performed several experiments at the University of Michigan; among them was the following.

Three hundred and eighty-four students in an introductory course in psychology were divided into a control group (206 students) and an experimental group (178 students). Three problems were presented to both groups. The experimental group also received a 20-minute lecture followed by general hints on "How to Reason" (see Box 95) before being presented with the problems. The three problems included the "string" problem, which we have already described (see Box 91), and two other similar "reasoning" problems.

The results seemed fairly clear. Within the hour that was allowed for solution of the problems the experimental group earned a total correct-solution score of 49.2 per cent, while the control group earned only 39.7 per cent. These results indicate that a *20-minute general lecture* improved the problem-solving of the students of the experimental group. A second experiment on different students (testing their reasoning ability before and after the lecture) gave similar results and Maier concluded, in part:

"The results of both experiments indicate that when subjects are carefully instructed to guard against habitual activities and persistent directions, but to be alert for new points of view, there is a decided increase in reasoning ability as measured by the increase in solutions found to difficult problems. . . . One cannot equip a person with the ability to form solution-patterns, but one can train him to clear the ground so that the solution-pattern is not prevented from appearing."

We must, however, avoid overgeneraliz-

BOX 94

If at First You Don't Succeed—Don't Try Again, Try Another Problem

In his book *How to Solve It* the mathematician Polya of Stanford University gives many valuable hints to college students on how to deal with mathematical problems. Among other suggestions he stresses the importance of analogies, "auxiliary problems," and "related" problems:

"People often use vague, ambitious, incomplete, or incompletely clarified analogies, but analogy may reach the level of mathematical precision. All sorts of analogy may play a role in the discovery of the solution and so we should not neglect any sort. . . . We may consider ourselves lucky when, trying to solve a problem, we succeed in discovering a *simpler analogous problem.*

"*Auxiliary problem* is a problem which we consider, not for its own sake, but because we hope that its consideration may help us to solve another problem, our original problem. . . . The auxiliary problem may appear more accessible than the original problem; or it may appear instructive; or it may have some sort of aesthetic appeal. Sometimes the only advantage of the auxiliary problem is that it is new and offers unexplored possibilities; we choose it because we are tired of the original problem all approaches to which seem to be exhausted.

"We can scarcely imagine a problem absolutely new, unlike and unrelated to any formerly solved problem. . . . In fact, when solving a problem, we always profit from previously solved problems. . . . Hence the question: *Do you know a related problem?* . . . The intention of using a certain formerly solved problem influences our conception of the present problem. Trying to link up the two problems, the new and the old, we introduce into the new problem elements corresponding to certain important elements of the old problem."

All these practical suggestions from a teacher of mathematics add up to methods of enlarging the range of stimuli that play upon us as we go about the business of trying to solve problems. And it may be this that lies behind the *Inventor's Paradox,* i.e., "The more ambitious plan may have more chances of success than the more limited one." As Polya points out:

". . . when passing from one problem to another, we may often observe that the new, more ambitious problem is easier to handle than the original problem. More questions may be easier to answer than just one question. . . . The more ambitious plan may have more chances of success provided it is not based on mere pretension but on some vision of the things beyond those immediately present."

POLYA, G. 1946. *How to solve it.* Princeton: Princeton Univ. Press.

---

ing from the results of Maier's experiment. In the first place, as Maier himself specifically points out, his experiments do not prove that we can "equip a person with the ability to form solution-patterns." In part this ability is dependent upon the person's basic intelligence, and no amount of well-designed lectures or "how-to-think" books can do very much to change that. In the second place, "clearing the ground so that the solution-pattern is not prevented from appearing" may sometimes make very little difference. Successful problem-solving necessitates a store of *previously acquired knowledge.* If the store of knowledge is not there, or if the knowledge was acquired in ways that make it unavailable for novel and creative problems, no amount of "ground clearing" can help. Finally, Maier's findings do not imply that all we need do to get rid of "habitual activities and persistent directions" is to listen to a general lecture. Personality and motivational factors may effectively inhibit the development of "new points of view." We cannot say to a person who gets emotionally upset by ambiguous stimulus-patterns, "Be alert to new points of view, guard against habitual directions," and expect any more success than we can from saying to a neurotically anxious person, "Stop worrying!" In either case much more fundamental difficulties are present than can be remedied by general lectures and admonitions.

To state the case more positively what Maier's experiment does tend to prove is that all other things being equal, general training on the theme "Do Not Be Stimulus-Bound" may facilitate creative problem-solving.

Knowledge and Creativity. Every discussion of creative problem-solving, whether by the practical inventor who generalizes from his own experiences or by the psychologist who theorizes on the basis of laboratory experiment, stresses the intimate relation between knowledge and creativity. This relationship, expressed in different words and with different emphases, can be summarized in two contradictory statements: (1) the *more* knowledge an individual has acquired in the past, the greater is the possibility that he will be creative with new problems; and (2) the *less* knowl-

---

BOX 95

A Psychologist's Lecture Notes on How to Reason

Maier's lecture that was successful in improving the problem-solving scores for 178 students covered the following points:

(1) The solution of a problem, when it is the product of reasoning, consists of a pattern that is made up of parts of different past experiences.

(2) The pattern forms suddenly as does the hidden face in a picture puzzle.

(3) Meanings of elements depend on the pattern of which they are a part. The sudden formation of a pattern therefore results in sudden changes of meaning.

(4) The solution-pattern overcomes a difficulty.

(5) The difficulty is what one sees it to be. It is not in the problem. (Illustrations were given that show how the same problem can be solved in different ways, each solution being the conquering of a different difficulty.)

(6) The particular difficulty one sees determines what one will do about it, i.e., what direction one will take (e.g., one doctor will seek a serum to immunize man to certain germs, another will seek a means of preventing the germ from traveling).

(7) All difficulties cannot be overcome.

Hence one must find a difficulty that can be overcome.

(8) Most people see the same difficulty.

(9) The difficulties we see are often determined by our past contact with problems (e.g., other diseases have been conquered by the discovery of serums). Such difficulties are habitual difficulties and give rise to habitual directions.

(10) Habitual directions do not solve difficult problems. Problems are difficult when a successful direction is not obvious.

Maier then summarized his lecture with the following "Hints on How to Reason":

Locate a difficulty and try to overcome it. If you fail, get it completely out of your mind and seek an entirely different difficulty.

Do not be a creature of habit and stay in a rut. Keep your mind open for new meanings.

The solution-pattern appears suddenly. You cannot force it. Keep your mind open for new combinations and do not waste time on unsuccessful attempts.

MAIER, N. R. F. 1933. An aspect of human reasoning. *Brit. J. Psychol.*, 24, 144–55.

edge an individual has acquired in the past, the greater is his creativity. The reason for this apparent contradiction is that *both* statements are valid—when properly specified as to meaning.

No amount of "flexibility" in creative problem-solving can be helpful, of course, if the person does not have the specific knowledge required for the solution. But facts can be restrictive. In many instances the novel and creative use of objects is directly traceable to the person's possession of so *few* facts about the object that "bizarre" meanings and ingenious uses are encouraged. Frequently the physiognomic properties of an object suggest all manner of novel uses, but with increased knowledge about an object, the physiognomic properties play a minor role. As we have noted in Chapter 3 when discussing the world of the child, the spontaneity of "childlike" perceptions has creative value. The knowledgeable astronomer who has learned that the moon is a dead mass of matter which can only reflect light from the sun, and has no source of radiant energy within itself, will rarely see in the moon the "ignorant" child's perception of "a hot bird flying through the night sky." Yet this is the stuff of creative poetry.

Facts may be restrictive for quite another reason. Much of the "knowledge" we acquire—whether through experience or formal education—is just simply wrong. Insofar as this is true, the ability to do creative problem-solving is damaged by the acquisition of this "knowledge." This is probably what Charles Kettering, the famous inventor, had in mind when he said, "The inventor is a fellow who doesn't take his education too seriously."

AVAILABILITY OF KNOWLEDGE. Knowledge that *can* be helpful, once acquired may (as many of us know) be forgotten and thus no longer be available for use. This merely emphasizes the point that sheer memory may be a very important determinant of the creative problem-solving ability of the person. However, as we shall see in the next chapter, memory is not an all-or-nothing affair. What we have memorized may be more or less available for use. Thus, while we may not be able to recall the name of a former acquaintance, we may easily recognize it among other names on a list. In the same way we may learn a great deal about objects—but we may remember the various attributes of the objects with different degrees of "functional availability." In general, the more numerous the different meanings we have learned to attach to an object and the more readily available these different meanings are, the better our problem-solving performance. (See Box 96 for an experimental illustration of the relationship between different degrees of availability of meanings of common objects and problem-solving.)

THE USES OF KNOWLEDGE. The availability of knowledge, then, is of crucial importance in problem-solving. Once available, the knowledge may be used in three different ways when we are engaged in creative problem-solving: (a) We may *reproduce* a bit of knowledge in a new situation directly and without change. For example, in Figure 94 we apply directly to the new problem, without any change, our previously learned knowledge that the area of a square is equal to the square of one of its sides. (b) We may *transform* an experience so that it becomes applicable to the solution of a problem (see Box 97). (c) We may combine many specific experiences into one *abstraction*. This generalized knowledge is now applicable to the solution of a problem in which the *specific* knowledge (which was included in the generalization) is not helpful in solving the problem. (See Box 98.)

Any specific piece of knowledge can, of course, appear in any one of the above

BOX 96

"Availability" of Meanings and Problem-Solving

Saugstad and Raaheim at the University of Oslo tested the hypothesis that problem-solving may depend on the general availability of specific meanings for certain objects.

Among the subjects tested were 95 Oslo high school boys. *The task:* Using anything on the table, transfer the balls from the glass "G" to the container "O" without stepping beyond the chalk line. (See sketch.) *Solution:* With the pliers the nail is bent into a hook, tied to the string, and thrown so as to catch the wooden frame "F," which is then pulled around the obstruction "B" to within reach of the subject. The newspapers are then rolled into tubes and with the aid of the rubber bands are made into one continuous tubing. The balls can now be rolled through this long paper tube into the container "O."

At a previous time the subjects had been given a "functional availability" test. For example: They had been told that a nail could be used to fasten, catch, stick, and hang things. They had then been asked to write down three illustrations for each function. The same was done for the other objects to be used in the later problem.

To solve the problem, two "unusual" meanings are involved: the nail as a "hook" and the newspapers as "tube." Particular attention was therefore paid to the mention of "hook" and "tube" (or "funnel") in the subjects' illustrations of the functions of a nail and a newspaper respectively. This permitted distinguishing three groups: (1) subjects who had mentioned both "hook" and "tube"; (2) those who had mentioned one *or* the other; (3) those who had mentioned neither. On the Saugstad problem these three groups performed as follows:

Function Available	No. of Subjects	Per Cent of Solutions
Hook *and* Tube	18	89
Hook *or* Tube	40	42
Neither	37	19

Success in problem-solving may sometimes be determined by the availability of a specific meaning for a specific object.

SAUGSTAD, P., and RAAHEIM, K. 1956. Problem-solving as dependent on availability of functions. Manuscript. Univ. of Oslo, Oslo, Norway.

BOX 97

Simple Knowledge Creatively Transformed

Székely demonstrated how a very simply acquired experience may be used in creative problem-solving. The subject was given three columns of match sticks, with three sticks in each column, and three more sticks with which to work. His task was to distribute the three extra sticks among the three columns in such a way that every vertical and horizontal row would have four sticks in it (see fig.). Few subjects solved the problem.

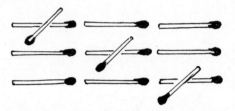

Some subjects, while carrying out these instructions, suddenly asked for some match sticks, saying that they wanted to try out an idea. They then solved yesterday's problem as shown in the figure below.

One day later the subjects were asked to serve in an entirely separate experiment. In this new experiment a horizontal row of lines was shown and the subject was *instructed* to draw a perpendicular through every third line (see fig.).

Two things should be noted: (1) The subjects returned to yesterday's unsolved problem of their "own accord." (2) The newly acquired experience was transformed a bit before it was applied to a new problem.

Try this experiment on your friends.

SZÉKELY, L. 1945. *Zur Psychologie des geistigen Schaffens. Schweitzer Zeitsch. f. Psychologie, 4,* 110–24.

---

three forms. Thus the knowledge that "wood floats," when stated in this way, is a reproduction. When stated in the form, "a-wooden-pellet-when-released-at-the-bottom-of-a-container-of-water-will-shoot-up-to-the-surface," it is a transformation. When stated in terms of the Hydrostatic Principle, it is an abstraction. It is obvious that any specific piece of knowledge that is available to the person in *all three forms* will be more useful than the same piece of knowledge available in only one form.

REPRODUCTION VS. TRANSFORMATION. When we are able to reproduce a bit of knowledge, on demand, we say that we have remembered (or retained) what we have learned. What determines whether we will remember? This question has been subjected to intensive experimental analysis, as we shall see in the next chapter, and the an-

swer is a fairly complex one. We will anticipate the discussion there by noting that, up to a certain point, and with diminishing returns, the more frequent the drill, the better the retention.

Many psychologists and educators believe that drill can be carried to the point where it becomes an inhibiting factor in creative problem-solving. However the experimental evidence for this remains rather sketchy. Experiments such as that of Luchins (Box 93) do indicate that practice may have a harmful effect on the solution of novel problems, since the well-practiced bit of knowledge may be applied uncritically. As we have already pointed out, when the person performs a habitual, well-drilled act, he is no longer *coping* with the problem (see p. 277).

Some psychologists have suggested that

BOX 98

Specific Knowledge vs. Abstraction

An abstract principle is often more useful in solving problems than are concrete statements of specific knowledge. We will try to demonstrate this with you as a subject. If you are too sophisticated for this experiment, try it on your less sophisticated friends.

On an inclined plane stands a cart attached to a string. The string runs over a pulley to a block of wood which is just barely touching the surface of water in a container. The whole arrangement is so balanced that the cart remains stationary. Standing on the table is a beaker of water. Nothing else is available. (See sketch.) Your task is to set the cart in motion so that it will move *down* the inclined plane. You are not permitted to touch the cart or put anything in it; nor may you lift the wooden block with your hands. Here is a bit of knowledge which helps to solve the problem: WOOD FLOATS.

Second problem. Everything remains as formerly, *except* that in place of the wooden block you now have a small lead weight. Again the arrangement is so balanced that the cart is at rest. (Same sketch will do exactly.) Same problem: Cause the cart to move *down*. Here is a bit of knowledge which helps solve the problem: LEAD SINKS.

If you don't understand the solution to this second problem, let us review your Freshman physics a bit, and take the two bits of specific knowledge, "wood floats, lead sinks," and see them as specific instances of an abstract generalization: *Whether a body floats or sinks depends upon the ratio between the body's weight and the weight of the displaced quantity of water.* If this Hydrostatic Principle doesn't seem to help you, let us state it in still another manner—in terms of Archimedes' Principle: All bodies, when immersed in water, appear to lose a certain part of their weight. The "lost weight" corresponds to the quantity of water displaced.

Now can you solve the second problem —and *understand* its solution? (The above "experiment" is a revision of one performed by Székely.)

We see how an abstract principle may help where specific knowledge fails.

SZÉKELY, L. 1950. Knowledge and thinking. *Acta Psychologica*, 7, 1–24.

---

although "blindly memorized" knowledge may be well retained, it is not available for transformation. On the other hand, "understood" knowledge may be even better retained and can be transformed. In this analysis the *teaching* method is usually stressed. We can teach the very same fact in a "senseless" manner, or we can teach it so that the person *understands* what he is memorizing.

CONCRETE VS. ABSTRACT KNOWLEDGE. It is sometimes assumed that the best kind of

teaching attaches concrete meanings to operations rather than stressing abstract principles. The attempt is frequently made, for example, to make the teaching of mathematics more "pupil-oriented," to "relate" mathematical problems more closely to Youngster Anyman's own everyday activities in order to "motivate" him. But motives, as we have seen in Chapter 8, do not always depend upon activities closely related to the self. Whatever "pupil-oriented" teaching may do to Youngster's motives, it is clear that teaching which neglects abstract principles may hinder Youngster's problem-solving. We have already seen that the acquisition of such concrete facts as "wood floats, metal sinks," instead of, say, the Hydrostatic Principle, may actually prevent problem-solving.

BY WAY OF SUMMARY. It is clear that "knowledge" is a two-edged sword. Without extensive knowledge of specific facts and general principles, no significant creative problem-solving can take place. But there are "good" and there are "bad" ways of acquiring knowledge. This points to the primary importance of sound educational methods if we are to help to develop creative problem-solvers. It also emphasizes the importance of inculcating in the learner the proper problem-solving principles, such as we have described. In other words, we must not only provide the student with the basic *materials* ("knowledge") with which he can solve problems, but with the *methods* that will enable him to make effective use of these basic materials.

Motivation, Personality, and Creativity. To arrange an "ideal" stimulus-pattern and to equip the person with all the knowledge he needs, even doing so in a proper manner, may still not be sufficient to enable us to understand, predict, and control his problem-solving behavior. For Mr. Anyman comes to a problem with definite motives and a well-established personality structure. We must understand how both of these will influence his problem-solving behavior if we are to write the complete story of problem-solving.

Some experimental evidence on the effects of motivational and emotional states on problem-solving has already been discussed. Attempting to solve a difficult problem takes on many aspects of frustration, and with frustration people (at least school children—see Box 72, p. 317) regress to lower levels of complexity and integration. We have also seen (Box 73, p. 319) that frustration in animals leads to stereotyped and maladaptive attempts at solution.

DEGREE OF MOTIVATION. More specific information on the effects of *degree* of motivation upon problem-solving comes from experimental work with chimpanzees. See Box 99. The data obtained there are consistent with general observations of the problem-solving behavior of human beings under varying degrees of stress.

The relationship between effectiveness in problem-solving and intensity of motivation can be described as an inverted "U curve." That is, as the intensity of the problem-solver's motivation increases, his problem-solving effectiveness also increases, *up to an optimal point.* Beyond that point any increase in intensity of motivation will result in a *decrease* in problem-solving efficiency (see Fig. 95).

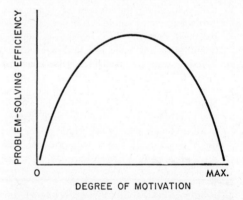

FIG. 95. A hypothetical curve representing the suggestion that the relationship between degree of motivation and problem-solving efficiency is curvilinear. As the degree of motivation increases from zero, the problem-solving efficiency first increases and then decreases.

The optimal point on the curve will vary tremendously from individual to individual. Some people have greater "frustration tolerance" than others. Moreover, different individuals have different patterns of frustration responses. One person's frustration behavior may consist of aggressive, violent attacks; another's may involve withdrawal from all external contact; still another's

may include regression. Each of these patterns will have a different effect on problem-solving behavior; some may be more harmful than others; and certainly each

---

BOX 99

Intensity of Motives and Problem-Solving in the Chimpanzee

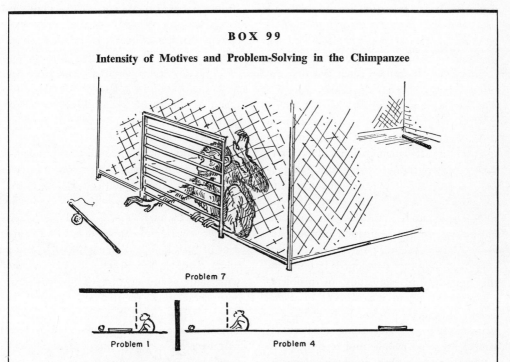

Problem 7

Problem 1   Problem 4

In 1945 Birch investigated the relationship between motivation and problem-solving in young chimpanzees. He used the "stick problems," which require the animal to rake in food with a stick. The problems differ in spatial patterning and complexity (see fig.). In problem 1 the stick is next to the food; in 4 the stick is *behind* the animal as he faces the food; in 7 the animal has to take the *short* stick behind him, with it pull the string attached to the *long* stick into reach, pull in the long stick by the string, and finally sweep in the food with the long stick. Motivation was varied by depriving the animals of food for 2, 6, 12, 24, 36, and 48 hours before testing.

The results are best described in Birch's own summary:

"When motivation is very low the animals are easily diverted from the problem by extraneous factors and behavior tends

to deteriorate into a series of non-goal-directed acts. Under conditions of very intense motivation, the animals concentrated upon the goal to the exclusion of other features of the situation which were essential to the solution of the problem. Also, the frequent occurrence of frustration responses, such as tantrums and screaming, when a given stereotyped pattern of response proved to be inadequate, hindered the animals in their problem-solving efforts. Those animals who worked . . . under intermediate conditions of motivational intensity . . . were not so dominated by the desire to obtain the food that they were incapable of responding to other relevant features of the problem situation. Their behavior was characterized by both direction and flexibility in response."

BIRCH, H. G. 1945. The role of motivational factors in insightful problem-solving. *J. comp. Psychol.*, 43, 259–78.

will result in a qualitatively different pattern of creative problem-solving.

"INTOLERANCE OF AMBIGUITY." Psychoanalytic concepts have played an important role in the approach to the study of problem-solving which emphasizes personality factors. For example, Otto Fenichel, the psychoanalyst who did much work on the neurotic personality, suggested that the problem-solving behavior of the compulsive person is in keeping with his whole personality pattern. In conformity with such a personality the neurotically compulsive person, according to Fenichel's observations, ". . . tends to make false generalizations, to classify hastily all ideas into certain mutually exclusive categories and then to get into a state of doubt concerning the nature and evaluation of the categories." (Fenichel, 1945.)

Perhaps the best-developed instance of this approach to the study of problem-solving is found in the concept of *ambiguity tolerance* proposed by Frenkel-Brunswik (1949). According to Frenkel-Brunswik, some people find it difficult to tolerate or cope with ambiguities, inconsistencies, and surprises. Such a person, therefore, will stick to the "tried and true" rather than venture forth on new paths. When he is unavoidably confronted with an ambiguous situation, he will quickly arrive at one concrete interpretation and stay with it as long as possible. This way of dealing with an ambiguous situation characterizes all of his behavior—his emotions, his relations with other people, his perceptions, and his problem-solving behavior. Such a person is said to be "intolerant of ambiguity."

Presumably all people can be described in terms of this personality pattern. That is, some of us are more, and some less, able to tolerate ambiguity. We should therefore expect to find definite relationships existing between people's general "inflexibility"

and their perceptual, learning, and creative problem-solving behavior. Some experimental evidence is now available to support this expectation. For example, Frenkel-Brunswik in experiments with children found that the degree to which prior experience with a problem "fixates" the child on one solution to a problem (as measured by the Luchins technique) correlated fairly well with children's "rigidity." Rigidity was determined by clinical ratings based on the children's attitudes toward parents, sex, self, and moral values.

The approach to the study of problem-solving which emphasizes personality factors and the experimental research on it are still rather new, and we cannot be certain that such an analysis will stand up under further investigation. No doubt the concept of "ambiguity tolerance" will undergo some change. Nevertheless, we can say with some assurance that our clinical, experimental, and theoretical observations strongly suggest that creative problem-solving ability is determined in considerable part by some general, emotional, and personality traits of the problem solver.

Creative Problem-Solving— a Process Description

So far we have devoted ourselves to an analysis of the factors that influence problem-solving. We will now present a brief description of the process of problem-solving as it occurs over time. Such a description will have to be a generalized one. The "natural history" of one creative problem-solving process differs from that of almost every other one. The difficulty and complexity of the problem, the capacity of the problem solver, his work habits, his store of knowledge, his motivation, his personality, all influence the sequence of events which, taken together, we call the creative problem-solving process.

Not only the psychologist, but all creative workers have been interested in the description of the problem-solving process. Each one brings somewhat different testimony, but one descriptive schema appears again and again. This is the classical four stages of creative thought: *preparation, incubation, illumination,* and *verification.* Though this neat schema occasionally does violence to the actual sequence of events, it will do as a general framework, and we will briefly describe these four phases.

The Four Stages. The first stage, *preparation,* can be briefly described as the period when the problem solver becomes acquainted with the various features of the problem and begins to "play" with ideas. The stimulus-pattern evokes first this and then that association. Often these associations seem to be random and "free" in nature, directed by the demands of the problem, but not completely restricted by these demands. Gradually a more disciplined attitude is taken. Certain suggestions and ideas are discarded, others are examined more carefully, and problem-solving in earnest gets underway. Frequently this stage merges rapidly and without any noticeable "break" into the illumination and verification stages, and the problem is solved.

The second stage, *incubation,* varies greatly in its nature and its duration. It may last a few minutes, several days, weeks, months or even years. It is a stage in which the problem is laid aside and no "conscious" work done upon it, but after which renewed attention to the problem results in prompt solution or at least a prompt advance beyond the previous degree of mastery. The testimony of creative thinkers is full of accounts of the incubation period. Mathematicians, inventors,

poets, scientists, and artists have testified that this or that solution unaccountably occurred while shaving, or while bathing, or while listening to a concert, or while rounding the corner of Hampstead Heath. There can be no doubt of its reality.

We have already seen some possible factors that might account for the facilitating effect of a rest period on problem-solving, when we considered the advantages of taking "breaks" (see p. 385). There still remains the possibility that creative problem-solving may go on *during* this rest period —without conscious effort. This points to an important consideration. An analysis of creative problem-solving which restricts itself to the person's reports of "what he is thinking about" may not be adequate. Much may occur without any conscious experience. We must supplement the person's reports with other kinds of observations and analyses.

Illumination was described in the last chapter when we discussed "insight." Often the person, as soon as he has hit upon what appears to him to be the general solution, will assume that the problem has been solved and will do no further work on it. This may mean that he ends his problem-solving prematurely. His "general idea" may not work.

Verification is the last stage. The proposed solution may be worked out in more specific detail, and it may be applied and tested. If it meets the test, the problem is solved.

A Three-Level Description. Duncker has suggested a somewhat different and more detailed description. This description is based on a careful observation of people actively solving problems under laboratory conditions. It fills out the more general four-stage picture and gives a "play-by-play" account of how solutions seem to arise. We will conclude our discussion of creative problem-solving with Duncker's description of the developmental history of a solution.

Duncker's analysis of problem-solving is couched in perceptual terms; each step in the process is equivalent to a new perceptual organization. He describes the creative problem-solving process as consisting of *a related series of organizations*, each influenced by what preceded it. This series, his analysis shows, can be grouped into three major levels.

When a person first tackles a problem, the initial organization that he achieves can be described as a "general range." This is a very general restatement of the original problem which indicates the "direction" of a possible solution. This initial organization may emphasize some general property of the sought-after solution, or some general method that might bring about the solution. The "general range" is followed by the "functional solution," which reformulates and narrows the "general range." "Functional solutions" have the typical form: "If such and such could be achieved, the problem would be solved."

The next step, "specific solution," can be described as a reformulation and a further specification of the "functional solution." If a given "specific solution" is found to be unsatisfactory, the subject may revert to the stage of the preceding "functional solution" and seek some other "specific solution." Failing in that, he may revert to the "general range" and start out on other "functional solutions" and go on from there. He may even, of course, try out different "general ranges."

AN EXPERIMENTAL ILLUSTRATION. Duncker's description can be clarified through specific illustration from his classic study of problem-solving. In one of his experiments he presented his subjects (University of Berlin students) with the schematic sketch shown in Figure 96 and the following prob-

lem: "Given, a human being with an inoperable stomach tumor. We know that if we apply certain rays, with sufficient intensity, the tumor can be destroyed. The problem is: how can these rays, at the required high intensity, be applied to the tumor without at the same time destroying the healthy tissue which surrounds the tumor?"

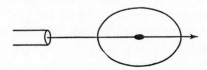

FIG. 96. This schematic sketch used by Duncker in his cancer problem is intended to represent a cross section through the body with the tumor in the middle and the radiation apparatus on the left. The line with the arrow represents the course of the rays. (After Duncker, 1945.)

Read the problem as presented in the text and see if you can solve it.

Duncker asked his subjects to "think out loud" while they worked at this problem. Figure 97 presents a diagrammatic summary of the thinking of one subject as he attempted to solve the problem. It will be seen that his problem-solving process consisted of several "general ranges," "functional solutions," and "specific solutions."

The first "general range" adopted by this student was: "I must find some way of avoiding contact between the rays and the healthy tissue." This "general range" could and did lead to several more specific restatements of the problem ("functional solutions"): use a free path to the stomach; remove healthy tissue from path of rays; insert a protecting wall between rays and healthy tissue; displace tumor toward the surface. From each of these "functional solutions" a "specific solution" suggested itself to the subject. These in turn were either rejected by the experimenter as inadequate, or were seen to be inadequate by the subject himself. As each "specific solu-

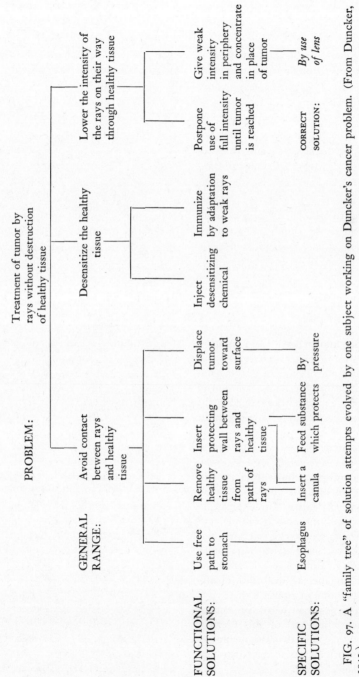

FIG. 97. A "family tree" of solution attempts evolved by one subject working on Duncker's cancer problem. (From Duncker, 1945.)

tion" was rejected, the subject would go on to a different "functional solution," and to different "general ranges," until he finally adopted the one, "Lower the intensity of the rays on their way through healthy tissue." This third "general range" finally did lead to the correct solution. Let us quote the student as he approached this last lap and went through the "functional solution" into the "specific": "Somehow divert . . . diffuse rays . . . disperse . . . stop! Send a broad and weak bundle of rays through a lens in such a way that the tumor lies at the focal point and thus receives intensive radiation." (This solution is closely related to the best solution: Send several weak bundles of rays from various points outside the body, all these weak bundles to meet at the tumor; thus the intensity of the rays necessary for destruction is attained only at the tumor. The rays could not be deflected by ordinary lenses, as suggested by the student, but nevertheless the experimenter accepted this as a solution.) The total duration of this problem-solving attempt was about half an hour.

This description of the problem-solving process is, like the four-stage description, generalized from many observations. Not every problem solver goes through the three levels of "general range," "functional solution," "specific solution," in that order. Almost every conceivable "exception to the rule" is found if a large enough group of subjects is examined. Nevertheless, Duncker's description, insofar as it does represent an accurate picture of the *typical* or modal problem-solving process, helps to fill out the more global description given by the traditional four-stage analysis. Both together, then, provide us with a description of the problem-solving process.

Glossary

abstraction of knowledge. Combining a number of specific experiences into a single generalization. Frequently this generalization is applicable to the solution of new problems in which any one of the specific experiences alone would not be helpful.

ambiguity tolerance. A concept intended to describe a basic personality trait. According to this concept, people differ in their capacity to tolerate, or cope with, conflicting emotions, unstructured percepts, unclear relationships among people, etc. A person low in ambiguity tolerance will seek to avoid inconsistencies and change; a person high in ambiguity tolerance will show less reluctance to deal with changing, unstructured situations.

Einstellung. The German word for "mental set." The common use of this German word reflects the fact that the mental-set experiments originated in German psychological laboratories.

explanation. A category of creative problem-solving. Refers to those problems in which the person seeks to understand why a certain event has occurred.

functional availability. A term that refers to the ease with which a specific meaning or use of an object can be recalled.

functional fixity. A term that refers to the fact that seeing an object being used in one way may inhibit seeing other ways in which the same object may be employed.

functional solution. A term proposed by Karl Duncker, a German psychologist, to refer to the second step in problem-solving. The functional solution is characterized by a narrowing of the "general range," and thus specifies the nature of the final, but not-yet-achieved, "specific solution." (See also "general range" and "specific solution.")

general range. A term referring to the step occurring first in problem-solving. It is a very general restatement of the original problem. This restatement indicates the direction of the to-be-sought-for solution.

illumination. The third stage of problem-solving. Identical with the "Aha!" experience and refers to the sudden recognition of how a problem is to be solved.

incubation. The second stage that may occur in the problem-solving process. During this stage no "conscious" work is done on the problem, but when the person returns to it, a prompt advance beyond the previous degree of mastery is noted. It has been suggested that during the "silent" or incubation period creative problem-solving goes on despite the lack of conscious effort.

invention. A category of creative problem-solving. Refers to problems in which the person seeks to discover and arrange the objects that will be necessary to bring about a desired end. He must also understand why these objects will bring about the desired end.

"mental dazzle." A term coined by the German psychologist, David Katz, to refer to the disturbing effect of irrelevant or unfamiliar attributes of objects upon problem-solving.

prediction. A category of creative problem-solving. Refers to problems in which the person seeks to anticipate what will happen, given certain conditions. He must also understand why these specified conditions will bring about the anticipated event.

preparation. The first stage of the problem-solving process. This is the period when the person becomes acquainted with the problem and "plays" with ideas for its solution.

reproduction of knowledge. Applying previously acquired knowledge, directly and without change, to solve a problem.

specific solution. A term that pertains to the final step in problem-solving. This step involves a further specification of the "functional solution" and, if successful, is the final, correct solution. (See also "general range" and "functional solution.")

stimulus-bound. Behavior displaying great dependence upon the specific stimulus-pattern confronting the person. To be stimulus-bound is to be inflexible.

transformation of knowledge. Revising previously acquired knowledge so that it becomes applicable to the solution of a new problem.

verification. The fourth stage of problem-solving. At this stage the proposed general solution may be specified or it may be applied and tested.

Suggestions for Further Reading

DUNCKER, K. 1945. (Trans. by L. S. Lees.) On problem-solving. *Psychol. Monogr.*, 58, No. 270.

A series of experiments on creative thinking together with a searching analysis of the psychological processes involved. Not easy reading, but rewarding.

HUMPHREY, G. 1948. *Directed thinking.* New York: Dodd, Mead.

An interestingly written, nontechnical account of many experiments in the field of creative thinking, by a former professor of psychology at Oxford University. Contains many sound suggestions for improving one's thinking.

KÖHLER, W. 1925. *The mentality of apes.* New York: Harcourt, Brace.

A classic account of problem-solving in the primates, written by one of the founders of Gestalt psychology. Has served as the basis for much of the subsequent work in the field.

POLYA, G. 1946. *How to solve it.* Princeton: Princeton Univ. Press.

This little book, widely reprinted, contains many helpful suggestions on how to solve problems. Written by a distinguished mathematician.

WERTHEIMER, M. 1945. *Productive thinking.* New York: Harper.

Essays and demonstration experiments in creative thinking. Of special interest is Wertheimer's account of what constitutes good and bad teaching in the field of mathematics.

BRUNER, J. S., GOODNOW, J. J. and AUSTIN, G. A. 1956. *A study of thinking.* New York: Wiley.

An account of many original experiments on the strategy of problem-solving performed in the Harvard laboratories.

JOHNSON, D. M. 1955. *The psychology of thought and judgment.* New York: Harper.

A systematic presentation of experimental work in the area of thinking. Clearly written and showing wide coverage.

CHAPTER XV

Simple Learning

THE IMPORTANCE of learning was made clear in the last chapter where we saw that significant creative problem-solving is possible only when the individual can apply old knowledge to new problems in novel and original ways. Such previously learned knowledge ranges from familiarity with the use of forks and knives to the generalizations of atomic physics.

The many kinds of learning which man and beast display can be grouped into three categories of increasing complexity. These are (1) conditioned-response learning, (2) rote learning, and (3) trial-and-error learning.

In *conditioned-response learning* the individual is presented with an original stimulus (one that calls forth a fairly simple response) and a neutral stimulus (one that does *not* call forth that response). After sufficient repetitive pairings of these two stimuli, the individual acquires the tendency to make a response to the neutral stimulus—a response which formerly was not evoked by that stimulus.

In *rote learning* the person merely has to commit to memory a series of words, letters, numbers, sentences, sounds, or movements that are clearly defined for him.

Finally, in *trial-and-error learning* the person faces a more complex task. He must *select* out certain "correct" responses from a range of possible responses and retain the responses thus selected.

It is clear that as we go from the simpler conditioned-response type of learning to the more complex trial-and-error learning we approach creative problem-solving. There are no sharp dividing lines among the various forms of adaptive behavior. For purposes of convenience we will discuss the simpler forms of learning—conditioned-response and rote learning—in this chapter; the more complex form of trial-and-error learning, in the next chapter.

Conditioned Response Learning

The term "conditioned response" is variously used. It is sometimes used to cover every possible type of learning, thinking, and problem-solving. Such usage reflects a *theory* about conditioned responses—the theory that conditioned responses are the basic elements of which all learning is composed. We shall use the term in a purely *descriptive* sense, to refer to a training technique and a learning process which, taken together, differ in some important respects from all other kinds of learning.

The classical work in conditioned responses was done in the laboratory of the Russian physiologist, Ivan Petrovich Pavlov, during the first years of the present century. Pavlov, who was primarily interested in the study of the digestive glands (for which he was awarded the Nobel Prize), noted, as a laboratory curiosity, that the secretions from the salivary glands of the dog could be controlled by learning as well as by direct physiological or biochemical means. Becoming interested in what he called the "psychic influences" on the salivary gland, he soon devoted most of the facilities of his laboratory to their systematic investigation, and the era of "conditioned responses" in psychology, physiology, philosophy, literature, and science-fiction was initiated.

Pavlov and his coworkers very early isolated and named the three basic phenomena of conditioned response: (1) *conditioning*, that is, the acquisition of a stimulus-response relationship; (2) *generalization*, that is, the ability of the organism to transfer its acquisition to other situations; (3) *extinction*, that is, the loss of the acquisition.

Conditioning. The fundamental facts of acquisition are easily described. When a weak acid is placed in a dog's mouth, his salivary glands are stimulated and saliva flows. The flow of saliva under these circumstances is automatic and unlearned, and is therefore known as an *unconditioned response*, abbreviated UR. The acid that elicits this UR is called an *uncondi-*

tioned stimulus, or US. Suppose we now take some other stimulus—such as a bright light—that has no influence on the action of the salivary glands, and shine it in the dog's eyes just before we place the acid (US) on his tongue. Each time a conditioned stimulus is paired with an unconditioned stimulus we speak of *reinforcement.* After a number of such joint presentations of acid and light, the light stimulus when presented alone will elicit the flow of saliva. The action of the glands under these circumstances is a new response and is known as a *conditioned response,* or CR. The light that can now call forth this CR is known as the *conditioned stimulus,* or CS. A new stimulus-response relationship has been established in the dog. Where formerly he had only US → UR, he now has in addition CS → CR.

Closely allied with original conditioning is the process known as *higher-order conditioning.* This refers to the establishment of a second conditioned response based upon a previously established one. Thus, to carry forward our example, if after the dog is conditioned to salivate to the light stimulus we now couple the light with a bell, the dog will soon salivate to the bell alone. In this case it is "as if" the light were now the US, and the bell the CS. Presumably this can go on for several more steps. We can couple the bell with a touch on the nose, and soon the dog will salivate to a touch on the nose, etc. (We will later see, in Box 102, an illustration of the use of higher-order conditioning in man.)

TEMPORAL PATTERNING. The temporal patterning of events is as important in conditioning as it is in perception and creative problem-solving. The crucial factor is the time relation between the US and CS. There are four major time patterns normally used in conditioned-response training: (1) *Simultaneous conditioning.* Here the CS may begin from a fraction of a second to 5 seconds before the US and continue along with it until the response occurs. (2) *Delayed conditioning.* The CS begins from 5 seconds to several minutes before the US and then continues with it. (3) *Trace conditioning.* The CS is given first and then *removed* before the US starts. (Presumably only some neural "trace" remains when the US starts, hence the name.) (4) *Backward conditioning.* The US is given *first* and then removed before the CS starts. (See Fig. 98.)

In most instances the time interval between the onset of the CS and the appearance of the CR is longer than that between the US and the UR. In other words, it takes a *longer* time for the conditioned response to appear than it does for the unconditioned response. Thus, in the *delayed* and *trace* methods the conditioned stimulus appears appreciably before the unconditioned stimulus, and the conditioned response is therefore given an opportunity to appear before the unconditioned stimulus enters the scene. In the *simultaneous* method, the conditioned response does not have as good an opportunity to appear prior to the unconditioned stimulus. Finally, in the *backward* technique there is, of course, *no* opportunity for the CR to appear before the US.

The experimental findings are that the delayed and trace techniques are more efficient than the simultaneous technique, and that it is almost impossible to obtain backward conditioning. This suggests that the conditioned response may be interpreted as a *preparatory adjustment* in anticipation of the soon-to-arrive unconditioned stimulus. The individual behaves *as if* the CS is a signal or a warning that the US is about to take place, and his response prepares him for the oncoming US. For example: The light can be understood as a signal for "acid is coming." The dog now reacts with a flow of saliva so that when the acid actually appears, he is ready for it. If the CS occurs too shortly before the US (as in the *simultaneous* technique), the individual does not have time to give a preparatory reaction; and if the CS occurs *after* the US (as in *backward* conditioning), no "preparatory" reaction is possible.

Generalization. The newly acquired relationship, CS → CR, is capable of what Pavlov called *generalization*. This means that once a CS → CR relationship is established, stimuli that are *similar* to the CS can evoke the CR even though these similar stimuli have *never* appeared in the original training. Thus the dog, after conditioning, will salivate to the intense light that was used in the original training. But he will also give the same reaction to a much less intense light.

CHARACTERISTICS OF GENERALIZATION. How does the degree of similarity between

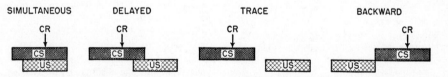

FIG. 98. Temporal patterning, conditioned-response learning, and preparatory responses. In this figure the time relationships between the onset of the unconditioned and of the conditioned stimuli for the four temporal patterns are illustrated together with the point of onset of the conditioned response. The most efficient temporal patterning for conditioning is one that permits the CR to appear before the US appears. This is most easily satisfied in the delayed and trace techniques. Under these circumstances when the unconditioned stimulus finally does make its appearance, the animal has already made his conditioned response and is thus "prepared" for the unconditioned stimulus.

the stimuli relate to the degree of generalization? Though the answer is still in some dispute, it appears that the more similar the new stimulus is to the original CS, the more effective it will be. This has been labeled the "gradient of generalization." (For an experiment that illustrates and defines this relationship more specifically, see Box 100.) There is also evidence indicating that generalization is somewhat more extensive when the original CS is a complex pattern of stimuli than when it is a relatively simple stimulus.

One way to limit the degree of generalization is by specific training. For example: every time a light of intensity "A" is presented, it is reinforced with the unconditioned stimulus of acid; when a light of intensity "B" is presented, no acid is placed on the animal's tongue. Eventually, the animal will acquire a *conditioned discrimination* so that he will salivate to a light of intensity "A" and not to a light of intensity "B."

The number of reinforcements influences the degree of the original conditioning as well as the degree of generalization. In Figure 99 are given the corresponding curves of the amplitude of the conditioned galvanic skin response after varying number of reinforcements to the original stimulus (a tone of a certain loudness) and to a new but similar stimulus (of different loudness). It will be seen that with added reinforcements the conditioned response increases in amplitude for both the original conditioned stimulus and the similar stimulus. However this increase in amplitude proceeds at different rates for the two curves.

BOX 100

Generalization of Conditioned Responses

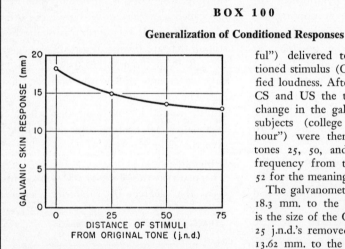

DISTANCE OF STIMULI
FROM ORIGINAL TONE (j.n.d.)

In 1937 Hovland of Yale University reported what has become one of the most-quoted experiments in this field. He used the *galvanic skin response* (see p. 338) as the unconditioned response (UR). The subject has no awareness of this response and it is beyond his voluntary control. The unconditioned stimulus (US) was a slight electric shock ("unpleasant but not painful") delivered to the wrist. The conditioned stimulus (CS) was a tone of a specified loudness. After 16 combinations of the CS and US the tone alone called forth a change in the galvanic skin response. The subjects (college students "paid by the hour") were then tested with three new tones 25, 50, and 75 j.n.d.'s removed in frequency from the original tone (see p. 52 for the meaning of a "j.n.d.").

The galvanometer showed a deflection of 18.3 mm. to the original tone (this, then, is the size of the CR); 14.9 mm. to the tone 25 j.n.d.'s removed from the original tone; 13.62 mm. to the tone 50 j.n.d.'s removed; and 12.89 to the tone 75 j.n.d.'s removed. (See fig.) The less the similarity between the new and the original stimulus, the less effective is the new stimulus in calling forth the conditioned response. However, it should be pointed out that the exact shape of the generalization curve is still in dispute.

HOVLAND, C. I. 1937. The generalization of conditioned responses. *J. gen. Psychol., 17,* 125–48.

SIGNIFICANCE OF GENERALIZATION. A stimulus that is generalized gives the individual "room," as it were, to move about. This has definite adaptive value, for stimulus situations are never *exactly* repeated in nature. If a conditioned response could be evoked only when the conditioned stimulus occurs in the identical form that it had during the original training, the conditioned response would have little value in coping with environmental problems. On the other hand, the fact that generalization is more and more limited as the new stimuli are less similar to the original one also has its adaptive value. It would benefit the in-

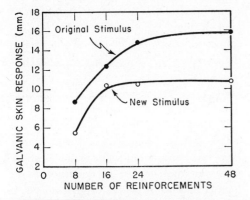

FIG. 99. The magnitude of the galvanic skin response—as measured by the deviation from zero of a galvanometer indicator—to the original conditioned stimulus after varying number of reinforcements is shown by the upper curve. The magnitude of this response to a new stimulus, 150 j.n.d.'s removed in loudness from the original CS, is shown by the lower curve. Each pair of points is the average for 32 subjects. (Adapted from Hovland, 1937.)

dividual little if he gave a "preparatory" response indiscriminately to stimuli which were so different that the response was no longer appropriate.

The fact that similarity of stimuli, complexity of stimulus-pattern, and frequency of practice all influence the degree of generalization points again to the continuity between conditioning and other forms of behavior. We found in perception and in creative problem-solving that similarity of stimuli, complexity of stimulus-patterns and frequency of occurrence of stimulus situations all help to determine the nature and effectiveness of the resultant behavior.

Extinction. Once a conditioned response has been established, the CS will elicit the response without the US. The presentation of CS without US is called *non-reinforcement*. For example, the light is presented, without the acid on the tongue. What will happen as non-reinforced responses (e.g., salivation) continue to be elicited? Typically, the strength of the response gradually decreases until a point is reached where the CS fails to evoke the response at all. When this occurs, we say that *extinction* has taken place.

RECOVERY FROM EXTINCTION. After extinction has occurred, the CS → CR relationship may *reappear without any additional training*. For example, after the dog's conditioned response to the light has been "extinguished" and he has been removed from the experimental room, if we return him there at some later time, we may find that the light will elicit the flow of saliva all over again! This reappearance of a CS → CR relationship is called *spontaneous recovery*.

There is, of course, an end to the recovery from extinction possible in this way. Successive spontaneous recoveries follow a law of diminishing returns. That is, if spontaneous recovery is tested day after day, the extent of spontaneous recovery will grow less and less.

RATE OF EXTINCTION. The speed with which extinction takes place is determined by many of the same factors that determine the speed of acquisition of a conditioned response, e.g., temporal patterning of stimuli and number of reinforcements. In general it has been found that the stronger the original conditioned response, the slower the extinction process. (Some experimenters actually use the rate of extinction as a measure of the strength of the conditioned response.)

Other factors also influence the rate of extinction. As we shall soon see, certain conditioned responses (primarily those of an "emotional" nature, and those involving verbal stimuli) are very resistant to extinction. In some of these cases no extinction seems possible. Finally, it has almost invariably been found that no matter how complete the extinction may seem to be, some aftereffect always remains. Thus, after "complete" extinction has taken place, it is easier to *re-establish* the conditioned response by further reinforcements than it was to establish it initially.

SIGNIFICANCE OF EXTINCTION. The facts of extinction can be understood in terms of its adaptive function. If time after time the US failed to follow the CS, it would be of little value for the organism to continue giving a "preparatory" reaction. In some instances such continuation could even prove to be a handicap. On the other hand, too rapid or permanent extinction of a conditioned response that had been reinforced frequently in the past life of the individual might also be dangerous. Such extinction could be "premature."

We have been stressing the adaptive value of conditioned responses. Obviously, however, not all the characteristics of their acquisition, generalization, or extinction are perfectly adaptive. An appreciation of *both* the adaptive and nonadaptive features of conditioned responses must be gained if we are to understand the role of conditioning in adaptive behavior.

Conditioned Responses and Behavior. If conditioning is restricted to the very simple, involuntary responses we have thus far examined, it might be argued that condi-

tioning can have but little importance in the total adaptive economy of the individual. We must therefore know something about the range and complexity of conditioned responses.

Conditioned and unconditioned responses are rarely identical. In some cases the conditioned response consists merely of a *part* of the unconditioned response. Thus an increased flow of saliva may occur as a conditioned response, whereas the original unconditioned response consisted of salivation, chewing, and swallowing movements. In other cases the *form* of the conditioned response differs so radically from the form of the unconditioned response that there is only a very general kind of similarity between them. For example, in conditioning guinea pigs, when the sounding of a tone is the CS and electric shock the US, the unconditioned response to electric shock is a *sharp inspiration* of breath, whereas the conditioned response to the tone is a *smooth restrained* breathing, shallower than normal. Almost every experiment can serve to demonstrate that even the simplest of conditioned responses have some degree of generality and variability about them. *They are rarely mere copies of an automatic response.*

In addition to relatively simple responses, complexly integrated patterns of uncontrollable responses can be conditioned. This is especially true of emotionally toned behavior and persistent (sometimes pathologically persistent) reactions to "neutral" stimuli. On the basis of experimental work in these fields it has been suggested (as a hypothesis) that many of our allergy reactions, "irrepressible" outbursts, and complex visceral and glandular responses which accompany intense feelings and emotion can best be understood as acquired conditioned responses. (For an illustrative experiment, see Box 101.) Perhaps the presence in emotional behavior of

BOX 101

Conditioned Nausea

Kleitman and Crisler of the University of Chicago have reported the conditioning of a complexly integrated pattern of responses which was, at the same time, involuntary in nature.

Using 8 dogs as subjects, the experimenters first prepared the animals by cutting a permanent opening (fistula) into the animals' salivary glands. This made it possible to collect and measure the saliva as it was secreted. As a conditioned stimulus the dog was harnessed into place in a stock, and a tube was tied around the lower jaw so that all the saliva secreted could be collected and measured. The animals were left in the stock for a constant period of time (from 15 minutes to 2 hours for different dogs) without anything being done to them. Thus the CS was "being placed in the experimental situation." The unconditioned stimulus was an injection of about 40 mg. of morphine which was administered to the animal after the lapse of the predetermined waiting time. This procedure was repeated daily for many months.

Morphine, when injected subcutaneously, does not act upon some single localized receptor, but upon many centers in the nervous system. The unconditioned response is best described as "general nausea." It includes panting, profuse salivation, shivering, vomiting, and other signs of distress.

Very soon after the experiment was started, a complex "conditioned response" began to appear. In many instances, as soon as the dog was placed in the stock—and long before the morphine was injected—the animal showed all the behavior characteristic of nausea: excessive salivation (in some dogs as much as 300 to 400 c.c. of saliva was secreted in an hour), shivering, retching, panting, and vomiting. As a consequence of conditioning, then, the dog "learned" to become nauseated at the sight of the "hospital room."

KLEITMAN, N., and CRISLER, G. 1927. A quantitative study of a salivary conditioned reflex. *Amer. J. Physiol.*, 79, 571–614.

---

conditioned components not easily available to consciousness or control is exactly why we find it so difficult to change that behavior. This may also be the reason the reacting individual does not himself understand why he feels or behaves the way he does under some circumstances.

This brings us to a second main question—the relation of conditioning to voluntary behavior.

CR—VOLUNTARY OR INVOLUNTARY? For Mr. Anyman, "voluntary" means acts that are conscious and over which he has control. A detailed examination of conditioned responses, however, will show that it is difficult to distinguish sharply between those that are voluntary and those that are involuntary. At one extreme we have the situation described in Box 100 in which the response has no attribute of awareness or of control. But it has also been demonstrated experimentally that there can be situations in which there is no "awareness" of the response but there *is* voluntary control. For instance, there is some evidence that a person can learn to dilate or contract the pupils of his eyes "at will" although, of course, he cannot feel his pupils dilating or contracting. (See Box 102.) It is also evident from other experiments that verbal instructions can influence the degree of conditioning, *even though the response is not completely under voluntary control.* (See Box 103.)

All of this suggests that an analysis of conditioning may give us some help in understanding how we acquire voluntary control over much of our behavior. Something like the following may occur: (1) Automatic, involuntary responses (e.g.,

BOX 102

Making the Involuntary Voluntary

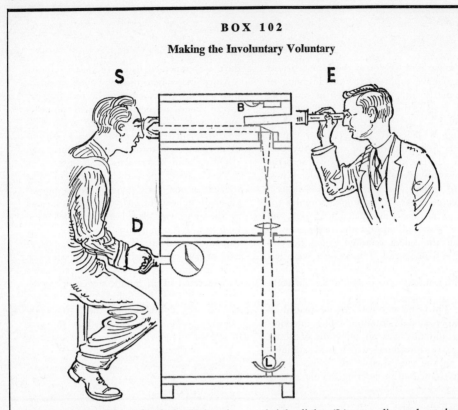

In 1933 Hudgins of Clark University brought the pupillary response (which cannot be felt) under voluntary control. This was accomplished in "three easy stages."

In Stage I a bell (B) sounded and a bright light (L) was directed at the subject's (S) eyes through the aperture into which he was looking. (See fig.) When the bell was turned off, the bright light was also turned off. Thus the coming *on* of the

---

micturition) may become conditioned to a perceived stimulus-object (e.g., a toilet). (2) As the child acquires language, a specific word becomes attached to the perceived stimulus-object so that eventually the word itself evokes the same reactions that the stimulus-object did. (3) By higher-order conditioning (as in the Hudgins experiment) the word alone will come to evoke the conditioned response. We now have the situation in which the child's originally "automatic" response can be controlled by commands given by another person, or by *self-initiated instructions;* thus has been achieved "voluntary" con-

trol over a formerly "involuntary" response.

By way of summary. The conditioned response, relatively simple as it is, resembles other forms of learning in many ways. It is adaptive; it generalizes to new stimulus situations; it disappears when no longer reinforced. On the other hand there are clear points of difference between the conditioned response and other forms of learning. Perhaps the most significant derives from the relative lack of awareness and control which is characteristic of conditioning. Moreover, intent or motivation plays a much more decisive role in the per-

---

BOX 102 (continued)

Making the Involuntary Voluntary

sound and of the light were the CS and US respectively for the *contraction* of the pupil. When the sound of the bell alone brought forth a contraction, the subjects (college students, professors, and two secretaries) were ready for Stage II.

The subjects were now given these instructions:

"Place the right hand on the dynamometer switch (D) and at the command 'Contract' squeeze the handle until the light and bell appear. . . . When you hear the bell and see the light, hold the contraction until you hear the command 'relax.'"

After 200 trials Stage III was introduced. The same procedure as in Stage II was followed except that the bell was not used, and the subject was asked to "Repeat the verbal commands subvocally each time you hear me give them." Again 200 trials were given and then the following tests were made: the experimenter (E) would say "Contract" (or "Relax") and measure the pupillary response. In the next test the subject whispered these words himself, and in the final test the subject said these words "subvocally." Throughout these tests, of course, *the light was never turned on.*

The results showed that the pupillary re-

sponses had been successively transferred from the light, to the sound of the bell, then to the movement of the hand in squeezing the dynamometer switch, then to the spoken words, and at the end of this process, without further training, the subject could, by "inner speech" alone, cause his pupil to contract or dilate—"at will"!

Additional tests indicated that *no experimental extinction occurred with the verbal stimuli,* and even after 15 days the responses were still present. The conditioned responses to the bell, however, showed the usual experimental extinction.

One word of caution: Some attempts to repeat this experiment have reported negative results. The interested reader is referred to the article by Steckle and Renshaw, to Hudgins' 1935 reply, and to Steckle's 1936 counterreply.

HUDGINS, C. V. 1933. Conditioning and the voluntary control of the pupillary light reflex. *J. gen. Psychol., 8,* 3–51.

STECKLE, L. C., and RENSHAW, J. 1934. An investigation of the conditioned iridic reflex. *J. gen. Psychol., 11,* 3–23.

HUDGINS, C. V. 1935. Steckle and Renshaw on the conditioned iridic reflex: a discussion. *J. gen. Psychol., 12,* 208–14.

STECKLE, L. C. 1936. Two additional attempts to condition the pupillary reflex. *J. gen. Psychol., 15,* 369–77.

---

formance of other kinds of learned behavior than it does in conditioning.

These similarities and differences between conditioning and other types of adaptive behavior suggest two areas of psychological inquiry which can be illuminated by a study of conditioning: (1) the facts of conditioning may help us to understand many of the facts of "irrational" and pathologically persistent patterns of responses; (2) conditioning may give us some insight into the development of voluntary behavior.

But knowledge of conditioning alone is inadequate for a complete understanding

of the tremendously complex processes which we call adaptive behavior. Not all learned behavior, thinking, and problem-solving can be reduced to a chain or collection of conditioned responses.

Rote Learning

In *rote learning,* as we have already indicated, the individual is presented with a set of clearly specified items, and his problem is to commit these items to memory. It is for this reason that this type of learning is sometimes called rote *memorizing.*

BOX 103

Effect of Verbal Instructions on Conditioned Responses

It has been demonstrated that verbal instructions, although they do not completely prevent conditioning or extinction, nevertheless have an important influence upon the behavior.

In an experiment by Miller, light was the conditioned stimulus, and an air-puff directed at the eyelid, the unconditioned stimulus. The response was a blinking of the eyelid. He used 6 groups of subjects; the results of 3 of the groups are given in the graphs below. The "noncommittal" group was given only the minimum instructions necessary for photographic recording of the eye-blink. The "inhibitory" group was told "Be sure that you do not wink or

start to wink before you have felt the puff." The "facilitatory" group was told: "In case you feel your eyes closing or starting to close, do nothing to prevent it."

Although all 3 groups showed conditioning and extinction, the different instructions had different effects. The facilitatory group showed the quickest conditioning and the slowest extinction, next came the noncommittal group, and finally, the inhibitory group. (See fig.)

MILLER, J. 1940. The effect of facilitatory and inhibitory attitudes on eyelid conditioning. In Hilgard, E. R., and Marquis, D. G., *Conditioning and learning.* New York: Appleton-Century-Crofts.

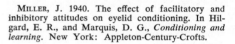

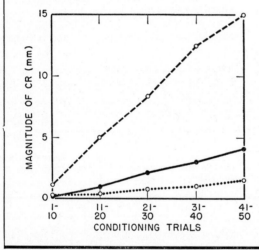

Mr. Anyman and some educators regard learning by "rote" as a somewhat "low" form of adaptive behavior, something only bad teachers insist on and dull people do. Such an evaluation seriously underestimates the importance of rote learning. *Most* of our adaptive behavior is intimately dependent upon knowledge acquired via rote learning.

Because of the obvious importance of language in modern civilization, it is not at all surprising that the major part of the

psychologist's work on rote learning has been concerned with *verbal* material rather than, say, with motor skills. Indeed, most of the experimental work *in the entire field of learning* has been devoted to the study of rote learning of verbal material. This has been true ever since the first experiment on learning was performed by the German psychologist, Hermann Ebbinghaus, in the late nineteenth century.

Ebbinghaus, whose initial training was in philosophy, was much impressed with the work on psychophysics which was putting the study of sensations on a scientific and experimental basis (see p. 49). Inspired by this, he set out to do the same for the "higher mental processes." Without any predecessors to learn from, he invented a whole new experimental field. The problems he attacked and the methods he developed are still, today, among the basic problems and methods used in the study of rote learning. The similarity between the origin of conditioning studies and that of rote-learning studies is striking. In each instance a new approach to a problem of psychology came into being, full-blown, through the genius and industry of one man—Pavlov for conditioning, Ebbinghaus for rote learning. (We will later see another such instance in Freud's creation of psychoanalysis.)

The study of rote learning can be organized in terms of three major problems: (1) *acquisition*, that is, the conditions that influence the memorizing of the specified items; (2) *retention*, that is, the subsequent availability of the items once they have been memorized; (3) *transfer*, that is, the influence which the memorizing of one set of items can have upon memorizing subsequent sets as well as upon the retention of previous ones.

However, these three problems are intimately interrelated. Indeed, it is sometimes difficult to distinguish, for example, between the acquisition and the retention processes.

Basic Methods. To study rote learning, we must make both *quantitative* and *qualitative* analyses. To do this requires a systematic way of recording the learner's performance as well as his conscious experiences. Performance is recorded in terms of speed and accuracy, and is represented in curves of learning and forgetting. No formal systematic method has been developed for the recording of conscious ex-

perience during learning, and in many instances we have to depend upon inference and general introspective reports.

THE LEARNING AND FORGETTING CURVES. The learning and forgetting curves are pictorial devices that tell us at a glance how a person's quantitative performance changes with the passage of time or trials. The curves are constructed in a simple manner. We first mark off on the horizontal baseline or axis (the abscissa) of a graph the units of *time* or number of *trials*. On the vertical axis (the ordinate) of the graph we mark off *performance* units (e.g., number of items correctly recalled, number of items missed, the speed with which the performance takes place, etc.) By counting off the proper number of units on each axis, we can indicate by *one point* two bits of information: the time or trials that have elapsed, and the efficiency of performance at that time or trial. If we now do this for various trials (or times) and connect the points so made by a line (curve), we get a quantitative picture of the performance as an ongoing process. The *height*, the *slope*, and the *shape* of the curve are the significant variables here. (See Box 104 for further explanations and illustrations of learning and forgetting curves.)

NONSENSE SYLLABLES. One of the most commonly used kinds of materials in rote learning is the "nonsense syllable," invented by Ebbinghaus. Ebbinghaus felt that in studying the acquisition of verbal behavior he would need a new kind of verbal material, since the use of already familiar and meaningful words would not permit us to study learning "from scratch." He took two consonants and a vowel at random and put them together—for example, *zat, bok, bif*—and in that way built up a supply of over 2,000 nonsense syllables. Memorizing a list made up of such items would presumably be uninfluenced by previous learning. We will later see that Ebbinghaus' belief

BOX 104

Learning and Forgetting Curves

In an experiment reported by Kingsley the subject was required to learn the English equivalents of ten Hebrew words. The experimenter first read the Hebrew word and gave the English equivalent. In the following trials, after pronouncing each Hebrew word, the experimenter paused and the subject gave the English equivalent if he could remember it. If he could not, the subject was told the answer, and then the next word was given. This is called the "paired associate" method of testing for learning.

In the figure below are shown two simple ways of graphing the same acquisition performance. Note the *positive slope* (curve goes *up*) of the curve when the performance score is number of items recalled correctly, and the *negative slope* (curve goes *down*) when the score is items missed.

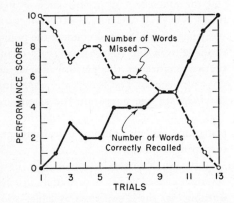

The *height* of the curve, at any one point, tells us the *absolute achievement* (e.g., at trial 4 the subject could recall 2 items; at trial 11, 7 items). The *slope* of the curve tells us the *rate of change* in performance; the steeper the slope, the greater the change. The *shape* of the curve gives us a general picture of *changes in rate* over time. Thus in the above figure the speed of change *increases* as time goes on. (Note the difference in slope between the first 9 trials, when a total of only 4 words was learned, and the last 3 trials, when 5 words were learned.) This is called a *positively*

accelerated *curve* (a relatively slow start but a fast finish).

In the next figure we have Ebbinghaus' classical "forgetting curve." Here the shape indicates that forgetting is very rapid at

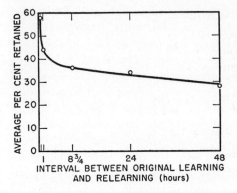

first, and then much more slow. A curve of this shape is called a *negatively accelerated curve*.

Ebbinghaus learned several lists of nonsense syllables. He recorded the *time* required for the original learning, and then *relearned* these lists after 40 minutes. (This was done separately for each list.) He then learned other lists, and relearned them after 60 minutes, etc. The relearning took less time than the original learning. The average *difference* in time (expressed as a percentage) was taken as a measure of retention. Thus, for an interval of 40 minutes the average time for *relearning* his lists was only 42 per cent of the time of original learning. This means that he had retained 58 per cent of the material—as measured by this *savings method*.

Each point on the curve can be considered as a "still" picture; attention to the height, slope, and shape of the connecting lines gives us a perception analogous to seeing a successive series of "stills," a "moving" picture of what has been going on over time.

KINGSLEY, H. L. 1946., *The nature and conditions of learning.* New York: Prentice-Hall.

EBBINGHAUS, H., 1913. *Memory: A contribution to experimental psychology.* (Trans. by H. A. Ruger and C. E. Bussenius.) New York: Columbia Univ. Press.

that nonsense syllables are "meaningless" was not altogether justified, but nonsense syllables have so many advantages that they still remain among the most popular of laboratory materials for the study of rote learning.

Acquisition. The factors that determine rote acquisition have been studied with respect to their influence on (1) the *shape* of the acquisition curve, and (2) the *efficiency* of acquisition. By efficiency we mean the total work required to reach a specified level of mastery—the trials or time required to memorize a set of words, say, to the point of one perfect recitation.

THE SHAPE OF THE ACQUISITION CURVE. Much effort has gone into the quest for *the* shape of *the* acquisition curve, but thus far with only limited success. For one thing, rote learning under different conditions and with different material results in different shapes of curves. Secondly, the learning curve, like any other index of complicated behavior, reflects the person's momentary changes in fatigue, boredom, emotional state, and motivation. Consequently individual learning curves are typically jagged, contain both positive and negative slopes, and periods of no progress, and they usually defy simple characterization. To overcome these unsystematic fluctuations, attempts have been made to combine the performance scores of several individuals into *group* curves.

A group curve has two major difficulties. In the first place there is the technical problem of how to combine individual curves. For example, after the first ten trials, say, some people will have completed their learning, others will not. The shape of the group curve before trial ten will be determined by both the slow and fast learners; *after* trial ten, only by the slow learners. It is questionable, therefore, whether we can consider these two segments of the curve as a *single* curve. Attempts have been made to meet this difficulty, but with questionable success. (We will soon see one of the more commonly used procedures.)

In the second place, there is the basic question whether a group curve (which is, after all, a statistical average and may not faithfully reflect the performance of *any* single person) can legitimately be used as a description of a psychological process. Because of this, generalizations about learning curves (especially group curves) must be regarded with caution. Nevertheless certain generalizations about the shape of rote-learning curves can be made with some confidence.

NEGATIVELY ACCELERATED CURVES. Most acquisition curves in rote learning are negatively accelerated. A possible reason for this can be seen from certain perceptual considerations.

Both *ends* of a list of items, simply because of their temporal positions, are differentiated from the rest of the list, and therefore "stand out" in perception. The items in the middle of the list, on the other hand, tend to become assimilated into one perceptually undifferentiated group of items. This is especially true if the items are all equally unfamiliar. This means that at the beginning of the rote-learning process, the person can make considerable progress by first learning the "easy" (because perceptually dominant) items at the end points on the list. But after "cleaning off" these items, his progress will slow down because he now has the more difficult task of memorizing the perceptually undifferentiated items in the middle of the list. The net result will be a negatively accelerated acquisition curve—a quick start and a slow finish.

This analysis seems to be supported by the so-called "serial position effect." Thus, if we examine the rate at which *specific* items in a list are learned, we discover that the items toward the beginning and toward the end of the series are usually learned more quickly than the items in the middle. (See Box 105 for an experiment that illustrates the kinds of data considered here.)

THE LINEAR CURVE. The acquisition curve for a relatively short list of familiar items tends to be linear. A linear slope (straight line) indicates, of course, that the rate of progress is constant from trial to trial. Again the reason for this can be understood in terms of a "perceptual analysis."

When every item on a list is a familiar

BOX 105

An Experiment in Rote Learning

Postman of the University of California has reported an extensive series of experiments in rote learning, from which the following is taken.

In one experiment 90 students learned a 12-item list of nonsense syllables; another 90 students, a 12-item list of common words. The standard "memory drum" (see sketch) and the "anticipation" method of learning were used. The items were successively exposed in the window of the drum for 2 seconds each. Beginning with

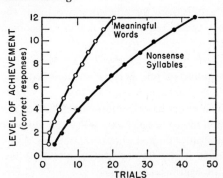

the second time around, the subject was required to call out the *next* item on the list before it appeared in the window. The lists were repeated until the subject could "anticipate" every item during a given run.

For the nonsense syllables the fastest learner required 13 runs of the list; the slowest learner, 93 runs. To derive a "group" curve, the *average* number of trials required to achieve one correct anticipation was calculated, then the average to achieve 2 correct anticipations, etc. From these averages an acquisition curve was plotted, as shown in the first figure. By this method every subject is included in every point on the curve. Note that the curve for the meaningful material has a steeper slope.

To analyze the serial-position effect, the average number of failures in anticipations was determined for each item separately and plotted as shown below. The middle items of the nonsense list (items 6, 7, 8)

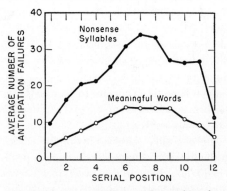

were much more difficult to learn than the end items (1 and 12). This is not true to the same extent for the meaningful material.

POSTMAN, L., and RAU, L. 1957. Retention as a function of the method of measurement. *Univ. Calif. Publ. Psychol.*, 8, No. 3.

word with its distinctive meaning, the end items do not have as great a perceptual advantage over the middle items as in the case of lists of unfamiliar items. The meaning of each item differentiates it from all other items. Furthermore, there is less tendency for the middle items to become assimilated into one perceptually undifferentiated grouping. As a consequence of this we should expect a constant and relatively rapid acquisition process. Here, too, this analysis is congruent with the results obtained from an analysis of the serial-position effect. It will be recalled that with familiar items the serial position effect is not as pronounced as with unfamiliar items (see Box 105 again).

A linear curve, however, will be found only if the list is relatively short. With very long lists we again find negative acceleration.

POSITIVELY ACCELERATED CURVES. Where the material consists of extremely unfamiliar and difficult items, we usually find positively accelerated acquisition curves. Thus we saw in Box 104, where the learning of so unfamiliar a language as Hebrew was involved, an instance of a positively accelerated acquisition curve.

In terms of our analysis we would say that with very unfamiliar or strange items, a long time may elapse before *any* item can be differentiated from any other item. In addition we must take into account emotional and motivational factors, such as discouragement, which may inhibit our learning efforts. Under these circumstances a relatively long adjustment period may elapse before any substantial progress can be made. This would be reflected, of course, in a period of little or no progress followed by a period of relatively fast learning, that is, a positively accelerated acquisition curve.

EFFICIENCY OF ACQUISITION. Because of the theoretical and practical importance of the subject, a considerable amount of research has been done on the problem of efficiency of acquisition. The following statements, which summarize much of this research, may therefore have some value to the student as guides for improving his memorizing ability, as well as in giving him insight into the rote-learning process.

1. *The more meaningful the material, the less difficult it is to learn.* We have already indicated one reason for this in terms of the greater perceptual differentiability of meaningful items over meaningless ones. Another factor derives from the following consideration. Seeing many relationships and many implications of any one item may help in its retention and in the retention of items related to it. The generalization holds even for random sequences of meaningful words. It is most pronounced with highly integrated material such as prose passages. Whatever the learner can do to increase the meaningfulness of the material may help speed up his acquisition process. There are various (and curious) ways in which this can be done, and we will discuss some of them later.

2. *Distributed practice is generally more efficient than massed practice.* This effect of temporal patterning seems to hold for meaningless or meaningful material, and long or short lists. For example, Ebbinghaus, in 1885, found it more efficient, in learning nonsense syllables, to *distribute* his learning trials over three days rather than to *mass* all his practice in one day; and Bumstead, in 1943, found that learning a prose passage with a 48-hour interval between each reading resulted in faster learning (in terms of total time actually spent on the task) than when only one hour intervened between the readings. (It is interesting to note here a possible similarity between the value of distributed practice in rote learning, and that of "incubation periods" in creative problem-solving.)

3. *Active performance during rote learning is more efficient than passive performance.* Reciting aloud the words to be memorized, or writing them down as we proceed with our learning, results in more rapid acquisition than a silent and passive reading. (For an interesting application of this, see Box 106.) Again the factors of motivation and perceptual organization are important. As each item is recited or written down, the learner concretely indicates, as it were, that he has reached a subgoal on his way to complete mastery. We have already seen that a series of subgoals has value in providing evidence of progress and thus increasing the motivational level of a person engaged in an extended task.

On the perceptual side there is evidence that doing something active with an item helps differentiate it from the other items and thus contributes to more efficient acquisition. This suggests that the advantage of recitation over silent reading would be greater for nonsense syllables than for meaningful material, since the latter are already differentiated to a considerable de-

---

BOX 106

"A" for "Active," "P" for "Passive"

The relative effectiveness of active and passive rote learning was tested by Hovland, Lumsdaine, and Sheffield in teaching soldiers the phonetic alphabet in which word equivalents are learned for letters (e.g., "Dog" for "D," "Oboe" for "O").

Two film strips were used, each with a different group of recruits. In both films each letter and corresponding phonetic name was presented in an individual frame showing a picture to illustrate the phonetic name, with accompanying sound effects and narration designed to aid the memorizing of the name. After every 6 frames was a review list. When the entire alphabet had been run through, two complete review lists were shown.

The two film strips were identical in all respects *except* that in the "passive" strip *all review lists* presented each phonetic name with its corresponding letter and these were *pronounced by the narrator,* whereas in the "active" strip the letters in the review lists were followed by question marks and the names were to be *recalled and pronounced by the audience.* Immediately after this training, soldiers from each group were given individual tests to determine how much they had learned. The time required to give the correct response to each letter was recorded; no subject was permitted more than 15 seconds to recall any one name.

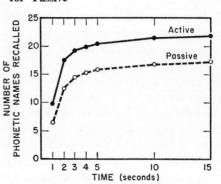

The results, presented in the figure as a cumulative curve, show a marked superiority of the "active" group. Thus, within two seconds after the test letter was shown, the "passive" group recalled an average of 12.6 names (48 per cent of all 26 alphabet names); the "active" group, 17.6 names (68 per cent). The "active" group had learned about 20 per cent more letters than the "passive" group.

For the active group, 10 words took one second each for recall; for the passive group, the comparable figure was about 6 words. The total numbers of words correctly recalled by the two groups within the time limit of 15 seconds were 22 for the active and 17 for the passive.

HOVLAND, C. I., LUMSDAINE, A. A., and SHEFFIELD, F. D. 1949. *Experiments on mass communication.* Princeton: Princeton Univ. Press.

gree. And this is exactly what seems to happen. In his 1917 study Gates found that the advantage of recitations over reading was *greatest for nonsense syllables, less great for lists of words,* and *still less great for connected prose or poetry.* Gates cites an illuminating introspective report on the value of recitation in perceptual differentiation. One of his subjects had this to say:

"In reading it was so easy to glide through the series that I did not take the trouble to note any special points of interest. It seemed that I could do more if I just looked hard at the syllables, covering up my ears so that I could do nothing but look. But when I began to recite I found that I had to note certain syllables specially, which I afterwards used as starting and stopping places."

Throughout this section we have emphasized the importance of perceptual organization in rote learning. This factor plays so great a role that we can formalize it into the fourth and last "efficiency factor."

4. *Organizing items into distinctive perceptual groups facilitates acquisition in rote learning.* Investigators of rote learning have, from the beginning, been very much concerned with the problem of spatial and temporal groupings as aids to memorizing. The results of their studies can be summarized by saying that any device that aids grouping, no matter how "inane," may aid the acquisition process. Thus a singsong or melodic reading of items, a rhythmic accenting of every third or fourth item, finding that adjacent items rhyme with each other and can thus be made into a group (e.g., 607 and 411), finding that a sequence of numbers combine to make a "familiar" larger number (e.g., 17 and 76)—all can aid in the learning process. The good memorizer not only combines and conquers, but is also on the alert for anything that will add *meaning*—even to

nonsense syllables. Thus the syllable sequence *zat-bok* may be given the temporary meaning of "sat on a rock," and this will speed up the learning of the two syllables.

Closely related to grouping is the question of part learning vs. whole learning, i.e., whether it is more efficient to learn an entire sequence from beginning to end, or to break the whole into parts and learn each part separately. The experimental answer is that *either* method may be better, depending upon such factors as the size, structure, and meaningfulness of the "whole" and the "part." Thus Hovland (1951), after reviewing much of the experimental work in this field, concludes:

"In a practical situation, factors like fatigue, interest, etc., may play an important part in the relative advantage of whole or part learning. But, if these are held reasonably constant, the best advice seems to be to learn by using the largest units that are meaningful and within the individual's capacity. The older the individual, the higher his intelligence, the more practice he has had, the greater is the size of the unit he is able to handle."

QUALITATIVE DESCRIPTION OF ACQUISITION. Modern psychological research has emphasized the quantitative study of learning. Since the early part of the century very little has been added to our knowledge of the *experiences* that accompany rote learning. We have already indicated some of the findings—the major one being that the learner, from the very first, attempts to impose organization and meaning upon his material, no matter how "nonsensical" the material may at first appear. A description of the experiences of a person attempting to commit a list of items to memory is a description of a man discovering or inventing meaningful relations where no meaning exists, successively trying out now this perceptual organization and now that, emphasizing distinctive physiognomic attributes of various items. In brief, he is trying to put some sense and interest into the problem facing him. His final achievement may be "officially" classified as "rote memory"—but his experiences have attributes of genuine problem-solving, even of creative problem-solving. (See Box 107 for one of William James' statements on this question.)

After material has been memorized many of the organized units and meanings may disappear as experienced attributes, and what is left in consciousness is a series of "bare" image-pairs (as in the multiplication table) or "automatic" image-sequences (as in the alphabet).

Retention. Retention deals with the subsequent availability of a list of items once they have been learned. In a strict sense all rote-learning studies that use performance scores for their data are "retention" studies. Thus, we construct an *acquisition curve* by recording the number of items recalled immediately after each presentation of the stimulus-items, and we construct a *retention curve* by recording the number of items recalled after the lapse of a longer interval of time. Frequently, indeed, the term "immediate recall" is applied to the first type of performance and "delayed recall" to the second type.

METHODS OF MEASURING RETENTION. Methods of measurement always play an important role in determining the results of any scientific experiment. They are particularly important in retention studies. While there are many methods available for measuring retention, we will list and describe only the three major ones. (1) In the *recognition* method the person is shown a large collection of items, among which are the ones he has previously

---

BOX 107

Remembering Is Thinking

A qualitative analysis of the "thinking process" and the "remembering process" led William James to identify the two in one of his famous passages—passages that are among the great heritages of psychological literature.

"In mental terms, *the more other facts a fact is associated with in the mind, the better possession of it our memory retains.* Each of its associates becomes a hook to which it hangs, a means to fish it up by when sunk beneath the surface. Together they form a network of attachments by which it is woven into the entire tissue of our thought. . . . But this forming of associations with a fact, what is it but *thinking about* the fact as much as possible. . . . The reason why *cramming* is such a bad mode of study is now made clear. . . . Things learned thus in a few hours, on one occasion, for one purpose, cannot possibly have formed many associations with other things in the mind. . . . Speedy oblivion is the almost inevitable fate of all that is committed to memory in this simple way. Whereas, on the contrary, the same materials taken in gradually, day after day, recurring in different contexts, considered in various relations, associated with other external incidents, and repeatedly reflected on, grow into such a system, form such connections with the rest of the mind's fabric, lie open to so many paths of approach, that they remain permanent possessions. . . . Of course there is no moral turpitude in cramming. If it led to the desired end of secure learning it would be infinitely the best method of study. But it does not; and students themselves should understand the reason why."

JAMES, W. 1890. *Principles of psychology.* New York: Holt.

learned as well as new items. His score is determined by the number of items which he can identify correctly as those he has learned. If an equal number of old and new items are presented for the subject to choose from, sheer guessing alone would give him a 50 per cent "correct" score. Therefore, conventionally, a correction for chance guessing is introduced, i.e., the score is determined by subtracting the number of wrong choices from the number of correct choices. This score is sometimes expressed as a percentage, i.e., the number identified correctly divided by the total number learned. (2) In *recall* he is merely asked to reproduce the items learned. Again, the number of items he can reproduce correctly is divided by the number of items originally learned, to give him a recall score expressed as a percentage. (3) The third method is the *relearning* method that we have already described and illustrated in the Ebbinghaus forgetting curve (Box 104). The score ("savings score") is the amount saved in relearning and is also expressed as a percentage of the original learning.

The stimulus-patterns that each of the above methods presents to the subject to test his retention differ widely. The different results that are obtained with these measurement methods clearly show that the ability of the person to demonstrate how much he has retained of previously learned material depends very much upon the *current* stimulus situation. In some instances a person may seem to have "forgotten" everything in the sense that he cannot *recall* a single item, and yet he may be able to *recognize* many of the items correctly, or to *relearn* the items with a sizable saving. It is clear that in measuring retention we do not tap the remains of a bygone learning process, but, rather, we observe a performance determined by an *ongoing process as it responds to new stimulus-patterns*. When we test a person's memory, we do not discover what he *has* remembered—we determine what he *is* remembering.

SHAPE OF THE FORGETTING CURVE. The most general thing we can say about the shape of the forgetting curve is that it is a negatively accelerated one—a great deal is forgotten soon after learning, and then forgetting proceeds more slowly. However there are many important variations within this general shape.

Sometimes retention curves show a *positive* slope immediately after the cessation of practice; the person earns a better score after an interval of time than he did immediately after the last learning period. This is called *reminiscence*. While many such observations have been reported in the experimental literature ever since 1913, few of these experiments can be unambiguously interpreted as demonstrating genuine reminiscence. Either the original experiments cannot be repeated in other laboratories, or proper controls have not been employed so as to eliminate various artifacts of measurement, fatigue, or the possibility of "silent practice" between the learning period and the retention testing. However in the case of "motor learning" (where the subject learns to perform a defined series of movements) there seems to be little doubt of the genuineness of reminiscence.

A common deviation from the negatively accelerated retention curve is found with meaningful material. English, Welborn, and Killian (1934) presented their subjects with a 1,100-word article that they were to memorize, and then subgroups of their subjects were tested for retention at various intervals thereafter. One form of the tests measured the retention of specific items; another, of general comprehension of the passage. The results of the specific memory tests gave a negative acceleration curve, whereas the general comprehension test showed no loss in retention at all.

EFFICIENCY OF RETENTION. The factors that determine efficiency of retention have also been extensively studied and can be summarized in the following four "efficiency principles" of retention:

1. *The higher the degree of acquisition, the higher is the retention.* The more "firmly" a list is learned, the better it will be retained over time; but this seems to follow a law of diminishing returns, especially with meaningful material. That is, if a set of material has been learned, let us say, to a criterion of one perfect recitation, it will not be retained as well as if it had been *overlearned* (i.e., if practice had continued well beyond that point). But as the amount of overlearning is increased, the improvement in retention does not keep corresponding pace.

Closely related to this is the relative retention of meaningful versus meaningless material. Many experimenters have reported that meaningful material is better retained in rote learning than meaningless material. However the validity of such a generalization is open to serious question, since it is difficult to disentangle *degree of learning* from *degree of meaningfulness* when the usual material is compared, e.g., nonsense syllables *versus* words.

Words are not only "meaningful," but each individual word has already been *overlearned* long before the subject sits down in front of the psychologist's memory drum. When the degree of learning is equated for the two sets of material, it appears that the higher the degree of meaningfulness, the *less* lasting is the retention. In an experiment by Underwood and Richardson (1956) two lists of 10 nonsense syllables were used. One list was "meaningful." This list contained such nonsense syllables as *soc, pur, wak*, which have high "association values" in the sense that they

remind people of many meaningful words. The other list was "meaningless," containing such syllables as *gah, yil, cef*, which have low "association values." The experimenters found that while the high meaningful list was *learned* more rapidly than the low meaningful list, the high meaningful list was not better retained than the low meaningful list. (See Table 3.)

TABLE 3

Acquisition and retention scores (after 24 hours) for two lists of nonsense syllables, one high in "association values" (meaningful) and one low (meaningless).

List	Trials to Learn	Recall Score (No. Correct)
Meaningful	19.27	6.90
Meaningless	29.18	7.10

This paradox has important implications. If we conceive of the retention process as a *continuous* process, meaningful items memorized in rote learning will become enmeshed in larger and larger organizations. In this continuing process the specific items may become altered in meaning as time goes on. The general *sense* of what has been learned will be retained well (see the study of English, Welborn, and Killian to which we referred above), but the *verbatim* recall of the specific items may be interfered with. On the other hand, if the material is relatively "meaningless," there is less possibility of the specific items becoming embedded in larger units. Therefore the verbatim memory for such items may be maintained.

2. *The higher the degree of perceptual differentiation, the higher is the retention.* We have seen in our chapter on perception that the degree of "isolation" of an item is an important determinant of its perceptual vividness (p. 90), and we have already used this principle in interpreting the serial-position effect. In an experiment by

von Restorff (1933) it was specifically demonstrated that "isolated" items are not only learned better than "crowded" ones, but are also retained better. In one of her experiments a list composed of nine syllables and one number was used. The number thus isolated in the midst of the syllables was remembered about twice as well as the same number when it was part of a more varied list—e.g., one including other numbers, syllables, and nonsense figures. The same result was obtained when the list consisted of nine numbers and one syllable; in this case the syllable was remembered better.

In 1954 Postman and Phillips extended these findings as follows. (1) The isolation effect occurs even when the total number of syllables and digits in the list are equal, but are so distributed that within one list several *relatively* isolated digits and syllables occur. (2) The relative isolation of an item is a function of the *over-all* temporal patterning of the list, and is not dependent merely on the immediate neighbors of the "isolated" item. (3) The isolation effect occurs much more strongly when there is directed attention to the stimulus-items. Thus, for instance, when the subject was exposed to the list without having a specific intention to learn it, there was very little evidence for the isolation effect in retention. (See Box 108.)

3. *The more efficient the methods of acquisition, the higher is the retention.* Material that is learned by the distributed method seems to be retained better than material learned by the massed method. This holds even though more practice is required for the massed method. But here again we have some contradictory evidence and at present we must accept this as a probable hypothesis.

In the Gates study to which we referred earlier, it was demonstrated that material learned with the active method (recitation) is retained better than material learned passively. The retention process benefits from the conditions that held for the initial acquisition process.

4. *The degree of "ego involvement" in original learning may influence the degree of retention.* Many experiments have been done on the question of whether material closely related to central attitudes and beliefs of the person are remembered better than neutral material, or whether material learned under high motivation is better retained than material learned under low motivation. The results of these experiments are somewhat contradictory, but in general the findings indicate that material which is congruent with the beliefs of the person, or important to him, or learned under high motivation is the better retained.

There are difficulties with most of these experiments, however. Usually the two groups of subjects (the "ego-involved" and the "non-ego-involved") are not strictly equated in the degree of original learning. The possibility also exists that the higher motivated group engaged in more "silent rehearsal" during the period between original learning and retention testing. It may be, therefore, that the first three retention principles we have listed are sufficient to account for the apparent superiority of "ego-involved" material in retention. At the present time we must list this fourth principle as a very tentative one.

Closely related to "ego involvement" is the question whether pleasant or unpleasant experiences are remembered better. Here again the data are somewhat contradictory, some experimenters reporting no difference; some, that unpleasant experiences are remembered better; but most, that the pleasant experiences show the best retention. Freudian theory suggests that it is not the pleasantness or unpleasantness of the material which is important, but

---

BOX 108

Retention of the Perceptually Different

Postman and Phillips have reported two experiments that compared the effectiveness of "isolated" material for intentional and incidental learning.

To obtain "incidental" learning, the following strategem was employed: pairs of psychology students were informed that one of them was to act as a "subject" and the other as an "experimenter" in a special investigation, because this would help out the professor and would give the "experimenter" useful training!

One of the lists used consisted of 10 syllables and 10 numbers arranged as follows: GUB, KEV, *406*, DAC, RUL, HOF, 763, VOM, 581, WAJ, 341, 258, *SIH*, 179, 417, 562, FIP, 738, TER, 269. A "reverse" list, 341, 258, *SIH*, 179, 417, 562, FIP, 738, TER, 269, GUB, KEV, *406*, DAC, RUL, HOF, 763, VOM, 581, WAJ, was used with other pairs of subjects. It will be noted that the items we have italicized (*406* and *SIH*) are relatively isolated ones for both lists.

As the items appeared in the window of a memory drum, the "experimenter" read them aloud to the "subjects." The "subject" then repeated the item. The students sat side by side so that both saw the items, each pronounced them once, and each heard them once. The only difference was that the "subject" *was instructed to learn* the items; the "experimenter" was merely there to get "training"—presumably.

Immediately after a single presentation of the list, *both* students were given a recall test. They were then given a 20-minute reading task (Plato's *Dialogues*) to prevent "silent rehearsal," and were then tested again for the recall of the list. The results of this second test are summarized in Figure 100. Items *406* and *SIH* (in serial positions 3 and 13) were recalled much better than their surrounding neighbors by the intentional learner, but not by the incidental learner. The isolation effect occurs, then, even when the total number of syllables and numbers in the list are equal, but so distributed that within the list a relatively isolated number and syllable occur simultaneously. This effect seems to be restricted to intentional learners.

In the second experiment the same list and the same procedures were used, except that for half the subjects the syllables were printed in black and the numbers in red; for the other half, the colors were reversed. Now, even for the intentional learners, the isolation effect begins to break down. Figure 101 shows that it is present for the first isolated item, and not for the second. The introduction of the color difference may have grouped the second "isolated" item to the other same-colored items and robbed it of its "isolation." The perceptual vividness of an item, in other words, depends upon the stimulus characteristics of the entire series of which it is a part—and not only upon the stimulus characteristics of its immediate neighbors.

POSTMAN, L., and PHILLIPS, L. W. 1954. Studies in incidental learning. *J. exp. Psychol., 48,* 48–56.

---

whether the material is *anxiety provoking.* Thus there seems to be evidence, obtained from the clinical psychologist's case histories, that material which evokes anxiety is "repressed" (see Chapter 24), that is, the person cannot bring the material to conscious awareness.

QUALITATIVE CHANGES DURING RETENTION. Perhaps the most dramatic evidence that the retention process is very much akin

to the acquisition process comes from a *qualitative* analysis of retention. One of the most famous experiments in this area is that of Bartlett (1932). Bartlett had his subjects (English university students) read a North American Indian folk tale twice to themselves. Fifteen minutes later, and at various intervals after that, he tested them for recall. He found that (1) the general *form* of the student's first recall was preserved throughout his reproductions; (2) elements of the original story which seemed unconnected or meaningless to the English student were changed so as to make them more *meaningful;* (3) various new details were *invented* by the subject so as to make the story more coherent and more in keeping with English speech-patterns, customs, and values. The final story "remembered" was frequently quite different from the original story heard, but "forgetting" did not consist of a gradual dropping out of items; rather, there was a definite, consistent *reworking* of the materials into a "new" story, one that the

subjects had really never heard before. It is for this reason that Bartlett speaks of *"creative forgetting."* The important implications of this for the growth of rumors and the reliability of testimony are obvious.

Bousfield (1955) and his associates have demonstrated, in an extensive series of experiments, that after various retention periods, material may be recalled in meaningful groupings even when the stimulus list consists of unconnected words. In their experiments words belonging to various categories are presented in a *random* order (e.g., bayonet, ferret, mandolin, cow, carbine, piano). When the subjects are tested

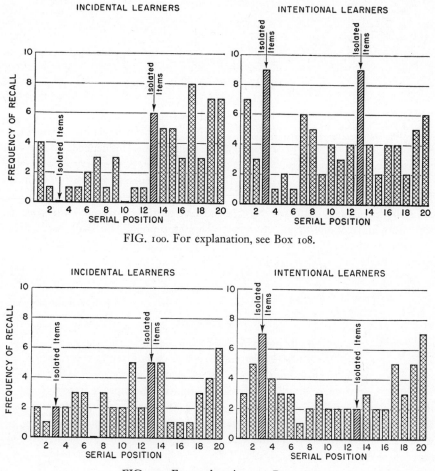

FIG. 100. For explanation, see Box 108.

FIG. 101. For explanation, see Box 108.

for retention (after various intervals), these words tend to be recalled in a sequence that is organized into related categories (e.g., bayonet, carbine; ferret, cow; mandolin, piano) rather than in the original randomized fashion. This tendency has been termed *"associative clustering."* The retention performance, then, shows grouping behavior analogous to that described for the acquisition process. Not only are adjacent items grouped together as an aid to learning, but during the retention process as well items from one part of the list are grouped with items from a distant part to make meaningful clusters.

This organizing and generalizing achievement of retention sometimes plays a very important part in determining the recall performance. The process of recalling a specific name, for example, is guided by the *general form* of the name that the retention process has abstracted and retained. Woodworth (1938) gives several illustrations from his own studies. For the name *Richards*, the name first recalled is *Rogers;* for *Ranelaugh, Casenaugh;* for *Fishberg, Hirschberg*, etc. The first attempts are related to the correct names in similarity of initial sounds, in rhythm, or in the "atmosphere" of the name, e.g., both may be elegant, or commonplace, or foreign, etc. The reader will remember William James' vivid description of the state of consciousness which corresponds to this process (see Box 81, p. 363).

BY WAY OF SUMMARY. A quantitative analysis of retention, as well as a qualitative study, seems to show that retention and acquisition have the following things in common: (1) acquisition and retention performances are determined by the current stimulus situation, as well as by past events; (2) acquisition and retention are sensitive to similar stimulus-patterning factors and probably to much the same motivational, attitudinal, and personality factors; and

(3) in both, the material is continuously organized and reorganized into meaningful clusters and groupings.

Transfer

Suppose we learn "A" and then "B." The major transfer problems are: How will the learning of "A" influence the *learning* of "B"? And how will the learning of "B" influence the *retention* of "A"? The transfer problem, thus defined, is involved in almost every acquisition study, since we always come to a new acquisition task with an extensive series of previously learned acquisitions.

Similarly, every retention study is a study of transfer. Immediately after the acquisition of any "A" the person continues, uninterruptedly, to start new learning processes and to get new experiences as he perceives the world around him. Certainly the process of retaining "A" does not run its course in quarantined isolation, rather it is constantly being influenced by the effects of innumerable new experiences.

Our discussion of transfer, then, will continue the examination of the material we have partially covered, but from a different vantage point. We shall concern ourselves primarily with an analysis of the *interaction* between the processes of retention and acquisition.

The net effect of interaction between acquisition and retention processes may be "beneficial" or "harmful." When the previous learning speeds up new learning, we speak of *positive transfer*; when the effect is harmful, of *negative transfer*. When new acquisitions improve retention of the old, the term *reproductive facilitation* is frequently applied; and when the effect is negative, *reproductive interference*.

POSITIVE AND NEGATIVE TRANSFER. We have seen that in rote learning the memorizer, by a process of trial-and-error and with many of the characteristics of creative problem-solving, achieves a number of very simple concepts about how to memorize. No matter how simple the learning task we give our subject, he frequently learns more than we had bargained for. Thus, when he has completed his memorizing of a nonsense-syllable list, he has not only acquired *specific* information (a list of nonsense syllables), but *general* information as well; he has had practice in the *method of memorizing* nonsense syllables.

When a person comes to a second rote-learning task, the specific and the general information he acquired from the first task can have differential effects; one kind of information may hamper and the other may aid in the new learning. Which does which depends upon the relationships between the first and second tasks and certain other things. With this in mind, we can now summarize many of the transfer experiments.

Transfer of General Information. Positive transfer is frequently cumulative; that is, the more rote tasks we learn, the more transfer there is, up to a point. The reason for this is quite simple. Since in any rote learning the person is given an opportunity to practice the methods of rote learning, we would expect that the more practice he has, the more he learns about the method of memorizing. In other words, many instances of transfer are due to the transfer of general information. This leads to a first transfer principle: *General information acquired in rote learning may result in positive transfer among similar learning tasks.*

An experiment by Ward (1937) presents some relevant and interesting data. Ward had his subjects (university students) learn sixteen different 12-item nonsense-syllable lists at the rate of one list per day (Saturdays and Sundays excluded). Practice on each list (using the anticipation method)

was continued until the criterion of one complete, successful anticipation was achieved. Figure 102 presents the average results for a group of 12 students. It will be seen that with each successive list the number of trials required to reach the criterion decreased, but these savings from list to list slowed up after the first few lists. Transfer from list to list, in other words, is negatively accelerated. It will be remembered that most acquisition curves also show negative acceleration from trial to trial. The similarity between the two curves is in keeping with the suggestion that the positive transfer often found among similar tasks is

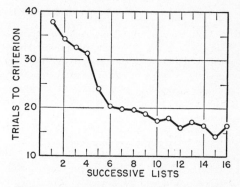

FIG. 102. Average number of trials required by a group of 12 subjects to learn 16 successive lists of 12-item nonsense syllables. (After Ward, 1937.)

really an acquisition function. *The subjects learn to learn.*

There are always individual differences in behavior and some people may acquire relatively little general information from rote learning, and others, a great deal. In the usual rote-learning task the person is told to learn only the specific items. His acquisition of the general information is, in a sense, incidental (even if important) to the task at hand. And yet, as we have just seen, it is this "by-product" that can be responsible for positive transfer. This suggests that if the "incidental" task were made more important, the value of "memory practice" should be increased; a larger degree of positive transfer should result. Experiments testing this conclusion have almost uniformly found it to be true. (For one such experiment, see Box 109.) We can state the following as a corollary of our first "transfer principle": Emphasizing the general information aspect of rote learning will tend to increase the degree of positive transfer among similar rote-learning problems.

Transfer of Specific Information. Paired associates and serial lists make up the major types of material in rote learning. In the first, the task is to learn to associate one item with another; in the second, a series of items must be memorized in successive order. Let us first consider transfer in paired associates.

The relationships between one list of paired associates and another can be of three types, and the transfer effects differ accordingly.

PAIRED ASSOCIATES, TYPE I. In type I, the *first* members of the corresponding pairs in list A differ from those of list B, but the

---

BOX 109

Transfer of General Information in Rote Learning

Woodrow at the University of Minnesota posed the following question: How can training in one rote-learning task be given so as to maximize transfer to other *kinds* of rote-learning tasks? To answer this question, the following experiment was performed.

The *control group* (106 students) was tested in six different forms of memorizing (poetry, prose, facts, dates, Turkish-English vocabulary, and consonants) at the beginning and end of a 33-day period, with no intervening practice. The *practice group* (34 students) was given the same tests, but during the interim it was given a total of 177 minutes of practice in memorizing poetry and nonsense syllables. The *training group* (42 students), also tested at the beginning and end of the period, spent 76 minutes listening to an exposition of the technique of memorizing and 101 minutes in practicing the memorizing of poetry and nonsense syllables. The rules which were taught to the training group, *and which they were told were the important things to learn*, included the following: learning by wholes, use of rhythm and groupings, attention to meaning.

First the differences in scores made by the three groups on the initial and end tests were calculated. The gains made by the *control group* were then subtracted from the gains made by the *practice* and *training*

groups to discover how much the practice and training had contributed. The results are presented in the following table:

PERCENTAGE GAINS IN THE END TESTS AFTER SUBTRACTION OF PERCENTAGE GAINS OF THE CONTROL GROUP

Material	Gains Practice Group	Gains Training Group
Poetry	3.7	22.2
Prose	—3.2	22.0
Facts	8.1	17.7
Dates	8.5	58.7
Vocabulary	4.0	55.8
Consonants	—1.0	14.4

It is clear that drill on such simple things as memorizing nonsense syllables and poetry, *when the methods of memorizing are stressed*, can result in sizable amounts of transfer to *various* rote-learning tasks, and that the amounts of transfer are uniformly larger than when the methods of memorizing are not stressed.

Note: In the light of the negative acceleration transfer curve found by Ward, can you account for the relatively small positive transfer found by Woodrow for the *practice* group?

WOODROW, H. 1927. The effect of type of training upon transference. *J. educ. Psychol., 18,* 159–72.

second members of the pairs are identical. This is similar to the situation in which you have two lists of foreign words, the English equivalents of which you are to memorize, and they are set up as follows:

LIST A

Chien	—	Dog
Homme	—	Man
Garçon	—	Boy
Assez	—	Enough
	etc.	

LIST B

Hund	—	Dog
Mann	—	Man
Knabe	—	Boy
Genug	—	Enough
	etc.	

If in learning list A you have the *French* words before you, and you cover up the English equivalents while you attempt to give them correctly, and for List B, the same words are given in *German*, and you attempt to respond with the correct English equivalent, you have satisfied the conditions for the type 1 situation. For this situation the experimental evidence is clear that learning list A *facilitates* the later learning of list B. The more similar the first members of the pairs in list A are to the first members of the corresponding pairs in list B, the greater is the facilitation (as would be the case in Italian and French). We can now state a general principle: *In paired-associate learning, when the first members of the corresponding pairs are different, but the second members are the same, the transfer effect is positive; the magnitude of the positive transfer is greater, the greater the similarity between the first members.*

PAIRED ASSOCIATES, TYPE 2. In type 2, the situation is reversed. Here the first members of the corresponding pairs are the same, but the second members differ, as in the following situation:

LIST A

Dog	—	*Chien*
Man	—	*Homme*
Boy	—	*Garçon*
Enough	—	*Assez*
	etc.	

LIST B

Dog	—	*Hund*
Man	—	*Mann*
Boy	—	*Knabe*
Enough	—	*Genug*
	etc.	

If in learning list A you have the English words before you, and your task is to respond with the correct French word, and in list B if you have the English word before you, your task is to respond with the German word, then learning list A will *interfere with and slow down* the subsequent learning of list B. This interference is less the more similar are the second members of the corresponding pairs. The formal statement of this is: *In paired-associate learning, when the first members of the corresponding pairs are the same, but the second members are different, the transfer effect is negative; the magnitude of the negative transfer is less, the greater the similarity among the second members.*

The significant thing to be pointed out is that while each corresponding pair of associates is made up of *identical elements* in both types, the *temporal patterning* of these elements differs (e.g., in type 1 we have "Chien–Dog," "Hund–Dog"; in type 2 we have "Dog–Chien," "Dog–Hund"), and this makes for entirely different transfer effects. Here we have a dramatic illustration of the role that stimulus-*patterning* can play, the importance of which we have already seen in perception, creative problem-solving, conditioning, rote learning, and retention. (The alert student who has two language vocabularies to memorize in an evening will no doubt see the practical value of these two laws in arranging his material for study.)

PAIRED ASSOCIATES, TYPE 3. In type 3, *both* the first and second items of the corresponding pairs are different. This is similar to the situation in which the first task requires the learning of the English equivalents of French words, and the second, the names of various statistical symbols:

LIST A

Chien	—	Dog
Homme	—	Man
Garçon	—	Boy
Assez	—	Enough
	etc.	

LIST B

σ	—	Standard deviation
r	—	Correlation coefficient
Σ	—	Sum
M	—	Average
	etc.	

Here the specific information learned in list A has no demonstrable effect on the learning of the specific information of list B. Stated formally: *In paired-associate learning, when the first and second members of the corresponding pairs are entirely different, the transfer effect of specific information is zero.*

SERIAL LEARNING. When we have two *serial* lists to learn, the items of the two lists may differ in similarity. For instance, here are two sets of lists with different degrees of similarity between them:

HIGH DEGREE OF SIMILARITY

Passage A	*Passage B$_1$*
My	Our
Tough	Rough
Drowsy	Sleepy
Kind	Gentle
Little	Tiny
Fellow	Boy

LOW DEGREE OF SIMILARITY

Passage A	*Passage B$_2$*
My	The
Tough	Pigeons
Drowsy	On
Kind	The
Little	Grass
Fellow	Alas

In these instances the learning of A will *interfere* with the later learning of B$_1$ but will have little effect on the learning of B$_2$. The generalization covering these cases can be simply stated: *In serial learning, the negative transfer is greater, the greater the similarity among the corresponding items in serial position.*

Reproductive Facilitation and Interference. The retention process may be affected by other processes that start *after* it does. In this case we speak of *retroactive* effects. The following diagram illustrates the experimental design used to investigate retroactive effects:

Experimental Group:
    Learn A → Learn B → Recall A
Control Group:
    Learn A —————————→ Recall A

If the *experimental* group does *better* on its recall test than the control group, we assume that this improvement is due to its having learned B *after* A; then we have an instance of *retroactive facilitation*. If the recall score of the experimental group is *worse* than that of the control group, we speak of *retroactive interference* (sometimes called "retroactive inhibition").

The retention process may also be affected by processes that start *before* it does. In this case we speak of *proactive* effects. The following diagram illustrates the experimental design used to investigate proactive effects:

Experimental Group:

    Learn B → Learn A → Recall A

Control Group:

        Learn A → Recall A

If the experimental group does better on its recall than the control group, we assume that this improvement is due to the previous learning of B; we call this *proactive facilitation* (i.e., B works *forward* on the A process). If the recall score of the experimental group is *worse* than that of the control group, we have an instance of *proactive interference*.

SUSPENDED ANIMATION. For an ideally controlled study of reproductive facilitation and interference, we would have to have a completely "brain-washed" person learn A, put him into a state of "suspended animation," and then introduce one or another specified process and see what would happen to his retention of A. Thus far we have found this impossible to do. The nearest approximation is a study by Minami and Dallenbach (1946), who taught cockroaches to avoid a certain corner of their cage which was wired for electric shock, then immobilized half of the cockroaches by

---

BOX 110

Retention During Sleep

Van Ormer and his wife, acting alternately as subject and experimenter, found that memorized material is retained better during sleep than during waking hours.

At each sitting three lists of 12-item nonsense syllables were learned. Half of the sittings occurred in the mornings (between 9:00 A.M. and 10:15 A.M.) and half at night (11:00 P.M. to 12:30 A.M.) Retention was

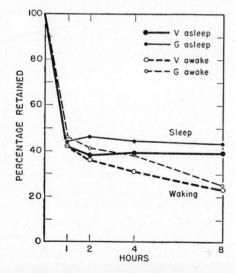

tested by the relearning method. The retention tests for the lists learned in the mornings came 1, 2, 4, or 8 hours after

learning, and these intervals were filled with the "usual activities of a graduate student and his wife living in New York City." Immediately after learning the three lists at night, the subject went to bed and was allowed to sleep 1, 2, 4 or 8 hours, when he was awakened by an alarm clock, dashed cold water on his face, and began the relearning test. This experiment was repeated 8 times for each time interval for both the waking and sleeping conditions.

The results are shown in the figure ("V" refers to Van Ormer, "G" to his wife): (1) forgetting during the first hour of sleep is as rapid as for the first hour of waking; (2) there is practically no forgetting during sleep after the first hour, while during waking, forgetting continues; (3) after 8 hours of sleep the average amount retained is about 41 per cent; after 8 hours of waking activity, 24 per cent. Forgetting seems to be a function of interference with the retention process by the various new processes that are initiated during waking hours.

Van Ormer ends with an encouraging word for the night owls: "Assuming that there is little or no decrease in learning efficiency at the late evening hours (and he found none) the advantage of night study becomes evident." (!)

VAN ORMER, E. B., 1932. Retention after intervals of sleep and waking. *Arch. Psychol., 21*, #137.

placing them for some time in a dark box in bodily contact with tissue paper which inhibits their movements. The other half were permitted freedom of movement. When the immobilized cockroaches were later released and tested, they showed very little forgetting of which corner was to be avoided, while the other cockroaches showed considerable forgetting.

With human subjects the effects of sleep, rather than immobilization, have been studied. Jenkins and Dallenbach in 1924, and Van Ormer in 1932, compared retention during intervals spent in sleep with retention during intervals of waking activities. Both experiments found that retention was better during sleep, when the *general* level of activity is presumably lower than during waking. (For Van Ormer's experiment, see Box 110, on preceding page.)

These experiments support the general statement that retention processes interact with *many* other kinds of processes.

Two GENERALIZATIONS. We can summarize the results of the many facilitation and interference experiments with the following two major generalizations:

1. *Retroactive facilitation and interference depend upon the nature of the relationships between the tasks.* The same relationships hold for retention as for transfer. That is, if the A and B tasks are of type 1 (Chien–Dog; Hund–Dog), the learning of B (Hund–Dog) improves the retention of A (Chien–Dog). *Retroactive facilitation* has occurred. In type 2 (Dog–Chien; Dog–Hund) the learning of B (Dog–Hund) lowers the retention of A (Dog–Chien). *Retroactive interference* has occurred. In type 3 (Chien–Dog; σ–Standard deviation) there is neither retroactive facilitation nor interference. In serial learning the retroactive effect may be zero or interfering, depending upon the degree of similarity between the two tasks.

2. *The degree of retroactive and proac-*

tive effects is in part determined by the degree of differentiation between the tasks. The degree of differentiation between tasks A and B is governed by several factors. One such factor is the *context* within which the tasks A and B occur. For example, it has been found that if the A and B tasks are tackled in the same room, there are more interaction effects between the tasks than if the tasks are done in different rooms.

Another factor determining differentiation of tasks is the degree of learning of each task. As the degree of mastery of A increases, the effect of B upon the retention of A decreases. A well-practiced task will show little retroactive interference by an intervening task. The degree of mastery of the *intervening* task is also important. Thus as the degree of the mastery of B increases, the interfering effect of B upon the retention of A at first increases, then it begins to decrease (see Fig. 103). With *extended* practice the materials of both tasks become more clearly differentiated from each other and hence are less likely to interact.

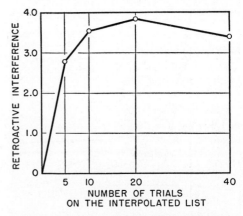

FIG. 103. Retroactive interference effect on the A list as a function of the degree of practice on the interpolated B list. Note that with increased practice on the interpolated list there is an increased retroactive interference effect. This follows the law of diminishing returns, and with overlearning (40 trials of practice) the interference effect begins to decrease. (Data from Melton and Irwin, 1940.)

Glossary

abscissa. The horizontal base line of a graph.

"active" performance. A method in rote learning by which the person recites aloud the items to be memorized, or writes them down *as he proceeds with his memorizing*. To be compared with "passive" performance. Usually the "active" method is the more efficient.

acquisition. The process of attaining a new response, memory, knowledge, etc.

anticipation method. A training procedure in rote learning according to which the subject is required to produce the next correct item when he is presented with the preceding item.

association value. The capacity of a word or nonsense syllable to evoke associations. Thus a nonsense syllable that reminds people of many meaningful words has *high* association value; one that reminds people of none or very few meaningful words has *low* association value.

associative clustering. The tendency to reproduce items in meaningfully related groups, even though these items had originally been learned in a random order.

backward conditioning. Training procedure in which the US is presented first and the CS is presented after the cessation of the US. The least efficient method of conditioned-response training.

conditioned discrimination. When an organism, after appropriate conditioned-response training, is capable of responding in two different ways to two different stimuli, we speak of conditioned discrimination. Thus if after conditioned-response training a dog salivates to the tone of a bell, but not to the noise of a click, we have an instance of conditioned discrimination.

conditioned response. The response that is evoked by the conditioned stimulus after conditioning has occurred. Abbreviated to CR. The CR is usually different from

the UR and normally has a longer latency.

conditioned stimulus. The stimulus to which a new response becomes related through the process of conditioning. Abbreviated to CS.

conditioning. The process of training which results in the formation of conditioned responses.

delayed conditioning. Training procedure in which the CS begins from 5 seconds to several minutes prior to the US and continues until the response occurs. One of the most efficient conditioned-response training methods.

distributed practice. A training procedure in which successive trials are separated by relatively long time intervals. To be compared with "massed practice." In rote learning the distributed method is usually more efficient than the massed method.

efficiency (in acquisition). Refers to the total work required to reach a specified level of mastery. E.g., the trials or time required to memorize a set of words to the point of one perfect recitation.

extinction. The training procedure of presenting the CS unaccompanied by the US. This term is also used to refer to the loss of conditioning as a result of this procedure. Sometimes called "experimental extinction."

forgetting curve. A graphic method of presenting the change in the amount retained as a function of the passage of time between the end of the acquisition process and the time of testing for retention. In such a curve the successive time units are usually plotted on the abscissa and the performance units on the ordinate. Sometimes called a "retention curve."

generalization (in conditioning). The fact that a conditioned response may be elicited by stimuli that have not been used in the conditioning training. The more similar the new stimuli are to the stimulus used in the training, the greater is the probability that generalization will be evident. This is sometimes referred to as the "gradient of generalization."

group curve. A curve based upon the combined performance or scores of two or more individuals.

higher-order conditioning. Training procedure in which the CS is paired with a *previously* established CS instead of a US. Conditioning based upon previous conditioning.

incidental learning. Refers to acquisition that takes place when the learner has received no instructions from the experimenter to learn the material, or when no explicit set to learn seems to be present. To be compared with intentional learning.

intentional learning. Refers to acquisition that takes place when the learner has received instructions from the experimenter to learn the material, or when there is an explicit set to learn.

isolation effect. In rote learning, the observation that the perceptually differentiated item in a group of items will be more quickly acquired and better retained than items that are less perceptually differentiated. Originally demonstrated by the German psychologist, von Restorff.

latency. The time interval elapsing between the onset of the stimulus and the onset of the response.

learning curve. A graphic method of presenting the change in performance of an individual or group of individuals during the acquisition process. In such a curve the successive time or trial intervals are usually plotted on the abscissa and the performance units on the ordinate. Sometimes called an "acquisition curve."

linear slope; linear curve. A curve that shows a *constant rate of change* with passage of time or trials (steady progress, or steady deterioration).

massed practice. A training procedure in which successive trials are separated by relatively short time intervals. To be compared with "distributed practice." In rote learning the massed method is usually less efficient than the distributed method.

memory drum. An apparatus, used in rote-learning experiments, designed to present one set of items at a time with a predetermined exposure time and at a predetermined interval between exposures of items.

negatively accelerated curve. A curve that shows a *decrease in rate of change* with passage of time or trials (a fast start, but a slow finish).

non-reinforcement. The failure to accompany the CS with the US.

nonsense syllable. A combination of consonants and syllables presumed to be meaningless. Invented by Ebbinghaus, a German psychologist, and used extensively as items in rote-learning experiments.

ordinate. The vertical axis of a graph.

overlearning. A training procedure in which practice is continued beyond some previously agreed-upon level of mastery.

paired-associates. Material used in rote learning, consisting of a list of pairs of items in which one serves as "stimulus" and the other as "response." *Paired-associate learning* refers to the learning to respond with a *second* item of a paired associate when the *first* item is presented.

part method. A training procedure in which the entire task is subdivided into parts, and each part is practiced independently before the entire task is practiced as a whole. To be compared with the "whole method."

"passive" performance. A method in rote learning by which the person silently observes the items to be memorized. To be compared with "active" performance. Usually the active method is the more efficient.

positively accelerated curve. A curve that shows an *increase in rate of change* with passage of time or trials (a slow start, but a fast finish).

preparatory adjustment. A response interpreted as one that puts the subject in readiness for the appearance of a forth-coming stimulus. Conditioned responses are believed by some to have this characteristic.

proactive facilitation. The facilitative effect upon the recall of A by the acquisition of B *previous* to the learning of A.

proactive interference. The disruptive effect upon recall of A by the acquisition of B *previous* to the learning of A.

recall method. A method of measuring retention by which the person is required to reproduce the items previously learned. The number of items reproduced divided by the number of items originally learned is his "recall score" expressed in percentage terms.

recognition method. A method of measuring retention by which the person is required to identify the set of items previously learned from among a larger collection of items. The number of items identified correctly divided by the total number of items originally learned is taken as the person's "recognition score."

reinforcement. The training procedure of accompanying the CS by the US.

relearning. A method of measuring retention in which a task originally learned is learned again after a lapse of time. The difference in time or number of trials between original learning and relearning is used to determine the amount retained, and is referred to as the "savings score."

reminiscence. The phenomenon when a person earns a better score after an interval of time has elapsed after learning than he did *immediately* after learning.

retention. The process of or capacity for remembering things whereby responses or knowledge once acquired become available for use by the organism on later occasions.

retroactive facilitation. The facilitative effect upon recall of A by a new acquisition (B) interpolated between the original acquisition of A and its later recall.

retroactive interference (**inhibition**). The disruptive effect upon recall of A by a new acquisition (B) interpolated between the original acquisition of A and its later recall.

rote learning. Committing to memory a clearly specified set of items. Sometimes called "rote memorizing."

savings method. A measure of retention based upon the relearning method. The difference in time or number of trials between original learning and relearning, expressed as a percentage, is taken as a measure of retention, i.e., the time or trials "saved" in the relearning.

serial lists. Material used in rote learning consisting of a list of single items. In the learning of serial lists, the items are presented in the same order on every trial.

serial-position effect. The observation that in rote learning the items toward the beginning and end of the series to be learned are more quickly memorized than the items in the middle of the list.

simultaneous conditioning. Training procedure in which the CS begins simultaneously with or up to 5 seconds before the US and continues until the response occurs. Not a very efficient conditioning procedure.

slope of curve. Refers to the direction and degree of incline of a curve. Thus a *positive* slope refers to a curve (or a section of the curve) that slants upward; a *negative* slope, that slants downward; *zero* slope, that remains horizontal; steep slope, that slants sharply; shallow slope, that slants gently.

spontaneous recovery. The return in strength of an extinguished CR after a lapse of time and with no additional conditioning.

trace conditioning. Training procedure in which the CS is presented first but is removed prior to the onset of the US. A fairly efficient method of conditioning.

transfer. Refers to the effect upon the learning of one task (B) by the previous learning of another task (A). When the learning of A has a facilitating effect on the learning of B, we speak of *positive* *transfer;* when it has a deleterious effect, we speak of *negative transfer.*

unconditioned response. The original response evoked by the unconditioned stimulus without training. Abbreviated to UR.

unconditioned stimulus. The stimulus that evokes the unconditioned response without training. Abbreviated to US.

whole method. A training procedure in which the entire task is performed at each successive trial until acquisition has been achieved. To be compared with the "part method."

Suggestions for Further Reading

BARTLETT, F. C. 1932. *Remembering.* Cambridge: Cambridge Univ. Press.

An original treatment of remembering as a creative and dynamic process, written by a former professor of psychology at Cambridge University. Presents some experiments that have become classics in the field.

HILGARD, E. R., and MARQUIS, D. G. 1940. *Conditioning and learning.* New York: Appleton-Century-Crofts.

A useful, systematic presentation of the facts and theories of conditioning. A standard reference.

OSGOOD, C. E. 1953. *Method and theory in experimental psychology.* New York: Oxford Univ. Press.

A detailed systematic presentation of the data and theories in experimental psychology. See especially Chapters 12, 13.

STEVENS, S. S. (ed.) 1951. *Handbook of experimental psychology.* New York: Wiley.

Chapter 17 of this standard reference book presents a useful summary of rote learning in man. Written by C. I. Hovland of Yale University who has contributed much to this research field.

CHAPTER XVI

Complex Learning and Skills

THE STUDY of the more complex forms of learning is continuous with the study of the more simple types of learning. In considering complex learning, we shall be concerned with two major problems: an analysis of trial-and-error learning and an analysis of the development of skills.

As we study trial-and-error learning, we shall find that some instances of such learning approach creative problem-solving in their complexity and very nature. This becomes especially clear when we take up the problem of skills. Indeed the development of skills involves every type of learning and problem-solving we have thus far investigated.

Trial-and-Error Learning

"Trial and error," like "conditioned response," is an ambiguous term. It describes a *specific type of learning situation*, and it also refers to a *general theory about learning*. We shall use the term in the first, more specific sense. As such, trial-and-error learning has three characteristics. (1) The responses to be acquired are not narrowly defined by the presented stimulus-pattern. The individual must *select* out the correct response from a number of possible responses to the stimulus situation. (2) Typically, the correct response is within the well-practiced repertoire of the individual before he comes to the learning situation. (3) The "correctness" of the response is *specific to the presented problem* and can be verified only by *actual trial*. No amount of abstract thinking can possibly lead to the selection of the correct response in a genuine trial-and-error problem situation.

Trial-and-error learning differs from conditioning and rote learning, in that in these the stimulus-pattern is less ambiguous and the individual does not have to *discover* the correct responses. It also differs from creative problem-solving, in which the to-be-discovered "correct" response is a novel one and in which *general* knowledge can lead to a solution of a given problem prior to concrete verification. That is, one can "think through" a solution.

Trial-and-error learning, both as an analysis of a specific kind of problem situation and as a general theory, is associated with the name of Edward Lee Thorndike, the great American psychologist whose work on cats in a puzzle box (first published in 1898) had such a profound influence on American educational theory and practice as well as on psychological experimentation and theory. Thorndike, while still working for his degree at Columbia University (having previously studied with William James at Harvard) undertook to study the intelligence of chicks, rabbits, and cats. Confining his cats in "puzzle boxes" (from which they could escape by clawing down loops of string, pushing on levers, turning buttons), Thorndike observed what the animals did and plotted learning curves showing how long it took the cats to get out of the boxes on successive trials. The significant observations he made were these: (1) the animal first tries everything—squeezing through the bars, clawing and biting at any loose object within the box, thrusting its paws out, etc.; (2) gradually the "errors" (responses that do not release the animal from the box) are eliminated, and only the successful responses remain—the animal has learned "by trial and error, and accidental success."

These observations, made in a controlled experimental situation, describe behavior which, on the face of it, characterizes the haphazard adaptive behavior of so many of us. Elaborated into several "laws of learning," they launched the experimental and theoretical research on trial-and-error learning in American psychology and education. This research still continues, and Thorndike's laws, frequently under different names and with different elaborations, are still being investigated, "proved" and "disproved." Many theorists, outstanding

among whom was Clark Hull of Yale University, have shown ingenuity in revising and elaborating Thorndike's original laws in an attempt to encompass all the experimental data. Other theorists have tended to question the general validity of these laws, regarding them as too limited to account for all aspects of animal or human learning.

Two Major Stages of Trial-and-Error Learning. It may be helpful for the discussion that follows if we summarize the characteristics of trial-and-error learning by a simple diagram (see Fig. 104.)

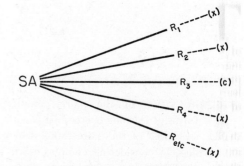

FIG. 104. For explanation, see text.

R_1, R_2, R_3, R_4, etc., represent an array of responses which the stimulus-situation, SA, can elicit from the individual even before any learning has taken place. The x's after R_1, R_2, and R_4 represent the fact that these are "incorrect" responses; and the c after R_3 indicates that it is the "correct" response.

We can, very roughly, distinguish two major stages in trial-and-error learning: the "presolution" period and the "solution" period. In studying the first period, we concern ourselves with the factors that determine the occurrence of R_3—(c), the correct response. In studying the solution period, we analyze the factors that determine the dropping out of R_1—(x), R_2—(x), R_4—(x), etc., i.e., the elimination of the incorrect responses or errors. It is obvious that these two sets of problems are closely interrelated.

The Presolution Period. We have already seen that Thorndike's answer to the question of how R_3—(c) comes about in the first instance is a seemingly very simple one: the animal in the stimulus situation reacts with a large number of responses. One of these responses, by chance alone, will be correct. However, later research has indicated that in the "spelling out" of this general answer, the simplicity is lost.

DISCRIMINATION LEARNING. Ever since Thorndike's original work, animal experimentation has been of particular importance in the analysis of trial-and-error learning. Prominent in this experimentation has been the study of "discrimination learning." One of the most common types of apparatus used in such studies is the Lashley jumping stand (see Fig. 105). In the typical discrimination-learning situation the animal faces a set of two cards, one of which is "correct" and the other "wrong." The animal is permitted to choose these cards until he finally jumps to the "correct" card almost every time. Here seems to be an ideal experimental setup to study pure trial-and-error learning, since there is no "logical" reason why one card rather than the other should be correct.

A perceptual analysis of the discrimination-learning situation would suggest that the animal's task is first to discover which stimulus-dimension of the situation is the relevant one. Within this stimulus-dimension he must next discover which is the cor-

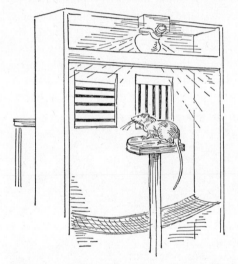

FIG. 105. Pictured here is the discrimination apparatus (adapted from Lashley's original design, 1930) used in the University of California Psychological Laboratory. The rat is perched on the jumping stand and can jump at either the card in the left window or the card in the right window. These cards are shifted from trial to trial so that the horizontally striped card is sometimes in the left window, sometimes in the right.

Let us assume that we wish the rat to choose the horizontally striped card every time. We would set up the locks behind the cards so that if the rat jumps at the vertically striped card, the card would remain immovable, and the rat would fall into the net. He would then be picked up and put back on the jumping stand for another try. On the other hand, if the rat jumps at the horizontal stripes, the card would fall at the impact of the rat's body, and the rat would be carried through to the landing platform where he would receive several nibbles of food. After a sufficient number of "successes" (jumping at the horizontal stripes) and "failures" (jumping at the vertical stripes), the animal learns to discriminate between the two and will always jump at the horizontally striped card, whether it is on the left or the right side.

Any number of other pairs of cards can be used, of course, to test the learning of other perceptual discriminations.

rect stimulus-object, and then he must learn to respond to this object consistently. Thus, in the illustration given in Figure 105 the animal must first discover whether it is the *spatial location* of the card which is the relevant stimulus-dimension, or whether it is the visual attribute of the card. If it is the former, there are various possible correct responses: the card on the *right side* may be correct, or the one on the *left side;* or the right-hand and the left-hand cards may be *alternately* correct, first right, then left, then right again, etc. If the visual characteristics are the important cues, the card with the *horizontal* lines may be correct, or the cards with the *vertical* lines, or they may be alternately correct.

This analysis seems to make of trial-and-error learning a systematic and "logical" affair, quite similar to Duncker's analysis of creative problem-solving (see Chapter 14). But how do we know that this is actually the way the animal attacks the discrimination-learning problem? The answer is that,

although we do not really know directly, we know that the animal's responses, observed under various experimental conditions, are *consistent* with such a description. These experimental data can be summarized as follows:

1. *The animal's discrimination-learning behavior consists of a series of systematic responses to various aspects of the total situation.* The discrimination-learning curve, unlike most other learning curves, is usually a *positively* accelerated one. That is, the animal starts off showing no progress in the number of correct responses and then the correct responses begin to appear *at an increasing rate* until complete mastery is achieved. An analysis of what the animal has been doing during the presolution period (when he is not jumping consistently to the correct stimulus-object) shows that he is responding to *other* stimulus-dimensions of the situation. For example, in one experiment (Krechevsky, 1932) laboratory rats were presented with a hurdle-

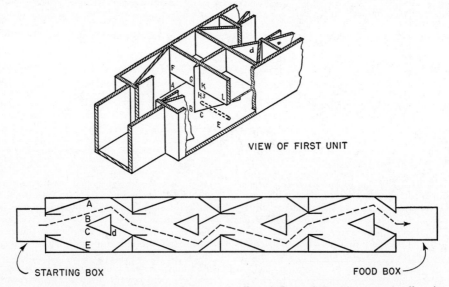

FIG. 106. Floor plan and elevation of Krechevsky's multiple-unit discrimination box. The dotted figure (C-E) represents the hurdle that can be withdrawn and placed in position B-A. The door *d* can swing so as to block either alley A-B or C-E. Above each alley in each unit (in chambers F-G and K-L) are electric lamps that can flood either alley with light, making of this box a light-dark discrimination box. (After Krechevsky, 1932.)

discrimination problem to solve (see Fig. 106). A typical learning curve obtained in this experiment is presented in Figure 107. Two points should be noticed here. (1) The correct-response curve shows the typical *positive* acceleration of discrimination learning. For the first 70 trials the animal chooses the hurdle-alley only about 50 per cent of the time. Starting with the 70th trial however, he begins to choose the hurdle consistently, and within 20 trials he has mastered the problem. (2) During the pre-

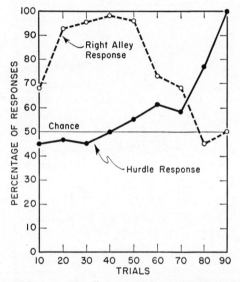

FIG. 107. Hurdle responses (correct) and right-alley responses (wrong) during hurdle-discrimination learning. These curves represent the performance of a single rat. (After Krechevsky, 1932.)

solution period he has been choosing the *right-side* alley quite consistently. The animal, in other words, *first* responded on the basis of the spatial location of the alleys, *then* on the basis of the presence or absence of a hurdle. The same kind of data has been obtained in the Lashley jumping stand with visual discrimination, and in learning by chimpanzees (Spence, 1934).

2. *The stimulus-pattern can accelerate or retard the occurrence of the correct response in accordance with perceptual prin-*

ciples. Patterns that increase the saliency of the relevant stimulus-dimension speed up the occurrence of the correct responses. Thus, if the stimulus-pattern is such as to "isolate" the correct stimulus-object, correct responses will appear rapidly. If the correct stimulus-object is "lost in the perceptual shuffle," the presolution period is prolonged while the animal responds to other characteristics (see Box 111).

3. *There are characteristic individual differences in responses to stimulus-dimensions.* In addition to the *stimulus*-patterns, factors *within* the individual also determine which stimulus-dimension will be responded to. Some animals, in the very same discrimination situation, start off with one type of response (e.g., spatial) and some with another (e.g., visual). Which animals do which depends upon the past experience and the heredity of the animal. Lawrence (1949, 1950) has shown that the learning of a discrimination serves to make the relevant stimulus-objects more distinctive and hence facilitates any subsequent discriminations in which those stimulus-objects may be involved. And Krechevsky (1933) has shown that rats of one genetic strain will respond to the spatial differences among the alleys; rats of another strain, to the visual differences.

4. *Differences in the ease with which responses shift from one stimulus-dimension to another are determined by the motivation, experience, and capacity of the organism.* Quite aside from stimulus-patterns and selective attention there seem to be factors that determine the ease with which different individuals can *shift* their responses from one stimulus-dimension to another until the problem is finally mastered. Many of the same factors that we have already treated in our study of perception, motivation, and creative problem-solving are involved here. (1) With excessive motivation, intense emotional stimulation, or

BOX 111

Apparatus, Perceptual Principles, and Learning Capacity

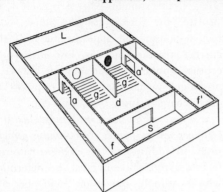

S, starting box; d, choice point; g, g', electrified grids; a, a', doors leading from alleys to food boxes, f, f'; L, lighting chamber, which can illuminate either patch facing the animal.

The development of discrimination-learning apparatus provides an interesting footnote in the history of psychology. The original apparatus used in discrimination-learning was the Yerkes box (see fig.). Using this apparatus, researchers found that the rat was (a) incapable of discriminating any visual patterns and (b) an exceedingly slow learner of simple brightness discriminations (requiring well over a hundred trials). In 1930 Lashley devised his jumping apparatus (see Fig. 105), and using it researchers now found that the rat (a) was

capable of discriminating complex visual patterns and (b) could learn black-white discriminations in 10 or less trials. Why this striking difference?

The clue may be found in Köhler's guesses (writing in 1925) as to why the Yerkes box was "perceptually unfair" to the rat: "The electric shock, for instance, applied to the legs, is not intimately connected to the task of getting a red spot as 'the negative stimulus.' There is only a very loose connection between them in space and time. If that spot *itself* would make a sudden movement against the animal and so frighten it . . . we should certainly have a situation much nearer the animal's learning in common life and a more efficient one."

In Lashley's apparatus the relevant stimulus-object, the response, and the consequence are all grouped together and make a "perceptual whole." The "correct" card *is* the door opening to food and the incorrect card *itself* is what the rat jumps against and what gives him the bump on the nose. The spatial and temporal stimulus-patterning in the apparatus plays an important role in the speed with which the animal begins to respond to the relevant stimulus-object.

KÖHLER, W., 1925. Intelligence in apes. In *Psychologies of 1925*. (C. Murchison, ed.) Worcester: Clark University Press.
LASHLEY, K. S., 1930. The mechanism of vision. *J. genet. Psychol., 37,* 453–60.

---

conflict, the ease of shift is decreased. In extreme cases, as we have seen (see Box 73, p. 319), the animal becomes so abnormally "fixated" upon one stimulus-dimension that it is almost impossible for him to respond to other dimensions. (2) With excessive past training on one set of stimulus-objects, the ease of shift to another stimulus-object is decreased. (3) Some animals seem to have the capacity to respond to several stimulus-dimensions *simultaneously*, while other animals do not. The former find it easy to shift their responses when the experimental

situation is changed, while the latter seem "stuck" with their initial solution attempts. For an experiment that provides evidence on many of these factors, see Box 112.

BY WAY OF SUMMARY. The occurrence of the solution in trial-and-error learning, whether for the rat or the human being, is not altogether a "random" affair in which haphazard trial follows haphazard trial. It is determined in accordance with the well-established laws of perception. The more we know about perception, motivation, and personality, the more we can predict about

BOX 112

Breadth of Learning in the Rat

Bruner, Matter, and Papenek of Harvard University investigated the effect of overlearning and motivation on the range of cues to which rats "attend" in discrimination learning.

Fifty-two experimental and control rats were run in a three-stage training program. In Stage I the experimental animals were trained on a four-unit discrimination apparatus (similar to the one in Fig. 106) to go to a white card for food and to avoid a black one. The white card was sometimes on the right, sometimes on the left—in a random pattern. (1) One subgroup was run for 30 trials under a 12-hour food deprivation. (2) Another was run for 30 trials with a 36-hour food deprivation. (3) A third was run for 100 trials with a 12-hour deprivation. (4) The final subgroup was run for 100 trials with a 36-hour deprivation.

In Stage II all the experimental animals were given 20 trials in which the white card was first on the right, then on the left, then on the right, in a *regular alternating pattern.*

There were 4 corresponding control groups. They received the black-white training in Stage I, but in Stage II the doors *continued* to be randomly positioned.

In Stage III *all* doors were gray. *All* animals were tested on the *regular alternating*

pattern. The animals now *had* to respond in terms of the spatial dimension.

Did the experimental animals take advantage of the opportunity that had been given to them in Stage II? If so, they should perform better in Stage III than the controls, since in Stage III the correct response is a *regular alternating one.* Another question: What effect did overlearning and higher motivation have on the ability to take advantage of what they had experienced in Stage II?

The following table presents the error records of the animals on the first 10 trials of Stage III.

It will be seen that the experimental animals did learn about spatial alternation in Stage II (compare the error scores for the experimental and control groups).

The authors conclude that "breadth of learning" is an important characteristic in discrimination learning; that a "dose of overlearning" inhibits shift to a new dimension (compare savings scores for Groups 1, 2 *vs.* 3, 4); and that high motivation similarly slows down the rate of shift (compare Groups 1, 3 *vs.* 2, 4).

BRUNER, J. S., MATTER, J., and PAPANEK, M. L., 1955. Breadth of learning as a function of drive level and mechanization. *Psychol. Rev., 62,* 1–10.

| | Errors | | Savings |
Conditions	Control	Experimental	Control Minus Experimental
1. Learn (30 trials)—12 hr.	13.6	7.8	5.8
2. Learn (30 trials)—36 hr.	12.3	6.8	5.5
3. Overlearn (100 trials)—12 hr.	11.5	7.8	3.7
4. Overlearn (100 trials)—36 hr.	10.3	9.5	.8

the presolution period of trial-and-error learning. Trial-and-error learning seems to be as complexly determined as the so-called "higher" forms of problem-solving.

The Solution Period. The Laws of Exercise and Effect were the experimentalist's

first answers to the problems connected with the solution period. Let us first consider the Law of Exercise. In its simplest formulation this law states that when differences in *frequency* and in *recency* between R_3 and all other R's is large enough (see Fig. 104, p. 436), R_3 will become the most probable response to be elicited by the stimulus situation at any future time.

The usual trial-and-error learning situation is so set up that R_3 will occur *at least once on every trial*, since the trial continues until R_3 *is* performed (the cat finally does get out of the puzzle box, or the rat finally does go through the correct door). Also, R_3 will always be the most recently performed response at the start of any new trial, since it is the *last* response of the previous trial. Therefore, over a large series of trials, R_3 will have occurred more frequently and more recently than any other response.

If the Law of Exercise is valid, R_3 will be automatically "stamped in" by frequency and recency quite aside from any "intentions" of the animal.

Thorndike, however, insisted that the Law of Exercise was not enough to account for learning. He pointed out that another important reason why R_3 gets stamped in and the other responses do not is that R_3 is usually followed by some *good effect* (the cat escapes from confinement), while the other responses are usually followed by a *bad effect* (the cat remains imprisoned). This relationship he called the Law of Effect.

The apparent simplicity of these laws and their ability to summarize many experimental results as well as "real-life" observations without recourse to "complex mental processes" appealed to many psychologists and educators. The result has been that these laws and their implications have permeated much of our thinking about learning and have influenced many of the educational practices in our schools. It is highly probable that Mr. Anyman, if asked how his dog, his son, or his neighbor learns, would appeal to some sort of Law of Exercise (he might use the word "practice") and Law of Effect (he might use the phrase "reward and punishment").

In 1932 Edward C. Tolman published *Purposive Behavior in Animals and Men*— a book that was destined to influence psychological theory greatly. The publication of this book started experimental and theoretical questioning and reformulation of the Laws of Exercise and Effect. The issue is still very much alive, experimental work in trial-and-error learning is extensive, and the most that can be done here is to present a very few of the relevant basic studies and point up their implications.

MAZE LEARNING. The most popular device for studying trial-and-error learning in animals has been the *maze*. In 1901 W. S. Small at Clark University published his study of the "mental processes of the rat" in which he used a small-scale reproduction of the Hampton Court Palace hedge maze. Since then thousands of laboratory rats, hamsters, guinea pigs, mice, ants, cockroaches, cats, fish, and even college sophomores have been running, hopping, crawling, swimming, and shuffling their way through various kinds of mazes, under the worried and wearied eyes of experimental psychologists. In essence, the maze consists of a series of discrimination-learning problems. At each choice point (see Box 113) the subject must discover which alley is the correct one and which the wrong; then he must "string together" or organize these various choice-point discriminations, memorize them, and run them off in proper sequence. The maze situation thus combines many of the elements of trial-and-error learning and rote memory. Experiments with the maze and the discrimination box have provided most of the data for the various learning analyses.

THE LAW OF EXERCISE. There are many experiments in which the subject performs the *wrong* act as frequently as the correct act, and yet finally learns to do the correct one! Tolman's book is replete with experimental illustrations of this. (See Box 114

BOX 113

Mazes

Goal Box

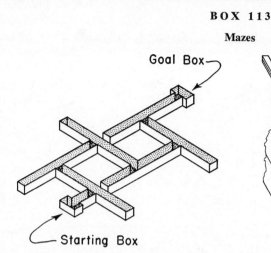

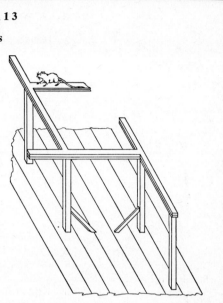

Starting Box

A 6-unit alley maze. (After Blodgett, 1929.)

Section of elevated maze. (After Honzik, 1936.)

The maze can be defined as a problem which requires for its solution the selection of the shortest route to a goal. The maze may have walled alleys, in which case it is called an "alley maze" (left fig.), or it may be an "elevated maze" (right fig.). The particular sequence of turnings and correct alleys varies from maze to maze. It has been estimated that over 150 different maze patterns have been used to study learning in animals. In almost all mazes it is possible for visual, auditory, tactual, olfactory, and other stimuli emanating from the alleys, from the environment outside the maze, or from the choice point itself to serve as cues differentiating the correct pathway from the blind alley.

BLODGETT, H. C., 1929. The effect of the introduction of reward upon the maze performance of rats. *Univ. Calif. Publ. Psychol., 4,* 113–34.

HONZIK, C. H., 1936. The sensory basis of maze learning in rats. *Comp. Psychol. Monogr., 13,* #64.

---

for one such experiment.) The experimental evidence—from both animals and men—seems to show clearly that the sheer frequency or recency of performing an act cannot, by itself, account for stamping in that act. And yet despite these experiments it is clear from many other experiments, as well as from everyday observations, that many trials are required before trial-and-error learning takes place. Practicing the correct act *does* seem to be necessary.

Tolman's answer to this paradox is phrased somewhat like this: What happens during trial-and-error learning is that the individual is given an opportunity to discover what response leads to what consequence. The more opportunities he has for this, the quicker and more firm will be his learning. *But this holds for the wrong acts as well as for the correct acts.* He must learn, in other words, that R_1 leads to (x) as well as that R_3 leads to (c). It is not *differential* frequency or recency of R_3 over R_1 that is the deciding factor, but the *total* frequency of R_1—(x) *and* R_2—(x) *and* R_3—(c) *and* R_4—(x), etc., which is important. Thus in the Blodgett "latent-learning" experiment (see Box 114) the rat

---

BOX 114

Hidden Learning in the Rat

In 1929 Blodgett of the University of California reported his now famous experiment on "latent learning" in the rat.

Using the 6-unit alley maze shown in Box 113, he ran three groups of hungry rats, each animal being given one trial per day. Group I (*control*) always found food in the food box and were allowed to eat there for 3 minutes, after which they were removed to another cage for the remainder of their rations. Group II for the first 6 days did not find food in the food box. When they arrived there, they were confined for 2 minutes, removed to another cage, and *one hour later* were given their daily ration. From the seventh day on these animals did find food in the food box and thenceforth were run under the same conditions as the control group. Group III ran the maze for the first *two* days without food, and from the third day on found food.

During the no-food periods Groups II and III showed no signs of learning, i.e., they chose the wrong alley about as frequently as the correct alley. (See fig.) The control group did show a decrease in errors. But on the first day *after* food was found, Groups II and III showed tremendous improvement, cutting their error

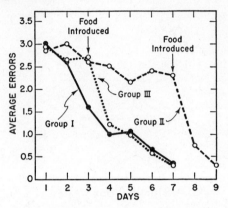

scores by about 50 per cent, and on the second day, they had caught up with the control group! Despite the fact that during the first period they had not been practicing the correct responses more than the wrong responses, they had been learning something about the maze, as is indicated by their performance *immediately after the introduction of food*. The evidence of their learning was "latent" or hidden until it had become "worthwhile" to show it!

BLODGETT, H. C. 1929. The effect of the introduction of reward upon the maze performance of rats. *Univ. Calif. Publ. Psychol.*, 4, 113–34.

---

is given many opportunities to learn this alley is a blind, that alley leads on to other alleys, etc. Then when he finds food in the food box, and "knows" that R_3 leads to the food box, he will choose R_3 in preference over the other responses. The learning process becomes one of *learning the consequences of every response*. In essence, then, trial-and-error learning is *discovery*—discovery of the meaning of cues, or what leads to what. And frequent experience with *the entire situation* makes discovery possible.

THE LAW OF EFFECT. The Law of Effect has suffered a similar fate at the hands of

experimentalists. The evidence soon became clear that the speed with which a response is "stamped in," or the "strength" of a habit, does not depend merely upon the number of times R_3 has been followed by "good consequences," or the number of times an individual has been "rewarded" for performing a certain act.

One modern formulation of the Law of Effect, for instance, runs something like this: the strength of a response is a function of the number of times that response has resulted in some decrease in the need-state of the individual. Thus, every time the hungry rat jumps through the white card and receives a bit of food, his need-state is somewhat reduced. The more frequently this happens, the stronger will be his habit of jumping to the white card. But it has been shown that this relationship does not always hold; in fact, we often get just the opposite results.

PARTIAL REINFORCEMENT. Perhaps the most significant experiments in this field are the "partial reinforcement" studies. These studies indicate that rewarding an animal only occasionally for performing a certain act ("partial reinforcement") will establish that act more strongly, as measured by resistance to extinction, than rewarding him every time he performs the act. For an illustrative experiment, see Box 115. Partial reinforcement is certainly more

---

BOX 115

Occasional vs. Continuous Rewards

At Indiana University, Jenkins and Rigby measured the relative strengths of responses that were periodically, or continuously reinforced.

The apparatus used (somewhat like the sketch above) was a modified "Skinner box," originally designed by B. F. Skinner. Among their experimental procedures they had two groups of thirsty rats who were taught to press a lever to get a drink of water. After preliminary training the animals of Group I were placed in the box for a total of 180 minutes (divided into ½ hour sessions) and were permitted to press the lever as frequently as they wished, but they were rewarded with water only every

two minutes, for a total of 90 rewards. Group II rats were in the box 180 minutes (in ½ hour sessions) and were rewarded *every time* they pressed the lever. They piled up 2,400 reinforcements. In terms of number of reinforcements, then, the cards were heavily stacked in favor of Group II.

Immediately after this training, "extinction" tests were started. The animals were allowed to press the lever—but no reward was ever given. They were tested this way for three daily 1-hour periods. The following table summarizes the experimental conditions and gives the results.

Group I, given *90 intermittent rewards,* pressed the bar 129 times during the extinction period—just slightly over 140 per cent of the number of previous reinforcements. Group II, given *2,400 continuous reinforcements* in the original training, yielded only 100 responses during the "extinction" period—or just slightly over 4 per cent. Partial reinforcement is a far more potent basis for resistance to extinction than continuous reinforcement. The less consistently you reward, the *stronger* the habit!

JENKINS, W. O., and RIGBY, M. K. 1950. Partial (periodic) versus continuous reinforcement in resistance to extinction. *J. comp. physiol. Psychol., 43,* 30–40.

SKINNER, B. F. 1938. *The behavior of organisms.* New York: Appleton-Century-Crofts.

Group	Minutes in Box	No. and Conditions of Reinforcement	No. of Lever-Pressings During Extinction Period
I	180	90; 2-min. periodic	129
II	180	2,400; continuous	100

like the everyday situation than 100 per cent or continuous reinforcement. In our daily life it is rarely the case that a specified act *invariably* leads to the reward. More typically the correct act will frequently get us our anticipated reward, but the same act will sometimes fail to get us our reward. When the situation changes so that our act will *never* be rewarded, we will persist with our act for some time before we discover that fact. For the continuously rewarded act, a *single* failure stands out saliently against the background of uniform successes. Thus we can understand why partial reinforcement is more resistant to extinction than continuous reinforcement.

Taken together, the experimental data indicate clearly that if we want to train a person or an animal to persist in certain behavior, it is better to reward the person occasionally rather than every time. Occasional *failure* to reward an act helps "stamp it in."

This conclusion is quite contrary to the Law of Effect and certainly does not jibe with Mr. Anyman's belief in the efficacy of "rewards and punishments." However, Mr. Anyman cannot be altogether wrong. It is clear that rewards and punishments, and motivation in general, *are* important in adaptive behavior. How can this apparent contradiction be resolved?

LEARNING AND PERFORMANCE. One way of dealing with this problem is to distinguish between "learning" and "performance." We have already seen in the Blodgett experiment that an animal may have *learned* something, but may not reveal it in its *performance* until it becomes "worthwhile" to do so. We have here an experimental demonstration that learning and performance are not the same.

The proposal has been made that the function of reward and punishment is different for learning from what it is for performance. In *learning*, the function of reward and punishment is to enable the individual to discover what acts are rewarded and what acts are punished. The fact that one response is rewarded and another punished does not stamp in one response or eliminate the other. On the other hand, in *performance*, the function of reward and punishment is to determine which response will be displayed, and with what efficiency and speed. With a "better" reward or with a higher degree of motivation the individual will perform what he has previously learned with more efficiency or speed. Therefore when Mr. Anyman notes that with better rewards there is better "learning," what he really observes is that better rewards lead to better *performance*. In many of our studies we measure *performance* and not learning. The laws that relate degree of rewards and motives to *learning* are really, according to this view, "Laws of Performance."

The Nature of Skills

As people muddle through their world of problems, they gradually accumulate a larger and larger collection of creative solutions, conditioned reactions, memorized sets of items, and selected responses; and they acquire something else. Many of these bits and pieces of adaptive behavior become integrated into patterns and sequences of performance which we call *skills*.

Skills vary tremendously, of course, in their nature and complexity. Serving as an efficient chairman of a meeting is a "social skill." Reading, writing, and speaking are "verbal skills." Painting, playing the piano, and arranging flowers involve "artistic skills." Performing appendectomies, making diagnoses, prescribing placebos at the proper time are "medical skills." Rewiring an "electronic brain," repairing a leaky faucet, and operating a lathe are valuable "mechanical skills." There is no end to the variety of skills, and just as we are all constantly called upon to be creative problem-solvers and learners, so must we develop a repertoire of skills.

When a skill is developed, something new is added to our bits and pieces of adaptive behavior. A skill is not merely a collection of previously acquired responses put together in a sequence that can then be run off as a sort of chain reaction. Although a skill is composed of conditioned reactions, memorizations, and selected responses, each of these when integrated into a skill *becomes modified*, and the pattern, taken as a whole, acquires distinctive attributes of its own. Two major attributes of a skill differentiate it from a collection of discrete adjustive responses: (1) its integration and (2) its flexible serial ordering.

Skills as Integrated Wholes. As a person acquires a skill, his movements and responses become more sure, are executed with more precision and speed. An analysis of this simple observation demonstrates that a skill involves a unique *reorganization* of the component parts. Piano-playing is a good illustration of what we mean.

Anyone who has played the piano knows that piano-playing does not consist of a series of discrete responses to discrete sets of stimulus-patterns. Although when Youngster Anyman first begins to take piano lessons the playing of each note is a response to a specific visual cue, at a later stage these specific stimulus-response sequences seem to disappear. At least in terms of perception, playing a composition on the piano does *not* consist of seeing one note on the music sheet, making the proper response to that note, seeing the next note, making the proper response to that note, etc. The perception is more "global" (see Box 116).

This phenomenological observation is fully supported by neurological considera-

tions. It takes time for a neural pattern to travel from the retina of the eye to the brain, and from the brain to the arm, wrist, and finger muscles. It takes time for the muscles to react. And there just is not time enough for all this to happen, note after note, to make possible the playing of

---

BOX 116

The Phenomenologist as a Piano Player

Bentley has described the experiences of the novice-turning-pianist in the following terms. Just about the time the piano student begins to make rapid progress in the smoothness of his performance, he finds that:

"The perception shrinks. Individual notes upon the staff are no longer apprehended as individuals. They come in groups and their meanings are group-flashes. Again, the individual determination which leads from this or that note upon the score to this or that movement toward the appropriate black or white key disappears. After the group-flash comes, without intermediation, a sequence of rapid movements. Still later, the score may wholly drop out of clear perception and serve as a vague and obscure cue to a complicated series of movements. The sound itself as it flows along may be the controlling object and then we have the curious fact of an action where the perceived object is the result of the action and not its antecedent. This stage informs us that the action is becoming automatized."

BENTLEY, M. 1925. *The field of psychology.* New York: Appleton-Century-Crofts.

---

a swift cadenza by a skillful pianist. Lashley (1951) has made this point very clear:

"The finger strokes of a musician may reach sixteen per second in passages which call for a definite and changing order of successive finger movements. The succession of movements is too quick even for visual reaction time. In rapid sight reading it is impossible to read the individual notes of an arpeggio. The notes must be seen in groups, and it is actually easier to read chords simultaneously and to translate them into temporal sequence than to read successive notes in the arpeggio as usually written."

We must conclude that the neurological control of the movements of a skillful musician is different from the control of a discrete response or even of a series of discrete responses. Both perceptual and neurological facts argue that when a sequence of acquired responses becomes a skilled performance, *the increase in the speed and smoothness of the temporal sequence reflects some genuine reorganization.*

Skills as Flexible Patterns. Sometimes a skill involves a fairly rigid sequence of actions in which response A always precedes B, which always precedes C, and so on. But most skills demand a less rigid kind of pattern; for these skills, the increase in the precise control of a *flexible* ordering of the component parts is even more impressive than the increase in smoothness which accompanies their development. Language skills provide an excellent illustration of this.

In the development of speech the person must learn many specific words. He must learn to spell them, to pronounce them, to define them, to recognize them when they are spoken, etc. But this is not enough. Each language has a predetermined orderly sequence, and the skilled "speaker" must be able to arrange the specific words appropriately, rapidly, and smoothly. Thus, in English the adjective usually precedes the noun, the verb comes as early as possible after the subject, etc. The same word may be an adverb, an adjective, a verb, or a noun, as is true of the word "right" in the sentence, "The man right before me thinks it is right to right wrongs as a matter of simple right." The *meaning* of each "right"

is determined in part by its serial order. A change in the serial order of a single word, therefore, can change the meaning of a phrase or sentence completely. For example:

(a) The man right before me. . . .
(b) The right man before me. . . .

The serial order in which a word is used in speech cannot be learned as a specific attribute of that word. Word positioning is too flexible for that. What differentiates a verbal *skill* from mere verbal behavior is the *generalized pattern, systematic yet flexible, that is imposed upon the discrete responses.* Verbal behavior without such flexible control of serial ordering no more resembles language than a dictionary resembles Shakespeare's sonnets.

Control of serial ordering is not restricted to language. Such skills as running, sawing a board, driving a car, and chasing a ball out in left field present problems in sequences of action which cannot be explained in terms of successions of discrete responses to discrete stimuli.

Skills as Knowledge. A medical student who has seen many operations and has memorized, letter-perfect, the full and detailed procedure for removing a cataract but has never himself held a surgical instrument in his hand would, of course, be a menace if let loose on a patient in an operating room. Why? To say that "he has the knowledge but lacks the skill" implies that all he needs is appropriate "muscle practice." But a skill is not only the "muscle translation" of some previously acquired knowledge; it also involves a specific kind of *additional knowledge*—kinesthetic knowledge. And kinesthetic knowledge is just as genuine knowledge as is any other kind. Because this *knowledge* attribute of skills is so frequently missed, this point merits further discussion.

Most adaptive behavior depends upon knowledge gained through the visual and auditory senses. There are, of course, other senses through which knowledge can be gained. Frequently the knowledge provided by one sense may serve the same end as knowledge provided by another sense (see Box 117). Thus we may learn a piece of poetry by reading it or hearing it. However, each sensory system also contributes its own unique knowledge.

The knowledge provided us by the kinesthetic system cannot be provided by our eyes and ears. Just as the only way of receiving visual knowledge is via patterned visual stimulation of the retina, so there is only one way of receiving kinesthetic knowledge—via patterned stimulation of the spindle cells (see Chapter 7). The spindle cells can be stimulated only by actual muscle movements. Herein lies one

of the most important functions of "action" or practice. It is not merely muscular *exercise*, it is a method of perceiving via the kinesthetic system. When you listen to your typing instructor and look at the diagrams he draws on the blackboard, you are not "exercising" your ears and your eyes. You are *perceiving* by ear and by eye and thus obtaining knowledge about typing. Similarly, when you practice typing "Now is the time for all good men to come to the aid of their party," you are perceiving kinesthetically and obtaining additional knowledge about typing. Without this additional knowledge the development of skillful typing is impossible, just as it is impossible without the visual or auditory knowledge.

A skill, to repeat, is not merely "muscle facility"; nor is it to be described as a "muscular translation" of previous knowl-

---

BOX 117

Every Sensory System Contributes

In 1936 Honzik of the University of California reported what still remains the most exhaustive experimental analysis of the sensory control of a patterned series of responses.

Twenty-three groups of rats deprived of various sense organs were trained on a 14-unit elevated maze (a section of which was illustrated in Box 113). Some groups were (1) *anosmic* (animals whose sense of smell had been destroyed by cutting through their olfactory bulbs), or (2) blinded, or (3) deafened and blinded, or (4) anosmic and deafened, or (5) anosmic and deafened and blinded.

An analysis of the behavior of some 1,100 rats who learned the maze under these conditions led to the following conclusions:

(1) The motor responses constituting the maze habit are made, not to individual stimuli, but to complexes or patterns of stimuli.

(2) The rat can make use of *various*

sensory modalities in acquiring and performing the maze habit. In normal animals vision plays the dominant role, with olfaction next. When he is deprived of one sense, he leans more heavily on information obtained from the other senses. Thus olfaction and audition can serve fairly well in place of vision, but there is a limit to this interchangeability.

(3) The blind-anosmic-deaf group showed almost no learning. Honzik points out "that only after learning on the basis of the other senses has begun does kinesthesis take some part in perfecting the habit."

Apparently the rat, very much like the human being, gets his information where he can, via his eyes, his ears, his nose, and his kinesthetic system; but not all modes are equally useful, nor are they completely interchangeable.

HONZIK, C. H., 1936. The sensory basis of maze learning in rats. *Comp. Psychol. Monogr.*, 13, #64.

edge acquired via reading or listening. A skill involves actual performance, and hence knowledge that does not include the "knowledge of performance" is only *part* of the knowledge that makes up a skill. The execution of a skilled performance may reflect knowledge acquired via reading, listening, smelling, tasting, *and* kinesthesis.

Since very few (if any) processes of acquisition or retention live out their lives in isolation, it is clear that as a series of discrete responses to specific visual and auditory stimuli develop into a skill, each discrete response becomes altered by the additional kinesthetic information acquired during this development. Here, then, is another way in which a series of discrete responses is changed as they develop into a skill, as more knowledge is added, and the previous knowledge is changed.

FEEDBACK. Performance edits, disciplines, and evaluates knowledge acquired *via* other senses. We may not recognize vagueness when we "think about" doing a thing, but this vagueness dramatically reveals itself when we begin to perform. The main reason for this, of course, is that the consequences of performance are immediately made clear to us. In other words, when we practice a response (instead of merely "thinking" about it), *feedback* occurs. In practicing typing, the movement of our fingers stimulates the muscle-spindle cells, and they in turn send sensory messages back to the brain (see Chapter 7). We move our muscles, and our muscles report back. But not all feedback need be initiated within our own bodies. Although the introverted person who has acquired the "social graces" purely from reading books and seeing plays may be able to imagine how he would act skillfully, he may be quite clumsy in his actual dealings with other people. The reason is frequently that that such a person simply lacks vital information, information that he can obtain only

through feedback from *others*. Social skill requires, among other knowledge, the ability to predict how others will react to any one of your acts, how you will feel when he reacts that way; it requires the ability to perceive correctly the other's feelings, and to perceive correctly how the other will perceive your feelings. And there is no conceivable way of learning these sub-skills except by getting a feedback from the other to your responses.

Feedback not only makes the learning of a skill possible; it is also essential for the performance itself. The execution of a skilled performance is a continuous process of behavior in which each step is governed by what went before, what will happen next, and the final goal aimed at. This is another way of saying, of course, that a skill always has a temporal organization involving a flexible sequence of acts. For such a continuously changing pattern of adjustments and readjustments, *moment-by-moment feedback of information is absolutely essential*. Without it, most skilled performances would be impossible.

The Development of Skills

The course of the development of a skill, like that of other forms of learning, is depicted in performance curves. The typical curve obtained in the development of a skill is similar in shape to the learning curve. It is negatively accelerated, and occasionally shows several periods of stalemate or lack of progress. These level portions of the curve are called *plateaus*.

In Figure 108 is shown a curve portraying the acquisition of typewriting skill. Three stages can be differentiated in this curve. (1) There is a rapid and continuous rise from the first practice period to about the forty-second day. (2) From about the 42nd to the 80th day there is no apparent improvement. The subject has reached a plateau. (3) From the 80th day to about the 110th day the subject's performance begins to rise again, and then at the 110th it starts leveling off for a second time. There is some indication that after about the 160th session the subject (now a skilled typist) is beginning to show additional improvement.

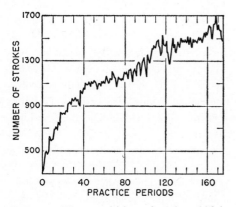

FIG. 108. The acquisition of typing skill by subject "x" in the study by Book. This subject had never used a typewriter prior to the experiment. The curve represents 174 consecutive daily half-hour practice periods (with time out "owing to trouble with apparatus, sickness, and other unavoidable causes"). The measure of progress in the skill is the total number of correct strokes made on the typewriter during each practice session. Punctuation marks, carriage shifts, space shifts, etc., were all counted as strokes. (Based on data from Book, 1925.)

ACQUISITION AND CONSOLIDATION. The first two stages, the initial rise and the leveling off in improvement, may be seen as the acquisition and consolidation of the component parts of the skill. The beginning typist must first learn to hit the correct key for the corresponding letter or symbol on the manuscript. An analysis of his performance shows that he attends to each letter as he types out each word. As time goes on, there is an improvement in performance, but this improvement soon reaches a plateau and additional practice

does not seem to result in corresponding gains. However something very important does occur during this plateau period.

In discussing rote learning, we pointed out that at the beginning of the process the person seeks out and attends to all kinds of meanings, associations, and groupings as he attempts to memorize a list of nonsense syllables. After he has mastered this task, these associations and other "aids" tend to disappear, and "what is left in consciousness is a series of 'bare' image-pairs (as in the multiplication table) or 'automatic' image-sequences (as in the alphabet)." This simplification and automatization in the acquisition of discrete responses shows itself on the motor side as well. As discrete responses are practiced, they become more "automatic" and require less directed awareness (refer back to Bentley's description in Box 116). When this stage is reached, the individual's attention is released, as it were, for "bigger and better things." He can now pay attention to relationships among his discrete responses, to patterns, and to the more complex phases of his task. He is no longer *coping* (see p. 276) with each letter. And this is the point where the plateau ends and the series of discrete performances is ready to be transformed into a skill.

THE THIRD PHASE OF THE CURVE. Just as the skilled musician will read a whole series of notes simultaneously and translate them into temporal sequence, so the typist will begin to read and type *words*, rather than successive letters. A skill is now in the making. When this occurs, the performance curve will leave the plateau and begin to rise again. Occasionally the typist will then show another plateau and another rise. What seems to happen here is that the typist begins to read and type *phrases* rather than words. After the end of the first plateau the organized nature of his responses achieves higher and higher levels of integration, until he has mastered the skill.

The above description is an "idealized" one; the acquisition process does not always show neatly divided phases. Thus Book (1925) observed that in learning typewriting, the beginner sometimes successfully attempted to read and type words before the discrete letter-responses were firmly learned. Furthermore, even after the curve leaves the plateau continued improvement in discrete responses can take place. Finally, many skill acquisition curves show no plateaus. This is especially true, as we shall soon see, when the learner, from the very beginning, practices on the pattern rather than on the discrete responses.

Part-Whole Training. All of this suggests that some practice on the components of the skill is essential before a series of discrete responses can become the integrated skill. The question is obviously raised as to whether *part training* (practice on the components) or *whole training* (practice on the complex task) is more effective in the development of skills. On theoretical grounds it would appear that either method may be more efficient, depending on circumstances.

The arguments favoring whole training derive from the fact that the essence of a skill lies in the *integrated* nature of its component parts. The experimental evidence is clear that in an integrated task the performance of a single component by itself is different from the performance of the same component when it is embedded in the entire task (see Box 118 for an illustrative experiment). This difference may make it inefficient to train on the discrete responses first, and then to attempt a combination, since we learn to do different things with the "same" response under these two conditions.

The arguments that favor part training

would suggest that where the discrete responses are novel and difficult, the part method may speed up the acquisition of the discrete responses. Further, it is also possible that the more practice given on the discrete responses, the quicker they become "automatized" and therefore the more quickly ready for integration into a skill. (For an experimental demonstration of this see Box 119.) These considerations would suggest that in certain instances the part method, or a combination of part method and whole method, may be superior to the whole method alone.

While all skills involve patterning, they vary in the degree of integration involved. Thus some "skills" are actually composed of several relatively independent activities. Carpentry is a good example. The skillful carpenter can saw, nail, fit materials together, plane, etc. Training in sawing may be carried on independently of training in nailing without any loss due to lack of integration. The same is true of surgery, which can also be broken down into a number of relatively independent component skills. However a skill whose performance involves simultaneous components will be more efficiently taught by the whole method. In driving an automobile, we must operate the brakes, the throttle, the clutch, and the steering wheel more or less simultaneously. Training on steering alone, or shifting gears alone, etc., may not be as efficient as training on the whole complex.

The general rule would then be that whole training increases in effectiveness as the integration of the component parts of the skill increases in importance.

Variety of Practice Material. One of the distinguishing attributes of a skill is the precise control over a flexible serial ordering of the components. This would suggest that in training for a skill we should present the trainee with as many variations in the

BOX 118

Relation of Part to Whole in Motor Skills

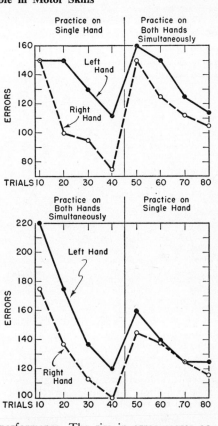

Beeby at the University of London demonstrated that when a well-practiced simple movement is combined into a larger act, the simple movement may show a loss in efficiency.

The task was to follow the 1/16-inch brass strips around the squares with a stylus as rapidly as possible without breaking contact between the stylus tip and the strips. Both hands were to move in a counterclockwise direction. Each slip of the stylus off the brass strip was recorded as an error. All of this was to be done *blindfolded*. (See sketch.)

Group A started by practicing with one hand, then with the other, then was tested on both hands simultaneously. Group B started with both hands simultaneously, then was tested on one hand alone. The results show that the transition from the simple to the complex, *or from complex to simple*, resulted in a loss of skill. In Group A the error scores for each hand increased when they attempted to combine the two movements into one simultaneous act. In Group B the left (or right) hand did *better* when it was part of the two-handed movement than when it was shifted to a solo

performance. The rise in error scores occurred when the shift was from the "easy" to the "difficult" task (Group A) or from the "difficult" to the "easy" (Group B). The learning and performance of a single component task is significantly different from the learning and performance of the "same" task when it is part of a larger whole.

BEEBY, C. E. 1930. An experimental investigation into the simultaneous constituents of an act of skill. *Brit. J. Psychol.*, 20, 336–53.

stimulus-conditions as possible. When this principle is neglected, the development of a skill can be delayed, or even prevented. According to one psychologist, Wolfle (1951), a number of military schools during

World War II violated this rule with the result that the men they sent out to the field were inadequately trained. He says,

"Men in training were given an inadequate variety of targets to track, casualties

BOX 119

From Components to Skills

Gagné and Foster of Connecticut College measured transfer of training to a complex motor skill with varying amounts of practice on a component part.

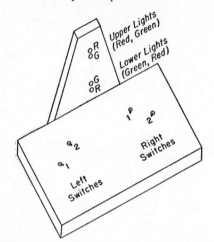

The task was to learn to throw the appropriate toggle switches *as rapidly as possible* when certain lights went on.

COMPONENT TASK

(Only 1 upper and 1 lower light of the same color was used, and 1 switch on the left and the right.)

Stimulus	*Response*
Lower Red Light	Left Switch #1
Upper Red Light	Right Switch #1

COMPLEX TASK

(For this task all four lights and all four switches were used.)

Stimulus	*Response*
Lower Red Light	Left Switch #1
Lower Green Light	Left Switch #2
Upper Red Light	Right Switch #1
Upper Green Light	Right Switch #2

Using 120 Navy enlisted men, three *experimental* groups were first trained on the

"Component Task" and then on the "Complex Task"; the *control* group had only the complex task. One experimental group was given 10 trials on the component task before being transferred to the complex task; the second, 30 trials; and the third, 50 trials. Performance was measured by the time it took to make a correct choice. The learning curves for all groups on the complex task (see fig.) indicate that the more prac-

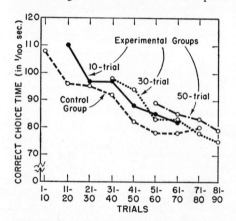

tice one has on the component task, the greater is the transfer to the complex skill. Thus the control group's starting average on the complex task was 108; the starting averages for the 10-, 30-, and 50-trial practice groups were, respectively: 110, 98, 89. It will be seen, however, that the control group, which spent all of its time on the complex task, learned more quickly than any other group. Thus while practice on a component part helped the learning of a complex skill, the most efficient method for this particular skill is working on the complex skill from the very beginning.

GAGNÉ, R. M., and FOSTER, H., 1949. Transfer of training from practice on components in a motor skill. *Jour. exp. Psychol., 39,* 47–68.

to repair, messages to record, or radar images to interpret. The result was that, although they learned to respond correctly to the particular materials used in training,

they were not able to respond adequately to the somewhat different situations encountered later on the job."

The general rule that follows from all

BOX 120

2.42 minus 0.71 does NOT always equal 1.71

Ghiselli and Brown, at the University of California, tested the time-and-motion method of analysis with the following experiment: With telegraph keys arranged as shown, subjects learned to tap the keys in a certain sequence (e.g., A, B, C, D, C, E, F, A). The time between each pair of keys was recorded automatically. After the subjects had reached their maximum speed, they were instructed to eliminate some superfluous steps in the sequence (e.g., they now tapped A, B, C, E, F, A) and were permitted enough practice until they had again reached a maximum speed. Two examples of the results are given below:

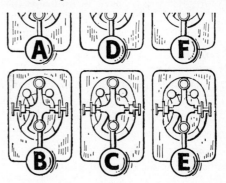

SEQUENCES AND TIME (IN SECONDS) REQUIRED TO MAKE EACH MOVEMENT

EXAMPLE I

First Sequence		Second Sequence	
A-B	0.40	A-B	0.44
B-C	0.28	B-C	0.30
C-D	0.39 ⎫ 0.71	(Eliminated)	
D-C	0.32 ⎭	(Eliminated)	
C-E	0.30	C-E	0.29
E-F	0.39	E-F	0.41
F-A	0.34	F-A	0.37
Total Time:	2.42	Total Time:	1.81

EXAMPLE II

B-C	0.23	B-C	0.21
C-D	0.30 ⎫ 0.59	(Eliminated)	
D-C	0.29 ⎭	(Eliminated)	
C-E	0.17	C-E	0.11
E-A	0.31	E-A	0.30
Total Time:	1.30	Total Time:	.62

In the first example the seven movements required 2.42 seconds. Elimination of movements C-D and D-C should have reduced the time to 1.71 seconds (2.42 − 0.71 = 1.71). This did not happen. Most of the movements of the second sequence required *more time* than they had originally. The "savings" was 0.61 seconds instead of the "predicted" 0.71 seconds.

In the second example elimination of C-D and D-C *reduced* the individual times of the remaining ones. A saving of 0.68 sec-

onds resulted instead of the "predicted" 0.59 seconds.

This simple experiment testifies to an important psychological principle: Human activity consists of integrated patterns, and in an integrated pattern we cannot add (or subtract) elements and expect simple additive changes.

GHISELLI, E. E., and BROWN, C. W. 1955. *Personnel and industrial psychology*. New York: McGraw-Hill.

this can be stated somewhat as follows: In training for a skill, drill on limited practice material should be avoided. The practice material should vary in as many dimensions and over as wide a range as will the situations to be encountered by a skillful operator.

Time-and-Motion Studies. While we cannot, in this book, devote much space to specific practical problems, we might indicate one important implication of the psychology of skills for certain industrial practices. The development of methods of work in industrial organizations is largely in the hands of the industrial engineer and the efficiency expert. These specialists have developed a technique of speeding up the performance of skilled operations which is known as time-and-motion analysis.

In time-and-motion analysis the industrial engineer gets a detailed picture of each movement involved in a particular task. He then identifies the movements that seem essential and those that seem superfluous. On the basis of such an analysis the industrial engineer trains the worker to change the sequence of his movements so as to eliminate the superfluous ones.

Such an approach sometimes reflects a fallacious assumption about the nature of skilled acts. We have already seen that the individual components of a complex task cannot be considered as unrelated units. Yet some efficiency engineers assume that if one movement is eliminated from a task, the total time for completing the task should be reduced proportionately, and they expect the efficient worker to behave that way after being "properly taught." As a concrete experimental demonstration of the inadequacy of such reasoning, Ghiselli and Brown (see Box 120) have shown that the person performing even a simple motor task integrates all the movements into a whole pattern, and the elimination of any one movement, *even if such an elimination results in a simpler task*, may increase the time per unit for the remaining movements. The pattern of the whole is changed and the "efficiency" gained is less than the time-and-motion analyst would expect. Proper training for improvement of a skill must rest upon a sound psychological analysis of skill.

Such an analysis also permits us to understand the development of *language*, the skill that differentiates man from all other forms of animal life. And it is to that which we now turn.

Glossary

blind alley. The wrong pathway in a maze —one ending in a block.

discrimination learning. A form of trial-and-error learning in which the individual must learn to make differential responses to different stimuli.

feedback. A general term referring to the process whereby action initiated by a subject provides further source of stimulation. Thus the *consequences* of action become apparent to the performer and influence his succeeding acts.

Lashley jumping stand. An apparatus used in visual discrimination studies on the rat in which the animal jumps (from a platform) against one of a number of stimulus cards. If the animal jumps against the correct card, the card falls and the animal lands on the food platform. If against the wrong one, the card remains standing and the animal falls into a net.

latent learning. Learning that does not display itself in performance until some later time.

law of effect. This law, in its simplest form, states that when one response is followed by some good effect, and other responses by bad effects, the former will become the most probable response to be elicited by the stimulus situation at any future time. This law has been proposed to hold for all trial-and-error learning.

law of exercise. This law, in its simplest form, states that when differences in frequency and recency between one response and all others become large enough, that response will become the most probable response to be elicited by the stimulus situation at any future time. This law has been proposed to hold for all trial-and-error learning.

maze. An apparatus used to study trial-and-error learning. Consists of a series of choice points at each of which the subject must learn to make the correct choice. To master the maze, he must memorize the sequence of correct choices so that he can run them off without error.

partial reinforcement. The training procedure in which reinforcement occurs on only some of the trials. *Periodic* reinforcement is partial reinforcement according to a fixed and regular schedule, e.g., every 5th trial, or every 2nd minute.

plateau. A portion of a learning curve showing no change in efficiency of performance. Often found in a curve depicting the acquisition of a motor skill.

presolution period. The period (in discrimination learning) during which the frequency of the correct response shows no increase.

puzzle boxes. Apparatus used in the study of learning and problem-solving in animals. Usually the animal is confined in the box, from which he can escape (in order to reach food on the outside) by learning how to manipulate levers or buttons or strings within the box.

skill. An organized sequence of actions, proficiently executed and usually displaying a flexible but systematic temporal patterning.

solution period. The period (in discrimination learning) during which the frequency of the correct response increases. See also "presolution period."

time-and-motion analysis. A method of analyzing a skilled motor performance in terms of specific movements; designed to identify "superfluous" movements in such performance.

trial-and-error learning. Discovering and consistently performing the "correct" response in a situation that permits a number of different responses. The correct response can be verified to be correct only by actual trial.

Suggestions for Further Reading

GHISELLI, E. E., and BROWN, C. W. 1955. *Personnel and industrial psychology.* New York: McGraw-Hill.

Chapter 11 of this standard text in industrial psychology presents a lucid analysis of skills in industry and the design of equipment in terms of learning and perceptual principles.

HILGARD, E. R. 1956. *Theories of learning.* New York: Appleton-Century-Crofts.

An excellent summary of the current theories of learning. Especially valuable for its discussion of trial-and-error learning.

OSGOOD, C. E. 1953. *Method and theory in experimental psychology.* New York: Oxford Univ. Press.

A detailed systematic presentation of the data and theories in experimental psychology. See particularly Chapter 10.

TOLMAN, E. C. 1932. *Purposive behavior in animals and men.* New York: Appleton-Century-Crofts.

The book that has been described as marking the coming of age of "Behaviorism." Contains an account of many important experiments in animal learning as well as a presentation of Tolman's system of behavior. Part V of the book, dealing with motivation and learning, is of special interest for the material of this chapter.

CHAPTER XVII

Language

THE DEVELOPMENT of language involves every form of learning and every principle of perception, organization, and serial patterning. "Certainly language," wrote the American neurological psychologist Lashley, "presents in most striking form the integrative functions that are characteristic of the cerebral cortex and that reach their highest development in human thought processes." Through the study of language much basic understanding about behavior and neurology can be gained. Obviously we cannot, in a general textbook, present a complete outline of what is already known about language. The most we shall attempt here is to *suggest* what is known about its development and function in the individual and to indicate the nature of the problems upon which current work is being done.

The first part of the chapter will be concerned with the development of language. We shall deal with some of the experimental problems involved in studying the most obvious function of language: communication. Quite aside from this social function, language also plays an important part in thinking, and the last part of the chapter is devoted to that topic.

Development of Language

Spoken language from a "brutishly materialistic" view, as Osgood (1953) has pointed out, "is nothing more than a complexly integrated series of skilled movements of the diaphragm, vocal cords, jaws, lips, and tongue, with air being driven through the varied openings at appropriate moments and pressures." This complex is built up from a series of relatively simple and automatic muscle twitches. The very first sound produced by the speech musculature is the "birth cry"—the sound which announces the triumphant entry of Youngster Anyman into this world. The explanation of the birth cry seems simple enough. When the umbilical cord is severed, the infant's source of oxygen (his mother's blood) is shut off. The resulting increase in the carbon dioxide content of his own

458

blood automatically stimulates the muscles of his lung cavity so that the cavity expands. When that happens and the air rushes into his lungs, it is drawn rapidly over the vocal cords, and Youngster Anyman's birth-cry is produced. From this first simple noise develops the marvelous variety of sounds which makes up raucous football cheers, sweet lullabies, droning lectures, and inspiring speeches. Let us trace briefly the development of this repertoire of sounds that are essential for speech.

Development of Sound Patterns. One of the characteristics of infant life is undifferentiated mass activity. Almost every muscle of the infant is exercised in random fashion: legs, arms, eyes, fingers, toes. The vocal apparatus is also a muscular system and it joins in this random activity. In the course of this nondirected and uncontrolled movement of the jaws, lips, tongue, and vocal cords, various sounds are produced. When the baby's general body musculature is relaxed, the muscles of its vocal apparatus are also relaxed and the sounds produced then are quite different from when the body musculature is under tension. In other words, different sounds and random combinations appear as the result of purely chance conditions of the physiological state of the infant (see Box 121).

Some investigators have suggested that within the first two or three months of life babies make all of the sounds that the human voice can produce, including French trills and German gutturals. In the beginning are the universal sounds! All normal babies, no matter what their culture or "race" produce the same speech sounds. (See Box 122.) In this connection it is interesting to note that a study of 3- to 6-year-old-children made at the Clarke School for the Deaf (Heider, 1940) showed that "with the exception of five consonants, the range of vowels, diphthongs, and consonants recorded for the group of deaf children included all those of standard English speech."

However this universal pattern soon

BOX 121

Momentary Physiological States and Infant Sounds

At Yale University, Osgood made a transcription (via mechanical recording devices) of the sounds produced by a single infant during the first year of life. Approximately 10 minutes of "vocal activity" were recorded each week, partly of sounds produced spontaneously by the infant and partly in response to specific stimulation by the experimenter. These recordings indicated:

1. Within the first two months of life babies make all the sounds of the human voice. "This," concludes Osgood, "is in flat contradiction to the notion that the infant gradually 'becomes capable' of making various sounds. A more accurate statement would be that the comparative *frequencies* of various speech sounds change as development proceeds."

2. Soft, open vowels occurred most frequently during and after feeding or when the baby's cheeks were stroked. On the other hand, if the nipple was withdrawn while the baby was still feeding or if the baby's arm or head movements were forcibly restrained, then the sounds became explosive and hard, such as ". . . erh! . . . errah! . . . erh! erh! erh!" and were accompanied by many vigorous bodily movements.

Osgood concludes: "It seems likely that the same efferent neural patterns that produce relaxation of the gross bodily musculature also serve to relax the muscles that participate in vocalizing, whereas increasing tension in the bodily musculature is paralleled by increasing tension in the vocal muscles."

Osgood, C. E. 1953. *Method and theory in experimental psychology.* New York: Oxford Univ. Press.

BOX 122

Sound Patterns in the Infant and Young Child

Irwin at the University of Iowa has long studied sound patterns among children. In one study the sounds of 95 infants were sampled each month until they were 30 months old. In another, 50 newborn white infants were compared with 30 newborn Negro infants. The frequency of the more *prominent* elemental speech sounds was noted and "sound profiles" were constructed in the following manner: A given consonant may constitute, for example, 35 per cent of the total number of consonants which a child produces. The percentages are determined for each of the consonants and the results are then plotted as a "consonant profile." The same thing can be done to determine a vowel profile. From these profiles Irwin has drawn the following conclusions (among many others):

(1) Racial differences at birth are not present. The vowel and consonant profiles for white and Negro infants show almost complete identity.

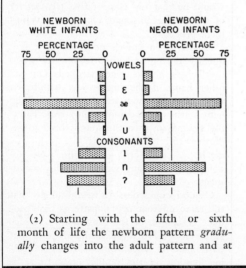

(2) Starting with the fifth or sixth month of life the newborn pattern *gradually* changes into the adult pattern and at

the age of 30 months the infant's pattern reflects his adult environment.

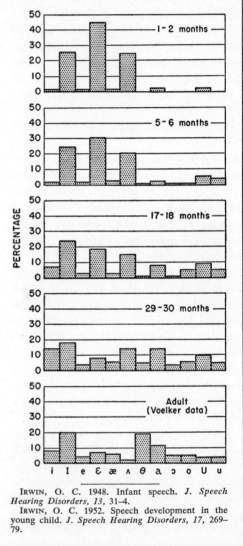

IRWIN, O. C. 1948. Infant speech. *J. Speech Hearing Disorders, 13,* 31–4.

IRWIN, O. C. 1952. Speech development in the young child. *J. Speech Hearing Disorders, 17,* 269–79.

becomes differentiated, and one baby's pattern of sounds differs from another's.

DIFFERENTIAL PATTERNS. Although it appears that the young infant can make all speech sounds, it makes some of them more

frequently than others. After a few months of life the typical infant's frequency-pattern starts to change, soon beginning to resemble the pattern of sounds made by the people around him. The child born into an English-speaking environment begins to drop out the German gutturals and the French trills, and the "typical" English sounds appear more and more frequently until within a relatively short time the vocalizations of the child, as far as the frequency-pattern of sound is concerned, reflect his cultural environment—he begins to "conform." This shift toward the adult pattern is noticeable as early as the fifth or sixth month (see Box 122).

From this account it would appear that we *start* with everything that is required and progress consists of eliminating the "useless" sounds. However, this is only part of the story. For while it may be that we start with all the necessary elemental sound responses, the change from the ability to produce these discrete sound responses to the *skillful control* and patterning of these sounds does develop with age and does indicate a gradual change in capacity. To indicate the degree of skillful control required for speech let us consider the following facts.

CONTROL OF SOUNDS. There are approximately 39 different sounds used in spoken English. These 39 sounds can appear in an astronomically large number of different *sequences*. In an adult, speech musculature works at a speed of approximately five syllables per second and the best estimates indicate that each syllable contains, on the average, 2.5 sounds. Thus we can produce about 12.5 sounds per second. Shannon, a mathematical physicist, has calculated that an English talker can have a choice of any *one* of about 100,000,000,000,000,000 *different sequences* of sound each second! In addition the 39 different basic sounds and the large number of different sequences can vary in intensities, pitch, and other characteristics of the auditory stimulus. Out of this astronomical number of different sound sequences we unerringly pick the "correct" ones. How does this magnificent control

develop? Let us first describe the chronological sequence of the development of control.

(1) The first aspect of sounds over which control is achieved seems to be *volume*. Thus (according to Osgood's records) during the second month of life the same sound appears repeatedly, but with *varied* volume. A sound is pronounced by the baby (by chance, perhaps) and then he "practices" it again and again, first with this volume, and then with that. To do this, the infant must exercise in his practice some control over the muscles of the diaphragm, a control which is essential for skillful speech.

(2) Within the third or fourth month the same thing happens to the *pitch* of the sounds. The infant repeats a sound initially produced at random, and then he varies the pitch with each repetition. Here he is exercising some control over the vocal cord muscles.

(3) About the fifth month control over the *sequence* of sounds seems to begin. Certain combinations of sounds are repeated again and again for a fairly long period; then another combination is chosen for repeated practice, and so on. This is the so-called "syllabic babbling" stage.

What initiates such practice is not known with any certainty. It seems that the baby's discovery that he can produce a sound is sufficient reason for its practice. We are reminded here of the point made in Chapter 13 that some problems are tackled and work done on them without any specific extrinsic rewards, but merely for the pleasure of it. When the infant finds that he can produce the same sound in different volumes or pitches, he does seem to behave as if he has discovered a new game, and he zestfully joins in exploring all possibilities. One investigator, C. H. Bean (1932), who kept daily sound and speech records of the first four years of a child, refers to the babblings of the child as "vocal playthings" and points out that the "variety of its own vocalizations is sufficient to interest a baby in its sounds . . . The number of sounds that ultimately find a place in this self-imposed practice is astonishing. One cannot fail to hear all the vowels and consonants, diphthongs, aspirates, sub-vocals, nasals, German umlauts and tongue trills, French throaty trills and grunts, and even the Welsh *l.* Then these syllables are rehearsed in grotesque mixtures."

Acquisition of Meanings. Obviously, however, the development of differential patterns of sound is not done altogether as "sheer play" without any attention to environmental consequences or extrinsic rewards delivered from the outside. We have already pointed out that the frequency-pattern of sound is a selective one. The child ends up with a pattern which conforms to that of the adults around him, and this happens well before the child really begins to speak. Even when Youngster's "speech" consists of such creations as "uggle-uggle," "aduh-duhdehduhe-ooh" and "oddle-oddle" (syllabic babbles solemnly recorded by investigators as appearing at the age of 5 months), he is already discriminating one combination of sounds from another in terms of some kind of *environmental consequences.* This is how a child in one culture develops a different pattern from a child in another. The encouragement and rewards of the adult help the child to select for permanent retention only certain sounds from the repertoire with which he is initially endowed.

THE ROLE OF THE BABBLE. The syllabic-babble stage provides the opportunity for satisfying the prerequisites for the learning of speech. The child not only hears his own sounds but at the very same time he receives kinesthetic stimuli from his speech musculature. He thus has an opportunity

to learn how to produce a specific sound, and with continued practice the child soon achieves voluntary control over a fairly large repertoire of sounds. This also means that he now has the ability to reproduce the sounds in his repertoire whenever he hears those sounds (or a reasonable facsimile thereof) *produced by someone else.* Repeating someone else's sounds, as we shall see, is essential for "verbal conditioning" to take place.

But why should he *wish* to reproduce the sounds of others? The reason is not altogether clear. It may be that the child "imitates" because repeating sounds that he hears from outside provides still another opportunity for "verbal play" or for increasing the range of varied experience, another instance of the basic stimulation motive (Chapter 10). In any event, the child does tend to repeat the sounds he hears, and after the syllabic stage has extended over some time, he has a repertoire of self-initiated verbal responses under voluntary and fairly skillful control, and a tendency to reproduce sounds initiated by others.

LEARNING WORDS. In the first stages of language learning it is probable that each of the three kinds of learning is effective: conditioned-response learning, rote learning, and trial-and-error learning. F. H. Allport (1924) has given the classical description of how *conditioning* may play a role. The mother holds up a doll and at the same time pronounces "doll." The child *sees* the doll and *hears the sound* "doll." The sound "doll" coming from the mother is considered the unconditioned stimulus which evokes from the child the "imitative" response "doll" (or "dah"). The sight of the doll serves as the conditioned stimulus. Upon frequent repetition, the sight of the doll alone comes to evoke the word "doll" from the child. We might then assume that *generalization* takes place (see p. 403).

Any object which is visually similar to a doll will therefore also evoke the response "doll" and soon, perhaps, all dolls, pictures of dolls, and small children will be called "doll."

Phrases and sentences can be learned, presumably, via the *rote-memory* process. The child is not given his piece of candy until he repeats after his mother "Thank you very much." In this way he may learn "by heart" a number of appropriate social formulas, nursery rhymes, songs and religious hymns, all part of learning language. Frequently, of course, the *meanings* he attaches to these sentences and phrases have no relationship to the meanings which the adult has in mind, as when the hymnal phrase "Gladly the Cross I'd bear" was learned as "Gladly, the cross-eyed bear."

Opportunities for *trial-and-error learning* also abound. When the child wants a particular toy (let us say a ball) he may babble any number of what appear to him to be appropriate sounds until he finally receives his toy. Eventually he learns that such-and-such a sound will produce the toy, and the problem, "How do I get a ball?" is solved by the acquisition of a specific verbal response. Again he has learned a word.

FUNCTIONS OF WORDS. Words, once learned, do not function only as signs for objects or events, although that may be their most common function. Actually we can distinguish three different ways in which words are used—as *signs*, as *attributes* of objects, and as *objects* themselves.

A word, when it is used as a *sign* for an object or event, elicits reactions which *are related to* the object or event signified. These reactions may be anticipatory, the word preparing us for the real object's coming. Or the word may evoke the image of the object, permitting the "combinatory play" of images which we have previously described in Chapter 13.

According to both the Swiss psychologist Piaget and the Russian psychologist Vigotsky the young child frequently tends to perceive a word as an inalienable *attribute* of the object referred to, just as he does the color of the object. (For an illustration taken from Vigotsky's analysis, see Box 123.) Words which are merely attributes

---

BOX 123

A Cow Is a Cow Is a Cow

Work with preschool children shows that the name of an object cannot be separated from the object's other qualities. An animal is *called* "cow" *because it has horns.* When the children were asked whether it is possible to call a cow "ink," and ink a "cow," they answered that it was impossible because ink is used for writing and the cow gives milk. In one study the children were instructed to change the names of some objects and then they were asked questions about these objects. Here are some notes from one such interview. The child was told to call a dog by the word "cow." Experimenter: "Has a cow horns?" Child: "Yes, it has." Experimenter: "But the 'cow' is really a dog." Child: "Of course, if a dog is a cow, if it is called a cow, then there must be horns. Such a dog which is called cow must have *little* horns."

Vigotsky quotes in this connection a story about a peasant who listened to two students of astronomy talking about the stars. Finally the peasant said to them: "I can see that with the help of instruments men could measure the distance from the earth to the remotest stars and find their position and motion. But what puzzles me is: How in the devil did you find out the *names* of the stars!?"

VIGOTSKY, L. S. 1939. Thought and speech. *Psychiat.*, 2, 29–52.

---

of specific objects presumably cannot be manipulated as flexibly as words which are signs or symbols; they are "tied down" to specific objects. The ability to see a word as a *sign* for an object seems to develop with age.

Finally, a word may be treated as an *object* in its own right. Many "magic" words or "holy" words are of this nature. What, for example, is the word "abracadabra" a sign for? In this case the word itself is a potent object which can open locked doors and perform many other wondrous things. It does not "stand for" anything, it is not an attribute of anything. Words function as objects not only for the young child, but for some adults as well. A dramatic instance is found among some primitives where a man never reveals his real name for fear that an enemy might harm the name itself and this would, in turn, harm the owner of the "name-object."

Of the three functions of words—signs, attributes, and objects—the sign function is the most significant in the development of language, and much research has been done on it. One of the firmest conclusions which has come out of this work is that a word very quickly (and perhaps from the beginning) comes to be a sign for *several* objects. A child does not have to be taught to generalize but, on the contrary, has to be trained to brake his natural tendency to generalize. Generalizing may be understood as a reflection of our basic tendency to group and organize objects perceptually. And it is this which makes it possible for language to have such useful abstract words as "man," "house," "book,"— single words which encompass a large number of different instances of a class of objects. Almost all sign-words, except proper names, are signs for groups of objects, and thus they all refer to *generalizations*. In psychology the term "concept" is usually used to refer to such generalizations. The achievement of the correct meaning of a word is usually, then, dependent upon the achievement of a "concept." What are concepts and how are they achieved?

Concept Formation. Concept *formation* refers to the process of discovering some characteristic that is common to a series of discrete objects, and that sets off these objects from all other objects. A *concept* refers to the description of this common element. If we discover that mice, elephants, human beings, and whales all have mammary glands and that this common characteristic differentiates them from pigeons, trout, snakes, and most other animals, then we have formed a concept. The concept "mammal" is defined as all-animals-who-have-mammary-glands.

The processes involved in concept formation are the perceptual, learning, and creative problem-solving processes discussed in previous chapters. It has been found, for example, that the speed of the formation of a concept is a function of mental set, of the number of specific objects to be included in the group, of the ambiguity of the stimulus-patterns provided by the specific objects, etc. The process of concept formation has been described by one investigator (Reed, 1946) as involving the following three steps:

1. A period of doubt and orientation.
2. A period of search and trial solutions.
3. A period of evaluation and checking.

This sequence the reader will recognize as being almost identical to the one found for all problem-solving. (For an illustrative experiment in concept formation see Box 124.)

All of this can be summarized by saying that the meanings of sign-words are best described as "concepts," and "concepts" are embodied in specific words. But one word of caution must be sounded. Words not only have meanings, but they also have a *formal grammatical* function. The child may be able to use words correctly, in the formal sense, without having any notion

BOX 124

Problem-Solving—Word Learning—Concept Formation

Reed of Fort Hays Kansas State College has reported various studies on the acquisition and retention of concepts. The material consisted of cards with four common words printed on each one. The cards were grouped so that every card of one group, say, would have the name of an animal among its four words—the other words having nothing in common. Six such groupings were made up, and to each group Reed gave a nonsense-syllable name. Thus all the cards with an animal word on them were called KUN; the cards with a vegetable name, BEP; cards with a color name, DAX, etc. We shall here discuss one of his many experiments.

One group of subjects was told that their task was to learn the *names of the cards*. Thus they would be shown card 1 with the words *"horn leaf monkey debt"* and were told that this was a KUN. Card 2 was then shown with the words *"club picnic reaches beet"* which the experimenter called a BEP. Card 3 had *"answer highest airplane red"* and was called DAX. Card 4 had *"fame ought tiger saucer"* and was also called KUN, etc., until all 42 cards had been run through. Then the run of 42 was repeated. This was continued until the subject could name each card. The subjects were also asked such questions as: "What is KUN?" "In what ways have you tried to learn the names of these cards?"

A second group was told that its task was not only to learn the names of the card but also to discover the "meaning" of the name.

Among Reed's conclusions were: (1) All subjects "tried out" various concepts before arriving at the correct one. The process was very similar to problem-solving. (2) Subjects with the set to learn the name *also* learned the concept. (3) When the subject had the set to look for the *meaning* of the nonsense syllable, he learned the name of the card and the meaning more quickly than if he had the set only to learn the name. (4) Retention of names thus learned was extremely good (for both groups) and even after 40 days the subjects retained over 90 per cent of the names.

This experiment can be variously described: It is an experiment in problem-solving; in learning the "meaning of strange words"; in "concept formation." All three seem identical—in this instance at least.

REED, H. B. 1946. Factors influencing the learning and retention of concepts. *J. exp. Psychol.*, 36, 71–87.

of what they mean. Thus Piaget has shown that the child can use such conjunctions as "because," "therefore," "on account of," —and in a grammatically proper way— long before he has achieved the concept of causation. We cannot take the presence of a word in a person's vocabulary as indicating an understanding of the concept involved. Indeed, many words are no more than meaningless "verbal tics"—mere time-fillers.

By Way of Summary. The development of speech involves both a "narrowing down" and an acquisition process. Shortly after birth the child is capable of producing every possible speech sound. With self-induced practice he learns to bring these various sounds under voluntary and skillful control. As a consequence of being rewarded for certain specific sounds he makes, and as a result of his tendency to repeat the sounds of the adults he hears about him, the child very soon eliminates the "superfluous" sounds and ends with the sound-pattern characteristic of the culture in which he lives. By a process of conditioning, rote-memory, and trial-and-error learning, the child comes to attach meanings to various sounds and sound combinations. He is now beginning to acquire a language—to learn words. Words, once learned, function as *signs* for objects, as *attributes* of objects, and even as *objects themselves*. Very quickly in the development of language single words come to be signs for groups of objects, and thus *concept* formation is initiated.

Serial Ordering. Before a person can be said to have the skill of language he must know and be able to control the proper serial ordering of the discrete words. The rules of serial ordering in a language (sentence structure) are what is meant by the "syntax" or, more loosely, the "grammar" of a language. With the growth in mastery of the meanings of words goes a growth in mastery of complex sentence structure, but it is a long, slow growth. (See Fig. 109.)

Unfortunately, while grammar is of crucial importance in understanding language skill, very little experimental work has been done on the "psychology of grammar." A great deal is already known, and much more is being discovered, about the *effects* of syntax upon the production and perception of word sequences, but relatively little is known about the psychological process whereby this occurs.

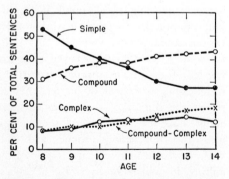

FIG. 109. These curves are based on 817 compositions written by Massachusetts school children of different ages in response to a request to give an account of a short motion picture they had just seen. The data present the proportions of different kinds of sentences found in these compositions. (After Heider, 1940.)

THE FREQUENCY COUNT. Much of the work in language and communication makes use of the statistical approach. Here the question asked is: What words and sequences are most frequently spoken? The answer to this question can provide us with the basic descriptive data for our major problem. Once we know what words and word sequences do appear most frequently, we are in a better position to seek the reasons.

The most comprehensive dictionaries of modern English reveal a total vocabulary of well over a million words. The supply of English words is so generous that Mr. or Mrs. Anyman could talk away for weeks before either one would have to use the same word a second time. But statistical counts of word usage have indicated that they do repeat themselves—and at an astonishingly great rate. Mr. Anyman repeats himself in every 10 or 15 words. The 50 most commonly used words make up about 60 per cent of all the words we speak, and 45 per cent of all the words we write. This repetitious use of a very few words (arranged and rearranged in a large number of patterns) to express an infinite number of ideas is characteristic of most languages. Here we have a striking demonstration of the importance of patterning in language.

Why should we be so niggardly in our usage of words? Several answers can be immediately suggested. In the first place a good number of the words (it has been estimated as much as three quarters of all of our words) are the specialized words of the sciences, technology, and trade jargons. In the second place most of us do not know more than a very small portion of even the general words; we simply have not acquired all the discrete responses possible. The average adult is said to have a use-and-recognition vocabulary of 30,-000–60,000 words, and a highly literate adult is not likely to go much beyond 100,-000. But our word usage is not constrained by the size of our vocabulary alone. It is also constrained by syntax and verbal context. That is, once we have spoken one word, what the next word will be is to some degree determined or restricted by the rules of grammar and by the meaning or rhythm or sound of the previous word spoken.

VERBAL CONTEXT AND FREQUENCY COUNT. A fairly precise quantitative measurement of the constraints upon our language has been developed in analyzing the sequences of *letters* constituting printed English. Letters, even more than words, occur with differential frequencies, e.g., the letter *e* appears much more frequently than any of the remaining 25 letters of the alphabet. The letters in one part of a sequence limit the possibilities and influence the probabilities of the appearance of another letter in a later part of the sequence. For example: once we have written the letter *q* it must almost invariably be followed by the letter *u;* once we have written the two letters *th*, the third letter can be only one of eight or nine letters (see Box 125).

Presumably one could discover the frequencies of different letter sequences in the English language by taking large samples of printed English and tabulating all

---

BOX 125

53‡‡†305))6*;4826)4‡.)4‡);806*;48†8¶60))85;1‡(;:‡*8†83(8
8)5*†;46(;88*96*?;8)*‡(;485);5*†2:*‡(;4956*2(5*—4)8¶8*;4
069285);)6†8)4‡‡;1(‡9;48081;8:8‡1;48†85;4)485†528806*8
1(‡9;48;(88;4(‡?34;48)4‡;161;:188;‡?;

Edgar Allan Poe's short story, *The Gold-Bug*, makes romantic use of the systematic patterning of letter sequences in language.

Poe's hero, Legrand, while rummaging around Sullivan's Island, found an old piece of parchment which he used to wrap up the "gold bug"—a curious beetle which attracted his fancy. Later, in his cabin, he discovered that on this parchment, "rudely traced, in a red tint" were the characters reproduced above. For Legrand this was an easy message to decode.

"My first step," he smugly explains to the obligingly bewildered narrator of the story, "was to ascertain the predominant letters, as well as the least frequent . . . Now in English, the letter which most frequently occurs is *e* . . . *e* predominates so remarkably, that an individual sentence of any length is rarely seen, in which it is not the prevailing character . . . As our predominant character is 8, we will commence by assuming it as the *e* . . . Now of all *words* in the language 'the' is most usual; let us see therefore, whether there are not repetitions of any three characters, in the same

order of collocation, the last of them being 8 . . . Upon inspection, we find no less than seven such arrangements, the characters being ; 4 8. We may therefore, assume that ; represents *t*, 4 represents *h*, and 8 represents *e*—the last being now well confirmed. Thus a great step has been taken."

From this first "great step," the rest followed easily and within two more pages of Poe's story Legrand had the solution:

"A good glass in the bishop's hostel in the devil's seat—forty-one degrees and thirteen minutes—northeast and by north—main branch seventh limb east side—shoot from the left eye of the death's head—a bee-line from the tree through the shot fifty feet out."

And thus, because all who would use language must operate within the structured confines of language patterns, William Legrand could easily understand the dead Captain Kidd's message, and a buried treasure chest, "filled to the brim" was the reward.

Elementary, my dear Watson, elementary!

the different letter sequences. Thus we can count the number of times the following (and every other conceivable sequence) occur: *th, tha, the, thi, tho, thr, ah, aha, aho.* We could then, from such a count, be able to estimate the *constraining influence* of *th,* say, upon the third letter. That is, we would be able to predict with what probabilities certain letters would follow the combination *th.*

The ordering of the letters, however, is so complex and the number of different sequences is so great, that the only adequate statistical "machine" to deal with the problem is the skilled human talker! A literate person already "knows" the constraints which the occurrence of a letter in one part of the sequence will have upon a later part. He obeys these constraints in his language behavior even though he cannot formulate the rules. Shannon (1951) therefore developed the following technique of getting that knowledge from the skilled person. He showed a subject a succession of ten letters (making up part of a meaningful passage taken from Dumas Malone's *Jefferson the Virginian*) and asked the subject to guess what the eleventh letter had originally been. The subject was instructed to continue guessing until he got the correct answer. From the number of guesses required to get the correct letter, Shannon could then estimate the *degree* to which the occurrence of a sequence of ten letters determined what the eleventh letter would be. For example, suppose that the person's *first* guess was correct and that this happened again and again with different guessers and different ten-letter passages. This would mean that the English language functions in such a manner that given the first ten letters, the eleventh letter is completely determined. In other words, the constraining influence of a sequence of ten letters upon the eleventh is 100 per cent. If the subjects in such an ex-

periment are skilled in language their "guesses" are really summary statements reflecting what the English language itself has taught the subjects.

REDUNDANCY. But if a literate person, given the first ten letters can accurately predict what the eleventh letter must be, the eleventh letter need never have been printed at all, as far as its information value is concerned. The person already knew what it would be once he had read the preceding ten letters. (Remember the high predictability of the letter *u* once *q* has appeared.) This consideration has led to the important concept of *redundancy* of language. Redundancy refers to the fact that certain letters and words occurring in certain contexts carry little *new* information.

Suppose, however, that given the first ten letters, we cannot predict with complete accuracy what the next letter will be, but we can still do better than chance. (Remember our ability to predict, with better than chance accuracy, which letter will follow *th*). Then we can say that the eleventh letter is redundant, but not completely so. In other words, redundancy is not an all-or-nothing affair. Obviously, the more rigidly the sequences are determined by the preceding letters, syntax, spelling, etc., the more redundant will a language be. With the use of Shannon's technique we can take a *random sample* of sequences, of varying lengths, and see, *on the average,* how much the letters of the English language are determined by these constraining factors. From this average we can estimate the average redundancy of the language, and the average strength of the constraining forces.

Shannon's data, and other confirming studies (see Box 126), clearly indicate that the English language is highly redundant. The average English letter is approximately three quarters determined by what has pre-

BOX 126

Long-Range Verbal Constraints

Burton and Licklider of the Massachusetts Institute of Technology argued that "printed English might turn out to be, say, 95% redundant if very-long-range constraints were taken into account. Since long-range constraints include the influences of subject matter, style, level of presentation, and the dynamics of the situation reported or described, it is possible *a priori* that they might be quite strong." Here is how they checked on this possibility.

They used ten paper-backed novels of about equal reading difficulty, from each of which they selected 100 randomly chosen passages. These passages were of ten different lengths: 0, 1, 2, 4, 8, 16, 32, 64, 128, and 10,000 letters. The subjects' task was to guess what letter came next. They con-

tinued guessing until they had named the letter correctly.

Ten graduate students were used as subjects. They were carefully chosen because the experimenters wanted verbally skilled subjects. (See text for the reasons for this.)

From the number of guesses required for each passage, the *relative redundancy* of each sequence was determined. (This measure of redundancy is too complicated mathematically to describe here, but suffice it to say that a score of 1.00 indicates complete redundancy.) The results are given in terms of upper and lower limits of relative redundancy. It can be seen that the constraints imposed by preceding letters increase rapidly as the number of preceding letters increase, up to about 32 letters (predicting what the 33d letter would be was more accurate than what the 4th letter would be, etc). *From then on additional letters do not seem to make much difference.* In general their conclusions agree with Shannon's. Since printed English usually consists of passages of more than 30 letters, the constraining influences in printed English are such that any letter is between 66 and 80 per cent determined by what has preceded it.

BURTON, N. G., and LICKLIDER, J. C. R. 1955. Long-range constraints in the statistical structure of printed English. *Amer. J. Psychol., 68,* 650–3.

ceded it. Such studies provide *quantitative measures* of the constraints upon serial ordering of letters, constraints which the skillful talker must learn.

Unlike many skills, speech not only involves an "active" phase, but also a "passive" one. The skillful speaker must not only be able to produce speech, but he must also, of course, be able to understand speech produced by others. Redundancy in language is of great help here. While a redundant language may be inefficient in that it uses more symbols than are absolutely necessary, it is efficient in that it decreases

the probability of error in perception. Speech is almost always delivered against some distracting background of noise, competing stimuli, inattention, etc. If there were *zero* redundancy in language, there would be no verbal context effect. In order to comprehend speech under those circumstances we would have to perceive *every sound* accurately. This would make of speech a highly inadequate communication system. (See experiment in Box 127.)

Perception of Speech. Almost every generalization made about the production of

BOX 127

Information, Freedom of Choice, and Perception of Speech

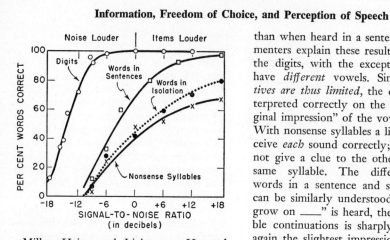

Miller, Heise, and Lichten at Harvard University sought an answer to the question of why a word is heard correctly in one context and incorrectly in another when perceptual conditions are difficult.

Digits, nonsense syllables, words (in random order), and sentences (consisting of the same words connected by "of's," "the's," etc., to make meaningful statements) were spoken against noisy backgrounds varying in intensities. Each item was heard with the background noise sometimes louder and sometimes softer than the item by 18, 12, and 6 decibels.

The results indicate that (1) intelligibility is highest for digits, and lowest for nonsense syllables; and (2) a word is harder to understand when it is heard in isolation

than when heard in a sentence. The experimenters explain these results as follows. All the digits, with the exception of 5 and 9, have *different* vowels. Since *the alternatives are thus limited,* the digits can be interpreted correctly on the basis of a "marginal impression" of the vowel sound alone. With nonsense syllables a listener must perceive *each* sound correctly; one sound does not give a clue to the other sounds in the same syllable. The difference between words in a sentence and scrambled words can be similarly understood. When "apples grow on ____" is heard, the range of possible continuations is sharply restricted, and again the slightest impression of the fourth word is enough to permit a good "guess."

Most words consist of several sounds. Each sound can be considered as one bit of "information." The above data are summarized as follows: the amount of information necessary for the correct perception of a word depends upon the range of alternative possibilities (the listener's freedom of choice). As the range of alternatives increases, the amount of information necessary per word also increases, and so the noise level must be decreased to permit the correct perception of the whole word.

MILLER, G. A., HEISE, G. A., and LICHTEN, W. 1951. The intelligibility of speech as a function of the context of test material. *J. exp. Psychol.,* 41, 329–35.

speech also holds for the perception of speech. Just as the skillful speaker must be able to produce systematically patterned sounds, so must he be able to perceive patterns of sounds; and just as learning the meanings of words shares many aspects of problem-solving, so does the hearing of words.

PERCEIVING SPEECH PATTERNS. Much of the work on the perception of speech has been done by the engineers at the Bell Telephone Laboratories who are primarily interested in determining the adequacies of

their communication devices. Among their techniques is that of changing or distorting speech sounds to determine the intelligibility of speech under difficult conditions of transmission. Let us give some illustrative findings.

(1) Wide changes in the *intensity* of speech have but little effect on perception. Thus, as the intensity is raised from about 50 decibels to 140, no significant change in intelligibility of heard words occurs (see Fig. 110).

(2) Wide changes in the "spectrum" of

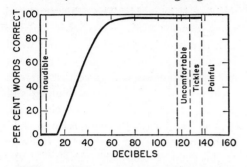

FIG. 110. The curve shows the relation between the per cent of English monosyllabic words which can be recorded correctly and the intensity of the speech at the listener's ear. Changes in intensity of almost 100 decibels (see Chapter 4 for meaning of "decibels") do not change a listener's ability to hear correctly, even though the intensity may reach the stage where it is actually painful. Over the range of 50 to 140 decibels, therefore, intensity does not seem to be a crucial determinant of intelligibility of speech. (After Miller, 1951.)

speech sounds can be tolerated without any significant loss in understanding. The speech "spectrum" refers to the range of different sound frequencies and amplitudes which are found in ordinary speech sounds. Male voices, speaking at a conversational level, can range in frequency from 100 cycles per second to about 8000 cycles, and in intensity from about 20 to 120 decibels. By the use of appropriate instrumentation the normal spectrum can be radically altered. Thus, recorded speech may be passed through a transmission system which will "clip off" all the upper, or all the lower frequencies and pass on only the remaining sounds. What happens when we mutilate normal speech sounds in this way? The data indicate that with meaningful words perception is still adequate even if we hear the frequencies above 1900 c.p.s. *only*, or the frequencies below 1900 c.p.s. *only*. We not only can clip off certain frequencies, we can do the same for amplitude, so that only the loud or only the soft components of the normal spectrum are heard. Again, violent distortions have remarkably

little effect on the intelligibility of such speech. (See Fig. 111.)

(3) Another type of distortion of the normal speech pattern is to produce intermittent interruptions. By the use of telephonic equipment we can arrange a situation where the recorded speech is interrupted, say, 10 times every second, so that out of a speech sequence which lasts ten minutes, the sound is actually on for only five minutes of that time. Yet, under these conditions, the listener's ability to understand what is being said is not interfered with (Miller and Licklider, 1950).

The significance of these experiments is this: The sound waves produced by spoken speech may undergo extensive changes in many of their characteristics—frequency, amplitude, harmonics, duration—but a careful physical analysis of what is left indicates that the essential *pattern of the total sound wave* remains constant. As long as a specific organization is maintained, we can understand what the sound waves are saying. In part this dependence upon patterning reflects the general biological tend-

Undistorted Speech Wave

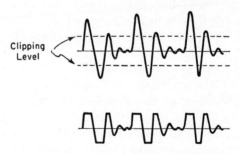

FIG. 111. Distortion of speech wave by amplitude selectivity. The usual wave form at the top is clipped electronically along the dotted lines so that only the center of the wave (the lower form) gets through to the listener's ears. Such "peak clipping" has practically no effect on intelligibility. The lower clipped wave will be just as intelligible to the listener as will the undistorted wave. (Adapted from Miller, 1951.)

ency to organize discrete stimuli in perception, but in part it also reflects a long and complex skill-training process.

PERCEPTION OF SPEECH AS PROBLEM-SOLVING. We are bound by the rules of syntax in producing speech, and we are helped by these rules in perceiving speech. Thus, as we have seen in the experiment described in Box 127, verbal context plays an exceedingly important role in the very perception of sounds and words. Miller (1951) in dicussing such experiments couches his description of the perception of speech almost entirely in terms of intelligent problem-solving:

"If enough of the discourse is perceived to reveal the basic pattern of the sentence, the range of possible words that can be substituted into the pattern is greatly decreased. Thus the probability of a correct guess is increased. For example, in the sentence 'He threw the . . . out the window,' we can immediately reject all parts of speech except nouns. Then we can reject all the nouns that are associated with unthrowable objects. Then we can give preference to certain things that people are known to throw—balls, rocks, bombs, etc. So we get down to a rather small number of possibilities. . . . Because the elimination of unlikely possibilities occurs so quickly and so automatically, it is difficult to imagine how the process takes place. The nature of the situation somehow influences what a listener expects, and from this relatively narrow range of expected events he chooses one that seems to him the most probable."

Language and Thinking

The images most frequently used in thinking are words. The most common way of communicating the solution of a problem is in words. The achievement of a new concept often results in the coining of a new word, or of giving an old word new meanings. For these and other reasons most psychologists will agree that there is a close relationship between thinking and language, so close that some psychologists, such as Jean Piaget, the famous Swiss child psychologist, use the analysis of *language* of the child to study the *thinking* of the child.

But while agreeing that there is a close relationship between the two, psychologists disagree on the nature of the relationship. The major question upon which they disagree can be stated simply: *What role do the vocabulary and grammar of a language play in thinking?*

Language: Vehicle or Mold? One analysis suggests that the nature and content of thinking is very little dependent upon the nature and content of language. According to this analysis, though thinking is *expressed* in words, it is not greatly influenced by the structure of the language. In many instances, problem-solving consists of the interplay of purely visual or auditory or kinesthetic images. As a *secondary* process we may then seek to find words to express our thoughts, but by then "thinking" or problem-solving has already been completed. (See Einstein's comments on his own thinking process, Box 83, p. 366.) According to this position, the development of thinking and of language in a child go along concurrently, but more or less separately. As the child learns new words he can better communicate his thoughts, and better remember his conclusions, but that is all. Language is a convenient "vehicle" for thinking.

The second position maintains that as thought turns into speech it is inevitably molded by it. A number of linguistic studies have been cited to support this view. Thus the studies of the language and thinking of different societies and cultural groups have been interpreted to show that the nature of the thinking of a group corresponds to the nature of its grammar and vocabulary (see Box 128). There have been some clinical studies which indicate that the disturbance in the thinking of the schizophrenic patient, for example, corresponds to the disturbance in his language.

According to this second formulation, the development of language and thought must be seen as a highly interdependent process. As the child learns new words and new ways of putting words together, the very nature of his thinking is changed; and as he achieves new concepts the very structure of his language is affected.

The proponents of the first position have countered these arguments by pointing out that since language is used to *express* thinking, there will inevitably be a correspondence between the two, but that does not prove an interaction. A particular language and a particular kind of thinking may both reflect the influence of some third factor, such as different environments, or diseased nervous systems. What is needed is not a correlational study but carefully controlled experimental studies.

At the present time it is difficult to choose among these (and other) formulations. Very little experimental research on the relationship between thinking and language has been done. Perhaps this relationship cannot be studied experimentally, but

---

BOX 128

It Houses

Benjamin Lee Whorf, a student of linguistics, argues that ". . . the background linguistic system [the grammar] of each language is not merely a reproducing instrument for voicing ideas but rather is itself the shaper of ideas." He supports his arguments, in part, by comparing the way various languages "dissect nature." He points out that we tend to differentiate between "things" and "events" in a hard and fast way because in English we divide most of our words into nouns and verbs. "Our language thus gives us a bipolar division of nature. But nature herself is not bipolarized. If it be said that strike, turn, run, are verbs because they denote temporary or short-lasting events, i.e., actions, why then is fist a noun? It is also a temporary event. Why are lightning, spark, wave, eddy, pulsation, flame, storm, phase, cycle, spasm, noise, emotion, nouns? . . . It will be found that an 'event' to *us* means 'what our language classes as a verb'. . . . In the Hopi language, lightning, wave, flame, meteor, puff of smoke, pulsation, are verbs—events of necessarily brief duration cannot be anything but verbs. Cloud and storm are at about the lower limit of duration for nouns. Hopi, you see, actually has a classification of events . . . by duration type, something strange to our modes of thought . . . in Nootka, a language of Vancouver Island . . . we have as it were, a monistic view of nature that gives us only one class of words for all kinds of events. 'A house occurs' or 'it houses' is the way of saying 'house' exactly like 'a flame occurs' or 'it burns.'"

Thus Whorf would maintain that because of our grammar (nouns and verbs) we divide the world into "events" and "things," while the Hopis use quite another basis (their grammar classifies words by "duration" type), and the Vancouver Islanders make no division at all between a "thing" and an "event." Thus *grammar* determines the perception of the world around us, and that, in turn, will determine the content and direction of our thinking.

WHORF, B. L. 1956. *Language, thought and reality.* New York: Wiley. Copyright 1956, Wiley & Sons, N.Y.

must be studied by observing correlations as found "in nature"; perhaps we have not yet been able to formulate the questions specifically enough to permit experimental attack. The best we can do, therefore, is to present some of the more plausible (or perhaps they are merely more "interesting") speculations, paying due regard to the available data. But again the student should be warned—or promised, depending on whether the student is upset by or thrives upon problems—that here we are in a field that is as confused as it is important.

Dual Function of Language. It may be profitable to begin by dividing the thinking process into two stages: the "silent thinking" stage, and the "communicative" stage.

That words make up a good part of our experiences during the first stage seems clear from the introspective reports of many observers. Some objective experimental evidence is available which suggests the same thing. It has been shown that when a person is "thinking," minimal movements of the throat and tongue can sometimes be detected by sensitive instruments. These movements are of such a nature as to permit the interpretation that the person is really "talking to himself." (For one such experiment see Box 129.)

But a more detailed analysis indicates that language plays two different roles in these two stages. In the "silent thinking" stage the specific grammar and vocabulary of the language seem to play a relatively minor role in determining the nature and content

---

BOX 129

Thinking—Speech Without Sound?

Jacobson of the University of Chicago has reported an experiment demonstrating that "During . . . thinking involving words or numbers, muscular contractions appear . . . in at least some of the muscles which participate when the same words or numbers are actually whispered or uttered out loud."

Since even the most minute muscular contractions are accompanied by electrical potential changes, Jacobson used an instrument to detect and record such changes. Two fine platinum-iridium wire electrodes were inserted about one centimeter into the tip of the tongue and the underlip of the subject. The electrodes led off to an amplifier and a string galvanometer. Only well-trained subjects were used.

The subject, lying relaxed upon a couch in a darkened, quiet room with eyes closed, was instructed to *imagine* or to recall certain poems, multiply (mentally) certain numbers, to think of such abstract matters as "eternity," etc. Throughout, the vibra-

tions of the string of the galvanometer were photographed. We quote from Jacobson's statement of results:

"When the electrodes are connected in the speech musculature of the trained subject, the string shadow is practically quiet . . . But promptly after the signal is sounded to engage in mental activity . . . marked vibrations appear, indicating action-potentials. Soon after the subject hears the signal to relax . . . the vibrations cease . . . The series of vibrations during mental activity occur in patterns evidently corresponding with those present during actual speech . . . but of considerably less voltage."

This experiment and many similar ones by other workers gave support to the so-called "motor theory of thinking," i.e., that all thinking involves minimal speech movements.

JACOBSON, E. 1938. *Progressive relaxation.* Chicago: Univ. of Chicago Press.

of the thought. In the "communicative" stage, language serves what might be termed a "policing" and "editing" function, and here the specific structure of the language may play a more significant role.

"Egocentric" speech. One of Piaget's earliest findings was that the small child engages in self-centered monologues. This he called "egocentric" speech which has no communicative function. The child is merely "playing" with words as he babbles away in short, incomplete, self-addressed sentences.

Vigotsky, the Russian psychologist, while confirming Piaget's description of the young child's speech, has, on the basis of various experimental investigations, come to a different conclusion concerning the significance of such speech. The child, Vigotsky argues, does use this egocentric speech as communication to others. For example, when a child who shows all the external signs of egocentric speech is placed in a group of deaf-and-dumb children, or among strangers, or off in a corner by himself, he speaks less than under other conditions. Vigotsky considers the egocentric nature of the child's speech as resulting from the child's insufficient differentiation of his own inner world from the outer social world. That is, the child feels that everyone else perceives what he perceives, and understands what he understands.

Inner vs. external speech. If this is so, the child's egocentric speech provides the psychologist with a unique tool in the study of the relations between thinking and language. When we "think" and engage in "inner speech" we, too, are talking to ourselves. Unfortunately for science, however, an outside observer cannot record and study what we are saying to ourselves. Should the experimenter request us to "think out loud," we may, under these "unnatural" circumstances completely alter the content and form of our "inner speech." But if the child's egocentric speech is not mere verbal play but is really "inner speech" spoken aloud because it is meant by the child to be heard and understood, then the scientist has here a splendid opportunity to gain some insights into the nature of inner speech of the adult.

Working on this assumption Vigotsky came to the following conclusion. Inner speech of the adult (1) is abrupt and incomplete; (2) makes many assumptions about the "self-evident" nature of the facts and relationships involved in any line of reasoning; (3) is relatively independent of the rules of grammar. This is the nature of speech in the "silent thinking" stage.

However, when we reach the second stage—communication—we realize that we cannot be so abrupt and elliptical. We must "spell out" our steps, we must use words more precisely, we must pay some attention to grammatical construction, else we run the risk of not communicating at all. We realize all this because we, unlike the child, have learned that *our* private world is not shared by others.

Context and speech forms. The differences between the speech used in the "silent thinking" stage and the "communication" stage do not represent sharp breaks. The degree of difference depends, in part, upon the relationship between the speaker and the listener. In general, the more common the sympathies and context shared by the listener and speaker, the more elliptical, abrupt, unfinished, and grammatically unrestrained speech can be. At one extreme is the instance where we are talking to ourselves; at the other extreme is the formal, written communication addressed to an unknown audience.

Talking to ourselves we have a perfect friend, a completely sympathetic and understanding "audience" which shares our context completely. We use the vaguest of words without any fear that we will be misunderstood. We use the "felt sense" of words, rather than the dictionary meanings. We are not constrained by grammatical rules. We skip steps in our reasoning, feeling that we "understand" what we have not spoken.

Conversation among good friends of like mind may be only slightly removed from talking to oneself. Such conversations may also consist of somewhat abbreviated speech. Often we find that no sooner does one friend begin to speak than the other will immediately anticipate the purport of the speech and begin his reply, only to be understood immediately and to be interrupted by the beginning of another reply. Such a conversation may well include mere beginnings of sentences, snatches of phrases, and elliptical exclamations.

Increasing formalization of speech can be illustrated in the difference between the professor's language when he lectures and when he writes. The former is apt to be more informal, sentences are not completed, tenses are mixed, plural nouns are coupled with singular verbs, participles are left hanging, and such phrases as "the what-not" abound. Yet this garbled and grammatically "barbarous" spoken language may be perfectly understood by most listeners whereas the same words, read in a manuscript, may cause confusion and bewilderment. Why? One of the reasons seems to be that in spoken speech the audience not only hears the words which are spoken, but it sees the facial expressions of the speaker, hears stresses and emphases, sees gestures, and all of it takes place in a very specific context. When reading a manuscript, however, the reader is mostly dependent upon the written words. He does not have the multitude of *non*-verbal cues

which the listener has when he not only hears but also sees the speaker.

Speech, then, becomes more formal as we attempt to communicate with others, and it increases in formality as the "psychological distance" between the speaker and listener increases.

COMMUNICATION AND THINKING. When we prepare to communicate our thoughts —when we attempt to "dress up" our thoughts for public display—we often find that we cannot do so. In the light of day, as it were, we find that we have assumed too much, that our thinking process has *not* been completed. The reason we sometimes cannot find the word for our thoughts is that we really did not have the thought clearly in the first place, we had only *assumed* that we had it. Thus the second stage is not merely a stage of "expression," it is very frequently a continuation of the stage of creation. We correct, fill in, revise, and even completely alter our "thinking" as we attempt to express it. *But now we are doing our "thinking" under the constraints imposed upon us by the dictionary meaning of words and by the rules of grammar.*

BY WAY OF SUMMARY. The above analysis suggests that language and thinking are intimately related, but in a complex manner. The constraints imposed upon us by our vocabulary and grammar may be very light at one stage of our thinking, and quite important at a later stage. The "thinking" process is not completed when expression of it begins. It continues to take shape and form and to undergo change as we attempt to express our thoughts.

Logic. One kind of thinking where the solution is arrived at almost entirely through the aid of words or symbols is the formal syllogism of the logician. The "laws of logic" which have come down

BOX 130

Nonlogical Factors in "Logical Thinking"

In Burt's investigation (reported in Woodworth, 1938) of syllogistic reasoning in children, it was clear that the *temporal sequence of the premises and words can affect such reasoning*. An example:

1) Three boys are sitting in a row: Harry is to the left of Willie; George is to the left of Harry. Which boy is in the middle?

2) Three boys are sitting in a row: George is to the left of Harry; Harry is to the left of Willie. Which boy is in the middle?

The first form is passed correctly by 50 per cent of 9-year-old children, the second form, by 61 per cent.

In 1935 Woodworth and Sells of Columbia University advanced the hypothesis that *the over-all "atmosphere" of the syllogisms influences the conclusions drawn*. For example, a *universal* ("all") premise creates a universal atmosphere and results in a universal conclusion; a *particular* ("some") premise creates a particular atmosphere and results in a particular conclusion. Sells and Koob tested 134 college students who were asked to fill in the blanks with the correct conclusions to such syllogisms as the following:

1) All x's are y's;
   And all x's are z's;
   Therefore ____ y's ____ z's.
2) Some x's are y's;
   And some y's are z's;
   Therefore ____ x's ____ z's.

In the first syllogism the *correct* conclusion is "*some* y's are z's." The conclusion favored by the "atmosphere effect" is "*all* y's are z's." Seventy-eight of the students gave the *atmosphere* conclusion, 9 gave the correct conclusion, and the rest gave other incorrect conclusions. In the second syllogism, no valid conclusion can be drawn, but the "atmosphere effect" would predispose toward "*some* x's are z's." This time 90 students gave the atmosphere conclusion, 9 said that no conclusion was possible, and the others scattered among various wrong conclusions.

Psychological laws and logical laws may lead to different results.

WOODWORTH, R. S. 1938. *Experimental psychology.* New York: Holt.
WOODWORTH, R. S., and SELLS, S. B. 1935. An atmospheric effect in formal syllogistic reasoning. *J. exp. Psychol., 18,* 451–60.
SELLS, S. B., and KOOB, H. E. 1937. A classroom demonstration of "atmospheric effect" in reasoning. *J. educ. Psychol., 28,* 514–18.

from Aristotle also impose constraints on thinking.

The rules and principles of logic are the "distilled" products of man's thinking as perceived and categorized by the logician. The "laws of logic," in other words, are the "laws of *human* logic." However, they are not (nor are they intended to be) adequate summary statements concerning human thinking, because they omit entirely many factors which we now know do influence thinking. Let us give two simple perceptual examples. We know that the *temporal order* in which stimuli are presented will determine the problem-solving of people. We also know that the *part-whole* relationships among objects influence problem-solving. These two principles are not recognized as factors in any set of laws of formal logic. Yet they can influence, tremendously, so-called "logical thinking," as is demonstrated by the experimental material in Box 130. It is precisely because of this that the rules and principles of logic have great value. They afford good checks on the validity of our reasoning. They are not laws of thought, they are laws *for* thought.

Glossary

"atmosphere" effect. The over-all effect of specific words and word sequences upon the conclusions drawn in any reasoning process. Refers to *extra*-logical influences on reasoning.

attribute function of word. When a word is perceived as an inalienable part of an object, the word is said to have an attribute function. Characteristic of the speech of young children.

"communicative" stage—in thinking. Refers to the *communication* of one's thoughts to others—either in writing or in vocal speech.

concept. Refers to the description of an element common to a class of objects or events.

concept formation. The process of discovering a characteristic common to a series of objects such that this series can be differentiated from all other objects.

egocentric speech. A term first used by Piaget, the Swiss psychologist, to describe the apparently self-centered "monologues" of the child. This speech is characterized by short, incomplete, elliptical sentences. Believed by Piaget not to be intended as social communication by the child. Vigotsky, the Russian psychologist, believes this speech *is* intended as social communication.

inner speech. The speech used when "talking to one's self." According to Vigotsky the "inner speech" of the adult is similar to the "egocentric speech" of the child.

logic. The principles governing correct or valid inferences. The laws and principles of logic assert what inferences man *may* validly draw, but do not describe *how* he draws them. They are laws *for* thought, not laws *of* thought.

object function of word. A word is said to have an object function when the word is treated as an object in its own right, not as a sign for an object. Such "magic" words as "abracadabra" are frequently used in this way.

redundancy in language. Refers to the fact that certain letters and words, occuring in certain contexts, carry varying degrees of *new* information. A word with 100 per cent redundancy contributes *no* information; a word with zero redundancy contributes completely new information.

sign (function of word). When a word elicits a response which is related to an object or event, the word is said to function as a sign for that object or event. These responses may be anticipatory, preparing the person for the real object's coming, or may be the occurrence of an image of the object.

"silent thinking" stage. The stage in the thinking process which does not involve *communicating* the thoughts (either in writing or in vocal speech). Frequently characterized by "inner speech."

sound profiles. A graphic representation of the *relative* frequencies of occurrence of all the different consonants (consonant profile) or of all the different vowels (vowel profile).

speech spectrum. The range of sound frequencies and sound amplitudes found in speech.

"syllabic babbling" stage. The stage in the infant's development of speech when typically certain combinations of sounds are repeated over and over again in different pitches and with different volumes.

syntax. The rules of serial ordering of words in a language (sentence structure).

verbal conditioning. Refers to a special instance of conditioning where the conditioned response is a word, or a combination of sounds.

verbal context effect. The effect on the probability of appearance of a given word or letter of preceding words or letters. If the preceding words or letters completely determine what the next letter will be, we speak of a large verbal context effect.

Suggestions for Further Reading

HAYAKAWA, S. I. 1949. *Language in thought and action.* New York: Harcourt, Brace.

An interestingly written account of how words get in our way in thinking and communicating, by one of the outstanding students in semantics. Directed toward helping us overcome these difficulties.

MILLER, G. A. 1951. *Language and communication.* New York: McGraw-Hill.

A standard textbook on the subject, written by a Harvard psychologist who has done considerable experimental work on the subject. Especially interesting in its application of "information theory" to problems of language.

OSGOOD, C. E. 1953. *Method and theory in experimental psychology.* New York: Oxford Univ. Press.

A detailed systematic presentation of the data and theories in experimental psychology. See particularly Chapters 15, 16.

PIAGET, J. 1925. *The language and thought of the child.* New York: Harcourt.

Written by the eminent Swiss psychologist who has contributed more to our understanding of the development of thinking in the child than any other single investigator. This book, his first of more than twenty books, deals largely with children between 3 and 12 years of age. It is here that he traces the development of social speech from egocentric speech.

CHAPTER XVIII

Physiological Basis of Adaptive Behavior

THE SEARCH for the physiological bases of learning and problem-solving has, almost from the very beginning, concentrated on the brain. It is impossible to say when this search began. According to Professor J. H. Breasted (1930), the eminent Egyptologist, the term "brain" is recorded for the first time in an ancient Egyptian text (known as the Edwin Smith Surgical Papyrus) which may go back to 3000 B.C. Not only does this ancient document contain the earliest known reference to the brain, but, according to Breasted, "the observation of effects on the lower limbs of injuries to the skull and brain, noted by the ancient surgeon with constant reference to *that side of the head which has been injured*, shows an astonishingly early discernment of localization of function in the brain . . ."

But aside from ancient observations, systematic experimental studies that sought to understand the mind by understanding the brain are of fairly recent origin. Perhaps the best date to give would be 1824 when the French physiologist, Pierre Flourens, published his *Experimental Researches on the Properties and the Functions of the Nervous System in Vertebrate Animals.* This report is an important one for several reasons:

(1) It is the first *experimental* study relating behavior to the brain. This was in sharp contrast to the phrenologists who had jumped to their wild conclusions on the basis of uncontrolled observations of pathological behavior and on collections of anecdotes (see Box 131).

(2) In this report Flourens described *a new experimental procedure*—the ablation technique. As we have seen in Chapter 7, this technique still is one of our major experimental procedures.

(3) The *conclusions* of the report set

480

BOX 131

Phrenology

While Flourens's book marks the beginning of experimental work on the brain-mind problem, the general question had been dramatically raised 14 years earlier by two German physicians, Gall and Spurzheim. In their 6-volume *Anatomy and Physiology of the Nervous System* (1810) they laid the basis for phrenology by asserting that (1) the brain is the organ of the mind; (2) different kinds of behavior are controlled by separate parts of the brain (see illustration); and (3) the external shape of the skull reflects the shape of the brain underneath. (Protuberances and dips on the skull presumably reflected over- or underdevelopment of the brain underneath.)

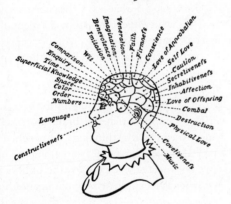

Gall's System.

Science has treated Gall and Spurzheim with ridicule. Yet, their anatomy and neurology were sound, and their general theoretical position was a reasonable one for the time. Why, then, did their contemporaries

and history treat them so meanly? One might venture two reasons: (1) Phrenology seemed to be an easy way of "finding out about people"—just feel the bumps on their heads! In the hands of the uncritical and the charlatans phrenology became a morass of pseudoscientific nonsense. (2) The supporting *data* Gall and Spurzheim used fell far short of scientific standards. Here is how Spurzheim relates the "discovery" that physical love is controlled by the cerebellum:

"Being physician to a widow who was subject to very strong hysterical fits, during which she drew her head backward with great violence, Gall sometimes supported her head with his hand, and, in doing so, observed that her neck was very large and hot. He was acquainted with her character [Gall's case history of this patient makes it clear why she is sometimes referred to as 'Gall's passionate widow'] . . . and he accordingly considered in connection her passion, this magnitude of the neck, and the consequent development of the cerebellum."

Often in science, when a reasonable theory is wildly overstated, the good in an idea is thrown out with the bad.

Nevertheless, as Boring (1950), the historian of psychology, reminds us, phrenology accomplished two things: ". . . it forced the problem of correlation of mind and brain to the fore . . . [and] by going to extremes, Gall made a radical but less extreme view actually seem conservative. Without a Gall, Flourens might never have conceived the problem of finding different functions for the cerebrum, the cerebellum, the medulla and the cord."

the pattern of thought and research in this field of investigation for many years to come. Among his major conclusions were the following: (a) The brain as a whole is composed of several organs, each with its own functions. The cerebrum is the "seat

of intelligence" and the cerebellum is the "seat of the principle which coordinates locomotor motions." (We still believe this to be a relatively sound distinction.) (b) The cerebrum is functionally indivisible, "The unity of the cerebrum proper . . . is one of the most important results of my experiments . . . all the intellectual faculties reside exclusively in this organ . . . without any one being separable from the others." In other words, it was not true, as the phrenologists had argued, that different intellectual functions were controlled by different parts of the brain. (However, there is still some dispute among experimentalists on this.) (c) The more cortical tissue that is destroyed, the greater the loss of function, but if sufficient tissue is left intact, the remaining tissue may take over the functions of the entire brain, even if inefficiently. (This has not been completely dropped as a hypothesis by modern researchers.)

Since the time of Flourens, literally thousands of man-hours have been spent and thousands upon thousands of rats, dogs, cats, monkeys, and other animals have given their lives to a continued search for the physiological mechanisms behind the "higher mental processes." A great deal of ingenuity in experimental attack has been shown. Many new techniques have been evolved. A number of novel hypotheses have been put forth, disproven, revived, and have again been subjected to rigorous test. As a result of all this we have learned a great deal.

What we shall do in this chapter is to sketch some of this knowledge within the framework of the material presented in the preceding five chapters. Specifically we shall deal with the following three questions: (1) Images play an important role in our experiences when we solve problems. What are the physiological correlates of these mental phenomena? (2) Man reacts to a problem by acquiring adaptive responses. What neurological mechanisms make such acquisition possible? (3) Once acquired, a response can be retained. Where in the nervous system does the retention persist?

Mental Phenomena and Physiological Correlates

We will start our physiological analysis as we did our psychological one, with the mental experiences that accompany thinking and problem-solving.

To look at Mr. Anyman while he is "deep in thought" is often to see an inactive, motionless, and silent man (remember the famous statue of *The Thinker*). It is a reasonable guess that during this period of outward bodily rest Mr. Anyman's nervous system (and particularly his brain) is far from inactive. This "reasonable guess" has been amply supported by experimental investigations. By the use of various electrophysiological techniques, it has been shown that as we change from sleep to wakefulness, or from a "mentally relaxed" state to one of "mental activity," the pattern of neural activity in the brain undergoes observable and measurable changes. This general finding is, of course, hardly surprising in the light of the universal assumption that the brain has something to do with thinking. Experiments have also demonstrated something a bit more unexpected. Not only is the brain active when we experience mental images but *so are our muscles*—legs, arms, trunk, neck, and most of the rest of our musculature. This complicates an already complicated picture, for it appears that we not only think with our brain, *we also think with our muscles!* (See Box 132.) In seeking the physiological correlates of images and other mental phenomena we cannot restrict ourselves to the brain alone. We must examine the muscular reactions as well as the neurological ones. The data will show that the muscles of our body cannot be conceived of as merely the brain's "handmaidens," ready to serve in response to its command,

BOX 132

Thought and Action

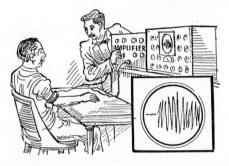

In his book, *Directed Thinking*, George Humphrey of Oxford University, gives a delightful description of an "informal and completely impromptu experiment" in which he served as a subject. We have here slightly paraphrased his account.

"Some years ago I was in an English laboratory with a young friend. He fastened an electrode to the upper part of my arm, and arranged wires so that they ran through a set of amplifying tubes to an oscilloscope. Now an oscilloscope has a small circular screen on which a line of light shows. When no current is passing, the line is straight. When there is a current, the line is disturbed. When my young friend, Dr. Rawdon Smith, threw in the switch, at once little spurts shot up, jags of disturbance, changing from instant to instant.

"The spurts came from small currents caused by contractions of muscle fibers so small that to our eyes they were entirely invisible. What we saw was a bare arm to all appearances entirely relaxed and resting on a table. What the apparatus registered was muscle fibers slightly thickening, first one, then another, helter-skelter, and producing electric disturbances as they did so.

"But the really dramatic part was to come. The experimenter said: 'When I say go, imagine you are knocking out the heavyweight champion. You are really letting yourself go. Let him have it on the chin . . . Ready . . . GO!'

"The result was astonishing. The line seemed to explode instantaneously, filling the screen with smashes of light and darting needlepoints. The whole four-inch circle seemed to be lit up for a fraction of a second, and the line completely blotted out. I am not a heavy man. Any blow of mine would doubtless feel like a playful punch to a heavyweight champion; so that I was gratified at the tempestuous effect of my effort—even if it was, as my young friend irreverently remarked, 'a storm in an electrical teapot.' Through it all, an onlooker would have seen two people quite motionless, in a roomful of apparatus, one with his arm resting quietly on a table. There was not a visible quiver from the muscles that had caused the four-inch cataclysm.

"This experiment showed that when I was merely *thinking* of doing something, my muscles were still acting, though on a small scale. *Thought never wholly frees itself from action.*"

HUMPHREY, G. 1948. *Directed thinking*, New York: Dodd, Mead. Copyright 1948 by Dodd, Mead & Co., New York.

but that the muscles, in addition to responding to neural stimulation from the brain, help serve as regulators and determiners of the brain's functions.

Brain Waves and Mental Phenomena. In 1929, the psychiatrist Hans Berger first demonstrated that the electrical activity of the human brain could be recorded through the unopened skull, and thus gave us an electronic "window" into the brain.

The passage of a nerve impulse along a nerve fiber causes a brief change in the electrical charge on the surface of the fiber. This change in electrical charge (which travels along the fiber as an aspect of the nerve impulse) creates an electrical wave and is known as the "action potential." These electrical waves are so highly correlated with other aspects of the nerve impulse that, for all practical purposes, they can be taken as a measure of the nervous activity of the fibers. Such electrical waves, when they come from the cerebral cortex, are called *brain waves.*

The voltages normally developed at the surface of man's cortex by these brain waves range from 100 to 1,000 microvolts (millionths of a volt). Berger discovered that these waves "get through" the skull and scalp and can be picked up and recorded on the surface of the head. By the time these waves reach the surface of the head, however, their voltages are reduced to between 20 and 60 microvolts! To obtain records of such minute voltages requires a highly sensitive instrument. With the use of vacuum tube methods of amplification (as developed in radio engineering) it is a relatively easy matter to magnify these small electrical waves by one or two million times, without distorting them in any way. (Here we have a nice illustration of how advancement in one area of science or engineering can have profound effects on an entirely different field of investigation.)

Brain waves are not "broadcast" but must be picked up by special electrodes which are cemented to the surface of the scalp at various points. From these electrodes the brain waves are led through wires to an amplifier, and then are passed on to an oscilloscope which makes the brain waves visible, or through an ink-writing oscillograph so that the brain waves move an inked pen on continuously running paper. In this way the brain waves literally write the record of their own activity.

It can now be seen why the scientific world was so excited by Berger's discovery; for the first time we could "look in on" the intact human brain in action!

The great expectations first aroused by Berger's discovery have not yet been fulfilled. A tremendous amount of work has been done, but beyond a few basic facts the major value of *electroencephalography* (as this technique came to be known) has been to help detect the locus of tumors and other pathologies of the brain. Indeed the brain surgeon would find it impossible to get along without the E.E.G. (the abbreviation for "electroencephalograph"). However, the few facts which have been established are of fundamental importance in advancing our understanding of the physiological basis of mental phenomena.

INCESSANT NATURE OF BRAIN WAVES. One of the first important facts discovered by this technique was that spontaneous electrical activity may be recorded from the human brain whether a person is awake or asleep, excited or relaxed, and even during moderately deep anesthesia. The amplitude and form of the brain waves may change with these various conditions, *but activity is incessant* (see Fig. 112). Only the most extreme conditions of deficient blood supply to the brain or near lethal anesthesia will abolish all signs of electrical activity in the cortex. The brain is an ever-active organ.

THE ALPHA WAVE. Another important fact which was soon discovered is that the most prominent electrical activity of the normal human cortex consists of a constant and rhythmic series of waves occurring at about 10 per second (see the "relaxed" E.E.G. in Fig. 112). These waves are referred to as the *alpha waves.* This feature of the normal E.E.G. is constant enough so that any sharp deviation from it is a positive indication that something is happening in the brain. What causes the appearance of the alpha rhythm?

In the cortex of the brain there are thousands and thousands of nerve cells interconnected by an exceedingly complex network of nerve fibers. Therefore each cell acts not as an independent unit, but only as a part of a large system. The first fact to remember is that these cells are almost never at "rest" for any long period of time. As we have already pointed out several times in Chapter 7, nerve cells (whether in the retina, the cochlea, the nose, etc.) are not just passive instruments waiting to be discharged by some stimulus, but show intermittent spontaneous activity; they are almost always firing "on their own." Because the cells of the cortex are so interrelated, the firing of one cell affects the state of many hundreds of other cells. Apparently what happens is that, through this closely knit interrelationship, many different cortical cells tend to get into step and fire together in organized synchrony. This spontaneous electrical activity from a given brain area may thus appear as a series of simple rhyth-

mic waves, even though each wave represents the change in electrical energy occurring among thousands of individual cells.

BRAIN WAVES, CONSCIOUSNESS, AND ATTENTION. Any drop in general consciousness is almost immediately reflected in a change in the E.E.G. (see Fig. 112 again.) As we enter a drowsy and then a deep sleep stage, the characteristic rhythm of the alpha wave disappears and is replaced by slower, irregular waves.

Changes in the brain waves, similar to those brought about by sleep, can also be induced by damage to the ascending reticular system as has been demonstrated by the experiments of Lindsley, Bowden, and Magoun (1949). It will be remembered from Chapter 7 that the functions of the neural impulses from the ascending reticu-

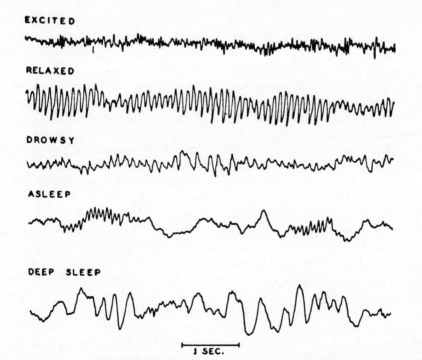

EXCITED

RELAXED

DROWSY

ASLEEP

DEEP SLEEP

⊢ 1 SEC. ⊣

FIG. 112. Brain waves typical of various states of alertness. Note the change in shape and frequency of the brain waves as the relaxed individual becomes excited or as he falls asleep. The frequency can be judged with the help of the one-second marker. (From Jasper, 1941.)

lar system were to *alert* the cortex so that it could make a normal perceptual response to stimuli.

Thus the results of E.E.G. records taken during sleep and the experiments on the ascending reticular formation both testify that the state of the brain waves is related to the state of the consciousness or awareness of the person and his ability to maintain a normal perception of the world about him. A normal Alpha wave indicates an alert, conscious individual ready for mental activity.

BRAIN WAVES AND MENTAL ACTIVITY. As soon as such an alert person engages in sustained mental activity, there is an immediate change in his alpha rhythm. If a person is told to attend to a visual stimulus, if he is given a "mental arithmetic" problem to solve (Davis and Davis, 1936), or even if he is told, while under hypnosis, to "see a light" (Jasper, 1941), the alpha wave is normally reduced in amplitude. But perhaps the most dramatic evidence that the E.E.G. gives an indication of the neurological events that accompany mental activity is found in the so-called "conditioning" studies. It has been demonstrated that as a person learns that one stimulus (e.g., sound) always precedes another (e.g., light), his brain waves change: when the *sound* comes on, the alpha wave from his *visual* cortex drops in amplitude. The E.E.G. permits us to "see," as it were, what happens in the brain when a person anticipates a perception! (See Box 133.)

It may seem queer, at first, that attending to a visual stimulus, thinking through a mental arithmetic problem, imagining a light, anticipating a percept, should *reduce* the amplitude of the alpha rhythm rather than enhance it. But when we remember that the alpha wave represents the spontaneous and synchronized discharge of thousands of cortical cells, we can understand why the alpha wave will be of maximum amplitude and regularity only when the cortex is relatively free from neural impulses originating from the outside. Neural impulses coming from sensory cells in the eye, ear, etc. will disturb or "desynchronize" the spontaneously established rhythm of the "resting" brain. In any event, the evidence is clear that mental activity (perceiving, imagining, thinking, anticipating) is accompanied by a change in the alpha wave.

Muscular Activity and Mental Phenomena. As we have already pointed out, the changes in the brain waves which accompany images, attention, and mental work of all kinds are only part of the story. Muscular activity also plays a significant role in "pure thought."

Experimental evidence suggests that we can differentiate at least two kinds of such muscular activity: a *general* over-all increase in muscular tension which seems to involve the whole body; and a *localized* increase in tension limited to that particular muscle-group closely related to the content of the accompanying mental activity. Each of these seems essential for thinking, problem-solving, and learning, and each may play a somewhat different role.

GENERAL MUSCLE TENSION. Some degree of general tension accompanies all mental activity. It is true that Mr. Anyman sometimes sits "quietly" as he thinks, but he sometimes paces restlessly or insistently drums with his fingers until Mrs. Anyman is driven to distraction. And we have all observed Youngster Anyman as he laboriously writes out his spelling lesson. He grimaces, screws his head sideways, wraps one leg about the other; he is "thinking." But whether the person goes through these more noticeable contortions or not, experimental observations would seem to suggest that *some degree of general tension is always present during thinking.*

BOX 133

Brain Waves and Anticipation

Jasper and Shagass of McGill University have demonstrated (in a "conditioned response" experiment) that learning is accompanied by changes in the alpha-wave pattern.

The following procedure was used with 34 subjects: Two electrodes were cemented to the subject, one on the scalp, immediately over the right occipital area of the brain, and the other to the ear (this was the "neutral" wire). Wires led from the electrodes to an ink-writing oscillograph so that the brain waves from the *occipital (visual) area of the cortex* could be recorded. The subject lay on a bed in a completely dark, sound-proof, electrically shielded room. Several *sound stimuli* were presented and brain wave records taken. Then after 5 or 6 such trials, a *light stimulus* came on about .7 seconds after the sound stimulus had started. The sound and light overlapped for 5.3 seconds.

The sound stimulus alone produced no noticeable effect on the rhythm or amplitude of the alpha waves *from the occipital area.* The light stimulus, of course, showed a very strong effect. After very few combinations of sound followed by light, the sound alone resulted in the very same change in the alpha wave previously evoked by the light. The subject had learned that shortly after the sound came on, the light would appear, and this *expectation* of a light resulted in the typical brain wave that accompanies an *actual light stimulus.*

In the next column are shown three brain wave records from this experiment: the first shows the brain waves in response to the sound alone; the second shows the brain waves after two trials of light *plus* sound; and the third shows the brain waves after nine such trials.

CONTROL

Sound

TRIAL 2

Sound

Light

TRIAL 9 CR

Sound

10 SEC.

Note that at first (curve labelled "control") the onset of sound alone does not change the occipital alpha wave. When light and sound are on, the alpha wave is depressed in amplitude. In trial 9, the onset of sound *alone* depresses the alpha wave.

JASPER, H., and SHAGASS, C. 1941. Conditioning the occipital alpha rhythm in man. *J. exp. Psychol., 28,* 373–88.

This has best been demonstrated by Jacobson (1938) who, through an elaborate training process (called "progressive relaxation") was able to relax his subjects to the point where practically no action potentials could be picked up from any muscles, i.e., muscle tension was at a minimum. When completely relaxed, his subjects did not fall asleep but their imagery and thinking processes "dwindled and disappeared."

Several of his subjects found it impossible to imagine or recollect anything without showing some increase in muscle tension.

LOCALIZED MUSCLE TENSION. Evidence indicates that the *localized* muscle tensions which accompany images differ, in a systematic manner, according to the *modality, content,* and *vividness* of the image.

On the basis of an extensive series of action-potential studies, many of which have been duplicated in other laboratories by other experimenters, Jacobson (1938) has shown that the *content* of the image is reflected in the *specific pattern* of muscular tensions. For example, when the person imagines looking at the Eiffel Tower, the activity-pattern of the muscles that move the eye is practically identical with the pattern for actually looking upward. When the person imagines or recalls the performance of a "muscular" task, contraction occurs in those muscles which would naturally engage in the actual performance of the act. And the pattern is quite specific: if the person imagines that he is pumping a tire, the minute muscular contractions of his arm show a rhythmic pattern; if he imagines he is throwing a baseball, there is only one burst of microscopic muscular contractions in his right arm.

Other experimenters have found that the more *vividly* an image is experienced, the *greater is the muscular tension* of the appropriate muscle-group (see Box 134). In general, then, the evidence seems fairly clear that there is a high correlation between subjective experience and muscular tension-patterns.

Brain and Muscle. A correlation, we know, does not necessarily indicate anything about cause-and-effect. Do these muscular contractions have any effect on what goes on in the brain, or are they merely "useless" by-products of brain action? Do they contribute anything to imagining, re-membering, thinking, or are they without functional significance in adaptive behavior? Before we can indicate the significance of the correlation between muscular tension and experience we must know something about the anatomy and physiology of muscular contraction.

NEURAL CONTROL OF MUSCULAR CONTRACTION. As we have already seen in Chapter 12, muscles fall into two groups: striated and smooth. Since most of the research on muscle tonus and mental activity has concerned itself with the striated muscles, we shall restrict our discussion to this group.

In the healthy organism, striate muscle tissue, even when the individual is "relaxed," is normally in a state of slight contraction called *muscle tonus.* Such muscle tonus disappears completely when all neural connections to the muscles are cut. The reason for this is clear. The muscle fiber will contract only when stimulated by a neural impulse which comes to it via a motor nerve. *The tonus of striate muscles depends upon the activity of the motor nerves which supply them.*

Numerous investigations indicate that the *motor area* of the cerebral cortex and the cerebellum are in primary control of the motor nerves. These two parts of the brain, through integrated action, initiate neural impulses in motor cells. These impulses then travel down the motor nerves to the muscles, which react with slight contractions (tonus), or major contractions (movement).

Let us first see how the cerebellum and the cerebrum are interrelated to permit a cooperative control of muscle action. In the first place, both of them receive a large neural input from the various sense organs of the body. The cerebellum, for example, receives not only kinesthetic and vestibular impulses, but also tactual, visual, and auditory impulses. In the second place, the cerebral hemispheres and the cerebellum are

BOX 134

Imaginal Weight Lifting

Shaw at Columbia University investigated whether the amount of muscular tension varied with the magnitude of an *imagined* performance and with the *vividness* of the image.

The subject sat at a table with his arm resting comfortably on the top. Electrodes from his arm led off to an oscillograph. When the oscillograph indicated that the subject's arm was relaxed, the tests were begun. The experimenter presented the subject with one of 5 boxes to lift. Although all the boxes looked alike, their weights varied from 100 to 500 grams. After lifting the weight, he again received instructions to relax. When the oscillograph indicated relaxation, the subject was asked "to image lifting the weight just lifted." He was then asked whether his image had been vague, fair, clear or vivid. He was given another weight, and the cycle continued, each weight being tested several times. During the imagined lifting the subject's arm was, of course, lying in complete rest.

Some sample results:

1. The activity of the muscle of the arm (as measured by the oscillograph) during imagined weight lifting *increases in magnitude as the imagined weight increases*. (See top fig.)

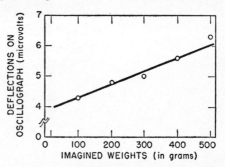

2). The greater the reported *vividness* of the image, the greater the amount of *muscular activity*. (See fig. below.)

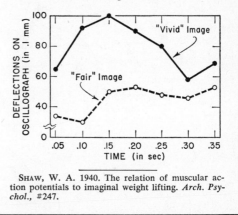

SHAW, W. A. 1940. The relation of muscular action potentials to imaginal weight lifting. *Arch. Psychol.*, #247.

connected by nerve fibers which carry messages from one to the other. For example, the auditory and visual areas of the cerebellum are connected with the auditory and visual areas of the cerebrum, and the motor area of the cerebral cortex is connected with most areas of the cerebellum. Thus the cerebellum and cerebral cortex receive somewhat the same sensory signals, and are so well interconnected that they can coordinate the motor messages they send to the muscles. How do they transmit such messages?

In and around the motor area of the cerebral cortex are found large pyramid-shape cells called *Betz cells*. These Betz cells together with other cortical cells send their fibers, bunched together into one large bundle called the *pyramidal tract*, down to the spinal cord. Here connections are made with other motor cells which, leaving the cord, end in the various muscles of the body (see Fig. 113). Therefore, whenever a cell or group of cells in the motor area is stimulated, some muscle or other will eventually contract.

In addition to the "pyramidal system" there is a so-called *extrapyramidal system*. It also originates in the motor and adjacent areas of the cortex and ends finally in the

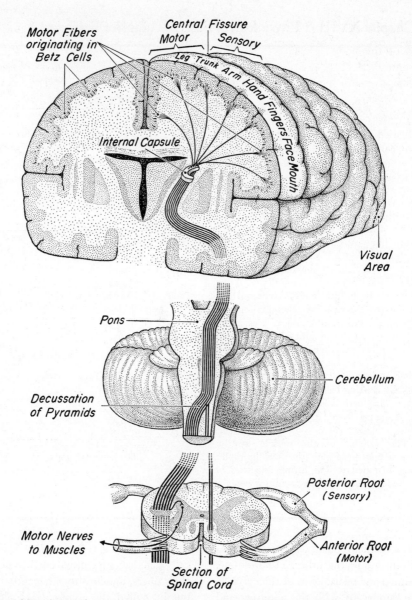

Motor Fibers
originating in
Betz Cells

Central Fissure
Motor   Sensory

Leg Trunk Arm Hand Fingers Face Mouth

Internal Capsule

Visual
Area

Pons

Cerebellum

Decussation
of Pyramids

Posterior Root
(Sensory)

Motor Nerves
to Muscles

Anterior Root
(Motor)

Section of
Spinal Cord

FIG. 113. Motor area of cortex and pyramidal tract. The major *motor area* of the cortex lies on the surface of the brain just in front of the central fissure of the brain. As the diagram indicates, different parts of this area are responsible for the control of different parts of the body musculature. Thus the very top part sends fibers to the leg, the side part, to the mouth, etc. (The motor cortex for only the left hemisphere is shown in the diagram. The right hemisphere has a similar motor area.) Lying fairly deep in this cortical area are the giant *Betz cells* from which originate fibers collected together in a bundle, called the *internal capsule*, deep within the brain. From here the fi-

bers, called the *pyramidal tract*, travel down the brain and into the brain stem. Before entering the spinal cord most of the fibers (between 75 and 80 per cent) decussate (cross over) to the other side, while some of the fibers continue down the same side. Once the pyramidal tract enters the spinal cord, fibers from the tract "peel off" at various levels to make connections with motor nerves. These motor nerves leave the spinal cord through the *anterior root* and connect with various skeletal muscles of the body.

This is the major pathway over which motor impulses travel from the motor cortex of the brain to the musculature of the body.

muscles of the body. These two systems have somewhat different functions. The pyramidal system controls the discrete, fine, movements (such as are typical of motor skills), while the extrapyramidal system controls grosser movements as well as the inhibition of movements.

The cerebellar cortex also contains large specialized cells called *Purkinje cells*. The fibers from these cells go deep into the cerebellum where they make connections with other cells which send on their fibers, via various connections, to the musculature of the body.

The musculature is even more complexly controlled than would be indicated by Figure 113. For example, one experimenter (Sperry, 1947) inflicted a large number of crisscrossed cuts across a monkey's motor cortex, thus destroying some motor cells and many of their cross connections, which presumably controlled the monkey's muscles. The monkey, after first showing some loss in control of voluntary movement, soon regained muscular control—in a surprisingly short time. If the whole motor cortex is cut away, the animal loses *fine* motor control permanently—but not gross motor control. This, and other work on the recovery of voluntary movement after injury to the motor areas, strongly suggests that gross muscular contractions are to a considerable degree under the control of the *brain as a whole*. Whether a muscle will be sent a neural impulse or not depends, in part, upon what is going on in the entire brain, and is not a function only of the "motor cells." *In an intact individual, the maintenance of tonus as well as the initiation of voluntary movements is controlled by the integrative action of the higher brain centers.*

From the E.E.G. data we have seen that the brain is an ever-active organ whose patterned neural activity reflects changes in mental activity. And we have now seen that the patterned neural activity of the brain as a whole controls muscular activity. Here then is an outline of the anatomical and physiological mechanisms which make the correlation between *muscular tension* and *mental activity* possible and understandable.

MUSCULAR CONTROL OF NEURAL ACTIONS. We have seen in Chapter 7 that when a muscle contracts it stimulates the spindle cells and immediately sends neural impulses back to the brain. We have already mentioned at least two different effects of such a feed-back process: In the first place, a neural impulse coming to the brain, from whatever source, will change the pattern of neural activity in the cortex. This we have seen when considering the change in the alpha rhythm as a consequence of incoming sensory stimulation (see p. 486). We know that the mental states of a person (his images, percepts, expectations) are related to the pattern of neural activity in his cortex. Therefore, a change in muscle tension, by changing the pattern of neural activity in the cortex, may change the content of the person's experience. We have here a highly complicated pattern of brain-muscle interaction. The neural activity of the brain results in muscle contractions; muscle contractions change the pattern of the neural activity in the brain; and the attributes of our mental experience are determined by the resultant.

In the second place, we have seen in Chapter 7 that a sensory neural impulse, no matter what its source, sends some signals to the cortex through the ascending reticular formation, and thus has an overall alerting effect on the brain. Muscular contractions, especially of the more extensive general type and perhaps to a lesser degree of the localized type as well, may therefore, through stimulating the reticular formation, increase the alertness of the cortex to all environmental stimuli. Again we have a highly complicated pattern of brain-muscle interaction. The neural activity of the brain results in muscle contractions; muscle contractions result in an increased readiness of the brain to respond; and the adaptive behavior of the person is influenced by the resultant.

The above analysis is in part speculative. We lack information on many crucial points, both psychological and neurological. Nevertheless, the available data are consistent with this analysis. The correlations already discovered between brain waves and muscular tension encourage the belief that we may someday succeed in writing the story of the physiological correlates of mental states.

Problem-Solving and Physiological Correlates

In this section we shall consider the physiological correlates of creative problem-solving and learning, with special attention to acquisition. Research in this field has sought to answer two basic questions: (1) What lasting changes take place in the nervous system during acquisition? (2) Which part of the nervous system is primarily concerned in acquisition?

Changes in the Nervous System. The pattern of cortical activity in response to a stimulus is different after a person has acquired a new expectation or a new habit from what it was prior to such acquisition. This changed pattern lasts for a considerable time. This leads us to the conclusion that during training or problem-solving the nervous system is *altered in some lasting way.*

Much work has been devoted to the search for such lasting changes in the nervous system. It has been suggested that as an individual repeatedly responds in a systematic manner to a stimulus-pattern, *new connections are formed in the brain.* That is, the fibers of some brain cells may elongate or grow so that parts of the nervous system which formerly were indirectly connected become more firmly connected. This would help explain why behavior once executed is more readily performed at a later time. On the other hand, it may be that no such new growths occur. Rather, already existing connections may become more efficient through the *lowering of the thresholds* at the synapses, the point of functional contact between fibers from two nerve cells. In this way a pattern of neural impulses can travel more readily from one area of the nervous system to another.

Evidence for these hypotheses, and others, has been sought by the neurologist, the histologist (who examines the microscopic structure of nerve cells), and the experimental psychologist. But so far the answer to the question "What lasting changes take place in the nervous system during acquisition?" has eluded us. It may well be that the next great "breakthrough" in the biological science of behavior will be the discovery of how the nervous system is physically changed as learning goes on.

The positive findings resulting from all the experimental work which has been done concern themselves with the second question—which part of the nervous system is primarily concerned in acquisition?

Most attention on this problem has been paid to the highest level of the nervous system—the cerebral cortex of the brain. Some research has been done on the subcortical levels of the brain (the parts of the brain underneath the cortex), and some even on the spinal level (the question being whether any learning can take place without involving the brain).

Spinal Learning. Learning on the spinal level has been investigated with the simplest kind of acquisition—conditioned-response learning. Such experimentation has been restricted to animals, since we must have a subject whose brain has been surgically "disconnected" from the part of the body to be trained, although human paraplegic patients (in whom the lower half of the body has been "disconnected" from the brain by a spinal injury) could also be studied.

The basic technique in these studies is fairly simple. Under surgical anesthesia the spinal cord of the animal is cut completely through, thus severing the neural connections between the lower part of his body and the brain. Such an animal is called a "spinal" animal, and with proper care can be kept alive for years. During the postoperative period conditioned-response training is instituted. Both the stimuli and the responses for the conditioning training must be carefully chosen so as to involve only the lower part of the body. (Visual and auditory stimuli cannot, of course, be used in such training since this would involve the brain.) If the spinal animal, under these circumstances, is able to acquire a conditioned response we would have evidence that simple acquisition is possible without the help of the brain. In this case, presumably, the integration of the incoming sensory stimuli and the outgoing motor impulses would be wholly under the control of the spinal cord.

The results from such experiments are somewhat ambiguous. One group of experimenters (Culler and Shurrager, 1940) have reported that with appropriate training, isolated muscles in the dog's leg can be conditioned to "twitch" when the dog's tail is shocked. Other experimenters have failed to find evidence for conditioning (see Box 135). More research is obviously needed before we can answer the question.

In any event, if acquisition can take place under the control of the spinal cord

alone, it is most probably restricted to the simplest kind of "muscle twitches." Certainly for acquisition of the complex responses involved in the adaptive behavior of man and beast, the spinal cord is not enough. We must therefore look to the brain for the locus of most learning.

Subcortical Learning. The levels next above the spinal cord where we might find the locus of the control of learning are the subcortical structures of the brain. Can learning take place there, without the help of the cerebral cortex?

Here again we must restrict our experimental work to animals, since we must have "decorticated" subjects. Under deep anesthesia the animal's skull is opened and the *entire* cortex is either cauterized, or stripped away. Usually this requires several successive operations. Rats, cats, and dogs can be kept alive and fairly healthy for long periods of time after such an operation, and their learning capacities can therefore be tested. Monkeys and the higher primates cannot survive these operations and so we simply have no information on them.

Almost all experimenters agree that decorticate animals can show some signs of learning in simple problem-situations. One experimenter (Bromiley, 1948) was able to train a completely decorticate dog to avoid a shock to his leg by flexing it when a whistle was sounded. He was also then able to extinguish this response and retrain the dog to flex his leg to the onset of a light. The dog survived 33 months without a cerebral cortex but his behavior remained at a very low level of complexity. For the first twenty post-operative days he had to be given water by means of a stomach tube before he could learn to lap it from a pan held under his nose. He was able to swallow pieces of meat placed on the back of his tongue, but it took him more than four months to relearn to eat food from a pan.

BOX 135

Can the Spine Learn?

Kellogg and his associates at Indiana University attempted to condition 4 spinal dogs —with negative results.

During conditioning the dog was placed in a "stock" where his chin rested upon a shelf and his chest in a hammock. The *unconditioned* stimulus was a 2-second electric shock to his *right* hind foot calling forth an automatic flexor movement of that limb. The *conditioned* stimulus was a similar shock to his *left* hind foot; it preceded the unconditioned stimulus by 1 second.

Prior to the operation the dogs were given 400 conditioning trials. Long before the end of this training, the animals flexed their *right* limb when their *left* foot was shocked. They were then operated on, their spinal cord was severed, and after complete recovery from the anesthetic (about 2 or 3 hours) the conditioning training was continued.

Was the conditioned response *retained* after the spinal cord was cut, and if not, could the animal re-acquire it with further training?

The answer to both questions was "No." *After 1,000 post-operative trials* (spread over 5 days) *there was no evidence of any conditioning.*

An additional fact was noted which might help explain Culler and Shurrager's "contradictory" results (see text). When the spinal dog's *left* foot was shocked, not only did that limb automatically flex, but muscles in *various* parts of the dog's body would also twitch. Therefore Kellogg suggests that what Culler and Shurrager *thought* was a conditioned response in the isolated muscle of the leg, was merely a part of the automatic, *unlearned* spread of muscle twitches in response to a shock on the tail.

The life of the experimenter is beset with pitfalls.

KELLOGG, W. N., DEESE, J., PRONKO, N. H., and FEINBERG, M. 1947. An attempt to condition the chronic spinal dog. *J. exp. Psychol., 37,* 99–117.

"Late in his career he showed some evidence of cleaning his chest but had to be bathed regularly. No behavior which could be interpreted as pleasure or fear reactions was noted."

It would appear then, that at least among such animals as dogs and cats, the cortex is not needed for the acquisition of the most primitive kinds of problem-solving— very simple conditioned responses and sensory discriminations. For these the subcortical mechanisms alone may be sufficient. But the subcortical mechanisms alone do not seem sufficient for the acquisition, retention, and control of the more complex patterns of behavior which characterize the adaptive organism.

Cortical Learning. It appears obvious that we will, in the cerebral cortex, find the major locus of complex adaptive behavior.

For we are at the end of the road, there is no place else to go. The very complexity of the cortex suggests that we have found the right spot. The number of neural cells in the cerebral cortex has been estimated to be greater than nine billion. These nine billion cells can fire in an astronomical number of different groupings and sequences. We have here all the complexity needed for integrative action. It would seem that the cerebral cortex *must* be the locus of learning and problem-solving.

But this is not necessarily so. All that we have demonstrated is that the centers below the cerebral cortex cannot *alone* provide the neurological basis for acquisition. It is still possible that even the most complex forms of learning and problem-solving depend upon these lower centers *in conjunction with the cerebral cortex.*

Actually this possibility is the one favored

by many contemporary workers in the field. The long search for the "place" where learning occurs is no longer directed toward finding a specific, sharply delimited "point-locus." Any acquisition may involve simultaneous changes in the cerebral cortex, subcortical bodies, spinal cord, and perhaps even peripheral nerve-endings in the sensory organs and muscles. What the experimenter does when he studies the relation between the cerebral cortex and learning is to "tap" *one point of a complex circuit.* Keep this clearly in mind as you study the following paragraphs.

THE PROBLEM OF CORTICAL LOCALIZATION. Are different kinds of learning and problem-solving dependent upon different areas of the cortex? In a sense we are asking the same question which Gall and Spurzheim asked (and answered affirmatively) in 1810.

Experimental work in the last 100 years has led to various suggestions concerning cortical localization of intellectual functions. These have ranged from specificity hypotheses (in the tradition of Gall and Spurzheim) to complete nonspecificity ones (in the tradition of Flourens).

"EQUIPOTENTIALITY" AND "MASS ACTION." Shepard Ivory Franz and Karl S. Lashley, American psychologists, are the two men most closely associated with contemporary "nonspecificity" theory. Lashley has proposed two principles which he believes describe the way that problem-solving is related to the cerebral cortex.

(1) The principle of "equipotentiality" asserts that, except for the primary sensory and motor areas of the brain, any one part of the cerebral cortex can do whatever any other part can do. That is, all parts are potentially equal in function. (2) The "mass action" principle asserts that the adaptive capacity of a brain-injured animal is determined by the total amount of cerebral cortex he has left. (See the conclusion of Flourens in 1824—p. 482.)

These two principles add up to the assertion that *all parts of the cortex are equally involved in learning and problem-solving.* Lashley supports his views with the results of his extensive cortical-ablation (destruction) experiments in the rat. In these experiments he found that as far as the rat's learning ability was concerned, the *specific part* of the cortex destroyed was of little consequence. A lesion in one part of the brain had the same effect as an equally large lesion in another part of the brain (the "equipotentiality" principle). The animal's learning was retarded in proportion to the *amount* of cortex destroyed. A large lesion had a more profound deteriorating effect than a small lesion (the "mass action" principle). For a brief summary of this experimental work, see Box 136.

These two principles seem to hold for the various subsidiary processes involved in problem-solving. For example, as we have seen, the ability of the individual to *vary* his responses is extremely important in problem-solving. Many clinical observations on brain-injured people have shown that the ability to vary responses is interfered with when parts of the cerebral cortex are destroyed. Experimental work with animals has further shown that there is no one part of the cortex upon which this ability is dependent, but, again, the animal's variability is decreased in proportion to the *amount* of the cortex destroyed, irrespective of the location of the destruction. (See Box 137.)

To the question: "Which part of the cerebral cortex is the locus of learning and problem-solving?", Lashley would answer: "Every part."

ALTERNATIVE INTERPRETATIONS. Most biologists agree that the excision technique is not ideally designed to enable us to investigate the function of the part excised or removed. This is due, primarily, to the great power of *compensation* inherent in all living organisms. For example, we have

BOX 136

The Brain-Injured Rat

In 1929 Lashley published his major research report, *Brain Mechanisms and Intelligence*, which rapidly became the most influential book in the field. We shall give a very brief summary of one part of its contents.

Using 1-, 3-, and 8-unit alley mazes, Lashley tested 37 rats with brain lesions differing in *size* (from 1.5 per cent to 81.2 per cent of the cortex) and in *locus* (every part of the cortex being explored). Normal animals were also tested for comparison data.

His results indicated that:

1) As the mazes increase in complexity, the difference between the learning ability of the normal rats and the brain-injured rats becomes more and more significant. The same lesions which have a relatively slight effect upon solving the simplest maze,

have a strikingly large effect upon the complex maze (see first figure). A small injury to the cortex may not be detected, therefore, except where the injured individual attempts to cope with a complex problem.

2) The efficiency of learning the maze is reduced in proportion to the extent of the cortex destroyed, *regardless of the locus of injury.* (See second figure.)

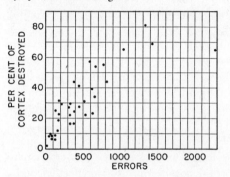

Each point on the graph represents one rat. Note that *in general,* the larger the lesion suffered by the rat, the greater the number of errors he made. Note also that there are wide individual differences in the effect of cortical lesions upon error scores.

Learning and problem-solving cannot be localized in any one part of the brain—in the rat.

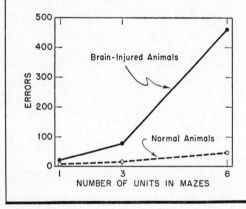

LASHLEY, K. S. 1929. *Brain mechanisms and intelligence.* Chicago: Univ. of Chicago Press.

seen that normal rats, in learning a maze, depend primarily upon vision. (See Box 117, p. 449.) But suppose, *not knowing this,* we excise the rat's eyes and test his maze learning. What do we find? The blind rat can quite readily learn the maze. We might be tempted to say, therefore, that vision plays no special role in maze learning. But of course it does. What happens is that when an animal is blinded, other senses (in this instance, olfaction) may take over the "guiding" functions formerly performed

by the visual sense. Much the same may be true for the cortex. In the intact person, learning and problem-solving may *normally* be localized in quite specific areas of the cortex. Removing these areas need not, however, completely demolish the acquisition *capacity* of the person. Almost any part of the brain *may* be able to function in learning or problem-solving even if normally it would not. This means that so-called "equipotentiality" results obtained in acquisition studies cannot be unambigu-

BOX 137

The Cortex and Variability in Behavior

Krechevsky while at the University of Chicago asked: "Suppose we have a problem with a simple *general* solution, permitting a large number of alternative specific solutions within it. How will a cortical injury affect the display of the alternative specific solutions?" (Note how this question is related to the description of creative problem-solving given on p. 396.)

Krechevsky tested 26 normal and 30 brain-injured rats in the Dashiell maze (see figure). Here a general "forward-going" response always brings the rat to the food-

box, but there are 20 different and equally long such paths. (The figure shows 3 of these paths.) Each rat was given 14 test trials (1 per day) and the number of *different* paths taken and the shifts among paths on consecutive days were used as measures of variability.

Lesions of various sizes and in various parts of the cortex were inflicted upon the 30 experimental animals. The results in the table below indicate that: (1) Brain-injured rats show a loss in the variety and flexibility of specific solutions displayed; and (2) the degree of loss is correlated with the *size* of the lesion, regardless of *locus*.

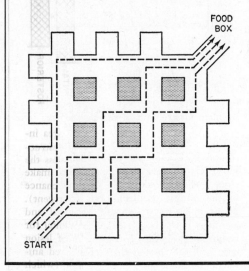

FOOD
BOX

START

	Av. No. of Diff. Paths Chosen	Av. No. of Shifts on Consecutive Days
Normal	5.46	5.77
Injured	3.00	2.19
Correlation	−.63	−.73

(The correlations are between the size of the lesion and the measures of variability. The −.63, for example, means that as the size of the lesion *increased*, the number of different paths taken *decreased*.) Thus variability, so important in problem-solving, is seen to be intimately dependent upon the functioning of the *entire* cortex.

KRECHEVSKY, I. 1936. Brain mechanisms and variability. *J. comp. Psychol.*, 23, 121–38.

ously interpreted. They may mean that there is no specific part of the cortex primarily involved in acquisition; or they may mean that *normally* there *is* a specific part of the cortex primarily involved in acquisition, but other parts of the cortex can substitute.

In addition, there are experimental findings which have cast doubt on the generality of Lashley's findings, and which have supported a partial specificity theory.

PARTIAL SPECIFICITY. The "equipotentiality" and "mass action" hypotheses were based primarily on the results of experi-

mental work with rats. But what is true of the rat brain may not be true of the more highly developed brains of monkeys and men. As Herrick, the eminent neurologist was wont to point out, "Men are bigger and better than rats."

Shortly after Lashley's work was published, ablation experiments were extended to the monkey. It was soon discovered that the monkey's cortex seemed to have more specificity of function than did the cortex of the rat. For example, a task necessitating a high degree of directed attention is greatly interfered with when lesions are

BOX 138

The Brain-Injured Monkey

Harlow, at the University of Wisconsin, was one of the pioneers in the use of monkeys for neurobehavioral research. In one series of studies either the anterior or posterior association areas (see figure below)

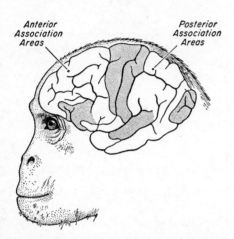

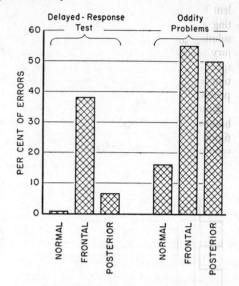

were destroyed in 8 monkeys who were then, together with 4 normal monkeys, tested on an extended series of problems. Among them were the "delayed-response" and "oddity" problems.

In the delayed-response problem the monkey, in his cage, watches the experimenter place food in one of two identical boxes. Then a screen is lowered between the monkey and the boxes. After several seconds the screen is raised and the monkey makes his choice. Here the monkey must pay strict attention while the box is baited and remember the position of that box during the delay. In the oddity problem, a tray, containing two identical and one odd object, is presented to the monkey and he is allowed to lift one. Underneath the *odd* object is a bit of food. The objects are changed from time to time and the monkey, in order to find the food, must learn always to choose the odd object of the three.

Some of the results are shown in the following figure. In the delayed-response problem, destruction of the *frontal* area increases the errors much more than destruction of the posterior area. Nevertheless the frontal-lesion animals do learn to make fewer errors than they would by chance alone (which would be about 50 per cent). In the oddity problem, both frontal and posterior lesions are equally detrimental for learning; but although either type of lesion results in the same scores, the injured animals still do better than chance (which would be about 67 per cent errors). Harlow concludes: ". . . different kinds of intellectual functions are differentially susceptible to lesions located in the frontal and posterior association areas . . . In no cortical association area have we found a lesion that completely destroys any intellectual function."

Some kinds of problem-solving can be localized to *some* degree, but no kind of problem-solving can be localized completely.

HARLOW, H. F. 1952. Functional organization of the brain in relation to mentation and behavior. In *The biology of mental health and disease.* New York: Paul B. Hoeber, Inc.

produced in the frontal areas of the monkey's brain. Lesions in other areas do not show the same degree of interference with this kind of problem-solving. (See Box 138.)

In addition to experimental work with the higher animals, numerous human cases have been studied during the last several decades. These cases include people with accidental brain injuries, World War II soldiers suffering from gunshot wounds in the brain, and patients who for one reason or another (e.g., tumors, schizophrenia) have had large parts of their cortex surgically removed or the connections of whole areas with the rest of the brain severed. The study of these people has corroborated, in general, the results of the work on the subhuman primates. The results point to some degree of specificity in the cerebral cortex. The exact nature of this specificity is in dispute. Some research workers believe that in the frontal lobes are to be found the centers for "reasoning," or for the "elaboration of conscious thought," or for "attentiveness." Other experimenters refuse to commit themselves to such specificity.

BY WAY OF SUMMARY. Perhaps the safest way of summarizing the present status of the question of brain localization is by the two following propositions:

1) *No one kind of learning or problem-solving is dependent solely upon one area of the cortex.* Almost every part of the cortex seems to be involved in every kind of learning and problem-solving. This is especially true of complex adaptive behavior. To this extent the original "equipotentiality" hypothesis is corroborated.

2) *The different areas of the cortex seem to play unequal roles for different kinds of problem-solving.* The various parts of the cortex do not contribute equally to every different learning task or problem-solution. We can "spare" certain cortical areas more readily than others. To this extent, the "equipotentiality" hypothesis is contradicted.

It appears, in short, that the ancient dispute between Gall and Flourens is going to end in a compromise. But the terms of the compromise cannot, at this date, be specified. They are being worked out in the laboratories and in the clinics.

Retention and Cortical Localization

Much the same neurological questions are asked about memory which are asked of learning and problem-solving: *What* and *where* in the nervous system is the "memory process?"

The answer to the *what* remains as before. We have no answer except to restate our belief that an acquisition that is retained must be represented by some sort of lasting structural change in the nervous system. Such structural changes must, furthermore, be susceptible to alteration by other neurological events. For retention, as we have seen, is influenced by other acquisitions and memories. But just what the neurological structural changes are which will meet the requirements we do not know.

The answer to the *where* has a somewhat different character when dealing with retention than when dealing with acquisition. The "specificity" point of view has a somewhat better case in the study of memory than in acquisition. This is especially true for the cerebral cortex of man.

While many psychologists and neurologists are wary of pointing to one area of the cortex (e.g., the frontal lobes) as the "seat of reasoning" they are somewhat more willing to point to specific cortical areas as playing special roles in retention.

"Psychic Blindness." The part of the cortex which has received much attention in this connection is the temporal lobe, the area of the cortex covering the side of the brain. Some experimenters have reported that the extirpation of the temporal lobes results in what might be called "psychic blindness": the animal suffers no visual disturbances, he can see all the objects about him, but he seems to have completely forgotten the *meanings* of the objects. For example, Klüver and Bucy (1939) reported that a monkey, whose two temporal cortexes had been removed, had only one way of determining whether or not an object was edible—by picking it up and tasting it. Visual "recognition" of the object was lost entirely. Thus such a monkey would pick up a live snake (the very sight of which had formerly terrified him) and put it in his mouth to see if it were fit to eat. This was true only of monkeys with *both* temporal lobe cortexes removed. Monkeys suffering other lesions showed no such "psychic blindness."

Aphasia. Data collected in the clinics from patients suffering from brain tumors and cerebral strokes which destroy cortical tissue have also been studied intensively. Many of these patients show very specific forms of memory-loss as a consequence of brain injury. (See Box 139.) When these specific memory losses are checked against the cortical damage suffered by the patients, the story is less clear. Two patients with quite similar lesions within the temporal lobes frequently show different behavioral symptoms.

Nevertheless almost all research workers and clinicians are willing to subscribe to a certain degree of localization as far as the retention of man's major skills and accumulated knowledge is concerned. Most of the work has been done with *aphasia* (the loss of memory for the *meaning* of words, see

Box 139) among brain-injured patients. From this work it appears that

1. The skill of speech is not represented equally in both cerebral cortexes. There seems to be "hemispheric localization." In some people (those who are right-handed) the left cortex may be dominantly involved in this highly integrated skill. In left-handed people, the *right* cortex may be dominant.

2. There is also area localization *within* the hemisphere. Aphasia seems to be correlated primarily with fairly localized injuries within the temporal lobe of the dominant hemisphere. Thus a right-handed man who suffers a cortical injury to the middle part of the temporal lobe on his left hemisphere may irretrievably "forget" the meaning of words.

Functional Organization of the Cortex

If we add together the experimental and clinical data for both acquisition and retention tests, we find considerable ambiguity and even inconsistency. Nevertheless, the data seem to bear the same general testimony: The cortex of man is highly integrated, but it is also differentiated. The brain is not one homogeneous "catch-all." *There is a measurable degree of functional specialization.*

But we should be clear as to what this specialization means. It does *not* mean that we have special parts of the brain serving as "problem-solving centers" (e.g., the frontal lobes), and other parts as "memory storehouses" (e.g., the temporal lobes). The psychological analysis in Chapter 15 of the interrelation between acquisition and retention would not lead us to expect, and the neurological data examined in this chapter do not support, such a differentiation.

BOX 139

The Brain-Injured Man

One of the most pathetic effects of a sizable injury to the human cortex is a disturbance in memory. Such disturbance need not be accompanied by any severe loss in sensory or general intellectual capacity. The patient can hear, see, and move, but *he has forgotten the meanings and uses of the objects in his perceived world.*

The neurologist divides such memory losses into three general types: agnosia, aphasia, apraxia.

1) *Agnosia* is the inability to recognize the formerly familiar. Seven different types (e.g., bodily, spatial, color, etc.) have been described. For example, in "bodily agnosia" the patient seems to have lost his own "body image," and, in addition, cannot recognize feet, ankles, shoulders, although other objects may offer no difficulties in recognition.

2) *Aphasia* refers to language disturbance. In "sensory aphasia" the patient has forgotten how to *formulate* words (although he can recognize them and knows their meanings as soon as he sees or hears them); or else he has forgotten the *meanings* of words and numbers. In "motor aphasia" he cannot *speak* the words. He understands what people are saying, he knows the words he wants to speak in reply, but he has simply forgotten how to make his vocal mechanism do what he wishes. He sits and utters monosyllables, or

a single word, or one name over and over again until he breaks down in frustration and defeat.

3) *Apraxia* refers to the inability to perform certain *purposeful* movements, aside from speech. For example, a patient when asked to put his tongue out tries to obey; he opens his mouth, but the tongue remains inert. In "spontaneous" movements (such as in licking his lips) the tongue may move about freely. The patient has "forgotten" how to bring his tongue under *voluntary* control.

The *specificity* of these disturbances has suggested that these lost meanings, skills, and responses must be localized in different parts of the cortex. Injuries to different parts could then result in different (yet quite specific) patterns of memory disturbances.

While this argument seems perfectly reasonable, the data do not support it. When patients suffering from agnosia, aphasia, and apraxia die, their brains are examined and the locus of their brain injuries are carefully described. Thus far we have failed to find any consistent relationship between the specific nature of the memory disturbance and the locus or size of the brain injury. However, such autopsies have given some support for a localization theory. Most of these patients are found to have injuries in the central part of their temporal lobes.

A General Formula and a Map. Perhaps the most general summarizing statement we can tentatively make about the specificity of the human cortex would be something like this: For some kinds of adaptive behavior (e.g., speech), acquisition and retention may be *primarily* centered in a specified part of the cortex. But most adaptive behavior is composed of many different sub parts and involves the integration of many other "bits" of adaptive behavior. Therefore, no one complex form of adaptive behavior can be *entirely* localized in such a

center, but probably extends over much of the cortex. How many major centers or "focal localization points" there are in the cortex, we do not know.

It should be clear, of course, that the statement refers only to the more complex adaptive behaviors. There can be very little doubt that the cortex is highly specialized as far as our *simple sensory* experiences are concerned. (See Chapter 7.)

If we are willing to combine tentative conclusions about adaptive behavior together with firm ones about sensory experience, we can draw a functional "map" of the human cortex which will look somewhat like Figure 114. It is perhaps a more conservative map than some scientists would be willing to draw, and, on the other hand, might be irreverently labeled a "phrenological chart" by a few extreme nonspecificists. It does, however, represent the conception held by many research

complexly interrelated structures. Much of the future research will no doubt be directed at these subcortical levels, especially the reticular formation. Such research may considerably change our view of the neurological control of behavior. Figure 114 may someday be regarded as a quaint construction.

The cortex by itself, apart from the rest

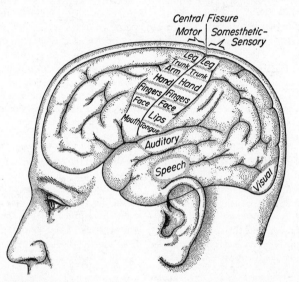

FIG. 114. The functional map of the cortex. Represented here are some of the more definitely established functional areas of the human cortex—both sensory (the areas which *receive* impulses from our sense organs) and motor (the areas which *initiate* impulses to the muscles)—together with the speech area in the temporal lobe. Note the vast extent of the motor area given over to the control of the movements of our arms, hands, and fingers—the organs of our body which are capable of the

finest manipulation. It should also be mentioned that the initiation of motor movements is not entirely restricted to the motor areas indicated here. There is some evidence that motor movements may be initiated from numerous other parts of the cortex as well. However, the motor areas labeled here are the most important for such initiation of impulses.

It might be of interest to compare this figure with the Gall and Spurzheim map of the brain as shown in the figure of Box 131.

workers of the functional organization of the human cortex, and may thus serve as a helpful tentative summary.

By Way of Summary. Regardless of the details, such a "brain-map" seems to justify the view that the seat of the mind is in the gray matter of the cortex. However we might end this chapter by reminding the reader that beneath the cortex are many

of the brain, is certainly not enough to provide the physiological basis for learning, problem-solving, thinking, and remembering. The brain itself, apart from the rest of the nervous system is not enough; the nervous system, by itself, apart from the musculature, is not enough. All biological phenomena show integration, but nowhere is this more profoundly true than in the adaptive behavior of living organisms.

Glossary

action potential. Changes in electrical energy (electrical waves) accompanying neural or muscular activity.

agnosia. The inability, following cortical injury (usually in the temporal lobe), to recognize the formerly familiar object. Thus in "bodily agnosia" the patient cannot recognize feet, ankles, shoulders, for what they are.

alpha wave. A constant and rhythmic series of brain waves occurring at about 10 per second in the normal relaxed person. Sometimes referred to as the "alpha rhythm" or the "Berger rhythm"—after the name of its discoverer.

anterior association area. The part of the cortex lying in front of the motor area.

aphasia. Language disturbance following cortical injury, usually in the temporal lobe. *Sensory* aphasia refers to the forgetting how to formulate words, or the meaning of words. *Motor* aphasia refers to the forgetting how to speak words.

apraxia. The inability, following cortical injury, to perform certain purposeful movements, aside from speech.

Betz cells. Large pyramid-shaped cells lying fairly deep in and around the motor cortex and from which originate the fibers that transmit neural impulses to the skeletal muscles of the body.

brain waves. Changes in action potentials, or electrical charges, accompanying neural activity in the brain. These changes can be detected by use of appropriate electrodes cemented to the skull and connected with an oscilloscope. On the oscilloscope these changes take the form of "waves." First described by Hans Berger, a neurologist in Jena.

decorticate animal. An animal whose entire cerebral cortex has been destroyed or removed.

electroencephalograph (E.E.G.). A record of brain waves. The technique of obtaining such records is called electroencephalography.

equipotentiality. The principle of equipotentiality, proposed by Lashley, asserts that, except for the primary sensory and motor areas of the brain, any one part of the cerebral cortex can do whatever any other part can do. All cortical areas are potentially equal in function.

extrapyramidal system. A system of fibers originating in the motor and adjacent areas of the cortex and ending in the muscles of the body. This system complements the pyramidal system and controls gross movements as well as the inhibition of movements.

mass action. The principle of mass action proposed by Lashley asserts that the capacity for learning and retention of a brain-injured animal is determined by the total amount of cerebral cortex the animal has remaining.

motor area of cortex. A strip of the cortex lying just in front of the central fissure. Different parts of this area are responsible for the major control of different parts of the bodily musculature. From this area neural impulses are sent to the various skeletal muscles of the body.

muscle tension or tonus. A state of muscular contraction. Sometimes this contraction is so slight as to be detectible only through the amplification of the accompanying action potentials. Most muscles are always in some slight degree of tension.

phrenology. A doctrine originally advanced by the physicians Gall and Spurzheim (1810) relating skull formations to behavior and character attributes of a person. Rests on 3 assumptions: (1) Different traits of a person are controlled by different areas of the cortex; (2) the larger the area of the cortex, the more pronounced is its associated behavior trait in the person; (3) the external shape of the skull reflects the shape of the brain underneath. Therefore by studying the shape of the skull the phrenologist believed he could discover the capacities and character of the person.

posterior association areas. The areas of the cortex lying between the sensory-somesthetic area and the occipital area.

psychic blindness. Refers to the inability of an animal (whose temporal lobes have been removed) to remember the "meaning" of objects. Such an animal seems to suffer very little visual disturbance, but cannot, through seeing the object, recognize its meaning.

Purkinje cells. Large specialized cells found in the cerebellar cortex which play an analogous role to the Betz cells. The fibers from the Purkinje cells go deep into the cerebellum where they synapse with other cells that send their fibers to the bodily musculature. Named after Johannes Purkinje, a Bohemian physician who first described these cells.

pyramidal tract. The motor fibers originating from the pyramid-shaped Betz cells in the motor area of the cortex and travelling down through the spinal cord. The major motor pathway from the brain. Controls the fine voluntary movements of the body.

spinal animal. An animal whose spinal cord has been cut through, thus severing all neural connections between the lower part of his body and the brain. A human patient who has suffered such an accident is called a "paraplegic."

subcortical levels. The areas of the cerebrum underneath the cerebral cortex.

temporal lobe. The lower side area of the cortex, lying just below the lateral fissure. Injuries in the temporal lobe frequently lead to various kinds of memory disturbances, "psychic blindness," aphasia, agnosia, etc.

Suggestions for Further Reading

HEBB, D. O. 1949. *The organization of behavior.* New York: Wiley.

An interesting attempt to construct a theory of brain function.

LASHLEY, K. S. 1929. *Brain mechanisms and intelligence.* Chicago: Univ. of Chicago Press.

The book that initiated the very active field of neurobehavioral studies among American psychologists. A clearly written experimental report.

STEVENS, S. S. (ed.) 1951. *Handbook of experimental psychology.* New York: Wiley.

Chapter 20 of this standard reference book presents a summary of the studies in the physiological bases of learning. Written by C. T. Morgan.

Part Four

THE INDIVIDUAL

CHAPTER XIX

Psychological Measurement

THE THEME of individual differences has recurred repeatedly throughout this book. We have discussed many measurable aspects of man: the speed with which he can learn nonsense syllables—and blissfully forget them; the facility of his creative problem-solving; the acuity of his pitch discrimination; the strength of his needs. These can be measured in behavioral indices or in physical units. But no matter what we measure, whenever two or more men are gathered together to be measured, there will be individual differences among them.

Perhaps nowhere is the *fact* of individual differences more accepted and its *interpretation* more disputed than in intelligence and personality. No one denies that some children learn their lessons more readily than others, that some men achieve more than their neighbors, that people differ from their fellows in character and temperament. On the basis of these differences in ability and personality a number of contradictory doctrines of man have been built.

There are those who would argue that all men are created equal in potential capacity. The fact of individual differences and differences among racial or national groups, or between the sexes, are interpreted to mean that *environmental* differences are all important. Equal opportunities for all will equate achievements and personality.

At the other extreme there are those who interpret individual differences to mean that *hereditary* influences are all important. The bright are born bright, the stupid, stupid, and the wicked, wicked; and no environmental manipulation can change them. There are, according to this view, biologically superior individuals, groups, nationalities, and races.

Between these two extremes, arguments have raged for centuries, and their outcome has influenced political, educational, and social policy. These matters are still being argued—but with one possible difference. We can now subject them to scientific inquiry.

To answer these questions scientifically, we must first have some way of *measuring* people's personality and intelligence. We must be able to do so reliably and validly. With measurement tools permitting us to do this, we can discuss rationally some of the bitterly fought social questions of the day. Without these simple statistical tools we cannot understand the scientific evidence on these problems and we can only revert to the same dreary prejudices and arguments that have held sway for so long.

To Mr. Anyman, the word "statistics" often means simple enumeration. The number of people killed on our highways annually or the number of births per year are the kinds of things which are usually called "statistics." But enumeration of events makes up only a very small part of statistics. The major part is made up of carefully worked-out *methods of analyzing numerical data.* Statistical methods permit us to summarize such data, to assess their reliability and validity, to generalize from observed events to new events. Statistical methods properly used are among the most powerful analytical tools of physics, astronomy, medicine, genetics, psychology, economics, sociology, political science, business, and almost every other human enterprise that can state its data in numbers. An understanding of simple statistics is almost as necessary for modern man as is the ability to read and write. And for the study of individual differences among men it is, of course, of *absolute* importance.

Quantifying Individual Differences

Our first task is to quantify the extent of individual differences. People differ in intelligence, but do they differ over a large or a small range? And how large does large have to be before it is "large"? We need measurement techniques that will per-

mit *numerical* statements if we are to carry out statistical operations.

Measurement techniques are not necessarily restricted to a narrow field of application. For example, the method of obtaining an "average" is the same whether we are interested in getting the average grade-point for the senior class, or the average number of cells in the occipital lobe of monkeys, or the average height of Russian soldiers.

People differ in height and weight as well as in personality. Measurement of individual differences in the former involves many of the same techniques as in the latter. Let us therefore start with the measurement of individual differences in height and weight. This is a relatively simple problem since our units of measurement (inches, pounds) are already familiar to us. We can then apply what we learn here to the more complex problems involved in the measurement of intelligence and personality.

Frequency Distribution. In 1923–24, there were 629 freshmen entering the University of Washington, and in due course they were weighed and measured. Their weights were recorded to the nearest full pound, and their heights to the nearest half inch. (See Box 140 for an explanation of "grouped" data.) The shortest freshman was 60.5 inches; the tallest, 76 inches. The lightest was 100 pounds; the heavyweight tipped the scales at 216 pounds. Here, then, are 1,258 numbers—inches and pounds—telling us a story of individual differences. If we are to read and understand this story, we must arrange these numbers in a simple and orderly way. The first step toward achieving this is to array them in *frequency tables.*

FREQUENCY TABLES. A frequency table is just what its name implies—a table that tells us how frequently certain values oc-

BOX 140
Grouped Data

In every investigation involving numerical quantities a "degree of accuracy" must be established, and every item must be recorded to this degree of accuracy. For example, in measuring the height of a freshman, should we record our measurement to the nearest ½ inch, $\frac{1}{100}$ inch, $\frac{1}{10,000}$ inch, or what? There is no end to the number of parts an inch can be divided into, yet we must stop somewhere if for no other reason than that the acuity of our instruments and eyes will soon fail us. Our stopping place (degree of accuracy) is determined, among other things, by the use we plan to make of the measurements. For some purposes it is

sufficient to know the freshman's height to the nearest inch (we "round off" the measurement to the nearest inch); for other purposes, to the nearest ½ inch, etc. .

Once we have recorded our measurements to the previously determined degree of accuracy, it is frequently desirable (for purposes of convenience and especially when dealing with large numbers of measurements) to group these "rounded off" values into *class intervals.*

Let us illustrate with some of our freshman data. Here we have rounded off to the nearest half inch, then made another grouping into *class intervals* of 1½ inches

Observed Measurements	Rounded Values	Class Interval	Number of Cases in Interval
76.2 inches	76.0		
75.8 "	76.0	76.0–75.0	3
74.9 "	75.0		
74.7 "	74.5		
74.2 "	74.0		
74.2 "	74.0	74.5–73.5	5
73.6 "	73.5		
73.5 "	73.5		

cur. Thus, from the array of data in Table 4 we can see that the heights between 71.5 and 70.5 inches occurred 64 times among the 629 freshmen, while heights between

68.5 and 67.5 occurred 156 times. The interval 68.5 to 67.5 is the "most popular" interval in the distribution, and is therefore called the *modal* class interval.

TABLE 4
Frequency Distribution of Heights of Entering Freshmen, University of Washington, 1923–24 (Gavett, 1925)

Inches	Number
76.0–75.0	3
74.5–73.5	5
73.0–72.0	43
71.5–70.5	64
70.0–69.0	148
68.5–67.5	156
67.0–66.0	115
65.5–64.5	51
64.0–63.0	33
62.5–61.5	8
61.0–60.0	3
	N = 629

TABLE 5
Frequency Distribution of Weights of Entering Freshmen, University of Washington, 1923–24 (Gavett, 1925)

Pounds	Number
220–210	1
209–199	3
198–188	5
187–177	16
176–166	35
165–155	82
154–144	129
143–133	162
132–122	138
121–111	44
110–100	14
	N = 629

FREQUENCY GRAPHS. We have already seen, in discussing the learning curve, that a graph has many perceptual advantages over a table. We can transform frequency tables into frequency graphs. There are two commonly used types of frequency graphs: *histograms* and *frequency curves.*

Figures 115 and 116 show how Tables 4 and 5 look when made into *histograms.*

Here the measurements are indicated along the horizontal base line; and frequencies, along the vertical axis. Figures 117 and 118 show the same data as *frequency curves* (or, more technically, "frequency polygons"). The only difference between histograms and frequency curves is that in constructing a frequency curve, instead of representing the data with a bar, a point is

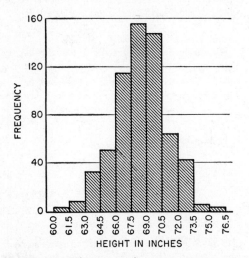

FIG. 115. Histogram of the distribution of heights among the 629 freshmen entering the University of Washington in 1923–24.

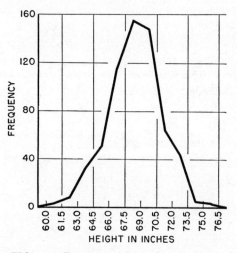

FIG. 117. Frequency curve for the data of Table 4. Note that each point is placed in the *middle* of the interval.

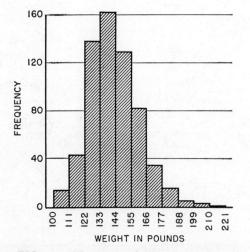

FIG. 116. Histogram of the distribution of weights among the 629 freshmen entering the University of Washington, 1923–24.

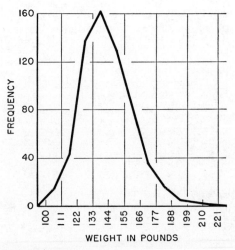

FIG. 118. Frequency curve for the data of Table 5. As in Fig. 117, each point is placed in the middle of the interval.

placed in the middle of each interval at the appropriate frequency value; then these points are connected.

SHAPES OF DISTRIBUTION CURVES. We now have a useful tool for describing the distribution of individual differences. Human traits, capacities, and behavior are distributed in *many* different ways. The *shape* of the frequency curve can tell us several interesting things about the nature of the individual differences portrayed. Sometimes the curve looks like an L, sometimes it looks like a rectangle, and sometimes it is so irregular as to defy a simple description (see Fig. 119). However the most com-

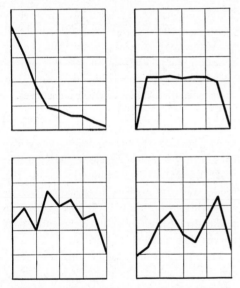

FIG. 119. Four less common shapes of distribution curves.

monly found shape looks somewhat like Figures 117 and 118.

The curves of Figures 117 and 118 can be described as more or less symmetrical: high toward the middle and tapering off gradually at either end. The curve for freshmen heights, however, is more symmetrical than that for their weights. A curve that departs from the symmetrical shape is called a *skewed* curve. Since curves can depart from perfect symmetry to a greater or lesser degree, we can speak of "degree of skewness" of a curve. The symmetry, or the degree of skewness of a frequency distribution curve, plays a very important part in statistical analysis of data.

Almost all measurements of behavior, learning performance, memory, intelligence, or sensory capacity give skewed frequency-distribution curves. This basic fact has significant implications for our understanding of the nature of individual differences among men. For one thing it emphasizes the caution with which we should use such concepts as the "average man" or "average intelligence."

Measures of Central Tendency. The word "average" is used by many of us as synonymous with "typical," "most frequent," or "representative." All these words refer to some kind of *central tendency*—a middle value between two extremes. When we attempt to give these words exact mathematical meaning, however, we find that they are synonymous *only when the distribution curve is perfectly symmetrical.* These "averages" can mean quite different things when the distribution curve is skewed—and we have just pointed out that almost all measurements of behavior give skewed curves.

MEAN, MODE, MEDIAN. There are three frequently used mathematical measures of central tendency. First, there is the familiar *arithmetic mean.* It is the arithmetic sum of all the values in a distribution divided by the number of cases. Put as a formula, it is written $M = \dfrac{\Sigma X}{N}$. M stands for the arithmetic mean; the Greek capital letter Σ, for "sum of"; X, for the individual values; and N, for the number of cases. Thus, the 629 freshmen, all told, weighed 89,475 pounds. ΣX is therefore 89,475; N is 629; and M, the arithmetic mean, is found by dividing

ΣX by N, which gives us 142.25 pounds. Rounding this off to the nearest pound we get 142 pounds. The same kind of calculation for the freshmen heights gives us an arithmetic mean of 68.0 inches.

The second measure of central tendency is the *mode*. When we say that Jim McGraw is a freshman of "average height," we may mean that Jim is of that height which occurs most frequently among freshmen. This meaning of "average" (the typical) is quite common. We can get a good estimate of the modes for the freshmen's heights and weights from either the histograms or the frequency curves. The histograms (Figs. 115 and 116) suggest that the mode for height will fall somewhere in the class interval between 67.5 and 68.5 inches (as can also be seen from Table 4, and as is represented in Figure 115 by the bar on the 67.5-69.0 position), while that for weight, between 133 and 143 pounds. But we can approximate the modes a bit closer than that. We assume that they will fall halfway along their respective modal class intervals. This will give us for height, 68.0 inches (which is halfway between 67.5 and 68.5 inches) and for weight, 138 pounds (which is halfway between 133 and 143 pounds).

The third measure is called the *median*. When we say that Tony Morales is of "average" height, we may mean that he is neither short nor tall, but exactly in the middle. Thus, if the 629 freshmen were lined up in order of height with the shortest man at one end and the tallest at the other, Morales would be the 315th man—314 men being shorter and 314 taller. His height would be called the median height. It is a simple matter to array, count up, and find the median of a distribution. Doing this, with our material, we find the median for weight (rounded off) to be 141 pounds; for height (rounded off), 68.0 inches.

We now have three different "average

freshmen" entering the University of Washington in 1923, as indicated in Table 6.

TABLE 6

The "Average Freshman" as a Function of the Central Tendency Measure Used

Measure Used	Height	Weight
Arithmetic Mean	68.0 inches	142 pounds
Mode	68.0 "	138 "
Median	68.0 "	141 "

Two points should be noted from the data in Table 6. First, whether Jim McGraw or Tony Morales or some third person is the "perfect average freshman" as far as *weight* is concerned, depends upon which measure of central tendency we use. Second, as far as *height* is concerned, all three measures give the same value (after rounding off). The reason for this difference between weight and height is found in the shapes of the two distribution curves.

The height curve is fairly close to a symmetrical shape; the weight curve is definitely skewed. It is clear that in a symmetrical curve the mid-point along the base line *must* represent the arithmetic mean, the mode, and the median. In a skewed curve these three values can be at three different points. In Figure 120 we have presented two curves that make this clear.

The meaning of "average man" or "average intelligence," therefore, may refer to any one of three different measures of central tendency, each with a different value and each mathematically correct. Each measure has certain advantages and certain disadvantages. The arithmetic mean is strongly influenced by the values of the extreme items, whereas this is not true for the mode and the median. And sometimes the extreme values are "unnatural" ones and should not be allowed to play their full influence. For example, suppose four students earn scores of 75, 80, 80, and 85 on an examination. The mean, mode, and me-

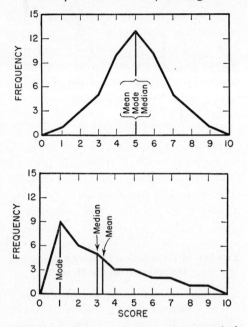

FIG. 120. These two curves, one symmetrical and one skewed, indicate the different locations of the 3 measures of central tendency. Note that in the symmetrical curve the mean, mode, and median must be at the same point (value 5), whereas in the skewed curve they occupy 3 different points: the mode has a value of 1; the median, 3; and the mean, about 3.4.

dian for this group is 80. Now suppose a fifth brother joins the group—an unfortunate brother who overslept, came late to the examination and earned only 15 points on the examination. The mean of this group of five is now 67; the mode and median, however, remain at 80. To say that this fraternity group of five "averaged" 67 seems a bit misleading. This low average is due to the accidental fault of one man. If we wish to get an average that will reflect every score including the extremes, we use the arithmetic mean; if we wish one that will not be influenced by extreme scores, we use either the mode or the median.

CENTRAL TENDENCY AND DISPERSION. If the *only* thing we know about a group is its average, our best guess as to what the group is like would have to be stated in terms of

the average. But this can sometimes lead to serious errors. For example, suppose we have the following two sets of scores made by two groups of contestants in a dart-throwing game:

8,8,9,9,9,9,10,10 and 3,5,7,9,9,11,13,15.

Both distributions are symmetrical, and for both groups the average is 9, whether measured by the mean, mode, or the median. It is clear, however, that the two groups are quite dissimilar in one very important respect. In the first group the scores cluster closely together; in the second, the individual scores are widely scattered or dispersed. An average is not enough, we must also have information on the degree of dispersion of the scores in the group.

Measures of Dispersion. For a quick, qualitative impression of the degree of dispersion, a look at the frequency distribution curves is usually enough. For example, in Figure 121 are two distributions having the

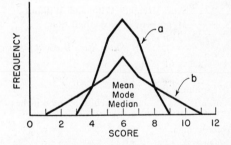

FIG. 121. Two distribution curves, both symmetrical, both having the same mean, median, and mode, but differing in dispersion. The scores of curve *b* are obviously more scattered (have greater dispersion) than those of curve *a*.

same averages but different dispersions. It is obvious that distribution *a* has a smaller dispersion about the average than distribution *b*, and therefore the average is more representative of *a* than of *b*.

If we wish to state the degree of dispersion more precisely in *numerical* terms, we must use one of the many available quantitative measures of dispersion. Let us consider some of the more common ones.

THE RANGE. The *range*, or the distance between the highest and lowest scores, is the simplest numerical measure of dispersion. Thus, to return to our dart-throwing scores, the range for the first set of scores is 2 (i.e., 10 minus 8); for the second set it is 12 (15 minus 3).

For many purposes, and with many distributions, the range is an adequate measure of dispersion and tells us what we wish to know. However it is too easily influenced by a single extreme value. For example, let us suppose that in 1923 a basketball star, measuring 7 feet, 1 inch, had decided to enter the University of Washington. Being merely one freshman among 630, he would have affected the mean height very little—not even in the decimal place. He would, however, have changed the range considerably, as shown in Table 7.

TABLE 7

Freshman Heights With and Without Hypothetical Basketball Star

Measures	With the Star	Without the Star
N (Number of students)	630	629
M (Arithmetic mean)	68.0 inches	68.0 inches
Tallest man	85.0 "	76.0 "
Shortest man	60.5 "	60.5 "
Range	24.5 "	15.5 "

It seems clear that a measure of dispersion so unstable as to be seriously changed (from 15.5 to 24.5) by *one* score out of 630 cannot be a very good measure of the degree of dispersion of scores for the entire group. Because of this and other considerations, slightly more complicated but more stable measures of dispersion have been developed.

THE AVERAGE DEVIATION. We can minimize the influence of a single extreme score by calculating a dispersion measure that takes account of *every* score in the distribu-

tion, not just the two extremes. To do this we first determine by how much *each* score differs from the group average, and then we can calculate the *average* of these differences to get a simple measure of dispersion. Let us return to our dart-throwing example.

There are 8 scores and the arithmetic mean of each distribution is 9. Now let us see how much each score deviates (differs) from the arithmetic mean. The values for these individual deviations are listed in the *d* column of Table 8. For example, in

TABLE 8

Two Sets of Hypothetical Individual Scores and Deviations from the Mean

	Group I		Group II	
	Scores	d	Scores	d
	8	1	3	6
	8	1	5	4
	9	0	7	2
	9	0	9	0
	9	0	9	0
	9	0	11	2
	10	1	13	4
	10	1	15	6
Σ (Sum)	72	4	72	24
M (Mean)	9		9	

$$\text{A.D.} = \frac{\Sigma d}{N} = \frac{4}{8} = .50 \quad \text{A.D.} = \frac{\Sigma d}{N} = \frac{24}{8} = 3.00$$

Group II the score of 3 deviates from the group mean by 6 points, the score of 5 by 4 points, etc. If we sum the individual deviations, we get a total of 4 for the first group and 24 for the second group. Therefore the *average deviation* for the 8 scores in Group I is .50 (4 divided by 8). For Group II, the average deviation is 3.00. The scores of the second group have a larger average deviation (are more widely dispersed) than do the scores of the first group.

The formula for the average deviation is simply $\text{A.D.} = \frac{\Sigma d}{N}$. A.D. stands for "average deviation," Σd for the sum of the individual deviations from the group mean, and N for the total number of cases.

STANDARD DEVIATION. Another measure of dispersion, and one much more useful for various statistical purposes, is the *standard deviation*. The logic of the standard deviation is similar to that of the average deviation. Again we obtain the individual deviations from the mean. But this time we square each of the deviations, sum the squared deviations, and divide by the number of cases. The reason for squaring the deviations before getting their average lies in certain mathematical considerations that need not concern us here. However, since the average was obtained by squaring the individual deviations in the first place, we end up with a dispersion measure expressed in squared units instead of in the original units (e.g., in "inches squared" instead of "inches"). If we wish to express the dispersion measure in terms of the original units, all we need do is remove the square. This is done by simply taking the *square root* of the result, and we now have a measure of dispersion expressed in terms of the original units, e.g., inches, pounds.

TABLE 9

Calculation of Standard Deviation for Two Sets of Hypothetical Scores

Score	d	d²		Score	d	d²
8	1	1		3	6	36
8	1	1		5	4	16
9	0	0		7	2	4
9	0	0		9	0	0
9	0	0		9	0	0
9	0	0		11	2	4
10	1	1		13	4	16
10	1	1		15	6	36

$\Sigma = 72$ 4 $\Sigma = 72$ 112

$M = 9$ $M = 9$

$N = 8$ $\Sigma d^2 = 4$ $N = 8$ $\Sigma d^2 = 112$

$$\sigma = \sqrt{\frac{\Sigma d^2}{N}} = \sqrt{\frac{4}{8}} = \sqrt{.50} = .70$$

$$\sigma = \sqrt{\frac{\Sigma d^2}{N}} = \sqrt{\frac{112}{8}} = \sqrt{14} = 3.74$$

This final result, the standard deviation, is usually symbolized by the letters S.D., or by the Greek letter, sigma (σ), and its formula is $\sigma = \sqrt{\dfrac{\Sigma d^2}{N}}$.

Returning again to our dart-throwing example, we would calculate the σ as shown in Table 9.

The statistics we have learned here can be applied to the measurement of many things—the heights and weights of people, intelligence test scores, reading-ability tests, or personality measurements. However, some of these psychological measurements create special problems, and it is to these special problems that we now turn.

Units of Measurement

If Shirley Cohen weighs 120 pounds, Tony Morales 150 pounds, and Jim Mc-Graw 180 pounds, there are several simple comparisons we can make. We can *rank* the three and say that Jim is the heaviest, Tony next, and Shirley the lightest. We can make *quantitative* comparisons and say that Jim weighs 50 per cent more than Shirley, or that the difference in weight between Jim and Tony is equal to the difference in weight between Tony and Shirley. All this seems quite obvious. But now let us take a second set of measurements and see what happens.

Suppose that we give intelligence tests to the same three people and find that Shirley gets a score of 100, Tony 110, and Jim 120. Again we can *rank* the three and say that Jim is the most intelligent, Tony next, and Shirley the least intelligent. We can also make a quantitative statement to the effect that Jim has scored 10 points more than Tony; and Tony, 10 points more than Shirley. But we *cannot* conclude that Tony is 10 per cent more intelligent than Shirley, or that Jim is 20 per cent more intelligent, or that the amount of difference in intelligence between Jim and Tony is the same as between Tony and Shirley! To understand why this is so we must consider various problems of measurement.

The Absolute Zero. Length is measured with a calibrated ruler of some sort. The numbers on the ruler start, of course, at zero. Suppose we measure the length of three arrows and find that one arrow extends from zero to 10 inches along the ruler; another, from zero to 20 inches; and the third, from zero to 40 inches. Since the ruler, in each case, starts at the zero point, the second arrow must be twice as long as the first one, and the third, twice as long as the second.

Let us suppose, however, that we had a ruler whose numbered units did not start at the zero point, but at some *unspecified distance from the zero point,* as in Figure 122, and that we again measured three arrows (different ones, this time), and

again found that the first arrow ended at the 10-inch mark interval, the second at the 20-inch mark, and the third at the 40-inch mark. Even with this very queer measuring stick we could still rank the three arrows with complete accuracy and say that the second arrow was longer than the first, and the third, the longest of all. We could *not* say, however, that the second arrow was twice as long as the first, or that the third was twice as long as the second. A little reflection will make it clear that in order to make quantitative comparative statements (e.g., "This is twice as long . . ." or "He is 10 per cent brighter than . . ."), *we must have measuring instruments that have a real zero starting point.*

Most measurement instruments with which we are familiar have a real zero (*absolute zero*) starting point. Thus a reading of zero on a reliable scale literally means *no* weight. Not all of our physical measurement instruments are of this kind. For example, on the familiar Fahrenheit or

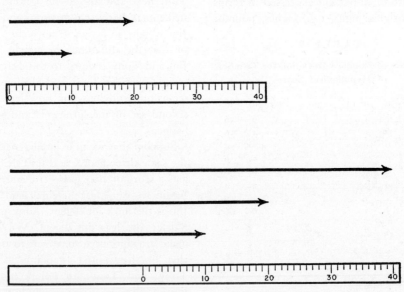

FIG. 122. Here we have a pictorial representation of the difficulties that exist when we use a measuring instrument that does not have an absolute zero point of origin (lower figure).

Centigrade temperature scale the zero on the thermometer is not at the absolute zero of heat, and a temperature of 80° F. is *not* twice that of 40° F. When we turn to psychological measurement instruments, we find that very few of our tests have a real zero starting point. We have no tests in which a score of zero means that the person has absolutely no intelligence, or absolutely no honesty, cowardice, shyness, neuroticism. It is even difficult to conceive what zero intelligence or honesty could mean.

It is because our mental and personality tests have no absolute zeros that we cannot make ratios of our scores, and say that Tony is 10 per cent more intelligent than Shirley. Direct comparisons of this sort are not justified. This raises many problems of psychological measurement. But before turning to some of the suggested solutions to these problems, let us consider a second difficulty with many psychological measuring instruments.

Equal Units. Another important characteristic of the usual physical measuring instrument is that all units are equal in magnitude—an inch is the same length whether it is the first inch on the ruler or the last. This permits us to say that the difference in length between 20 inches and 30 inches is the same as between 10 and 20.

Suppose, however, that we had a measuring instrument on which the units of measurement were not equal in size—the "inches" becoming progressively longer. It is clear that now the distance between 20 and 30 "inches" would be greater than the distance between 10 and 20 "inches."

For no intelligence or personality tests do we know whether the units of measurement are of equal magnitude. For example: in most tests it is essential to *add* scores from many subtests to get one total score.

A "reasoning ability" test may consist of "verbal reasoning" problems and "arithmetic reasoning" problems. We do not know, however, whether each arithmetic problem is equal in difficulty to each verbal problem. That is, we do not know whether a score of 10 points on the arithmetic problem is equal to a score of 10 points on the verbal problem. Let us assume that Shirley Cohen and Tony Morales have earned the scores shown in Table 10.

TABLE 10

Hypothetical Scores on Two Subtests

	Verbal Problems	Arithmetic Problems	Total
Shirley Cohen	98	22	120
Tony Morales	90	25	115

From these scores it appears that Shirley's general reasoning ability is *higher* than Tony's (120 vs. 115). But since neither test has an absolute zero point or equal units, this does *not* necessarily follow. It is quite possible that a difference of 3 points on the arithmetic reasoning subtest is much more significant than a difference of 8 points on the verbal reasoning subtest. Therefore Tony's *total* score may actually indicate a *higher* reasoning ability than does Shirley's score!

In order to meet this and similar problems, several statistical devices have been developed which, within limits, do permit numerical comparisons among scores obtained on different subtests. Almost all of these devices require that the original scores (sometimes called "raw scores") first be changed into one or another kind of "converted score." The simplest kind and the one most commonly used is the *percentile score.*

Percentile Score. A percentile score tells us the person's standing, in any one test, *relative to the rest of the group.* As its name implies, the *percentile points* divide the total distribution of scores into 100 parts, each containing 1 per cent of all the cases. For example: suppose that 1,500 people took the verbal reasoning subtest. Let us now array these 1,500 raw scores from highest to lowest. To convert these raw scores into percentile scores, we first determine how many scores should be placed into each percentile (or each 100th part). This is done by dividing 1,500 by 100, which gives us 15. We now take the lowest fifteen scores and these comprise the cases of the first percentile. The top value of these fifteen cases is the point above which lie 99 per cent of the cases, and below which lie 1 per cent of the cases. We do the same for the second, third, etc., percentile until we have 100 percentile points. We can then easily transform any raw score into its percentile equivalent by reference to these points. A score with a percentile value of 50 would mean that 50 per cent of the 1,500 people who took the test scored above that point and 50 per cent scored below that point. A percentile value of 90 would mean that only 10 per cent of the people scored above that point and 90 per cent scored below.

Percentile scores vary from zero to 100 *no matter what the range of the raw scores.* This makes it possible to compare the performance of different people on quite diverse tests having quite different "raw" units of measurement.

Despite the undoubted value of percentile scores and other kinds of converted scores (such as "standard scores"), we must nevertheless remember that all comparisons of scores made on psychological tests must be treated with caution. At best the comparisons are only relative (e.g., relative to the group that took the test). Where we have neither absolute zero nor equal units of measurement, we cannot make comparisons in absolute terms.

Correlation

The description of individual differences not only involves comparing one person with his fellows, but also comparing two aspects of the same person. For example, what relation exists between being good in arithmetic and being good in music? Is there such a thing as an all-around able person, or are most of us good in some things, average in others, and poor in still others? To answer these and other questions, we must have some way of expressing the degree of co-relation of say, ability in arithmetic with ability in music.

The Correlation Plot. A *correlation plot* is a simple graphic device picturing the relationship between two sets of scores.

Let us start with some hypothetical data. Suppose we give ten students three tests: a Verbal Reasoning Test, an Arithmetic Reasoning Test, and a Maze-Learning Test, and also record the students' weights to the nearest pound. Suppose that for the first two tests the score for each student is determined by the number of problems correctly solved, while the score for the third test is recorded in terms of the number of errors made prior to one perfect run through the maze. These hypothetical results are shown in Table 11.

THE POSITIVE CORRELATION. A *positive correlation* refers to two sets of measures whose values go together. Let us start by taking two sets of the scores from Table 11: the Verbal Reasoning scores and the Arithmetic Reasoning scores. To make a "picture" of these two sets of scores, we construct a graph with the Verbal Reasoning scores on the horizontal axis, the Arithmetic Reasoning scores on the vertical axis. It does not matter which axis we use for which test. In this graph (see Fig. 123) a student's scores on both tests are repre-

TABLE 11

**Hypothetical Scores on Four Sets of Measures
for Ten Students**

Student	No. Correct Verbal Reasoning Test	No. Correct Arithmetic Reasoning Test	No. Errors Maze Test	Weight (in pounds)
A	98	24	40	135
B	82	21	46	130
C	90	20	48	160
D	95	26	36	125
E	85	23	42	145
F	100	27	34	165
G	80	22	44	143
H	78	19	50	157
J	102	28	32	140
K	91	25	38	150

sented by *one* point. For example, the point representing student A's performance tells us that he scored 98 on the Verbal Reasoning Test and 24 on the Arithmetic Reasoning Test.

An inspection of Figure 123 shows a clear trend among the ten subjects. The higher the person's Verbal Reasoning Score, the higher his Arithmetic Reasoning Score tends to be. We have here a positive correlation. *Whenever the correlation plot*

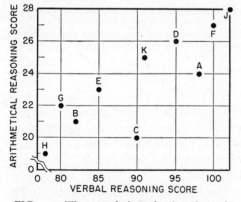

FIG. 123. The correlation plot based on the data in Table 11 and indicating a positive correlation. Each point represents the scores of the subject on each of the two tests. For purposes of clarity, the subject's "name" (A, B, C, etc.) has been placed next to the point. Ordinarily the names of the subjects are not indicated, merely the score points.

shows a trend from the lower left-hand corner to the upper right-hand corner, a positive correlation exists. But it will also be noted that there are some exceptions to this trend. Subject C, for example, is definitely out of line. Although he did better than subjects G, B, and E on the Verbal Test, he did worse than they did on the Arithmetic Test. We can conclude, then, that although there is a positive correlation, it is not a perfect positive correlation.

THE NEGATIVE CORRELATION. In Figure 124 the data are plotted for the Verbal Reasoning Test and the Maze Test. Now we find that the *higher* the score in the Verbal Test, the *fewer* the errors made on the maze. We have here a *negative correlation* between the two sets of scores. *Whenever the correlation plot shows a trend from the upper left-hand corner to the lower right-hand corner, a negative correlation exists.* But again we do not have a perfect negative correlation; note, for instance, the scores made by subjects A and C.

This negative correlation, however, can be interpreted as a positive relationship. In our reasoning test we have recorded the number of solutions achieved, while in our Maze Test we have recorded the number of *errors* made. Obviously, the more errors

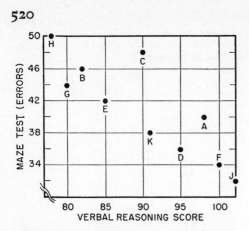

FIG. 124. A correlational plot based on the data in Table 11 and indicating a negative correlation.

made, the poorer the performance. Therefore this negative correlation between *scores* really means that a good performance on the maze test is associated with a good performance on the reasoning test. The sign of a correlation (whether positive or negative) merely tells us the relationship between the *scores* on the two tests. The *meaning* of the correlation depends upon the *meaning* of the scores.

THE ZERO CORRELATION. In Figure 125 we have constructed the correlation plot for the Verbal Reasoning Test and the body weights of the subjects. The correlation between body weight and Verbal Reasoning scores is very close to zero. *When the points on the correlation plot do not fall in any specific trend but are found scattered haphazardly, a zero correlation exists.*

It is clear from the above examples that a positive or negative correlation can be something less than perfectly positive or perfectly negative. In many instances we need to know the *magnitude* or size of correlation as well as the sign. This requirement has been satisfied by the development of the *correlation coefficient*—a single index that gives us both the sign and the magnitude of the correlation.

By general agreement, it has been decided to call a perfect positive correlation +1.00 and a perfect negative correlation −1.00. Thus, the correlation coefficient can range from +1.00 to −1.00. For example, a correlation coefficient of +0.14 is low positive; a correlation coefficient of −0.90 is high negative. Note that a −0.90 correlation would thus be considered higher than a +0.14. The *size* of the correlation refers to the distance from zero (whether positive or negative), *not* to its positiveness or negativeness.

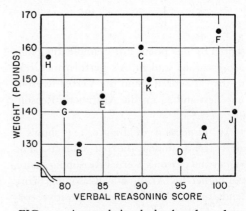

FIG. 125. A correlational plot based on data in Table 11 (indicating a zero correlation) between the weight of the subjects and their performance on the Verbal Reasoning Test. Note that the points do not arrange themselves in any special form but are found scattered all over the correlational plot. This therefore represents a *zero* correlation.

RANK-ORDER CORRELATION. There are several ways of determining the magnitude of a correlation coefficient. The simplest of these ways is the *rank-order correlation coefficient*, the symbol for which is ρ (the Greek letter rho).

The basic logic behind the formula for ρ is readily grasped, and we shall sketch it here through an example.

The first step in obtaining ρ is to *rank* the subjects in terms of their performances on each of the two tests being analyzed. We then compare the ranks and from that derive the value of ρ. Table 12 presents the necessary steps for getting a ρ for our illustrative data from the Verbal and Arithmetic test of Table 11.

In column 4 we have ranked the performance of the ten subjects on the Verbal Reasoning Test. The highest score, 102, was earned by subject J, and he is given the top rank of 1; the next best score was 100, earned by F, and he receives the rank of 2; A is ranked 3, etc. In column 5 we have ranked the ten subjects according to their scores on the Arithmetic Reasoning Test.

If there were a *perfect positive* correlation, there would be no difference between the two sets of ranks. For example, subject J, who received rank 1 in the Verbal Test, would also receive rank 1 in the Arithmetic Test. The man who received rank 2 in the Verbal Test would also receive rank 2 in the Arithmetic Test, and so on down to the man who would be ranked 10th in both lists. If in this case we obtained the differences between the scores of column 5 and those of column 4, we would get a column of zeros.

However if the correlation were something less than perfect, the differences between the ranks (column 5 minus column 4) would not all be zero. A man receiving the 3rd rank in one test could get the 5th rank in the second test, etc. The greater the discrepancies in ranks, the lower would be the positive relation between the two sets of scores. Therefore the average of the rank differences obviously provides a way of measuring the degree of correlation—the larger the average, the lower the positive correlation.

Again, for various mathematical reasons, we do not deal with the differences among the ranks, but with the squares of these differences. In other words, we square each value in column 6 to give us the values in column 7.

Since a $+1.00$ is the highest positive correlation possible, to obtain the correlation coefficient we should *subtract* from 1.00 the average of the differences between the ranks. The higher the average of the differences between the ranks, the lower will be the correlation coefficient.

We now end up with the following formula: the size of the correlation should be

TABLE 12

Rank-Order Correlation Between VR and AR Tests

1	2	3	4	5	6	7
	No. Correct	No. Correct	Rank on	Rank on		
Subject	VR Test	AR Test	VR Test	AR Test	D	D²
A	98	24	3	5	2	4
B	82	21	8	8	0	0
C	90	20	6	9	3	9
D	95	26	4	3	1	1
E	85	23	7	6	1	1
F	100	27	2	2	0	0
G	80	22	9	7	2	4
H	78	19	10	10	0	0
J	102	28	1	1	0	0
K	91	25	5	4	1	1

$$\Sigma D^2 = 20$$

$$\rho = 1 - \frac{6\Sigma D^2}{N(N^2 - 1)} = 1 - \frac{120}{10(99)} = 1 - \frac{120}{990} = 1 - .12 = +.88$$

1.00 *minus* the average of the differences between the ranks, or $\rho = 1 - \dfrac{\Sigma D^2}{N}$. And this "logically" derived formula is similar in structure to the mathematically derived for-

from 1.00, we would end up as far away from a +1.00 as we could get, i.e., at −1.00. The student is urged to work through the example given in Table 13, in which the coefficient is negative (and, by

TABLE 13

Rank-Order Correlation Between VR and Maze Test

Subject	No. Correct VR Test	No. Correct Maze	Rank on VR Test	Rank on Maze	D	D²
A	98	40	3	6	3	9
B	82	46	8	3	5	25
C	90	48	6	2	4	16
D	95	36	4	8	4	16
E	85	42	7	5	2	4
F	100	34	2	9	7	49
G	80	44	9	4	5	25
H	78	50	10	1	9	81
J	102	32	1	10	9	81
K	91	38	5	7	2	4

$$\Sigma D^2 = 310$$

$$\rho = 1 - \frac{6\Sigma D^2}{N(N^2 - 1)} = 1 - \frac{1860}{10(99)} = 1 - \frac{1860}{990} = 1 - 1.879 = -.88$$

mula. For various mathematical reasons that need not concern us at this time, the actual formula is: $\rho = 1 - \dfrac{6\Sigma D^2}{N(N^2 - 1)}$.

Applying this latter formula, we get a ρ of +0.88 for the correlation coefficient between Verbal and Arithmetic Reasoning scores among our ten hypothetical subjects. We have now expressed in numerical terms the positive correlation indicated in Figure 123.

A NEGATIVE RANK-ORDER CORRELATION. The same reasoning is involved in the negative rank-order correlation. In a perfect negative correlation the top man in one test would be the worst man in the second test; the subject who received a rank of 2 in the first test would receive a rank of 9 in the second, etc. In this case the differences between the two sets of ranks would be at their maximum. If we subtracted the average of the differences between the ranks

sheer coincidence, of the same value as the coefficient in Table 12).

PRODUCT-MOMENT CORRELATION. The correlation coefficient that is most commonly used is the *product-moment correlation coefficient*. The formula for this correlation coefficient (which is symbolized by the letter r) is $r = \dfrac{\Sigma xy}{N\sigma_x\sigma_y}$; x and y are the deviations of the individual scores from the group means; σ_x is the standard deviation of the scores on test X; and σ_y is the standard deviation of the scores on test Y. An example of how a product-moment correlation coefficient is calculated is given in Box 141.

As a general rule, the rank-order correlation coefficient is preferred when the number of cases is small (about 15 to 20), and when there are few ties in ranks. In other cases the product-moment correlation is a more desirable measure.

BOX 141

$$r = \frac{\Sigma xy}{N \sigma_X \sigma_Y}$$

The product-moment correlation coefficient was developed by the English mathematician, Karl Pearson, and is sometimes referred to as "Pearson's coefficient of correlation." There are seven steps involved. Using the hypothetical data of the table shown below:

Subject	Score on X	Score on Y
A	126	120
B	123	100
C	122	60
D	100	50
E	80	25
F	67	23

1) We obtain the group means for test X and test Y, which are 103.0 and 63.0 respectively.

2) Then we determine for each subject the amount by which his score deviates from the group mean. We do this for each test separately. Thus subject A with 126 points is 23 points away from the group mean on the X test. This gives subject A an x score of 23. (When the letters are in lower case type, they refer to deviations from the average.) He is 57 points away from the group mean on the Y test. This gives him a y score of 57. In the same manner we obtain the x and y scores for *each* subject.

3) We then multiply each person's x score by his y score. E.g., for subject A we multiply 23 by 57 to get the product of 1,311.0. We do the same for each of the other 5 subjects.

4) We then sum all of these 6 products, and get 4,461.0. This is the value for Σxy.

5) We then obtain the σ's of the X scores and the Y scores. These turn out to be 22.8 for the X scores and 36.1 for the Y scores.

6) We now multiply the σ of the X scores by the σ of the Y scores and by the number of subjects. This gives us a product of 4,938.48. This is the value for $N \sigma_X \sigma_Y$.

7) Finally, we divide this last product into the sum of the xy products (step 4). This gives us the product-moment correlation coefficient, which, in this illustration, is + .88.

By Way of Summary. One of the major problems in dealing with several sets of data is to determine the interrelationships among them. Perhaps the most useful technique for this purpose is the correlation coefficient, which permits us to state in quantitative terms the degree of relationship between two variables.

A logical error that is frequently made in the *interpretation* of the correlation coefficient is the cause-and-effect argument. It is often assumed that if two variables are highly correlated, one is the *cause* of the other. (The psychological basis for this kind of logical error was discussed on page 374). However a high correlation between two events may mean merely that *both* events are caused by some *third* factor, not that one event causes or influences the other. In statistical work the correlation coefficient is often used where we *know* there is no causal relationship between the two sets of measurements we are correlating. We shall see some examples of this in the following pages.

Errors of Measurement

Whenever we measure anything—the length of a table or the personality of a patient in a mental hospital—our measure suffers from some degree of error. The error may be due to an imperfect measuring instrument, to an imperfect method of applying the instrument, to our careless reading of the instrument or recording, or to any one of a number of other factors.

Since so much of our reasoning in science depends upon the results of measurement, a great deal of concern has been shown for errors of measurement, and we have learned much about their nature, source, and control. Where we have been unable to eliminate them, we have developed techniques that permit us to estimate the degree of error. Knowing the magnitude of our error, we can state the degree of our confidence in any conclusions based on measurements. The study of errors of measurement is one of the basic studies in statistics.

We shall concern ourselves here with two types of error-problems: the *reliability* and the *validity* of our instruments.

Reliability. There exists no absolutely perfect measuring instrument. Even the simplest kind of measuring instrument, the ruler, is not without built-in error. It is impossible to construct a ruler whose inches, for example, will be absolutely uniform in length. Even if they vary as little as $\frac{1}{1,000,000}$ of an inch, the ruler is fallible to that extent. Furthermore, to measure objects, we must actually *apply* the measuring stick to the objects. The way we apply it may differ ever so slightly from one time to another and thus contribute to the error. And finally, since there is a limit to the smallness of the unit in which we can read off any measure, we *must* always "round off" our readings. (See Box 140.)

We all know that some measuring instruments give us larger errors than others. A metal ruler, for example, may give us larger errors than a wooden one, because metal expands or shrinks as the room temperature rises or falls. Obviously, a ruler that expands and shrinks would be "unreliable," since if we used it to measure the same object twice, it might give us two different readings, depending upon the temperature of the room. A "reliable" ruler would give us the same answer no matter how many times we measured the same object.

This simple consideration gives us the definition of reliable and unreliable measuring instruments. Reliability of a measurement device (*including its method of application*) can be defined as *the degree to which repeated measurement with the instrument will give the same or similar readings*.

RELIABILITY MEASURED BY CORRELATION. Let us suppose that we want to determine the degree of reliability of a new intelligence test. We could administer the test to a group of children and record their scores. One week later we could give them the same test, and again record their scores. We would now have two sets of scores for the same group of children on the same test. If the test and its method of application are reliable, the children should receive the same, or very similar, scores on both occasions. This would be true, of course, only if the children's intelligence had not changed during the one-week interval. If the test is not reliable, the children would receive widely different scores at the two testing periods. Let us assume, in an illustrative case, that we have obtained the data shown in Table 14.

How reliable is this test? On the first testing child K was tops; on the second testing he was tops again. On the first testing J was 2nd, as he was also on the second testing. But not every child achieved the same rank on both occasions. For example, child G was 4th on the first testing, but came out 5th the second time around. The test is not perfectly reliable. If it were perfectly reliable, we would get a correlation of +1.00 between the first and second testing. The actual correlation (rank-order) is +.98. (The reader is invited to work out

TABLE 14

**Hypothetical Scores for 10 Children on
Test X Taken Twice**

Children	Scores on Test X First Week	Scores on Test X Second Week	Rank on 1st Testing	Rank on 2nd Testing
A	100	110	7	6
B	110	100	6	7
C	90	90	8	8
D	120	130	5	4
E	140	140	3	3
F	80	80	9	9
G	130	120	4	5
H	70	70	10	10
J	150	150	2	2
K	160	160	1	1

this rank-order correlation coefficient for himself.) Obviously, if the test had been a very unreliable one, the correlation would have been very low. The correlation coefficient, therefore, gives us *a numerical index expressing the degree of reliability of a test*. When a correlation coefficient is used for this purpose, it is called a *reliability coefficient*.

It is not always desirable, however, to repeat the same test at two different times. There is always the possibility, for example, that the child may remember what he did the previous week and merely repeat his performance on the basis of memory. The correlation between the first set of scores and the second, in that event, would give us a measure of the *child's memory* rather than of the *test's reliability*. Or there is the possibility that the child's intelligence itself may actually have changed during the interval, and we would therefore have no way of knowing whether a low correlation between first and second testing was due to the change in intelligence or lack of testing reliability. Or there is the possibility that the child is bored with the test the second time, and the low test-retest correlation may be caused by lack of motivation rather than by any unreliability of the test or the testing procedure.

Several techniques have been developed

in an attempt to avoid these problems in determining the reliability of a test. Among these techniques is that known as *comparable-forms reliability*.

COMPARABLE-FORMS RELIABILITY. Most psychological tests consist of a large number of items, problems, and questions. Let us assume an Arithmetic Reasoning Test made up of 100 different arithmetic-reasoning problems. We then proceed to construct another 100-item test of arithmetic reasoning. The correlation between the two comparable forms would give us the reliability of either form. We can therefore give a group of subjects the first 100 items at one time, and at a later time, the second group of 100 items. What we have here are two comparable forms of the same test.

The comparable-forms method avoids the "memory" problem and perhaps the "boredom" problem discussed above, but it still leaves the problem of timing. The two forms are given at different times. Many things can happen during the interval to make difficult the interpretation of the correlation between the two comparable forms. Partly to meet this problem, the *split-half reliability* method has been developed.

SPLIT-HALF RELIABILITY. The reasoning behind the split-half reliability method is identical with that behind the comparable-form method. Let us return to our 100-item

Arithmetic Reasoning Test. Instead of constructing two comparable forms and giving each form at a different time, we can give our subjects the 100-item test at one sitting and then split the 100-item test into two 50-item tests. For example, for each subject we have a record of his performance on 100 items. Suppose we now take these 100 items and split them so that the performance on the odd-numbered items (1,3,5,7, etc.) makes up one subscore for each subject, and the performance on the even-numbered items (2,4,6,8, etc.) makes up another subscore for each subject. For all practical purposes we have scores on two comparable forms of the test for each subject. We next correlate the subject's score on all the odd-numbered items with his score on all the even-numbered items, and in this way determine the reliability coefficient of either half, and from this, the reliability of the whole. That is why this method is sometimes called the "odd-even reliability coefficient."

This method has the following advantages over the comparable-forms method: (1) Both subtests (even and odd) are taken at the same time, under the same conditions of motivation, same conditions of testing, same state of alertness, of the subject. (2) Since we have split the test by the odd-even method, we have ensured comparability of forms—not only in content, but also in manner of administration. That is, each subtest contains items that come both early and late in the total sitting so that such factors as fatigue and lagging interest are presumably equated for both subtests.

These and other methods can give us valuable information on the adequacy of a test as a measurement instrument. However, knowing that a test is reliable is not enough to enable us to assess its value as a measurement instrument. It may be highly reliable and still a very poor measurement instrument because it lacks *validity*.

Validity. The terms "reliability" and "validity" are used fairly interchangeably in common speech. In measurement theory, however, these terms have different meanings. The statistician, concerned with the question of the *reliability* of an instrument, asks how consistently the instrument measures whatever it measures. When he is concerned with the question of *validity*, he asks whether the instrument is measuring what he wants it to measure. An instrument may give consistent measurements (have high reliability), but it may not be measuring what we think it measures (it may have low validity). For example, weekly quizzes in your psychology course may give consistent results, in that week after week you earn a gentleman's 75. The quizzes are reliable indicators. But indicators of what? If your psychology instructor intends them as measures of your understanding of the principles of psychology, he may be wrong. They may be measuring mainly rote memory. Thus, they would have low validity as indicators of psychological understanding.

For many measurement instruments, of course, there are no serious problems of validity. Thus, a ruler is a valid measuring instrument of length, simply by definition. A quiz designed to determine whether you can give the definitions of specific psychological terms is, again by definition, a valid test of whether you can do so. Such tests are said to have *face validity*—they are valid on the face of it!

But most tests that seek to measure more complex phenomena are not that easily "validated." For one thing, validity, like reliability, is not an all-or-nothing affair. A test may have degrees of validity. Your quiz grades may be influenced *only* by your understanding of psychological principles. In that case we would say that the quiz has perfect validity as a measure of understanding of psychological principles. But more probably your score on it is the resultant of your psychological understanding *plus* rote-memory ability. The test still has some validity for psychological understanding and some validity for rote-memory capacity, but it is no longer a "pure" test of either. As was true of reliability, we must have some way of expressing the *degree* of the validity of a measuring instrument. And again, as with reliability, the correlation coefficient provides us with just such a way.

VALIDITY MEASURED BY CORRELATION. It is clear that a test is valid to the degree that its measurements correlate with the actual thing it is supposed to measure. For example, suppose you wished to determine the validity of a test designed to measure the ability of students to get high grades in school work. We would give the test to a large number of students and see whether the scores they made on the test correlated highly with the actual grades they received in their school work. Their school grades would, of course, be the final *criteria* of the validity of the test. If the correlation between the test scores and the criterion scores is high, the test obviously measures what it is intended to measure and it has high validity. If the correlation is low, the test has low validity. When the correlation coefficient is used in this way, it is called a *validity coefficient*.

The general principle is simple enough: To determine the validity of a test, we correlate the scores of the test with the criterion. The difficulty is that frequently we cannot find a criterion against which to correlate the test scores. Suppose we want to measure the validity of an intelligence test. We can get the intelligence test scores easily enough, but what will serve as our criterion of "intelligence"? Grades in school? Money earned in "real life"? Originality and creativity? Leadership in social affairs? Different people might suggest different criteria, and some of the criteria would themselves pose problems of meas-

urement. For example, even if we all agreed that "intelligence" refers to originality and creativity, we would still have the problem of finding scores of originality and of creativity to correlate with our intelligence test scores.

There have been many attempts to solve the criterion problem. Among the more common techniques is the so-called "known-group" method of validity determination.

KNOWN GROUPS AND VALIDITY. There are no easily available criterion scores for originality and creativity. There are, however, certain well-known people whom most of us would regard as "highly original and creative." Thus, a group of inventors, scientists, and artists might be picked who *exemplify* originality and creativity. These people could then be considered as a "known group" of creative people.

Presumably this "known group" is more creative than the average run of men. We would then give our test to this known group and also to a large unselected group of people and compare the results. If the test has any validity as a measure of "originality and creativity," the average member of the "creative" group should score higher than the average member of the control group, and the greater the difference between the scores, the more valid the test.

Sometimes it is easy to choose the proper "known group"; sometimes it is quite difficult. Nevertheless, in many instances we have no better way of determining the validity of tests than by the "known-group" method. Whichever method we use, we must have some information on the validity of a test before we can interpret its results sensibly.

By Way of Summary. Every measurement instrument together with its method of application, whether it measures simple physical attributes or complex psychological ones, *is subject to error*. Before we can adequately assess any measurement, we must know something about its reliability and validity. That is the beginning of all statistical wisdom. A test may have *high reliability,* but *low validity.* However, a test of *low reliability* cannot have *high validity;* if a test is capricious in its measurement, now giving a high reading, now a low one, for the same unchanging object, its measurements are being determined by "chance" factors (i.e., it has low reliability) and they cannot consistently correlate highly with any set of criteria scores (it must have low validity).

Reliability and validity pertain to errors of measurement due to the inadequacy of the measurement instrument and its method of application. But quite aside from this, there is still another major source of error in any investigation that uses measurement. We may make a *sampling error.*

Sampling the "Average" Man

Whenever we measure a specific group of people, we have one of two reasons for choosing them for our attention. We may be interested in these particular people themselves, or we may be interested in a specific category of people of which the particular group is supposed to be a sample.

In the former instance there are no measurement problems aside from those we have already considered—reliability and validity. Thus, if we wish to know what West Bicycle State freshmen will score on our scholastic aptitude test, we measure all the freshmen at W.B.S., and that is all there is to it.

However, if we want to know what the "American Freshmen" will score on our test, we immediately run into a whole new set of measurement problems. We cannot, or do not wish to, test every American freshman. We therefore test a *sample* of freshmen, and from their results we generalize to the all-American freshman. But how do we know that the results of our sample freshmen reliably portray the American freshmen? Perhaps our sample freshmen are brighter than the average American freshman—or duller. As soon as we measure a sample of a group instead of the entire group, we introduce the possibility of "sampling errors."

The Uses of Samples. In scientific investigations we are not primarily interested in the specific individuals we are measuring. For example, when the physiologist studies the heart of Pluto, he is not interested in how the heart of *Pluto* behaves, he is interested in how the hearts of dogs the world over behave. When the psychologist studies how quickly a group of sophomores can learn a list of nonsense syllables using the recitation method, he is not interested in that specific group of sophomores. He is not even interested in sophomores in general. He is interested in how *people*—all people, of all colors, of all educational levels, of all cultures—respond to active versus passive learning methods. Most scientific investigations are in theory concerned with infinitely large groups.

In most studies it would be literally impossible to test and measure every member of the group. We are therefore *forced* to use a sampling technique. Usually, however, we are being "forced" to do what is good for us. Even if we had the facilities to test and measure every member of the group in which we are interested, it would be a wasteful and foolish thing to do. In many instances we can obtain almost as adequately precise an estimate of the group score by measuring a *sample,* as we can by measuring the total group. It is therefore more sensible and economical to use our limited resources for study on samples. And a sample need not be very large to be a "good" sample. A group of 3,000 carefully chosen Americans can make up a better sample of all 175,000,000 Americans than can 1,000,000 chosen in an inadequate fashion.

Biased and Unbiased Samples. While the technique of obtaining a good sample is a highly technical one, the guiding principle is simple. Ideally, in drawing a sample from a large population, we must use a procedure permitting every member of the entire population *an equal opportunity to be included in the sample.* In other words, our technique must not be systematically *biased* in favor of any kind of person. For example, suppose we want to determine the average body weight of all the residents of New York City. To do this, we must first obtain a representative sample of New York residents and then weigh them. How do we get such a representative sample?

THE BIASED SAMPLE. One method, used in the past, was to take the city telephone directory and draw, say, every 500th name. But this inevitably results in a "systematically biased sample" since it has systematically drawn only those New Yorkers who have telephones and has systematically excluded all those who do not. Obviously this is not a good sample of New Yorkers for our purpose. It may be, for instance, that New Yorkers who have telephones are in the higher income brackets, eat more, and therefore weigh more than non-telephone subscribing New Yorkers. Or, one might argue, the telephone subscribers are the more harried people, the people with Madison Avenue ulcers, and therefore eat less and weigh less than the "poor but relaxed" non-telephone subscribers.

Once we have a systematically biased sample, there is very little we can do to correct the sample mathematically. Whatever measurements we make on telephone-subscribing New Yorkers cannot safely be generalized to all New Yorkers. Every study that works with a systematically biased sample may, therefore, lead to erroneous conclusions when the attempt is made to generalize the results to the rest of the population.

THE RANDOM SAMPLE. The best way to avoid systematic bias is to draw the sample in a random fashion, permitting no systematic preferences. Thus, if we could write the name of each New Yorker on a standard-sized slip of paper, place all the papers in a huge bin, shake the bin vigorously, and then blindly pick out, say, 3,000 names at random, we would have avoided all possible systematic tendencies. We would have chosen what is called a *random sample.*

Frequently, of course, it is not feasible to use such an ideal "random" method, so we attempt to approximate the ideal method. We might, for example, take every 3rd city block and choose every 10th family in the chosen blocks for our sample. This would give us an approximation to a random sample.

While we may thus avoid systematic bias or error in our sample, there still remains the possibility that our sample would deviate from the population because of unsystematic or "chance" events. For example, it might be that *just by sheer chance* we would include, say, many more names of women, or of older people, proportionally, than there are in New York City. If we were to weigh these people, the average we would obtain would differ from the true average of all the residents of New York City. However, unlike the situation in which there are "systematic biases," we *can* do something about "chance" errors. We can predict their magnitude! To understand how this is possible, it is necessary to make a rather long detour and discuss the question of *probability.*

Probability. One of the most important mathematical achievements in the field of probability theory was the discovery that "chance events" behave lawfully! That is, if we record all our observations of recurring chance events and make a distribution curve of these observations, the distribution curve will take the shape of what is called a *normal curve*.

The phrase *chance event* is used in the mathematical sense and means an event that has so many completely interrelated causes that it is impossible to predict (at the time) the exact nature of the occurrences. "Chance" does not mean *uncaused*. For example, suppose we toss ten dimes into the air. What determines how many heads and how many tails will fall? Many things: the force of the toss, the weight of the dimes, their position in the hand when tossed, the spin given to the coins, etc. It is impossible to predict whether a particular dime will fall heads or tails, and this is therefore said to be a chance event.

While we do not know, for any single throw, how many heads will show, we do know, for many throws, the approximate final distribution of heads and tails that we will get. That is, we can calculate, from the mathematical theory of probability, the approximate number of times we will get 10, 9, 8, 7, 6, 5, 4, 3, 2, 1, and 0 heads in, say, 10,000 throws. Let us see how this is accomplished.

MUTUALLY EXCLUSIVE EVENTS. Let us start with one dime. It may either show a head or a tail when it is tossed and comes to rest. Knowing nothing about the forces that determine how it will fall, we can say that the probability that we will get a head is 1 out of 2, or, as it is usually written, $h = \frac{1}{2}$ (where h stands for "head"). The same is, of course, true for tail, i.e., $t = \frac{1}{2}$. The probability that the coin will fall *either* a head or tail is 1, i.e., $(\frac{1}{2} h + \frac{1}{2} t) = 1$. (Certainty, in probability nomenclature, is represented by the value of 1.) This simple operation is an illustration of an important

general probability rule: *The probability of occurrence of two or more mutually exclusive events is obtained by adding the probabilities of the individual events.*

INDEPENDENT EVENTS. Now let us throw *two* dimes at a time. The probability that one dime will fall heads is $\frac{1}{2}$; the probability that the other dime will fall heads is also $\frac{1}{2}$. What is the probability that *both* dimes will fall heads? When we have two dimes, the events are *not* mutually exclusive. That is, one dime can show a head but this does not exclude the other dime from also showing a head. The falls of the two dimes are *independent events*.

For independent events the following rule holds: *The probability of the occurrence of independent events is obtained by multiplying the probabilities of the individual events.* For example: With two coins the probability of getting 2 heads is found by multiplying $\frac{1}{2}$ (i.e., the probability of one dime showing a head) by $\frac{1}{2}$ (the probability of the other dime showing a head). Expressed mathematically it is $(\frac{1}{2} h \times \frac{1}{2} h)$ or $\frac{1}{4} h$. The same is, of course, true for two tails $(\frac{1}{2} t \times \frac{1}{2} t)$ or $\frac{1}{4} t$.

We can now make a probability prediction. If we were to throw two dimes 10,000 times, we would expect to find that 2 heads would come up about $\frac{1}{4}$ of the time, or 2,500 times; and that two tails would come up about $\frac{1}{4}$ of the time, or 2,500 times; and for the remaining 5,000 throws we would expect one head and one tail. The predicted distribution is shown in Figure 126 as a frequency histogram. From this figure it will be seen that *the most probable event is 1 head and 1 tail*, but, *by chance alone*, we would get 2 heads in 25 per cent of the throws and two tails in 25 per cent of the throws.

By similar reasoning we can determine the probabilities for 3, 4, 5, or any number of coins. In Table 15 and Figure 127 are presented the data for 10 coins. The most

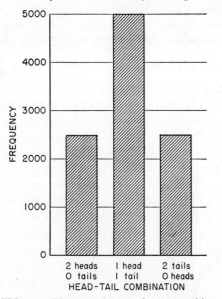

FIG. 126. Here we have a frequency histogram of the theoretically derived distribution of head-tail combinations which we might expect to find if we flipped 2 coins 10,000 times.

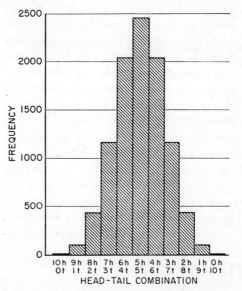

FIG. 127. Here we have a frequency histogram of the theoretically derived distribution of head-tail combinations which we might expect to find if we flipped 10 coins 10,000 times.

probable event—the one we would expect would occur 24.6 per cent of the time (in 2,460 throws out of 10,000, see Table 15) —is 5 heads and 5 tails. Buy *by chance alone*, without any special twist being applied to the coins, or any other manipulation, we might expect to find 10 heads showing up in 0.1 per cent of the time (or

TABLE 15

Theoretical Expectations of Head-Tail Combinations for 10 Coins Tossed 10,000 Times

Combinations of h(eads) and t(ails)	Frequency
10h and 0t	10
9h and 1t	98
8h and 2t	439
7h and 3t	1,172
6h and 4t	2,051
5h and 5t	2,460
4h and 6t	2,051
3h and 7t	1,172
2h and 8t	439
1h and 9t	98
0h and 10t	10
	10,000

in 10 out of 10,000 throws). Another way of phrasing this is to say that the chances are 1 in 1,000 that we will get 10 heads showing at one throw.

THE NORMAL CURVE. Note one very important characteristic of the two histograms shown in Figures 126 and 127. They are perfectly symmetrical around the most probable event. As the number of coins is increased, the histograms maintain their perfect symmetry, but their shapes gradually change from the sharp, angular shape of the two-coin histogram, to the somewhat bell-shaped appearance of the ten-coin histogram. As the number of coins increases, the number of head-tail combinations to be plotted necessarily increases and the histogram becomes smoother and smoother, ultimately approaching in form the normal-distribution curve. This is what we meant by saying that chance events behave lawfully—they give a beautifully smoothed bell-shaped distribution curve.

Since the normal curve was constructed

through the application of mathematical theory (some of the basic aspects of which we have just worked through), a great deal is known about its mathematical properties. It is these properties that make the normal curve of such great value in estimating sampling errors. The most important of these properties, and the one immediately relevant to our problem, is the fixed relationship that the standard deviation bears to the curve. The relationship is such that *the standard deviation measures off constant proportions of the curve from the mean.* An example will make this clear.

First let us calculate the standard devia-

tion for the theoretically derived distribution shown in Table 15 and Figure 127. Using the formula we have already developed on page 515 ($\sigma = \sqrt{\dfrac{\Sigma d^2}{N}}$), we find that the standard deviation is 1.58. The most probable outcome of a throw of 10 dimes will be 5 heads and 5 tails. This is the mean of the distribution. Let us therefore start at 5 on the base line of Figure 128 (which portrays the data of Figure 127 as a smooth curve rather than as a histogram) and measure off a distance of 1σ on either side. This will bring us to 3.42 on one side and 6.58 on the other. Between 5 (the mean) and

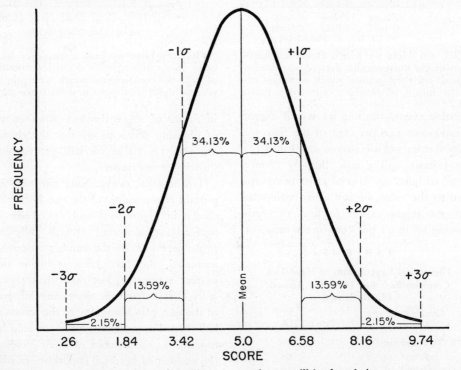

FIG. 128. Here we have the data of the histogram in Fig. 127 portrayed as a "smooth curve" with the mean at 5. The percentage values shown are characteristic of every normal distribution curve; thus within the area marked off by $+1\sigma$ and -1σ will be found 68.26 per cent of all the scores in the distribution; within the area marked off by $+2\sigma$ and -2σ will be found 95.44 per cent of all the scores in the distribution; and between the area marked off by $+3\sigma$

and -3σ will be found about 99.75 per cent of all the scores in the distribution. The theoretical normal distribution curve will never hit the base line, although it will continue to approach it. This means that no matter how many sigma-distances we go from the mean (on both sides), we will never encompass 100 per cent of the cases. Of course, a curve representing actual data does hit the base line on either end, since we have a limited number of cases.

6.58 (the mean plus 1σ) will be found approximately 34.13 per cent of the 10,000 throws; and, similarly, between 5 and 3.42 (the mean minus 1σ) will be found approximately 34.13 per cent of the 10,000 throws. Since Figure 128 is only a close approximation to a normal curve, the qualification "approximate" is used. In a perfectly *normal curve* exactly 34.13 per cent of all cases will be found to fall between the mean value and the value 1σ away from the mean. Let us now mark off another σ distance. This brings us to 1.84 and 8.16. Between 3.42 and 1.84 will be found approximately 13.59 per cent of the cases, and the same is true for the interval between 6.58 and 8.16. *These relationships between the standard deviation and the distribution of cases in a normal distribution are always true, no matter what the absolute size of the mean or the size of the standard deviation.*

The significance of this relationship lies in this extraordinary fact: If we know the number of cases, the arithmetic mean, and the standard deviation of a set of measurements that are approximately normally distributed, *we can reconstruct from these three bits of information alone all the scores of the original distribution.* Let us see how this works out with our freshman-height data.

AN ILLUSTRATION. While the freshman-height data are somewhat skewed, the distribution curve is close enough to a normal one to permit us to use these data for a demonstration. The three facts we must have are the number of cases, which is 629; the arithmetic mean, which 68.0 inches; and the standard deviation, which can be calculated by our formula to be 2.5. Since 68.26 per cent of the cases of a normal distribution curve fall within the limits of plus 1σ and minus 1σ on either side of the mean (see Fig. 128) that would mean that 429 freshmen (which is 68.26 per cent of

all the freshmen) should fall within the limits of 70.5 (which is the mean plus 1σ) and 65.5 inches (which is the mean minus 1σ). Looking back at Table 4 we find that actually within the limits of 70.0 inches and 66.0 inches (the nearest class intervals to the ones we want) there were 419 freshmen. This is a fairly close fit between theory and actual observation.

Another example: Since 13.59 per cent of the cases should fall between the first and second standard deviations on either side of the mean, 85 freshmen (which is 13.59 per cent of all the freshmen) should fall between 70.5 inches and 73.0 inches, and a similar number should fall between 65.5 inches and 63.0 inches. Again checking with the data in Table 4 we see that the actual figures are 107 and 84. This gives us a poor fit in the first case, an excellent one in the second. The reason for the relatively poor agreement between theory and actual results in the first case is accounted for by the fact that our height curve is *not* a perfectly normal distribution curve.

Finally: If we measure off three sigmas above and below the mean (60.5 inches to 75.5 inches), we should expect to include within those limits 99.75 per cent of all the freshmen. Actually we find that 100 per cent of the freshmen fall within limits very close to this.

The value of the standard deviation in describing the individual differences found in a group of measurements can hardly be exaggerated. Together with the mean it gives us the information that is carried by the discrete scores, by a frequency-distribution table, or by a frequency-distribution curve. But as we have just seen, *this information will be accurate only to the extent that the set of measurements approximates a normal distribution curve.*

Chance Errors. We have now completed our detour and are ready to return to New

York City, the weights of its residents, and sampling errors.

Let us suppose that we have the names and weights of each New Yorker on a separate slip of paper, that we have drawn from this collection of papers a random selection of, say, 100 names, and that we have found the mean weight of this sample of 100 New Yorkers to be 120 pounds. We can now determine how reliable an estimate 120 pounds is of the true average weight of all New Yorkers! To indicate how this is done, let us continue with our hypothetical experiment.

We first throw the 100 slips of paper back into the huge bin that is New York, shake it up again, and draw a *new* sample of 100 names. Calculating the mean of this new sample, we may find it to be 122 pounds. Again we throw the 100 names back, and again we draw a new sample. Now suppose we do this 10,000 times. We will end up, of course, with 10,000 means. But even *before* we do this laborious experiment, we can predict something about what we will find.

It is clear that for each draw of 100 names it is a matter of pure *chance* which 100 names we get. It is therefore a matter of pure chance (within the limits of all New Yorkers' weights) what the mean weight of each sample will be. We have a situation strictly comparable to that in the coin-throwing experiment we discussed on page 531, in which the head-tail combination of each toss was a matter of pure chance.

It will be recalled that when we record repeated chance events and throw these observations into a distribution curve, we obtain a normal distribution curve with the most probable value in the center. Therefore we know in advance that were we actually to calculate the 10,000 means, they would distribute themselves in a normal curve. In addition, we have a way of

estimating the standard deviation of that normal curve.

The standard deviation of such a curve is called the *standard error of the mean* and is symbolized by σ_M. The formula for σ_M is $\sigma_M = \dfrac{\sigma}{\sqrt{N-1}}$; in which σ is the standard deviation of our sample and N is the number of cases in our sample. Thus knowing only these two facts about our *sample*, we can estimate the standard deviation of the 10,000 means we have not bothered to get! To return to our illustration: If we assume that our sample σ was 19.5, then the σ_M 1.97. This is shown in Figure 129.

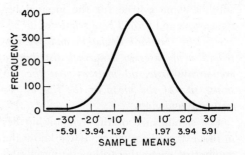

FIG. 129. A normal distribution curve representing the theoretically expected distribution of the means of 10,000 random samples of 100 cases each, taken from the same population. The standard deviation of one obtained sample is 19.5 and the σ_M is 1.97.

THE STANDARD ERROR. This standard deviation of the 10,000 means is called the standard error of the mean because it enables us to say something very important about the size of error we are likely to have in our sample mean.

Let it be recalled that neither the *shape* of the curve in Figure 129 nor its σ of 1.97 would change a bit even if we took 20,000, or 30,000, or any number of samples of 100 and their means. This curve encompasses *all possible* averages obtainable from groups of 100 New Yorkers, just as the curve in Figure 128 encompassed all possible head-tail combinations obtainable from throws of 10 dimes.

Let us further recall that in the dime-throwing experiment the *true* mean number of heads which would fall was five (5 heads and 5 tails). But we saw that *by chance alone* we would sometimes get as many as 6, 7, 8, 9, or even 10 heads. We also know the frequency with which we can expect to get these various combinations. This frequency is given to us by the standard deviation. That is, by chance alone 68.26 per cent of all the throws will fall within the range of plus or minus one σ from the average throw of 5 heads. Or, put in another way, the *probability is 68.26 out of a 100 that a toss of dimes will give us a result that is within the range of plus or minus one σ from the true mean.*

We now come back to our New Yorkers. We have found that our sample mean was 120 pounds. How far away is this sample mean of 120 pounds from the true mean? The answer is clear. Since the sigma of the means is 1.97, there are about *68 chances out of 100* that our sample mean is not more than plus or minus 1.97 pounds away from the true mean. In statistical language this statement is written as follows: "The mean is 120 ± 1.97."

We can state the probabilities with even more confidence. Since we know that 99.74 per cent of all the cases fall within plus and minus 3σ of the mean, we can say that there are *over 99 chances out of 100* that our sample mean is not more than plus or minus 5.91 pounds away from the true mean.

PRECISION AND SIZE OF SAMPLE. This is a high level of confidence (one that any betting man would be willing to risk his all on), but the range of ±5.91 pounds is pretty wide. Is there any way we can reduce this range and still maintain the same level of confidence? There is a relatively simple way in which this can be attempted. When we recall that the standard error of of the mean is determined by the formula

$\sigma_M = \dfrac{\sigma}{\sqrt{N-1}}$, it is clear that by increasing the N (number of cases in our sample) the σ_M is reduced. For instance, if our sample had 200 cases, we would have obtained a standard error of the mean of something less than 1.97 pounds, say 1.30. With a sample of 200 cases we can state our conclusions with the same degree of confidence but with more precision, i.e., there are over 99 chances out of 100 that our sample mean is not more than plus or minus 3.90 pounds (three times the new standard error of the mean) away from the true mean.

While every increase in sample size decreases the standard error of the mean, this increase follows the law of diminishing returns since the N in the σ_M formula is under the square root sign. That is, an increase in N from 100 to 200 may show a sizable drop in the standard error; an increase of another 100 cases will show a smaller decrease in the standard error; an increase of another 100 will show a still smaller increase; and soon the point will be reached where an additional number of cases will show very little decrease in the size of the standard error of the mean. The determination of what size sample we should use rests mainly upon two considerations: (a) the desired precision of the results and (b) the available time, money, and energy. For some measures we wish a highly precise result, and in such cases we must have a large N; for some measures, however, a less highly precise estimate of the true mean is sufficient.

CHANCE ERRORS OF OTHER STATISTICS. Everything we have said about the *mean* of a sample is equally true for other measurements we obtain from samples. For example, suppose we determine that the correlation coefficient between the size of a cortical lesion in our experimental rats and their learning ability is .70. This correlation was based, obviously, on a *sample* of rats—not on all of laboratory ratdom—and therefore may suffer from sampling. But again we can determine the *standard error of the correlation coefficient* (symbolized by σ_r) and indicate what the probabilities are that the obtained correlation coefficient is within a certain distance from the true correlation coefficient for all laboratory ratdom. (But *only* if our original sample of rats was randomly chosen from the population "laboratory ratdom.") Thus, a correlation coefficient written as .70 ± .09 for example, means that there are about 68 chances out of 100 that our sample correlation is not more than plus or minus .09 away from the true correlation for laboratory ratdom.

Another example: Suppose we have two groups of people, one of which has learned a list of nonsense syllables by the "active" method, the other by the "passive" method. Let us assume that the "active" group made an average of 18 errors in learning the list; the "passive" group, 24 errors. The difference between the two means is thus 6 errors. But this difference of 6 errors was obtained from the means of two *samples* of people; therefore, this difference of 6 is uncertain. Again we can work out the *standard error of the difference* between the two groups (symbolized by $\sigma_{\text{diff.}}$), and indicate what the probabilities are that the obtained difference of 6 errors is within a certain distance of the true difference. Thus when we see the statement, "The difference between the means of the two groups was 6 ± 2," this signifies that there are about 68 chances out of 100 that the difference obtained from the samples is not more than plus or minus 2 errors away from the true difference. Suppose we wanted to state our case with a higher level of confidence. Instead of being content with the odds of 68 out of 100, we want odds of 99 out of 100. Then we would say that the chances are 99 out of 100 that the difference obtained from the sample is not more than plus or minus 9 errors (3σ) away from the true difference. But since the obtained difference was only 6 errors to begin with, the true difference could very well be zero. The difference of 6 errors may be just a chance deviation from a true difference of zero. Therefore if we insist on making a statement with a high degree of confidence, we cannot say that the "active" group has been shown to make fewer errors than the passive group.

We take account in these ways of the errors inherent in all measurements based on samples. We can never be *certain* that our obtained means are the true means, that our obtained correlation coefficients are the true correlation coefficients, or that our obtained differences between groups are the real differences. We can only state the *probabilities* that our obtained measurements are within a specified distance from the true values. Sometimes the probabilities are high enough so that we are willing to go ahead as if we really did know the truth. Most scientists will not accept confidence limits of anything less than 95 chances out of 100 before they "go ahead." But even when we demand such high odds, we are still betting on probabilities. The scientist is a gambling man. He has no choice.

Glossary

absolute zero. A measuring instrument that starts numbering its units from a real zero is said to have an absolute zero as its point of origin. Such an instrument is contrasted with a measurement instrument whose numbered units start at some unspecified distance from the zero point. The Fahrenheit and Centigrade thermometers and most intelligence and personality scales are illustrations of the latter type of measurement instruments. When a measurement instrument does not have an absolute zero as its point of origin, we cannot make direct ratio comparisons of scores, i.e., we cannot say that a score of 50 on such an instrument is twice the value of a score of 25, etc.

average deviation (A.D.) A measure of dispersion based on the average of the deviations of every score in the distribution from the mean of all the scores of the distribution. The formula for the average deviation is A.D. $= \frac{\Sigma d}{N}$. The average deviation is less influenced by extreme scores than is the range or the standard deviation.

biased sample. The result of a sampling procedure that systematically excludes certain kinds of people, or systematically under-represents certain kinds of people who should be included. Contrasted with a "random sample."

central tendency. A middle value between the extremes of a set of measures. There are many different kinds of central-tendency measures. Among the more common are the mean, median, and mode. These three measures of central tendency, even when based on the same scores, need not give identical values. They will do so only in a perfectly symmetrical frequency curve. Each measure of central tendency has a somewhat different meaning.

chance errors. Errors due to random factors as opposed to systematic factors. Thus a sampling error occurring from a random sampling procedure is called a chance error.

chance event. An event that has so many complexly interrelated causes that it is impossible (at the time) to predict the exact nature of the occurrences.

class interval. The range of values treated within one group. Thus if we were to treat all values from 10 to 20 as one group, and from 21 to 30 as another group, these ranges would be called "class intervals."

comparable-forms reliability. A method of determining the reliability coefficient for a measuring instrument by obtaining the correlation coefficient between two comparable forms of the same test, administered to the same group of subjects.

converted scores. When a raw score is changed into another kind of score, it is referred to as a converted score. The simplest, and the most commonly used, converted score is the *percentile* score.

correlation coefficient. A single index that gives both the sign and magnitude of a correlation. A correlation coefficient can vary from $+1.00$ (a perfect positive correlation) to -1.00 (a perfect negative correlation). Two common correlation coefficients are the rank-order correlation coefficient (ρ) and the product-moment correlation coefficient (r).

correlation plot. A graphic device picturing the relationship between two sets of scores. In such a graph a person's scores on two different tests are represented by one point. When the scores of a number of people are thus plotted on the graph, we can determine, by inspection, the *sign* of the correlation. When the points on a correlation plot show a trend from the lower left-hand corner to the upper right-hand corner, a *positive correlation* exists; when the trend is from the upper left-hand corner to the lower right-hand corner, a *negative correlation* exists; and when no specific trend is apparent, a *zero correlation* exists.

dispersion. Refers to the degree of scatter among the individual scores of a set of scores. If the scores all cluster closely together around some measure of central tendency, we speak of a low degree of dispersion; if the scores are widely scattered around the central tendency, we speak of a high degree of dispersion. There are a number of quantitative measures of degree of dispersion, among them the range, the average deviation, and the standard deviation.

equal units. An important characteristic of the usual physical measuring instrument is that all units are equal in magnitude, i.e., the distance from 4 inches to 7 inches is equal to the distance from 10 inches to 13 inches. This is to be contrasted with many psychological tests (intelligence, personality) in which we do not know whether the units of measurement (scores) are of equal magnitude, i.e., the difference between a score of 100 and 110 I.Q. points may *not* be equal to the difference between a score of 110 and 120 I.Q. points.

face validity. Tests that are assumed to be valid simply by definition. E.g., a ruler is a valid measuring instrument of length, by definition of what constitutes length.

frequency curve. A graphic representation of the data from a frequency table. The measurement values are represented along the horizontal base line of the graph; the number of cases for each value, along the vertical axis. For each class interval a point, in the middle of the interval, is placed at the appropriate height to indicate the frequency of the occurrence of cases in that interval. These points are then connected by lines to give a frequency "curve." The more technical name for this kind of frequency graph is "frequency polygon."

frequency tables. An orderly arrangement of discrete values in terms of the frequency of occurrence of the different values. Usually the different values are grouped together into class intervals and the frequency table presents the number of cases falling into each class interval.

histogram. A bar diagram that presents the data from a frequency table. Each class interval is represented by a separate bar, and the height of each bar indicates the number of cases falling within that class interval. The bars are usually arranged so that the bar representing the class interval with the lowest measurement value is at the extreme left of the diagram and the one with the highest measurement value, at the extreme right. The histogram is sometimes referred to as a "frequency graph."

independent events. Two events are said to be independent when the occurrence of one does not influence, in any degree, the probability of the occurrence of the other. E.g., when two coins are flipped, the fact that one may fall heads does not influence at all the probability of the other also falling heads—or tails. The probability of the occurrence of independent events is obtained by multiplying the probabilities of the individual events.

"known group" validity. A method for determining the validity of a test by comparing the scores made on the test by a group previously "known" to be high on a certain trait, with the scores of a group "known" to be lower on that trait.

mean (M). The arithmetic mean, frequently referred to as the arithmetic average, is the most commonly used measure of central tendency. It is the arithmetic sum of all the values in a set of data divided by the number of cases. The formula for the mean is written $M = \dfrac{\Sigma X}{N}$. The value of the mean can be strongly influenced by a few extreme values found in the set.

median. A measure of central tendency. It refers to that value, in an array of values arranged from the lowest to the highest, which occupies the middle point. Thus, in such an array the median value would have as many cases below it as above it. The value of the median is not very strongly influenced by extreme items in the set of values.

mode. A measure of central tendency. It refers to the *most frequent* value occurring in a set of values. The terms "most popular" and "most frequent" can be seen as synonymous. The value of the mode is not at all influenced by a few extreme items found in the set of values.

mutually exclusive events. Two events are said to be mutually exclusive when the occurrence of one makes impossible the simultaneous occurrence of the other. E.g., when a coin is flipped, the showing of a *head* makes impossible the simultaneous showing of a tail. The showing of head and the showing of tail are thus mutually exclusive events. The probability of occurrence of two or more mutually exclusive events is obtained by adding the probabilities of the individual events.

negative correlation. Refers to two sets of measures whose values are *inversely* related to each other. Thus if we found that children who are good in arithmetic are *poor* in reading, and those who are poor in arithmetic are *good* in reading, we would have a negative correlation.

normal curve. A perfectly symmetrical, bell-shaped frequency curve having certain well-defined mathematical characteristics. Among these are the following: within the area of the curve marked off by $\pm 1\sigma$ (from the mean) will be found 68.26 per cent of all the scores in the distribution; within the area marked off by $\pm 2\sigma$ will be found 95.44 per cent of the scores; and within the area marked off by $\pm 3\sigma$ will be found 99.75 per cent of the scores. A distribution curve made up of many chance events will approximate a normal distribution curve.

percentile score. One type of a converted score expressing a person's score relative to his group in percentile points. A percentile point divides the total distribution of scores into 100 parts each containing 1 per cent of all the cases. Thus a percentile score of 90 means that 10 per cent of the people in the group scored above that point and 90 per cent scored below. Percentile scores vary from zero to 100 no matter what the range of the raw scores. This makes it possible to compare the performance of people on diverse tests having quite different raw units of measurement.

population. Refers to *all* the objects or people of a given class. E.g., a population of test items would refer to all the items included in any test.

positive correlation. Refers to two sets of measures whose values go together. Thus if we found that children who are good in arithmetic are also good in reading, and those who are poor in the one are poor in the other, we would have a positive correlation.

product-moment correlation coefficient (r). The product-moment correlation coefficient, symbolized by the small letter r is based on the values of the individual deviations and the standard deviations of the two sets of scores. The formula for the product-moment correlation coefficient is $r = \dfrac{\Sigma xy}{N\sigma_x\sigma_y}$. The product-moment correlation coefficient is sometimes called "Pearson's coefficient of correlation" after its inventor, Karl Pearson, an English mathematician. This coefficient is commonly used where N is relatively large.

random sample. The result of a sampling procedure permitting every member of the population an equal opportunity to be included. Contrasted with a "biased sample."

range. The simplest numerical measure of dispersion. It is calculated by obtaining the difference between the two extreme (or end) values of a distribution, and thus the value of the range is greatly influenced by one extreme score.

rank-order correlation coefficient (ρ). A correlation coefficient symbolized by the Greek letter ρ (rho) based on a comparison of the ranks of people on two sets of scores. The formula for the rank-order correlation coefficient is $\rho = 1 - \dfrac{6\Sigma D^2}{N(N^2-1)}$. The rank-order correlation coefficient is usually employed where the number of cases (N) is relatively small (about 15 to 20 cases).

raw scores. The original scores obtained from a measuring instrument. To be contrasted with *converted scores*.

reliability coefficient. Refers to the degree to which repeated measurement of an instrument will give the same or similar readings. This is determined by getting the correlation coefficient between two sets of measurements of the same object by the same measuring instrument. The higher the correlation, the more *reliable* is the instrument.

sampling error. When we measure a *sample* of subjects and attempt to generalize to the total population, we may make wrong generalizations because our sample was not perfectly representative of the population. Errors contributing to the lack of representativeness of a sample are called sampling errors.

skewness. Refers to the deviation of the shape of a frequency curve from a normal curve. A skewed curve, therefore, is a frequency curve that departs from the symmetrical normal curve either by having more cases on the right of the mean than on the left or vice versa. In a skewed curve the values for the mean, median, and mode are not identical.

split-half reliability. A method for determining the reliability coefficient for a measuring instrument by obtaining the correlation coefficient between two equal halves of the same test. By splitting a test into two halves, the scores on the odd-numbered items are grouped together to form one subscore, and the scores on the even-numbered items to form the second subscore. For this reason the split-half reliability method is sometimes referred to as the odd-even method.

standard deviation (S.D., σ). A measure of dispersion based on the average of the deviations *squared* of every score in the distribution, from the mean of all the scores of the distribution. The formula for the standard deviation is $\sigma = \sqrt{\dfrac{\Sigma d^2}{N}}$ The standard deviation is the most commonly used measure of dispersion.

standard error of correlation coefficient (σ_r). The standard deviation of a theoretical frequency curve made up of many sample correlation coefficients. Used in estimating the degree to which the obtained sample correlation deviates from the true correlation of the population.

standard error of the difference. (σ_{diff}). The standard deviation of a theoretical frequency curve made up of many sample differences. Used in estimating the degree to which the obtained sample difference deviates from the true difference of the population.

standard error of the mean (σ_M). The standard deviation of a theoretical frequency curve made up of many sample means. Called the "standard error" because it is useful in estimating the degree to which the obtained sample mean deviates from the true mean of the population.

statistics. The mathematical discipline relating to the analysis of numerical data. Statistical methods are designed to summarize such data, to assess their reliability and validity, to determine the nature and magnitude of relationships among sets of data, and to guide us in our attempts to generalize from observed events to new events.

validity coefficient. Refers to the degree to which the measurements obtained with an instrument correlate with the criterion measures. When we ask whether an instrument is *valid*, we ask whether it measures what we think it measures. The higher the correlation coefficient between the scores on a test and the criterion scores, the more valid is the test.

zero correlation. Refers to the absence of a relationship between two sets of scores. Thus if we found that some children who are good in arithmetic are poor in reading, while other children who are good in arithmetic are also good in reading, we would have a zero correlation.

Suggestions for Further Reading

WALLIS, W. A., and ROBERTS, H. V. 1956. *Statistics: a new approach*. Glencoe: The Free Press.

A clearly written general approach to statistics, explaining the basic ideas with scarcely more than high school mathematics.

UNDERWOOD, B. J., DUNCAN, C. P., TAYLOR, J. A., and COTTON, J. W. 1955. *Elementary statistics*. New York: Appleton-Century-Crofts.

An introductory textbook to the study of statistics with special application to problems of psychological measurement.

CHAPTER XX

Intelligence and Ability

WE HAVE studied different aspects of man: man the perceiver, man the needful, and man the adaptive. But it has always been clear that this tripartite division is merely one of convenience—for analytic purposes—and that man, functioning in his social and physical world, is an indivisible unity who perceives and desires and learns *simultaneously*. We now turn to the task of synthesis—to the task of describing the whole man.

One of the first things to become apparent as we turn our attention to the whole man is that he manifests himself in infinite variety. There has never been a person exactly like you, and there never will be. And one of the major factors which distinguishes you from your neighbor is the way your perceptual, motivational, and learning processes are organized into *unique patterns of capacities:* intelligence, abilities, talents, and aptitudes. It is this patterning and synthesis which helps make you, *you;* which makes you Jim McGraw, or Shirley Cohen, or Tony Morales instead of Mr. Anyman.

Intelligence

The study of the abilities of man has been intimately tied up with intelligence testing. Literally millions of people, representing different ages, economic groups, cultures, nationalities, and races have been subjected to intelligence testing of one kind or another. There are *individual tests* (where one person at a time is tested) and *group tests* (where hundreds of people at a time are tested); *speed tests* (where the scores are determined by the rapidity with which correct answers can be given) and *power tests* (where the difficulty of the tasks successfully completed determines the score); *verbal tests* (requiring verbal responses to questions) and *performance tests* (involving such nonverbal responses as stringing variously colored beads in a specified order).

From these tests we have accumulated much useful information. We can fairly quickly and reliably determine where a person stands in relation to any reference group of his fellows, and on the basis of this we can predict a number of things about his performance in various situations. But the question of what it is we are testing, the question of what is "intelligence," remains unanswered.

The Meaning of Intelligence. Intelligence is a concept variously used and variously defined. Some people define it as the ability to adapt to new circumstances, others as the ability to learn, and still others as the capacity to deal with complex and abstract material.

Different psychologists have championed these (and other) definitions of intelligence, and much research has been addressed to these questions. However, none of this research has resulted in a clear definition of intelligence. For this reason many psychologists today have reached the point where they no longer ask "*What* is intelligence?" They have decided that they can do a useful job in measuring intelligence without defining it. In this respect they are doing what the early physicists did when they studied heat. Long before the physicists could agree on a sound definition of heat they had invented reliable thermometers to measure changes in temperature and with these instruments they were able to discover many important physical laws.

A PRACTICAL APPROACH. That mental testers can work effectively without defining intelligence reflects the fact that from its very beginnings intelligence testing has concerned itself with practical problems rather than theoretical ones.

About the year 1900, at the request of the school authorities of Paris, the eminent French psychologist, Alfred Binet, undertook to develop a set of tests which would identify mentally deficient school children so that they could be placed in schools where they would not be held to the standard curriculum. From that time on, intelligence tests have been used primarily to help predict the capacity of children and students to profit from "intellectual" training. With this orientation, it does not matter what intelligence is, so long as the tests can predict success in intellectual performance.

Intelligence tests usually consist of a relatively large collection of different *test items*, or tasks, and an intelligence test *score* is based on the total number of those tasks completed successfully. In constructing a test all sorts of items are tried out: word definitions, arithmetic problems, perceptual tasks, following of complex directions, etc. The final inclusion or exclusion of a test item is not determined by any very explicit psychological theory of intelligence; the question of what constitutes a good test item is primarily a practical one: "Does it work?"

"INTELLIGENCE" BY DEFINITION. In selecting items for an intelligence test, the psychologist does, however, follow some guiding principles. Since an intelligence test is designed to measure the "intellect" rather than, say, temperament or motor skills, it seems clear that the items in the test should be of an "intellectual" nature. When an item is being considered for inclusion in an intelligence test, its content is examined with a common-sense definition of "intellectual" in mind. If the psychologist is satisfied that it is an intellectual task, it is included. A test made up of such items is, *by definition*, an "intelligence test." We have here a kind of "face validation" (see p. 526).

However, face validity is not enough. An intelligence test must meet several other validating criteria before it can be accepted.

Intelligence and Age. Most of us assume that children become "brighter" as they grow older, since it is obvious that older children can cope with more problems than can younger children. If we accept this common-sense assumption, older children should receive higher scores on intelligence tests than younger children. We have here a kind of "known group" validating method (see p. 527).

The usual method of constructing intelligence tests (first designed by Binet) attempts to guarantee that the tests will meet this criterion. A number of diverse intellectual tasks are collected (sampling widely the mental abilities presumed to be typical of the various age levels) and then the children of different ages are tested on these items. An item is kept or dropped according to how well it can discriminate among children of different ages.

For example: In preparing the 1937 revision of the Stanford-Binet Intelligence test, Terman and Merrill (1937) tested the ability of children of various ages to define such words as "connection," "carrying," etc. They found that almost no eight- or nine-year-olds could pass this item. About 10 per cent of the ten-year-olds was successful. Beyond that age the percentage of children passing this item increased rather regularly. Thirty per cent of the 11-year-olds, 50 per cent of the 12-year-olds, over 60 per cent of the 13-year-olds, and 70 per cent of the 14-year-olds were able to pass the item. At the age of 17 years over 90 per cent of the individuals could pass it. This item, therefore, was considered a good item since *an increasing number of children were able to pass it with each higher age level.* An item which does not clearly show this relationship is thrown out as unrelated to the growth of mental ability.

THE DEVELOPMENTAL CURVE. It comes as no surprise therefore that "intelligence" (as measured by these tests) will show a *developmental curve,* that is, show growth with age. This is not simply arguing in circles. The significant thing is that we have been able to find intellectual tasks which

do give us such growth curves. Presumably if intelligence did not grow with age, we would not be able to discover such test items. This becomes clear when we look at the results of testing intelligence at later ages.

Although it has been possible to construct tests which give us a developmental curve up to the ages of 13 or 14 years, it has been much more difficult to find intellectual tasks which show a developmental trend *after* the age of 16 (see Fig. 130).

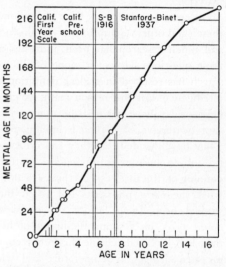

FIG. 130. This curve represents the average mental ages of children studied in the Berkeley Growth Study. In this study the same children were measured regularly, over a long period of years, for various characteristics, among them, intelligence. Four different forms of intelligence tests were used (appropriate for each age range): The California First Year Scale, The California Pre-School Test, the 1916 form of the Stanford-Binet Intelligence Test, and the 1937 revision of the Stanford-Binet Test. It will be noted that there is a diminished rate of growth in mental age after 14 years. (Adapted from Bayley, 1951.)

While most recent research suggests that mental growth (especially among "mentally gifted" people) may continue up to the age of 50 or 60 (see Fig. 131), in general the evidence seems clear that the rate of growth of intelligence is fairly rapid

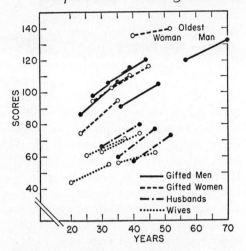

FIG. 131. Average scores earned on a Concept Mastery Test by 422 "gifted men," 346 "gifted women," and their spouses. The Concept Mastery Test was designed by Terman. It consists of difficult vocabulary items and analogies items dealing chiefly with abstract ideas. The subjects have been grouped according to the age of their first testing. The first and second tests for each group (12 years apart) are connected. For example: In the lower left-hand corner we have the scores of a group of wives who were first tested when they were 20 years old, and then re-tested when they were about 32 years old. Note that all groups show similar tendencies to increase in scores over the 12-year period. "Gifted," as used here, refers to men and women who, while still children, were shown to have I.Q.'s ranging from 140 to 200. Note also the scores made by the oldest woman in the group (40 years at first testing, 52 at second) and the oldest man (56 years at the first testing and about 70 at the second). (Adapted from Bayley and Oden, 1955.)

up to the age of puberty and from then on growth continues at a decreasing rate.

MENTAL AGE. In Figure 130 the scores of the children taking the intelligence tests are presented in terms of *mental age*. This unit is a converted score (see p. 518), and derives directly from the developmental curve of intelligence. It will be remembered that the Terman-Merrill task of defining words was passed by about 60 per cent of the 13-year-old children. Such an item, because it can be passed by a majority of the 13-year-olds, is therefore placed at

year 13 on the intelligence test scale. Similarly, every item in an intelligence test can be given its appropriate *age level* value. When a single child is tested, his score, based on the number of items passed, can then be described *in terms of age*.

For example: Suppose Youngster Anyman can pass *all* the items that had been passed by at least 60 per cent of all the 10-year-olds taking this test, and *some* of the 11- and 12-year-old items. Youngster Anyman would then get credit for all the items up to and including the 10-year items, plus those he passed above the 10-year age level. Thus if he passed half the items for year 11, and one fourth of the items for year 12, he would receive an additional 6 months credit for the 11-year items, and 3 months credit for the 12-year items. This would give him a total mental age (abbreviated to M.A.) of 10 years and 9 months. This method of scoring is illustrated in the following listing which gives some of the tests for the years 6 and 14 in the 1937 Stanford-Binet revision, together with the scoring credits:

Year 6 (6 items, 2 months credit for each item passed)
1. Giving meanings of such words as *orange, envelope, puddle*.
2. Stringing a chain of seven differently shaped beads in a specified order.
3. Discovering missing details or absurdities in pictures.
4. Counting up to nine blocks.
5. Pointing out similarities and differences in pictured objects.
6. Tracing the correct path through a pictured maze.

Year 13 (6 items, 2 months credit for each item passed)
1. Vocabulary of more difficult words.
2. Discovering the rule followed in a series of paper-foldings.
3. Telling how to measure 3 pints, using a 4-pint and a 9-pint can.

4. Pointing out absurdities in pictures.
5. Directional orientation: "Suppose you were going west, then turn to your right, then . . . ," etc.
6. Giving the meaning of abstract words.

INTELLIGENCE QUOTIENT. If Youngster Anyman has a mental age of 10 years and 9 months, then he has passed the same number of items as most of the 10-year-nine-month-old children who have taken this intelligence test. But suppose that Youngster Anyman is only 9 years and 6 months old chronologically. Obviously he is somewhat brighter than the average child of this age. In order to indicate this, we must have a score which will express his *mental age as related to his chronological age.* Such a score is called the *intelligence quotient,* or the *I.Q.*

On the Binet test the I.Q. is simply a ratio of mental age over chronological age (multiplied by 100 in order to remove decimal points): $I.Q. = \frac{M.A.}{C.A.} \times 100$. Thus a child with a chronological age of 9 years 6 months (9.5 years) who obtained a mental age of exactly 9 years 6 months would have an I.Q. of 100, i.e., $I.Q. = \frac{9.5}{9.5} \times 100 = 100$. Youngster Anyman who has a chronological age of 9 years 6 months, and a mental age of 10 years 9 months (10.75 years) has an I.Q. of approximately 113, i.e.,

$I.Q. = \frac{10.75}{9.5} \times 100 = 113.2$.

It can be seen that an I.Q. of 100 will be characteristic of the average child, an I.Q. greater than 100 will indicate a somewhat superior child, an I.Q. lower than 100 will indicate a child of somewhat less than average brightness. (See Box 142 for a further discussion of the meanings of I.Q. scores.)

STANDARDIZATION OF INTELLIGENCE TESTS. But all of the above statements are *relative to the group on which the test was stand-ardized.* To say that the "average" ten-year-old can pass certain items of an intelligence test implies, of course, that we have previously tested a *representative* sample of the entire population of ten-year-old children. This procedure is called standardizing the test items. As we have seen in Chapter 19, the problem of obtaining a sample truly representative of the entire population is beset with difficulties. If the sample used in standardizing an intelligence test is unrepresentative of the entire population of children (see p. 529 for a discussion of *biased samples*) the intelligence test has limited usefulness. Thus if the intelligence test was standardized on a sample which did not adequately include children of the lower economic groups, or of certain racial stocks, we cannot legitimately use this test to measure the I.Q. for these children. This is but a reflection of the fact that the I.Q. is a *relative* score, not an absolute score (see p. 518).

ADULT I.Q.'S. We have seen that intelligence, as measured by our available tests, does not grow at the same rate after puberty as it does prior to that age. This means, of course, that the concept of I.Q. cannot have the same meaning for an adult as it does for a person younger than about 16. In order to use the I.Q. unit for adults, several simplifying assumptions have been made. In computing a Stanford-Binet I.Q. for anyone over the age of 15 the person is given a chronological age of 15—no matter how old he really is. This is done because it is assumed that the average adult has stopped growing in intelligence at that age. Thus the formula for I.Q. for an adult becomes $\frac{M.A.}{15} \times 100$.

Since the Stanford-Binet test has been standardized on children and very young adults (up to the age of 18) many psychologists do not consider it an adequate test for older adults. In response to these diffi-

---

BOX 142

The Genius and the Moron

We all have a strong urge to translate I.Q. scores into such descriptive and colorful terms as "genius," "moron," and "idiot." For the most part, however, psychologists have shied away from such translations primarily because the I.Q. scores for large populations show a normal distribution curve. That is, there is no sharp break between an I.Q. of say 50 or 70 (the I.Q. scores which are conventionally taken as the limits defining the moron) and lower or higher I.Q.'s. Moreover we know full well that whether an individual's performance justifies the honorific term of "genius" depends as much upon other factors as it does upon I.Q.—Upon *special* skills, abilities, motivation, and other personality factors.

Since I.Q.'s are relative scores, the most helpful guide to understanding the meaning of an I.Q. score is in terms of the number of children in the total population who equal or exceed such a score. The following values are based on such estimates made by Pintner, Dragositz, and Kushner for the revised Stanford-Binet Intelligence Test:

The child whose I.Q. is:	*Is equaled or excelled by:*				
160	1 child out of 10,000				
152	8 children out of 10,000				
140	70	"	"	"	"
130	300	"	"	"	"
120	1,100	"	"	"	"
110	2,700	"	"	"	"
100	5,000	"	"	"	"
90	7,300	"	"	"	"
80	8,900	"	"	"	"
70	9,700	"	"	"	"
60	9,900	"	"	"	"

The above data tell the important story of individual differences in intelligence test scores. A test of 2,904 children shows a range of about 140 I.Q. points, from a low of 34 to a high of 174, with a standard deviation of 16.4. In intelligence, as elsewhere among the abilities of man, pronounced individual differences are the striking fact.

PINTNER, R., DRAGOSITZ, A., and KUSHNER, R. 1944. *Supplementary guide for the revised Stanford-Binet*. Stanford: Stanford Univ. Press.

---

culties a number of tests have been developed especially for adults. Among the most commonly used of these is the Wechsler Adult Intelligence Scale which consists of two parts—a verbal part and a performance part, each consisting of five kinds of items. The verbal part includes *information, comprehension, vocabulary, memory span* for digits forwards and backwards, *arithmetical reasoning*, etc. The performance scale includes tasks involving *object assembly* (putting together cut-out parts to complete a figure such as a human profile—very much like a jig-saw puzzle), *picture completion, picture arrangement*, etc. It is of interest to note that the correlation between the Stanford-Binet and the Wechsler Adult Intelligence Scale is about .85.

BY WAY OF SUMMARY. In selecting items to differentiate the more intelligent from the less intelligent children, intelligence-test constructors usually follow several guiding principles: in the first place, the content of the items must, on the face of it, be "intellectual" in nature; secondly, items must discriminate between children of different ages, such that the percentage of children passing the item must increase with increase in age. Other considerations also have been taken into account: the items should be reasonably easy to administer and score, should sample a wide variety of tasks, and should reflect the experiences common to all children.

The use of such items when standardized on representative samples, enables us then to convert the raw scores earned on intelligence tests into mental age scores and I.Q. scores. When this is done we find that intelligence shows a fairly constant developmental growth up to the age of approximately 14 years. This can be taken as a "known group" validation of the intelligence test. But this very fact makes for difficulties in using the I.Q. concept when measuring adult intelligence.

Intelligence and Performance. The mere fact that an intelligence test results in a developmental curve is not adequate for complete validation. The intelligence test must meet the final criterion of correlating with intellectual performance in "real life."

The usual performance measured for determining the validity of an intelligence test is success in school. This is, as we have seen, a reflection of the history of intelligence testing. Other criteria have also been used, such as success in various occupations and professions. Together these criteria testify to the practical usefulness of intelligence tests.

INTELLIGENCE AND SCHOOL SUCCESS. Two kinds of measures of school success have been correlated with intelligence test scores —*grades* earned in school, and *achievement tests*. In the first case subjective factors are involved, since the determination of a student's grades can obviously reflect a teacher's judgment of and attitudes toward the student. In the second case such biasing factors play no role, since achievement tests are usually objectively scored, comprising the familiar true-false, multiple-choice, matching, and completion items, and are designed to measure how much of the subject matter of the course has been mastered by the student.

In both cases the correlations are positive. Correlations between intelligence tests and school grades average about .50, with some school subjects showing higher and some lower correlation coefficients. Thus,

knowing the child's I.Q. permits us to predict (with something better than chance accuracy) the grades that the child will earn from the beginning of his schooling through graduation from college. Such predictions over long periods of time are not as accurate as predictions made over short periods of time.

Correlations of intelligence test scores with achievement test scores tend to be somewhat higher than with school grades. Again we find differences according to subject-matter. Learned and Wood (1938) list the following correlations between achievement tests in various subjects and scores on the Otis Intelligence Test among high-school students in a large city:

Otis Test and English	.74
" " " Algebra	.68
" " " General Science	.64
" " " Biology	.52
" " " Physics	.48
" " " French	.46
" " " History	.42

Correlations between intelligence test scores taken in early life and achievement in college range from .21 to .58. For instance, the fairly low correlation of .21 was obtained between intelligence scores earned in *first grade* and achievement scores later earned in college.

Studies of college drop-outs and graduates have indicated that it is unlikely that a person with an I.Q. below 100 will be able to graduate from college and also that a person with an I.Q. below 125 will succeed at a first-rate graduate school in any subject. These statements, of course, are merely statements of *probabilities*.

It is clear that the performance of students in their school work is not entirely determined by "intelligence" nor entirely predictable by intelligence tests. But it is equally clear from the available data that intelligence tests do measure some lasting intellectual capacity of a person, a capacity which is fairly important for success in school.

INTELLIGENCE AND OCCUPATIONAL APTITUDE. When psychological testing was first tried in industry, intelligence tests were used almost exclusively in selecting workers for various occupations. This was based on the belief that intelligence is a general factor important in the performance of all types of work. Later research cast some doubt on this assumption and specialized *aptitude tests* were designed for each major occupational category. Nevertheless, intelligence test scores do correlate highly with most kinds of work proficiency.

Two kinds of occupational-proficiency measures have commonly been used. One is the proficiency shown by an employee during his *training period* for his job. This measure of his performance is apt to be fairly objective and reliable, since he is being rated by skilled teachers and training personnel under standard conditions. The second measure is the worker's actual *performance on the job* after he has completed his training period. Here such measures as productivity or ratings by supervisors can be used. Two major conclusions can be drawn from a comprehensive survey by Ghiselli (1955) of the validity coefficients of almost every conceivable aptitude test:

1) There is a wide range in the degree to which intelligence test scores correlate with occupational proficiency. With the training performance the correlations range from —.03 for "gross manual workers" to .61 for "personal service occupations." With the actual work on the job, the correlations range from —.10 for sales clerks to .47 for electrical workers. (See Table 16 for some further illustrative findings.)

2) For all the jobs examined the overall correlation between intelligence test scores and job proficiency is almost as high as any other single kind of aptitude test. The average correlation for *all* the tests with training performance on all the jobs was .27, while for *intelligence tests* with all the jobs it was .38. With actual work on the job, the average correlation for all the tests was .16, for the intelligence tests it was .19.

Man's diverse abilities, whether expressed in school or in work, are reflected to some degree in "intelligence" as measured by intelligence tests.

Generality of Intelligence. The fact that intelligence test scores correlate with such a variety of performance scores might be taken as evidence that "intelligence" is a *general and unitary* capacity of the individual. And indeed some psychologists have maintained just that position. However,

TABLE 16

Correlation Coefficients Between Intelligence Tests and Various Occupations (Data from Ghiselli, 1955)

Occupation	Training Performance	Job Performance
Managerial work	.46	.28
Mechanical repairmen	.38	.18
Complex machine operators	.34	.28
Computing clerks	.23	.18
Vehicle operators	.18	.14
Agricultural workers	.05	.00
Bench workers and assemblers	.02	.22
Salesmen	(No data)	.31

other psychologists have argued that intelligence test scores represent the composite of many *different and separate* mental abilities such as reasoning, memory, and learning. Much research has been done on this question, leading to the present view that intelligence tests measure neither a single unitary quality of a person nor a simple composite of separate unrelated traits. The major research approach to this question has been through the correlating of various mental tests with each other.

INTERCORRELATIONS OF MENTAL ABILITIES. We have pointed out that intelligence tests can be verbal or nonverbal. Both types correlate to about the same degree with school and work performance. But how do these two types of tests correlate with each other? The results of many studies agree: Individuals' performances on verbal and nonverbal tests correlate positively, but seldom do these correlations run higher than about .50 or .60. Thus, these studies suggest that though there is *something* in common between verbal intelligence test scores and nonverbal intelligence test scores, each is also measuring something which is peculiar to itself.

Correlations among the different kinds of test items normally found within an intelligence test provide additional arguments against the hypothesis that intelligence tests measure only a unitary capacity of the person. (See Box 143 for an extreme example of different capacities found within one person.) Such studies indicate, for example, that correlations between performance on items involving definitions of words and those involving arithmetic problems do not correlate highly enough to assure us that both kinds of items are measuring exactly the same capacity of the person. In these studies a special technique, called *factor analysis*, has been used.

FACTOR ANALYSIS. While factor analysis is a rather complicated statistical and mathematical affair, the rationale for it can be illustrated in a simple example.

Suppose we give a group of subjects two tests: an arithmetic-reasoning test and a vocabulary test, and we find that the two tests correlate positively. This single correlation, no matter how high, does not permit us to decide whether the two tests are measuring a general capacity related to "intelligence," or a specific capacity related to "verbal comprehension"—since even an arithmetic-reasoning test must be read and the words understood to be solved. We need more information. Suppose we now give the same subjects another test—a performance intelligence test that requires no reading—and then examine the resulting correlations obtained among all three tests. If we now find that the performance test correlates more highly with the arithmetic-reasoning test than with the vocabulary test, it might be argued that there are at least two abilities involved—one ability which is reflected in both the arithmetic-reasoning test and the performance test, and another which is reflected in the vocabulary and the arithmetic-ability test. If all the correlations among the three tests are about the *same* size, then some overall general ability seems to be at work.

By adding more and more different kinds of tests to our battery and studying the resulting correlations we may eventually be able to discover the minimum number of different abilities we have to postulate in order to account for all of the mental capacities of man. However when we add many tests to our battery we run into a major difficulty. The study of the interrelations of even a small number of tests involves a large number of correlations. Thus, among two tests there is only one correlation; among three tests, there are three different correlations; among four tests, there are six correlations; among twenty tests, 190 correlations; and among

---

BOX 143

Idiot Savant

From time to time there arise in the human population so-called "idiot-savants" —feeble-minded persons with one or several highly developed specialties. The most intensively studied case is that of "L" reported by Scheerer, Rothmann and Goldstein. "L" was first brought in by his mother, for psychological and neuropsychiatric examination, when he was 11 years old. His case was studied from 1937 to 1943.

Medical examination throughout the six-year period showed him to be healthy and physically well-developed with no signs of neurological disturbance. His EEG was normal. But his mental examination revealed a world of paradoxes.

He could tell the day of the week for any given date between 1880 and 1950. He could add up correctly the totals of ten to twelve 2-place numbers just as quickly as one could call them out. He could spell correctly many words *forwards and backwards,* and never forgot the spelling of a word, once having been told how to spell it. He could play *by ear only* such musical compositions as the "Largo" from Dvorak, and could sing, from beginning to end, the "Credo," "Si Ciel," and the "Adagio Pathétique" from the opera *Othello.*

On the other hand: He was unable to follow the regular school curriculum. His general information was extremely substandard. He knew the meanings of very few words. He was almost completely deficient in logical reasoning, and was at a total loss in any problem involving abstractions. His I.Q. on the Binet was 50!

"L" seems to bear dramatic testimony against the notion that intellectual activities are determined by a unitary quality or capacity. Neither, however, does his case permit us to assume that intellectual activities are determined by a host of separate and independent capacities—one for each type of performance.

In the first place, as Scheerer, Rothmann and Goldstein point out, "L"'s superiority in a few narrowly specialized activities does not necessarily indicate special *endowment* in those capacities. Rather, what "L" seems to show is the effect of special motivation and practice in a highly narrowed field of activities. Any normal child *could* do what "L" did—and much more. These writers suggest the following analysis of the idiot savant:

There are both general and specific intellectual capacities. Abstract capacity and intelligence is essential for the normal functioning of *all* intellectual activities. Where abstract intelligence is impaired, the person may be driven, in an abnormal degree, to exercise and develop those specific functions which are less impaired. But since there is a close *interdependence* between all functions of the person, this can result only in atypical forms of expression in his relatively intact capacities. He therefore develops "queer" performance patterns. He can add 2-place numbers, but cannot understand the logic and rules of arithmetic. He can spell, but he cannot understand the meanings of words.

The performance of the idiot savant, no less than that of the normal person, is determined by the interaction of special capacities and general capacities.

SCHEERER, M., ROTHMANN, E., and GOLDSTEIN, K. 1945. A case of "idiot savant": an experimental study of personality organization. *Psychol. Monogr.,* 58, #4.

---

50 tests, 1,225 correlations. To deal with so many correlations simultaneously and to see which tests tap the same abilities requires some method of arranging the many correlations into groups, so that the correlations within any one group have about the same interrelations. The mathematical technique of factor analysis is designed to do just that. Factor analysis enables us to deal with a large number of correlations simultaneously, and in this way it is hoped we can discover whether the correlations

can be accounted for by a single mental factor or whether we must postulate several different kinds of factors.

THURSTONE'S PRIMARY MENTAL ABILITIES. Perhaps the best known study which used the factor analysis method in intelligence testing is that of Thurstone at the University of Chicago (1938). On the basis of a factor analysis examination of the results of a battery of sixty tests, Thurstone came to the conclusion that most of the mental capacity of man could be accounted for by postulating seven primary mental abilities. These are:

1) *Number:* The ability to add, subtract, multiply, and divide. This is not the same as arithmetic-reasoning ability because it involves only the four fundamental arithmetic processes.

2) *Word fluency:* The ability to write and speak with ease. This is not the same as verbal meaning (the next primary ability) since a person who knows but very few words may be able to use them fluently, while a person who knows many words may be halting in his speech.

3) *Verbal meaning:* The understanding of ideas in word form.

4) *Memory:* The ability to retain and revive impressions, or of recalling and recognizing past experiences.

5) *Reasoning:* The ability to solve complex problems, profit from experience, and plan new activities based on past experience.

6) *Spatial perception:* The ability to perceive size and spatial relationships correctly.

7) *Perceptual speed:* The ability to identify stimulus objects quickly. Thus, in developing reading skill it is necessary to identify entire words without carefully examining each letter in the word.

However, Thurstone did not find that these primary mental abilities were independent abilities. Each of these, in fact, correlates positively with every other one. For example: *Number* correlates .46 with word fluency, .38 with verbal meaning, .18 with memory, etc.; *Verbal meaning* correlates .51 with word fluency, .39 with memory, and .54 with reasoning.

BY WAY OF SUMMARY. It appears that an intelligence test score does not reflect a single unitary capacity, nor does it represent the simple summation or average of several different and independent mental abilities. People can be good in arithmetic and poor in word definitions, creative and imaginative in music and relatively uncreative in science. But normally, those of us who are superior in one mental activity tend to be somewhat superior in many other activities. Among almost all the abilities of man there tend to be positive correlations. The mental organization that determines the abilities of man seems to be a rather complex one and has thus far defied adequate description.

Aptitudes

The recognition that a highly intelligent individual may turn out to be a good musician but a poor scientist, a mediocre streetcar conductor but an excellent electrician, has led to the development of *aptitude tests.* Aptitude refers to the *potential* ability of a person to perform a specific kind of activity. This is to be distinguished from proficiency achievement, which refers to the person's *present performance.* An aptitude test, therefore, is designed to detect some dormant or undeveloped ability within a person and to predict how well he will perform after he has had proper training in that activity.

Such tests, it was believed, would be of great value to many people. For industry, aptitude tests could be helpful in selecting people for various kinds of jobs; for the individual, they could be helpful in selecting the type of education, or training, or work which would be proper for him. The usefulness of aptitude tests rests on the assumption, then, that different occupations require different abilities and that people differ in their ability patterns.

Occupational Ability Patterns. The evidence seems clear that different occupations require different proficiencies. Thus the office clerk must be more proficient at number work than must the garage mechanic. But experience during the two World Wars has shown that people from various walks of life could learn highly specialized military duties with about the same efficiency. Retail tradesmen, for example, learned to be engine-room mechanics about as easily as did civilian machinists. This experience together with continued research (recall the fact that intelligence tests correlate positively with almost *every* occupation) has suggested a revision of the original belief that there exists a specialized type of work ideally suited to the specialized aptitudes of each person. Rather it appears that we can divide people into three broad groups in this respect.

Some people have no special aptitude which stands out above the rest, and the general level of all of their aptitudes is so *low* that they can only carry on relatively unskilled or semiskilled work. Aptitude tests could be of no help in directing them into specific occupations. For other people, the general level of all of their aptitudes is so *high* that they can be successful in almost any occupation or profession. Aptitude tests can be of no great help to them either. But most people have an *intermediate* level of general ability. For them it is important to know which aptitudes stand

out above the rest, so that they will be able to capitalize on their strongest points. For these people aptitude tests might make the difference between success and failure.

Psychologists have thus been spurred on to devise a multitude of aptitude tests. These many kinds of tests have been used for many different objectives and with varying degrees of success.

Varieties of Aptitude Tests. Some aptitude tests are designed to measure a general aptitude. Thus there are tests of general mechanical aptitude and tests of general scientific aptitude which are supposed to predict future success in any kind of job involving mechanical ability, or in any scientific field. There are also tests of specific aptitudes, designed, for example, to predict success in work as a garage mechanic, or as a lathe operator; as a physicist, or as a geologist.

In designing aptitude tests a purely practical and common-sense approach was first attempted. Test items were selected primarily on the basis of the nature of the performance to be predicted, and ranged from intellectual items to measures of quickness of muscular response. The various aptitude tests thus designed can be classified into four broad categories.

INTELLECTUAL TESTS. We have already seen that intelligence tests have been used with some success in predicting proficiency in the various trades and crafts, and in the more "scholarly" occupations. In addition to the usual items found in general intelligence tests, aptitude tests occasionally have "tailor-made" items for the specific occupations involved. Thus an arithmetic item in a test for cashiers may take the form of a series of transactions involving the making of change.

SPATIAL-PERCEPTUAL TESTS. Tests of this type are designed to measure speed and accuracy of perceiving spatial relations.

Frequently these spatial relations are presented in the context of mechanical problems and their solution requires the application of mechanical principles as well as accurate perception of spatial relations (see Fig. 132).

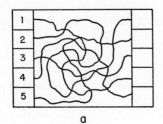

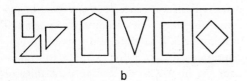

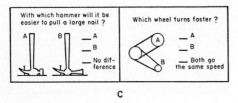

FIG. 132. Examples of items found in spatial-perceptual aptitude tests. In *a* ("pursuit test") the person is required, by eye alone, to follow the winding path from each of the five points of departure and to indicate where the path terminates. In *b* (spatial relations) the several smaller forms in the square on the left can be assembled to make one of the four forms on the right. Item *c* is self-explanatory.

MOTOR TESTS. The motor tests are designed to measure speed and dexterity of simple movements. Included as items in such tests are dotting and tapping tasks measuring speed and accuracy (see Fig. 133); dexterity tasks in which the individual is required, for example, to pick up very small pegs and insert them into holes (finger dexterity), or to pick up a block in each hand, turn the blocks over, and replace them in their original location (hand

dexterity); and reaction-time tasks in which the quickness of response is measured. In simple reaction-time tasks the person is required to depress a telegraph key with his finger as soon as a signal light goes on, and the time between the appearance of the stimulus and the onset of the response is measured. In complex reaction-time tasks, several different stimuli are presented serially and the person is required to make a different response to each. Sometimes the score is determined by his speed of reaction, sometimes by the number of errors made.

TALENT TESTS. A number of tests have been designed to measure such special aptitudes as musical or artistic "talent." One of the earliest of these is the Seashore test for musical talent designed in 1919. It makes use of a number of phonograph records which present musical notes or patterns of notes differing in pitch, intensity, time, rhythm, and timbre. On each record the person has to make a number of comparisons between the patterns of notes. With pitch, for example, pairs of notes are sounded which differ from each other in frequency from 24 vibrations per second to ½ vibration per second. The person has

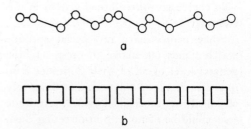

FIG. 133. Examples of items found in motor aptitude tests. In *a* ("dotting") the individual is required to make a single dot in each of the series of irregularly placed small circles. Speed and precision of movement is important here. In *b* (tapping) the squares which the person must tap with his pencil are relatively large so that precision of movement is relatively less important than in the dotting test. Speed of movement is emphasized here.

to choose which of the pair has the higher pitch.

Validity of Aptitude Tests. Any one of these aptitude tests yields disappointingly low validity coefficients. When used in industry, the spatial-perceptual tests show the highest correlation with proficiency at work; the intellectual tests rank next; and the motor tests, last. (See Table 17.) For

TABLE 17

Average Validity Coefficients for Various Types of Aptitude Tests for Various Jobs
(After Ghiselli, 1955)

Type of Test	*Correlation*
Intellectual	.19
Spatial-Perceptual	
Spatial relations....................	.14
Pursuit..........................	.19
Perceptual speed...................	.27
Mechanical principles..............	.26
Motor	
Dotting..........................	.15
Tapping..........................	.14
Finger dexterity...................	.19
Hand dexterity...................	.14
Arm dexterity....................	.17

all tests investigated and for many different jobs, the highest average validity coefficient is found with the perceptual speed test, a correlation of .27.

The rather low validity of aptitude tests may have more serious consequences when they are used to counsel a person about his future career than when they are used to assign employees to certain kinds of jobs. In the latter instance even a test with low validity might still be better than no test at all. The fact that an employment office on the basis of aptitude tests makes errors in, say, 20 per cent of the people allocated to jobs may be of minor importance to the industry, and perhaps even to the individual. Changes can be made. But the situation is quite different in the counseling office. If an aptitude test for

nursing has a very low validity coefficient and if the counselor misdirects even one student into taking the nursing course— where she may fail miserably after a year or two of trying—a fairly grave error has been committed. Counseling offices are fully aware of the low validity of most aptitude tests and are therefore reluctant to let final decisions of what people should do with their lives rest upon these test results alone.

The low validities of most aptitude tests (including the so-called "talent" tests) has led to a reorientation in aptitude test construction. Instead of depending solely upon a common-sense appraisal of the requirements for any specific occupation, factor-analysis methods are now being used in an attempt to determine which abilities are important for which occupations. Instead of testing for distinctive "vocational aptitudes," more general and perhaps more basic aptitudes are being investigated. This has meant two things: First, rather than single specialized tests, *batteries* of tests are now used for each occupation. Second, other general factors such as the individual's personality and *interests* are being measured in an attempt to help determine his vocational aptitudes. This is a reflection, again, of the basic principle we have observed at work throughout this book. The behavior of the person is determined by many factors—perceptual, intellectual and motivational—operating simultaneously.

Interests

It is instructive to note that it was the applied psychologists who were concerned with the occupational abilities of men, who made the first attempts to study and measure the interests of men. It is only recently that their work has been incorporated into the general body of psychological knowledge.

The initial work on measuring occupational interests was done by Strong of Stanford University who first published the Strong Vocational Interest Blank in 1927. Since that date the interests of thousands of people, in various professions and occupations, have been measured and tabulated by psychologists.

The Strong Vocational Interest Blank. The method of constructing this interest test was purely empirical. Strong collected several hundred items of many kinds—statements about occupations, school subjects, recreational activities, personality characteristics—and then asked his subjects to indicate their degree of interest in each item on a three-point scale. For example, one occupational item was "Actor" and the respondent was asked to indicate whether he *liked,* was *indifferent* to, or *disliked* "Actors." A recreational item was "Collecting postage stamps" and again the respondent was asked to signify whether he liked, was indifferent to, or disliked stamp collecting. Strong then gave these tests to hundreds of people from various professions and occupations. He found that people from certain occupations tended to respond to certain items in a similar way. For example, 60 per cent of successful engineers said that they disliked "Actors," whereas only 47 per cent of men in general responded *dislike* for "Actors."

On the basis of such an analysis Strong was able, by 1954, to determine various patterns of likes, dislikes, and indifferences, which characterized 45 different occupational groups for men, and 25 for women. It should be clear that this represents a purely empirical, descriptive analysis. It does not tell us why morticians, for example, have the interest they do, nor does it even tell us that they are interested in

being morticians. All it tells us is that the average successful mortician likes certain things, dislikes others, and is indifferent to still others.

Validity of Interests Inventories. The mere fact that people of one occupational group have different interests than people of other groups has some practical value for vocational counseling. A test based on such preference patterns has *face validity.* When any individual receives a high "engineering" score on an interest inventory, we can, by definition, say that such a person has an interest-pattern similar to that found among most engineers. We have, therefore, one more bit of information about the person which will enable us to advise him on his vocational choice. Thus if his pattern of interests is similar to that of real estate salesmen, and if other tests are consistent with this finding, he may be well-advised to become a real estate salesman.

Our confidence in the usefulness of interests inventories does not rest only upon this point. A consistent research finding has been that the patterns of likes and dislikes which characterize a person as a member of a given occupational group remain constant over the years. By now there are a number of groups of people who were first tested on the Strong test during their high school and college days and have been retested many years later. The correlations between their test and retest scores are consistently high. (See Table 18.) The pattern of interests seems to be a rather permanent characteristic of the person.

Another line of corroborative evidence comes from the studies which show that occupational experience seems not to be important in the development of interest-patterns. That is, it appears that a person's interest pattern develops *before* he selects an occupation, and this pattern remains rel-

TABLE 18

Permanence of Interest Scores (Data from Strong, 1951)

No. of Subjects	Educational Level	Age at Time of Test	Age at Time of Retest	Median Correlation
50	College Freshman	19	20	.88
50	College Freshmen	19	38	.72
50	College Seniors	22	27	.84
228	College Seniors	22	44	.75

atively constant thereafter. Thus undergraduates who show a high interest score characteristic of physicians tend to remain in the medical professions for a longer period of time than undergraduates who do not show as high an interest score. The latter tend to drift away from medicine even after they have completed their medical training. The same is true of engineering and other professions.

It should be remembered, of course, that though these studies indicate that *most* people change very little in their interest patterns, this does not mean that *all* people are stable in their preferences. As a matter of fact there are great individual differences in stability of interests, even among adults. Some people show radical changes in their interests as measured by any of the available interest tests.

By Way of Concern. One point which merits a great deal of thought and concern should be mentioned. The interest test is used in counseling centers and in employment offices to help recruit new members for the various occupations and professions. This is done in a negative as well as in a positive fashion. The college student whose interest pattern is not similar to that of the typical "successful engineer," for example, may be discouraged from entering that profession. But this may have unfortunate consequences for society and the welfare of that profession. It may very well be that in some professions there is need for different kinds of people with patterns of interest different from the present practitioners. This may be especially true in a changing world where new demands are being made on all professions and occupations. But what seems to be happening is a "freezing" of the *status quo*. We are recruiting only *conformers*.

As we learn more about the abilities of man we learn to *predict* better. In this instance, our ability to predict is put to use in *selecting*, and by selecting we eventually *control*. But since we are selecting on the basis of our past experience, we may be "controlling out" possibilities for change. This must raise grave questions of social policy.

Abilities and Age

Most studies of the abilities of man have been carried out on the relatively young. This reflects our deep-seated attitude that youth is the period of achievement, the glorious age of man. The heroes of our novels and short stories tend to be within the 20–30 year-old age range; our advertisers make their appeals to the young man and woman—or to the men and women who would seek to retain their youth; and employment offices are reluctant to hire people over forty. Until recently, of course, America has been a nation of the young. But with developments in medicine which have increased the life span of people, and with a decrease in emigration of young people from Europe, the composition of our population is changing fairly rapidly. Thus in 1850 about 88 per cent of the people in the United States were under 45 years of age. In 1900 this percentage dropped to 82; in 1920, to 79 per cent; and in 1940 to about 75 per cent. Today we have more than twice as many people in the 45–64 age-range, in proportion to our total population, as we had in 1850.

One of the consequences of this change has been an increased interest in *gerontology*—the scientific study of older people. And this has become evident in the study of abilities as well.

Age and Intelligence. There are two major difficulties in the way of studying the change in intelligence in the older age ranges. In the first place there is no easy way of obtaining a representative sample of older people. A "captive sample" readily available for testing, such as our school population gives us for children, does not exist for adults. In the second place, and partly as a consequence of the first difficulty, we do not have appropriate and adequately standardized tests.

Ideally what we should have are *longitudinal studies*—that is, measurements made on the same people at different ages. Because large groups of adults are difficult to keep track of for long periods of time this approach has not been attempted until recently. As a substitute method the *cross-sectional study* has been used. Here *different* groups of people, of different ages, are compared. But with this method we frequently find that we are comparing nonequivalent samples of people. It is not surprising therefore, that the data accumulated by these two methods show many contradictions.

CROSS-SECTIONAL STUDIES. In general, the cross-sectional studies have indicated a drop in intelligence test scores with age. The scores increase up to the age of 18,

maintain the 18-year-old level through the 20's, show a slight drop during the 30's, a slightly greater drop during the 40's, and an increasingly greater fall from then on. It has been estimated that by the age of 50, over one year of mental age has been lost; by the age of 60, two years.

LONGITUDINAL STUDIES. The more recent longitudinal studies tell a quite different story. We have already referred to Bayley's study which showed that the "mentally gifted" do not show a decline with age, but, rather, that intelligence *increases* with age from the 20's up to the 50's—and perhaps even beyond (see Fig. 131). Similar results have been reported by other investigators. Thus Owens (1953) retested 127 men thirty years after they had taken the Army Alpha Intelligence Examination at the time of their entrance to college, and found that these men scored significantly higher on the second testing than they had on the first.

These contradictory results cannot be easily explained. One hypothesis that has been suggested is that intelligence does drop for the average person as he grows older, but not for those who were mentally superior to begin with. This may indicate some biological difference between the mentally superior and the less superior, or differences due to life experiences. The superior younger man may lead a more stimulating life than his duller brother and this continued stimulation may reflect itself in his higher score in later age. A major difficulty with the data which seem to support the hypothesis of a difference between the two groups (whatever may be the *reason* for the difference) is that the mentally superior people have been tested by the longitudinal method, while the "average person" has been tested by the cross-sectional method. Obviously more longitudinal studies must be made before we can settle this question. In any event, the formerly accepted conclusion that after the 20's intelligence drops with age is open to serious question.

Age and Other Capacities. Some studies have investigated the effect of age upon various *special* capacities and abilities. These studies are of current interest since the useful employment of older people is becoming an increasingly important social problem. But here again, carefully planned studies carried out on adequate samples are rare.

Tyler (1956), after reviewing the available studies, suggests that the following four conclusions seem to be warranted at our present stage of knowledge:

1) There is a gradual decline in all types of measurable abilities after the age of thirty. This decline, however, does not become marked until well after fifty.

2) Simple sensory abilities and even fairly complex perceptual capacities decline most and earliest. Thus deafness to high pitches is very commonly found among middle-aged people; sensitivity to taste, smell, and even to pain decreases with age. Dark adaptation and color vision show the same trend. Speed of perception of fairly complex material as measured by tachistoscopic studies also show deterioration with age.

3) Motor abilities hold up fairly well until middle age, but then decline. Interestingly enough the *patterning* of the time required for the performance of skilled tasks show the greatest changes. Thus the speed and quality of the specific movements involved in any skilled performance show relatively little change with age, but the time needed to grasp the meaning of a stimulus, and to decide what to do about it, increases sharply with age.

4) Older people learn a little less rapidly than younger people. But here the rate of decline varies with the nature of the learning task involved. Some studies suggest, for example, that this decline is more marked in learning tasks which involve interference with old habits, than in tasks in which old habits can be used to advantage.

5) Finally, here as in all studies of the abilities of man, wide individual differences exist. In any age group some people are superior to the average for groups much younger.

Age and Achievement. In the light of all this the question has been raised as to the age at which man's best work is accomplished. Perhaps the best-known work on this problem is the analysis which Lehman (1953) has made. With the aid of expert judges, Lehman ascertained the ages at which leaders in various fields achieved their "outstanding accomplishments." The following list summarizes some of his findings in terms of the age ranges when the peaks of achievement occurred:

Fiction writing	30–39
Games and sports	25–29
Medicine and surgery	35–39
Painting	30–45
Philosophy	35–39
Poetry	25–29
Science	30–34

It seems clear that the peaks come during the thirties and, according to Lehman's data, this has been true throughout recent history and in various countries. However, here again great individual differences have been noted and some outstanding achievements have occurred well past the age of forty.

At the present time we do not know whether the relatively early age of achievement is due to the biological processes of aging, the motivational differences between the old and the young, or the sheer lack of opportunity for the older people to engage in creative activity. Complex behavior, as we have seen throughout this book, is determined by the interaction of many factors. As medical and psychological gerontology advance, the *healthy* life span of people may increase considerably. With this increase the "peak of achievement" may also move up. An increase in the healthy life span may not only slow down the rate of the biological processes of aging, but may also change the motivational structure of the older person, and both of these may help maintain his abilities at his formerly high level.

As the composition of our population continues to change, the study of the abilities of men will encompass his whole life span. Society is becoming as interested in the capacities and aptitudes of the 60-year-old as of the 6- and 16-year-old. And science will study what interests society.

Glossary

achievement tests. Objective tests designed to measure how much a person has learned or knows about a specific subject.

aptitude. Refers to the *potential* ability of a person to perform a specific kind of activity. To be distinguished from "proficiency" or "achievement" which refers to the person's *present* performance capacity.

chronological age (C.A.). Age from birth.

cross-sectional study. A study in which different groups of people, of different ages, are measured for the same trait. Designed to give information about the affects of age upon the trait concerned. This method, the validity of which depends heavily upon the comparability of the different samples of people at the different ages, is usually not as good a method as the longitudinal study.

factor analysis. A statistical method permitting us to deal with a large number of correlations simultaneously. It is designed to determine the number of "factors" required to account for the intercorrelations among the scores of different tests.

gerontology. The science that treats with the problems connected with aging.

group tests. Tests designed to measure the general intelligence or specialized aptitudes of people and which are administered to large groups simultaneously. The Army General Classification Test (AGCT), used in World War II to measure the mental capacity of the American soldier, is one such test.

idiot savants. Feeble-minded persons (usually with I.Q.'s of 50) who show one or several highly developed special mental proficiencies.

individual tests. Tests designed to measure the general intelligence or specialized aptitudes of people and which are administered to one person at a time. The Stanford-Binet test is one such test.

intelligence quotient (I.Q.). A converted score based on performance on an intelligence test which expresses the individual's mental age (M.A.) in relation to his chronological age (C.A.). The formula for this relationship is $I.Q. = \dfrac{M.A.}{C.A.} \times 100$. The average I.Q., is therefore *necessarily* 100, since the average 10-year-old will receive an M.A. of 10, etc. For persons over 15 years the formula is revised to $I.Q. = \dfrac{M.A.}{15} \times 100$.

longitudinal study. A study in which repeated measurements of some trait are made on the same people at different ages. Designed to give information about the change in the trait as a function of age. See also *cross-sectional study*.

mental age (M.A.). A converted score based on performance on a mental test, and determined by the level of difficulty of the test items passed. Thus if an individual child, no matter how old he is, can pass only those items passed by the *average* ten-year-old, he will be given a mental age score of 10. This unit was first proposed by Binet and is fairly widely used today. Because of the nature of the developmental curve, the M.A. unit is difficult to apply after the age of 15. See also *intelligence quotient.*

performance tests. Tests designed to measure the general intelligence or specialized aptitudes of people and consisting primarily of motor or perceptual test items in which verbal facility plays a minimal role. To be contrasted with "verbal tests."

power tests. Tests designed to measure the general intelligence or specialized aptitudes of people in which the difficulty of the tasks successfully completed determines the score. To be contrasted with "speed tests."

primary mental abilities. According to L. L. Thurstone, the "statistical psychologist," most of man's mental capacity can be accounted for by postulating seven primary mental abilities. These are: *Number, Word fluency, Verbal meaning, Memory, Reasoning, Spatial perception,* and *Perceptual speed.* These seven abilities, however, correlate among themselves to a considerable degree, i.e., they are not wholly independent of one another.

speed tests. Tests designed to measure the general intelligence or specialized aptitudes of people in which the scores are determined primarily by the rapidity with which correct answers can be given.

standardization. When used in connection with tests this term refers to the procedure of administering a new test to a representative sample of people to determine the scale values for the scores. Thus before we can assign a test item to a given age level (in the Binet test), we must give this item to a large number of children to determine its age level.

Stanford-Binet test. One of the most commonly used general intelligence tests—especially for children. The current Stanford-Binet test represents Terman's revision of the French psychologist's, Binet's, test. L. M. Terman, perhaps the most famous psychologist in the field of mental testing, was a professor of psychology at Stanford University. Hence the name "Stanford-Binet."

Strong Vocational Interest Blank. A test designed to measure a person's pattern of interests. Since it appears that members of different occupational groups have different interest-patterns, this test has been used in counseling centers and job assignment work. Developed by E. K. Strong of Stanford University.

verbal tests. Tests designed to measure the general intelligence or specialized aptitudes of people, and consisting primarily of verbal test items. To be contrasted with "performance tests."

Wechsler Adult Intelligence Scale. An intelligence test specially devised for adults. Consists of two parts—a verbal part and a performance part. The Wechsler correlates about .85 with the Stanford-Binet. For measuring children's intelligence there is also available the Wechsler Intelligence Scale for Children.

Suggestions for Further Reading

ANASTASI, A., and FOLEY, J. P. 1949. *Differential psychology* (rev. ed.). New York: Macmillan.

A standard text that covers the field of psychological differences among groups of people.

CRONBACH, L. J. 1949. *Essentials of psychological testing.* New York: Harper.

An elementary text on the construction and application of psychological tests. A sound, lucid, and highly readable account.

GHISELLI, E. E., and BROWN, C. W. *Personnel and industrial psychology* (2nd ed.). New York: McGraw-Hill.

A standard text in industrial psychology with a very good account of the theory and use of aptitude tests in industry.

TYLER, L. E. 1956. *The psychology of human differences* (2nd ed.). New York: Appleton-Century-Crofts.

A well-written, comprehensive account of the extent and nature of individual and group differences in psychological traits among people.

CHAPTER XXI

Heredity and Environment

WE STARTED Part IV by pointing to one of the major problems to which the study of individual differences can contribute: Is it heredity or environment, nature or nurture, that makes us what we are? This is, of course, a major issue when studying the intelligence and abilities of man. People vary tremendously in intelligence, in abilities, in interests, in achievements. Is this variation due to heredity or to environment?

To answer this question we must first understand the mechanisms of heredity.

Hereditary Mechanisms

We can all say that "heredity runs in our family," but what is it that "runs"? The answer is that both similarities *and* differences are inherited. The facts of the genetic mechanism demand that there be not only resemblances between parents and offspring, but that there also be differences.

Life Begins. The life of every person begins when a *sperm cell* from the father penetrates the wall of an *ovum* (or egg) from the mother. Each of these *germ cells* (sperm and ova) contains within it *chromosomes,* the "carriers of heredity."

Until very recently it was believed that normal human cells contained 24 pair of chromosomes, or a total of 48. Recent research seems to indicate that the number may be 23 pairs, or 46 chromosomes. When germ cells are being formed, the cell destined to become a sperm or ovum first divides in two and each germ cell ends up with only one member of each pair of chromosomes, i.e., with a total of 23 chromosomes instead of 46. When a sperm unites with an ovum, the resulting *zygote* (fertilized ovum) contains the full complement of 23 complete pairs, or 46 chromosomes. (See Fig. 134.) Thus exactly half of the zygote's chromosomes come from the father and half from the mother.

Relatives Are the Same and Different. Chromosomes are the "carriers" of heredity only in the "transportation" sense. Each chromosome bears many separate complex molecules called *genes*. And it is these

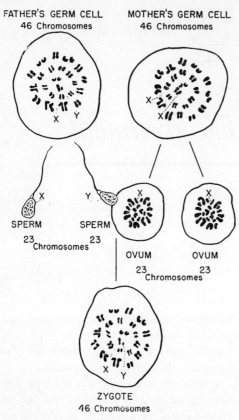

FATHER'S GERM CELL
46 Chromosomes

MOTHER'S GERM CELL
46 Chromosomes

X   Y   X

SPERM   SPERM
23   23
  Chromosomes

X   X

OVUM   OVUM
23   23
  Chromosomes

X   Y

ZYGOTE
46 Chromosomes

FIG. 134. Relationships between the mature parental germ cells and the zygote. Each mature germ cell of both the father and mother (top of illustration) has the full number of chromosomes (which consists of 23 pairs or 46 chromosomes). When these germ cells reach full maturity they undergo division and become ova (for the female) and sperm (for the male). During such division the chromosomes are assorted so that each sperm (and ovum) has only one member of each pair, i.e., 23 chromosomes all told. When one sperm enters through the cell body of one ovum, a zygote is formed, and the zygote, of course, will have the full number of 46 chromosomes. From the zygote a new organism develops.

One pair of the chromosomes is a special kind—consisting of the X and Y chromosomes. The mature *male* cell has one X and one Y chromosome; the mature *female* cell has two X chromosomes. When the mature male germ cell divides into sperm one of the resulting sperm gets the X and the other the Y. Each ovum, of course, must get an X. If the sperm with the Y chromosome happens to unite with the ovum, then the zygote will have an X–Y pair (as in the zygote illustrated); if the sperm with the X chromosome fertilizes the ovum, then the zygote will have an X–X pair. A zygote with an X–Y pair will develop into a male while a zygote with an X–X pair will develop into a female. Thus our zygote of the above figure will develop into a boy.

genes which are the "determiners" of inherited bodily traits. The genes do not always stay put in their own chromosomes. There is a phenomenon known as *crossing-over*, which refers to the fact that occasionally one segment of a chromosome will break off and be exchanged with a corresponding segment from a parallel chromosome. Thus a chromosome containing genes A, B, C, D, E, etc., may, after crossing over, contain genes A, B, C, d, e, etc. (See Fig. 135.)

If the 46 chromosomes in the germ cell always divided in the same way, with one combination going to one sperm (or ovum) and the other to another sperm, we would have available, for any one mating, two different kinds of sperm and two different kinds of ova. Therefore any two parents could give birth to only four ge-

netically different kinds of children—depending upon which sperm united with which ova. We would thus expect to find many *identical* brothers and sisters.

But chromosomes do not divide that way. They seem to divide at random. Thus, one sperm might contain chromosomes A, b, c, D, e, . . . , another sperm might get a, B, C, d, e, . . . , and still another might consist of a, b, c, D, E, . . . , etc. (See Fig. 136.) Theoretically, the number of different chromosome combinations possible is 2^{23}, on the assumption that there are 23 different *pairs* of chromosomes. In other words, a single human male can produce 8,388,608 *genetically different* sperm, and similarly, a single human female, 8,388,608 genetically different ova. In a single mating, any one of these 8 million chromosome combinations in the sperm might join with

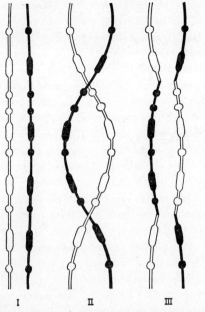

I   II   III

FIG. 135. At one period of development of the mature germ cell, the two members of a pair of chromosomes (see I above), approach each other and become intimately intertwined (see II). During this period one section of one chromosome may become exchanged with a corresponding section of the other chromosome, so that when they are separated again (see III), we have a recombination of genes in the two chromosomes (compare I and III). This phenomenon is referred to as the "crossing-over of genes."

any one of the 8 million chromosomes combinations in the ovum to form a single zygote.

The probabilities are even more bewildering than that. We have noted that chromosomes can exchange genes. This means that the number of different kinds of *gene* combinations is vastly greater than 8,388,-608. This increases tremendously the already astronomically large number of genetically different zygotes which can eventuate from matings between the same parents. The number of possible combinations of chromosomes in the zygote is practically infinite and our reproductive system practically guarantees that, except in the case of identical twins who develop from a sin-

gle zygote, no two brothers or sisters can ever be genetically the same. *Heredity means individual differences.*

On the other hand, no matter which combination of the chromosomes ends up in the zygote, nothing can be there which was not contributed by either parent. For example, if both parents are homozygous for brown eyes (have *only* "brown-eyed genes") then no recombination can make the offspring blue-eyed. In this sense there is a definite limit to the individual differences possible in a family. *Heredity means similarity.*

IDENTICAL TWINS. Identical twins, because they are *genetically identical,* are of great interest to the psychologist who is concerned with the problem of heredity. How do identical twins come about?

When an ovum becomes fertilized it multiplies by division. With fertilization a process known as *mitosis* (or cell division) begins. The zygote first divides into two daughter cells, each of which is a complete and faithful replica of the other. We have seen that the single zygote has within it the full complement of chromosomes. *This means that each daughter cell has within it the potentialities of becoming a complete individual.* However, in most cases, this cell division does not mean cell separation. The two cells remain as parts of a single organism. If the two cells remain together, each one of these divides, and subdivides until thousands and millions of cells have been formed. As the number of cells increases, the mass of subdivided cells begins to become differentiated into bone cells, nerve cells, skin cells, etc. The embryo which at first resembles an expanding ball begins to take shape and the first suggestions of a head, eyes, trunk, and limbs appear.

In some instances, however, the first two daughter cells, do not stay together, but *actually separate.* Now, these can develop into two separate individuals, through the process of mitosis occurring separately in the two daughter cells. Indeed, this actual separation can continue, so that three or four or more individuals can develop. (See Fig. 137.) These individuals are known as identical twins, because, as can readily be seen, they have been developed from the same *zygote* and therefore must be genetically identical.

The mother may sometimes produce more than one ovum. If she produces two

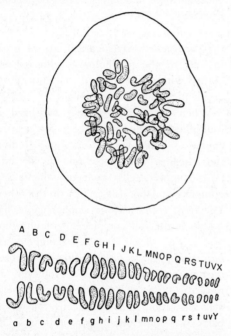

FIG. 136. This figure presents a semi-diagrammatic view of an egg cell with the chromosomes clustered in pairs in the middle of the cell. The lower part of the figure represents the pairs of chromosomes spread out for inspection. Each chromosome contains many genes.

and each of these is fertilized (by two different sperm, of course), then *genetically* the twins are completely separate individuals and can be expected to be no more similar than any set of brothers or sisters. They are known as *fraternal twins.*

According to available statistics, twins

occur in the United States about once in 86 births. Identical twins are much rarer than fraternal twins. It seems fairly clear that the likelihood of giving birth to twins is hereditarily determined to a considerable extent. Thus, twinning is found more often in some families than in others, and even in some races than in others. The age of the parents at the time of conception seems also to be important. Older fathers, regardless of the age of the mother, are more apt to conceive twins than are younger fathers. Women between the ages of 30 and 38 are also more likely to give birth to twins than are women of any other age.

While the genetic difference between identical and fraternal twins is well established, there are no clear-cut, practical tests that enable us to be absolutely certain whether a pair of twins is identical or fraternal. Of course if one twin is a male and the other a female, they are clearly fraternal. But if both are of the same sex, it is often difficult to know whether they are identical or fraternal, since even fraternal twins of the same sex may look very much alike.

Though many criteria have been suggested for distinguishing between fraternal and identical twins, each criterion lacks complete validity. Most authorities now demand that at least four tests be met before we can assume that a pair of like-sex twins is identical: (1) the two children must have the same blood type; (2) they must have the same eye coloring; (3) they must have the same hair color; and (4) they must have similar fingerprints. There does exist a foolproof test as to whether twins are identical or not, but this test is obviously impractical for general application to human beings. It is known that only genetically identical individuals can undergo successful skin transplantation. Thus if the skin from one twin is transplanted to the skin of the other, and if the

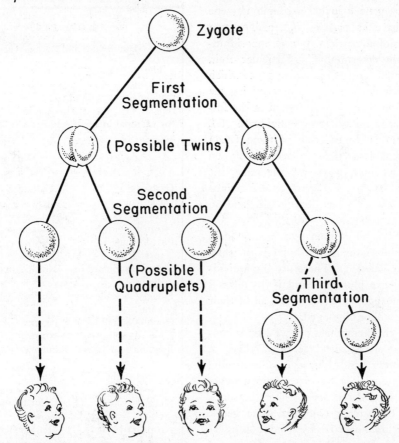

Zygote

First
Segmentation

(Possible Twins)

Second
Segmentation

(Possible
Quadruplets)

Third
Segmentation

FIG. 137. The above figure diagrams the process by which identical multiple births may occur. If the zygote, during the first cell division, does not segment, only one child will develop. If, at the first division, actual segmentation takes place, so that we now have two zygotes and if no further actual separation occurs, then identical twins will be developed. If, however, at the first cell division of these two identical zygotes another separation takes place, we have the possibilities for more than two identical children. In the figure above we have carried out the process until *identical quintuplets* become possible.

transplanted skin "takes" and continues to grow in the host twin, then we have conclusive evidence that the donor twin and the host twin are genetically identical.

Multiple Determiners. We have said that genes are the determiners of inherited traits or characteristics (e.g., of eye color, hair structure, body length). But this does not mean that one gene is responsible for each trait. Actually, any one gene produces a multitude of effects, and each trait is determined by the interaction of many factors from several genes—often from genes found in separate chromosomes. The multifactorial determination of traits is, as we shall see, of major importance in understanding the inheritance of abilities in man.

Perhaps the simplest illustration of multiple determination is found in the interplay between *dominant* and *recessive* genes. Every gene in any one chromosome has its corresponding partner in the paired chromosome. Thus Gene *A* in chromosome 1, will have gene *a* in chromosome 1', gene *B* will have its partner, *b*, etc. The two members of any pair may have opposite influence in determining a particular trait. For example, one of the sets of genes which plays an important part in determining the color of the eyes may be found in the following pairs for different individuals: *AA*, or *aa*, or *Aa*. In the first of these (*AA*) either gene is such as to produce brown eyes. Since both genes are the same, the person is said to be *homozygous* for these genes. He will have brown eyes and so must all his progeny.

In the second combination, *aa*, we again have homozygous genes. Now both genes make for blue eyes. Therefore the individual will have blue eyes and if his mate is also homozygous for blue eyes, all of their progeny will be blue-eyed.

In the third combination, we have a conflict. *A* tends to produce brown eyes, *a*, on the other hand, blue eyes. Genetically, the individual is a mixture of brown-eyes and blue-eyes determiners. Such a person is said to be *heterozygous* for these genes. But *A* is dominant over *a* (it "suppresses" the effect of *a*), and therefore the person will develop brown eyes. But he continues to carry within his germ cells the *a* genes. Now suppose an *Aa* father and an *Aa* mother (both showing brown eyes) mate. The progeny may get an *a* from the father and an *a* from the mother, i.e., *aa*, and thus show blue eyes, even though both parents were brown-eyed. (See Box 144 for a partial list of dominant and recessive characters in man.)

But we must emphasize again that very few traits are determined by a single set of genes. (See Fig. 138.) Each chromosome of the organism, perhaps even each gene in the zygote, influences the whole body. And each part or process is influenced by all the others. Genetics teaches us the same lesson as does psychol-

---

BOX 144

Dominance and Recessiveness

The following table lists some of the dominant and recessive characters in human inheritance. Note that the "dominant" trait is not always the "desirable" one, as for example in fused fingers or limb dwarfing.

Dominant Characters	Recessive Characters
Curly hair	Straight hair
Dark hair	Light or red hair
Brown eyes	Blue eyes
Normal coloring	Albinism
Fused fingers or toes	Normal digits
Supernumerary digits	Normal number
Fingers lacking one joint	Normal length
Double-jointedness	Normal joints
Limb dwarfing	Normal proportion
Immunity to poison ivy	Susceptibility to poison ivy
Normal sight	Night blindness
Normal hair	Baldness
Normal color vision	Color-blindness
Normal blood	Hemophilia
Normal hearing	Deaf-mutism

---

ogy—the individual is a complex *interrelated* unity of parts.

The Continuity of Man. The inherited characteristics that are produced by genes are passed along from one generation to another unchanged (with relatively rare exceptions). But it is *not* true that the experiences of the adult can be passed on to his progeny by heredity. The only things which are passed on are the genes, and they remain unchanged by life experiences. (See Fig. 139.)

The "rare exceptions" occur when genes themselves are changed through some "chemical accident" or through stimulation

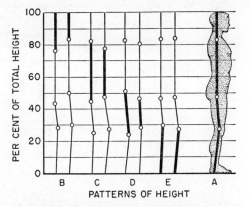

FIG. 138. An illustration of "multiple factors" in determination of a "single" trait. Tallness or shortness in man is hereditarily determined to a considerable extent. However, the characteristic of height may be due to four sets of independent factors—one group of factors responsible for the head-neck length (B), one, for the trunk (C), one, for the thighs (D), and one for the legs (E). Any one of these sets of factors may be inherited independently of the others, so that a person may inherit a tendency to a relatively long head-neck length and a short thigh length (see the line on the extreme left in above graph). One does not inherit shortness or tallness as a simple trait. The above lines indicate Davenport's estimate of the typical combinations of these four factors as found in man. (Adapted with permission from *Biology and man* by B. C. Gruenberg and N. E. Bingham. Copyright 1944 by Ginn & Co., New York.)

by such radiant energies as X-rays and cosmic rays. These changes we call *mutations* and they have been used to account for evolutionary changes in organisms. Not only is man an integrated unity, he is— except as he is transformed by bombardment of cosmic rays, X-rays, and fallouts from hydrogen and cobalt bombs—a *continuous unity*.

Environment. Each fertilized egg, then, carries within it hereditary determinants from the father and the mother, and thus each zygote differs from all other zygotes at the very moment of conception. These differences become magnified and more easily detectable as we grow in our moth-

er's womb, as we are born, and as we enter into the activities of the outside world. The continuous unity which is man is an ever-changing one.

These changes, however, do not take place in a biological organism suspended in a vacuum. From the very moment of fertilization, through the development of the zygote, the embryo, and the fetus, the organism is immersed in an environment which is unique to him. Just as it is true that each zygote differs from all other zygotes, so is it true that the *environment* of each zygote differs from that of every other zygote. We have known for a long time that the condition of the zygote's environment—the uterus—can help shape the *physical* development of the offspring, and we now have some experimental evidence to suggest that it may also help shape the later *behavior* of the individual. (See Box 145 for an account of one such experiment.)

Environmental differences among organisms become far more pronounced, of course, after birth.

We therefore have two sets of factors which differentiate one organism from another: heredity *and* environment. And both of these play their roles *from the very moment of conception*.

Formulation of the Nature-Nurture Problem

The recognition that our behavioral traits result from the interaction of heredity and environment has changed the formulation of the nature-nurture problem. We no longer speak of the nature-nurture *controversy* (is it heredity *or* environment?) and the questions we ask assume, at the very outset, that *both* heredity and environment are involved. The three major

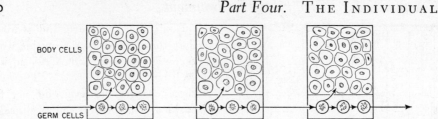

BODY CELLS

GERM CELLS

FIG. 139. This figure represents, diagrammatically, the continuity of germ cells and indicates "what is inherited." We start as a fertilized germ cell—a zygote. The zygote, through the process of cell division (mitosis), gives rise to two kinds of cells: the somatic cells and the germ cells. The somatic (body) cells soon change and become specialized—into nerve cells, muscle cells, skin cells, etc.—until we end up with a complete and mature person. (Each rectangle above represents a person.) The germ cells do not change in any important respect. They continue to reproduce germ cells. A sperm descendant of the original zygote combines with the ovum of a female organism to start another zygote and thus another person. It is the germ cell which "runs in a family," not the somatic cells. When a person dies, there are no descendants of his body cells. If he has progeny, they are "descendants" of his germ cells only. The germ cells alone can claim "immortality." No matter what happens to the body cells during the life of the father or mother, *such changes cannot be transmitted to the offspring.* The athlete who develops his muscles (body cells) during his life-time cannot transmit his well-developed muscles to his son. The mother who learns to appreciate art during her pregnancy (thus bringing about changes in her nervous system—body cells) cannot transmit a love for beauty and art to her daughter.

The *biological* inheritance you can transmit to your children has already been determined by your parents. No program of "right living" can change that.

questions of concern to research workers in the field are: (1) What proportion of any given trait (such as intelligence) is determined by heredity and what proportion by environment? (2) What is the specific nature of the genetic mechanism responsible for the inheritance of behavior tendencies or traits? (3) How much difference can variations in the environment make in traits that are partly determined by heredity?

To answer these questions various types of investigations have been carried out. Among them are animal experimentation, identical-twin studies, research on foster children, comparison of intelligence test scores of people from different stock, correlation of intelligence test scores of children with their parents, and study of the effect of schooling on performance. The results of these various investigations are quite consistent.

Experimental Behavior Genetics. The field of experimental behavior genetics, though now a very active one, has a rather short history. The first extensive experiment was that of Tryon who initiated his now famous *selective breeding* experiment with rats in 1927.

Selective breeding consists of mating animals that display certain traits, selecting from among their offspring those that express the trait and then breeding their offspring. If the trait is regulated by heredity, continued selection for a number of generations will result in a strain that breeds more or less true for that trait.

Tryon's results were clear. Bright maze-learners breed bright progeny, dull maze-learners breed dull progeny. (See Box 146.) Other experimenters have corroborated Tryon's results, and various additional traits have been shown to be inherited. Thus Rundquist (1933) after 12 generations of selective breeding obtained groups of active and inactive rats; Hall (1937) within 8 or 9 generations produced strains of rats differing in emotionality (using the open-field test of emotionality, see

BOX 145

Prenatal Influences on Offspring

Thompson at Weslyan University has tested the hypothesis that emotional upset undergone by female rats during pregnancy can affect the emotional characteristics of the offspring.

Thompson trained five female rats in a double-compartment shuttlebox, first to expect strong shock at the sound of a buzzer, and then to avoid the shock by opening a door between the compartments and running through to the safe side. When the rats had learned this they were mated. As soon as they became pregnant, they were exposed to the buzzer three times every day in the shock side of the shuttlebox, but with shock turned off and the door to the safe side locked. This was continued until the females gave birth to their pups. Thus during pregnancy the mother rats were exposed to an anxiety-arousing situation, but their accustomed means to escape was blocked. Thompson's assumption was that this would generate strong "free-floating" anxiety in the pregnant females and that any resulting endocrine changes would be transmitted via the blood stream to the fetuses. Will this create emotional offspring?

The emotionality of the offspring (there were 30 of them) was measured by two tests given at 30 to 40 and 130 to 140 days of age and compared with 30 offspring of control animals who had not been subjected to this stress. In Test A, the offspring of the experimental and control animals were placed in a large open area for three daily sessions of ten minutes each and their activity was measured, on the assumption that the more timid or emotional the animal, the less the activity in an open area. In Test B, emotionality was measured by the time elapsing before the rat left the home cage to reach food at the end of an alley leading out from the cage. For this test the animals were first deprived of food for 24 hours. Both of these tests (especially Test A, which is sometimes called the "open-field" test), are used fairly commonly to measure emotionality in rats.

The results are shown in the table below. It is clear that the offspring of the experimental animals differ strikingly from offspring of the control animals. Further, it appears that these differences persist to a great extent into adulthood.

However, while these differences are statistically reliable there is some ambiguity regarding their cause. It is possible that the buzzer was strong enough to act on the fetuses directly rather than indirectly through causing release of hormones in the mother. For this reason Thompson concludes cautiously: ". . . there are some grounds for supposing that prenatal maternal anxiety does actually increase the emotionality of offspring."

Whatever the mechanism may finally be shown to be, it seems that *differences in the prenatal environment of the rat make for differences in later behavior.*

THOMPSON, W. R. 1957. Influence of prenatal maternal anxiety on emotionality in young rats. *Science, 125,* 698–9.

	TEST A	TEST B
	Amount of activity (Distance Moved)	*Time to leave home cage (Minutes)*
	Tests given at age 30 to 40 days	
Experimental	86.0	14.9
Control	134.5	5.2
	Tests given at age 130 to 140 days	
Experimental	114.5	4.8
Control	162.3	2.1

BOX 146

Inheritance of Learning Ability

Tryon's experiment at the University of California had as its purpose the establishment, by selective breeding, of a line of maze-bright and a line of maze-dull rats.

Tryon started with a "parental" generation of 142 male and female rats. Each animal was run for 19 trials through a 17-unit maze. The brightest animals made a total of approximately 14 errors in learning the maze, the dullest, about 174. The bright females were then mated with the bright males, the dull females with the dull males —the other animals being discarded. Then the offspring of these matings were tested on the same maze. On the basis of their performance, the brightest rats within each of the bright litters were mated, and the dullest within each of the dullest litters were mated. This testing and selective breeding procedure was followed for 18 generations. The results are summarized in the distribution curves of Fig. 140 showing the errors made by the parental group, the third generation (F_2), the seventh generation (F_6) and the ninth generation (F_8). With successive generations the two strains of rats pull apart, until by the F_8 generation the dullest of the bright rats were about as bright or brighter than the brightest of the dulls.

Rigorous environmental controls were employed in this experiment. All animals were given identical care. In some cases, indeed, a dull mother would be given the pups of a bright mother to raise, and a bright mother, the pups of a dull mother. This was done to rule out the possibility of different "maternal care" as an environmental factor. The maze used was highly reliable and the scoring of the errors was done automatically, by an electrical recorder, so as to eliminate any possible "unconscious bias" of the experimenter in scoring the rats.

A number of years later, Searle, working in Tryon's laboratory, tested the two strains on various other learning tests. He did not find that the "bright" were bright on everything, nor the "dulls" altogether dull. Instead, the rats from each strain showed different *patterns* of abilities. Here we have evidence indicating that Tryon's strains were not *generally* bright and *generally* dull.

Opposed to Searle's conclusions, however, are data obtained some 27 years after Tryon's experiment was begun. In 1954, Krech, Rosenzweig, Bennett, and Krueckel, also at the University of California, examined the descendants of Tryon's two strains for the level of their *cholinesterase* activity. Cholinesterase is an enzyme found in the brain and other nervous tissue which is important in the efficient transmission of neural impulses. Their assumption was that if brightness and dullness reflected a *general* biochemical characteristic of the nervous system, the bright animals should show a higher level of cholinesterase activity than the dull animals. A biochemical analysis indicated that the brights had a higher level of cholinesterase than did the lows *in every part of the cerebral cortex tested*. These findings suggest two things: (1) Tryon did succeed in breeding a generally bright strain and a generally dull strain; (2) the inheritance of brightness and dullness may be via the genes which determine the level of cholinesterase activity in the nervous system. Here we have a first approach to determining the biological mechanism of the inheritance of abilities. Later selective breeding experiments showed that the level of cholinesterase activity could indeed be inherited.

No matter how the question of the generality of the learning ability of Tryon's two strains will eventually be answered— and more research is still being done on this question—the minimal conclusion is clear: *Some kinds of learning ability can be inherited*.

TRYON, R. C. 1940. Genetic differences in maze learning in rats. National Society for the Study of Education, *The thirty-ninth yearbook*. Bloomington, Illinois: Public School Publishing Co.

SEARLE, L. V. 1949. The organization of hereditary maze-brightness and maze-dullness. *Genet. Psychol. Monogr., 39,* 279–325.

KRECH, D., ROSENZWEIG, M. R., BENNETT, E. C., and KRUECKEL, B. 1954. Enzyme concentrations in the brain and adjustive behavior-patterns. *Science, 120,* 994–6.

Box 145); and Fuller and Scott (1954) have shown that such traits as aggressiveness and timidity are inherited in dogs.

These animal experiments, involving carefully controlled selective breeding and carefully controlled environmental factors, have established beyond any doubt that behavior traits can be inherited. Both kinds of behavior are involved: adaptive behavior (such as maze-learning ability), and motivational-emotional behavior. It is also important to note that most experimenters agree that such traits seem to be deter-

mined by *multiple* genetic factors, just as are most physical traits (see Fig. 138). There is no one gene for maze-learning ability, or for emotionality, but, rather, a whole host of genes are involved in determining each of these traits.

Human Behavioral Genetics. In the study of human behavioral genetics control of matings is, of course, not feasible. Recourse has therefore been had to comparisons of the abilities among identical twins, among fraternal twins, among children and par-

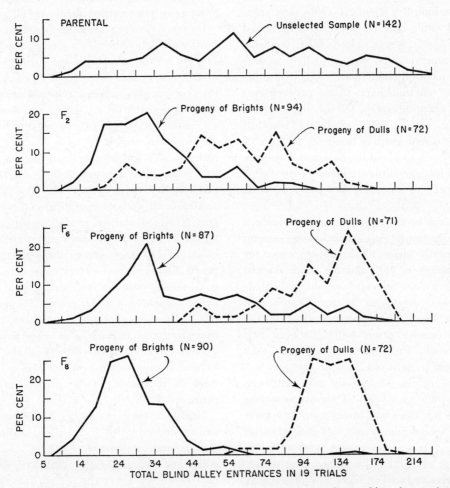

FIG. 140. Error scores made by animals of successive generations. On the vertical axis is indicated the per cent of the total group of rats of any one generation making the number of errors indicated on the horizontal axis. For further explanation, see Box 146.

ents, etc. In other words, family resemblances in traits and abilities have been investigated.

IDENTICAL TWINS REARED APART. Much attention has been paid to identical twins in studies seeking to analyze the contribution of heredity and environment to ability. The reasons for this derive from the fact that identical twins, as we have seen, are *genetically* identical and therefore differences in ability between one child and his identical twin brother must presumably be due to environmental differences rather than genetic factors.

Occasionally, identical twins are separated while still very young, and reared in different homes. Here, then, we have an "experiment in nature" where genetically identical children are subjected to different environments. And psychologists have taken advantage of this opportunity.

The most careful study of identical twins reared apart is based on 19 pairs of such twins analyzed by Newman, Freeman, and Holzinger (1937). Table 19 presents a summary of some of the data from that study.

As can be seen from the table, difference in educational opportunity, even among genetically identical people, can make for differences in I.Q., and the more marked the difference between the educational advantages, the bigger is the difference in I.Q.'s. The largest difference shown in the table (case 11) was found between two sisters who had been separated when they were 18 months old. One of the girls was reared in the backwoods and had been given only two years of formal schooling while her sister was brought up in a good farming community and had gone through college. When these twins were tested at the age of 35 the girl who had gone to college received an I.Q. score 24 points higher than her sister.

However the data of Table 19 make it also perfectly clear that environmental factors play a relatively minor role in determining the I.Q. On the *average* the differences found among identical twins reared apart is only 8 I.Q. points, and this is barely statistically significant. In some instances, indeed, better educational opportunities go along with *decreased* I.Q. (See cases 3, 14, 7, and 19 in Table 19.) Even the most extreme effect of good educational opportunities in I.Q. (24 points) is not enough to account for the range of differences in I.Q. in the general population where, it will be remembered, individual I.Q.'s ranged from 34 to 174 (see Box 142, p. 547).

IDENTICAL AND FRATERNAL TWINS. The importance of hereditary factors is further brought out by comparing the correlations in I.Q. scores among identical twins with the correlations among fraternal twins. Since identical twins are genetically identical, while fraternal twins are not, one identical twin should be more like his genetically identical brother than one fraternal twin like his genetically *different* brother.

Almost all such comparative studies report greater similarities in abilities between identical twins than between fraternal twins. In I.Q. the average difference between identical twins (reared together) is 5.9 points; between fraternal twins (also reared together) it is 9.9 points. The correlation between identical twins is .88, between fraternal twins, .63. In other words a bright identical twin is very likely to have an equally bright brother. This is not true to the same extent for fraternal twins.

Much the same results are found when we examine abilities and capacities other than general intelligence. Thus on motor-skill tests, identical twins correlate with each other to the extent of .79, fraternal twins, .43.

Again we must conclude that hereditary

factors are very important determinants of individual differences in the abilities of man.

FAMILY RESEMBLANCES. If intelligence and other abilities are inherited we should expect family resemblances in these traits. However, as was emphasized in the section on genetics, heredity also means family *differences*. Both of these effects of heredity should result in *positive but not perfect* correlations between members of the same families. But we can make a somewhat more precise prediction than that. On the basis of genetic facts and principles we can also predict the *order* of the correlations among various family members. The order,

to be expected, starting with the highest correlation is:

1. Between siblings (brothers and sisters)
2. Between parents and children
3. Between grandparents and grandchildren
4. Between uncles (or aunts) and nephews (or nieces)
5. Between first cousins

The above prediction rests on several basic assumptions, among them the assumption that intelligence reflects the action of *a large number of separate genes*. We have seen that this assumption of multiple factors in the determination of a "single"

TABLE 19

Identical Twins Reared Apart
(Data from Newman, Freeman, and Holzinger, 1937)

Case Number	Sex	Age at Separation	Age at Testing	Differences in Educational Advantages [1]	Differences in I.Q. between Twins [2]
11	f	18 mo.	35	37	24
2	f	18 mo.	27	32	12
18	m	1 yr.	27	28	19
4	f	5 mo.	29	22	17
12	f	18 mo.	29	19	7
1	f	18 mo.	19	15	12
17	m	2 yr.	14	15	10
8	f	3 mo.	15	14	15
3	m	2 mo.	23	12	−2
14	f	6 mo.	39	12	−1
5	f	14 mo.	38	11	4
13	m	1 mo.	19	11	1
10	f	1 yr.	12	10	5
15	m	1 yr.	26	9	1
7	m	1 mo.	13	9	−1
19	f	6 yr.	41	9	−9
16	f	2 yr.	11	8	2
6	f	3 yr.	59	7	8
9	m	1 mo.	19	7	6

[1] The differences in educational advantages were obtained in the following way: From the case material each of five judges rated the educational advantages of every twin on a scale of ten points, and then these five ratings were summed. Therefore the highest score any one twin could get would be 50. The difference between any two twins is the value given in the table. Thus, in case 11, one sister was rated as having 37 points better educational advantages than her twin.

[2] A minus sign before the I.Q. difference means that the twin who received the higher rating for educational advantages obtained a lower I.Q. score. Thus, in case 19 one sister was rated as having a 9 points educational advantage over her twin, yet she scored nine points *less* in her I.Q. test.

trait is in accordance with the available data and apparently holds for the determination of such physical traits as stature. (See Fig. 138.)

Stature of people was the first measurable characteristic used to test theories of human inheritance (by Galton in the latter part of the nineteenth century), and for which the most extensive data are available. It is therefore interesting to compare the corresponding correlations among different members of families for both stature and intelligence. Table 20 presents these cor-

TABLE 20

Correlations Among Relatives
(Data from Burt and Howard, 1956)

	Stature	Intelligence
Between siblings	.54	.51
Between parents and children	.51	.49
Between grandparents and grandchildren	.32	.34
Between uncles (or aunts) and nephews (or nieces)	.29	.35
Between first cousins	.24	.29

relations and it will be seen that not only do intelligence measures and stature measures show the same rank-order in the correlations between different relatives, but both of these orders fit the theoretical predictions almost perfectly.

The data from studies of family resemblances, then, are also consistent with the view that intelligence test scores are determined in large measure by heredity.

HEREDITARY AND ENVIRONMENTAL CONTRIBUTIONS. We have also seen that environment plays its part. This has led to many attempts to determine what proportion of individual variation in intelligence is due to hereditary factors, and what proportion to environmental factors.

The most recent attempt has been made by the English psychologist and statistician, Burt (1956). Previous estimates usually were based on the extent of resemblances between relatives and overlooked the fact that *differences* among members of the same families may also be due to genetic influences. Burt attempted to take full account of both kinds of hereditary influences and on the basis of his analysis he estimates that as much as 77 per cent of individual variance is due to genetic influences.

However we must remember that we still do not know what intelligence really is. (See p. 543.) Burt's estimate, therefore, should not be taken as an indication of how much heredity contributes to "intelligence." As Burt himself points out his estimate holds only for "test-results supplied by 'group tests' of the kind most psychologists use" and moreover ". . . our analysis holds only for a population of the particular type we have sampled, brought up in an environment [England] of a certain definite and restricted character."

While Burt's conclusions, therefore, must be accepted as provisional, it seems highly probable that well over half of a person's score on our present intelligence tests is determined by hereditary factors.

Sex, Race, National, and Class Differences

Closely tied in with the study of individual differences in ability as a function of heredity is the analysis of *group* differences in abilities. Do men excel women in reasoning capacity? Are Negroes less intelligent than non-Negroes? Are the higher economic groups more capable people than the lower economic groups? These questions have often aroused Mr. Anyman's emotions and the psychologists' interests. And the answer to these questions have just as often reflected prejudices as they have careful observation. But during the last fifty years a great deal of quantitative data has been accumulated and some *tentative* scientific answers to some of these questions can now be suggested.

Sex Differences. Not even the most dedicated feminist denies that in the outside world men have achieved more than women. Not only in the sciences, business, engineering, exploration, and the arts do men excel, but even in the traditional "feminine" fields of dress-designing, interior decorating, and cooking do we find men as the leaders.

Two explanations have been offered for this. On the one hand there is the hypothesis that in general intelligence and in specific aptitudes men are biologically superior to women. On the other hand there is the cultural and social explanation: Women are the equals of men in all these traits, but they are not given the same opportunities to develop and display their abilities.

ACHIEVEMENT MEASURES. In contrast to achievement in the "outside world," girls make better achievement scores in school than do boys. While the differences between boys and girls are rather small, they are consistently found in almost every type of measure used. Thus girls receive better grades from their teachers and also do better on objective achievement tests. While in general girls are better in such school subjects as English, spelling, writing, and art, and boys tend to achieve more in arithmetic, geography, and science, even with the latter subjects girls are frequently reported as doing better in school.

GENERAL INTELLIGENCE TESTS. Perhaps the best study on the question of sex difference in intelligence is the one done under the supervision of the Scottish Council for Research in Education (1939) where *all* the children in Scotland who were born on the first of February, May, August, and November of one year were given the Stanford-Binet test. The average I.Q. for the boys was found to be 100.5, and for the girls, 99.7. This slight difference was not statistically significant and could be explained as due to errors of measurement (see p. 523).

SPECIFIC ABILITIES. It must be remembered, however, that the Binet test score is based on the sum of the scores earned on a large number of test items involving arithmetic reasoning, word definitions, memory, perceptual performances, etc. If we look at tests designed to measure each of these specific abilities, we do find significant differences between boys and girls. Thus girls are usually found to be superior to boys on verbal fluency and straight memory tests, while boys are superior in mathematical ability—especially in mathematical *reasoning* as opposed to the straightforward manipulation of numbers.

In the more specialized aptitudes we again find differences between the sexes. In judgment and manipulation of spatial relationships and in most mechanical aptitude tests the boys are better. On the other hand, in tasks requiring dexterity of the fingers or perceptual speed women seem to excel.

In all these measures, however, there is a great deal of overlap in the distribution of scores earned by boys and girls. Though the above statements are valid when speaking of the *average* boy or girl, we find many girls excelling many boys in mathematical reasoning, just as we find many boys who are superior to many girls in memory and verbal fluency.

ORIGINS OF DIFFERENCE. Are these differences due to biological factors or to social and cultural factors? It is obvious that boys and girls are different in their anatomical structures and hormonal composition. It is therefore conceivable that their intellectual and aptitude capacities are also genetically determined. The basis for this hypothesis becomes clear when we remember that any one behavior trait is determined by a host of genes, and perhaps by the interaction of most of the genes. The fact that performance differences between the sexes have also been reported for the lower animals further supports the biological argument, since here "cultural and social" influences can play very little role. On the other hand it is equally clear that social and cultural influences are different for boys and girls and this might account for the observed differences in test performance. And even the animal studies are not clear-cut, since the different biological structures and functions of the two sexes might result in their having different environmental experiences.

Our present data do not allow an unequivocal answer to the question of the origins of the observed differences in performance between male and female.

Racial and National Differences. The attempt to measure and explain racial or national differences in abilities faces three major difficulties. In the first place it is almost impossible to study *pure* races. Wherever people of originally different racial stock live together, considerable race mixture occurs. It has been estimated, for example, that in the United States about 20 per cent of the people classified as "whites" have Negro parentage in their family line.

One might grant this and still argue that the members of the so-called "Negro group" would have a different *average* racial composition than those of the so-called "white group." But here we run into the second difficulty. People who are labeled as being of "different" racial or national or religious groups often are not subjected to the same environmental influences as are other people. We often find discriminatory practices employed by the majority groups. Thus in the United States the Ne-

gro does not have the same educational advantages as does the white person; the recent immigrant does not have the same social and economic opportunities as the "native" American. Any differences in test scores we might find among such groups would therefore be difficult to interpret.

Finally, it might be suggested that we could avoid the discrimination problem by testing people of different nationalities in their own countries where they are the majority groups. But here we come up against the third difficulty. Intelligence tests and aptitude tests, standardized on specified populations, cannot validly be used for other populations (see p. 546). Since we do not know what I.Q. scores really mean, there is almost no way, at present, for designing tests that can be equally valid for people of widely different cultures.

Despite these difficulties a great deal of useful data on this question of racial and national difference has been accumulated. In these studies no attempt was made to define these groupings biologically; "common sense" or social definitions have been used.

THE AMERICAN NEGRO. Perhaps more studies have been directed toward comparing the intellectual capacities of Negro and white children in America than toward any other single comparison. On the basis of many studies three firm conclusions can be stated:

1) *Negro children, on the average, earn lower intelligence test scores than do white children.* One of the most carefully controlled comparative studies is that of Tanser (1939). Tanser's study of the Negroes in Kent County (Ontario, Canada) took advantage of an unusually favorable research opportunity. Kent County (on the north shore of Lake Erie near Detroit) is almost unique in that it is one of the few parts of Canada in which extensive attempts have been made to establish Negro settle-

ments. The ancestors of the present Negro population moved to Kent County before the Civil War, during the days of the underground railroad. Most of the schools there are integrated, and racial discrimination is at a minimum. The socioeconomic status of the Negro and white groups are more nearly comparable in Kent County than anywhere else in North America.

In Tanser's study carefully chosen samples of 386 white and 103 Negro pupils were tested with four different intelligence tests, both verbal and non-verbal. On all tests the average white child surpassed the average Negro child. For instance, on the National Intelligence Test the mean I.Q. for the white children was 103.6, for the Negro children, 89.2. This difference held whether rural Negro and rural white children, or urban Negro and urban white children, were compared.

2) *I.Q. scores for Negro and white children show a large degree of overlap.* It is clear that the difference between the *average* Negro child and the *average* white child does not adequately describe the difference between the mental capacities of the two groups: Thus, to return to Tanser's study, Figure 141 presents the distribution curves of I.Q. scores for the Negro and white children. It can be seen that about 18 per cent of the white children earned *lower* I.Q.'s than did the *average Negro child;* and about 22 per cent of the Negro children earned *higher* I.Q.'s than did the *average white child.* The shaded area of the two curves represents the degree of overlap between the two groups. With this high degree of overlap (a finding that is characteristic of most studies on this question) and with the realization that Negro children in the public schools of this country have earned I.Q. scores as high as 200, one conclusion is inescapable: Any decision to use differences in the *average* I.Q. scores of the two "racial" groups as a basis

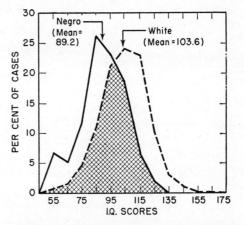

FIG. 141. Distribution of I.Q. scores for 386 white children and 103 Negro children of Kent County, Ontario, Canada (data from Tanser, 1939).

for classifying in advance *any individual child,* Negro or white, is scientifically unjustified.

3) *The Negro child's I.Q. score shows a consistent rise when his educational opportunities are improved.* A number of studies have demonstrated that Negro children who leave the South and enter Northern schools (where presumably they have better educational opportunities) show an increase in I.Q. Table 21 shows the results of one such study performed in the city of Philadelphia. Here it can be seen that the longer the Southern-born Negro children remained in the Philadelphia schools, the more did their I.Q. scores increase. Thus the children whose I.Q.'s averaged 86.5 when they entered the first grade earned 89.3 in the second grade, 91.8 in the fourth grade, and 93.3 in the sixth grade. The children who entered later, never did catch up with the children who had moved to the North earlier. The available evidence seems to indicate, then, that some of the observable differences between the Negro and white children may be adequately explained in terms of environmental differences.

But there still remains a difference be-

TABLE 21

Mean I.Q.'s on Philadelphia Tests of Mental and Verbal Ability
(Based on data from Lee, 1951)

		Grade in which Test Was Taken			
Grade Entered	*Number of Children*	1A	2B	4B	6B
1A	182	86.5	89.3	91.8	93.3
1B–2B	109		86.7	88.8	90.9
3A–4B	199			86.3	87.2
5A–6B	221				88.2

tween the two groups, as we have seen in Tanser's study. While the three conclusions we have listed are amply supported by scientific evidence, no unequivocal answer can be given to the question whether the remaining differences in the I.Q. scores between the Negro and white children are due to biological or environmental factors. Because it is almost impossible to find sizeable groups of Negro and white children who have equally good home environments, equally good schooling, equally good social and occupational opportunities (these requirements are not met in our Northern states, nor even in Kent County), no definitive study has yet been made on this question. The only valid conclusion we can draw is a negative one: There is no scientific *proof* that the differences in the I.Q. scores between Negro and white children are due to inherited biological factors, nor is there any scientific *proof* that these differences are due to environmental influences. Science has not yet provided even an acceptable tentative answer to this question.

NATIONALITY DIFFERENCES. Because the United States has been a "melting pot" for so long, there has been a great deal of interest in comparing the intellectual levels of the different national groups who have emigrated to this country.

A number of studies of immigrants and their children seem to agree that Jews, Scandinavians, Germans, and English-speaking groups earn higher I.Q.'s than South Europeans of all nationalities. How-

ever, when these various nationalities are tested in their "home grounds," this ordering seems to change somewhat. For example, using a non-language test, Franzblau (1935) found that the Danes and the Italians in Europe did not differ, although the Danish-Americans received significantly higher scores than did the Italian-Americans. The results of this study, and of similar ones, have been interpreted to mean that differences among nationality groups in this country result from "selective immigration" rather than from innate differences among the parent populations. Thus it might be argued that the Danes who emigrated to this country had higher I.Q.'s than was true for the Italians who emigrated.

We have already indicated some of the difficulties in the way of such comparative studies. Until we can develop a better understanding of what intelligence test scores really reflect, and on the basis of that understanding develop better tests for comparative purposes, no definite conclusions can be drawn as to the biological basis of the observed nationality differences.

Class Differences. Mr. Anyman and the sociologists of this country disagree on whether we live in a "class society." It is part of the popular American credo that in the United States we have a classless society—where every man is every other man's equal (except for the Negro). While this may be more or less *legally* true, it does not seem to be *sociologically* valid.

Various communities in this country have been carefully studied by a number of social scientists and they all seem to agree that our societies are definitely "class structured" as far as sociological measures and behavior of people are concerned. For example, in "Yankee City," the name given to a New England community studied by Warner and Lunt (1941), and "Oldtown," the name used by Davis, Gardner, and Gardner (1941) for their Southern community, six distinct classes seem to exist: The *Upper Upper,* the *Lower Upper,* the *Upper Middle,* the *Lower Middle,* the *Upper Lower* and the *Lower Lower.* People in each of these classes have parties together, marry into each other's families, differ from the other classes in education and occupation.

MENTAL ABILITIES. The undoubted existence of different classes, defined in terms of differences in wealth, influence, educational level, occupation, and social behavior, immediately raises the question whether these classes also differ in "native ability." Most of the research here has involved a comparison of the I.Q.'s of people from different socioeconomic levels. Tyler (1956) after reviewing the many studies in this field, concludes that ". . . the relationship of I.Q. to socioeconomic level is one of the best documented facts in mental test history." It seems quite clear that higher I.Q.'s are found among the families of the upper socioeconomic levels than among the lower levels. (See Box 147.)

ORIGINS OF DIFFERENCES. Here, as in our previous comparisons, the same kinds of questions relative to the origin of these average differences have arisen. Do people tend to become members of certain socioeconomic groups *because* of native differences in capacity, or are their I.Q. scores determined by their socioeconomic levels?

It is clear, as we have seen in our discussion of aptitude testing, that different occupations require different levels of general intelligence. Given equal opportunities this means that people will eventually find the occupational level suited for their intellectual level. While a condition of completely equal opportunity does not exist, nevertheless there is "enough" equal opportunity to expect us to find a trend in that direction. We have also seen that intelligence test scores are determined by hereditary factors to a considerable degree. It therefore seems highly probable that, to some extent at least, the differences in I.Q.'s among the children of the different occupational groups reflect native biological differences in capacity. The people of the different occupational groups are not only *sociologically* unequal, but they may also be *biologically* unequal.

On the other hand we must remember that I.Q. scores also reflect educational opportunities. Since the educational facilities (home environments, schools, etc.) of the lower socioeconomic groups tend to be inferior to those of the upper socioeconomic groups, a part of the difference in I.Q. scores is undoubtedly due to environmental differences.

SOCIAL IMPLICATIONS. These facts have very important implications for the functioning of a democratic society. But before these implications can be spelled out we must recall several additional facts.

We have seen that heredity means *differences* between offspring and parents as well as similarities. This is especially true for any trait, such as "intelligence," which is determined by a large number of genes or hereditary factors. Because of this we must expect to find children who are brighter than their parents, and children who are duller. This expectation, based on genetic grounds, is amply confirmed by our statistical findings. The demonstrated differences in I.Q. among the children of parents from various occupational groups

BOX 147

Occupational Level and Intelligence—U.S., England, U.S.S.R.

Johnson at the University of Illinois has examined a number of studies made on children and adults from various occupational groups. The data of these studies, using different intelligence tests and carried out in three different countries, were made comparable by converting all the scores into standard scores (see Chapter 9). The results of this analysis tell a convincing story of a high relationship between occupational level and intelligence. In comparing England and the United States Johnson obtained the following results:

wise described and hence Johnson could not place them in the same table with the data for the American and English children. But the range of occupational levels is apparently the same among the three studies. After converting the scores into standard I.Q. scores Johnson found that the Russian children from the six different occupational levels earned the following I.Q.'s: 117, 109, 105, 101, 97, and 92.

Apparently, then, the hierarchy of intelligence of children in Russia, in the United States, and in England is remarkably simi-

OCCUPATIONAL LEVEL	CHILDREN		ADULTS	
	U.S.	*England*	*U.S.*	*England*
Professional	116	115	120	132
Semi-professional and managerial	112	113	113	117
Clerical, skilled trades, retail business	107	106	108	109
Rural owners, farmers	95	97	94	(No data)
Semiskilled, minor clerical, minor business	105	102	104	105
Slightly skilled	98	97	96	84
Day laborers, rural and urban	96	95	95	96

For the Russian comparison Johnson used the data published in 1929 by a member of the Labor Institute at Kharkov, Russia. The intelligence test scores for more than 2,300 children in a large Ukrainian city were presented in that report. The children had been classified into six occupational groups, the highest of which was composed of "children of officials having university education," and the lowest, of "workmen's children of whom one or both parents were illiterate." The categories were not other-

lar. The day laborer and his child—no matter under what flag and in what society he lives—has a lower I.Q. than the professional man and his child.

But one word of caution: These results are based on *average* figures. Again the variability within each group and the overlap among the groups were large and significant.

JOHNSON, D. M. 1948. Application of the standard-score I.Q. to social statistics. *J. soc. Psychol.*, 27, 217–27.

are based on *average* figures. While these average differences are statistically reliable, we also find wide individual differences within each group and considerable overlap among the groups. The difference in capacity of a parent and his children is also reflected in the fact that class structure

in the United States is not a rigid one. The variability in native capacities and the democratic structure of our society have permitted people to move from one class to another.

One of the most important implications of this *genetically determined variability* is this: If we wish to maximize the human resources of our society it becomes essential to create conditions in which each *individual*, no matter what his parentage or socioeconomic background, will be given an opportunity to achieve up to the limit of his potentialities. The son of the lawyer or doctor may be limited in his capacity, and the son of the day laborer may have the capacity to become our most brilliant scientist. We cannot classify in advance. The highly capable person may come from almost any source.

The science of genetics and the scientific study of the abilities of man provide strong support for a social policy that is in harmony with the democratic credo and aspirations of our society.

Glossary

cell segmentation. Refers to the fact that in some instances a zygote, when undergoing mitosis (or cell division) will be split or "segmented" into two separate and complete daughter cells. Cell segmentation makes possible the identical multiple births as in identical twins.

chromosomes. Threadlike bodies of different sizes and shapes appearing in like pairs, found within animal cell bodies. Normal human cells seem to contain 23 pairs of chromosomes or a total of 46 chromosomes. Chromosomes are believed to carry the genes.

crossing-over of genes. Refers to the fact that occasionally one segment of a chromosome will break off and be exchanged with a corresponding segment from the paired chromosome. Thus genes do not always "stay put" in their original chromosomes.

dominant gene. A gene assumed to have greater biochemical activity than another termed the "recessive gene." In the heterozygous condition, therefore, the dominant gene will more or less completely mask the effects of the recessive gene in determining the hereditary traits of the individual. A dominant gene is usually symbolized by a capital letter, as "A." A "dominant character" refers to a hereditary trait which reflects the activities of a dominant gene.

fraternal twins. Two individuals who have developed from *two different* fertilized ova (zygotes). To be contrasted with "identical twins." Fraternal twins may both be male, or both female, or one of each. Fraternal twins are no more genetically similar than any two brothers or sisters.

gene. The unit of inheritance, biochemical in nature, which is located on the chromosomes. The gene, as it reacts with the environment and other genes, is assumed to be a factor in determining the hereditary traits and structures of the developing individual.

germ cells. Refers to the ova (female) and sperm (male) cells. Changes in the germ cells, occurring during the lifetime of the individual, are transmitted to the offspring. To be contrasted with "somatic cells."

heterozygous genes. Refers to a pair of genes (one on each member of a pair of chromosomes) which are *different* with respect to their effects on any one hereditary trait. Thus a pair of genes, one dominant and one recessive (A, a), are heterozygous genes.

homozygous genes. Refers to a pair of genes (one on each member of a pair of chromosomes) which are *identical* with respect to their effects on any one hereditary trait. Thus a pair of dominant genes (A, A) or a pair of recessive genes (a, a) are homozygous genes.

identical twins. Two complete individuals who have developed from *one* segmented fertilized ovum (zygote). To be contrasted with "fraternal twins." Identical twins are therefore *genetically* identical and are of great interest to the psychologist who is concerned with the problem of the hereditary factors in behavior.

mitosis. The process of cell division of a zygote. In most cases the cells do not separate completely, but the subdivided cells remain as parts of a single organism.

multi-factorial determination. In genetics refers to the hypothesis that any one trait (e.g., stature) is determined by the interaction effects of many genes.

mutation. A change in genes that causes a sudden departure from the parent type, as when an individual differs from its parents in one or more heritable characteristics.

ovum (egg). The female germ (or reproductive) cell produced by the ovaries. The ovum contains within it *one* member of each pair of chromosomes from the mother, or a total of 23 chromosomes. After fertilization by the sperm the ovum can develop into a new individual.

recessive gene. A gene assumed to have lesser biochemical activity than another gene termed the "dominant gene." In the heterozygous condition, therefore, the recessive gene will be suppressed, more or less completely, by the dominant gene and the hereditary trait controlled by these two genes will not show the effects of the recessive gene. A recessive gene is usually symbolized by a small letter, as "a." In the homozygous condition (where *both* genes are recessive) the effects of the recessive genes will be apparent in the hereditary trait of the individual. A "recessive character" refers to a hereditary trait which reflects the activities of a recessive gene.

selective breeding. A technique used in experimental genetics. Consists of mating animals that display certain traits and selecting for breeding from among their offspring those that express the trait. If the trait is regulated by heredity, continued selection for a number of generations will result in a strain that breeds true for that trait.

somatic cells. Refers to the non-germ cells of the body—the cells making up the nerves, muscles, skin, and other structures of the body. Changes in the somatic cells, occurring during the lifetime of the individual, are not transmitted to the offspring. To be contrasted with "germ cells."

sperm. The male germ (or reproductive) cell produced by the testes. The sperm carries within it *one* member of each pair of chromosomes from the father, or a total of 23 chromosomes.

uterus. That part of the female reproductive system in which the fertilized ovum (zygote) implants itself and develops during the prenatal developmental period. The *womb.*

X–Y chromosomes. The chromosomes which, it is assumed, determine the sex of the new individual. A fertilized egg (zygote) with two X chromosomes will develop into a female; a zygote with one X chromosome and one Y chromosome will develop into a male.

zygote. The fertilized ovum, or the cell produced by the union of an ovum and a sperm. The normal human zygote contains 23 complete pairs of chromosomes (or 46 chromosomes), one member of each pair coming from the ovum, the other from the sperm.

Suggestions for Further Reading

ANASTASI, A., and FOLEY, J. P. 1949. *Differential psychology* (rev. ed.). New York: Macmillan.

This standard text in the field of psychological differences has several chapters on racial and socioeconomic differences which are of interest here.

DOBZHANSKY, T. 1955. *Evolution, genetics, and man.* New York: Wiley.

While primarily oriented toward the

problem of evolution, the first third of this book is devoted to genetics, covering many topics from contemporary research as well as from classical genetics. The last two chapters on "Human Evolution" and "Choice, Guidance, and Freedom in Evolution" may be of particular interest to the student of psychology.

STERN, C. 1949. *Principles of human genetics*. San Francisco: Freeman.

A well-written, authoritative, and comprehensive book. It starts at the beginning and makes no assumptions about previous study in the field on the part of the reader. An excellent introduction to human genetics.

TYLER, L. E. 1956. *The psychology of human differences* (2nd ed.). New York: Appleton-Century-Crofts.

A comprehensive account of individual and group differences in psychological attributes of people. Of special interest in the present connection are Parts Three and Four dealing with "Varieties of Group Differences" and "Factors Producing Differences."

CHAPTER XXII

Growth and Development

MAN does not come into this world with a full-blown set of abilities. Man grows, and as he grows he develops his intelligence and his aptitudes. The pattern of these capacities can best be understood, as we have indicated in the previous chapter, as the outcome of a continuously changing organism interacting with a continuously changing environment. This process of growth and development has been intensively studied by psychologists. Indeed, a separate field of *child psychology* has been devoted to this enterprise.

Child Psychology

There are various reasons why child psychology has flourished. In the first place, there is the belief that the key to the understanding of the adult personality will be found by studying the growth of personality in the child. For this reason many "personality psychologists" have concerned themselves with problems of child psychology. In the second place, so many kinds of adult skills and behavior are acquired during childhood that if we are to study the acquisition of much of adult behavior we must study the child. A good example is found in the development of language (see Chapter 17). And so we find psychologists interested in learning and perception going to the child for their information. Finally, there is the necessity of studying the child in his own right, regardless of what light he can throw on adult personality or adult skills. While the child may be father of the man, he is quite a different organism from the adult.

Child vs. Adult. Much of the experimentation and theory of psychology which we have thus far examined is concerned with adult behavior. Can we, on the basis of that knowledge and theory, say anything about the behavior of the child? The answer is not an unqualified "Yes." While it may be true that the child is intimately related to the adult and eventually develops into one, it takes a great deal of "doing" before such development occurs. The child is *not* an adult cut small; the child is a different biological organism from the adult. His skeletal structure is differently proportioned, his nervous system is different, his hormonal and biochemical make-up are different. And these differences are significant enough to prevent our generalizing from the behavior of the adult to the behavior of the child. The first problem of the child psychologist, therefore, is to describe the behavior of the child and to seek for the understanding of his behavior.

Child into Adult. But the child psychologist has still another task, for he is not only a child psychologist, he is also a "developmental psychologist." He is dealing with a rapidly changing organism. He starts with something called a *neonate* (newborn), who, in two to four weeks becomes an infant, then in a short while a child, and in 13 years or so an adolescent. He must trace the development of this changing organism and write the story of how the body and behavior of the newborn change into those of the infant, the two-year-old, the school child, the young adolescent, and the late teenager. (At this point the "adult" psychologist takes over.)

Research in child psychology since about 1920 has given us a large body of facts about the behavior of the child and several serviceable principles of growth and development. We cannot here, of course, review all the facts, but we can list the major developmental principles and illustrate each with some of the facts from child behavior.

Growth Patterns and Behavior

The behavior of an organism is always limited and directed by its anatomical structure, neurological organization, and bio-

chemical composition. Because of this, the study of the *behavior* of growing children has gone hand in hand with the study of the growth, development, and maturation of the child's *body*. Out of these studies have come several developmental principles relating function to structure.

Over-all Growth Rates. Data on the over-all bodily growth rate of man have been accumulating for many years and the general shape of the physical growth curve of man is well established. The over-all mental growth rate has also been studied and comparison between bodily and mental growth is now possible.

PHYSICAL GROWTH OF MAN. The two simplest measures of over-all bodily growth in man are total height and total weight. These measures tell similar stories.

Figure 142 depicts the growth of man

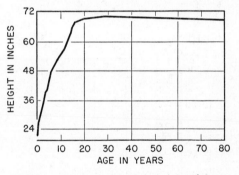

FIG. 142. Average growth in height of American males from birth to 80 years. (Adapted from Bayley in *Theoretical foundations of psychology*, H. Helson (ed.), Copyright 1951 by D. Van Nostrand Company, Inc., Princeton, New Jersey.)

as represented by total height. The most rapid changes—those occurring during the prenatal period from conception to birth —are not indicated in the figure. Immediately after birth the growth rate continues to be rapid, more so than at any other time after birth. Toward the end of "childhood" at about age 11, there is another spurt of growth which lasts into the adolescent years. After puberty, the rate of growth slows down considerably until the final height is reached. Then comes a fairly stable period, after which there begins an actual shrinking in over-all height —senescence has begun to set in.

There are large individual variations from this average picture, in terms of both the age at which puberty is reached and the maximum growth attained. Some girls reach their adult height by the time they are 14 years old; some boys, not until they are 22 or 23 years old.

Figure 143 tells the story of the growth of man and other animals in terms of total weight. The period between conception and birth, and that immediately after birth, again show the most rapid increase. Then, for human beings there is a long juvenile

period (from about 3 to 12) when weight accumulates rather slowly. With puberty, when growth in height has begun to taper off, growth in weight again increases and continues at a fairly rapid rate of gain until maturity is reached. The chart does not go beyond the age of 24, the outside limit for the period of physical growth. After the beginning of decline in our physical powers (about 25 years or so) there is an increasing tendency to corpulence, but this increase in weight indicates senescence rather than growth. It may be due to the change in hormonal composition of the body which accompanies decline in physical powers.

In comparing man with other animals two conspicuous points stand out: (1) For human beings the pubertal age has a special significance in weight growth. With the beginning of puberty, the rate of weight

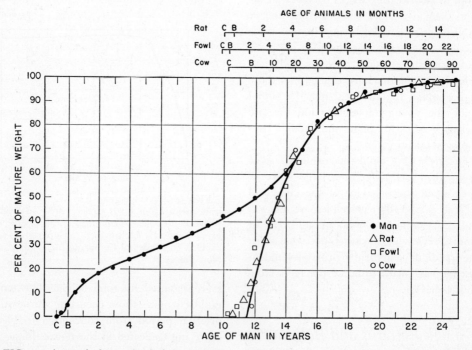

FIG. 143. An equivalence chart of the growth in weight for man and three other species. The curves have been so equated as to make the age of maturity coincide for all animals (see the data at the top of the chart). The letter "C" represents the point of conception; "B" the point of birth. (Adapted from W. J. Robbins, S. Brody, A. G. Hogan, C. M. Jackson, and C. W. Greene, in *Growth*, Copyright 1928 by Yale University Press.)

gain shows a definite change. From that point on the difference between man and other animals, as far as the shape of the growth curve is concerned, disappears. (2) While other species go through a juvenile period corresponding to man's, the length of this period in animals is relatively insignificant when compared to that of man. Man's long juvenile period makes the human family group unique among all animals. The human family is the only family where there is the *simultaneous presence of dependent offspring of different ages*. This fact has important consequences for the personality development of the child and the adult.

MENTAL GROWTH OF MAN. Mental growth data are difficult to collect and even more difficult to interpret. However, as we have already shown in another chapter, some fairly satisfactory approximations to mental growth curves are available, making comparisons between body growth and mental growth possible. The curve shown in Figure 130, page 544, represents average scores on intelligence tests made up of several different types of items and in that sense shows an "over-all intellectual growth."

From that curve, and many other similar studies, the evidence seems clear that intelligence grows at a rapid rate up to the age of 13 to 15, and from then on the growth continues at a decreasing rate. The correspondence between the rates of growth of body and of over-all intelligence is striking.

Our first developmental generalization can thus be stated as follows: *The over-all bodily and mental growth curves run parallel courses, with the rate of growth showing a drop at the age of puberty.*

Differential Growth Rates. An over-all growth rate is the sum of several quite different growth rates. The different parts of the body do not grow at the same speed.

The head, the trunk, and the legs, for example, lengthen out at different times and at different rates. Some of the organs of the body grow very rapidly at first, then slow down; others start off slowly, then accelerate. In some instances, one part of a single organ (e.g., the brain) matures faster than another part of the same organ.

Because of these differences in rates of growth and varying times of maturation of parts, it might be expected that psychological development would also progress at differential rates, e.g., some capacities appearing before others, and some emotions preceding other emotions. We shall see that this is indeed the case.

DEVELOPMENTAL DIRECTION. One of the most striking characteristics of the growing human body is the change in the form and proportions of its various parts. Look at Figures 144 and 145. At two months after conception you were about 50 per cent head. At birth you were 25 per cent head and the rest evenly divided between trunk and legs. Eventually, you have developed into the "average" adult who is 50 per cent legs, about one-third trunk, and only about 12–14 per cent head (Fig. 144). (Here again we must make allowances for individual differences. Look around you at your neighbors.)

These changes come about through very different growth rates for the different parts of the body. The head starts growing at a very rapid rate almost immediately after conception. By the time the baby is born, the head has already achieved over 60 per cent of its adult size (Fig. 145). The trunk is next in growth rate, and by the end of the second year, it has reached the halfway point to its final length. During the second year, the legs and arms begin to grow in earnest, reaching the 50 per cent point at about the fourth year. This progressive differential growth—first the head, then the trunk, then the legs—has been

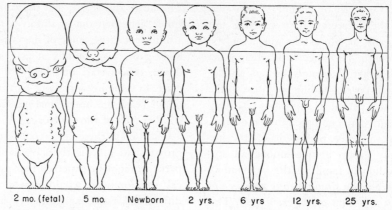

2 mo. (fetal)   5 mo.   Newborn   2 yrs.   6 yrs   12 yrs   25 yrs.

FIG. 144. Changes in form and proportion of the human body during the fetal period and the postnatal period up to maturity. (Adapted from W. J. Robbins, S. Brody, A. G. Hogan, C. M. Jackson, and C. W. Greene, in *Growth*, Copyright 1928 by Yale University Press.)

designated by the term *cephalocaudal* (head-to-foot).

While the body has been growing in length, it has also been growing in a *proximodistal* direction, that is, from the central part out to the peripheral part. For example, the trunk and shoulders develop first and then the arms, fingers, and toes begin their real growth.

Correlated with these physical growth directions, the sensorimotor *behavior* of the infant also shows a head-to-foot and central-to-peripheral development. Nursing is the earliest and best organized behavior in the neonate. It is, of course, primarily localized in the head. According to Gesell (1947), the "normal" infant (again allowing for individual differences) shows the following sequence of sensorimotor development:

4 weeks......Control of eye movements; ability to follow an object visually, etc.

16 weeks......Ability to balance head.

28 weeks......The hands can be used to grasp and manipulate objects.

40 weeks......The trunk is under control, enabling the child to sit and crawl.

52 weeks......The legs and feet are under control, enabling the child to stand and cruise about.

It is clear that we have here a cephalocaudal direction of development.

In the development of locomotion and movement the proximodistal tendency is also apparent. At first the child's purposeful movements stem from the shoulder and pelvic girdles. Later in infancy, movements appear at the elbows, wrists, knees, and ankles. For example, in reaching for some-

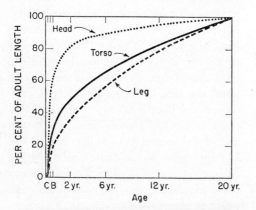

FIG. 145. Differential growth of the human head, torso, and legs from conception to maturity. (Based on data from various sources.)

thing, the infant first moves his shoulders and elbows toward the object, and only later does he begin to use his wrists and fingers.

All of the above can be summarized in a second developmental generalization: *Development of sensorimotor behavior in the infant follows the cephalocaudal and proximodistal directions of body growth.*

DIFFERENCES AMONG ORGANS. Not only do the chief divisions of the body (head, trunk, and limbs) show variable growth rates, but so do the different organs within the body. Moreover, the different parts within the individual organ grow at different rates. A consideration of both of these differential growth patterns—*among* organs and *within* organs—will lead us to other important developmental principles.

The various organs of man can be grouped into four different growth types, as shown in Figure 146. The genital organs show a *positive acceleration*: very slow growth during childhood and then extremely rapid acceleration at puberty. Just the opposite is true of the brain and its parts. Here we have a *negatively accelerated* growth curve, with rapid growth during the first six years of life and then a sharp slowing down. The lymphoid group shows a growth *reversal*, increasing very rapidly at first, then actually decreasing in size. Finally the "general" type shows an *S-shaped* curve—starting and ending with rapid growth periods separated by a long period of very little gain.

DIFFERENCES WITHIN ORGANS. Different parts of some of the endocrine glands (especially of the pituitary) develop at different rates. Perhaps the most interesting

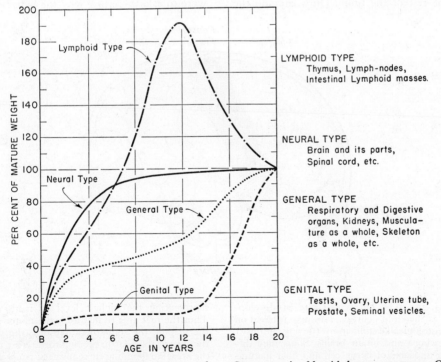

FIG. 146. Curves showing growth rates of the four major categories of organs or tissue types in the human body. (Adapted from Scammon, in *Morris' human anatomy*. Copyright 1923 by P. Blakiston's Sons & Co., New York.)

and important example of differential
growths within a single organ is provided
by the cerebral cortex.

At birth the cortex has all the neural cells
it is ever going to get. However, as the
body grows, certain changes occur in the
brain. Among them are changes in the size
and chemical composition of the nerve
cells, and in the length and state of development of the nerve fibers. These changes
occur at different rates for different areas
of the cortex. For example, the pyramidal
Betz cells (important for motor control,
see p. 489), are more advanced in over-all
development than any other type of cell in
the cortex from birth to the age of 6
months. During the first 6 months of life
the circumference, length, compactness of
structure, and protective covering of the
nerve fibers in the primary motor and sensory areas are far advanced over the fibers
in the rest of the brain. Only later do the

other areas of the brain develop to the
mature level (see Fig. 147).

Thus, while the human infant is born
with a brain, *it is a brain whose parts and
functions mature at different rates.* (See
Figure 148 for an illustration of the gradual
development of the alpha rhythm in the
brain.) The sensory and motor areas can
begin to function relatively early and simple conditioning may be possible, but the
association areas (presumably those im-
portantly involved in complex percepts
and problem-solving, see p. 498) are just
not ready to go to work until some later
time.

Maturation and Learning. The story of
bodily growth suggests that the development of behavior will show a successive unfolding of functions and capacities as their
underlying bodily structures develop. If we
were to ask, therefore, why the behavior of

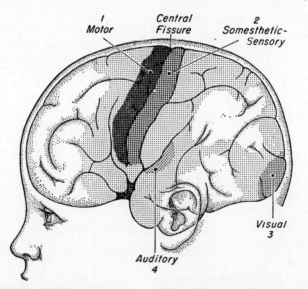

FIG. 147. The differential rate of development of the child's cortex. This map is based on
the histological examination (during autopsy)
of newborn and infant brains. Some nine different measures of nerve cell and fiber maturation have been used in arriving at this picture.
Different degrees of shading represent different
stages of development, with the darkest shading

representing the highest level of maturation.
Thus the first area to mature is the motor area;
the second, the somesthetic-sensory; the third,
the visual; the fourth, the auditory. Next come
the areas surrounding these primary sensory and
motor areas. The areas shown in white are the
last to mature. (Based on data from Conel,
1952.)

the older child is much more complex than that of the infant, we cannot merely say "learning" or "experience." The recognition of this has led to the maturation-learning principle which we can list as our third developmental generalization: *The development of behavior reflects maturation through growth as well as the cumulative effects of learning through experience.*

We have a good illustration of this principle in the development of the child's learning ability itself. There are, of course, no sudden changes in learning ability with age. Nevertheless when we compare the newborn with even the three-month-old infant, striking differences appear.

NEONATE LEARNING. There have been many attempts to study learning in the first week or two of life. The simplest conditioning tasks have been used. For example, Marquis (1931) attempted to condition the sucking response of infants to the sound of a buzzer, and Wickens and Wickens (1940) tried to train the infant to withdraw his foot (in order to escape an electric shock) whenever a buzzer was sounded. Of the

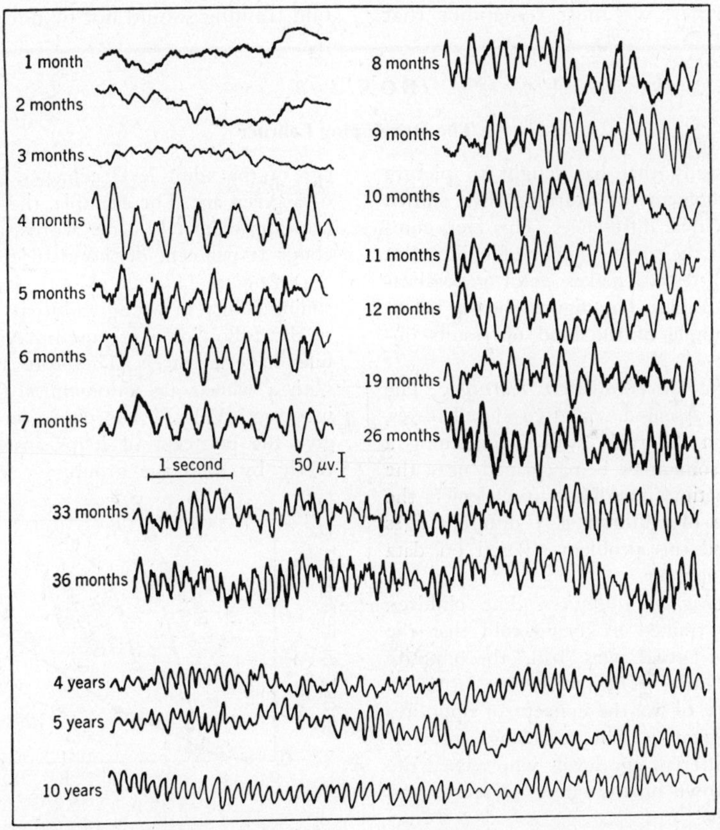

FIG. 148. Records showing the development of the alpha rhythm (taken from the occipital area) in a boy from 1 month of age to 10 years. For the first three months there appears no uniform pattern. About the 4th month a persistent rhythm begins to develop (about 3 per second) and by the end of the first year the rhythm increases to about 6 per second. From that point on there is a slow increase in rhythm until about the age of 10 or 12 years where it reaches the adult frequency of 10 per second. These records were taken by the psychologist Lindsley from his own son. (Reproduced with permission from *Cerebral mechanisms in behavior*, L. A. Jeffress, ed. Copyright 1951 by John Wiley & Sons, Inc., New York.)

many attempts to establish conditioning, only that of Marquis showed any success. The best other experimenters have been able to do is to get occasional indications of conditioning, and these were extremely erratic and unstable.

When we recall that the cortex of the neonate is quite undeveloped and that we do not even have clear evidence that his cortical cells can conduct impulses at all, the "stupidity" of the newborn becomes understandable. *No amount of training can make up for an immature cortex.* The most impatient of parents have to wait for growth. Further, we must remember that

as the child grows older his cortex first becomes a motor cortex, then a motor-sensory one, and only later do the various association areas mature. We can then see why the learning ability of the child develops only very gradually from the stage where following a moving object with his eyes is the height of his intellectual accomplishment, through that of learning to coo at the sight of his mother, to the more complex achievements of the older child (see Box 148).

"READINESS" FOR TRAINING. The maturation-learning principle suggests that certain training should not be undertaken until

---

BOX 148

The Developing Learner

Every study that has sought to picture the development of learning has shown large individual differences. This fact, combined with the small number of children at each level tested, makes valid generalizations impossible. The figure shown below gives a sample of the kind of results obtained.

1) *Simple discrimination learning.* The child was presented with two closed boxes, the one on the right always containing a doll, but sometimes being placed near the child, sometimes far. The curve depicts the percentage of children at 3 different ages who solved this problem. (Based on data from Heidbreder.)

2) *Meaning of opposites.* The children were first trained by being told that the opposite of "good" was "bad," the opposite of "big," "little." They were then tested on their ability to use the concept of opposites after this training. The percentages of children of different age levels who passed the test are shown on the curve. (Kreezer and Dallenbach)

3) *Vocabulary.* Based on "smoothed" data from several sources and represents the number of different words in *actual use* at different ages. On the assumption that the average adult uses about 11,500 words, each point on the curve represents the percent-

age of the adult level achieved by a child of a given age. For example, the 6-year-old uses approximately 2,500 words, and this is about 22 per cent of the mature level.

4) *Logical fallacies.* Moore studied reasoning ability in young children. Such items as the following were used: "All automobiles have 4 wheels. Therefore all vehicles with 4 wheels are automobiles. Correct or incorrect? Why?" The points on the curve give the per cent of items answered correctly by each age group.

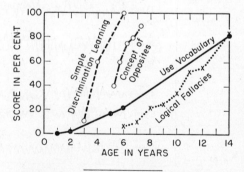

HEIDBREDER, E. F., 1928. Problem-solving in children and adults. *J. genet. Psychol., 35,* 522–45.

KREEZER, G., and DALLENBACH, K. M., 1929. Learning the relation of opposition. *Amer. J. Psychol., 41,* 432–41.

MOORE, T. V., 1929. The reasoning ability of children in the first years of school life. *Catholic Univ. Stud. Psychol. & Psychiat.*

the child is specifically ready for such training. Pushing the child ahead of his maturation level may impose harmful stresses and strains on the child, not to mention the parent and teacher. But even if one were willing to pay this price, the educational objectives might still not be reached, or reached only with great inefficiency of time and effort. (See Box 149.)

It might therefore be thought that the

BOX 149

Maturation, Ladder-Climbing, Language Development

The maturation-learning principle has been tested on various forms of behavior, from locomotion skills to the learning of language. The following figure is taken from a study by Hilgard at the Merrill-Palmer nursery school with 28-month-old children, of whom 8 were trained for 12 weeks on climbing up and down a 3-step ladder, 2½ ft. high, and 8 others were not. Both groups, on a preliminary test, earned equivalent scores. The untrained group, after *one* week of practice caught up with the 12-week-trained group. As far as this skill is concerned, "premature" practice shows considerable waste. (The "score in seconds" is the average time taken to climb up and down the ladder.)

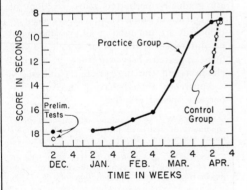

Strayer at Yale compared the effectiveness of vocabulary training at two different maturation periods, using the "co-twin control" method. Here one of a pair of identical twins is given training, the other is reserved as a control, thus insuring that both subjects are genetically identical and therefore, it is assumed, equally mature.

The subjects were identical twin sisters, *T* and *C*, 84 weeks of age. *T* was given intensive vocabulary training for 5 weeks, while *C* lived in an isolated "nonverbal" environment where the child's attendants carefully avoided speaking in her presence. Then *C* was given a 4-week training period, and *T* was returned to a normal language environment of other children and adults.

Among the results were the following: (a) *C*'s learning rate was faster; after an equal amount of training (4 weeks) she had a larger vocabulary than did *T*. (b) In a picture-pointing test, *C*, by the end of 4 weeks, was making *no* errors, while *T* could not pass a single test after 5 weeks of training. (c) *T*'s vocabulary continued to increase after training was discontinued, and because of this it was several months before *C* caught up with *T*.

"Premature" learning is not efficient, but neither is it always entirely wasted.

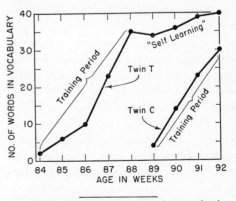

Hilgard, J. R., 1932. Learning and maturation in pre-school children. *J. genet. Psychol.*, 41, 36–56.
Strayer, L. C., 1930. Language and growth. *Genet. Psychol. Monogr.*, 8, #3.

child psychologist could draw up a list of the ages at which the child becomes ready for different kinds of training, and this list could be used to guide both parents and teacher. Some lists have been attempted, but there are two major considerations which limit the applicability of such "readiness" guides:

(1) From the moment the ovum is fertilized until the time of death, the individual lives in a constantly changing environment, whether it be the fluid bathing the embryo in its mother's womb, the noises and cooings surrounding the baby in its cradle, or the welter of stimuli bombarding the child as soon as he begins to sit up and take notice. Although some performances develop despite restricted stimulation (see Box 150), the amount and kind of general stimulation may affect some of the "innate" growth factors. For example, there are some data to suggest that the continued transmission of impulses through the nervous system speeds up the maturation of the nerve fibers. In other words, although learning may not be very effective until maturation has taken place, *the very attempt to learn and the stimulation of the child in that attempt may speed up the maturation process.*

2) There are large individual differences in maturation rates. This holds true whether we use such measures as body weight or length, bone structure development, and the onset of puberty, or the more subtle measures of sensitivity to various emotional, social, and "intellectual" situations (see Fig. 149). The maturation-learning principle, as a guide to the educational program for a child, must be applied with full allowance for such individual differences.

Differentiation of Structure and Function.
As the major parts of the body, its organs and its systems develop, greater and

---

BOX 150

You Can't Keep a Good Baby Down

Dennis, in both experimental and field studies, has accumulated evidence that the development of sitting, standing, and walking is determined by growth changes and maturational development of the neural and muscular systems rather than by practice.

In one drastic study he kept a pair of girl twins on their backs for the first 36 weeks of their lives, thus preventing any practice in sitting or standing. Several weeks later they were able to sit alone. At 52 weeks the twins were given their first opportunity to stand with support. They were unable to do so, but within three days they had succeeded. One twin, indeed, suffered no retardation in crawling, standing alone, or walking independently, while the other twin soon caught up with the normal developmental rate.

In his field study of the development of walking among Hopi Indian children Dennis compared the effects of cradleboard restriction as against no restriction. Most Hopi children are bound to cradleboards almost immediately after birth and are kept bound for three months, after which they are gradually permitted more freedom of movement. In some Hopi villages the cradleboards are not used at all. Yet he found no difference in the age at which walking first appeared between the cradleboard children and the unrestricted children.

Apparently these behaviors develop without any special practice.

DENNIS, W., 1941. Infant development under conditions of restricted practice and of minimum social stimulation. *Genet. Psychol. Monogr.*, 23, 143–91.
DENNIS, W., and DENNIS, M. G., 1940. The effect of cradling practices upon the onset of walking in Hopi children. *J. genet. Psychol.*, 56, 77–86.

---

greater precision of function within any one system becomes possible. For example, at first the entire upper half of the child's body—starting with the shoulder region and involving the arms, hands, and fingers—moves spasmodically and excitedly toward a desired object. With development,

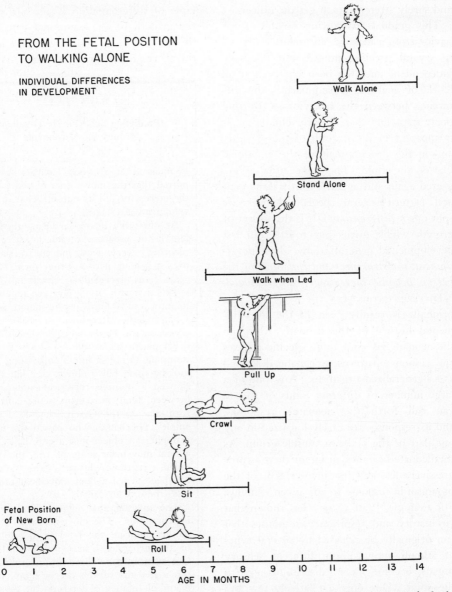

FROM THE FETAL POSITION
TO WALKING ALONE

INDIVIDUAL DIFFERENCES
IN DEVELOPMENT

Walk Alone

Stand Alone

Walk when Led

Pull Up

Crawl

Sit

Fetal Position
of New Born

Roll

0   1   2   3   4   5   6   7   8   9   10   11   12   13   14
AGE IN MONTHS

FIG. 149. One indication of the extent of in-dividual differences in maturation rate is seen in the development of walking. Although the *order* in which children progress from one stage to another is similar, the *age* at which the different stages are reached vary greatly. Shown here are the age *zones* within which 95 per cent of a group of 215 infants, studied at a well-baby clinic in Rochester, Minnesota, reached the various stages of performance. In general there was more than a four-month spread for any one stage. For example, some children were able to stand alone at about eight and a half months, other children, not until they were thirteen months of age. (Data from Aldrich and Nerval, 1946.)

more and more limited movements are called forth until finally only the fingers —or even only one finger—may languidly and surely stretch out to get the object.

This gradual "narrowing down" of behavior from a massive, all-inclusive pattern to several precise, limited, and relatively independent ones has been observed at all levels of analysis. It summarizes the difference between the behavior of the neonate stage and that of early childhood. It is apparent in the growth of motor skills, and in the development of the emotional life of the child. The same story is repeated again and again: From a large general pattern several specialized ones are split off or *differentiated.* It is this aspect of growth which forms our fourth and last developmental generalization: *With development, the structures and functions of the person become increasingly differentiated.*

DIFFERENTIATION AND THE NEONATE. This principle is readily seen in the developmental history of the neonate. Although the neonate has some quite specific reflexes and response patterns, it can be described as a "generalized organism." Any one of a large number of different kinds of stimuli can call forth the neonate's responses, and its responses are rarely localized in any one part of the body or muscle group. As the neonate becomes an infant there is progressively less and less involvement of the organism in response to any given stimulus. For example, Pratt (1937) has shown that circulatory and respiratory responses that can originally be released by several types of stimuli acting upon different sensory organs, become more "discriminating," to the point where only a relatively few and quite specific stimuli are effective. These early specialized movements of the infant derive from and are definitely related to the preceding massive ones. This has led to the suggestion that the generalized *active* fetus is the one who most quickly develops

the finer specialized movements when he becomes an infant (see Box 151).

DIFFERENTIATION OF EMOTIONS. This principle of differentiation is also apparent in the growth of the emotional behavior of the child. The newborn has but one emotional response for everything. Whether

---

BOX 151

Predicting Behavior Development from Fetal Movements

Richards and Newberry of the Fels Foundation at Antioch College have reported that the movements of the fetus in the uterus foretell its rate of behavioral development after birth.

At one-week intervals, during the last 2 months of pregnancy, each of 12 women recorded every fetal movement she felt over a 5-hour period. From these records each fetus received a "fetal movement score" in terms of the average number of minutes it was active per 10-minute period.

Six months after birth the babies were tested on the Gesell schedule of behavioral development consisting of such tasks as dropping an object into a cup, sitting alone, looking for a fallen object, etc. The results showed a positive correlation (about .65) between fetal movement score and performance on the Gesell schedule. For example: The babies who passed the test of dropping an object into a cup, had earned a fetal movement score of 5.76, those who failed, 3.31; those who passed the "sit alone" test had earned a fetal movement score of 4.88, those who failed, 2.90.

The investigators suggest the following interpretation: The movements felt by the mother indicate the level of development of the generalized behavior of the fetus. Out of this generalized behavior are differentiated the various precise motor movements of infancy. Therefore, the more advanced the organism is in the development of his *generalized* behavior, the sooner his *precise* motor movements become differentiated.

RICHARDS, T. W., and NEWBERRY, H., 1938. Studies in fetal behavior. *Child Develop., 9,* 79–86.

the stimulus is a loud noise, sudden loss of support, pain, wet diaper, hunger, or tickle, the response is a fairly diffuse emotional outburst which can best be labeled "general excitement." In the course of development, this generalized excitement becomes more and more differentiated until by the end of the first two years the baby's emotional life has become a more discriminating and a "richer" one. He shows fewer outbursts, but the kinds of situations which lead to emotional episodes increase in variety and the nature of his response becomes more specifically adapted for those situations. (See Fig. 150.)

According to Bridges (1932) there is a definite temporal pattern in the differentiation of the emotions. The generalized response of excitement first becomes differentiated into a general negative and a general positive response called "distress" and "delight" respectively. As time goes on these still quite general responses split into more and more specific ones. Distress comes to find expression in a variety of emotions: anger, disgust, fear, or jealousy. Delight also becomes differentiated and can express itself as appreciation and joy in numerous pursuits. The rate at which these emotions become differentiated varies from infant to infant and the exact age of appearance of the various emotions is difficult to determine. Figure 151 presents one developmental history based on Bridges' observations of 62 infants in the Montreal Foundling Hospital. It is probable that the emotional development of children brought up in normal family surroundings, with the constant attention of parents and other adults, would be different.

This process of differentiation does not, of course, cease in infancy. The arousing situations and the forms of emotional response may become more and more differentiated throughout the lifetime of the person. With added maturity the "emo-

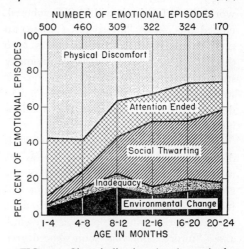

FIG. 150. Chart indicating the change in frequency of emotional outbursts in children and the nature of the exciting situation. It is based on data collected by Blatz and Millichamp (1935) in their observations of the behavior of 5 children. Over the two-year period some 2095 emotional outbursts were observed and recorded in these infants. It will be noted that the *number* of emotional episodes drops from a total of 500 during the 1–4 month age period to 170 during the 20–24 month period. At first most of the episodes (over 60 per cent) were initiated by physical discomfort—wet diaper, pins sticking in skin, illness, etc., or by the cessation of adult attention. As time went on, other situations called forth an emotional response. "Social thwarting" refers to such stimuli as teasing the child, laughing at him, refusing him a request. "Inadequacy" includes such situations as the child's inability to reach for desired objects, inability to do something. "Environmental change" includes being placed into an unfamiliar physical or social environment, being exposed to loud and sudden noises.

tional value" of objects and situations change. Figure 152 illustrates the changing patterns of fear-arousing situations as the child grows older. As the emotional value of the stimulus-pattern changes, so does the nature of the response. Eventually we end up with an exceedingly large supply of differentiated fears and hatreds, joys and loves.

DIFFERENTIATION AND THE LIFE-SPACE. We not only perceive the world about us, but we also perceive ourselves as objects in this world. Kurt Lewin, it will be remembered, coined the phrase "life-space" (p. 210) to refer to the percept which includes *both* the self and the environment. In his many studies of child psychology, he and his students have been primarily interested in describing the life-space of the developing child.

The life-space of the newborn child is described by Lewin as "a field which has relatively few and only vaguely distinguished areas." Few objects seem to be differentiated from each other, and "time" is not differentiated into a "past," a "present," and a "future." But very soon some degree of differentiation begins. As early as the first week the child begins to react differentially to the *objects* of nursing, and to the *time* of nursing. Within the first few months he begins to study his own body and his immediate physical surroundings.

Over the years, the child's life-space shows a continuous increase in its *scope* and in its *differentiation*. By increase in scope Lewin referred to the fact that the child's life-space begins to contain much that is not physically present and his time-perspective

increases in the directions of the past and the future (he remembers past events, anticipates future ones, and even creates imaginary episodes).

Differentiation is reflected in his ability to distinguish between his inner and outer world, and in the variety of emotions he can display. This growing complexity of the child is shown also by his increased *socialization*. The development of the child's social relations is best illustrated and studied in his play. Before the age of six months children show little awareness of their "play-pen pals." Beginning with that age they initiate contacts by touching, cooing at, and interfering with the other child's movements. From that stage their play gradually develops until the age of about 5 or 6 years when group and associative play among children become the rule. (See Box 152.)

Individual Differences in Development. Behavior does not always show a constant progression in complexity or integration. There seem to be lapses in development and even apparent regressions. In addition there

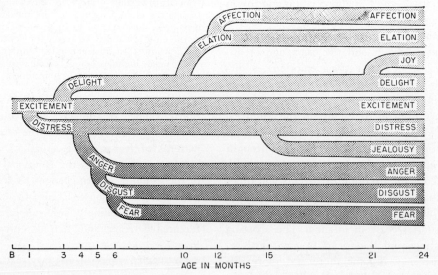

FIG. 151. A diagrammatic representation of the progressive differentiation of emotions in the child during his first two years. (After Bridges, 1932.)

are tremendous individual differences in growth and development, some children showing a much longer "infantile" period, both bodily and mentally, than other children. The fact that skeletal, hormonal, and mental age do not always correspond to chronological age may make for difficulties —for both parent and child.

People expect, for example, that a certain height and body-build will go along with a correspondingly developed maturity of interests and emotions. The child who is larger than the average ten-year-old is expected to be more mature than the average ten-year-old. And when he behaves like a typical ten-year-old, or shows the muscular coordination typical of a ten-year-old, the observer may feel that the child is "backward" or "awkward." The child who is retarded (as against the average) in his body growth, or emotional maturity, also runs against adjustment prob-

lems. He differs from his schoolmates and does not live up to the expectations of his teachers and the adults surrounding him. The fact that he may later catch up is of little help at the moment. We must always be ready to allow for great individual differences in growth rates.

By Way of Summary. By and large, the story of the development of the human being is a story of integrated changes in structure and function. It is a story of a gradual, orderly unfolding of more and more complex systems, with a simultaneous differentiation and specialization within each system. Accompanying this growth in specialization and independence, there is an increase in integration.

The unfolding of structure and function, however, is not always perfectly integrated. Individual differences play a prominent role in the developmental story.

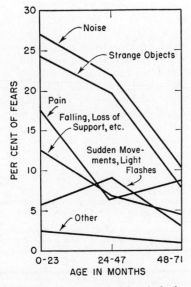
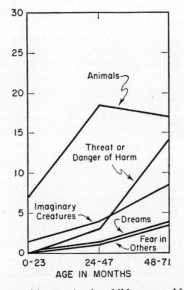

FIG. 152. Relative frequency of fear-inducing situations as described by parents and teachers, including direct observations of 263 children. The figure on the left portrays those situations which *decrease* in importance as fear-evoking stimuli with age. The figure on the right presents those situations which *increase* in impor-

tance with age. As the child grows older, then, he adapts to simple situations which once frightened him, but learns to recognize the potential danger in more subtle stimuli. (Adapted from A. T. Jersild, from *Manual of child psychology*, L. Carmichael, ed. Copyright 1946 by John Wiley & Sons, Inc., New York.)

BOX 152

From Solitary to Co-operative Play

The increasing socialization of the child's play from the age of 6 months to 5 years can be illustrated by two studies. Maudry and Nekula reported on the play of 92 children, aged 6 to 25 months, where each child was observed in his play when paired with an age-mate. For some observation periods the partners were without playthings; for others, a toy was given to each child; for still others, only one toy was available to both children. Between 6 and 8 months the babies paid little attention to each other or the playthings. Between 9 and 13 months, they neglected each other and responded primarily to the playthings. However, when only one toy was present some fighting did occur for possession of the toy. From 14 months on, awareness of the "other one" played an increasing role, and at 22 months social responsiveness began to appear in earnest.

Parten, of the University of Minnesota Nursery School, reported an investigation of 30 children aged 2 to 5 years. One-minute samples of the behavior of each child during the free-play hour were taken. Four major types of play were found: (1) *Solitary* play—playing alone with toys different from those used by the children within speaking distance. (2) *Parallel* play—independent activity bringing the child among other children and involving toys similar to theirs; the child plays *beside* rather than *with* others. (3) *Associative* play—active participation with other children; borrowing and lending of play materials, following one another with trains and wagons, etc., but no organization or "division of labor." (4) *Co-operative* play—the group of children have a goal; "leaders" and "organizers" appear, and there is a division of activity.

The following figure indicates the change in relative frequencies of these four types of play with increasing age. It is clear that

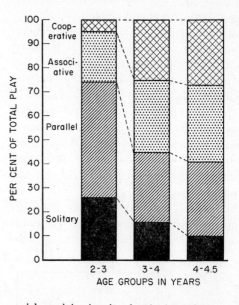

social participation in play is dependent to a large extent upon the age of the children. It is of interest to note that length of nursery school attendance did not correlate with the degree of social participation. Again we have an indication of the maturation principle at work. Socialization, like ladder-climbing, must wait upon the child's growing older.

MAUDRY, M. and NEKULA, M., 1939. Social relations between children of the same age during the first two years of life. *J. genet. Psychol.*, 54, 193–215.

PARTEN, M. B., 1932. Social participation among pre-school children. *J. abn. soc. Psychol.*, 27, 243–69.

The Adolescent

Throughout the story of growth, one age range recurs as the most crucial—the age of puberty. We have seen that at this age the rate of bodily and intellectual growth decelerates, as if the end of the growth process were now in sight. Everything seems to slow down, everything except the development of the sexual system.

With the onset of pubescence sexual development is speeded up. The age of adolescence, marking the tapering off of bodily and intellectual growth and the beginning of sexual maturity, is perhaps the chief and only dramatic landmark in an otherwise gradual developmental sequence. (For a minority report on this view, see Box 153.) Adolescence has received special attention by psychologists, physiologists, educators, and child welfare groups.

Physiological Onset of Adolescence. Pubescence refers to the achievement of the state of sexual maturity. Its onset involves several kinds of physiological changes—hormonal, primary sexual, and secondary sexual.

Before the onset of puberty, the secretions of the anterior pituitary gland stimulate the growth of the gonads—ovaries and testes. When the gonads mature, they produce ova (in the female) and sperm (in the male). As we have seen in Chapter 12, the gonads also produce estrogen (female sex hormone) and androgen (male sex hormone). With these primary sexual changes the reproductive organs are now mature and the individual is capable of reproducing his kind. At the same time, it will be

---

BOX 153

The Middle-Aged Child

Fritz Redl, child psychoanalyst, believes that the pre-adolescent age is unique in the developmental process and has not received its proper attention. He writes: "The period of pre-adolescence is a stretch of no-man's land in child-study work. By pre-adolescence I mean the phase when the nicest children begin to behave in a most awful way. This definition cannot exactly be called scientific, but those who have to live with children of that age will immediately recognize what I am talking about. This phase lies somewhere between childhood and adolescence—roughly speaking, between about nine and thirteen . . ."

This age, he believes, is the most baffling phase of child development. Most referrals to child-guidance clinics occur around this age, and yet "whatever may happen within the glands is certainly not dramatic enough to explain the undoubtedly dramatic behavior of the child."

Redl's explanation for "this peculiar phenomenon of human growth" is that this is the "breaking-up-of-the-child-personality period." Through his early years the child absorbs many experiences which he integrates into his "child personality." But now he must rid himself of this personality. Long forgotten or repressed impulses of early childhood come to the surface again before they are discarded for good; childhood standards and values are being dropped with loud bangs, and new ones have not yet been achieved.

This would explain the return to infantile habits, the silly antics, the lack of self-control, and the lowering of standards which Redl thinks are so characteristic of this age.

How can the *parent* survive all this? Redl has several suggestions, concluding with: "The one thing the pre-adolescents don't want to be reminded of is of themselves as small children. . . . If you punish, don't repeat ways you used when they were little. If you praise, don't use words that would please a three-year-old. . . . Whether you promise or reward, threaten or blackmail, appeal to their sense, morals, or anything else, always avoid doing it in the same way you did when they were little. . . . There are developmental levels of parental control as well as developmental levels of child behavior. The two have to be matched or there will be fireworks."

REDL, F. 1952. Pre-adolescents: What makes them tick? In *Our children today*, S. M. Gruenberg, ed. New York: Viking Press. Copyright 1952 by Viking Press.

remembered, patterns of over-all bodily changes, the secondary sexual characteristics, occur as a consequence of the various hormonal changes. (See p. 345.)

THE PUBESCENT GIRL. The appearance of the first menstruation is generally taken as the onset of puberty. The age at which this occurs varies widely and is in considerable part determined by nutritional and other general health factors. (There is very little evidence to substantiate the commonly held belief that girls in the tropical countries reach puberty before girls in the temperate zones.) In the United States the average age of puberty for girls is about 13 years, and ranges from 9 to 17.

THE PUBESCENT BOY. The problem of determining the exact onset of puberty in boys is much more difficult than that for girls, since here we have no such clear-cut event as menstruation to mark the change. Various measures have been suggested, such as the appearance of pigmented hairs in the pubic region and the occurrence of the first ejaculation. Using this last measure Kinsey, Pomeroy, and Martin (1948) have found the average age of puberty in boys in the United States to be somewhere between the age of 13.7 and 14.6. The age of ejaculation seems to depend in part upon nutritional factors. Thus the first ejaculation for boys who go on to college (and who, therefore, tend presumably to come from higher socioeconomic and better fed families than the boys who do not go to college) occurs at the age of 13.7; for boys who do not go beyond high school, 14.0; and for boys who stop at the 8th grade, 14.6. The range for the onset of puberty in boys seems to extend from the 11th to the 18th year.

Psychological End of Adolescence. The beginnings of adolescence, then, can be defined in purely physiological terms. But when does adolescence end? Here physiological measures are not very helpful. Once puberty is achieved, the last major physiological growth change has taken place and from now on the person continues along a fairly smooth curve to the culmination of his growth. Presumably adolescence ends when the person achieves "psychological maturity" and puts away childish things to take on the responsibilities and attitudes of adulthood. While everyone might accept this definition, it is not very useful since we have no certain way of knowing what "psychological maturity" is, nor how to measure it. By general agreement the early twenties have been set aside as the terminal point for adolescence, as the "maturity" point. But this is a fairly arbitrary figure.

There are several reasons why any period set aside as the end of adolescence must be arbitrary. In the first place, here, as elsewhere there are wide individual differences. In the second place, "psychological maturity" cannot be a unitary event. A person may mature in one respect much more rapidly than in others, and, no doubt, some of us go through life without ever maturing in some areas. But more important than these reasons—or perhaps underlying these reasons—is the influence of the cultural pattern.

MATURITY AND CULTURE. We all live under the confines of the cultural pattern specific to our part of the world, our national boundaries, our socioeconomic class, our religious congregation, and our familial group. Each of these groupings establishes its own rules-of-the-game, its own demands and expectations for its members.

Perhaps the most important psychological characteristics of the adolescent are an awakening of primary sexual interest accompanied by an ability to do something about it, and a desire to achieve status as an adult among adults. And it is at both these points that the culture within which the adolescent lives becomes important.

If the culture permits the adolescent to recognize his awakened sexual urges and, further, has worked out some satisfactory way of dealing with these urges, then one set of adolescent problems is considerably mitigated. If, in addition, the culture allows the adolescent to exercise responsibility early and to assume the role of the adult, the maturity of the adolescent is hastened. On the other hand, if the culture handles these two needs of the adolescent in a confused and frequently contradictory way, then emotional conflict may result and maturity be delayed.

THREE PATTERNS. In some American subcultures it is relatively easy, and perhaps too easy, to enter adulthood. The seventeen-year-old is accepted as an adult. He is required to earn all, or a large part, of his livelihood. He may stay out late, is responsible for his own leisure time, and his sexual life is bound by much the same rules and conventions in force for the adults of his culture.

In some American subcultures the other extreme seems to be the rule. The adolescent is denied any major responsibility and is sheltered almost throughout his teens. His money is provided for, his living arrangements, leisure-time activity, and even companionship are arranged for him. He is a "kept child," long beyond his time.

However, most American subcultures fall in between, and present the adolescent with contradictory rules taken from both extremes. He is given some of the responsibilities of adulthood, he is allowed to drive a car, to handle his own money, and even to earn at least part of it. He may stay out a bit later than formerly. But at the same time, his parents seem ready to apply a strong restraining hand on the very freedom they have granted. The psychiatrist, Josselyn, has stated the situation in the following terms:

". . . This contradictory attitude is nicely illustrated in the common struggle over the hour of coming in at night. The adolescent is not only allowed to date, but he is usually encouraged to do so. Dating may involve an elaborately planned social engagement, such as a party, or it may mean only going out for a movie or a drive or a walk, or mixing with other couples in a home to listen to records, to talk and "neck." All of these dates are acceptable—if the child returns at a stated hour. . . . The magical hour, be it midnight, eleven, or one, must be respected or something is lost. The girl's virginity is symbolically destroyed and the boy is prematurely initiated into manhood. Of course nothing can be done after the magical hour that cannot be done before; the magic lies in the implied continued control by the parent figures. To respect a stipulated hour implies obedience to all rules. Through what is actually a superstition, the parent thus handles his own anxiety . . . to the adolescent reality has become a confusing picture of opportunities dangled before him but frequently snatched away by anxious parents before he enjoys them." (Quoted with permission from *Our Children Today*, S. M. Gruenberg, ed. Copyright 1952. The Viking Press, Inc.)

The parents, of course, have some justification for anxiety. The adolescent frequently *is* confused about what is happening to him, his body, and his relations to other people. He wants freedom of action, yet in many instances he does not have the knowledge, wisdom, or courage to make decisions without guidance—and he knows it. He needs help—and he wants it. He is interested in sex, thinks about it, dreams about it, yet he may fear it and may not really know how to handle all of its manifestations. For example, the boy who masturbates—as almost all boys do—may at first regard himself as uniquely depraved or wicked. He needs advice, information, and support, and again he knows it. The adolescent, no less than the parent, is full of anxieties and contradictory impulses.

Mitigating Adolescence. The period of adolescence, even under the best of circumstances, usually involves some difficult problems of adjustment on the part of the boy or girl. However, this period of transition from childhood to adulthood need not be the awful period of storm and stress it is so frequently and luridly dramatized as being. Whether adolescence is painful and long-drawn out, or pleasant, exciting, and decently short depends in part upon the early childhood experiences of the adolescent, the culture within which he lives, and parental attitudes. We might therefore end our section on adolescence and our chapter on development, with a word of advice to the parents of the adolescent.

FOR PARENTS ONLY. Many parents of adolescents find it difficult to accept the fact that they have lost a child and gained an adult offspring. But this is one of the inevitabilities of life and the sooner the parent realizes that he cannot retain a child forever, the easier will life be for both parent and adolescent. However, as Josselyn (1952) points out, the problem is much more complicated than adopting a "Now-You-Are-A-Man" attitude on the part of the parent. The parent must be ready, on call, to revert to the previous child-parent relationship. The adolescent is *maturing*; he is not yet mature. We have seen that the adolescent is frequently confused and needs help. We have also seen that under emotional stress "regression" can take place (see p. 318). This means that on occasion

the adolescent will need the comfort and support of a somewhat "immature" parent-child relationship. The parent must be flexible enough so that when occasion demands he can forget that his "adult offspring" is supposed to be grown up, and give his *child* the kind of support he had given him in days not yet quite beyond recall. The parent who is eager to force his child out on his own cannot be of much help in what must be a *maturation process*.

The good parent begins his "adolescent training" while his child is still very young. The adolescent will find it easier to attain adulthood if he has learned, during childhood, how to exercise independence. We have stressed in Chapter 16 the importance of performance in learning. The learning of decision making, the assumption of responsibility, the postures of independence necessitate practice no less than does the learning of piano-playing or writing. But here, too, the parent needs a word of caution. We have previously pointed out that the child is not a miniature man, and what may seem like a responsibility from the perceptual vantage point of an adult may be an irritating nuisance to the child.

For example, too many parents are under the impression that making the child dry the dishes after meals teaches the child "responsibility." It may do nothing of the sort. If a boy or girl grudgingly dries dishes every day of his life, this exercise teaches him little except, perhaps, to improve his technique of dish-drying. If this task is presented—*and* performed—in a different spirit, it may teach a child that the family is a cooperative enterprise. And he may well carry over this sense of responsibility to other groups of which he later becomes a member—his living group at college, his working group on the job. But even here we cannot assume that developing responsibility of one sort will carry over to other fields where judgment and responsibility of a different sort are demanded.

We have yet to demonstrate that drying dishes nourishes self-confidence in decision making. On the other hand, permitting freedom in the expenditure of a regular allowance may provide an important training opportunity for *both parent and child* to build up the attitudes and capacities which can make the adolescent period a pleasant and interesting period of awakening. For with all the strain and stress and self-doubt, adolescence *is* a time of excitement and discovery and promise. Though parents must sometimes simply watch from the sidelines, they can take comfort in the fact that, once their sons and daughters reach adulthood, new and satisfying relationships will be possible between the generations.

Glossary

adolescence. Refers to the age between puberty and adulthood. It is said to extend from about 14 to 25 years of age in man and from about 12 to 21 in woman. While the beginning of adolescence can be set quite accurately (since it is defined by the specific physiological criterion of sexual maturity), the terminal point of adolescence can only be approximated, since there is no sharp differentiation between adolescence and adulthood.

associative play. Play where active participation with other children (borrowing and lending of play materials, etc.) is present but no group organization or common "group goal" is apparent.

cephalocaudal direction. Refers to the progressive growth of the body parts from the head end to the legs, characteristic of the developing human being. From the Greek word *kephale* (denoting head) and the Latin word *cauda* (denoting tail). From head to tail.

cooperative play. Group play among children where "leaders" and "organizers" appear and a common "group goal" seems to be present.

co-twin control method. A method sometimes used in experimental studies in child psychology whereby one of a pair of identical twins is placed in the experimental group and the other in the control group. In this way the experimental and control groups are equated genetically.

differentiation. In growth studies the term refers to the gradual narrowing down of behavior from a massive, simultaneous pattern of many responses to several more limited and independently controlled responses.

embryo. A young animal during the early stages within its mother's body. For man the term "embryo" is used to describe the developing individual up to the end of the seventh week after conception.

fetus. Refers to the young of an animal in the womb, especially in its later stages.

maturation. Refers to the progressive or successive unfolding of various bodily and mental functions and capacities as their underlying bodily structures develop through the normal growth process.

maturation-learning principle. The generalization which states that the development of behavior shows the effects of interaction between maturational and learning processes.

neonate. The newborn. For man the term is used to describe the developing individual for the first few days after birth.

parallel play. Play in which *independent* activity brings the child among other children and involves toys similar to the toys of other children. The child plays *beside* rather than *with* others.

proximodistal direction. Refers to the progressive growth of the body parts from the central part out to the peripheral or terminal parts, a direction of growth characteristic of the developing human being. Thus the shoulders develop first, then the arms, then the hands and fingers.

puberty. Puberty refers to the earliest age at which a person is capable of procreating offspring. The term *pubescence* refers to the achievement of sexual maturity. In the U.S. the average age of pubescence for boys is about 14 years and for girls about 13 years. It is interesting to note that in English common law the age

of puberty is presumed to be 14 years in the male and 12 years in the female.

sensorimotor development. The development of behavior showing co-ordination between perception and action. E.g., the ability to direct the hand to the point in space where an object is visually perceived.

socialization. Refers to the process whereby socially determined factors become influential in controlling the behavior of the person.

solitary play. Playing alone with toys different from those used by children within speaking distance.

Suggestions for Further Reading

CARMICHAEL, L. (ed.) 1954. *Manual of child psychology* (2nd ed.). New York: Wiley.

A standard reference book for research methods and results in child development.

GESELL, A., and ILG, F. L. 1943. *Infant and child in the culture of today.* New York: Harper.

GESELL, A., and ILG, F. L. 1946. *The child from five to ten.* New York: Harper.

These two books, based on studies in Yale's Clinic of Child Development, present norms of what to expect from the "average" child at various ages. Unfortunately the sample on which these norms are based is not representative of American children. Should be read with that in mind.

GRUENBERG, S. M. (ed.) 1952. *Our children today.* New York: Viking Press.

A symposium by twenty-six authorities in a number of applied and research fields

related to child development, child guidance, parent-child relationships, and social psychology.

LANDRETH, C. 1958. *The psychology of early childhood.* New York: Knopf.

Covers the behavior of the child during the first five years of life. Although written for those primarily interested in the application of child psychology, careful attention is given to the scientific research in the field. Of particular value for nursery-school teachers, pediatricians, and child-welfare workers.

MUSSEN, P. H., and CONGER, J. J. 1956. *Child development and personality.* New York: Harper.

An introductory text integrating data from clinical psychology, sociology, and cultural anthropology. The main focus is on the ways in which social factors influence the development of the child's personality.

CHAPTER XXIII

Personality

THE STUDY of personality is the apex of psychology. All psychological knowledge ultimately contributes to the understanding of personality—what shapes it, why it differs from individual to individual, how it develops and changes throughout the course of life.

In the Roman theater the mask worn by the actor to depict a role was called a *persona*, and this may be the source of our present term *personality*. In this sense, personality is taken to refer to the outward aspect of the individual and how it is perceived by and affects other people—in short, the "social stimulus value" of the individual. This is but one of a great many different ways of speaking of personality. (Allport, 1937, lists no less than fifty definitions, drawn from philosophy, theology, law, and sociology, as well as from psychology.)

The psychologist's definition of personality tends to be broad, encompassing the totality of the psychological make-up of the individual, of which the social stimulus value is but one limited aspect. It includes the individual's traits, abilities, beliefs, attitudes, values, motives, habitual modes of adjustment. It includes what we call *temperament*—the typical emotional reactions, mood states, and energetic attributes of the person—as well as what in older terminology was called *character*—the moral outlook and conduct of the person. And more than this, it includes the synthesis of all these—the particular manner in which traits, abilities, motives, and values are organized within the person. In short, it includes the *structure* of personality, that unique patterning of characteristics that constitutes an Emerson, a Beethoven, a Hitler, a Madame Curie, a corner grocer in Terre Haute, a sweeper in Calcutta, a Gaucho in the Argentine.

In the study of personality we are concerned with the *whole individual as our unit of analysis*. We seek to understand what characterizes the individual as a unified entity as he reacts to and copes with his environment. Our concern is not with the "disembodied" processes of perception, learning, thinking, emotion, motivation, but with the *person* who perceives, learns, thinks, feels, acts.

Thus, in studying personality, individual differences in the psychological processes become crucially important. But it should be stressed that the basic nature of these processes and the general principles describing them are presumably the same in all persons; it is the particular manner in which the various processes combine and interact in specific individuals that is unique for each person.

The Description of Personality

When Mr. Anyman is asked to describe the personality of an acquaintance, he may say that he is "quiet, shy, co-operative, optimistic, punctual, and intelligent." These terms represent the generalizations Mr. Anyman has made from observations of the other person's behavior in a variety of situations. That is, they are Mr. Anyman's perceptions of the other person's *traits*.

Traits. A *trait* is an enduring characteristic of the individual which is manifested in a consistent way of behaving in a wide variety of situations. To ascribe the trait of "punctuality" to Mr. Anyman's acquaintance implies that he tends regularly to arrive on time—at work, at parties, in meeting trains. A trait is not, of course, an all-or-nothing affair. It exists in the individual in some given amount. Mr. Anyman's friend was presumably called "punctual" not because he is perfectly punctual in all possible circumstances, but because he is highly punctual as compared with other people. When we talk about a personality trait, therefore, we mean to signify a trait *dimension* along which people vary in the amount of the trait exhibited, from those showing a great deal of the trait to those showing very little.

As we compare people and seek to specify what differentiates their personalities,

we naturally focus attention on the traits in which behavioral differences are most marked; such traits stand out saliently as "figure" on "ground." But this may lead to neglect of other trait dimensions in regard to which people of a given population do not differ appreciably in amount. And the traits that most people of a given group share equally may often be as important for our understanding of their personalities as the traits in which they differ. For example, the native psychologist among his own Dobu people might never ascribe to them the trait of "suspiciousness," for everyone in that culture is excessively suspicious. A visiting psychologist may at once pick out this trait as the most noteworthy of Dobu personality, even though Dobuans do not differ individually in the amount of it they exhibit. The reason the visiting psychologist notices the trait is that he views it in a larger frame of reference, comparing it with the degrees of suspiciousness found in other cultures.

Thus, one reason why we may be blind to certain basic traits of personality that play a vital role in the whole "meaning" of personality structure is that we tend to view man within the fairly narrow milieu of our own society or culture. In principle, a full-fledged personality description should include *all* the identifiable traits that exist in an individual. In practice, however, we must be satisfied with something less than this.

VARIETIES OF TRAITS. Traits are of many different kinds or classes. Some pertain to temperamental characteristics; some to typical ways of adjusting; some to abilities, interests, values; some to social relations. Some traits are narrow in scope, others broad; some are superficial, others deep-seated.

REDUCING THE TRAITS. Through an assiduous search of the English language, Allport and Odbert (1936) compiled a list of

17,953 adjectives used to describe distinctive and personal forms of people's behavior. About 4,500 of these terms clearly designate consistent and stable modes of an individual's adjustment to his environment; each of these words, in a sense, represents a potential trait to be measured and analyzed.

Obviously, what is needed is some method for *reducing* the number of trait dimensions to manageable proportions, eliminating those that overlap or are not susceptible to measurement and retaining only those likely to be of greatest significance in accounting for personality differences among people.

We have already seen, in our discussion of the *factor analysis* of mental tests (Chapter 20, p. 550), how such a task of reduction can be accomplished. An example of how the method has been applied to the "boiling down" of personality traits is given in Box 154.

Such factor-analysis methods in personality research are of utmost importance in the parsimonious ordering of trait variables. But they are a tool and not a solution to the problem of understanding personality organization. The primary trait factors that result from a factor analysis depend greatly upon the trait dimensions originally included in the test battery. A factor analysis of test results will never discover what was not included in the tests in the first place. And the selection of the original dimensions to be tested inevitably reflects the beliefs of the investigator concerning the basic nature of personality and what aspects are central. It is not surprising, therefore, that different factor-analysis studies do not entirely agree on the "primary" trait factors that they distill out.

TRAIT PROFILES. Once a set of basic trait dimensions has been established, through factor analysis or other means, we wish to be able to summarize the description of each individual with respect to all these dimensions. One convenient way is to plot a *trait profile*. This requires that on each dimension the person's standing relative to that of the general population be ascertained. (The methods for such measurement will be discussed later in the chapter.) Figure 153 gives profiles for three individuals on eight traits.

The trait profile facilitates our inspection of the pattern of an individual's traits. It permits us to see how that pattern, as a whole and in detail, compares and contrasts with the trait patterns of other people. By computing an "index of profile similarity," it is possible to state in quantitative terms the degree of similarity or dissimilarity in the personalities of two individuals *as measured on these traits*.

Personality Types. Confronted with the bewildering complexity and diversity of individual characteristics, man has, from the beginning of recorded history, "solved" the problem of describing people's personalities by assigning them to simple *types*. The type categories have been legion: good man vs. bad man, dominant vs. submissive, tough-minded vs. tender-minded, optimistic vs. pessimistic, thin-skinned vs. thick-skinned, man-of-action vs. man-of-thought.

Historical accounts of type theories begin with Hippocrates (circa 400 B.C.), who postulated that there were four types of temperament, associated with four main kinds of fluids, or "humors," of the body:

Body "humor"	Temperament
Blood	Sanguine: optimistic, hopeful
Black Bile	Melancholic: sad, depressed
Yellow Bile	Choleric: irascible
Phlegm	Phlegmatic: apathetic

Needless to say, the specific "humors" postulated by Hippocrates are not consist-

BOX 154

Twelve "Primary" Traits of Personality

Starting with the Allport-Odbert list of 17,953 dictionary words (see text), Cattell at the University of Illinois pruned it down to 171 terms by eliminating synonyms, rare words, etc. The 171 trait-names were further reduced to 35 main "trait clusters" by combining all the traits that correlated fairly highly with one another. The 35 trait clusters were used as the basis for constructing 35 rating scales. About 200 men (soldiers, professional and business men, artists, skilled workers, etc.), divided into a number of small groups of intimate ac-

These are presumably *source* traits, which through complex dynamics come to determine the more familiar *surface* traits. The precise names given by Cattell to these 12 factors are merely convenient identifying labels. Their actual natures must be discovered by further study.

How "primary" are these factors? Some of them (Nos. 1, 2, 5, 7, 9, and 11) Cattell regards as "repeatedly confirmed and unmistakable"; others are not uniformly found in other studies. Moreover, other factor analyses have identified additional factors

1. *Cyclothymia*
   Emotionally expressive, frank, placid
   vs. *Schizothymia*
   Reserved, close-mouthed, anxious
2. *General mental capacity*
   Intelligent, smart
   vs. *Mental defect*
   Unintelligent, dull
3. *Emotionally stable*
   Free of neurotic symptoms, realistic about life
   vs. *Neurotic emotionality*
   Variety of neurotic symptoms, evasive, immature
4. *Dominance*
   Self-assertive, confident, aggressive
   vs. *Submissiveness*
   Submissive, unsure, complaisant
5. *Surgency*
   Cheerful, joyous, humorous, witty
   vs. *Desurgency*
   Depressed, pessimistic, phlegmatic
6. *Positive character*
   Persevering, attentive to people
   vs. *Dependent character*
   Fickle, neglectful of social chores
7. *Adventurous cyclothymia*
   Likes meeting people, strong interest in opposite sex
   vs. *Withdrawn schizothymia*
   Shy, little interest in opposite sex
8. *Mature, tough poise*
   Independent-minded, self-sufficient
   vs. *Sensitive, infantile emotionality*
   Dependent, immature, attention-seeking
9. *Socialized, cultured mind*
   Polished, composed, introspective
   vs. *Boorishness*
   Awkward, socially clumsy, crude
10. *Trustful cyclothymia*
    Trustful, understanding
    vs. *Paranoia*
    Suspicious, jealous
11. *Bohemian unconcernedness*
    Unconventional, eccentric, fitful hysterical upsets
    vs. *Conventional practicality*
    Conventional, unemotional
12. *Sophistication*
    Logical mind, cool, aloof
    vs. *Simplicity*
    Sentimental mind, attentive to people

quaintances, served as subjects. Two members from each group were first trained in the rating technique, and then rated their fellows independently. The two ratings were averaged to get the final rating for each man.

The ratings were then subjected to a factor analysis. It was found that 12 factors were adequate to account for most of the individual differences among the men in the rated traits. These 12 were named and characterized by Cattell as listed above.

not represented here. Differences in these factor studies may be due to the type of measurement used, the breadth of behavioral information on which ratings are made, the sample of persons measured, etc. We must reserve judgment on this list as anything approaching a "final" definitive set of the "primary" traits of human personality.

CATTELL, R. B. 1946. *Description and measurement of personality.* Yonkers, N.Y.: World Book Co.

ent with our modern knowledge of physiology, but his temperamental types still flourish in our thinking. His theory was the classical forerunner of modern theories correlating temperament with glandular secretions (see Chapter 12, page 351). And it was the beginning of a long line of type theories in which personality make-up was conceived to be intimately related to body constitution and physique.

ASTHENIC VS. PYKNIC. The most influential of modern theories relating physique and personality was that of Kretschmer (1921, 1936). He presented evidence that there was a characteristic body type for each of the two main kinds of mental illness—schizophrenia and manic-depressive psychosis (see Chapter 24). The schizophrenic tended to have a thin, long-limbed, narrow-chested body, which Kretschmer

called the *asthenic* type; the manic-depressive tended to have a short, fattish, barrel-chested body, called the *pyknic* type. Kretschmer generalized this typology to the normal population, asserting that there were distinctly different patterns of personality traits biologically linked with these two body types. The asthenic type person was said to be shy, sensitive, aloof, and withdrawn. The pyknic type was said to be jovial, lively, outgoing, and inclined to mood fluctuations.

This typology has been repudiated by empirical evidence, but it has served to stimulate further attempts to establish physique-personality relationships (see p. 630).

INTROVERT VS. EXTROVERT. Probably the most widely known typology is that of introversion-extroversion advanced by Jung

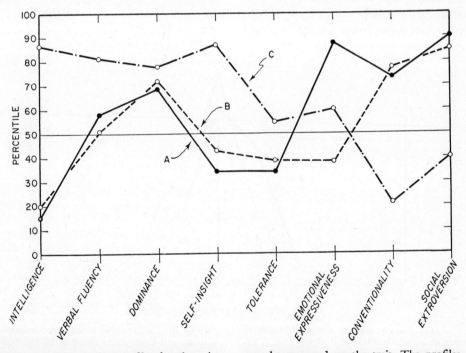

FIG. 153. Comparative profiles for three individuals on a set of eight traits. The ordinate indicates the amount of each trait exhibited by the individual in terms of his percentile standing relative to the entire population of people measured on the trait. The profiles of A and B are obviously very similar except for a difference in *emotional expressiveness*. C's profile differs markedly from the other two. (After Arbuthnot, 1948.)

(1923). The *introvert* was described as subjective in orientation; as primarily interested in ideas, imagination, and inner life; as tender-minded and idealistic. The *extrovert* was described as having an orientation directed outward to the objective world of things and events; as primarily interested in social activities and practical affairs; as tough-minded and realistic.

The simple introvert-extrovert dichotomy has become solidly entrenched in our popular thinking; but in its overly simplified form at least, the evidence does not support such a dichotomy. Attempts to measure people along the introversion-extroversion dimension have shown that rather than falling into two distinct types, people are distributed all along the dimension with most around the center (see Fig. 154).

Actually, Jung's conception was far more complex than as here represented, and the introversion-extroversion variable was not regarded by him as a simple one. That it is not a simple affair has been confirmed by factor-analytic studies that identify as many as five separate introversion-extroversion factors: social introversion, thinking introversion, depression, tendency to mood swings, and happy-go-lucky disposition (Guilford, 1940).

EIDETIC TYPES. A rather interesting typology was that proposed by Jaensch (1930) on the basis of study of eidetic imagery (see Chapter 13, p. 367). He concluded that people fall into several main, distinctly different types, on the basis of the forms of eidetic imagery they experience. These differences in experience were related, he thought, to basic differences in styles of perceptual and cognitive functioning, and thus to differences in over-all personality patterns. Jaensch's theory, though not confirmed by experimental evidence, initiated the modern research that seeks to find relationships between personality var-

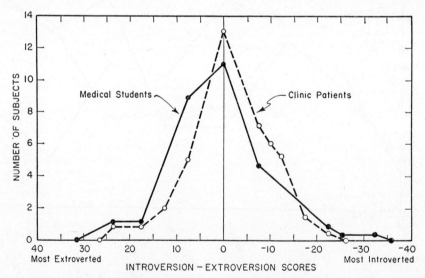

FIG. 154. Curve showing the distribution of scores of 44 senior medical students and 44 patients on the *Neymann-Kohlstedt Introversion-Extroversion Test* (a 50-item paper-and-pencil test). Despite the difference in age, educational level, etc., between the patients and medical students there is no difference in the distribution of their scores. Note that most individuals fall in the middle of the range of scores, and are not concentrated at the two extremes, as would be implied by a simple type theory which would categorize people as being either extroverted or introverted. (After Neymann and Yacorzynski, 1942.)

iables and habitual modes of perceiving.

VALUE TYPES. Numerous typologies have been built around the notion that people can be classified into discrete *value* types. Here the conception is that each person has some sort of unifying philosophy of life—a dominant value—which shapes and structures his entire personality. One such theory was that of Spranger (1928), who sought to classify all people into six "ideal" value types:

1. *The Theoretical.* Dominant interest in discovery of *truth.* Seeks to observe and to reason. Chief aim in life is to order and systematize his knowledge.

2. *The Economic.* Dominant interest in what is *useful.* Concerned with the production of wealth. Believes in practice rather than theory, utility rather than aesthetics.

3. *The Aesthetic.* Dominant interest in *form and harmony.* Believes beauty is the greatest truth, and each experience is judged on its aesthetic merits.

4. *The Social.* Dominant interest is *love of people.* Concerned with other people's affairs and with their welfare. A warm and humane outlook.

5. *The Political.* Dominant interest in *power.* Whether in politics or in other activities, the aim is to gain influence and control over people and events, to become a leader.

6. *The Religious.* Dominant interest in comprehending the *unity* of the universe. Concern with mystical experiences and with what is divine in every phenomenon.

Very few people would seem to fit such "ideal" value types in a pure fashion. Most people would have a mixture of these values, with one or more primary, and the others secondary. This is demonstrated in the results of personality tests that are designed to measure people on these six value dimensions (see p. 636).

EVALUATION OF TYPE THEORIES. The difficulties with type theories are effectively stated in the following passage by Allport (1937):

"Every typology is based on the abstraction of some segment of the total personality, and the forcing of this segment to unnatural prominence. All typologies place boundaries where boundaries do not belong. They are artificial categories.

"This harsh judgment is unavoidable in the face of the conflicting claims of various typologies. Many of them pretend to embrace the total personality, and to follow the cleavages that occur in nature. But the very typologies that have proclaimed themselves 'basic,' contradict one another. Compare, for example, the supposedly foundational types of Kretschmer, Spranger and Jaensch. Certainly not one of these typologies, so diverse in conception and scope, can be considered final, for none of them overlaps any other. Each theorist slices nature in any why he chooses, and finds only his own cuttings worthy of admiration."

The above criticisms are directed particularly at "pure" type theories, in which it is assumed that all people can be neatly pigeonholed into one of several qualitatively different categories. But people are not that "pure." Most people are "mixed" types. On all the many trait dimensions that have been investigated it turns out that people distribute themselves in a continuous way from one extreme to the other, with the greater proportion falling in the middle, and the curve often approximating the form of a normal distribution curve (see Chapter 19, p. 531). It is more meaningful to speak of a trait dimension, along which there is quantitative variation, than to speak of types.

An important implication of typologies is their assumption that the structure of personality is a simple affair. In effect, they assert that an individual's placement on a single trait dimension can permit us to understand all that is most basic about his personality.

Such an assumption flies in the face of all that we have already discovered about the complexity and interaction of psychological processes. Simple typologies are not equipped to deal with the intricate structure of human personality.

COMPLEX TYPES. What we have been discussing so far are simple typologies, usually consisting of two or three main categories alleged to accommodate all people. But there can also be much more complex typologies in which the defining of each type depends upon the individual's placement with respect to many dimensions. Thus, the number of different types might run to dozens or scores or even more—with each type being a "pure" type, and with no individual left to fall into the void separating the types.

The evidence on the existence of such complex types is far more difficult to obtain, and as of now it is not conclusive.

The existence of such complex types would imply that the several trait dimensions defining each type are not randomly or accidentally combined, but are combined in certain unique ways because of an underlying "necessity" for certain particular organizations. That is, of the mathematically possible combinations of the trait dimensions, some would be much more probable, some much less probable, and some downright impossible.

TRAIT SYNDROMES. The suggestion that there may be certain patterns of traits that "intrinsically" belong together has led to the concept of *trait syndromes.* For example, empirical research has demonstrated that such traits as orderliness, obstinacy, stinginess, punctuality, and excessive cleanliness tend to go together in people. This has been referred to as the *compulsive* syndrome.

On the face of it there would seem to be no compelling reason why these particular traits *should* go together. A possible explanation of the origin of this pattern comes from psychoanalytic theory (see p. 619). As a result of severe parental pressures on toilet training the child comes to develop permanent drives toward conformity and overcontrol, which are manifested in the various traits making up the compulsive syndrome. In the light of this theory the syndrome has been dubbed the *anal character.* But it remains to be proved that this explanation is the correct one. (See the later discussion on the research findings on child-rearing practices.)

Another striking example of trait patterning is the *authoritarian* syndrome discussed in Box 155.

The Structure of Personality. We see that much of the individual's behavior can be summed up in terms of certain enduring and consistent behavior characteristics, that is, traits. Through factor analysis there can be achieved a drastic reduction in the number of traits necessary to describe the behavioral consistencies. And the traits are found to be organized in patterns and syndromes.

These facts have led to the inference that there is within each person an underlying *personality structure* that provides the basis for the orderly organization we observe. This structure is made up most centrally of the person's chief motives, his principal beliefs, attitudes, and values, his basic emotional dispositions; and of the *particular manner in which all these are dynamically interrelated.*

An understanding of structure is inseparable from an understanding of the developmental processes through which the

BOX 155

The Authoritarian Personality

Authoritarianism has always been one of the most basic problems of human society. It is seen in its most spectacular form in political dictatorships, but it can be found in less dramatic and often more insidious form in almost every type of interpersonal relationship and social organization. One of its aspects that has especially interested psychologists is the role of personality in authoritarian behavior.

For instance, an extensive study by Adorno and his associates provides evidence that a syndrome of "authoritarian" traits can be identified as a central and enduring part of some people's personalities. The main traits making up the syndrome appear to be:

1. Great concern with authority relationships with people; extreme deference to superior authority, and exercise of one's authority over those in subordinate positions.

2. Heavy stress on conventional behavior, values, and morality; close conformity to group norms.

3. Overcontrol and denial of own "immoral" impulses and feelings, and projection of these onto the out-group; exaggerated sense of own moral "rightness"; lack of self-insight.

4. Depersonalization of social relations; tendency to manipulate and exploit people as objects, rather than treating them as human beings, and an expectation of being exploited in turn; sadistic tendencies (enjoyment in hurting other people) together with masochistic tendencies (enjoyment in being hurt.)

5. Rigidity of thought processes; excessive stereotyped thinking; prejudice and intolerance toward minority groups.

The Adorno study suggests that the development of this syndrome comes from severe disciplinary treatment of the child, typically involving excessive stress on the rightness of parental rules and values, with insistence on complete obedience to them, reinforced by punishment. Often such severe discipline is accompanied by a parental attitude of emotional rejection of the child, and by exploitative manipulation of the child.

The consequences are that the child develops extreme submissiveness to parental authority, which later extends to all authority figures. This is accompanied by an unquestioning acceptance of the rightness of the values of the authorities. But there is also aroused a strong hostility toward the parents or other authorities. This hostility cannot be readily expressed in direct aggression against the authority figure; for one thing, there is fear of punishment by the all-powerful authority, and for another, such aggression would be incompatible with belief in the complete rightness of the authority. Thus, the hostility is repressed (see p. 648) and the aggression displaced toward safer targets, such as minority groups and those in positions of inferior status, and sometimes toward the self.

Evidence for this general picture is found by Adorno and his associates—and by numerous other investigators—through studies of many groups of subjects, using many kinds of techniques, such as psychiatric interviews, attitude questionnaires, laboratory tests, sociological surveys.

It should be emphasized that the "authoritarian" syndrome is not the exclusive characteristic of any single ideological movement, social class, or occupation. "Authoritarian personalities" can be found everywhere—in the labor union as well as in industrial management; in social clubs as well as in government bureaucracy; and they are by no means unknown in the church and even in the classroom.

ADORNO, T. W., FRENKEL-BRUNSWIK, E., LEVINSON, D. J., and SANFORD, R. N. 1950. *The authoritarian personality*. New York: Harper.

structure evolved. As we now turn to the discussion of personality theories, we shall see that it is with these questions of structure and development that the theorists are mainly concerned.

Theories of Personality

There is no single generally accepted theory of personality. Nor is any one of the leading theories regarded as sufficiently comprehensive to cover all that is embraced within human personality. Indeed, no theory of personality has yet been formulated in sufficiently detailed and rigorous form to permit clear empirical validation or refutation. At most there has been a certain amount of experimental research devoted to testing some of the hypotheses incorporated in some of the theories.

The situation as it stands—no matter how unsatisfactory from the point of view of a science of psychology, or of Mr. Anyman's desire to get the answer—is not surprising. The complexity of the elements of human personality, the profusion of personality patterns, the multiplicity of determinants—biological as well as social—make the task of developing an adequate theory of personality an insuperable one until our knowledge about psychology shall have become much less fragmentary. Contemporary theories of personality must, therefore, be regarded simply as tentative maps of a generally uncharted wilderness. All the maps are doubtless in error, and at a future stage of psychology they will look as "queer" as the ancient maps of the world do to us now. The specific regions of the wilderness emphasized by the different theorists tend to vary widely, reflecting the theoretical bias of the particular theorist. And it is around these theorists that our following review will be built. No attempt can be made here to give a comprehensive account of the theories. All that is intended is a brief description, serving to highlight the unique contributions of each approach.

Freud and Psychoanalysis. By far the most influential theory of personality has been that advanced by Sigmund Freud during the years from 1900, when he was a Viennese physician treating mental disorders, to his death in 1939. Psychoanalysis is many things—a theory of personality, a method of psychotherapy (treatment of the mentally ill), and, for many, a philosophical view of life. Its effects on man's thought during the first half of this century have been incalculable, and its force is far from spent. Our concern here is only with the psychoanalytic theory of personality. In the following chapter we will discuss its contributions to psychotherapy.

ID, EGO, SUPEREGO. Freud conceived of man as a dynamic system of energies. The personality is constructed of three main systems—the id, the ego, and the superego. These three systems of psychological forces, dynamically interacting with one another, produce the individual's behavior.

The *id* is the original system, out of which gradually evolve the other two. The id is the sole source of all psychic energy (*libido*). The energy takes the form of unconscious instincts that drive the organism. The instincts derive from the inherited, biological nature of the organism. The two main classes of instincts are those concerned with survival (the "life instincts"), such as hunger, thirst, and especially sex; and those concerned with destructive impulses (the "death instincts"), taking the form of aggression. The id-impulses are "primitive, blind, irrational, brutish" demands for immediate gratification (the "pleasure principle").

In seeking to satisfy id-impulses, the organism must cope with the realities of the external world. As a consequence, there emerges the *ego*, a system of forces having the function of conscious control and redirecting of the id-impulses in such a way that gratifications can be achieved in the organism's specific environment (the "reality principle"). Thus, the ego is the system of cognitive processes—perceiving, thinking, planning, deciding.

In expressing basic impulses, the individual may run afoul of the rules and values of his society. These rules and values are made clear to the child by the rewards and punishments delivered by his parents for his conduct. As a consequence, there gradually evolves in the child the *superego*, a system of restraining and inhibiting forces upon those basic impulses—especially sex and aggression—which are regarded as dangerous or detrimental by society. The superego in time becomes the internal substitute for the external forces of parental and societal control. It becomes, in short, the child's conscience and moral sense. A well-developed superego tends to result in automatic and unconscious control of id-impulses.

When blocked of immediate and direct expressions, the libidinal energies are *displaced* in other directions, toward substitute means and objects of satisfaction. The flexibility in the directions of such displacements and in attachments of energies to various substitute means and objects accounts for the rich diversity in people's patterns of specific interests, motives, attitudes, and habits. However, the critical thing to note is that such displacements do not mean a change in the motivational energies. The basic energies of all action from life to death are the original id-instincts.

The forces of id, ego, and superego are often in conflict, and this leads to the arousal of anxiety. The person develops characteristic ways of reducing the anxieties (such *defense mechanisms* will be discussed in the following chapter), and these char-

acteristic ways constitute a distinctive aspect of the personality structure of the individual.

PSYCHOSEXUAL STAGES. Freud conceived of the process of personality development as a continuous one. The most critical stages of development occur during the first five years of life, when the permanent structure is largely established. He believed that there is a characteristic sequence of psychosexual stages through which the child passes. Individual differences in adult personality, he assumed, are mainly traceable to the specific manner in which the person experiences and handles the conflicts aroused in these stages.

In the *oral stage*, the first year of life, the infant's attention is centered mainly on the erogenous zones of the mouth. He is pleasure bent on sucking. If there is inadequate gratification, or anxiety and insecurity surrounding the nursing situation, there may be a permanent *fixation* of some libidinal energy on oral activities. This may give rise, in the adult personality, to the so-called *oral character*, a syndrome of traits including dependence, passivity, greediness, and excessive tendencies toward oral behavior, as in smoking or garrulous speech.

In the *anal stage*, the second and third years, the infant's concern centers mainly on anal activity, particularly emphasized through parental demands for toilet training and the taboos on anal eroticism. Here again there may be enduring anal fixations, resulting from punishments for failure to control elimination, from excessive rewards for successful control, or generally from the induced anxieties surrounding the anal activities. The *anal character* associated with such fixation has already been described (p. 616).

In the *phallic stage* the child's interest turns to the sexual organs and to the pleasures associated with their manipulation.

(Freud scandalized Victorian society by the assertion that childhood sexuality, with its sexual fantasy and masturbation, is universal, a view that is now more generally accepted.) At this stage typically occurs what Freud called the *Oedipus complex* (after the classical myth of King Oedipus, who unwittingly killed his father and married his mother). This is the "childhood romance" in which the boy normally directs his erotic feelings toward the mother, and the girl toward the father. And by thus placing themselves in the fantasied roles of father and mother respectively, the boy and the girl come to establish the primary identifications, out of which later derive all the complex male and female social identifications that constitute a great part of the adult personality. But vicissitudes in the usual course of growth and decay of the Oedipus complex may lead to aberrations of later personality development, such as are manifested in latent homosexuality, authority problems, rejection of appropriate masculine and feminine roles.

These three so-called pregenital stages are followed at puberty by the *genital stage,* during which the adolescent experiences a shift in interest away from himself as the primary object, to other people and things as the important objects. Thus, heterosexual attachments emerge, and the person gradually comes to acquire interests in mature life-activities.

AFTER FREUD WHAT? Viewed in this most general perspective, it is readily seen why the Freudian conception of personality has been widely influential. It gives a sense of continuity and pattern to the course of personality development. It gives a place to biological determinants and to social determinants. And it has bravely (often recklessly) sought to face up to those fundamental questions about personality with which a proper theory must deal.

All of these features commend themselves to most psychologists, as well as to Mr. Anyman. But it is in the matter of certain basic assumptions, of specific concepts, of relative emphases, that the arguments begin. Is all motivation basically of the same unchanging instinctual "stuff," or may it not change in essential nature? Are the first five years of life so fatally crucial for permanent personality make-up, or may not later childhood and adult experiences play even more decisive roles? Are social influences given a sufficiently heavy emphasis? Are sex and aggression really the main motives? Are the Oedipus complex, the oral-anal-phallic-genital stages really universal, or are they merely found among some people in some cultures? Is unconscious motivation so all-important?

In raising and trying to answer such questions, most other theorists of personality show—either in building further upon Freud's theories, or in developing alternative theories aimed at least in part at rectifying or demolishing psychoanalysis—that their debt to him is great. To some of these other main theories we now proceed.

Adler and Striving for Superiority. Alfred Adler, also Viennese, was originally a disciple of Freud, but later broke away from him. The central characteristics of Adler's theory lie in his stress on the social rather than the biological determinants of personality, and in his conception of the eternally upward drive of the self.

In his view, the prime source of man's motivation is the innate *striving for superiority*. That is, the main aim of life is to perfect oneself; all other motives are expressions of this aim. As Adler put it in 1930:

"I began to see clearly in every psychological phenomenon the striving for superiority. It runs parallel to physical growth and is an intrinsic necessity of life itself. It lies at the root of all solutions of life's problems and is manifested in the way in which we meet these problems. All our functions follow its direction. They strive for conquest, security, increase, either in the right or in the wrong direction. The impetus from minus to plus never ends. The urge from below to above never ceases. Whatever premises all our philsophers and psychologists dream of—self-preservation, pleasure principle, equalization—all these are but vague representations, attempts to express the great upward drive."

COMPENSATION. The directions taken in the strivings for superiority are in the nature of *compensations*. According to Adler each one of us, very early in life, becomes aware of some weakness or deficiency within himself. The perception of such a deficiency or inferiority calls into play strivings to overcome, or compensate for, the imperfection. Thus, paradoxically, the person may ultimately distinguish himself in the very area where he was most deficient—the painfully stuttering child works hard at overcoming his defect and ends by becoming the fluent orator, Demosthenes. The compensatory strivings may also take *indirect* forms—the bodily handicapped child may devote himself to the pursuit of ideas, the homely girl may become a business tycoon.

The course of personality development, according to this view, is a continuous process of reactions to inferiority—real or fancied. And inasmuch as inferiority can occur in so many spheres, and certainly in some form in every person's experiences, there is endless fuel for striving. Adler sees the stage of childhood as especially important, not as in Freud's theory because of the pressures of childhood sexuality, but because the intrinsic weakness of the child in the world of adults inevitably makes for strivings to overcome these weaknesses. Thus, inferiority feelings are essential requirements of psychological growth. It is only when there is excessive stress laid upon

the inferiority, or when the strivings repeatedly fail, that an *inferiority complex* may develop, with all of its detrimental consequences for further adjustment.

UNIQUENESS OF PERSONALITY. Adler stresses the uniqueness of each personality, reflecting the particular direction of strivings for superiority that the individual has taken. This basic direction tends to be established in childhood as a consequence of the particular inferiorities perceived by the child and the particular methods of coping with them. And this basic direction serves to guide all his behavior and to engender the distinctive goals, interests, and values that uniquely characterize him.

The paths to perfection vary widely among people. For one man, perfection may be sought in the complete knowledge of a certain field of science, for another in religious revelation. Or it may mean perfection in artistic creation, or in athletic prowess, or in raising a family. What is for one individual the goal of perfection may for other people be anything but "perfect"—a Hitler striving for mastery of the "master race," a psychotic obsessed with the goal of committing the "perfect murder." But despite examples of socially detrimental aims, it was Adler's view that under optimal circumstances of development, strivings for superiority take socially constructive forms, having to do with co-operative relations with people, identifications with the group, and efforts to bring about the ideal society.

Adler's emphasis on social factors and on the conscious functioning of the self in adjusting to such factors is echoed in varying ways and degrees in certain other personality theories that derive from Freud, for instance, in the theories of Horney, Fromm, and Sullivan.

Horney and "Basic Anxiety." In her descriptions of the "neurotic personality of our time" Karen Horney (1937) makes *basic anxiety* the primary concept. It is the arousal and fate of this anxiety, rather than of the sexual and aggressive impulses à la Freud, that is central for our understanding of the individual personality.

Basic anxiety stems from anything that causes insecurity in the child, especially in relation to his parents: being dominated by parents, being inconsistently treated, being given too much or too little responsibility, being treated with coldness or indifference, being involved in parental conflicts, etc. The child tries to cope with the feelings of anxiety by various adjustive and largely irrational acts; if the anxieties are intense and prolonged, these adjustment methods become crystallized into enduring motivational patterns, in the form of "neurotic needs."

By "neurotic needs" Horney means those that are excessive, insatiable, and unrealistic. She lists "neurotic needs" (1) for affection and approval, (2) for someone to depend on, (3) to restrict one's life within narrow borders, (4) for power, (5) to exploit others, (6) for prestige, (7) for personal admiration, (8) for personal achievement, (9) for self-sufficiency and independence, and (10) for perfection and unassailability. These needs may appear in everyone and many of the needs are "desirable." But they are called "neurotic" to the extent that they come to dominate the person.

Neurotic needs interfere with the person's life adjustments inasmuch as many of them are inherently incompatible—some require the person to seek love and close relations with other people, while others require him to aggress against people. Conflict is the inevitable result.

The basic anxiety, the "neurotic needs," and the conflicts to which they ultimately lead are not, according to Horney, biological or instinctual in origin. They are social; they arise from culturally induced disturb-ances in the child's developmental experiences.

Fromm and "Escape from Freedom." Like Horney, Erich Fromm (1941) considers personality to be a product of the manner in which social conditions provide or fail to provide what the growing person needs. But Fromm considers social conditions that reach far beyond the family influences. In his view, the individual's personality is shaped by his relation to the whole society of which he is part. To understand personality, therefore, it is essential to study the nature of the particular society in which the person develops.

Fromm's main thesis is that as the child develops he gradually gains freedom from the control of parents and other primary groups, and that this new-won independence may, by separating him emotionally from others, result in loneliness and fear. The child is then driven to "escape from freedom" and attempt to restore his security by seeking new and productive relations with other people and groups. On the other hand, he may attempt to regain feelings of security through submission to authority and through excessive conformity to the dictates of society.

Whether the constructive or the detrimental effects occur depends upon the nature of the particular society and its adequacy or inadequacy in meeting man's basic needs. The innate human needs, distinguishing man from animals, are to achieve a sense of personal identity, to create, to attain a stable and consistent way of perceiving and understanding the world, and to establish a secure position in the world. The individual's personality is the product of these basic human needs and the specific constraints and opportunities of his society.

Fromm undertakes to show how each different type of society—communist, fascist, feudal, socialist, capitalist—may be expected to lead to the formation of a particular kind of personality. The "sane society" is one in which the basic human needs are optimally met so that feelings of loneliness, isolation, and despair are avoided.

Sullivan and Interpersonal Relations. An even bigger stride toward stress on social determinants of personality is taken in the theories of Harry Stack Sullivan (1953). Indeed, for him, personality *is* "the relatively enduring pattern of recurrent interpersonal situations which characterize a human life." There is no personality apart from its relations with other people; all that is distinctly human is a product of social interactions from birth onward. Thus, the study of personality is really the study of the whole interpersonal situation, not of an isolated individual.

The regular stages of personality development are not due to a gradual unfolding of instinctual tendencies, as implied by Freud and some others, but to the fact that there is a fairly regular sequence of interpersonal events that are likely to occur, at least in our society. The first important interpersonal event is the infant's feeding by the mother, an event that may be productive of security or anxiety in the infant. This experience determines how the individual will later tend to approach and perceive other interpersonal situations that have similar elements, and in turn these experiences modify what comes after.

In preadolescence the earlier forms of interpersonal relations—dependence upon people—give way to relations of equality, reciprocity, and intimacy with people. Adolescence confronts the person with the special problems of developing patterns of heterosexual relationships, and of somehow integrating the simultaneous demands for sexual gratification, security, and intimacy. Later adolescence involves the development and refinement of all the complex interpersonal relations that have to do with the duties and responsibilities of social living.

Thus, we see that to Sullivan personality is not fully set during early childhood, but develops continuously as new kinds of interpersonal situations arise.

Murray and Psychological Needs. Most of the theories of personality reviewed so far have in common a "monistic" view of the sources of motivation. That is, they postulate one major instinct or need (possibly accompanied by other minor ones), the developmental elaboration and expression of which account for the differences among personalities. Thus, we have Freud's libido, Adler's striving for superiority, Horney's basic anxiety.

Prominent among certain other theories that substantially multiply the number of postulated motivational energies is that of Henry Murray (1938). In place of a limited set of motivational categories he has constructed a far more extended list, which he believes to be minimally adequate to do justice to the rich diversity of human behavior. His tentative list of basic motivational energies—which he calls *psychological needs*—is given in Table 22. This list is a distillation of intensive clinical and experimental study of the behavior of groups of subjects at the Harvard Psychological Clinic.

It is assumed that all of these needs are to be found in some degree in every person. It is the relative amounts of each need and the manner in which the needs become dynamically organized during the individual's development that characterize his personality.

Allport and Functional Autonomy. The multiplication of motives reaches its extreme in the personality theory of Gordon Allport (1937). He argues that motives are

TABLE 22

Murray's Tentative List of Psychological Needs

Need	*Brief definition*
Abasement	To submit passively to external force. To accept injury, blame, criticism, punishment. To become resigned to fate.
Achievement	To accomplish something difficult. To rival and surpass others.
Affiliation	To seek out and enjoy close and co-operative relationships with other people. To adhere and remain loyal to a friend.
Aggression	To overcome opposition forcefully. To attack, injure, or punish another.
Autonomy	To get free, shake off restraint, break out of confinement. To be independent and free to act according to impulse. To defy convention.
Counteraction	To master or make up for a failure by renewed striving. To overcome weaknesses. To maintain self-respect and pride on a high level.
Defendance	To defend the self against assault, criticism, and blame. To conceal or justify a misdeed, failure, or humiliation.
Deference	To admire and support a superior. To yield readily to the influence of others. To conform to custom.
Dominance	To control one's human environment. To influence or direct the behavior of others by suggestion, seduction, persuasion, or command.
Exhibition	To make an impression. To be seen and heard. To excite, entertain, shock, or entice others.
Harmavoidance	To avoid pain, physical injury, illness, and death.
Infavoidance	To avoid humiliation. To refrain from action because of fear of failure.
Nurturance	To give sympathy to and gratify the needs of weak and helpless persons. To feed, help, support, console, protect, nurse.
Order	To put things in order. To achieve cleanliness, arrangement, balance, neatness, and precision.
Play	To act for "fun" without further purpose. To like to laugh and make jokes. To seek enjoyable relaxation of stress.
Rejection	To separate oneself from a disliked object. To exclude, abandon, or remain indifferent to an inferior person.
Sentience	To seek and enjoy sensuous impressions.
Sex	To form and further an erotic relationship. To have sexual intercourse.
Succorance	To have one's needs gratified by the sympathetic aid of another person. To be nursed, supported, protected, loved, guided, forgiven, consoled.
Understanding	To ask or answer general questions. To be interested in theory. To speculate, formulate, analyze, and generalize.

Adapted from Murray (1938).

virtually limitless in number and variety. To account for this diversity, he proposes his basic concept of the *functional autonomy* of motives. This asserts that activities serving an original motive may later become motivating *in their own right*, after the original motive has subsided. The man who goes to sea in order to earn a living may continue to go to sea, for its "own sake," even after he becomes rich. The meaning of his "sea-going motive" as it is expressed in his later life may have no re-lation to its original meaning of a "money-earning" activity. Its nature is to be understood entirely in terms of its present function in the person. (See Box 156.)

This view is obviously at sharp variance with Freud's notion of innate id-instincts, whose outward guise can change, but whose fundamental nature is permanent. In numerous respects Allport's personality theory is at the opposite end of the spectrum from psychoanalytic theory. His stress is upon conscious, rather than unconscious, proc-

---

BOX 156

Functional Autonomy and Acquired Drives

Direct experimental evidence for or against the concept of functional autonomy of motives is hard to obtain. However, one line of indirect evidence comes from the studies of so-called *acquired drives*. An early example is a study by Williams in which rats were first trained to find food in a black-white discrimation box. The rats were then placed in an unfamiliar maze with the discrimination box at the end of it, *but empty of food*. The rats proceeded to learn the maze in order to get to the discrimination box "reward" even though this did not satisfy their original hunger drive (or any other apparent drive). Thus, it might be said that the activity of getting to the discrimination box had become an "autonomous" function.

Even more impressive results were obtained later by Wolfe with chimpanzees. A "Chimp-o-mat" vending machine was designed to deliver a grape when the chimp placed a poker chip in the slot. After a time the poker chip came to possess value "in its own right." This could be demonstrated by making the chimp do hard work (pull in a heavy box) in order to get the poker chip as sole reward, *even though the poker chip could not immediately be used to get food* because the vending machine had been removed from the cage. Moreover, the chimp would continue to accumulate and hoard poker chips.

Here then would seem to be evidence of activities becoming "functionally autonomous." But it is not at all sure from the above findings that getting to the discrimination box, or collecting poker chips, was actually "autonomous" in Allport's sense. There may simply have been a lag in perceiving the new fact that the box or poker chip no longer "paid off" in food. If this is the explanation, the acquired positive value

should soon wear off, and this is what was found. For instance, the poker chips gradually lost their "value" unless the chimp was occasionally permitted to use them to buy food from the Chimp-o-mat.

On the other hand, some acquired drives *do* persist without further reinforcement by the original motivation. This is especially the case with negative drives, that is, acquired tendencies to avoid or escape noxious stimuli. For example, Miller confined rats to a white compartment of a two-compartment box and administered electric shocks for ten trials. The rats made strenuous but unavailing efforts to escape. From the 11th trial on, the electric shock was never administered. Yet when placed in the white compartment the rats continued their efforts to escape, and were able to learn how to get from the white compartment into the other compartment through a door by manipulating a lever. The escape behavior persisted for hundreds of trials even though the electric shock was never experienced after the initial ten trials.

Here again, however, it cannot be safely concluded that the escape action had become "functionally autonomous." For the animals may still have perceived the white compartment as dangerous and frightening, the fright persisting because there was not sufficient opportunity for them to discover that the shock was gone—each time they were placed in the compartment they promptly got out, thus "avoiding" the shock and "confirming" their fear of it.

WILLIAMS, K. A. 1924. The reward value of a conditioned stimulus. *Univ. Calif. Publ. Psychol., 4,* 31–55.

WOLFE, J. B. 1936. Effectiveness of token-rewards for chimpanzees. *Comp. Psychol. Monogr., 12,* No. 60.

MILLER, N. E. 1948. Fear as an acquired drive. *J. exp. Psychol., 38,* 89–101.

---

esses; upon normal personality rather than abnormal; upon the contemporaneous structure of personality as found in the adult rather than upon its past history of development from early childhood.

Allport makes *traits* the center of his theory. In his use of the term (broader than ours) a trait is an enduring predisposition to respond in a particular and consistent, adaptive way to certain general classes of stimuli. Thus each person's traits are entirely unique.

Some traits are central in the person's make-up, others more peripheral. It is the particular way the traits are ordered and patterned that gives the distinctive character to the individual personality. With growth toward psychological maturity there goes an increasing unification of the trait pattern. Such unification is attained most fully in the rare cases in which a master trait emerges to govern all others, and to render wholly consistent all of the person's activities.

Maslow and Self-actualization. In some theories of personality development there is a "forward-going" orientation, contrasting with the "backward-looking" perspective of Freudian theories. For example, Carl Jung, an eminent Swiss psychiatrist, stresses the *ends* toward which personality development is directed. There is, he thinks, a basic tendency toward the end of making actual what is potential in the self, toward maximal realization of one's potentialities. This concept of *self-actualization* occupies an important place also in many other theories of personality. We have already seen, for instance, that Adler's striving for superiority implies just such a basic trend toward self-perfection.

One of the more recent theories that centers on the concept of self-actualization is that of Abraham Maslow (1954). He decries what he takes to be the pessimistic and limited view of human nature implied in the Freudian and other theories that concentrate on the abnormal person rather than the normal in trying to understand personality. There is too much attention on fear, conflict, anxiety, aggression, deprivation, and too little on gratification, joy, curiosity, and creativity. (Recall the distinction between "deficiency" and "abundancy" motivation in Chapter 10.)

Rather than studying what happens to personality when something goes wrong in the process of development, he would focus on what the outcomes are when all goes well. In his view the "natural" course of development involves a gradual "unfolding" of the essential needs and attributes of human nature, a sequential series of stages through which the person passes, progressing toward higher and higher levels of motives and organization.

Specifically, Maslow conceives of the following five levels of needs, arranged in a ladder from "lower needs" to "higher needs":

> *Physiological needs*, e.g., to satisfy hunger, thirst
> *Safety needs*, e.g., security, order, stability
> *Belongingness and love needs*, e.g., affection, identification
> *Esteem needs*, e.g., prestige, success, self-respect
> *Need for self-actualization*

The terms "lower" and "higher" merely indicate that certain needs manifest themselves earlier in the developmental process, are more closely linked to biological necessities, and are narrower in scope. Most important of all, a "lower" need must be adequately satisfied before the next "higher" need can fully emerge in the person's development. The person cannot devote himself to ensuring his safety until his insistent physiological requirements are met. A basic sense of security must be attained before love and belongingness relations with people can reach their full power. Full-fledged strivings for achievement require that the person feel an adequate degree of satisfaction of his demands for love. And, finally, if the tendency toward self-actualization is to reach its height, all of the preceding levels must have been successively surmounted.

Psychological growth is not, of course, a matter of sharp, discontinuous steps—each "lower" need does not have to be completely gratified before the next "higher" emerges. It is more in the nature of a succession of waves, in which the relative salience of the different needs gradually shifts (see Fig. 155). The optimal physical and social environment is one that makes possible the gratification of each level of needs as it reaches its crest in the individual.

The "natural" course of development can go wrong when there is insufficient gratification of needs at any given level. The next higher needs are thereby prevented from full emergence, and the highest may never appear. The man whose life-long environment provides the barest essentials for physical survival is not likely to develop pressing needs for achievement, prestige, beauty. The chronically hungry man will never seek to build a brave new world. He is much too concerned with satisfying his immediate and pressing hunger needs. It is perhaps partly for this reason that revolutionary movements are initiated not by the completely downtrodden classes, but by groups

of people whose most primitive needs have been satisfied and who are now prepared to seek the achievement of more complex goals.

Once the person has "graduated" from a lower level of needs through their adequate gratification, the needs do not disappear, but simply come to assume a less important place in the whole motivational structure. They may, of course, become temporarily salient again, but never as obsessive and overpowering of the entire individual as they once were. In short, after an individual has passed through the various stages of development, there is a personality structure in which the many kinds of needs are organized into a well-governed hierarchical pattern. The person is freed of the domination of lower needs, freed to allow his rich potentialities to flourish, freed to become self-actualized.

The number of persons who approach complete self-actualization must be very small. Through a study of certain historical figures (e.g., Beethoven, Lincoln) and certain contemporary persons (e.g., Einstein, Schweitzer) judged to be markedly distinguished by self-actualization, Maslow has

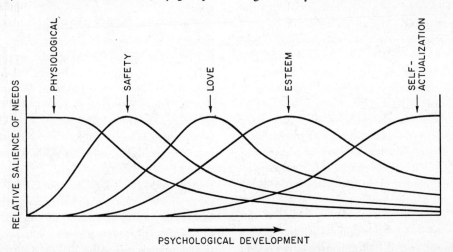

FIG. 155. A schematic portrayal of the progressive changes in relative saliency of the five main classes of needs as described by Maslow. Note that the peak of an earlier main class of needs must be passed before the next "higher" need can begin to assume a dominant role.

isolated what he takes to be the essential common characteristics of the self-actualized personality:

1. Realistic perception of the world
2. Acceptance of self, others, and the world for what they are
3. Spontaneity in behavior and inner experience
4. Centered on problems rather than self
5. Capable of detachment
6. Independent and self-contained
7. Freshness of appreciation of people and things
8. Subject to profound mystical experiences
9. Identification with the human race
10. Deep emotional relations with small circle of friends
11. Democratic attitudes and values
12. Ability to discriminate between means and ends
13. Philosophical rather than hostile sense of humor
14. Creativeness
15. Resistance to cultural conformity

By Way of Summary. We have reviewed a number of the more influential theories of personality. If the reader is not by now confused, he has not been reading faithfully. Some of the theories make the first five years of life all-important; others regard personality formation and reformation as occurring continuously through adulthood. Some conceive of a few basic motivational sources, others of many. Some see personality development as a mere circumstantial ramification of "accidental" events; others, as an organized progression toward positive ends.

Though we are not in a position at this stage of psychological knowledge to accept or reject any of these theories in toto, light on the problems they raise can be given by a brief review of some of the empirical research that has been carried out on personality determinants.

Research on Personality Determinants

Much of the theorizing about personality has been based on clinical observation—of children in behavior clinics, of disturbed and worried people in the psychiatrist's office. Carefully controlled research studies are needed to evaluate these clinical observations and the theories to which they lead. A great deal of such research has been carried out. Here we can do no more than illustrate some of the kinds of research results that have been obtained in studying the main classes of personality determinants —hereditary factors, somatic factors, childhood experiences, social influences, and cultural context.

Hereditary Factors. As we have seen in Chapter 21, there is convincing evidence of the role of genetic constitution in determining individual differences in intelligence.

The data on genetic determination of the nonintellective aspects of personality are not as clear. For one thing, the available measures of intelligence are better validated and more widely accepted than the measures of most other personality attributes, and in general there has been less work done on the inheritance of personality. Nevertheless, the available evidence does seem to point to heredity's playing a powerful role in influencing the temperamental aspects of personality. Animal breeders have long been aware, of course, of the marked differences in temperamental characteristics of animals of various breeds and strains. Some breeds of dogs are placid, others skittish and easily upset. Carefully controlled studies in behavioral genetics confirm this picture. As we have already seen (p. 570), Hall carried out a program of selective breeding for "emotionality" in rats. After a number of generations of such selective breeding, he obtained two populations differing markedly in their "emotionality."

Inherited temperamental differences in human beings can be studied by observing the early emotional characteristics of infants and how these characteristics endure. For instance, in a study by Gesell and his associates (1939) a large group of children were periodically observed from early infancy to adolescence. There was strong indication that temperamental qualities such as energy output and emotional expressiveness remained fairly constant in certain individuals, thus giving support to the hypothesis of their origin in innate predisposition.

Somatic Factors. There is no doubt that differences among people in bodily constitution and physiological functioning can have effects on personality. For instance, we have noted in Chapter 12 that unusual glandular conditions may markedly affect the individual's development—as in the case of cretinism resulting from undersecretion of thyroid hormone. Serious diseases occurring at crucial stages of development, or chronic ill health in general, may often be associated with personality changes.

But the causal connections are difficult to disentangle. Not only may bodily (somatic) factors influence behavior and personality, but the reverse may also be true. For instance, there are many kinds of *psychosomatic disorders*, that is, bodily disorders caused by psychological factors, e.g., stomach ulcers caused by chronic anxiety (see Box 78, p. 341).

Moreover, the effect of somatic factors on personality may be *indirect*, mediated by other people's reaction to the person.

A physically crippled person treated by others as wholly helpless may come to develop a dependent personality; regarded with obvious pity by others, he may become the victim of inferiority feelings, excessive shyness and so on.

The intrusion of this factor of social appraisal and reaction immensely complicates the problem of interpreting correlations found between personality traits and types of body physique. *If* it is true that fat men are jolly, is this because of a direct effect of physical constitution on temperament, or simply because the fat man comes to accommodate himself to society's stereotype that all fat man are jolly? (See Box 157.)

Childhood Experiences. Most personality theories place heavy stress on the role of childhood experiences, and this has led to voluminous research on the effects of various childhood experiences upon personality. But there are sharp contradictions in the findings and interpretations of this research.

CHILD TRAINING PRACTICES. Perhaps the greatest interest and most heated controversies have centered on the "proper" and "improper" methods of feeding, weaning, and toilet training, and their alleged consequences for personality formation. There have been shifting fads and fashions in these practices, often governed by ill-tested assumptions. The facts are complex, to say the least. There is no final decision regarding the relative merits of bottle feeding or breast feeding, late or early weaning, fixed or flexible feeding schedules, early or late toilet training. Especially when we look at anthropological evidence, it becomes clear that the same practice in different cultures may have quite different consequences for personality.

The point seems to be that it is not the precise *form* of the practice that is significant, but the particular *meaning* it has for the infant. The "same" practice can be quite

BOX 157

Physique and Temperament

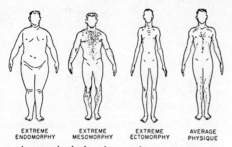

EXTREME ENDOMORPHY   EXTREME MESOMORPHY   EXTREME ECTOMORPHY   AVERAGE PHYSIQUE

A particularly interesting attempt to show relations between physique and temperament has been made by Sheldon at Harvard University. After studying and measuring thousands of photographs of nude male bodies, he concluded that every physique can be identified in terms of the respective amounts of three components: *endomorphy*, the fatty, visceral component; *mesomorphy*, the muscular and bony component; *ectomorphy*, the "skinny" component. A person's somatotype is stated by a three-digit number indicating the amount of each component. For each component the figure may range from 7 at maximum to 1 at minimum.

The figure illustrates persons extreme in a given component, with minimum amounts of the other two components. It also shows a person of average physique, that is having the mean value of 4 on all three components.

As a second step Sheldon, by studying correlations among temperament traits, isolated three main clusters that he considered adequate to account for all the important individual differences in temperament. These were:

Viscerotonia. Relaxed posture, love of physical comfort, slow reaction, indiscriminate amiability, deep sleep, need of people when troubled, etc.

Somatotonia. Assertiveness of posture and movement, love of physical adventure, competitive aggressiveness, general noisiness, need of action when troubled, etc.

Cerebrotonia. Restraint and tightness in posture and movement, overly fast reactions, inhibited social response, poor sleep habits, chronic fatigue, need of solitude when troubled, etc.

A person's temperament could then be described (in a manner analogous to somatotyping) by assigning him a three-digit number, indicative of the respective amounts of the three components, ranging from 7 at maximum to 1 at minimum.

As the final step Sheldon somatotyped 200 college students and then rated each of them on the three temperamental components on the basis of prolonged observation of their behavior. The correlations between somatotype and temperament proved to be astonishingly high, in the direction hypothesized by Sheldon. Thus, the correlation between endomorphy and viscerotonia was .79, that between mesomorphy and somatotonia .82, and that between ectomorphy and cerebrotonia .83.

Unfortunately, as critics have pointed out, these correlations are simply too good to be true; sources of measurement error and complexity of personality determinants being what they are, we cannot expect to find simple relationships of this magnitude. There is reason to surmise that Sheldon's ratings of his subjects' temperaments were unconsciously influenced by his knowledge of their physiques. Other later investigations have failed to find such high correlations as Sheldon reported, and when objective tests rather than ratings were used to measure temperament traits, the correlations of temperament with physique sank to zero.

Evidence has also shown that nutritional differences, ill health, etc., may make for pronounced changes in an individual's somatotype. Sheldon has come, therefore, to modify his conception of somatotype to allow for such variations. He recommends that somatotyping be done on the basis of a series of photographs taken over considerable time periods, and with respect to the individual's history of diet and environment. This modification, however, robs the somatotyping concept of much of its attractive economy and simplicity.

SHELDON, W. H., STEVENS, S. S., and TUCKER, W. B. 1940. *The varieties of human physique.* New York: Harper.

SHELDON, W. H., and STEVENS, S. S. 1942. *The varieties of temperament.* New York: Harper.

different psychologically, depending upon the manner in which it is carried out, the emotions engendered. Early weaning may be disruptive for the child or not, depending on how the parent handles it. The same is true of every other practice. In short, what we need to investigate is the effects on personality of the different kinds of emotional experiences attached to practices of infant care.

INFANTILE INSECURITY. Especially important appears to be the degree of feelings of anxiety and insecurity experienced by the infant in connection with various training practices. These feelings may be aroused by deprivation or frustration of the infant's needs for food, comfort, and affection. It has been argued that such feelings of infantile insecurity may leave deep marks on adult personality; the infant whose feeding is repeatedly and abruptly interrupted before satisfaction is complete may come to develop permanent beliefs that the world is unreliable, that people cannot be trusted. Some evidence on this important notion is given in Box 158.

PARENT-CHILD RELATIONS. Above all else, it is the parents' *attitudes* toward the child that seem to be the crucial determinants. Even for the young infant these attitudes make themselves felt, and as infant becomes child, and child becomes adolescent, the parental attitudes continue to play their powerful role. The attitudes determine the main patterns of parent-child relations, some beneficial for optimal personality development of the child, others detrimental. Some of the latter are as follows:

1. *Rejection* of the child tends to lead to feelings of insecurity and self-devaluation, often combined with hostile, negativistic, and rebellious behavior, or with apathy and indifference. The rejected child may later find it difficult to give and receive affection in his interpersonal relationships.

2. *Maternal overprotection,* or "mom-ism," may lead to quite different deleterious effects, depending upon the form it takes. When the overprotection is *indulgent,* the child is likely to show tendencies to be selfish, egocentric, and irresponsible and to have a low level of frustration tolerance. When it is *dominating,* the child is more likely to develop in the direction of submissiveness, obedience, inadequacy, lack of initiative, passive dependence on others.

3. *Excessively severe discipline* may lead to strong needs for social approval or feelings of self-condemnation for one's conduct. The hostility that is often generated toward the punishing parents may break through in the form of socially deleterious behavior.

4. *Inconsistent or insufficient discipline* may lead to inadequate development of self-control, vacillations in making decisions and meeting problems.

5. *Excessively strict moral standards* enforced by the parents, especially in connection with sexual activities, may lead to a rigid personality, and tendencies to experience feelings of conflict and guilt.

FAMILY ENVIRONMENT. There are all manner of defects in family environment that may make for feelings of insecurity and anxiety in the child. Such disturbed consequences often stem from marital discord, broken homes, immoral behavior of parents, or severe mental disturbances in parents.

BIRTH ORDER. It has often been asserted that whether the child is eldest or youngest or in between may have significant consequences for his personality development. But the research findings do not confirm this. There may, indeed, be important consequences for a given individual arising from his birth order, but the nature, direction, and amount of the effect will depend upon his whole psychological situation, not just the sheer fact of seniority or juniority. The evidence that does show a slight differ-

---

BOX 158

Deprived Infant—Adult Hoarder

J. McV. Hunt used white rats to test the following psychoanalytic hypothesis: Food deprivation during infancy promotes stinginess and greed in the adult. He justified using rats as his subjects on the grounds that "If the experiences considered important by psychoanalysts belong among fundamental biological processes, their effects should be demonstrable upon lower animals as well as human beings."

Two experimental and two control groups were used. Each control group consisted of littermates of the corresponding experimental group. The two control groups were allowed unlimited feeding from birth until the test periods, which occurred when the animals were seven months old—long after they had reached adulthood. The two experimental groups underwent privation during infancy. When the animals of Experimental Group I reached the age of 24 days, their food was removed from their cages and during the next 15 days they were allowed 10-minute feedings at randomly spaced intervals varying from 9 to 36 hours. Thus during this infant food-frustration period these animals were fed irregularly and were forced to go without food for as long as 36 hours, and never less than 9 hours. The animals of the Experimental Group II underwent the same frustration period beginning when they were 32 days old.

When all the animals—experimental and control—were 210 days old, they were tested for "hoarding behavior." For these tests the rat's living cage was connected to a 39-inch-long alley at the end of which was a supply of food pellets. The animal was allowed to transfer as many pellets as he wished from the food supply to his home cage. The measure of "hoarding" (Hunt used this as the rat equivalent to human greed) was the number of pellets which the animal cached in his cage. A trial consisted of a 30-minute period of hoarding opportunity.

The first set of tests took place at a time when unlimited supplies of food had been available in the animal's home cage for several months. Under these conditions very little hoarding occurred. Each of the four groups hoarded an average total of less than two pellets over a period of three trials. Infantile feeding frustration seemed to have no effect on the adult's hoarding when the animal had enjoyed a plentiful food supply over a long period.

For the second set of tests all the animals were first made hungry by being put on a markedly reduced diet. After five days of this "subsistence diet" all four groups were given four hoarding trials. Now the effect of infant deprivation became clear. Experimental Group I, the rats that had suffered food deprivation at the age of 24 days, hoarded an average of 37.7 pellets, while their control brothers and sisters hoarded an average of only 14.0 pellets. However the 32-day experimental group averaged 15.1 pellets and did not differ from its control group, which averaged 18.0. Thus it appears that hunger experience during adulthood will result in greater hoarding behavior for rats that have suffered food deprivation during infancy than it will for rats that have not suffered infant food deprivation. Further, it appears that this infant feeding frustration, to be effective in adult behavior, must come early in the rat's infancy—before the rat is 32 days old.

"These results," concludes Hunt, "tend to substantiate the psychoanalytic claim that infantile experience is an effective determinant of adult behavior."

HUNT, J. McV. 1941. The effects of infant feeding-frustration upon adult hoarding in the albino rat. *J. abnorm. soc. Psychol.,* 36, 338–60.

---

ence between the elder child and the younger, seems to confirm the common notion that the elder tends to be more oriented toward adult perspective, more serious, and less socially at ease, whereas the younger tends to be more easy-going, cheerful, and less serious-minded.

Findings on the *only child* are equally

indecisive. Though there is some indication that the only child in a family is somewhat different from other children, the differences are not large and do not go in a consistent direction.

SIBLING RIVALRY. The presence of other children in the family may have effects on the child in connection with the arousal of *sibling rivalry*, that is, the feelings of jealousy and competition among siblings. Often this occurs when a baby is born, and the child feels that he is being displaced in his parents' affection. The result may be aggressive acts toward the intruder—overt or covert—or regressive behavior, such as resumption of baby talk or bed wetting. This regressive behavior has been interpreted as the older child's attempt to re-establish himself in a dependent role with the parents. But sibling rivalry is by no means universal or inevitable. It seems to depend in part upon how the parents handle the situation and the whole context of family relationships.

BY WAY OF SUMMARY. In discussing the effects of childhood experiences on personality, we repeatedly stressed that what is important is not the particular form of infant care, the particular act of parental control, the particular detail of family environment, but the manner in which these events and circumstances are perceived and understood by the child.

What is important for optimal personality growth is an adequate gratification of needs and desires—not only those that have to do with food, rest, affection, and the like, but also those that have to do with seeking of stimulation and self-development. Such needs can be gratified in a multitude of ways, under a multitude of external circumstances, both favorable and unfavorable. What is vital is that the situation, and especially the parental attitudes, be such as to assure the child of love, security, scope for exploration, opportunity for assuming responsibility. These do not depend upon bottle versus breast, but upon what the parent believes and tries to do. There is no formula for "correct" child rearing. The act must fit the situation and the needs of the specific child, and the only "formula" to remember is to cherish the child without smothering him, to be firm without being rigid, and above all to "relax and enjoy" being a parent.

Personality Measurement

In order to do research on personality, we need adequate measuring instruments. We will now describe the various approaches to this problem. It would be well for the reader first to review the general principles of psychological measurement presented in Chapter 19, and their application to the measurement of motives (Chapter 11) and of intelligence and abilities (Chapter 20).

The assumption in measuring any given personality characteristic (trait, ability, attitude, value, or motive) is that people vary in amount of the characteristic, and that with respect to it each person can be assigned a specific numerical score based on behavioral data. The behavioral data may be simple (e.g., check marks on a sheet of paper) or very complex (e.g., patterns of interpersonal response in a group problem-solving situation).

Whether simple or complex, the data may be scored in one of two main ways. (1) *Objective* scoring involves the mechanical counting of responses. For example, a true-false examination is objectively scored by counting the number of correct choices. (2) *Subjective* scoring requires the scorer to study the behavioral data and *judge* what score to assign; the so-called "essay examination" is so scored.

The value of a personality measuring

technique rests on the reliability and validity it possesses (see Chapter 19, p. 524), that is, the extent to which it *consistently* taps behavior of the individual *relevant* to the personality attribute in question. Other things being equal, objectively scored tests are preferred to those subjectively scored, owing to their greater economy and mechanical processing. For personality attributes that manifest themselves in simple and uncomplicated ways in behavior, objective methods are especially suitable. But when the attribute is complex and subtle in its manifestations, it may be necessary to rely on subjective ratings of the behavioral data, in which the rater can weigh multiple factors and synthesize his impressions. However, even for complex and elusive variables there is a constant effort by psychologists to discover test techniques that will permit objective scoring without sacrifice of essential validity. And these efforts have, as we shall see, met with some success.

For convenience of discussion, methods of personality measurement may be classified as performance tests, personality inventories, projective techniques, situational tests, and ratings.

Performance Tests. Performance tests are those that require the person to achieve tasks set for him, such as solving problems. Generally they call for the person to *perform at his best*. In other words, they are measures of his abilities. In Chapter 20 we discussed some tests of this type, for example, tests of intelligence and special mental functions.

We wish to measure, in addition to intellectual abilities, many other kinds of abilities that help constitute the personality. There are performance tests designed to measure areas of competence such as the following:

GENERAL INFORMATION. The amount of knowledge the person has about the world he lives in. A measure of sheer cognitive differentiation of his life-space. Made up of items of information drawn from all spheres of human activity but not weighted with "book" knowledge to the exclusion of "practical" knowledge.

SOCIAL ACUITY. The degree to which the person accurately perceives other people. In one such test the subject is shown film sequences of a person behaving, and he is asked to make predictions of how the person would behave in certain other specified situations (the actual facts being known to the tester).

PERCEPTUAL EFFICIENCY. The person's perceptual speed, accuracy, flexibility, synthesizing power, and other characteristic modes of perception related to more general aspects of personality. An example is the test requiring the setting of a rod to the vertical in a darkroom (Box 14, p. 47).

"CREATIVITY." The originality of the person's thought processes as he attempts to solve problems. For example, the battery of "creativity" tests developed by Guilford and his associates (1951) includes tests of the person's ability to think of "unusual uses" of common objects, his ability to think of various possible "consequences" of a particular event, e.g., lengthening of the human life-span to 200 years.

Personality Inventories. Perhaps the principal approach to personality measurement is through *personality inventories*, which are aimed at a great variety of traits. Some have to do with interests (e.g., the *Strong Vocational Interest Blank*, see p. 556). Others have to do with emotional adjustment, social relations, attitudes, and values.

An inventory consists of a large number of statements or questions, each to be answered in one of several specified categories, such as "Agree" or "Disagree," "Like" or "Dislike." The score on a particular trait dimension is not based on the answer to a single item, but on answers on several items, all intended to reveal the trait in question. A given scale may be composed of as many as 20 to 50 items, relating to various traits. One inventory may provide measures of a dozen or more traits at the same time.

There are two quite different methods of establishing the direction in which the answers to an item are to be scored. In the *a priori* method the test constructor designs an item whose meaning on the very face of it, clearly indicates how the item is to be scored. This method is used in the *Allport-Vernon-Lindzey Study of Values* (see Box 159). In the *empirical* method the direction in which the item is to be scored is established by pretesting a large collection of items on criterion groups known to be high and low on the trait in question (see p. 527 for a discussion of the "known group" method of validation). The items on which the answers of the two groups differ significantly are included in the final inventory scale. The direction of scoring is empirically based on the direction of difference in the answers of the criterion groups, regardless of the "obvious" meaning of the item.

An example of this method is the *Minnesota Multiphasic Personality Inventory* (abbreviated MMPI). It consists of 550 simple statements to each of which the person is to answer "True," "False," or "Cannot say." The items refer to such diverse topics as bodily complaints ("I am troubled by discomfort in the pit of my stomach every few days or oftener"), fears and anxieties ("I am afraid when I look down from a high place"), behavior characteristics ("Often I cross the street in order not to meet someone I see"), social and moral attitudes ("I do not blame a person for taking advantage of someone who lays himself open to it").

The test is scored on a number of standard scales, plus many other special scales. The standard scales are measures of traits that, if possessed in excess, are likely to be symptomatic of disturbances of personality, e.g., "depression," "hysteria," "paranoia," etc. The MMPI is one of the devices most widely used by clinicians for the diagnosis of personality disorders.

Another inventory, constructed in somewhat the same manner but aimed at the measurement of more favorable and positive traits having significance for social living and behavior in general, is the *California Psychological Inventory* (Gough, 1957). It includes 18 scales grouped under four broad categories: (a) measures of poise, ascendancy, and self-assurance; (b) measures of socialization, maturity, and responsibility; (c) measures of achievement-potential and intellectual efficiency; and (d) measures of style of thinking and orientation to life.

Personality inventories are easily scored and can be economically administered to large groups of subjects. Although the person may "fake" his answers in order to give a good impression, such "faking" can be at least partially detected by answers to certain items deliberately built into the inventory. And inasmuch as the empirical scales are made up of items whose significance is often not obvious to the person, he may not be successful in his efforts to "fake."

A disadvantage of inventories may be their difficulty in getting at deeper-lying aspects of personality. However, there is no reason in principle why the inventory approach if properly applied cannot be used to measure deeper aspects as well as the more obvious ones.

Projective Techniques. It is mainly to get at the deeper and subtler aspects of personality that *projective techniques* are used. The essence of these techniques is the pres-

BOX 159

Measuring Personal Values

The notion of six "ideal" value types proposed by Spranger (see p. 615) later led to the development of an inventory designed to measure the relative importance of each of these six values to the individual. This inventory, called the *Study of Values*, was constructed by Allport and Vernon at Harvard University, and later revised with the help of Lindzey. It consists of 45 items pertaining to the person's attitudes and preferences. The items were selected on the basis of their apparent relevance to one or more of the six value areas—Theoretical, Economic, Aesthetic, Social, Political, Religious.

An example of one type of item is the following statement, to which the person is to answer "yes" or "no."

"Are our modern industrial and scientific developments signs of a greater degree of civilization than those attained by any previous society, the Greeks, for example?"

A "yes" answer gives a point toward the Economic value, a "no" answer a point toward the Aesthetic value.

Another type of item is a multiple-choice question, such as the following:

"If you could influence the educational policies of the public schools of some city, would you undertake—

a. to promote the study and participation in music and fine arts;

b. to stimulate the study of social problems;

c. to provide additional laboratory facilities;

d. to increase the practical value of courses."

(Can you figure out which of the six values each of the four possible answers is meant to reveal?)

Total scores are computed for the person on each of the six values, and a profile is plotted with the midpoint of each scale at 40. This provides a quick picture of the pattern of his values.

The graph shows two "averaged" profiles for a group of male students of business administration and a group of theological students. Note the differences.

ALLPORT, G. W., VERNON, P. E., and LINDZEY, G. 1951. *A study of values: a scale for measuring the dominant interests in personality.* (Revised). Boston: Houghton Mifflin.

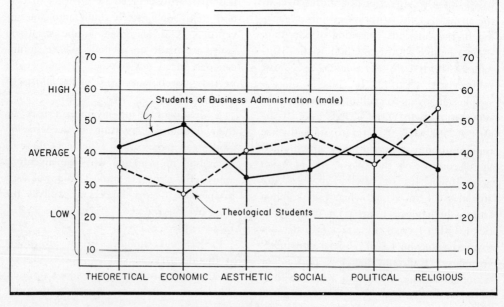

entation of weakly structured or ambiguous stimulus materials to which the person responds. It is assumed that this method will permit a greater degree of "projection" of his deep-lying tendencies than will more direct methods, as he perceives and interprets the stimuli, without being aware himself of what he is revealing. In this connection we should recall that a person's set has a greater influence on the perception of a weakly structured stimulus than of a well-structured stimulus (see p. 100).

RORSCHACH INK BLOT TEST. This widely used projective technique, designed in 1911 by the Swiss psychiatrist, Herman Rorschach, consists in the presentation of 10 standard ink blots, some black-and-white, some colored. (One application of the test has already been described in Box 13, page 46, where one of the blots is reproduced.) The subject is asked to describe the various things he sees in the blots, and his responses are scored in a number of categories, pertaining to (1) the location in the blot of the thing seen, (2) the kind of stimulus-characteristic emphasized, e.g., form, color, shading, texture, movement, (3) the content of the percept, e.g., animal, human being, inanimate object, etc., and (4) the originality of the response.

These various scores are taken to be "indicators" of specific tendencies in the person. For instance, seeing the blot as a whole is regarded as an indication of tendencies toward abstract and theoretical orientations, whereas concentration on many small details of the blots indicates compulsive attention to trivial things; "color" responses are considered to be related to emotional expression; "human movement" responses to richness of inner life. *Ratios* of the separate scores are also considered highly diagnostic. Thus, a high ratio of color to form responses is supposed to signify a tendency to uncontrolled emotional behavior; a high ratio of human movement to color re-

sponses is taken to mean a withdrawn, introversive tendency, and so on.

Although the scoring of the Rorschach is more or less standard, the interpretation is decidedly not. It requires a highly skilled tester to synthesize the information from the entire pattern of test scores and to arrive at a conception of the structure of the personality. Such conceptions are "intuitive," and the same test scores may be quite differently interpreted by different experts. This raises doubts concerning the basic validity of the technique, and studies directed at the question of validation have not dispelled these doubts.

THEMATIC APPERCEPTION TEST. This is the other most widely used projective technique. Known as the TAT, it was designed by Morgan and Murray (1935), especially for the purpose of measuring the various "psychological needs" postulated in Murray's theory of personality (see p. 624).

There is a standard set of 20 test pictures, each depicting a simple scene of ambiguous meaning, e.g., an old woman looking past the averted face of a younger woman, a man standing with head bowed beside a bed on which a partially undressed woman is lying. The subject is asked to tell a story about each picture, indicating what is happening, how it came about, what will happen next. The stories are then analyzed by a TAT expert, who looks for certain consistencies and recurrent themes in the natures of the plots, the types of heroes, the kinds of outcomes, etc. Such characteristics in the stories are taken to reveal important aspects of the person's needs, attitudes, conflicts, identifications, aspirations, self-conception. (We have already seen in Box 68, page 305, the application of a very similar technique to measurement of the achievement motive.)

Situational Tests. Another valuable approach to personality measurement is to place the person in a standard test situation that is an approximate replica of a "real life" situation and to record data on his behavior. The assumption is that his behavior in the test situation may coincide fairly closely with his general behavioral traits. This is likely to be more true the more "real" the test situation is for the person. Sometimes, indeed, he may not realize that it is a test at all. For instance, MacKinnon (1938) measured "honesty" in a sample of subjects by placing each one alone in a standard test situation where he was to solve a series of numerical problems. An answer booklet was available but he was instructed not to look. The experimenter observed him through a one-way screen, recording whether or not he violated the prohibition.

The situational test may often be one involving interpersonal behavior among several subjects being tested. For example, a group of five subjects may be assigned a topic to discuss, being left free to choose their own leader, set their own rules, and proceed as they see fit. The behavior of each person as he interacts with the others is recorded by observers and scored on one or more personality variables, such as dominance, poise, leadership, negativism, tolerance, originality. The scores may be objectively derived through the counting of behavior items (e.g., the number of times the person initiated suggestions during the discussion), or they may be subjectively rated by the observers.

Some situational tests are deliberately contrived to confront the individual with conditions of stress, or with conflicts to be overcome in the assigned task. Thus, he may be required to work on a problem in co-operation with another person who is actually a confederate of the experimenter, and who deliberately causes well-timed interferences in the subject's attack on the problem. The distinctive manner in which he reacts to the stress and handles the interpersonal conflict provides data for measuring various dimensions of personality.

Ratings. Perhaps the most generally used approach to personality measurement is through *ratings,* in which the person's score on a given dimension is determined by the place on a rating scale that he is assigned by a rater. Ratings may be made on the basis of direct observations of the person's behavior, either in a limited setting, such as ratings of children's traits from their behavior on the school playground, or in much broader settings, such as ratings of workers by their supervisors on the basis of behavior occurring in many diverse situations, formal and informal.

Ratings may also be made on the basis of personal interviews with the individual, or on the basis of a study of various sources of information about him, life-history documents, work records, test scores, etc., from all of which the rater seeks to gain an over-all impression of the individual's traits. Rating scales take many forms. An example is given in Table 23.

TABLE 23

An Illustrative Rating Scale for the Measurement of the Trait of Dominance-Submission

Instructions: Place a check mark before the category that best describes the behavior of the individual.

_____ 1. Takes the lead in all his relations with other people; is always dominant and assertive.

_____ 2. Usually takes the ascendant role in his relations with others, but occasionally may follow rather than lead.

_____ 3. Is about equally likely to take the dominant role or the submissive role in his relations with others.

_____ 4. Usually takes the submissive role, but occasionally is ascendant over others.

_____ 5. Takes the submissive role in all his relations with other people; is always led and dominated.

Ratings have been made on a great many different personality attributes, and they have proved indispensable for much of the research on personality. But they are fraught with dangers. Some traits cannot be rated in a reliable and valid fashion. It is the general rule that wherever possible ratings should be made by several different raters, so that the degree of agreement of their judgments can be checked.

SELF-RATINGS. The person may also rate *himself* on various traits. There are obvious pitfalls in the use of self-ratings, inasmuch as they are susceptible to distortions caused by lack of frankness, limitation of perspective, and self-deception. Thus, the self-rating may disagree markedly with ratings made by objective observers.

But it should be recognized that the most important use of self-ratings is to provide measures of different aspects of self-perception, which, of course, constitute a central part of personality structure. Assuming that the person reports frankly, his self-ratings are presumably the best evidence we can get on what the person believes about himself. And the fact that self-ratings may often deviate from the objective appraisals of observers is itself a fertile source of information about degrees of self-deception and self-insight in the person. For example, in one testing procedure a list of 300 adjectives is checked by the person for terms descriptive of himself. The same list is checked about him by a team of expert observers. The degree of agreement between his description and theirs is then computed. High agreement presumably indicates more self-insight; and low agreement, less self-insight.

Assessment of Personality. The many different types of measurement reviewed above may be combined in an *intensive assessment* of a sample of individuals. The ideal aim of such assessment is to obtain all the information necessary to describe the whole personality of each individual. Performance tests, personality inventories, projective techniques, situational tests, and ratings, all contribute to this end. And, typically, each main dimension of personality is measured through not one but a combination of different techniques.

Moreover, beyond the measurement and description of the personality of the individual, the ultimate purpose is to relate the personality attributes to various determinants, and to various behavioral outcomes. Thus, intensive assessment also includes the collection of numerous data having to do with the person's body characteristics, physiological functioning, life history, work history, social background, and the like. Since the amount of information collected on each individual is enormous, serious problems arise in synthesizing and interpreting the data. Despite these problems, assessment methods are proving to be highly effective in the study of the whole person.

Glossary

anal stage. In Freudian theory, the second stage of psychosexual development, occurring during the second and third years, when the child's bodily concerns are mainly on anal activity, especially in relation to the demands of toilet training. Fixation at the anal stage is assumed to lead to development of the anal, or compulsive, character.

asthenic type. The type of physique characterized by a thin, long-limbed, narrow-chested body, which was asserted by Kretschmer to be associated with being shy, sensitive, aloof, withdrawn, and—

in cases of mental disease—with schizophrenia. Contrasted with the pyknic type.

authoritarian syndrome. A constellation of traits often found together in some individuals. It includes excessive conformity, authoritarian behavior and values, overcontrol of impulses and feelings, rigidity of thought processes, prejudice toward minority groups, etc. Assumed to derive from excessively severe forms of disciplinary treatment by parents, against whom repressed hostility develops.

basic anxiety. A term used by Horney to denote the main source of adjustment problems in personality development. Arises from anything that causes insecurity in the child, especially in relations with the parents.

character. That aspect of personality which in earlier terminology referred to the moral outlook and conduct of the individual.

compensation. Efforts made to overcome a weakness or inferiority. May take the direct form of striving for superiority in the very area of defect, or may be indirect, that is, in the form of substitute strivings.

compulsive syndrome. A constellation of traits frequently found associated in individuals. It includes orderliness, obstinacy, stinginess, punctuality, excessive cleanliness, etc. Assumed to relate to the aftermath in personality of fixations occurring at the anal stage of psychosexual development; thus sometimes referred to as the anal character.

ectomorphy. The "skinny" component in Sheldon's classification of body types.

ego. In Freudian theory, one of the three main systems making up the personality. It is the system of cognitive processes—perceiving, thinking, planning, deciding—which makes possible the realistic channeling and satisfaction of the id-instincts.

endomorphy. The fatty, visceral component in Sheldon's classification of body types.

extrovert. In Jung's typology, the type of person who has an orientation directed outward to the objective world of things and events; primarily interested in social activities and practical affairs; tough-minded and realistic. Contrasted with the introvert.

functional autonomy of motives. The notion advanced by Allport that activities serving an original motive may later become motivating in their own right, after the original motive has subsided.

genital stage. In Freudian theory, the final stage of psychosexual development, occurring at puberty, when the adolescent experiences a shift of interest away from himself as primary object to other people and things as important objects; the period during which heterosexual attachments emerge.

id. In Freudian theory, one of the three main systems making up the personality. It is the source of the basic and unconscious instinctive energies that underly all the person's behavior.

inferiority complex. Strong and generalized feelings of inferiority and inadequacy which tend to block the person's successful achievement.

introvert. In Jung's typology, the type of person who is subjective in orientation; primarily interested in ideas, imagination, and inner life; tender-minded and idealistic. Contrasted with the extrovert.

libido. In Freudian theory, the term for basic psychic energy. Though popularly defined as sexual in nature, it is more broadly intended to refer to all pleasure-seeking impulses.

mesomorphy. The muscular, bony component in Sheldon's classification of body types.

Oedipus complex. In Freudian theory, the directing of the boy's erotic feelings toward the mother, and the girl's toward the father. Allegedly the source of the primary identifications with parents, out of which later life-identifications develop.

oral stage. In Freudian theory, the first stage of psychosexual development, occurring during the first year when the infant's interest centers on the erogenous zones of the mouth. Fixations at the oral stage are hypothesized to lead to development of the oral character.

performance tests. Tests of personality, especially of intelligence and abilities, which are aimed at measuring the individual as he performs at his best.

personality inventory. A method for the measurement of traits of personality, such as those having to do with interests, attitudes, emotional adjustment, social relations. An inventory consists of a large number of simple statements or questions, each to be answered in terms of specified categories. A given trait is measured by the total score on a large number of items.

personality structure. The particular manner in which the individual's traits, abilities, motives, values, etc., are dynamically organized to form his unique personality.

personality types. The qualitatively different categories into which personalities may allegedly be divided. There are simple type theories, which postulate a very limited number of categories, and complex type theories, involving classification of persons on a large number of dimensions.

phallic stage. In Freudian theory, the third stage of psychosexual development, during which the child's bodily interest turns to the sexual organs and to the pleasures associated with their manipulation, and during which the so-called Oedipus complex occurs.

projective technique. A method intended for the measurement of deeper-lying tendencies in the person not readily ascertainable through more direct methods. Consists in the presentation of weakly structured or ambiguous stimulus materials (e.g., ink blots), into the perception and interpretation of which the perceiver is said to "project" tendencies of which he may be unaware.

psychoanalysis. The theory of personality and the method of psychotherapy invented by Sigmund Freud.

psychosomatic disorders. Bodily disorders caused by psychological factors, e.g., stomach ulcers caused by chronic anxiety.

pyknic type. The type of physique characterized by a short, fattish, barrel-chested body, which was asserted by Kretschmer to be associated with being jovial, lively, outgoing, inclined to mood fluctuations, and—in cases of mental disease—with manic-depressive psychosis. Contrasted with the asthenic type.

ratings. Perhaps the most widely used method of measuring personality traits. The person's score on a given trait dimension is determined by his placement on a rating scale by a rater. There may also be self-ratings.

self-actualization. The notion, embodied in various theories of personality, of a basic human tendency toward the end of making actual what is potential in the self, that is, toward maximal realization of one's potentialities.

sibling rivalry. Feelings of jealousy and competition among siblings. Often aroused in a child when a baby is born in the family, leading the child to aggressive and sometimes regressive behavior.

situational tests. A method for measuring personality traits in which the subject is observed in a standard test situation that is an approximate replica of a "real life" situation. The test situation often involves interpersonal behavior among several subjects being tested.

somatotype. The body type of an individual as measured in Sheldon's three-component system of endomorphy, mesomorphy, and ectomorphy.

striving for superiority. Adler's conception that the primary source of human motivation is the innate upward drive to self-perfection. The directions taken by the strivings are in the nature of compensations for particular weaknesses or inferiorities that the person perceives.

superego. In Freudian theory, one of the three main systems making up the personality. It is a system of restraining and inhibiting forces, derived from social rules and regulations, which serve to curb and channel basic impulses—especially sex and aggression—regarded as dangerous or detrimental by society. It is the child's conscience or moral sense.

temperament. That aspect of personality pertaining to the typical emotional reactions, mood states, and energetic attributes of the individual.

trait. An enduring characteristic of the individual which is manifested in a consistent way of behaving in a wide variety of situations. Traits are of many varieties; some are broad in scope, some narrow; some are on the surface and others are deep-seated.

trait profile. An individual's standing on each of a set of trait dimensions, relative to the population of people.

trait syndrome. A pattern of traits often found associated in individuals, presumably owing to certain critical events in the developmental process. For example, the compulsive syndrome.

Suggestions for Further Reading

ALLPORT, G. W. 1937. *Personality.* New York: Holt.

A scholarly presentation of a distinctive theory of personality, focusing on the concepts of individual traits and functional autonomy of motives.

ANSBACHER, H. L., and ANSBACHER, R. R. (eds.) 1956. *The individual psychology of Alfred Adler.* New York: Basic Books.

A skillfully annotated selection of significant passages from Adler's writings.

FREUD, S. 1938. *The basic writings of Sigmund Freud.* New York: Modern Library.

Edited by A. A. Brill, this volume provides an introduction to some of the many classic writings of Freud, including, for instance, *The psychopathology of everyday life.*

HALL, C. S., and LINDZEY, G. 1957. *Theories of personality.* New York: Wiley.

An extremely valuable description and critique of a dozen major theories of personality, including all those discussed in this chapter.

KLUCKHOHN, C., MURRAY, H. A., and SCHNEIDER, D. M. (eds.) 1953. *Personality in nature, society, and culture* (rev. ed.). New York: Knopf.

Contributions on the topic of personality by psychologists and anthropologists.

MASLOW, A. H. 1954. *Motivation and personality.* New York: Harper.

Argues for a positive approach to personality, in which growth rather than deprivation is the keynote.

MURPHY, G. 1947. *Personality.* New York: Harper.

A thoughtful and highly informed account of the structure and development of personality, stressing both biological and social factors.

OFFICE OF STRATEGIC SERVICES, ASSESSMENT STAFF. 1948. *Assessment of men.* New York: Rinehart.

A detailed account of methods of personality assessment used for the selection of psychologically qualified agents delegated to carry out secret missions behind enemy lines in World War II.

WHITE, R. W. 1952. *Lives in progress: a study of the natural growth of personality.* New York: Dryden.

Detailed studies of the personality development of three normal individuals—from their college years until ten years later.

CHAPTER XXIV

Conflict and Adjustment

WE SAW in the previous chapter that conflict is an inevitable and perhaps indispensable feature of personality development. For it is the particular manner in which the individual has met and resolved, or failed to resolve, his conflicts that gives the unique stamp to his personality.

In this chapter we go on to examine the sources of the individual's conflicts and the nature of his defensive reactions to them. We describe the forms of mental disorder, both mild and severe, that may arise from a breakdown of defenses. And, finally, we review the methods of psychotherapy for such disorders.

Sources of Conflict

The specific forms in which conflicts are cast in the various personality theories described in the last chapter vary widely: opposing forces among id, ego, and superego (Freud); inferiority feelings versus striving for perfection (Adler); incompatible "neurotic needs" driving the person to seek to be with others, to aggress against them, and to be independent of them, all at the same time (Horney); desires for freedom and self-expression versus fears of isolation (Fromm); conflicting requirements of complex interpersonal relationships (Sullivan). Yet common to all these theories are certain main classes of conflict, presumably found in varying degrees among all people.

Conflict of Motives. Owing to the diversity of motives impelling the individual, it is inevitable that he experience continuous conflicts among them. Four of the more significant classes of such conflicts are:

1. PLEASURE VS. PUNISHMENT. The individual is driven by many impulses that society seeks to control and suppress. He has desires connected with sex, with aggression, etc., and these are subject to social threats and punishments that aim at preserving the society and its mores. Thus, the person feels many basic conflicts between his desires for various forms of action and his fear of social censure and downright punishment.

2. PERSONAL GAIN VS. PRINCIPLE. When the standards of society are well "internalized" in the form of the individual's moral and ethical principles, there may be conflicts between his desires for personal gain and the need to avoid a sense of sin and evil-doing, a sense of violating the principles he holds, and of disturbing the ideal self-conception he maintains. A businessman wants to make a quick dollar but feels that the deal would be unethical. The young man and young woman want to satisfy their desire for premarital intercourse but feel that it is sinful. The man wants to preserve his life but feels that he is patriotically obliged to risk himself in battle.

3. ACHIEVEMENT VS. FEAR OF FAILURE. The individual is driven to achieve, to accomplish, to create. But at the same time the need to enter into achievement activities may be in serious conflict with the fear of failing in these endeavors, with a consequent loss of self-esteem and prestige in the eyes of others.

4. INDEPENDENCE VS. BELONGING. The individual feels powerful needs and desires to be independent and autonomous, to strike out for himself, to form and express his own opinions, to be a "lone wolf"; but at the same time he feels equally strong and competing needs and desires—to be a member of a group, to be loved and accepted, to conform.

Conflict of Roles. One of the most critical aspects of personality development is the individual's coming to fit the various *roles* that society defines for him. The process of adjusting to and reconciling the roles is fraught with conflict.

One important source of such *role conflicts* is the discrepancy that may often exist between the requirements of the role and the capabilities of the person. We have seen that some aspects of personality, especially temperament and intelligence, may

be heavily determined by genetic factors, and as a consequence of this an individual may be basically and permanently unsuited for what is demanded of him by society. In most, if not all, cultures, there are individuals who appear ill-suited to the conventional masculine and feminine roles defined by the specific culture. Though biologically a male or a female, the person may be psychologically more suited to the opposite role. This may stem from physiological deviation from the average (see p. 345), or it may have to do with an abnormal direction of development in the early states of personality formation, due to a host of circumstantial events. In most cultures there are built-in "safety devices" for handling such deviant personalities. And in complex societies, such as our own, the problem can often be handled, as there are available many special subcultures in which the deviant person may find a better "fit." Yet, in general, the discrepancy between the individual's constitution and what is generally required of him by the culture is a potent source of conflict for the person.

There are many other forms that this discrepancy can take. For instance, the abilities of an individual may not be commensurate with the special requirements of his role. A child of highly intellectual parents may turn out to possess no better than average intelligence, and hence not fit the "proper" role of an intellectual that his parents expect and demand of him. The son of a famous athlete may be physically puny; the son of an army officer, temperamentally timid; the son of a musician, "tone deaf." All these situations can lead to acute conflict between expectations and potentialities.

Incompatible Roles. But an even more serious source of role conflicts stems from the fact that the person is required to fit *many diverse roles* at the same time or in quick succession. In simpler and highly stabilized cultures the demand that an individual fit many roles has become minimized so that the person can with greater ease fulfill the total requirements of society as he grows. But in highly complex societies such as our own, the incompatibility of roles can be enormous. The individual is typically in many overlapping situations at once, and each presents different role demands. Moreover as he develops from stage to stage, from childhood to adolescence, from adolescence to adulthood, the changing role definitions present acute problems of adjustment for him.

Many cases of marital and family discord can be traced to such conflicts of roles. The educated woman may experience severe conflict between the nurturant role of wife and mother and the role of an independent woman creating and achieving in the "outside world." The woman who tacks her college diploma over her kitchen sink is a graphic instance of this type of conflict. The man may feel a conflict between his role as the dependable breadwinner and his role as the carefree "man about town."

ROLE DIFFUSION. In addition to direct conflicts because of incompatible requirements of roles, there may also be severe conflict because the *diffusion* of roles required of the individual prevents him from achieving a stable and clear-cut self-identity. Erikson (1956) describes the process of formation of self-identity as one in which the various roles with which the adolescent identifies gradually become harmonized and organized so that a coherent and workable pattern of beliefs, values, motives, abilities, and temperament is achieved. With such organization, the individual establishes and identifies himself as a *person;* he becomes *himself*, rather than the mere aggregate of diffuse roles and identifications which he

had previously been. Erikson has stressed the particular importance of this problem of achieving self-identity which is faced by the adolescent as he approaches adult status.

Defensive Reactions to Conflict

As we have seen in Chapter 11, the consequences of conflict may be constructive or disruptive for the person's adjustment, depending on the nature of the conflict, the situation in which it arises, and the frustration tolerance of the individual. We have also seen that there are indirect effects of conflict, most important of which is the arousal of anxiety stemming from threats to self-esteem, from feelings of guilt, and from fear of punishment.

The crucial significance of the anxiety induced by conflict is that it leads the person to show various defensive reactions serving to allay or avoid the anxiety. We turn now to a discussion of these so-called *defense mechanisms* or mechanisms of self-defense.

Rationalization. Our earlier discussions of processes of perception and thinking stressed the individual's constant striving to make "sense" of his world of experience. He seeks an explanation not only of external phenomena but also of his own behavior, his own feelings. The cognitive processes involved in achieving such explanations are subject to the distorting influences of emotional and motivational factors. Thus the individual may come to "explain" his behavior and feelings in conflict situations in such a way that self-esteem is maintained and anxiety avoided. Such cognitive accommodation to conflict is called *rationalization.*

Rationalization takes many forms. In cases of personal failure or of violation of moral principles, the individual may find false but "good reasons" to justify his conduct. He failed the quiz "because the questions were unfair"; he need not feel guilty about riding on the train without a ticket "because the railroad is a big corporation that would never miss the money," "the fares they charge are too high," and besides "everybody does it."

The frustrated fox who called the unreachable grapes sour finds many human counterparts: the man who says the job he was fired from was not a desirable one anyway, that the girl who turned him down was not really attractive, and so on. Serving the same function as the "sour grapes" reaction is the "sweet lemon" phenomenon —the person forced into a distasteful situation rationalizes that it is really desirable.

Rationalizations usually involve a complex web of "explanations" rather than a single one, and this helps make them less pervious to attack. The person has defenses "in depth" so that if one rationalization breaks down, others are in reserve. The man accused of returning a borrowed pot in a damaged condition asserts that he never borrowed the pot, that he returned it in perfect condition, that it already had the hole in it when he borrowed it.

In mild form, rationalization may have the beneficial function of permitting the person to remain in the anxiety-producing situation and possibly to achieve an adaptive solution because rationalization provides protective armor while he tries to cope. In extreme forms, however, rationalization is likely to lead to worse failures of adjustment in that the person becomes so enmeshed in a web of deluded self-justification that he is hindered from realistic attack on his problem.

Rationalizations may not always, of course, succeed in allaying anxiety. The real facts of the situation may be so crystal-clear that there is little room for the protective, cognitive distortions to occur.

Rationalizations are not simply lies; the person may not deliberately set out to deceive. Typically, he is unaware of the distortions in his thinking, even though they are patent to people around him.

There is, moreover, no *sharp* dividing line between rationalization and reason. We have seen (p. 370) that reason, too, can be affected by emotional and motivational factors. But in rationalizing the person seems to devote special effort toward justifying himself and may become emotionally upset when his "explanations" are questioned by other people. Inasmuch as the very purpose of rationalization is defensive, it is to be expected that threats to the defenses themselves will be emotionally resisted.

Insulation. The processes of reasoning are especially differentiated from those of rationalization in the degree to which rationalizations tend to be relatively impervious to contradictory evidence. The human mind seems capable, under some circumstances, of entertaining two logically incompatible concepts side by side, without awareness of the obvious discrepancy. This phenomenon has been dubbed "logic-tight compartments." For example, an outraged antivivisectionist wrote a denunciatory letter to a psychiatrist who had described his experiments with animals involving electric shocks:

". . . I am surprised that anyone as well educated as you must be . . . would stoop to such a depth as to torture helpless little cats in the pursuit of a cure for alcoholics. . . . Instead . . . why not torture the drunks . . . if such people are weaklings the world is better off without them. . . . My greatest wish is that you have brought home to you a torture that will be a thousand fold greater than what you are doing to the little animals. . . . I'm glad I am just an ordinary human being . . . with a clear conscience, knowing I have not hurt any living creature." (Masserman, 1946.)

This instance of a complete contradiction between the denunciation of torture and the advocacy of it is doubtless the product of an unbalanced mind. But less bizarre examples of "logic-tight compartments" in people's thinking are constantly encountered by all of us—though not, of course, in ourselves!

There is, in short, the process of insulating one part of the mental contents from other parts, in such a way that the normal interactions that would occur among them are reduced, and hence conflicts may be resolved. We saw earlier that such "separation of systems" is a general phenomenon and can even be found in simple perception (see p. 113).

Insulation may pertain to emotional as well as to cognitive processes. The feelings normally connected with a given percept, or thought, or action, may fail to be experienced. (We noted in Chapter 8 an example of such a phenomenon in the case in which a physical pain may be experienced by the person as not "his" own pain.)

A common form of insulation is the excessive "intellectualization" indulged in by some people as they approach all kinds of life problems. By attending only to the "intellectual" aspects of a problem, the person may protect himself against the anxieties that might stem from the emotions customarily attached to the problem.

It is largely by virtue of such "separation of systems" in psychological processes that other defense mechanisms, such as projection, repression, and fantasy, can work.

Projection. One obvious way to defend against anxiety arising from failure or guilt is by *projection* of the blame onto someone else. The tennis player who muffs a stroke and looks critically at his racket is engaging in a primitive perceptual projection. On a more profound scale, the person who sees his own hostile impulses as being possessed by *other* people who hate and persecute *him* is also projecting.

The essence of projection is a cognitive distortion of such a nature that attributes that would normally be perceived as attached to or arising out of the self are displaced away from the self toward other objects. We have already seen (p. 315) that there can be such displacements, for instance, of aggression. And we have encountered a practical application of the phenomenon in the projective techniques of personality measurement (p. 635).

The direction of projection is not haphazard; rather it tends to go toward objects whose perceptual properties are already best suited to "fit" the displaced material. Frenkel-Brunswik and Sanford (1945) found, for instance, that extremely rigid and conventionally moralistic college girls, unable to acknowledge their own "unworthy" sexual impulses, tended to project them onto certain "inferior" minority groups, such as lower-class Mexicans and "zoot-suiters." That is, they perceived these "others" as indulging in loose, rampant, and enviable sexuality. This projection served to maintain the girls' self-conception of superior "purity."

It should be stressed that projection is not at all the same thing as a mere tendency to overgeneralize one's own attributes to everyone else. Typically, the projection occurs to the extent that the person is *unaware of the undesirable trait in himself.* This is clearly brought out in an experiment by Sears (1936) in which 97 members of a college fraternity rated each other and themselves on a number of undesirable traits, e.g., stinginess, obstinacy, disorderliness. Some of the men who were rated very high on the undesirable traits by the consensus of their fellows showed little self-insight, rating themselves *low* on the traits; and they exhibited a significant amount of projection of these same traits, rating their fraternity fellows as exceptionally high on them.

Repression. When the person experiences extreme difficulties in recognizing his anxiety-producing impulses or in remembering deeply emotional and traumatic past events, this is termed *repression*. For example, a person with hostile impulses may not realize that he has such impulses; a person who has suffered a mortifying personal failure may be unable to recall the experience.

The *deliberate* suppression of painful feelings or recollections is a very commonplace affair, but this is not repression. Repression is not deliberate, but somehow occurs "automatically" as a reaction in certain situations of conflict.

Repression is assumed to be more than forgetting. In support of this view is the observation that some experiences seem to be so deeply repressed that intensive psychotherapy, hypnosis, or treatment by drugs may be required to recover the "lost" material. Moreover, there may be difficulty not only in reinstating memory of the painful events themselves; the repression may also extend to neutral events that were associated with the traumatic event. In cases of *amnesia*, for example, a person suffering an emotional crisis may not only "forget" the conflict besetting him, but also everything that reminds him of it, including his own name and identity. And when the amnesia attack begins to wear off, the memories that first return are those most remote from the precipitating emotional crisis. For these reasons repression has been termed a "motivated forgetting."

The precise nature of the processes underlying repression is still a considerable mystery. Laboratory experiments on the phenomenon are not easily carried out. The principal evidence for it rests upon a large body of clinical observation by psychiatrists and others.

If repression were a simple matter of "blotting out" the conflict and all its attendant anxieties, it would, of course, be the "ideal" defensive reaction. But this does not seem to happen. The relief from anxiety "bought" by repression is "paid for" in other ways—for example, in reaction-formation.

Reaction-Formation. Repression of strong impulses, for instance sexual and hostile impulses, is often accompanied by a counteracting tendency that takes the form of behavior and feelings exactly *opposed* to the repressed tendencies. This is known as *reaction-formation*. Thus, a fanatical crusader against vice may have become "that way" because he is driven by his own impulses toward the very "sinful" activities he denounces. It has been suggested that excessive manifestations of concern for the child may mask the mother's repressed hostility toward him; extreme politeness toward a person may really mean concealed disdain; bravado, hidden fear.

Reaction-formation can be regarded as a particularly powerful defense mechanism inasmuch as it serves to remove the individual most effectively from the very activities in which he is basically most vulnerable to anxiety. On the other hand, it is also likely to have dangerous social consequences because of the irrational intensity of the reaction.

Knowing about the phenomenon of reaction-formation, it would be easy for Mr. Anyman to come to develop a thoroughly skeptical attitude toward *all* of people's motives. If things can sometimes mean just the opposite of what they seem on the surface, how can one distinguish the real motivation in any given case? The answer is that reaction-formation, like every defense mechanism, is found only under fairly special circumstances. Most zealous reformers are not secret sinners; most overmaternal mothers are not hiding hatred of their children. One difference is likely to be found in the degree of obvious exaggeration of the behavior. As Shakespeare pithily summed it up, "The lady doth protest too much, methinks." But the intensity of the behavior is not a certain proof of reaction-formation. We must know a great deal about the person and all the attendant circumstances before we can safely interpret an intense feeling or behavior as indicating a reaction-formation. Psychodiagnosis is not a simple matter.

Defensive Identification. The importance of identification in personality development has already been made clear. In addition to its other functions, identification can serve as a defense. The individual may reduce or avoid his anxiety by identifying himself with other persons or groups in such a way that he is protected. For instance, the person who suffers threats of personal failure may counteract these effects by identifying himself with the successes of others.

Moreover, external threats to self are likely to be reduced to the extent that the person can perceive the threat as aimed not solely at himself but at the larger group with which he identifies. It is a common observation that individuals undertake antisocial actions, or actions for which they fear reprisals, more easily in groups than when acting alone. It is not merely that the person feels stronger in the group than when alone; it is even more that his sense of guilt or anxiety is diluted.

As with the other mechanisms of defense, identification may have greater or lesser adjustive value depending upon circumstances. To the extent that the identification permits the person to gain a sense of confidence, it is likely to help him in his further adjustments. On the other hand, excessive reliance on identifications may hinder his coping with his problems.

A great many identifications are entirely removed from reality—the identification of the insecure child with the great athlete, of the movie-goer with the "glamorous" star, etc. Much of such identification occurs in a world of fantasy. There are also many identifications with antisocial persons or groups, and these, though serving an immediate defensive purpose, may in the long run lead to even more serious adjustmental difficulties.

IDENTIFICATION WITH THE AGGRESSOR. Paradoxically, there can be defensive identification with the very individual or group that threatens the person. Such "identification with the aggressor," as it has been called, serves to transform the person from the one threatened to the one making the threat. Wishing on her birthday cake, four-year-old Lila was overheard to say in reference to her six-year-old brother, "I wish I were Paul so that I could beat up on Lila." How far such defensive identification with the aggressor can go under severe stress is indicated by Bettelheim (1943) in his reports of how some prisoners in German concentration camps finally came to identify with the Gestapo guards:

"The identifications with the Gestapo did not stop with the copying of their outer appearance and behavior. Old prisoners accepted their goals and values too. . . . It was appalling to see how far formerly well-educated prisoners would go in this identification."

Fantasy. We often find in the realm of fantasy and daydreams ways of maintaining our self-esteem and defending ourselves against various threats and anxieties. We "see" ourselves achieving great successes, engaging in heroic acts, confounding our critics who "laughed as we sat down at the piano," triumphantly vindicating ourselves from accusations of guilty conduct.

Though fantasies tend to take a self-enhancing and self-defensive course, there are also "bad" fantasies. A person may engage in prolonged "morbid introspection" on his shortcomings and difficulties, often more imagined than real.

Fantasy in mild doses serves an adjustive function in that it may permit anxiety to dispel, enabling the person to try again to cope with his problem. But a steady diet of fantasy is likely to have serious repercussions on one's adjustment, for it takes one away from the realities of the situation and provides a spurious and transient feeling of "success." There are constant reality-pressures stemming from the objective world which challenge the fantasies, and the rude awakening to reality can be exceedingly painful.

DREAMS. The forces of external reality are at their minimum strength when we sleep (see Box 160). It follows that nocturnal dreams are likely to give fullest scope to the tendencies of defensive wish-fulfillment. But there is also the fact that when a person is asleep his normal defenses cannot operate with their customary power, and this may permit intrusion into the drama of all sorts of anxiety-provoking influences. For this reason, as Freud and others have argued, the dream may provide a specially revealing source of repressed anxieties and conflicts.

Withdrawal. Insofar as fantasy serves to remove a person from the realities of a situation, it can be regarded as a kind of *withdrawal* reaction. There are various more extreme forms of withdrawal reactions.

Withdrawal is perhaps the most insidious of all defense mechanisms. In the other defensive reactions the individual remains more or less within the conflict situation, seeking through rationalization to adjust himself to it, warding off dangerous thoughts and feelings through repression. But in withdrawal reactions the person "gives up" and avoids the conflict situation altogether. This means that he excludes the possibility of an effective solution to the problem.

The most obvious form of withdrawal is actually to remove oneself from situations where the conflict is likely to occur. The student may leave college because he feels he can no longer face the fear of academic failure; the man may desert his family.

SECLUSION. In the case of deep-seated conflicts pertaining to basic self-conceptions the range of situations capable of arousing conflict feelings is very wide. As the individual gradually withdraws from all such potential situations—especially those involving people—he is driven into a state of seclusiveness and isolation, often becoming excessively shy and timid. Although this may serve the more immediate purpose of reducing conflicts, its detrimental effects on the larger life-adjustments of the person are obvious.

APATHY. Frequently the person is required by circumstances to remain in the actual situation that is engendering the conflict—the child is forced to go on with school even though he may feel completely inadequate, the incompatible husband and wife go on living together for the sake of the children. What may happen under these circumstances is a kind of "encapsulation," that is, the building up of a wall around the person which cuts him off from the impact of the actual situation.

This often results in a condition of *apathy*. The child sits listlessly in the schoolroom; the husband and wife fall into a routine of bored inaction, he reading his newspaper while she does her silent knit-

BOX 160

The Dream World

A substantial portion of our lives is spent in the dream world, a world that bears many resemblances to the waking world, but also differs from it in striking respects. Though our nocturnal dreams are composed of the same cognitive elements that occur in our waking fantasies, our day dreams, they often involve bizarre combinations and weird transformations of these familiar elements. The expressive, dynamic, and physiognomic qualities of things are accentuated or exaggerated, and these are often the most salient aspects of our recollection of dreams upon awakening. We were "escaping from something horrible," but cannot remember exactly what it was. We may fill in the concrete details as we recount the dream—a form of "creative forgetting" discussed earlier (p. 423).

But dreams are not of a basically different "stuff" from other mental experiences. They are—like all other complex mental experiences—organizations of the person's *percepts, thoughts, feelings.* And the general principles of organization are the same as for the waking forms of mental life. We see this in connection with studies of the determinants of dream structure and contents.

As to the *perceptual* side, for instance, many experimental studies have shown that the nature of a dream is greatly influenced by the immediate external stimuli playing upon the sleeper: attaching a piece of adhesive tape to the cheek of the sleeping person may evoke a dream of being kissed; tipping the bed slightly may produce a dream of falling from an airplane.

As to the *cognitive* side, there is ample evidence that what the person has been thinking about shortly before going to sleep tends to play a significant role in governing the dream contents. One study of nightmares, for instance, showed that the majority of them had obvious reference to pressing problems that the person had experienced during the day.

It has been especially in connection with the *motivational* and *emotional* side that

Freud's theoretical contributions have been so influential. In his classic work, *The Interpretation of Dreams,* first published in 1900, he proposed the important distinction between the *manifest* content of dreams, that is, the literal meanings of the dream images, and the *latent* content, that is, the "hidden" meanings, pertaining to repressed impulses, sexual and otherwise. Thus, Freud conceived of dreams as mainly "wish fulfilling" in function. The manifest content of the dream takes a form that permits a symbolic gratification of the repressed desires and impulses, and the manifest form is innocuous in its outward meaning and thus does not "threaten the ego defenses" of the dreamer in such a way as to awaken him.

In short, the dream requires interpretation, for the manifest content merely symbolizes and to some degree "disguises" the underlying dynamic meaning.

Such symbolization follows the basic principles governing all cognitive processes. It is, for example, the fact that there are certain commonly shared physiognomic properties of the thing in both the manifest and the latent dream contents that makes the symbolization possible. An example is the not uncommon symbolization of sexual intercourse as "climbing stairs."

However, it should be strongly stressed that there is no justification for the popular view that there is a necessary or *fixed* symbolic meaning to concrete dream images. "Climbing stairs" may symbolize entirely different motives from the sexual ones— e.g., desires for promotion in one's job, etc. —or may symbolize nothing at all. For, to repeat, the specific form taken by a given dream depends upon the synthesis of *all* the factors operating at the moment—immediate physical stimuli and recent patterns of thoughts, as well as underlying emotional and motivational tendencies.

FREUD, S. 1933. *The interpretation of dreams.* (Trans. by A. A. Brill). New York: Macmillan.

ting. Sometimes what is apparently extreme apathy in a person may really come from the fact that he is burdened with conflict, for instance, the outward "laziness" of some groups of people who live under conditions of excessive deprivation.

NEGATIVISM. A generalized withdrawal, or giving up, may have another significant effect on the person's behavior. He may come to develop bitter negativistic attitudes toward everyone and everything. It is as though he can only rationalize his own defeat by cynicism and defeatism—he has failed because nothing is any good anyway.

Generalizations About Defense Mechanisms. 1. The various defense mechanisms we have just reviewed are common to everyone. As with any form of behavior, they become symptoms of abnormality only when they occur in a person in excessive amounts.

2. The mechanisms are not consciously selected and exercised by the individual. That is, he does not *decide* to repress or rationalize or project. The particular pattern of defensive behavior that occurs is an "automatic" outcome of the total set of psychological factors working in the given situation—the processes of perception, motivation, and learning.

3. Which particular mechanism operates at a given moment depends upon the nature of the specific situation and upon characteristics of the given person. For example, some situations lend themselves more readily to rationalization, others to withdrawal, etc. Moreover, the same situation may call forth quite different defensive reactions in different people. There are large individual differences in the thresholds for elicitation of the various mechanisms.

4. The pattern of mechanisms most readily evoked in a given individual constitutes a distinctive aspect of his unique personality. This characteristic organization of adjustment tendencies is, presumably, learned and gradually fixated in the individual as he develops. The mechanisms found most successful in handling past conflicts tend to be the ones exhibited in future conflicts.

5. The defense mechanisms may have both beneficial and detrimental effects for the person's adjustment (as we noted in Chapter 11 was the case concerning the direct consequences of frustration). They are beneficial in allaying anxiety and maintaining and enhancing self-esteem, which in turn helps to protect the individual against future threats and anxieties. As a consequence of this protection the person may be able to withstand conflict long enough to bring about a more realistic and effective adjustment to the problem. But the long-run effects of prolonged and excessive occurence of defense mechanisms may be detrimental to proper life-adjustment. In this respect some of the mechanisms are "worse" than others—withdrawal prevents the person from ever being able to cope with the problem, repression may blind him to the nature of the problem.

6. Aside from purely adjustmental implications, defensive behavior may often have incidental value for the person and for society. Creative work may stem from the person's being forced into fantasy; the search for convincing rationalizations may produce insightful reorganizations of problems. Indeed, it has been argued that many systems of philosophical, social, political, economic, and religious thought are elaborate rationalizations of the personality conflicts of their creators. But even if this argument is valid, the systems of thought so created may have intrinsic merit.

7. The defensive mechanisms may themselves be frustrated! The rationalization may be disproved, the identification repudiated, the withdrawal prevented, the repression revealed. And this means that the

conflicts become even further intensified.

8. When the defensive mechanisms are not, for whatever reason, adequate to allay the anxiety, much more drastic upheavals of behavior may occur. These take the form of severe psychological disturbances, breakdowns of the self, acute mental disorders of various kinds. To these phenomena we now turn.

Mental Disorders

On the basis of a study of statistical trends it has been estimated (Goldhamer and Marshall, 1953) that *one out of every ten* persons born in the United States today will at some time during his life be hospitalized for mental illness. At present about half of all hospital beds in the United States are occupied by persons with mental illness. In addition there are a large number of people with mental disturbances that are not severe enough to require hospital care, yet are sufficiently severe to interfere significantly with their life-adjustment. It has been suggested by several surveys that upward of 30 per cent of the population may be so affected.

Two Classes of Mental Disorders. There are two main classes of mental disorders. The milder is called *psychoneurosis;* the more severe, *psychosis.* It is not entirely clear whether these two classes are qualitatively different, as are two entirely different physical diseases, or whether they merely differ in degree of deviation from normality, with psychoneuroses shading into psychoses.

In comparing the two, it may be said that the psychoneurotic person shows less severe cognitive, emotional, and behavioral disturbances; rarely loses his orientation to his environment; remains more or less in contact with reality; has some insight into the nature of his behavior; is unlikely to behave in ways actually dangerous to himself or to others; and only rarely requires hospitalization. The psychotic person, on the other hand, shows far more severe cognitive, emotional, and behavioral disturbances; may suffer hallucinations and delusions; tends to lack insight into his behavior; may be completely disoriented in his environment and out of touch with reality; may engage in extremely deviant and sometimes dangerous actions; and is generally so incapacitated in social functioning as to require at least temporary hospitalization.

Psychoneuroses. In general, psychoneuroses (often called simply *neuroses*) are disturbances in which the person's conflicts are not adequately handled by the various defense mechanisms, with the result that he becomes overwhelmed by anxiety and unable to cope effectively with his problems and his everyday life. As White (1948) has put it, ". . . the core of the neurosis lies at the point where anxiety has blocked or distorted the learning process so that new learning essential to adjustment cannot take place."

In earlier practice it was customary to classify psychoneurotic persons into a number of different types, on the assumption that the different patterns of symptoms exhibited represented separate disorders. It now seems doubtful, however, that such a psychoneurotic typology is valid. The neurotic person's symptoms may shift from time to time, even though his underlying problem remains the same. There are, indeed, "fashions" in symptoms; the hysterical blindnesses and paralyses common at one time are much rarer today.

There is still value, nevertheless, in some classification of the behavioral symptoms found in the psychoneurotic person. It is highly likely that the specific form taken by behavioral and mental disturbances tells us something about the nature of the individual and of his problems, just as the characteristic pattern of defense mechanisms in the individual tells us something about his personality. Some of the generally recognized forms of psychoneurotic reactions are:

ANXIETY REACTIONS. These are characterized by generalized and persistent feelings of intense anxiety, often accompanied by such bodily effects as tenseness, palpitation of the heart, sweating, nausea.

PHOBIC REACTIONS. These are characterized by excessive and groundless fears of external objects and conditions. The specific form taken may vary widely—fear of closed places (claustrophobia), fear of heights, fear of animals, fear of darkness, fear of contamination by germs.

OBSESSIVE-COMPULSIVE REACTIONS. These are characterized by obsessive and unavoidable thoughts, often unpleasant and unwelcome to the person, and by compulsive irrational acts, which follow from irresistible urges. The person's obsessive thoughts may have to do with fear that he is "losing his mind," that his child is "going to have an accident," or with the persistent idea that he is "going to strike someone," or with insistent thoughts of an erotic nature. The compulsive acts frequently take the form of repetitive ritualistic behavior, such as highly routinized ways of moving, dressing, or eating. The compulsive act often appears to be a "magic" way of warding off the unpleasant obsessive thought. An adolescent boy, for example, was characterized by a neurotic compulsion to wash himself repeatedly during the day, spending much time in a series of acts relating to body cleanliness. Investigation indicated that he suffered obsessive guilt feelings, stemming from masturbation, which he regarded as "unclean."

NEURASTHENIC REACTIONS. These are characterized by chronic physical and mental fatigue, general listlessness and inability to concentrate, tendency to arise in the morning feeling tired and dispirited despite long sleep. There may be other hypochondriacal complaints as well. It is notable that the fatigue becomes most marked when the neurotic person is faced with an unpleasant task or conflict situation, and may evaporate when he turns to pleasurable pursuits.

CONVERSION REACTIONS. These are characterized by the appearance of incapacitating bodily ailments, such as blindness, loss of sensitivity of parts of the body, and paralysis of the limbs. The ailments tend to be of such a nature as to protect the individual from having to face his anxiety-inducing conflicts. There is, so to say, a *conversion* of the anxiety into the form of the physical symptoms that allow the person to avoid or reduce the anxiety. For example, a battle-shocked soldier suffering acute anxiety finds that his arm is paralyzed and he cannot hold a rifle. It is not a case of malingering; the soldier is actually unable to move his arm. Yet the disorder will disappear completely when the conflict is resolved.

Psychoses. The problem of classifying the psychoses is complicated by the fact that some psychoses are said to be *organic*, that is, originating in identifiable bodily disease or defect; whereas others are thought to be *functional*, that is, originating in the psychological problems of the individual. (However, as we shall see presently, even the distinction between organic and functional is by no means clear-cut.)

The three main classes of functional psychoses are the *manic-depressive reactions*, the *schizophrenic reactions*, and the *paranoid reactions*.

MANIC-DEPRESSIVE REACTIONS. These disorders are characterized by extreme fluctuations in mood states. For instance, the person may shift from normal moods to excessive elation, and with this going too far he may explode into violent and unrestrained behavior, sometimes dangerous to other people or to himself (thus the popular term "maniac"). Conversely, the person may shift from normal mood states to extreme depression, sometimes of suicidal intensity, sometimes so deep that he is thrown into a condition of bodily immobility. Some psychotic persons show alternations of extreme elation and depression; others may have only periodic depressions, or only periodic manic states.

SCHIZOPHRENIC REACTIONS. This most prevalent of all psychoses is characterized by a wide variety of symptoms, not all found in any one schizophrenic person. In general, there appears to be a peculiar distortion of the emotions and feelings of the person; he may become apparently completely insensitive to things that would normally be expected to evoke emotional response, such as news of the death of a member of the family. His standards of conduct, dress, social relations, may show severe deterioration. He may become excessively withdrawn, out of all touch with the external world, even to the point where he may sit completely immobile for hours, during which his limbs can be moved about by someone else and will remain in the positions in which they are placed. He may often be subject to hallucinations (see p. 46) in which he "hears voices" or "sees visions." He may exhibit bizarre behavior, confused thought processes, chaotic speech.

PARANOID REACTIONS. This form of psychosis is characterized by serious delusions (that is, false beliefs) in the person. The delusions are usually organized into a systematic and "logical" whole. This tends to make them strongly impervious to rational disproof by other people and to the logic of contradictory evidence.

The delusions may take many specific forms. Most common are *delusions of persecution* and *delusion of grandeur*. In the former the paranoid person constructs an elaborate delusional edifice "proving" that people are "out to get him," that his enemies are everywhere, that his food is poisoned, that invisible deadly "rays" are being showered on him by people who pass innocently by. It can readily be appreciated how difficult a job the paranoid's family and friends, as well as his psychotherapist, will have in convincing him that they, too, are not in the "plot."

Delusions of grandeur, such as the person's belief that he is Napoleon or the Messiah, may be the product of a "logical" extension of paranoid thinking from the delusion that he is being persecuted. "For why," he may ask himself, "are they persecuting me? It must be that I am a very important and powerful person, whom they fear! I am the Messiah!" (Q.E.D.)

The paranoid person is likely to show much less general behavioral deterioration than a person with other psychoses. He is often perfectly able to carry on his affairs successfully at home and in business and to avoid hospitalization. He may, of course, be succeeding at the expense of damage to his family and associates, and occasionally, in cases of extreme paranoia, he may resort to murderous action against his "persecutors."

ORGANIC PSYCHOSES. A great many varieties of psychotic behavior are specifically connected with deterioration of the brain and nervous system due to accident or disease. Some of the more important organic factors are syphilitic invasion of brain tissue, brain tumors, degeneration of nerve tissue in senility, excessive uses of alcohol and drugs.

Causes of Mental Illness. We are still far from an understanding of the causes of mental illness. The psychological processes are extremely complex, and their physiological bases are but dimly understood. The origins of the disorders may lie in remote and relatively inaccessible life experiences of the patient and in subtle biochemical and neural disturbances. To carry out controlled study on the genesis, development, and change of mental illness presents the most formidable of research problems.

We can briefly review some of the suggestions about causation which come from work on hereditary determinants, physiological and organic determinants, and life-history determinants.

HEREDITARY DETERMINANTS. The notion that "insanity is inherited" has long been popular. But the belief has been based on uncritical acceptance of "evidence" that several members of the same family have mental illness. The actual incidence of mental disease in families is very difficult to ascertain, and even where there are clear indications of multiple cases of mental disorder in a family group, there is usually no way to disentangle the effects of similar environment from those of similar heredity.

As we saw earlier (p. 574), one approach to this problem is to compare the degree of resemblance between identical twins with that between fraternal twins. In such a study by Kallmann (1953) it was reported that if one identical twin had schizophrenia, in 86 per cent of the cases the other twin also had it, whereas if one fraternal twin had schizophrenia, it occurred also in his twin in only 14 per cent of the cases.

Somewhat the same picture has been reported for other psychoses, and perhaps even for psychoneurotic tendencies.

There would thus seem to be support for the idea that *susceptibility* to mental illnesses may be markedly influenced by innate genetic constitution. But to what extent and just how such genetic factors work is entirely unknown.

PHYSIOLOGICAL DETERMINANTS. Aside from the organic psychoses—which by definition are those based on pathological conditions in the brain and nervous system—there is the critical question of the physiological concomitants of the so-called "functional" psychoses.

Most of the research on this question has centered on the possibility that there are special biochemical elements in the psychotic individual, resulting from genetic or other causes, that somehow have the effect of producing the mental disorder. For instance, injection of a form of lysergic acid into a normal person may produce hallucinatory experiencs akin to those found in schizophrenia (Hoch, 1955). Moreover, some drugs that neutralize lysergic acid have given indication that they can reduce schizophrenic reactions. Some very recent studies appear to show that if blood serum taken from a schizophrenic patient is injected into the blood stream of a normal person, the normal person may temporarily manifest some schizophrenic symptoms. But the interpretation of all such biochemical studies is at present highly conjectural.

LIFE-HISTORY DETERMINANTS. Extensive studies have been made of the life histories of mentally disturbed persons as compared with normal persons. Many differences have been found, especially concerning family experiences during childhood. There is significantly greater incidence among the mentally ill of the kinds of faulty relationships with parents that we reviewed in the last chapter—overdomination, brutal discipline, lack of affection. Poor home and social environments in childhood—broken homes, marital discord, poverty, slum neighborhoods, psychosis or neurosis in parents or other members of the family—

are also much more frequent in the backgrounds of the mentally ill. There also appears to be a childhood history of more severe physical illness in the mentally disturbed persons than in normal persons. Traumatic emotional events of various kinds—traumas having to do with sexual assault by adults, physical beatings, death of loved parents at critical periods in development—tend to be found often in the childhood histories of the mentally ill.

But the interpretation of such findings is not easy. Traumatic events are far from universal in the histories of the mentally ill, and even more striking is the fact that a great many of these deleterious circumstances can be found in the life histories of persons who prove to be entirely normal or even superior in achievement and adjustment. Most of the time psychiatrists deal with abnormal people, but if for research purposes they come to look at the life histories of perfectly normal people, they find widespread incidence among them of just the factors that they have "found" as predisposing factors in the histories of the mentally ill. That a man who was raised in the slums, rejected by his parents, and beset by physical illness, turns out mentally ill, may not surprise us; but what about another man raised in the same unfavorable circumstances who turns out to be perfectly normal? Perhaps we must search for an unknown x factor that makes the difference in the two men. The nature of such a mysterious x factor might ultimately prove to be hereditary or organic; or it might prove to relate to some vital aspect of psychological development that is as yet wholly unsuspected.

INTERACTION OF DETERMINANTS. Doubtless whatever the principal determinants are found to be, there will also be found a complex *interaction* among them. The extent to which hereditary predispositions toward mental disorder actually produce mental disorder will be partly determined by the particular experiences of the individual. The extent to which life-history factors operate will depend upon the physiological factors characteristic of the person. And there is "feedback" of one kind of effect on others. Thus, the person who shows signs of mental disorder may be responded to by other people in ways that serve to accentuate the disorder; failures of adjustment by the emotionally incapacitated person will make the original conflicts even more intensified and disruptive.

Psychotherapy and Mental Health

The psychological treatment of mental disorders is called *psychotherapy*. Psychotherapists are of several different kinds. The *psychiatrist* is an M.D., specializing in mental disease. Some psychiatrists are known as *psychoanalysts*, having been trained in methods of therapy developed by Freud. *Clinical psychologists* are not medically trained, but customarily are Ph.D.'s in psychology. Certain kinds of *social workers*, especially trained in psychiatric problems, also participate in some aspects of psychotherapy. This profusion of kinds of experts treating mental disease tends to confuse the layman, but it is natural since mental disorders are of many different kinds and are related to medical, psychological, and sociological factors. Thus, these various specialities are all required for therapy, and whenever possible there is a coordination of the efforts of all these experts in dealing with patients.

Mr. Anyman, too, is frequently cast into the role of a psychotherapist. He listens sympathetically to the emotional outpourings of his troubled friend, offers advice, arranges for his friend to take a needed vacation or to change a job to which he is ill-suited, does his best to make the friend feel loved and appreciated; he may even dispense "medicine" in the form of a regular "night-cap" that allays the friend's intense anxiety and provides a good sleep. These are all elements in the more professional practice of psychotherapy.

The techniques of psychotherapy vary widely, partly because there are different prevailing theories about the nature and cause of mental disorders and about the proper method of treating them, and partly because the techniques used depend upon the particular kind and severity of disorder, and the particular circumstances of the individual. We shall briefly review some of the more important techniques of psychotherapy—counseling, client-centered therapy, psychoanalytic therapy.

Counseling. For the milder psychological maladjustments, such as worries and confusions arising in connection with marital discord, job difficulties, school problems, academic failure, and the like, psychological *counseling* is often most suitable. The aim is to provide help to the person in seeing what the sources of his difficulties are, and to give guidance toward ways of solving the problems, or at least of becoming able to cope with them without being disrupted emotionally by them. Almost everyone has experienced such counseling, by professional counselors or by others less professional, and its general nature is well known.

Counseling is not mere giving of *advice,* for "advice is cheap." What counts is the ability of the counselor to ascertain what the person's problem really is, and what kind of "information" is likely to get the person himself to see what he should do. Often, the real problem besetting the person is not what he comes to the counselor

about, and only gradually during the counseling process may he become aware of what is basically troubling him. Sometimes the counseling goes beyond the person himself; the counselor may talk to the marriage partner, or to the parents, or to work associates, in an effort to improve the interpersonal situations experienced by the person. Indeed, it is often the case that the individual who comes for counseling is not the one who most needs help; the source of his disturbance may be in the emotional problems of his family members or associates rather than in himself.

Nor is counseling merely the providing of *reassurance* to the person. To help the person regain self-confidence is, of course, often vital, but superficial assurance may simply serve temporarily to strengthen the person's inadequate modes of adjustment. Clearly the disturbed person will seek out the very kind of advice and reassurance that he wants to get, but such advice and reassurance may be "wrong" for the correction of his ills.

Client-Centered Therapy. The importance of enabling the person himself to come to achieve insight on his own problems and on the proper remedial action is stressed in *client-centered therapy,* originally developed by Carl Rogers (1951) at the University of Chicago. In this method the patient (client) takes the primary role in the psychotherapy. The patient is encouraged to do most of the talking. The therapist assumes the role of a sympathetic "reflector," enabling the patient to keep talking, and—from time to time—summarizing what has been said in order to *clarify* the patient's feelings but not to judge or explain them. It is for this reason that the method is labelled *non-directive.*

The basic assumption underlying this approach is that the person is fully capable of coming, through ventilation of his feelings, to see what his problems are and what might be done about them. The aim of the therapist is to provide the right interpersonal "atmosphere" to facilitate this process of self-insight.

Obviously the method requires great skill by the therapist, in avoiding the temptation of authoritative advice-giving (of being "directive"). The therapeutic sessions usually occur for an hour once or twice weekly; the pace of the therapy is largely dictated by the patient.

Criticism made of the method has argued that it can deal only with superficial aspects of mild adjustmental problems, not with deep-seated conflicts. However, the merits of this criticism are undecided, owing largely to the difficulties in objective evaluation of therapeutic success (see below).

Psychoanalytic Therapy. Freudian psychoanalysis, as we have previously mentioned, is not only a theory of personality, but also a method of treating psychological disturbances.

The therapy is based on Freud's conceptions of the primary role of early childhood experiences in the establishing of the seeds of lifelong conflicts and disturbances, and on his conception of the unconscious manner in which much of the individual's behavior is governed.

FREE ASSOCIATION. In light of these two conceptions, psychoanalysts devote their main efforts toward the uncovering of deep-hidden, "repressed" dynamics in the person, and the tracing of these back to their origins in the person's childhood. The main method is that of *free association*. The patient is urged to talk freely about whatever comes into his mind, regardless of how trivial, stupid, or shameful it seems, and to let this flow of thoughts take whatever course his free associations may dictate. (The process is thought to be facili-

tated by having the patient relax on a couch.) It is assumed that the free associations may reflect relationships and conflicts of which the person is unaware, and the psychoanalyst's aim is to search among these associations for hidden meanings, which gradually become clearer and clearer as the person repeatedly reflects these basic themes.

The process is regarded as necessarily a very long one. A psychoanalysis may involve spending four or five 50-minute sessions a week in the psychoanalyst's office, over a period of many months or even of several years.

TRANSFERENCE. It is also assumed that important changes may gradually take place in the individual as the interpersonal relation with the psychoanalyst continues. Particularly there is the phenomenon of *transference* in which the person is said to transfer his unconscious emotional feelings, positive and negative, from other objects or people to the psychoanalyst himself. Through this means, it is felt, there is greater opportunity for the feelings to become consciously manifest and open to discussion and analysis. This transference process is regarded as the very core of the therapy, and makes possible the emotional re-education of the person: ". . . the pathological effect of earlier emotional experiences is corrected by exposing the patient to the same type of emotional conflicts in the therapeutic situation. The therapist, however, reacts differently, not as the parents, teachers, relatives, or friends in the past. This difference between the therapist's reaction and the original parental reactions is the most fundamental therapeutic factor" (Alexander, 1946).

Thus in the course of a successful analysis the patient is presumably able, through free association and the questions and interpretations of the analyst, to gain insight into repressed feelings and conflicts, to modify emotional attitudes, and to get free of disabling symptoms.

There are, it should be added, many varieties of psychoanalytic therapy, reflecting the many revisions of Freudian theorizing by others. Although originally psychoanalysis was restricted largely to the treatment of neurotics, it is now also applied to the treatment of some psychotics, and even to groups as well as to individuals.

Special Techniques in Psychotherapy. Client-centered counseling and psychoanalysis are the two main forms of psychotherapy. Certain other special techniques are often used in conjunction with them.

GROUP THERAPY. Patients with somewhat similar neurotic complaints may be treated in groups rather than singly. They meet and discuss their problems under the guidance of a psychotherapist. Thus the therapist is able to handle more patients, and the method also has the advantage that people in groups will often find emotional support from the other members, especially when they find that they are not alone in their "peculiar" difficulties. This is, of course, one of the basic reasons for the success of Alcoholics Anonymous.

PSYCHODRAMA. The group therapy method may include the acting out of roles, fantasies, and problem situations by the patients in little playlets. It has been found that such *psychodramas* (Moreno, 1946) often serve to release pent-up feelings through effectively reactivating the kind of real-life problem situation besetting the person.

PLAY THERAPY. An effective method of therapy with children is to encourage the child to play with toys and other materials in the presence of the therapist. A wide range of play materials is provided, including objects that can be smashed, paints that can be smeared, dolls that can be set up in miniatures of real-life family situations. In using this approach, the assumption is made that the child tends to express his emotional problems in his manner of play. The therapist makes opportune uses of this emotional release to enter into a favorable interpersonal relationship with the child, and to proceed—either more directively or less directively—to aid in resolving his conflicts.

HYPNOTHERAPY. *Hypnosis* of the patient as an aid to psychotherapy has a long history, and its use in this connection seems to have been growing recently. (See Box 161).

Physical Treatments of Mental Illness. In addition to the more strictly psychological therapies that we have described, there are, of course, those involving the use of drugs and other physiological methods of a medical nature. For a long time, severely disturbed hospitalized patients (especially the mentally depressed) have been given *shock therapy*. This includes the administering of insulin or of electric current sufficient to cause brief convulsive seizures and subsequent periods of lucidity. The purpose is to bring the patient for a short while into a state of mental clarity and greater contact with reality, so that the therapist can communicate with him. This method is fast being supplanted, however, by the more recent and highly promising methods of administration of "tranquilizing" and other drugs. (see Box 76, p. 333, and Box 162).

There are also far more drastic methods of psychosurgery, used in cases of certain long-standing psychoses, especially those involving deep chronic anxiety. One example is the operation known as *prefrontal lobotomy*. Nerve fibers are cut between the frontal lobes of the cortex and the thalamic regions that are important in arousal and control of emotions (see Chap. 12, p. 333). Such operations have had success in reducing the anxiety, some-

BOX 161

Hypnosis and Hypnotherapy

The phenomena of *hypnosis*—a topic of considerable popular interest, and often misconception—have been the subject of a great deal of theoretical speculation and controversy. Briefly stated, the main facts as determined by psychological investigation are as follows:

1. Induction of a hypnotic state, or trance, requires the assent and cooperation of the person. Generally speaking, he cannot be hypnotized "against his will."

2. Almost everyone can be hypnotized under some circumstances. But there are great individual differences in susceptibility.

3. The effects produced in a hypnotic state do not flow from the "power" of the hypnotist; they are the result of operation of psychological processes in the person himself. The hypnotist may, of course, play a crucial role in giving various suggestions with which the person seeks to comply.

4. Various pronounced changes in behavior can be produced by such hynotic suggestion. For instance, the person can be induced to withstand extremely painful stimulation without apparent signs of feeling the pain, as witness the successful use of hypnosis in difficult childbirth and in surgery without anaesthetics. And numerous demonstrations and experiments show that the hypnotized person will follow instructions and convincingly act out roles suggested to him.

5. Yet there are definite limits to what he will do under suggestion. Thus, he may "stab" a friend with a rubber knife after being instructed that the other person is an "enemy." But, if given a steel knife, he will balk at the suggestion. Though the evidence is not absolutely clear on this point, the consensus of expert opinion is that a person cannot be brought by hypnotic suggestion to commit a crime or other act that he regards as immoral or repugnant (unless perhaps his own "normal" inclinations really predispose him that way to begin with.)

In general, then, it appears that hypnotic behavior is a kind of "as if" behavior. The person really knows that the situation is not what the hypnotist suggests it to be, but he is highly susceptible to behaving "as if" it were.

Hypnotherapy. Inasmuch as the hypnotized person does show this far greater readiness to cooperate with the hypnotist's suggestions, it is obvious how the phenomenon may contribute to psychotherapy. In cases where there is severe emotional blockage of the recall of deeply "repressed" material, the recall may sometimes be facilitated by placing the patient in a hypnotic state and instructing him to talk about the problem. This, indeed, was the method with which Freud began his work, but he soon abandoned it in favor of the free association technique.

Such *hypnotherapy* has had success in some cases. For example, in cases of breakdown through combat exhaustion during World War II, hypnosis was sometimes effectively used to help amnesic patients recall the details of their traumatic battle experiences, thus paving the way for treatment.

But hypnotherapy is not a method of therapy in itself. It is merely a therapeutic *aid*, which, by inducing a particularly receptive attitude and emotional state in the patient, may facilitate the progress of the actual psychotherapy that is being conducted.

times permitting discharge of the patients. But the damage to the brain is irreversible and there are many critics who doubt the wisdom and justification for such drastic treatment, especially inasmuch as the objective evaluation of the results of therapy methods is so difficult.

The Effectiveness of Psychotherapy. Many people who suffer incapacitating mental illness and undergo psychotherapy eventually get better. Thus it might appear to be a straightforward matter to ascertain which of the several different kinds of therapies is most effective and just how

BOX 162

"Tranquilizing" Drugs and Psychotherapy

Within the past several years there have been optimistic predictions of sensational new advances to be made in the treatment of mental illness through drugs. These predictions are based particularly on some striking successes in the use of the so-called "tranquilizing" drugs, for instance, reserpine and chlorpromazine (see p. 332).

These drugs have come into sudden and widespread use in mental hospitals, especially in the treatment of schizophrenic patients and those with acute anxieties. Their function in such treatment of mental disturbance is apparently to calm the patient and reduce anxiety thus rendering him more amenable to psychotherapy. Though some remarkable "cures" have been reported, it is far too early for an adequate scientific appraisal of the effects of the drugs—for what disorders they are beneficial, how permanent the benefits are, etc.

By what means these drugs achieve their beneficial effects is also not at all clear. Some indications concerning the possible brain mechanisms have been given previously in our discussion of the hypothalamus and the reticular formation (see p. 332).

Unfortunately, the enthusiasm for these "tranquilizers," as yet unsupported by adequate medical research, has spread to the chronically "tense" general public. More than *30 billion* tablets of one such "tranquilizing" drug were sold in the United States in 1956! Indiscriminate use of these drugs to reduce people's everyday anxieties is a source of alarm to doctors and mental health authorities of the nation.

What is needed is a great deal of research to determine just what the psychological effects of such drugs are, not alone in the treatment of mental disease but in the wider use for the allaying of the emotional stresses and strains common in our "age of anxiety."

---

great its effect is. But as a matter of fact, despite a considerable body of research on evaluating psychotherapy, the issue is still almost entirely unresolved. There are a number of reasons for this:

1. Many mentally ill persons may show recovery *without* any psychotherapy. Some investigators (e.g., Eysenck, 1952) have gone so far as to assert that the recovery rate among the untreated is as good as that among the treated, thus denying any proved value to psychotherapy whatsoever. Other studies, however, do seem to indicate that there are substantial benefits.

2. There is the difficult problem of finding *comparable* groups of treated and untreated among the mentally ill. The fact that some people do seek and get treatment and others do not, itself probably reflects some psychological differences between them.

3. Though there may be temporary improvement after psychotherapy, much of this may be lost after a short time.

4. To compare the relative merits of several different types of psychotherapy is exceedingly difficult because the exact method used by the given therapist may not be identical with another presumably using the "same" method, and because the samples of patients treated by the various therapies may be different.

5. Most difficult of all is the question of what shall constitute the *criterion of improvement* following therapy. Is it that the person stops coming, or that he *says* he feels better, or that his friends and associates report that he gets along better with them, or what?

In general, we must conclude that we do not yet know just how much good psychotherapy does, nor just how it is supposed to work. But, owing to the urgency of the problem, this state of ignorance is not likely to impede the immense and growing use of psychotherapy. What *can* be said with assurance is that the problem of mental illness should best be tackled before it starts. *Preventive* therapy is more likely to help than any amount of attempted cure. And the more we learn about the basic processes of personality development, the more effective can we be in our preventive therapy. For mental illness, no matter how defined, reflects a disturbance in personality development.

Glossary

amnesia. Loss of memory, sometimes so complete as to include forgetting of own identity. Often results from a severe emotional upset, and the "repressed" memories are likely to be restored when the conflict subsides.

anxiety reaction. A form of psychoneurosis, characterized by intense "free-floating" feelings of anxiety and accompanied by such bodily signs as tenseness, palpitation of the heart, sweating, etc.

client-centered therapy. One of the main methods of psychotherapy, involving a non-directive approach by the therapist, who provides sympathetic "reflection" of the patient's expressed feelings rather than direct interpretation and evaluation of them. Thus, the patient is encouraged to arrive at his own insights concerning his problems and the proper course of remedial action. The method is primarily associated with the name of Carl Rogers.

conversion reaction. A form of psychoneurosis, characterized by incapacitating bodily ailments, such as blindness, loss of sensitivity of parts of the body, paralysis of the limbs, etc. Presumably the person's anxiety is "converted" into the form of these bodily symptoms, thus making it possible for him to avoid the conflict situation.

counseling. A form of psychotherapy dealing with the milder maladjustments in marriage, vocation, school, etc. Generally more directive than deeper forms of psychotherapy, with the counselor cast more into the role of the expert guide and "information" giver.

defense mechanisms. Various forms of reaction to the anxiety aroused by conflict, which serve to protect and enhance the self-picture. The "mechanisms" are not deliberately chosen by the person. They are common to everyone, and raise serious problems for adjustment only when they occur in excessive amount and thus prevent the person from coping realistically with his difficulties.

defensive identification. A mechanism of defense in which the person avoids threats to self and achieves feelings of success through identifying with powerful and successful persons and groups. May sometimes assume the paradoxical form of identifying with the very persons or groups who are the source of the threats to the individual.

fantasy. Activity of the imagination, as in daydreaming, which tends to be out of full contact with reality. Fantasy often serves as a defense mechanism by giving the person a temporary feeling of having "solved" his problems. Under some circumstances fantasy may, of course, serve a creative function.

free association. The method employed in psychoanalytic therapy, in which the person is encouraged to report freely everything that comes into his mind.

group therapy. A technique of psychotherapy in which groups of patients are treated simultaneously, in group discussions under the supervision of the therapist.

hypnosis. A state of extreme suggestibility during which the person is highly susceptible to the suggestions offered by the hypnotist.

hypnotherapy. A technique sometimes useful as an aid to psychotherapy in which the patient is hypnotized and through suggestion is enabled to recall "repressed" material.

insulation. A defense mechanism involving a "separation of systems"—either cognitive or emotional—such that protective rationalizations can be preserved, and disturbing thoughts and feelings can be cut off.

manic-depressive reaction. One of the main forms of psychosis, characterized by wide swings in mood state, from normal to conditions of excessive elation and violent excited behavior, or from normal to deep depression.

neurasthenic reaction. A form of psychoneurosis characterized by chronic physical and mental fatigue, listlessness, and lack of "will-power." Often accompanied by hypochondriacal complaints.

obsessive-compulsive reaction. A form of psychoneurosis involving insistent and unavoidable thoughts, often unpleasant, and recurrent and irresistible urges. The latter appear to be "ritualistic" ways of escaping from the obsessive thoughts.

paranoid reaction. A form of psychosis characterized by a fixed and highly organized set of delusions, most commonly delusions of persecution or of grandeur.

phobic reaction. A form of psychoneurosis involving intense fears of common objects and situations, e.g., fear of closed places, which the person recognizes as irrational but is unable to overcome.

play therapy. A technique of psychotherapy with children in which the therapist observes the child as he plays with toys and other play materials permitting him freely to express aggression and emotional feelings and conflicts.

prefrontal lobotomy. An operation in which nerve fibers are cut between the frontal lobes and the thalamic areas of the brain, important in the control and expression of emotion. The surgery is intended to relieve the deep chronic anxiety in extremely ill mental patients who have failed to respond to other forms of treatment.

projection. A defense mechanism involving the attribution to other people of impulses and traits that the person has but cannot accept. Especially likely to occur to the extent that the person lacks insight into his own impulses and traits.

psychoanalytic therapy. A principal method of psychotherapy first developed by Freud. It involves long and intensive exploration of the person's conflicts, repressed memories, childhood experiences, etc. The main technique is *free association,* and an essential part of the psychotherapy is the process of *transference,* in which the patient's emotional attitudes toward parents and other people become temporarily attached to the psychoanalyst. Through this means emotional reeducation of the person is achieved.

psychodrama. A technique of psychotherapy in which the patients—alone or in groups—play roles which represent their emotional problems, and in so doing come to gain emotional release and insight.

psychoneurosis. The class of the milder forms of mental illness, usually not requiring hospitalization. The psychoneurotic person retains his orientation to the environment and considerable contact with reality, but suffers disruption of cognitive and emotional processes sufficient to interfere with his effective life-adjustments.

psychosis. The class of the more severe mental diseases, such as schizophrenic reaction, manic-depressive reaction, and paranoid reaction. Involves serious disruptions of cognitive and emotional processes, often necessitating at least temporary hospitalization.

psychotherapy. The psychological treatment of mental disorders, for instance, client-centered therapy and psychoanalytic therapy.

rationalization. A defense mechanism in which the person, through cognitive distortion, finds false but "good reasons" to justify his questionable acts, failure, or unpleasant situation.

reaction-formation. A defense mechanism characterized by the exaggerated expression of behavioral tendencies exactly opposed to the underlying "repressed" impulses of the person.

repression. The inability to recall strongly emotional and anxiety-arousing experiences. Serves as a defensive protection against the anxiety.

role conflict. The simultaneous demand upon the individual to fulfill two or more social roles that are contradictory and incompatible. For instance, the conflicting female roles of homemaker and career-woman.

role diffusion. The experiencing by a person of the requirements of a great many diverse and confusing roles, which—in failing to form a unified pattern—make it difficult for the person, for instance an adolescent, to establish a clear self-identity.

schizophrenic reaction. The most common form of psychosis. Characterized by a wide variety of symptoms, varying from patient to patient, including a marked blunting of emotional sensitivity, hallu-cinatory and delusional experiences, bizarre behavior, depression, withdrawal from full contact with reality, etc.

shock therapy. A psychotherapeutic aid involving the induction of a convulsive seizure in the psychotic patient, through the administration of insulin or electric shock. The result is a temporary period of lucidity during which the therapist can communicate with the patient.

transference. The process, especially important in psychoanalytic therapy, in which the patient comes to transfer his disturbed emotional attitudes toward parents and other important persons in his life and attach them to the psychotherapist. This provides an opportunity for these basic emotional attitudes to be re-educated with the aid of the therapist.

withdrawal. A defense mechanism involving a retreat by the person from the conflict situation. The withdrawal may take the form of actual removal from the situation, or of an apathetic "encapsulation" of the person from contact with the emotion-provoking features of the situation.

Suggestions for Further Reading

CAMERON, N. A. 1947. *Psychology of the behavior disorders.* Boston: Houghton Mifflin.

    A standard textbook of abnormal psychology.

DOLLARD, J., and MILLER, N. E. 1950. *Personality and psychotherapy.* New York: McGraw-Hill.

    A discussion of psychotherapy in terms of learning theory and experiment.

HADLEY, J. M. 1958. *Clinical and counseling psychology.* New York: Alfred A. Knopf.

    A description of counseling techniques useful in the milder adjustmental problems.

McKINNEY, F. 1949. *Psychology of personal adjustment.* (rev. ed.) New York: Wiley.

    A text on the personal adjustment problems of those of college age.

ROGERS, C. R. 1951. *Client-centered therapy.* Boston: Houghton Mifflin.

    An account of the theory and methods of non-directive, client-centered psychotherapy, by its foremost proponent.

SHAFFER, L. F., and SHOBEN, E. J., JR. 1956. *The psychology of adjustment.* (2nd ed.) Boston: Houghton Mifflin.

    A basic text on adjustment, including extensive discussion of the defense mechanisms.

SYMONDS, P. M. 1949. *Dynamic psychology.* New York: Appleton-Century-Crofts.

    A full-fledged treatment of the defense mechanisms.

WHITE, R. W. 1948. *The abnormal personality.* New York: Ronald.

    A thoughtful and well-written textbook of abnormal psychology.

CHAPTER 25

The Individual in Society

EVERY human being is born into a going society. Thus the social environment —people and the products of people —is a significant part of the world to which man responds. The obvious importance of studying man's actions as related to his social environment (his "social behavior") has given rise to a specialized branch of psychology, known as *social psychology*.

The Individual and the Group. The social behavior of man can be studied at two somewhat different levels: (1) the level of the *individual;* (2) the level of *groups* of individuals.

In studying social behavior at the individual level we are mainly concerned with Mr. Anyman's *social perceptions*—how he perceives other people and social events; and with Mr. Anyman's *social attitudes*— his enduring emotional and motivational dispositions with respect to various aspects of his social world.

But instead of being primarily interested in Mr. Anyman's behavior as an individual, we may focus our attention on his behavior as a member of the groups to which he belongs: the family, the fraternal organization, the labor union, the political party, the church. Here we are concerned with questions of how the nature of the group influences the individual's behavior, and how in turn his behavior affects the behavior of the other group members.

Obviously the study of social behavior at the individual level and at the group level cannot be carried on independently. To understand Mr. Anyman's social perceptions, attitudes, and roles, we must know a great deal about the groups to which he belongs; to understand the functioning of groups, we must know a great deal about Mr. Anyman and each of his colleagues individually.

The first part of the chapter, therefore, will concern itself with the individual level of analysis, and the second part with the group level of analysis.

Social Perception

How we perceive the world about us is determined by all the influences which play upon us—physical, physiological, and social (see Part I). Here we might note one important implication of the data reported in the earlier discussion: The isolated individual is a fiction. Whether we study Mr. Anyman in the psychophysicist's laboratory, or in the politician's audience, we are studying Mr. Anyman as a member of society. And his perceptions will reflect that fact. All psychology, in the strict sense, is "social psychology."

In its attempt to understand social perception, therefore, social psychology builds upon the findings of the experimental laboratory. The same general perceptual principles are involved whether we look at a revolving color wheel or at a milling crowd. In either case we have the same perceiver and the same nervous system. This generality of perceptual principles becomes particularly clear when we seek to understand the determinants of our perception of other people.

Perceiving People. We spend a good part of our time observing people in action. We see them at work and at their leisure. We note their appearance, expressive traits, kind acts and thoughtless ones, stupidities and intelligence. All of these observations, taken together, are what we call our "perception" of the person. Such a perception does not consist of a series of discrete and unrelated observations; we integrate the discrete observations into a unified impression of the "complete" personality—even inventing attributes, when necessary, to fill out this complete impression. (See Box 163.)

FIRST IMPRESSIONS. This full impression does not wait for all the "returns" to come in. As soon as we observe anything at all about a person we begin to form an integrated impression. Our "hasty judgments" about people, our "jumping to conclusions," are but reflections of the basic perceptual tendency to organize the stimulus-field. Later observations will be influenced by these very first observations. (See Box 164). It is this which makes "first impressions" so very important in our perceptions and judgments of people's personalities. Here we have another instance of the importance of temporal ordering of the stimulus pattern in perception.

A person as a social object is the source of a host of stimuli for the perceiver. Out of this wealth of stimuli the perceiver selects only the more salient ones upon which he builds his first impression. For some people clothes are the most salient aspects of a person, for others, the physical stature, or the skin coloring, or the mode of speech. The saliency of these various aspects is, in turn, dependent upon the cultural norms and values of the perceiver, and may also reflect his immediate emotional and motivational states as well as his role relationship to the person being perceived. All of this means that the same person may create quite different first impressions in different perceivers. To know what kind of an impression a man will make we must know not only the man, but also his perceiver—and the social relations between the two.

STABILITY OF FIRST IMPRESSIONS. First impressions may become lasting ones, and this is partly due to the process of mutual adjustment which occurs between the perceiver and the perceived. The first impression we have of a person may determine our behavior toward him. The other person will then behave in a way consistent with our own behavior, and this will, in turn, reinforce our initial impression. Thus, if Mr. Anyman perceives a new acquaintance

---

BOX 163

Forming Impressions of Personality

Here are some terms descriptive of a certain person: *energetic, assured, talkative, cold, ironical, inquisitive, persuasive.* What is your impression of this person?

Asch at Brooklyn College posed this question to a large number of college students. He found that the students were readily able to write down a full-bodied impression of the unknown person, with nothing but this series of trait words to go on. For instance, one student wrote the following description:

"He impresses people as being more capable than he really is. He is popular and never ill at ease. Easily becomes the center of attraction at any gathering. He is likely to be a jack-of-all-trades. Although his interests are varied, he is not necessarily well versed in any of them. He possesses a sense of humor. His presence stimulates enthusiasm and very often he does arrive at a position of importance."

Not only are the given trait terms organ-ized to produce a unified picture of the person, but additional traits are created in order to give the picture its full character. Thus, the person is described as possessing a "sense of humor," or as being "not necessarily well versed" in his varied interests. These traits seem to follow from the over-all impression that the original list produced in this particular perceiver, and so they are ascribed to the unknown person.

As Asch summarizes it:

"When a task of this kind is given, a normal adult is capable of responding to the instruction by forming a unified impression. Though he hears a sequence of discrete terms, his resulting impression is not discrete. All subjects . . . of whom there were over 1,000 fulfilled the task in the manner described . . . Starting from the bare terms, the final account is completed and rounded."

ASCH, S. E. 1946. Forming impressions of personality. *J. abnorm. soc. Psych. 41,* 258–90.

---

as being an "important" man, he will behave toward this new acquaintance in a manner appropriate to this perceived role. The acquaintance, noting Mr. Anyman's deference, will tend to play the role expected of him. Because we are dealing with objects (people) which are capable of mutual adjustments, the process of feedback may sometimes "confirm" and stabilize an originally inaccurate perception. And because we frequently strive to live up to others' expectations of us, our very personalities may be shaped by what others *mis*-perceive in us.

STEREOTYPING PEOPLE. People are almost never perceived as isolated individuals. We perceive them as being members of this or that aggregate—as Baptists or Catholics, as Republicans or Democrats, as Egyptians or Englishmen. And when we see a person as a member of a group, the personality we perceive is influenced by what we believe about his group. In other words, our perception of a person is not only determined by the person's own traits, but by the larger *context* within which we perceive him. The part-whole principle (p. 94) and the phenomena of assimilation and contrast (p. 86) operate as much in our perception of personality as in our perception of physical objects. These perceptual principles help us to understand why our judgments of people are so frequently couched in stereotyped terms, and unjust.

For example: Many Americans believe that the Chinese are "inscrutable orientals." When meeting a shy and somewhat bewildered Chinese, we may therefore perceive him as "mysterious and inscrutable." Here we have an instance of the perceived attributes of the individual being affected by his group membership in the direction of

BOX 164

First Impressions Make a Difference

To study the effect of the first piece of information about a person on the manner in which the later impressions of him develop, Kelley performed the following experiment at the Massachusetts Institute of Technology.

Appearing before three sections comprising 55 students of a course numbered Economics 70 Kelley announced: "Your regular instructor is out of town today, and since we of Economics 70 are interested in the general problem of how various classes react to different instructors, we're going to have an instructor today you've never had before . . . Then, at the end of the period, I want you to fill out some forms about him. In order to give you some idea of what he's like, we've had a person who knows him write up a little biographical note about him."

He then passed out mimeographed sheets to the students. One half of the students in each section received a description which included the following sentence: "People who know him consider him to be a rather cold person, industrious, critical, practical and determined." The other half of the students found the following sentence: "People who know him consider him to be a rather warm person, industrious, critical, practical and determined."

The "guest lecturer" then entered the room and led a 20-minute discussion. Records were kept of which students participated in the discussion. After the "guest lecturer" left, the students were asked to write a description of him, and to rate him on 15 different attributes. The ratings given by the two halves of the class differed significantly on a number of dimensions, de-spite the fact that they had all observed the very same man, in the very same performance. Among the differences were the following: The students who had received the "warm" description, tended to rate the lecturer as: Considerate of others; informal; sociable; popular; humorous. The students who had received the "cold" description rated him as: Self-centered; formal; unsociable; unpopular; humorless. It was also found that 56 per cent of the students receiving the "warm" description participated in the class discussion, while only 32 percent of the "cold" students participated.

It seems clear that an initial set toward perceiving the person as "warm" or as "cold," had a marked effect on the subsequent organization of the whole impression of the person, and tended to influence the behavior of the perceiver toward the person.

Of course, not every initial piece of information can exercise such a strong directive force on the developing impression of a person. This has been shown by Asch's studies of the impressions of fictitious persons formed on the basis of lists of adjectives read to the subjects. He found that though "warm" versus "cold" produced large differences in total impressions, adjectives such as "polite" versus "blunt" produced much smaller differential effects. The explanation may be that these latter terms refer to a less central dimension of personality.

KELLEY, H. H. 1950. The warm-cold variable in first impressions of persons. *J. Person., 18,* 431–9.

ASCH, S. E. 1952. *Social Psychology.* New York: Prentice-Hall.

---

assimilation—shyness becomes "inscrutability." Another example: Some Americans believe that Negroes are unintelligent. When such Americans meet a Negro of obvious intellectual achievement, they may tend to *over*estimate his intellectual capacity and see him as an exceptionally bright person. Here we have an instance of the perceived attributes of the individual being affected by his group membership in the direction of *contrast*.

PERSISTENCE OF PERCEPTIONS. The fixity of our impressions of people—even in the face of contradictory evidence—is notorious. Again a review of some basic perceptual principles may help us to understand this characteristic of social perception.

Our perceptions of people can be described as well-structured organizations in which individuals are related to subgroups, and subgroups to larger groups. Such perceptual structures are subject to change, especially if the external stimuli are changed. However it will be remembered that a change in the external stimulus-pattern will often not result in a change in the percept —as is the case in the constancy phenomenon (see p. 142). Changes in the external stimulus-pattern may often result in a separation of the parts of the perceptual fields into isolated fragments rather than in a change of the perceived attributes of the major structure in the field (see p. 112). Let us examine how each of these effects help preserve our original perceptions of people and groups.

1. CONSTANCY. Suppose you believe that the political leaders of a certain foreign nation have a policy of war and aggression, and suppose that you were to listen to one of their diplomats, on the podium of the United Nations, appealing for peace and good will. Under these conditions you may "perceive" all kinds of indications of insincerity in his speech, "cynical smiles," a "sneering tone," etc. You will interpret what you hear as "diplomatic doubletalk" and your original perception of him as an aggressive war-like person will remain unchanged. An external stimulus pattern (his appeal for peace and good will) which is inconsistent with a well-established prior percept has been so absorbed as to permit a constant perception of the diplomat to remain. (See Box 165.)

2. SEPARATION OF SUBSYSTEMS. Sometimes, however, we cannot "re-interpret away" the changes in the external stimulus pattern. We then may display the second phenomenon of the separation of subsystems. Sup-

pose that you firmly believe that Englishmen are insufferable snobs, and suppose that you meet an Englishman who is as democratic and "homespun" as one might wish. It is highly probable the you will set this Englishman apart as an "exception"— an "exception that proves the rule"—and your very strong percept of Englishmen-in-general will remain unaltered. By reorganizing your perceptual field so as to "break off" the subsystem of this particular Englishman, a change in the stimulus-field has been absorbed so as to bring about minimal change to the structured whole.

BY WAY OF SUMMARY. Many of the basic principles which help us to describe the perception of physical objects are equally useful in analyzing our perception of social phenomena. All of our perceptions of the behavior and attributes of people quickly become integrated perceptions of personality. We do this even with "inadequate" data. We tend to interpret later observations of the person in terms of our first observations, in terms of the total context within which we meet the person, and in terms of our own motivational and emotional states. These first impressions can easily become lasting ones, and may show a remarkable resistance to change. But because we are here dealing with people, our perceptions affect not only our own behavior, but may also affect the behavior and personality of the person being perceived. For these and other reasons the understanding of social psychology requires an understanding of the processes of how we perceive other people.

Social Attitudes

When the social psychologist wishes to describe a person's significant perceptions of and behavioral dispositions toward the social order, he does so in terms of the

---

BOX 165

How Not to See a Factory Worker as Intelligent

The various ways in which a pre-existing stereotype in the perception of a person can be maintained despite contradictory information is well demonstrated in a study performed by Haire and Grunes at the University of California. They presented two groups of subjects (179 students in the introductory psychology course) with the following terms descriptive of "a certain working-man":

Group I.: Works in a factory; reads a newspaper; goes to movies; average height; cracks jokes; strong; active.

Group II.: Works in a factory; reads a newspaper; goes to movies; average height; cracks jokes; intelligent; strong; active.

The subjects were then asked to write a paragraph describing the sort of person they thought this worker was. Subjects in Group II experienced greater difficulty than those in Group I in forming a unified impression of the person because of the term "intelligent." This was, for many of the students, inconsistent with their stereotype of factory workers. However, most of them, through various forms of cognitive suppression and distortion, were able to maintain their stereotype unimpaired. Among these forms (and some illustrative comments from the students) were the following:

1. *Denial of the existence of the disturbing element.* "He is intelligent, but not too much so, since he works in a factory."
2. *Placing the disturbing element in a context so as to render it harmless to the original stereotype.* "He is intelligent, but doesn't possess the initiative to rise above his group."
3. *Recognizing the incongruity, but maintaining the original stereotype anyway.* "The traits seem to be conflicting . . . most factory workers I have heard about aren't too intelligent."

HAIRE, M., and GRUNES, W. F. 1950. Perceptual defenses: processes protecting an original perception of another personality. *Hum. Relat., 3,* 403–12.

---

person's attitudes. An *attitude* may be defined as an enduring organization of perceptual, motivational, emotional, and adaptive processes centering on some object in the person's world. Thus, if Mr. Anyman perceives Germans as overbearing, insensitive, ruthless, if he feels antipathy in their presence, if he seeks to avoid them or to harm them, we say that he has a *negative attitude* toward Germans. And if Mr. Anyman perceives Italians as friendly, lively, helpful, if he enjoys being with them, and if he seeks them out and aids them, we say that he holds a *positive attitude* toward Italians.

Attitudes pertain not only to individual persons and to groups of people, but also to social institutions, social issues, and so on. Mr. Anyman may have attitudes toward the Baptist Church, the Rotary Club, the Labor Union, war, Communism, birth control, and fluoridation of the city water supply.

Almost every object in man's life-space can become the object of an attitude. But, as we have seen earlier, the scope and contents of the life-space vary greatly among men. Not every individual, therefore, has an attitude with respect to every possible object. Not every American, for instance, has an attitude about the Middle East, or trade barriers, or the cobalt bomb—either because the object may simply not exist in his life-space, or because the object is not psychologically significant enough to result in a crystallization of his emotional and motivational dispositions around it. We will soon see that this creates a major problem for the measurement of attitudes and for public opinion polling.

A complete picture of man's attitudes toward the objects of his social world can yield highly reliable predictions about his behavior in many situations. It is for this reason that some psychologists regard the study of attitudes—their nature, function, development and change, and their measurement—as the central problem of social psychology.

The Nature of Attitudes. The nature of attitudes can be described in terms of five major attributes: extremeness, content, differentiation, isolation, and strength. And it is only when we can adequately describe an attitude in terms of these attributes that we can use it for predictive purposes.

EXTREMENESS. The most obvious thing that can be said about any attitude is how positive or negative it is. Mr. Anyman may hold an extremely favorable attitude toward the United Nations, a moderately favorable attitude toward the pastor of his church, and a barely positive attitude toward the proposal to raise the postage rate. He may have a slightly negative attitude toward Frenchmen, and an extremely negative attitude toward Communists.

COGNITIVE CONTENTS. Different people may agree in voting for the Democratic party, or in expressing a dislike of vivisection, or in taking action to insure that Negroes are not segregated in the schools. But the mere fact that they manifest the same degree of positive or negative disposition toward a given object or issue may not really mean that the attitude is the "same" in all these people. Further investigation of the precise cognitive contents of the attitudes they hold may reveal that their percepts of the object differ markedly. Indeed, psychologically speaking, the "object" may not be the same for all of them. For one person, the Democratic party may be

seen as the champion of the "common man"; for another it may be seen as the party of Negro-white segregationists; for another it may be seen as the source of political patronage.

The implication of this point for the understanding of attitudes is obvious. We cannot safely combine all these people who express favorable dispositions toward the Democratic party in the same category of attitude. What determines their attitudes differs; so does the way that their attitudes will change or fail to change under the impact of new information or new motivational pressures. Moreover, this diversity in the cognitive contents of the "same" attitude among different people raises perplexing problems for the *measurement* of attitudes, as we shall presently see.

DIFFERENTIATION. Not only may the contents of the "same" attitudes vary, there is also variation in their degree of differentiation. Some attitudes are clear, explicitly focused, highly structured; others are vague, diffuse, and poorly structured. For example, Mr. Anyman may have a clearly formulated and higly differentiated attitude toward the Republican party. He knows exactly why he approves of the party and what its principles and practices are. He makes various distinctions about the party —he is favorable to the moderate wing and hostile to the reactionary wing; he supports the party's policy of cutting the budget but not its policy of cutting off federal funds for schoolrooms; he makes a distinction between the Republican party on the national level, which he favors, and the Republican party in his own state, which he regards as imcompetent.

In contrast to this, Mr. Anyman's strongly positive attitude toward "science" may be quite undifferentiated. He may have very little real grasp of the nature of science, the distinctions between applications and theories of science, the distinctions between one field of science and another, etc.—he is merely "for science," regarding it as something valuable and to be supported.

ISOLATION. Attitudes also differ in the degree to which they are related and integrated with other attitudes in the person. Thus, Mr. Anyman's positive attitude toward science may exist more or less in isolation; it has no close relations with his attitudes toward business, or toward politics, or toward his religion. It does not "communicate" with or influence his other attitudes. On the other hand, the same kind of positive attitude toward science in another person may be very highly integrated with his attitudes toward education, toward ethics, toward the ideal of human progress, toward a whole complex of objects in his life-space.

STRENGTH. Some attitudes endure for long periods of time, despite evidence that contradicts them and despite other pressures operating against their maintenance. They are *strong* attitudes. Other attitudes are *weak*, shifting readily under stress.

An attitude is likely to be stronger the more extreme the person's feeling, the more differentiated its cognitive contents, and the more integrated it is with other attitudes. It is also likely to be more resistant to change the more central its value in the personality structure of the individual and the more firmly anchored it is in the beliefs of the person's group. This leads us to consider the *functions* which attitudes serve for the individual.

The Functions of Attitudes. Attitudes serve many functions. Man's ability to deal in a consistent way with various psychological situations is made possible primarily by the enduring pattern of his attitudes which holds together his many diverse experiences in a sort of continuing "super-organization." In addition to serving this general organizing role, attitudes help man to achieve many of his specific goals and to defend his self-image from attack.

ATTITUDES AND MEANING. Many psychologists have pointed to man's search for meaning as one of his most insistent strivings. This striving after meaning can sometimes result in rigidly held attitudes—both positive and negative ones. An instance of this is seen in the development of prejudices during periods of social crisis. During economic depression, war, riots, or plagues, when people see their well-being threatened by forces beyond their comprehension, they actively seek for some understandable explanation. If at such times they are told that their ill-fate is due to the evil machinations of a particular religious, or political, or ethnic group, *and if they are offered no alternative explanation*, they may readily accept the interpretation. People in a crisis cannot long tolerate ambiguity. But such an acceptance is not a "cold intellectual" affair. It frequently means the development of a strong and unyielding prejudice against the "guilty" group, since the "explanation" integrates cognitive and perceptual processes in a context of intense emotional crisis. Even the emotionally mature person, with no more than the "normal" share of aggressive impulses, may develop racial or national or class hatreds and prejudices in such a situation. *The context within which we strive after meanings plays an important role in determining the nature of the meaning we finally achieve.*

ATTITUDES AND PERSONAL GOALS. The expression of attitudes often aids a person to achieve social and economic goals. By announcing certain attitudes he may thereby assert his conformity to the ideals and beliefs of his society—and the pressure toward conformity, as we know, is great. By expressing certain "approved" attitudes Mr. Anyman may meet the "entrance requirements" of social groups he desires to join, or he may be appointed to a job he seeks. These attitudinal entrance requirements are often just as rigidly adhered to by informal groups as they are by the more formal religious, political, and economic organizations.

ATTITUDES AND SELF-DEFENSE. Attitudes often reflect aggression born of frustration, or rationalization born of feelings of self-failure and conflict. The need for self-justification, or for finding a scapegoat, provides excellent opportunities for the development of strongly organized negative attitudes. Once developed these prejudices serve vital functions for the person, as we have seen in Chapter 24. They channel his aggressions in a "reasonable" manner ("the Negro *is* bad, therefore aggressing against him is not wicked, or unchristian"); and they make palatable his own failures ("I can't make a go of my business as long as those thieving labor racketeers carry on their extortion practices").

The manner in which the individual's characteristic self-defenses may be reflected in his social attitudes is well demonstrated in a study by Smith, Bruner, and White (1956) of the personalities of ten persons with strong pro-Russian or strong anti-Russian attitudes. For example, men who were likely to *project* blame on other people for their own personal failures also were more likely to regard Russia as wholly to blame for international tensions.

And Festinger (1957) offers various experimental demonstrations that when there is what he calls *cognitive dissonance* (i.e., perceived incongruity) between the person's own attitudes and his behavior, the person may tend to reduce the dissonance by appropriate changes in attitudes. Thus, the heavy smoker "rationalizes" his behavior in the face of the disturbing scientific evidence linking smoking and lung cancer by developing an attitude of skepticism and disbelief about the scientific data.

Development of Attitudes. The varied functions of attitudes make it clear that many different kinds of factors shape the development of attitudes. In tracing such determinants we must examine man's cultural environment, his membership in such primary groups as his family, his personality.

CULTURAL DETERMINANTS. Many social scientists have emphasized the importance of the individual's cultural influences as a determinant of his attitudes. This is reflected in the large number of studies which seek to discover a correlation between the attitudes a man holds and the religious, ethical, political, and economic institutions under which he lives. For example, it has been found that Jewish college students hold the most liberal attitudes toward the concept of a personal God, toward war, and toward birth control; Protestants are intermediate; and Catholics, the most conservative.

But cultural influences are varied and often contradictory. The church, the schools, the neighborhood, the business community do not always promote the same or even similar attitudes. Two people living in the same general culture have many influences from which to "choose." Culture sets the *limits* for the attitudes which may develop, but within these limits there is a great deal of room for individual variation. And which attitudes a man will pick up from his culture depends in great part upon his immediate primary group as well as upon his unique personality.

PARENTAL AND GROUP INFLUENCES. The most direct and powerful agents of attitude formation are the parents and other members of the family. Studies of the development of racial prejudice in the growing child, for example, show clearly that these attitudes are not present in the very young child, and only gradually develop as the child comes to be more and more cognizant of parental beliefs, and more and more subject to direct parental "guidance"—in the form of instruction, and rewards and punishment. In one study of college students (Allport and Kramer, 1946), for example, 69 per cent of the students report having been affected by their parents' ethnic attitudes, and the percentage is even higher among the most prejudiced students.

PERSONALITY. Parents also have an *indirect* influence in shaping a child's attitudes through the kinds of child-rearing practices in which they engage. We have seen in Chapter 23 how specific forms of child-rearing may influence the personality of the child, and how, in turn, the particular structure of personality may help predispose the child toward the development of certain attitudes. For example, the "authoritarian" personality predisposes the person to hostile attitudes toward racial minority groups, to rigid moralistic attitudes, etc. (See Box 155, p. 617).

However, here again we must be careful not to overgeneralize. An "authoritarian" Mr. Anyman, in the context of his specific cultural environment, may develop "reactionary" political attitudes; his son, with the same personality traits, but growing up in a different cultural environment and knowing different facts, may develop "radical" political attitudes. The same or similar personality structure may eventuate in quite different attitudes as far as the direction and content of the attitudes are concerned.

Change of Attitudes. Changes in attitudes may be brought about in various ways. Some involve shifts in group membership, or changes in the individual's situation. Others have to do with the impact of persuasive efforts of educators and propagandists.

CHANGES IN GROUP MEMBERSHIP. The attitudes of the person's groups help determine his own attitudes. If his group identifications or memberships shift, there may be an associated change in his own attitudes. Several studies show this effect. In a study of Bennington College girls from their freshman to their senior years, Newcomb (1943) found that the attitudes of the girls shifted in the liberal direction as they became socially assimilated into that very liberal college community. The attitudes of those girls who failed to be assimilated tended to show less change in the liberal direction, or no change at all. Sims and Patrick (1936) found that Northern college students enrolled in a Southern university tended to take on the attitudes of their fellow white students, becoming less favorable in their attitudes toward Negroes.

SITUATIONAL CHANGE. Attitudes are often modified by changes in the person's situation. For example, economic improvement or removal of political restraint may eventuate in a reduction of frustration and of hostile attitudes as well. Conversely, a worsening of the person's situation may produce changes in the other direction. The person on a low-level fixed income may become increasingly jaundiced toward labor unions as he sees the cost of living rising and his own income becoming less adequate.

ENFORCED CHANGES IN BEHAVIOR. Under some circumstances legal or other force may be applied to require the person to change his behavior toward an object for which he has a negative attitude. Society's purpose in this enforced change in behavior is to prevent harm to the object. But an important additional result may be a change in attitude. For example, Deutsch and Collins (1951) found that white housewives who were forced to live in an integrated interracial public housing project due to a shortage of other housing soon displayed much more favorable attitudes toward the Negroes than did housewives who lived in segregated projects. Thus 53 per cent of the former women voted for a policy of interracial integration for city housing in general, whereas only 5 per cent of the latter women favored that policy. The experience of interracial living also made the former women more willing to accept Negroes as fellow workers, as schoolmates for their children, and as fellow members of an informal social club than were the women who had not been forced to live in close contact with the Negro families.

CONTACT WITH OBJECT. Part of the reason that the change occurs is presumably that the prejudiced person comes to have new perceptions of the object of his prejudice. He comes to learn that his stereotype about the Negro is incorrect. This discovery may be encouraged by the fact that since he is forced to remain in contact with the Negro, he will actively seek out the most desirable traits in his "enforced neighbor." He will, in other words, try to "make the best of it," and in this process, he will achieve new perceptions of the Negro. He may also come to learn that other members of his group are also ready to accept a more tolerant attitude toward the Negro.

Though it is often true that the more information about people a person gains from contact with them, the more favorable his attitudes are likely to be, this obviously is not always the case. The added information may make him see the people in a worse light than before. Thus Watson (1950) reports that of persons who came into new contacts with Jews and Negroes of status at least equal to their own, the great majority changed to more favorable attitudes; on the other hand, of those who came into contact with Jews and Negroes of *lower* status positions, the majority changed in the direction of less favorable attitudes.

And Mussen (1950) found that though a four-week period of interracial contact in a summer camp for boys did produce significant change in attitudes of white boys toward Negroes, the changes were in *both*

directions. Boys with strong aggressive needs tended to become more anti-Negro as a result of camp experience, while boys without such aggressive needs tended to become more favorable toward Negroes.

CHANGES IN THE OBJECT. Sometimes, through enforced behavioral changes, the object of the attitude itself undergoes change, which—if perceived by the person—may result in a change in his attitudes. For instance, as a result of desegregation the Negro may become better educated and thus modify some of the undesirable traits which had supported prejudice against him.

THE ROLE OF INFORMATION. The most obvious way in which attitudes are changed is through changes in the facts or information about the object available to the person. In the complex world in which we live no person can hope to ascertain, at first hand, all the facts essential to achieve understanding about the objects which concern him. He must depend upon what "experts" tell him. Frequently the facts provided by these "experts" are contradictory, and often relevant facts are just not available. Where this is so, "facts" may be invented in order to make meaning out of those situations which are important for the person. Here we have a process analogous to the creation of "stimuli" in simple perception (see p. 89) and in the perception of personality traits (see p. 667).

Facts, as we have pointed out repeatedly, must be interpreted. It is therefore essential to understand how a person acquires his facts—who his authorities are and how these authorities present the information to him. Clearly the incidence of superstitions, delusions, stereotypes, and prejudices (all of which are attitudes which incorporate "facts" widely divergent from reality) will be related to the adequacy of the authorities we depend upon and to their methods of presenting their "facts." In other words, we must examine the processes of persuasion.

Who are the experts we depend upon for our facts? For the child, the experts are mainly his parents and older children; for the student, they are his teachers and books; for the religious person, his priests and ministers; for the scientists, they are other specialists in his field; and for all of us, they include newspaper writers, movie producers, radio and television broadcasters, politicians, businessmen, doctors, lawyers, engineers, etc. Almost anyone may serve as an authority for some one else. And every one of these authorities can be influential in changing some one's attitudes —whether we refer to them as propagandists or educators. (See Box 166.)

The effectiveness of new information in changing the person's attitudes is dependent upon the *way the source of the information is perceived, the manner in which the information is presented,* and *the characteristics of the perceiver.*

Illustrative experimental findings on these factors are as follows:

1. Even though information from a source perceived as biased and untrustworthy is *remembered* as well as information from a source perceived as unbiased and credible, it has less effect on changing the *attitude* of the person. Hovland and Weiss (1951) gave college students excerpts allegedly from newspapers and magazines arguing for the feasibility of developing an atomic submarine. For half the subjects the article was attributed to the noted American physicist, Robert Oppenheimer, and for the other half, to the Russian newspaper, *Pravda.* In the first group the net percentage of cases in which the subjects' opinions changed in the direction of the communication was 36, whereas in the second group, the net percentage change was zero. Despite this difference in effect on attitudes, the amount of information acquired

from the communication was about equal in the two groups.

After four weeks had passed there was found to be a "sleeper" effect—that is, those who had had the untrustworthy source and had originally shown no change in attitude now showed a delayed change in the direction of the communication. (See Fig. 156.)

2. Is a fear-arousing approach more effective or less effective than one which minimizes fear? Janis and Feshbach (1953) compared the effects of three versions of an illustrated lecture on dental hygiene in three matched groups of high school students. Version I included a strong appeal to fear, showing unpleasant slides of diseased gums, etc. Version II used a moderate appeal to fear, and version III minimized the fear element. The effects in pro-

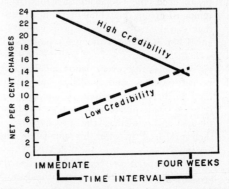

FIG. 156. Curves showing the net per cent change of attitude toward that of a communication, when the communication is ascribed to a high-credibility source and when ascribed to a low-credibility source. Immediately after the communication, the group of subjects exposed to the high-credibility source shows a much larger positive effect than does the group exposed to the low-credibility source. After four weeks have passed, the difference between the two groups has disappeared. The high-credibility group has suffered some loss in the effect, whereas the low-credibility group has actually gained some effect. This latter "sleeper" phenomenon is apparently due to the fact that with the passage of time the low-credibility source becomes "detached" from the communication in the minds of these subjects, and no longer inhibits their acceptance of the communication. (Hovland and Weiss, 1951.)

BOX 166

Persuasion Through Propaganda

The term propaganda is often used as an epithet to characterize persuasive techniques which we believe to be harmful or undesirable. But quite aside from the *ends* to which propaganda may be put, the fundamental nature of its processes is the same as that found in any form of "education." Thus the effectiveness of propaganda depends upon the degree to which it observes the basic principles of perception, motivation, and learning. The nature of the effective propagandist's suggestions have been summarized in a book by Krech and Crutchfield under the following six "guides to the propagandist":

1. *The suggestion should seem to meet an existing need.* Where there is no appropriate need, the propagandist will first attempt to create one. Thus if no need exists that can be tied in with propaganda for anti-labor legislation, the propagandist will seek to have news sources and political discussions magnify every labor incident—especially strikes and violence—no matter how small. If this strategy is successful in creating widespread public fear of labor tie-ups and violence, the propagandist is then prepared to offer his anti-labor suggestions.

2. *The suggestion should seem to clarify an ambiguous situation.* The propagandist must be ready to take advantage of every social crisis—when man's needs for new and clearer meanings are great. He will offer his suggestions as "clarifying explanations" and, if possible, prevent alternative suggestions from coming to the attention of the people. Where no confusion exists, he may first seek to create confusion. He fishes in muddy waters.

3. *The suggestion should seem to fit already existing attitudes.* To a religious group he may present Communism (for example) as congruent with the ideals of Christianity; to an anti-religious group, as congruent with a purely materialistic and atheistic philosophy.

4. *The suggestion must emphasize the at-tributes of the objects which are least controversial.* This is sometimes called *indirect propaganda.* Thus instead of offering a direct suggestion that the public support a universal conscription bill, the propagandist may discuss and emphasize the educational opportunities offered in Army service, or the health benefits of Army training, or the morale values of Army discipline. He may avoid any mention of universal conscription.

5. *The suggestion should fit the people's needs to be in harmony with other people.* He will "plant" his suggestions around prestige figures. He will use the "bandwagon" technique with issues of general social import ("*Most* people buy Bledsoes"), and the "expert" technique with technical issues ("18 California doctors recommend Ginger"). If necessary he may first direct his efforts to establish identifications between the public and the individual who will later be used to "sell" his wares or ideas. This is sometimes known as *public relations.*

6. *The suggestion should be congruent with the principles of effective stimulus patterning.* He makes his suggestions brief, simple, and repetitious. He makes use of figure-ground relations, of the "isolation effect," and even of the possible effectiveness of subliminal stimulation.

Social scientists have been concerned with protecting people against the "power of propaganda" and various educational approaches to the problem have been explored. But if people accept suggestions that seem harmful or dangerous to society, this is due in large part to the failure of the existing social institutions to meet the needs and desires of the people. It would seem, therefore, that the best kind of counter-propaganda is a social and economic system that satisfies most of the needs and desires of most of the people most of the time.

KRECH, D., and CRUTCHFIELD, R. S. 1948. *Theory and problems of social psychology.* New York: McGraw-Hill.

ducing adherence to the recommended hygienic dental practice were *inversely* related to the degree of fear arousal. Version III produced a 37 per cent net effect, version II, a 22 per cent net effect, and version I, only an 8 per cent net effect. Although fear may sometimes be effective in changing attitudes, this study indicates some very severe limitations to its effectiveness. The investigators suggest that intense fear may have had adverse effects in this instance by inducing hostility toward the communicator, and thus encouraging the rejection of his communication.

3. The intelligence of the person is related to the extent to which he is influenced by information. But the relationship is a highly complex one. The more intelligent person is better able to grasp the content of the communication, but at the same time he is more likely to be resistant to the propaganda. Thus Cantril (1940) found that a much higher proportion of those with grammar school education than those with college education were "panicked" by the famous radio broadcast on October 30, 1938, purporting to describe an invasion from Mars, because they believed the broadcast to be an authentic news report.

The tendency to be influenced by a communication is also related to other personality factors. Thus Janis (1954) found that those subjects who were more readily influenced by communications tended to be characterized by feelings of social inadequacy, inhibition of aggression, and depression. The possible explanation is that such persons with low self-esteem are more likely to fear social disapproval for deviancy of opinions, and therefore are more ready to accept the propagandist's suggestion. (See also the findings on personal factors in conformity tendencies, p. 690).

Self-preservation of Attitudes. In discussing general perception in Part I of this book, and the perception of people in this chapter, we have already considered some of the major factors which help maintain constancy in the way we see and react to our world. But the resistance of attitudes to change, even in the face of contradictory evidence, is so compelling a fact in social behavior, and so important for our understanding of social events, that we might here summarize some of these "self-preservative" factors in the maintenance of attitudes.

WITHDRAWAL. The person with a strong attitude often withdraws himself, *physically*, from the necessity to face contradictory evidence. The anti-Catholic usually will not listen to a Catholic radio broadcast; and the typical anti-Communist will not read Communist newspapers and pamphlets. Attitudes, by encouraging this withdrawal behavior, drop a "silent curtain" against the intrusion of possible embarrassing facts.

PERCEPTUAL SELECTIVITY. Actual physical withdrawal is not always necessary. We have seen that perception is selective and that this selectivity is determined in large measure by our mental sets and attitudes (see p. 100). Because of this, though the person may be exposed to data which are contradictory to a strong attitude, he may simply not perceive them. Here attitudes may be said to drop a "perceptual curtain" to shut out conflicting facts.

Even when people are *forced* to observe contradictory data (as when children, for example, are forced to hear tolerance lectures) the effect of such perceptions may be fleeting. For not only is perception selective, the *retention* of what is perceived is also selective in content. Very soon after exposure, people will have forgotten the contradictory facts and their attitudes will remain unchallenged. In selective memory, as in selective perception, attitudes have "built-in" self-protective devices.

REINTERPRETING DATA. Facts rarely speak for themselves; they must be interpreted. And the understanding and interpretation of facts are determined by the on-going mental sets and attitudes, just as are perceptions and memory. This becomes particularly evident where strong attitudes are involved (see Box 167). Thus attitudes may be preserved by a "derailment of understanding."

SELF-REINFORCEMENT. The above processes do not merely serve to preserve our original attitudes, they also strengthen them. A pro-Israeli attitude, by determining that the individual will perceive only the virtues of Israelis, provides ever-fresh data that all Israelis are models of the good and the virtuous. An anti-Catholic attitude that results in the withdrawal from all contact with things Catholic can lead to distorted thinking about Catholics. As this autistic thinking goes on, unchecked by reality, the Catholics become worse and worse

and the anti-Catholic attitudes become more intense. Attitudes not only tend to select and twist data and thus maintain themselves, but can create the fuel upon which they grow in intensity.

Measurement of Attitudes. To do research on the psychology of attitudes and to make practical applications, as in public opinion surveys, we must have methods of measuring attitudes. The principles of attitude measurement are no different from the principles involved in measuring motives (Chap. 11), abilities (Chap. 20), and traits (Chap. 23). Throughout, the aim is to place the individual at some point along a dimension indicating the amount of the motive, ability, trait, or attitude that he has relative to a population of people.

Thus, in attitude measurement the primary objective is to determine the position of the person on a continuum varying from the most extreme favorable attitude to the

---

BOX 167

Mr. Biggott Interprets Propaganda

Cooper and Jahoda, at the Bureau of Applied Social Research of Columbia University, undertook to answer the question of what happens to a prejudiced person when he is involuntarily confronted with anti-prejudice propaganda.

In these studies prejudiced people were presented with a series of cartoons lampooning a character named "Mr. Biggott" who was depicted as holding the same prejudices as the subject. The producers of the cartoon assumed that the prejudiced person would perceive that Mr. Biggott's ideas were similar to his own; that Mr. Biggott was an absurd character; and that therefore, the subject would reject or at least begin to question his own prejudices in order to avoid identifying himself with the absurd Mr. Biggott. But the study showed quite different results from what the cartoonist had hoped for.

In one cartoon Mr. Biggott is shown lying in a hospital bed and saying to the doctor that he wants only "sixth-generation American blood" for his blood transfusion. This cartoon was shown to anti-Semitic subjects and then they were interviewed and asked what they thought of Mr. Biggott and his attitudes. One of the subjects said that obviously Mr. Biggott was a socially inferior person, and that one who was *only a sixth-generation American* had no right to pretensions! In this way the point of the cartoon was reinterpreted to deal with snobbishness rather than with prejudice, and thus the subject's own absurd racial prejudices remained unaffected by the absurd Mr. Biggott.

COOPER, E., and JAHODA, M. 1947. The evasion of propaganda: how prejudiced people respond to anti-prejudice propaganda. *J. Psychol.*, 23, 15–25.

most extreme negative attitude. There are three main methods available: *scales, ratings*, and *projective techniques*.

ATTITUDE SCALES. The attitude scale is merely a special case of the more general class of scales for the measurement of personality, as described in Chapter 23, p. 634. It consists of a large number of items, each designed to elicit an answer indicating a favorable or unfavorable disposition toward a specific object.

There are several ways of constructing attitude scales. Thurstone's method (1929) is the following: Hundreds of items representing possible attitudes toward a specific object are written. A large group of judges sorts these into eleven piles, varying from those items expressing the most favorable attitudes to those expressing the least favorable attitudes. Only those items on which the judges clearly agree as to scale position are retained, and each such item is given a scale value in terms of the judges' placement. Thus scale values for any one item can vary from 1 to 11. The final scale is usually made up of about 20 items, selected so that the entire range of attitudes is represented. A few items from such a scale are given in Table 24. In being measured on the scale, an individual's score is determined by the average scale

TABLE 24

Illustrative Items from a Thurstone-Type Scale for Measuring Attitudes Toward War (Adapted from Droba, 1930)

Item

Scale Value

1.3   1. A country cannot amount to much without a national honor, and war is the only means of preserving it.

2.5   2. When war is declared we must enlist.

5.2   3. Wars are justifiable only when waged in defense of weaker nations.

8.4   4. The disrespect for human life and rights involved in war is a cause of crime waves.

10.6   5. All nations should disarm immediately.

values of the items with which he expresses agreement.

Another method has been developed by Likert (1932). Hundreds of statements pertaining to the attitude in question are collected. These items are then administered to a trial group of subjects who indicate for each item whether they *strongly agree, agree, are undecided, disagree*, or *strongly disagree*. Each of these responses is scored 5, 4, 3, 2, or 1 respectively. Each item is then studied to see how well its answers agree with the total scores on all the items. Items are eliminated whose individual scores do not correlate highly with the total score. Thus it can be assumed that the remaining items that make up the final score are all measuring the same or similar attitude.

The Thurstone and Likert methods are widely used and give fairly comparable results. While there are other kinds of scales which are mathematically too technical to describe here, there is a special type of scale—the *social distance scale* (Bogardus, 1925) which does deserve mention. It is primarily directed at the measurement of ethnic attitudes. The items permit the respondent to indicate the "social distance" that he wants to keep between himself and the given ethnic group. Table 25 gives the percentages of 1725 native-born Americans who would "willingly admit" members of the ethnic groups listed to each one of the various Bogardus classifications. Thus 97 per cent of the group was willing to admit Englishmen to their street as neighbors, but only 26 per cent was willing to admit Jews.

ATTITUDE RATINGS. Another quite different approach to the measurement of attitudes is the rating method. Here the score assigned to a person on an attitude dimension is based upon the judgment of the person's friend, or of an expert rater. The sources for making this judgment are various: general familiarity with the person, interviews, examination of personal docu-

TABLE 25
Responses (in percentages) of Native-Born Americans on the Bogardus Social Distance Scale
(Adapted from Bogardus, 1928)

Scale Item	Englishmen	Germans	Jews	Negroes
1. To close kinship by marriage	94	54	8	1
2. To my club as personal chums	97	67	22	9
3. To my street as neighbors	97	79	26	12
4. To employment in my occupation	95	83	40	39
5. To citizenship in my country	96	87	54	57

ments (such as letters and speeches), test scores, and controlled observations of behavior. In a typical rating scale the rater may indicate in which category of a five-point scale the person falls. For example, a person may be rated as having one of the following attitudes toward birth control:

1. Very much in favor of birth control
2. Moderately in favor of birth control
3. Uncertain about birth control
4. Moderately opposed to birth control
5. Very much opposed to birth control

There can also be *self*-ratings of one's attitudes. Such self-ratings are, of course, susceptible to serious distortions when the attitudes are such that the person wishes to conceal them from others, or when he is unclear about his own attitudes.

PROJECTIVE TECHNIQUES. The information upon which the person's attitudes are scored or rated is sometimes obtained through projective techniques (see p. 635). Such methods are particularly important when it is desired to conceal the intent of the measurement from the subject, or when the subject desires to conceal his attitudes, or when the subject cannot clearly phrase his attitude. Thus, the child's attitudes toward Negroes may be ascertained by such techniques as presenting him with pictures of Negro children at play, and asking him whether he would like to join in such a game.

The projective technique can even be used outside the laboratory. An ingenious approach to market research was pioneered by Haire (1950) in seeking to measure the elusive attitudes of consumers toward the purchase and use of "instant coffee." In a door-to-door survey housewives were presented with a list of grocery items bought by a fictitious woman and then they were asked to give their impression of the woman's personality. In some cases the item "instant coffee" was included in the list, while in other cases it was not. By analyzing the differences in personality descriptions thus obtained, Haire was able to show that housewives tend to perceive a woman who uses instant coffee as lazy, spendthrift, and a poor planner. Such negative attitudes toward the buying of instant coffee ascertained by this projective technique could not so readily be elicited by direct questioning.

PUBLIC OPINION RESEARCH. The most extensive measurement of attitudes occurs in public opinion polls and surveys. Their applications are legion—to determine public opinion on current issues, to ascertain voter preferences, to collect information on people's spending habits, on their television viewing, etc. Two of the most important technical problems involved in such research have to do with (1) the kinds of questions asked, and (2) the choice of people to be interviewed.

TYPES OF QUESTIONS. The simplest form of question is the *fixed-alternative*, or poll-type question. It is a question which the person can answer by a choice among two or more alternative responses. For example, the question may be: "Are you in favor of or opposed to the admission of

Communist China to the United Nations?" Or it may be: "Which of the following plans do you think best for solving the shortage of school teachers?", with five alternatives specified from which the respondent must choose one.

The advantages of this type of question are obvious. It takes very little time to administer, the answers are readily classified into opinion categories, the interviewers need not be as highly trained as in other types of interviewing. But its shortcomings emerge when the attitudes being measured are complex or not crystallized. Thus the person may be constrained to give a simple answer which does not correspond in a meaningful way with the attitude he holds. Or he may even be tempted to give an answer when he has *no* attitude on the subject. As we have previously noted, not every person has an attitude on every subject that interests the public-opinion poller. Anyone who has taken a true-false examination knows that it is more tempting to respond "yes" or "no" to a question than to say "I don't know." Thus the fixed-alternative question runs the danger of recording non-existent attitudes.

It is particularly in this connection that the *open-ended* question shows its value. The person may be asked "What do you think about the proposal to admit Communist China to the United Nations?", and be encouraged to answer as freely as possible in his own terms. The answers are taken down by the interviewer more or less verbatim, and later are studied and rated for the attitudes they reveal.

By this means it is possible to get essential data about the person's way of perceiving the issue, the reasons he holds his opinions, the qualifications he feels—in short, the specific and detailed cognitive content and degree of differentiation of his attitudes. And this is a highly important require-ment of attitude measurement, for, as we have already pointed out, the nature of different people's attitudes toward the "same" object may vary so widely that they cannot be meaningfully compared on a single dimension.

SAMPLING. In public opinion research our interest is ordinarily not in the attitudes of a single person, but in the attitudes of a specified population of people. We wish to know how registered American voters feel about the candidates, how white-collar workers feel about inflation, how the residents of a housing project feel about Puerto Ricans as neighbors.

As we have seen in Chapter 19, it is not usually feasible or necessary to measure every person in the population being studied. Instead we measure a sample of persons from the population. Such a sample, it will be remembered, must be *large enough* so that the estimates of the entire population are as reliable as needed (see p. 535), and must be *representative* of the entire population (see p. 529).

Group Behavior

We have many times pointed to the truism that man is born into a going society and lives his life through as a member of many groups. The existence of groups has at least two important implications for the study of man's behavior. In the first place the group makes possible, and perhaps even necessary, certain forms of behavior which would otherwise be non-existent. Thus it is obvious that leadership can emerge as a form of behavior only when people live in groups. In the second place, the group has certain important and unique effects on the more general and universal behavior of man.

Consider the problem of four or five people in the process of making a "group decision." The opinions, behavior, facial expressions, and prestige of any one person in the group affect the behavior of all the others. These effects rebound on the original person, who in turn influences all the others anew, and this complex of effects takes place simultaneously among all the members of the group. To understand how the group decision is finally arrived at, we must pay attention to these complex, simultaneous, multiple feed-back effects. This means that we must study the problem-solving behavior of people *in the context of groups.* Studying the problem-solving behavior of the *individual* alone—as we did in Part III of this book—will not enable us to understand group problem-solving.

For both these major reasons, social psychology and many of the other social sciences have set aside the study of group behavior as a special experimental and theoretical field of inquiry. This field of study is sometimes called *group dynamics.*

Leadership. One of the most obvious aspects of group behavior is that some people become leaders, and others, followers. The main psychological problems concerning leadership have to do with the functions of leaders, the manner in which leaders emerge, the personality characteristics associated with the "trait" of leadership, and the effects of leadership on group functioning.

FUNCTIONS OF LEADERS. Most leaders must play many roles. They partake of the functions of executive, planner, policy maker, expert, external group representative, controller of internal group relations, purveyor of rewards and punishments, arbitrator and mediator, exemplar, father-figure and— when things go wrong—scapegoat. In informal, temporary groups—such as a group of hikers—most of these functions have no opportunity to emerge in the "leader"; in

a more stable group—such as people living together in a dormitory—more of these functions must be assumed by the leader; in the most stable and formal organization —such as the political party—all of these roles must be played at one time or another by the leader.

EMERGENCE OF LEADERS. In some types of formal groups the leaders are designated officially from the outside, or by tradition. In other cases, however, there is at first no designated leader, but if the group persists long enough, some member will usually emerge as the leader.

What determines, in these latter cases, who will emerge as leader? For one thing, the leader is someone who is perceived by the others as likely to further their goals. And when these goals change, so may their leadership. Often the leader is not highly "accepted" or liked by the followers, but he will be chosen as leader if he is perceived as being able to help the members achieve their goals.

Quite aside from the perceived power of the leader, the personalities of the *followers* may also help determine who shall emerge as leader. Sanford (1952) has found, for example, that group members having an "authoritarian" outlook prefer and demand strong directive leadership; conversely, members having an "equalitarian" outlook are more likely to prize traits of good "human relations" in the leader rather than directive leadership. Hollingworth (1942) has shown that when there is *too great* a discrepancy between the intelligence of the followers and of the leader, the leader may be repudiated.

TRAITS OF THE LEADER. Are some men "born leaders" and others not—or is leadership something any person can exhibit, given the appropriate situation? This controversial question has not been entirely answered. The weight of the evidence seems to show that (1) the amount of leadership behavior exhibited by any one person varies widely with the situation, the group structure, the group goals, and the personality of the group members; (2) there is, nonetheless, a substantial amount of *generality* of leadership proclivity in individuals. That is, some people tend to be the leaders in most situations; some people, in very few.

With what personality traits is such leadership ability connected? On the basis of a large number of studies of leaders in all kinds of groups it appears that such traits as intelligence, dominance, self-confidence, high drive for achievement, and a strong sense of self-identity are important. But these general findings are by no means consistent. For each one of these traits there can be found instances where it fails to go with leadership, or may even be negatively related—as we have seen in Hollingworth's study where high intelligence may be a handicap to the person who would be the leader of people who themselves are of very low intelligence.

EVALUATION OF LEADERSHIP. The problem of determining who is a "good" or a "poor" leader is an extremely difficult one. For one thing it depends upon whose perspective is taken. There is often a difference in evaluation of a leader "from above" and "from below." Thus, the middle-echelon military officer or business executive may be appraised as "good" by his *superiors* to the extent that he gets his group to produce, maintains discipline, and upholds the official values and ideology of the organization; whereas his subordinates may regard him as "good" to the extent that he is warm and sensitive to "human relations," and protects his followers from the "higher ups."

This discrepancy in the perceptions of the "good leader" is well illustrated by a study of the attitudes of U.S. Army privates, noncoms, and officers toward good leadership (Stouffer, 1949). For example,

to the statement "A noncom should not let the men in his squad forget that he is a noncom even when off-duty," the following percentages of agreement were obtained: Officers, 81 per cent; noncoms, 54 per cent; privates, 39 per cent. Obviously the private and the officer have quite a different view of what makes a good noncom. The noncom, it will be noted, is right "in the middle."

Because of this discrepancy the leader is often placed in a serious conflict of roles, especially in our democratic culture which tends to value "getting things done" but at the same time is suspicious of leadership and dominance.

Our traditional suspicion of leadership is reflected in the curious fact that until the year 1896 not a single book on leadership was listed in the Library of Congress. Recently, however, research on leadership has come to occupy a prominent place in the work of behavioral scientists.

TYPES OF LEADERSHIP. There are many ways in which different kinds of leadership behavior can be described, but the one which has received the most experimental attention is in terms of the "authoritarian-democratic" dimension. From a series of experiments (Lippitt, 1940) designed to investigate the functioning of groups under these two types of leadership we can draw a fairly clear picture of their differences and their effects on group activity.

In these experiments groups of ten-year old Iowa boys (of five members each) met, under adult supervision, to assemble toy airplanes, make soap carvings and plaster models, etc. In some groups the adult supervisor adopted the role of an authoritarian leader, in others, of a democratic leader. Some groups, however, had an opportunity to work under each type of leader—first one, then the other.

For the authoritarian groups the leader himself decided what the boys were to do;

he dictated, one at a time, the techniques and steps of accomplishing each project so that the boys were uncertain, to a large degree, of the future direction of their work; the particular task and work companion of each boy was determined by the supervisor. Except when demonstrating what was to be done, the leader remained aloof from group activities.

In the democratic group the decisions as to what to work on were determined in group discussion, with the leader seeking to draw each boy into the discussion. The general steps involved in each project were outlined by him at the first meeting so that the boys could get some idea of where they were headed. Where advice was needed, he tried to point out two or three alternatives from which the boys could choose. The boys were free to work with whomever they chose, and the division of tasks was left up to the group. Throughout, the leader tried to be a participating group member without, however, doing the work for the boys.

Lippitt reports the following differences in the behavior of the groups:

1. The authoritarian groups tended to be more aggressive or more apathetic than the democratic groups. The aggression was usually directed toward "scapegoats" within the group—not against the leader. The lack of aggression in the apathetic groups was due to the restraining influence of the leader, for when he left the room, aggressive outbursts occurred.

2. In the authoritarian groups there were more attention-demanding approaches to the leader than in the democratic groups.

3. Group unity was higher in the democratic groups.

4. When the situation was manipulated so that the boys became bogged down in their work, the democratic group responded by organized attempts to deal with the apparent difficulty; the authoritarian

groups tended to bicker and blame each other for the lack of progress.

One caution should be kept in mind. This study was conducted in our democratic culture. A similar study, in another culture, might yield different results. As a matter of fact, not all the children reacted poorly to the authoritarian leadership. It is significant that some of the children who preferred the authoritarian group to the democratic one came from homes which were autocratic in structure. (See also Sanford's study, p. 684).

GROUP MORALE. It seems clear that the authoritarian and democratic leaders, as defined by their differing roles in the Lippitt experiment, make for significant differences in group behavior. Perhaps the simplest summary of these differences can be made by saying that the democratic groups showed a higher *group morale* than did the authoritarian groups. By group morale we usually mean the level of effectiveness of group functioning, and the unity and solidarity of the group. Indeed, insuring group morale is one of the major responsibilities of a leader.

Among the differences between high- and low-morale groups are that the latter fall apart more easily under stress, or break up into antagonistic subgroups or cliques, and that their members have little feeling of mutual friendliness and often have negative attitudes toward the group leader. In essence the difference between the groups is found in the difference in types of personal interrelationships that exist among the group members.

SOCIOMETRY. To measure the network of interrelationships within a group, Moreno (1934) developed what he called the "sociometric" method. This method, in its simplest form, involves asking each member of a group to specify (privately) which other members he likes, or wishes to work, eat, or live beside, and which ones he dislikes or wishes to avoid. From these responses it is possible to construct a *sociogram* which pictures the various patterns of likes and dislikes within the group (see Fig. 157). Such sociograms have proven to be of great value in studying the relation of group structure to group function.

Group Problem-Solving. The morale of a group is indicated not only by the quality of interpersonal relations among the members, but also by the effectiveness of the group in coping with and solving problems. Even in "group problem-solving," of course, *individuals* solve the problems, but, as we have already indicated, because of feedback effects individual problem-solving in the context of a group is significantly different from individual problem-solving when the person is working alone. Moreover, in the group situation there is the necessity of arriving at *agreements* on solution attempts. This itself introduces new psychological problems.

Various experimental studies have been made of the comparative effectiveness of problem-solving by individuals alone, and individuals working together in groups. Some tentative generalizations have already emerged from these studies.

NATURE OF PROBLEM. Whether group or individual problem-solving is superior depends upon the nature of the problem. If there are subproblems that can be distributed among the members, the group may be more efficient. If the problem requires a single over-all insight, then an individual may often do better than the group. When the problem requires "rational" checking or a large fund of information and skills, the group may do better; but when it calls for an original or novel set of responses, this advantage may not hold true.

NATURE OF GROUP. The nature of the group and the group situation is also important. For example, *size of group* is a critical factor. As the group gets larger, the amount of individual participation is lowered, and the most active or aggressive person, rather than the most capable person may play a more and more disproportionate role. Even-numbered groups (4, 6) are less effective

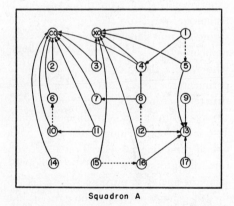

Squadron A

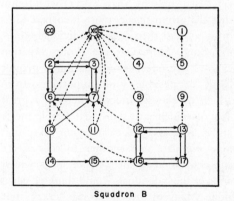

Squadron B

FIG. 157. Sociograms of a high-morale group (Squadron A) and a low-morale group (Squadron B). The flying personnel (indicated by numbered circles) of these two naval air squadrons were asked to state anonymously which men in their own squadron they would like to have fly beside them, and which men they would not like to have fly beside them. A solid line indicates a positive choice, and a

dotted line, a rejection. Note in Squadron B the isolation of the commanding officer (CO), the rejection of the executive officer (XO), and the two strong cliques (2, 3, 6, 7; and 12, 13, 16, 17) each of which constitutes a little "mutual admiration society," isolated from the rest of the group. None of these deleterious interpersonal relationships is true of Squadron A. (Adapted from Jenkins, 1947).

than odd-numbered groups (3, 5, 7), presumably because odd-numbered groups run less of a risk in falling into a dead lock which can paralyze action (Bales and Borgatta, 1955).

The kind of "group motivation" which exists can be important. If the members of the group are self-oriented—competitive among themselves—the group problem-solving is less effective than if the members are *group*-oriented—cooperative—where the solution of a problem rebounds to the benefit of all the members equally (Deutsch, 1949). Another factor which determines the effectiveness of group problem-solving is the *range* of differences in personality in the group. Thus, paradoxical as it may seem, a group composed of like personalities may not be as effective as a group showing diversity of personalities. (See Box 168.)

SPECIFIC FACTORS AFFECTING GROUP SOLUTIONS. One obvious reason that the group may often do better is that there is a "pooling" of the individual answers, and thus any one person's errors may be more readily cancelled out. Another reason is indicated in a study by Shaw (1932) who found that the group rejects more incorrect ideas or hypotheses than does an individual working alone. Moreover, the group situation exposes any one person to a much greater range of possible valid hypotheses from which to choose. Indeed, there is a great deal of evidence to show that people meeting in free and informal group discussion may stimulate one another to the release and expression of all sorts of ideas which none of the individuals would think of when alone. Many of these ideas are "crazy" but some may be quite creative. For this to be effective it is critical that the full range of ideas be aired in the group, even if the opinions are held by only a minority of the members and run counter to the majority beliefs. It is in guaranteeing that such deviant minority ideas shall be heard by the group that the role of the leader is often most vital in facilitating group problem-solving.

This points to one of the most important of all questions bearing on the relation of individual to group creativity: What effect does *conformity pressure* from the group have on inhibiting the creative solutions of the individual? The very fact that a person is in a group whose ideas differ from his may prevent him from airing his ideas because he does not want to appear to be deviant. We now turn to this problem of group pressure for individual conformity.

Conformity to Group Pressure. What happens when an individual, in trying to make a judgment on a matter, is confronted with strong pressure from the group in a contradictory direction? And, especially, what happens when he feels that his perceptions are valid, his judgment correct, his solution the right one, and yet there is a *unanimous* consensus of his fellows against him?

Asch (1956) has carried out a series of experimental studies on this question. His technique was to make up groups consisting of one genuine subject and various numbers (from 3 to 10) of other "subjects" who were actually confederates of the experimenter. These confederates were instructed beforehand to give *unanimously wrong* judgments at certain points during a series of visual judgments as to which one of three lines projected on a screen before the group was equal in length to a standard line. The purpose was to see how the one genuine subject (who gave his judgment as the last one in the group) would respond—whether he would yield to the group pressure. Would he give an answer contradictory to his own judgment, or would he remain independent of the group pressure, and call them as he saw them?

The effects of group pressure proved to

BOX 168

Pattern of Personalities in Effective Groups

That the *pattern* of the different personalities in a group is of crucial importance in determining the effectiveness of the group's performance has been shown by Ghiselli and Lodahl.

Ninety subjects first took a "decision-making" test. On this test persons who see themselves as capable of making decisions rapidly and with full confidence in their own resourcefulness, earn high scores; those who see themselves as careful planners who require full information and review of the facts before making a decision, earn low scores.

The ninety subjects were then divided into thirty *groups*, and given the Ghiselli "railroad problem." This consists of an electric miniature railroad laid out in a square with rounded corners. At opposite corners are passing sidings, with a station on the main line at one corner and on the siding at the other. There are two identical sets of panels with separate switch controls, speed controls, and reversing switches. The two sets of panels are interrelated so that if current is fed into one track segment from one panel, it cannot be turned off from the other; similarly if a reversal switch is thrown from one panel, it cannot be turned to the other position from the other panel. Each panel is operated by one or two people. The task is to run two trains (a freight train and a passenger train) in opposite directions, as many times as possible during a three-minute trial. Since part of the right-of-way consists of a single track, the operation of the railroad requires a high degree of coordination and rapid decision-making among the persons comprising the group operating the two panels.

The results indicated that groups containing members all of whom were quick decision-makers (scoring high on the decision-making test) performed no better on the railroad task than groups containing members all of whom made low scores on the decision-making test. However, the groups which did best on the railroad task always contained *one* person who had made a high score on the decision test. The groups which contained several people who made high scores on the decision test and only one person who had made a low score, did most poorly on the railroad problem.

Ghiselli concludes that in a group task requiring coordination and cooperation among its members, performance will be better if most of the group members are cautious and careful in their decision making, but *one* member possesses a substantial measure of decisiveness and self-assurance. If the reverse is true, and the group contains many decisive persons and only a few cautious ones, performance will be poorer.

GHISELLI, E. E., and LODAHL, T. M. 1958. Patterns of managerial traits and group effectiveness. *J. abnorm. soc. Psychol.* (In press).

be very large. Thus about one third of all the genuine subjects gave judgments markedly distorted in the direction of the false group consensus. And this was true even though the difference between the correct line and the line picked by the confederates was so large that anyone free from the group pressure would never make a mistake. Further, experimental variations showed that the *size* of the unanimous group consensus was a significant factor. When the group consisted of only one confederate and a genuine subject, the subject remained completely independent. With two against him, there was appreciable conformity, and with three against him, the conformity reached a high level. Beyond that point—even with 15 confederates—there was no increase in conformity. If a "partner" were introduced who consistently gave the *correct* answer, this virtually abolished conformity in the subject. Having the social support of just one other fellow group-member was apparently sufficient to

BOX 169

The Measurement of Conformity

In work at the University of California's Institute of Personality Assessment and Research, Crutchfield has developed a technique that reproduces the essential conditions of the Asch group-pressure procedure (see text) but avoids the necessity of confederates, and makes all subjects in the group situation genuine subjects. This is accomplished through use of an electrical communication network (see photograph).

Five persons engage in a task in which they express their individual judgments of various kinds of stimuli, such as judging the relative length of lines, choosing the

answer to simple arithmetic problems, stating their opinions on social issues. The stimuli are presented by slides projected on the wall in front of the group. Each person is seated in his own open cubicle, facing a switchboard. The group members are not permitted to talk directly with one another, but only to communicate indirectly through these switchboards. Each person indicates his judgment by closing one of the numbered switches on his board, and this turns on certain signal lights on the switchboards of the other members. Thus, each person in the group can see what judgments their fellows make on each item.

The five persons are instructed by the experimenter to respond in a pre-established order, that is, one person is designated to give his judgment first, another second, and so on. This order of responding is rotated throughout the session, so that each person responds in each of the five serial positions.

Now, though this is what the subjects believe to be the situation, they are being grossly deceived by the experimenter. Actually, there is *no* electrical connection among their switchboards; all the signals

---

strengthen resistance to an otherwise overpowering group pressure. Strength of stimulus structure was also a factor. As the perceptual difference between the correct and "false" lines was diminished, the amount of conformity greatly increased.

PERSONALITY FACTORS IN CONFORMITY. Studies by Crutchfield (1955) show that there are large and consistent individual differences in tendency to conform or to remain independent under such group pressure. The experimental technique used by him to measure conformity behavior is described in Box 169.

More than 450 persons, varying in age, education, social background, intelligence, and personality characteristics have been

tested in this "standard group pressure" procedure. Included have been samples of military officers, college undergraduates, medical students, and middle-aged alumnae of a woman's college. In all these samples the range of individual differences in total conformity scores has been enormous, extending from virtually complete independence on all items exhibited by some persons to virtually complete conformity on all items in other persons.

Many of these persons were tested as part of a larger intensive assessment of their personalities. Analysis of those personality variables found to correlate significantly with conformity scores revealed the following main characteristics of the individual

BOX 169 (continued)

The Measurement of Conformity

that allegedly show the judgments of their fellow members are really being "fed" to them by the experimenter. All five subjects always get the same information; for instance, at a given point each is falsely told that he is answering second and each is told the same (non-existent) answer for his (non-existent) predecessor.

Through this deception, the experimenter can confront the subjects at certain points in the session with deliberately contrived conflicts. This he does by making it appear that all the other four members agree on a false answer. The individual's conformity tendency can thus be measured by determining the number of items on which he expresses agreement with this false group consensus and the number on which he gives the correct answer, or the judgment which he privately believes.

The amount of conformity behavior elicited by this technique is remarkably high. On easy perceptual comparisons and simple arithmetical problems as many as 30 per cent of the subjects will conform to the false group consensus. When the arithmetical problem is made highly ambiguous (by being actually insoluble), as many as

80 per cent of the subjects can be induced to accept the clearly illogical answer allegedly agreed upon by the rest of the group. And the conformity tendencies on social issues are equally striking. For example, an expression of agreement or disagreement by the person was called for on the following statement: "Free speech being a privilege rather than a right, it is proper for a society to suspend free speech whenever it feels itself threatened." Among control subjects answering outside the group-pressure situation, only 19 per cent expressed agreement. But among the experimental subjects confronted with a unanimous group consensus purporting to agree with the statement, *58 per cent* expressed agreement.

As many as fifty different items on which there is such group pressure may be included in a single session. Thus, it is readily possible to determine a total conformity score for each individual. These scores can then be used to study the relations of individual differences in conformity behavior to personality factors (see text).

CRUTCHFIELD, R. S. 1955. Conformity and character. *Amer. Psychol., 10,* 191–198.

---

able to withstand the group pressure and remain independent:

1. Intelligence, as measured by standard mental tests.

2. Originality, as manifested in thought processes and problem-solving.

3. "Ego strength," that is, the ability to cope effectively despite stressful circumstances.

4. Self-confidence, and absence of anxiety and inferiority feelings.

5. Optimal social attitudes and behavior, such as tolerance, responsibility, dominance, and freedom from disturbed and dependent relations with other people.

It is also found that on the average, females are more conforming than males.

And there are indications that the basis for conforming or for remaining independent of group pressure in the females lies not mainly in the types of factors listed above for the males, but lies rather in their acceptance of or rejection of the culturally stereotyped feminine role of passivity, dependence, and compliance.

The data also clearly reveal that there are different *kinds* of conforming behavior. Some persons conform in the group-pressure situation in an "expedient" way. They express outward agreement with the false group consensus though inwardly they do not believe it to be correct. This is shown by the fact that when they are tested privately on the attitude items after the group session, they revert completely to their own initial personal opinion, showing no after-effect of their compliance to the group consensus. Other subjects, on the other hand, seem to conform mainly out of the doubts about their own judgments engendered in them by the contrary group opinion. Thus, they continue to show some of the after-effects of the group pressure when tested privately even some weeks after the group session.

Those persons who remain independent of the group pressure may also be divided into several types. Some of them seem to resist the group pressure because they are rebellious and hostile toward other people; they may even move away from their own initial opinion in the direction *opposite* to the group consensus. They are, in a word, deliberate *non*-conformists. Others of the independent subjects may be regarded as "true" independents. That is, they are able to resist the group pressure toward a false answer apparently because of their intelligence, self-confidence, and "ego-strength."

Finally, it should be stressed that though these patterns of personality factors related to conformity tendencies do prove quite consistent, the conformity behavior of the individual is governed by more than these personality factors alone. Whether he conforms and how much are determined also by his perception of the particular group situation, the consequences he foresees for conforming or failing to conform, the nature of the items being judged, and the strength of conviction he feels.

The Individual and the Group. Most of the many problems that man faces and the decisions he must make, occur in the context of groups. This, as we have seen, is not an unmitigated blessing as far as man's effectiveness in coping with his world is concerned. The group can help the individual, but it can also inhibit his creativity and hinder his rational decision-making.

Nevertheless we must accept the universe. Man is a social animal, and he must forever remain so. The major problem facing a socially oriented psychology, therefore, is to discover how to enable each one of us to maximize his freedom of choice and to release his individual creativity while still remaining an integrated member of his group. The central problem toward which the study of man must be directed is how man can remain an *individual* in *society*.

Glossary

attitude. An enduring organization of perceptual, motivational, emotional, and adaptive processes centering on some object in the person's world. Attitudes may be positive or negative, that is, the person may be favorably disposed or unfavorably disposed toward the object.

attitude ratings. Consist of a number of descriptive categories (usually 5) ranging from one extreme to the other on a given dimension. The score assigned to a person is based upon the judgment of a rater who indicates in which descriptive category the person best fits.

attitude scale. A special case of the more general class of scales used in the measurement of personality. Consists of a large number of items, each designed to elicit an answer indicating a favorable or unfavorable disposition toward a specific object.

authoritarian leadership. Behavior characteristic of a leader who himself determines the policies and plans of the group, is the only one in the group cognizant of the succession of future steps in the group's activities, dictates the pattern of interrelations among the members, serves as the ultimate judge and agent of rewards and punishments of the group members.

Bogardus social distance scale. A scale primarily directed at the measurement of ethnic attitudes. The items permit the respondent to indicate the "social distance" that he wishes to keep between himself and the members of the ethnic group in question.

cognitive dissonance. Refers to a perceived incongruity between the person's own attitudes and his behavior. E.g., the man who fears the possible effect of smoking upon the development of lung cancer, and yet continues to smoke.

democratic leadership. Behavior characteristic of a leader who seeks to evoke the maximum involvement of every member in the determination of policies, seeks to spread responsibilities, encourages interpersonal contacts, and seeks to avoid a group structure in which special privilege and status differentials predominate.

fixed-alternative question. Used in public opinion polls, these questions can be answered by a choice among two or more alternative responses, such as "yes"-"no." Sometimes called "poll-type" questions, and very similar to the true-false or multiple-choice questions of "objective" examinations.

group dynamics. A term used to refer to the study of group behavior. The term is intended to emphasize the complex feed-back effects which influence the mutual behavior of individuals in groups.

group morale. A general term that refers to the level of effectiveness of group functioning and the unity and solidarity of the group. The higher the morale, the more productive the group, and the more resistant it is to break-up in the form of cliques and internal conflicts.

Likert scale. An empirically derived attitude scale consisting of many items referring to the same attitude. To each item the respondent indicates whether he strongly agrees, agrees, is undecided, disagrees, or strongly disagrees. These

responses are scored 5, 4, 3, 2, and 1, respectively. His attitude measure is given by the sum of all the scores.

open-ended question. Used in public opinion surveys, these questions permit the respondent to express his opinions in his own words and to indicate any qualifications he wishes. This type of question makes possible the collection of data concerning the cognitive content and degree of differentiation of the person's attitudes. Similar to the "essay type" questions found in examinations.

prejudice. Refers to attitudes that tend to place the objects of the attitude at an advantage or disadvantage without respect to all the available data. Thus one may be prejudiced *in favor of* Frenchmen and *against* Englishmen. In the former instance, the prejudiced person's perceptions of the Frenchman will tend to accentuate the good characteristics of the French and will tend to neglect any unfavorable data. In the latter instance, the perceptions will be selective in such a way that only the unfavorable traits of the Englishman will be observed, remembered and incorporated into the person's cognitive content. Such biased perceptions will be accompanied by behavior appropriate to them.

role. A pattern of behavior characteristic of an individual occupying a given niche in society, or fulfilling a specified function. The same individual may display many roles. For example, a person may be expected to behave in one manner *vis a vis* his children (the role of a father), in another manner in his job (the role of a worker), and in still another manner in the office of the doctor (the role of the patient).

sociometry. A method of determining the interrelationships among the members of a group in terms of feelings of attraction and rejection. Each member privately specifies which other members he likes, or wishes to work, eat, or live with, and which ones he wishes to avoid. From these responses it is possible to construct a "social map" of the group called a *sociogram.*

stereotype. May refer to two related phenomena. As a sociological and statistical concept it refers to a belief or attitude which is widespread in a society (e.g., the belief that blondes are less intellectual than brunettes). As a psychological concept it refers to a belief or attitude which is oversimplified in content, in which the unique attributes of the object are not observed, and which is resistant to change.

Thurstone scale. One type of attitude scale, usually consisting of about 20 items, each one of which has been assigned a scale value on the basis of ratings made by a set of judges. The 20 items represent the entire range of extremeness of attitudes. The person's attitude score is given by the sum of all the scale values of the items with which he agrees.

Suggestions for Further Reading

CARTWRIGHT, D., and ZANDER, A. F. (eds.) 1953. *Group dynamics: research and theory.* Evanston, Ill.: Row, Peterson.

A collection of 41 papers in the field of group dynamics written by some of the outstanding experimenters and theoreticians in the field.

HARE, P., BORGATTA, E. F., and BALES, R. F. (eds.) 1955. *Small groups: studies in social interaction.* New York: Alfred A. Knopf.

Fifty-eight social scientists are the contributors to this book which is concerned with social interaction in small groups. Both theoretical papers and experimental reports are included.

HOVLAND, C. I., JANIS, I. L., and KELLEY, H. H. 1953. *Communication and persuasion.* New Haven: Yale University Press.

A report of a series of studies performed at Yale University on the problem of attitude change via communication and persuasion.

HYMAN, H. H. 1955. *Survey design and analysis.* Glencoe, Ill.: Free Press.

One of the most thorough textbooks in the field of public opinion surveys. Deals with both the theoretical problems and the practical problems of such research.

KRECH, D., and CRUTCHFIELD, R. S. 1948. *Theory and problems of social psychology.* New York: McGraw-Hill.

A standard textbook. Covers in some detail all of the topics referred to in the present chapter.

LINDZEY, G. (ed.) 1954. *Handbook of social psychology* (2 vols.). Cambridge, Mass.: Addison-Wesley.

This handbook, written by authorities in the field, provides detailed coverage of the experimental facts in all major fields of social psychology.

General Glossary:
Review Index to Chapter Glossaries

Index to Works Cited

Subject and Name Index

Index to Works Cited

THE NUMBERS in **bold face** following each reference give the pages in the text on which that reference is cited, described, or discussed.

ADAMSON, R. E. 1952. Functional fixedness as related to problem-solving. *J. exp. Psychol.*, *44*, 288–91. —**379**

ADLER, A. 1930. Individual psychology. In Murchison, C. (ed.), *Psychologies of 1930*. Worcester, Mass.: Clark Univ. Press. Pp. 395–405. —**620**

ADORNO, T. W., FRENKEL-BRUNSWIK, E., LEVINSON, D. J., and SANFORD, R. N. 1950. *The authoritarian personality*. New York: Harper. —**617**

ALDRICH, C. A., and NORVAL, M. A. 1946. A developmental graph for the first year of life. *J. Pediat.*, *29*, 304–8. —**597**

ALEXANDER, F. 1946. Individual psychotherapy. *Psychosom. Med.*, *8*, 110–15. —**659**

ALLPORT, F. H. 1924. *Social psychology*. Boston: Houghton Mifflin. —**462**

ALLPORT, F. H. 1955. *Theories of perception and the concept of structure*. New York: Wiley. —**117**

ALLPORT, G. W. 1937. *Personality*. New York: Holt. —**609, 615, 623, 642**

ALLPORT, G. W., and KRAMER, B. M. 1946. Some roots of prejudice. *J. Psychol.*, *22*, 9–39. —**675**

ALLPORT, G. W., and ODBERT, H. S. 1936. Traitnames: a psycho-lexical study. *Psychol. Monogr.*, *47*, No. 211. —**610**

ALLPORT, G. W., VERNON, P. E., and LINDZEY, G. 1951. *A study of values: a scale for measuring the dominant interests in personality* (rev. ed.). Boston: Houghton Mifflin. —**636**

ANASTASI, A., and FOLEY, J. P. 1949. *Differential psychology* (rev. ed.). New York: Macmillan. —**561, 584**

ANDERSON, B. 1952. Polydipsia caused by intrahypothalamic injections of hypertonic NaCl solutions. *Experientia*, *8*, 157. —**331**

ANSBACHER, H. L., and ANSBACHER, R. R. (eds.). 1956. *The individual psychology of Alfred Adler*. New York: Basic Books. —**642**

ASCH, S. E. 1946. Forming impressions of personality. *J. abnorm. soc. Psychol.*, *41*, 258–90. —**668**

ASCH, S. E. 1952. *Social psychology*. New York: Prentice-Hall. —**669**

ASCH, S. E. 1956. Studies of independence and submission to group pressure: I. A minority of one against a unanimous majority. *Psychol. Monogr.*, *70*, No. 416. —**688**

ATTNEAVE, F. 1954. Some informational aspects of visual perception. *Psychol. Rev.*, *61*, 183–93. —**92**

BALES, R. F., and BORGATTA, E. F. 1955. Size of group as a factor in the interaction profile. In Hare, A. P., Borgatta, E. F., and Bales, R. F. (eds.). *Small groups*. New York: Alfred A. Knopf. Pp. 396–413. —**688**

BARKER, R., DEMBO, T., LEWIN, K. 1941. Frustration and regression: an experiment with young children. *Univ. of Iowa Studies in Child Welfare*, *18*, No. 1. —**317**

BARTLETT, F. C. 1932. *Remembering*. Cambridge: Cambridge Univ. Press. —**422, 434**

BARTLEY, S. H. 1951. The psychophysiology of vision. In Stevens, S. S. (ed.), *Handbook of experimental psychology*. New York: Wiley. —**164**

BATTERSBY, W. S., TEUBER, H. L., and BENDER, M. B. 1953. Problem-solving behavior in men with frontal or occipital brain injuries. *J. Psychol.*, *35*, 329–51. —**380**

BAYER, E. 1929. *Beiträge zur Zweikomponotentheorie des Hungers*. Z. Psychol., *112*, 1–54. —**295**

BAYLEY, N. 1951. Development and maturation. In Helson, H. (ed.), *Theoretical foundations of psychology*. New York: Van Nostrand. —**544, 587**

BAYLEY, N., and ODEN, M. H. 1955. The maintenance of intellectual ability in gifted adults. *J. Gerontology*, *10*, 91–107. —**545**

BEACH, F. A. 1948. *Hormones and behavior*. New York: Hoeber. —**355**

BEACH, F. A. 1951. Instinctive behavior: reproductive activities. In Stevens, S. S. (ed.), *Handbook of experimental psychology*. New York: Wiley. —**347, 348**

BEAN, C. H. 1932. An unusual opportunity to investigate the psychology of language. *J genet. Psychol.*, *40*, 181–202. —**461–2**

BEEBY, C. E. 1930. An experimental investigation into the simultaneous constituents of an act of skill. _Brit. J. Psychol., 20,_ 336–53. —**453**

BENTLEY, M. 1925. _The field of psychology._ New York: Appleton-Century-Crofts. —**447**

BETTELHEIM, B. 1943. Individual and mass behavior in extreme situations. _J. abnorm. soc. Psychol., 38,_ 417–52. —**649**

BIRCH, H. G. 1945. The role of motivational factors in insightful problem-solving. _J. comp. Psychol., 38,_ 259–78. —**393**

BLAKE, R. R., and RAMSEY, G. V. (eds.). 1951. _Perception: an approach to personality._ New York: Ronald. —**48**

BLATZ, W. E., and MILLICHAMP, D. A. 1935. The development of emotion in the infant. _Univ. of Toronto Studies, Child Development Series,_ No. 4. —**599**

BLEULER, M., and BLEULER, R. 1935. Rorschach's ink-blot tests and racial psychology. _Charact. and Personal., 4,_ 97–114. —**46**

BLOCK, J. 1957. Studies in the phenomenology of emotion. _J. abnorm. soc. Psychol., 54,_ 358–63. —**232**

BLODGETT, H. C. 1929. The effect of the introduction of reward upon the maze performance of rats. _Univ. Calif. Publ. Psychol., 4,_ 113–34. —**443, 444**

BOGARDUS, E. S. 1925. Measuring social distance. _J. appl. Sociol., 9,_ 299–308. —**681**

BOGARDUS, E. S. 1928. _Immigration and race attitudes._ Boston: Heath. —**682**

BOOK, W. F. 1925. _The psychology of skill._ New York: Gregg. —**451**

BORING, E. G. 1942. _Sensation and perception in the history of experimental psychology._ New York: Appleton-Century-Crofts. —**82**

BORING, E. G. 1943. The moon illusion. _Amer. J. Physics, 11,_ 55–60. —**5**

BORING, E. G. 1950. _A history of experimental psychology_ (2nd ed.). New York: Appleton-Century-Crofts. —**481**

BORING, E. G., LANGFELD, H. S., and WELD, H. P. (eds.). 1948. _Foundations of psychology._ New York: Wiley. —**24, 54, 132**

BOUSFIELD, W. A., and COHEN, B. H. 1955. General review of a program of research on associative clustering. Storrs, Conn.: Univ. of Conn., Technical Report, No. 11, O. N. R. —**423**

BREASTED, J. H. 1930. _The Edwin Smith surgical papyrus._ Chicago: Univ. of Chicago Press. —**480**

BRIDGES, K. M. B. 1932. Emotional development in early infancy. _Child Develop., 3,_ 324–41. —**599**

BROMILEY, R. B. 1948. Conditioned responses in a dog after removal of neocortex. _J. comp. physiol. Psychol., 41,_ 102–10. —**493–4**

BROWN, D. R. 1953. Stimulus similarity and the anchoring of subjective scales. _Amer. J. Psychol., 66,_ 199–214. —**95**

BROWN, J. F. 1931. The visual perception of velocity. _Psychol. Forsch., 14,_ 199–232. —**125**

BROWN, J. S. 1948. Gradients of approach and avoidance responses and their relation to motivation. _J. comp. physiol. Psychol., 41,_ 450–65. —**310**

BROWN, R. W., BLACK, A. H., and HOROWITZ, A. E. 1955. Phonetic symbolism in natural languages. _J. abnorm. soc. Psychol., 50,_ 388–93. —**30**

BRUNER, J. S., GOODNOW, J. J., and AUSTIN, G. A. 1956. _A study of thinking._ New York: Wiley. —**400**

BRUNER, J. S., MATTER, J., and PAPENEK, M. L. 1955. Breadth of learning as a function of drive level and mechanization. _Psychol. Rev., 62,_ 1–10. —**441**

BRUNER, J. S., and POSTMAN, L. J. 1949. On the perception of incongruity: a paradigm. _J. Person., 18,_ 206–23. —**103**

BRUNSWIK, E. 1956. _Perception and the representative design of psychological experiments._ Berkeley: Univ. of California Press. —**152**

BUMSTEAD, A. P. 1943. Finding the best method for memorizing. _J. educ. Psychol., 34,_ 110–14. —**415**

BURT, C., and HOWARD, M. 1956. The multifactorial theory of inheritance and its application to intelligence. _Brit. J. statist. Psychol., 9,_ 95–131. —**576**

BURTON, N. G., and LICKLIDER, J. C. R. 1956. Long-range constraints in the statistical structure of printed English. _Amer. J. Psychol., 68,_ 650–3. —**469**

CAMERON, N. A. 1947. _Psychology of the behavior disorders._ Boston: Houghton Mifflin. —**665**

CANNON, W. B. 1927. The James-Lange theory of emotions: a critical examination and an alternative theory. _Amer. J. Psychol., 39,_ 106–24. —**343**

CANNON, W. B. 1929. _Bodily changes in pain, hunger, fear, and rage_ (2nd ed.). New York: Appleton-Century-Crofts. —**264**

CANNON, W. B. 1931. Again the James-Lange and the thalamic theories of emotion. _Psychol. Rev., 38,_ 281–95. —**343**

CANNON, W. B. 1939. _The wisdom of the body_ (rev. ed.). New York: Norton. —**324**

CANNON, W. B., and BRITTON, S. W. 1925. Studies on the conditions of activity in endocrine glands. _Amer. J. Physiol., 72,_ 283–94. —**331**

CANNON, W. B., and WASHBURN, A. C. 1912. An explanation of hunger. _Amer. J. Physiol., 29,_ 441–54. —**329**

CANTRIL, H. 1940. _The invasion from Mars._ Princeton: Princeton Univ. Press. —**679**

CARMICHAEL, L. (ed.). 1954. Manual of child psychology (2nd ed.). New York: Wiley. —**608**

CARR, H. A. 1935. *An introduction to space perception.* New York: Longmans, Green. —**154**

CARR, H. A., and HARDY, M. C. 1920. Some factors in the perception of relative motion. *Psychol. Rev., 27,* 24–37. —**120**

CARTWRIGHT, D., and ZANDER, A. F. (eds.). 1953. *Group dynamics: research and theory.* Evanston, Ill.: Row, Peterson. —**694**

CASON, H. 1930. Common annoyances: a psychological study of every-day aversions and irritations. *Psychol. Monogr., 40,* No. 2, 1–218. —**241**

CATTELL, R. B. 1946. *Description and measurement of personality.* Yonkers, N.Y.: World Book Co. —**612**

CLARK, K. B., and CLARK, M. K. 1939. The development of consciousness of self and the emergence of racial identification in Negro pre-school children. *J. soc. Psychol., 10,* 591–9. —**214**

COHEN, L. D., KIPNIS, D., KUNKLE, E. C., and KUBZANSKY, P. E. 1955. Observations of a person with congenital insensitivity to pain. *J. abnorm. soc. Psychol., 51,* 333–8. —**42**

CONEL, J. L. 1952. Histologic development of the cerebral cortex. In *The biology of mental health and disease.* New York: Hoeber. —**592**

COOK, T. H. 1942. The application of the Rorschach test to a Samoan group. *Rorsch. Resch. Exch., 6,* 51–60. —**46**

COOPER, E., and JAHODA, M. 1947. The evasion of propaganda: how prejudiced people respond to anti-prejudice propaganda. *J. Psychol., 23,* 15–25. —**680**

CRONBACH, L. J. 1949. *Essentials of psychological testing.* New York: Harper. —**561**

CROZIER, W. J., and PINCUS, G. 1926. The geotropic conduct of young rats. *J. gen. Physiol., 10,* 257–69. —**269**

CROZIER, W. J., and PINCUS, G. 1927. On the equilibration of geotropic and phototropic excitation in the rat. *J. gen. Physiol., 10,* 419–24. —**269**

CRUTCHFIELD, R. S. 1955. Conformity and character. *Amer. Psychol., 10,* 191–8. —**690, 691**

CRUTCHFIELD, R. S., WOODWORTH, D. G., and ALBRECHT, R. E. 1955. *Perceptual performance and the effective person.* San Antonio: Air Force Personnel and Training Research Center. —**152**

DALLENBACH, K. M. 1927. The temperature spots and end organs. *Amer. J. Psychol., 39,* 417. —**71**

DAVIS, A., GARDNER, B. B., and GARDNER, M. B. 1941. *Deep South.* Chicago: Univ. Chicago Press. —**581**

DAVIS, H. (ed.). 1947. *Hearing and deafness.* New York: Rinehart. —**82**

DAVIS, H., and DAVIS, P. A. 1936. Action potentials of the brain. *Arch. Neurol. & Psychiat., 36,* 1214–24. —**486**

DEMPSEY, E. W. 1951. Homeostasis. In Stevens, S. S. (ed.), *Handbook of experimental psychology.* New York: Wiley. —**355**

DENNIS, W. 1941. Infant development under conditions of restricted practice and of minimum social stimulation. *Genet. psychol. Monogr., 23,* 143–91. —**596**

DENNIS, W., and DENNIS, M. G. 1940. The effect of cradling practices upon the onset of walking in Hopi children. *J. genet. Psychol., 56,* 77–86. —**596**

DEUTSCH, M. 1949. An experimental study of the effects of cooperation and competition upon group process. *Hum. Relat., 2,* 199–232. —**688**

DEUTSCH, M., and COLLINS, M. E. 1951. *Interracial housing: a psychological evaluation of a social experiment.* Minneapolis: Univ. of Minnesota Press. —**675**

DOBZHANSKY, T. 1955. *Evolution, genetics, and man.* New York: Wiley. —**584**

DOLLARD, J., DOOB, L. W., MILLER, N. E., MOWRER, O. H., SEARS, R. R., FORD, C. S., HOVLAND, C. I., and SOLLENBERGER, R. T. 1939. *Frustration and aggression.* New Haven: Yale Univ. Press. —**324**

DOLLARD, J., and MILLER, N. E. 1950. *Personality and psychotherapy.* New York: McGraw-Hill. —**665**

DOOB, L. W. 1956. In *Quarterly Report,* Carnegie Corporation of New York, 4, No. 1. —**44**

DROBA, D. D. 1930. *A scale for measuring attitude toward war.* Chicago: Univ. of Chicago Press. —**681**

DUNBAR, F. 1954. *Emotions and bodily changes* (4th ed.). New York: Columbia Univ. Press. —**264**

DUNCKER, K. 1938. Induced movement. In Ellis, W. D., *A sourcebook of Gestalt psychology.* New York: Harcourt, Brace. —**121**

DUNCKER, K. 1945. On problem-solving. *Psychol. Monogr., 58,* No. 5. —**374, 396, 399**

DUNLAP, K. 1927. The role of eye-muscles and mouth-muscles in the expression of the emotions. *Genet. Psychol. Monogr., 2,* No. 3. —**261**

DURKIN, H. 1937. Trial-and-error, gradual analysis, and sudden re-organization. *Arch. Psychol., 30,* No. 210. —**364**

EBBINGHAUS, H. 1913. *Memory: a contribution to experimental psychology.* (Trans. by H. A. Ruger and C. E. Bussenius). New York: Columbia Univ. Press. —**412**

ELLIOTT, M. H. 1928. The effect of change of reward on the maze performance of rats. *Univ. Calif. Publ. Psychol., 4,* 19–30. —**303**

ELLIS, W. D. 1938. *A sourcebook of Gestalt psychology.* New York: Harcourt, Brace. —33, 117

ENGLISH, H. B., WELBORN, E. L., and KILLIAN, C. D. 1934. Studies in substance memorization. *J. gen. Psychol. 11,* 233–60. —419

ERIKSON, E. H. 1956. The problem of ego identity. *J. Amer. Psychoanal. Assn., 4,* 56–112. —645

EVANS, R. M. 1948. *An introduction to color.* New York: Wiley. —82

EYSENCK, H. J. 1952. The effects of psychotherapy: an evaluation. *J. consult. Psychol., 16,* 319–24. —662

FENICHEL, O. 1945. *Psychoanalytic theory of neurosis.* New York: Norton. —394

FESTINGER, L. 1957. *A theory of cognitive dissonance.* Evanston, Ill.: Row, Peterson. —674

FLOURENS, P. 1824. *Recherches expérimentales sur les propriétés et les fonctions du système nerveux dans les animaux vertébrés.* Paris: Librairie de l'Académie Royale de Médecine. —480–2

FLUGEL, J. C. 1954. Humor and laughter. In Lindzey, G. (ed.), *Handbook of social psychology.* Cambridge, Mass.: Addison-Wesley. —254

FORD, C. S., and BEACH, F. A. 1951. *Patterns of sexual behavior.* New York: Hoeber. —290

FRANZBLAU, R. N. 1935. Race differences in mental and physical traits studied in different environments. *Arch. Psychol.,* No. 177. —580

FRENKEL-BRUNSWIK, E. 1949. Intolerance of ambiguity as an emotional and perceptual personality variable. *J. Personal., 18,* 108–43. —394

FRENKEL-BRUNSWIK, E., and SANFORD, R. N. 1945. Some personality factors in anti-Semitism. *J. Psychol., 20,* 271–91. —647

FREUD, S. 1933. *The interpretation of dreams.* (Trans. by A. A. Brill.) New York: Macmillan. —651

FREUD, S. 1938. *The basic writings of Sigmund Freud.* New York: Modern Library. —642

FROMM, E. 1941. *Escape from freedom.* New York: Rinehart. —622

FULLER, J. L., and SCOTT, J. P. 1954. Heredity and learning ability in infrahuman mammals. *Eugen. Quart., 1,* 28–43. —573

GAGNÉ, R. M., and FOSTER, H. 1949. Transfer of training from practice on components in a motor skill. *J. exp. Psychol., 39,* 47–68 —454

GARDNER, E. 1952. *Fundamentals of neurology.* Philadelphia: Saunders. —197

GATES, A. I. 1917. Recitation as a factor in memorizing. *Arch. Psychol., 7,* No. 40. —417

GAVETT, G. I. 1925. *A first course in statistical method.* New York: McGraw-Hill. —509

GELDARD, F. A. 1953. *The human senses.* New York: Wiley. —83

GESELL, A., ET AL. 1939. *Biographies of child development.* New York: Hoeber. —629

GESELL, A., and AMATRUDA, C. S. 1947. *Developmental diagnosis: normal and abnormal child development.* New York: Hoeber. —590

GESELL, A., and ILG, F. L. 1943. *Infant and child in the culture of today.* New York: Harper. —608

GESELL, A., and ILG, F. L. 1946. *The child from five to ten.* New York: Harper. —608

GHISELLI, E. E. 1955. The measurement of occupational aptitude. *Univ. Calif. Publ. Psychol., 8,* 101–216. —549, 555

GHISELLI, E. E., and BROWN, C. W. 1955. *Personnel and industrial psychology.* New York: McGraw-Hill. —455, 456, 457, 562

GHISELLI, E. E., and LODAHL, T. M. 1958. Patterns of managerial traits and group effectiveness. *J. abnorm. soc. Psychol.* (In press.) —689

GIBSON, J. J. 1950. *The perception of the visual world.* Boston: Houghton Mifflin. —154

GLANVILLE, A. D., and DALLENBACH, K. M. 1929. The range of attention. *Amer. J. Psychol., 41,* 207–36. —104

GOLDHAMER, H., and MARSHALL, A. W. 1953. *Psychosis and civilization.* Glencoe, Ill.: Free Press. —635

GOLTZ, F. 1892. *Der Hund ohne Grosshirn. Arch. ges. Physiol., 51,* 570–614. —331

GOTTSCHALDT, K. 1926; 1929. *Über den Einfluss der Erfahrung auf die Wahrnehmung von Figuren. Psychol. Forsch., 8,* 261–317; *12,* 1–87. —97

GOUGH, H. G. 1957. *Manual for the California Psychological Inventory.* Palo Alto: Consulting Psychologists Press. —635

GRUENBERG, B. C., and BINGHAM, N. E. 1944. *Biology and man.* New York: Ginn & Co. —569

GRUENBERG, S. M. (ed.). 1952. *Our children today.* New York: Viking Press. —608

GUILFORD, J. P. 1940. An inventory of factors STDCR. Beverly Hills, Calif.: Sheridan Supply Co. —614

GUILFORD, J. P., WILSON, R. C., CHRISTIANSEN, P. R., and LEWIS, D. J. 1951. *A factor-analytic study of creative thinking: I. Hypotheses and descriptions of tests.* Report from the Psychol. Lab., No. 3. Los Angeles: Univ. of Southern California. —634

GUYTON, A. C. 1956. *Textbook of medical physiology.* Philadelphia: Saunders. —338

HADAMARD, J. 1949. *Psychology of invention in the mathematical field.* Princeton: Princeton Univ. Press. —363, 366, 371

HADLEY, J. M. 1958. *Clinical and counseling psychology.* New York: Alfred A. Knopf. —665

HAIRE, M. 1950. Projective techniques in market research. *J. Marketing*, 649–56. —**682**

HAIRE, M., and GRUNES, W. F. 1950. Perceptual defenses: processes protecting an original perception of another personality. *Hum. Relat.*, *3*, 403–12. —**671**

HALL, C. S. 1937. Emotional behavior in the rat. *J. comp. Psychol.*, *24*, 369–75. —**570**

HALL, C. S., and LINDZEY, G. 1957. *Theories of personality*. New York: Wiley. —**642**

HARE, P., BORGATTA, E. F., and BALES, R. F. (eds.). 1955. *Small groups: studies in social interaction*. New York: Alfred A. Knopf. —**694**

HARLOW, H. F. 1950. Learning motivated by a manipulation drive. *J. exp. Psychol.*, *40*, 228–34. —**9**

HARLOW, H. F. 1952. Functional organization of the brain in relation to mentation and behavior. In *The biology of mental health and disease*. New York: Hoeber. —**498**

HARROWER, M. R. 1937. *The psychologist at work*. New York: Harper. —**33**

HAYAKAWA, S. I. 1949. *Language in thought and action*. New York: Harcourt, Brace. —**479**

HEBB, D. O. 1946. On the nature of fear. *Psychol. Rev.*, *53*, 259–76. —**237**

HEBB, D. O. 1949. *The organization of behavior*. New York: Wiley. —**504**

HEIDBREDER, E. F. 1928. Problem-solving in children and adults. *J. genet. Psychol.*, *35*, 522–45. —**594**

HEIDER, F. 1940. Report of Research Department: Clarke School for the Deaf. *Psychol. Monogr.*, *52*, No. 232. —**459, 466**

HELSON, H. 1947. Adaptation-level as a frame of reference for prediction of psychophysical data. *Amer. J. Psychol.*, *60*, 1–29. —**95**

HENLE, M. 1942. An experimental investigation of dynamic and structural determinants of substitution. *Contrib. psychol. Theory*, *2*, No. 3. —**313**

HENLE, M. 1942. An experimental investigation of past experience as a determinant of visual form perception. *J. exp. Psychol.*, *30*, 1–21. —**96**

HENNING, H. 1916. *Der Geruch. Z. Psychol.*, *75*, 177–230; *76*, 1–127. —**69**

HERNÁNDEZ-PEÓN, R., SCHERRER, H., and JOUVET, M. 1956. Modification of electrical activity in cochlear nucleus during "attention" in unanesthetized cats. *Science*, *123*, 331–2. —**172**

HERON, W., DOANE, B. K., and SCOTT, T. H. 1956. Visual disturbances after prolonged perceptual isolation. *Canad. J. Psychol.*, *10*, 13–8. —**8**

HERTZ, M. 1929. *Die Organisation des optischen Feldes bei der Biene. Zeitschr. f. vergl. Physiol.*, *8*, 693–748. —**38**

HESS, E. H. 1950. Development of the chick's responses to light and shade cues of depth. *J. comp. physiol. Psychol.*, *43*, 112–22. —**140**

HILGARD, E. R. 1956. *Theories of learning*. New York: Appleton-Century-Crofts. —**457**

HILGARD, E. R., and MARQUIS, D. G. 1950. *Conditioning and learning*. New York: Appleton-Century-Crofts. —**410, 434**

HILGARD, J. R. 1932. Learning and maturation in pre-school children. *J. genet. Psychol.*, *41*, 36–56. —**595**

HIMWICH, H. E. 1955. The new psychiatric drugs. *Scientific American*, *193*, 80–6. —**333**

HOCH, P. H. 1955. Experimental psychiatry. *Amer. J. Psychiat.*, *111*, 787–90. —**656**

HOLLINGWORTH, L. S. 1942. *Children above 180 I.Q.* New York: World Book Co. —**684**

HOLWAY, A. H., and BORING, E. G. 1941. Determinants of apparent visual size with distance variant. *Amer. J. Psychol.*, *54*, 21–37. —**148**

HONZIK, C. H. 1936. The sensory basis of maze learning in rats. *Comp. Psychol. Monogr.*, *13*, No. 64. —**443, 449**

HORNEY, K. 1937. *The neurotic personality of our time*. New York: Norton. —**622**

HOVLAND, C. I. 1937. The generalization of conditioned responses. *J. gen. Psychol.*, *17*, 125–48. —**404**

HOVLAND, C. I. 1937. The generalization of conditioned responses. *J. exp. Psychol.*, *21*, 261–76. —**405**

HOVLAND, C. I. 1951. Human learning and retention. In Stevens, S. S. (ed.), *Handbook of experimental psychology*. New York: Wiley. —**417, 434**

HOVLAND, C. I., JANIS, I. L., and KELLEY, H. H. 1953. *Communication and persuasion*. New Haven: Yale Univ. Press. —**694**

HOVLAND, C. I., LUMSDAINE, A. A., and SHEFFIELD, F. D. 1949. *Experiments on mass communication*. Princeton: Princeton Univ. Press. —**416**

HOVLAND, C. I., and WEISS, W. 1951. The influence of source credibility on communication effectiveness. *Publ. Opin. Quart.*, *15*, 635–50. —**677**

HOWELLS, T. H. 1944. The experimental development of color-tone synesthesia. *J. exp. Psychol.*, *34*, 87–103. —**31**

HUDGINS, C. V. 1933. Conditioning and the voluntary control of the pupillary light reflex. *J. gen. Psychol.*, *8*, 3–51. —**409**

HUDGINS, C. V. 1935. Steckle and Renshaw on the conditioned iridic reflex: a discussion. *J. gen. Psychol.*, *12*, 208–14. —**409**

HUMPHREY, G. 1948. *Directed thinking*. New York: Dodd, Mead. —**366, 399, 483**

HUNT, J. MCV. 1941. The effects of infant feeding-frustration upon adult hoarding in the albino rat. *J. abnorm. soc. Psychol.*, *36*, 338–60. —**632**

HYMAN, H. H. 1955. *Survey design and analysis*. Glencoe, Ill.: Free Press. —**694**

KRECH, D., and CRUTCHFIELD, R. S. 1948. *Theory and problems of social psychology.* New York: McGraw-Hill. —**678**

KRECH, D., ROSENZWEIG, M. R., BENNETT, E. C., and KRUECKEL, B. 1945. Enzyme concentrations in the brain and adjustive behavior-patterns. *Science, 120,* 994-6. —**572**

KRECHEVSKY, I. 1932. "Hypotheses" versus "chance" in the pre-solution period in sensory discrimination-learning. *Univ. Calif. Publ. Psychol., 6,* No. 3—**438**

KRECHEVSKY, I. 1933. Hereditary nature of "hypotheses." *J. comp. Psychol., 16,* 99-116. —**439**

KRECHEVSKY, I. 1937. Brain mechanisms and variability. *J. comp. Psychol., 23,* 121-38. —**497**

KREEZER, G., and DALLENBACH, K. M. 1929. Learning the relation of opposition. *Amer. J. Psychol., 41,* 432-41. —**594**

KRETSCHMER, E. 1921. *Körperbau und Charakter.* Berlin: Springer. (Trans., 1936, as *Physique and character.* New York: Harcourt, Brace). —**613**

LANDIS, C. 1924. Studies of emotional reactions. II. General behavior and facial expression. *J. comp. Psychol., 4,* 447-501. —**261**

LANDRETH, C. 1958. *The psychology of early childhood.* New York: Alfred A. Knopf. —**608**

LANGFELD, H. S. 1914. Note on a case of chromaesthesia. *Psychol. Bull., 11,* 113-4. —**31**

LASHLEY, K. S. 1929. *Brain mechanisms and intelligence.* Chicago: Univ. of Chicago Press. —**496, 504**

LASHLEY, K. S. 1930. The mechanism of vision. *J. genet. Psychol., 37,* 453-60. —**440**

LASHLEY, K. S. 1951. The problem of serial order in behavior. In Jeffress, L. A. (ed.), *Cerebral mechanisms in behavior.* New York: Wiley. —**447-8, 458**

LASHLEY, K. S., and RUSSELL, J. T. 1934. The mechanism of vision. XI. A preliminary test of innate organization. *J. genet. Psychol., 45,* 136-44. —**139**

LAWRENCE, D. H. 1949, 1950. Acquired distinctiveness of cues. *J. exp. Psychol., 39,* 770-84; *40,* 175-88. —**439.**

LAWRENCE, M. 1949. *Studies in human behavior.* Princeton: Princeton Univ. Press. —**155**

LEARNED, W. S., and WOOD, B. D. 1938. *The student and his knowledge.* New York: Carnegie Foundation for the Advancement of Teaching. —**548**

LEE, E. S. 1951. Negro intelligence and selective migration. *Amer. sociol. Rev., 16,* 227-33. —**580**

LEEPER, R. W. 1935. A study of a neglected portion of the field of learning: the development of sensory organization. *J. genet. Psychol., 46,* 41-75. —**101**

LEHMAN, H. C. 1953. *Age and achievement.* Princeton: Princeton Univ. Press. —**559**

LEWIN, K. 1935. *Dynamic theory of personality.* New York: McGraw-Hill. —**229, 313, 324**

LEWIS, H. B., and FRANKLIN, M. 1944. An experimental study of the role of the ego in work. II. The significance of task-orientation in work. *J. exp. Psychol., 34,* 195-215. —**321**

LICHTEN, W., and LURIE, S. 1950. A new technique for the study of perceived size. *Amer. J. Psychol., 63,* 281-2. —**148**

LILLY, J. C. 1956. Mental effects of reduction of ordinary levels of physical stimuli on intact healthy persons. *Psychiat. Resch. Repts., 5,* 1-9. —**8**

LINDSLEY, D. B. 1951. Discussion. In Jeffress, L. A. (ed.), *Cerebral mechanisms in behavior.* New York: Wiley. —**593**

LINDSLEY, D. B. 1951. Emotions. In Stevens, S. S. (ed.), *Handbook of experimental psychology.* New York: Wiley. —**355**

LINDSLEY, D. B., BOWDEN, J., and MAGOUN, H. W. 1949. Effect upon EEG of acute injury to the brain stem activating system. *EEG clin. Neurophysiol., 1,* 475-86. —**485**

LINDZEY, G. (ed.). 1954. *Handbook of social psychology* (2 vols.). Cambridge, Mass.: Addison-Wesley. —**694**

LIPPITT, R. 1940. An experimental study of the effect of democratic and authoritarian group atmospheres. *Univ. Ia. Stud., 16,* No. 3, 43-198. —**685**

LUCHINS, A. S. 1942. Mechanization in problem-solving. *Psychol. Monogr., 54,* No. 6. —**384**

MCCLELLAND, D. C. (ed.). 1955. *Studies in motivation.* New York: Appleton-Century-Crofts. —**324**

MCCLELLAND, D. C., and ATKINSON, J. W. 1948. The projective expression of needs. I. The effect of different intensities of hunger drive on perception. *J. Psychol., 25,* 205-22. —**98**

MCCLELLAND, D. C., ATKINSON, J. W., CLARK, R. A., and LOWELL, E. L. 1953. *The achievement motive.* New York: Appleton-Century-Crofts. —**305**

MCDOUGALL, W. 1923. *An introduction to social psychology* (15th ed.). Boston: Luce. —**290**

MCKINNEY, F. 1949. *Psychology of personal adjustment* (rev. ed.). New York: Wiley. —**665**

MACKINNON, D. W. 1938. Violation of prohibitions. In Murray, H. A., *Explorations in personality.* New York: Oxford Univ. Press. Pp. 491-501. —**638**

MAIER, N. R. F. 1933. An aspect of human reasoning. *Brit. J. Psychol., 24,* 144-55. —**387**

MAIER, N. R. F. 1949. *Frustration: a study of behavior without a goal.* New York: McGraw-Hill. —**324**

MAIER, N. R. F., GLASER, N. M., and KLEE, J. B. 1940. Studies of abnormal behavior in the rat. III. The development of behavior fixations through frustration. *J. exp. Psychol.*, *26*, 521–46. —**319**

MARAÑON, G. 1924. In *Revue française d'endocrinologie*, *2*, 301. —**234**

MARQUIS, D. P. 1931. Can conditioned responses be established in the newborn infant? *J. genet. Psychol.*, *39*, 479–92. —**594**

MASLOW, A. H. 1954. *Motivation and personality.* New York: Harper. —**290, 626, 642**

MASSERMAN, J. H. 1946. *Principles of dynamic psychiatry.* Philadelphia: Saunders. —**647**

MAUDRY, M., and NEKULA, M. 1939. Social relations between children of the same age during the first two years of life. *J. genet. Psychol.*, *54*, 193–215. —**602**

MELTON, A. E., and IRWIN, J. MCQ. 1940. The influence of degree of interpolated learning on retroactive inhibition and overt transfer of specific responses. *Amer. J. Psychol.*, *53*, 173–203. —**430**

METZGER, W. 1953. *Gesetze des Sehens.* Frankfurt am Main: Waldemar Kramer. —**117**

MICHOTTE, A. 1954. *La perception de la causalité* (2nd ed.). Louvain: Publication Universitaires de Louvain. —**127, 155**

MILLER, G. A. 1951. *Language and communication.* New York: McGraw-Hill —**471, 472, 479**

MILLER, G. A., HEISE, G. A., and LICHTEN, W. 1951. The intelligibility of speech as a function of the context of test material. *J. exp. Psychol.*, *41*, 329–35. —**470**

MILLER, G. A., and LICKLIDER, J. C. R. 1950. The intelligibility of interrupted speech. *J. acoust. Soc. Amer.*, *22*, 167–73. —**471**

MILLER, N. E. 1944. Experimental studies of conflict. In Hunt, J. McV. (ed.), *Personality and the behavior disorders.* New York: Ronald, 431–65. —**310**

MILLER, N. E. 1948. Fear as an acquired drive. *J. exp. Psychol.*, *38*, 89–101. —**625**

MILLER, N. E., and BUGELSKI, R. 1948. Minor studies of aggression. II. The influence of frustrations imposed by the in-group on attitudes expressed toward out-groups. *J. Psychol.*, *25*, 437–52. —**316**

MILLER, R. E., MURPHY, J. V., and MIRSKY, I. A. 1955. The modification of social dominance in a group of monkeys by interanimal conditioning. *J. comp. physiol. Psychol.*, *48*, 392–6. —**285**

MINAMI, H., and DALLENBACH, K. M. 1946. The effect of activity upon learning and retention in the cockroach. *Amer. J. Psychol.*, *59*, 1–58. —**429**

MOORE, T. V. 1929. The reasoning ability of children in the first years of school life. *Cathol. Univ. Stud. Psychol. Psychiat.* —**594**

MORENO, J. L. 1934. *Who shall survive? A new approach to the problem of human interrelations.* Washington: Nervous and Mental Disorders Publishing Co. —**686**

MORENO, J. L. 1946. *Psychodrama.* New York: Beacon House. —**660**

MORGAN, C. D., and MURRAY, H. A. 1935. A method for investigating fantasies: the thematic apperception test. *Arch. Neurol. Psychiat.*, *34*, 289–306. —**637**

MORGAN, C. T. 1951. The psychophysiology of learning. In Stevens, S. S. (ed.), *Handbook of experimental psychology.* New York: Wiley. —**504**

MORGAN, C. T., and STELLAR, E. 1950. *Physiological psychology.* New York: McGraw-Hill. —**197, 355**

MOSS, F. A. 1924. Study of animal drives. *J. exp. Psychol.*, *7*, 165–85. —**302**

MURPHY, G. 1947. *Personality: a biosocial approach to origins and structure.* New York: Harper. —**229, 642**

MURRAY, H. A. 1933. The effect of fear upon estimates of the maliciousness of other personalities. *J. soc. Psychol.*, *4*, 310–29. —**98**

MURRAY, H. A. 1938. *Explorations in personality.* New York: Oxford Univ. Press. —**623, 624**

MUSSEN, P. H. 1950. Some personality and social factors related to changes in children's attitudes toward Negroes. *J. abnorm. soc. Psychol.*, *45*, 423–41. —**676**

MUSSEN, P. H., and CONGER, J. J. 1956. *Child development and personality.* New York: Harper. —**608**

NEWCOMB, T. M. 1943. *Personality and social change.* New York: Dryden. —**675**

NEWMAN, H. H., FREEMAN, F. N., and HOLZINGER, K. J. 1937. *Twins: a study of heredity and environment.* Chicago: Univ. of Chicago Press. —**574**

NEYMANN, C. A. and YACORZYNSKI, G. K. 1942. Studies of introversion-extroversion and conflict of motives in the psychoses. *J. gen. Psychol.*, *27*, 241–55. —**614**

OFFICE OF STRATEGIC SERVICES, ASSESSMENT STAFF. 1948. *Assessment of men.* New York: Rinehart. —**642**

OLDS, J., and MILNER, P. 1954. Positive reinforcement produced by electrical stimulation of septal area and other regions of rat brain. *J. comp. physiol. Psychol.*, *47*, 419–27. —**335**

OSGOOD, C. E. 1953. *Method and theory in experimental psychology.* New York: Oxford Univ. Press. —**434, 457, 458, 459, 461, 479**

OSTERBERG, G. 1935. Topography of the layer of rods and cones in the human retina. *Acta Opthal. Suppl.*, *61*, 1–102. —**164**

OWENS, W. A. 1953. Age and mental abilities: a longitudinal study. *Genet. Psychol. Monogr.*, *48*, 3–54. —**558**

PARTEN, M. B. 1932. Social participation among pre-school children. *J. abnorm. soc. Psychol.*, 27, 243–69. —**602**

PENFIELD, W., and RASMUSSEN, T. 1950. *The cerebral cortex of man.* New York: Macmillan. —**175**

PERKY, C. W. 1910. An experimental study of imagination. *Amer. J. Psychol.*, 21, 422–52. —**368**

PIAGET, J. 1925. *The language and thought of the child.* New York: Harcourt, Brace. —**479**

PIAGET, J. 1929. *The child's conception of the world.* New York: Harcourt, Brace. —**48**

PIAGET, J. 1930. *The child's conception of physical causality.* New York: Harcourt, Brace. —**48**

PINTNER, R., DRAGOSITZ, A., and KUSHNER, R. 1944. *Supplementary guide for revised Stanford-Binet scale.* Stanford: Stanford Univ. Press. —**547**

PIRENNE, M. H. 1949. *Vision and the eye.* London: Chapman and Hall. —**83**

POLYA, G. 1946. *How to solve it.* Princeton: Princeton Univ. Press. —**386, 399**

POSTMAN, L., BRUNER, J. S., and MCGINNIES, E. 1948. Personal values as selective factors in perception. *J. abnorm. soc. Psychol.*, 43, 142–54. —**98**

POSTMAN, L., and CRUTCHFIELD, R. S. 1952. The interaction of need, set, and stimulus-structure in a cognitive task. *Amer. J. Psychol.*, 65, 196–217. —**99**

POSTMAN, L., and EGAN, J. P. 1949. *Experimental psychology.* New York: Harper. —**83**

POSTMAN, L., and PHILLIPS, L. W. 1954. Studies in incidental learning. *J. exp. Psychol.*, 48, 48–56. —**421, 422**

POSTMAN, L., and RAU, L. 1957. Retention as a function of the method of measurement. *Univ. Calif. Publ. Psychol.*, 8, No. 3. —**414**

PRATT, K. C. 1937. The organization of behavior in the newborn infant. *Psychol. Rev.*, 44, 470–90. —**598**

PRINCE, M. 1930. *The dissociation of personality* (2nd ed.). New York: Longmans, Green. —**209**

REDL, F. 1952. Pre-adolescents: what makes them tick? In Gruenberg, S. M. (ed.), *Our children today.* New York: Viking Press. —**603**

REED, H. B. 1946. Factors influencing the learning and retention of concepts. *J. exp. Psychol.*, 36, 71–87. —**464, 465**

REYMERT, M. L. (ed.) 1950. *Feelings and emotions.* New York: McGraw-Hill. —**264**

RICHARDS, T. W., and NEWBERG, H. 1938. Studies in fetal behavior. *Child Develop.*, 9, 79–86. —**598**

RICHTER, C. P. 1932. Symposium: Contributions of psychology to the understanding of problems of personality and behavior. IV. Biological foundations of personality differences. *Amer. J. Orthopsychiat.*, 2, 345–54. —**294**

RICHTER, C. P., HOLT, L. E., and BARELARE, B. 1937. Vitamin B₁ craving in rats. *Science*, 86, 354–5. —**282**

ROBBINS, W. J., BRODY, S., HOGAN, A. G., JACKSON, C. M., and GREENE, C. W. 1928. *Growth.* New Haven: Yale Univ. Press. —**588, 590**

ROGERS, C. R. 1951. *Client-centered therapy.* Boston: Houghton Mifflin. —**658, 665**

ROSENZWEIG, M. R. 1954. Cortical correlates of auditory localization and of related perceptual phenomena. *J. comp. physiol. Psychol.*, 47, 269–76. —**181**

RUCKMICK, C. A. 1936. *The psychology of feeling and emotion.* New York: McGraw-Hill. —**264**

RUNDQUIST, E. A. 1933. Inheritance of spontaneous activity in rats. *J. comp. Psychol.*, 16, 415–38. —**570**

SANFORD, F. H. 1952. Research on military leadership. In Flanagan, J. C. (ed.), *Psychology in the world emergency.* Pittsburgh: Univ. of Pittsburgh Press. Pp. 17–74. —**684**

SANFORD, R. N. 1937. The effects of abstinence from food upon imaginal processes: a further experiment. *J. Psychol.*, 3, 145–59. —**98**

SAUGSTAD, P., and RAAHEIM, K. 1956. Problem-solving as dependent on availability of functions. Oslo: Univ. of Oslo Library. —**389**

SAWREY, W. L., CONGER, J. J., and TURREL, E. S. 1956. An experimental investigation of the role of psychological factors in the production of gastric ulcers in rats. *J. comp. physiol. Psychol.*, 49, 457–61. —**341**

SAWREY, W. L., and WEISZ, J. D. 1956. An experimental method of producing gastric ulcers. *J. comp. physiol. Psychol.*, 49, 269–70. —**341**

SCAMMAN, R. E. 1923. Developmental anatomy. In *Morris' Human anatomy* (7th ed.). Philadelphia: P. Blakiston's Sons & Co. —**591**

SCHAFER, R., and MURPHY, G. 1943. The role of autism in a visual figure-ground relationship. *J. exp. Psychol.*, 32, 335–343. —**88**

SCHEERER, M., ROTHMANN, E., and GOLDSTEIN, K. 1945. A case of "idiot savant": an experimental study of personality organization. *Psychol. Monogr.*, 58, No. 4. —**551**

SCHREINER, L., and KLING, A. 1953. Behavioral changes following rhinencephalic injury in cat. *J. Neurophysiol.*, 16, 643–59. —**347**

SCOTT, E. M., and VERNEY, E. L. 1949. Self-selection of diet. IX. The appetite for thiamine. *J. Nutrition*, 37, 81–92. —**282**

SCOTTISH COUNCIL FOR RESEARCH IN EDUCATION. 1939. *The intelligence of a representative group of Scottish children.* London: Univ. of London Press. —**577**

SEARLE, L. V. 1949. The organization of hereditary maze-brightness and maze-dullness. *Genet. Psychol. Monogr.*, *39*, 279–325. —**572**

SEARS, P. S. 1940. Levels of aspiration of academically successful and unsuccessful children. *J. abnorm. soc. Psychol.*, *35*, 498–536. —**221**

SEARS, R. R. 1936. Experimental studies of projection. I. Attribution of traits. *J. soc. Psychol.*, *7*, 151–63. —**647**

SELLS, S. B., and KOOB, H. F. 1937. A classroom demonstration of "atmosphere effect" in reasoning. *J. educ. Psychol.*, *28*, 514–18. —**477**

SENDEN, M. V. 1932. *Raum und Gestaltauffassung bei operierten Blindgeborenen vor und nach Operation.* Leipzig: Barth. —**143**

SHAFFER, L. F., and SHOBEN, E. J., JR. 1956. *The psychology of adjustment* (2nd ed.). Boston: Houghton Mifflin. —**665**

SHANNON, C. E. 1951. Prediction and entropy in printed English. *Bell System Tech. Jour.*, *30*, 50–64. —**468**

SHAW, M. E. 1932. A comparison of individuals and small groups in the rational solution of complex problems. *Amer. J. Psychol.*, *44*, 491–504. —**688**

SHAW, W. A. 1940. The relation of muscular action potentials to imaginal weight lifting. *Arch. Psychol.*, No. 247. —**489**

SHELDON, W. H., and STEVENS, S. S. 1942. *The varieties of temperament.* New York: Harper. —**630**

SHELDON, W. H., STEVENS, S. S., and TUCKER, W. B. 1940. *The varieties of human physique.* New York: Harper. —**630**

SHERIF, M., and CANTRIL, H. 1947. *The psychology of ego-involvements.* New York: Wiley. —**229**

SHERRINGTON, C. S. 1897. On reciprocal action in the retina as studied by means of some rotating discs. *J. Physiol.*, *21*, 33–54. —**75**

SHURRAGER, P. S., and CULLER, E. 1940. Conditioning in the spinal dog. *J. exp. Psychol.*, *26*, 133–59. —**493, 494**

SIIPOLA, E. M. 1935. A study of some effects of preparatory set. *Psychol. Monogr.*, *46*, No. 210. —**102**

SIMMEL, M. L. 1956. Phantoms in patients with leprosy and in elderly digital amputees. *Amer. J. Psychol.*, *69*, 529–45. —**203**

SIMS, V. M. and PATRICK, J. R. 1936. Attitude toward the Negro of northern and southern college students. *J. soc. Psychol.*, *7*, 192–204. —**675**

SKINNER, B. F. 1938. *The behavior of organisms.* New York: Appleton-Century-Crofts. —**445**

SMALL, W. S. 1901. An experimental study of the mental processes of the rat. *Amer. J. Psychol.*, *12*, 206–39. —**442**

SMITH, M. B., BRUNER, J. S., and WHITE, R. W. 1956. *Opinions and personality.* New York: Wiley. —**674**

SNYDER, F. W., and PRONKO, N. H. 1952. *Vision with spatial inversion.* Wichita, Kansas: Univ. of Wichita Press. —**141**

SOLOMON, R. L., and HOWES, D. H. 1951. Word frequency, personal values, and visual duration thresholds. *Psychol. Rev.*, *58*, 256–70. —**98**

SPENCE, K. W. 1934. Systematic versus random responses in the solution of multiple choice problems by the chimpanzee. *Proc. Amer. Psychol. Assoc.*, 42nd meeting. —**439**

SPERRY, R. W. 1947. Cerebral regulation of motor coordination in monkeys following multiple transection of sensorimotor cortex. *J. Neurophysiol.*, *10*, 275–94. —**491**

SPRAGG, S. D. S. 1940. Morphine addiction in chimpanzees. *Comp. Psychol. Monogr.*, *15*, No. 7. —**293**

SPRANGER, E. 1928. *Types of men.* New York: Stechert. —**615**

STECKLE, L. C. 1936. Two additional attempts to condition the pupillary reflex. *J. gen. Psychol.*, *15*, 369–77. —**409**

STECKLE, L. C., and RENSHAW, J. 1934. An investigation of the conditioned iridic reflex. *J. gen. Psychol.*, *11*, 3–23. —**409**

STERN, C. 1949. *Principles of human genetics.* San Francisco: Freeman. —**585**

STEVENS, S. S. (ed.). 1951. *Handbook of experimental psychology.* New York: Wiley. —**197, 355, 434, 504**

STRATTON, G. M. 1897. Vision without inversion of the retinal image. *Psychol. Rev.*, *4*, 341–60. —**141**

STRAYER, L. C. 1930. Language and growth. *Genet. Psychol. Monogr.*, *8*, No. 3, 209–317. —**595**

STRONG, E. K., JR. 1951. Permanence of interest scores over 22 years. *J. appl. Psychol.*, *35*, 89–91. —**557**

SULLIVAN, H. S. 1953. *The interpersonal theory of psychiatry.* New York: Norton. —**623**

SUPA, M., COTZIN, M., and DALLENBACH, K. M. 1944. Facial vision: the perception of obstacles by the blind. *Amer. J. Psychol.*, *57*, 133–83. —**40**

SYMONDS, P. M. 1949. *Dynamic psychology.* New York: Appleton-Century-Crofts. —**665**

SYMONDS, P. M. 1951. *The ego and the self.* New York: Appleton-Century-Crofts. —**229**

SZÉKELY, L. 1945. *Zur Psychologie des geistigen Schaffens. Schweitzer Zeitsch. f. Psychologie*, *4*, 110–124; 332–47. —**390**

SZÉKELY, L. 1950. Knowledge and thinking. *Acta Psychologica*, *7*, 1–24. —**374, 391**

TANSER, H. A. 1939. *The settlement of Negroes in Kent County, Ontario.* Chatham, Ontario: Shephard Publ. Co. —**578–9**

TERMAN, L. M., and MERRILL, M. A. 1937. *Measuring intelligence.* Boston: Houghton Mifflin. —**544**

THIGPEN, C. H., and CLECKLEY, H. M. 1957. *The three faces of Eve.* New York: McGraw-Hill. —**209**

THOMPSON, W. R. 1957. Influence of prenatal maternal anxiety on emotionality in young rats. *Science, 125,* 698–9. —**571**

THORNDIKE, E. L. 1898. Animal intelligence. *Psychol. Monogr., 1,* No. 8. —**436**

THURSTONE, L. L. 1938. *Primary mental abilities.* Chicago: Univ. of Chicago Press. —**552**

THURSTONE, L. L., and CHAVE, E. J. 1929. *The measurement of attitudes.* Chicago: Univ. of Chicago Press.— **681**

TINBERGEN, N. 1951. *The study of instincts.* London: Oxford Univ. Press. —**290**

TOLMAN, E. C. 1932. *Purposive behavior in animals and men.* New York: Century. —**442, 457**

TOLMAN, E. C., and HONZIK, C. H. 1930. "Insight" in rats. *Univ. Calif. Publ. Psychol., 4,* 215–32. —**373**

TRYON, R. C. 1940. Genetic differences in maze learning in rats. In, National Society for the Study of Education. *The thirty-ninth yearbook.* Bloomington, Ill.: Public School Publ. Co. —**572**

TYLER, L. E. 1956. *The psychology of human differences.* New York: Appleton-Century-Crofts. —**558, 562, 581, 585**

UEXKÜLL, J. 1927. *Atlas zur Bestimmung der Orte in den Sehraümen der Tiere. Z. vergl. Physiol., 5,* 167–78. —**36**

UNDERWOOD, B. J., DUNCAN, C. P., TAYLOR, J. A., and COTTON, J. W. 1955. *Elementary statistics.* New York: Appleton-Century-Crofts. —**541**

UNDERWOOD, B. J., and RICHARDSON, J. 1956. The influence of meaningfulness, intralist similarity, and serial position on retention. *J. exp. Psychol., 52,* 119–26. —**420**

VAN ORMER, E. B. 1932. Retention after intervals of sleep and waking. *Arch. Psychol., 21,* No. 137. —**429, 430**

VIGOTSKY, L. S. 1939. Thought and speech. *Psychiat., 2,* 29–52. —**463**

VON FREY, M., and GOLDMAN, A. 1915. *Der zeitliche Verlauf der Einstellung bei den Druckempfindungen. Z. Biol., 65,* 183–202. —**77**

VON RESTORFF, H. 1933. *Über die Wirkung von Bereichsbildung im spurenfeld. Psychol. Forsch., 18,* 299–342. —**421**

WALLACH, H. 1935. *Über visuell wahrgenommene Bewegungsrichtung. Psychol. Forsch., 20,* 325–80. —**110**

WALLACH, H. 1940. The role of head movements and vestibular and visual cues in sound localization. *J. exp. Psychol., 27,* 339–68. —**133**

WALLACH, H. 1948. Brightness constancy and the nature of achromatic colors. *J. exp. Psychol., 38,* 310–24. —**150**

WALLIS, W. A., and ROBERTS, H. V. 1956. *Statistics: a new approach.* Glencoe: The Free Press. —**541**

WANGENSTEEN, O. H., and CARLSON, H. A. 1931. Hunger sensation in a patient after total gastrectomy. *Proc. Soc. Exp. Biol. & Med., 28,* 545–7. —**329**

WARD, L. B. 1937. Reminiscence and rote learning. *Psychol. Monogr., 49,* No. 4. —**425**

WARDEN, C. J. 1931. *Animal motivation studies: the albino rat.* New York: Columbia Univ. Press. —**302**

WARNER, W. L., and LUNT, P. S. 1941. *The social life of the modern community.* New Haven: Yale Univ. Press. —**581**

WATSON, J. 1950. Some social and psychological situations related to change in attitude. *Hum. Relat., 3,* 15–56. —**676**

WATSON, J. B. 1924. *Psychology from the standpoint of a behaviorist* (2nd ed.). Philadelphia: Lippincott. —**238**

WERTHEIMER, M. 1923. *Untersuchungen zur Lehre von der Gestalt. Psychol. Forsch., 4,* 301–50. —**91**

WERTHEIMER, M. 1945. *Productive thinking.* New York: Harper. —**213, 371, 399**

WHITE, R. W. 1948. *The abnormal personality.* New York: Ronald. —**653, 665**

WHITE, R. W. 1952. *Lives in progress: a study of the natural growth of personality.* New York: Dryden. —**642**

WHORF, B. L. 1956. *Language, thought and reality.* New York: Wiley. —**473**

WICKENS, D. D., and WICKENS, C. 1940. A study of conditioning in the neonate. *J. exp. Psychol., 26,* 94–102. —**593**

WIESNER, B. P., and SHEARD, N. M. 1933. *Maternal behavior in the rat.* London: Oliver and Boyd. —**298**

WILLIAMS, K. A. 1924. The reward value of a conditioned stimulus. *Univ. Calif. Publ. Psychol., 4,* 31–55. —**625**

WILLIAMS, R. J. 1956. *Biochemical individuality.* New York: Wiley. —**351**

WITKIN, H. A., LEWIS, H. B., HERTZMAN, M., MACHOVER, K., MEISSNER, P. B., and WAPNER, S. 1954. *Personality through perception.* New York: Harper. —**47**

WOLF, A. V. 1956. Thirst. *Scientific American, 194,* 70–80. —**331**

WOLFE, J. B. 1936. Effectiveness of token-rewards for chimpanzees. *Comp. Psychol. Monogr., 12,* No. 60. —**625**

WOLFLE, D. 1951. Training. In Stevens, S. S. (ed.), *Handbook of experimental psychology*. New York: Wiley. —**453**

WOODROW, H. 1927. The effect of type of training upon transference. *J. educ. Psychol.*, *18*, 159–72. —**426**

WOODWORTH, R. S. 1938. *Experimental psychology*. New York: Holt. —**424, 477**

WOODWORTH, R. S., and SCHLOSBERG, H. 1954. *Experimental psychology* (rev. ed.). New York: Holt. —**83, 155**

WOODWORTH, R. S., and SELLS, S. B. 1935. An atmospheric effect in formal syllogistic reasoning. *J. exp. Psychol.*, *18*, 451–60. —**477**

WORCHEL, P., and DALLENBACH, K. M. 1947. Facial vision: perception of obstacles by the deaf-blind. *Amer. J. Psychol.*, *60*, 502–53. —**40**

YOSHIOKA, J. G. 1929. Weber's law in the discrimination of maze distance by the white rat. *Univ. Calif. Publ. Psychol.*, *4*, 155–84. —**55**

YOUNG, P. T. 1936. *Motivation of behavior*. New York: Wiley. —**324**

YOUNG, P. T. 1943. *Emotion in man and animal*. New York: Wiley. —**264**

ZEIGARNIK, B. 1927. *Über das Behalten von erledigten und unerledigten Handlungen*. *Psychol. Forsch.*, *9*, 1–85. —**321**

Subject and Name Index

A NOTE ON THE TYPE

The text of this book was set on the Linotype in JANSON, *a recutting made direct from the type cast from matrices made by Anton Janson. Whether or not Janson was of Dutch ancestry is not known, but it is known that he purchased a foundry and was a practicing type-founder in Leipzig during the years 1660 to 1687. Janson's first specimen sheet was issued in 1675. His successor issued a specimen sheet showing all of the Janson types in 1689.*

His type is an excellent example of the influential and sturdy Dutch types that prevailed in England prior to the development by William Caslon of his own incomparable designs, which he evolved from these Dutch faces. The Dutch in their turn had been influenced by Garamond in France. The general tone of Janson, however, is darker than Garamond and has a sturdiness and substance quite different from its predecessors. It is a highly legible type, and its individual letters have a pleasing variety of design. Its heavy and light strokes make it sharp and clear, and the full-page effect is characterful and harmonious.

Designed by HARRY FORD.